Quantitative
Analysis
for Management

Quantitative Analysis for Management

Seventh Edition

Barry Render

Charles Harwood Professor of Management Science
Roy E. Crummer Graduate School of Business, Rollins College

Ralph M. Stair, Jr.

Professor of Information and Management Sciences
Florida State University

Prentice Hall
Upper Saddle River, New Jersey 07458

Acquisitions Editor: Tom Tucker
Editorial Assistant: Kerri Limpert
Editor-in-Chief: Natalie Anderson
Marketing Manager: Debbie Clare
Associate Managing Editor: Cynthia Regan
Permissions Coordinator: Monica Stipanov
Manufacturing Supervisor: Arnold Vila
Manufacturing Manager: Vincent Scelta
Senior Designer: Cheryl Asherman
Design Manager: Patricia Smythe
Interior/Cover Design: Jill Little
Cover Photo: Ralph Mercer Photography
Composition/Illustrator (Interior): UG / GGS Information Services, Inc.

Microsoft Excel, Solver, and Windows are registered trademarks of the Microsoft Corporation in the U.S.A. and other countries. Screen shots and icons reprinted with permission from the Microsoft Corporation. This book is not sponsored or endorsed by or affiliated with the Microsoft Corporation.

Library of Congress Cataloging-in-Publication Data
Render, Barry.
    Quantitative analysis for management / Barry Render, Ralph M.
        Stair, Jr. — 7th ed.
        p.   cm.
        Includes bibliographical references.
        ISBN 0-13-021538-4
        1. Management science.   2. Operations research.   I. Stair, Ralph
        M.   II. Title.
T56.R544   1999
658.4′03—dc21   99-21605
                                                                                    CIP

Prentice-Hall International (UK) Limited, London
Prentice-Hall of Australia Pty. Limited, Sydney
Prentice-Hall Canada, Inc., Toronto
Prentice-Hall Hispanoamericana, S.A., Mexico
Prentice-Hall of India Private Limited, New Delhi
Prentice-Hall of Japan, Inc., Tokyo
Prentice-Hall (Singapore) Pte. Ltd.
Editora Prentice-Hall do Brasil, Ltda., Rio de Janeiro

Printed in the United States of America

10 9 8 7 6 5 4 3

To Donna, Charlie, and Jesse

To Lila and Leslie

Brief Contents

CHAPTER 1   Introduction to Quantitative Analysis 1

SUPPLEMENT 1   Game Theory 21

CHAPTER 2   Probability Concepts and Applications 39

CHAPTER 3   Fundamentals of Decision Theory Models 81

CHAPTER 4   Decision Trees and Utility Theory 117

CHAPTER 5   Forecasting 155

CHAPTER 6   Inventory Control Models 203

CHAPTER 7   Linear Programming Models: Graphical and Computer Methods 253

CHAPTER 8   Linear Programming Modeling Applications: With Computer Analyses in Excel and QM for Windows 305

CHAPTER 9   Linear Programming: The Simplex Method 345

CHAPTER 10   Transportation and Assignment Models 407

CHAPTER 11   Integer Programming, Goal Programming, Nonlinear Programming, and Branch and Bound Models 473

SUPPLEMENT 11   Analytic Hierarchy Process 519

CHAPTER 12   Network Models 537

CHAPTER 13   Project Management 567

CHAPTER 14   Waiting Lines and Queuing Theory Models 615

CHAPTER 15   Simulation Modeling 655

CHAPTER 16   Markov Analysis 705

CD-ROM MODULES

1   Statistical Quality Control M1-1

2   Dynamic Programming M2-1

3   Decision Theory and the Normal Distribution M3-1

4   Material Requirements Planning and Just-In-Time Inventory M4-1

5   Mathematical Tools: Determinants and Matrices M5-1

6   The Binomial Distribution M6-1

Contents

Preface xix

CHAPTER 1 **Introduction to Quantitative Analysis 1**

1.1 *Introduction 2*

1.2 *What Is Quantitative Analysis? 2*

1.3 *The Quantitative Analysis Approach 2*

Defining the Problem 3
Developing a Model 3
Acquiring Input Data 4
Developing a Solution 5
Testing the Solution 5
Analyzing the Results and Sensitivity Analysis 5
Implementing the Results 6
The QA Approach and Modeling in the Real World 7

1.4 *How To Develop A Quantitative Analysis Model 7*

The Advantages of Mathematical Modeling 8
Mathematical Models Categorized by Risk 9

1.5 *The Role of Computers and Spreadsheet Models in the Quantitative Analysis Approach 9*

1.6 *Possible Problems in the QA Approach 12*

Defining the Problem 13
Developing a Model 13
Acquiring Input Data 14
Developing a Solution 14
Testing the Solution 15
Analyzing the Results 15

1.7 *Implementation—Not Just the Final Step 16*

Lack of Commitment and Resistance to Change 16
Lack of Commitment by Quantitative Analysts 16
Summary 17 Glossary 17 Key Equations 17 Self-Test 18 Discussion Questions 19 Bibliography 19

SUPPLEMENT 1 **Game Theory 21**

S1.1 *Introduction 22*

S1.2 *Language of Games 22*

S1.3 *Pure Strategy Games 24*

S1.4 *Minimax Criterion 25*

S1.5 *Mixed Strategy Games 25*

S1.6 *Dominance 29*

Summary 31 Glossary 31 Solved Problems 31 Self-Test 33 Discussion Questions and Problems 34 Data Set Problem 36 Bibliography 37

Appendix S1.1 Game Theory with QM for Windows 37

CHAPTER 2 **Probability Concepts and Applications 39**

2.1 *Introduction 40*

2.2 *Fundamental Concepts 41*
Types of Probability 42

2.3 *Mutually Exclusive and Collectively Exhaustive Events 42*

Adding Mutually Exclusive Events 44
Law of Addition for Events That Are Not Mutually Exclusive 45

2.4   *Statistically Independent Events 45*

2.5   *Statistically Dependent Events 47*

2.6   *Revising Probabilities with Bayes' Theorem 48*

General Form of Bayes' Theorem 50

2.7   *Further Probability Revisions 51*

2.8   *Random Variables 52*

2.9   *Probability Distributions 54*

Probability Distribution of a Discrete Random Variable 54
Expected Value of a Discrete Probability Distribution 55
Variance of a Discrete Probability Distribution 56
Probability Distribution of a Continuous Random Variable 57

2.10   *The Normal Distribution 58*

Area Under the Normal Curve 58
Using the Standard Normal Table 60
Haynes Construction Company Example 63

2.11   *The Exponential Distribution 66*

2.12   *The Poisson Distribution 66*

Summary 67   Glossary 68   Key Equations 69   Solved Problems 70   Self-Test 73   Discussion Questions and Problems 74   Case Study: Century Chemical Company 79   Bibliography 80

Appendix 2.1   Derivation of Bayes' Theorem 80

CHAPTER 3   **Fundamentals of Decision Theory Models 81**

3.1   *Introduction 82*

3.2   *The Six Steps in Decision Theory 82*

3.3   *Types of Decision-Making Environments 84*

3.4   *Decision Making Under Risk 85*

Expected Monetary Value 85
Expected Value of Perfect Information 87
Opportunity Loss 88
Sensitivity Analysis 89

3.5   *Decision Making Under Uncertainty 90*

Maximax 90
Maximin 91
Equally Likely (Laplace) 91
Criterion of Realism (Hurwicz Criterion) 92
Minimax 93
Using Excel QM to Solve Decision Theory Problems 93

3.6   *Marginal Analysis with a Large Number of Alternatives and States of Nature 95*

Marginal Analysis with Discrete Distributions 95
Marginal Analysis with the Normal Distribution 98
Summary 100   Glossary 100   Key Equations 101   Solved Problems 101 Self-Test 104   Discussion Questions and Problems 105   Data Set Problem 111 Case Study: Starting Right Corporation 112 Case Study: Ski Right 113   Bibliography 114

Appendix 3.1   Decision Theory with QM for Windows 114

CHAPTER 4   **Decision Trees and Utility Theory 117**

4.1   *Introduction 118*

4.2   *Decision Trees 118*

A More Complex Decision for Thompson Lumber 119
Expected Value of Sample Information 123
Using TreePlan to Solve the Thompson Lumber Problem 124

4.3   *How Probability Values Are Estimated by Bayesian Analysis 125*

Calculating Revised Probabilities 126
Potential Problem in Using Survey Results 128

4.4   *Utility Theory 129*

Measuring Utility and Constructing a Utility Curve 129
Utility as a Decision-Making Criterion 132

4.5   Sensitivity Analysis 134

        Summary 135   Glossary 135   Key
        Equations 136   Solved Problems 136
        Self-Test 141   Discussion Questions and
        Problems 142   Data Set Problem 149
        Case Study: Blake Electronics 150   Internet
        Case Studies 152   Bibliography 152

Appendix 4.1   Decision Trees with QM for
                Windows 152

Appendix 4.2   Using TreePlan to Solve
                Decision Tree Problems 153

CHAPTER 5   Forecasting 155

5.1   Introduction 156

5.2   Types of Forecasts 156

        Time-Series Models 157
        Causal Models 157
        Qualitative Models 157

5.3   Scatter Diagrams 158

5.4   Time-Series Forecasting Models
        159

        Decomposition of a Time Series 159
        Moving Averages 161
        Exponential Smoothing 163
        Trend Projections 169
        Seasonal Variations 173

5.5   Causal Forecasting Methods 176

        Using Regression Analysis to Forecast 176
        Standard Error of the Estimate 178
        Correlation Coefficients for Regression
          Lines 180
        Multiple Regression Analysis 181

5.6   Monitoring and Controlling
        Forecasts 182

        Adaptive Smoothing 184

5.7   Using the Computer
        to Forecast 184

        Summary 185   Glossary 185   Key
        Equations 186   Solved Problems 187
        Self-Test 190   Discussion Questions and
        Problems 191   Data Set Problem 197
        Case Study: North–South Airline 198   Case
        Study: Akron Zoological Park 199   Internet
        Case Studies 200   Bibliography 200

Appendix 5.1   Forecasting with QM for
                Windows 200

CHAPTER 6   Inventory Control Models 203

6.1   Introduction 204

6.2   Importance of Inventory
        Control 205

        Decoupling Function 205
        Storing Resources 205
        Irregular Supply and Demand 205
        Quantity Discounts 206
        Avoiding Stockouts and Shortages 206

6.3   Inventory Decisions 207

6.4   Economic Order Quantity
        (EOQ): Determining How Much
        to Order 208

        Inventory Costs 209
        Finding the Economic Order Quantity 210
        Sumco Pump Company Example 211
        Purchase Cost of Inventory Items 212

6.5   Reorder Point: Determining When
        to Order 214

6.6   EOQ Without the Instantaneous
        Receipt Assumption 215

        Determining the Annual Carrying Cost 216
        Finding the Annual Setup Cost or the
          Annual Ordering Cost 216
        Determining the Optimal Order Quantity
          and Production Quantity 217
        Brown Manufacturing 217

6.7   Quantity Discount Models 220

6.8   Use of Safety Stock 223

        Reorder Point with Known Stockout
          Costs 225
        Safety Stock with Unknown Stockout
          Costs 228

6.9   ABC Analysis 231

6.10   Sensitivity Analysis 232

        Summary 233   Glossary 234   Key
        Equations 234   Solved Problems 235
        Self-Test 238   Discussion Questions and
        Problems 239   Data Set Problems 246
        Case Study: Sturdivant Sound Systems 247
        Case Study: Martin–Pullin Bicycle
        Corporation 248   Case Study: Professional
        Video Management 248   Internet Case
        Studies 250   Bibliography 250

Appendix 6.1   Inventory Control with QM for
                Windows 250

CHAPTER 7 **Linear Programming Models: Graphical and Computer Methods 253**

7.1 *Introduction 254*

7.2 *Requirements of a Linear Programming Problem 254*

Basic Assumptions of LP 255

7.3 *Formulating Linear Programming Problems 256*

Flair Furniture Company 256

7.4 *Graphical Solution to a Linear Programming Problem 257*

Graphical Representation
  of Constraints 257
Isoprofit Line Solution Method 263
Corner Point Solution Method 266

7.5 *Solving Flair Furniture's LP Problem Using QM for Windows and Excel 267*

Using QM for Windows 267
Using Excel's Solver Command to Solve LP
  Problems 268

7.6 *Solving Minimization Problems 269*

Holiday Meal Turkey Ranch 271

7.7 *Summary of the Graphical Solution Methods 275*

7.8 *Four Special Cases in Linear Programming 277*

Infeasibility 277
Unboundedness 278
Redundancy 278
Alternate Optimal Solutions 279

7.9 *Sensitivity Analysis 280*

High Note Sound Company 281
Using QM for Windows for Sensitivity
  Analysis 284
Using Excel for Sensitivity
  Analysis 284
*Summary 287   Glossary 287   Solved
Problems 288   Self-Test 292   Discussion
Questions and Problems 293   Case Study:
Mexicana Wire Works 301   Internet Case
Studies 302   Bibliography 303*

CHAPTER 8 **Linear Programming Modeling Applications: With Computer Analyses in Excel and QM for Windows 305**

8.1 *Introduction 306*

8.2 *Marketing Applications 306*

Media Selection 306
Marketing Research 307

8.3 *Manufacturing Applications 310*

Production Mix 310
Production Scheduling 312

8.4 *Employee Scheduling Applications 316*

Assignment Problems 316
Labor Planning 318

8.5 *Financial Applications 320*

Portfolio Selection 320

8.6 *Transportation Applications 321*

Shipping Problem 321
Truck Loading Problem 324

8.7 *Ingredient Blending Applications 326*

Diet Problems 326
Ingredient Mix and Blending Problems 327
*Summary 329   Self-Test 330   Problems
331   Case Study: Red Brand Canners 340
Case Study: Chase Manhattan Bank 342
Bibliography 343*

CHAPTER 9 **Linear Programming: The Simplex Method 345**

9.1 *Introduction 346*

9.2 *How to Set Up the Initial Simplex Solution 346*

Converting the Constraints
  to Equations 347
Finding an Initial Solution
  Algebraically 348
The First Simplex Tableau 348

9.3 *Simplex Solution Procedures 352*

9.4 *The Second Simplex Tableau 352*

Interpreting the Second Tableau 355

9.5   Developing the Third Tableau 357

9.6   Review of Procedures for Solving
       LP Maximization Problems 360

9.7   Surplus and Artificial
       Variables 360

       Surplus Variables 361
       Artificial Variables 361
       Surplus and Artificial Variables in the
          Objective Function 362

9.8   Solving Minimization
       Problems 362

       Graphical Analysis 363
       Converting the Constraints and Objective
          Function 364
       Rules of the Simplex Method for
          Minimization Problems 365
       First Simplex Tableau for the Muddy River
          Chemical Corporation Problem 365
       Developing a Second Tableau 367
       Developing a Third Tableau 368
       Fourth Tableau for the Muddy River
          Chemical Corporation Problem 370

9.9   Review of Procedures for Solving
       LP Minimization Problems 371

9.10   Special Cases 372

       Infeasibility 372
       Unbounded Solutions 372
       Degeneracy 373
       More Than One Optimal Solution 374

9.11   Sensitivity Analysis with the
       Simplex Tableau 375

       High Note Sound Company Revisited 375
       Changes in the Objective Function
          Coefficients 376
       Changes in Resources or Right-Hand-Side
          Values 378
       Sensitivity Analysis by Computer 380

9.12   The Dual 381

       Dual Formulation Procedures 382
       Solving the Dual of the High Note Sound
          Company Problem 382

9.13   Karmarkar's Algorithm 384

       Summary 384   Glossary 385   Key
       Equation 386   Solved Problems 386
       Self-Test 391   Discussion Questions and
       Problems 392   Data Set Problem 403

Case Study: Coastal States Chemicals and
Fertilizers 404   Bibliography 405

CHAPTER 10   Transportation and Assignment
              Models 407

10.1   Introduction 408

       Transportation Model 408
       Assignment Model 408
       Special-Purpose Algorithms 408

10.2   Setting Up a Transportation
       Problem 409

10.3   Developing an Initial Solution:
       Northwest Corner Rule 411

10.4   Stepping-Stone Method: Finding a
       Least-Cost Solution 413

       Testing the Solution for Possible
          Improvement 414
       Obtaining an Improved Solution 416

10.5   MODI Method 421

       How to Use the MODI Approach 421
       Solving the Executive Furniture Corporation
          Problem with MODI 422

10.6   Vogel's Approximation Method:
       Another Way to Find an Initial
       Solution 424

10.7   Unbalanced Transportation
       Problems 427

       Demand Less Than Supply 427
       Demand Greater Than Supply 428

10.8   Degeneracy in Transportation
       Problems 430

       Degeneracy in an Initial Solution 430
       Degeneracy during Later Solution
          Stages 431

10.9   More Than One Optimal
       Solution 432

10.10 Facility Location Analysis 432

       Locating a New Factory for Hardgrave
          Machine Company 433

10.11 Approach of the Assignment
       Model 436

       The Hungarian Method
          (Flood's Technique) 437
       Making the Final Assignment 441

10.12   *Dummy Rows and Dummy Columns 442*

10.13   *Maximization Assignment Problems 442*

   Glossary 446   Key Equations 446 Solved Problems 447   Self-Test 452 Discussion Questions and Problems 453 Data Set Problems 464   Case Study: Andrew–Carter, Inc. 465   Case Study: Custom Vans, Inc. 466   Case Study: Old Oregon Wood Store 468   Internet Case Studies 469   Bibliography 469

Appendix 10.1   Using QM For Windows 469

CHAPTER 11   Integer Programming, Goal Programming, Nonlinear Programming, and Branch and Bound Models 473

11.1   *Introduction 474*

11.2   *Integer Programming 474*

   Harrison Electric Company Example of Integer Programming 474
   Cutting Plane Method 476
   Using Software to Solve the Harrison Integer Programming Problem 478
   Types of Integer Programming Problems 478
   Mixed-Integer Programming Problem Example 480
   Zero-One Integer Programming Problem Example 482

11.3   *Branch and Bound Method 483*

   Assignment Problem Example 484
   Solving an Integer Programming Problem with Branch and Bound 488
   Harrison Electric Company Revisited 488

11.4   *Goal Programming 491*

   Example of Goal Programming: Harrison Electric Company Revisited 492
   Extension to Equally Important Multiple Goals 493
   Ranking Goals 494
   Solving Goal Programming Problems Graphically 495
   Modified Simplex Method for Goal Programming 498

11.5   *Nonlinear Programming 501*

   Nonlinear Objective Function and Linear Constraints 502
   Both Nonlinear Objective Function and Nonlinear Constraints 502
   Linear Objective Function with Nonlinear Constraints 504
   Computational Produres for Nonlinear Programming 506
   Summary 506   Glossary 506   Solved Problems 507   Self-Test 509   Discussion Questions and Problems 510   Data Set Problem 514   Case Study: Schank Marketing Research 515   Case Study: Oakton River Bridge 516   Case Study: Puyallup Mall 516   Bibliography 518

SUPPLEMENT 11   Analytic Hierarchy Process 519

S11.1   *Introduction 520*

S11.2   *Multifactor Evaluation Process 520*

S11.3   *Analytic Hierarchy Process 521*

   Judy Grim's Computer Decision 522
   Using Pairwise Comparisons 523
   Evaluations for Hardware 525
   Determining the Consistency Ratio 525
   Evaluations for the Other Factors 527
   Determining Factor Weights 528
   Overall Ranking 528
   Using the Computer to Solve AHP Problems 529

S11.4   *Comparison of MFEP and AHP 529*

   Summary 530   Glossary 531   Key Equations 531   Solved Problems 531 Self-Test 533   Discussion Questions and Problems 534   Bibliography 536

CHAPTER 12   Network Models 537

12.1   *Introduction 538*

12.2   *Minimal-Spanning Tree Technique 538*

12.3   *Maximal-Flow Technique 542*

12.4   *Shortest-Route Technique 545*

   Summary 549   Glossary 549   Solved Problems 549   Self-Test 553

Discussion Questions and Problems 554
Data Set Problem 560   Case Study:
Ranch Development Project 561   Case
Study: Binder's Beverage 563
Bibliography 564

Appendix 12.1   Network Models with QM for
Windows 564

CHAPTER 13   Project Management 567

13.1   Introduction 568
Framework of PERT and CPM 568

13.2   PERT 569
General Foundry Example of PERT 569
Drawing the PERT Network 571
Activity Times 572
How to Find the Critical Path 573
Probability of Project Completion 578
What PERT Was Able to Provide 581
Dummy Activities in PERT 581
Sensitivity Analysis and Project
Management 581

13.3   PERT/Cost 583
Planning and Scheduling Project Costs:
Budgeting Process 584
Monitoring and Controlling Project
Costs 586

13.4   Critical Path Method 589
Project Crashing with CPM 589
Project Crashing with Linear
Programming 591
Summary 593   Glossary 594   Key
Equations 595   Solved Problems 595
Self-Test 598   Discussion Questions and
Problems 599   Data Set Problem 607
Case Study: Haygood Brothers Construction
Company 608   Case Study: Family
Planning Research Center of Nigeria 610
Internet Case Studies 611   Bibliography 611

Appendix 13.1   Project Management with QM
for Windows 612

**CHAPTER 14   Waiting Lines and Queuing Theory
Models 615**

14.1   Introduction 616
14.2   Waiting Line Costs 616

14.3   Characteristics of a Queuing
System 618
Arrival Characteristics 618
Waiting Line Characteristics 620
Service Facility Characteristics 620

14.4   Single-Channel Queuing Model
with Poisson Arrivals and
Exponential Service Times 623
Assumptions of the Model 624
Queuing Equations 624
Arnold's Muffler Shop Case 625

14.5   Multiple-Channel Queuing Model
with Poisson Arrivals and
Exponential Service Times 629
Equations for the Multichannel Queuing
Model 629
Arnold's Muffler Shop Revisited 630

14.6   Constant Service Time Model
633
Equations for the Constant Service Time
Model 633
Garcia-Golding Recycling, Inc. 634

14.7   Finite Population Model 634
Equations for the Finite Population
Model 636
Department of Commerce Example 636

14.8   More Complex Queuing Models
and the Use of Simulation 638
Summary 638   Glossary 639   Key
Equations 640   Solved Problems 642
Self-Test 645   Discussion Questions
and Problems 646   Case Study: New
England Castings 651   Case Study:
Winter Park Hotel 652   Internet Case
Studies 652   Bibliography 653

Appendix 14.1   Using QM for Windows 653

CHAPTER 15   Simulation Modeling 655

15.1   Introduction 656
15.2   Advantages and Disadvantages of
Simulation 657
15.3   Monte Carlo Simulation 658
Using QM for Windows for
Simulation 663
Simulation with Excel Spreadsheets 664

15.4 *Simulation and Inventory Analysis 664*

Simkin's Hardware Store 666
Analyzing Simkin's Inventory Costs 670

15.5 *Simulation of a Queuing Problem 671*

Port of New Orleans 671
Using Excel to Simulate the Port of New Orleans Queuing Problem 673

15.6 *Simulation Model for a Maintenance Policy 675*

Three Hills Power Company 675
Cost Analysis of the Simulation 678
Building an Excel Simulation Model for Three Hills Power Company 679

15.7 *Two Other Types of Simulation Models 679*

Operational Gaming 681
Systems Simulation 681

15.8 *Role of Computers in Simulation 682*

Crystal Ball 683
Summary 683   Glossary 683   Solved Problems 684   Self-Test 687   Discussion Questions and Problems 688   Case Study: Alabama Airlines 697   Case Study: Abjar Transport Company 698   Internet Case Study 699   Bibliography 698

Appendix 15.1 *Using the* Crystal Ball *Excel Add-In 699*

Installing and Starting *Crystal Ball* 699
Textbook Profitability Analysis Model 699
Steps in Using *Crystal Ball* 701

CHAPTER 16

Markov Analysis 705

16.1 *Introduction 706*

16.2 *States and State Probabilities: Grocery Store Example 706*

16.3 *Matrix of Transition Probabilities 708*

Transition Probabilities for the Three Grocery Stores 708

16.4 *Predicting Future Market Shares 709*

16.5 *Markov Analysis of Machine Operations 710*

16.6 *Equilibrium Conditions 711*

16.7 *Absorbing States and the Fundamental Matrix: Accounts Receivable Application 714*

Summary 719   Glossary 719   Key Equations 719   Solved Problems 720   Self-Test 724   Discussion Questions and Problems 725   Data Set Problems 728   Case Study: Rentall Trucks 730   Internet Case Studies 731   Bibliography 731

Appendix 16.1 *Markov Analysis with QM for Windows 732*

APPENDICES

APPENDIX A   Areas Under the Standard Normal Curve 736

APPENDIX B   Unit Normal Loss Integral 738

APPENDIX C   Values of $e^{-\lambda}$ for Use in the Poisson Distribution 740

APPENDIX D   Using QM for Windows 741

APPENDIX E   Using Excel QM 744

APPENDIX F   Solutions to Selected Problems 745

APPENDIX G   Solutions to Self-Tests 748

Index 753

CD-ROM MODULES

Module 1   Statistical Quality Control M1-1

M1.1 *Introduction M1-2*

M1.2 *Defining Quality and TQM M1-2*

M1.3 *Statistical Process Control M1-3*

Variability in the Process M1-3

M1.4 *Control Charts for Variables M1-5*

The Central Limit Theorem M1-5
Setting $\overline{X}$-Chart Limits M1-6
Setting Range Chart Limits M1-8

M1.5   Control Charts for Attributes M1-9

p-Charts M1-10
c-Charts M1-11
Summary M1-13   Glossary M1-14   Key Equations M1-14   Solved Problems M1-15   Self-Test M-17   Discussion Questions and Problems M1-18   Case Study: Bayfield Mud Company M1-21   Case Study: Morristown Daily Tribune M1-23   Bibliography M1-24

Appendix M1.1   Using QM for Windows for SPC M1-25

Module 2   Dynamic Programming M2-1

M2.1   Introduction M2-2

M2.2   Shortest-Route Problem Solved by Dynamic Programming M2-2

M2.3   Dynamic Programming Terminology M2-5

M2.4   Dynamic Programming Notation M2-7

M2.5   Knapsack Problem M2-9

Types of Knapsack Problems M2-9
Roller's Air Transport Service
  Problem M2-10
Summary M2-16   Glossary M2-16   Key Equations M2-17   Solved Problem M2-17   Self-Test M2-20   Discussion Questions and Problems M2-21   Case Study: United Trucking M2-24   Internet Case Study M2-24   Bibliography M2-24

Module 3   Decision Theory and the Normal Distribution M3-1

M3.1   Introduction M3-2

M3.2   Break-Even Analysis and the Normal Distribution M3-2

Barclay Brothers New Product
  Decision M3-2
Probability Distribution of Demand M3-3
Using EMV to Make a Decision M3-5

M3.3   EVPI and the Normal Distribution M3-6

Opportunity Loss Function M3-6
Expected Opportunity Loss M3-7

Summary M3-8   Glossary M3-8   Key Equations M3-8   Solved Problems M3-9   Self-Test M3-10   Discussion Questions and Problems M3-11   Bibliography M3-12

Appendix M3.1   Derivation of the Break-Even Point M3-13

Module 4   Material Requirements Planning and Just-in-Time Inventory M4-1

M4.1   Introduction M4-2

M4.2   Dependent Demand: The Case for Material Requirements Planning M4-2

Material Structure Tree M4-2
Gross and Net Material Requirements
  Plan M4-3
Two or More End Products M4-6

M4.3   Just-in-Time Inventory Control M4-8

Summary M4-10   Glossary M4-10   Solved Problems M4-10   Self-Test M4-13   Discussion Questions and Problems M4-14   Internet Case Study M4-14   Bibliography M4-15

Module 5   Mathematical Tools: Determinants and Matrices M5-1

M5.1   Introduction M5-2

M5.2   Determinants M5-2

M5.3   Matrices M5-4

Matrix Addition and Subtraction M5-5
Matrix Multiplication M5-5
Matrix Transpose M5-8
Matrix of Cofactors and Adjoint M5-9
Finding the Inverse of a Matrix M5-9
Summary M5-11   Glossary M5-11   Self-Test M5-12   Problems M5-13   Bibliography M5-14

Module 6   The Binomial Distribution M6-1

M6.1   Introduction M6-2

M6.2   Solving Problems with the Binomial Formula M6-2

M6.3   Solving Problems with Binomial Tables M6-4

Discussion Questions and Problems M6-6   Case Study: WTVX M6-6

Preface

OVERVIEW

The seventh edition of *Quantitative Analysis for Management* looks to the future with the latest software and pedagogy. With over 20 years of service to the management science and quantitative analysis discipline, this edition builds on the traditions and strengths of past successes, while keeping an eye on the needs of future managers and decision makers.

The seventh edition continues to provide the reader with the skills to apply the techniques of quantitative analysis in all kinds of organizational decision-making situations. The chapters, supplements, and CD modules cover every major topic in the quantitative analysis/management science field. There is probably more material included than most instructors can cover in a typical first course, but we have found that the resulting flexibility of topic selection is appreciated by instructors who need to tailor their courses to different audiences and curricula.

We show how each technique works, discuss the assumptions and limitations of the models, and illustrate the real-world usefulness of each technique with many applications in both profit and nonprofit organizations. We have kept the notation, terminology, and equations standard with other books. As in the first six editions, we have tried to write a text that is easy to understand and use. Algebra is the only mathematics prerequisite.

FEATURES RETAINED FROM THE PREVIOUS EDITION

This book is student oriented; the following features have proved to be effective aids to the learning process.

- *QA in Action* boxes summarize published articles illustrating how real organizations have used quantitative analysis to solve problems. There are a dozen new *QA in Action* boxes in the seventh edition

- *Solved problems*, included at the end of chapters, serve as models for students in solving their own homework problems.

- *Problems*, included in every chapter, are applications-oriented and test the student's ability to solve exam-type problems. They are graded by three levels: introductory (one bullet), moderate (two bullets), and challenging (three bullets).

- *INFORMS* videos are available for classroom use. The INFORMS videos are edited versions of award-winning presentations at the annual meeting.

- *Data set problems*, found in most chapters, require the computer to solve problems with larger amounts of data. These real-world problems are also available to instructors on data disks.
- *Modeling in the Real World* boxes help students apply the steps of the quantitative analysis approach, first presented in Chapter 1, to every technique discussed in the book.
- *Procedure Boxes* describe quantitative analysis techniques as a series of steps.
- *Margin Notes*, sentences or short paragraphs, are used to make it easier for students to understand important points.
- *Self Tests* allow students to test their knowledge of important terms and concepts to help them prepare for quizzes and examinations.
- *History* boxes briefly describe how a technique was developed.
- *Glossaries*, at the end of each chapter, define important terms.
- *Key equations*, which summarize the mathematical material, are listed at the end of each chapter.
- *Discussion questions*, at the end of each chapter, test the student's understanding of concepts.
- *Case studies*, at the end of each chapter, provide challenging managerial applications.
- *End-of-chapter bibliographies* provide a current selection of more advanced books and interesting articles.
- *QM for Windows* uses the full capabilities of Windows to solve quantitative analysis problems and is described either in the chapter or in an appendix at the end of the chapter.

 KEY CHANGES IN THE TEXT

The seventh edition of *Quantitative Analysis for Management* has many new and exciting enhancements. In the text, you will find an increased emphasis on modeling, computer integration, and a variety of new features. In addition, new CD ROM modules, an extensive Companion Web Site, and a comprehensive set of supplements accompany and support the text.

Increased Emphasis on Modeling

The seventh edition stresses the use of modeling. Chapter 1 has been rewritten to introduce the importance of modeling in quantitative analysis. The title of Chapter 1 has been changed to *Introduction to Quantitative Analysis and Modeling* to emphasize this new orientation. This modeling emphasis has been incorporated into the other chapters. Modeling in the Real World boxes have been retained and enhanced. Many chapter titles have also been changed to reflect this new emphasis.

Computer Integration

The integration of the computer can be seen in the first chapter and throughout the book. The software features include Excel, Crystal Ball, TreePlan, Excel QM, and a new version of QM for Windows.

Excel.   Excel is the featured software tool for the seventh edition. There is an increased use of Solver in the optimization chapters. Students are shown how Solver can be used to model a variety of quantitative analysis problems. In addition, the seventh edition has incorporated Crystal Ball and TreePlan into the simulation and decision-modeling chapters. These powerful Excel add-ins show students how Excel can be extended to solve simulation and decision-modeling problems. In addition, Chapter 1 shows how Goal Seek can be used to model a break-even problem.

Excel QM.   Excel QM, a new program from Professor Howard Weiss, author of *QM for Windows*, solves many of the problems and examples found in the text. The use of Excel QM is integrated into most chapters. Students can see the power of this new software package in modeling and solving quantitative analysis problems. Excel QM is menu driven and easy to use. All of the power and convenience of Excel can be used to solve quantitative analysis problems.

QM for Windows.   QM for Windows, our popular decision-support software for solving homework problems, has been upgraded and enhanced. Appendices at the end of most chapters show how this software tool can be used to solve quantitative analysis problems.

Free Software and Data Files on the Student CD-ROM.   As a convenience to students, Excel QM, Crystal Ball, TreePlan, QM for Windows, and data files for examples will be conveniently packaged into a CD-ROM and included free to students as part of the text. Formerly, there was an additional charge for QM for Windows.

New Features in the Text

The text includes a number of new and exciting features to make teaching and learning easier. The new features in the text include:

- *New Student CD-ROM.* A new student CD-ROM accompanies every text. Included are Excel QM, QM for Windows, Crystal Ball, TreePlan, example data files, and new CD-ROM modules.
- *Example Data Files.* Data files used to solve the examples presented in this book and solved using Excel QM are included with the student CD-ROM.
- *Upgraded QA in Action Boxes.* The QA in Action boxes have been upgraded with many new applications.
- *Upgraded Modeling in the Real World Boxes.* Modeling in the Real World boxes have been upgraded to include new examples of how real companies have benefited from the modeling approach.
- *New Problems and Cases.* Most chapters have new problems and/or cases.
- *Updated Bibliographies.* The bibliographies at the end of the chapters have been updated to include newer applications of quantitative analysis. The classic references have been retained to give students a flavor of the history and development of the quantitative analysis field.

 CD-ROM MODULES

To streamline the book, some chapters and supplements are now CD-ROM modules included with the student CD-ROM. These new CD-ROM modules have the same format and features of any chapter or supplement found in the text. The six CD-ROM modules are:

- Statistical Quality Control
- Dynamic Programming
- Decision Theory and the Normal Distribution

- Material Requirements Planning and Just-In-Time Inventory
- Mathematical Tools: Determinants and Matrices
- The Binomial Distribution

COMPANION WEB SITE

Our updated companion Web site uses the latest features of the Internet and the World Wide Web (WWW) with new content and features. Students can benefit from the updated Web site by seeing up-to-the-minute examples and real-world companies using the quantitative analysis approach. As with past editions, this edition also contains interesting Internet links, additional assignments, and numerous additional cases. The address for the Web site is *http://www.prenhall.com/render*.

SUPPLEMENTS

The supplements have been updated to reflect the new emphasis of the text and to provide students and instructors with the best teaching package possible. Here is a brief list of the supplements available with the text.

- *New Instructor CD-ROM.* A new instructor CD-ROM includes the complete Instructor's Solution Manual, the PowerPoint slides, and data files for end-of-chapter problems.
- *New PowerPoint Slides.* New PowerPoint slides are included with the Instructor CD-ROM.
- *Instructor's Solution Manual.* Available to adopters.
- *Updated Test Item File.* An updated test item file is available to adopters.
- *Prentice Hall's Test Manager for Windows.* This powerful test manager software is available to adopters.
- *Videos.* We have selected the best INFORMS videos from past editions and included them in a video package for this edition.

ACKNOWLEDGMENTS

We gratefully thank the users of previous editions and the reviewers who provided valuable suggestions and ideas for this edition. As in the past, we truly value your needs and feedback. The long-term success of *Quantitative Analysis for Management* is a direct result of instructor and student feedback. Your feedback has enabled our success in the past and will shape the future of our discipline.

The Roy E. Crummer School of Business at Rollins College and the Department of Information and Management Sciences at The Florida State University provided support and a conducive environment for the development of this text. Professors Jerry Kinard, F. Bruce Simmons III, Khala Chand Seal, Victor E. Sower, Michael Ballot, Curtis P. McLaughlin, and Zbigniew H. Przanski have contributed excellent cases.

In addition, the authors were thrilled to have partnered with three wonderful professionals who helped us on this project. Professor Howard Weiss, at Temple University, did an outstanding job in developing QM for Windows and Excel QM and providing their screen captures. We believe these programs are the best educational quantitative analysis tools available. Madeline S. Thimmes, at Utah State University, was our overall error checker and problem consultant. Professor John Swearingen, at Bryant College, developed the PowerPoint slides, Test Item File, and Companion Website On-line Study Guide.

We would also like to express our appreciation to the reviewers of the present and past editions.

Present Edition:

Ephrem Eyob, *Virginia State University*
Madeline Thimmes, *Utah State University*
Peter Miller, *University of Windsor*
Richard Slovacek, *North Central College*
Ike Ehie, *Southeast Missouri State*
Hooshang Beheshti, *Radford University*
Shahriar Mostashari, *Campbell University*

Past Editions:

Stephen Achtenhagen, *San Jose University*
M. Jill Austin, *Middle Tennessee State University*
Raju Balakrishnan, *Clemson University*
Rodney L. Carlson, *Tennessee Technological University*
Edward Chu, *California State University, Dominguez Hills*
John Cozzolino, *Pace University-Pleasantville*
Shad Dowlatshahi, *University of Wisconsin, Platteville*
Wade Ferguson, *Western Kentucky University*
Robert Fiore, *Springfield College*
Frank G. Forst, *Loyola University of Chicago*
Ed Gillenwater, *University of Mississippi*
Irwin Greenberg, *George Mason University*
Michael E. Hanna, *University of Houston-Clear Lake*
Robert R. Hill, *University of Houston-Clear Lake*
Gordon Jacox, *Weber State College*
Bharat Jain, *Towson State University*
Darlene R. Lanier, *Louisiana State University*
Jooh Lee, *Rowan College*
Richard D. Legault, *University of Massachusetts–Dartmouth*
Douglas Lonnstrom, *Siena College*
Daniel McNamara, *University of St. Thomas*
Robert C. Meyers, *University of Louisiana*
Ralph Miller, *California State Polytechnic University*
David Murphy, *Boston College*
Robert Myers, *University of Louisville*
Barin Nag, *Towson State University*
Harvey Nye, *Central State University*
Alan D. Olinsky, *Bryant College*
Savas Ozatalay, *Widener University*
Young Park, *California University of Pennsylvania*
Cy Peebles, *Eastern Kentucky University*
Ranga Ramasesh, *Texas Christian University*
William Rife, *West Virginia University*
Bonnie Robeson, *John Hopkins University*
Grover Rodich, *Portland State University*
L. Wayne Shell, *Nicholls State University*

John Swearingen, *Bryant College*
F.S. Tanaka, *Slippery Rock State University*
Jack Taylor, *Portland State University*
M. Keith Thomas, *Olivet College*
Chris Vertullo, *Marist College*
James Vigen, *California State College, Bakersfield*
William Webster, *The University of Texas at San Antonio*
Larry Weinstein, *Eastern Kentucky University*

Finally, we are grateful to all the people at Prentice Hall who worked so hard to bring the book through the publication process. They are Cynthia Regan, our top-notch production editor, Patricia Smythe, Cheryl Asherman, and Jill Little, our outstanding design team; Arnold Vila, handling manufacturing and prepress; UG / GGS Information Services, Inc. for electronic formatting; Danielle Meckley for project management; Howard Weiss for creating the screen captures; Kristen Imperatore for managing all text supplements; Tom Tucker our editor; and Reva Shader, at First Printing, for creating the excellent index and proofreading the Solution Manual. Thank you all!

INFORMS. The Institute for Operations Research and Management Science, a leading international association in the field of management science, contributed to the video component of this package. The work in the videotapes, representing the best in management science practice, has been excerpted from videotapes of complete presentations from the Institute's Annual Franz Edelman Award for Management Science Achievement. For further information or a complete catalog of videos, write to INFORMS, 290 Westminster St. Providence, RI 02903

Barry Render
407-646-2657 (Phone)
407-646-1550 (Fax)
brender@rollins.edu (e-mail)

Ralph Stair
850-644-8232 (Phone)
rstair@cob.fsu.edu (e-mail)

CHAPTER 1

Introduction to Quantitative Analysis

LEARNING OBJECTIVES

After completing this chapter, students will be able to:

1. Describe the quantitative analysis approach.
2. Understand the application of quantitative analysis in a real situation.
3. Describe the use of modeling in quantitative analysis.
4. Use computers and spreadsheet models to perform quantitative analysis.
5. Discuss possible problems in using quantitative analysis.

CHAPTER OUTLINE

1.1 Introduction

1.2 What Is Quantitative Analysis?

1.3 The Quantitative Analysis Approach

1.4 How to Develop a Quantitative Analysis Model

1.5 The Role of Computers and Spreadsheet Models in the Quantitative Analysis Approach

1.6 Possible Problems in the QA Approach

1.7 Implementation—Not Just the Final Step

Summary • Glossary • Self-Test • Discussion Questions • Bibliography

1.1 INTRODUCTION

Quantitative analysis uses a scientific approach to decision making.

People have been using mathematical tools to help solve problems for thousands of years; however, the formal study and application of quantitative techniques to practical decision making is largely a product of the twentieth century. The techniques we study in this book have been applied successfully to an increasingly wide variety of complex problems in business, government, health care, education, and many other areas. Many such successful uses are discussed throughout this book.

It isn't enough, though, just to know the mathematics of how a particular quantitative technique works; you must also be familiar with the limitations, assumptions, and specific applicability of the technique. The successful use of quantitative techniques usually results in a solution that is timely, accurate, flexible, economical, reliable, and easy to understand and use.

1.2 WHAT IS QUANTITATIVE ANALYSIS?

Both qualitative and quantitative factors must be considered.

Quantitative analysis is the scientific approach to managerial decision making. Whim, emotions, and guesswork are not part of the quantitative analysis approach. This approach starts with data. Like raw material for a factory, these data are manipulated or processed into information that is valuable to people making decisions. This processing and manipulating of raw data into meaningful information is the heart of quantitative analysis. Computers have been instrumental in the increasing use of quantitative analysis.

In solving a problem, managers must consider both qualitative and quantitative factors. For example, we might consider several different investment alternatives, including certificates of deposit at a bank, investments in the stock market, and an investment in real estate. We can use quantitative analysis to determine how much our investment will be worth in the future when deposited at a bank at a given interest rate for a certain number of years. Quantitative analysis can also be used in computing financial ratios from the balance sheets for several companies whose stock we are considering. Some real estate companies have developed computer programs that use quantitative analysis to analyze cash flows and rates of return for investment property.

In addition to quantitative analysis, *qualitative* factors should also be considered. The weather, state and federal legislation, new technological breakthroughs, the outcome of an election, and so on may all be factors that are difficult to quantify.

Because of the importance of qualitative factors, the role of quantitative analysis in the decision-making process can vary. When there is a lack of qualitative factors and when the problem, model, and input data remain the same, the results of quantitative analysis can *automate* the decision-making process. For example, some companies use quantitative inventory models to determine automatically *when* to order additional new materials. In most cases, however, quantitative analysis will be an *aid* to the decision-making process. The results of quantitative analysis will be combined with other (qualitative) information in making decisions.

FIGURE 1.1

The Quantitative Analysis Approach

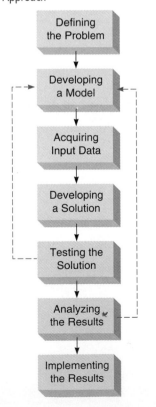

1.3 THE QUANTITATIVE ANALYSIS APPROACH

The quantitative analysis approach consists of defining a problem, developing a model, acquiring input data, developing a solution, testing the solution, analyzing the results, and implementing the results (see Figure 1.1). One step does not have to be finished com-

HISTORY   **The Origin of Quantitative Analysis**

Quantitative analysis has been in existence since the beginning of recorded history, but it was Frederick W. Taylor who in the early 1900s pioneered the principles of the scientific approach to management. During World War II, many new scientific and quantitative techniques were developed to assist the military. These new developments were so successful that after World War II many companies started using similar techniques in managerial decision making and planning. Today, many organizations employ a staff of operations research or management science personnel or consultants to apply the principles of scientific management to problems and opportunities. In this book, we use the terms *management science*, *operations research*, and *quantitative analysis* interchangeably.

The origin of many of the techniques discussed in this book can be traced to individuals and organizations that have applied the principles of scientific management first developed by Taylor; they are discussed in *History* boxes scattered throughout the book.

pletely before the next is started; in most cases one or more of these steps will be modified to some extent before the final results are implemented. This would cause all of the subsequent steps to be changed. In some cases, testing the solution might reveal that the model or the input data are not correct. This would mean that all steps that follow defining the problem would need to be modified.

Defining the Problem

The first step in the quantitative approach is to develop a clear, concise statement of the *problem*. This statement will give direction and meaning to the following steps.

In many cases, defining the problem is the most important and the most difficult step. It is essential to go beyond the symptoms of the problem and identify the true causes. One problem may be related to other problems; solving one problem without regard to other related problems can make the entire situation worse. Thus, it is important to analyze how the solution to one problem affects other problems or the situation in general.

Defining the problem can be the most important step.

It is likely that an organization will have several problems. However, a quantitative analysis group usually cannot deal with all of an organization's problems at one time. Thus, it is usually necessary to concentrate on only a few problems. For most companies, this means selecting those problems whose solutions will result in the greatest increase in profits or reduction in costs to the company. The importance of selecting the right problems to solve cannot be overemphasized. Experience has shown that bad problem definition is a major reason for failure of management science or operations research groups to serve their organizations well.

Concentrate on only a few problems.

When the problem is difficult to quantify, it may be necessary to develop *specific*, *measurable* objectives. A problem might be inadequate health care delivery in a hospital. The objectives might be to increase the number of beds, reduce the average number of days a patient spends in the hospital, increase the physician-to-patient ratio, and so on. When objectives are used, however, the real problem should be kept in mind. It is important to avoid obtaining specific and measurable objectives that may not solve the real problem.

Developing a Model

Once we select the problem to be analyzed, the next step is to develop a *model*. Simply stated, a model is a representation (usually mathematical) of a situation.

Even though you might not have been aware of it, you have been using models most of your life. You may have developed models about people's behavior. Your model might be that friendship is based on reciprocity, an exchange of favors. If you need a favor such as a small loan, your model would suggest that you ask a good friend.

IN ACTION   **The Indispensable Role of Management Science at Reynolds**

As the title of this box implies, quantitative approaches can be indispensable in helping companies such as the Reynolds Metals Company. Headquartered in Richmond, Virginia, Reynolds Metals Company is a Fortune 75 metals producer. Its aluminum operation includes production, mining, and the use of recycled aluminum. Of the company's $6 billion in sales in a recent year, more than 94% was in value-added fabricated products, including aluminum cans, flexible packaging, and a variety of consumer products.

In order to provide a more effective shipping operation, Reynolds decided to use management science to control shipping and reduce transportation costs. The result was the use of an integer programming model (see Chapter 11) that had the minimization of central dispatch freight cost as a primary objective. Using the annual shipping demand patterns, this quantitative analysis technique was able to improve on-time delivery of shipments and reduce freight costs by more than $7 million annually. As a company spokesperson said: "The confidence and respect I have for the management science discipline gave me the resolve to stick to the project plan when others doubted it could be done. I am very pleased to report today that the results that were predicted are being achieved. Management science made the difference between success and failure for this venture."

Source: W. Moore, J. Warmke, and L. Gorban. *Interfaces* 21, 1 (January–February 1991): 107–129.

The types of models include physical, scale, schematic, and mathematical models.

Of course, there are many other types of models. Architects sometimes make a *physical model* of a building that they will construct. Engineers develop *scale models* of chemical plants, called pilot plants. A *schematic model* is a picture, drawing, or chart of reality. Automobiles, lawn mowers, gears, fans, typewriters, and numerous other devices have schematic models (drawings and pictures) that reveal how these devices work. What sets quantitative analysis apart from other techniques is that the models that are used are mathematical. A *mathematical model* is a set of mathematical relationships. In most cases, these relationships are expressed in equations and inequalities, as they are in a spreadsheet model that computes sums, averages, or standard deviations.

Although there is considerable flexibility in the development of models, most of the models presented in this book contain one or more variables and parameters. A *variable*, as the name implies, is a measurable quantity that may vary or is subject to change. Variables can be *controllable* or *uncontrollable*. A controllable variable is also called a *decision variable*. An example would be how many inventory items to order. A *parameter* is a measurable quantity that is inherent in the problem. The cost of placing an order for more inventory items is an example of a parameter. In most cases, variables are unknown quantities, while parameters are known quantities. All models should be developed carefully. They should be solvable, realistic, and easy to understand and modify, and the required *input data* should be obtainable. The model developer has to be careful to include the appropriate amount of detail to be solvable, yet realistic.

Acquiring Input Data

Garbage in, garbage out means that improper data will result in misleading results.

Once we have developed a model, we must obtain the data that are used in the model (input data). Obtaining accurate data for the model is essential, since even if the model is a perfect representation of reality, improper data will result in misleading results. This situation is called garbage in, garbage out (GIGO). For a larger problem, collecting accurate data can be one of the most difficult steps in performing quantitative analysis.

There are a number of sources that can be used in collecting data. In some cases, company reports and documents can be used to obtain the necessary data. Another source is interviews with employees or other persons related to the firm. These individuals can sometimes provide excellent information, and their experience and judgment can be invaluable. A production supervisor, for example, might be able to tell you with a great degree of accuracy the amount of time that it takes to produce a particular product. Sampling and direct measurement provide other sources of data for the model. You may need to know how many pounds of a raw material are used in producing a new photochemical product. This information can be obtained by going to the plant and actually measuring with scales the amount of raw material that is being used. In other cases, statistical sampling procedures can be used to obtain data.

Developing a Solution

Developing a solution involves manipulating the model to arrive at the best (optimal) solution to the problem. In some cases, this requires that an equation be solved for the best decision. In other cases, you can use a *trial and error* method, trying various approaches and picking the one that results in the best decision. For some problems, you may wish to try all possible values for the variables in the model to arrive at the best decision. This is called *complete enumeration*. This book will also show you how to solve very difficult and complex problems by repeating a few simple steps until you find the best solution. A series of steps or procedures that are repeated is called an *algorithm*, named after Algorismus, an Arabic mathematician of the ninth century.

The accuracy of the solution depends on the accuracy of the input data and the model. If the input data are accurate to only two significant digits, then the results can be accurate to only two significant digits. For example, the results of dividing 2.6 by 1.4 should be 1.9, not 1.857142857.

The input data and model determine the accuracy of the solution.

Testing the Solution

Before a solution can be analyzed and implemented, it needs to be tested completely. Because the solution depends on the input data and the model, both require testing.

Testing the input data and the model includes determining the accuracy and completeness of the data used by the model. Inaccurate data will lead to an inaccurate solution. There are several ways to test input data. One method of testing the data is to collect additional data from a different source. If the original data were collected using interviews, perhaps some additional data can be collected by direct measurement or sampling. These additional data can then be compared with the original data, and statistical tests can be employed to determine whether there are differences between the original data and the additional data. If there are significant differences, more effort is required to obtain accurate input data. If the data are accurate but the results are inconsistent with the problem, the model may not be appropriate. The model can be checked to make sure that it is logical and represents the real situation.

Testing the data and model is done before the results are analyzed.

Although most of the quantitative techniques discussed in this book have been computerized, you will probably be required to solve a number of problems by hand. To help detect both logical and computational mistakes, you should check the results to make sure that they are consistent with the structure of the problem. For example (1.96) (301.7) is close to (2) (300), which is equal to 600. If your computations are significantly different from 600, you know you have made a mistake.

Analyzing the Results and Sensitivity Analysis

Analyzing the results starts with determining the implications of the solution. In most cases, a solution to a problem will result in some kind of action or change in the way an organization is operating. The implications of these actions or changes must be determined and analyzed before the results are implemented.

Because a model is only an approximation of reality, the sensitivity of the solution to changes in the model and input data is a very important part of analyzing the results. This type of analysis is called *sensitivity analysis* or *postoptimality analysis*. It determines how much the solution will change if there were changes in the model or the input data. When

Sensitivity analysis determines how the solutions will change with a different model or input data.

the solution is sensitive to changes in the input data and the model specification, additional testing should be performed to make sure that the model and input data are accurate and valid. If the model or data are wrong, the solution could be wrong, resulting in financial losses or reduced profits.

The importance of sensitivity analysis cannot be overemphasized. Because input data may not always be accurate or model assumptions may not be completely appropriate, sensitivity analysis can become an important part of the quantitative analysis approach. Most of the chapters in the book cover the use of sensitivity analysis as part of the decision-making and problem-solving process.

Implementing the Results

The final step is to *implement* the results. This is the process of incorporating the solution into the company. This can be much more difficult than you would imagine. Even if the solution is optimal and will result in millions of dollars in additional profits, if managers

---

MODELING IN THE REAL WORLD   **Planning China's Coal and Electricity Delivery System**

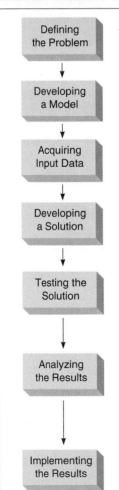

China produces about 1.1 billion tons of coal each year. Demand, however, is estimated to be about 1.6 billion tons. In addition, China faced air pollution problems that could threaten its high gross national product (GNP) growth rate. These problems were identified by the Chinese State Planning Commission and the World Bank as important to the continued growth of the GNP.

In order to analyze some of the problems associated with the delivery of coal and electricity, the Chinese State Planning Commission developed a comprehensive model, called the Coal Transport Study (CTS) model. The model specified key components in the generation, transmission, and demand for electricity.

In addition to historical data, the model requires forecasts of future demand and the potential environmental impact of various energy sources and uses. In addition, specific data concerning the various stages of coal and electricity production are needed.

Instead of developing and reporting one solution, the quantitative analysis team analyzed 16 different solutions or possibilities. These solutions revealed that the investment in new coal–electricity systems could be as high as $250 billion over a ten-year period. The new system would have to deliver about 2 billion tons of coal.

Assumptions of the model and the solution were carefully tested. About a half-a-year was spent in testing the data, the model, and the solutions. This included running a series of tests on the data and model using known data to make sure that the data and model produced results consistent with the current situation. This testing resulted in fine tuning the data and model to make them more accurate. After testing, corrections and adjustments were made to make sure that the results were as accurate as possible.

The solutions also resulted in major findings. First, the government should plan on an 8% to 9% growth in power needs. Second, railways will continue to be the dominant transportation system for coal. Next, coal distribution can be greatly increased by increasing the volume and length of coastal and inland waterways. The chance of building and using slurry pipelines was slim. In addition, there were a number of specific findings on how coal should be handled and processed into energy to reduce pollution and negative environmental consequences.

Implementation of the CTS model resulted in a new steam coal-washing procedure, the construction of improved railway systems and a new port, and the use of coal imports. In addition, the planning commission has developed a sophisticated model for strategic-level investment planning. The model will be extended to perform energy planning to the year 2010.

Source: M. Kuby, et al. "Planning China's Coal and Electricity Delivery System," *Interfaces* 25 (January–February 1995): 41.

resist the new solution, all of the efforts of the analysis are of no value. Experience has shown that a large number of quantitative analysis teams have failed in their efforts because they have failed to implement a good, workable solution properly.

After the solution has been implemented, it should be closely monitored. Over time, there may be numerous changes that call for modifications of the original solution. A changing economy, fluctuating demand, and model enhancements requested by managers and decision makers are only a few examples of changes that might require the analysis to be modified.

The QA Approach and Modeling in the Real World

The quantitative analysis approach is not a series of theoretical steps that are not used in the real world. These steps, first seen in Figure 1.1 and described in this section, are the building blocks of any successful use of quantitative analysis. As seen in our first *Modeling in the Real World* box, the steps of the quantitative analysis approach can be used to help a large country such as China plan for critical energy needs now and for decades into the future. Throughout this book, you will see how the steps of the quantitative analysis approach are used to help countries and companies of all sizes save millions of dollars, plan for the future, increase revenues, and provide higher-quality products and services. The *Modeling in the Real World* boxes in every chapter will demonstrate to you the power and importance of quantitative analysis in solving real problems for real organizations. Using the steps of quantitative analysis, however, does not guarantee success. These steps must be applied carefully.

1.4   HOW TO DEVELOP A QUANTITATIVE ANALYSIS MODEL

Developing a model is an important part of the quantitative analysis approach. Let's see how we can use the following mathematical model, which represents profits:

Profits = Revenue − Expenses

In many cases, we can express revenues as price per unit multiplied times the number of units sold. Expenses can often be determined by summing fixed costs and variable cost. Variable cost is often expressed as variable costs per unit multiplied times the number of units. Thus, we can also express profits as the following mathematical model:

Expenses include fixed and variable costs.

Profits = (Price per Unit)(Number of Units Sold) − Fixed Costs
  − (Variable Costs per Unit)(Number of Units Sold).   **(1-1)**

We will use the Bill Pritchett clock repair shop example to demonstrate the use of mathematical models. Bill's company, Pritchett's Precious Time Pieces, buys, sells, and repairs old clocks and clock parts. Bill sells rebuilt springs for a price per unit of $10. The fixed cost of the equipment to build the springs is $1,000. The variable cost per unit is $5 for spring material. If we represent the number of springs (units) as the variable X, we can restate the profit model as follows:

Profits = $10X − $1,000 − $5X

If sales are 0, Bill will realize a $1,000 loss. If sales are 1,000 units, he will realize a profit of $4,000. ($4,000 = ($10)(1,000) − $1,000 − ($5)(1,000)). See if you can determine the profit for other values of units sold.

The BEP results in $0 profits.

In addition to the profit models shown here, decision makers are often interested in the **break-even point (BEPs)**. The break-even point is the number of units sold that will result in $0 profits. We set profits equal to $0 and solve for X, the number of units at the breakeven point:

0 = (Price per Unit)(Number of Units) − Fixed Costs
− (Variable Costs per Unit)(Number of Units)

This can be rewritten as

(Price per Unit)(Number of Units) − (Variable Costs per Unit) (Number of Units)
= Fixed Costs

or

(Price per Unit − Variable Costs per Unit)(Number of Units)
= Fixed Costs

Dividing both sides by **(Price per Unit − Variable Costs per Unit)**, we can compute the BEP as follows:

Number of Units (BEP) = Fixed Costs/(Price per Unit − Variable
Costs per Unit)   **(1-2)**

For the Pritchett's Precious Time Pieces example, the BEP can be computed as follows:

BEP = $1,000/($10 − $5) = 200 units or springs at the break-even point

The Advantages of Mathematical Modeling

There are a number of advantages of using mathematical models:

1. Models can accurately represent reality. If properly formulated, a model can be extremely accurate. A **valid model** is one that is accurate and correctly represents the problem or system under investigation. The above profit model is accurate and valid for many business problems.

2. Models can help a decision maker formulate problems. In the profit model, for example, a decision maker can determine the important factors or contributors to revenues and expenses, such as sales, returns, selling expenses, production costs, transportation costs, and so on.

3. Models can give us insight and information. For example, using the profit model from the preceding section, we can see what impact changes in revenues and expenses will have on profits. As discussed in the previous section, studying the impact of changes in a model, such as a profit model, is called sensitivity analysis.

4. Models can save time and money in decision making and problem solving. It usually takes less time, effort, and expense to analyze a model. We can use a profit model to analyze the impact of a new marketing campaign on profits, revenues, and expenses. In most cases, using models is faster and less expensive that actually trying a new marketing campaign in a real business setting and observing the results.

5. A model may be the only way to solve some large or complex problems in a timely fashion. A large company, for example, may produce literally thousands of sizes of nuts, bolts, and fasteners. The company may want to make the highest profits possible given its manufacturing constraints. A mathematical model may be the only way to determine the highest profits the company can achieve under these circumstances.

6. A model can be used to communicate problems and solutions to others. A decision analyst can share his or her work with other decision analysts. Solutions to a mathematical model can be given to managers and executives to help them make final decisions.

Mathematical Models Categorized by Risk

Some mathematical models, like the profit and breakeven models previously discussed, do not involve risk or chance. We assume that we know all values used in the model with complete certainty. These are called **deterministic models**. A company, for example, might want to minimize manufacturing costs while maintaining a certain quality level. If we know all these values with certainty, the model is deterministic.

Deterministic means complete certainty.

Other models involve risk or chance. For example, the market for a new product might be "good" with a chance of 60% (a probability of 0.6) or "not good" with a chance of 40% (a probability of 0.4). Models that involve chance or risk, often measured as a probability value, are called **probabilistic models**. In this book, we will investigate both deterministic and probabilistic models.

1.5 THE ROLE OF COMPUTERS AND SPREADSHEET MODELS IN THE QUANTITATIVE ANALYSIS APPROACH

Developing a solution, testing the solution, and analyzing the results are important steps in the quantitative analysis approach. Because we will be using mathematical models, these steps require mathematical calculations. Fortunately, we can use the computer to make these steps easier. Four programs that allow you to solve many of the problems found in this book are provided in the attached CD-ROM:

1. **QM for Windows**, which is an easy-to-use decision support program developed specifically for this text. Program 1.1 shows the main menu of QM for Windows.

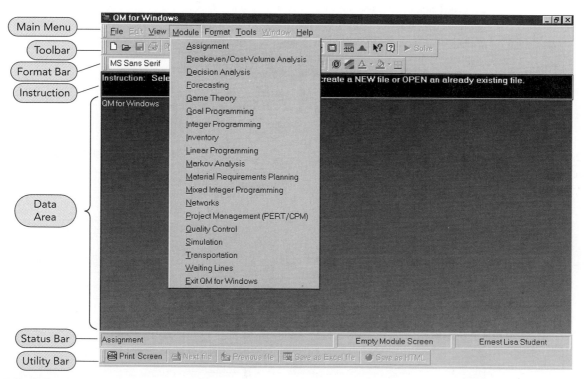

PROGRAM 1.1

QM for Window's Main Menu of Quantitative Models

Appendix D and appendices at the end of many chapters show how this powerful computer program can be used to solve quantitative analysis problems.

2. **Excel QM**, which can also be used to solve many of the problems discussed in this book works automatically within Excel spreadsheets. Excel QM makes using a spreadsheet even easier by providing custom menus and solution procedures that guide you through every step. Program 1.2 shows the main menu for Excel QM and the quantitative models this program can solve. Appendix E also provides further details on how to install and use this program. To solve the breakeven problem discussed in Section 1.4, we illustrate Excel QM features in Program 1.3A and 1.3B.

3. **Crystal Ball**, also an Excel add-in, can be used to solve simulation problems. This topic is addressed in Chapter 15.

4. **Treeplan**, another Excel add-in, is used in Chapter 4 to solve certain decision-making problems.

Add-in programs make Excel, which is already a wonderful tool for modeling, even more powerful in solving quantitative analysis problems. Excel QM, Crystal Ball, Treeplan, and the Excel files used in the examples used throughout this text are also included with the CD-ROM that accompanies this text. There are two other powerful Excel built-in features that make solving quantitative analysis problems easier:

1. **Solver.** Solver is an optimization technique that can maximize or minimize a quantity given a set of limitations or constraints. We will be using Solver throughout the text to solve optimization problems. It is described in detail in the appendix to Chapter 7 and used in Chapters 7, 8, 9, 10, 11, 12, and 13.

2. **Goal Seek.** This feature of Excel allows you to specify a goal or target (Set Cell) and what variable (Changing Cell) that you want Excel to change in order to achieve a desired goal. Bill Pritchett, for example, would like to determine what price he would need to lower the BEP from 200 springs to 175 springs. Program 1.4 shows how Goal Seek can be used to make the necessary calculations.

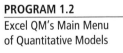

PROGRAM 1.2

Excel QM's Main Menu of Quantitative Models

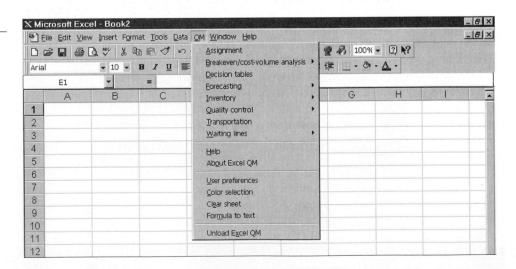

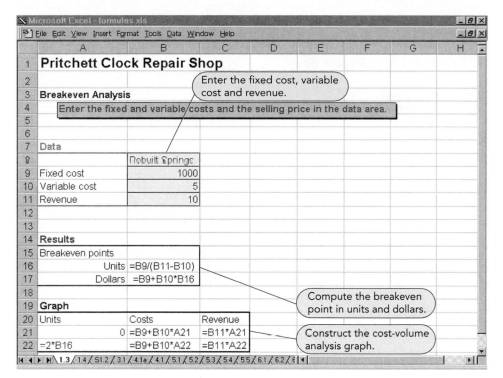

PROGRAM 1.3A

The Input Data for the
Breakeven Problem

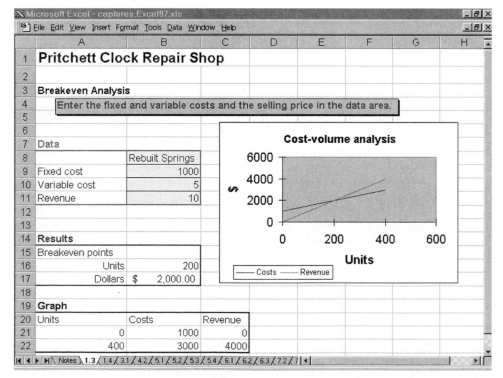

PROGRAM 1.3B

The Solution to the
Breakeven Problem

PROGRAM 1.4

Using Goal Seek in the
Breakeven Problem

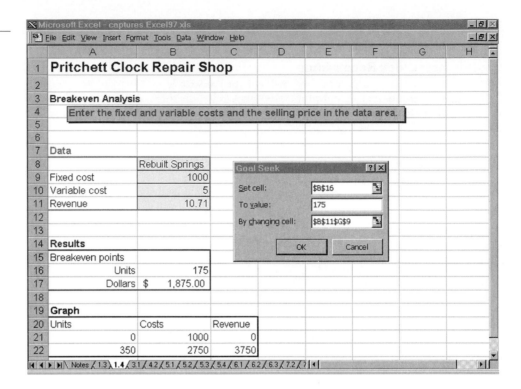

   1.6   **POSSIBLE PROBLEMS IN THE QA APPROACH**

We have presented the quantitative analysis approach as a logical, systematic means of tackling decision-making problems. Even when these steps are followed carefully, there are many difficulties that can hurt the chances of implementing solutions to real-world problems. We now take a look at what can happen during each of the steps.

IN ACTION   **Better Modeling for Better Pollution Control**

It is often difficult to balance economic returns with pollution control. When pollution is a problem, modeling industrial facilities can maintain high profitability while achieving pollution control guidelines and laws. This was the situation in Chile.

Chile is the world's largest producer of copper, producing 2.2 million tons of the metal in 1994. This large copper production represents about 8% of the country's gross domestic product (GDP). Although private businesses operate about 50% of copper mining operations, Chile controls most of the refining. Unfortunately, the production of copper produces solid, liquid, and gas by-products that end up in the environment. As a result, the Chilean government decided to enact pollution and air quality standards for many of the by-products of the copper mining process.

To help meet pollution and air quality standards, a quantitative optimization model was developed. The objective of the model was to minimize the costs of copper mining while maintaining pollution and air quality standards set by the Chilean government. The model resulted in a number of changes. First, the model solution was substantially different from the clean-up plans that were developed before the model solution. As a result, many of the early clean-up plans were delayed, redone, or scrapped. In addition, some previously developed pollution and air quality clean-up plans were approved because they were consistent with the solution from the model. Furthermore, the model provided critical input to a computerized decision support system to analyze the impact of various copper mining strategies on total costs and pollution control. The result of this optimization model is a cleaner environment at minimal cost.

Source: Mondschein, et al. "Optimal Investment Policies for Pollution Control in the Copper Industry," *Interfaces 27* (November–December 1997): 69.

Defining the Problem

One view of decision makers is that they sit at a desk all day long waiting until a problem arises and then stand up and attack the problem until it is solved. Once it is solved, they sit down, relax, and wait for the next big problem. In the worlds of business, government, and education, problems are, unfortunately, not easily identified. There are four roadblocks that quantitative analysts face in defining a problem. We use an application, inventory analysis, throughout this section as an example.

Conflicting Viewpoints The first difficulty is that quantitative analysts must often consider conflicting viewpoints in defining the problem. For example, there are at least two views that managers take when dealing with inventory problems. Financial managers usually feel that inventory is too high, as inventory represents cash not available for other investments. Sales managers, on the other hand, often feel that inventory is too low, as high levels of inventory may be needed to fill an unexpected order. If analysts assume either one of these statements as the problem definition, they have essentially accepted one manager's perception and can expect resistance from the other manager when the "solution" emerges. So it's important to consider both points of view before stating the problem.

Impact on Other Departments The next difficulty is that problems do not exist in isolation and are not owned by just one department of a firm. Inventory is closely tied with cash flows and various production problems. A change in ordering policy can seriously hurt cash flows and upset production schedules to the point that savings on inventory are more than offset by increased costs for finance and production. The problem statement should thus be as broad as possible and include the input from all departments that have a stake in the solution.

Beginning Assumptions The third difficulty is that people have a tendency to state problems in terms of solutions. The statement that inventory is too low implies a solution that inventory levels should be raised. The quantitative analyst who starts off with this assumption will probably indeed find that inventory should be raised. From an implementation standpoint, a "good" solution to the *right* problem is much better than an "optimal" solution to the *wrong* problem.

Solution Outdated Even with the best of problem statements, however, there is a fourth danger. The problem can change as the model is being developed. In our rapidly changing business environment, it is not unusual for problems to appear or disappear virtually overnight. The analyst who presents a solution to a problem that no longer exists can't expect credit for providing timely help.

Developing a Model

Fitting the Textbook Models One problem in developing quantitative models is that a manager's perception of a problem won't always match the textbook approach. Most inventory models involve minimizing the total of holding and ordering costs. Some managers view these costs as unimportant; instead, they see the problem in terms of cash flow, turnover, and levels of customer satisfaction. Results of a model based on holding and ordering costs are probably not acceptable to such managers.

Understanding the Model A second major concern involves the trade-off between the complexity of the model and ease of understanding. Managers simply will not use the results of a model they do not understand. Complex problems, though, require complex models. One trade-off is to simplify assumptions in order to make the model easier to understand. The model loses some of its reality but gains some acceptance by management.

One simplifying assumption in inventory modeling is that demand is known and constant. This means that probability distributions are not needed and it allows us to build simple, easy-to-understand models. Demand, however, is rarely known and constant, so the model we build lacks some reality. Introducing probability distributions provides more realism but may put comprehension beyond all but the most mathematically sophisticated managers. One approach is for the quantitative analyst to start with the simple model and make sure that it is completely understood. Later, more complex models can be introduced slowly as managers gain more confidence in using the new approach.

Acquiring Input Data

Gathering the data to be used in the quantitative approach to problem solving is often no simple task. One-fifth of all firms in a recent study had difficulty with data access.

Using Accounting Data One problem is that most data generated in a firm come from basic accounting reports. The accounting department collects its inventory data, for example, in terms of cash flows and turnover. But quantitative analysts tackling an inventory problem need to collect data on holding costs and ordering costs. If they ask for such data, they may be shocked to find that the data were simply never collected for those specified costs.

Gene Woolsey, former editor of the journal *Interfaces*, tells a story of a young quantitative analyst sent down to accounting to get "the inventory holding cost per item per day for part 23456/AZ." The accountant asked the young man if he wanted the first-in, first-out figure, the last-in, first-out figure, the lower of cost or market figure, or the "how-we-do-it" figure. The young man replied that the inventory model required only one number. The accountant at the next desk said, "Hell, Joe, give the kid a number." The kid was given a number and departed.[1]

Validity of Data A lack of "good, clean data" means that whatever data are available must often be distilled and manipulated (we call it "fudging") before being used in a model. Unfortunately, the validity of the results of a model is no better than the validity of the data that go into the model. You cannot blame a manager for resisting a model's "scientific" results when he or she knows that questionable data were used as input.

Developing a Solution

Hard-to-understand mathematics and one answer can be a problem in developing a solution.

Hard-to-Understand Mathematics The first concern in developing solutions is that although the mathematical models we use may be complex and powerful, they may not be completely understood. Fancy solutions to problems may have faulty logic or data. The aura of mathematics often causes managers to remain silent when they should be critical. The well-known operations researcher C. W. Churchman cautions that "because mathematics has been so revered a discipline in recent years, it tends to lull the unsuspecting into believing that he who thinks elaborately thinks well."[2]

---

[1] R. E. D. Woolsey. "The Measure of MS/OR Application or Let's Hear It for the Bean Counters," *Interfaces* 5, 2 (February 1975).

[2] C. W. Churchman. "Relativity Models in the Social Sciences," *Interfaces* 4, 1 (November 1973).

Only One Answer Is Limiting The second problem is that quantitative models usually give just one answer to a problem. Most managers would like to have a *range* of options and not be put in a take-it-or-leave-it position. A more appropriate strategy is for an analyst to present a range of options, indicating the effect that each solution has on the objective function. This gives managers a choice as well as information on how much it will cost to deviate from the optimal solution. It also allows problems to be viewed from a broader perspective, since nonquantitative factors can be considered.

Testing the Solution

The results of QA often take the form of predictions of how things will work in the future if certain changes are made now. To get a preview of how well solutions will really work, managers are often asked how good the solution looks to them. The problem is that complex models tend to give solutions that are not intuitively obvious. And such solutions tend to be rejected by managers. The quantitative analyst now has the chance to work through the model and the assumptions with the manager in an effort to convince the manager of the validity of the results. In the process of convincing the manager, the analyst will have to review every assumption that went into the model. If there are errors, they may be revealed during this review. In addition, the manager will be casting a critical eye on everything that went into the model, and if he or she can be convinced that the model is valid, there is a good chance that the solution results are also valid.

Assumptions should be reviewed.

Analyzing the Results

Once the solution has been tested, the results must be analyzed in terms of how they will affect the total organization. You should be aware that even small changes in organizations are often difficult to bring about. If the results indicate large changes in organization policy, the quantitative analyst can expect resistance. In analyzing the results, the analyst should ascertain who must change and by how much, if the people who must change will be better or worse off, and who has the power to direct the change.

 IN ACTION   **Bellcore's SONET Decision Support System**

Bellcore is a company that provides high-capacity fiber-optic technologies. Its primary clients are the regional Bell operating companies that provide local phone service. These regional Bell operating companies are expected to purchase tens of billions of dollars of fiber-optic equipment and systems in the future to replace and supplement existing copper-based phone cables.

In order to make best use of fiber-optic systems, Bellcore developed the Synchronous Optical NETwork (SONET) standard. The SONET toolkit is a decision support system used to help in planning and designing a telecommunications network. The decision support system uses a number of models to help in planning and designing activities. As discussed in this chapter, model development is an important step in the quantitative analysis approach. The SONET model includes network, demand, equipment, and architecture models. The network model is a schematic model that is usually represented as a graph. The demand module is a mathematical model that estimates future demand for channels and networks. The equipment model is used to plan the needed equipment, and the architecture model is used to specify an overall structure for the telecommunications system.

The SONET decision support system has saved up to 30% in better designed systems compared with traditional design approaches on telecommunications networks. In addition, the toolkit can save a substantial amount of time. Network planning and design, which could take months to complete, can now be completed with SONET in a few days.

Source: S. Cosares, et al. "SONET Toolkit: A Decision Support System for Designing Robust and Cost-Effective Fiber-Optic Networks," *Interfaces* 25 (January–February 1995): 20.

1.7   IMPLEMENTATION—NOT JUST THE FINAL STEP

We have just presented some of the many problems that can affect the ultimate acceptance of the quantitative analysis approach and use of its models. It should be clear now that implementation isn't just another step that takes place after the modeling process is over. Each one of these steps greatly affects the chances of implementing the results of a quantitative study.

Lack of Commitment and Resistance to Change

Even though many business decisions can be made intuitively, based on hunches and experience, there are more and more situations in which quantitative models can assist. Some managers, however, fear that the use of a formal analysis process will reduce their decision-making power. Others fear that it may expose some previous intuitive decisions as inadequate. Still others just feel uncomfortable about having to reverse their thinking patterns with formal decision making. These managers often argue against the use of quantitative methods.

Many action-oriented managers do not like the lengthy formal decision-making process and prefer to get things done quickly. They prefer "quick and dirty" techniques that can yield immediate results. Once managers see some quick results that have a substantial payoff, the stage is set for convincing them that quantitative analysis is a beneficial tool.[3]

Management support and user involvement are important.

We have known for some time that management support and user involvement are critical to the successful implementation of quantitative analysis projects. A Swedish study found that only 40% of projects suggested by quantitative analysts were ever implemented. But 70% of the quantitative projects initiated by users, and fully 98% of projects suggested by top managers, *were* implemented.

Lack of Commitment by Quantitative Analysts

Just as manager attitudes are to blame for some implementation problems, analysts' attitudes are to blame for others. When the quantitative analyst is not an integral part of the department facing the problem, he or she sometimes tends to treat the modeling activity as an end in itself. That is, the analyst accepts the problem as stated by the manager and builds a model to solve only that problem. When the results are computed, he or she hands them back to the manager and considers the job done. The analyst who does not care whether these results help make the final decision is not concerned with implementation.

Successful implementation requires that the analyst not *tell* the users what to do, but work with them and take their feelings into account. An article in *Operations Research* describes an inventory control system that calculated reorder points and order quantities. But instead of insisting that computer-calculated quantities be ordered, a manual override feature was installed. This allowed users to disregard the calculated figures and substitute their own. The override was used quite often when the system was first installed. Gradually, however, as users came to realize that the calculated figures were right more often than not, they allowed the system's figures to stand. Eventually, the override feature was used only in special circumstances. This is a good example of how good relationships can aid in model implementation.

---

[3] R. Nebike. "Five Suggestions to Save OR," *OR/MS Today* (August 1995): 10–11.

Summary

Quantitative analysis is the scientific approach to decision making. The quantitative analysis approach includes defining the problem, developing a model, acquiring input data, developing a solution, testing the solution, analyzing the results, and implementing the results. In using the quantitative approach, however, there can be potential problems, including conflicting viewpoints, the impact of quantitative analysis models on other departments, beginning assumptions, outdated solutions, fitting textbook models, understanding the model, acquiring good input data, hard-to-understand mathematics, obtaining only one answer, testing the solution, and analyzing the results. In using the quantitative analysis approach, implementation is not the final step. There can be a lack of commitment to the approach and resistance to change.

Glossary

Quantitative Analysis or **Management Science.** A scientific approach using quantitative techniques as a tool in decision making.

Problem. A statement, which should come from a manager, that indicates a problem to be solved or an objective or goal to be reached.

Model. A representation of reality or of a real-life situation.

Mathematical Model. A model that uses mathematical equations and statements to represent the relationships within the model.

Input Data. Data that are used in a model in arriving at the final solution.

Algorithm. A set of logical and mathematical operations performed in a specific sequence.

Sensitivity Analysis. Determining how sensitive a solution is to changes in the formulation of a problem.

Key Equations

(1-1)   Profits = (Price per Unit)(Number of Units Sold) − Fixed Costs − (Variable Costs per Unit)(Number of Units Sold).

An equation to determine profits as a function of the price per unit, number of units sold, fixed costs, and variable costs.

(1-2)   Number of Units (BEP) = Fixed Costs/(Price per Unit − Variable Costs per Unit)

An equation to determine the break-even point in units as a function of fixed costs, variable costs, and the price per unit.

SELF-TEST

- Before taking the self-test, refer back to the learning objectives at the beginning of the chapter, the notes in the margins, and the glossary at the end of the chapter.
- Use the key at the back of the book to correct your answers.
- Restudy pages that correspond to any questions that you answered incorrectly or material you feel uncertain about.

1. In analyzing a problem you should normally study
   a. the qualitative aspects.
   b. the quantitative aspects.
   c. both a and b.
   d. neither a nor b.
2. Quantitative analysis is
   a. a logical approach to decision making.
   b. a rational approach to decision making.
   c. a scientific approach to decision making.
   d. all of the above.
3. Frederick Winslow Taylor
   a. was a military researcher during World War II.
   b. pioneered the principles of scientific management.
   c. developed the use of the algorithm for QA.
   d. all of the above.
4. The most important and often the most difficult step in the scientific method is
   a. developing a model.
   b. acquiring input data.
   c. defining the problem.
   d. developing a solution.
5. A physical model is an example of
   a. an iconic model.
   b. a schematic model.
   c. a mathematical model.
   d. a stochastic model.

6. The term algorithm
   a. is named after Algorismus.
   b. is named after a ninth-century Arabic mathematician.
   c. describes a series of steps or procedures to be repeated.
   d. all of the above.
7. An analysis to determine how much a solution would change if there are changes in the model or the input data is called
   a. sensitivity or postoptimality analysis.
   b. schematic or iconic analysis.
   c. futurama conditioning.
   d. both b and c.
8. Decision variables are
   a. controllable.
   b. uncontrollable.
   c. parameters.
   d. constant numerical values associated with any complex problem.
9. _____ is the scientific approach to managerial decision making.
10. _____ is the first step in quantitative analysis.
11. A _____ is a picture, drawing, or chart of reality.
12. A series of steps that are repeated until a solution is found is called a(n) _____ .

Discussion Questions

1-1 What is the difference between quantitative and qualitative analysis? Give several examples.

1-2 Define *quantitative analysis*. What are some of the organizations that support the use of the scientific approach?

1-3 What is the quantitative analysis process? Give several examples of this process.

1-4 Briefly trace the history of quantitative analysis. What happened to the development of quantitative analysis during World War II?

1-5 Give some examples of various types of models. What is a mathematical model? Develop two examples of mathematical models.

1-6 List some sources of input data.

1-7 What is implementation, and why is it important?

1-8 Describe the use of sensitivity analysis and postoptimality analysis in analyzing the results.

1-9 Managers are quick to claim that quantitative analysts talk to them in a jargon that does not sound like English. List four terms that might not be understood by a manager. Then explain in nontechnical terms what each term means.

1-10 Why do you think many quantitative analysts don't like to participate in the implementation process? What could be done to change this attitude?

1-11 Should people who will be using the results of a new quantitative model become involved in the technical aspects of the problem-solving procedure?

1-12 C. W. Churchman once said that "mathematics — tends to lull the unsuspecting into believing that he who thinks elaborately thinks well." Do you think that the best QA models are the ones that are most elaborate and complex mathematically? Why?

Bibliography

Ackoff, R. L. *Scientific Method: Optimizing Applied Research Decisions.* New York: John Wiley & Sons, Inc., 1962.

Churchman, C. W. "Relativity Models in the Social Sciences," *Interfaces* 4, 1 (November 1973).

Churchman, C. W. *The Systems Approach.* New York: Delacort Press, 1968.

Clements, Dale, et al. "Analytical MS/OR Tools Applied to a Plant Closure," *Interfaces* (March 1994): 1.

Cosares, S., et al. "SONET Toolkit: A Decision Support System for Designing Robust and Cost-Effective Fiber-Optic Networks," *Interfaces* 25 (January 1995): 20.

Davis, Joyce. "How to Nurture Creative Sparks," *Fortune* (January 10, 1994): 94. Also see K. MacCrimmon and C. Wagner. "Stimulating Ideas through Creativity Software," *Management Science* (November 1994): 1514.

Ginzberg, M. J. "Finding an Adequate Measure of OR/MS Effectiveness," *Interfaces* 8, 4 (August 1978).

Grayson, C. J. "Management Science and Business Practice," *Harvard Business Review* 51 (1973).

Harris, Carl, "Could You Defend Your Model in Court?" *OR/MS Today* (April 1997): 6.

Kuby, M., et al. "Planning China's Coal and Electricity Delivery System," *Interfaces* 25 (January 1995): 41.

Lancaster, Hal. "Re-engineering Authors Reconsider Re-engineering," *The Wall Street Journal* (January 17, 1995): B1.

Moore, William E., Jr., Janice M. Warmke, and Lonny R. Gorban. "The Indispensable Role of Management Science in Centralizing Freight Operation at Reynolds Metals Company," *Interfaces* 21, 1 (January–February 1991): 107–129.

Salveson, Melvin, "The Institute of Management Science: A Prehistory and Commentary," *Interfaces* 27, 3 (May–June 1997): 74.

Vazsoni, Andrew. "The Purpose of Mathematical Models Is Insight, Not Numbers," *Decision Line* (January 1998): 20.

Venkatakrishnan, C. S. "Optimize Your Career Prospects," *OR/MS Today* (April 1997): 28.

Game Theory

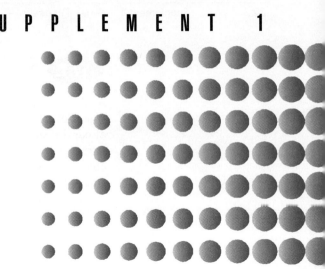

LEARNING OBJECTIVES

After completing this supplement, students will be able to:

1. Understand the principles of zero-sum, two-person games.
2. Analyze pure strategy games and use dominance to reduce the size of a game.
3. Solve mixed strategy games when there is no saddle joint.

SUPPLEMENT OUTLINE

S1.1 Introduction

S1.2 Language of Games

S1.3 Pure Strategy Games

S1.4 Minimax Criterion

S1.5 Mixed Strategy Games

S1.6 Dominance

Summary • Glossary • Solved Problems • Self-Test • Discussion
Questions and Problems • Data Set Problem • Bibliography

Appendix S1.1: Game Theory with QM for Windows

S1.1   INTRODUCTION

As discussed in Chapter 1, competition can be an important decision-making factor. The strategies taken by other organizations or individuals can dramatically affect the outcome of our decisions. In the automobile industry, for example, the strategies of competitors to introduce certain models with certain features can dramatically affect the profitability of other carmakers. Today, businesses cannot make important decisions without considering what other organizations or individuals are doing or might do.

Game theory is one way to consider the impact of the strategies of others on our strategies and outcomes. A *game* is a contest involving two or more decision makers, each of whom wants to win. *Game theory* is the study of how optimal strategies are formulated in conflict.

The study of game theory dates back to 1944, the year in which John von Neumann and Oscar Morgenstern published their classic book, *Theory of Games and Economic Behavior*.[1] Since then, game theory has been used by army generals to plan war strategies, by union negotiators and managers in collective bargaining, and by businesses of all types to determine the best strategies given a competitive business environment.

Game theory continues to be important today. In 1994, John Harsanui, John Nash, and Reinhard Selten jointly received the *Nobel Prize in Economics* from the Royal Swedish Academy of Sciences.[2] In their classic work, these individuals developed the notion of *noncooperative game theory*. After the work of John von Neumann, Nash developed the concepts of the Nash equilibrium and the Nash bargaining problem, which are the cornerstones of modern game theory.

Game models are classified by the *number of players*, the *sum of all payoffs*, and the *number of strategies* employed. Owing to the mathematical complexity of game theory, we limit the analysis in this module to games that are two-person and zero-sum. A *two-person game* is one in which only two parties can play—as in the case of a union and a company in a bargaining session. For simplicity, X and Y represent the two game players. *Zero sum* means that the sum of losses for one player must equal the sum of gains for the other player. Thus, if X wins 20 points or dollars, Y loses 20 points or dollars. With any zero-sum game, the sum of the gains for one player is always equal to the sum of the losses for the other player. When you sum the gains and losses for both players, the result is zero. This is why these games are called *zero-sum games*.

S1.2   LANGUAGE OF GAMES

To introduce you to the notation used in game theory, let us consider a simple game. Suppose that there are only two lighting fixture stores, X and Y, in Urbana, Illinois (this is called a *duopoly*). The respective market shares have been stable up until now, but the situation may change. The daughter of the owner of store X has just completed her MBA and has developed two distinct advertising strategies, one using radio spots and the other newspaper ads. Upon hearing this, the owner of store Y also proceeds to prepare radio and newspaper ads.

The 2×2 payoff matrix in Table S1.1 shows what will happen to current market shares if both stores begin advertising. By convention, payoffs are shown only for the first game player, X in this case. Y's payoffs will just be the negative of each number. For this game, there are only two strategies being used by each player. If store Y had a third strategy, we would be dealing with a 2×3 payoff matrix.

---

[1] J. von Neumann and O. Morgenstern. *Theory of Games and Economic Behavior*, Princeton, NJ: Princeton University Press, 1944.

[2] Rita Koselka. "The Games Businesses Play," *Forbes* (November 7, 1994): 12.

TABLE S1.1   **Store X's Payoff Matrix**

		GAME PLAYER Y's STRATEGIES	
		Y_1 (Use radio)	Y_2 (Use newspaper)
GAME PLAYER X's STRATEGIES	X_1 (Use radio)	2	7
	X_2 (Use newspaper)	6	−4

A positive number in Table S1.1 means that X wins and Y loses. A negative number means that Y wins and X loses. It is obvious from the table that the game favors competitor X, since all values are positive except one. If the game had favored player Y, the values in the table would have been negative. In other words, the game in Table S1.1 is biased against Y. However, since Y must play the game, he or she will play to minimize total losses.

Game Outcomes		
STORE X'S STRATEGY	STORE Y'S STRATEGY	OUTCOME (% CHANGE IN MARKET SHARE)
X_1 (use radio)	Y_1 (use radio)	X wins 2 and Y loses 2
X_1 (use radio)	Y_2 (use newspaper)	X wins 7 and Y loses 7
X_2 (use newspaper)	Y_1 (use radio)	X wins 6 and Y loses 6
X_2 (use newspaper)	Y_2 (use newspaper)	X loses 4 and Y wins 4

 IN ACTION   **Game Theory in the Brewing Business**

Companies that understand the principles and importance of game theory can often select the best competitive strategies. Those companies that don't can face financial loss or even bankruptcy. The successful and unsuccessful selection of competitive gaming strategies can be seen in most industries, including the brewing industry.

In the 1970s, Schlitz was the second-largest brewer in the United States. With its slogan "the beer that made Milwaukee famous", Schlitz was chasing after the leader in beer sales, Anheuser-Busch, maker of Budweiser. Schlitz could either keep its current production output or attempt to produce more beer to compete with Anheuser-Busch. It decided to get more beer to the market in a shorter amount of time. In order to accomplish this, Schlitz selected a strategy of distributing "immature" beer. The result was a cloudy beer that often contained a slimy suspension. The beer and Schlitz's market share and profitability went down the drain. Anheuser-Busch, Miller, and Coors became the market leaders.

Similarly when Miller decided to first market Miller Lite, with the slogan "tastes great—less filling," Busch had two possible gaming strategies: to develop its own low-calorie beer or to criticize Miller in its advertising for producing a watered down beer. The strategy it selected was to criticize Miller in its advertising. The strategy didn't work, Miller gained significant market share, and Busch was forced to come out with its own low-calorie beer—Bud Light.

Today, Anheuser-Busch, Miller, Coors, and other large beer manufacturers face new games and new competitors that produce micro-brews, dry beer, and ice beer. Although it is too early to tell what the large beer makers will do and how successful their strategies will be, it appears that their strategy will be to duplicate what these smaller brewers are doing. What is clear, however, is that a knowledge of the fundamentals of game theory can make a big difference.

Source: Philip Van Munching. "American Brewing, Unreal," *The Economist* (September 6, 1997): 24.

S1.3   PURE STRATEGY GAMES

In some games, the strategies each player follows will always be the same regardless of the other player's strategy. This is called a *pure strategy*. A *saddle point* is a situation where both players are facing pure strategies. Strategies for *saddle point games* can be determined without performing any calculations.

Consider the following game. Does it have a saddle point?

| | | SECOND PLAYER's (Y) STRATEGIES | |
		Y_1	Y_2
FIRST PLAYER's (X) STRATEGIES	X_1	3	5
	X_2	1	−2

The answer is *yes*. Here is how we can determine the strategies for *X* and *Y*.

1. *X* will always play strategy X_1. The worst outcome for *X* playing strategy X_1 is +3 points. The best outcome for *X* playing X_2 is +1.

2. Knowing that *X* will always play strategy X_1, *Y* will always play strategy Y_1. *Y* will lose three points by playing Y_1. If Y_2 is played, *Y* will lose five points.

3. Both players have a dominant or pure strategy, and therefore the game has a saddle point. The numerical value of the saddle point is the game outcome. For this example, the saddle point is 3.

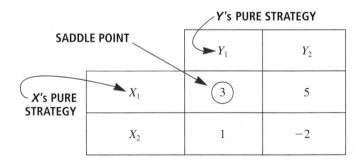

Why do we have a saddle point for this situation? Looking at the payoffs, we can see that *X* will always play strategy X_1. The lowest, or worst, outcome for playing this strategy is better than the best outcome for playing the other strategy, X_2. Thus, player *X* will always play strategy X_1. Knowing this, to minimize losses, *Y* will always play strategy Y_1. The loss for playing strategy Y_1 is 3, while the loss for playing Y_2 is 5.

In reality, players *X* and *Y* may not see the saddle point at first. After the game is played for some time, however, each player will realize that there is only one strategy that should be played. From then on, these players will play only one strategy, which corresponds to the saddle point.

The *value of the game* is the average or expected game outcome if the game is played an infinite number of times. The value of the game for this example is 3. If a game has a saddle point, the value of the game is equal to its numerical value.

You will note that the saddle point in this example, 3, is the largest number in its column and the smallest number in its row. This is true of all saddle points. There is a convenient way of determining whether a game has a saddle point. A saddle point exists if both of the following conditions exist for a number in the table: if it is the largest number in its column, and if it is the smallest number in its row.

S1.4 MINIMAX CRITERION

Minimizing one's maximum losses is identical to maximizing one's minimum gains. In game theory, this is called the *minimax criterion*. This criterion is one approach to selecting strategies that will minimize losses for each player.

The minimax procedure is accomplished as follows. Find the smallest number in each row. Pick the largest of these numbers. This number is called the *lower value* of the game, and the row is X's maximin strategy. Next, find the largest number in each column. Pick the smallest of these numbers. This number is called the *higher value* of the game, and the column is Y's minimax strategy.

If the upper value and lower value of the game are the same, there is a saddle point that is equal to the upper or lower value. This is an alternative method of determining whether or not a saddle point exists. Table S1.2 illustrates how we can determine if there is a saddle point using the minimax criterion. Since the upper value equals the lower value of the game, the saddle point is 6. X's strategy is to play X_1, and Y's strategy is to play Y_2.

T A B L E S 1 . 2   **Example of the Minimax Criterion**

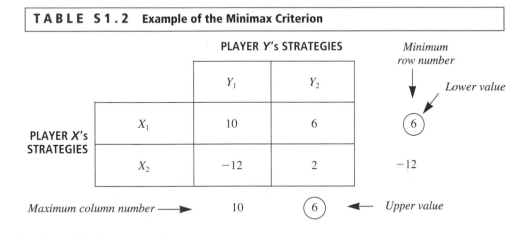

S1.5 MIXED STRATEGY GAMES

When there is no saddle point, players will play each strategy for a certain percentage of the time. This is called a *mixed strategy game*, and the rest of this supplement investigates ways to determine the percentage of the time that each strategy will be played.

For 2×2 games (where both players have only two possible strategies), an algebraic approach can be used to solve for the percentage of the time each strategy is played. The following diagram can be helpful:

	P	$1 - P$
Q		
$1 - Q$		

where

$Q, 1 - Q$ = fraction of the time X plays strategies X_1 and X_2, respectively

$P, 1 - P$ = fraction of the time Y plays strategies Y_1 and Y_2, respectively

The overall objective of each player is to determine the fraction of the time that each strategy is to be played to maximize winnings. Each player desires a strategy that will result in the most winnings no matter what the other player's strategy happens to be.

The solution to the mixed strategy 2×2 game may be found by equating a player's expected winnings for one of the opponent's strategies with his or her expected winnings for the opponent's other strategy. With this approach, X wants to divide his or her plays between the two rows in such a way that the expected winnings from playing the first row will be exactly equal to the expected winnings from playing the second row despite what Y does. In other words, X wants to determine the best possible strategy that is independent of the strategy that player Y will adopt. Thus, it is necessary to equate the expected winnings of strategy X_1, which is row 1, and strategy X_2, which is row 2.

The same approach used to determine X's strategy can be used to determine Y's strategy. Y will want to divide his or her time between the columns in such a way that no matter what X does, Y will minimize his or her losses or maximize its winnings.

Steps for a 2 × 2 Game

1. To find X's best strategy, multiply Q and $1 - Q$ times the appropriate game outcome numbers and solve for Q and $1 - Q$ by setting column 1 equal to column 2 in the game.
2. To find Y's best strategy, multiply P and $1 - P$ times the appropriate game outcome numbers and solve for P and $1 - P$ by setting row 1 equal to row 2 in the game.

 IN ACTION   **Using Game Theory to Shape Strategy at General Motors**

Game theory often assumes that one player or company must lose for another to win. In the auto industry, car companies typically compete by offering rebates and price cuts. This allows one company to gain market share at the expense of other car companies. Although this win-lose strategy works in the short term, competitors quickly follow the same strategy. The result is lower margins and profitability. Indeed, many customers wait until a rebate or price cut is offered before buying a new car. The short-term win-lose strategy turns into a long-term lose-lose result.

By changing the game itself, it is possible to find strategies that can benefit all competitors. This was the case when

General Motors (GM) developed a new credit card that allowed people to apply 5% of their purchases to a new GM vehicle, up to $500 per year with a maximum of $3,500. The credit card program replaced other incentive programs offered by GM. Changing the game helped bring profitability back to GM. In addition, it also helped other car manufacturers who no longer had to compete on price cuts and rebates. In this case, the new game resulted in a win-win situation with GM. Prices, margins, and profitability increased for GM and some of its competitors.

Source: Adam Brandenburger, et al. "The Right Game: Use Game Theory to Shape Strategy," *Harvard Business Review* (July–August 1995): 57.

Here is how you would determine the optimal strategies for X and Y in the following game:

Y's STRATEGIES

X's STRATEGIES		Y_1	Y_2
	X_1	4	2
	X_2	1	10

Step 1: X's Optimal Strategy

	P	$1 - P$
Q	4	2
$1 - Q$	1	10

(a) Column 1 is $4Q + 1(1 - Q)$.

(b) Column 2 is $2Q + 10(1 - Q)$.

(c) Equating column 1 and column 2 gives:
$$4Q + 1(1 - Q) = 2Q + 10(1 - Q).$$

(d) Solving for Q and $1 - Q$ yields the following:
$$4Q - Q - 2Q + 10Q = -1 + 10. \quad Q = \tfrac{9}{11}, \text{ and thus } 1 - Q = 1 - \tfrac{9}{11} = \tfrac{2}{11}.$$

(e) $\tfrac{9}{11}$ and $\tfrac{2}{11}$ represent the fraction of the time X should play X_1 and X_2, respectively.

Handwritten: $4Q + 1 - Q = 2Q + 10 - 10Q$
$3Q + 1 = -8Q + 10$
$11Q = 9$
$Q = \tfrac{9}{11}$
$1 - Q: \ 1 - \tfrac{9}{11} = \tfrac{2}{11}$

Step 2: Y's Optimal Strategy

(a) Row 1 is $4P + 2(1 - P)$.

(b) Row 2 is $1P + 10(1 - P)$.

(c) Equating row 1 and row 2 gives: $4P + 2(1 - P) = 1P + 10(1 - P)$.

(d) Solving for P and $1 - P$ yields the following: $4P - 2P - P + 10P = -2 + 10$.
$P = \tfrac{8}{11}$; $1 - P = \tfrac{3}{11}$.

(e) $\tfrac{8}{11}$ and $\tfrac{3}{11}$ represent the fraction of the time Y should play Y_1 and Y_2, respectively.

Handwritten: $4P + 2(1 - P) = 1P + 10(1 - P)$
$4P + 2 - 2P = 1P + 10 - 10P$
$2P + 2 = -9P + 10$
$11P = 8 \quad P = \tfrac{8}{11}$
$1 - P = 1 - \tfrac{8}{11} = \tfrac{3}{11}$

Once this procedure is understood, it is possible to write the appropriate equations directly from the game. This is shown in the following example game:

	Y_1	Y_2
X_1	-6	-1
X_2	-2	-8

Step 1:

	P	$1 - P$
Q	-6	-1
$1 - Q$	-2	-8

The equation for X's strategy is

$-6Q - 2(1 - Q) = -1Q - 8(1 - Q)$

$-6Q + 2Q + Q - 8Q = 2 - 8$

$Q = \frac{6}{11}, 1 - Q = \frac{5}{11}$

[handwritten marginal notes:]
$-6q - 2(1-q) = -1 - 8(1-q)$
$-6q - 2 + 2q = -1 - 8 + 8q$
$-6q + 2q + q$

Step 2: The equation for Y's strategy is

$-6P - 1(1 - P) = -2P - 8(1 - P)$

$-6P + P + 2P - 8P = +1 - 8$

$P = \frac{7}{11}, 1 - P = \frac{4}{11}$

Once player strategies have been determined, the value of the game can be calculated. The value of the game is the average or expected game outcome after a large number of plays. It can be computed by multiplying each game outcome times the P and Q factors of respective strategies. The results are then added up to obtain the value of the game. The following example shows how the exact calculations are performed:

	Y_1	Y_2
X_1	4	2
X_2	1	10

$Q = \frac{9}{11}$

$1 - Q = \frac{2}{11}$

$P = \frac{8}{11}$

$1 - P = \frac{3}{11}$

The next diagram is usually helpful:

	$P = \frac{8}{11}$	$1 - P = \frac{3}{11}$
$Q = \frac{9}{11}$	4	2
$1 - Q = \frac{2}{11}$	1	10

To get a game outcome of 4, strategies X_1 and Y_1 must be played. The P and Q factors are $\frac{9}{11}$ and $\frac{8}{11}$. Therefore, we multiply 4 times $\frac{9}{11}$ times $\frac{8}{11}$. We do the same for all game outcomes and add the results. The calculations are displayed in the accompanying table.

GAME OUTCOME	P FACTOR	Q FACTOR	
4	$\times \ \frac{9}{11}$	$\times \ \frac{8}{11}$	= 2.38
2	$\times \ \frac{9}{11}$	$\times \ \frac{3}{11}$	= 0.45
1	$\times \ \frac{2}{11}$	$\times \ \frac{9}{11}$	= 0.13
10	$\times \ \frac{2}{11}$	$\times \ \frac{3}{11}$	= 0.50
		Value of the game	= 3.46

Thus, on the average, X will win 3.46 points and Y will lose 3.46 points per game if the game is played many times.

Although this procedure will give the expected value of the game, a shortcut method does exist. Since optimal strategies are obtained by equating expected gains of both strategies for each player, the value of the game may be computed by multiplying game outcomes times their probabilities of occurrence for any row or column. The following illustration reveals the computational procedures:

		COLUMN 1	COLUMN 2
		$P = \frac{8}{11}$	$1 - P = \frac{3}{11}$
ROW 1	$Q = \frac{9}{11}$	4	2
ROW 2	$1 - Q = \frac{2}{11}$	1	10

Row 1: Value of the game = $(4)(\frac{8}{11}) + (2)(\frac{3}{11}) = \frac{38}{11}$

Row 2: Value of the game = $(1)(\frac{8}{11}) + (10)(\frac{3}{11}) = \frac{38}{11}$

Column 1: Value of the game = $(4)(\frac{9}{11}) + (1)(\frac{2}{11}) = \frac{38}{11}$

Column 2: Value of the game = $(2)(\frac{9}{11}) + (10)(\frac{2}{11}) = \frac{38}{11}$

Thus, the value of the game can be computed using any row or column. The value of this game, which was computed to be 3.46, is $\frac{38}{11}$.

S1.6 DOMINANCE

The principle of *dominance* can be used to reduce the size of games by eliminating strategies that would never be played. A strategy for a player can be eliminated if the player can always do as well or better playing another strategy. In other words, a strategy can be eliminated if all its game's outcomes are the same or worse than the corresponding game outcomes of another strategy.

Using the principle of dominance, we reduce the size of the following game:

	Y_1	Y_2
X_1	4	3
X_2	2	20
X_3	1	1

In this game, X_3 will never be played because X can always do better by playing X_1 or X_2. The new game is

	Y_1	Y_2
X_1	4	3
X_2	2	20

Here is another example:

	Y_1	Y_2	Y_3	Y_4
X_1	-5	4	6	-3
X_2	-2	6	2	-20

In this game, Y would never play Y_2 and Y_3 because Y could *always* do better playing Y_1 or Y_4. The new game is

	Y_1	Y_4
X_1	-5	-3
X_2	-2	-20

Summary

Game theory is the study of how optimal strategies are formulated in conflict. Because of the mathematical complexities of game theory, this module was limited to two-person and zero-sum games. A two-person game allows only two people or two groups to be involved in the game. *Zero sum* means that the sum of the losses for one player must equal the sum of the gains for the other player. The overall sum of the losses and gains for both players, in other words, must be zero.

Depending on the actual payoffs in the game and the size of the game, a number of solution techniques can be used. In a pure strategy game, strategies for the players can be obtained without making any calculations. When there is *not* a pure strategy, also called a saddle point, for both players, it is necessary to use other techniques, such as the mixed strategy approach, dominance, and a computer solution for games larger than 2 × 2.

Glossary

Two-Person Game. A game that has only two players.

Zero-Sum Game. A game where the losses for one player equal the gains for the other player.

Pure Strategy. A game where both players will always play just one strategy.

Saddle Point Game. A game that has a pure strategy.

Value of the Game. The expected winnings of the game if the game is played a large number of times.

Minimax Criterion. A criterion that minimizes one's maximum losses. This is another way of solving a pure strategy game.

Mixed Strategy Game. A game where the optimal strategy for both players involves playing more than one strategy over time. Each strategy is played a given percentage of the time.

Dominance. A procedure that is used to reduce the size of the game.

Solved Problems

Solved Problem S1-1

George Massic (player X) faces the following game. Using dominance, reduce the size of the game if possible.

	Y_1	Y_2
X_1	6	5
X_2	20	23
X_3	15	11

Solution

After carefully analyzing the game, George realizes that he will never play strategy X_1. The best outcome for this strategy (6) is worse than the worst outcome for the other two strategies. In addition, George would never play strategy X_3, for the same reason. Thus, George will always play strategy X_2. Given this situation, player Y would always play strategy Y_1 to minimize his losses. This is a pure strategy game with George playing X_2 and person Y playing strategy Y_1. The value of the game for this problem is the outcome of these two strategies, which is 20.

Solved Problem S1-2

Using the solution procedure for a mixed strategy game, solve the following game:

	Y_1	Y_2
X_1	4	2
X_2	0	10

Solution

This game can be solved by setting up the mixed strategy table and developing the appropriate equations.

	P	$1 - P$
Q	4	2
$1 - Q$	0	10

The equations for Q are

$$4Q + 0(1 - Q) = 2Q + 10(1 - Q)$$

$$4Q = 2Q + 10 - 10Q$$

$$12Q = 10 \text{ or } Q = {}^{10}\!/_{12} \text{ and } 1 - Q = {}^{2}\!/_{12}$$

The equations for P are

$$4P + 2(1 - P) = 0P + 10(1 - P)$$

$$4P + 2 - 2P = +10 - 10P$$

$$12P = 8 \text{ or } P = {}^{8}\!/_{12} \text{ and } 1 - P = {}^{4}\!/_{12}$$

SELF-TEST

- Before taking the self-test, refer back to the learning objectives at the beginning of the supplement and the glossary at the end of the supplement.
- Use the key at the back of the book to correct your answers.
- Restudy pages that correspond to any questions that you answered incorrectly or material you feel uncertain about.

1. A popular game theory solution procedure is
   a. maximax.
   b. minimax.
   c. maximin.
   d. equally likely.
   e. equal flow.
2. What happens when the upper and lower values of the game are the same?
   a. There is no solution.
   b. There is a mixed solution.
   c. There is a saddle point.
   d. There is an equally likely solution.
   e. There is a maximax solution.
3. The solution to the mixed strategy 2 $\times$ 2 game can be found by
   a. equating a player's expected winnings for one of the opponent's strategies with the opponent's other strategy.
   b. equating the value of the game for player X with the value of the game for player Y.
   c. setting Q equal to P and solving.
   d. setting $1 - Q$ equal to $1 - P$ and solving.
   e. none of the above.
4. What can be used to reduce the size of a game?
   a. game value reduction
   b. rotation reduction
   c. game transpose
   d. game inversion
   e. dominance
5. _____ means that the sum of the losses for one player must equal the sum of the gains for the other player.
6. When the strategies that each player follows will always be the same regardless of the other player's strategy, the game is called a _____ game.

Discussion Questions and Problems

Discussion Questions

S1-1 What is a two-person, zero-sum game?

S1-2 How do you compute the value of the game?

S1-3 What is a pure strategy, and how is dominance used?

S1-4 What is a mixed game, and how is it solved?

Problems*

S1-5 Determine the strategies for X and Y given the following game. What is the value of the game?

	Y_1	Y_2
X_1	2	−4
X_2	6	10

S1-6 What is the value of the following game and the strategies for A and B?

	B_1	B_2
A_1	19	20
A_2	5	−4

S1-7 Determine each player's strategy and the value of the game given the following table:

	Y_1	Y_2
X_1	86	42
X_2	36	106

----

*Note: 🖳 means the problem may be solved with QM for Windows; ✖ means the problem may be solved with Excel QM; and 🖳 means the problem may be solved with QM for Windows and/or Excel QM.

S1-8 What is the value of the following game?

	S_1	S_2
R_1	21	116
R_2	89	3

S1-9 Player A has a \$1 bill and a \$20 bill, while player B has a \$5 bill and a \$10 bill. Each player will select a bill from the other player without knowing what bill the other player selected. If the total of the bills selected is odd, player A gets both of the two bills that were selected, but if the total is even, player B gets both bills.
  (a) Develop a payoff table for this game. (Place the sum of both bills in each cell.)
  (b) What are the best strategies for each player?
  (c) What is the value of the game? Which player would you like to be?

S1-10 Resolve Problem S1-9. If the total of the bills is even, player A gets both of the bills selected, but if the total is odd, player B gets both bills.

S1-11 Solve the following game:

	Y_1	Y_2
X_1	-5	-10
X_2	12	8
X_3	4	12
X_4	-40	-5

S1-12 Shoe Town and Fancy Foot are both vying for more share of the market. If Shoe Town does no advertising, it will not lose any share of the market if Fancy Foot does nothing. It will lose 2% of the market if Fancy Foot invests \$10,000 in advertising, and it will lose 5% of the market if Fancy Foot invests \$20,000 in advertising. On the other hand, if Shoe Town invests \$15,000 in advertising, it will gain 3% of the market if Fancy Foot does nothing; it will gain 1% of the market if Fancy Foot invests \$10,000 in advertising; and it will lose 1% if Fancy Foot invests \$20,000 in advertising.
  (a) Develop a payoff table for this problem.
  (b) Determine the various strategies using the computer.
  (c) How would you determine the value of the game?

S1-13 Assume that a 1% increase in the market means a profit of \$1,000. Resolve Problem S1-12 using monetary value instead of market share.

S1-14 Solve for the optimal strategies and the value of the following game:

A \ B	STRATEGY B1	STRATEGY B2	STRATEGY B3
Strategy A1	−10	5	15
Strategy A2	20	2	−20
Strategy A3	6	2	6
Strategy A4	−13	−10	44
Strategy A5	−30	0	45
Strategy A6	16	−20	6

Data Set Problem

S1-15 Petroleum Research, Inc. (*A*), and Extraction International, Inc. (*B*), have both developed a new extraction procedure that will remove metal and other contaminants from used automotive engine oil. The equipment is expensive, the extraction process is complex, but the approach provides an economical way to recycle used engine oil. Both companies have developed unique technical procedures. Both companies also believe that advertising and promotion are critical to their success. Petroleum Research, with the help of an advertising firm, has developed 15 possible strategies. Extraction International has developed 5 possible advertising strategies. The economic outcome in millions of dollars is shown in the following table. What strategy do you recommend for Petroleum Research? How much money can they expect from their approach?

A \ B	STRATEGY B1	STRATEGY B2	STRATEGY B3	STRATEGY B4	STRATEGY B5
Strategy A1	1	2	2	1	4
Strategy A2	−1	3	−6	7	5
Strategy A3	10	−3	−5	−20	12
Strategy A4	6	−8	5	2	2
Strategy A5	−5	3	3	7	5
Strategy A6	−1	−1	−3	4	−2
Strategy A7	−1	0	0	0	−1
Strategy A8	3	6	−6	8	3
Strategy A9	2	6	−5	4	−7
Strategy A10	0	0	0	−5	7
Strategy A11	4	8	−5	3	3
Strategy A12	−3	−3	0	3	3
Strategy A13	1	0	0	−2	2
Strategy A14	4	3	3	5	7
Strategy A15	4	−4	4	−5	5

Bibliography

Bowen, Kenneth Credson, with contributions by Janet I. Harris. *Research Games: An Approach to the Study of Decision Process.* New York: Halstead Press, 1978.

Brandenburger, A., et al. "The Right Game: Use Game Theory to Shape Strategy," *Harvard Business Review* (July–August 1995): 57–71.

Bushko, David, et al., "Consulting's Future, Game Theory, and Storytelling,"*Journal of Management Consulting* (November 1997): 3.

Davis, M. *Game Theory: A Nontechnical Introduction.* New York: Basic Books, Inc., 1970.

Ichiishi, Tatsuro. *Game Theory for Economic Analysis.* New York: Academic Press, Inc., 1983.

Koselka, Rita. "Playing Poker with Craig McCaw," *Forbes* (July 3, 1995): 62–64.

Lan, Lim, et al. "Property Acquisition and Negotiation Styles," *Real Estate Finance* (Spring 1998): 72.

Lucas, W. "An Overview of the Mathematical Theory of Games," *Management Science* 8, 5, Part II (January 1972): 3–19.

Luce, R. D., and H. Raiffa. *Games and Decisions.* New York: John Wiley & Sons, Inc., 1957.

Shubik, M. *The Uses and Methods of Game Theory.* New York: American Elsevier Publishing Company, 1957.

Sinha, Arunava. "The Value Addition Game," *Business Today* (February 7, 1998): 143.

von Neumann, J., and O. Morgenstern. *Theory of Games and Economic Behavior.* Princeton, NJ: Princeton University Press, 1944.

APPENDIX S1.1: GAME THEORY WITH QM FOR WINDOWS

In this supplement we showed you how to solve 2×2 games using a variety of techniques. In Section S1.5, for example, we discussed how a mixed strategy game could be solved using straightforward algebraic techniques. In this game, player X will receive 4 and 2 by playing strategy X_1 when player Y played strategies Y_1 and Y_2, respectively. Values of 1 and 10 are the results when player X plays strategy X_2.

To illustrate QM for Windows, let's use these data. Program S1.1 shows the mix that each player should play for each strategy. The value of the game, 3.45, is displayed at the bottom right of the decision table.

Game Theory Results				
Game 1 Solution				
	Col strat 1	Col strat 2	Row Mix	
Row strategy 1	4.	2.	0.8182	
Row strategy 2	1.	10.	0.1818	
Column Mix—>	0.7273	0.2727	3.4545	

PROGRAM S1.1

QM for Windows Output for Game Theory

Probability Concepts and Applications

CHAPTER 2

LEARNING OBJECTIVES

After completing this chapter, students will be able to:

1. Understand the basic foundations of probability analysis.
2. Describe statistically dependent and independent events.
3. Use Bayes' theorem to establish posterior probabilities.
4. Describe and provide examples of both discrete and continuous random variables.
5. Explain the difference between discrete and continuous probability distributions.
6. Calculate expected values and variances and use the normal table.

CHAPTER OUTLINE

2.1   Introduction
2.2   Fundamental Concepts
2.3   Mutually Exclusive and Collectively Exhaustive Events
2.4   Statistically Independent Events
2.5   Statistically Dependent Events
2.6   Revising Probabilities with Bayes' Theorem
2.7   Further Probability Revisions
2.8   Random Variables
2.9   Probability Distributions
2.10 The Normal Distribution
2.11 The Exponential Distribution
2.12 The Poisson Distribution

Summary • Glossary • Key Equations • Solved Problems • Self-Test • Discussion Questions and Problems • Case Study: Century Chemical Company • Bibliography

Appendix 2.1: Derivation of Bayes' Theorem

2.1   INTRODUCTION

Life would be simpler if we knew without doubt what was going to happen in the future. The outcome of any decision would depend only on how logical and rational the decision was. If you lost money in the stock market, it would be because you failed to consider all of the information or to make a logical decision. If you got caught in the rain, it would be because you simply forgot your umbrella. You could always avoid building a plant that was too large, investing in a company that would lose money, running out of supplies, or losing crops because of bad weather. There would be no such thing as a risky investment. Life would be simpler, but boring.

It wasn't until the sixteenth century that people started to quantify risks and to apply this concept to everyday situations. Today, the idea of risk or probability is a part of our lives. "There is a 40% chance of rain in Omaha today." "The Florida State University Seminoles are favored 2 to 1 over the Louisiana State University Tigers this Saturday." "There is a 50-50 chance that the stock market will reach an all-time high next month."

A probability is a numerical statement about the chance that an event will occur.

A probability is a numerical statement about the likelihood that an event will occur. In this chapter we examine the basic concepts, terms, and relationships of probability and probability distributions that are useful in solving many quantitative analysis problems. Table 2.1 lists some of the topics covered in this book that rely on probability theory. You can see that the study of quantitative analysis would be quite difficult without it.

TABLE 2.1	Chapters In This Book That Use Probability
CHAPTER	TITLE
S1	Game Theory
3	Fundamentals of Decision Theory Models
4	Decision Trees and Utility Theory
5	Forecasting Models
6	Inventory Control Models
13	Project Management Models
14	Waiting Lines and Queuing Theory Models
15	Simulation Modeling
16	Markov Analysis
CD Module 1	Statistical Quality Control
CD Module 3	Decision Theory and the Normal Distribution
CD Module 6	The Binomial Distribution

2.2   FUNDAMENTAL CONCEPTS

There are two basic statements about the mathematics of probability:

1. The probability, P, of any event or state of nature occurring is greater than or equal to 0 and less than or equal to 1. That is,

$$0 \leq P(\text{event}) \leq 1 \tag{2-1}$$

A probability of 0 indicates that an event is never expected to occur. A probability of 1 means that an event is always expected to occur.

2. The sum of the simple probabilities for all possible outcomes of an activity must equal 1. Both of these concepts are illustrated in Example 1.

People often misuse the two basic rules of probabilities by such statements as, "I'm 110% sure we're going to win the big game."

Example 1: Two Laws of Probability Demand for white latex paint at Diversey Paint and Supply has always been 0, 1, 2, 3, or 4 gallons per day. (There are no other possible outcomes and when one occurs, no other can.) Over the past 200 working days, the owner notes the following frequencies of demand:

QUANTITY DEMANDED (GALLONS)	NUMBER OF DAYS
0	40
1	80
2	50
3	20
4	10
	Total 200

If this past distribution is a good indicator of future sales, we can find the probability of each possible outcome occurring in the future by converting the data into percentages of the total

QUANTITY DEMANDED	PROBABILITY
0	0.20 (= 40/200)
1	0.40 (= 80/200)
2	0.25 (= 50/200)
3	0.10 (= 20/200)
4	0.05 (= 10/200)
	Total 1.00 (= 200/200)

Thus the probability that sales are 2 gallons of paint on any given day is $P(2 \text{ gallons}) = 0.25 = 25\%$. The probability of any level of sales must be greater than or equal to 0 and less than or equal to 1. Since 0, 1, 2, 3, and 4 gallons exhaust all possible events or outcomes, the sum of their probability values must equal 1.

Types of Probability

There are two different ways to determine probability: the *objective approach* and the *subjective approach*.

Objective Probability   Example 1 provided us with an illustration of objective probability assessment. The probability of any paint demand level was the *relative frequency* of occurrence of that demand in a large number of trial observations (200 days in this case). In general,

$$P(\text{event}) = \frac{\text{number of occurrences of the event}}{\text{total number of trials or outcomes}}$$

Objective probability can also be set using what is called the *classical* or *logical method*. Without performing a series of trials, we can often logically determine what the probabilities of various events should be. For example, the probability of tossing a fair coin once and getting a head is

$$P(\text{head}) = \frac{1}{2} \quad \overset{\textstyle\nearrow \textit{ number of ways of getting a head}}{\textstyle\searrow \textit{ number of possible outcomes (head or tail)}}$$

Similarly, the probability of drawing a spade out of a deck of 52 playing cards can be logically set as

$$P(\text{spade}) = \frac{13}{52} \quad \overset{\textstyle\nearrow \textit{ number of chances of drawing a spade}}{\textstyle\searrow \textit{ number of possible outcomes}}$$

$$= \frac{1}{4} = 0.25 = 25\%$$

Subjective Probability   When logic and past history are not appropriate, probability values can be assessed *subjectively*. The accuracy of subjective probabilities depends on the experience and judgment of the person making the estimates. A number of probability values cannot be determined unless the subjective approach is used. What is the probability that the price of gasoline will be more than $4 in the next few years? What is the probability that our economy will be in a severe depression in 2005? What is the probability that you will be president of a major corporation within 20 years?

There are several methods for making subjective probability assessments. Opinion polls can be used to help in determining subjective probabilities for possible election returns and potential political candidates. In some cases, experience and judgment must be used in making subjective assessments of probability values. A production manager, for example, might believe that the probability of manufacturing a new product without a single defect is 0.85. In the Delphi method, a panel of experts is assembled to make their predictions of the future. This approach is discussed in Chapter 5.

Where do probabilities come from? Sometimes they are subjective and based on personal experiences. Other times they are objectively based on logical observations such as the roll of a die. Often, probabilities are derived from historical data.

2.3   **MUTUALLY EXCLUSIVE AND COLLECTIVELY EXHAUSTIVE EVENTS**

Events are said to be *mutually exclusive* if only one of the events can occur on any one trial. They are called *collectively exhaustive* if the list of outcomes includes every possible outcome. Many common experiences involve events that have both of these properties. In tossing a coin, for example, the possible outcomes are a head or a tail. Since both of them cannot

---

| MODELING IN THE REAL WORLD | **Liver Transplants in the U.S.** |

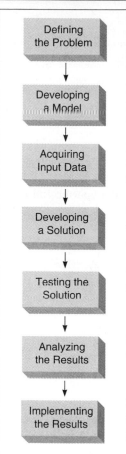

Defining the Problem

The scarcity of liver organs for transplants has reached critical levels in the U.S.; 1,131 individuals died in 1997 while waiting for a transplant. With only 4,000 liver donations per year, there are 10,000 patients on the waiting list, with 8,000 being added each year. There is a need to develop a model to evaluate policies for allocating livers to terminally ill patients who need them.

Developing a Model

Doctors, engineers, researchers, and scientists worked together with Pritsker Corp. consultants in the process of creating the liver allocation model, called ULAM. One of the model's jobs would be to evaluate whether to list potential recipients on a national basis or regionally.

Acquiring Input Data

Historical information was available for the United Network from Sharing Organs (UNOS), from 1990 to 1995. The data were then stored in ULAM. "Poisson" probability processes described the arrivals of donors at 63 organ procurement centers and arrival of patients at 106 liver transplant centers.

Developing a Solution

ULAM provides probabilities of accepting an offered liver, where the probability is a function of the patient's medical status, the transplant center, and the quality of the offered liver. ULAM also models the daily probability of a patient changing from one status of criticality to another.

Testing the Solution

Testing involved a comparison of the model output to actual results over the 1992–1994 time period. Model results were close enough to actual results that ULAM was declared valid.

Analyzing the Results

ULAM was used to compare more than 100 liver allocation policies and was then then updated in 1998, with more recent data, for presentation to Congress.

Implementing the Results

Based on the projected results, the UNOS committee voted 18-0 to implement an allocation policy based on regional, not national, waiting lists. This decision is expected to save 2,414 lives over an eight-year period.

Source: A. A. B. Pritsker. "Life and Death Decisions," *OR/MS Today* (August 1998): 22–28.

---

occur on any one toss, the outcomes head and tail are mutually exclusive. Since obtaining a head and a tail represent every possible outcome, they are also collectively exhaustive.

Example 2: Rolling a Die Rolling a die is a simple experiment that has six possible outcomes, each listed in the following table with its corresponding probability:

OUTCOME OF ROLL	PROBABILITY
1	$\frac{1}{6}$
2	$\frac{1}{6}$
3	$\frac{1}{6}$
4	$\frac{1}{6}$
5	$\frac{1}{6}$
6	$\frac{1}{6}$
	Total 1

These events are both mutually exclusive (on any roll, only one of the six events can occur) and are also collectively exhaustive (one of them must occur and hence they total in probability to 1).

Example 3: Drawing a Card You are asked to draw one card from a deck of 52 playing cards. Using a logical probability assessment, it is easy to set some of the relationships, such as

$$P(\text{drawing a 7}) = {}^4/_{52} = {}^1/_{13}$$

$$P(\text{drawing a heart}) = {}^{13}/_{52} = {}^1/_4$$

We also see that these events (drawing a 7 and drawing a heart) are *not* mutually exclusive since a 7 of hearts can be drawn. They are also *not* collectively exhaustive since there are other cards in the deck besides 7s and hearts.

You can test your understanding of these concepts by going through the following cases:

This table is especially useful in helping to understand the difference between mutually exclusive and collectively exhaustive.

DRAWS	MUTUALLY EXCLUSIVE?	COLLECTIVELY EXHAUSTIVE?
1. Draw a spade and a club	Yes	No
2. Draw a face card and a number card	Yes	Yes
3. Draw an ace and a 3	Yes	No
4. Draw a club and a nonclub	Yes	Yes
5. Draw a 5 and a diamond	No	No
6. Draw a red card and a diamond	No	No

Adding Mutually Exclusive Events

Often we are interested in whether one event *or* a second event will occur. When these two events are mutually exclusive, the law of addition is simply as follows:

$$P(\text{event } A \text{ or event } B) = P(\text{event } A) + P(\text{event } B)$$

or more briefly,

$$P(A \text{ or } B) = P(A) + P(B) \tag{2-2}$$

For example, we just saw that the events of drawing a spade or drawing a club out of a deck of cards are mutually exclusive. Since $P(\text{spade}) = {}^{13}/_{52}$, and $P(\text{club}) = {}^{13}/_{52}$, the probability of drawing either a spade or a club is

$$P(\text{spade or club}) = P(\text{spade}) + P(\text{club})$$
$$= {}^{13}/_{52} + {}^{13}/_{52}$$
$$= {}^{26}/_{52} = {}^1/_2 = 0.50 = 50\%$$

The *Venn diagram* in Figure 2.1 depicts the probability of the occurrence of mutually exclusive events.

FIGURE 2.1

Addition Law for Events that Are Mutually Exclusive

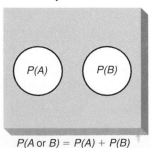

$P(A \text{ or } B) = P(A) + P(B)$

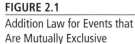

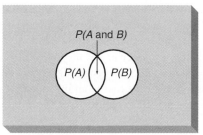

FIGURE 2.2
Addition Law for Events that
Are Not Mutually Exclusive

$$P(A \text{ or } B) = P(A) + P(B) - P(A \text{ and } B)$$

Law of Addition for Events That Are Not Mutually Exclusive

When two events are not mutually exclusive, Equation 2-2 must be modified to account for double counting. The correct equation reduces the probability by subtracting the chance of both events occurring together:

$$P(\text{event } A \text{ or event } B) = P(\text{event } A) + P(\text{event } B)$$
$$- P(\text{event } A \text{ and event } B \text{ both occurring})$$

This can be expressed in shorter form as

$$P(A \text{ or } B) = P(A) + P(B) - P(A \text{ and } B) \qquad (2\text{-}3)$$

The formula for adding events that are not mutually exclusive is $P(A \text{ or } B) = P(A) + P(B) - P(A \text{ and } B)$. Do you understand why we subtract $P(A \text{ and } B)$?

Figure 2.2 illustrates this concept of subtracting the probability of outcomes that are common to both events. When events are mutually exclusive, the area of overlap, called the *intersection*, is 0, as shown in Figure 2.1.

Let us consider the events drawing a 5 and drawing a diamond out of the card deck. These events are not mutually exclusive, so Equation 2-3 must be applied to compute the probability of either a 5 or a diamond being drawn.

$$P(\text{five } or \text{ diamond}) = P(\text{five}) + P(\text{diamond})$$
$$- P(\text{five } and \text{ diamond})$$
$$= \tfrac{4}{52} + \tfrac{13}{52} - \tfrac{1}{52}$$
$$= \tfrac{16}{52} = \tfrac{4}{13}$$

2.4 STATISTICALLY INDEPENDENT EVENTS

Events may be either *independent* or *dependent*. When they are *independent*, the occurrence of one event has no effect on the probability of occurrence of the second event. Let us examine four sets of events and determine which are independent:

1. (a) Your education ⎱ *Dependent events.*
   (b) Your income level ⎰ Can you explain why?

2. (a) Draw a jack of hearts from a full 52-card deck ⎱ *Independent events*
   (b) Draw a jack of clubs from a full 52-card deck ⎰

3. (a) Chicago Cubs win the National League pennant ⎱ *Dependent events*
   (b) Chicago Cubs win the World Series ⎰

4. (a) Snow in Santiago, Chile ⎱ *Independent events*
   (b) Rain in Tel Aviv, Israel ⎰

A marginal probability is the probability of an event occurring.

A joint probability is the product of marginal probabilities.

The three types of probability under both statistical independence and statistical dependence are (1) marginal, (2) joint, and (3) conditional. When events are independent, these three are very easy to compute, as we shall see.

A *marginal* (or a *simple*) *probability* is just the probability of an event occurring. For example, if we toss a fair die, the marginal probability of a 2 landing face up is P(die is a 2) = $\frac{1}{6}$ = 0.166. Because each separate toss is an independent event (that is, what we get on the first toss has absolutely no effect on any later tosses), the marginal probability for each possible outcome is $\frac{1}{6}$.

The *joint probability* of two or more independent events occurring is the product of their marginal or simple probabilities. This may be written as

$$P(AB) = P(A) \times P(B) \tag{2-4}$$

where

$P(AB)$ = joint probability of events A and B occurring together, or one after the other

$P(A)$ = marginal probability of event A

$P(B)$ = marginal probability of event B

The probability, for example, of tossing a 6 on the first roll of a die and a 2 on the second roll is

P(6 on first and 2 on second roll)

= P(tossing a 6) $\times$ P(tossing a 2)

= $\frac{1}{6} \times \frac{1}{6} = \frac{1}{36}$

= 0.028

A conditional probability is the probability of an event occurring given that another event has taken place.

The third type, *conditional probability*, is expressed as $P(B|A)$, or "the probability of event B, given that event A has occurred." Similarly, $P(A|B)$ would mean "the conditional probability of event A, given that event B has taken place." Since events are independent the occurrence of one in no way affects the outcome of another, $P(A|B) = P(A)$ and $P(B|A) = P(B)$.

Example 4: Probabilities When Events Are Independent A bucket contains 3 black balls and 7 green balls. We draw a ball from the bucket, replace it, and draw a second ball. We can determine the probability of each of the following events occurring:

1. A black ball is drawn on the first draw.

    $P(B)$ = 0.30 *(This is a marginal probability.)*

2. Two green balls are drawn.

    $P(GG) = P(G) \times P(G) = (0.7)(0.7) = 0.49$

    (This is a joint probability for two independent events.)

3. A black ball is drawn on the second draw if the first draw is green.

    $P(B|G) = P(B)$ = 0.30 *(This is a conditional probability but equal to the marginal because the two draws are independent events.)*

4. A green ball is drawn on the second draw if the first draw was green.

    $P(G|G) = P(G)$ = 0.70 *(This is a conditional probability as above.)*

2.5 STATISTICALLY DEPENDENT EVENTS

When events are statistically dependent, the occurrence of one event affects the probability of occurrence of some other event. Marginal, conditional, and joint probabilities exist under dependence as they did under independence, but the form of the latter two are changed.

A *marginal probability* is computed exactly as it was for independent events. Again, the marginal probability of the event *A* occurring is denoted $P(A)$.

Calculating a *conditional probability* under dependence is somewhat more involved than it is under independence. The formula for the conditional probability of *A*, given that event *B* has taken place, is now stated as

$$P(A \mid B) = \frac{P(AB)}{P(B)} \tag{2-5}$$

The use of this important formula, often referred to as *Bayes' law* or *Bayes' theorem*, is best defined by an example.

A Presbyterian minister, Thomas Bayes (1702–1761), did the work leading to this theorem.

Example 5: Probabilities When Events Are Dependent Assume that we have an urn containing 10 balls of the following descriptions:

4 are white (*W*) and lettered (*L*).

2 are white (*W*) and numbered (*N*).

3 are yellow (*Y*) and lettered (*L*).

1 is yellow (*Y*) and numbered (*N*).

You randomly draw a ball from the urn and see that it is yellow. What, then, we may ask, is the probability that the ball is lettered? (See Figure 2.3.)

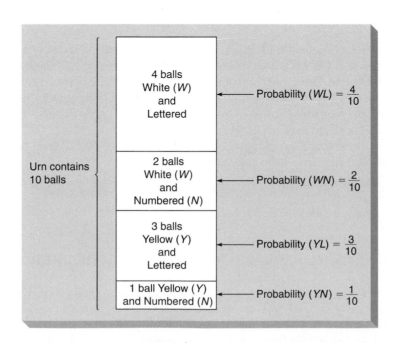

FIGURE 2.3

Dependent Events of Example 5

Since there are 10 balls, it is a simple matter to tabulate a series of useful probabilities.

$$P(WL) = \tfrac{4}{10} = 0.4 \qquad P(YL) = \tfrac{3}{10} = 0.3$$

$$P(WN) = \tfrac{2}{10} = 0.2 \qquad P(YN) = \tfrac{1}{10} = 0.1$$

$$P(W) = \tfrac{6}{10} = 0.6, \;\; \text{or} \;\; P(W) = P(WL) + P(WN) = 0.4 + 0.2 = 0.6$$

$$P(L) = \tfrac{7}{10} = 0.7, \;\; \text{or} \;\; P(L) = P(WL) + P(YL) = 0.4 + 0.3 = 0.7$$

$$P(Y) = \tfrac{4}{10} = 0.4, \;\; \text{or} \;\; P(Y) = P(YL) + P(YN) = 0.3 + 0.1 = 0.4$$

$$P(N) = \tfrac{3}{10} = 0.3, \;\; \text{or} \;\; P(N) = P(WN) + P(YN) = 0.2 + 0.1 = 0.3$$

We may now apply Bayes' law to calculate the conditional probability that the ball drawn is lettered, given that it is yellow.

$$P(L \mid Y) = \frac{P(YL)}{P(Y)} = \frac{0.3}{0.4} = 0.75$$

This equation shows that we divided the probability of *yellow* and *lettered* balls (3 out of 10) by the probability of yellow balls (4 out of 10). There is a 0.75 probability that the yellow ball that you drew is lettered.

You may recall that the formula for a joint probability under statistical independence was simply $P(AB) = P(A) \times P(B)$. When events are *dependent*, however, the joint probability is derived from Bayes' conditional formula. Equation 2-6 reads "the joint probability of events A and B occurring is equal to the conditional probability of event A, given that B occurred, multiplied by the probability of event B."

$$P(AB) = P(A \mid B) \times P(B) \tag{2-6}$$

We can use this formula to verify the joint probability that $P(YL) = 0.3$, which was obtained by inspection in Example 5 by multiplying $P(L \mid Y)$ times $P(Y)$.

$$P(YL) = P(L \mid Y) \times P(Y) = (0.75)(0.4) = 0.3$$

Example 6: Joint Probabilities When Events Are Dependent Your stockbroker informs you that if the stock market reaches the 12,500-point level by January, there is a 70% probability that Tubeless Electronics will go up in value. Your own feeling is that there is only a 40% chance of the market average reaching 12,500 points by January. Can you calculate the probability that *both* the stock market will reach 12,500 points *and* the price of Tubeless Electronics will go up?

Let M represent the event of the stock market reaching the 12,500 level, and let T be the event that Tubeless goes up in value. Then

$$P(MT) = P(T \mid M) \times P(M) = (0.70)(0.40) = 0.28$$

Thus, there is only a 28% chance that *both* events will occur.

2.6   **REVISING PROBABILITIES WITH BAYES' THEOREM**

Bayes' theorem can also be used to incorporate additional information as it is made available and help create revised or *posterior probabilities*. This means that we can take new or recent data and then revise and improve upon our old probability estimates for an event (see Figure 2.4). Let us consider the following example.

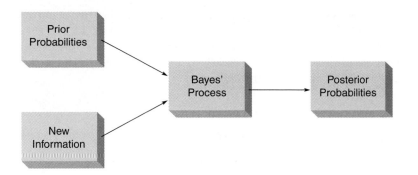

FIGURE 2.4
Using Bayes' Process

Example 7: Posterior Probabilities A cup contains two dice identical in appearance. One, however, is fair (unbiased) and the other is loaded (biased). The probability of rolling a 3 on the fair die is ⅙ or 0.166. The probability of tossing the same number on the loaded die is 0.60.

We have no idea which die is which, but select one by chance and toss it. The result is a 3. Given this additional piece of information, can we find the (revised) probability that the die rolled was fair? Can we determine the probability that it was the loaded die that was rolled?

The answer to these questions is yes, and we do so by using the formula for joint probability under statistical dependence and Bayes' theorem. First, we take stock of the information and probabilities available. We know, for example, that since we randomly selected the die to roll, the probability of it being fair or loaded is 0.50.

$$P(\text{fair}) = 0.50 \qquad P(\text{loaded}) = 0.50$$

We also know that

$$P(3 \mid \text{fair}) = 0.166 \qquad P(3 \mid \text{loaded}) = 0.60$$

Next, we compute joint probabilities $P(3 \text{ and fair})$ and $P(3 \text{ and loaded})$ using the formula $P(AB) = P(A \mid B) \times P(B)$.

$$P(3 \text{ and fair}) = P(3 \mid \text{fair}) \times P(\text{fair})$$

$$= (0.166)(0.50) = 0.083$$

$$P(3 \text{ and loaded}) = P(3 \mid \text{loaded}) \times P(\text{loaded})$$

$$= (0.60)(0.50) = 0.300$$

A 3 can occur in combination with the state "fair die" or in combination with the state "loaded die." The sum of their probabilities gives the unconditional or marginal probability of a 3 on the toss, namely, $P(3) = 0.083 + 0.300 = 0.383$.

If a 3 does occur, and if we do not know which die it came from, the probability that the die rolled was the fair one is

$$P(\text{fair} \mid 3) = \frac{P(\text{fair and } 3)}{P(3)} = \frac{0.083}{0.383} = 0.22$$

The probability that the die rolled was loaded is

$$P(\text{loaded} \mid 3) = \frac{P(\text{loaded and } 3)}{P(3)} = \frac{0.300}{0.383} = 0.78$$

These two conditional probabilities are called the *revised* or *posterior probabilities* for the next roll of the die.

Before the die was rolled in the preceding example, the best we could say was that there was a 50-50 chance that it was fair (0.50 probability) and a 50-50 chance that it was loaded. After one roll of the die, however, we are able to revise our *prior probability* estimates. The new posterior estimate is that there is a 0.78 probability that the die rolled was loaded and only a 0.22 probability that it was not.

General Form of Bayes' Theorem

Another way to compute revised probabilities is with Bayes' theorem.

Revised probabilities can also be computed in a more direct way using a general form for Bayes' *theorem*. We originally saw in Equation 2-5 that Bayes' law for the conditional probability of event A, given event B, is

$$P(A \mid B) = \frac{P(AB)}{P(B)}$$

However, in Appendix 2.1 we will go through the mathematical steps to show that

$$P(A \mid B) = \frac{P(B \mid A)P(A)}{P(B \mid A)P(A) + P(B \mid \overline{A})P(\overline{A})} \tag{2-7}$$

where

$\overline{A}$ = the complement of the event A; for example,
    if A is the event "fair die," then $\overline{A}$ is "unfair" or "loaded die"

Now let's return to Example 7.

Although it may not be obvious to you at first glance, we used this basic equation to compute the revised probabilities. For example, if we want the probability that the fair die was rolled given the first toss was a 3, namely, $P(\text{fair die} \mid 3 \text{ rolled})$, we can let

event "fair die" replace A in Equation 2-7.

event "loaded die" replace $\overline{A}$ in Equation 2-7.

event "3 rolled" replace B in Equation 2-7.

We can then rewrite Equation 2-7 and solve as follows:

$P(\text{fair die} \mid 3 \text{ rolled})$

$$= \frac{P(3 \mid \text{fair})P(\text{fair})}{P(3 \mid \text{fair})P(\text{fair}) + P(3 \mid \text{loaded})P(\text{loaded})}$$

$$= \frac{(0.166)(0.50)}{(0.166)(0.50) + (0.60)(0.50)}$$

$$= \frac{0.083}{0.383} = 0.22$$

This is the same answer that we computed in Example 7. Can you use this alternative approach to show that $P(\text{loaded die} \mid 3 \text{ rolled}) = 0.78$? Either method is perfectly acceptable, but when we deal with probability revisions again in Chapter 4, we may find that Equation 2-7 is easier to apply.

2.7 FURTHER PROBABILITY REVISIONS

Although one revision of prior probabilities can provide useful posterior probability estimates, additional information can be gained from performing the experiment a second time. If it is financially worthwhile, a decision maker may even decide to make several more revisions.

Example 8: A Second Probability Revision Returning to Example 7, we now attempt to obtain further information about the posterior probabilities as to whether the die just rolled is fair or loaded. To do so, let us toss the die a second time. Again, we roll a 3. What are the further revised probabilities?

To answer this question, we proceed as before, with only one exception. The probabilities $P(\text{fair}) = 0.50$ and $P(\text{loaded}) = 0.50$ remain the same, but now we must compute $P(3,3 \mid \text{fair}) = (0.166)(0.166) = 0.027$ and $P(3,3 \mid \text{loaded}) = (0.6)(0.6) = 0.36$. With these joint probabilities of two 3s on successive rolls, given the two types of dice, we may revise the probabilities.

$$P(3,3 \text{ and fair}) = P(3,3 \mid \text{fair}) \times P(\text{fair})$$

$$= (0.027)(0.5) = 0.013$$

$$P(3,3 \text{ and loaded}) = P(3,3 \mid \text{loaded}) \times P(\text{loaded})$$

$$= (0.36)(0.5) = 0.18$$

Thus, the probability of rolling two 3s, a marginal probability, is $0.013 + 0.18 = 0.193$, the sum of the two joint probabilities.

$$P(\text{fair} \mid 3,3) = \frac{P(3,3 \text{ and fair})}{P(3,3)}$$

$$= \frac{0.013}{0.193} = 0.067$$

$$P(\text{loaded} \mid 3,3) = \frac{P(3,3 \text{ and loaded})}{P(3,3)}$$

$$= \frac{0.18}{0.193} = 0.933$$

What has this second roll accomplished? Before we rolled the die the first time, we knew only that there was a 0.50 probability that it was either fair or loaded. When the first die was rolled in Example 7, we were able to revise these probabilities:

probability the die is fair $= 0.22$

probability the die is loaded $= 0.78$

Now, after the second roll in Example 8, our refined revisions tell us that

probability the die is fair $= 0.067$

probability the die is loaded $= 0.933$

This type of information can be extremely valuable in business decision making.

IN ACTION   Flight Safety and Probability Analysis

With catastrophic crashes, such as the TWA 800 and Swissair 111 flights, airline safety is an important international issue. Is airline travel safe? What should be done, if anything, to reduce accidents? How can countries around the world reduce the impact of terrorism on air safety? These and similar questions can only be answered by investigating the costs of improving air safety and the use of probability analysis to determine how many lives can be saved with improved safety measures.

Determining airline safety is a matter of applying the concepts of objective probability analysis. The chance of getting killed in a scheduled domestic flight is about 1 in 5 million. This is a probability of about .0000002. Another measure is the number of deaths per passenger mile flown. The number is about 1 passenger per billion passenger miles flown, or a probability of about .000000001. Without question, flying is safer than many other forms of transportation, including driving. For a typical weekend, more people are killed in car accidents than a typical air disaster. Even so, air crashes and airline safety continue to get more national attention than fatalities on our highways.

Analyzing new airline safety measures involves costs and the subjective probability that lives will be saved. One airline expert proposed a number of new airline safety measures. When the costs involved and probability of saving lives were taken into account, the result was about a $1 billion cost for every life saved on average. In addition, some proposed safety issues are not completely certain. For example, a Thermal Neutron Analysis (TNA) device to detect explosives at airports had a probability of .15 of giving a false alarm, resulting in a high cost of inspection and long flight delays. Furthermore, the accident with the highest probability of occurrence is a plane flying into a mountain or the ground. The probability of a crash from a mid-air collision or terrorism is significantly lower.

Without question, the use of probability analysis to determine and improve flight safety is indispensable. Many transportation experts hope that the same rigorous probability models used in the airline industry will some day be applied to the much more deadly system of highways and the drivers who use them.

Source: Robert Machol. "Flying Scared," *OR/MS Today* (October 1997): 32–37.

2.8   RANDOM VARIABLES

We have just discussed various ways of assigning probability values to the outcomes of an experiment. Let us now use this probability information to compute the expected outcome, variance, and standard deviation of the experiment. This can help select the best decision among a number of alternatives.

A *random variable* assigns a real number to every possible outcome or event in an experiment. It is normally represented by a letter such as X or Y. When the outcome itself is numerical or quantitative, the outcome numbers can be the random variable. For example, consider refrigerator sales at an appliance store. The number of refrigerators sold during a given day can be the random variable. Using X to represent this random variable, we can express this relationship as follows:

X = number of refrigerators sold during the day

In general, whenever the experiment has quantifiable outcomes, it is beneficial to define these quantitative outcomes as the random variable. Examples are given in Table 2.2.

When the outcome itself is not numerical or quantitative, it is necessary to define a random variable that associates each outcome with a unique real number. Several examples are given in Table 2.3.

There are two types of random variables: *discrete random variables* and *continuous random variables*. Developing probability distributions and making computations based on these distributions depends on the type of random variable.

TABLE 2.2 **Examples of Random Variables**

EXPERIMENT	OUTCOME	RANDOM VARIABLES	RANGE OF RANDOM VARIABLES
Stock 50 Christmas trees	Number of Christmas trees sold	X = number of Christmas trees sold	$0, 1, 2, \ldots, 50$
Inspect 600 items	Number of acceptable items	Y = number of acceptable items	$0, 1, 2, \ldots, 600$
Send out 5,000 sales letters	Number of people responding to the letters	Z = number of people responding to the letters	$0, 1, 2, \ldots, 5,000$
Build an apartment building	Percent of building completed after 4 months	R = percent of building completed after 4 months	$0 \leq R \leq 100$
Test the lifetime of a lightbulb (minutes)	Length of time the bulb last up to 80,000 minutes	S = time the bulb burns	$0 \leq S \leq 80,000$

A random variable is a *discrete random variable* if it can assume only a finite or limited set of values. Which of the random variables in Table 2.2 are discrete random variables? Looking at Table 2.2, we can see that stocking 50 Christmas trees, inspecting 600 items, and sending out 5,000 letters are all examples of discrete random variables. Each of these random variables can assume only a finite or limited set of values. The number of Christmas trees sold, for example, can only be integer numbers from 0 to 50. There are 51 values that the random variable X can assume in this example.

A *continuous random variable* is a random variable that has an infinite or an unlimited set of values. Are there any examples of continuous random variables in Tables 2.2 or 2.3? Looking at Table 2.2, we can see that testing the lifetime of a lightbulb is an experiment that can be described with a continuous random variable. In this case, the random variable, S, is the time the bulb burns. It can last for 3,206 minutes, 6,500.7 minutes, 251.726 minutes, or any other value between 0 and 80,000 minutes. In most cases, the range of a continuous random variable is stated as: lower value $\leq S \leq$ upper value, such as $0 \leq S \leq 80,000$. The random variable R in Table 2.2 is also continuous. Can you explain why?

Try to develop a few more examples of discrete random variables to be sure you understand this concept.

TABLE 2.3 **Random Variables for Outcomes That Are Not Numbers**

EXPERIMENT	OUTCOME	RANDOM VARIABLES	RANGE OF RANDOM VARIABLES
Students respond to a questionnaire	Strongly agree (SA) Agree (A) Neutral (N) Disagree (D) Strongly disagree (SD)	$X = \begin{cases} 5 \text{ if SA} \\ 4 \text{ if A} \\ 3 \text{ if N} \\ 2 \text{ if D} \\ 1 \text{ if SD} \end{cases}$	1, 2, 3, 4, 5
One machine is inspected	Defective Not defective	$Y = \begin{cases} 0 \text{ if defective} \\ 1 \text{ if not defective} \end{cases}$	0, 1
Consumers respond to how they like a product	Good Average Poor	$Z = \begin{cases} 3 \text{ if good} \\ 2 \text{ if average} \\ 1 \text{ if poor} \end{cases}$	1, 2, 3

2.9 PROBABILITY DISTRIBUTIONS

Earlier we discussed the probability values of an event. We now explore the properties of *probability distributions*. We see how popular distributions, such as the normal, Poisson, and exponential probability distributions, can save us time and effort. Since selection of the appropriate probability distribution depends partially on whether the random variable is *discrete* or *continuous*, we consider each of these types separately.

Probability Distribution of a Discrete Random Variable

When we have a *discrete random variable*, there is a probability value assigned to each event. These values must be between 0 and 1, and they must sum to 1. Let's look at an example.

The 100 students in Pat Shannon's statistics class have just completed the instructor evaluations at the end of the course. Dr. Shannon is particularly interested in student response to the textbook because he is in the process of writing a competing statistics book. One of the questions on the evaluation survey was: "The textbook was well written and helped me acquire the necessary information."

5. Strongly agree

4. Agree

3. Neutral

2. Disagree

1. Strongly disagree

The students' response to this question in the survey is summarized in Table 2.4. Also shown is the random variable X and the corresponding probability for each possible outcome. This discrete probability distribution was computed using the relative frequency approach presented earlier.

The distribution follows the three rules required of all probability distributions: (1) the events are mutually exclusive and collectively exhaustive, (2) the individual probability values are between 0 and 1 inclusive, and (3) the total of the probability values sum to 1.

While listing the probability distribution as we did in Table 2.4 is adequate, it can be difficult to get an idea about characteristics of the distribution. To overcome this problem,

TABLE 2.4   Probability Distribution for Textbook Question

OUTCOME	RANDOM VARIABLE (X)	NUMBER RESPONDING	PROBABILITY $P(X)$
Strongly agree	5	10	0.1 = 10/100
Agree	4	20	0.2 = 20/100
Neutral	3	30	0.3 = 30/100
Disagree	2	30	0.3 = 30/100
Strongly disagree	1	10	0.1 = 10/100
		Total 100	1.0 = 100/100

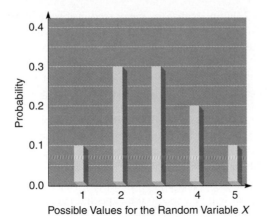

FIGURE 2.5
Probability Function
for Dr. Shannon's Class

the probability values are often presented in graph form. The graph of the distribution in Table 2.4 is shown in Figure 2.5.

The graph of this probability distribution gives us a picture of its shape. It helps us identify the central tendency of the distribution, called the *expected value*, and the amount of variability or spread of the distribution, called the *variance*.

Expected Value of a Discrete Probability Distribution

Once we have established a probability distribution, the first characteristic that is usually of interest is the *central tendency*, or average of the distribution. The expected value, a measure of central tendency, is computed as a weighted average of the values of the random variable:

The expected value of a discrete distribution is a weighted average of the values of the random variable.

$$E(X) = \sum_{i=1}^{n} X_i P(X_i)$$

$$= X_1 P(X_1) + X_2 P(X_2) + \cdots + X_n P(X_n) \qquad \text{(2-8)}$$

where

$\qquad X_i$ = random variable's possible values

$\qquad P(X_i)$ = probability of each of the random variable's possible values

$\qquad \displaystyle\sum_{i=1}^{n}$ = summation sign indicating we are adding all *n* possible values

$\qquad E(X)$ = expected value of the random variable

The expected value of any discrete probability distribution can be computed by multiplying each possible value of the random variable, X_i, times the probability, $P(X_i)$, that outcome will occur, and summing the results, Σ. Here is how the expected value can be computed for the textbook question:

$$E(X) = \sum_{i=1}^{5} X_i P(X_i)$$

$$= X_1 P(X_1) + X_2 P(X_2) + X_3 P(X_3)$$

$$+ X_4 P(X_4) + X_5 P(X_5)$$

$$= (5)(0.1) + (4)(0.2) + (3)(0.3)$$

$$+ (2)(0.3) + (1)(0.1)$$

$$= 2.9$$

The expected value of 2.9 implies that the mean response is between disagree (2) and neutral (3), and that the average response is closer to neutral, which is 3. Looking at Figure 2.5, this is consistent with the shape of the probability function.

Variance of a Discrete Probability Distribution

In addition to the central tendency of a probability distribution, most people are interested in the variability or the spread of the distribution. If the variability is low, it is much more likely that the outcome of an experiment will be close to the average or expected value. On the other hand, if the variability of the distribution is high, which means that the probability is spread out over the various random variable values, there is less chance that the outcome of an experiment will be close to the expected value.

A probability distribution is often described by its mean and variance. Even if most of the men in class (or the United States) have heights between 5 feet 6 inches and 6 feet 2 inches, there is still some small probability of outliers.

The *variance* of a probability distribution is a number that reveals the overall spread or dispersion of the distribution. For a discrete probability distribution, it can be computed using the following equation:

$$\text{variance} = \sum_{i=1}^{n} [X_i - E(X)]^2 P(X_i) \qquad \text{(2-9)}$$

where

$$X_i = \text{random variable's possible values}$$

$$E(X) = \text{expected value of the random variable}$$

$$[X_i - E(X)] = \text{difference between each value of the random variable and the expected value}$$

$$P(X_i) = \text{probability of each possible value of the random variable}$$

To compute the variance, each value of the random variable is subtracted from the expected value, squared, and multiplied times the probability of occurrence of that value. The results are then summed to obtain the variance. Here is how this procedure is done for Dr. Shannon's textbook question:

$$\text{variance} = \sum_{i=1}^{5} [X_i - E(X)]^2 P(X_i)$$

$$\text{variance} = (5 - 2.9)^2(0.1) + (4 - 2.9)^2(0.2) + (3 - 2.9)^2(0.3) + (2 - 2.9)^2(0.3) \\ + (1 - 2.9)^2(0.1)$$

$$= (2.1)^2(0.1) + (1.1)^2(0.2) + (0.1)^2(0.3) + (-0.9)^2(0.3) + (-1.9)^2(0.1)$$

$$= 0.441 + 0.242 + 0.003 + 0.243 + 0.361$$

$$= 1.29$$

A related measure of dispersion or spread is the *standard deviation*. This quantity is also used in many computations involved with probability distributions. The standard deviation is just the square root of the variance.

$$\sigma = \sqrt{\text{variance}} \qquad \text{(2-10)}$$

where

$$\sqrt{} = \text{square root}$$

$$\sigma = \text{standard deviation}$$

The standard deviation for the textbook question is

$$\sigma = \sqrt{\text{variance}}$$
$$= \sqrt{1.29} = 1.14$$

Probability Distribution of a Continuous Random Variable

There are many examples of *continuous random variables*. The time it takes to finish a project, the number of ounces in a barrel of butter, the high temperature during a given day, the exact length of a given type of lumber, and the weight of a railroad car of coal are all examples of continuous random variables. Since random variables can take on an infinite number of values, the fundamental probability rules for continuous random variables must be modified.

As with discrete probability distributions, the sum of the probability values must equal 1. Because there are an infinite number of values of the random variables, however, the probability of each value of the random variable must be 0. If the probability values for the random variable values were greater than 0, the sum would be infinitely large.

With a continuous probability distribution, there is a continuous mathematical function that describes the probability distribution. This function is called the *probability density function* or simply the *probability function*. It is usually represented by *f(X)*.

A probability density function, f(x), is a mathematical way of describing the probability distribution.

We now look at the sketch of a sample density function in Figure 2.6. This curve represents the probability density function for the weight of a particular machined part. The weight could vary from 5.06 to 5.30 grams, with weights around 5.18 grams being the most likely. The shaded area represents the probability the weight is between 5.22 and 5.26 grams.

If we wanted to know the probability of a part weighing exactly 5.1300000 grams, for example, we would have to compute the area of a slice of width 0. Of course, this would be 0. This result may seem strange, but if we insist on enough decimal places of accuracy, we are bound to find that the weight differs from 5.1300000 grams *exactly*, be the difference ever so slight.

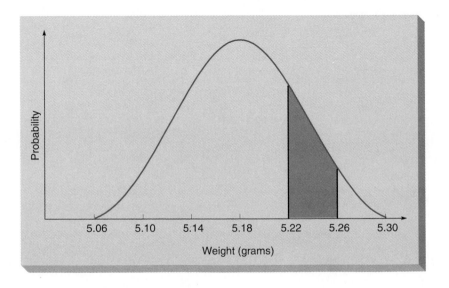

FIGURE 2.6

Sample Density Function

In this section we have investigated the fundamental characteristics and properties of probability distributions in general. In the next three sections we introduce two important continuous distributions—the normal distribution and the exponential distribution—and a useful discrete probability distribution—the Poisson distribution.

2.10 THE NORMAL DISTRIBUTION

The normal distribution affects a large number of processes in our lives (for example, filling boxes of cereal with 32 ounces of corn flakes). Each normal distribution depends on the mean and standard deviation.

One of the most popular and useful continuous probability distributions is the *normal distribution*. The probability density function of this distribution is given by the rather complex formula

$$f(X) = \frac{1}{\sigma\sqrt{2\pi}} e \left[\frac{-\frac{1}{2}(X - \mu)^2}{\sigma^2} \right] \tag{2-11}$$

The normal distribution is specified completely when values for the mean, μ, and the standard deviation, σ, are known. Figure 2.7 shows several different normal distributions with the same standard deviation and different means. As shown, differing values of μ will shift the average or center of the normal distribution. The overall shape of the distribution remains the same. On the other hand, when the standard deviation is varied, the normal curve either flattens out or becomes steeper. This is shown in Figure 2.8.

As the standard deviation, σ, becomes smaller, the normal distribution becomes steeper. When the standard deviation becomes larger, the normal distribution has a tendency to flatten out or become broader.

Area under the Normal Curve

Because the normal distribution is symmetrical, its midpoint (and highest point) is at the mean. Values on the X axis are then measured in terms of how many standard deviations they lie from the mean. As you may recall from our earlier discussion of the uni-

FIGURE 2.7

Normal Distribution with Different Values for μ

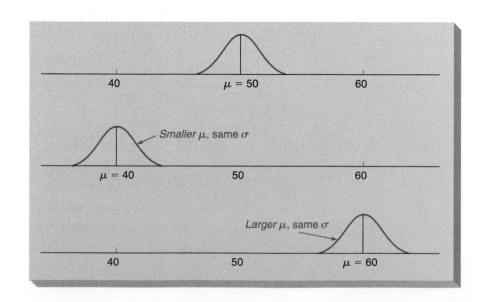

IN ACTION   Using Probability Distributions to Search for Sunken Gold

In 1857, most people traveling from California to New York sailed by steamer from San Francisco to the west coast of Panama, crossed the isthmus by train, and took a steamship to New York. The *Central America* operated on the Atlantic side of the Panama route, taking passengers and gold from California to New York. She sank 200 miles off the coast of South Carolina in a hurricane in 1857, taking gold bars and coins worth an estimated $400 million to the ocean bottom almost 8,000 feet below. Some 425 people lost their lives.

In 1985, Lawrence Stone was hired by the Columbus-America Discovery Group to develop a probability distribution map for the location of the *Central America*. The work was to be based on historical information from survivors and ships in the area at the time. The objective was to use the map to design an efficient search plan that would produce a high probability of finding the target. It would provide specific directions for performing a search and serve as a basis for estimating the amount of time, effort, and money necessary to assure a high probability of success.

Stone's work first involved quantifying all relevant information. He then assigned each scenario a probability distribution and developed the "probability map" as the estimate of the wreck's location from each scenario.

The project was successful. In 1989, the group recovered 1 ton of gold bars and coins from the wreck. Some 39 insurance companies then filed claims to the recovered gold, but all claims were settled in favor of the Columbus-America Discovery Group.

Source: Lawrence D. Stone. "Search for the SS *Central America*," *Interfaces* 22, 1 (January–February 1992): 32-54.

form distribution, the area under the curve (in a continuous distribution) describes the probability that a random variable has a value in a specified interval. When dealing with the uniform distribution, it was easy to compute the area between any points *a* and *b*. The normal distribution requires mathematical calculations beyond the scope of this book, but tables that provide areas or probabilities are readily available. For example, Figure 2.9 illustrates three commonly used relationships that have been derived from standard normal tables (to be discussed shortly). The area from point *a* to point *b* in the first drawing represents the probability, 68%, that the random variable will be within 1 standard deviation of the mean. In the middle graph, we see that about 95.4% of the area lies within plus or minus 2 standard deviations of the mean. The third figure shows that 99.7% lies between $\pm 3\sigma$.

95% confidence is actually ± 1.96 standard deviations, whereas ± 3 standard deviations is actually a 99.7% spread.

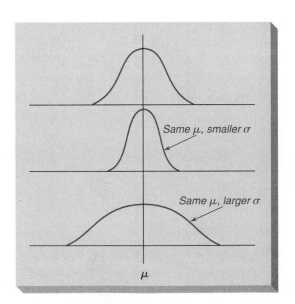

FIGURE 2.8

Normal Distribution with Different Values for σ

FIGURE 2.9

Three Common Areas
under Normal Curves

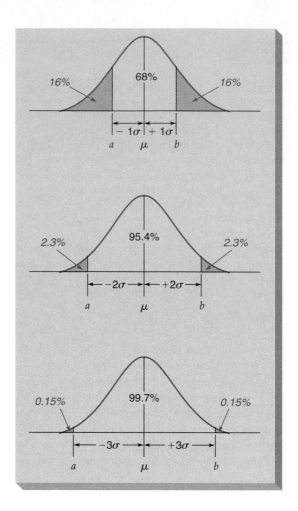

*Figure 2.9 is very important,
and you should comprehend
the meanings of ±1, 2, and 3
standard deviation
symmetrical areas.
Managers often speak of
95% and 99% confidence
interval, which roughly refer
to ±2 and 3 standard
deviation graphs.*

Translating Figure 2.9 into an application implies that if the mean IQ in the United States
is $\mu = 100$ points, and if the standard deviation is $\sigma = 15$ points, we can make the following statements:

1. 68% of the population have IQs between 85 and 115 points (namely, $\pm 1\sigma$).

2. 95.4% of the people have IQs between 70 and 130 points ($\pm 2\sigma$).

3. 99.7% of the population have IQs in the range from 55 to 145 points ($\pm 3\sigma$).

4. Only 16% of the people have IQs greater than 115 points (from first graph, the
   area to the right of $+1\sigma$).

Many more interesting remarks could be drawn from these data. Can you tell the probability that a person selected at random has an IQ of less than 70? Greater than 145? Less
than 130?

Using the Standard Normal Table

To use a table to find normal probability values, we follow two steps.

Step 1: Convert the normal distribution to what we call a *standard normal distribution*. A
standard normal distribution is one that has a mean of 0 and a standard deviation of 1. All
normal tables are set up to handle random variables with $\mu = 0$ and $\sigma = 1$. Without a

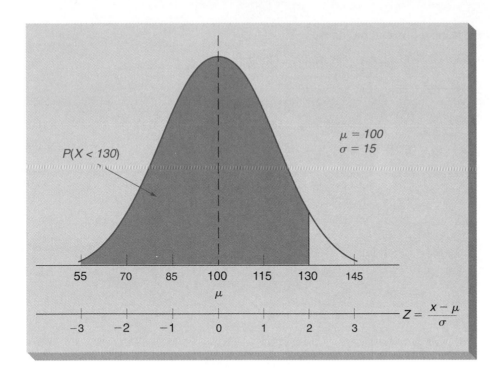

FIGURE 2.10

Normal Distribution Showing the Relationship between Z Values and X Values

standard normal distribution, a different table would be needed for each pair of μ and σ values. We call the new standard random variable Z. The value for Z for any normal distribution is computed from this equation:

$$Z = \frac{X - \mu}{\sigma} \qquad (2\text{-}12)$$

where

$X =$ value of the random variable we want to measure

$\mu =$ mean of the distribution

$\sigma =$ standard deviation of the distribution

$Z =$ number of standard deviations from X to the mean, μ

For example, if $\mu = 100$, $\sigma = 15$, and we are interested in finding the probability that the random variable X is less than 130, we want $P(X < 130)$.

$$Z = \frac{X - \mu}{\sigma} = \frac{130 - 100}{15}$$

$$= \frac{30}{15} = 2 \text{ standard deviations}$$

This means that the point X is 2.0 standard deviations to the right of the mean. This is shown in Figure 2.10.

Step 2: Look up the probability from a table of normal curve areas. Table 2.5, which also appears as appendix A, is such a table of areas for the standard normal distribution. It is set up to provide the area under the curve to the left of any specified value of Z.

TABLE 2.5   Standardized Normal Distribution Function

	AREA UNDER THE NORMAL CURVE									
Z	0.00	0.01	0.02	0.03	0.04	0.05	0.06	0.07	0.08	0.09
0.0	.50000	.50399	.50798	.51197	.51595	.51994	.52392	.52790	.53188	.53586
0.1	.53983	.54380	.54776	.55172	.55567	.55962	.56356	.56749	.57142	.57535
0.2	.57926	.58317	.58706	.59095	.59483	.59871	.60257	.60642	.61026	.61409
0.3	.61791	.62172	.62552	.62930	.63307	.63683	.64058	.64431	.64803	.65173
0.4	.65542	.65910	.66276	.66640	.67003	.67364	.67724	.68082	.68439	.68793
0.5	.69146	.69497	.69847	.70194	.70540	.70884	.71226	.71566	.71904	.72240
0.6	.72575	.72907	.73237	.73536	.73891	.74215	.74537	.74857	.75175	.75490
0.7	.75804	.76115	.76424	.76730	.77035	.77337	.77637	.77935	.78230	.78524
0.8	.78814	.79103	.79389	.79673	.79955	.80234	.80511	.80785	.81057	.81327
0.9	.81594	.81859	.82121	.82381	.82639	.82894	.83147	.83398	.83646	.83891
1.0	.84134	.84375	.84614	.84849	.85083	.85314	.85543	.85769	.85993	.86214
1.1	.86433	.86650	.86864	.87076	.87286	.87493	.87698	.87900	.88100	.88298
1.2	.88493	.88686	.88877	.89065	.89251	.89435	.89617	.89796	.89973	.90147
1.3	.90320	.90490	.90658	.90824	.90988	.91149	.91309	.91466	.91621	.91774
1.4	.91924	.92073	.92220	.92364	.92507	.92647	.92785	.92922	.93056	.93189
1.5	.93319	.93448	.93574	.93699	.93822	.93943	.94062	.94179	.94295	.94408
1.6	.94520	.94630	.94738	.94845	.94950	.95053	.95154	.95254	.95352	.95449
1.7	.95543	.95637	.95728	.95818	.95907	.95994	.96080	.96164	.96246	.96327
1.8	.96407	.96485	.96562	.96638	.96712	.96784	.96856	.96926	.96995	.97062
1.9	.97128	.97193	.97257	.97320	.97381	.97441	.97500	.97558	.97615	.97670

Source: Richard I. Levin and Charles A. Kirkpatrick. *Quantitative Approaches to Management*, 4th ed. Copyright © 1978, 1975, 1971, 1965 by McGraw-Hill, Inc. Used with permission of the McGraw-Hill Book Company.

Let's see how Table 2.5 can be used. The column on the left lists values of Z, with the second decimal place of Z appearing in the top row. For example, for a value of $Z = 2.00$ as just computed, find 2.0 in the left-hand column and 0.00 in the top row. In the body of the table, we find that the area sought is 0.97725, or 97.7%. Thus,

To be sure you understand the concept of symmetry in Table 2.5, try to find the probability such as **P(X < 85).** *Note that the standard normal table shows only right-hand-side Z values.*

$$P(X < 130) = P(Z < 2.00) = 97.7\%$$

This suggests that if the mean IQ score is 100, with a standard deviation of 15 points, the probability that a randomly selected person's IQ is less than 130 is 97.7%. By referring back to Figure 2.9, we see that this probability could also have been derived from the middle graph. (Note that $1.0 - 0.977 = 0.023 = 2.3\%$, which is the area in the right-hand tail of the curve.)

AREA UNDER THE NORMAL CURVE

Z	0.00	0.01	0.02	0.03	0.04	0.05	0.06	0.07	0.08	0.09
2.0	.97725	.97784	.97831	.97882	.97932	.97982	.98030	.98077	.98124	.98169
2.1	.98214	.98257	.98300	.98341	.98382	.98422	.98461	.98500	.98537	.98574
2.2	.98610	.98645	.98679	.98713	.98745	.98778	.98809	.98840	.98870	.98899
2.3	.98928	.98956	.98983	.99010	.99036	.99061	.99086	.99111	.99134	.99158
2.4	.99180	.99202	.99224	.99245	.99266	.99286	.99305	.99324	.99343	.99361
2.5	.99379	.99396	.99413	.99430	.99446	.99461	.99477	.99492	.99506	.99520
2.6	.99534	.99547	.99560	.99573	.99585	.99598	.99609	.99621	.99632	.99643
2.7	.99653	.99664	.99674	.99683	.99693	.99702	.99711	.99720	.99728	.99736
2.8	.99744	.99752	.99760	.99767	.99774	.99781	.99788	.99795	.99801	.99807
2.9	.99813	.99819	.99825	.99831	.99836	.99841	.99846	.99851	.99856	.99861
3.0	.99865	.99869	.99874	.99878	.99882	.99886	.99899	.99893	.99896	.99900
3.1	.99903	.99906	.99910	.99913	.99916	.99918	.99921	.99924	.99926	.99929
3.2	.99931	.99934	.99936	.99938	.99940	.99942	.99944	.99946	.99948	.99950
3.3	.99952	.99953	.99955	.99957	.99958	.99960	.99961	.99962	.99964	.99965
3.4	.99966	.99968	.99969	.99970	.99971	.99972	.99973	.99974	.99975	.99976
3.5	.99977	.99978	.99978	.99979	.99980	.99981	.99981	.99982	.99983	.99983
3.6	.99984	.99985	.99985	.99986	.99986	.99987	.99987	.99988	.99988	.99989
3.7	.99989	.99990	.99990	.99990	.99991	.99991	.99992	.99992	.99992	.99992
3.8	.99993	.99993	.99993	.99994	.99994	.99994	.99994	.99995	.99995	.99995
3.9	.99995	.99995	.99996	.99996	.99996	.99996	.99996	.99996	.99997	.99997

To feel comfortable with the use of the standard normal probability table, we need to work a few more examples. We now use the Haynes Construction Company as a case in point.

Haynes Construction Company Example

Haynes Construction Company builds primarily three- and four-unit apartment buildings (called triplexes and quadraplexes) for investors, and it is believed that the total construction time in days follows a normal distribution. The mean time to construct a triplex is 100 days, and the standard deviation is 20 days. Recently, the president of Haynes Construction signed a contract to complete a triplex in 125 days. Failure to complete the

FIGURE 2.11

Normal Distribution
for Haynes Construction

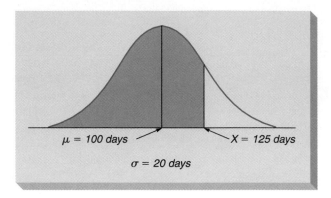

triplex in 125 days would result in severe penalty fees. What is the probability that Haynes Construction will not be in violation of their construction contract? The normal distribution for the construction of triplexes is shown in Figure 2.11.

To compute this probability, we need to find the shaded area under the curve. We begin by computing Z for this problem:

$$Z = \frac{X - \mu}{\sigma}$$

$$= \frac{125 - 100}{20}$$

$$= \frac{25}{20} = 1.25$$

Looking in Table 2.5 for a Z value of 1.25, we find an area under the curve of 0.89435. (We do this by looking up 1.2 in the left-hand column of the table and then moving to the 0.05 column to find the value for $Z = 1.25$.) Therefore, the probability of not violating the contract is 0.89435, or about an 89% chance.

Now let us look at the Haynes problem from another perspective. If the firm finishes this triplex in 75 days or less, it will be awarded a bonus payment of $5,000. What is the probability that Haynes will receive the bonus?

Figure 2.12 illustrates the probability we are looking for in the shaded area. The first step is again to compute the Z value:

$$Z = \frac{X - \mu}{\sigma}$$

$$= \frac{75 - 100}{20}$$

$$= \frac{-25}{20} = -1.25$$

This Z value indicates that 75 days is -1.25 standard deviations to the left of the mean. But the standard normal table is structured to handle only positive Z values. To solve this problem, we observe that the curve is symmetric. The probability that Haynes will finish in *less than 75 days* is *equivalent* to the probability that it will finish in *more than 125 days*. A

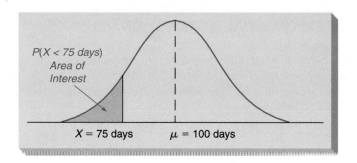

FIGURE 2.12
Probability That Haynes Will Receive the Bonus by Finishing in 75 Days

moment ago (in Figure 2.11) we found the probability that Haynes will finish in less than 125 days. That value was 0.89435. So the probability it takes more than 125 days is

$$P(X > 125) = 1.0 - P(X < 125)$$
$$= 1.0 - 0.89435 = 0.10565$$

Thus, the probability of completing the triplex in 75 days or less is 0.10565, or about 10%.

One final example: What is the probability that the triplex will take between 110 and 125 days? We see in Figure 2.13 that

$$P(110 < X < 125) = P(X < 125) - P(X < 110)$$

That is, the shaded area in the graph can be computed by finding the probability of completing the building in 125 days or less *minus* the probability of completing it in 110 days or less.

Recall that $P(X < 125$ days$)$ is equal to 0.89435. To find $P(X < 110$ days$)$, we follow the two steps developed earlier.

1. $Z = \dfrac{X - \mu}{\sigma} = \dfrac{110 - 100}{20} = \dfrac{10}{20}$

   $= 0.5$ standard deviations

2. From Table 2.5, the area for $Z = 0.50$ is 0.69146. So the probability the triplex can be completed in less than 110 days is 0.69146. Finally,

   $$P(110 < X < 125) = 0.89435 - 0.69146 = 0.20289$$

The probability that it will take between 110 and 125 days is about 20%.

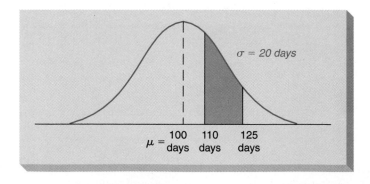

FIGURE 2.13
Probability of Haynes' Completion between 110 and 125 Days

2.11 THE EXPONENTIAL DISTRIBUTION

The *exponential distribution*, also called the *negative exponential distribution*, is used in dealing with queuing problems. The exponential distribution describes the number of customers serviced in a time interval. The exponential distribution is a continuous distribution. Its probability function is given by

$$f(X) = \mu e^{-\mu x} \tag{2-13}$$

where

    X = random variable (service times)

    μ = average number of units the service facility can handle in a specific period of time

    e = 2.718 (the base of natural logarithms)

The general shape of the exponential distribution is shown in Figure 2.14. Its expected value and variance can be shown to be

$$\text{expected value} = \frac{1}{\mu} \tag{2-14}$$

$$\text{variance} = \frac{1}{\mu^2} \tag{2-15}$$

The exponential distribution will be illustrated again in Chapter 14.

2.12 THE POISSON DISTRIBUTION

An important *discrete* probability distribution is the *Poisson distribution*.[1] We examine it because of its key role in complementing the exponential distribution in queuing theory in Chapter 14. The distribution describes situations in which customers arrive independently

FIGURE 2.14

Negative Exponential Distribution

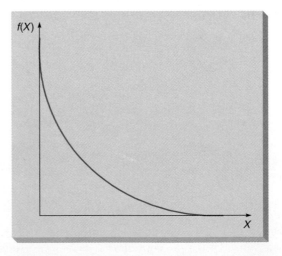

---

[1] This distribution, derived by Simeon Poisson in 1837, is pronounced "pwah-sahn."

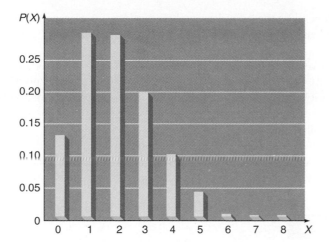

FIGURE 2.15
Sample Poisson Distribution
with $\lambda = 2$

during a certain time interval, and the number of arrivals depends on the length of the time interval. Examples are patients arriving at a health clinic, customers arriving at a bank window, passengers arriving at an airport, and telephone calls going through a central exchange.

The formula for the Poisson distribution is

$$P(X) = \frac{\lambda^x e^{-\lambda}}{X!}$$ (2-16)

where

$P(X)$ = probability of exactly X arrivals or occurrences

λ = average number of arrivals per unit of time (the mean arrival rate), pronounced "lambda"

e = 2.718, the base of the natural logarithms

X = specific value (0, 1, 2, 3, and so on) of the random variable

The mean and variance of the Poisson distribution are equal and are computed simply as

expected value = λ (2-17)

variance = λ (2-18)

A sample distribution for $\lambda = 2$ arrivals is shown in Figure 2.15 (the values plotted are derived from tables in appendix C).

Summary

This chapter presented the fundamental concepts of probability and probability distributions. Probability values can be obtained objectively or subjectively. A single probability value must be between 0 and 1, and the sum of all probability values for all possible outcomes must be equal to 1. In addition, probability values and events can have a number of properties. These properties include mutually exclusive, collectively exhaustive, statistically independent, and statistically dependent events. Rules for computing probability values depend on these fundamental properties. It is also possible to revise probability values when new information becomes available. This can be done using Bayes' theorem.

We also covered the topics of random variables, discrete probability distributions (such as Poisson), and continuous probability distributions (such as normal and exponential). A probability distribution is any statement of a probability function having a set of collectively exhaustive and mutually exclusive events. All probability distributions follow the basic probability rules above.

The topics presented here will be very important in many of the chapters to come. Basic probability concepts and distributions are used for decision theory, inventory control, Markov analysis, quality control, project management, and simulation.

Glossary

Probability. A statement about the likelihood of an event occurring. It is expressed as a numerical value between 0 and 1, inclusive.

Relative Frequency Approach. An objective way of determining probabilities based on observing frequencies over a number of trials.

Classical or Logical Approach. An objective way of assessing probabilities based on logic.

Subjective Approach. A method of determining probability values based on experience or judgment.

Mutually Exclusive Events. A situation in which only one event can occur on any given trial or experiment.

Collectively Exhaustive Events. A collection of all possible outcomes of an experiment.

Independent Events. The situation in which the occurrence of one event has no effect on the probability of occurrence of a second event.

Dependent Events. The situation in which the occurrence of one event affects the probability of occurrence of some other event.

Marginal Probability. The simple probability of an event occurring.

Joint Probability. The probability of events occurring together (or one after the other).

Conditional Probability. The probability of one event occurring given that another has taken place.

Revised or Posterior Probability. A probability value that results from new or revised information and prior probabilities.

Prior Probability. A probability value determined before new or additional information is obtained. It is sometimes called an a priori probability estimate.

Bayes' Theorem. A formula that allows us to compute conditional probabilities when dealing with statistically dependent events.

Random Variable. A variable that assigns a number to every possible outcome of an experiment.

Discrete Random Variable. A random variable that can only assume a finite or limited set of values.

Continuous Random Variable. A random variable that can assume an infinite or unlimited set of values.

Probability Distribution. The set of all possible values of a random variable and their associated probabilities.

Discrete Probability Distribution. A probability distribution with a discrete random variable.

Continuous Probability Distribution. A probability distribution with a continuous random variable.

Expected Value. The (weighted) average of a probability distribution.

Variance. A measure of dispersion or spread of the probability distribution.

Standard Deviation. The square root of the variance.

Probability Density Function. The mathematical function that describes a continuous probability distribution. It is represented by $f(X)$.

Normal Distribution. A continuous bell-shaped distribution that is a function of two parameters, the mean and standard deviation of the distribution.

Negative Exponential Distribution. A continuous probability distribution that describes the time between customer arrivals in a queuing situation.

Poisson Distribution. A discrete probability distribution used in queuing theory.

Key Equations

(2-1) $0 \leq P(\text{event}) \leq 1$
A basic statement of probability.

(2-2) $P(A \text{ or } B) = P(A) + P(B)$
Law of addition for mutually exclusive events.

(2-3) $P(A \text{ or } B) = P(A) + P(B) - P(A \text{ and } B)$
Law of addition for events that are not mutually exclusive.

(2-4) $P(AB) = P(A) \times P(B)$
Joint probability for independent events.

(2-5) $P(A \mid B) = \dfrac{P(AB)}{P(B)}$
Bayes' law for conditional probabilities.

(2-6) $P(AB) = P(A \mid B) \times P(B)$
Joint probability for dependent events: a restatement of Bayes' law.

(2-7) $P(A \mid B) = \dfrac{P(B \mid A)P(A)}{P(B \mid A)P(A) + P(B \mid \overline{A})P(\overline{A})}$
A restatement of Bayes' law in general form.

(2-8) $E(X) = \sum\limits_{i=1}^{n} X_i P(X_i)$
This equation computes the expected value of a discrete probability distribution.

(2-9) $\text{Variance} = \sum\limits_{i=1}^{n} [X_i - E(X)]^2 \, P(X_i)$
This equation computes the variance of a discrete probability distribution.

(2-10) $\sigma = \sqrt{\text{variance}}$
This equation computes the standard deviation from the variance.

(2-11) $f(X) = \dfrac{1}{\sigma\sqrt{2\pi}} \ e^{\left[\dfrac{-^1\!/_2(X - \mu)^2}{\sigma^2}\right]}$
This is the density function for the normal probability distribution.

(2-12) $Z = \dfrac{X - \mu}{\sigma}$
This equation computes the number of standard deviations, Z, the point X is from the mean μ.

(2-13) $f(X) = \mu e^{-\mu x}$
The exponential distribution.

(2-14) $\text{Expected value} = \dfrac{1}{\mu}$
The expected value of an exponential distribution.

(2-15) Variance $= \dfrac{1}{\mu^2}$

The variance of an exponential distribution.

(2-16) $P(X) = \dfrac{\lambda^x e^{-\lambda}}{X!}$

The Poisson distribution.

(2-17) Expected value $= \lambda$

The mean of a Poisson distribution.

(2-18) Variance $= \lambda$

The variance of a Poisson distribution.

Solved Problems

Solved Problem 2-1

In the past 30 days, Roger's Rural Roundup has sold either 8, 9, 10, or 11 lottery tickets. It never sold fewer than 8 nor more than 11. Assuming that the past is similar to the future, find the probabilities:

Solution

SALES	NO. DAYS	PROBABILITY
8	10	0.333
9	12	0.400
10	6	0.200
11	2	0.067
Total	30	1.000

Solved Problem 2-2

A class contains 30 students. Ten are female (F) and U.S. citizens (U); 12 are male (M) and U.S. citizens; 6 are female and non-U.S. citizens (N); 2 are male and non-U.S. citizens.

A name is randomly selected from the class roster and it is female. What is the probability that the student is a U.S. citizen?

Solution

$$P(FU) = {}^{10}\!/_{30} = 0.333$$

$$P(FN) = {}^{6}\!/_{30} = 0.200$$

$$P(MU) = {}^{12}\!/_{30} = 0.400$$

$$P(MN) = {}^{2}\!/_{30} = 0.067$$

$$P(F) = P(FU) + P(FN) = 0.333 + 0.200 = 0.533$$

$$P(M) = P(MU) + P(MN) = 0.400 + 0.067 = 0.467$$

$$P(U) = P(FU) + P(MU) = 0.333 + 0.400 = 0.733$$

$$P(N) = P(FN) + P(MN) = 0.200 + 0.067 = 0.267$$

By Bayes' law,

$$P(U \mid F) = \frac{P(FU)}{P(F)} = \frac{0.333}{0.533} = 0.625$$

Solved Problem 2-3

Your professor tells you that if you score an 85 or better on your midterm exam, then you have a 90% chance of getting an A for the course. You think you have only a 50% chance of scoring 85 or better. Find the probability that *both* your score is 85 or better *and* you receive an A in the course.

Solution

$$P(\text{A and }85) = P(\text{A} \mid 85) \times P(85) = (0.90)(0.50) =$$

$$= 45\%$$

Solved Problem 2-4

A statistics class was asked if it believed that all tests on the Monday following the football game win over their archrival should be postponed automatically. The results were:

Strongly agree	40
Agree	30
Neutral	20
Disagree	10
Strongly disagree	0
	100

Transform this into a numeric score, using the following random variable scale and find a probability distribution for the results.

Strongly agree	5
Agree	4
Neutral	3
Disagree	2
Strongly disagree	1

Solution

OUTCOME	PROBABILITY, $P(X)$
Strongly agree (5)	0.4 = 40/100
Agree (4)	0.3 = 30/100
Neutral (3)	0.2 = 20/100
Disagree (2)	0.1 = 10/100
Strongly disagree (1)	0.0 = 0/100
Total	1.0 = 100/100

Solved Problem 2-5

Compute the expected value for the question in Solved Problem 2-4

Solution

$$E(x) = \sum_{i=1}^{5} x_i P(x_i) = x_1 P(x_1) + x_2 P(x_2)$$

$$+ x_3 P(x_3) + x_4 P(x_4) + x_5 P(x_5)$$

$$= 5(0.4) + 4(0.3) + 3(0.2) + 2(0.1) + 1(0)$$

$$= 4.0$$

Solved Problem 2-6

Compute the variance and standard deviation for the question in Solved Problem 2-4

Solution

$$\text{Variance} = \sum_{i=1}^{5} (x_i - E(x))^2 P(x_i)$$

$$= (5 - 4)^2(0.4) + (4 - 4)^2(0.3) + (3 - 4)^2(0.2) + (2 - 4)^2(0.1) + (1 - 4)^2(0.0)$$

$$= (1)^2(0.4) + (0)^2(0.3) + (-1)^2(0.2) + (-2)^2(0.1) + (-3)^2(0.0)$$

$$= 0.4 + 0.0 + 0.2 + 0.4 + 0.0 = 1.0$$

The standard deviation is

$$\sigma = \sqrt{\text{variance}} = \sqrt{1} = 1$$

Solved Problem 2-7

The length of the rods coming out of our new cutting machine can be said to approximate a normal distribution with a mean of 10 inches and a standard deviation of 0.2 inch. Find the probability that a rod selected randomly will have a length

(a) of less than 10.0 inches

(b) between 10.0 and 10.4 inches

(c) between 10.0 and 10.1 inches

(d) between 10.1 and 10.4 inches

(e) between 9.9 and 9.6 inches

(f) between 9.9 and 10.4 inches

(g) between 9.886 and 10.406 inches

Solution

First compute the standard normal distribution, the Z-value:

$$Z = \frac{x - \mu}{\sigma}$$

Next, find the area under the curve for the given Z-value by using a standard normal distribution table.

(a) $P(x < 10.0) = 0.50000$

(b) $P(10.0 < x < 10.4) = 0.97725 - 0.50000 = 0.47725$

(c) $P(10.0 < x < 10.1) = 0.69146 - 0.50000 = 0.19146$

(d) $P(10.1 < x < 10.4) = 0.97725 - 0.69146 = 0.28579$

(e) $P(9.9 < x < 9.6) = 0.97725 - 0.69146 = 0.28579$

(f) $P(9.9 < x < 10.4) = 0.19146 + 0.47725 = 0.66871$

(g) $P(9.886 < x < 10.406) = 0.47882 + 0.21566 = 0.69448$

SELF-TEST

- Before taking the self-test, refer back to the learning objectives at the beginning of the chapter and the glossary at the end of the chapter.
- Use the key at the back of the book to correct your answers.
- Restudy pages that correspond to any questions that you answered incorrectly or material you feel uncertain about.

1. Discrete probability distributions require that
   a. the events are mutually inclusive.
   b. the probability values total 1.
   c. the individual probability values are between 0 and 1.
   d. all of the above.
2. A measure of central tendency is
   a. expected value.
   b. variance.
   c. standard deviation.
   d. all of the above.
3. The distributions that deal with queuing problems do *not* include
   a. exponential distributions.
   b. Poisson distributions.
   c. normal distributions.
   d. all of the above deal with queuing problems.
4. To compute the variance, you need to know the
   a. variable's possible values.
   b. expected value of the variable.
   c. probability of each possible value of the variable.
   d. all of the above.
5. The square root of the variance is the
   a. expected value.
   b. standard deviation.
   c. area under the normal curve.
   d. all of the above.
6. The Poisson distribution is a _____ distribution.
7. Total probability of the discrete probability distribution is found by _____ .
8. Total probability of the continuous probability distribution is found by _____ .
9. In either type of probability distribution, total probability must equal _____ .
10. The probability of two or more independent events occurring is the
    a. marginal probability.
    b. simple probability.
    c. conditional probability.
    d. joint probability.
    e. all of the above.
11. In the normal distribution, 95.45% of the population lies within _____ standard deviations of the mean.
12. If a normal distribution has a mean of 200 and a standard deviation of 10, 99.7% of the population falls within what range of values?
    a. 170-230
    b. 180-220
    c. 190-210
    d. 175-225
    e. 170-220
13. Two types of random variables are
    a. binomial and Poisson.
    b. normal and continuous.
    c. discrete and expected value.
    d. continuous and discrete.
    e. uniform and continuous.
14. If $P(A) = 0.4$ and $P(B) = 0.5$ and $P(A$ and $B) = 0.2$, then $P(B \mid A) =$
    a. 0.80.
    b. 0.50.
    c. 0.10.
    d. 0.40.
    e. none of the above.
15. If $P(A) = 0.4$ and $P(B) = 0.5$ and $P(A$ and $B) = 0.2$, then $P(A$ or $B) =$
    a. 0.7.
    b. 0.9.
    c. 1.1.
    d. 0.2.
    e. none of the above.

Discussion Questions and Problems

Discussion Questions

2-1 What are the two basic laws of probability?

2-2 What is the meaning of mutually exclusive events? What is meant by collectively exhaustive? Give an example of each.

2-3 Describe the various approaches used in determining probability values.

2-4 Why is the probability of the intersection of two events subtracted in the sum of the probability of two events?

2-5 What is the difference between events that are dependent and events that are independent?

2-6 What is Bayes' theorem, and when can it be used?

2-7 How can probability revisions assist in managerial decision making?

2-8 What is a random variable? What are the various types of random variables?

2-9 What is the difference between a discrete probability distribution and a continuous probability distribution? Give your own example of each.

2-10 What is the expected value, and what does it measure? How is it computed for a discrete probability distribution?

2-11 What is the variance, and what does it measure? How is it computed for a discrete probability distribution?

2-12 Name three business processes that can be described by the normal distribution.

2-13 After evaluating student response to a question about a case used in class, the instructor constructed the following probability distribution. What kind of probability distribution is it?

RESPONSE	RANDOM VARIABLE, X	PROBABILITY
Excellent	5	0.05
Good	4	0.25
Average	3	0.40
Fair	2	0.15
Poor	1	0.15

Problems

2-14 A student taking Management Science 301 at East Haven University will receive one of five possible grades for the course: A, B, C, D, or F. The distribution of grades over the past two years is as follows:

GRADE	NUMBER OF STUDENTS
A	80
B	75
C	90
D	30
F	25
	Total 300

If this past distribution is a good indicator of future grades, what is the probability of a student receiving a C in the course?

• **2-15** A silver dollar is flipped twice. Calculate the probability of each of the following occurring.
   (a) A head on the first flip
   (b) A tail on the second flip given that the first toss was a head
   (c) Two tails
   (d) A tail on the first and a head on the second
   (e) A tail on the first and a head on the second or a head on the first and a tail on the second
   (f) At least one head on the two flips

• **2-16** An urn contains 8 red chips, 10 green chips, and 2 white chips. A chip is drawn and replaced, and then a second chip drawn. What is the probability of
   (a) a white chip on the first draw?
   (b) a white chip on the first draw and a red on the second?
   (c) two green chips being drawn?
   (d) a red chip on the second, given that a white chip was drawn on the first?

• **2-17** Evertight, a leading manufacturer of quality nails, produces 1-, 2-, 3-, 4-, and 5-inch nails for various uses. In the production process, if there is an overrun or if the nails are slightly defective, they are placed in a common bin. Yesterday, 651 of the 1-inch nails, 243 of the 2-inch nails, 41 of the 3-inch nails, 451 of the 4-inch nails, and 333 of the 5-inch nails were placed in the bin.
   (a) What is the probability of reaching into the bin and getting a 4-inch nail?
   (b) What is the probability of getting a 5-inch nail?
   (c) If a particular application requires a nail that is 3 inches or shorter, what is the probability of getting a nail that will satisfy the requirements of the application?

• **2-18** Last year, at Northern Manufacturing Company, 200 people had colds during the year. One hundred fifty-five people who did no exercising had colds, while the remainder of the people with colds were involved in a weekly exercise program. Half of the 1,000 employees were involved in some type of exercise.
   (a) What is the probability that an employee will have a cold next year?
   (b) Given that an employee is involved in an exercise program, what is the probability that he or she will get a cold?
   (c) What is the probability that an employee that is not involved in an exercise program will get a cold next year?
   (d) Are exercising and getting a cold independent events? Explain your answer.

• **2-19** The Springfield Kings, a professional basketball team, has won 12 of its last 20 games and is expected to continue winning at the same percentage rate. The team's ticket manager is anxious to attract a large crowd to tomorrow's game but believes that depends on how well the Kings perform tonight against the Galveston Comets. He assesses the probability of drawing a large crowd to be 0.90 should the team win tonight. What is the probability that the team wins tonight and that there will be a large crowd at tomorrow's game?

• **2-20** David Mashley teaches two undergraduate statistics courses at Kansas College. The class for Statistics 201 consists of 7 sophomores and 3 juniors. The more advanced course, Statistics 301, has 2 sophomores and 8 juniors enrolled. As an example of a business sampling technique, Professor Mashley randomly selects, from the stack of Statistics 201 registration cards, the class card of one student and then places that card back in the stack. If that student was a sophomore, Mashley draws another card from the Statistics 201 stack; if not, he randomly draws a card from the Statistics 301 group. Are these two draws independent events? What is the probability of
   (a) a junior's name on the first draw?
   (b) a junior's name on the second draw, given that a sophomore's name was drawn first?
   (c) a junior's name on the second draw, given that a junior's name was drawn first?
   (d) a sophomore's name on both draws?

(e) a junior's name on both draws?

(f) one sophomore's name and one junior's name on the two draws, regardless of order drawn?

2-21 The oasis outpost of Abu Ilan, in the heart of the Negev desert, has a population of 20 Bedouin tribesmen and 20 Farima tribesmen. El Kamin, a nearby oasis, has a population of 32 Bedouins and 8 Farima. A lost Israeli soldier, accidentally separated from his army unit, is wandering through the desert and arrives at the edge of one of the oases. The soldier has no idea which oasis he has found, but the first person he spots at a distance is a Bedouin. What is the probability that he wandered into Abu Ilan? What is the probability that he is in El Kamin?

2-22 The lost Israeli soldier mentioned in Problem 2-21 decides to rest for a few minutes before entering the desert oasis he has just found. Closing his eyes, he dozes off for 15 minutes, wakes, and walks toward the center of the oasis. The first person he spots this time he again recognizes as a Bedouin. What is the posterior probability that he is in El Kamin?

2-23 Ace Machine Works estimates that the probability their lathe tool is properly adjusted is 0.8. When the lathe is properly adjusted, there is a 0.9 probability that the parts produced pass inspection. If the lathe is out of adjustment, however, the probability of a good part being produced is only 0.2. A part randomly chosen is inspected and found to be acceptable. At this point, what is the posterior probability that the lathe tool is properly adjusted?

2-24 The Boston South Fifth Street Softball League consists of three teams: Mama's Boys, team 1; the Killers, team 2; and the Machos, team 3. Each team plays the other teams just once during the season. The win—loss record for the past five years is as follows:

WINNER	(1)	(2)	(3)
Mama's Boys (1)	X	3	4
The Killers (2)	2	X	1
The Machos (3)	1	4	X

Each row represents the number of wins over the past five years. Mama's Boys beat the Killers three times, beat the Machos four times, and so on.

(a) What is the probability that the Killers will win every game next year?

(b) What is the probability that the Machos will win at least one game next year?

(c) What is the probability that Mama's Boys will win exactly one game next year?

(d) What is the probability that the Killers will win less than two games next year?

2-25 The schedule for the Killers next year is as follows (refer to Problem 2-24):

Game 1: the Machos

Game 2: Mama's Boys

(a) What is the probability that the Killers will win their first game?

(b) What is the probability that the Killers will win their last game?

(c) What is the probability that the Killers will break even—win exactly one game?

(d) What is the probability that the Killers will win every game?

(e) What is the probability that the Killers will lose every game?

(f) Would you want to be the coach of the Killers?

2-26 The Northside Rifle team has two markspersons, Dick and Sally. Dick hits a bull's-eye 90% of the time, and Sally hits a bull's-eye 95% of the time.

(a) What is the probability that either Dick or Sally or both will hit the bull's-eye if each takes one shot?

(b) What is the probability that Dick and Sally will both hit the bull's-eye?

(c) Did you make any assumptions in answering the preceding questions? If you answered yes, do you think that you are justified in making the assumption(s)?

⁝ **2-27** In a sample of 1,000 representing a survey from the entire population, 650 people were from Laketown, and the rest of the people were from River City. Out of the sample, 19 people had some form of cancer. Thirteen of these people were from Laketown.

    (a) Are the events of living in Laketown and having some sort of cancer independent?

    (b) Which city would you prefer to live in, assuming that your main objective was to avoid having cancer?

⁝ **2-28** Compute the probability of "loaded die, given that a 3 was rolled," as shown in Example 7, this time using the general form of Bayes' theorem from Equation 2-7.

• **2-29** Which of the following are probability distributions? Why?

(a)

RANDOM VARIABLE X	PROBABILITY
−2	0.1
−1	0.2
0	0.3
1	0.25
2	0.15

(b)

RANDOM VARIABLE Y	PROBABILITY
1	1.1
1.5	0.2
2	0.3
2.5	0.25
3	−1.25

(c)

RANDOM VARIABLE Z	PROBABILITY
1	0.1
2	0.2
3	0.3
4	0.4
5	0.0

• **2-30** Harrington Health Food stocks 5 loaves of Neutro-Bread. The probability distribution for the sales of Neutro-Bread is listed in the following table. How many loaves will Harrington sell on average?

NUMBER OF LOAVES SOLD	PROBABILITY
0	0.05
1	0.15
2	0.20
3	0.25
4	0.20
5	0.15

- **2-31** What are the expected value and variance of the following probability distribution?

RANDOM VARIABLE X	PROBABILITY
1	0.05
2	0.05
3	0.10
4	0.10
5	0.15
6	0.15
7	0.25
8	0.15

- **2-32** Sales for Fast Kat, a 16-foot catamaran sailboat, have averaged 250 boats per month over the last five years, with a standard deviation of 25 boats. Assuming that the demand is about the same as past years and follows a normal curve, what is the probability sales will be less than 280 boats?

- **2-33** Refer to Problem 2-32. What is the probability that sales will be more than 265 boats during the next month? What is the probability that sales will be less than 250 boats next month?

- **2-34** Precision Parts is a job shop that specializes in producing electric motor shafts. The average shaft size for the E300 electric motor is 0.55 inch, with a standard deviation of 0.10 inch. It is normally distributed. What is the probability that a shaft selected at random will be between 0.55 and 0.65 inch?

- **2-35** Refer to Problem 2-34. What is the probability that a shaft size will be greater than 0.65 inch? What is the probability that a shaft size will be between 0.53 and 0.59 inch? What is the probability that a shaft size will be under 0.45 inch?

- **2-36** An industrial oven used to cure sand cores for a factory manufacturing engine blocks for small cars is able to maintain fairly constant temperatures. The temperature range of the oven follows a normal distribution with a mean of 450°F and a standard deviation of 25°F. Leslie Larsen, president of the factory, is concerned about the large number of defective cores that have been produced in the last several months. If the oven gets hotter than 475°F, the core is defective. What is the probability that the oven will cause a core to be defective? What is the probability that the temperature of the oven will range from 460 to 470°F?

- **2-37** Steve Goodman, production foreman for the Florida Gold Fruit Company, estimates that the average sale of oranges is 4,700 and the standard deviation is 500 oranges. Sales follow a normal distribution.
  (a) What is the probability that sales will be greater than 5,500 oranges?
  (b) What is the probability that sales will be greater than 4,500 oranges?
  (c) What is the probability that sales will be less than 4,900 oranges?
  (d) What is the probability that sales will be less than 4,300 oranges?

- **2-38** Susan Williams has been the production manager of Medical Suppliers, Inc., for the past 17 years. Medical Suppliers, Inc., is a producer of bandages and arm slings. During the past five years, the demand for No-Stick bandages has been fairly constant. On the average, sales have been about 87,000 packages of No-Stick. Susan has reason to believe that the distribution of No-Stick follows a normal curve, with a standard deviation of 4,000 packages. What is the probability that sales will be less than 81,000 packages?

2-39 Armstrong Faber produces a standard number two pencil called Ultra-Lite. Since Chuck Armstrong started Armstrong Faber, sales have grown steadily. With the increase in the price of wood products, however, Chuck has been forced to increase the price of the Ultra-Lite pencils. As a result, the demand for Ultra-Lite has been fairly stable over the past six years. On the average, Armstrong Faber has sold 457,000 pencils each year. Furthermore, 90% of the time sales have been between 454,000 and 460,000 pencils. It is expected that the sales follow a normal distribution with a mean of 457,000 pencils. Estimate the standard deviation of this distribution. (*Hint*: Work backward from the normal table to find Z. Then apply Equation 2-12.)

2-40 Patients arrive at the emergency room of Costa Valley Hospital at an average of 3 per day. The demand for emergency room treatment at Costa Valley follows a Poisson distribution.
(a) Using Appendix C, compute the probability of exactly 0, 1, 2, 3, 4, and 5 arrivals per day.
(b) What is the sum of these probabilities, and why is the number less than 1?

2-41 Using the data in Problem 2-40, determine the probability of more than 3 visits for emergency room service on any given day.

2-42 Cars arrive at Carla's Muffler shop for repair work at an average of 3 per hour, following an exponential distribution.
(a) What is the expected time between arrivals?
(b) What is the variance of the time between arrivals?

Case Study

Century Chemical Company

Century Chemical Company, formed in 1975 as a result of the merger of three smaller firms, produces chlorine and caustic soda through the electrolysis of brine. Century's largest plant, located in St. Gabriel, Louisiana, produces approximately 1,500 tons of chlorine and 1,700 tons of caustic soda daily. The St. Gabriel plant operates at capacity; its entire output is sold.

A major problem confronting Century Chemical Corporation is associated with its chlorine collection and handling system. The system incorporates headers that collect chlorine gas from the electrolytic cells. The gas then passes through heat exchangers for cooling and condensation of water entrapped in the chlorine. Residual water in the chlorine gas is removed by "scrubbing" with concentrated sulfuric acid. Thereafter, the dry chlorine gas is chilled by being bubbled through liquid chlorine before being fed to the chlorine compressor. The chlorine compressor is the "heart" of the handling system. It pulls the gas from the cells through the cooling and drying system. Then it compresses the gas for liquefaction and storage as liquid chlorine.

A major problem for the production manager of Century Chemical is the gradual deterioration of the plant's compressor capacity because of the fouling of component parts. The reliability of Century's centrifugal compressor at its St. Gabriel complex is 0.92. The 8% downtime includes cleaning and restoration of capacity as well as other mechanical/electrical failures. Heretofore, management at Century has chosen to incur the downtime and lost sales associated with compressor failures. However, from time to time, management considers the installation of a spare compressor. Currently, the cost of such an installation is estimated to total $800,000. The spare compressor is also projected to have a 0.92 reliability factor.

Approximately 12 hours of downtime are required to change over to an installed spare compressor. Profit and overhead contribution for chlorine is estimated at $50 per ton; the profit and overhead contribution for caustic soda is $40 per ton. Century's cost of capital or opportunity cost is estimated to equal 20%. The useful life of the compressor is estimated to be 10 years. Salvage is assumed to be zero. The effective tax rate is 40%.

Discussion Question

Should management of Century Chemical install the spare compressor? Why or why not? (*Hint:* The present value factor of 20% over 10 years is 4.192.)

Source: Professor Jerry Kinard, Western Carolina University.

Bibliography

Campbell, S. *Flaws and Fallacies in Statistical Thinking*. Upper Saddle River NJ: Prentice Hall, 1974.

Feller, W. *An Introduction to Probability Theory and Its Applications*, Vols. 1 and 2. New York: John Wiley & Sons, Inc., 1957 and 1968.

Hamburg, Morris and Margaret Young. *Statistical Analysis for Decision Making*, 6th ed. San Diego: Harcourt Brace & Company, 1993.

Hanke, J. E. and A. G. Reitsch. *Business Forecasting*, 6th ed. Upper Saddle River, NJ: Prentice Hall, 1998.

Huff, D. *How to Lie with Statistics*. New York: W. W. Norton & Company, Inc., 1954.

Levin, R. I., and D. S. Rubin. *Statistics for Management*, 6th ed. Upper Saddle River, NJ: Prentice Hall, 1994.

APPENDIX 2.1: DERIVATION OF BAYES' THEOREM

We know that the following formulas are correct:

$$P(A \mid B) = \frac{P(AB)}{P(B)} \tag{1}$$

$$P(B \mid A) = \frac{P(AB)}{P(A)}$$

[which can be rewritten as $P(AB) = P(B \mid A)P(A)$] and $\qquad$ (2)

$$P(B \mid \overline{A}) = \frac{P(\overline{A}B)}{P(\overline{A})}$$

[which can be rewritten as $P(\overline{A}B) = P(B \mid \overline{A})P(\overline{A})$]. $\qquad$ (3)

Furthermore, by definition, we know that

$$P(B) = P(AB) + P(\overline{A}B)$$

$$= P(B \mid A)P(A) + P(B \mid \overline{A})P(\overline{A}) \tag{4}$$

 from (2)   from (3)

Substituting Equations 2 and 4 into Equation 1, we have

$$P(A \mid B) = \frac{P(AB)}{P(B)}$$

from (2)

$$= \frac{P(B \mid A)P(A)}{\underbrace{P(B \mid A)P(A) + P(B \mid \overline{A})P(\overline{A})}} \tag{5}$$

from (4)

This is the general form of *Bayes'* theorem, shown as Equation 2-7 in this chapter.

CHAPTER 3

Fundamentals of Decision Theory Models

LEARNING OBJECTIVES

After completing this chapter, students will be able to:

1. List the steps of the decision-making process.

2. Describe the types of decision-making environments.

3. Use probability values to make decisions under risk.

4. Make decisions under uncertainty, where there is risk but probability values are not known.

5. Use computers to solve basic decision-making problems.

CHAPTER OUTLINE

3.1 Introduction

3.2 The Six Steps in Decision Theory

3.3 Types of Decision-Making Environments

3.4 Decision Making under Risk

3.5 Decision Making under Uncertainty

3.6 Marginal Analysis with a Large Number of Alternatives and States of Nature

Summary • Glossary • Key Equations • Solved Problems • Self-Test • Discussion Questions and Problems • Data Set Problem • Case Study: Starting Right Corporation Ski Right

Appendix 3.1: Decision Theory with QM for Windows

3.1   INTRODUCTION

Decision theory is an analytic and systematic way to tackle problems.

To a great extent, the successes or failures that a person experiences in life depend on the decisions that he or she makes. The person who managed the ill-fated space shuttle *Challenger* is no longer working for NASA. The person who designed the top-selling Mustang became president of Ford. Why and how did these people make their respective decisions? In general, what is involved in making good decisions? One decision may make the difference between a successful career and an unsuccessful one. *Decision theory* is an analytic and systematic approach to the study of decision making. In this and the next chapter, we present the mathematical models useful in helping managers make the best possible decisions.

A good decision is based on logic.

What makes the difference between good and bad decisions? A good decision is one that is based on logic, considers all available data and possible alternatives, and applies the quantitative approach we are about to describe. Occasionally, a good decision results in an unexpected or unfavorable outcome. But if it is made properly, it is *still* a good decision. A bad decision is one that is not based on logic, does not use all available information, does not consider all alternatives, and does not employ appropriate quantitative techniques. If you make a bad decision but are lucky and a favorable outcome occurs, you have *still* made a bad decision. Although occasionally good decisions yield bad results, in the long run, using decision theory will result in successful outcomes.

3.2   THE SIX STEPS IN DECISION THEORY

Whether you are deciding about getting a haircut today, building a multimillion-dollar plant, or buying a new camera, the steps in making a good decision are basically the same. These six steps are:

Six Steps of Decision Making

1. Clearly define the problem at hand.

2. List the possible alternatives.

3. Identify the possible outcomes.

4. List the payoff or profit of each combination of alternatives and outcomes.

5. Select one of the mathematical decision theory models.

6. Apply the model and make your decision.

We use the Thompson Lumber Company case as an example to illustrate these decision theory steps. John Thompson is the founder and president of Thompson Lumber Company, a profitable firm located in Portland, Oregon.

The first step is to define the problem.

Step 1. The problem that John Thompson identifies is whether to expand his product line by manufacturing and marketing a new product, backyard storage sheds.

The second step is to list alternatives.

Step 2. Thompson's second step is to generate the alternatives that are available to him. In decision theory, an *alternative* is defined as a course of action or a strategy that may be chosen by the decision maker. John decides that his alternatives are to construct: (1) a large new plant to manufacture the storage sheds, (2) a small plant, or (3) no plant at all (that is, he has the option of not developing the new product line).

One of the biggest mistakes that decision makers make is to leave out some important alternatives. Although a particular alternative may seem to be inappropriate or of little value, it might turn out to be the best choice.

Step 3. The third step involves identifying the possible outcomes of the various alternatives. The criteria for action are established at this time. Thompson determines that there are only two possible outcomes: the market for the storage sheds could be favorable, meaning that there is a high demand for the product, or it could be unfavorable, meaning that there is a low demand for the sheds.

The third step is to identify possible outcomes.

A common mistake is to forget about some of the possible outcomes. Optimistic decision makers tend to ignore bad outcomes, while pessimistic managers may discount a favorable outcome. If you don't consider all possibilities, you will not be making a logical decision, and the results may be undesirable. If you do not think the worst can happen, you may design another Edsel automobile. In decision theory, those outcomes over which the decision maker has little or no control are called *states of nature*.

Step 4. Thompson's next step is to express the payoff resulting from each possible combination of alternatives and outcomes. Because in this case he wants to maximize his profits, he can use *profit* to evaluate each consequence. Not every decision, of course, can be based on money alone—any appropriate means of measuring benefit is acceptable. In decision theory, we call such payoffs or profits *conditional values*.

The fourth step is to list payoffs.

John Thompson has already evaluated the potential profits associated with the various outcomes. With a favorable market, he thinks a large facility would result in a net profit of $200,000 to his firm. This $200,000 is a *conditional value* because Thompson's receiving the money is conditional upon both his building a large factory and having a good market. The conditional value if the market is unfavorable would be a $180,000 net loss. A small plant would result in a net profit of $100,000 in a favorable market, but a net loss of $20,000 would occur if the market was unfavorable. Finally, doing nothing would result in $0 profit in either market.

The easiest way to present these values is by constructing a *decision table*, sometimes called a *payoff table*. A decision table for Thompson's conditional values is shown in Table 3.1. All of the alternatives are listed down the left side of the table and all of the possible outcomes or states of nature are listed across the top. The body of the table contains the actual payoffs.

During the fourth step the decision maker can construct decision or payoff tables.

Steps 5 and 6. The last two steps are to select a decision theory model and apply it to the data to help make the decision. Selecting the model depends on the environment in which you're operating and the amount of risk and uncertainty involved.

The last two steps are to select and apply the decision theory model.

TABLE 3.1   Decision Table with Conditional Values for Thompson Lumber

	STATE OF NATURE	
ALTERNATIVE	**FAVORABLE MARKET ($)**	**UNFAVORABLE MARKET ($)**
Construct a large plant	200,000	−180,000
Construct a small plant	100,000	−20,000
Do nothing	0	0

Note: It is important to include all alternatives, including "do nothing."

3.3   TYPES OF DECISION-MAKING ENVIRONMENTS

The types of decisions people make depend on how much knowledge or information they have about the situation. Three decision-making environments are defined and explained as follows.

Type 1: Decision Making under Certainty In the environment of *decision making under certainty*, decision makers know with certainty the consequence of every alternative or decision choice. Naturally, they will choose the alternative that will maximize their well-being or will result in the best outcome. For example, let's say that you have $1,000 to invest for a one-year period. One alternative is to open a savings account paying 6% interest and another is to invest in a government Treasury bond paying 10% interest. If both investments are secure and guaranteed, there is a certainty that the Treasury bond will pay a higher return. The return after one year will be $100 in interest.

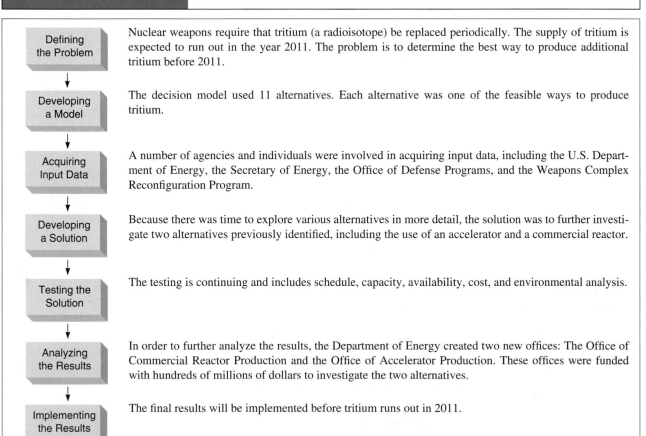

| MODELING IN THE REAL WORLD | Critical Decisions in a Nuclear World |

Defining the Problem

Nuclear weapons require that tritium (a radioisotope) be replaced periodically. The supply of tritium is expected to run out in the year 2011. The problem is to determine the best way to produce additional tritium before 2011.

Developing a Model

The decision model used 11 alternatives. Each alternative was one of the feasible ways to produce tritium.

Acquiring Input Data

A number of agencies and individuals were involved in acquiring input data, including the U.S. Department of Energy, the Secretary of Energy, the Office of Defense Programs, and the Weapons Complex Reconfiguration Program.

Developing a Solution

Because there was time to explore various alternatives in more detail, the solution was to further investigate two alternatives previously identified, including the use of an accelerator and a commercial reactor.

Testing the Solution

The testing is continuing and includes schedule, capacity, availability, cost, and environmental analysis.

Analyzing the Results

In order to further analyze the results, the Department of Energy created two new offices: The Office of Commercial Reactor Production and the Office of Accelerator Production. These offices were funded with hundreds of millions of dollars to investigate the two alternatives.

Implementing the Results

The final results will be implemented before tritium runs out in 2011.

Source: Detlof von Winterdeldt, et al. "An Assessment of Tritium Supply Alternatives in Support of the US Nuclear Weapons Stockpile," *Interfaces* (January–February 1998): 92.

Type 2: Decision Making under Risk In *decision making under risk*, the decision maker knows the probability of occurrence of each outcome. We know, for example, that the probability of being dealt a club is 0.25. The probability of rolling a 5 on a die is ⅙. In decision making under risk, the decision maker attempts to maximize his or her expected well-being. Decision theory models for business problems in this environment typically employ two equivalent criteria: maximization of expected monetary value and minimization of expected loss.

Probabilities are known.

Type 3: Decision Making under Uncertainty In *decision making under uncertainty*, the decision maker does not know the probabilities of the various outcomes. As an example, the probability that a Democrat will be president of the United States 25 years from now is not known. Sometimes it is impossible to assess the probability of success of a new undertaking or product. The criteria for decision making under uncertainty are explained in Section 3.5.

Probabilities are not known.

Let's see how decision making under certainty (the type 1 environment) could affect John Thompson. Here we assume that John knows exactly what will happen in the future. If it turns out that he knows with certainty that the market for storage sheds will be favorable, what should he do? Look again at Thompson Lumber's conditional values in Table 3.1. Because the market is favorable, he should build the large plant, which has the highest profit, $200,000.

Few managers would be fortunate enough to have complete information and knowledge about the states of nature under consideration. Decision making under risk, discussed next, is a more realistic situation—and slightly more complicated.

3.4 DECISION MAKING UNDER RISK

Decision making under risk is a probabilistic decision situation. Several possible states of nature may occur, each with a given probability. In this section we consider one of the most popular methods of making decisions under risk: selecting the alternative with the highest expected monetary value. We also look at the concepts of perfect information and opportunity loss.

Expected Monetary Value

Given a decision table with conditional values (payoffs) and probability assessments for all states of nature, it is possible to determine the *expected monetary value* (EMV) for each alternative if the decision could be repeated a large number of times. The EMV for an alternative is just the sum of possible payoffs of the alternative, each weighted by the probability of that payoff occurring.

EMV is the weighted sum of possible payoffs for each alternative.

$$
\begin{aligned}
\text{EMV (alternative } i) = \; &(\text{payoff of first state of nature}) \\
&\times (\text{probability of first state of nature}) \\
&+ (\text{payoff of second state of nature}) \\
&\times (\text{probability of second state of nature}) \\
&+ \ldots + (\text{payoff of last state of nature}) \\
&\times (\text{probability of last state of nature}) \qquad \textbf{(3-1)}
\end{aligned}
$$

TABLE 3.2   Decision Table with Probabilities and EMVs for Thompson Lumber

| | STATE OF NATURE | | |
ALTERNATIVE	FAVORABLE MARKET ($)	UNFAVORABLE MARKET ($)	EMV COMPUTED ($)
Construct a large plant	200,000	−180,000	10,000
Construct a small plant	100,000	−20,000	40,000
Do nothing	0	0	0
Probabilities	0.50	0.50	

Suppose that John Thompson now believes that the probability of a favorable market is exactly the same as the probability of an unfavorable market; that is, each state of nature has a 0.50 probability. Which alternative would give the greatest expected monetary value? To determine this, John has expanded the decision table, as shown in Table 3.2. His calculations are:

EMV(large plant) = (0.50)($200,000) + (0.50)(−$180,000) = $10,000

EMV(small plant) = (0.50)($100,000) + (0.50)(−$20,000) = $40,000

EMV(do nothing) = (0.50)($0) + (0.50)($0) = $0

The largest expected value results from the second alternative, "construct a small plant." Thus, Thompson should proceed with the project and put up a small plant to manufacture storage sheds. The EMVs for the large plant and for doing nothing are $10,000 and $0, respectively.

IN ACTION   Planning KLM's Aircraft Maintenance

KLM Royal Dutch Airlines has been the major Dutch airline since the early twentieth century. The company owns almost 100 aircraft and flies to about 150 cities in about 80 different countries. One of the primary concerns of KLM is the safety of its aircraft and reliable service for its customers.

To help KLM achieve its quality and safety objectives, a comprehensive maintenance program was developed. Developing such a program involves a careful analysis of a large number of alternatives and possible outcomes. How often should various pieces of equipment be maintained? What is the chance that a piece of equipment or a structural element of an aircraft will break or malfunction given various maintenance programs? These and related decision theory factors had to be considered.

The maintenance function of KLM relies on about 3,000 employees. In addition, about 30 other airline companies have maintenance contracts with KLM and use KLM employees and procedures to maintain their aircraft. The actual maintenance of aircraft for KLM includes both major and minor maintenance procedures. The major maintenance procedures can take from several hours to several days. Minor maintenance includes servicing arriving aircraft, departure checks, and platform maintenance, which involves checking the technical status of the aircraft.

To perform important maintenance functions, KLM has developed a computerized decision support system (DSS) that helps in determining the size and organization of the maintenance workforce or staff. The DSS has benefited KLM by increasing the quality of decision making. The computerized system provides information to KLM managers that was either not available or too time-consuming to gather.

Source: M. Dijkstra, et al. "Planning the Size and Organization of KLM's Aircraft Maintenance Personnel," *Interfaces* 24 (November–December 1994): 47.

Expected Value of Perfect Information

John Thompson has been approached by Scientific Marketing, Inc., a firm that proposes to help John make the decision about whether to build the plant to produce storage sheds. Scientific Marketing claims that its technical analysis will tell John with certainty whether the market is favorable for his proposed product. In other words, it will change his environment from one of decision making under risk to one of decision making under certainty. This information could prevent John from making a very expensive mistake. Scientific Marketing would charge Thompson $65,000 for the information. What would you recommend to John? Should he hire the firm to make the marketing study? Even if the information from the study is perfectly accurate, is it worth $65,000? What would it be worth? Although some of these questions are difficult to answer, determining the value of such *perfect information* can be very useful. It places an upper bound on what you would be willing to spend on information such as that being sold by Scientific Marketing. In this section, two related terms are investigated: the *expected value of perfect information* (EVPI) and the *expected value with perfect information* (EVwPI). These techniques can help John make his decision about hiring the marketing firm.

EVPI places an upper bound on what to pay for information.

The expected value *with* perfect information is the expected or average return, in the long run, if we have perfect information before a decision has to be made. To calculate this value, we choose the best alternative for each state of nature and multiply its payoff times the probability of occurrence of that state of nature.

Expected value *with* perfect information (EVwPI)

= (best outcome or consequence for first state of nature)

  × (probability of first state of nature)

  + (best outcome for second state of nature)

  × (probability of second state of nature)

  + ... + (best outcome for last state of nature)

  × (probability of last state of nature)   **(3-2)**

The expected value of perfect information, EVPI, is the expected outcome *with* perfect information minus the expected outcome *without* perfect information: namely, the maximum EMV.

EVPI is the expected value with perfect information minus the maximum EMV.

EVPI = expected value *with* perfect information—maximum EMV   **(3-3)**

By referring back to Table 3.2, Thompson can calculate the maximum that he would pay for information, that is, the expected value of perfect information, or EVPI. He follows a two-stage process. First, the expected value *with* perfect information is computed. Then, using this result, EVPI is calculated. The procedure is outlined as follows.

1. The best outcome for the state of nature "favorable market" is "build a large plant" with a payoff of $200,000. The best outcome for the state of nature "unfavorable market" is "do nothing," with a payoff of $0. Expected value with perfect information = ($200,000)(0.50) + ($0)(0.50) = $100,000. Thus, if we had perfect information, we would expect, on average, $100,000 if the decision could be repeated many times.

2. The maximum EMV is $40,000, which is the expected outcome without perfect information.

    EVPI = expected value *with* perfect information—maximum EMV

        = $100,000 − $40,000 = $60,000

Thus, the *most* Thompson would be willing to pay for perfect information is $60,000. This, of course, is again based on the assumption that the probability of each state of nature is .50.

Opportunity Loss

EOL is the cost of not picking the best solution.

An alternative approach to maximizing expected monetary value (EMV) is to minimize *expected opportunity loss* (EOL). Opportunity loss, sometimes called *regret*, refers to the difference between the optimal profit or payoff and the actual payoff received. In other words, it's the amount lost by not picking the best alternative.

The minimum expected opportunity loss is found by constructing an opportunity loss table and computing EOL for each alternative. Let's see how the procedure works for the Thompson Lumber case.

The first step is to create the opportunity loss table.

Step 1. The first step is to create the opportunity loss table. This is done by determining the opportunity loss for not choosing the best alternative for each state of nature. Opportunity loss for any state of nature, or any column, is calculated by subtracting each outcome in the column from the *best* outcome in the same column. For a favorable market, the best outcome is $200,000 as a result of the first alternative, "construct a large plant." For an unfavorable market, the best outcome is $0 as a result of the third alternative, "doing nothing." Table 3.3 illustrates these comparisons.

Using Table 3.3, an opportunity loss table can be constructed. The values in Table 3.4 represent the opportunity loss for each state of nature for not choosing the best alternative.

The second step is to compute EOL.

Step 2. EOL is computed by multiplying the probability of each state of nature times the appropriate opportunity loss value.

$$\text{EOL(construct large plant)} = (0.5)(\$0) + (0.5)(\$180,000)$$

$$= \$90,000$$

$$\text{EOL(construct small plant)} = (0.5)(\$100,000) + (0.5)(\$20,000)$$

$$= \$60,000$$

$$\text{EOL(do nothing)} = (0.5)(\$200,000) + (0.5)(\$0)$$

$$= \$100,000$$

Using minimum EOL as the decision criterion, the best decision would be the second alternative, "construct a small plant."

TABLE 3.3   Determining Opportunity Losses for Thompson Lumber

STATE OF NATURE	
FAVORABLE MARKET ($)	UNFAVORABLE MARKET ($)
200,000 − 200,000	0 − (−180,000)
200,000 − 100,000	0 − (−20,000)
200,000 − 0	0 − 0

TABLE 3.4   Opportunity Loss Table for Thompson Lumber

ALTERNATIVE	STATE OF NATURE	
	FAVORABLE MARKET ($)	UNFAVORABLE MARKET ($)
Construct a large plant	0	180,000
Construct a small plant	100,000	20,000
Do nothing	200,000	0
Probabilities	0.50	0.50

It is important to note that minimum EOL will always result in the same decision as maximum EMV, and that the following relationship always holds: EVPI = minimum EOL. Referring to the Thompson case, EVPI = $60,000 = minimum EOL.

EOL will always result in the same decision as the maximum EMV.

Sensitivity Analysis

In previous sections we determined that the best decision for Thompson Lumber was to construct the small plant, with an expected value of $40,000. This conclusion depends on the values of the economic consequences and the two probability values of a favorable and an unfavorable market. *Sensitivity analysis* investigates how our decision might change given a change in the problem data. In this section we investigate the impact that a change in the probability values would have on the decision facing Thompson Lumber. We first define the following variable:

Sensitivity analysis investigates how our decision might change with different input data.

P = probability of a favorable market

We can now express the expected monetary values (EMVs) in terms of P. This is done below. A graph of these EMV values is shown in Figure 3.1.

$$\text{EMV(large plant)} = \$200,000P - \$180,000(1 - P)$$

$$= \$380,000P - \$180,000$$

$$\text{EMV(small plant)} = \$100,000P - \$20,000(1 - P)$$

$$= \$120,000P - \$20,000$$

$$\text{EMV(do nothing)} = \$0P + \$0(1 - P) = \$0$$

As you can see in Figure 3.1, the best decision is to do nothing as long as P is between 0 and point 1, where the EMV for doing nothing is equal to the EMV for the small plant. When P is between points 1 and 2, the best decision is to build the small plant. Point 2 is where the EMV for the small plant is equal to the EMV for the large plant. When P is greater than point 2, the best decision is to construct the large plant. Of

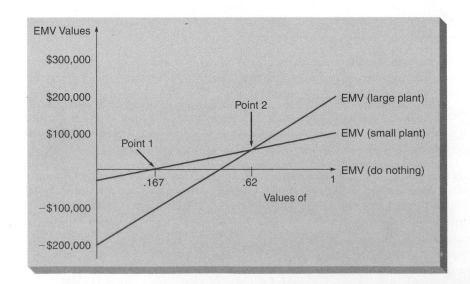

FIGURE 3.1

Sensitivity Analysis

course, this is what you would expect as P increases. Points 1 and 2 can be computed as follows:

Point 1: EMV(nothing) = EMV(small plant)

$$0 = \$120{,}000P - \$20{,}000 \quad P = \frac{20{,}000}{120{,}000} = 0.167$$

Point 2: EMV(small plant) = EMV(large plant)

$$\$120{,}000P - \$20{,}000 = \$380{,}000P - \$180{,}000$$

$$260{,}000P = 160{,}000 \quad P = \frac{160{,}000}{260{,}000} = 0.62$$

The results of this sensitivity analysis are displayed in the following table:

ALTERNATIVE	RANGE OF P VALUES
Do nothing	Less than 0.167
Construct a small plant	0.167 − 0.62
Construct a large plant	Greater than 0.62

3.5   DECISION MAKING UNDER UNCERTAINTY

Probability data are not available.

When the probability of occurrence of each state of nature can be assessed, the EMV or EOL decision criteria are usually appropriate. When a manager *cannot* assess the outcome probability with confidence or when virtually no probability data are available, other decision criteria are required. This type of problem has been referred to as *decision making under uncertainty*. The criteria that we cover in this section include:

1. Maximax
2. Maximin
3. Equally likely
4. Criterion of realism
5. Minimax

The first four criteria can be computed directly from the decision table, whereas the minimax criterion requires use of the opportunity loss table. Let's take a look at each of the five models and apply them to Thompson Lumber. It is now assumed that no probability information about the two outcomes is available to Thompson.

Maximax

Maximax is an optimistic approach.

The *maximax* criterion finds the alternative that *max*imizes the *max*imum outcome or consequence for every alternative. You first locate the maximum outcome within every alternative, and then pick that alternative with the maximum number. Since this decision criterion locates the alternative with the *highest* possible gain, it has been called an *optimistic decision criterion*. In Table 3.5 we see that Thompson's maximax choice is the first alternative, "construct a large plant." This is the maximum of the maximum number within each row or alternative.

TABLE 3.5	Thompson's Maximax Decision		
	STATES OF NATURE		
ALTERNATIVE	FAVORABLE MARKET ($)	UNFAVORABLE MARKET ($)	MAXIMUM IN ROW ($)
Construct a large plant	200,000	−180,000	200,000 ← Maximax
Construct a small plant	100,000	20,000	100,000
Do nothing	0	0	0

Maximin

The *maximin* criterion finds the alternative that *max*imizes the *min*imum outcome or consequence for every alternative. You first locate the minimum outcome within every alternative and then pick that alternative with the maximum number. Since this decision criterion locates the alternative that has the least possible *loss*, it has been called a *pessimistic decision criterion*.

Maximin is a pessimistic approach.

Thompson's maximin choice, "do nothing," is shown in Table 3.6. This is the maximum of the minimum number within each row or alternative.

Equally Likely (Laplace)

The *equally likely*, also called *Laplace*, decision criterion finds the alternative with the highest average outcome. You first calculate the average outcome for every alternative, which is the sum of all outcomes divided by the number of outcomes. Then pick the alternative with the maximum number. The equally likely approach assumes that all probabilities of occurrence for the states of nature are equal, and thus each state of nature is equally likely.

Equally likely computes the highest average outcome.

The equally likely choice for Thompson Lumber is the second alternative, "construct a small plant." This strategy, shown in Table 3.7, is the maximum of the average outcome of each alternative.

TABLE 3.6	Thompson's Maximin Decision		
	STATES OF NATURE		
ALTERNATIVE	FAVORABLE MARKET ($)	UNFAVORABLE MARKET ($)	MINIMUM IN ROW ($)
Construct a large plant	200,000	−180,000	−180,000
Construct a small plant	100,000	−20,000	−20,000
Do nothing	0	0	0 ← Maximin

	STATES OF NATURE		
ALTERNATIVES	**FAVORABLE MARKET ($)**	**UNFAVORABLE MARKET ($)**	**ROW AVERAGE ($)**
Construct a large plant	200,000	−180,000	10,000
Construct a small plant	100,000	−20,000	40,000 — Equally likely
Do nothing	0	0	0

TABLE 3.7   Thompson's Equally Likely Decision

Criterion of Realism (Hurwicz Criterion)

Criterion of realism uses the weighted average approach.

Often called the *weighted average*, the *criterion of realism* (*the Hurwicz criterion*) is a compromise between an optimistic and a pessimistic decision. To begin with, a *coefficient of realism*, α, is selected. This coefficient is between 0 and 1. When α is close to 1, the decision maker is optimistic about the future. When α is close to 0, the decision maker is pessimistic about the future. The advantage of this approach is that it allows the decision maker to build in personal feelings about relative optimism and pessimism. The formula is as follows:

$$\text{criterion of realism} = \alpha(\text{maximum in row}) + (1 - \alpha)(\text{minimum in row})$$

IN ACTION   Decision Analysis Helps Allocate Health Care Funds in the United Kingdom

Individuals and companies have often used decision-making techniques to help them invest or allocate funds to various projects. In some cases, decision-making techniques can be used to determine how millions of dollars are to be spent. This same type of analysis can also be used on a larger scale for countries or governments. This was the case in the allocation of health care funds for the United Kingdom (UK).

Over the years, the United States has debated the possible implementation of a comprehensive national health care program. Although this does not seem likely for the United States in the near future, other countries, such as the UK, have been using some form of national health care system for decades. For the UK, the question is not whether to have a national health care system, but how funds from such a system are to be allocated.

The United Kingdom's National Health Service (NHS) is funded through general tax revenues. The funds are dispersed to about 105 different local health authorities. The annual funding for the NHS is approximately $35 billion. With such a large sum of national funds going to such an important area,

the decision-making process to justly allocate funds can be difficult indeed.

Starting in the 1970s, a formula, based partly on a standardized mortality ratio, was developed to distribute health funds to the local authorities. This formula, however, failed to take into account social deprivation and general health care needs. As a result, the NHS decided to seek a better way to allocate health care dollars to the local authorities.

A team from York University spent about 4 months developing the original allocation model and another 14 months refining the decision-making model. Using decision theory, the team identified a set of key variables to explain health care needs and usage in the UK. This resulted in modifications to the decision-making approach regarding health care funds. Many believe that the new model will more fairly and justly allocate the UK's important national health care funds to those who truly need the assistance.

Source: Nancy Bistritz. "Rx for UK Healthcare Woes," *OR/MS Today* (April 1997): 18.

TABLE 3.8	Thompson's Criterion of Realism Decision (also called Hurwicz criterion)		
	STATES OF NATURE		
ALTERNATIVE	**FAVORABLE MARKET ($)**	**UNFAVORABLE MARKET ($)**	**CRITERION OF REALISM OR WEIGHTED AVERAGE ($\alpha = 0.8$) $**
Construct a large plant	200,000	−180,000	124,000 ← Realism
Construct a small plant	100,000	−20,000	76,000
Do nothing	0	0	0

If we assume that John Thompson sets his coefficient of realism, α, to be 0.80, the best decision would be to construct a large plant. As seen in Table 3.8, this alternative has the highest weighted average: $124,000 = (0.80)(\$200,000) + (0.20)(-\$180,000)$.

Minimax

The final decision criterion that we discuss is based on opportunity loss. *Minimax* finds the alternative that *min*imizes the *max*imum opportunity loss within each alternative. You first develop an opportunity loss table and then find the maximum opportunity loss within each alternative. Then pick that alternative with the minimum (or smallest) number.

Thompson's opportunity loss table is shown as Table 3.9. We can see that the minimax choice is the second alternative, "construct a small plant." Doing so minimizes the maximum opportunity loss.

Minimax is based on opportunity loss.

Using Excel QM to Solve Decision Theory Problems

Excel QM can be used to solve a variety of decision theory problems discussed in this chapter. Programs 3.1A and 3.1B show the use of Excel QM to solve the Thompson lumber case. Program 3.1A provides the formulas needed to compute the EMV, maximin, maximax, and other measures. Program 3.1B shows the results of these formulas.

TABLE 3.9	Thompson's Minimax Decision Using Opportunity Loss		
	STATES OF NATURE		
ALTERNATIVE	**FAVORABLE MARKET ($)**	**UNFAVORABLE MARKET ($)**	**MAXIMUM IN ROW ($)**
Construct a large plant	0	180,000	180,000
Construct a small plant	100,000	20,000	100,000 ← Minimax
Do nothing	200,000	0	200,000

PROGRAM 3.1A

Input Data for the Thompson Lumber Problem

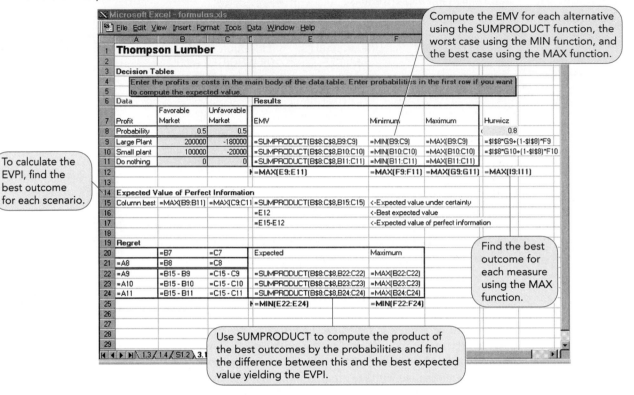

PROGRAM 3.1B

Output Results for the
Thompson Lumber Problem

mot doing

3.6 MARGINAL ANALYSIS WITH A LARGE NUMBER OF ALTERNATIVES AND STATES OF NATURE

So far, we have considered cases in which there are only a few alternatives and states of nature. What happens when we have a large number of alternatives and states of nature? For example, a large restaurant might be able to stock from 0 to 100 cartons of doughnuts. Furthermore, demand could also range from 0 to 100 cartons per day. In this case we have to analyze 101 possible alternatives and states of nature. This would require a very large decision table if we used the decision theory approaches discussed so far in this chapter. When we can identify a marginal profit and loss, it is possible to use *marginal analysis* to obtain the best decision without using a large decision table.

Marginal analysis is a decision-making approach that can help select the optimal inventory level. It involves two new terms: *marginal profit* and *marginal loss*. Let's say that you are a newspaper distributor; each daily paper costs you 19 cents and can be sold for 35 cents. But if a paper is not sold at the end of the day, it is completely worthless (a 0 cent salvage value). In this case the *marginal profit* (MP) is the profit made by selling each additional paper, namely, 16 cents (= 35 cents − 19 cents). The *marginal loss* (ML) is the loss caused by stocking, but not selling, each additional newspaper—it would be 19 cents for every paper remaining at the end of the day.

When there are a manageable number of alternatives and states of nature and we know the probabilities for each state of nature, *marginal analysis with discrete distributions* can be used. When there are a very large number of possible alternatives and states of nature and the probability distribution of the states of nature can be described with a normal distribution, *marginal analysis with the normal distribution* is appropriate. Both of these techniques are discussed in the following sections.

Marginal analysis can be used to obtain the best decision with a large number of alternatives.

Marginal Analysis with Discrete Distributions

Finding the best inventory level to stock is not difficult when we follow the marginal analysis procedure. Given any inventory level, we would only add an additional unit to our inventory level if its expected marginal profit equals or exceeds its expected marginal loss. This relationship is expressed symbolically as follows. First, we let

P = probability that demand will be greater than or equal to a given supply (or the probability of selling at *least* one additional unit)

$1 - P$ = probability that demand will be less than supply

The expected marginal profit is then found by multiplying the probability that a given unit will be sold by the marginal profit, $P(\text{MP})$. Similarly, the expected marginal loss is the probability of not selling the unit multiplied by the marginal loss, or $(1 - P)(\text{ML})$.

The optimal decision rule is

$$P(\text{MP}) \geq (1 - P)(\text{ML})$$

We only add inventory when expected MP is greater than or equal to expected ML.

With some basic mathematical manipulations, we can determine the level of P that will help solve marginal analysis problems:

$$P(\text{MP}) \geq \text{ML} - P(\text{ML})$$

or

$$P(\text{MP}) + P(\text{ML}) \geq \text{ML}$$

or

$$P(\text{MP} + \text{ML}) \geqslant \text{ML}$$

or

$$P \geqslant \frac{\text{ML}}{\text{MP} + \text{ML}} \qquad \text{(3-4)}$$

In other words, as long as the probability of selling one more unit (P) is greater than or equal to ML/(MP + ML), we would stock the additional unit.

Steps of Marginal Analysis with Discrete Distributions

1. Determine the value of P for the problem.

2. Construct a probability table and add a cumulative probability column.

3. Keep ordering inventory as long as the probability of selling at least one additional unit is greater than P.

An inventory example will illustrate the concept. Café du Donut is a popular New Orleans dining spot on the edge of the French Quarter. Its specialty is coffee and doughnuts; it buys the doughnuts fresh daily from a large industrial bakery. The café pays $4 for each carton (containing two dozen doughnuts) delivered each morning. Any cartons not sold at the end of the day are thrown away, for they would not be fresh enough to meet the café's standards. If a carton of doughnuts is sold, the total revenue is $6. Hence, the marginal profit per carton of doughnuts is

MP = marginal profit = $6 − $4 = $2

The marginal loss is ML = $4, since the doughnuts cannot be returned or salvaged at day's end.

From past sales, the café's manager estimates that the daily sales will follow the probability distribution shown in Table 3.10. Management then follows three steps to find the optimal number of cartons of doughnuts to order each day.

TABLE 3.10	**Café du Donut's Probability Distribution**
DAILY SALES (CARTONS OF DOUGHNUTS)	**PROBABILITY SALES WILL BE AT THIS LEVEL**
4	0.05
5	0.15
6	0.15
7	0.20
8	0.25
9	0.10
10	0.10
	Total 1.00

TABLE 3.11	Marginal Analysis for Café du Donut	
DAILY SALES (CARTONS OF DOUGHNUTS)	PROBABILITY THAT SALES WILL BE AT THIS LEVEL	PROBABILITY THAT SALES WILL BE AT THIS LEVEL OR GREATER
4	0.05	$1.00 \geqslant 0.66$
5	0.15	$0.95 \geqslant 0.66$
6	0.15	$0.80 \geqslant 0.66$
7	0.20	0.65
8	0.25	0.45
9	0.10	0.20
10	0.10	0.10
	Total 1.00	

Step 1. Determine the value of P for the decision rule.

$$P \geqslant \frac{ML}{ML + MP} = \frac{\$4}{\$4 + \$2} = \frac{4}{6} = 0.66$$

$$P \geqslant 0.66$$

Step 2. Add a new column to the table to reflect the probability that doughnut sales will be at each level *or greater*. This is shown in the right-hand column of Table 3.11. For example, the probability that sales will be 4 cartons or greater is 1.00 (= 0.05 + 0.15 + 0.15 + 0.20 + 0.25 + 0.10 + 0.10) since sales have always been between 4 and 10 cartons per day. Similarly, the probability that sales will be 8 cartons or greater is 0.45 (= 0.25 + 0.10 + 0.10): namely, the sum of probabilities for sales of 8, 9, or 10 cartons.

Step 3. Keep ordering additional cartons as long as the probability of selling at least one additional carton is greater than P, which is the indifference or break-even probability. If Café du Donut orders 6 cartons, marginal profits will still be greater than marginal loss.

$$P \text{ at 6 cartons} \geqslant \frac{ML}{ML + MP}$$

since $0.80 \geqslant 0.66$.

If 7 cartons are ordered, however, the probability of selling 7 or more cartons (0.65) is *not* greater than 0.66. Thus, the expected marginal loss will be greater than the expected marginal profit if seven cartons are ordered. In other words, the café can expect to lose money on the seventh carton if it is purchased. The optimal decision is to order 6 cartons each day.

This problem *could* have been placed in a decision table and solved, but the table would require seven rows and seven columns (one for each sales level). Although marginal analysis with discrete distributions is very efficient compared with decision tables, in which there are more than 15 or 20 different alternatives and states of nature, marginal analysis with the normal distribution may be more appropriate.

Marginal Analysis with the Normal Distribution

When product demand or sales follow a normal distribution, which is a common business situation, marginal analysis with the normal distribution can be applied. First we need to find four values:

1. The average or mean sales for the product, μ
2. The standard deviation of sales, σ
3. The marginal profit for the product, MP
4. The marginal loss for the product, ML

Once these quantities are known, the process of finding the best stocking policy is somewhat similar to marginal analysis with discrete distributions.

Steps of Marginal Analysis with the Normal Distribution

1. Determine the value of *P*. With the normal distribution, *P* is equal to ML/(ML + MP):

$$P = \frac{ML}{ML + MP}$$

2. Locate *P* on the normal distribution. For a given area under the curve, we can find *Z* from the standard normal table (Appendix A). Then, using the relationship

$$Z = \frac{X^* - m}{s} \tag{3-5}$$

we can solve for X^*, the optimal stocking policy.

An illustration will help explain. Demand for copies of the *Chicago Tribune* newspaper at Joe's Newsstand is normally distributed and has averaged 50 papers per day, with a standard deviation of 10 papers. With a marginal loss of 4 cents and a marginal profit of 6 cents, what daily stocking policy should Joe follow?

Step 1. Joe should stock *Tribunes* until the probability of having a demand at a given level or greater is at least ML/(ML + MP).

$$P = \frac{ML}{ML + MP} = \frac{4 \text{ cents}}{4 \text{ cents} + 6 \text{ cents}} = \frac{4}{10} = 0.40$$

Step 2. Figure 3.2 shows the normal distribution. Since the normal table has cumulative areas under the curve between the left side and any point, we look for 0.60 ($= 1.0 - 0.40$) in order to get the corresponding *Z* value.

$Z = 0.25$ standard deviations from the mean

In this problem, $\mu = 50$ and $\sigma = 10$, so

$$0.25 = \frac{X^* - 50}{10}$$

or

$$X^* = 10(0.25) + 50 = 52.5 \text{ or } 53 \text{ newspapers}$$

Thus, Joe should order 53 *Chicago Tribunes* daily.

This same procedure can be used when *P* is greater than 0.50. Let's say that Joe's Newsstand also stocks the *Chicago Sun-Times* and its marginal loss is 8 cents and mar-

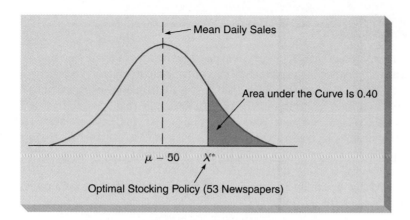

FIGURE 3.2
Joe's Stocking Decision for
Chicago Tribunes

ginal profit is 2 cents. The daily sales have averaged 100 *Sun-Times* with a standard deviation of 10 papers. The optimal stocking policy is as follows:

$$P = \frac{ML}{ML + MP} = \frac{8 \text{ cents}}{8 \text{ cents} + 2 \text{ cents}} = \frac{8}{10} = 0.80$$

Step 3. The normal curve is shown in Figure 3.3. Since the normal curve is symmetrical, we find Z for an area under the curve of 0.80 and multiply this number by -1.

$Z = -0.84$ standard deviation from the mean for an area of 0.80

With $\mu = 100$ and $\sigma = 10$,

$$-0.84 = \frac{X^* - 100}{10}$$

or

$$X^* = -8.4 + 100 = 91.6 \text{ or } 92 \text{ papers}$$

So Joe should order 92 *Sun-Times* every day.

The optimal stocking policies in these two examples are intuitively consistent. When marginal profit is *greater* than marginal loss, we would expect X^* to be *greater than* the average demand, μ, and when marginal profit is *less* than marginal loss, we would expect the optimal stocking policy, X^*, to be *less than* μ.

*Optimal stocking policies
should be intuitively
consistent.*

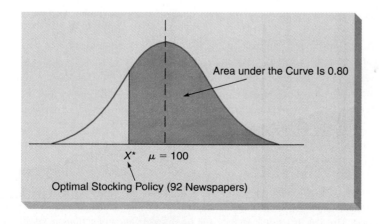

FIGURE 3.3
Joe's Stocking Decision for
Chicago Sun-Times

Summary

Decision theory is an analytic and systematic approach to studying decision making. Six steps are usually involved in making decisions in three environments: decision making under certainty, risk, and uncertainty. Such methods as determining expected monetary value (EMV), expected value of perfect information (EVPI), expected opportunity loss (EOL), and sensitivity analysis are used in decision making under risk. In decision making under uncertainty, decision tables are constructed to compute such criteria as maximax, maximin, equally likely, minimax, and criterion of realism. In solving problems with a large number of alternatives and states of nature, marginal analysis can be used. Software such as QM for Windows and Excel QM (see Appendix 3.1) are also used to solve decision theory problems.

Glossary

Alternative. A course of action or a strategy that may be chosen by a decision maker.

State of Nature. An outcome or occurrence over which the decision maker has little or no control.

Conditional Value or Payoff. A consequence or outcome, normally expressed in a monetary value, that occurs as a result of a particular alternative and state of nature.

Decision Making under Certainty. A decision-making environment in which the future outcomes or states of nature are known.

Decision Making under Risk. A decision-making environment in which several outcomes or states of nature may occur as a result of a decision or alternative. The probabilities of the outcomes or states of nature are known.

Decision Making under Uncertainty. A decision-making environment in which several outcomes or states of nature may occur. The probabilities of these outcomes, however, are not known.

Expected Monetary Value (EMV). The average or expected monetary outcome of a decision if it can be repeated many times. This is determined by multiplying the monetary outcomes by their respective probabilities. The results are then added to arrive at the EMV.

Expected Value of Perfect Information (EVPI). The average or expected value of information if it were completely accurate. The information is perfect.

Expected Value with Perfect Information. The average or expected value of the decision if you knew what would happen ahead of time. You have perfect knowledge.

Expected Opportunity Loss. The amount you would lose by not picking the best alternative. For any state of nature, this is the difference between the consequences of any alternative and the best possible alternative.

Maximax. An optimistic decision-making criterion. This is the alternative with the highest possible return.

Maximin. A pessimistic decision-making criterion. This alternative maximizes the minimum outcome. It is the best of the worst possible outcomes.

Equally Likely. A decision criterion that places an equal weight on all states of nature.

Coefficient of Realism (α). A number from 0 to 1. When the coefficient is close to 1, the decision criterion is optimistic. When the coefficient is close to zero, the decision criterion is pessimistic.

Minimax. A criterion that minimizes the maximum opportunity loss.

Marginal Analysis. A decision-making technique that uses marginal profit and marginal loss in determining optimal decision policies. Marginal analysis is used when the number of alternatives and states of nature is large.

Marginal Profit. The additional profit that would be realized by stocking and selling one more unit.

Marginal Loss. The loss that would be incurred by stocking and not selling an additional unit.

Key Equations

(3-1) EMV (Alternative i) = (payoff of first state of nature) $\times$ (its probability) + (payoff of second state of nature) $\times$ (its probability) + . . . + (payoff of last state of nature) $\times$ (its probability)

This equation computes expected monetary values.

(3-2) Expected value *with* perfect information = (best outcome for first state of nature) $\times$ (its probability) + (best outcome for second state of nature) $\times$ (its probability) + . . . + (best outcome for last state of nature) $\times$ (its probability)

(3-3) EVPI = expected value *with* perfect information— maximum EMV

This equation calculates the expected value of perfect information.

(3-4) $P \geq \dfrac{ML}{MP + ML}$

Equation used in marginal analysis to compute stocking policies.

(3-5) $Z = \dfrac{X^* - m}{s}$

Equation used in marginal analysis to compute the optimal stocking policy, X^*, when demand follows a normal distribution.

Solved Problems

Solved Problem 3-1

Maria Rojas is considering the possibility of opening a small dress shop on Fairbanks Avenue, a few blocks from the university. She has located a good mall that attracts students. Her options are to open a small shop, a medium-sized shop, or no shop at all. The market for a dress shop can be good, average, or bad. The probabilities for these three possibilities are 0.2 for a good market, 0.5 for an average market, and 0.3 for a bad market. The net profit or loss for the medium-sized and small shops for the various market conditions are given below. Building no shop at all yields no loss and no gain. What do you recommend?

ALTERNATIVE	GOOD MARKET ($)	AVERAGE MARKET ($)	BAD MARKET ($)
Small shop	75,000	25,000	−40,000
Medium-sized shop	100,000	35,000	−60,000
No shop	0	0	0

Solution

The problem can be solved by developing a payoff table that contains all alternatives, states of nature, and probability values. The expected monetary value (EMV) for each alternative is also computed. See the following table:

ALTERNATIVE	STATE OF NATURE			
	GOOD MARKET ($)	AVERAGE MARKET ($)	BAD MARKET ($)	EMV ($)
Small shop	75,000	25,000	−40,000	15,500
Medium-sized shop	100,000	35,000	−60,000	19,500
No shop	0	0	0	0
Probabilities	0.20	0.50	0.30	

$$\text{EMV(small shop)} = (0.2)(\$75,000) + (0.5)(\$25,000)$$
$$+ (0.3)(-\$40,000) = \$15,500$$
$$\text{EMV(medium-sized shop)} = (0.2)(\$100,000) + (0.5)(\$35,000)$$
$$+ (0.3)(-\$60,000) = \$19,500$$
$$\text{EMV(no shop)} = (0.2)(\$0) + (0.5)(\$0) + (0.3)(\$0) = \$0$$

As can be seen, the best decision is to build the medium-sized shop. The EMV for this alternative is $19,500.

Solved Problem 3-2

Cal Bender and Becky Addison have known each other since high school. Two years ago they entered the same university and today they are taking undergraduate courses in the business school. Both hope to graduate with degrees in finance. In an attempt to make extra money and to use some of the knowledge gained from their business courses, Cal and Becky have decided to look into the possibility of starting a small company that would provide word processing services to students who needed term papers or other reports prepared in a professional manner. Using a systems approach, Cal and Becky have identified three strategies. Strategy 1 is to invest in a fairly expensive microcomputer system with a high-quality laser printer. In a favorable market, they should be able to obtain a net profit of $10,000 over the next two years. If the market is unfavorable, they can lose $8,000. Strategy 2 is to purchase a less expensive system. With a favorable market, they could get a return during the next two years of $8,000. With an unfavorable market, they would incur a loss of $4,000. Their final strategy, strategy 3, is to do nothing. Cal is basically a risk taker, while Becky tries to avoid risk.

(a) What type of decision procedure should Cal use? What would Cal's decision be?

(b) What type of decision maker is Becky? What decision would Becky make?

(c) If Cal and Becky were indifferent to risk, what type of decision approach should they use? What would you recommend if this were the case?

Solution

The problem is one of decision making under uncertainty. Before answering the specific questions, a decision table should be developed showing the alternatives, states of nature, and related consequences.

ALTERNATIVE	FAVORABLE MARKET ($)	UNFAVORABLE MARKET ($)
Strategy 1	10,000	−8,000
Strategy 2	8,000	−4,000
Strategy 3	0	0

(a) Since Cal is a risk taker, he should use the maximax decision criteria. This approach selects the row that has the highest or maximum value. The $10,000 value, which is the maximum value from the table, is in row 1. Thus Cal's decision is to select strategy 1, which is an optimistic decision approach.

(b) Becky should use the maximin decision criteria. The minimum or worst outcome for each row, or strategy, is identified. These outcomes are −$8,000 for strategy 1, −$4,000 for strategy 2, and $0 for strategy 3. The maximum of these values is selected. Thus, Becky would select strategy 3, which reflects a pessimistic decision approach.

(c) If Cal and Becky are indifferent to risk, they should use the equally likely approach. This approach selects the alternative that maximizes the row averages. The row average for strategy 1 is $1,000 [$1,000 = ($10,000 − $8,000)/2]. The row average for strategy 2 is $2,000, and the row average for strategy 3 is $0. Thus, using the equally likely approach, the decision is to select strategy 2, which maximizes the row averages.

Solved Problem 3-3

Rick Miller has just opened a new bakery in Frisco, Colorado, called Morning Fresh. In performing an economic analysis, Rick has determined that the marginal cost or loss for each dozen doughnuts sold is $4. The marginal profit is estimated to be $2.75 per dozen doughnuts. At this time, Rick is considering stocking 10, 15, 20, 25, or 30 dozen doughnuts. The probability of selling 10 dozen doughnuts is 10%. The chance of selling 15 dozen doughnuts is 20%. There is a 30% chance that Morning Fresh will sell either 20 or 25 dozen doughnuts. Finally, there is a 10% chance of selling 30 dozen doughnuts, which is considered by Rick to be the most that Morning Fresh would be able to accommodate. What is your recommendation to Rick?

Solution

The problem facing Rick Miller involves the use of marginal analysis. First, we need to know the marginal loss and the marginal profit. This information was given in the problem: The marginal loss is $4, while the marginal profit is $2.75. Now we can compute the probability of selling one more unit (P):

$$P \geq \frac{ML}{ML + MP} = \frac{\$4}{\$4 + \$2.75} = 0.59$$

The probability of selling one more unit, which in this case is a dozen doughnuts, is 0.59. The next step is to develop a table showing the probability of selling doughnuts at a particular level or greater. The solution is to stock additional doughnuts as long as P is greater than or equal to 0.59. As seen in the table, the solution is to stock 20 dozen doughnuts.

DEMAND	PROBABILITY AT THIS LEVEL	PROBABILITY AT THIS LEVEL OR GREATER
10	0.1	1.00 ≥ 0.59
15	0.2	0.90 ≥ 0.59
20	0.3	0.70 ≥ 0.59
25	0.3	0.40
30	0.1	0.10
Total 1.0		

SELF-TEST

- Before taking the self-test, refer back to the learning objectives at the beginning of the chapter, the notes in the margins, and the glossary at the end of the chapter.
- Use the key at the back of the book to correct your answers.
- Restudy pages that correspond to any questions that you answered incorrectly or material you feel uncertain about.

1. A bad decision is one that
   a. is not based on logic.
   b. produces an unfavorable outcome.
   c. produces an unexpected outcome.
   d. is difficult to make.
   e. all of the above.
2. A good decision is one that
   a. considers all available data and possible alternatives.
   b. will occasionally yield bad results.
   c. is based on logic.
   d. will produce successful results in the long run.
   e. all of the above.
3. Which of the following is not a type of decision making?
   a. decision making under chance
   b. decision making under risk
   c. decision making under certainty
   d. decision making under uncertainty
4. A conditional value is
   a. the value you will receive if that particular state of nature occurs.
   b. a value that can be received only after the three assumptive conditions are met.
   c. a value that, when received, conditions the answer.
5. A payoff table
   a. lists states of nature on one axis and alternatives on the other axis.
   b. is also called a decision table.
   c. is a matrix (table) of conditional values.
   d. all of the above.
6. A type of decision-making environment is
   a. certainty.
   b. risk.
   c. uncertainty.
   d. both a and c.
   e. all of the above.
7. Which of these models is valid under conditions of uncertainty.
   a. maximax
   b. maximin
   c. equally likely
   d. minimax
   e. all of the above
8. Probabilities are needed under conditions of
   a. certainty.
   b. risk.

   c. uncertainty.
   d. both a and c.
9. The minimum EOL is
   a. the minimum expected opportunity loss.
   b. the minimum regret.
   c. equivalent to the EVPI.
   d. the alternative to select.
   e. all of the above.
10. The sum of the products of the probabilities of mutually exclusive and exhaustive states of nature and the conditional values of those same states of nature is called the
    a. EOL.
    b. EMV.
    c. EVPI.
11. EVPI is
    a. the expected value with perfect information.
    b. equal to maximum EOL.
    c. equal to expected value with perfect information minus maximum EMV.
12. An α value is needed to indicate the decision maker's optimism when using the
    a. maximax.
    b. equally likely.
    c. criterion of realism.
    d. minimax.
13. The decision model that utilizes the opportunity loss table is the
    a. maximax.
    b. maximin.
    c. equally likely.
    d. criterion of realism.
    e. minimax.
14. Marginal loss
    a. is caused by stocking a perishable item that you should not have stocked.
    b. is caused by stocking a perishable item that you did not sell.
    c. is the negative of EVPI.
    d. is the cost of an item, regardless of whether there is a scrap value or salvage value.
15. We would add a perishable item to our inventory if
    a. its expected marginal profit equals or exceeds its expected marginal loss.
    b. its EMV is any negative value or zero.
    c. MP $\leq$ ML.

Discussion Questions and Problems

Discussion Questions

3-1   Give an example of a good decision that you made that resulted in a bad outcome. Also give an example of a bad decision that you made that had a good outcome. Why was each decision good or bad?

3-2   Describe what is involved in the decision process.

3-3   What is an alternative? What is a state of nature?

3-4   Discuss the differences between decision making under certainty, decision making under risk, and decision making under uncertainty.

3-5   Mary Lillich is trying to decide whether to invest in real estate, stocks, or certificates of deposit. How well she does depends on whether the economy enters a period of recession or inflation. Develop a decision table (excluding the conditional values) to describe this situation.

3-6   State the meanings of EMV and EVPI.

3-7   What techniques are used to solve decision-making problems under uncertainty? Which technique results in an optimistic decision? Which technique results in a pessimistic decision?

Problems*

3-8   Kenneth Brown is the principal owner of Brown Oil, Inc. After quitting his university teaching job, Ken has been able to increase his annual salary by a factor of over 100. At the present time, Ken is forced to consider purchasing some more equipment for Brown Oil because of competition. His alternatives are shown in the following table.

EQUIPMENT	FAVORABLE MARKET ($)	UNFAVORABLE MARKET ($)
Sub 100	300,000	−200,000
Oiler J	250,000	−100,000
Texan	75,000	−18,000

For example, if Ken purchases a Sub 100 and if there is a favorable market, he will realize a profit of $300,000. On the other hand, if the market is unfavorable, Ken will suffer a loss of $200,000. But Ken has always been a very optimistic decision maker.
(a)   What type of decision is Ken facing?
(b)   What decision criterion should he use?
(c)   What alternative is best?

3-9   Although Ken Brown (discussed in Problem 3-8) is the principal owner of Brown Oil, his brother Bob is credited with making the company a financial success. Bob is vice president of finance. Bob attributes his success to his pessimistic attitude about business and the oil industry. Given the information from Problem 3-8, it is likely that Bob will arrive at a different decision. What decision criterion should Bob use, and what alternative will he select?

---

*Note: ▭ means the problem may be solved with QM for Windows; ✖ means the problem may be solved with Excel QM; and ▭ means the problem may be solved with QM for Windows and/or Excel QM.

*when is
Risk ⟶ Do a Decision Tree*

3-10 The *Lubricant* is an expensive oil newsletter to which many oil giants subscribe, including Ken Brown. In the last issue, the letter described how the demand for oil products would be extremely high. Apparently, the American consumer will continue to use oil products even if the price of these products doubles. Indeed, one of the articles in the *Lubricant* states that the chances of a favorable market for oil products was 70%, while the chance of an unfavorable market was only 30%. Ken would like to use these probabilities in determining the best decision. (See Problem 3-8 for details.)

(a) What decision model should be used?

(b) What is the optimal decision?

(c) Ken believes that the $300,000 figure for the Sub 100 with a favorable market is too high. How much lower would this figure have to be for Ken to change his decision made in part (b)?

3-11 Allen Young has always been proud of his personal investment strategies and has done very well over the past several years. He invests primarily in the stock market. Over the past several months, however, Allen has become very concerned about the stock market as a good investment. In some cases it would have been better for Allen to have his money in a bank than in the market. During the next year, Allen must decide whether to invest $10,000 in the stock market or in a certificate of deposit (CD) at an interest rate of 9%. If the market is good, Allen believes that he could get a 14% return on his money. With a fair market, he expects to get an 8% return. If the market is bad, he will most likely get no return at all—in other words, the return would be 0%. Allen estimates that the probability of a good market is 0.4, the probability of a fair market is 0.4, and the probability of a bad market is 0.2.

(a) Develop a decision table for this problem.

(b) What is the best decision?

3-12 Janet Kim, president of Kim Manufacturing, Inc., is considering whether to build more manufacturing plants in Wisconsin. Her decision is summarized in the following table:

ALTERNATIVES	FAVORABLE MARKET ($)	UNFAVORABLE MARKET ($)
Build a large plant	400,000	−300,000
Build a small plant	80,000	−10,000
Don't build	0	0
Probabilities	0.4	0.6

(a) Construct an opportunity loss table.

(b) Determine EOL and the best strategy.

(c) What is the expected value of perfect information?

3-13 Helen Murvis, hospital administrator for Portland General Hospital, is trying to determine whether to build a large wing onto the existing hospital, a small wing, or no wing at all. If the population of Portland continues to grow, a large wing could return $150,000 to the hospital each year. If the small wing were built, it would return $60,000 to the hospital each year if the population continues to grow. If the population of Portland remains the same, the hospital would encounter a loss of $85,000 if the large wing were built. Furthermore, a loss of $45,000 would be realized if the small wing were constructed and the population remains the same. Unfortunately, Helen does not have any information about the future population of Portland.

(a) What type of decision problem is this?

(b) Construct a decision table.

(c) Using the equally likely criterion, determine the best alternative.

3-14 In Problem 3-11 you helped Allen Young determine the best investment strategy. Now, Young is thinking about paying for a stock market newsletter. A friend of Young said that these types of letters could predict very accurately whether the market would be good, fair, or poor. Then, based on these predictions, Young could make better investment decisions.

(a) What is the most that Young would be willing to pay for a newsletter?

(b) Young now believes that a good market will give a return of only 11% instead of 14%. Will this information change the amount that Young would be willing to pay for the newsletter? If your answer is yes, determine the most that Young would be willing to pay, given this new information.

3-15 Hardie Lord, Helen Murvis's boss, is not convinced that Helen used the correct decision technique. (Refer to Problem 3-13.) Hardie believes that Helen should use a coefficient of realism of 0.75 in determining the best alternative. Hardie thinks of himself as a realist.

(a) Develop a decision table for this problem.

(b) Using the criterion of realism, what is the best decision?

(c) Did Hardie's decision technique result in a decision that was different from Helen's?

3-16 Brilliant Color is a small supplier of chemicals and equipment that are used by some photographic stores to process 35-mm film. One product that Brilliant Color supplies is BC-6. John Kubick, president of Brilliant Color, normally stocks 11, 12, or 13 cases of BC-6 each week. For each case that John sells he receives a profit of $35. Like many photographic chemicals, BC-6 has a very short shelf life, so if a case is not sold by the end of the week, John must discard it. Since each case costs John $56, he loses $56 for every case that is not sold by the end of the week. There is a probability of 0.45 of selling 11 cases, a probability of 0.35 of selling 12 cases, and a probability of 0.2 of selling 13 cases.

(a) Construct a decision table for this problem. Include all conditional values and probabilities in the table.

(b) What is your recommended course of action?

(c) If John is able to develop BC-6 with an ingredient that stabilizes it so that it no longer has to be discarded, how would this change your recommended course of action?

3-17 Today's Electronics specializes in manufacturing modern electronic components. It also builds the equipment that produces the components. Phyllis Weinberger, who is responsible for advising the president of Today's Electronics on electronic manufacturing equipment, has developed the following table concerning a proposed facility:

| | PROFIT ($) | | |
	STRONG MARKET	FAIR MARKET	POOR MARKET
Large facility	550,000	110,000	−310,000
Medium-sized facility	300,000	129,000	−100,000
Small facility	200,000	100,000	−32,000
No facility	0	0	0

(a) Develop an opportunity loss table.

(b) What is the minimax decision?

3-18 Megley Cheese Company is a small manufacturer of several different cheese products. One of the products is a cheese spread that is sold to retail outlets. Jason Megley must decide how many cases of cheese spread to manufacture each month. The probability that the demand will be six cases is 0.1, for 7 cases is 0.3, for 8 cases is 0.5, and for 9 cases is 0.1. The cost of every case is $45, and the price that Jason gets for each case is $95. Unfortunately, any cases not sold by the end of the month are of no value, due to spoilage. How many cases of cheese should Jason manufacture each month?

3-19 Even though independent gasoline stations have been having a difficult time, Susan Solomon has been thinking about starting her own independent gasoline station. Susan's problem is to decide how large her station should be. The annual returns will depend on both the size of her station and a number of marketing factors related to the oil industry and demand for gasoline. After a careful analysis, Susan developed the following table:

SIZE OF FIRST STATION	GOOD MARKET ($)	FAIR MARKET ($)	POOR MARKET ($)
Small	50,000	20,000	−10,000
Medium	80,000	30,000	−20,000
Large	100,000	30,000	−40,000
Very large	300,000	25,000	−160,000

For example, if Susan constructs a small station and the market is good, she will realize a profit of $50,000.

(a) Develop a decision table for this decision.

(b) What is the maximax decision?

(c) What is the maximin decision?

(d) What is the equally likely decision?

(e) What is the criterion of realism decision? Use an α value of 0.8.

(f) Develop an opportunity loss table.

(g) What is the minimax decision?

3-20 Dorothy Stanyard has three major routes to take to work. She can take Tennessee Street the entire way, she can take several back streets to work, or she can use the expressway. The traffic patterns are very complex, however. Under good conditions, Tennessee Street is the fastest route. When Tennessee is congested, one of the other routes is usually preferable. Over the past two months, Dorothy has tried each route several times under different traffic conditions. This information is summarized in minutes of travel time to work in the following table:

	NO TRAFFIC CONGESTION (minutes)	MILD TRAFFIC CONGESTION (minutes)	SEVERE TRAFFIC CONGESTION (minutes)
Tennessee Street	15	30	45
Back roads	20	25	35
Expressway	30	30	30

In the past 60 days, Dorothy encountered severe traffic congestion 10 days and mild traffic congestion 20 days. Assume that the last 60 days are typical of traffic conditions.

(a) Develop a decision table for this decision.

(b) What route should Dorothy take?

(c) Dorothy is about to buy a radio for her car that would tell her the exact traffic conditions before she started to work each morning. How much time in minutes on the average would Dorothy save by buying the radio?

3-21 Farm Grown, Inc., produces cases of perishable food products. Each case contains an assortment of vegetables and other farm products. Each case costs $5 and sells for $15. If there are any cases not sold by the end of the day, they are sold to a large food processing company for $3 a case. The probability that daily demand will be 100 cases is 0.3, the probability that daily demand will be 200 cases is 0.4, and the probability that daily demand will be 300 cases is 0.3. Farm Grown has a policy of always satisfying

customer demands. If its own supply of cases is less than the demand, they buy the necessary vegetables from a competitor. The estimated cost of doing this is $16 per case.
  (a) Draw a decision table for this problem.
  (b) What do you recommend?

3-22 Teresa Granger is the manager of Chicago Cheese, which produces cheese spreads and other cheese-related products. E-Z Spread Cheese is a product that has always been popular. The probability of sales, in cases, is as follows:

DEMAND IN CASES	PROBABILITY
10	0.2
11	0.3
12	0.2
13	0.2
14	0.1

A case of E-Z Spread Cheese sells for $100 and has a cost of $75. Any cheese that is not sold by the end of the week is sold to a local food processor for $50. Teresa never sells cheese that is more than a week old. How many cases of E-Z Spread Cheese should Teresa produce each week?

3-23 Harry's Hardware does a brisk business during the year, but during Christmas, Harry's Hardware sells Christmas trees for a substantial profit. Unfortunately, any trees not sold at the end of the season are totally worthless. Thus, the number of trees that are stocked for a given season is a very important decision. The following table reveals the demand for Christmas trees.

DEMAND FOR CHRISTMAS TREES	PROBABILITY
50	0.05
75	0.1
100	0.2
125	0.3
150	0.2
175	0.1
200	0.05

Harry sells trees for $15 each, but his cost is only $6.
  (a) How many trees should Harry stock at his hardware store?
  (b) If the cost increased to $12 per tree and Harry continues to sell trees for $15 each, how many trees should Harry stock?
  (c) Harry is thinking about increasing the price to $18 per tree. Assume that the cost per tree is $6. It is expected that the probability of selling 50, 75, 100, or 125 trees will be 0.25 each. Harry does not expect to sell more than 125 trees with this price increase. What do you recommend?

3-24 In addition to selling Christmas trees during the Christmas holidays, Harry's Hardware sells all of the ordinary hardware items. (Refer to Problem 3-23.) One of the most popular items is Great Glue HH, a glue that is made just for Harry's Hardware. The selling price is $2 per bottle, but unfortunately, the glue gets hard and unusable after one month. The cost of the glue is 75 cents. During the past several months, the mean sales of glue have been 60 units, and the standard deviation is 7. How many bottles of glue should Harry's Hardware stock? Assume that sales follow a normal distribution.

3-25 The marginal loss on Washington Reds, a brand of apples from the state of Washington, is $35 per case. The marginal profit is $15 per case. During the past year, the mean sales of Washington Reds in cases was 45,000 cases, and the standard deviation was 4,450. How many cases of Washington Reds should be brought to market? Assume that sales follow a normal distribution.

3-26 Linda Stanyon has been the production manager for Plano Produce for over eight years. Plano Produce is a small company located near Plano, Illinois. On the average, 400 cases of tomatoes are sold each day. In addition, 85% of the time the sales are between 350 and 450 cases. Each case sells for $3. All cases that are not sold must be discarded. A case costs approximately $2. How many cases of tomatoes should Linda stock?

3-27 Paula Shoemaker produces a weekly stock market report for an exclusive readership. She normally sells 3,000 reports per week, and 70% of the time her sales range from 2,990 to 3,010. The report costs Paula $15 to produce, but Paula is able to sell reports for $350 each. Of course, any reports not sold by the end of the week have no value. How many reports should Paula produce each week?

 3-28 After buying a computer system, Sim Thomas must decide whether to purchase (1) a complete maintenance (or service) policy at a cost of $500, which would cover all maintenance costs; (2) a partial maintenance policy at a cost of $300, which would cover some of the costs of any maintenance; or (3) no maintenance policy. The consequences, costs, and probabilities are given in the following table:

	MAINTENANCE REQUIRED	NOT REQUIRED
No Service Agreement	$3,000	$0
Partial Service Agreement	$1,500	$300
Complete Service Agreement	$500	$500
Probabilities	0.2	0.8

(a) What do you recommend?
(b) If the probability of needing maintenance is 0.8 (instead of 0.2) and the probability of not needing maintenance is 0.2, how does this change Sim's decision?

3-29 Bob Welch, a famous divorce attorney, is facing a decision with four options (alternatives) and four scenarios (states of nature). The options relate to furniture in his client's house. The options range from a cash settlement for the furniture (Option 1) to aggressively litigating the issue (Option 4), where his client could get $30,000 or suffer a $20,000 loss from fees and related costs. He does not know the probabilities of the states of nature, which include Scenario 1 (favorable judge), Scenario 2 (jury trial), Scenario 3 (out of court settlement), and Scenario 4 (arbitration). (See the following table.) Help Bob by determining the maximax and maximin decisions. What is the equally likely decision?

	SCENARIO 1	SCENARIO 2	SCENARIO 3	SCENARIO 4
Option 1	$5,000	$5,000	$5,000	$5,000
Option 2	$10,000	$5,000	$2,000	$0
Option 3	$20,000	$7,000	$1,000	−$5,000
Option 4	$30,000	$15,000	−$10,000	−$20,000

Data Set Problem

3-30   Chris Dunphy, executive vice president for marketing and sales of Sumu Electronics, is considering the possibility of introducing a new line of inexpensive wristwatches, which would be oriented primarily toward young adults. The watch would have a plastic face-plate and wristband and a variety of features, including an alarm, a chronograph, and the ability to store and retrieve various split times. The watch has been designed to come in a variety of colors and styles. The retail price of the watch is expected to be $19. At this price, Chris feels that there is a substantial market for the watch. To help gain further information, Chris has hired a marketing research firm to study the market potential for this new venture.

The marketing research team conducted a survey and a pilot study to determine the potential market for the new watch being considered by Sumu. The team, realizing that there is market risk associated with any new product, looked at the potential market on a five-point scale. The number 1 represents the poorest or weakest market for the new product, while the number 5 represents the most optimistic market for the new watches. Using the five-point scale, the marketing research team looked at a variety of production, or stocking, policies related to each of the marketing segments. The stocking policies involve producing 100,000 to 500,000 watches.

The worst market scenario for Sumu was still expected to bring profitability through all stocking ranges. (Remember, the worst-case marketing scenario was assigned a value of 1 on the five-point scale.) The probability of having a 1-type market was estimated to be 0.10. A stocking policy of 100,000 units was expected to return a net profit of $100,000 for Sumu. A stocking policy of 150,000 units was expected to return only $90,000. Similarly, higher stocking policies for a market potential of 1 were expected to yield lower profits. A stocking policy of 200,000 was expected to return $85,000 in net profits. The stocking policies of 250,000, 300,000, 350,000, 400,000, 450,000, and 500,000 were expected to yield net profits of $80,000, $65,000, $50,000, $45,000, $30,000, and $20,000, respectively.

The next-best market scenario was categorized by the number 2. This market potential was categorized as below average, and the marketing research team estimated that the chance of getting a below average market was 20%. The net profit for the beginning stocking policy of 100,000 units was estimated to be $110,000. The net profit for stocking 150,000 units was $120,000. If Sumu stocked 200,000 units, the net profit would be $110,000. A net profit of $120,000 would be realized if the stocking policy was 250,000 units. Stocking policies of 300,000, 350,000, 400,000, 450,000, and 500,000 would result in net profits of $100,000, $100,000, $95,000, $90,000, and $85,000, respectively.

The marketing research team estimated that the probability of an average market was 50%. This average market was coded with a 3 on the five-point scale. In general, profits were significantly higher for all stocking policies with this average market scenario. As before, profitability figures were estimated for all of the stocking policies, ranging from 100,000 to 500,000 units. The net profitabilities for this range are $120,000, $140,000, $135,000, $155,000, $155,000, $160,000, $170,000, $165,000, and $160,000.

A good market potential for the watches was given a 4 on the five-point scale. The probability, however, of a good market was relatively low. It was estimated to be 10%. Net profitability factors for stocking policies that range from 100,000 to 500,000 units were estimated to be $135,000, $155,000, $160,000, $170,000, $180,000, $190,000, $200,000, $230,000, and $270,000.

The probability of a very good market was estimated to be 10%. This market received a 5 on the scale. Profitability factors for this market, in general, were higher. The profitability factors for stocking policies that range from 100,000 to 500,000 were $140,000, $170,000, $175,000, $180,000, $195,000, $210,000, $230,000, $245,000, and $295,000.

(a) Determine the expected monetary values for each of the stocking policy alternatives. Which stocking policy do you recommend?

(b) What is the expected value of perfect information for this situation?

(c) Chris has just received information that the original probability estimations were not accurate. Market 2 has a probability of 0.28, while market 5 has a probability of 0.02. Does this new information change any decisions?

(d) Chris has also received new information about stocking 500,000 watches. The return given a very good market is now estimated to be $340,000. What is the impact of the new probability values [given in point (c)] and the new return for a very good market for stocking 500,000 units?

Case Study

Starting Right Corporation

After watching a movie about a young woman who quit a successful corporate career to start her own baby food company, Julia Day decided that she wanted to do the same. In the movie, the baby food company was very successful. Julia knew, however, that it is much easier to make a movie about a successful woman starting her own company than to actually do it. The product had to be of the highest quality, and Julia had to get the best people involved to launch the new company. Julia resigned from her job and launched her new company—Starting Right.

Julia decided to target the upper end of the baby food market by producing baby food that contained no preservatives but had a great taste. Although the price would be slightly higher than for existing baby food, Julia believed that parents would be willing to pay more for a high-quality baby food. Instead of putting baby food in jars, which would require preservatives to stabilize the food, Julia decided to try a new approach. The baby food would be frozen. This would allow for natural ingredients, no preservatives, and outstanding nutrition.

Getting good people to work for the new company was also important. Julia decided to find people with experience in finance, marketing, and production to get involved with Starting Right. With her enthusiasm and charisma, Julia was able to find such a group. Their first step was to develop prototypes of the new frozen baby food and to perform a small pilot test of the new product. The pilot test received rave reviews.

The final key to getting the young company off to a good start was to raise funds. Three options were considered: corporate bonds, preferred stock, and common stock. Julia decided that each investment should be in blocks of $30,000. Furthermore, each investor should have an annual income of at least $40,000 and a net worth of $100,000 to be eligible to invest in Starting Right. Corporate bonds would return 13% per year for the next five years. Julia furthermore guaranteed that investors in the corporate bonds would get at least $20,000 back at the end of five years. Investors in preferred stock should see their initial investment increase by a factor of 4 with a good market or have the investment worth only half of the initial investment with an unfavorable market. The common stock had the greatest potential. The initial investment was expected to increase by a factor of 8 with a good market, but investors would lose everything if the market was unfavorable. During the next five years, it was expected that inflation would increase by a factor of 4.5% each year.

1. Sue Pansky, a retired grade-school teacher, is considering investing in Starting Right. She is very conservative and is a risk avoider. What do you recommend?

2. Ray Cahn, who is currently a commodities broker, is also considering an investment, although he believes that there is only an 11% chance of success. What do you recommend?

3. Lila Battle has decided to invest in Starting Right. While she believes that Julia has a good chance of being successful, Lila is a risk avoider and very conservative. What is your advice to Lila?

4. George Yates believes that there is an equally likely chance for success. What is your recommendation?

5. Peter Metarko is extremely optimistic about the market for the new baby food. What is your advice for Pete?

6. Julia Day has been told that developing the legal documents for each fund-raising alternative is expensive. Julia would like to offer alternatives for both risk-averse and risk-seeking investors. Can Julia delete one of the financial alternatives and still offer investment choices for risk seekers and risk avoiders?

Case Study

Ski Right

After retiring as a physician, Bob Guthrie became an avid downhill skier on the steep slopes of the Utah Rocky Mountains. As an amateur inventor, Bob was always looking for something new. With the recent deaths of several celebrity skiers, Bob knew he could use his creative mind to make skiing safer and his bank account larger. He knew that many deaths on the slopes were caused by head injuries. Although old helmets have been on the market for some time, most skiers considered them boring and basically ugly. As a physician, Bob knew that some type of new ski helmet was the answer.

Bob's biggest challenge was to invent a helmet that was attractive, safe, and fun to wear. Multiple colors, using the latest fashion designs would be a must. After years of skiing, Bob knew that many skiers believed that how you looked on the slopes was more important than how you skied. His helmets would have to look good and fit in with current fashion trends. But attractive helmets were not enough. Bob had to make the helmets fun and useful. The name of the new ski helmet, Ski Right, was sure to be a winner. If Bob could come up with a good idea, he believed that there was a 20% chance that the market for the Ski Right Helmet would be excellent. The chance of a good market should be 40%. Bob also knew that the market for his helmet could be only average (30% chance) or even poor (10% chance).

The idea of how to make ski helmets fun and useful came to Bob on a gondola ride to the top of a mountain. A busy executive on the gondola ride was on his cell phone trying to complete a complicated merger. When the executive got off of the gondola, he dropped the phone and it was crushed by the gondola mechanism. Bob decided that his new ski helmet would have a built-in cell phone and an AM/FM Stereo radio. All of the electronics could be operated by a control pad worn on a skier's arm or leg.

Bob decided to try a small pilot project for Ski Right. He enjoyed being retired and didn't want a failure to cause him to go back to work. After some research, Bob found Progressive Products (PP). The company was willing to be a partner in developing the Ski Right and sharing any profits. If the market were excellent, Bob would net $5,000. With a good market, Bob would net $2,000. An average market would result in a loss of $2,000, and a poor market would mean Bob would be out $5,000.

Another option for Bob was to have Leadville Barts (LB) make the helmet. The company had extensive experience in making bicycle helmets. Progressive would then take the helmets made by Leadville Barts and do the rest. Bob had a greater risk. He estimated that he could lose $10,000 in a poor market or $4,000 in an average market. A good market for Ski Right would result in a $6,000 profit for Bob, while an excellent market would mean a $12,000 profit.

A third option for Bob was to use TalRad TR, a radio company in Tallahassee, Florida. TalRad had extensive experience in making military radios. Leadville Barts could make the helmets, and Progressive Products could do the rest. Again, Bob would be taking on greater risk. A poor market would mean a $15,000 loss, while an average market would mean a $10,000 loss. A good market would result in a net profit of $7,000 for Bob. An excellent market would return $13,000.

Bob could also have Celestial Cellular (CC) develop the cell phones. Thus, another option was to have Celestial make the phones and have Progressive do the rest of the production and distribution. Because the cell phone was the most expensive component of the helmet, Bob could lose $30,000 in a poor market. He could lose $20,000 in an average market. If the market were good or excellent, Bob would see a net profit of $10,000 or $30,000, respectively.

Bob's final option was to forget about Progressive Products entirely. He could use Leadville Barts to make the helmets, Celestial Cellular to make the phones, and TalRad to make the AM/FM stereo radios. Bob could then hire some friends to assemble everything and market the finished Ski Right helmets. With this final alternative, Bob could realize a net profit of $55,000 in an excellent market. Even if the market were just good, Bob would net $20,000. An average market, however, would mean a loss of $35,000. If the market were poor, Bob would lose $60,000.

Discussion Questions

1. What do you recommend?
2. What is the opportunity loss for this problem?
3. Compute the expected value of perfect information.
4. Was Bob completely logical in how he approached this decision problem?

Bibliography

Ahlbrecht, Martin, et al. "An Empirical Study on Intertemporal Decision Making under Risk," *Management Science* (June 1997): 813.

Bistritz, Nancy. "Rx for UK Healthcare Woes," *OR/MS Today* (April 1997): 18.

Borison, Adam. "Oglethorpe Power Corporation Decides about Investing in a Major Transmission System," *Interfaces* 25, 2 (March 1995): 25.

Brown, R. "Do Managers Find Decision Theory Useful?" *Harvard Business Review* (May–June 1970): 78–89.

Brown, R. V. "The State of the Art of Decision Analysis: A Personal Perspective," *Interfaces* 22, 6 (November—December 1992): 5–14.

Dantzig, G. B. "The Diet Problem," *Interfaces* 20, 4 (July–August 1990): 43–47.

Ferland, J., and C. Fleurent. "SAPHIR: A Decision Support System for Course Scheduling," *Interfaces* (March 1994): 105.

Gass, S. I. "Model World: Models at the OK Corral," *Interfaces* 21, 6 (November–December 1991): 80.

Green, A. E. S. "Finding the Japanese Fleet," *Interfaces* 23, 5 (September–October 1993): 62.

Hammond, J. S., R. L. Kenney, and H. Raiffa. "The Hidden Traps in Decision Making," *Harvard Business Review* (September–October 1998): 47–60.

Hess, S. W. "Swinging on the Branch of a Tree: Project Selection Applications," *Interfaces* 23, 6 (November–December 1993): 5–12.

Jbuedj, Coden. "Decision Making under Conditions of Uncertainty: A Wakeup Call for the Financial Planning Profession," *Journal of Financial Planning* (October 1997): 84.

Kirkwood, C. W. "An Overview of Methods for Applied Decision Analysis," *Interfaces* 22, 6 (November–December 1992): 28–39.

Lane, M. S., A. H. Mansour, and J. L. Harpell. "Operations Research Techniques: A Longitudinal Update 1973–1988," *Interfaces* 23, 2 (March–April 1993): 63–68.

Lev, B. "Airline Operations Research," *Interfaces* 20, 3 (May–June 1990): 99.

Luce, R., and H. Raiffa. *Games and Decisions*. New York: John Wiley & Sons, Inc., 1957.

Moore, E. W., Jr., J. M. Warmke, and L. R. Gorban. "The Indispensable Role of Management Science in Centralizing Freight Operations at Reynolds Metals Company," *Interfaces* 21, 1 (January–February 1991): 107–129.

Pratt, J. W., H. Raiffa, and R. Schlaifer. *Introduction to Statistical Decision Theory*. New York: McGraw-Hill Book Company, 1965.

Raiffa, H. *Decision Analysis*. Reading, MA: Addison-Wesley Publishing Co., Inc., 1968.

Render, B., and R. M. Stair. *Cases and Readings in Management Science*, 2nd ed. Boston: Allyn and Bacon, Inc., 1988.

Schlaifer, R. *Analysis of Decisions under Uncertainty*. New York: McGraw-Hill Book Company, 1969.

Strait, Scott. "Decision Analysis Approach to Competitive Situations with a Pure Infinite Regress," *Decision Sciences* (September 1994): 853.

Sullivan, Gerald, and Kenneth Fordyce. "IBM Burlington's Logistics Management System," *Interfaces* 20, 1 (January–February 1990): 43–64.

APPENDIX 3.1: DECISION THEORY WITH QM FOR WINDOWS

QM for Windows can be used to solve decision theory problems discussed in this chapter. In this appendix we show you how to solve straightforward decision theory problems that involve tables. In Appendix 4.1 we explore the use of QM for Windows to solve more sophisticated decision theory problems, where decisions are sequential.

In this chapter we solved the Thompson Lumber problem. The alternatives included constructing a large plant, a small plant, or doing nothing. The probabilities of an unfavorable and a favorable market, along with financial information, were presented in Figure 3.2.

To demonstrate QM for Windows, let's use these data to solve the Thompson Lumber problem. Program 3.2 shows the results. Note that the best alternative is to construct the medium-sized plant, with an EMV of $40,000.

PROGRAM 3.2

Computing EMV for Thompson Lumber Company Problem Using QM for Windows

This chapter also covered decision making under uncertainty, where probability values are not available or appropriate. Solution techniques for these types of problems were presented in Section 3.5. Program 3.2 shows these results, including the maximax, maximin, and Hurwicz solutions.

Chapter 3 also covered expected opportunity loss. To demonstrate the use of QM for Windows, we can determine the EOL for the Thompson Lumber problem. The results are presented in Program 3.3. Note that this program also computes EVPI.

PROGRAM 3.3

Opportunity Loss and EVPI for the Thompson Lumber Company Problem Using QM for Windows

Decision Trees and Utility Theory

LEARNING OBJECTIVES
....

After completing this chapter, students will be able to:

1. Develop accurate and useful decision trees.

2. Revise probability estimates using Bayesian analysis.

3. Understand the importance and use of utility theory in decision making.

4. Use computers to solve more complex decision problems.

CHAPTER OUTLINE
....

4.1 Introduction

4.2 Decision Trees

4.3 How Probability Values Are Estimated by Bayesian Analysis

4.4 Utility Theory

4.5 Sensitivity Analysis

Summary • Glossary • Key Equations • Solved Problems • Self-Test • Discussion Questions and Problems • Data Set Problem • Case Study: Blake Electronics • Internet Case Studies: Drink at Home, Inc.; Ruth Jones' Heart By-Pass Operation • Bibliography

Appendix 4.1: Decision Trees with QM for Windows

Appendix 4.2: Using TreePlan to Solve Decision Tree Problems

4.1   INTRODUCTION

In Chapter 3 we saw that problems with just a few alternatives and states of nature could be analyzed by using decision tables. This chapter moves us a step further in exploring decision theory by introducing the topics of decision trees, probability assessment, and utility theory.

4.2   DECISION TREES

Any problem that can be presented in a decision table can also be graphically illustrated in a *decision tree*. Let's take another look at the Thompson Lumber Company case first presented in Chapter 3. You may recall that John Thompson was trying to decide whether to expand his operation by building a new plant to produce storage sheds. A simple decision tree to represent John's decision is shown in Figure 4.1. Note that the tree presents the decision and outcomes in a sequential order. First, John decides whether to construct a large plant, a small plant, or no plant. Then, once that decision is made, the possible states of nature or outcomes (favorable or unfavorable market) will occur.

All decision trees are similar in that they contain *decision points* or *nodes* and *state-of-nature points* or *nodes*. These symbols are:

☐   A decision node from which one of several alternatives may be chosen

○   A state-of-nature node out of which one state of nature will occur

Analyzing problems with decision trees involves five steps:

Five Steps of Decision Tree Analysis

1. Define the problem.
2. Structure or draw the decision tree.
3. Assign probabilities to the states of nature.
4. Estimate payoffs for each possible combination of alternatives and states of nature.
5. Solve the problem by computing expected monetary values (EMVs) for each state of nature node. This is done by working backward, that is, starting at the right of the tree and working back to decision nodes on the left.

FIGURE 4.1

Thompson's Decision Tree

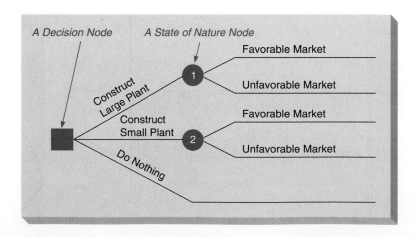

| MODELING IN THE REAL WORLD | Using Decision Tree Analysis on R&D Projects |

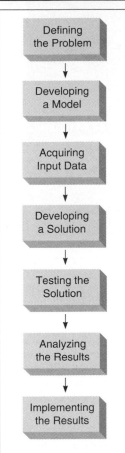

Defining the Problem

The Canadian subsidiary of ICI discovered a new unpatentable process for anthraquinone (AQ) to reduce paper mill pollution. The company had to decide whether to invest funds in research and development (R&D) for the new process.

Developing a Model

A traditional decision tree model was used. Instead of expected monetary values, the model used expected net present value, which converts future monetary flows into today's dollars.

Acquiring Input Data

ICI collected both probability and monetary values. The probability data included the probability of a technical success, the probability of a significant market for the new process, and the probability of a commercial success.

Developing a Solution

The solution was obtained using decision tree analysis like the ones performed in this chapter.

Testing the Solution

ICI tested the solution by analyzing various risks of the process, including whether the new process could be developed, the market for the new process, the accuracy of the conditional probabilities in the decision tree, and various expenses and monetary flows.

Analyzing the Results

The estimated net present value from decision tree analysis was $3.2 million. If the new project was successful, the net present value could be as high as $25 million.

Implementing the Results

The decision tree analysis moved this R&D project forward. As a result, it was decided to investigate the process further. After field testing, however, difficulty with pulp mills resulted in the project being canceled.

Source: Sidney Hess. "Swinging on the Branch of a Tree: Project Selection Applications," *Interfaces* 23, 6 (November–December 1993): 5–12.

A completed and solved decision tree for Thompson Lumber is presented in Figure 4.2. Note that the payoffs are placed at the right side of each of the tree's branches. The probabilities (first used by Thompson in Chapter 3) are placed in parentheses next to each state of nature. The expected monetary values for each state-of-nature node are then calculated and placed by their respective nodes. The EMV of the first node is $10,000. This represents the branch from the decision node to construct a large plant. The EMV for node 2, to construct a small plant, is $40,000. Building no plant or doing nothing has, of course, a payoff of $0. The branch leaving the decision node leading to the state-of-nature node with the highest EMV should be chosen. In Thompson's case, a small plant should be built.

A More Complex Decision for Thompson Lumber

When a *sequence of decisions* needs to be made, decision trees are much more powerful tools than decision tables. Let's say that John Thompson has two decisions to make, with the second decision dependent on the outcome of the first. Before deciding about building a new plant, John has the option of conducting his own marketing research survey, at

FIGURE 4.2

Completed and Solved Decision
Tree for Thompson Lumber

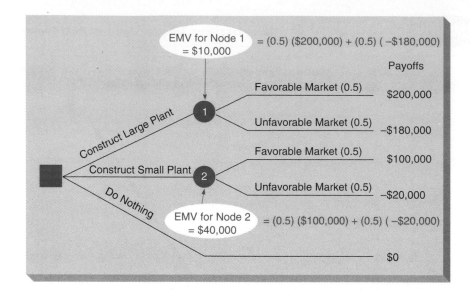

EMV for Node 1 = (0.5) ($200,000) + (0.5) (−$180,000)
= $10,000

Payoffs

Favorable Market (0.5) $200,000

1   Construct Large Plant

Unfavorable Market (0.5)   −$180,000

Construct Small Plant

Favorable Market (0.5) $100,000

2

Unfavorable Market (0.5)   −$20,000

Do Nothing

EMV for Node 2 = (0.5) ($100,000) + (0.5) (−$20,000)
= $40,000

$0

a cost of $10,000. The information from his survey could help him decide whether to construct a large plant, a small plant, or not to build at all. John recognizes that such a market survey will not provide him with *perfect* information, but it may help quite a bit nevertheless.

John's new decision tree is represented in Figure 4.3. Let's take a careful look at this more complex tree. Note that *all possible outcomes and alternatives* are included in their logical sequence. This is one of the strengths of using decision trees in making decisions. The user is forced to examine all possible outcomes, including unfavorable ones. He or she is also forced to make decisions in a logical, sequential manner.

All outcomes and alternatives must be considered.

Examining the tree, we see that Thompson's first decision point is whether to conduct the $10,000 market survey. If he chooses not to do the study (the lower part of the tree), he can either construct a large plant, a small plant, or no plant. This is John's second decision point. The market will either be favorable (0.50 probability) or unfavorable (also 0.50 probability) if he builds. The payoffs for each of the possible consequences are listed along the right side. As a matter of fact, the lower portion of John's tree is *identical* to the simpler decision tree shown in Figure 4.2. Why is this so?

The upper part of Figure 4.3 reflects the decision to conduct the market survey. State-of-nature node 1 has two branches. There is a 45% chance that the survey results will indicate a favorable market for storage sheds. We also note that the probability is 0.55 that the survey results will be negative.[1]

Most of the probabilities are conditional probabilities.

The rest of the probabilities shown in parentheses in Figure 4.3 are all *conditional probabilities*.[2] For example, 0.78 is the probability of a favorable market for the sheds given a favorable result from the market survey. Of course, you would expect to find a high probability of a favorable market given that the research indicated that the market was good. Don't forget, though, there is a chance that John's $10,000 market survey didn't result in perfect or even reliable information. Any market research study is subject

---

[1] An explanation of how these two probabilities can be obtained is the topic of Section 4.3. For now, let's assume that Thompson's experience provides them and accept them as reasonable.

[2] The derivation of these probabilities (0.78, 0.22, 0.27, and 0.73) is also discussed in the next section.

FIGURE 4.3
Larger Decision Tree with Payoffs and Probabilities for Thompson Lumber

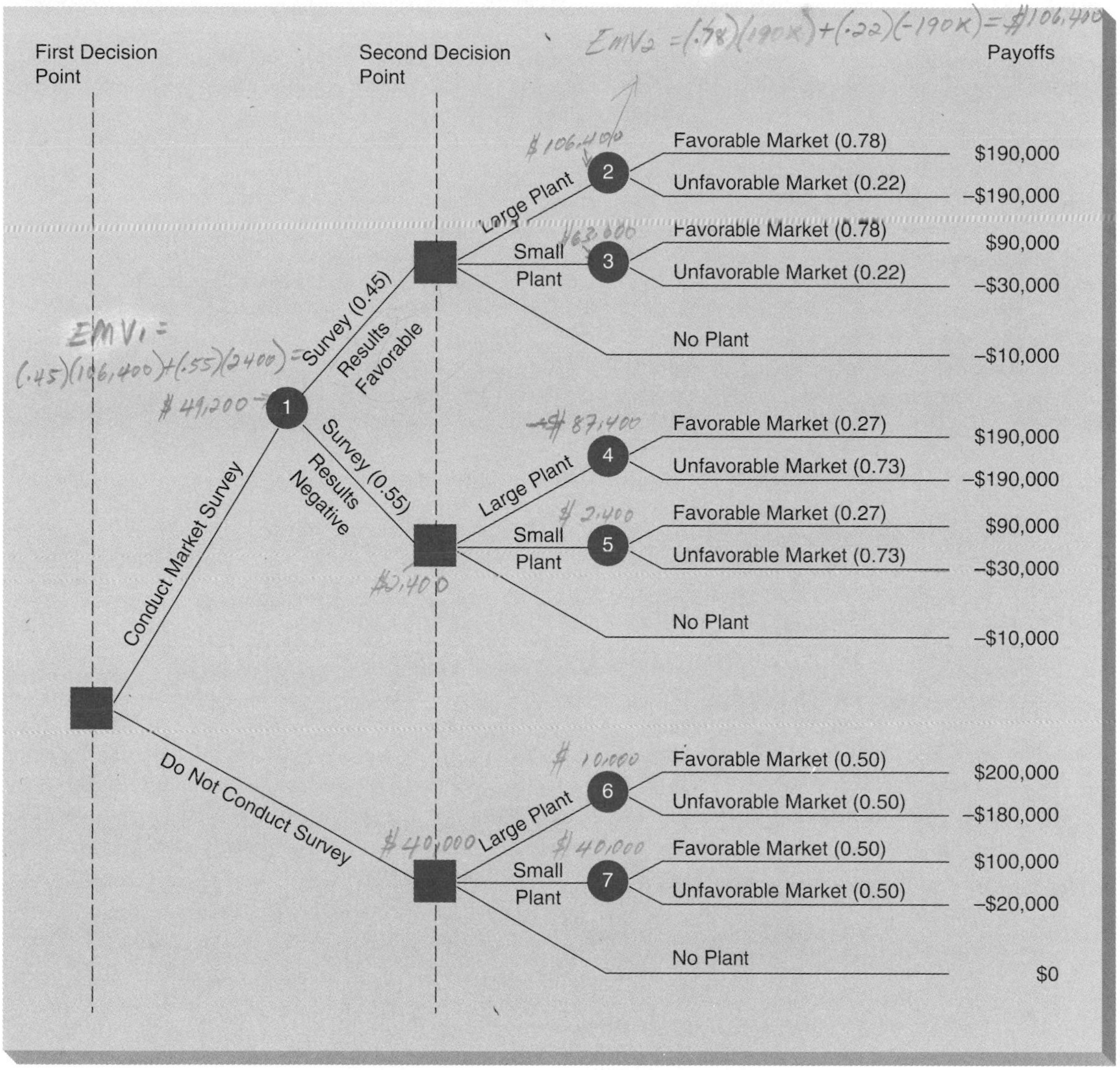

to error. In this case, there's a 22% chance that the market for sheds will be unfavorable given that the survey results are positive.

We note that there is a 27% chance that the market for sheds will be favorable given that John's survey results are negative. The probability is much higher, 0.73, that the market will actually be unfavorable given that the survey was negative.

The cost of the survey had to be subtracted from the original payoffs.

Finally, when we look to the payoff column in Figure 4.3, we see that $10,000, the cost of the marketing study, had to be subtracted from each of the top 10 tree branches. Thus, a large plant with a favorable market would normally net a $200,000 profit. But because the market study was conducted, this figure is reduced by $10,000 to $190,000. In the unfavorable case, the loss of $180,000 would increase to $190,000. Similarly, conducting the survey and building no plant now results in a −$10,000 payoff.

IN ACTION   **Electric Power at Oglethorpe**

Oglethorpe Power Corporation (OPC) is a cooperative that is involved with the generation and transportation of electric power. The cooperative supplies 39 Georgia counties with wholesale power. In 1990, OPC learned that Florida Power Corporation had a desire to install another transmission line to connect it to Georgia. This followed a trend where the whole-sale electric power market had become very active, with companies buying and selling excess power. In Georgia, due to larger nuclear and coal-fired power plants, there was a general surplus of electric power. At the same time, Florida had a need for additional electric power. OPC had to decide whether to build additional transmission capacity, an investment that could cost $100 million or more. The annual savings might be $20 million.

To help with this decision, OPC conducted a comprehensive analysis of the decision-making problem. The time frame was a short two weeks. OPC began by formulating the problem, which was stated as *"Should OPC go forward with the proposal to construct a 500-kV transmission line to Florida Power Corporation? If so, what should the framework of the business deal be?"* OPC next specified the major decisions,

uncertainties, and values of concern. The major decisions included (1) an integrated transmission as a joint venture with Georgia Power (another major supplier of power), (2) a go-it-alone strategy for installing the line, and (3) no line. This information was placed on several sequential decision trees, which investigated line, control, upgrade, construction cost, competitive situation, Florida demand, OPC share, and spot price issues. OPC also developed a spreadsheet model that examined savings and a final decision value. In addition, OPC used sensitivity analysis on the results.

The final recommendations based on decision tree analysis was—if a commitment regarding the transmission line is required immediately, OPC should choose between a high-risk, high-savings strategy (go-it-alone strategy) and a low-risk, low-savings (no-line) policy. If an immediate commitment is not needed, OPC should gather additional information on the competitive situation before a final decision is made.

Source: Adam Borison. "Oglethorpe Power Corporation Decides about Investing in a Major Transmission System," *Interfaces* 25, 2 (April 1995): 25.

We start by computing the EMV of each branch.

With all probabilities and payoffs specified, we can start calculating the expected monetary value of each of the branches. We begin at the end, or right side of the decision tree and work back toward the origin. When we finish, the best decision will be known.

EMV calculations for favorable survey results are made first.

1. Given favorable survey results,

$$\text{EMV(node 2)} = \text{EMV(large plant | positive survey)}$$

$$= (0.78)(\$190,000) + (0.22)(-\$190,000) = \$106,400$$

$$\text{EMV(node 3)} = \text{EMV(small plant | positive survey)}$$

$$= (0.78)(\$90,000) + (0.22)(-\$30,000) = \$63,600$$

The EMV of no plant in this case is $-\$10,000$. Thus, if the survey results are favorable, a large plant should be built.

EMV calculations for unfavorable survey results are done next.

2. Given negative survey results,

$$\text{EMV(node 4)} = \text{EMV(large plant | negative survey)}$$

$$= (0.27)(\$190,000) + (0.73)(-\$190,000) = -\$87,400$$

$$\text{EMV(node 5)} = \text{EMV(small plant | negative survey)}$$

$$= (0.27)(\$90,000) + (0.73)(-\$30,000) = \$2,400$$

The EMV of no plant is again $-\$10,000$ for this branch. Thus, given a negative survey result, John should build a small plant with an expected value of $2,400.

3. Continuing on the upper part of the tree and moving backward, we compute the expected value of conducting the market survey.

EMV(node 1) = EMV(conduct survey)

$$= (0.45)(\$106,400) + (0.55)(\$2,400)$$

$$= \$47,880 + \$1,320 = \$49,200$$

We continue working backward to the origin, computing EMV values.

4. If the market survey is *not* conducted,

EMV(node 6) = EMV(large plant)

$$= (0.50)(\$200,000) + (0.50)(-\$180,000)$$

$$= \$10,000$$

EMV(node 7) = EMV(small plant)

$$= (0.50)(\$100,000) + (0.50)(-\$20,000)$$

$$= \$40,000$$

The EMV of no plant is $0.

Thus, building a small plant is the best choice, given that the marketing research is not performed, as we saw earlier.

5. Since the expected monetary value of conducting the survey is $49,200, versus an EMV of $40,000 for not conducting the study, the best choice is to *seek* marketing information. If the survey results are favorable, John should construct a large plant; but if the research is negative, John should construct a small plant.

In Figure 4.4, these expected values are placed on the decision tree. Notice on the tree that a pair of slash lines / / through a decision branch indicates that a particular alternative is dropped from further consideration. This is because its EMV is lower than the best alternative. After you have solved several decision tree problems, you may find it easier to do all of your computations on the tree diagram.

Expected Value of Sample Information

With the market survey he intends to conduct, John Thompson knows that his best decision will be to build a large plant if the survey is favorable or a small plant if the survey results are negative. But John also realizes that conducting the market research is not free. He would like to know what the actual value of doing a survey is. One way of measuring the value of market information is to compute the *expected value of sample information* (EVSI).

EVSI measures the value of sample information.

$$\text{EVSI} = \begin{pmatrix} \text{expected value of best} \\ \text{decision } with \text{ sample} \\ \text{information, assuming} \\ \text{no cost to gather it} \end{pmatrix} - \begin{pmatrix} \text{expected value} \\ \text{of best decision} \\ without \text{ sample} \\ \text{information} \end{pmatrix} \qquad \textbf{(4-1)}$$

In John's case, his EMV would be $59,200 *if* he hadn't already subtracted the $10,000 study cost from each payoff. (Do you see why this is so? If not, add $10,000 back into each payoff, as in the original Thompson problem, and recompute the EMV of conducting the market study.) From the lower branch of Figure 4.4, we see that the EMV of *not* gathering the sample information is $40,000. Thus,

$$\text{EVSI} = \$59,200 - \$40,000 = \$19,200$$

FIGURE 4.4
Thompson's Decision Tree with EMVs Shown

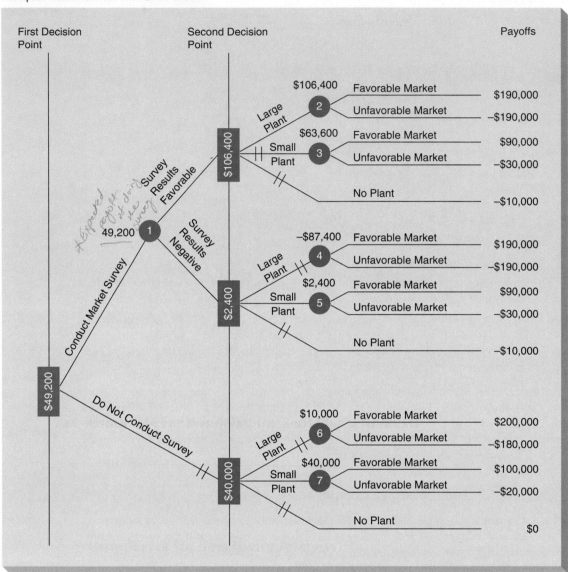

This means that John could have paid up to $19,200 for a market study and still come out ahead. Since it costs only $10,000, the survey is indeed worthwhile.

Using TreePlan to Solve the Thompson Lumber Problem

TreePlan, an Excel add-in provided on the CD-ROM in the back of the text, is a powerful decision tree-modeling tool. Appendix 4.2 at the end of the chapter describes the details of how to load and run the program. Program 4.1 shows the beginning tree in TreePlan.

PROGRAM 4.1

The Beginning Tree
from TreePlan

Program 4.2 is the final tree showing the solution to the Thompson Lumber Problem.

PROGRAM 4.2

The Solution to the Thompson
Lumber Problem Using
TreePlan

4.3 HOW PROBABILITY VALUES ARE ESTIMATED BY BAYESIAN ANALYSIS

There are many ways of getting probability data for a problem such as Thompson's. The numbers (such as 0.78, 0.22, 0.27, 0.73 in Figure 4.3) can be assessed by a manager based on experience and intuition. They can be derived from historical data, or they can be computed from other available data using Bayes' theorem. We discuss this last option in this section.

The Bayes' theorem approach recognizes that a decision maker does not know with certainty what state of nature will occur. It allows the manager to revise his or her initial or prior probability assessments. The revised probabilities are called *posterior probabilities*. (Before continuing, you may wish to review Bayes' theorem in Chapter 2.)

*Bayes' theorem allows
decision makers to revise
probability values.*

Calculating Revised Probabilities

In the Thompson Lumber case solved in Section 4.2, we made the assumption that the following four conditional probabilities were known:

$$P(\text{favorable market(FM)} \mid \text{survey results positive}) = 0.78$$

$$P(\text{unfavorable market(UM)} \mid \text{survey results positive}) = 0.22$$

$$P(\text{favorable market(FM)} \mid \text{survey results negative}) = 0.27$$

$$P(\text{unfavorable market(UM)} \mid \text{survey results negative}) = 0.73$$

We now show how John Thompson was able to derive these values with Bayes' theorem.

From discussions with market research specialists at the local university, John knows that special surveys such as his can either be positive (that is, predict a favorable market) or be negative (predict an unfavorable market). The experts have told John that, statistically, of all new products with a *favorable market* (FM), market surveys were positive and predicted success correctly 70% of the time. Thirty percent of the time the surveys falsely predicted negative results or an *unfavorable market* (UM). On the other hand, when there was actually an unfavorable market for a new product, 80% of the surveys correctly predicted negative results. The surveys incorrectly predicted positive results the remaining 20% of the time. These conditional probabilities are summarized in Table 4.1. They are an indication of the accuracy of the survey that John is thinking of undertaking.

Recall that without any market survey information, John's best estimates of a favorable and unfavorable market are

$$P(\text{FM}) = 0.50$$

$$P(\text{UM}) = 0.50$$

These are referred to as the *prior probabilities*.

We are now ready to compute Thompson's revised or posterior probabilities. These desired probabilities are the reverse of the probabilities in Table 4.1. We need the probability of a favorable or unfavorable market given a positive or negative result from the market study. The general form of Bayes' theorem presented in Chapter 2 was

$$P(A \mid B) = \frac{P(B \mid A) \cdot P(A)}{P(B \mid A) \cdot P(A) + P(B \mid \overline{A}) \cdot P(\overline{A})} \tag{4-2}$$

where

A, B = any two events,

$\overline{A}$ = complement of A

TABLE 4.1   Market Survey Reliability in Predicting Actual States of Nature

RESULT OF SURVEY	ACTUAL STATES OF NATURE	
	FAVORABLE MARKET (FM)	UNFAVORABLE MARKET (UM)
Positive (predicts favorable market for product)	$P(\text{survey positive} \mid \text{FM}) = 0.70$	$P(\text{survey positive} \mid \text{UM}) = 0.20$
Negative (predicts unfavorable market for product)	$P(\text{survey negative} \mid \text{FM}) = 0.30$	$P(\text{survey negative} \mid \text{UM}) = 0.80$

TABLE 4.2	Probability Revisions Given a Positive Survey				
				POSTERIOR PROBABILITY	
STATE OF NATURE	CONDITIONAL PROBABILITY P(SURVEY POSITIVE | STATE OF NATURE)	PRIOR PROBABILITY	JOINT PROBABILITY	$P\left(\dfrac{\text{STATE OF}}{\text{NATURE}}\right.\left\|\begin{array}{c}\text{SURVEY}\\\text{POSITIVE}\end{array}\right)$	
FM	0.70	× 0.50	= 0.35	0.35/0.45 = 0.78	
UM	0.20	× 0.50	= 0.10	0.10/0.45 = 0.22	
		P(survey results positive) = 0.45		1.00	

Substituting the appropriate numbers into this equation, we obtain the conditional probabilities, given that the market survey is positive:

P(FM | survey positive)

$$= \frac{P(\text{survey positive} \mid \text{FM}) \cdot P(\text{FM})}{P(\text{survey positive} \mid \text{FM}) \cdot P(\text{FM}) + P(\text{survey positive} \mid \text{UM}) \cdot P(\text{UM})}$$

$$= \frac{(0.70)(0.50)}{(0.70)(0.50) + (0.20)(0.50)} = \frac{0.35}{0.45} = 0.78$$

P(UM | survey positive)

$$= \frac{P(\text{survey positive} \mid \text{UM}) \cdot P(\text{UM})}{P(\text{survey positive} \mid \text{UM}) \cdot P(\text{UM}) + P(\text{survey positive} \mid \text{FM}) \cdot P(\text{FM})}$$

$$= \frac{(0.20)(0.50)}{(0.20)(0.50) + (0.70)(0.50)} = \frac{0.10}{0.45} = 0.22$$

An alternative method for these calculations is to use a probability table as shown in Table 4.2.

The conditional probabilities, given the market survey is negative, are

P(FM) | survey negative)

$$= \frac{P(\text{survey negative} \mid \text{FM}) \cdot P(\text{FM})}{P(\text{survey negative} \mid \text{FM}) \cdot P(\text{FM}) + P(\text{survey negative} \mid \text{UM}) \cdot P(\text{UM})}$$

$$= \frac{(0.30)(0.50)}{(0.30)(0.50) + (0.80)(0.50)} = \frac{0.15}{0.55} = 0.27$$

P(UM | survey negative)

$$= \frac{P(\text{survey negative} \mid \text{UM}) \cdot P(\text{UM})}{P(\text{survey negative} \mid \text{UM}) \cdot P(\text{UM}) + P(\text{survey negative} \mid \text{FM}) \cdot P(\text{FM})}$$

$$= \frac{(0.80)(0.50)}{(0.80)(0.50) + (0.30)(0.50)} = \frac{0.40}{0.55} = 0.73$$

These computations could have been performed in a table instead, as in Table 4.3.

The posterior probabilities now provide John Thompson with estimates of each state of nature if the survey results are positive or negative. As you know, John's *prior probability* of success without a market survey was only 0.50. Now he is aware that the probability of successfully marketing storage sheds will be 0.78 if his survey shows positive results. His chances of success drop to 27% if the survey report is negative. This is valuable management information, as we saw in the earlier decision tree analysis.

New probabilities provide valuable information.

TABLE 4.3   **Probability Revisions Given a Negative Survey**

STATE OF NATURE	CONDITIONAL PROBABILITY P(SURVEY POSITIVE | STATE OF NATURE)	PRIOR PROBABILITY	JOINT PROBABILITY	POSTERIOR PROBABILITY $P\left(\dfrac{\text{STATE OF NATURE}}{}\middle\vert\dfrac{\text{SURVEY POSITIVE}}{}\right)$
FM	0.30	× 0.50	= 0.15	0.15/0.55 = 0.27
UM	0.80	× 0.50	= 0.40	0.40/0.55 = 0.73
		P(survey results negative) = 0.55		1.00

Potential Problem in Using Survey Results

In many decision-making problems, survey results or pilot studies are done before an actual decision (such as building a new plant or taking a particular course of action) is made. As discussed earlier in this section, Bayes' analysis is used to help determine the correct conditional probabilities that are needed to solve these types of decision theory problems. In computing these conditional probabilities, we need to have data about the surveys and their accuracies. If a decision to build a plant or to take another course of action is actually made, we can determine the accuracy of our surveys. Unfortunately, we cannot get data about those situations in which the decison was not to build a plant or not to take some course of action. Thus, when we use survey results, we are basing our probabilities only on those cases in which a decision to build a plant or take some course of action is actually made. This means that conditional probability information is not quite as accurate as we would like. Even so, calculating conditional probabilities helps to refine the decision-making process and, in general, to make better decisions.

IN ACTION   Using Decision Nodes to Deter the Proliferation of Weapons of Mass Destruction

Weapons of Mass Destruction (WMD) have put fear in the hearts of people around the world and caused countries to take strong political stands. The production, storage, and use of chemical weapons that can kill or injure the populations of entire cities or regions has been a major concern of all democratic countries. Inspection teams have been used in countries to detect and eliminate these potent weapons. The testing and development of nuclear weapons is another concern. In the spring of 1998, for example, both India and Pakistan tested nuclear devices. Many political leaders were very concerned. Others called for stiff sanctions.

WMD has been a long-standing political issue in the United States and a concern for national security. In a 1993 speech about national security, President Clinton stated that "one of our most urgent priorities must be attacking the proliferation of weapons of mass destruction—nuclear, chemical, and biological. . . ." To help, the Department of Defense has launched a nonproliferation program based on four goals: (1)

to prevent countries from acquiring weapons of mass destruction, (2) to deter the use of WMD against the U.S. and its allies, (3) to destroy WMD before their use, and (4) to develop means to reduce the effectiveness of WMDs.

Decision theory has been employed to help develop sound counterproliferation policies and programs. One decision analysis included a decision tree with nodes to represent each of the possible decisions that can be made by the United States in this effort. These are called the Counterproliferation System Choices. A second set of decisions, called Use Offensive Counterproliferation, is used to determine if the United States should attack a country or group suspected of WMD storage and use. The decision analysis also incorporates sensitivity analysis to determine changes to results based on different assumptions or input data.

Source: Stanley Stafira et al. "A Methodology for Evaluating Military Systems in a Counterproliferation Role," *Management Science*. (October 1997): 1420.

4.4 UTILITY THEORY

So far we have used EMV to make decisions. In practice, however, using EMV could lead to bad decisions in many cases. For example, suppose that you are the lucky holder of a lottery ticket. Five minutes from now a fair coin could be flipped, and if it comes up tails, you would win $5 million. If it comes up heads, you would win nothing. Just a moment ago a wealthy person offered you $2 million for your ticket. Let's assume that you have no doubts about the validity of the offer. The person will give you a certified check for the full amount, and you are absolutely sure the check would be good.

EMV is not always the best approach.

A decision tree is shown in Figure 4.5. EMV indicates that you should hold on to your ticket, but what would you do? Just think, $2 million for *sure* instead of a 50% chance at nothing. Suppose you were greedy enough to hold on to the ticket, and then lost. How would you explain that to your friends? Wouldn't $2 million be enough to be comfortable for awhile?

Most people would sell for $2 million. Most of us, in fact, would probably be willing to settle for a lot less. Just how low we would go is, of course, a matter of personal preference. People have different feelings about seeking or avoiding risk. EMV is not a good way to make these types of decisions.

One way to incorporate your own attitudes toward risk is through *utility theory*. In the next section we explore first how to measure utility and then how to use utility measures in decision making.

Measuring Utility and Constructing a Utility Curve

Utility assessment begins by assigning the worst outcome a utility of 0 and the best outcome a utility of 1. All other outcomes will have a utility value between 0 and 1. In determining the utilities of all outcomes, other than the best or worst outcome, a *standard gamble* is considered. This gamble is shown in Figure 4.6.

Utility assessment assigns the worst outcome a utility of 0 and the best outcome, 1.

In Figure 4.6, p is the probability of obtaining the best outcome, and $(1 - p)$ is the probability of obtaining the worst outcome. Assessing the utility of any other outcome involves determining the probability, p, that makes you indifferent between alternative 1, which is the gamble between the best and worst outcomes, and alternative 2, which is ob-

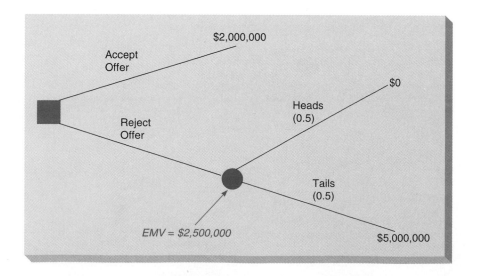

FIGURE 4.5

Your Decision Tree for the Lottery Ticket

FIGURE 4.6

Standard Gamble
for Utility Assessment

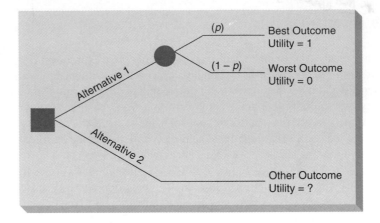

*When you are indifferent,
the expected utilities are
equal.*

taining the other outcome for sure. When you are indifferent between alternatives 1 and 2, the expected utilities for these two alternatives must be equal. This relationship is shown as

expected utility of alternative 2 = expected utility of alternative 1

utility of other outcome = (p)(utility of *best* outcome, which is 1)
$+ (1 - p)$(utility of the *worst* outcome, which is 0)

utility of other outcome $= (p)(1) + (1 - p)(0) = p$ **(4-3)**

Now all you have to do is to determine the value of the probability (p) that makes you indifferent between alternatives 1 and 2. In setting the probability, you should be aware that utility assessment is completely subjective. It's a value set by the decision maker that can't be measured on an objective scale. Let's take a look at an example.

Jane Dickson would like to construct a utility curve revealing her preference for money between $0 and $10,000. A *utility curve* is a graph that plots utility value versus monetary value. She can either invest her money in a bank savings account or she can invest the same money in a real estate deal.

If the money is invested in the bank, in three years Jane would have $5,000. If she invested in the real estate, after three years she could either have nothing or $10,000. Jane,

FIGURE 4.7

Utility of $5,000

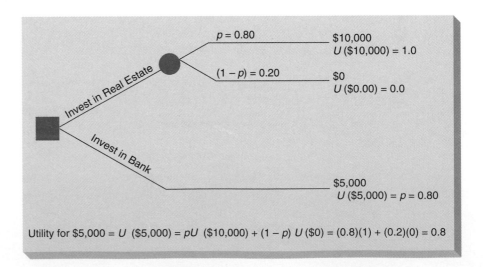

however, is very conservative. Unless there is an 80% chance of getting $10,000 from the real estate deal, Jane would prefer to have her money in the bank, where it is safe. What Jane has done here is to assess her utility for $5,000. When there is an 80% chance (this means that p is 0.8) of getting $10,000, Jane is indifferent between putting her money in real estate or putting it in the bank. Jane's utility for $5,000 is thus equal to 0.8, which is the same as the value for p. This utility assessment is shown in Figure 4.7.

Other utility values can be assessed in the same way. For example, what is Jane's utility for $7,000? What value of p would make Jane indifferent between $7,000 and the gamble that would result in either $10,000 or $0? For Jane, there must be a 90% chance of getting the $10,000. Otherwise, she would prefer the $7,000 for sure. Thus, her utility for $7,000 is 0.90. Jane's utility for $3,000 can be determined in the same way. If there were a 50% chance of obtaining the $10,000, Jane would be indifferent between having $3,000 for sure and taking the gamble of either winning the $10,000 or getting nothing. Thus, the utility of $3,000 for Jane is 0.5. Of course, this process can be continued until Jane has assessed her utility for as many monetary values as she wants. These assessments, however, are enough to get an idea of Jane's feelings toward risk. In fact, we can plot these points in a *utility curve*, as was done in Figure 4.8. In the figure, the assessed utility points of $3,000, $5,000, and $7,000 are shown by dots, and the rest of the curve is eyeballed in.

Once utility values have been determined, a utility curve can be constructed.

Jane's utility curve is typical of a *risk avoider*. A risk avoider is a decision maker who gets less utility or pleasure from a greater risk and tends to avoid situations in which high losses might occur. As monetary value increases on her utility curve, the utility increases at a slower rate.

Figure 4.9 illustrates that a person who is a *risk seeker* has an opposite-shaped utility curve. This decision maker gets more utility from a greater risk and higher potential payoff. As monetary value increases on his or her utility curve, the utility increases at an increasing rate. A person who is *indifferent* to risk has a utility curve that is a straight line. The shape of

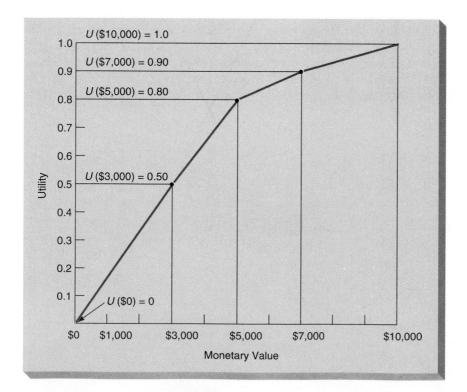

FIGURE 4.8

Utility Curve for Jane Dickson

FIGURE 4.9

Preferences for Risk

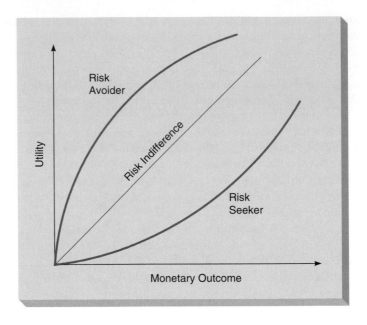

The shape of a person's utility curve depends on many factors.

a person's utility curve depends on the specific decision being considered, the person's psychological frame of mind, and how the person feels about the future. It may well be that you have one utility curve for some situations you face and completely different curves for others.

Utility as a Decision-Making Criterion

Utility values replace monetary values.

After a utility curve has been determined, the utility values from the curve are used in making decisions. Monetary outcomes or values are replaced with the appropriate utility values and then decision analysis is performed as usual. Let's take a look at an example in which a decision tree is used and expected utility values are computed in selecting the best alternative.

Mark Simkin loves to gamble. He decides to play a game that involves tossing thumbtacks in the air. If the point on the thumbtack is facing up after it lands, Mark wins

FIGURE 4.10

Decision Facing Mark Simkin

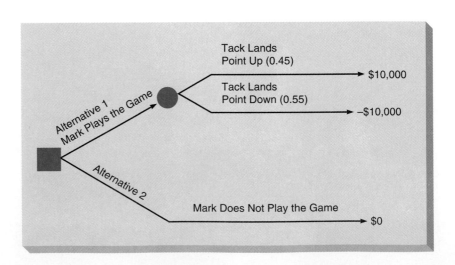

$10,000. If the point on the thumbtack is down, Mark loses $10,000. Should Mark play the game (alternative 1) or should he not play the game (alternative 2)?

Alternatives 1 and 2 are displayed in the tree shown in Figure 4.10. As can be seen, alternative 1 is to play the game. Mark believes that there is a 45% chance of winning $10,000 and a 55% chance of suffering the $10,000 loss. Alternative 2 is not to gamble. What should Mark do? Of course, this depends on Mark's utility for money. As stated previously, he likes to gamble. Using the procedure just outlined, Mark was able to construct a utility curve showing his preference for money. This curve appears in Figure 4.11.

We see that Mark's utility for −$10,000 is 0.05, his utility for not playing ($0) is 0.15, and his utility for $10,000 is 0.30. These values can now be used in the decision tree. Mark's objective is to maximize his expected utility, which can be done as follows:

Mark's objective is to maximize expected utility.

Step 1.

$$U(-\$10{,}000) = 0.05$$

$$U(\$0) = 0.15$$

$$U(\$10{,}000) = 0.30$$

Step 2. Replace monetary values with utility values. Refer to Figure 4.12. Here are the utilities for alternatives 1 and 2:

$$E(\text{alternative 1: play the game}) = (0.45)(0.30) + (0.55)(0.05)$$

$$= 0.135 + 0.027 = 0.1625$$

$$E(\text{alternative 2: don't play the game}) = 0.15$$

Therefore, alternative 1 is the best strategy using utility as the decision criterion. If EMV had been used, alternative 2 would have been the best strategy. The utility curve is a risk-seeker utility curve, and the choice of playing the game certainly reflects this preference for risk.

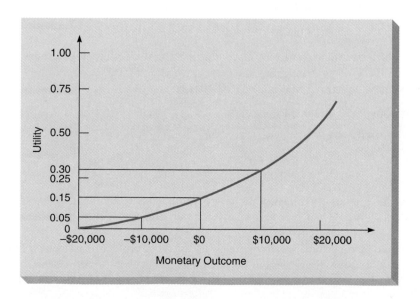

FIGURE 4.11

Utility Curve for Mark Simkin

FIGURE 4.12

Using Expected Utilities
in Decision Making

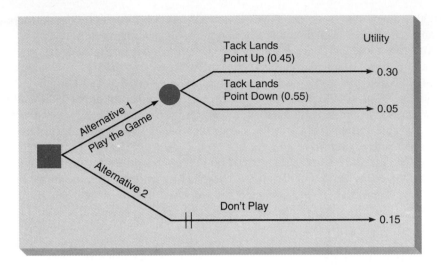

4.5 SENSITIVITY ANALYSIS

As in Chapter 3, sensitivity analysis can be applied to the decision theory concepts discussed in this chapter. The overall approach is the same. Consider the expanded Thompson Lumber problem solved in this chapter using decision tree analysis. The solution to this problem is to conduct the marketing survey. If the survey results are favorable, the decision is to build the large plant with an expected return of $106,400. If the survey results are negative, the decision is to build the small plant for an expected return of $2,400. In this problem we assumed that the probability of a favorable survey result was 0.45, while the probability of a negative survey result was 0.55. How sensitive is our decision to the probability of favorable survey results?

Let p be the probability of favorable survey results. Then $(1 - p)$ is the probability of negative survey results. Given this information, we can develop an expression for the expected monetary value of conducting the survey, which is node 1.

$$\text{EMV(node 1)} = (\$106{,}400)p + (1 - p)(\$2{,}400)$$

$$= \$104{,}000p + \$2{,}400$$

We are indifferent when the EMV of conducting the marketing survey, node 1, is the same as the EMV of not conducting the survey, which is $40,000. We can find the indifference point by equating EMV(node 1) to $40,000.

$$\$104{,}000p + \$2{,}400 = \$40{,}000.$$

$$\$104{,}000p = \$37{,}600$$

$$p = \frac{\$37{,}600}{\$104{,}000} = 0.36$$

As long as the probability of favorable survey results, p, is greater than 0.36, our decision will stay the same. When p is less than 0.36, our decision will be not to conduct the survey.

We could also perform sensitivity analysis for other problem parameters. For example, we could find how sensitive our decision is to the probability of a favorable market given favorable survey results. At this time, this probability is 0.78. If this value goes up, the large plant becomes more attractive. In this case, our decision would not change. What happens when this probability goes down? The analysis becomes more complex. As the probability of a favorable market given favorable survey results goes down, the small plant becomes more attractive. At some point, the small plant will result in a higher EMV (given favorable survey results) than the large plant. This, however, does not conclude our analysis. As the probability of a favorable market given favorable survey results continues to fall, there will be a point where not conducting the survey, with an EMV of $40,000, will be more attractive than conducting the marketing survey. We leave the actual calculations to you. It is important to note that sensitivity analysis should consider *all* possible consequences.

Summary

In this chapter we investigated a number of decision theory problems. Decision trees are used for larger decision problems, when one decision must be made before other decisions can be made. For example, a decision to take a sample or to perform market research is made before we decide to construct a large plant, a small one, or no plant. In this case we can also compute the expected value of sample information (EVSI). Bayesian analysis can be used to revise or update probability values. We can, for example, determine the probability of a favorable market given that we have received positive survey results using Bayesian analysis. When it is impossible or inappropriate to use monetary values, utility theory can be used to assign a utility value, which can range from 0 to 1, to each decision outcome. When utility values have been assigned, we compute the expected utility for the problem and select the alternative with the highest value. Decision making under uncertainty, decision making under risk, decision tree problems, and Bayesian analysis can be solved using QM for Windows and with TreePlan, as you can see in Appendix 4.1 and Appendix 4.2.

Glossary

Sequential Decisions. Decisions in which the outcome of one decision influences other decisions.

Utility Theory. A theory that allows decision makers to incorporate their risk preference and other factors into the decision-making process.

Utility Assessment. The process of determining the utility of various outcomes. This is normally done using a standard gamble between any outcome for sure and a gamble between the worst and best outcomes.

Utility Curve. A graph or curve that reveals the relationship between utility and monetary values. When this curve has been constructed, utility values from the curve can be used in the decision-making process.

Risk Avoider. A person who avoids risk. On the utility curve, as the monetary value increases, the utility increases at a decreasing rate. This decision maker gets less utility for a greater risk and higher potential returns.

Risk Seeker. A person who seeks risk. On the utility curve, as the monetary value increases, the utility increases at an increasing rate. This decision maker gets more pleasure for a greater risk and higher potential returns.

Key Equations

(4-1) Expected value of sample information (EVSI)

$$= \begin{pmatrix} \text{expected value of the best} \\ \text{decision } with \text{ sample} \\ \text{information, assuming} \\ \text{no cost to gather it} \end{pmatrix} - \begin{pmatrix} \text{expected value} \\ \text{of the best decision} \\ without \text{ sample} \\ \text{information} \end{pmatrix}$$

(4-2) $P(A \mid B) = \dfrac{P(B \mid A) \cdot P(A)}{P(B \mid A) \cdot P(A) + P(B \mid \overline{A}) \cdot P(\overline{A})}$

Bayes' theorem—it yields the conditional value of event A given that event B has occurred.

(4-3) Utility of other outcome $= (p)(1) + (1 - p)(0) = p$

The equation determining the utility of an intermediate outcome.

Solved Problems

Solved Problem 4-1

Monica Britt has enjoyed sailing small boats since she was 7 years old, when her mother started sailing with her. Today, Monica is considering the possibility of starting a company to produce small sailboats for the recreational market. Unlike other mass-produced sailboats, however, these boats will be made specifically for children between the ages of 10 and 15. The boats will be of the highest quality, and extremely stable, and the sail size will be reduced to prevent problems of capsizing.

Because of the expense involved in developing the initial molds and acquiring the necessary equipment to produce fiberglass sailboats for young children, Monica has decided to conduct a pilot study to make sure that the market for the sailboats will be adequate. She estimates that the pilot study will cost her $10,000. Furthermore, the pilot study can be either successful or not successful. Her basic decisions are to build a large manufacturing facility, a small manufacturing facility, or no facility at all. With a favorable market, Monica can expect to make $90,000 from the large facility or $60,000 from the smaller facility. If the market is unfavorable, however, Monica estimates that she would lose $30,000 with a large facility, while she would lose only $20,000 with the small facility. Monica estimates that the probability of a favorable market given a successful pilot study is 0.8. The probability of an unfavorable market given an unsuccessful pilot study result is estimated to be 0.9. Monica feels that there is a 50-50 chance that the pilot study will be successful. Of course, Monica could bypass the pilot study and simply make the decision as to whether to build a large plant, small plant, or no facility at all. Without doing any testing in a pilot study, she estimates that the probability of a successful market is 0.6. What do you recommend?

Solution

Before Monica starts to solve this problem, she should develop a decision tree that shows all alternatives, states of nature, probability values, and economic consequences. This decision tree is shown in Figure 4.13.

Once the decision tree has been developed, Monica can solve the problem by computing expected monetary values starting at the endpoints of the decision tree. The final solution is shown on the revised decision tree, Figure 4.14 on page 138. The optimal solution is to *not* conduct the study but to construct the large plant directly. The expected monetary value is $42,000.

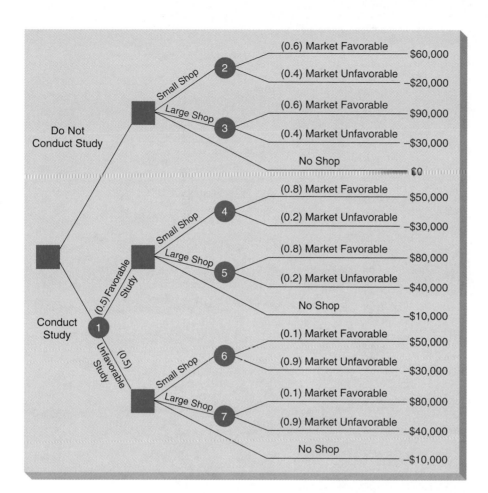

Within the figure, the following labels appear:

Do Not
Conduct Study

Conduct
Study

(0.5) Favorable Study

(0.5) Unfavorable Study

Small Shop

Large Shop

Node	Branch	Outcome
2	(0.6) Market Favorable	$60,000
	(0.4) Market Unfavorable	−$20,000
3	(0.6) Market Favorable	$90,000
	(0.4) Market Unfavorable	−$30,000
	No Shop	$0
4	(0.8) Market Favorable	$50,000
	(0.2) Market Unfavorable	−$30,000
5	(0.8) Market Favorable	$80,000
	(0.2) Market Unfavorable	−$40,000
	No Shop	−$10,000
6	(0.1) Market Favorable	$50,000
	(0.9) Market Unfavorable	−$30,000
7	(0.1) Market Favorable	$80,000
	(0.9) Market Unfavorable	−$40,000
	No Shop	−$10,000

FIGURE 4.13

Monica's Decision Tree, Listing Alternatives, States of Nature, Probability Values, and Financial Outcomes for Solved Problem 4-1

FIGURE 4.14

Monica's Revised Decision Tree, with EMVs

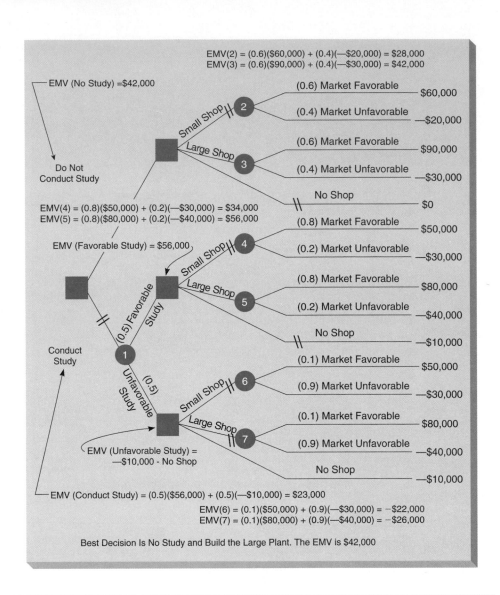

EMV(2) = (0.6)($60,000) + (0.4)(—$20,000) = $28,000
EMV(3) = (0.6)($90,000) + (0.4)(—$30,000) = $42,000

EMV (No Study) =$42,000

Do Not
Conduct Study

(0.6) Market Favorable — $60,000
(0.4) Market Unfavorable — —$20,000

(0.6) Market Favorable — $90,000
(0.4) Market Unfavorable — —$30,000

No Shop — $0

EMV(4) = (0.8)($50,000) + (0.2)(—$30,000) = $34,000
EMV(5) = (0.8)($80,000) + (0.2)(—$40,000) = $56,000

EMV (Favorable Study) = $56,000

(0.8) Market Favorable — $50,000
(0.2) Market Unfavorable — —$30,000

(0.8) Market Favorable — $80,000
(0.2) Market Unfavorable — —$40,000

No Shop — —$10,000

Conduct Study

(0.1) Market Favorable — $50,000
(0.9) Market Unfavorable — —$30,000

(0.1) Market Favorable — $80,000
(0.9) Market Unfavorable — —$40,000

No Shop — —$10,000

EMV (Unfavorable Study) =
—$10,000 - No Shop

EMV (Conduct Study) = (0.5)($56,000) + (0.5)(—$10,000) = $23,000

EMV(6) = (0.1)($50,000) + (0.9)(—$30,000) = —$22,000
EMV(7) = (0.1)($80,000) + (0.9)(—$40,000) = —$26,000

Best Decision Is No Study and Build the Large Plant. The EMV is $42,000

Solved Problem 4-2

Developing a small driving range for golfers of all abilities has long been a desire of John Jenkins. John, however, believes that the chance of a successful driving range is only about 40%. A friend of John's has suggested that he conduct a survey in the community to get a better feeling of the demand for such a facility. There is a 0.9 probability that the research will be favorable if the driving range facility will be successful. Furthermore, it is estimated that there is a 0.8 probability that the marketing research will be unfavorable if indeed the facility will be unsuccessful. John would like to determine the chances of a successful driving range given a favorable result from the marketing survey.

Solution

This problem requires the use of Bayes' theorem. Before we start to solve the problem, we will define the following terms:

$P(\text{SF})$ = probability of successful driving range facility

$P(\text{UF})$ = probability of unsuccessful driving range facility

$P(\text{RF} \mid \text{SF})$ = probability that the research will be favorable given a successful driving range facility

$P(\text{RU} \mid \text{SF})$ = probability that the research will be unfavorable given a successful driving range facility

$P(\text{RU} \mid \text{UF})$ = probability that the research will be unfavorable given an unsuccessful driving range facility

$P(\text{RF} \mid \text{UF})$ = probability that the research will be favorable given an unsuccessful driving range facility

Now, we can summarize what we know:

$$P(\text{SF}) = 0.4$$

$$P(\text{RF} \mid \text{SF}) = 0.9$$

$$P(\text{RU} \mid \text{UF}) = 0.8$$

From this information we can compute three additional probabilities that we need to solve the problem:

$$P(\text{UF}) = 1 - P(\text{SF}) = 1 - 0.4 = 0.6$$

$$P(\text{RU} \mid \text{SF}) = 1 - P(\text{RF} \mid \text{SF}) = 1 - 0.9 = 0.1$$

$$P(\text{RF} \mid \text{UF}) = 1 - P(\text{RU} \mid \text{UF}) = 1 - 0.8 = 0.2$$

Now we can put these values into Bayes' theorem to compute the desired probability:

$$P(\text{SF} \mid \text{RF}) = \frac{P(\text{RF} \mid \text{SF}) \cdot P(\text{SF})}{P(\text{RF} \mid \text{SF}) \cdot P(\text{SF}) + P(\text{RF} \mid \text{UF}) \cdot P(\text{UF})}$$

$$= \frac{(0.9)(0.4)}{(0.9)(0.4) + (0.2)(0.6)}$$

$$= \frac{0.36}{(0.36 + 0.12)} = \frac{0.36}{0.48} = 0.75$$

In addition to using formulas to solve John's problem, it is possible to perform all calculations in a table:

Revised Probabilities Given a Favorable Research Result

STATE OF NATURE	CONDITIONAL PROBABILITY		PRIOR PROBABILITY		JOINT PROBABILITY	POSTERIOR PROBABILITY
Favorable market	0.9	×	0.4	=	0.36	0.36/0.48 = 0.75
Unfavorable market	0.2	×	0.6	=	0.12	0.12/0.48 = 0.25
					0.48	

As you can see from the table, the results are the same. The probability of a successful driving range given a favorable research result is 0.36/0.48 or 0.75.

Solved Problem 4-3

Like many students before her, Anne Martin is facing a difficult and important career decision. While at school, Anne worked for a local accounting firm. She did a good job and the firm has given her a standing offer to work for them for $20,000. She can take as much time as she wants to make her decision. There are, however, two other companies that are interested in her. Barnes Accounting has given her an offer of $22,000. Unfortunately, Barnes has given her only two weeks to make a decision. The company that Anne would really like to work for is Ketchum Accounting Services. This company, she feels, may make her an offer of $28,000. Unfortunately, Anne is quite uncertain about whether Ketchum will offer her the position. Thus, Anne has to make a difficult decision. Should she accept the offer from Barnes for $22,000, or should she wait and hope to get the offer from Ketchum? If she waits and doesn't get the offer from Ketchum, she can always go back to her old job for $20,000. The worst situation would be her old job, while the best situation would be the job with Ketchum. For Anne to be indifferent between taking the job with Barnes and the gamble of waiting and trying to get the job with Ketchum, the probability of landing the job at Ketchum would have to be 0.6. Given this information, what utility should Anne place on the three jobs?

Solution

The problem facing Anne Martin is one of determining utility values. We begin by assigning a utility value of 1 to the best situation, which is obtaining a job from Ketchum. We also assign a utility value of 0 to the worst outcome in this situation, which is keeping the old job. Furthermore, the problem states that the probability for Anne to be indifferent between taking the job with Barnes and taking the gamble of waiting and trying to get the job with Ketchum is 0.6. This indifference situation can be shown in Figure 4.15.

Given the information and diagram, Anne can proceed to determine her indifference point. This point is where the utility (U) for getting the job with Barnes is equal to the gamble of getting the job with Ketchum, with a 0.6 probability, and her old job, with a 0.4 probability. The appropriate calculations are:

$$U \text{ (Ketchum)} = 1.0$$

$$U \text{ (old job)} = 0$$

$$U \text{ (Barnes)} = (0.6)U(\text{Ketchum}) + (0.4)U(\text{old job})$$

$$= (0.6)(1) + (0.4)(0) = 0.6$$

FIGURE 4.15

The Problem Facing
Anne Martin

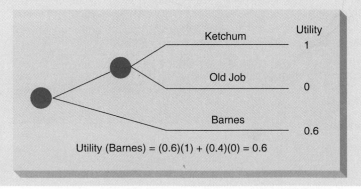

Utility (Barnes) = (0.6)(1) + (0.4)(0) = 0.6

SELF-TEST

- Before taking the self-test, refer back to the learning objectives at the beginning of the chapter, the notes in the margins, and the glossary at the end of the chapter.
- Use the key at the back of the book to correct your answers.
- Restudy pages that correspond to any questions that you answered incorrectly or material you feel uncertain about.

1. Bayes' theorem
   a. yields probabilities based strictly on historical data.
   b. allows the manager to develop posterior probabilities as revisions of his or her prior probability assessments.
   c. allows the decision maker to change the probability of the survey results.
   d. all of the above.
   e. none of the above.

2. An untrue statement about decision trees is
   a. they can be used to present graphically any problem that can be presented in a decision table.
   b. they present the decisions and outcomes in a sequential order.
   c. all decision trees contain two types of nodes: decision and state of nature.
   d. they are most useful in situations of uncertainty.
   e. they are used to find the maximum expected monetary value.

3. In calculating the expected monetary value on decision trees
   a. all probabilities and payoffs should be specified first.
   b. you begin at the right-hand side of each route and travel backward.
   c. the EMV at each decision node should be the highest of the choices from the succeeding branches.
   d. you assume a constantly increasing utility for constantly increasing amounts of money.
   e. all of the above.

4. The expected value of sample information (EVSI) equals
   a. the expected value of best decision with free sample information minus expected value of best decision without any sample information.
   b. an amount that should always be worthwhile saving as long as the value falls between zero and EMV.
   c. the expected value of the best alternative under conditions of risk minus the expected value of the best alternative under conditions of uncertainty.
   d. the value of eliminating all risk provided that the utility for money remains constant.
   e. all of the above.

5. Revised probabilities are calculated
   a. from a formula based entirely upon other conditional probabilities.
   b. only after you know whether the marketing survey results are positive.

   c. after you have first calculated the posterior probabilities.
   d. using Bayes' law instead of Bayes' theorem.
   e. all of the above.
   f. none of the above.

6. Constantly increasing utility for constantly increasing amounts of money
   a. is an attribute of a person who is risk indifferent.
   b. would eliminate your desire to gamble and also your desire to buy life insurance.
   c. is a fundamental assumption to EMV analysis.
   d. all of the above.
   e. none of the above.

7. The utility curves developed in this chapter
   a. varied in value from zero to 1.
   b. were valid among people of the same type (risk seekers or risk avoiders).
   c. required use of the standard gamble to compute the value of both the best and the worst outcome.
   d. are all objective.
   e. all of the above.

8. A utility curve
   a. can be used in the decision-making process.
   b. shows utility increasing at an increasing rate when the monetary value increases for a risk seeker.
   c. shows utility increasing at a decreasing rate when the monetary value increases for a risk avoider.
   d. all of the above.

9. In calculating the expected monetary value
   a. you are calculating the most likely outcome.
   b. you are calculating the median value.
   c. you are assuming that the utility of each additional dollar of income is equal to the utility of the preceding dollar.
   d. you assume that the decision maker is a betting person.
   e. all of the above.

10. _____ are typically used when a sequence of decisions needs to be made.

11. The revised probabilities computed using Bayesian analysis are called _____ .

12. In utility theory, _____ is used to determine utility values for various decision outcomes?

Discussion Questions and Problems

Discussion Questions

4-1 Under what conditions is a decision tree preferable to a decision table?

4-2 What information should be placed on a decision tree?

4-3 Describe how you would determine the best decision using the EMV criterion with a decision tree.

4-4 What is the difference between prior and posterior probabilities?

4-5 What is the purpose of Bayesian analysis? Describe how you would use Bayesian analysis in the decision-making process.

4-6 Discuss some of the problems with using the EMV criterion. Give an example of a situation in which it would be inappropriate.

4-7 What is the overall purpose of utility theory?

4-8 Briefly discuss how a utility function can be assessed. What is a standard gamble, and how is it used in determining utility values?

4-9 How is a utility curve used in selecting the best decision for a particular problem?

4-10 What is a risk seeker? What is a risk avoider? How does the utility curve for these types of decision makers differ?

4-11 Draw a utility curve for a decision maker that is indifferent to risk. If a decision maker is indifferent to risk, will using utility values give a different decision than using EMV?

Problems*

4-12 A group of medical professionals is considering the construction of a private clinic. If the medical demand is high (that is, there is a favorable market for the clinic), the physicians could realize a net profit of $100,000. If the market is not favorable, they could lose $40,000. Of course, they don't have to proceed at all, in which case there is no cost. In the absence of any market data, the best the physicians can guess is that there is a 50–50 chance the clinic will be successful.

Construct a decision tree to help analyze this problem. What should the medical professionals do?

4-13 The physicians in Problem 4-12 have been approached by a market research firm that offers to perform a study of the market at a fee of $5,000. The market researchers claim their experience enables them to use Bayes' theorem to make the following statements of probability:

probability of a favorable market given a favorable study $= 0.82$

probability of an unfavorable market given a favorable study $= 0.18$

probability of a favorable market given an unfavorable study $= 0.11$

probability of an unfavorable market given an unfavorable study $= 0.89$

probability of a favorable research study $= 0.55$

probability of an unfavorable research study $= 0.45$

---

*Note: ⌨ means the problem may be solved with QM for Windows; ✖ means the problem may be solved with Excel QM; and 🖥 means the problem may be solved with QM for Windows and/or Excel QM.

(a) Develop a new decision tree for the medical professionals to reflect the options now open with the market study.

(b) Use the EMV approach to recommend a strategy.

NO **(c)** What is the expected value of sample information? How much might the physicians be willing to pay for a market study?

4-14 Jerry Young is thinking about opening a bicycle shop in his hometown. Jerry loves to take his own bike on 50-mile trips with his friends, but he believes that any small business should be started only if there is a good chance of making a profit. Jerry can open a small shop, a large shop, or no shop at all. Because there will be a five-year lease on the building that Jerry is thinking about using, he wants to make sure that he makes the correct decision. Jerry is also thinking about hiring his old marketing professor to conduct a marketing research study. If the study is conducted, the results could be either favorable or unfavorable. Develop a decision tree for Jerry.

4-15 Jerry Young (of Problem 4-14) has done some analysis about the profitability of the bicycle shop. If Jerry builds the large bicycle shop, he will earn $60,000 if the market is favorable, but he will lose $40,000 if the market is unfavorable. The small shop will return a $30,000 profit in a favorable market and a $10,000 loss in an unfavorable market. At the present time, he believes that there is a 50–50 chance that the market will be favorable. His old marketing professor will charge him $5,000 for the marketing research. It is estimated that there is a 0.6 probability that the survey will be favorable. Furthermore, there is a 0.9 probability that the market will be favorable given a favorable outcome from the study. However, the marketing professor has warned Jerry that there is only a probability of 0.12 of a favorable market if the marketing research results are not favorable. Jerry is confused. What should he do?

Use probabilities here, do not calculate.

4-16 In Problem 4-15, Jerry Young determined whether he should seek marketing information from his marketing professor and whether he should open a bicycle shop. In this problem, Jerry's marketing professor estimated that there was a 0.6 probability that the marketing research would be favorable. Jerry, however, is not sure that this probability is correct. How sensitive is Jerry's decision, made in Problem 4-15, to this probability value? How far can this probability value deviate from 0.6 without causing Jerry to change his decision?

4-17 Karen Kimp would like to start a small dress shop. At the present time, she believes that the chances of a successful or unsuccessful dress shop are about the same (50%). In today's local paper, there was an article that described a study done on the potential of retail stores, which Karen believed applied to her. She found out that the probability of a favorable study given a successful shop (favorable study | SS) was 0.9, and the probability of an unfavorable study given a successful shop (unfavorable study | SS) was 0.1. Furthermore, the probability of an unfavorable study given an unsuccessful shop (unfavorable study | US) was 0.7, and the probability of a favorable study given an unsuccessful shop (favorable study | US) was 0.3. Help Karen by revising the probability that the dress shop will be successful.

4-18 Bill Holliday is not sure what he should do. He can either build a quadplex (that is, a building with four apartments), a duplex, gather additional information, or simply do nothing. If he gathers additional information, the results could be either favorable or unfavorable, but it would cost him $3,000 to gather the information. Bill believes that there is a 50–50 chance that the information will be favorable. If the rental market is favorable, Bill will earn $15,000 with the quadplex or $5,000 with the duplex. Bill doesn't have the financial resources to do both. With an unfavorable rental market, however, Bill could lose $20,000 with the quadplex or $10,000 with the duplex. Without gathering additional information, Bill estimates that the probability of a favorable rental market is 0.7. A favorable report from the study would increase the probability of a favorable rental market to 0.9. Furthermore, an unfavorable report from the additional information would decrease the probability of a favorable rental market to 0.4. Of course, Bill could forget all of these numbers and do nothing. What is your advice to Bill?

4-19 Before the marketing research was done, Peter Martin believed that there was a 50–50 chance that his brother's food store would be a success. The research team determined that there is a 0.8 probability that the marketing research will be favorable given a successful food store. Moreover, there is a 0.7 probability that the marketing research will be unfavorable given an unsuccessful food store. This information is based on past experience.

(a) If the marketing research is favorable, what is Peter's revised probability of a successful food store for his brother?

(b) If the marketing research is unfavorable, what is Peter's revised probability of a successful food store for his brother?

4-20 Mark Martinko has been a class A racquetball player for the past five years, and one of his biggest goals is to own and operate a racquetball facility. Unfortunately, Mark thinks that the chance of a successful racquetball facility is only 30%. Mark's lawyer has recommended that he employ one of the local marketing research groups to conduct a survey concerning the success or failure of a racquetball facility. There is a 0.8 probability that the research will be favorable given a successful racquetball facility. In addition, there is a 0.7 probability that the research will be unfavorable given an unsuccessful facility.

(a) Compute revised probabilities of a successful racquetball facility given a favorable and an unfavorable survey using the equations presented in this chapter.

(b) Compute revised probabilities of a successful racquetball facility given a favorable and an unfavorable survey using tables to make your computations.

4-21 Kuality Komponents buys on–off switches from two suppliers. The quality of the switches from the suppliers is as follows:

PERCENT DEFECTIVE	PROBABILITY FOR SUPPLIER A	PROBABILITY FOR SUPPLIER B
1	0.70	0.30
3	0.20	0.40
5	0.10	0.30

For example, the probability of getting a batch of switches that are 1% defective from supplier A is 0.70. Since Kuality Komponents orders 10,000 switches per order, this would mean that there is a 0.7 probability of getting 100 defective switches out of the 10,000 switches if supplier A is used to fill the order. A defective switch can be repaired for 50 cents. Although the quality of supplier B is lower, it will sell an order of 10,000 switches for $37 less than supplier A.

(a) Develop a decision tree.

(b) Which supplier should Kuality Komponents use?

(c) For how much less would supplier B have to sell an order of 10,000 switches than supplier A for Kuality Komponents to be indifferent between the two suppliers?

4-22 Jim Sellers is thinking about producing a new type of electric razor for men. If the market were favorable, he would get a return of $100,000, but if the market for this new type of razor were unfavorable, he would lose $60,000. Since Ron Bush is a good friend of Jim Sellers, Jim is considering the possibility of using Bush Marketing Research to gather additional information about the market for the razor. Bush has suggested that Jim either use a survey or a pilot study to test the market. The survey would be a sophisticated questionnaire administered to a test market. It will cost $5,000. Another alternative is to run a pilot study. This would involve producing a limited number of the new razors and trying to sell them in two cities that are typical of American cities. The pilot study is more accurate but is also more expensive. It will cost $20,000. Ron Bush has suggested that it would be a good idea for Jim to conduct either the survey or the pilot before Jim makes the decision concerning whether to produce the new razor. But Jim is not sure if the value of the survey or the pilot is worth the cost.

Jim estimates that the probability of a successful market without performing a survey or pilot study is 0.5. Furthermore, the probability of a favorable survey result given a favorable market for razors is 0.7, and the probability of a favorable survey result given an unsuccessful market for razors is 0.2. In addition, the probability of an unfavorable pilot study given an unfavorable market is 0.9, and the probability of an unsuccessful pilot study result given a favorable market for razors is 0.2.

(a) Draw the decision tree for this problem without the probability values.

(b) Compute the revised probabilities needed to complete the decision, and place these values in the decision tree.

(c) What is the best decision for Jim? Use expected monetary value as the decision criterion.

4-23 Jim Sellers has been able to estimate his utility for a number of different values. He would like to use these utility values in making the decision in Problem 4-22. The utility values are $U(-\$80,000) = 0$, $U(-\$65,000) = 0.5$, $U(-\$60,000) = 0.55$, $U(-\$20,000) = 0.7$, $U(-\$5,000) = 0.8$, $U(\$0) = 0.81$, U($\$80,000) = 0.9$, $U(\$95,000) = 0.95$, and $U(\$100,000) = 1$. Resolve Problem 4-22 using utility values. Is Jim a risk avoider?

4-24 In Problem 4-13, you helped the medical professionals analyze their decision using expected monetary value as the decision criterion. This group has also assessed their utility for money: $U(-\$45,000) = 0$, $U(-\$40,000) = 0.1$, $U(-\$5,000) = 0.7$, $U(\$0) = 0.9$, $U(\$95,000) = 0.99$, and $U(\$100,000) = 1$. Use expected utility as the decision criterion, and determine the best decision for the medical professionals. Are the medical professionals risk seekers or risk avoiders?

4-25 Rhonda Pearlman has just been approached by her investment counselor, Charlie Armstrong. Charlie has an investment that would cost Rhonda $500. If the investment is a success, Rhonda could double her money, but if it is a failure, she could lose the initial investment. Charlie believes that there is a 0.6 probability that Rhonda will double her investment and get $1,000. Charlie reasons that the expected return of this investment is $600 ($600 = $0 × 0.4 + $1,000 × 0.6). Because the cost is only $500, Charlie has urged Rhonda to make the investment. Rhonda, however, does not agree with Charlie. She would only consider investing the $500 if the probability of getting $1,000 is 0.8. Rhonda believes that the investment with a 0.6 probability of getting $1,000 is only worth $300. Plot a utility curve for Rhonda. What is Rhonda's preference for risk?

4-26 Charlie Armstrong cannot understand why Rhonda is not willing to make the investment (see Problem 4-25). Charlie believes that the investment is worth $600 with a probability of 0.6. Furthermore, Charlie believes that the investment is worth $800 if the probability of getting $1,000 is 0.8. Plot the utility curve for Charlie Armstrong. What is his preference for risk?

4-27 In this chapter a decision tree was developed for John Thompson (see Figure 4.3 for the complete decision tree analysis). After completing the analysis, John was not completely sure that he is indifferent to risk. After going through a number of standard gambles, John was able to assess his utility for money. Here are some of the utility assessments: $U(-\$190,000) = 0$, $U(-\$180,000) = 0.05$, $U(-\$30,000) = 0.10$, $U(-\$20,000) = 0.15$, $U(-\$10,000) = 0.2$, $U(\$0) = 0.3$, $U(\$90,000) = 0.5$, $U(\$100,000) = 0.6$, $U(\$190,000) = 0.95$, and $U(\$200,000) = 1.0$. If John maximizes his expected utility, does his decision change?

4-28 In the past few years, the traffic problems in Lynn McKell's hometown have gotten worse. Now, Broad Street is congested about half the time. The normal travel time to work for Lynn is only 15 minutes when Broad Street is used and there is no congestion. With congestion, however, it takes Lynn 40 minutes to get to work. If Lynn decides to take the expressway, it will take 30 minutes regardless of the traffic conditions. Lynn's utility for travel time is: $U(15 \text{ minutes}) = 0.9$, U($30 \text{ minutes}) = 0.7$, and $U(40 \text{ minutes}) = 0.2$.

(a) Which route will minimize Lynn's expected travel time?

(b) Which route will maximize Lynn's utility?

(c) When it comes to travel time, is Lynn a risk seeker or a risk avoider?

4-29 Jack Belkin considers himself an expert when it comes to fine food and beverage, and Jack is proud to tell his out-of-town friends that the best restaurant that he has encountered, Old Tavern, is located in his hometown. Big Burger, a national franchise, is the worst restaurant he has ever been to. Unfortunately, Jack's kids love the french fries at Big Burger, and when his family is deciding where to eat, his kids always say "Let's flip a coin to see if we go to Big Burger or Old Tavern." Jack hates Big Burger, but his kids hate Old Tavern. Jack's wife always has a compromise. She wants to go to Ralph's Diner instead of flipping a coin. But Jack is totally indifferent to these two alternatives. Once when Jack and his wife were alone, his wife suggested that they flip a coin to see if they would go to Old Tavern or Ralph's Diner. (Jack's wife did not like the rich food at Old Tavern.) When Jack demurred at this gamble, his wife proposed that they simply go to the Vacation Inn Restaurant, which was slightly more expensive than Ralph's Diner. Again, Jack was totally indifferent to this choice. Determine Jack's utility for restaurants.

4-30 Jack Belkin's kids love to play games while riding in the car, and this outing was no exception. (See Problem 4-29 for some additional details.) The entire family was about 50 miles from home, and Jack was looking forward to eating at the Vacation Inn Restaurant, which was a compromise restaurant choice. His oldest kid said, "Let's make a bet. If we see three red Volkswagens between here and home, we will eat at Big Burger. Otherwise, we will go to Old Tavern." Jack believes that the probability of seeing three red Volkswagens is very low—about 0.20. Should Jack take his kids' bet, or should he tell them that they are eating at Vacation Inn Restaurant and that is final?

4-31 After driving down the road and seeing one red Volkswagen, Jack Belkin had second thoughts about his probability assessment. (Refer to Problem 4-30.) In Problem 4-30, Jack estimated that the probability of seeing three red Volkswagens before the family got home was 0.20. How sensitive is Jack's decision in Problem 4-30 to his probability assessment? What probability would make him indifferent between the bet his kids proposed and eating at Vacation Inn Restaurant?

4-32 Coren Chemical, Inc., develops industrial chemicals that are used by other manufacturers to produce photographic chemicals, preservatives, and lubricants. One of their products, K-1000, is used by several photographic companies to make a chemical that is used in the film-developing process. To produce K-1000 efficiently, Coren Chemical uses the batch approach, in which a certain number of gallons is produced at one time. This reduces setup costs and allows Coren Chemical to produce K-1000 at a competitive price. Unfortunately, K-1000 has a very short shelf life of about one month.

Coren Chemical produces K-1000 in batches of 500 gallons, 1,000 gallons, 1,500 gallons, and 2,000 gallons. Using historical data, David Coren was able to determine that the probability of selling 500 gallons of K-1000 is 0.2. The probabilities of selling 1,000, 1,500, and 2,000 gallons are 0.3, 0.4, and 0.1, respectively. The question facing David is how many gallons to produce of K-1000 in the next batch run. K-1000 sells for $20 per gallon. Manufacturing cost is $12 per gallon, and handling costs and warehousing costs are estimated to be $1 per gallon. In the past, David has allocated advertising costs to K-1000 at $3 per gallon. If K-1000 is not sold after the batch run, the chemical loses much of its important properties as a developer. It can, however, be sold at a salvage value of $13 per gallon. Furthermore, David has guaranteed to his suppliers that there will always be an adequate supply of K-1000. If David does run out, he has agreed to purchase a comparable chemical from a competitor at $25 per gallon. David sells all of the chemical at $20 per gallon, so his shortage means that David loses the $5 to buy the more expensive chemical.

(a) Develop a decision tree for this problem.

(b) What is the best solution?

(c) Determine the expected value of perfect information.

4-33 The Jamis Corporation is involved with waste management. During the past 10 years it has become one of the largest waste disposal companies in the Midwest, serving primarily Wisconsin, Illinois, and Michigan. Bob Jamis, president of the company, is considering the possibility of establishing a waste treatment plant in Mississippi. From past experience, Bob believes that a small plant in northern Mississippi would yield a $500,000 profit regardless of the market for the facility. The success of a medium-sized waste treatment plant would depend on the market. With a low demand for waste treatment, Bob expects a $200,000 return. A medium demand would yield a $700,000 return in Bob's estimation, and a high demand would return $800,000. Although a large facility is much riskier, the potential return is much greater. With a high demand for waste treatment in Mississippi, the large facility should return a million dollars. With a medium demand, the large facility will return only $400,000. Bob estimates that the large facility would be a big loser if there is a low demand for waste treatment. He estimates that he would lose approximately $200,000 with a large treatment facility if demand was indeed low. Looking at the economic conditions for the upper part of the state of Mississippi and using his experience in the field, Bob estimates that the probability of a low demand for treatment plants is 0.15. The probability for a medium-demand facility is approximately 0.40, and the probability of a high demand for a waste treatment facility is 0.45.

Because of the large potential investment and the possibility of a loss, Bob has decided to hire a market research team that is based in Jackson, Mississippi. This team will perform a survey to get a better feeling for the probability of a low, medium, or high demand for a waste treatment facility. The cost of the survey is $50,000. To help Bob determine whether to go ahead with the survey, the marketing research firm has provided Bob with the following information:

P(survey results | possible outcomes)

	SURVEY RESULTS		
POSSIBLE OUTCOME	**Low Survey Results**	**Medium Survey Results**	**High Survey Results**
Low demand	0.7	0.2	0.1
Medium demand	0.4	0.5	0.1
High demand	0.1	0.3	0.6

As you see, the survey could result in three possible outcomes. Low survey results mean that a low demand is likely. In a similar fashion, medium survey results or high survey results would mean a medium or a high demand, respectively. What should Bob do?

4-34 Monetary values are sometimes inappropriate in decision theory. In such cases the concepts of utility theory can be used. Locate a friend or someone you know who has not worked Problem 4-33. Using a standard gamble for utility assessment, determine the utility values for all of the monetary outcomes for Problem 4-33. Then construct a utility curve. In some cases this may require several rounds of utility assessment to get an accurate and consistent utility curve. Then, using the utility values and the utility curve, resolve Problem 4-33. Is your friend a risk taker or a risk avoider? Did you have any difficulties in assessing a utility curve? If so, explain. Discuss the usefulness as well as the potential problems in the use of utility theory in making decisions.

4-35 Mary is considering opening a new grocery store in town. She is evaluating three sites: downtown, the mall, and out at the busy traffic circle. Mary calculated the value of successful stores at these locations to be: downtown, $250,000; the mall, $300,000; the circle, $400,000. Mary calculated the losses if unsuccessful to be $100,000 at either downtown or the mall and $200,000 at the circle. Mary figures her chance of success to be 50% downtown, 60% at the mall, and 75% at the traffic circle. Draw a decision tree for Mary and select her best alternative.

4-36 Mary has been approached by a marketing research firm. This firm has offered to study the area described in Problem 4-35 to see if it needs another grocery store for the sum of

$30,000. Mary believes there is a 60% chance that the survey results will be positive (show a need for another grocery store). SRP = survey results positive, SRN = survey results negative, SD = success downtown, SM = success at mall, SC = success at circle, $\overline{SD}$ = don't succeed downtown, and so on. For studies of this nature: $P(SRP \mid$ success$) = 0.7$; $P(SRN \mid$ success$) = 0.3$; $P(SRP \mid$ not success$) = 0.2$; and $P(SRN \mid$ not success$) = 0.8$. Calculate the revised probabilities for success (and not success) for each location, depending on survey results.

4-37 Draw a decision tree for Mary (Problems 4-35 and 4-36) and select her best alternative.

4-38 How much is the marketing research worth to Mary? Calculate the expected value of sample information (EVSI) from Problem 4-37 (which is based on Problems 4-35 and 4-36).

4-39 Sue Reynolds has to decide if she should get information (at a cost of $20,000) to invest in a retail store. If she gets the information, there is a 0.6 probability that the information will be favorable and a 0.4 probability that the information will not be favorable. If the information is favorable, there is a 0.9 probability that the store will be a success. If the information is not favorable, the probability of a successful store is only 0.2. Without any information, Sue estimates that the probability of a successful store will be 0.6. A successful store will give a return of $100,000. If the store is built but is not successful, Sue will see a loss of $80,000. Of course, she could always decide not to build the retail store.

(a) What do you recommend?

(b) What impact would a 0.7 probability of obtaining favorable information have on Sue's decision? The probability of obtaining unfavorable information would be 0.3.

(c) Sue believes that the probabilities of a successful and an unsuccessful retail store given favorable information might be 0.8 and 0.2, respectively, instead of 0.9 and 0.1 respectively. What impact, if any, would this have on Sue's decision and the best EMV?

(d) Sue had to pay $20,000 to get information. Would her decision change if the cost of the information increased to $30,000?

(e) Using the data in this problem and the following utility table, compute the expected utility. Is this the curve of a risk seeker or a risk avoider?

MONETARY VALUE	UTILITY
$100,000	1
$80,000	0.4
$0	0.2
−$20,000	0.1
−$80,000	0.05
−$100,000	0

(f) Compute the expected utility given the following utility table. Does this utility table represent a risk seeker or a risk avoider?

MONETARY VALUE	UTILITY
$100,000	1
$80,000	0.9
$0	0.8
−$20,000	0.6
−$80,000	0.4
−$100,000	0

Data Set Problem

4-40 Lane Bailey must decide how many large Christmas trees to stock. To simplify the problem, he is looking at the possibility of stocking 100, 200, 300, 400, or 500 trees. These stocking options are summarized in the following table:

Basic Decisions

NODES	DECISION NUMBER	STOCKING POLICY (NUMBER OF TREES)
1 → 2	1	100
1 → 3	2	200
1 → 4	3	300
1 → 5	4	400
1 → 6	5	500

For each decision alternative, there are five possible states of nature representing possible demand values. These values, along with their probabilities and expected profits, are summarized in the following tables:

Stocking 100 Trees

NODES	DEMAND	PROBABILITY	PROFITS ($)
2 → 7	100	0.10	1,000,000
2 → 8	200	0.30	1,000,000
2 → 9	300	0.40	1,000,000
2 → 10	400	0.10	1,000,000
2 → 11	500	0.10	1,000,000

Stocking 200 Trees

NODES	DEMAND	PROBABILITY	PROFITS ($)
3 → 12	100	0.10	800,000
3 → 13	200	0.30	900,000
3 → 14	300	0.40	1,000,000
3 → 15	400	0.10	1,100,000
3 → 16	500	0.10	1,200,000

Stocking 300 Trees

NODES	DEMAND	PROBABILITY	PROFITS ($)
4 → 17	100	0.10	700,000
4 → 18	200	0.30	800,000
4 → 19	300	0.40	1,000,000
4 → 20	400	0.10	1,200,000
4 → 21	500	0.10	1,300,000

Stocking 400 Trees

NODES	DEMAND	PROBABILITY	PROFITS ($)
5 → 22	100	0.10	600,000
5 → 23	200	0.30	800,000
5 → 24	300	0.40	1,000,000
5 → 25	400	0.10	1,100,000
5 → 26	500	0.10	1,300,000

Stocking 500 Trees

NODES	DEMAND	PROBABILITY	PROFITS ($)
6 → 27	100	0.10	500,000
6 → 28	200	0.30	600,000
6 → 29	300	0.40	1,000,000
6 → 30	400	0.10	1,200,000
6 → 31	500	0.10	1,300,000

(a) What is the best stocking policy given the information available?

(b) Lane believes that he may be able to get a quantity discount for stocking 500 trees. This would increase his profits. He believes that he may be able to make $100 more for each level of demand. Does this change the stocking decision?

(c) What if Lane receives $200 more for each level of demand for stocking 500 trees?

(d) What if Lane receives $400 more for each level of demand for stocking 500 trees?

Case Study

Blake Electronics

In 1947, Steve Blake founded Blake Electronics in Long Beach, California, to manufacture resistors, capacitors, inductors, and other electronic components. During World War II, Steve was a radio operator, and it was during this time that he became proficient at repairing radios and other communications equipment. Steve viewed his four-year experience with the army with mixed feelings. He hated army life, but this experience gave him the confidence and the initiative to start his own electronics firm.

Over the years, Steve kept the business relatively unchanged. By 1960, total annual sales were in excess of $2 million. In 1964, Steve's son, Jim, joined the company after finishing high school and two years of courses in electronics at Long Beach Community College. Jim was always aggressive in high school athletics, and he became even more aggressive as general sales manager of Blake Electronics. This aggressiveness bothered Steve, who was more conservative. Jim would make deals to supply companies with electronic components before he bothered to find out if Blake Electronics had

the ability or capacity to produce the components. On several occasions this behavior caused the company some embarrassing moments when Blake Electronics was unable to produce the electronic components for companies with which Jim had made deals.

In 1968, Jim started to go after government contracts for electronic components. By 1970, total annual sales had increased to more than $10 million, and the number of employees exceeded 200. Many of these employees were electronic specialists and graduates of electrical engineering programs from top colleges and universities. But Jim's tendency to stretch Blake Electronics to contracts continued as well, and by 1975 Blake Electronics had a reputation with government agencies as a company that could not deliver what it promised. Almost overnight, government contracts stopped, and Blake Electronics was left with an idle workforce and unused manufacturing equipment. This high overhead started to melt away profits, and in 1977, Blake Electronics was faced with the possibility of sustaining a loss for the first time in its history.

FIGURE 4.16
Master Control Center

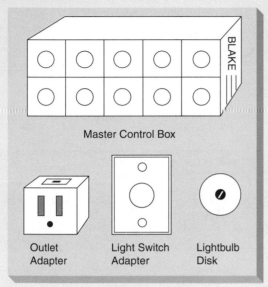

Master Control Box

Outlet
Adapter

Light Switch
Adapter

Lightbulb
Disk

In 1978, Steve decided to look at the possibility of manufacturing electronic components for home use. Although this was a totally new market for Blake Electronics, Steve was convinced that this was the only way to keep Blake Electronics from dipping into the red. The research team at Blake Electronics was given the task of developing new electronic devices for home use. The first idea from the research team was the Master Control Center. The basic components for this system are shown in Figure 4.16.

The heart of the system is the master control box. This unit, which would have a retail price of $250, has two rows of five buttons. Each button controls one light or appliance and can be set as either a switch or a rheostat. When set as a switch, a light finger touch on the bottom either turns a light or appliance on or off. When set as a rheostat, a finger touching the bottom controls the intensity of the light. Leaving your finger on the button makes the light go through a complete cycle ranging from off to bright and back to off again.

To allow for maximum flexibility, each master control box is powered by two D-sized batteries that can last up to a year, depending on usage. In addition, the research team has developed three versions of the master control box—versions A, B, and C. If a family wants to control more than 10 lights or appliances, another master control box can be purchased.

The lightbulb disk, which would have a retail price of $2.50, is controlled by the master control box and is used to control the intensity of any light. A different disk is available for each button position for all three master control boxes. By inserting the lightbulb disk between the lightbulb and the socket, the appropriate button on the master control box can completely control the intensity of the light. If a standard light

switch is used, it must be on at all times for the master control box to work.

One disadvantage of using a standard light switch is that only the master control box can be used to control the particular light. To avoid this problem, the research team developed a special light switch adapter that would sell for $15. When this device is installed, either the master control box or the light switch adapter can be used to control the light.

When used to control appliances other than lights, the master control box must be used in conjunction with one or more outlet adapters. The adapters are plugged into a standard wall outlet, and the appliance is then plugged into the adapter. Each outlet adapter has a switch on top that allows the appliance to be controlled from the master control box or the outlet adapter. The price of each outlet adapter would be $25.

The research team estimated that it would cost $500,000 to develop the equipment and procedures needed to manufacture the master control box and accessories. If successful, this venture could increase sales by approximately $2 million. But will the master control boxes be a successful venture? With a 60% chance of success estimated by the research team, Steve had serious doubts about trying to market the master control boxes even though he liked the basic idea. Because of his reservations, Steve decided to send requests for proposals (RFPs) for additional marketing research to 30 marketing research companies in southern California.

The first RFP to come back was from a small company called Marketing Associates, Inc. (MAI), which would charge $100,000 for the survey. According to its proposal, MAI has been in business for about three years and has conducted about 100 marketing research projects. MAI's major strengths appeared to be individual attention to each account, experienced staff, and fast work. Steve was particularly interested in one part of the proposal, which revealed MAI's success record with previous accounts. This is shown in Figure 4.17.

The only other proposal to be returned was by a branch office of Iverstine and Kinard, one of the largest marketing research firms in the country. The cost for a complete survey would be $300,000. While the proposal did not contain the same success record as MAI, the proposal from Iverstine and Kinard did contain some interesting information. The chance of getting a favorable survey result, given a successful venture, was 90%. On the other hand, the chance of getting an un-

FIGURE 4.17
Success Figures for MAI

OUTCOME	SURVEY RESULTS		
	FAVORABLE	UNFAVORABLE	TOTAL
Successful venture	35	20	55
Unsuccessful venture	15	30	45

favorable survey result, given an unsuccesful venture, was 80%. Thus, it appeared to Steve that Iverstine and Kinard would be able to predict the success or failure of the master control boxes with a great amount of certainty.

Steve pondered the situation. Unfortunately, both marketing research teams gave different types of information in their proposals. Steve concluded that there would be no way that the two proposals could be compared unless he got additional information from Iverstine and Kinard. Furthermore, Steve

wasn't sure what he would do with the information, and if it would be worth the expense of hiring one of the marketing research firms.

Discussion Questions

1. Does Steve need additional information from Iverstine and Kinard?
2. What would you recommend?

INTERNET CASE STUDIES

See our Internet home page at **http://www.prenhall.com/render** for these additional case studies:
Drink-at-Home Inc. and Ruth Jones' Heart By-Pass Operation.

Bibliography

Borison, Adam. "Oglethorpe Power Corporation Decides About Investing in a Major Transmission System," *Interfaces* 25 (March–April 1995): 25.

Derfler, Frank. "Use These Decision Trees and Our Questionnaire to Find the Best Way to Reduce Your Total Cost of Ownership," *PC Magazine* (May 5, 1998): 231.

Feinstein, Charles D. "Deciding Whether to Test Student Athletes for Drug Use," *Interface*s 20, 3 (May–June 1990): 80–87.

Freedman, J. S. "Decision-Tree Analysis: A Valuable Real Estate Investment Tool," *Pension World* 24 (November 1988): 20–22.

Fryar, E. O., et al. "Bayesian Evaluation of a Specific Hypothesis," *American Journal of Agricultural Economics* 70 (August 1988): 685–692.

Hammond, J. S., R. L. Kenney, and H. Raiffa. "The Hidden Traps in Decision Making," *Harvard*

Business Review (September–October 1998): 47–60.

Heian, B. C., and J. R. Gale. "Mortgage Selection Using a Decision-Tree Approach: An Extension," *Interfaces* 18 (July–August 1988): 72–83.

McDonald, John. "Decision Trees Clarify Novel Technology Applications," *Oil and Gas Journal* (February 24, 1997): 69.

Miller, Craig. "A Systematic Approach to Tax Controversy Management," *Tax Executive* (May 15, 1998): 231.

Stafira, Stanley, et al. "A Methodology for Evaluating Military Systems in a Counterproliferation Role," *Management Science* (October 1997): 1420.

Stone, Lawrence D. "Search for the SS *Central America:* Mathematical Treasure Hunting," *Interfaces* 21, 1 (January–February 1992): 32–54.

APPENDIX 4.1: DECISION TREES WITH QM FOR WINDOWS

We briefly described the use of QM for Windows for decision theory problems in Chapter 3. Note that the procedures for using QM for Windows discussed in Chapter 3 can be used for utility theory. After we convert the monetary values into utility values, the procedures are the same.

In this chapter we expanded the Thompson Lumber example to include a decision to conduct a marketing survey. This turned the example into one involving sequential decisions, requiring decision trees. The problem was diagrammed in Figure 4.4 and solved manually.

PROGRAM 4.3

QM for Windows for Sequential Decisions

Decision Analysis / Decision Trees								
Objective								
● Profits (maximize)								
○ Costs (minimize)								

Decision Tree Results								
Thompson Tree Upper Branch Solution								
	Start Node	Ending Node	Probabili	Profit	Use Branch?	Ending Node	Node Type	Node Value
Start	0.	1.	0.	0.		1.	Decision	106,400.
Branch 1	1.	2.	0.	0.	Yes	2.	Chance	106,400.
Branch 2	1.	3.	0.	0.		3.	Chance	63,600.
Branch 3	1.	0.	0.	-10,000.		0.	Final	-10,000.
Branch 4	2.	4.	0.78	190,000.		4.	Final	190,000.
Branch 5	2.	5.	0.22	-190,000.		5.	Final	-190,000.
Branch 6	3.	6.	0.78	90,000.		6.	Final	90,000.
Branch 7	3.	7.	0.22	-30,000.		7.	Final	-30,000.

To illustrate the use of QM for Windows, let's use these data to solve the Thompson decision tree problem. Program 4.3 shows the output results, including the original data, intermediate results, and the best decision, which has an EMV of $106,400.

APPENDIX 4.2: USING TREEPLAN TO SOLVE DECISION TREE PROBLEMS

TreePlan, an add-in for the Excel spreadsheet, can be used to structure and solve decision tree problems discussed in this chapter. The TreePlan program, TREEPLAN.XLA, can be found on the CD-ROM that accompanies this text. After you copy this program to your hard disk, you can install it by getting into Excel and clicking "Tools" from the menu bar and then clicking "add-ins" from the Tools menu. This will open the add-in menu. Click Browse and find TREEPLAN.XLA on your hard disk. Clicking OK from the "Browse" menu will add TreePlan to your Tools menu. When you have installed TreePlan, you can use the following steps to solve a decision tree problem:

1. Start Excel and enter the problem title and any other information that may be needed. Note that probability and monetary values can be entered directly onto TreePlan.

2. Place the cursor where you want the decision tree to start. Select "Tools" from the menu bar and then choose "Decision Tree." Select "New Tree." This will place a beginning decision tree with two branches in your spreadsheet. (Note: If you don't see Decision Tree as a selection in the Tools menu, you will have to install TreePlan as discussed previously.)

3. Add decision and state-of-nature (event) branches to the beginning decision tree to construct the appropriate decision tree for your problem. This can be done by selecting "Tools" and "Decision Tree" at the start or end of any branch. This will bring up the TreePlan menu. The TreePlan menu can also be obtained by pressing the T and Control (Ctrl) keys at the same time. Note that this menu is context-sensitive and will be different depending on the type of branch (decision or event) and the location in the decision tree.

4. Change the default titles for all branches to reflect your problem. Also change the default probability values on the event branches to the correct values. Finally, enter the correct monetary values at the end points of the tree. TreePlan will automatically make all calculations and solve the decision tree problem. At this stage, you can change the appearance of the tree if you desire.

Here is how TreePlan can be used to solve the Thompson Lumber Problem presented earlier:

1. We begin by opening Excel and typing "Thompson Lumber" near the top of the spreadsheet. All labels and values will be entered directly onto the decision tree.

2. Next, we move down a few cells from the top and insert a decision tree by selecting "Tools" from the Menu Bar and choosing "Decision Tree." Program 4.1, shown earlier in the chapter, illustrates this step.

3. The next step is to develop a decision tree for Thompson Lumber, as seen in Figure 4.1. We move the cursor to the beginning Node 1 and press the Ctrl and T keys at the same time. This will give us a decision tree menu. Select "Add Branch" at the top and click OK to get three decision branches like Figure 4.1. Put the cursor at the end of the Decision 1 branch and again press the Ctrl and T keys together. This will give you another decision tree menu. Select "Change to Event Node" and make sure Two is selected under Branches to add two event (state-of-nature) branches to the end of this decision node. Click OK to add the two-event branches. Do the same for the end of the Decision 2 branch. This will give you a decision tree similar to Figure 4.1.

4. The final step is to enter the appropriate data for the Thompson Lumber problem and do some minor formatting. You can start by selecting "Decision 1" and typing "Construct Large Plant." Do the same for the other branches to get the same appearance as Figure 4.1. Now enter the needed values. Note that the default probability values are 0.50, which is the same as the Thompson Lumber problem. Thus, we don't have to make any changes. To finish the problem, we will enter the monetary values at the end of each branch as seen earlier in Figure 4.2. As we saw in the chapter, Program 4.2 solves the Thompson Lumber Problem. Now, we can make optional formatting changes. All of the features of Excel can be used to make the diagram more attractive. For example, we can click the zoom drop-down box in the upper right-hand corner of the screen and change the zoom from 100% to 75% to see the entire tree on the screen. We can also change all of the monetary values to a currency format. Select each amount and click the $ button in the tool bar. We can also use the Decrease Decimal box on the tool bar to round off to the nearest dollar. Using the "Format" selection from the Menu Bar, we can even change the color or pattern of numbers. At this stage, we can also perform sensitivity analysis by changing probability or monetary values. As a practice exercise, see if you can develop a decision tree using TreePlan to include the market survey (as shown in Figure 4.3).

Forecasting

CHAPTER 5

LEARNING OBJECTIVES

After completing this chapter, students will be able to:

1. Understand and know when to use various families of forecasting models.
2. Compare moving averages, exponential smoothing, and trend time-series models.
3. Seasonally adjust data.
4. Understand Delphi and other qualitative decision-making approaches.
5. Identify variables and use them in a linear regression model.
6. Compute a variety of error measures.

CHAPTER OUTLINE

5.1 Introduction

5.2 Types of Forecasts

5.3 Scatter Diagrams

5.4 Time-Series Forecasting Models

5.5 Causal Forecasting Methods

5.6 Monitoring and Controlling Forecasts

5.7 Using the Computer to Forecast

Summary • Glossary • Key Equations • Solved Problems • Self-Test • Discussion Questions and Problems • Data Set Problem • Case Study: North-South Airline • Case Study: Akron Zoological Park • Internet Case Study • Bibliography

Appendix 5.1: Forecasting with QM for Windows

5.1   INTRODUCTION

Every day, managers make decisions without knowing what will happen in the future. Inventory is ordered though no one knows what sales will be, new equipment is purchased though no one knows the demand for products, and investments are made though no one knows what profits will be. Managers are always trying to reduce this uncertainty and to make better estimates of what will happen in the future. Accomplishing this is the main purpose of forecasting.

There are many ways to forecast the future. In numerous firms (especially smaller ones), the entire process is subjective, involving seat-of-the-pants methods, intuition, and years of experience. There are also many *quantitative* forecasting models, such as moving averages, exponential smoothing, trend projections, and least squares regression analysis.

Regardless of the method that is used to make the forecast, the same eight overall procedures that follow are used.

Eight Steps to Forecasting

1. Determine the use of the forecast—what objective are we trying to obtain?
2. Select the items or quantities that are to be forecasted.
3. Determine the time horizon of the forecast—is it 1 to 30 days (short term), one month to one year (medium term), or more than one year (long term)?
4. Select the forecasting model or models.
5. Gather the data needed to make the forecast.
6. Validate the forecasting model.
7. Make the forecast.
8. Implement the results.

These steps present a systematic way of initiating, designing, and implementing a forecasting system. When the forecasting system is to be used to generate forecasts regularly over time, data must be collected routinely, and the actual computations or procedures used to make the forecast can be done automatically. When a computer system is used, computer forecasting files and programs are needed.

No single method is superior—whatever works best should be used.

There is seldom a single superior forecasting method. One organization may find regression effective, another firm may use several approaches, and a third may combine both quantitative and subjective techniques. Whatever tool works best for a firm is the one that should be used.

5.2   TYPES OF FORECASTS

The three categories of models are time series, causal, and qualitative.

In this chapter we consider forecasting models that can be classified into one of three categories. These categories, shown in Figure 5.1, are time-series models, causal models, and qualitative models.

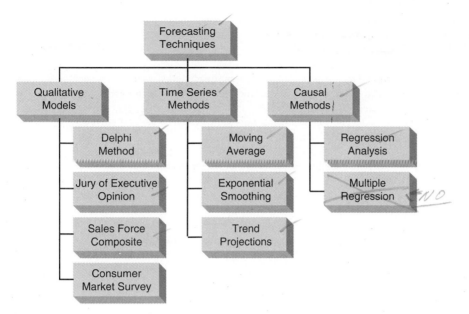

FIGURE 5.1

Forecasting Models Discussed

Time-Series Models

Time-series models attempt to predict the future by using historical data. These models make the assumption that what happens in the future is a function of what has happened in the past. In other words, time-series models look at what has happened over a period of time and use a series of past data to make a forecast. Thus, if we are forecasting weekly sales for lawn mowers, we use the past weekly sales for lawn mowers in making the forecast. The time-series models we examine in this chapter are moving average, exponential smoothing, and trend projections.

Causal Models

Causal models incorporate the variables or factors that might influence the quantity being forecasted into the forecasting model. For example, daily sales of a cola drink might depend on the season, the average temperature, the average humidity, whether it is a weekend or a weekday, and so on. Thus, a causal model would attempt to include factors for temperature, humidity, season, day of the week, and so on. Causal models may also include past sales data as time-series models do.

Qualitative Models

Whereas time-series and causal models rely on quantitative data, *qualitative models* attempt to incorporate judgmental or subjective factors into the forecasting model. Opinions by experts, individual experiences and judgments, and other subjective factors may be considered. Qualitative models are especially useful when subjective factors are expected to be very important or when accurate quantitative data are difficult to obtain.

IN ACTION Forecasting the Demand for HDTV Sales

Developing sales forecasts is an important component of any business plan, even for products that are in their infancy. Three especially challenging markets are personal digital assistants (e.g., the Palm Pilot by 3Com), multimedia and interactive television, and high-definition TV (called HDTV and considered the next generation of television). In all these cases, accurately estimating demand is extremely challenging because the products and services are so new—and hence, sales data are not yet observed. Still, demand estimates are important for critical decisions involving billions of dollars.

Qualitative forecasting methods, based on managerial judgment, are common in such conditions. Interestingly, though, we find that based on studies of previous products, this approach usually overestimates the future.

To deal with the U.S. market for the HDTV, historical data from three other products in the high-priced consumer segment were examined closely. Forecasters at the American Electronics Association looked to their experience with sales demand curves for color TV sets, refrigerators, and VCRs, using early estimates of price and costs to match these products' experiences.

Assumptions about government policy for funding the new HDTV industry complicate the forecasting process and accuracy. The head of the Congressional Budget Office "finds the forecast very optimistic about market size and certainly about timing." Yet by blending quantitative and qualitative modeling of potential demand, analysts can have a major impact on corporate decisions.

Source: Barry L. Bayus. "Charting Untamed Markets," *OR/MS Today* 22, 4 (August 1995): 36–38.

Here is a brief overview of four different *qualitative* forecasting techniques:

Overview of four qualitative or judgmental approaches: Delphi, jury of executive opinion, sales force composite, and consumer market survey.

1. *Delphi method.* This iterative group process allows experts, who may be located in different places, to make forecasts. There are three different types of participants in the *Delphi process*: decision makers, staff personnel, and respondents. The *decision making group* usually consists of five to ten experts who will be making the actual forecast. The *staff personnel* assist the decision makers by preparing, distributing, collecting, and summarizing a series of questionnaires and survey results. The *respondents* are a group of people whose judgments are valued and are being sought. This group provides inputs to the decision makers before the forecast is made.

2. *Jury of executive opinion.* This method takes the opinions of a small group of high-level managers, often in combination with statistical models, and results in a group estimate of demand.

3. *Sales force composite.* In this approach, each salesperson estimates what sales will be in his or her region; these forecasts are reviewed to ensure that they are realistic and are then combined at the district and national levels to reach an overall forecast.

4. *Consumer market survey.* This method solicits input from customers or potential customers regarding their future purchasing plans. It can help not only in preparing a forecast but also in improving product design and planning for new products.

5.3 SCATTER DIAGRAMS

A scatter diagram helps obtain ideas about a relationship.

To get a quick idea if any relationship exists between two variables, a *scatter diagram* may be plotted on a two-dimensional graph. The values of the independent variable (such as time) may be measured on the horizontal (X) axis and the proposed dependent variables (such as sales) placed on the vertical (Y) axis. Let us consider the example of a firm that needs to forecast sales for three different products.

Wacker Distributors notes that annual sales for three of its products—television sets, radios, and compact discs—over the past ten years are as shown in Table 5.1. One simple way

TABLE 5.1   Annual Sales of Three Products

YEAR	TELEVISION SETS	RADIOS	COMPACT DISCS
1	250	300	110
2	250	310	100
3	250	320	120
4	250	330	140
5	250	340	170
6	250	350	150
7	250	360	160
8	250	370	190
9	250	380	200
10	250	390	190

to examine these historical data, and perhaps to use them to establish a forecast, is to draw a scatter diagram for each product (see Figure 5.2). This picture, showing the relationship between sales of a product and time, is useful in spotting trends or cycles. An exact mathematical model that describes the situation can then be developed if it appears reasonable to do so.

5.4   TIME-SERIES FORECASTING MODELS

A time series is based on a sequence of evenly spaced (weekly, monthly, quarterly, and so on) data points. Examples include weekly sales of IBM personal computers, quarterly earnings reports of Microsoft Corp. stock, daily shipments of Eveready batteries, and annual U.S. consumer price indices. Forecasting time-series data implies that future values are predicted *only* from past values (such as we saw in Table 5.1) and that other variables, no matter how potentially valuable, are ignored.

Decomposition of a Time Series

Analyzing time series means breaking down past data into components and then projecting them forward. A time series typically has four components: trend, seasonality, cycles, and random variation.

1. *Trend* (*T*) is the gradual upward or downward movement of the data over time.
2. *Seasonality* (*S*) is a pattern of the demand fluctuation above or below the trend line that occurs every year.
3. *Cycles* (*C*) are patterns in the data that occur every several years. They are usually tied into the business cycle.
4. *Random variations* (*R*) are "blips" in the data caused by chance and unusual situations; they follow no discernible pattern.

Four components of a time series are trend, seasonality, cycles, and random variations.

Figure 5.3 shows a time series and its components.

FIGURE 5.2

Scatter Diagram for Sales

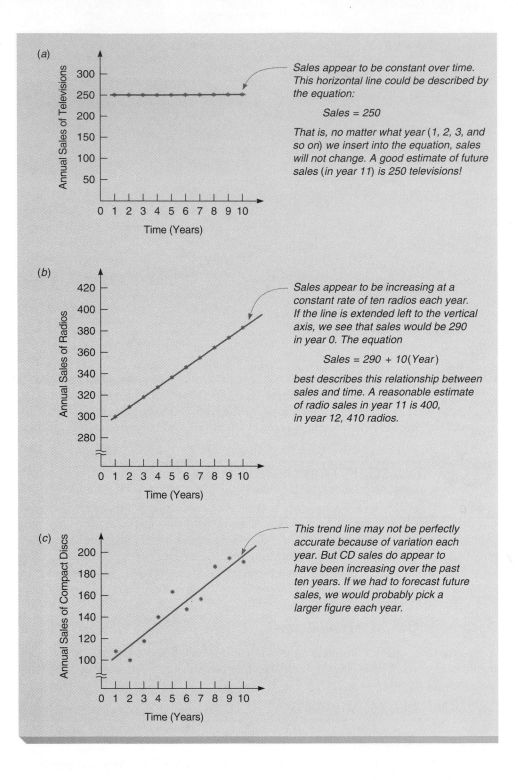

(a)

Sales appear to be constant over time. This horizontal line could be described by the equation:

Sales = 250

That is, no matter what year (1, 2, 3, and so on) we insert into the equation, sales will not change. A good estimate of future sales (in year 11) is 250 televisions!

(b)

Sales appear to be increasing at a constant rate of ten radios each year. If the line is extended left to the vertical axis, we see that sales would be 290 in year 0. The equation

Sales = 290 + 10(Year)

best describes this relationship between sales and time. A reasonable estimate of radio sales in year 11 is 400, in year 12, 410 radios.

(c)

This trend line may not be perfectly accurate because of variation each year. But CD sales do appear to have been increasing over the past ten years. If we had to forecast future sales, we would probably pick a larger figure each year.

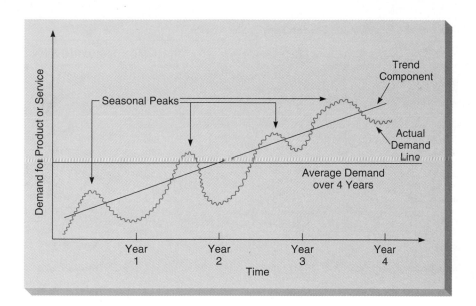

FIGURE 5.3

Product Demand Charted over Four Years with Trend and Seasonality Indicated

There are two general forms of time-series models in statistics. The most widely used is a multiplicative model, which assumes that demand is the product of the four components. It is stated as

$$\text{demand} = T \times S \times C \times R$$

An additive model adds the components together to provide an estimate. It is stated as

$$\text{demand} = T + S + C + R$$

In most real-world models, forecasters assume that the random variations are averaged out over time. They then concentrate on only the seasonal component and a component that is a combination of trend and cyclical factors.

Moving Averages

Moving averages are useful if we can assume that market demands will stay fairly steady over time. A four-month moving average is found simply by summing the demand during the past four months and dividing by 4. With each passing month, the most recent month's data are added to the sum of the previous three months' data, and the earliest month is dropped. This tends to smooth out short-term irregularities in the data series.

Mathematically, the moving average, which serves as an estimate of the next period's demand, is expressed as

$$\text{moving average} = \frac{\Sigma \text{ demand in previous } n \text{ periods}}{n} \tag{5-1}$$

where n is the number of period in the moving average: for example, four, five, or six months, respectively, for a four-, five-, or six-period moving average.

Wallace Garden Supply Example   Storage shed sales at Wallace Garden Supply are shown in the middle column of Table 5.2. A three-month moving average is indicated on the right.

When there is a trend or pattern, weights can be used to place more emphasis on recent values. This makes the techniques more responsive to changes because latter periods

Moving averages smooth out variations when forecasting demands are fairly steady.

Weights can be used to put more emphasis on recent periods.

TABLE 5.2   Wallace Garden Supply Shed Sales

MONTH	ACTUAL SHED SALES	THREE-MONTH MOVING AVERAGE
January	10	
February	12	
March	13	
April	16	(10 + 12 + 13)/3 = 11⅔
May	19	(12 + 13 + 16)/3 = 13⅔
June	23	(13 + 16 + 19)/3 = 16
July	26	(16 + 19 + 23)/3 = 19⅓
August	30	(19 + 23 + 26)/3 = 22⅔
September	28	(23 + 26 + 30)/3 = 26⅓
October	18	(26 + 30 + 28)/3 = 28
November	16	(30 + 28 + 18)/3 = 25⅓
December	14	(28 + 18 + 16)/3 = 20⅔

may be more heavily weighted. Deciding which weights to use requires some experience and a bit of luck. Choice of weights is somewhat arbitrary because there is no set formula to determine them. If the latest month or period is weighted too heavily, the forecast might reflect a large unusual change in the demand or sales pattern too quickly.

A weighted moving average may be expressed mathematically as

$$\text{weighted moving average} = \frac{\Sigma \, (\text{weight for period } n) \, (\text{demand in period } n)}{\Sigma \, \text{weights}} \qquad \text{(5-2)}$$

Wallace Garden Supply decides to forecast storage shed sales by weighting the past three months as follows:

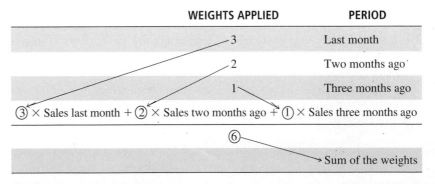

WEIGHTS APPLIED	PERIOD
3	Last month
2	Two months ago
1	Three months ago

③ × Sales last month + ② × Sales two months ago + ① × Sales three months ago

⑥ → Sum of the weights

The results of the Wallace Garden Supply weighted average forecast are shown in Table 5.3. In this particular forecasting situation, you can see that weighting the latest month more heavily provides a much more accurate projection.

Both simple and weighted moving averages are effective in smoothing out sudden fluctuations in the demand pattern in order to provide stable estimates. Moving averages do, however, have three problems. First, increasing the size of *n* (the number of periods

TABLE 5.3 Weighted Moving Average Forecast for Wallace Garden Supply		
MONTH	**ACTUAL SHED SALES**	**THREE-MONTH MOVING AVERAGE**
January	10	
February	12	
March	13	
April	16	$[(3 \times 13) + (2 \times 12) + (10)]/6 = 12\frac{1}{6}$
May	19	$[(3 \times 16) + (2 \times 13) + (12)]/6 = 14\frac{1}{3}$
June	23	$[(3 \times 19) + (2 \times 16) + (13)]/6 = 17$
July	26	$[(3 \times 23) + (2 \times 19) + (16)]/6 = 20\frac{1}{2}$
August	30	$[(3 \times 26) + (2 \times 23) + (19)]/6 = 23\frac{5}{6}$
September	28	$[(3 \times 30) + (2 \times 26) + (23)]/6 = 27\frac{1}{2}$
October	18	$[(3 \times 28) + (2 \times 30) + (26)]/6 = 28\frac{1}{3}$
November	16	$[(3 \times 18) + (2 \times 28) + (30)]/6 = 23\frac{1}{3}$
December	14	$[(3 \times 16) + (2 \times 18) + (28)]/6 = 18\frac{2}{3}$

averaged) does smooth out fluctuations better, but it makes the method less sensitive to *real* changes in the data. Second, moving averages cannot pick up trends very well. Because they are averages, they will always stay within past levels and will not predict a change to either a higher or a lower level. The third problem is that moving averages require extensive record keeping of past data.

Moving averages have three problems: larger number of periods may smooth out real changes; they don't pick up trends; and lots of past data must be kept.

Using Excel in Forecasting Excel and spreadsheets in general are frequently used in forecasting. Many forecasting techniques are supported by built-in Excel functions. You may also use Excel QM's forecasting module, which has five components: (1) moving averages, (2) weighted moving averages, (3) exponential smoothing, (4) regression (with one variable only), and (5) decomposition. Excel QM's error analysis is much more complete than that available with the Excel add-in.

Programs 5.1A and 5.1B illustrate Excel QM's formulas and output, respectively, using Wallace's weighted moving average data in Table 5.3.

Exponential Smoothing

Exponential smoothing is a forecasting method that is easy to use and is handled efficiently by computers. Although it is a type of moving average technique, it involves little record keeping of past data. The basic exponential smoothing formula can be shown as follows:

New forecast = last period's forecast
$\qquad\qquad + \alpha$ (last period's actual demand − last period's forecast) **(5-3)**

where α is a weight (or *smoothing constant*) that has a value between 0 and 1, inclusive.

PROGRAM 5.1A

Using Excel QM for Weighted Moving-Average Forecasting. Input data and formulas from Wallace Garden Supply are shown.

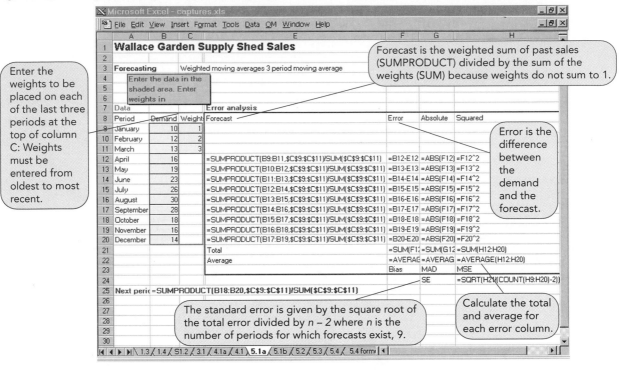

Enter the weights to be placed on each of the last three periods at the top of column C: Weights must be entered from oldest to most recent.

Forecast is the weighted sum of past sales (SUMPRODUCT) divided by the sum of the weights (SUM) because weights do not sum to 1.

Error is the difference between the demand and the forecast.

The standard error is given by the square root of the total error divided by n – 2 where n is the number of periods for which forecasts exist, 9.

Calculate the total and average for each error column.

PROGRAM 5.1B

Output of Excel QM's Weighted Moving-Average Program Using Data from Table 5.3 as Input.

	A	B	C	D	E	F	G	H
1	**Wallace Garden Supply Shed Sales**							
2								
3	**Forecasting**		Weighted moving averages 3 period moving average					
4	Enter the data in the shaded area. Enter							
5	weights in INCREASING order from top to							
6	bottom.							
7	Data				Error analysis			
8	Period	Demand	Weights		Forecast	Error	Absolute	Squared
9	January	10	1					
10	February	12	2					
11	March	13	3					
12	April	16			12.16667	3.833333	3.833333	14.69444
13	May	19			14.33333	4.666667	4.666667	21.77778
14	June	23			17	6	6	36
15	July	26			20.5	5.5	5.5	30.25
16	August	30			23.83333	6.166667	6.166667	38.02778
17	September	28			27.5	0.5	0.5	0.25
18	October	18			28.33333	-10.3333	10.33333	106.7778
19	November	16			23.33333	-7.33333	7.333333	53.77778
20	December	14			18.66667	-4.66667	4.666667	21.77778
21					Total	4.333333	49	323.3333
22					Average	0.481481	5.444444	35.92593
23						Bias	MAD	MSE
24							SE	6.796358
25	**Next period**	15.3333333						

Equation 5-3 can also be written mathematically as

$$F_t = F_{t-1} + \alpha(A_{t-1} - F_{t-1})$$ **(5-4)**

where

F_t = new forecast

F_{t-1} = previous forecast

α = smoothing constant $(0 \leq \alpha \leq 1)$

A_{t-1} = previous period's actual demand

The concept here is not complex. The latest estimate of demand is equal to our old estimate adjusted by a fraction of the difference between the last period's actual demand and the old estimate.

MODELING IN THE REAL WORLD — Forecasting at Tupperware International

Defining the Problem

To drive production at each of Tupperware's 15 plants in the United States, Latin America, Africa, Europe, and Asia, the firm needs accurate forecasts of demand for its products.

Developing a Model

A variety of statistical models are used, including moving averages, exponential smoothing, and regression analysis. Qualitative analysis is also employed in the process.

Acquiring Input Data

At world headquarters in Orlando, Florida, huge databases are maintained that map the sales of each product, the test market results of each *new* product (since 20% of the firm's sales come from products less than two years old), and where each product falls in its own life cycle.

Developing a Solution

Each of Tupperware's 50 profit centers worldwide develops computerized monthly, quarterly, and 12-month sales projections. These are aggregated by region and then globally.

Testing the Solution

Reviews of these forecasts take place in sales, marketing, finance, and production departments.

Analyzing the Results

Participating managers analyze forecasts with Tupperware's version of a "jury of executive opinion."

Implementing the Results

Forecasts are used to schedule materials, equipment, and personnel at each plant.

Source: Interviews by the authors with Tupperware executives.

The smoothing constant, α, allows managers to assign weight to recent data.

The *smoothing constant*, α, can be changed to give more weight to recent data when the value is high, or more weight to past data when it is low. For example, when $\alpha = 0.5$, it can be shown mathematically that the new forecast is based almost entirely on demand in the past three periods. When $\alpha = 0.1$, the forecast places little weight on recent demand and takes many periods (about 19) of historic values into account.[1]

In January, a demand for 142 of a certain car model for February was predicted by a dealer. Actual February demand was 153 autos. Using a smoothing constant of $\alpha = 0.20$, we can forecast the March demand using the exponential smoothing model. Substituting into the formula, we obtain

New forecast (for March demand) $= 142 + 0.2(153 - 142)$

$$= 144.2$$

Thus, the demand forecast for the cars in March is 144.

Suppose that actual demand for the cars in March was 136. A forecast for the demand in April, using the exponential smoothing model with a constant of $\alpha = 0.20$, can be made:

New forecast (for April demand) $= 144.2 + 0.2(136 - 144.2)$

$$= 142.6, \text{ or } 143 \text{ autos}$$

Selecting the Smoothing Constant The exponential smoothing approach is easy to use and has been applied successfully by banks, manufacturing companies, wholesalers, and other organizations. The appropriate value of the smoothing constant, α, however, can make the difference between an accurate forecast and an inaccurate forecast. In picking a value for the smoothing constant, the objective is to obtain the most accurate forecast. The overall accuracy of a forecasting model can be determined by comparing the forecasted values with the actual or observed values.

The forecast error is defined as

forecast error = demand − forecast

The forecast error tells us how well the model performed against itself using past data.

One measure of the overall forecast error for a model is the *mean absolute deviation* (MAD). This is computed by taking the sum of the absolute values of the individual forecast errors and dividing by the number of periods of data (n):

$$\text{MAD} = \frac{\Sigma \mid \text{forecast errors} \mid}{n}$$

(5-5)

Port of Baltimore Example Let us apply this concept with a trial-and-error testing of two values of α in the following example. The port of Baltimore has unloaded large quantities of grain from ships during the past eight quarters. The port's operations manager wants to test the use of exponential smoothing to see how well the technique works in predicting tonnage unloaded. He assumes that the forecast of grain unloaded in the first quarter was 175 tons. Two values of α are examined, $\alpha = 0.10$ and $\alpha = 0.50$. Table 5.4 shows the *detailed* calculations for $\alpha = 0.10$ only.

To evaluate the accuracy of each smoothing constant, we can compute the absolute deviations and MADs (see Table 5.5). Based on this analysis, a smoothing constant of $\alpha = 0.10$ is preferred to $\alpha = 0.50$ because its MAD is smaller.

---

[1] The term *exponential smoothing* is used because the weight that any one period's demand makes in a forecast demand decreases exponentially over time. See an advanced forecasting book for an algebraic proof.

TABLE 5.4 Port of Baltimore Exponential Smoothing Forecasts for $\alpha = 0.10$ and $\alpha = 0.50$

QUARTER	ACTUAL TONNAGE UNLOADED	ROUNDED FORECAST USING $\alpha = 0.10$*	ROUNDED FORECAST USING $\alpha = 0.50$*
1	180	175	175
2	168	176 = 175.00 + 0.10(180 − 175)	178
3	159	175 = 175.50 + 0.10(168 − 175.50)	173
4	175	173 = 174.75 + 0.10(159 − 174.75)	166
5	190	173 = 173.18 + 0.10(175 − 173.18)	170
6	205	175 = 173.36 + 0.10(190 − 173.36)	180
7	180	178 = 175.02 + 0.10(205 − 175.02)	193
8	182	178 = 178.02 + 0.10(180 − 178.02)	186
9	?	179 = 178.22 + 0.10(182 − 178.22)	184

* Forecasts rounded to the nearest ton.

Besides the mean absolute deviations, there are three other measures of the accuracy of historical errors in forecasting that are sometimes used. *Mean squared error* (MSE) is the average of the squared differences between the forecasted and observed values. *Mean absolute percent error* (MAPE) is the absolute difference between the forecasted and observed values expressed as a percentage of the observed values. *Bias* tells whether the

Three other measures of error, besides the commonly used MAD, are MSE, MAPE, and Bias.

TABLE 5.5 Absolute Deviations and MADs for Port of Baltimore Example

QUARTER	ACTUAL TONNAGE UNLOADED	ROUNDED FORECAST WITH $\alpha = 0.10$	ABSOLUTE DEVIATIONS FOR $\alpha = 0.10$	ROUNDED FORECAST WITH $\alpha = 0.50$	ABSOLUTE DEVIATION FOR $\alpha = 0.50$
1	180	175	5	175	5
2	168	176	8	178	10
3	159	175	16	173	14
4	175	173	2	166	9
5	190	173	17	170	20
6	205	175	30	180	25
7	180	178	2	193	13
8	182	178	4	186	4
		Sum of absolute deviations 84			100

$$\text{MAD} = \frac{\Sigma \,|\,\text{deviations}\,|}{n} = 10.50 \qquad\qquad \text{MAD} = 12.50$$

forecast is too high or too low, and by how much. In effect, bias provides the average total error and its direction.

Using Excel QM for Exponential Smoothing Programs 5.2A and 5.2B illustrate how Excel QM handles exponential smoothing. Input data and formulas appear in Program 5.2A, and output, using α of 0.1 for the Port of Baltimore, are in Program 5.2B. Note that the MAD in Program 5.2A (of 10.307) differs slightly from that in Table 5.5 because of rounding.

PROGRAM 5.2A

Excel QM Model of Port of Baltimore Exponential Smoothing Problem Using $\alpha = .10$. Input Data and Formulas are Shown.

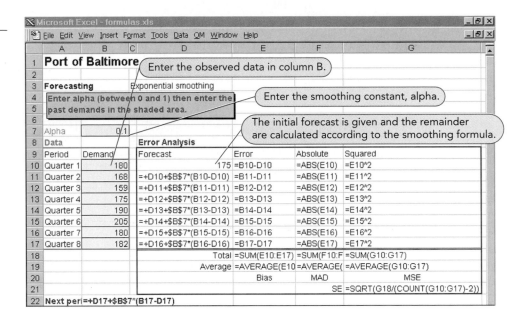

PROGRAM 5.2B

Output Screen for Port of Baltimore Exponential Smoothing Excel QM Example

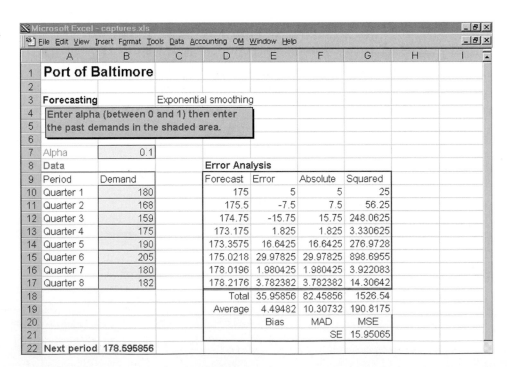

Exponential Smoothing with Trend Adjustment As with any moving average technique, simple exponential smoothing fails to respond to trends. A more complex exponential smoothing model can, at this point, be considered that adjusts for trend. The idea is to compute a simple exponential smoothing forecast and then adjust for positive or negative lag in trend. The formula is

forecast including trend (FIT_t) = new forecast (F_t) + trend correction (T_t)

To smooth out the trend, the equation for the trend correction uses a smoothing constant, β, in the same way the simple exponential model uses α. T_t is computed by

$$T_t = (1 - \beta)T_{t-1} + \beta(F_t - F_{t-1}) \qquad \textbf{(5-6)}$$

where

T_t = smoothed trend for period t

T_{t-1} = smoothed trend for preceding period

β = trend smoothing constant that we select

F_t = simple exponential smoothed forecast for period t

F_{t-1} = forecast for previous period

The value of the trend smoothing constant, β, resembles the α constant in that a high β is more responsive to recent changes in trend. A low β value gives less weight to the most recent trends to smooth out the trend present. Values of β can be found by the trial-and-error approach, with the MAD used as a measure of comparison.

β's responsiveness is like that of α—a low β gives less weight to more recent trends, while a high β gives higher weight.

Simple exponential smoothing is often referred to as *first-order smoothing*, and trend-adjusted smoothing is called *second-order*, or *double smoothing*. Other advanced exponential smoothing models are also in use; they include seasonal-adjusted and triple smoothing, but these are beyond the scope of this book.[2]

Trend Projections

The last time-series forecasting method we discuss in this section is *trend projection*. This technique fits a trend line to a series of historical data points and then projects the line into the future for medium- to long-range forecasts. There are several mathematical trend equations that can be developed (for example, exponential and quadratic), but in this section we look at linear (straight line) trends only.

Midwestern Manufacturing Company Example Let us consider the case of Midwestern Manufacturing Company; that firm's demand for electrical generators over the period 1993–1999 is shown in Table 5.6.

If we decide to develop a linear trend line by a precise statistical method, as opposed to "eyeballing" the line as we did in Figure 5.2(c), the *least squares method* may be applied. This approach results in a straight line that minimizes the sum of the squares of the vertical differences from the line to each of the actual observations. Figure 5.4 illustrates the least squares approach.

The least squares method finds a straight line that minimizes the sum of the vertical differences from the line to each of the data points.

[2] For more details, see E. S. Gardner. "Exponential Smoothing: The State of the Art," *Journal of Forecasting* 4, 1 (March 1985), or G. E. P. Box, G. M. Jenkins, and G. C. Reinsel. *Time Series Analysis: Forecasting and Control*, 3d ed., Upper Saddle River, NJ: Prentice Hall, 1994.

TABLE 5.6 **Midwestern Manufacturing's Demand**	
YEAR	**ELECTRICAL GENERATORS SOLD**
1993	74
1994	79
1995	80
1996	90
1997	105
1998	142
1999	122

A least squares line is described in terms of its Y-intercept (the height at which it intercepts the Y-axis) and its slope (the angle of the line). If we can compute the Y-intercept and slope, the line can be expressed by the following equation:

$$\hat{Y} = a + bX \qquad\qquad\qquad\qquad\qquad\qquad \textbf{(5-7)}$$

where

We need to solve for the Y-intercept and the slope to find the equation of the least squares line.

$\hat{Y}$ (pronounced "Y-hat") = computed value of the variable to be predicted
        (called the dependent variable)

$a = Y$-axis intercept

$b =$ slope of the least squares line (or the rate of change in Y
        for given changes in X)

$X =$ independent variable

FIGURE 5.4

Least Squares Method
for Finding the Best-Fitting
Straight Line

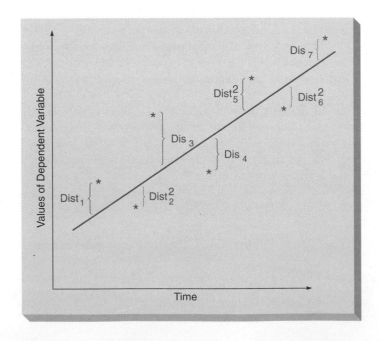

IN ACTION   **Forecasting Customer Demand at Taco Bell**

Like most quick service restaurants, Taco Bell understands the quantitative trade-off between labor and speed of service. More than 50% of the $5 billion company's daily sales come from the 3-hour lunch period. Customers don't like to wait more than 3 minutes for services, so it is critical that proper staffing is in place at all times.

Taco Bell tested a series of forecasting models to predict demand in specific 15-minute intervals during each day of the week. The company's goal was to find the technique that minimized the average square deviation between actual and predicted data. Because company computers only stored 6 weeks of transaction data, exponential smoothing was not considered. Results indicated that a 6-week moving average was best.

Building this forecasting methodology into each of Taco Bell's 6,500 stores' computers, the model makes weekly projections of customer transactions. These in turn are used by store managers to schedule staff, who begin in 15-minute increments, not one-hour blocks as in other industries. The forecasting model has been so successful that Taco Bell has documented more than $50 million in labor cost savings, while increasing customer service, in its first four years of use.

Source: J. Hueter and W. Swart. "An Integrated Labor-Management System for Taco Bell," *Interfaces* 28, 1 (January–February 1998): 75–91.

Statisticians have developed equations that we can use to find the values of *a* and *b* for any straight line. The slope, *b*, is found by

$$b = \frac{\Sigma\, XY - n\overline{X}\,\overline{Y}}{\Sigma\, X^2 - n\overline{X}^2}$$

(5-8)   *The slope equation* **b** *is found with Equation 5-8.*

where

b = slope of the straight line

Σ = summation sign for *n* data points

X = values of the independent variable (time here)

Y = values of the dependent variable (generator sales)

$\overline{X}$ = average of the values of the *X*'s

$\overline{Y}$ = average of the values of the *Y*'s

n = number of data points or observations (seven in this case)

The *Y*-intercept, *a*, is then computed as follows:

$$a = \overline{Y} - b\overline{X}$$

(5-9)   *The intercept equation* **a** *is found with the Equation 5-9.*

Transforming Time Variables With a series of data over time, we can minimize the computations by transforming the values of *X* (time) to simpler numbers. Thus, in the case of Midwestern Manufacturing's data, we can designate 1993 as year 1, 1994 as year 2, and so on. This is shown in Table 5.7.

$$\overline{X} = \frac{\Sigma\, X}{n} = \frac{28}{7} = 4 \qquad \overline{Y} = \frac{\Sigma\, Y}{n} = \frac{692}{7} = 98.86$$

$$b = \frac{\Sigma\, XY - n\overline{X}\,\overline{Y}}{\Sigma\, X^2 - n\overline{X}^2} = \frac{3{,}063 - (7)(4)(98.86)}{140 - (7)(4^2)} = \frac{295}{28} = 10.54$$

$$a = \overline{Y} - b\overline{X} = 98.86 - 10.54(4) = 56.70$$

TABLE 5.7   Midwestern Manufacturing's Trend Calculations

YEAR	TIME PERIOD	GENERATOR DEMAND	X^2	XY
1993	1	74	1	74
1994	2	79	4	158
1995	3	80	9	240
1996	4	90	16	360
1997	5	105	25	525
1998	6	142	36	852
1999	7	122	49	854
	$\Sigma X = 28$	$\Sigma Y = 692$	$\Sigma X^2 = 140$	$\Sigma XY = 3,063$

Hence, the least squares trend equation is $\hat{Y} = 56.70 + 10.54X$. To project demand in 2000, we first denote the year 2000 in our new coding system as $X = 8$:

$$(\text{sales in 2000}) = 56.70 + 10.54(8)$$

$$= 141.02, \text{ or } 141 \text{ generators}$$

We can estimate demand for 2001 by inserting $X = 9$ in the same equation:

$$(\text{sales in 2001}) = 56.70 + 10.54(9)$$

$$= 151.56 \text{ or } 152 \text{ generators}$$

To check the validity of the model, we plot historical demand and the trend line in Figure 5.5. In this case we may wish to be cautious and try to understand the 1998–1999 swings in demand.

FIGURE 5.5

Electrical Generators and the Computed Trend Line

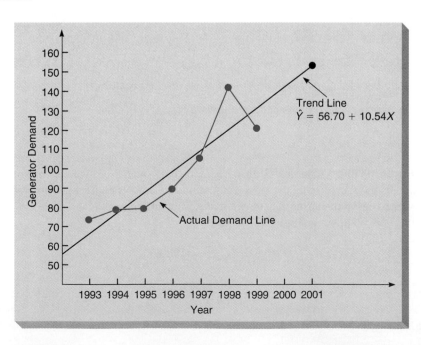

PROGRAM 5.3A

Excel QM's Trend Projection Model, Input Data, and Formulas Using Midwestern's Data in Table 5.7

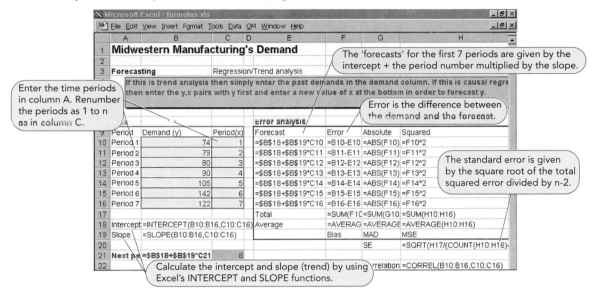

PROGRAM 5.3B

Output from Excel QM Trend Projection Model

Using Excel QM in Trend Analysis Programs 5.3A and 5.3B provide the Excel QM input/formulas and results, respectively, for Midwestern Manufacturing.

Seasonal Variations

Time-series forecasting such as that in the example of Midwestern Manufacturing involves looking at the *trend* of data over a series of time observations. Sometimes, however, recurring variations at certain seasons of the year make a *seasonal* adjustment in the trend line forecast necessary. Demand for coal and fuel oil, for example, usually peaks during cold winter months. Demand for golf clubs or suntan lotion may be highest in

TABLE 5.8   Answering Machine Sales and Seasonal Indices

MONTH	SALES DEMAND		AVERAGE TWO-YEAR DEMAND	AVERAGE MONTHLY DEMAND[a]	SEASONAL INDEX[b]
	YEAR 1	YEAR 2			
January	80	100	90	94	0.957
February	75	85	80	94	0.851
March	80	90	85	94	0.904
April	90	110	100	94	1.064
May	115	131	123	94	1.309
June	110	120	115	94	1.223
July	100	110	105	94	1.117
August	90	110	100	94	1.064
September	85	95	90	94	0.957
October	75	85	80	94	0.851
November	75	85	80	94	0.851
December	80	80	80	94	0.851
Total average demand = 1,128					

[a] Average monthly demand $= \dfrac{1,128}{12 \text{ months}} = 94$ [b] Seasonal index $= \dfrac{\text{average two-year demand}}{\text{average monthly demand}}$

summer. Analyzing data in monthly or quarterly terms usually makes it easy to spot seasonal patterns. Seasonal indices can then be developed by several common methods. The next example illustrates one way to compute seasonal factors from historical data.

Monthly sales of one brand of telephone answering machine at Eichler Supplies are shown in Table 5.8, for the two most recent years. Using the seasonal indices from Table 5.8, if we expected the third year's annual demand for answering machines to be 1,200 units, we would forecast the monthly demand as follows:

Jan.	$\dfrac{1,200}{12} \times 0.957 = 96$		July	$\dfrac{1,200}{12} \times 1.117 = 112$
Feb.	$\dfrac{1,200}{12} \times 0.851 = 85$		Aug.	$\dfrac{1,200}{12} \times 1.064 = 106$
Mar.	$\dfrac{1,200}{12} \times 0.904 = 90$		Sept.	$\dfrac{1,200}{12} \times 0.957 = 96$
Apr.	$\dfrac{1,200}{12} \times 1.064 = 106$		Oct.	$\dfrac{1,200}{12} \times 0.851 = 85$
May	$\dfrac{1,200}{12} \times 1.309 = 131$		Nov.	$\dfrac{1,200}{12} \times 0.851 = 85$
June	$\dfrac{1,200}{12} \times 1.223 = 122$		Dec.	$\dfrac{1,200}{12} \times 0.851 = 85$

For simplicity, trend calculations were ignored in the preceding example. The following example illustrates how indices that have already been prepared can be applied to adjust trend line forecasts and seasonal adjustments.

San Diego Hospital Example   A San Diego hospital used 66 months of adult inpatient hospital days to reach the following equation:

$$\hat{Y} = 8{,}091 + 21.5X$$

where

$\hat{Y}$ = patient days

X = time, in months

Based on this model, the hospital forecasts patient days for the next month (period 67) to be

Patient days = $8{,}091 + (21.5)(67) = 9{,}532$ (trend only)

As well as this model recognized the slight upward trend line in the demand for inpatient services, it ignored the seasonality that the administration knew to be present. Table 5.9 provides seasonal indices based on the same 66 months. Such seasonal data, by the way, were found to be typical of hospitals nationwide. Note that January, March, July, and August seem to exhibit significantly higher patient days on average, while February, September, November, and December experience lower patient days.

To correct the time-series extrapolation for seasonality, the hospital multiplied the monthly forecast by the appropriate seasonality index. Thus, for period 67, which was a January,

Patient days = $(9{,}532)(1.0436) = 9{,}948$ (trend and seasonal)

Using this method, patient days were forecasted for January through June (periods 67 through 72) as 9,948, 9,236, 9,768, 9,678, 9,554, and 9,547. This study led to better forecasts as well as to more accurate forecast budgets.

TABLE 5.9   **Seasonality Indices for Adult Inpatient Days at San Diego Hospital**

MONTH	SEASONALITY INDEX	MONTH	SEASONALITY INDEX
January	1.0436	July	1.0302
February	0.9669	August	1.0405
March	1.0203	September	0.9653
April	1.0087	October	1.0048
May	0.9935	November	0.9598
June	0.9906	December	0.9805

Source: W. E. Sterk and E. G. Shryock. "Modern Methods Improve Hospital Forecasting," *Healthcare Financial Management* (March 1987): 97. Reprinted with permission of author.

5.5   CAUSAL FORECASTING METHODS

Causal forecasting models usually consider several variables that are related to the variable being predicted. When these related variables have been found, a statistical model is built and used to forecast the variable of interest. This approach can be more powerful than time-series methods that use only the historic values of the forecasted variable.

The dependent variable is the item we are trying to forecast, and the independent variable(s) is an item (or items) we think might have a causal effect on the dependent variable.

Many factors can be considered in a causal analysis. For example, the sales of a product might be related to the firm's advertising budget, the price charged, competitor's prices, promotional strategies, and even the economy and unemployment rates. In this case, sales would be called the *dependent variable*, and the other variables would be called *independent variables*. Our job as quantitative analysts is to develop the best statistical relationship between sales and the set of independent variables. The most common quantitative causal forecasting model is *regression analysis*.

Using Regression Analysis to Forecast

Triple A Construction Company renovates old homes in Albany. Over time, the company has found that its dollar volume of renovation work is dependent on the Albany area payroll. The figures for Triple A's revenues and the amount of money earned by wage earners in Albany for the past six years are presented in Table 5.10.

Triple A wants to establish a mathematical relationship that will help predict sales. Just as we did with the least squares method of trend projection, we can let Y represent the dependent variable that we want to forecast, sales in this case. But now the independent variable, X, is not time; it is the Albany area payroll. Least squares regression analysis may now be used to establish the statistical model. The same basic model applies:

$$\hat{Y} = a + bX$$

where

$\hat{Y}$ = value of the dependent variable (sales here)

a = Y-axis intercept

b = slope of the regression line

X = independent variable (payroll)

TABLE 5.10   **Triple A Construction Company Sales**

Y TRIPLE A'S SALES ($100,000's)	X LOCAL PAYROLL ($100,000,000's)
2.0	1
3.0	3
2.5	4
2.0	2
2.0	1
3.5	7

The calculations for a and b follow:

SALES, *Y*	PAYROLL, *X*	*X*²	*XY*
2.0	1	1	2.0
3.0	3	9	9.0
2.5	4	16	10.0
2.0	2	4	4.0
2.0	1	1	2.0
3.5	7	49	24.5
$\Sigma Y = 15.0$	$\Sigma X = 18$	$\Sigma X^2 = 80$	$\Sigma XY = 51.5$

payroll # slope of .25 → sales are increasing by 25

$\hat{y} = 1.75 + 0.25 X$

*We determine **a** and **b** (the Y-intercept and slope) using the least squares formulas.*

$$\overline{X} = \frac{\Sigma X}{6} = \frac{18}{6} = 3$$

$$\overline{Y} = \frac{\Sigma Y}{6} = \frac{15}{6} = 2.5$$

$$b = \frac{\Sigma XY - n\overline{X}\,\overline{Y}}{\Sigma X^2 - n\overline{X}^2} = \frac{51.5 - (6)(3)(2.5)}{80 - (6)(3^2)} = 0.25$$

$$a = \overline{Y} - b\overline{X} = 2.5 - (0.25)(3) = 1.75$$

The estimated regression equation therefore is

$$\hat{Y} = 1.75 + 0.25X$$

or

sales $= 1.75 + 0.25$ (payroll)

If the local Chamber of Commerce predicts that the Albany area payroll will be $600 million next year, an estimate of sales for Triple A is found with the regression equation:

sales ($100,000's) $= 1.75 + (0.25)(6) = 1.75 + 1.50 = 3.25$

or

sales $= \$325,000$

The final part of Triple A's problem illustrates a central weakness of causal forecasting methods such as regression. We see that even after a regression equation is computed, it is necessary to provide a forecast of the independent variable, payroll, before estimating the dependent variable (*Y*) for the next time period. Although not a problem in the case of all forecasts, you can imagine the difficulty of determining future values of dependent and independent variables with *some* common independent variables (such as unemployment rates, gross national product, price indices).

One weakness of regression is that we need to know the values of the independent variable.

Using Excel QM for Regression Analysis Programs 5.4A and 5.4B show how Excel QM may be used in regression analysis. We note the similarity to the trend analysis in Programs 5.3A and 5.3B: This is because both models employ the least squares equations. Program 5.4A illustrates Triple A's input data and formulas, and the output is provided in Program 5.4B.

PROGRAM 5.4A

Excel QM's Regression Formulas and Input Using Triple A Data from Table 5.10

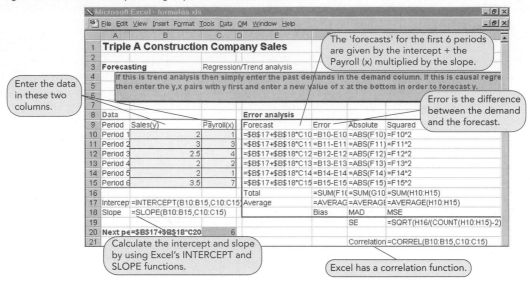

PROGRAM 5.4B

Output from Excel QM's Regression Analysis of the Triple A Construction Company Data

	A	B	C	D	E	F	G	H	I
1	**Triple A Construction Company Sales**								
2									
3	**Forecasting**		Regression/Trend analysis						
4	If this is trend analysis then simply enter the past demands in the demand column. If this								
5	is causal regression then enter the y,x pairs with y first and enter a new value of x at the								
6	bottom in order to forecast y.								
7									
8	Data				Error analysis				
9	Period	Sales(y)	Payroll(x)		Forecast	Error	Absolute	Squared	
10	Period 1	2	1		2	0	0	0	
11	Period 2	3	3		2.5	0.5	0.5	0.25	
12	Period 3	2.5	4		2.75	-0.25	0.25	0.0625	
13	Period 4	2	2		2.25	-0.25	0.25	0.0625	
14	Period 5	2	1		2	0	0	0	
15	Period 6	3.5	7		3.5	0	0	0	
16					Total	0	1	0.375	
17	Intercept	1.75			Average	0	0.166667	0.0625	
18	Slope	0.25				Bias	MAD	MSE	
19							SE	0.306186	
20	**Next period**	**3.25**	6						
21							Correlation	0.901388	

Standard Error of the Estimate

The forecast of $325,000 for Triple A's sales in the preceding example is called a *point estimate* of Y. The point estimate is really the mean, or expected value, of a distribution of possible values of sales. Figure 5.6 illustrates this concept.

To measure the accuracy of the regression estimates, we need to compute the *standard error of the estimate*, $S_{Y, X}$. This is called the *standard deviation of the regression*. Equation 5-10 is the expression found in most statistics books for computing the standard deviation of an arithmetic mean:

$$S_{Y, X} = \sqrt{\frac{\Sigma (Y - Y_c)^2}{n - 2}}$$

(5-10)

IN ACTION | **Forecasting Spare Parts at American Airlines**

To support the operation of its fleet of more than 400 aircraft, American Airlines maintains a vast inventory of spare repairable (rotatable) aircraft parts. Its PC-based forecasting system, the Rotatables Allocation and Planning System (RAPS), provides demand forecasts for spare parts, helps allocate these parts to airports, and computes the availability of each spare part. With 5,000 different kinds of parts, ranging from landing gear to wing flaps to coffeemakers to altimeters, meeting demand for each part at each station can be extremely difficult—and expensive. The average price of a rotatable part is about $5,000, with some parts (such as avionics computers) costing well over $500,000 each.

Before developing RAPS, American used only time-series methods to forecast the demand for spare parts. The time-series approach was slow to respond to even moderate changes in aircraft utilizations, let alone major fleet expansions. RAPS, instead, uses linear regression to establish a relationship between monthly part removals and various functions of monthly flying hours. Correlation coefficients and statistical significance tests are used to find the best regressions, which now take only one hour instead of the days that the old system needed.

The results? Using RAPS, American says that it had a one-time savings of $7 million and recurring annual savings of nearly $1 million.

Source: Mark J. Tedone. "Repairable Part Management," *Interfaces* 19, 4 (July–August 1989): 61–68.

where

Y = Y-value of each data point

Y_c = value of the dependent variable computed from the regression equation

n = number of data points

Equation 5-11 may look more complex, but it is actually an easier-to-use version of Equation 5-10. Either formula provides the same answer and can be used in setting up prediction intervals around the point estimate.[3]

$$S_{Y,X} = \sqrt{\frac{\Sigma Y^2 - a \Sigma Y - b \Sigma XY}{n-2}}$$ (5-11)

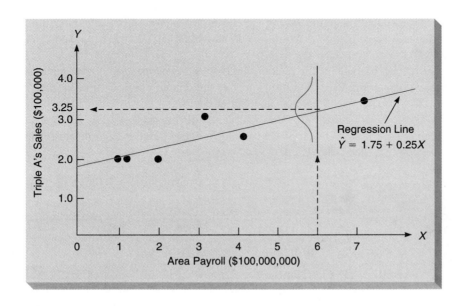

FIGURE 5.6

Distribution about the Point Estimate of $600 Million Payroll

---

[3] When the sample size is large ($n > 30$), the prediction interval for an individual value of Y can be computed using normal tables. When the number of observations is small, the *t*-distribution is appropriate. See any good statistics textbook for details, such as J. E. Hanke and A. G. Reitsch. *Business Forecasting,* 6th ed., Upper Saddle River, NJ: Prentice Hall, 1998.

TABLE 5.11   Triple A's Calculations, Including New Column for Y^2

Y	X	X^2	XY	Y^2
2.0	1	1	2.0	4.0
3.0	3	9	9.0	9.0
2.5	4	16	10.0	6.25
2.0	2	4	4.0	4.0
2.0	1	1	2.0	4.0
3.5	7	49	24.5	12.25
$\Sigma Y = 15.0$	$\Sigma X = 18$	$\Sigma X^2 = 80$	$\Sigma XY = 51.5$	$\Sigma Y^2 = 39.5$

Let us compute the standard error of the estimate for Triple A's data in the preceding section. The only number we need that is not available to solve for $S_{Y,X}$ is ΣY^2. Some quick addition in Table 5.11 reveals $\Sigma Y^2 = 39.5$. Therefore,

$$S_{Y,X} = \sqrt{\frac{\Sigma Y^2 - a \Sigma Y - b \Sigma XY}{n - 2}}$$

$$= \sqrt{\frac{39.5 - (1.75)(15.0) - (0.25)(51.5)}{6 - 2}}$$

$$= \sqrt{0.09375} = 0.306 \text{ (in hundreds of thousands of dollars)}$$

The standard error of the estimate is then $30,600 in sales.

Correlation Coefficients for Regression Lines

The regression equation is one way of expressing the nature of the relationship between two variables.[4] The equation shows how one variable relates to the value and changes in another variable.

The correlation coefficient helps measure the strength of the linear relationship.

Another way to evaluate the relationship between two variables is to compute the *coefficient of correlation*. This measure expresses the degree or strength of the linear relationship. It is usually identified as *r* and can be any number between and including $+1$ and -1. Figure 5.7 illustrates what different values of *r* might look like.

To compute *r* we use much of the same data needed earlier to calculate *a* and *b* for the regression line. The rather lengthy equation for *r* is

$$r = \frac{n \Sigma XY - \Sigma X \Sigma Y}{\sqrt{[n \Sigma X^2 - (\Sigma X)^2] [n \Sigma Y^2 - (\Sigma Y)^2]}} \tag{5-12}$$

Using the data in Table 5.11, we can compute the coefficient of correlation for Triple A Construction Company:

$$r = \frac{6(51.5) - (18)(15.0)}{\sqrt{[6(80) - (18)^2][6(39.5) - (15.0)^2]}} = \frac{309 - 270}{\sqrt{156(12)}} = \frac{39}{\sqrt{1,872}}$$

$$\text{or, } r = \frac{39}{43.3} = 0.901$$

---

[4] Regression lines are not always cause-and-effect relationships. In general, they describe the relationship between the movement of variables.

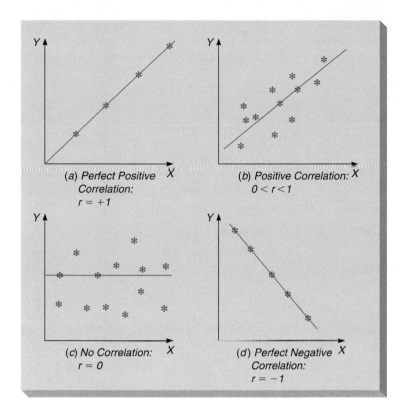

FIGURE 5.7
Four Values of the Correlation Coefficient

This r value of 0.901 appears to be a significant correlation and helps to confirm the closeness of the relationship of the two variables.

Although the coefficient of correlation is the most commonly used measure to describe the relationship between two variables, another measure does exist—the *coefficient of determination*. This is simply the square of the coefficient of correlation, namely, r^2. The value of r^2 will always be a positive number in the range $0 \leq r^2 \leq 1$. The coefficient of determination is the percent of variation in the dependent variable (Y) that is explained by the regression equation. In Triple A's case, the value of r^2 is 0.81, indicating that 81% of the total variation is explained by the regression equation.

Multiple Regression Analysis

Multiple regression is a practical extension of the model we just observed. It allows us to build a model with several independent variables. For example, if Triple A Construction wanted to include average annual interest rates in its model to forecast renovation sales, the proper equation would be

Adding another independent variable turns a simple regression model into a multiple regression model.

$$\hat{Y} = a + b_1X_1 + b_2X_2 \tag{5-13}$$

where

$$\hat{Y} = \text{dependent variable (sales)}$$

$$a = Y\text{-intercept}$$

$$X_1 \text{ and } X_2 = \text{values of the two independent variables (area payroll and interest rates),}$$
$$\text{respectively}$$

$$b_1 \text{ and } b_2 = \text{slopes for } X_1 \text{ and } X_2, \text{respectively}$$

The mathematics of multiple regression becomes quite complex, especially when more than two independent variables are considered, so we leave formulas for a, b_1, and b_2 to statistics texts. For now, let's assume that the new regression line, calculated by a computer, is

$$\hat{Y} = a + b_1 X_1 + b_2 X_2$$
$$= 1.80 + 0.30 X_1 - 5.0 X_2$$

Further, we find that the new coefficient of correlation is 0.96, implying that the inclusion of the variable X_2, interest rates, adds even more strength to the linear relationship.

We can now estimate Triple A's sales from Equation 5-13 if we substitute in values for next year's payroll and interest rates. If Albany's payroll will be \$600 million and interest rates will be 0.12 (12%), sales will be forecast as

The new forecast is made by filling in values of the two independent variables, X_1 and X_2.

$$\text{sales (\$100,000's)} = 1.80 + (0.30)(6) - (5.0)(0.12)$$
$$= 1.80 + 1.80 - 0.60$$
$$= 3.00$$
$$= \$300,000$$

Should interest rates drop to only 0.08, or 8%, can you see that the sales forecast would increase to \$320,000?

5.6   MONITORING AND CONTROLLING FORECASTS

After a forecast has been completed, it is important that it not be forgotten. No manager wants to be reminded when his or her forecast is horribly inaccurate, but a firm needs to determine why the actual demand (or whatever variable is being examined) differed significantly from that projected.[5]

One way to monitor forecasts to ensure that they are performing well is to employ a tracking signal. A *tracking signal* is a measurement of how well the forecast is predicting actual values. As forecasts are updated every week, month, or quarter, the newly available demand data are compared to the forecast values.

A tracking signal measures how well predictions fit actual data.

The tracking signal is computed as the *running sum of the forecast errors* (RSFE) divided by the mean absolute deviation:

$$\text{tracking signal} = \frac{\text{RSFE}}{\text{MAD}}$$
$$= \frac{\Sigma\,(\text{actual demand in period } i - \text{forecast demand in period } i)}{\text{MAD}} \quad \textbf{(5-14)}$$

where

$$\text{MAD} = \frac{\Sigma\,|\text{forecast errors}|}{n}$$

as seen earlier in Equation 5-5.

---

[5] If the forecaster is accurate, he or she usually makes sure that everyone is aware of his or her talents. Very seldom does one read articles in *Fortune, Forbes,* or the *Wall Street Journal,* however, about money managers who are consistently off by 25% in their stock market forecasts.

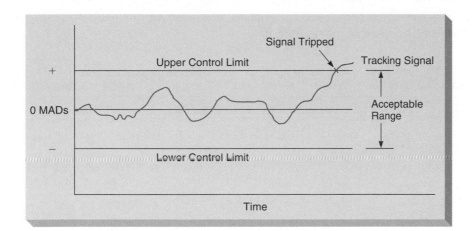

FIGURE 5.8
Plot of Tracking Signals

Positive tracking signals indicate that demand is greater than the forecast. Negative signals mean that demand is less than forecast. A good tracking signal, that is, one with a low RSFE, has about as much positive error as it has negative error. In other words, small deviations are okay, but the positive and negative deviations should balance so that the tracking signal centers closely around zero.

When tracking signals are calculated, they are compared to predetermined control limits. When a tracking signal exceeds an upper or lower limit, a signal is tripped. This means that there is a problem with the forecasting method and management may want to reevaluate the way it forecasts demand. Figure 5.8 shows the graph of a tracking signal that is exceeding the range of acceptable variation. If the model being used is exponential smoothing, perhaps the smoothing constant needs to be readjusted.

How do firms decide what the upper and lower tracking limits should be? There is no single answer, but they try to find reasonable values—in other words, limits not so low as to be triggered with every small forecast error and not so high as to allow bad forecasts to be regularly overlooked. George Plossl and Oliver Wight, two inventory control experts, suggested using maximums of ±4 MADs (for high-volume stock items) and ±8 MADs (for lower-volume items).[6] Other forecasters suggest slightly lower ranges. One MAD is equivalent to approximately 0.8 standard deviation, so that ±2 MADs = 1.6 standard deviations, ±3 MADs = 2.4 standard deviations, and ±4 MADs = 3.2 standard deviations. This suggests that for a forecast to be "in control," 89% of the errors are expected to fall within ±2 MADs, 98% within ±3 MADs, or 99.9% within ±4 MADs.[7]

Setting tracking limits is a matter of setting reasonable values for upper and lower limits.

Kimball's Bakery Example Here is an example that shows how the tracking signal and RSFE can be computed. Kimball's Bakery's quarterly sales of croissants (in thousands), as well as forecast demand and error computations, are in the following table. The

---

[6] See G. W. Plossl and O. W. Wight. *Production and Inventory Control*, Upper Saddle River, NJ: Prentice Hall, 1967.

[7] To prove these three percentages to yourself, just set up a normal curve for ±1.6 standard deviations (Z values). Using the normal table in Appendix A, you find that the area under that curve is 0.89. This represents ±2 MADs. Similarly, ±3 MADs = 2.4 standard deviations encompasses 98% of the area, and so on for ±4 MADs.

objective is to compute the tracking signal and determine whether forecasts are performing adequately.

QUARTER	FORECAST DEMAND	ACTUAL DEMAND	ERROR	RSFE	FORECAST ERROR	CUMULATIVE ERROR	MAD	TRACKING SIGNAL
1	100	90	−10	−10	10	10	10.0	−1
2	100	95	−5	−15	5	15	7.5	−2
3	100	115	+15	0	15	30	10.0	0
4	110	100	−10	−10	10	40	10.0	−1
5	110	125	+15	+5	15	55	11.0	+0.5
6	110	140	+30	+35	30	85	14.2	+2.5

$$\text{MAD} = \frac{\Sigma \, |\text{forecast errors}|}{n} = \frac{85}{6}$$

$$= 14.2$$

$$\text{tracking signal} = \frac{\text{RSFE}}{\text{MAD}} = \frac{35}{14.2}$$

$$= 2.5 \text{ MADs}$$

This tracking signal is within acceptable limits. We see that it drifted from −2.0 MADs to +2.5 MADs.

Adaptive Smoothing

A lot of research has been published on the subject of adaptive forecasting. This refers to computer monitoring of tracking signals and self-adjustment if a signal passes its preset limit. In exponential smoothing, the α and β coefficients are first selected based on values that minimize error forecasts and are then adjusted accordingly whenever the computer notes an errant tracking signal. This is called *adaptive smoothing*.

 5.7   USING THE COMPUTER TO FORECAST

The appendix to this chapter illustrates QM for Windows as an alternative way of developing forecasts.

Forecast calculations are seldom performed by hand in this day of computers. Numerous programs (such as SAS, SPSS, BIOMED, SYSTAB, and Minitab) are readily available to handle time-series and causal projections. Even spreadsheet software can effectively manage small to medium-sized forecasting problems, as we have seen with Excel QM.

Several mainframe-oriented packages, such as General Electric's Time Series Forecasting (called FCST1 and FCST2), are oriented toward organizations that need to perform large-scale regression and exponential smoothing projections. A large number of corporations use forecasting programs that also incorporate inventory control routines. Examples are IBM's IMPACT (Inventory Management Program and Control Technique) and COGS (Consumer Goods Program).

 **IN ACTION**   **Flood Forecasting at NOAA**

One of the major components of the National Oceanic and Atmospheric Administration (NOAA) is the National Weather Service, whose major objective is to save lives and reduce property damage. To accomplish this mission, an effective flood forecasting-response system is needed. The importance of an accurate and fast flood forecast cannot be overemphasized. Hundreds of lives and millions of dollars are at stake. In the United States, there are approximately 20,000 flood-prone areas.

The flood forecast-response system involves a number of steps. The first step is data collection. Data from the field regarding potential floods are collected and sent to river forecast centers. The second step is the actual forecasting procedure. This includes a number of mathematical models that transform rainfall, runoff, and a number of other factors into the flood forecasts. A flood forecast indicates the magnitude of the flood crest at specific points along rivers. The third step is the dissemination of the information to the appropriate points.

Radio, telephone, and television coverage are all used to inform the public of the potential of floods according to the forecast. The fourth step is the decision procedure step. Formal decision models are used to help formulate responses to various flood conditions. This includes the specific type of protective action to be taken. The fifth step is the implementation of actions to be taken both to prevent and to cope with flood conditions.

In many forecast situations, such as the flood forecast-response system described here, a lot more is involved than simply making the forecast. The appropriate data must be collected systematically, and the results must be carefully analyzed and disseminated so that the appropriate decisions can be made.

Source: R. Krzysztofowizz and D. Davis "Toward Improving Flood Forecast Response Systems," *Interfaces* 14, 3 (May–June 1984): 1–14.

Summary

Forecasts are a critical part of a manager's function. Demand forecasts drive the production, capacity, and scheduling systems in a firm and affect the financial, marketing, and personnel planning functions.

In this chapter we introduced three types of forecasting models: time series, causal, and judgmental. Moving averages, exponential smoothing, and trend projection time-series models were developed; a popular causal model, regression analysis, was illustrated; and four qualitative models were discussed. In addition, we explained the use of scatter diagrams, correlation coefficients, and the analysis of forecasting accuracy. In future chapters you will see the usefulness of these techniques in determining values for the various decision-making models.

As we learned in this chapter, no forecasting method is perfect under all conditions. Even when management has found a satisfactory approach, it must still monitor and control its forecasts to make sure that errors do not get out of hand. Forecasting can often be a very challenging but rewarding part of managing.

Glossary

Time-Series Models. Models that forecast using only historical data.

Causal Models. Models that forecast using variables and factors in addition to time.

Qualitative Models. Models that forecast using judgments, experience, and qualitative and subjective data.

Delphi. A judgmental forecasting technique that uses decision makers, staff personnel, and respondents to determine a forecast.

Decision-Making Group. A group of experts in a Delphi technique that has the responsibility of making the forecast.

Scatter Diagrams. Diagrams of the variable to be forecasted, plotted against another variable, such as time.

Moving Average. A forecasting technique that averages past values in computing the forecast.

Weighted Moving Average. A moving average forecasting method that places different weights on past values.

Exponential Smoothing. A forecasting method that is a combination of the last forecast and the last observed value.

Smoothing Constant. A value between 0 and 1 that is used in an exponential smoothing forecast. It is generally in the range from 0.1 to 0.3.

Mean Absolute Deviation (MAD). A technique for determining the accuracy of a forecasting model by taking the average of the absolute deviations.

Mean Squared Error (MSE). A technique for determining the accuracy of a forecasting model by taking the average of the squared error terms for a forecasting model.

Mean Absolute Percent Error (MAPE). A technique for determining the accuracy of a forecasting model by taking the average of the absolute errors as a percentage of the observed values.

Bias. A technique for determining the accuracy of a forecasting model by measuring the average total error and its direction.

Least Squares. A procedure used in trend projection and regression analysis to minimize the squared distances between the estimated straight line and the observed values.

Regression Analysis. A forecasting procedure that uses the least squares approach on one or more independent variables to develop a forecasting model.

Standard Error of the Estimate. A measure of the accuracy of regression estimates.

Coefficient of Correlation. A measure of the strength of the relationship between two variables.

Tracking Signal. A measure of how well the forecast is predicting actual values.

Key Equations

(5-1) $\text{Moving average} = \dfrac{\Sigma \text{ demand in previous } n \text{ periods}}{n}$

An equation for computing a moving average forecast.

(5-2) $\text{Weighted moving average} = \dfrac{\Sigma \text{ (weight for period } n\text{) (demand in period } n\text{)}}{\Sigma \text{ weights}}$

An equation for computing a weighted moving average forecast.

(5-3) New forecast = last period's forecast + α(last period's actual demand − last period's forecast)

An equation for computing an exponential smoothing forecast.

(5-4) $F_t = F_{t-1} + \alpha(A_{t-1} - F_{t-1})$

Equation 5-3 rewritten mathematically.

(5-5) $\text{MAD} = \dfrac{\Sigma \mid \text{forecast errors} \mid}{n}$

A measure of overall forecast error called mean absolute deviation.

(5-6) $T_t = (1 - \beta)T_{t-1} + \beta(F_t - F_{t-1})$

Trend component of an exponential smoothing model.

(5-7) $\hat{Y} = a + bX$

A least squares straight line used in trend projection and regression analysis forecasting.

(5-8) $b = \dfrac{\Sum XY - n\bar{X}\,\bar{Y}}{\Sum X^2 - n\bar{X}^2}$

An equation used to compute the slope, b, of a regression line.

(5-9) $a = \bar{Y} - b\bar{X}$

An equation used to compute the Y-intercept, a, of a regression line.

(5-10) $S_{Y,X} = \sqrt{\dfrac{\Sum (Y - Y_c)^2}{n - 2}}$

Standard error of the estimate.

(5-11) $S_{Y,X} = \sqrt{\dfrac{\Sum Y^2 - a\Sum Y - b\Sum XY}{n - 2}}$

Another way to express Equation 5-10.

(5-12) $r = \dfrac{n\Sum XY - \Sum X\Sum Y}{\sqrt{[n\Sum X^2 - (\Sum X)^2][n\Sum Y^2 - (\Sum Y)^2]}}$

Correlation coefficient.

(5-13) $\hat{Y} = a + b_1 X_1 + b_2 X_2$

The least squares line used in multiple regression.

(5-14) $\text{Tracking signal} = \dfrac{\text{RSFE}}{\text{MAD}}$

$$= \dfrac{\Sum (\text{actual demand in period } i - \text{ forecast demand in period } i)}{\text{MAD}}$$

An equation for monitoring forecasts.

Solved Problems

Solved Problem 5-1

Demand for patient surgery at Washington General Hospital has increased steadily in the past few years, as seen in the following table.

YEAR	OUTPATIENT SURGERIES PERFORMED
1	45
2	50
3	52
4	56
5	58
6	

The director of medical services predicted six years ago that demand in year 1 would be 42 surgeries.

Using exponential smoothing with a weight of $\alpha = 0.20$, develop forecasts for years 2 through 6. What is the MAD?

Solution

YEAR	ACTUAL	FORECAST (SMOOTHED)	ERROR	|ERROR|
1	45	42	−3	3
2	50	$42.6 = 42 + 0.2(45 - 42)$	−7.4	7.4
3	52	$44.1 = 42.6 + 0.2(50 - 42.6)$	−7.9	7.9
4	56	$45.7 = 44.1 + 0.2(52 - 44.1)$	−10.3	10.3
5	58	$47.7 = 45.7 + 0.2(56 - 45.7)$	−10.3	<u>10.3</u>
6	—	$49.8 = 47.7 + 0.2(58 - 47.7)$		38.9

$$\text{MAD} = \frac{\sum |\text{errors}|}{n} = \frac{38.9}{5} = 7.78$$

Solved Problem 5-2

Room registrations in the Toronto Towers Plaza Hotel have been recorded for the past nine years. Management would like to determine the mathematical trend of guest registration in order to project future occupancy. This estimate would help the hotel determine whether a future expansion will be needed. Given the following time-series data, develop a regression equation relating registrations to time. Then forecast year 11's registrations. Room registrations are in thousands:

Year 1: 17   Year 2: 16   Year 3: 16   Year 4: 21   Year 5: 20
Year 6: 20   Year 7: 23   Year 8: 25   Year 9: 24

Solution

YEAR (X)	REGISTRANTS (Y) (1,000's)	X^2	XY
1	17	1	17
2	16	4	32
3	16	9	48
4	21	16	84
5	20	25	100
6	20	36	120
7	23	49	161
8	25	64	200
9	24	81	216
$\sum X = 45$	$\sum Y = 182$	$\sum X^2 = 285$	$\sum XY = 978$

$$\bar{X} = \frac{45}{9} = 5 \qquad \bar{Y} = \frac{182}{9} = 20.22$$

$$b = \frac{\sum XY - n\bar{X}\,\bar{Y}}{\sum X^2 - n\bar{X}^2} = \frac{978 - (9)(5)(20.22)}{285 - (9)(25)} = \frac{978 - 909.9}{285 - 225} = \frac{68.1}{60} = 1.135$$

$$a = \overline{Y} - b\overline{X} = 20.22 - (1.135)(5) = 20.22 - 5.675 = 14.545$$

$$\hat{Y}\,(\text{registrations}) = 14.545 + 1.135X$$

The projection of registrations in year 11 is

$$\hat{Y} = 14.545 + (1.135)(11) = 27.03$$

or 27,030 guests in year 11.

Solved Problem 5-3

Quarterly demand for Jaguar XJ8's at a New York auto dealership is forecast with the equation

$$\hat{Y} = 10 + 3X$$

where

X = quarters: quarter I of last year   = 0

quarter II of last year   = 1

quarter III of last year = 2

quarter IV of last year = 3

quarter I of this year   = 4 and so on

and

$\hat{Y}$ = quarterly demand

The demand for luxury sedans is seasonal and the indices for quarters I, II, III, and IV are 0.80, 1.00, 1.30, and 0.90, respectively. Forecast the demand for each quarter of next year. Then seasonalize each forecast to adjust for quarterly variations.

Solution

Quarter II of this year is coded x = 5; quarter III of this year, x = 6; and quarter IV of this year, x = 7. Hence, quarter I of next year is coded x = 8; quarter II, x = 9; and so on.

$\hat{Y}(\text{next year quarter I}) = 10 + (3)(8) = 34$ Adjusted forecast = $(0.80)(34) = 27.2$

$\hat{Y}(\text{next year quarter II}) = 10 + (3)(9) = 37$ Adjusted forecast = $(1.00)(37) = 37$

$\hat{Y}(\text{next year quarter III}) = 10 + (3)(10) = 40$ Adjusted forecast = $(1.30)(40) = 52$

$\hat{Y}(\text{next year quarter IV}) = 10 + (3)(11) = 43$ Adjusted forecast = $(0.90)(43) = 38.7$

SELF-TEST

- Before taking the self-test, refer back to the learning objectives at the beginning of the chapter, the notes in the margins, and the glossary at the end of the chapter.
- Use the key at the back of the book to correct your answers.
- Restudy pages that correspond to any questions that you answered incorrectly or material you feel uncertain about.

1. Qualitative forecasting models include
   a. sales force composite.
   b. Delphi.
   c. consumer market survey.
   d. all of the above.
   e. none of the above.
2. A forecast that projects company's sales is a(n)
   a. economic forecast.   b. technological forecast.
   c. demand forecast.   d. none of the above.
3. Quantitative methods of forecasting include
   a. sales force composite.
   b. jury of executive opinion.
   c. consumer market survey.
   d. naive approach.
   e. all are quantifiable methods.
4. The method that considers several variables that are related to the variable being predicted is
   a. exponential smoothing.
   b. causal forecasting.
   c. weighted moving average.
   d. all of the above.
   e. none of the above.
5. Exponential smoothing is an example of a causal model.
   a. True   b. False
6. A time-series model incorporates the various factors that might influence the quantity being forecast.
   a. True   b. False
7. Decomposing a time series refers to breaking down past data into the components of
   a. constants and variations.
   b. trends, cycles, and random variations.
   c. strategic, tactical, and operational variations.
   d. long-term, short-term, and medium-term variations.
   e. none of the above.
8. In exponential smoothing, when the smoothing constant is high, more weight is placed on the more recent data.
   a. True   b. False
9. Three popular measures of forecast accuracy are
   a. total error, average error, and mean error.
   b. average error, median error, and maximum error.
   c. median error, minimum error, and maximum absolute error.
   d. mean absolute error, mean squared error, and mean absolute percent error.
   e. none of the above.
10. In a trend-adjusted exponential smoothing model, a high value for the trend smoothing constant, β, implies that we wish to make the model less responsive to recent changes in trend.
    a. True   b. False
11. Unfortunately, regression analysis can only be used to develop a forecast based on a single independent variable.
    a. True   b. False
12. A fundamental weakness of causal forecasting methods is that we must first forecast the value of the independent variable and *then* apply that value in the forecast of the dependent variable.
    a. True   b. False
13. With regard to a regression-based forecast, the *standard error of the estimate* gives a measure of
    a. the overall accuracy of the forecast.
    b. the time period for which the forecast is valid.
    c. the time required to derive the forecast equation.
    d. the maximum error of the forecast.
    e. none of the above.
14. One method of choosing among various smoothing constants when using exponential smoothing is to evaluate the mean absolute deviation (MAD) for each smoothing constant, and choose the smoothing constant that provides the minimum MAD.
    a. True   b. False
15. No single forecast methodology is appropriate under all conditions.
    a. True   b. False
16. The difference between a *dependent* and an *independent* variable is that _____ .
17. Quantitative forecasting methods include:
    1. _____   2. _____
    3. _____   4. _____
    5. _____
18. A time-series variable typically has the four components:
    1. _____   2. _____
    3. _____   4. _____
19. Qualitative forecast methods include:
    1. _____   2. _____
    3. _____   4. _____
20. The purpose of a *tracking signal* is to _____ .
21. The difference between a *moving average* model and an *exponential smoothing* model is that _____ .

Discussion Questions and Problems

Discussion Questions

5-1 Describe briefly the steps used to develop a forecasting system.

5-2 What is a time-series forecasting model?

5-3 What is the difference between a causal model and a time-series model?

5-4 What is a qualitative forecasting model, and when is it appropriate?

5-5 What is the meaning of least squares in a regression model?

5-6 What are some of the problems and drawbacks of the moving average forecasting model?

5-7 What effect does the value of the smoothing constant have on the weight given to the past forecast and the past observed value?

5-8 Describe briefly the Delphi technique.

5-9 What is MAD, and why is it important in the selection and use of forecasting models?

Problems*

• **5-10** John Smith has developed the following forecasting model:

$$\hat{Y} = 36 + 4.3X_1$$

where

$\hat{Y}$ = demand for K10 air conditioners
X_1 = the outside temperature (°F)

(a) Forecast the demand for K10 when the temperature is 70°F.
(b) What is the demand for a temperature of 80°F?
(c) What is the demand for a temperature of 90°F?

 5-11 Develop a four-month moving average forecast for Wallace Garden Supply. A three-month moving average forecast was developed in the section on moving averages in Table 5.2.

• **5-12** Using MAD, determine whether the forecast in Problem 5-11 or the forecast in the section concerning Wallace Garden Supply is more accurate.

5-13 Data collected on the yearly demand for 50-pound bags of fertilizer at Wallace Garden Supply are shown in the following table. Develop a three-year moving average to forecast sales. Then estimate demand again with a weighted moving average in which sales in the most recent year are given a weight of 2 and sales in the other two years are each given a weight of 1. Which method do you think is best?

YEAR	DEMAND FOR FERTILIZER (1,000's OF BAGS)	YEAR	DEMAND FOR FERTILIZER (1,000's OF BAGS)
1	4	7	7
2	6	8	9
3	4	9	12
4	5	10	14
5	10	11	15
6	8		

 5-14 Develop a two- and a four-year moving average for the demand for fertilizer in Problem 5-13.

*Note: ⌨ means the problem may be solved with QM for Windows; ✖ means the problem may be solved with Excel QM; and ⌨ means the problem may be solved with QM for Windows and/or Excel QM.

5-15 In Problems 5-13 and 5-14, four different forecasts were developed for the demand for fertilizer. These four forecasts are a two-year moving average, a three-year moving average, a weighted moving average, and a four-year moving average. Which one would you use? Explain your answer.

5-16 Use exponential smoothing with a smoothing constant of 0.3 to forecast the demand for fertilizer given in Problem 5-13. Assume that last period's forecast for year 1 is 5,000 bags to begin the procedure. Would you prefer to use the exponential smoothing model or the weighted average model developed in Problem 5-13? Explain your answer.

5-17 Sales of Cool-Man air conditioners have grown steadily during the past five years.

YEAR	SALES
1	450
2	495
3	518
4	563
5	584
6	?

The sales manager had predicted, before the business started, that year 1's sales would be 410 air conditioners. Using exponential smoothing with a weight of $\alpha = 0.30$, develop forecasts for years 2 through 6.

5-18 Using smoothing constants of 0.6 and 0.9, develop a forecast for the sales of Cool-Man air conditioners (see Problem 5-17).

5-19 What effect did the smoothing constant have on the forecast for Cool-Man air conditioners? (See Problems 5-17 and 5-18). Which smoothing constant gives the most accurate forecast?

5-20 Use a three-year moving average forecasting model to forecast the sales of Cool-Man air conditioners (see Problem 5-17).

5-21 Using the trend projection method, develop a forecasting model for the sales of Cool-Man air conditioners (see Problem 5-17).

5-22 Would you use exponential smoothing with a smoothing constant of 0.3, a three-year moving average, or a trend to predict the sales of Cool-Man air conditioners? Refer to Problems 5-17, 5-20, and 5-21.

5-23 The operations manager of a musical instrument distributor feels that demand for bass drums may be related to the number of television appearances by the popular rock group Green Shades during the preceding month. The manager has collected the data shown in the following table:

DEMAND FOR BASS DRUMS	GREEN SHADES TV APPEARANCES
3	3
6	4
7	7
5	6
10	8
8	5

(a) Graph these data to see whether a linear equation might describe the relationship between the group's television shows and bass drum sales.

(b) Use the least squares regression method to derive a forecasting equation.

(c) What is your estimate for bass drum sales if the Green Shades performed on TV nine times last month?

 5-24 Sales of industrial vacuum cleaners at R. Lowenthal Supply Co. over the past 13 months are as follows:

SALES (1000's)	MONTH	SALES (1000's)	MONTH
11	January	14	August
14	February	17	September
16	March	12	October
10	April	14	November
15	May	16	December
17	June	11	January
11	July		

(a) Using a moving average with three periods, determine the demand for vacuum cleaners for next February.

(b) Using a weighted moving average with three periods, determine the demand for vacuum cleaners for February. Use 3, 2, and 1 for the weights of the most recent, second most recent, and third most recent periods, respectively. For example, if you were forecasting the demand for February, November would have a weight of 1, December would have a weight of 2, and January would have a weight of 3.

(c) Evaluate the accuracy of each of these methods.

(d) What other factors might R. Lowenthal consider in forecasting sales?

 5-25 Passenger miles flown on Northeast Airlines, a commuter firm serving the Boston hub, are as follows for the past 12 weeks:

WEEK	ACTUAL PASSENGER MILES (1,000's)
1	17
2	21
3	19
4	23
5	18
6	16
7	20
8	18
9	22
10	20
11	15
12	22

(a) Assuming an initial forecast for week 1 of 17,000 miles, use exponential smoothing to compute miles for weeks 2 through 12. Use $\alpha = 0.2$.

(b) What is the MAD for this model?

(c) Compute the RSFE and tracking signals. Are they within acceptable limits?

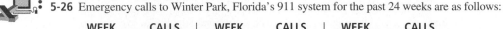

5-26 Emergency calls to Winter Park, Florida's 911 system for the past 24 weeks are as follows:

WEEK	CALLS	WEEK	CALLS	WEEK	CALLS
1	50	9	35	17	55
2	35	10	20	18	40
3	25	11	15	19	35
4	40	12	40	20	60
5	45	13	55	21	75
6	35	14	35	22	50
7	20	15	25	23	40
8	30	16	55	24	65

(a) Compute the exponentially smoothed forecast of calls for each week. Assume an initial forecast of 50 calls in the first week and use $\alpha = 0.1$. What is the forecast for the 25th week?

(b) Reforecast each period using $\alpha = 0.6$.

(c) Actual calls during the 25th week were 85. Which smoothing constant provides a superior forecast?

5-27 Using the 911 call data in Problem 5-26, forecast calls for weeks 2 through 25 using $\alpha = 0.9$. Which α is best? (Again, assume that actual calls in week 25 were 85 and use an initial forecast of 50 calls.)

5-28 Consulting income at Kate Walsh Associates for the period February–July has been as follows:

MONTH	INCOME ($1,000's)
February	70.0
March	68.5
April	64.8
May	71.7
June	71.3
July	72.8

Use exponential smoothing to forecast August's income. Assume that the initial forecast for February is $65,000. The smoothing constant selected is $\alpha = 0.1$.

5-29 Resolve Problem 5-28 with $\alpha = 0.3$. Using MAD, which smoothing constants provide a better forecast?

• **5-30** A study to determine the correlation between bank deposits and consumer price indices in Birmingham, Alabama, revealed the following (which was based on $n = 5$ years of data):

$$\Sigma X = 15$$
$$\Sigma X^2 = 55$$
$$\Sigma XY = 70$$
$$\Sigma Y = 20$$
$$\Sigma Y^2 = 130$$

Find the coefficient of correlation. What does it imply to you?

5-31 The accountant at O. H. Hall Coal Distributors, Inc., notes that the demand for coal seems to be tied to an index of weather severity developed by the National Weather Service. That is, when weather was extremely cold in the United States over the past five years (and hence the index was high), coal sales were high. The accountant proposes that one good forecast of next year's coal demand could be made by developing a regression equation and then consulting the *Farmer's Almanac* to see how severe next year's winter will be.

(a) Derive a least squares regression and compute the coefficient of correlation for the data in the following table.

(b) Also compute the standard error of the estimate.

COAL SALES (MILLIONS OF TONS) Y	WEATHER INDEX X
4	2
1	1
4	4
6	5
5	3

5-32 Bus and subway ridership in Washington, D.C. during the summer months is believed to be heavily tied to the number of tourists visiting the city. During the past 12 years, the following data have been obtained:

YEAR	NUMBER OF TOURISTS (1,000,000's)	RIDERSHIP (100,000's)
1	7	15
2	2	10
3	6	13
4	4	15
5	14	25
6	15	27
7	16	24
8	12	20
9	14	27
10	20	44
11	15	34
12	7	17

(a) Plot these data and decide if a linear model is reasonable.

(b) Develop a regression relationship.

(c) What is the expected ridership if 10 million tourists visit the city?

(d) If there are no tourists at all, explain the predicted ridership.

5-33 Accountants at the firm Walker and Walker believed that several traveling executives submit unusually high travel vouchers when they return from business trips. The accountants took a sample of 200 vouchers submitted from the past year; they then developed the following multiple regression equation relating expected travel cost ($\hat{Y}$) to number of days on the road (X_1) and distance traveled (X_2) in miles:

$$\hat{Y} = \$90.00 + \$48.50X_1 + \$0.40X_2$$

The coefficient of correlation computed was 0.68.

(a) If Thomas Williams returns from a 300-mile trip that took him out of town for five days, what is the expected amount that he should claim as expenses?

(b) Williams submitted a reimbursement request for $685; what should the accountant do?

(c) Comment on the validity of this model. Should any other variables be included? Which ones? Why?

 5-34 Jerilyn Ross, a New York City psychologist, specializes in treating patients who are phobic and afraid to leave their homes. The following table indicates how many patients Dr. Ross has seen each year for the past ten years. It also indicates what the robbery rate was in New York City during the same year.

YEAR	NUMBER OF PATIENTS	CRIME RATE (ROBBERIES PER 1,000 POPULATION)
1	36	58.3
2	33	61.6
3	40	73.4
4	41	75.7
5	40	81.1
6	55	89.0
7	60	101.1
8	54	94.8
9	58	103.3
10	61	116.2

Using trend analysis, how many patients do you think Dr. Ross will see in years 11, 12, and 13? How well does the model fit the data?

 5-35 Using the data in Problem 5-34, apply linear regression to study the relationship between the crime rate and Dr. Ross's patient load. If the robbery rate increases to 131.2 in year 11, how many phobic patients will Dr. Ross treat? If the crime rate drops to 90.6, what is the patient projection?

• **5-36** Management of Davis's Department Store has used time-series extrapolation to forecast retail sales for the next four quarters. The sales estimates are $100,000, $120,000, $140,000, and $160,000 for the respective quarters. Seasonal indices for the four quarters have been found to be 1.30, 0.90, 0.70, and 1.15, respectively. Compute a seasonalized or adjusted sales forecast.

 5-37 In the past, Judy Holmes's tire dealership sold an average of 1,000 radials each year. In the past two years, 200 and 250, respectively, were sold in fall, 300 and 350 in winter, 150 and 165 in spring, and 300 and 285 in summer. With a major expansion planned, Ms. Holmes projects sales next year to increase to 1,200 radials. What will the demand be each season?

 5-38 Thirteen students entered the undergraduate business program at Rollins College two years ago. The following table indicates what their grade-point averages (GPAs) were after being in the program for two years and what each student scored on the SAT exam when he or she was in high school. Is there a meaningful relationship between grades and SAT scores? If a student scores a 350 on the SAT, what do you think his or her GPA will be? What about a student who scores 800?

STUDENT	SAT SCORE	GPA	STUDENT	SAT SCORE	GPA
A	421	2.90	H	481	2.53
B	377	2.93	I	729	3.22
C	585	3.00	J	501	1.99
D	690	3.45	K	613	2.75
E	608	3.66	L	709	3.90
F	390	2.88	M	366	1.60
G	415	2.15			

Data Set Problem

5-39 Smith Savings and Loan is proud of its long tradition in Apopka, Florida. Begun by Laurie Shader-Smith eight years after World War II, the S&L has bucked the trend of financial and liquidity problems that have plagued the industry since 1988. Deposits have increased slowly but surely over the years, despite recessions in 1967, 1972, and 1987. Ms. Shader-Smith believes it necessary to have a strategic plan for her firm, including a one-year forecast of deposits. She examines the past deposit data and also peruses Florida's gross state product (GSP) over the same 44 years. [GSP is analogous to gross national product, (GNP) but on the state level.]

(a) Using exponential smoothing with $\alpha = 0.6$, trend analysis, and finally, linear regression, discuss which forecasting model fits best for Shader-Smith's strategic plan. Justify why one model should be selected over another.

(b) Examine the data carefully. Can you make a case for excluding a portion of the information? Why? Would that change your choice of model?

YEAR	DEPOSITS	GSP	YEAR	DEPOSITS	GSP	YEAR	DEPOSITS	GSP
1956	0.25	0.4	1971	2.3	1.6	1986	24.1	3.9
1957	0.24	0.4	1972	2.8	1.5	1987	25.6	3.8
1958	0.24	0.5	1973	2.8	1.6	1988	30.3	3.8
1959	0.26	0.7	1974	2.7	1.7	1989	36.0	3.7
1960	0.25	0.9	1975	3.9	1.9	1990	31.1	4.1
1961	0.30	1.0	1976	4.9	1.9	1991	31.7	4.1
1962	0.31	1.4	1977	5.3	2.3	1992	38.5	4.0
1963	0.32	1.7	1978	6.2	2.5	1993	47.9	4.5
1964	0.24	1.3	1979	4.1	2.8	1994	49.1	4.6
1965	0.26	1.2	1980	4.5	2.9	1995	55.8	4.5
1966	0.25	1.1	1981	6.1	3.4	1996	70.1	4.6
1967	0.33	0.9	1982	7.7	3.8	1997	70.9	4.6
1968	0.50	1.2	1983	10.1	4.1	1998	79.1	4.7
1969	0.95	1.2	1984	15.2	4.0	1999	94.0	5.0
1970	1.7	1.2	1985	18.1	4.0			

Note: Deposits in millions of dollars, GSP in billions of dollars.

Case Study

North-South Airline

In January 1999, Northern Airlines merged with Southeast Airlines to create the fourth largest U.S. carrier. The new North–South Airline inherited both an aging fleet of Boeing 727-300 aircraft and Stephen Ruth. Ruth was a tough former secretary of the navy who stepped in as new president and chairman of the board.

Ruth's first concern in creating a financially solid company was maintenance costs. It was commonly surmised in the airline industry that maintenance costs rise with the age of the aircraft. He quickly noticed that historically there had been a significant difference in the reported B727-300 maintenance costs (from ATA Form 41's) both in the airframe and engine areas between Northern Airlines and Southeast Airlines, with Southeast having the newer fleet.

On February 12, 1999, Peg Young, vice-president for operations and maintenance, was called into Ruth's office and asked to study the issue. Specifically, Ruth wanted to know whether the average fleet age was correlated to direct airframe maintenance costs, and whether there was a relationship between average fleet age and direct engine maintenance costs. Young was to report back by February 26 with the answer, along with quantitative and graphical descriptions of the relationship.

Young's first step was to have her staff construct the average age of Northern and Southeast B727-300 fleets, by quarter, since the introduction of that aircraft to service by each airline in late 1990 and early 1991. The average age of each fleet was calculated by first multiplying the total number of calendar days each aircraft had been in service at the pertinent point in time by the average daily utilization of the respective fleet to total fleet hours flown. The total fleet hours flown was then divided by the number of aircraft in service at that time, giving the age of the "average" aircraft in the fleet.

The average utilization was found by taking the actual total fleet hours flown at September 30, 1998, from Northern and Southeast data, and dividing by the total days in service for all aircraft at that time. The average utilization for Southeast was 8.3 hours per day, and the average utilization for Northern was 8.7 hours per day. Because the available cost data were calculated for each yearly period ending at the end of the first quarter, average fleet age was calculated at the same points in time. The fleet data are shown in the following table. Airframe cost data and engine cost data are both shown paired with fleet average age in that table.

Prepare Peg Young's response to Stephen Ruth.

Note: *Dates and names of airlines and individuals have been changed in this case to maintain confidentiality. The data and issues described here are actual.*

North–South Airline Data for Boeing 727-300 Jets

	NORTHERN AIRLINE DATA			SOUTHEAST AIRLINE DATA		
YEAR	AIRFRAME COST PER AIRCRAFT	ENGINE COST PER AIRCRAFT	AVERAGE AGE (HOURS)	AIRFRAME COST PER AIRCRAFT	ENGINE COST PER AIRCRAFT	AVERAGE AGE (HOURS)
1992	$51.80	$43.49	6,512	$13.29	$18.86	5,107
1993	54.92	38.58	8,404	25.15	31.55	8,145
1994	69.70	51.48	11,077	32.18	40.43	7,360
1995	68.90	58.72	11,717	31.78	22.10	5,773
1996	63.72	45.47	13,275	25.34	19.69	7,150
1997	84.73	50.26	15,215	32.78	32.58	9,364
1998	78.74	79.60	18,390	35.56	38.07	8,259

Case Study

Akron Zoological Park

During the late 1980s, the decline in Akron's tire industry, inflation, and changes in governmental priorities almost resulted in the permanent closing of the Akron Children's Zoo. Lagging attendance and a low level of memberships did not help matters. Faced with uncertain prospects of continuing, the city of Akron opted out of the zoo business. In response, the Akron Zoological Park was organized as a corporation to contract with the city to operate the zoo.

The Akron Zoological Park is an independent organization that manages the Akron Children's Zoo for the city. To be successful, the zoo must maintain its image as a high-quality place for its visitors to spend their time. Its animal exhibits are clean and neat. The animals, birds, and reptiles look well cared for. As resources become available for construction and continuing operations, the zoo keeps adding new exhibits and activities. Efforts seem to be working, because attendance increased from 53,353 in 1989 to an all-time record of 133,762 in 1994.

Due to its northern climate, the zoo conducts its open season from mid-April until mid-October. It reopens for 1 week at Halloween and for the month of December. Zoo attendance depends largely on the weather. For example, attendance was down during the month of December 1995, which established many local records for the coldest temperature and the most snow. Variations in weather also affect crop yields and prices of fresh animal foods, thereby influencing the costs of animal maintenance.

In normal circumstances, the zoo may be able to achieve its target goal and attract an annual attendance equal to 40% of its community. Akron has not grown appreciably during the past decade. But the zoo became known as an innovative community resource, and as indicated in the table, annual paid attendance has doubled. Approximately 35% of all visitors are adults. Children accounted for one-half of the paid attendance. Group admissions remain a constant 15% of zoo attendance.

The zoo does not have an advertising budget. To gain exposure in its market, then, the zoo depends on public service announcements, the zoo's public television series, and local press coverage of its activities and social happenings. Many of these activities are but a few years old. They are a strong reason that annual zoo attendance has increased.

Although the zoo is a nonprofit organization, it must ensure that its sources of income equal or exceed its operating and physical plant costs. Its continued existence remains totally dependent on its ability to generate revenues and to reduce its expenses.

Discussion Questions

1. The president of the Akron Zoo asked you to calculate the expected gate admittance figures and revenues for both 1999 and 2000. Would simple linear regression analysis be the appropriate forecasting technique?

2. What factors other than admission price influence annual attendance and thus should be considered in the forecast?

Source: Professor F. Bruce Simmons III, University of Akron.

YEAR	ATTENDANCE	ADMISSION FEE ($)		
		ADULT	CHILD	GROUP
1998	117,874	4.00	2.50	1.50
1997	125,363	3.00	2.00	1.00
1996	126,853	3.00	2.00	1.50
1995	108,363	2.50	1.50	1.00
1994	133,762	2.50	1.50	1.00
1993	95,504	2.00	1.00	0.50
1992	63,034	1.50	0.75	0.50
1991	63,853	1.50	0.75	0.50
1990	61,417	1.50	0.75	0.50
1989	53,353	1.50	0.75	0.50

INTERNET CASE STUDY

See our Internet home page at **http//www.prenhall.com/render** for this additional case study: Kwik Lube.

Bibliography

Chambers, J. C., C. Satinder, S. K. Mullick, and D. D. Smith. "How to Choose the Right Forecasting Technique," *Harvard Business Review* 49, 4 (July–August 1971): 45–74.

Clements, Dale W., and Richard A. Reid. "Analytical MS/OR Tools Applied to a Plant Closure," *Interfaces* 24, 2 (March–April 1994): 1–43.

De Lurgio, S. A. *Forecasting Principles and Applications*. New York: Irwin-McGraw-Hill, 1998.

Diebold, F. X. *Elements of Forecasting*. Cincinnati: South-Western College Publishing, 1998.

Gardner, E. S. "Exponential Smoothing: The State of the Art," *Journal of Forecasting* 4, 1 (March 1985).

Georgoff, D. M., and R. G. Murdick. "Manager's Guide to Forecasting," *Harvard Business Review* 64, 1 (January–February 1986): 110–120.

Hanke, J. E., and A. G. Reitsch. *Business Forecasting*, 6th ed. Upper Saddle River, NJ: Prentice Hall, 1998.

Heizer, J., and B. Render. *Operations Management*, 5th ed. Upper Saddle River, NJ: Prentice Hall, 1999.

Parker, G. C., and E. L. Segura. "How to Get a Better Forecast," *Harvard Business Review* (March–April 1971): 99–109.

Schnaars, S. P., and R. J. Bavuso. "Extrapolation Models on Very Short-Term Forecasts," *Journal of Business Research* 14 (1986): 27–36.

Weinberg, Charles B. "Arts Plan: Implementation, Evolution, and Usage," *Marketing Science* 5, 2 (Spring 1986).

Yurkiewicz, J. "Forecasting That Fits," *OR/MS Today* 25, 1 (February 1998): 42–55.

 APPENDIX 5.1: FORECASTING WITH QM FOR WINDOWS

In this section we look at our other forecasting software package, QM for Windows. QM for Windows can project moving averages (both simple and weighted), do simple and trend-adjusted exponential smoothing, handle least squares trend projection, and solve linear regression (causal) problems.

To illustrate QM for Windows, let's use the following data, shown earlier as Table 5.6.

YEAR	ELECTRICAL GENERATORS SOLD AT MIDWESTERN MANUFACTURING
1993	74
1994	79
1995	80
1996	90
1997	105
1998	142
1999	122

Program 5.5A shows the input for a three-year simple moving average analysis with QM for Windows. The method and the number of periods to average are selected by dragging your mouse or clicking on those respective screen areas. Output results, in Program 5.5B, include error terms as well as the ability to select a graph (through an icon on the bottom of the screen).

Similarly, Program 5.6 illustrates QM for Windows analysis of the same data using exponential smoothing with $\alpha = 0.3$. Finally, Program 5.7 uses least squares trend projection and produces the model

$$sales = 56.71 + 10.54(year)$$

If year $= 8$, the sales forecast is shown to be $56.71 + 10.54(8) = 141$ generators.

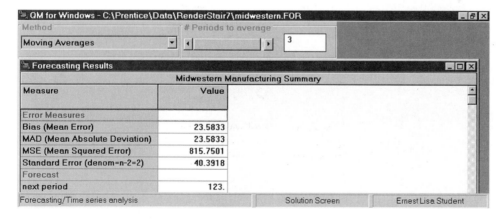

PROGRAM 5.5A

QM for Windows Input
for Moving Averages

PROGRAM 5.5B

QM for Windows Output
for Moving Averages
Using Program 5.5A Data

PROGRAM 5.6

QM for Windows Output Using Exponential Smoothing and $\alpha = 0.3$ for Midwestern Manufacturing

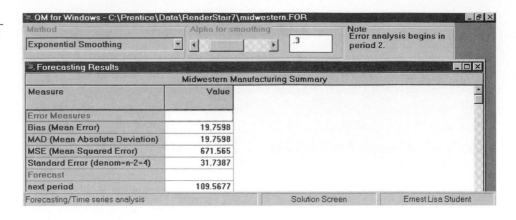

PROGRAM 5.7

QM for Windows Output Using Trend Analysis for Midwestern Manufacturing

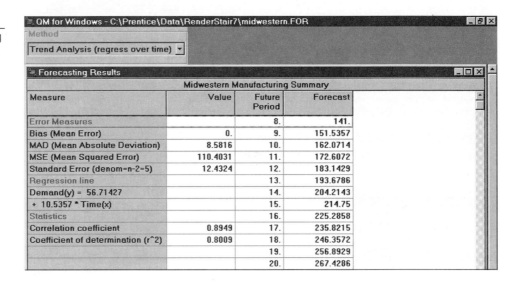

Inventory Control Models

CHAPTER 6

LEARNING OBJECTIVES

After completing this chapter, students will be able to:

1. Understand the importance of inventory control and ABC analysis.
2. Use the economic order quantity (EOQ) to determine how much to order.
3. Compute the reorder point (ROP) in determining when to order more inventory.
4. Handle inventory problems that allow quantity discounts or non-instantaneous receipt.
5. Understand the use of safety stock with known and unknown stockout costs.

CHAPTER OUTLINE

6.1 Introduction

6.2 Importance of Inventory Control

6.3 Inventory Decisions

6.4 Economic Order Quantity (EOQ): Determining How Much to Order

6.5 Reorder Point: Determining When to Order

6.6 EOQ without the Instantaneous Receipt Assumption

6.7 Quantity Discount Models

6.8 Use of Safety Stock

6.9 ABC Analysis

6.10 Sensitivity Analysis

Summary • Glossary • Key Equations • Solved Problems • Self-Test • Discussion Questions and Problems • Data Set Problems • Case Study: Sturdivant Sound Systems • Case Study: Martin-Pullin Bicycle Corporation • Case Study: Professional Video Management • Internet Case Studies • Bibliography

Appendix 6.1: Inventory Control with QM for Windows

6.1   INTRODUCTION

Inventory is one of the most expensive and important assets to many companies, representing as much as 50% of total invested capital. Managers have long recognized that good inventory control is crucial. On one hand, a firm can try to reduce costs by reducing on-hand inventory levels. On the other hand, customers become dissatisfied when frequent inventory outages, called *stockouts*, occur. Thus, companies must make the balance between low and high inventory levels. As you would expect, cost minimization is the major factor in obtaining this delicate balance.

Inventory is any stored resource that is used to satisfy a current or a future need. Raw materials, work-in-process, and finished goods are examples of inventory. Inventory levels for finished goods are a direct function of demand. When we determine the demand for completed clothes dryers, for example, it is possible to use this information to determine how much sheet metal, paint, electric motors, switches, and other raw materials and work-in-process are needed to produce the finished product.

All organizations have some type of inventory planning and control system. A bank has methods to control its inventory of cash. A hospital has methods to control blood supplies and other important items. State and federal governments, schools, and virtually every manufacturing and production organization are concerned with inventory planning and control. Studying how organizations control their inventory is equivalent to studying how they achieve their objectives by supplying goods and services to their customers. Inventory is the common thread that ties all the functions and departments of the organization together.

Inventory is any stored resource that is used to satisfy a current or future need.

Figure 6.1 illustrates the basic components of an inventory planning and control system. The *planning* phase is concerned primarily with what inventory is to be stocked and how it is to be acquired (whether it is to be manufactured or purchased). This information is then used in *forecasting* demand for the inventory and in *controlling* inventory levels. The feedback loop in Figure 6.1 provides a way of revising the plan and forecast based on experiences and observation.

Through inventory planning, an organization determines what goods and/or services are to be produced. In cases of physical products, the organization must also determine whether to produce these goods or to purchase them from another manufacturer. When this has been determined, the next step is to forecast the demand. As discussed in Chapter 5, there are many mathematical techniques that can be used in forecasting demand for a particular product. The emphasis in this chapter is on inventory control, that is, how to maintain adequate inventory levels within an organization.

FIGURE 6.1

Inventory Planning and Control

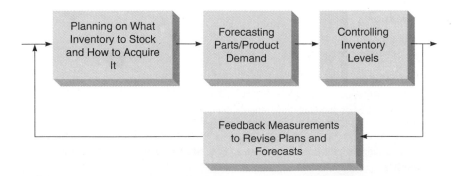

6.2 **IMPORTANCE OF INVENTORY CONTROL**

Inventory control serves several important functions and adds a great deal of flexibility to the operation of the firm. Five uses of inventory are:

1. The decoupling function
2. Storing resources
3. Irregular supply and demand
4. Quantity discounts
5. Avoiding stockouts and shortages

Decoupling Function

One of the major functions of inventory is to decouple manufacturing processes within the organization. If you did not store inventory, there could be many delays and inefficiencies. For example, when one manufacturing activity has to be completed before a second activity can be started, it could stop the entire process. If, however, you have some stored inventory between processes, it could act as a buffer.

Inventory can act as a buffer.

Storing Resources

Agricultural and seafood products often have definite seasons over which they can be harvested or caught, but the demand for these products is somewhat constant during the year. In these and similar cases, inventory can be used to store these resources.

In a manufacturing process, raw materials can be stored by themselves, in work-in-process, or in the finished product. Thus, if your company makes lawn mowers, you might obtain lawn mower tires from another manufacturer. If you have 400 finished lawn mowers and 300 tires in inventory, you actually have 1,900 tires stored in inventory. Three hundred tires are stored by themselves, and 1,600 (1,600 = 4 tires per lawn mower × 400 lawn mowers) tires are stored in the finished lawn mowers. In the same sense, *labor* can be stored in inventory. If you have 500 subassemblies and it takes 50 hours of labor to produce each assembly, you actually have 25,000 labor hours stored in inventory in the subassemblies. In general, any resource, physical or otherwise, can be stored in inventory.

Resources can be stored in work-in-process.

Irregular Supply and Demand

When the supply or demand for an inventory item is irregular, storing certain amounts in inventory can be important. If the greatest demand for Diet-Delight beverage is during the summer, you will have to make sure that there is enough supply to meet this irregular demand. This might require that you produce more of the soft drink in the winter than is actually needed to meet the winter demand. The inventory levels of Diet-Delight will gradually build up over the winter, but this inventory will be needed in the summer. The same is true for irregular *supplies*.

Quantity Discounts

Another use of inventory is to take advantage of quantity discounts. Many suppliers offer discounts for large orders. For example, an electric jigsaw might normally cost $10 per unit. If you order 300 or more saws in one order, your supplier may lower the cost to $8.75. Purchasing in larger quantities can substantially reduce the cost of products. There are, however, some disadvantages of buying in larger quantities. You will have higher storage costs and higher costs due to spoilage, damaged stock, theft, insurance, and so on. Furthermore, by investing in more inventory, you will have less cash to invest elsewhere.

Avoiding Stockouts and Shortages

Another important function of inventory is to avoid shortages or stockouts. If you are repeatedly out of stock, customers are likely to go elsewhere to satisfy their needs. Lost goodwill can be an expensive price to pay for not having the right item at the right time.

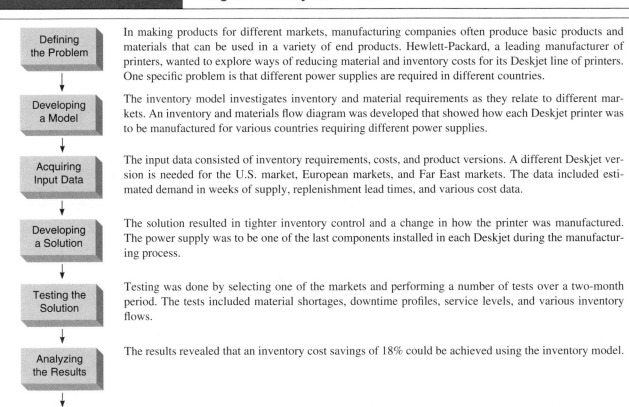

MODELING IN THE REAL WORLD   **Using an Inventory Model to Reduce Costs for a Hewlett-Packard Printer**

Defining the Problem

In making products for different markets, manufacturing companies often produce basic products and materials that can be used in a variety of end products. Hewlett-Packard, a leading manufacturer of printers, wanted to explore ways of reducing material and inventory costs for its Deskjet line of printers. One specific problem is that different power supplies are required in different countries.

Developing a Model

The inventory model investigates inventory and material requirements as they relate to different markets. An inventory and materials flow diagram was developed that showed how each Deskjet printer was to be manufactured for various countries requiring different power supplies.

Acquiring Input Data

The input data consisted of inventory requirements, costs, and product versions. A different Deskjet version is needed for the U.S. market, European markets, and Far East markets. The data included estimated demand in weeks of supply, replenishment lead times, and various cost data.

Developing a Solution

The solution resulted in tighter inventory control and a change in how the printer was manufactured. The power supply was to be one of the last components installed in each Deskjet during the manufacturing process.

Testing the Solution

Testing was done by selecting one of the markets and performing a number of tests over a two-month period. The tests included material shortages, downtime profiles, service levels, and various inventory flows.

Analyzing the Results

The results revealed that an inventory cost savings of 18% could be achieved using the inventory model.

Implementing the Results

As a result of the inventory model, Hewlett-Packard decided to redesign how its Deskjet printers are manufactured to reduce inventory costs in meeting a global market for its printers.

Source: H. Lee, et al. "Hewlett-Packard Gains Control of Inventory and Service through Design for Localization," *Interfaces* 23, 4 (July–August 1993): 1–11.

IN ACTION Using Expert Systems in Inventory Management and Logistics

Producing electronic chips and memory circuits is an interesting but often difficult process. Chip making begins with a silicon wafer and consists of approximately 200 complicated steps or procedures. Each silicon wafer, which is about 8 inches in diameter, will eventually be converted into hundreds of memory or logic chips that will become the heart of a new computer.

IBM's logistics management system (LMS) is a real-time expert system that assists with the dispatching function, inventory control, and monitoring of the flow of materials through IBM's semiconductor facility, located near Burlington, Vermont. This particular plant produces a variety of memory and logic chips that are used in a number of computer systems produced by IBM. LMS also allows managers to quickly update various databases and models as required.

The success of LMS can be traced to its ability to access, collect, organize, and deliver strategic data, knowledge, and model results quickly in a real-time fashion. This allows various IBM Burlington employees, including line technicians, process operators, maintenance technicians, industrial engineers, and managers to get the information they need to plan inventory control and scheduling functions. LMS is an example of a system that employs quantitative analysis to help in inventory control and management.

Source: G. Sullivan and K. Fordyce. *Interfaces* 20, 1 (January–February 1990): 43–64.

6.3 INVENTORY DECISIONS

Even though there are literally millions of different types of products produced in our society, there are only two fundamental decisions that you have to make when controlling inventory:

1. How much to order
2. When to order

The purpose of all inventory models and techniques is to determine rationally how much to order and when to order. As you know, inventory fulfills many important functions within an organization. But as the inventory levels go up to provide these functions, the cost of storing and holding inventory also increases. Thus, you must reach a fine balance in establishing inventory levels. A major objective in controlling inventory is to minimize total inventory costs. Some of the most significant inventory costs are:

The purpose of all inventory models is to minimize inventory costs.

1. Cost of the items
2. Cost of ordering
3. Cost of carrying, or holding, inventory
4. Cost of safety stock
5. Cost of stockouts

The inventory models discussed in the first part of this chapter assume that demand and the time it takes to receive an order are known and constant and that no quantity discounts are given. When this is the case, the most significant costs are the cost of placing an order and the cost of holding inventory items over a period of time (see Table 6.1 for a list of important factors making up these costs). Later in this chapter we discuss several more sophisticated inventory models.

TABLE 6.1 Inventory Cost Factors

ORDERING COST FACTORS	CARRYING COST FACTORS
Developing and sending purchase orders	Cost of capital
Processing and inspecting incoming inventory	Taxes
Bill paying	Insurance
Inventory inquiries	Spoilage
Utilities, phone bills, and so on, for the purchasing department	Theft
Salaries and wages for purchasing department employees	Obsolescence
Supplies such as forms and paper for the purchasing department	Salaries and wages for warehouse employees
	Utilities and building costs for the warehouse
	Supplies such as forms and paper for the warehouse

6.4   ECONOMIC ORDER QUANTITY (EOQ): DETERMINING HOW MUCH TO ORDER

The *economic order quantity* (EOQ) is one of the oldest and most commonly known inventory control techniques. Research on its use dates back to a 1915 publication by Ford W. Harris. EOQ is still used by a large number of organizations today. This technique is relatively easy to use, but it does make a number of assumptions. Some of the more important assumptions are:

1. Demand is known and constant.
2. The lead time, that is, the time between the placement of the order and the receipt of the order, is known and constant.
3. The receipt of inventory is instantaneous. In other words, the inventory from an order arrives in one batch, at one point in time.
4. Quantity discounts are not possible.
5. The only variable costs are the cost of placing an order, *ordering cost,* and the cost of holding or storing inventory over time, *holding* or *carrying cost.*
6. If orders are placed at the right time, stockouts or shortages can be avoided completely.

The inventory usage curve has a sawtooth shape.

With these assumptions, inventory usage has a sawtooth shape, as in Figure 6.2. In Figure 6.2, Q represents the amount that is ordered. If this amount is 500 dresses, all 500 dresses arrive at one time when an order is received. Thus, the inventory level jumps from 0 to 500 dresses. In general, an inventory level increases from 0 to Q units when an order arrives.

Because demand is constant over time, inventory drops at a uniform rate over time. (Refer to the sloped line in Figure 6.2.) Another order is placed such that when the inventory level reaches 0, the new order is received and the inventory level again jumps to Q units, represented by the vertical lines. This process continues indefinitely over time.

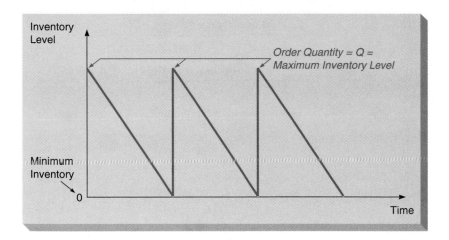

FIGURE 6.2
Inventory Usage over Time

Inventory Costs

The objective of most inventory models is to minimize the total costs. With the assumptions just given, the significant costs are the ordering cost and the carrying, or holding, cost. All other costs, such as the cost of the inventory itself, are constant. Thus, if we minimize the sum of the ordering and carrying costs, we are also minimizing the total costs. To help visualize this, Figure 6.3 graphs total costs as a function of the order quantity, Q. The optimal order size, Q^*, is the quantity that minimizes the total costs. As the quantity ordered increases, the total number of orders placed per year decreases. Thus, as the quantity ordered increases, the annual ordering cost decreases. But as the order quantity increases, the carrying cost increases due to larger average inventories that the firm has to maintain.

The objective of the simple EOQ model is to minimize ordering and carrying cost.

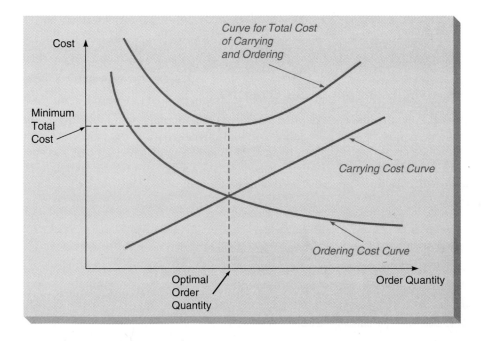

FIGURE 6.3
Total Cost as a Function of Order Quantity

TABLE 6.2   **Computing Average Inventory**

| | INVENTORY LEVEL | | |
DAY	BEGINNING	ENDING	AVERAGE
April 1 (order received)	10	8	9
April 2	8	6	7
April 3	6	4	5
April 4	4	2	3
April 5	2	0	1

Maximum level April 1 = 10 units
Total of daily averages = 9 + 7 + 5 + 3 + 1 = 25
Number of days = 5
Average inventory level = 25/5 = 5 units

The average inventory level is one-half the maximum level.

Note in Figure 6.3 that the optimal order quantity occurred at the point where the ordering cost curve and the carrying cost curve intersected. This was not by chance. With this particular type of cost function, the optimal quantity occurs at a point where the ordering cost is equal to the carrying cost. This is an important fact to remember.

Now that you have a better understanding of inventory costs, let's see how we can determine the optimal order quantity that minimizes these costs. In determining the *annual* carrying cost, it is convenient to use the average on-hand inventory level. We then multiply the average inventory level times a factor called *inventory carrying cost per unit per year* to determine the annual inventory cost. Table 6.2 illustrates how *average inventory* can be calculated. It is important to note that the average inventory level for this problem is equal to one-half of the maximum level of 10. (This is due to a constant demand, coupled with the fact that ending inventory is 0.) This maximum level is equal to the order quantity. Thus, the average inventory in units is simply calculated as one-half of the order quantity:

$$\text{average inventory level} = Q/2 \tag{6-1}$$

Finding the Economic Order Quantity

*We determine **Q*** by setting ordering cost equal to carrying cost.*

We pointed out that the optimal order quantity is the point that minimizes the total cost, where total cost is the sum of ordering cost and carrying cost. We also indicated graphically that the optimal order quantity was at the point where the ordering cost was equal to the carrying cost. Now, let's develop equations that directly solve for the optimum. To accomplish this, the following steps need to be performed.

Four Steps for Finding the Optimum Inventory
1. Develop an expression for the ordering cost.
2. Develop an expression for the carrying cost.
3. Set the ordering cost equal to the carrying cost.
4. Solve this equation for the optimum desired.

Using the following variables, we can determine ordering cost, carrying cost, and Q^*, the economic order quantity:

Q = number of pieces per order

Q^* = optimal number of pieces per order

D = annual demand in units for the inventory item

C_0 = ordering cost for each order

C_h = holding or carrying cost per unit per year

Here is the step-by-step procedure:

1. Annual ordering cost = (no. of orders placed per year) $\times$ (order cost per order)

$$= \frac{\text{annual demand}}{\text{no. of units in each order}} \times (\text{order cost per order})$$

$$= \left(\frac{D}{Q}\right) \times (C_0) = \frac{D}{Q}(C_0)$$

2. Annual holding or carrying cost = (average inventory level)
$$\times (\text{carrying cost per unit per year})$$

$$= \left(\frac{\text{order quantity}}{2}\right) \times (\text{carrying cost per unit per year})$$

$$= \left(\frac{Q}{2}\right) \times (C_h) = \frac{Q}{2} C_h$$

3. Optimal order quantity is found when ordering cost = carrying cost: namely,

$$\frac{D}{Q} C_0 = \frac{Q}{2} C_h$$

4. To solve for Q^*, simply cross-multiply terms and isolate Q on the left of the equal sign:

$$Q^* = \sqrt{\frac{2DC_0}{C_h}} \qquad \text{(6-2)}$$

Now that the equation for the optimal order quantity, Q^*, has been derived, it is possible to solve inventory problems directly.

Sumco Pump Company Example

Sumco, a company that sells pump housings to other manufacturers, would like to reduce its inventory cost by determining the optimal number of pump housings to obtain per order. The annual demand is 1,000 units, the ordering cost is \$10 per order, and the average carrying cost per unit per year is \$0.50. Using these figures, we can calculate the optimal number of units per order:

$$Q^* = \sqrt{\frac{2DC_0}{C_h}}$$

$$= \sqrt{\frac{2(1,000)(10)}{0.50}}$$

$$= \sqrt{40,000}$$

$$= 200 \text{ units}$$

The total annual inventory cost is the sum of the ordering costs and the carrying costs.

total annual cost = order cost + holding cost

In terms of the variables in the model, the total cost (TC) can now be expressed as

The total annual inventory cost is equal to ordering plus holding costs for the simple EOQ model.

$$TC = \frac{D}{Q}C_0 + \frac{Q}{2}C_h \qquad (6\text{-}3)$$

The total annual inventory cost for Sumco is computed as follows:

$$TC = \frac{D}{Q}C_0 + \frac{Q}{2}C_h$$

$$= \frac{1000}{200}(10) + \frac{200}{2}(0.5)$$

$$= \$50 + \$50 = \$100$$

As you might expect, the ordering cost is equal to the carrying cost. You may wish to try different values for Q, such as 100 or 300 pumps. You will find that the minimum total cost occurs when Q is 200 units. The economic order quantity, Q^*, is 200 pumps.

Using Excel QM for Basic EOQ Inventory Problems   The Sumco Pump Company example, and a variety of other inventory problems we address in this chapter, can be easily solved using Excel QM. Program 6.1A shows the input data for Sumco and the Excel formulas needed for the EOQ model. Program 6.1B contains the solution for this example, including the optimal order quantity, maximum inventory level, average inventory level, and the number of setups.

Purchase Cost of Inventory Items

Sometimes the total inventory cost expression is written to include the actual cost of the material purchased. The purchase cost does not depend on the particular order policy found to be optimal, because regardless of how many orders are placed each year, we still incur the same annual purchase cost of $D \times P$, where P is the price per unit and D is the annual demand in units.[1]

It is useful to know how to calculate the average inventory level in dollar terms when the price per unit is given. This can be done as follows. With the variable Q representing the quantity of units ordered, and assuming a unit price of P, we can determine the average dollar value of inventory:

$$\text{average dollar level} = \frac{(PQ)}{2} \qquad (6\text{-}4)$$

This formula is analogous to Equation 6-1.

I is the annual carrying cost as a percentage of the cost per unit.

Inventory carrying costs for many businesses and industries are also often expressed as an annual percentage of the unit cost or price. When this is the case, a new variable is introduced. Let I be the annual inventory holding charge as a percent of unit price or cost. Then the cost of storing one unit of inventory for the year, C_h, is given by $C_h = IP$, where P is the unit price or cost of an inventory item. Q^* can be expressed, in this case, as

$$Q^* = \sqrt{\frac{2DC_0}{IP}} \qquad (6\text{-}5)$$

---

[1] Later in this chapter, we discuss the case in which price can affect order policy, that is, when quantity discounts are offered.

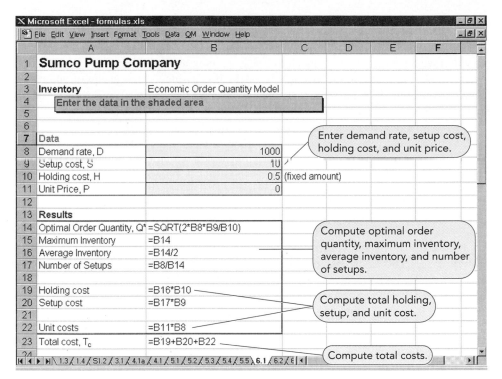

PROGRAM 6.1A

Input Data and Excel QM
Formulas for the Sumco Pump
Company Example

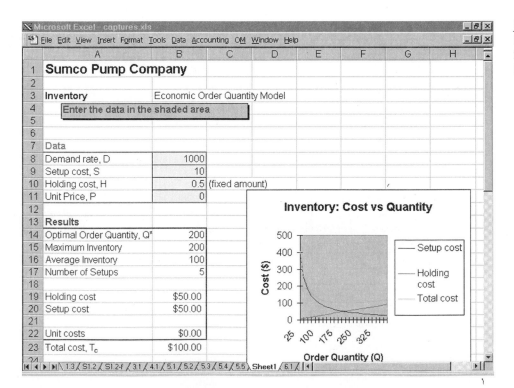

PROGRAM 6.1B

Excel QM Solution for the
Sumco Pump Company
Example

6.5   REORDER POINT: DETERMINING WHEN TO ORDER

Now that we have decided how much to order, we look at the second inventory question, when to order. In most simple inventory models, it is assumed that receipt of an order is instantaneous. That is, we assume that a firm waits until its inventory level for a particular item reaches 0, places an order, and receives the items in stock immediately.

As we all know, however, the time between the placing and receipt of an order, called the lead time or delivery time, is often a few days or even a few weeks. Thus, the *when to order* decision is usually expressed in terms of a *reorder point* (ROP), the inventory level at which an order should be placed. The reorder point, ROP, is given as

The reorder point (ROP) determines when to order inventory. It is found by multiplying the daily demand times the lead time in days.

ROP = (demand per day) × (lead time for a new order in days)

$$= d \times L \tag{6-6}$$

Figure 6.4 shows the reorder point graphically. The slope of the graph is the daily inventory usage. This is expressed in units demanded per day, *d*. The *lead time, L,* is the time that it takes to receive an order. Thus, if an order is placed when the inventory level reaches the ROP, the new inventory arrives at the same instant the inventory is reaching 0. Let's take a look at an example.

Procomp's Computer Chip Example Procomp's demand for computer chips is 8,000 per year. The firm has a daily demand of 40 units. On the average, delivery of an order takes three working days. The reorder point for chips is calculated as follows:

ROP = reorder point = $d \times L$ = 40 units per day × 3 days

= 120 units

Hence, when the inventory stock of chips drops to 120, an order should be placed. The order will arrive three days later, just as the firm's stock is depleted to 0. It should be mentioned that this calculation assumes that all of the assumptions listed previously are

FIGURE 6.4

Recorder Point (ROP) Curve

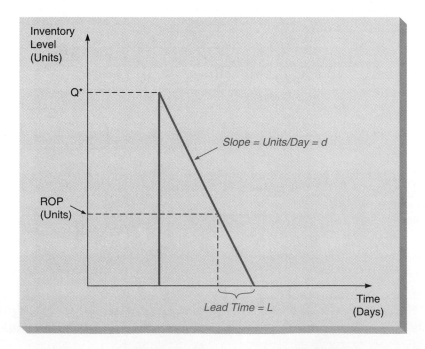

IN ACTION | **Inland Steel Uses Systems Contracts to Control Inventory Costs**

Sound inventory control involves much more than computing the economic order quantity. In most cases, other practical and financial considerations must be taken into account to minimize total inventory costs and to provide tighter control on inventory levels. Both practical and financial considerations led Inland Steel to consider several inventory policies, including systems contracts.

Inland Steel produces approximately 5.5 million tons of steel each year. The steel mill has two blast furnaces that supply steel to four casting operations. Yet, steel inventory is not the company's only inventory concern. For many large corporations, office equipment such as typewriters, printers, and fax machines can represent a substantial investment. Furthermore, all steel-processing facilities are controlled through computers, which are considered office equipment by Inland Steel.

Tricia Wynn, a project buyer for Inland Steel, was concerned about high costs and a lack of standardization for office equipment. To overcome these problems, she developed a comprehensive inventory ordering system that took advantage of standardization and contract buying. The result was a contract ordering system that provided superior equipment at substantial savings. Most of the equipment was leased or rented. The new system provided low monthly rates for office equipment, free installation, and a 30-day free trial. Another advantage was a floating systems contract. With this type of contract, there is no termination date, which helps reduce the time and costs of maintaining leasing agreements. The bottom line is that a systems contract approach allowed Inland Steel to order good-quality office equipment for fewer dollars.

Source: K. Evans-Correia. "All Systems Go," *Purchasing* (March 23, 1989): 106–107.

correct. When demand is not known with complete certainty, these calculations have to be modified. This is discussed later in this chapter.

6.6 EOQ WITHOUT THE INSTANTANEOUS RECEIPT ASSUMPTION

When a firm receives its inventory over a period of time, a new model is needed that does not require the *instantaneous inventory receipt* assumption. This new model is applicable when inventory continuously flows or builds up over a period of time after an order has been placed or when units are produced and sold simultaneously. Under these circumstances, the daily demand rate must be taken into account. Figure 6.5 shows inventory levels as a function of time. Because this model is especially suited to the production environment, it is commonly called the *production run model*.

The production run model eliminates the instantaneous receipt assumption.

In the production process, instead of having an ordering cost, there will be a *setup cost*. This is the cost of setting up the production facility to manufacture the desired product. It normally includes the salaries and wages of employees who are responsible for setting up the equipment, engineering and design costs of making the setup, paperwork,

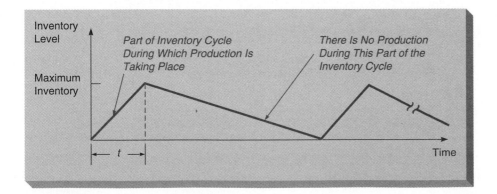

FIGURE 6.5

Inventory Control and the Production Process

Solving the production run model involves setting setup costs equal to holding costs and solving for Q.

supplies, utilities, and so on. The carrying cost per unit is composed of the same factors as the traditional EOQ model, although the annual carrying cost equation changes.

The production run model can be derived by setting setup costs equal to holding or carrying costs and solving for the order quantity. Let's start by developing the expression for carrying cost. You should note, however, that making setup cost equal to carrying cost does not always guarantee optimal solutions for models more complex than the production run model.

Determining the Annual Carrying Cost

Using the following variables, we can determine the expression for annual inventory carrying cost for the production run model:

Q = number of pieces per order or production run

C_h = holding or carrying cost per unit per year

p = daily production rate

d = daily demand rate

t = length of the production run in days

1. Annual inventory holding or carrying cost

   = (average inventory level) × (carrying cost per unit per year)
   = (average inventory level) × C_h

2. Average inventory level = ½(maximum inventory level)

3. Maximum inventory level

   = (total produced during the production run)
   − (total used during the production run)

   But Q = total produced = pt, and thus $t = Q/p$. Therefore, maximum inventory level = $p(Q/p) − d(Q/p) = Q − (d/p)Q = Q(1 − d/p)$.

4. Annual inventory carrying cost

   = ½ (maximum inventory level) × C_h

   = ½ × $Q(1 − d/p) × C_h$ **(6-7)**

   [*Note*: This is the same as the carrying cost developed in the EOQ model except that the factor $(1 − d/p)$ appears in the expression for carrying cost.]

Finding the Annual Setup Cost or the Annual Ordering Cost

When a product is being produced over time, setup cost replaces the ordering cost. Here is how *annual setup cost* and *annual ordering cost* can be determined:

1. Annual setup cost = (number of setups per year) × (setup cost per setup)

   $$= \frac{D}{Q_p} C_s$$ **(6-8)**

   where

   D = annual demand in units

   Q_p = quantity produced in one batch

   C_s = setup cost per setup

2. Annual ordering cost = $\dfrac{D}{Q} C_0$ **(6-9)**

As you can see, the form of the equation for the annual setup cost is identical to the form of the equation for the annual ordering cost. In determining the optimal order quantity, we use the variables presented in Equation 6-9 for the case where the inventory is ordered instead of produced. It should be noted, however, that the same optimal equation can be used in determining the optimal production quantity, Q_p^*, as well. Q_p and C_s would replace Q and C_0 in the equation.

Determining the Optimal Order Quantity and Production Quantity

With this model it is possible to determine the optimal quantity by setting the ordering cost equal to the carrying cost and solving for the desired quantity. Here is how this can be accomplished when the inventory is ordered.

Four Steps for Determining Optimal Order Quantity for the Production Run Model

1. Ordering cost $= \dfrac{D}{Q}\, C_0$.

2. Carrying cost $= \frac{1}{2}\, C_h Q \left(1 - \dfrac{d}{p} \right)$.

3. Set ordering cost equal to carrying cost.

$$\frac{D}{Q}\, C_0 = \frac{1}{2}\, C_h Q \left(1 - \frac{d}{p} \right)$$

4. Solve for Q^*. Optimal order quantity.

$$Q^2 = \frac{2DC_0}{C_h\left(1 - \dfrac{d}{p} \right)}$$

$$Q^* = \sqrt{\frac{2DC_0}{C_h\left(1 - \dfrac{d}{p} \right)}} \qquad \text{(6-10)}$$

Here is the formula for the optimal production quantity. Notice the similarity to the basic EOQ model.

The same calculations can be made to determine the optimal production quantity, Q_p^*. The results of these calculations are

$$Q_p^* = \sqrt{\frac{2DC_s}{C_h\left(1 - \dfrac{d}{p} \right)}} \qquad \text{(6-11)}$$

Brown Manufacturing

Brown Manufacturing produces commercial refrigeration units in batches. The firm's estimated demand for the year is 10,000 units. It costs about $100 to set up the manufacturing process, and the carrying cost is about 50 cents per unit per year. When the production process has been set up, 80 refrigeration units can be manufactured daily. The demand during the production period has traditionally been 60 units each day. Brown operates its refrigeration unit production area 167 days per year. How many

IN ACTION   Implementing Speed and Quality in the Production Run at Milton Bradley

Milton Bradley, a division of Hasbro, Inc., has been manufacturing toys for more than 100 years. Founded by Milton Bradley in 1860, the company started by making a lithograph of Abraham Lincoln. Using his printing skills, Bradley developed games, including the Checkered Game of Life, the Game of Life, Chutes and Ladders, Candy Land, Scrabble, and Lite Brite. Today, the company produces hundreds of games, requiring billions of plastic parts.

When Milton Bradley has determined the optimal quantities for its production run, it must implement these quantities. Some games require literally hundreds of plastic parts, including spinners, hotels, people, animals, cars, and so on. Getting the correct number of parts into each toy is critical. According to Garry Brennan, director of manufacturing at Hasbro, getting the right number of pieces to the right production line is the most important issue for the credibility of the company. Some companies, including Wal-Mart, can require 20,000 or more perfectly assembled games delivered to their warehouses and stores in a matter of days.

Not getting the correct number of parts or pieces is very frustrating for customers. It can also be time-consuming, expensive, and frustrating for Milton Bradley to supply the extra parts or get returned toys and games. If shortages are found during the assembly stage, the entire production run can be stopped until the problem is corrected. Counting parts by hand or machine was problematic and not always accurate. As a result, Milton Bradley decided to weigh the pieces and complete games to determine if the correct number of parts have been included. If the weight is not exactly correct, there is a problem that needs to be resolved before the game or toy is packaged and shipped. Using highly accurate digital scales, Milton Bradley has been able to get the right parts to the right production line at the right time. Without this simple implementation approach, the most sophisticated production run results would be meaningless.

Source: Doug Smock. "Games Tip the Scale at Milton Bradley," *Plastics World*, (March 1997): 22.

refrigeration units should Brown Manufacturing produce in each batch? How long should the production part of the cycle shown in Figure 6.5 last? Here is the solution:

$$\text{Annual demand} = D = 10{,}000 \text{ units}$$

$$\text{Setup cost} = C_s = \$100$$

$$\text{Carrying cost} = C_h = \$0.50 \text{ per unit per year}$$

$$\text{Daily production rate} = p = 80 \text{ units daily}$$

$$\text{Daily demand rate} = d = 60 \text{ units daily}$$

1. $Q_p^* = \sqrt{\dfrac{2DC_s}{C_h\left(1 - \dfrac{d}{p}\right)}}$

2. $Q_p^* = \sqrt{\dfrac{2 \times 10{,}000 \times 100}{0.5\left(1 - \dfrac{60}{80}\right)}}$

$= \sqrt{\dfrac{2{,}000{,}000}{0.5(^1/_4)}} = \sqrt{16{,}000{,}000}$

$= 4{,}000 \text{ units}$

If $Q_p^* = 4{,}000$ units and we know that 80 units can be produced daily, the length of each production cycle will be $Q/p = 4{,}000/80 = 50$ days. Thus, when Brown decides to produce refrigeration units, the equipment will be set up to manufacture the units for a 50-day time span.

Using Excel QM for Production Run Models The Brown Manufacturing production run model can also be solved using Excel QM. Program 6.2A contains the input data and

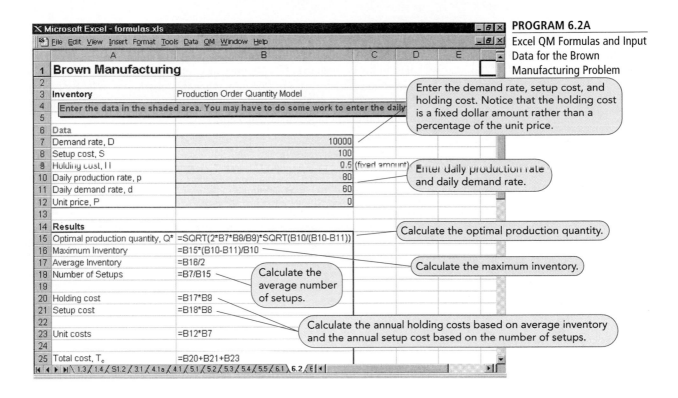

PROGRAM 6.2A

Excel QM Formulas and Input Data for the Brown Manufacturing Problem

the Excel formulas for this problem. Program 6.2B provides the solution results, including the optimal production quantity, maximum inventory level, average inventory level, and the number of setups.

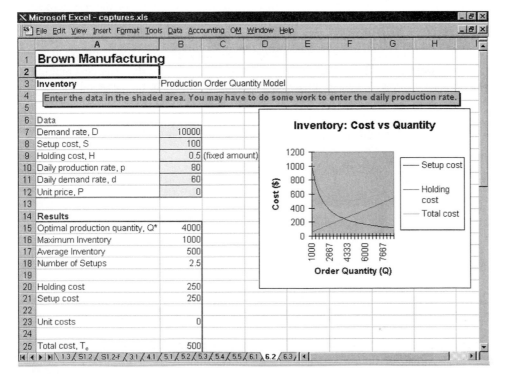

PROGRAM 6.2B

The Solution Results for the Brown Manufacturing Problem using Excel QM

6.7 QUANTITY DISCOUNT MODELS

To increase sales, many companies offer quantity discounts to their customers. A *quantity discount* is simply a reduced cost (*C*) for the item when it is purchased in larger quantities. It is not uncommon to have a discount schedule with several discounts for large orders. A typical quantity discount schedule appears in Table 6.3.

TABLE 6.3 **Quantity Discount Schedule**

DISCOUNT NUMBER	DISCOUNT QUANTITY	DISCOUNT (%)	DISCOUNT COST ($)
1	0 to 999	0	5.00
2	1,000 to 1,999	4	4.80
3	2,000 and over	5	4.75

As can be seen in the table, the normal cost for the item is $5. When 1,000 to 1,999 units are ordered at one time, the cost per unit drops to $4.80, and when the quantity ordered at one time is 2,000 units or more, the cost is $4.75 per unit. As always, management must decide when and how much to order. But with quantity discounts, how does the manager make these decisions?

The overall objective of the quantity discount model is to minimize total inventory costs, which now include actual material costs.

As with other inventory models discussed so far, the overall objective will be to minimize the total cost. Because the unit cost for the third discount in Table 6.3 is lowest, you might be tempted to order 2,000 units or more to take advantage of the lower material cost. Placing an order for that quantity with the greatest discount cost, however, might not minimize the total inventory cost. As the discount quantity goes up, the material cost goes down, but the carrying cost increases because the orders are large. Thus, the major trade-off when considering quantity discounts is between the reduced material cost and the increased carrying cost. When we include the cost of the material, the equation for the total annual inventory cost becomes

total cost = material cost + ordering cost + carrying cost

$$= DC + \frac{D}{Q}C_0 + \frac{Q}{2}C_h \qquad \text{(6-12)}$$

where

D = annual demand in units

C_0 = ordering cost per order

C = cost per unit

C_h = holding cost per unit per year

Now, we have to determine the quantity that minimizes the total annual inventory cost. This process involves four steps.

Four Quantity Discount Steps

1. For each discount, calculate a $Q*$ value using the following equation:

$$Q* = \sqrt{\frac{2DC_0}{IC}}$$

Note that the carrying cost is IC instead of C_h. Because the cost of the item is a factor in annual carrying cost, we cannot assume that the carrying cost is a constant when the cost per unit changes for each quantity discount. Thus, it is common to express the carrying cost (I) as a percentage of the unit cost (C) instead of as a constant cost per unit per year, C_h.

2. For any discount, if the order quantity is too low to qualify for the discount, adjust the order quantity upward to the lowest quantity that qualifies for the discount. For example, if $Q*$ for discount 2 in Table 6.3 were 500 units, you would adjust this value up to 1,000 units. Look at the second discount in Table 6.3. Order quantities between 1,000 and 1,999 qualify for the 4% discount. Thus, we adjust the order quantity to be 1,000 units if $Q*$ is below 1,000 units. The reasoning for step 2 may not be obvious. If the order quantity is below the quantity range that qualifies for a discount, a quantity within this range may still result in the lowest total cost.

   As seen in Figure 6.6 the total cost curve is broken into three different total cost curves. There is a total cost curve for the first ($0 \leq Q \leq 999$), second ($1,000 \leq Q \leq 1,999$), and third ($Q \geq 2,000$) discount. Look at the total cost (TC) curve for discount 2. $Q*$ for discount 2 is less than the allowable discount range, which is from 1,000 to 1,999 units. As seen in the figure, the lowest allowable quantity in this range, which is 1,000 units, is the quantity that minimizes the total cost. Thus, the second step is needed to ensure that we do not discard an order quantity that may indeed produce the minimum cost. It should be noted that an order quantity computed in step 1 that is greater than the range that would qualify it for a discount may be discarded.

3. Using the total cost equation (Equation 6-12), compute a total cost for every $Q*$ determined in steps 1 and 2. If you had to adjust $Q*$ upward because it was below the allowable quantity range, make sure to use the adjusted value for $Q*$.

4. Select that $Q*$ that has the lowest cost as computed in step 3. It will be the quantity that minimizes the total inventory cost.

Calculate **Q*** *values for each discount.*

IC *is used instead of* C_h.

Next, we adjust the **Q*** *values.*

The total cost curve is broken into parts.

Next, we compute total cost.

We select **Q*** *with lowest total cost.*

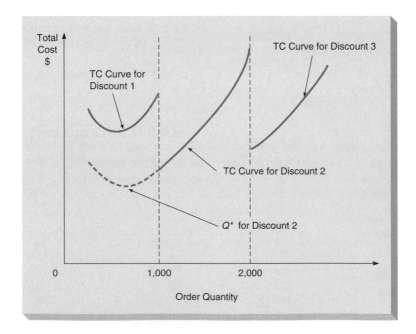

FIGURE 6.6

Total Cost Curve for the Quantity Discount Model

IN ACTION   Telephone Companies Analyze Price Quotations and Quantity Discounts

In many cases, companies buy inventory supplies from several suppliers. This was the case with Bellcore, formed in 1984 to allow the regional Bell operating companies to share common resources. The operating companies, which included Ameritech, Bell Atlantic, BellSouth Telecommunications, NYNEX, Pacific Bell, Southwestern Bell, and US West are often referred to as Bell client companies.

By pooling their resources, the Bell client companies have considerable power over their suppliers. As a result, they decided to select suppliers of required raw materials and inventory based on the availability and amount of quantity discounts and business volume discounts. Whereas a traditional quantity discount is based on the amount of a particular inventory item that is ordered, a business volume discount is based on the total dollar value of all items purchased. With a business volume discount, the supplier typically discounts each item by the same amount in an order.

One major inventory item needed by the Bell client companies is modular circuit boards, so managers of these firms inquired how they could purchase the boards from Bellcore under business volume discounts. The result was a quantitative analysis model, called the Procurement Decision Support System (PDSS), that determines the optimal ordering policy based on the most economical purchase of items under business volume discounts. PDSS was written to run on personal computers. The program allowed Bell client companies to move away from quantity discounts toward business volume discounts.

What is the result of using business volume discounts? PDSS now controls inventory and products worth more than $600 million. The savings for Bell client companies have ranged from about $5 million to $15 million per year.

Source: P. Katz, et al. "Telephone Companies Analyze Price Quotations with Bellcore's PDSS Software," *Interfaces* 24 (January–February 1994): 50–63.

Brass Department Store Example Let's see how this procedure can be applied by showing an example. Brass Department Store stocks toy race cars. Recently, the store was given a quantity discount schedule for the cars; this quantity discount schedule was shown in Table 6.3. Thus, the normal cost for the toy race cars is $5. For orders between 1,000 and 1,999 units, the unit cost is $4.80, and for orders of 2,000 or more units, the unit cost is $4.75. Furthermore, the ordering cost is $49 per order, the annual demand is 5,000 race cars, and the inventory carrying charge as a percentage of cost, I, is 20% or 0.2. What order quantity will minimize the total inventory cost?

The first step is to compute Q^* for every discount in Table 6.3. This is done as follows:

$$Q_1^* = \sqrt{\frac{(2)(5,000)(49)}{(0.2)(5.00)}} = 700 \text{ cars per order}$$

Q* *values are computed.*

$$Q_2^* = \sqrt{\frac{(2)(5,000)(49)}{(0.2)(4.80)}} = 714 \text{ cars per order}$$

$$Q_3^* = \sqrt{\frac{(2)(5,000)(49)}{(0.2)(4.75)}} = 718 \text{ cars per order}$$

Q* *values are adjusted.*

The second step is to adjust those values of Q^* that are below the allowable discount range. Since Q_1^* is between 0 and 999, it does not have to be adjusted. Q_2^* is below the allowable range of 1,000 to 1,999, and therefore, it must be adjusted to 1,000 units. The same is true for Q_3^*; it must be adjusted to 2,000 units. After this step, the following order quantities must be tested in the total cost equation:

$$Q_1^* = 700$$
$$Q_2^* = 1,000\text{—adjusted}$$
$$Q_3^* = 2,000\text{—adjusted}$$

The total cost is computed.   The third step is to use Equation 6-12 and compute a total cost for each of the order quantities. This is accomplished with the aid of Table 6.4.

TABLE 6.4 Total Cost Computations for Brass Department Store

DISCOUNT NUMBER	UNIT PRICE	ORDER QUANTITY	ANNUAL MATERIAL COST ($)	ANNUAL ORDERING COST ($)	ANNUAL CARRYING COST ($)	TOTAL ($)
1	$5.00	700	25,000	350.00	350.00	25,700.00
2	4.80	1,000	24,000	245.00	480.00	24,725.00
3	4.75	2,000	23,750	122.50	950.00	24,822.50

The fourth step is to select that order quantity with the lowest total cost. Looking at Table 6.4, you can see that an order quantity of 1,000 toy race cars minimizes the total cost. It should be recognized, however, that the total cost for ordering 2,000 cars is only slightly greater than the total cost for ordering 1,000 cars. Thus, if the third discount cost is lowered to $4.65, for example, this order quantity might be the one that minimizes the total inventory cost.

Q* is selected.

Using Excel QM for Quantity Discount Problems As seen in the previous analysis, the quantity discount model is more complex than the inventory models discussed so far in this chapter. Fortunately, we can use the computer to simplify the calculations. Program 6.3A shows the Excel formulas and input data needed for Excel QM for the Brass Department Store problem. Program 6.3B provides the solution to this problem, including adjusted order quantities and total costs for each price break.

6.8 USE OF SAFETY STOCK

Safety stock is additional stock that is kept on hand.[2] If, for example, safety stock for an item is 50 units, you are carrying an average of 50 units more of inventory during the year. When demand is unusually high, you dip into the safety stock instead of encountering a *stockout*. Thus, the main purpose of safety stock is to avoid stockouts when the demand is higher than expected. Its use is shown in Figure 6.7. Note that although stockouts can often be avoided by using safety stock, there is still a chance that they may occur. The demand may be so high that all the safety stock is used up, and thus there is still a stockout.

Safety stock helps in avoiding stockouts. It is extra stock kept on hand.

One of the best ways of maintaining a safety stock level is to use the reorder point, ROP. This can be accomplished by adding the number of units of safety stock as a buffer to the reorder point. As you recall,

$$\text{reorder point} = \text{ROP} = d \times L$$

$$d = \text{daily demand}$$

$$L = \text{order lead time or the number of working days it takes to deliver an order}$$

---

[2] Safety stock is used only when demand is uncertain, and models under uncertainty are generally much harder to deal with than models under certainty.

PROGRAM 6.3A

Excel QM's Formulas and the Input Data for the Brass Department Store Quantity Discount Problem

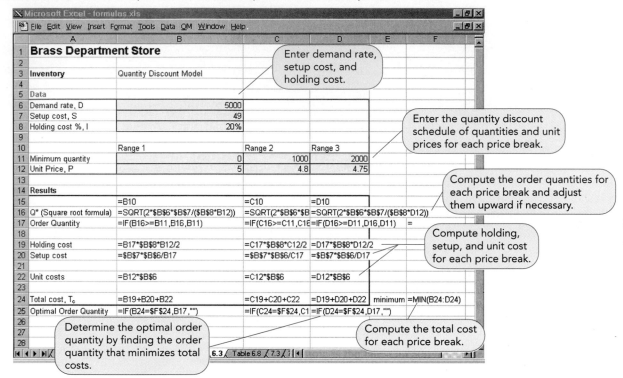

PROGRAM 6.3B

Excel QM's Solution to the Brass Department Store Problem

	A	B	C	D	E	F	G	H
1	**Brass Department Store**							
2								
3	**Inventory**	Quantity Discount Model						
4								
5	Data							
6	Demand rate, D	5000						
7	Setup cost, S	49						
8	Holding cost %, I	20%						
9								
10		Range 1	Range 2	Range 3				
11	Minimum quantity	0	1000	2000				
12	Unit Price, P	5	4.8	4.75				
13								
14	**Results**							
15		Range 1	Range 2	Range 3				
16	Q* (Square root formula)	700	714.434508	718.184846				
17	Order Quantity	700	1000	2000		=		
18								
19	Holding cost	$350.00	$480.00	$950.00				
20	Setup cost	$350.00	$245.00	$122.50				
21								
22	Unit costs	$25,000.00	$24,000.00	$23,750.00				
23								
24	Total cost, T_c	$25,700.00	$24,725.00	$24,822.50	minimum	$24,725.00		
25	Optimal Order Quantity		1000					

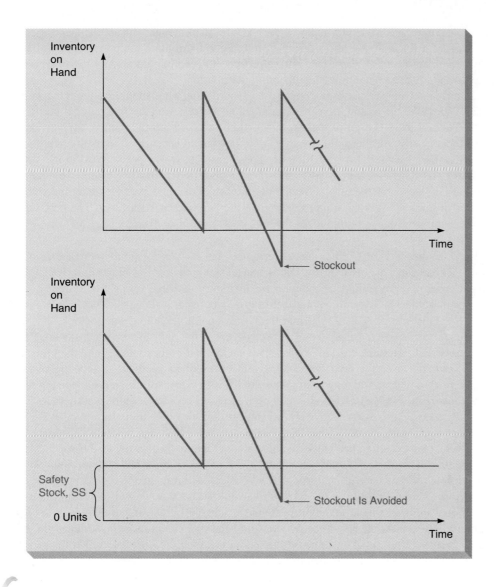

FIGURE 6.7
Use of Safety Stock

With the inclusion of safety stock, the reorder point becomes

$$\text{ROP} = d \times L + \text{SS}$$

where

$$\text{SS} = \text{safety stock} \tag{6-13}$$

Safety stock is included in the reorder point (ROP).

How to determine the correct amount of safety stock is the only remaining question. If cost data are available, the objective is to minimize total cost. If cost data are not available, it is necessary to establish a service level or policy.

Reorder Point with Known Stockout Costs

When the economic order quantity is fixed, and the reorder point is used to place orders, the only time that a stockout can occur is during the lead time. As you recall, the lead time is the time between when the order is placed and when it is received. In the techniques

It is necessary to know the probability of demand.

We use a stockout cost per unit.

The objective is minimizing total cost.

discussed here, it is necessary to know the probability of demand during the lead time and the cost of a stockout. We use a discrete probability distribution to describe the probability of demand over the lead time. This approach, however, could also be modified when the demand follows a continuous probability distribution.

In this section we use a stockout cost per unit. But what should be included in this cost? We make the assumption that if a stockout occurs, we lose forever that particular sale. Thus, if there is a profit margin of $0.10 per unit, we should include this as part of the stockout cost. Furthermore, we lose some customers because of stockouts and therefore lose their business for their lifetime. These costs must also be included in the stockout cost. In general, stockout costs should include all costs that are a direct or indirect result of a stockout. When we know the probability of demand over the lead time and the cost of a stockout, it is possible to determine the best safety stock level. The best safety stock level is the one that minimizes the total cost. Here is an example.

ABCO Example ABCO, Inc., has determined that its reorder point is 50 ($= d \times L$) units. Its carrying cost per unit per year is $5 and stockout cost is $40 per unit. ABCO has experienced the probability distribution for inventory demand during the reorder period shown in Table 6.5. The optimal number of orders per year is 6.[3]

The objective of ABCO is to find the reorder point, including safety stock, that will minimize total expected cost. Total expected cost is the sum of expected stockout cost plus expected additional carrying cost. When we know the stockout cost and the probability of demand over the lead time, the inventory problem becomes a decision making under risk problem. (You may wish to refer to Chapter 3 for a discussion of decision making under risk.) For ABCO, the alternatives are to use a reorder point of 30 (alternative 1), 40 (alternative 2), 50 (alternative 3), 60 (alternative 4), or 70 units (alternative 5). The states of nature are demand values 30 (state of nature 1), 40 (state of nature 2), 50 (state of nature 3), 60 (state of nature 4), or 70 units (state of nature 5) over the lead time.

Stockout and additional carrying costs will be zero when ROP = demand over lead time.

Determining the economic consequences for any alternative and state of nature combination involves a careful analysis of stockout and additional carrying cost. Consider a situation where the reorder point is 30 units. This means that we will place an order for additional units when the inventory on hand reaches 30 units. If the demand over lead time is also 30 units, there will be no stockouts and no extra units on hand when the new order arrives. Thus, stockouts and additional carrying costs will be 0. When the reorder point equals the demand over lead time, total cost will be 0.

TABLE 6.5   **Probability of Demand for ABCO, Inc.**

NUMBER OF UNITS	PROBABILITY
30	0.2
40	0.2
ROP ⟶ 50	0.3
60	0.2
70	0.1
	1.0

---

[3] We have assumed that we already know Q^* and ROP. If this assumption is not made, the values of Q^*, ROP, and safety stock would have to be determined simultaneously. This requires a more complex solution.

Consider what happens when the reorder point is 30 units but the demand is 40 units. In this case we will be 10 units short. The cost of this stockout situation is $2,400 ($2,400 = 10 units short × $40 per stockout × 6 orders per year). Note that we have to multiply the stockout cost per unit and the number of units short times the number of orders per year (6 in this case) to determine *annual* expected stockout cost. If the reorder point is 30 units and the demand over lead time is 50 units, the stockout cost will be $4,800 ($4,800 = 20 units short × $40 × 6). When the demand over lead time is 60 units, the stockout cost will be $7,200, and it will be $9,600 when demand over lead time is 70 units. In general, when the reorder point is less than demand over lead time, total cost is equal to stockout cost.

Total cost = stockout cost = number of units short × stockout cost per unit × number of orders per year (When the reorder point *is less than* demand over lead time).

Now consider a reorder point of 70 units. As before, if demand over lead time is also 70, the total cost is 0. If the demand over lead time is 60 units, we will have 10 additional units on hand when the new inventory is received. If this situation continues during the year, we will have 10 additional units on hand on average. The additional carrying cost is $50($50 = 10 additional units × $5 carrying cost per unit per year). If the demand over lead time is 50 units, we will have 20 additional units on hand when the new inventory arrives (20 = 70 − 50). If this situation continues during the year, the additional carrying cost will be $100 ($100 = 20 additional units × $5 per unit per year). When the reorder point is greater than the demand over lead time, total costs will be equal to total additional carrying costs.

Total cost = total additional carrying cost = number of surplus units × the carrying cost (When the reorder point *is greater than* the expected demand over the lead time).

Using the procedures described previously, we can compute the economic consequence for every alternative state of nature combination. The results are presented in Table 6.6.

Figure 6.8 graphically shows that the best alternative is a reorder point of 70 units with an EMV of $110.

TABLE 6.6 **ABCO's Stockout Costs: The Economic Consequences of Every Alternative and State of Nature**

PROBABILITY	0.20	0.20	0.30	0.20	0.10	
STATE OF NATURE ALTERNATIVE	30	40	50	60	70	EMV
30	$ 0	$2,400	$4,800	$7,200	$9,600	$4,320
40	50	0	2,400	4,800	7,200	$2,410
50	100	50	0	2,400	4,800	$990
60	150	100	50	0	2,400	$305
70	200	150	100	50	0	$110

FIGURE 6.8

EMVs for Each Reorder Point

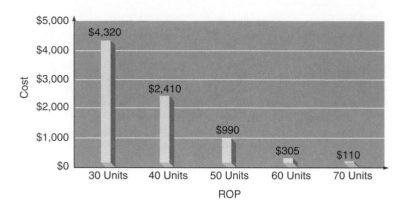

Safety Stock with Unknown Stockout Costs

Determining stockout costs may be difficult or impossible.

When stockout costs are not available or if they do not apply, the preceding type of analysis cannot be used. Actually, there are many situations when stockout costs are unknown or extremely difficult to determine. For example, let's assume that you run a small bicycle shop that sells mopeds and bicycles with a one-year service warranty. Any adjustments made within the year are done at no charge to the customer. If the customer comes in for maintenance under the warranty, and you do not have the necessary part, what is the stockout cost? It cannot be lost profit because the maintenance is done free of charge. Thus, the major stockout cost is the loss of goodwill. The customer may not buy another bicycle from your shop if you have a poor service record. In this situation, it could be very difficult to determine the stockout cost. In other cases, a stockout cost may simply not apply. What is the stockout cost for lifesaving drugs in a hospital? The drug may only cost $10 per bottle. Is the stockout cost $10? Is it $100 or $10,000? Perhaps the stockout cost should be $1 million. What is the cost when a life may be lost as a result of not having the drug?

An alternative approach to determining safety stock levels is to use a *service level*. In general, a service level is the percent of the time that you will not be out of stock of a particular item. Stated in other terms, the chance or probability of having a stockout is 1 minus the service level. This relationship is expressed as

service level $= 1 -$ probability of a stockout

or

probability of a stockout $= 1 -$ service level

An alternative to determining safety stock is to use service level and the normal distribution.

To determine the safety stock level, it is only necessary to know the probability of demand during the lead time and the desired service level. Here is an example of how the safety stock level can be determined when the probability of demand over the lead time follows a normal curve.

Hinsdale Company Example The Hinsdale Company carries an inventory item that has a normally distributed demand during the reorder period. The mean (average) demand is 350 units and the standard deviation is 10. Hinsdale wants to follow a policy that results in stockouts occurring only 5% of the time. How much safety stock should be maintained? Figure 6.9 may help you to visualize the example.

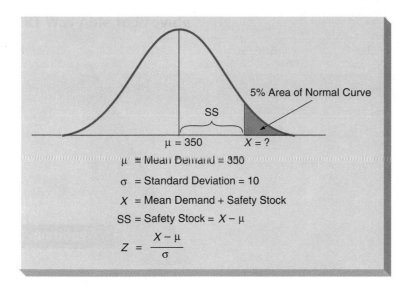

FIGURE 6.9
Safety Stock and the Normal
Distribution

We use the properties of a standardized normal curve to get a Z value for an area under the normal curve of $0.95 = (1 - 0.05)$. Using a normal table (see Appendix A), we find a Z value of 1.65.

$$Z = 1.65$$

Z is also equal to $\dfrac{X - \mu}{\sigma} = \dfrac{SS}{\sigma}$

$$Z = 1.65 = \frac{SS}{\sigma}$$

Solving for safety stock gives the following (because stock is usually in integer amounts):

SS = 1.65(10) = 16.5 units, or 17 units

Different safety stock levels will be generated for different *service levels*. The relationship between service levels and safety stock, however, is not linear. As the service level increases, the safety stock increases at an increasing rate. Indeed, at service levels greater than 97%, the safety stock becomes very large. Of course, high levels of safety stock mean higher carrying costs. If you are using a service level, you should be aware of how much your service level is costing you in terms of carrying the safety stock in inventory. Let's assume that Hinsdale has a carrying cost of $1 per unit per year. What is the carrying cost for service levels that range from 90% to 99.99%? This cost information is summarized in Table 6.7.

A safety stock level is determined for each service level.

Table 6.7 is developed by looking in the normal curve table for every service level. Finding the service level in the body of the table, we can obtain the Z value from the table in the standard way. Next, the Z values must be converted into the safety stock units. As you recall, the standard deviation of sales during lead time for Hinsdale is 10. Therefore, the relationship between Z and the safety stock can be developed as follows:

1. We know that $Z = \dfrac{X - \mu}{\sigma}$.

2. We also know that $SS = X - \mu$.

TABLE 6.7   **Cost of Different Service Levels**

SERVICE LEVEL (%)	Z VALUE FROM NORMAL CURVE TABLE	SAFETY STOCK (UNITS)	CARRYING COST ($)
90	1.28	12.8	12.80
91	1.34	13.4	13.40
92	1.41	14.1	14.10
93	1.48	14.8	14.80
94	1.55	15.5	15.50
95	1.65	16.5	16.50
96	1.75	17.5	17.50
97	1.88	18.8	18.80
98	2.05	20.5	20.50
99	2.33	23.3	23.20
99.99	3.72	37.2	37.20

FIGURE 6.10

Service Level versus Annual Carrying Costs

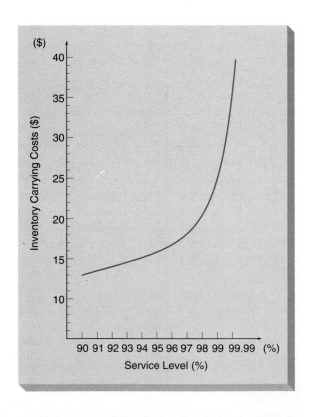

3. Thus, we can rewrite Z as $Z = \dfrac{SS}{\sigma}$.

4. By transposing terms, we have

$$SS = Z\sigma = (Z)(10) \tag{6-14}$$

Thus, the safety stock can be determined by multiplying the Z values by 10. Since the carrying cost is \$1 per unit per year, the carrying cost is the same numerically as the safety stock. A graph of the carrying cost as a function of service level is given in Figure 6.10.

As you can see from Figure 6.10, the carrying cost is increasing at an increasing rate. Moreover, the carrying cost gets extremely large when the service level is greater than 98%. Therefore, as you are setting service levels, you should be aware of the additional carrying cost that you will encounter. Although Figure 6.10 was developed for a specific case, the general shape of the curve is the same for all service-level problems.

Carrying cost increases at an increasing rate as the service level increases.

6.9 ABC ANALYSIS

Earlier, we showed how to develop inventory policies using quantitative techniques. There are also some very *practical* considerations that should be incorporated into inventory decisions, such as ABC analysis.

The purpose of ABC analysis is to divide all of a company's inventory items into three groups, the A group, the B group, and the C group. Then, depending on the group, it is necessary to decide how the inventory levels should be controlled in general. ABC analysis recognizes the fact that some inventory items are more important than others. A brief description of each group follows, with general guidelines as to which items are A, B, and C.

The inventory items in the A group are critical to the functioning and operation of the organization. As a result, their inventory levels must be monitored carefully. These items typically make up more than 70% of the company's *business in dollars.* Usually, they are only 10% of all inventory items. In other words, *a few inventory items are very important to the company.* As a result, the inventory control techniques discussed in this chapter should be used where appropriate for every item in the A group (refer to Table 6.8).

The items in the A group are critical.

The items in the B group are important to the organization, but they are not critical. Thus, it may not be necessary to monitor the levels of all of these items constantly. B-group items typically represent about 20% of the company's business and comprise about 20% of the items in inventory. Quantitative inventory models should be used on only some of the items. The cost of implementing and using a quantitative inventory control technique must be carefully balanced with the benefits of better inventory control. Usually, less than half of the B-group items are carefully controlled through the use of quantitative inventory control techniques.

The B-group items are important.

The items in the C group are not as important to the operation of the organization. These items represent perhaps only 10% of the company's business in dollars. They might, however, comprise 70% of the items in inventory. In other words, there are a large

The C-group items are not as important in terms of annual dollar value.

TABLE 6.8 **Summary of ABC Analysis**

INVENTORY GROUP	DOLLAR USAGE (%)	INVENTORY ITEMS (%)	ARE QUANTITATIVE CONTROL TECHNIQUES USED?
A	70	10	Yes
B	20	20	In some cases
C	10	70	No

number of inventory items that represent a small amount of business. Group C could include inexpensive items such as bolts, washers, screws, and so forth. They are not controlled using quantitative inventory techniques, for the cost of implementing and using these techniques would exceed the value gained.

6.10   SENSITIVITY ANALYSIS

Earlier in this chapter we developed formulas that can be used to solve directly for Q^*. The formulas for all of the inventory models assume that all input values are known with certainty. What would happen, though, if one of the input values changed—for example, the cost of placing an order rises by $5?

The answer is that if any of the values used in one of the formulas changes, the optimal value changes also. Determining the effect of these changes is called *sensitivity analysis*. One approach to sensitivity analysis is to recalculate the optimal quantity when one of the inputs changes.

In Section 6.4 we introduced Sumco, a company that sells pump housings. Let us use their data again to illustrate sensitivity analysis. For example, how would the order quantity be affected if Sumco's cost of placing an order were actually $40 instead of $10? Assume that the annual demand for Sumco pump housings is still the same, namely, $D = 1,000$ units and that the carrying cost is $0.50 per unit per year.

$$Q^* = \sqrt{\frac{2DC_0}{C_h}} = \sqrt{\frac{2(1,000)(40)}{0.50}} = \sqrt{160,000}$$

$$= 400 \text{ units}$$

When the ordering cost increases by a multiple of 4, the order quantity doubles.

Thus, when the ordering cost *increases* by a *multiple of 4*, the optimal order quantity *doubles*.

To determine how sensitive the optimal solution is to a change in one of the variables in an equation, it is not always necessary to recalculate the order quantity Q^* completely. Usually, it is possible to determine the effect of a change in the optimal quantity by inspecting the basic EOQ formula.

 IN ACTION   **Blue Bell Trims Its Inventory**

In the mid-1980s, the largest Blue Bell business was the Wrangler Group. Wrangler manufactures denim and corduroy jeans and several other product lines in sports and casual apparel. In basic styles of men's jeans, Wrangler makes 35 million pairs of jeans a year in 37 plants. There are over 10,000 individual stock-keeping units (called SKUs) manufactured and stocked.

One task Blue Bell faced was to find a better balance of the cost of carrying inventory against the risk of shortages. Data analysis showed that inventory had not been well balanced at the SKU level. Some SKUs showed months of supply, whereas others were out of stock. Thus, unless a systematic approach could be developed to achieve a "balanced" inventory consistently at the SKU level, it would be difficult for Blue Bell to attain a dramatic reduction in inventory.

When this effort began, the economic and competitive pressures that Blue Bell faced were severe. The high cost of carrying inventory had become particularly acute. Short-term interest rates were hovering at 20%, and as a result, net interest expenses for Blue Bell had ballooned. Financing inventory had dramatically pushed up Blue Bell's cost of doing business.

Management science provided the means for senior executives and other managers to take effective action swiftly to turn the situation around. A new production planning process was designed, tested, and implemented that reduced inventories more than 31% (from $371 million to $256 million) without a decrease in sales or customer service. The new process also reduced manufacturing costs by approximately $1 million. The strong support of top management was a major factor in this achievement, and that support was communicated down the line so that employees at every level became enthusiastically involved.

Source: J. R. Edwards, H. M. Wagner, and W. P. Wood. *Interfaces* 15, 1 (January–February 1985): 34–52.

Let us look at the formula for Q^* derived previously. What effect would the following individual changes have on the value of Q^*?

1. Ordering cost increases by a factor of 4.

2. Carrying cost increases by a factor of 4.

3. The total number of pieces of inventory sold per year (or the annual demand) decreases by a factor of 9.

The EOQ formula is given as

$$Q^* = \sqrt{\frac{2DC_0}{C_h}}$$

The following shortcuts can be used to test the effect of the changes listed.

1. The optimal order quantity will increase by a factor of 2 when C_0 increases by a factor of 4. To see this we simply replace C_0 in the formula by an ordering cost of 4 times that number, namely $4C_0$.

$$Q^* = 2\sqrt{\frac{2D(4)(C_0)}{C_h}}$$

Bringing the number 4 outside the square root sign yields

$$Q^* = 2\sqrt{\frac{2DC_0}{C_h}} = 2 \times \text{(previous optimal order quantity)}$$

2. The optimal order quantity will decrease by a factor of ½ when C_h increases by a factor of 4.

$$Q^* = \sqrt{\frac{2DC_0}{(4)(C_h)}}$$

$$= \frac{1}{2}\sqrt{\frac{2DC_0}{C_h}} = \frac{1}{2} \times \text{(previous optimal order quantity)}$$

3. The optimal order size will decrease by a factor of ⅓ (or become ⅓ of what it was before) when D decreases by a factor of 9.

$$Q^* = \sqrt{\frac{2(\frac{1}{9})(D)C_0}{C_h}}$$

$$= \frac{1}{3}\sqrt{\frac{2DC_0}{C_h}} = \frac{1}{3} \times \text{(previous optimal order quantity)}$$

In each of these, we note that the optimal value of Q^* changes by the square root of the change in a variable used in the formula.

Summary

In this chapter we introduced the fundamentals of inventory control theory. We showed that the two most important problems are (1) how much to order, and (2) when to order.

We investigated the economic order quantity, which determines how much to order, and the reorder point, which determines when to order. In addition, we explored the use of sensitivity analysis to determine what happens to computations when one or more of the values used in one of the equations changes.

The basic EOQ inventory model presented in this chapter makes a number of assumptions: (1) known and constant demand and lead times, (2) instantaneous receipt of inventory, (3) no quantity discounts, (4) no stockouts or shortages, and (5) the only variable costs are ordering costs and carrying costs. If these assumptions are valid, the EOQ inventory model provides optimal solutions. On the other hand, if these assumptions do not hold, the basic EOQ model does not apply. In these cases, more complex models are needed, including the production run, quantity discount, and safety stock models. We also presented ABC analysis to determine what inventory to control.

Glossary

Economic Order Quantity (EOQ). The amount of inventory ordered that will minimize the total inventory cost. It is also called the optimal order quantity, or Q^*.

Average Inventory. The average inventory on hand. In this chapter the average inventory is $Q/2$.

Reorder Point (ROP). The number of units on hand when an order for more inventory is placed.

Lead Time. The time it takes to receive an order after it is placed (called L in the chapter).

Instantaneous Inventory Receipt. A system in which inventory is received or obtained at one point in time and not over a period of time.

Production Run Model. An inventory model in which inventory is produced or manufactured instead of being ordered or purchased. This model eliminates the instantaneous receipt assumption.

Annual Setup Cost. The cost to set up the manufacturing or production process for the production run model.

Quantity Discount. The cost per unit when large orders of an inventory item are placed.

Safety Stock. Extra inventory that is used to help avoid stockouts.

Stockout. A situation that occurs when there is no inventory on hand.

Safety Stock with Known Stockout Costs. An inventory model in which the probability of demand during lead time and the stockout cost per unit are known.

Safety Stock with Unknown Stockout Costs. An inventory model in which the probability of demand during lead time is known. The stockout cost is not known.

Service Level. The chance, expressed as a percent, that there will not be a stockout. Service level = 1 − probability of a stockout.

ABC Analysis. An analysis that divides inventory into three groups. Group A is more important than group B, which is more important than group C.

Sensitivity Analysis. The process of determining how sensitive the optimal solution is to changes in the values used in the equations.

Key Equations

(6-1) Average inventory level = $Q/2$

(6-2) $Q^* = \sqrt{\dfrac{2DC_0}{C_h}}$

The economic order quantity.

(6-3) $\text{TC} = \dfrac{D}{Q}C_0 + \dfrac{Q}{2}C_h$

Total inventory cost.

(6-4) Average dollar level $= \dfrac{PQ}{2}$

(6-5) $Q^* = \sqrt{\dfrac{2DC_0}{IP}}$

The economic order quantity using the carrying cost, I, as a percentage of price, P.

(6-6) $\text{ROP} = d \times L$

The reorder point, where d is the daily demand and L is the lead time in days.

(6-10) $Q^1 = \sqrt{\dfrac{2DC_0}{C_h\left(1 - \dfrac{d}{p}\right)}}$

Order quantity when inventory is received over time.

(6-11) $Q_p^* = \sqrt{\dfrac{2DC_s}{C_h\left(1 - \dfrac{d}{p}\right)}}$

Optimal production quantity.

(6-12) $\text{TC} = DC + \dfrac{D}{Q}C_0 + \dfrac{Q}{2}C_h$

Total inventory cost with quantity discounts.

(6-13) $\text{ROP} = d \times L + \text{SS}$

Reorder point with safety stock.

(6-14) $\text{SS} = Z\sigma$

Safety stock using the normal curve.

Solved Problems

Solved Problem 6-1

Patterson Electronics supplies microcomputer circuitry to a company that incorporates microprocessors into refrigerators and other home appliances. Currently, Patterson orders components from various suppliers. One of the components is ordered in batches of 150 units. It has been estimated that annual demand for these components is 250. Furthermore, carrying cost is estimated to be $1 per unit per year. For the order policy to be optimal, determine what the ordering cost would have to be.

Solution

The data for Patterson Electronics can be summarized as follows:

$Q = 150$ units

$D = 250$ units

$C_h = \$1$

Given an annual demand of 250, a carrying cost of $1, and an order quantity of 150, Patterson Electronics must determine what the ordering cost would have to be for the order policy of 150 units to be optimal. To find the answer to this problem, we must solve the traditional economic order quantity equation for the ordering cost. As you can see in the calculations that follow, an ordering cost of $45 is needed for the order quantity of 150 units to be optimal.

$$Q = \sqrt{\frac{2DC_0}{C_h}}$$

$$C_0 = Q^2 \frac{C_h}{2D}$$

$$= \frac{(150)^2(1)}{2(250)}$$

$$= \frac{22,500}{500} = \$45$$

Solved Problem 6-2

Flemming Accessories produces paper slicers used in offices and in art stores. The minislicer has been one of its most popular items: Annual demand is 6,750 units. Kristen Flemming, owner of the firm, produces the minislicers in batches. On average, Kristen can manufacture 125 minislicers per day. Demand for these slicers during the production process is 30 per day. The setup cost for the equipment necessary to produce the minislicers is $150. Carrying costs are $1 per minislicer per year. How many minislicers should Kristen manufacture in each batch?

Solution

The data for Flemming Accessories are summarized as follows:

$D = 6,750$ units

$C_s = \$150$

$C_h = \$1$

$d = 30$ units

$p = 125$ units

This is a production run problem that involves a daily production rate and a daily demand rate. The appropriate calculations are shown here:

$$Q_p^* = \sqrt{\frac{2DC_s}{C_h(1 - d/p)}}$$

$$= \sqrt{\frac{2(6,750)(150)}{1(1 - 30/125)}}$$

$$= 1,632$$

Solved Problem 6-3

Dorsey Distributors has an annual demand for a metal detector of 1,400. The cost of a typical detector to Dorsey is $400. Carrying cost is estimated to be 20% of the unit cost, and the ordering cost is $25 per order. If Dorsey orders in quantities of 300 or more, it can get a 5% discount on the cost of the detectors. Should Dorsey take the quantity discount?

Solution

The solution to any quantity discount model involves determining the total cost of each alternative after quantities have been computed and adjusted for the original problem and every discount. We start the analysis with no discount:

$$\text{EOQ (no discount)} = \sqrt{\frac{2(1,400)(25)}{0.2(400)}}$$

$$= 29.6 \text{ units}$$

$$\text{Total cost (no discount)} = \text{material cost} + \text{ordering cost} + \text{carrying cost}$$

$$= \$400(1,400) + \frac{1,400(25)}{29.6} + \frac{29.6(\$400)(0.2)}{2}$$

$$= \$560,000 + \$1,183 + \$1,183 = \$562,366$$

The next step is to compute the total cost for the discount:

$$\text{EOQ (with discount)} = \sqrt{\frac{2(1,400)(25)}{0.2(\$380)}}$$

$$= 30.3 \text{ units}$$

$$\text{EOQ (adjusted)} = 300 \text{ units}$$

Because this last economic order quantity is below the discounted price, we must adjust the order quantity to 300 units. The next step is to compute total cost.

$$\text{Total cost (with discount)} = \text{material cost} + \text{ordering cost} + \text{carrying cost}$$

$$= \$380(1,400) + \frac{1,400(25)}{300} + \frac{300(\$380)(0.2)}{2}$$

$$= \$532,000 + \$117 + \$11,400 = \$543,517$$

The optimal strategy is to order 300 units at a total cost of $543,517.

SELF-TEST

- Before taking the self-test, refer back to the learning objectives at the beginning of the chapter, the notes in the margins, and the glossary at the end of the chapter.
- Use the key at the back of the book to correct your answers.
- Restudy pages that correspond to any questions that you answered incorrectly or material you feel uncertain about.

1. The following is not a basic component of an inventory control system.
   a. planning what inventory to stock and how to acquire it
   b. forecasting the demand for parts and products
   c. organizing the internal inventory users and explaining how they can help control inventory costs
   d. controlling inventory levels
   e. developing and implementing feedback measurements for revising plans and forecasts
2. The following is not a valid use of inventory.
   a. the decoupling function
   b. an inflation hedge
   c. smooth out irregular (cyclical) supply and demand
   d. the interlocutory function
   e. to achieve quantity discounts
3. The inventory decision may be summarized by two questions:
   a. to make or buy and how much
   b. how much and when to order
   c. how much to pay and when to order
   d. to make or buy and when to take quantity discounts
   e. none of the above
4. The economic order quantity (EOQ)
   a. has been around since 1915.
   b. is the same as the optimum order quantity ($Q*$).
   c. is designed to minimize the total of carrying costs and ordering costs per year (or similar time period).
   d. is that order quantity where the absolute value of the slopes of the ordering and the carrying cost curves are equal.
   e. all of the above.
5. The average inventory level in the basic EOQ model used in this chapter is
   a. one-half of the order quantity.
   b. that quantity on hand one-half of the way between order receipts.
   c. one-half way between the maximum inventory level and the minimum inventory level.
   d. all of the above.
6. For the production run model
   a. the quantity in inventory is presumed never to equal the order size.
   b. inventory is assumed to grow at a rate equal to the daily production rate minus the daily usage rate while the product is being produced.

c. a different optimum order size is computed from that which would have been calculated if the order were purchased from an outside supplier.
   d. all of the above.
   e. none of the above.
7. For both the basic economic order quantity model and for the production run model
   a. the average inventory is equal to one-half of the maximum inventory.
   b. the average inventory is equal to one-half of the order size.
   c. the total annual carrying cost will be identical if the optimum order size is identical.
   d. all of the above.
   e. none of the above.
8. The quantity discount model
   a. requires the minimization of the annual costs of the product and the annual ordering cost and the annual carrying cost.
   b. indicates that quantity at which it would be worthwhile taking advantage of the discount.
   c. indicates how much of a discount is necessary to save money by ordering enough to achieve the next quantity discount.
   d. can be used for only one or two quantity discount amounts.
9. The carrying cost per unit
   a. is calculated in the same manner (per unit cost times the number of units per year) for both the basic optimum order quantity model and for the production run model.
   b. is calculated as a percentage of the cost of the item in the quantity discount model.
   c. is calculated at zero for the stockout *periods* of time in the stockout model computation.
   d. all of the above.
10. _____ is additional stock that is kept on hand in case demand is greater than expected.
11. _____ is 1 minus the probability of a stockout.
12. The purpose of _____ is to divide all of a company's stock into three groups.

Discussion Questions and Problems

Discussion Questions

6-1 Why is inventory an important consideration for managers?

6-2 What is the purpose of inventory control?

6-3 Under what circumstances can inventory be used as a hedge against inflation?

6-4 Why wouldn't a company always store large quantities of inventory to eliminate shortages and stockouts?

6-5 Describe the major decisions that must be made in inventory control.

6-6 What are some of the assumptions made in using the economic order quantity?

6-7 Discuss the major inventory costs that are used in determining the economic order quantity.

6-8 What are some of the methods that are used in actually determining the equation for the economic order quantity?

6-9 What is the reorder point? How is it determined?

6-10 What is the purpose of sensitivity analysis?

6-11 What assumptions are made in the production run model?

6-12 What happens to the production run model when the daily production rate becomes very large?

6-13 In the quantity discount model, why is the carrying cost expressed as a percentage of the unit cost, I, instead of the cost per unit per year, C_h?

6-14 Briefly describe what is involved in solving a quantity discount model.

6-15 Discuss the methods that are used in determining safety stock when the stockout cost is known and when the stockout cost is unknown.

6-16 Briefly describe what is meant by ABC analysis. What is the purpose of this inventory technique?

Problems*

6-17 Lila Battle has determined that the annual demand for number 6 screws is 100,000 screws. Lila, who works in her brother's hardware store, is in charge of purchasing. She estimates that it costs $10 every time an order is placed. This cost includes her wages, the cost of the forms used in placing the order, and so on. Furthermore, she estimates that the cost of carrying one screw in inventory for a year is one-half of 1 cent. How many number 6 screws should Lila order at a time?

6-18 It takes approximately 8 working days for an order of number 6 screws to arrive once the order has been placed. (Refer to Problem 6-17). The demand for number 6 screws is fairly constant, and on the average, Lila has observed that her brother's hardware store sells 500 of these screws each day. Because the demand is fairly constant, Lila believes that she can avoid stockouts completely if she only orders the number 6 screws at the correct time. What is the reorder point?

6-19 Lila's brother believes that she places too many orders for screws per year. He believes that an order should be placed only twice per year. If Lila follows her brother's policy, how much more would this cost every year over the ordering policy that she developed in Problem 6-17? If only two orders were placed each year, what effect would this have on the reorder point (ROP)?

---

*Note: ⌨ means the problem may be solved with QM for Windows; ✖ means the problem may be solved with Excel QM; and ✖⌨ means the problem may be solved with QM for Windows and/or Excel QM.

6-20 Barbara Bright is the purchasing agent for West Valve Company. West Valve sells industrial valves and fluid control devices. One of the most popular valves is the Western, which has an annual demand of 4,000 units. The cost of each valve is $90, and the inventory carrying cost is estimated to be 10% of the cost of each valve. Barbara has made a study of the costs involved in placing an order for any of the valves that West Valve stocks, and she has concluded that the average ordering cost is $25 per order. Furthermore, it takes about two weeks for an order to arrive from the supplier, and during this time the demand per week for West valves is approximately 80.

    (a) What is the economic order quantity?

    (b) What is the reorder point?

    (c) What is the total annual inventory cost (carrying cost + ordering cost)?

6-21 Ken Ramsing has been in the lumber business for most of his life. Ken's biggest competitor is Pacific Woods. Through many years of experience, Ken knows that the ordering cost for an order of plywood is $25 and that the carrying cost is 25% of the unit cost. Both Ken and Pacific Woods receive plywood in loads that cost $100 per load. Furthermore, Ken and Pacific Woods use the same supplier of plywood, and Ken was able to find out that Pacific Woods orders in quantities of 4,000 loads at a time. Ken also knows that 4,000 loads is the economic order quantity for Pacific Woods. What is the annual demand in loads of plywood for Pacific Woods?

6-22 Shoe Shine is a local retail shoe store located on the north side of Centerville. Annual demand for a popular sandal is 500 sandals, and John Dirk, the owner of Shoe Shine, has been in the habit of ordering 100 sandals at a time. John estimates that the ordering cost is $10 per order. The cost of the sandal is $5. For John's ordering policy to be correct, what would the carrying cost as a percentage of the unit cost have to be? If the carrying cost were 10% of the cost, what would the optimal order quantity be?

6-23 In Problem 6-17 you helped Lila Battle determine the optimal order quantity for number 6 screws. She had estimated that the ordering cost was $10 per order. At this time, though, she believes that this estimate was too low. Although she does not know the exact ordering cost, she believes that it could be as high as $40 per order. How would the optimal order quantity change if the ordering cost were $20, $30, and $40?

6-24 Annual demand for the Doll two-drawer filing cabinet is 50,000 units. Bill Doll, president of Doll Office Suppliers, controls one of the largest office supply stores in Nevada. He estimates that the ordering cost is $10 per order. The carrying cost is $4 per unit per year. It takes 25 days between the time that Bill places an order for the two-drawer filing cabinets and the time when they are received at his warehouse. During this time, the daily demand is estimated to be 250 units.

    (a) What is the economic order quantity?

    (b) What is the reorder point?

    (c) What is the optimal number of orders per year?

6-25 Pampered Pet, Inc., is a large pet store located in Eastwood Mall. Although the store specializes in dogs, it also sells fish, turtle, and bird supplies. Everlast Leader, which is a leather lead for dogs, costs Pampered Pet $7 each. There is an annual demand for 6,000 Everlast Leaders. The manager of Pampered Pet has determined that the ordering cost is $10 per order, and the carrying cost as a percent of the unit cost is 15%. Pampered Pet is now considering a new supplier of Everlast Leaders. Each lead would cost only $6.65, but to get this discount, Pampered Pet would have to buy shipments of 3,000 Everlast Leaders at a time. Should Pampered Pet use the new supplier and take this discount for quantity buying?

6-26 Douglas Boats is a supplier of boating equipment for the states of Oregon and Washington. It sells 5,000 White Marine WM-4 diesel engines every year. These engines are shipped to Douglas in a shipping container of 100 cubic feet, and Douglas Boats keeps the warehouse full of these WM-4 motors. The warehouse can hold 5,000 cubic feet of boating supplies. Douglas estimates that the ordering cost is $10 per order, and the carrying cost is estimated to be $10 per motor per year. Douglas Boats is considering the possibility of expanding the warehouse for the WM-4 motors. How much should Douglas Boats expand, and how much would it be worth for the company to make the expansion?

6-27 Bill Doll (see Problem 6-24) now believes that the carrying cost may be as high as $16 per unit per year. Furthermore, Bill estimates that the lead time is 35 days instead of 25 days. Resolve Problem 6-24 using $16 for the carrying cost with a lead time of 35 days.

6-28 Northern Distributors is a wholesale organization that supplies retail stores with lawn care and household products. One building is used to store Neverfail lawn mowers. The building is 25 feet wide by 40 feet deep by 8 feet high. Anna Young, manager of the warehouse, estimates that about 60% of the warehouse can be used to store the Neverfail lawn mowers. The remaining 40% is used for walkways and a small office. Each Neverfail lawn mower comes in a box that is 5 feet by 4 feet by 2 feet high. The annual demand for these lawn mowers is 12,000, and the ordering cost for Northern Distributors is $30 per order. It is estimated that it costs Northern $2 per lawn mower per year for storage. Northern Distributors is thinking about increasing the size of the warehouse. The company can only do this by making the warehouse deeper. At the present time, the warehouse is 40 feet deep. How many feet of depth should be added on to the warehouse to minimize the annual inventory costs? How much should the company be willing to pay for this addition? Remember that only 60% of the total area can be used to store Neverfail lawn mowers.

6-29 Lisa Surowsky was asked to help in determining the best ordering policy for a new product. Currently, the demand for the new product has been projected to be about 1,000 units annually. To get a handle on the carrying and ordering costs, Lisa prepared a series of average inventory costs. Lisa thought that these costs would be appropriate for the new product. The results are summarized in the following table. These data were compiled for 10,000 inventory items that were carried or held during the year and were ordered 100 times during the last year. Help Lisa determine the economic order quantity.

COST FACTOR	COST ($)	COST FACTOR	COST ($)
Taxes	2,000	Inventory inquiries	450
Processing and inspection	1,500	Warehouse supplies	280
New product development	2,500	Research and development	2,750
Bill paying	500	Purchasing salaries	3,000
Ordering supplies	50	Warehouse salaries	2,800
Inventory insurance	600	Inventory theft	800
Product advertising	800	Purchase order supplies	500
Spoilage	750	Inventory obsolescence	300
Sending purchasing orders	800		

6-30 Melinda Sholer has spent the past few weeks determining inventory costs for Toco, a toy manufacturer located near Taos, New Mexico. She knows that annual demand will be 20,000 units per year and that carrying cost will be $0.50 per unit per year. Ordering cost, on the other hand, can vary from $40 per order to $50 per order. During the past 486 working days, Melinda has observed the following frequency distribution for the ordering cost. Melinda's boss would like Melinda to determine an EOQ value for each possible ordering cost and to determine an EOQ value for the expected ordering cost.

ORDERING COST ($)	FREQUENCY	ORDERING COST ($)	FREQUENCY
40	24	46	64
41	34	47	45
42	44	48	44
43	56	49	23
44	76	50	10
45	66		

6-31 Jan Gentry is the owner of a small company that produces electric scissors used to cut fabric. The annual demand is for 8,000 scissors, and Jan produces the scissors in batches. On the average, Jan can produce 150 scissors per day, and during the production process, demand for scissors has been about 40 scissors per day. The cost to set up the production process is $100, and it costs Jan 30 cents to carry one pair of scissors for one year. How many scissors should Jan produce in each batch?

6-32 Jim Overstreet, inventory control manager for Itex, receives wheel bearings from Wheel-Rite, a small producer of metal parts. Unfortunately, Wheel-Rite can only produce 500 wheel bearings per day. Itex receives 10,000 wheel bearings from Wheel-Rite each year. Since Itex operates 200 working days each year, the average daily demand of wheel bearings by Itex is 50. The ordering cost for Itex is $40 per order, and the carrying cost is 60 cents per wheel bearing per year. How many wheel bearings should Itex order from Wheel-Rite at one time? Wheel-Rite has agreed to ship the maximum number of wheel bearings that it produces each day to Itex when an order has been received.

6-33 North Manufacturing has a demand for 1,000 pumps each year. The cost of a pump is $50. It costs North Manufacturing $40 to place an order, and the carrying cost is 25% of the unit cost. If pumps are ordered in quantities of 200, North Manufacturing can get a 3% discount on the cost of the pumps. Should North Manufacturing order 200 pumps at a time and take the 3% discount?

6-34 Mr. Beautiful, an organization that sells weight training sets, has an ordering cost of $40 for the BB-1 set. (BB-1 stands for Body Beautiful Number 1.) The carrying cost for BB-1 is $5 per set per year. To meet demand, Mr. Beautiful orders large quantities of BB-1 seven times a year. The stockout cost for BB-1 is estimated to be $50 per set. Over the past several years, Mr. Beautiful has observed the following demand during the lead time for BB-1:

DEMAND DURING LEAD TIME	PROBABILITY
40	0.1
50	0.2
60	0.2
70	0.2
80	0.2
90	Total 0.1

The reorder point for BB-1 is 60 units. What level of safety stock should be maintained for BB-1?

6-35 Linder Lechner is in charge of maintaining hospital supplies at General Hospital. During the past year, the mean lead time demand for bandage BX-5 was 60. Furthermore, the standard deviation for BX-5 was 7. Ms. Lechner would like to maintain a 90% service level. What safety stock level do you recommend for BX-5?

6-36 Ralph Janaro simply does not have time to analyze all of the items in his company's inventory. As a young manager, he has more important things to do. The following is a table of six items in inventory along with the unit cost and the demand in units.

IDENTIFICATION CODE	UNIT COST ($)	DEMAND IN UNITS
XX1	5.84	1,200
B66	5.40	1,110
3CPO	1.12	896
33CP	74.54	1,104
R2D2	2.00	1,110
RMS	2.08	961

Which item(s) should be carefully controlled using a quantitative inventory technique, and what item(s) should not be closely controlled?

6-37 The demand for barbeque grills has been fairly large in the past several years, and Home Supplies, Inc., usually orders new barbeque grills five times a year. It is estimated that the ordering cost is $60 per order. The carrying cost is $10 per grill per year. Furthermore, Home Supplies, Inc., has estimated that the stockout cost is $50 per unit. The reorder point is 650 units. Although the demand each year is high, it varies considerably. The demand during the lead time appears in the following table:

DEMAND DURING LEAD TIME	PROBABILITY
600	0.3
650	0.2
700	0.1
750	0.1
800	0.05
850	0.05
900	0.05
950	0.05
1,000	0.05
1,050	0.03
1,100	0.02
	Total 1.00

The lead time is 12 working days. How much safety stock should Home Supplies, Inc., maintain?

6-38 Dillard Travey receives 5,000 tripods annually from Quality Suppliers to meet his annual demand. Dillard runs a large photographic outlet, and the tripods are used primarily with 35-mm cameras. The ordering cost is $15 per order, and the carrying cost is 50 cents per unit per year. Quality is starting a new option for its customers. When an order is placed, Quality will ship one-third of the order every week for three weeks instead of shipping the entire order at one time. Weekly demand over the lead time is 100 tripods.

(a) What is the order quantity if Dillard has the entire order shipped at one time?

(b) What is the order quantity if Dillard has the order shipped over three weeks using the new option from Quality Suppliers, Inc.? To simplify your calculations, assume that the average inventory is equal to one-half of the maximum inventory level for Quality's new option.

(c) Calculate the total cost for each option. What do you recommend?

6-39 Linda Lechner has just been severely chastised for her inventory policy. See Problem 6-35. Sue Surrowski, her boss, believes that the service level should be either 95% or 98%. Compute the safety stock levels for a 95% and a 98% service level. Linda knows that the carrying cost of BX-5 is 50 cents per unit per year. Compute the carrying cost that is associated with a 90%, a 95%, and a 98% service level.

6-40 Quality Suppliers, Inc., has decided to extend its shipping option. Refer to Problem 6-38 for details. Now, Quality Suppliers is offering to ship the amount ordered in five equal shipments once each week. It will take five weeks for this entire order to be received. What are the order quantity and total cost for this new shipping option?

 6-41 Xemex has collected the following inventory data for the six items that it stocks:

ITEM CODE	UNIT COST ($)	ANNUAL DEMAND (UNITS)	ORDERING COST ($)	CARRYING COST AS A PERCENTAGE OF UNIT COST
1	10.60	600	40	20
2	11.00	450	30	25
3	2.25	500	50	15
4	150.00	560	40	15
5	4.00	540	35	16
6	4.10	490	40	17

Lynn Robinson, Xemex's inventory manager, does not feel that all of the items can be controlled. What ordered quantities do you recommend for which inventory product(s)?

 6-42 Georgia Products offers the following discount schedule for its 4- by 8-foot sheets of good-quality plywood:

ORDER	UNIT COST ($)
9 sheets or less	18.00
10 to 50 sheets	17.50
More than 50 sheets	17.25

Home Sweet Home Company orders plywood from Georgia Products. Home Sweet Home has an ordering cost of $45. The carrying cost is 20%, and the annual demand is 100 sheets. What do you recommend?

6-43 Sunbright Citrus Products produces orange juice, grapefruit juice, and other citrus-related items. Sunbright obtains fruit concentrate from a cooperative in Orlando consisting of approximately 50 citrus growers. The cooperative will sell a minimum of 100 cans of fruit concentrate to citrus processors such as Sunbright. The cost per can is $9.90.

Last year, a cooperative developed the Incentive Bonus Program (IBP) to give an incentive to their large customers to buy in quantity. Here is how the incentive bonus program works. If 200 cans of concentrate are purchased, 10 cans of free concentrate are included in the deal. In addition, the names of the companies purchasing the concentrate are added to a drawing for a new personal computer. The personal computer has a value of about $3,000, and currently about 1,000 companies are eligible for this drawing. At 300 cans of concentrate, the cooperative will give away 30 free cans and will also place the company name in the drawing for the personal computer. When the quantity goes up to 400 cans of concentrate, 40 cans of concentrate will be given away free with the order. In addition, the company is also placed in a drawing for the personal computer and a free trip for two. The value of the trip for two is approximately $5,000. About 800 companies are expected to qualify and to be in the running for this trip.

Sunbright estimates that its annual demand for fruit concentrate is 1,000 cans. In addition, the ordering cost is estimated to be $10.00, while the carrying cost is estimated to be 10%, or about $1.00 per unit. The firm is intrigued with the incentive bonus plan. If the company decides that it will keep the car, the trip, or the computer if they are won, what should it do?

6-44 George Grim used to be an accounting professor at a state university. Several years ago, he started to develop seminars and programs for the CPA review course. The CPA review course is a course to help accounting students and others interested in passing the CPA exam. To develop an effective seminar, George developed a number of books and other related materials to help. The main product was the CPA review manual developed by George. The manual was an instant success for his seminars and other seminars and courses across the country. Today, George spends most of his time refining and distributing this CPA review manual. The price of the manual is $45.95. George's total cost to manufacture and produce the manual is $32.90. George wants to avoid stockouts or to develop a stockout policy that would be cost-effective. If there is a stockout on the CPA review manual, George loses the profit from the sale of the manual.

George has determined from past experience that the reorder point from his printer is 400 units, assuming no safety stock. The question that George must answer is how much safety stock he should have as a buffer. On average, George places one order per year for the CPA review manual. The frequency of demand for the CPA review manuals during lead time is as follows:

DEMAND	FREQUENCY	DEMAND	FREQUENCY
300	1	600	4
350	2	650	4
400	2	700	3
450	3	750	2
500	4	800	2
550	5		

George estimates that his carrying cost per unit per year is $7. What level of safety stock should George carry to minimize total inventory costs?

 6-45 George Lindsay sells disks that contain 25 software packages that perform a variety of financial functions, including net present value, internal rate of return, and other financial programs typically used by business students majoring in finance. Depending on the quantity ordered, George offers the following price discounts. The annual demand is 2,000 units on average. His setup cost to produce the disks is $250. He estimates holding costs to be 10% of the price or about $1 per unit per year.

PRICE RANGES	QUANTITY ORDERED		
	FROM	TO	PRICE
	1	500	$10.00
	501	1,000	9.95
	1,001	1,500	9.90
	1,500	2,000	9.85

(a) What is the optimal number of disks to produce at a time?

(b) What is the impact of the following quantity-price schedule on the optimal order quantity?

PRICE RANGES	QUANTITY ORDERED		
	FROM	TO	PRICE
	1	500	$10.00
	501	1,000	9.99
	1,001	1,500	9.98
	1,501	2,000	9.97

Data Set Problems

6-46 Rob Roller has been in charge of inventory policy at Cyclorama, a large retail bicycle shop in Orlando, Florida. He now orders Chrome-Moly frames from Frameco, a local frame supplier. Cyclorama builds each bike by adding different Shimano component groups to each frame. Currently, Cyclorama's annual demand for frames is 2,000 per year. The lead time is 10 days, and the ordering cost per order is $50. The holding cost is estimated to be 25% of the unit cost. Frameco offers the following discounts:

PRICE BREAK	LOWER QUANTITY UNITS	UPPER QUANTITY UNITS	UNIT PRICE ($)
1	0	10	220.00
2	11	20	219.99
3	21	30	219.98
4	31	40	219.97
5	41	50	219.96
6	51	60	219.95
7	61	70	219.94
8	71	80	219.93
9	81	90	219.92
10	91	100	219.91
11	101	110	219.90
12	111	120	219.89
13	121	130	219.88
14	131	140	219.87
15	141		219.86

(a) What are the optimal order quantity and the total inventory cost for Cyclorama given the data?

(b) Rob is optimistic about future demand. If annual demand becomes 3,000 frames, what is the impact on the optimal order quantity?

(c) What is the impact if the annual demand is 4,000 frames?

(d) In general, what happens to the order quantity and total inventory cost as demand increases?

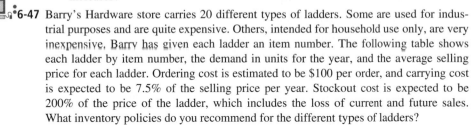 6-47 Barry's Hardware store carries 20 different types of ladders. Some are used for industrial purposes and are quite expensive. Others, intended for household use only, are very inexpensive. Barry has given each ladder an item number. The following table shows each ladder by item number, the demand in units for the year, and the average selling price for each ladder. Ordering cost is estimated to be $100 per order, and carrying cost is expected to be 7.5% of the selling price per year. Stockout cost is expected to be 200% of the price of the ladder, which includes the loss of current and future sales. What inventory policies do you recommend for the different types of ladders?

ITEM NUMBER	DEMAND	PRICE ($)	ITEM NUMBER	DEMAND	PRICE ($)	ITEM NUMBER	DEMAND	PRICE ($)
1	3,200	45	8	5,400	200	15	60	145
2	5,543	23	9	3,456	50	16	230	60
3	123	200	10	456	100	17	1,000	100
4	556	300	11	500	400	18	345	400
5	230	10	12	600	250	19	2,000	10
6	5,600	400	13	34	100	20	5,600	20
7	450	30	14	450	20			

Case Study

Sturdivant Sound Systems

Sturdivant Sound Systems manufactures and sells stereo and CD sound systems in both console and component styles. All parts of the sound systems, with the exception of speakers, are produced in the Rochester, New York, plant. Speakers used in the assembly of Sturdivant's systems are purchased from Morris Electronics of Concord, New Hampshire.

Jason Pierce, purchasing agent for Sturdivant Sound Systems, submits a purchase requisition for the speakers once every four weeks. The company's annual requirements total 5,000 units (20 per working day), and the cost per unit is $60. (Sturdivant does not purchase in greater quantities because Morris Electronics, the supplier, does not offer quantity discounts.) Rarely does a shortage of speakers occur because Morris promises delivery within one week following receipt of a purchase requisition. (Total time between date of order and date of receipt is 10 days.)

Associated with the purchase of each shipment are procurement costs. These costs, which amount to $20 per order, include the costs of preparing the requisition, inspecting and

storing the delivered goods, updating inventory records, and issuing a voucher and a check for payment. In addition to procurement costs, Sturdivant Sound Systems incurs inventory carrying costs, which include insurance, storage, handling, taxes, and so on. These costs equal $6 per unit per year.

Beginning in August of this year, management of Sturdivant Sound Systems will embark on a companywide cost control program in an attempt to improve its profits. One of the areas to be scrutinized closely for possible cost savings is inventory procurement.

Discussion Questions

1. Compute the optimal order quantity.
2. Determine the appropriate reorder point (in units).
3. Compute the cost savings that the company will realize if it implements the optimal inventory procurement decision.
4. Should procurement costs be considered a linear function of the number of orders?

Source: Professor Jerry Kinard, Western Carolina University.

Case Study

Martin-Pullin Bicycle Corporation

Martin-Pullin Bicycle Corp. (MPBC), located in Dallas, is a wholesale distributor of bicycles and bicycle parts. Formed in 1981 by cousins Ray Martin and Jim Pullin, the firm's primary retail outlets are located within a 400-mile radius of the distribution center. These retail outlets receive the order from Martin-Pullin within two days after notifying the distribution center, provided that the stock is available. However, if an order is not fulfilled by the company, no backorder is placed; the retailers arrange to get their shipment from other distributors, and MPBC loses that amount of business.

The company distributes a wide variety of bicycles. The most popular model, and the major source of revenue to the company, is the AirWing. MPBC receives all the models from a single manufacturer overseas, and shipment takes as long as four weeks from the time an order is placed. With the cost of communication, paperwork, and customs clearance included, MPBC estimates that each time an order is placed, it incurs a cost of $65. The purchase price paid by MPBC, per bicycle, is roughly 60% of the suggested retail price for all the styles available, and the inventory carrying cost is 1% per month (12% per year) of the purchase price paid by MPBC. The retail price (paid by the customers) for the AirWing is $170 per bicycle.

MPBC is interested in making the inventory plan for 2000. The firm wants to maintain a 95% service level with its customers to minimize the losses on the lost orders. The data collected for the past two years are summarized in the following table. A forecast for AirWing model sales in the upcoming year 2000 has been developed and will be used to make an inventory plan for MPBC.

Demands for AirWing Model			
MONTH	1998	1999	FORECAST FOR 2000
January	6	7	8
February	12	14	15
March	24	27	31
April	46	53	59
May	75	86	97
June	47	54	60
July	30	34	39
August	18	21	24
September	13	15	16
October	12	13	15
November	22	25	28
December	38	42	47
Total	343	391	439

Discussion Questions

1. Develop an inventory plan to help MPBC.
2. Discuss reorder points and total costs.
3. How can you address demand that is not at the level of the planning horizon?

Source: Professor Kala Chand Seal, Loyola Marymount University.

Case Study

Professional Video Management

Ever since the introduction of the first home video systems for television, Steve Goodman has dreamed about manufacturing his own video system for professionals. During the early years of home video, Steve watched a lot of his favorite old movies on his home video and planned the eventual development of his own video system. He intended it to be used primarily by television stations, advertising agencies, and other individuals and groups that wanted the best in video systems. The overall configuration of this system is shown in Figure 6.11.

The basic system includes a comprehensive control box, two separate videotape systems, a videodisk, and a professional-quality television set. All these devices are fully integrated. In addition, the basic system comes with an elaborate remote control device. This device can operate both video systems, the videodisk, and the TV system with ease. The remote control device works by sending infrared signals to the control box, which in turn controls the other devices in the system.

Steve's unique contribution to the video systems is the control box. The control box is an advanced microprocessor with the ability to coordinate the use and function of the other devices attached to it.

Steve's professional video system has numerous advantages over similar systems. To begin with, special effects can be introduced easily. Images from the videodisk, one of the video systems, and the television system can easily be placed on the other video system. In addition, it is possible to connect the control box to a MacIntosh or PC. This makes it possible to develop attractive graphics on the microcomputer and to transfer them directly to the video system. It is also possible to hook a stereo system to the control box to integrate the highest-quality stereo sound into the system and record it on one of the video systems.

FIGURE 6.11

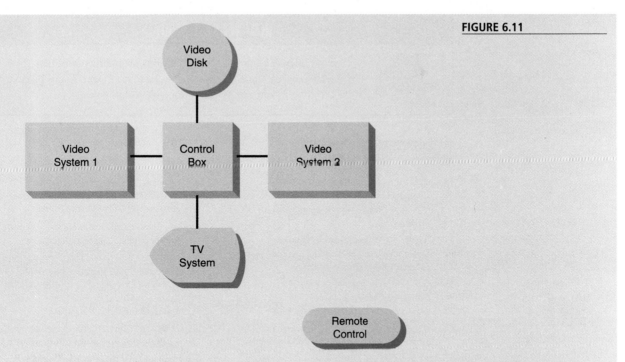

The two video systems also offer remarkable flexibility in editing. Several special editing buttons were placed on the remote control station. It is possible to record a program on one video system first and then edit it by using the other videotape system to add and delete sections. One of the best features of Steve's professional video system is the price. The basic system, including the control box, both video systems, the videodisk, and the television system, has a retail price of $1,995.

Steve found manufacturers for the television system, the control box, and the videodisk system in the United States. Because videotape systems are more popular, Steve had more choices. After extensive research, he was able to eliminate all of the potential suppliers but two. Both of these suppliers are Japanese companies. Toshiki is a new company located outside Tokyo, Japan. Like other suppliers, Toshiki offers quantity discounts. For quantities ranging from 0 to 2,000 units, Toshiki would charge Steve a price of $250 per video system. For quantities that ranged between 2,000 and 8,000 units, the per-unit cost would be $230. For quantities ranging from 8,000 to 20,000 units, the per-unit price of the video systems would be only $210.

The other Japanese supplier is Kony. Although Kony originally started in Japan, also outside Tokyo, it now has offices and manufacturing facilities around the world. One of these manufacturing facilities is located less than 100 miles north of Atlanta, Georgia. Like Toshiki, Kony offers quantity discounts for its videotape systems. For quantities ranging from 0 to 1,000, Kony's per unit cost is $250. For quantities that range from 1,000 to 5,000 units, the unit cost is $240; and for more than 5,000 units, the unit cost drops to $220.

Because Kony has manufacturing facilities located in the United States, the cost to place an order and the delivery time are much more favorable than they are with Toshiki. The estimated per order cost from Kony is $40, and the expected delivery time is two weeks. On the other hand, the ordering cost is higher and the delivery time is longer for Toshiki. The additional paperwork and problems associated with ordering directly from Japan would increase Steve's cost to $90 per order. Furthermore, the delivery time for Toshiki is three months. Steve estimates that his carrying cost would be 30%. This is due primarily to storage and handling costs as well as the potential for technological obsolescence.

For the first year or so of operations, Steve decided to sell only the basic unit: the control box, the television set, the videodisk, and the two videotape systems. The demand for the complete system was fairly constant during the past six months. For example, June sales were 7,970; July sales were 8,070; August sales were 7,950; and September were 8,070; August sales were 7,950; and September sales were 8,010. This demand pattern is expected to continue for the next several months.

Discussion Questions

1. What are the reorder points for Kony and Toshiki?
2. If you were Steve, which company would you choose to supply the videotape systems for your professional video system?
3. Steve is considering several alternative strategies. The first would be to sell all of the components separately. The second strategy would be to modify the control box to allow other videotape systems to be used as well as the videotape systems supplied by Steve. In general, what impact would the adoption of these strategies have on the reorder point and inventory control for Steve?

Bibliography

Badinetti, Ralph D. "Optimal Safety Stock Investment through Subjective Evaluation of Stockout Costs," *Management Science* 17, 3 (1986): 312–328.

Edds, Daniel, "The Real Costs of Quantity Discounts," *School Planning and Management* (March 1998): 37.

Emmons, Hamilton et al. "The Role of Return Policies in Pricing and Decisions," *Management Science* (February 1998): 276.

Gould, Eppen et al, "Backup Agreements in Fashion Buying," *Management Science* (November 1997): 1469.

Greis, Noel. "Assessing Service Level Targets in Production and Inventory Planning," *Decision Sciences* 25, 1 (January–February 1994): 15.

Millet, Ido. "How to Find Inventory by Not Looking," *Interfaces* (March 1995): 69.

Mitra, A., and J. F. Cox. "EOQ Formula: Is It Valid under Inflationary Conditions?" *Decision Sciences* 14, 4 (1983): 360–374.

Noori, A. Hamid, and Gerald Keller. "Lot Size Reorder Point," *Decision Sciences* 17, 3 (Summer 1986): 285–291.

Roundy, Robin. "98% Effective Inter-ration Lot-Sizing for One-Warehouse Multi-retailer Systems," *Management Science* 31, 11 (November 1985): 1416–1430.

Smock, Doug. "Games Tip the Scale at Milton Bradley," *Plastics World* (March 1997): 22.

Sox, Charles et al. "Coordinating Production and Inventory to Improve Service," *Management Science* (September 1997): 1189.

van der Duyn Schouten, Frank, et al. "The Value of Supplier Information to Improve Management of a Retailer's Inventory," *Decision Sciences* 25, 1 (January–February 1994): 1–14.

APPENDIX 6.1: INVENTORY CONTROL WITH QM FOR WINDOWS

A variety of inventory control models were covered in this chapter. Each model made different assumptions and used slightly different approaches. The use of QM for Windows is similar for these different types of inventory problems. As you can see in the inventory menu for QM for Windows, most of the inventory problems discussed in this chapter can be solved using your computer.

To demonstrate QM for Windows, we start with the basic EOQ model. Sumco, a manufacturing company discussed in the chapter, has an annual demand of 1,000 units, an ordering cost of $10 per unit, and a carrying cost of $0.50 per unit per year. With these data we can use QM for Windows to determine the economic order quantity. The results are shown in Program 6.4.

PROGRAM 6.4

QM for Windows Results for EOQ Model

Inventory Results				
Economic Order Quantity Solution				
PARAMETER	VALUE		PARAMETER	VALUE
Demand rate(D)	1000		Optimal order quantity (Q*)	200.
Setup cost(S)	10		Maximum Inventory Level	200.
Holding cost(H)	.5		Average inventory	100.
Unit cost	0		Orders per period(year)	5.
			Annual Setup cost	50.
			Annual Holding cost	50.
			Unit costs (PD)	0.
			Total Cost	100.

The production run inventory problem, which requires the daily production and demand rate in addition to the annual demand, the ordering cost per order, and the carrying cost per unit per year, was also covered in this chapter. Brown's Manufacturing example was used in this chapter to show how the calculations can be made manually. We can use QM for Windows on these data. Program 6.5 shows the results.

Inventory Results				
Production Run Model Solution				
PARAMETER	VALUE		PARAMETER	VALUE
Demand rate(D)	10000		Optimal order quantity (Q')	2,000.
Setup cost(S)	100		Maximum Inventory Level	2,000.
Holding cost(H)	.5		Average inventory	1,000.
Production rate(p)	80		Orders per period(year)	5.
Days per year (D/d)	0		Annual Setup cost	500.
Daily demand rate(d)	60		Annual Holding cost	500.
Unit cost	0			
			Unit costs (PD)	0.
			Total Cost	1,000.

PROGRAM 6.5
QM for Windows Results for the Production Run Model

The quantity discount model allows the material cost to vary with the quantity ordered. In this case the model must consider and minimize material, ordering, and carrying costs. This was done by examining each price discount. Program 6.6 shows how QM for Windows can be used to solve the quantity discount model discussed in the chapter. Note that the program output shows the input data in addition to the results.

Inventory Results					
Quantity Discount Solution					
PARAMETER	VALUE			PARAMETER	VALUE
Demand rate(D)	5000	xxxxxxx	xxxxxxx	Optimal order quantity	1,000.
Setup cost(S)	49	xxxxxxx	xxxxxxx	Maximum Inventory	1,000.
Holding		xxxxxxx	xxxxxxx	Average inventory	500.
				Orders per period(year)	5.
Price Ranges	From	To	Price	Annual Setup cost	122.5
	0	999.	5.	Annual Holding cost	950.
	1000	1,999.	4.8		
	2000	100,000.	4.75	Unit costs (PD)	24,000.
	0	0.	0.	Total Cost	24,725.

PROGRAM 6.6
QM for Windows Results for the Quantity Discount Model

When an organization has a large number of inventory items, ABC analysis is often used. As discussed in this chapter, total dollar volume for an inventory item is one way to determine if quantitative control techniques should be used. Performing the necessary calculations is done in Program 6.7, which shows how QM for Windows can be used to compute dollar volume and determine if quantitative control techniques are justified for each inventory item.

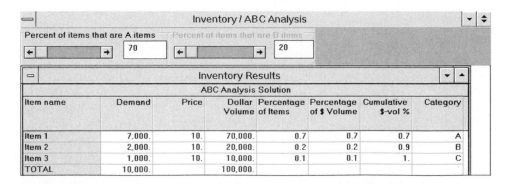

PROGRAM 6.7
QM for Windows Results for ABC Analysis

Inventory / ABC Analysis							
Percent of items that are A items 70				Percent of items that are B items 20			
Inventory Results							
ABC Analysis Solution							
Item name	Demand	Price	Dollar Volume	Percentage of Items	Percentage of $ Volume	Cumulative $-vol %	Category
Item 1	7,000.	10.	70,000.	0.7	0.7	0.7	A
Item 2	2,000.	10.	20,000.	0.2	0.2	0.9	B
Item 3	1,000.	10.	10,000.	0.1	0.1	1.	C
TOTAL	10,000.		100,000.				

CHAPTER 7

Linear Programming Models: Graphical and Computer Methods

LEARNING OBJECTIVES

After completing this chapter, students will be able to:

1. Understand the basic assumptions and properties of linear programming (LP).
2. Graphically solve any LP problem that has only two variables by both the corner point and isoprofit line methods.
3. Understand special issues in LP such as infeasibility, unboundedness, redundancy, and alternative optimal solutions.
4. Understand the role of sensitivity analysis.
5. Use Excel spreadsheets to solve LP problems.

CHAPTER OUTLINE

7.1 Introduction

7.2 Requirements of a Linear Programming Problem

7.3 Formulating LP Problems

7.4 Graphical Solution to an LP Problem

7.5 Solving Flair Furniture's LP Problem Using QM for Windows and Excel

7.6 Solving Minimization Problems

7.7 Summary of the Graphical Solution Methods

7.8 Four Special Cases in LP

7.9 Sensitivity Analysis

Summary • Glossary • Solved Problems • Self-Test • Discussion Questions and Problems • Case Study: Mexicana Wire Works • Internet Case Study • Bibliography

7.1   INTRODUCTION

Linear programming is a technique that helps in resource allocation decisions.

Many management decisions involve trying to make the most effective use of an organization's resources. Resources typically include machinery, labor, money, time, warehouse space, and raw materials. These resources may be used to produce products (such as machinery, furniture, food, or clothing) or services (such as schedules for shipping and production, advertising policies, or investment decisions). *Linear programming* (LP) is a widely used mathematical modeling technique designed to help managers in planning and decision making relative to resource allocation. We devote this and the next two chapters to illustrating how and why linear programming works.

Despite its name, linear programming, and the more general category of techniques called *"mathematical" programming*, have very little to do with computer programming. In the world of management science, *programming* refers to modeling and solving a problem mathematically. Computer programming has, of course, played an important role in the advancement and use of LP. Real-life LP problems are too cumbersome to solve by hand or with a calculator. So throughout the chapters on LP we give examples of how valuable a computer program can be in solving a linear programming problem.

7.2   REQUIREMENTS OF A LINEAR PROGRAMMING PROBLEM

In the past 50 years, LP has been applied extensively to military, industrial, financial, marketing, accounting, and agricultural problems. Even though these applications are diverse, all LP problems have four properties in common.

First LP property: Problems seek to maximize or minimize an objective.

1. All problems seek to *maximize* or *minimize* some quantity, usually profit or cost. We refer to this property as the *objective function* of an LP problem. The major objective of a typical manufacturer is to maximize dollar profits. In the case of a trucking or railroad distribution system, the objective might be to minimize shipping costs. In any event, this objective must be stated clearly and defined mathematically. It does not matter, by the way, whether profits and costs are measured in cents, dollars, or millions of dollars.

Second LP property: Constraints limit the degree to which the objective can be obtained.

2. The second property that LP problems have in common is the presence of restrictions, or *constraints*, that limit the degree to which we can pursue our objective. For example, deciding how many units of each product in a firm's product line to manufacture is restricted by available personnel and machinery. Selection of an advertising policy or a financial portfolio is limited by the amount of money available to be spent or invested. We want, therefore, to maximize or minimize a quantity (the objective function) subject to limited resources (the constraints).

Third LP property: There must be alternatives available.

3. There must be alternative courses of action to choose from. For example, if a company produces three different products, management may use LP to decide how to allocate among them its limited production resources (of personnel, machinery, and so on). Should it devote all manufacturing capacity to make only the first product, should it produce equal amounts of each product, or should it allocate the resources in some other ratio? If there were no alternatives to select from, we would not need LP.

4. The objective and constraints in linear programming problems must be expressed in terms of *linear* equations or inequalities. Linear mathematical relationships just mean that all terms used in the objective function and constraints are of the first degree (that is, not squared, or to the third or higher power, or appearing more than once). Hence, the equation $2A + 5B = 10$ is an acceptable linear function, while the equation $2A^2 + 5B^3 + 3AB = 10$ is not linear because the variable A is squared, the variable B is cubed, and the two variables appear again as a product of each other.

Fourth LP property: Mathematical relationships are linear.

You will see the term *inequality* quite often when we discuss linear programming problems. By inequalities we mean that not all LP constraints need be of the form $A + B = C$. This particular relationship, called an *equation*, implies that the term A plus the term B are together exactly equal to the term C. In most LP problems, we see inequalities of the form $A + B \leq C$ or $A + B \geq C$. The first of these means that A plus B is less than or equal to C. The second means that A plus B is greater than or equal to C. This concept provides a lot of flexibility in defining problem limitations.

An inequality has a $\leq$ or $\geq$ sign.

Basic Assumptions of LP

Technically, there are five additional requirements of an LP problem that you should be aware:

1. We assume that conditions of *certainty* exist; that is, numbers in the objective and constraints are known with certainty and do not change during the period being studied.

2. We also assume that *proportionality* exists in the objective and constraints. This means that if production of 1 unit of a product uses 3 hours of a particular scarce resource, then making 10 units of that product uses 30 hours of the resource.

3. The third technical assumption deals with *additivity*, meaning that the total of all activities equals the sum of the individual activities. For example, if an objective is to maximize profit = $8 per unit of first product made plus $3 per unit of second product made, and if 1 unit of each product is actually produced, the profit contributions of $8 and $3 must add up to produce a sum of $11.

4. We make the *divisibility* assumption that solutions need not be in whole numbers (integers). Instead, they are divisible and may take any fractional value. If a fraction of a product cannot be produced (for example, one-third of a submarine), an *integer programming problem* exists. Integer programming is discussed in more detail in Chapter 11.

5. Finally, we assume that all answers or variables are *nonnegative*. Negative values of physical quantities are impossible; you simply cannot produce a negative number of chairs, shirts, lamps, or computers.

Five technical requirements are (1) certainty, (2) proportionality, (3) additivity, (4) divisibility, and (5) nonnegativity.

HISTORY **How Linear Programming Started**

Linear programming was conceptually developed before World War II by the outstanding Soviet mathematician A. N. Kolmogorov. Another Russian, Leonid Kantorovich, won the Nobel Prize in Economics for advancing the concepts of optimal planning. An early application of linear programming, by Stigler in 1945, was in the area we today call "diet problems."

Major progress in the field, however, took place in 1947 and later when George D. Dantzig developed the solution procedure known as the *simplex algorithm*. Dantzig, then an Air Force mathematician, was assigned to work on logistics problems. He noticed that many problems involving limited resources and more than one demand could be set up in terms of a series of equations and inequalities. Although early LP applications were military in nature, industrial applications rapidly became apparent with the spread of business computers. In 1984, N. Karmarkar developed an algorithm that appears to be superior to the simplex method for many very large applications.

7.3   FORMULATING LINEAR PROGRAMMING PROBLEMS

Product mix problems use LP to decide how much of each product to make, given a series of resource restrictions.

One of the most common linear programming applications is the *product mix problem.* Two or more products are usually produced using limited resources such as personnel, machines, raw materials, and so on. The profit that the firm seeks to maximize is based on the profit contribution per unit of each product. (Profit contribution, you may recall, is just the selling price per unit minus the variable cost per unit.[1]) The company would like to determine how many units of each product it should produce so as to maximize overall profit given its limited resources.

Flair Furniture Company

The Flair Furniture Company produces inexpensive tables and chairs. The production process for each is similar in that both require a certain number of hours of carpentry work and a certain number of labor hours in the painting and varnishing department. Each table takes 4 hours of carpentry and 2 hours in the painting and varnishing shop. Each chair requires 3 hours in carpentry and 1 hour in painting and varnishing. During the current production period, 240 hours of carpentry time are available and 100 hours in painting and varnishing time are available. Each table sold yields a profit of $7; each chair produced is sold for a $5 profit.

Flair Furniture's problem is to determine the best possible combination of tables and chairs to manufacture in order to reach the maximum profit. The firm would like this production mix situation formulated as a linear programming problem.

We begin by summarizing the information needed to formulate and solve this problem (see Table 7.1). Further, let us introduce some simple notation for use in the objective function and constraints:

X_1 = number of tables to be produced

X_2 = number of chairs to be produced

Now we can create the LP objective function in terms of X_1 and X_2. The objective function is maximize profit = $7X_1 + $5X_2.

Our next step is to develop mathematical relationships to describe the two constraints in this problem. One general relationship is that the amount of a resource used is to be less than or equal to ($\leq$) the amount of resource *available.*

TABLE 7.1   Flair Furniture Company Data

DEPARTMENT	HOURS REQUIRED TO PRODUCE 1 UNIT		AVAILABLE HOURS THIS WEEK
	(X_1) TABLES	(X_2) CHAIRS	
Carpentry	4	3	240
Painting and varnishing	2	1	100
Profit per unit	$7	$5	

---

[1] Technically, we maximize total contribution margin, which is the difference between unit selling price and costs that vary in proportion to the quantity of the item produced. Depreciation, fixed general expense, and advertising are excluded from calculations. Problem 7-37 deals with these issues.

In the case of the carpentry department, the total time used is

(4 hours per table) (number of tables produced)
    + (3 hours per chair) (number of chairs produced)

So the first constraint may be stated as follows: Carpentry time used is $\leq$ carpentry time available.

$4X_1 + 3X_2 \leq 240$ (hours of carpentry time)

The resource constraints put limits on the carpentry labor resource and the painting labor resource mathematically.

Similarly, the second constraint is as follows: Painting and varnishing time used is $\leq$ painting and varnishing time available.

$2X_1 + 1X_2 \leq 100$ (hours of painting and varnishing time)

(This means that each table produced takes two hours of the painting and varnishing resource.)

Both of these constraints represent production capacity restrictions and, of course, affect the total profit. For example, Flair Furniture cannot produce 70 tables during the production period because if $X_1 = 70$, both constraints will be violated. It also cannot make $X_1 = 50$ tables and $X_2 = 10$ chairs. Why? Because this would violate the second constraint that no more than 100 hours of painting and varnishing time be allocated. Hence, we note one more important aspect of linear programming; that is, certain interactions will exist between variables. The more units of one product that a firm produces, the fewer it can make of other products. How this concept of interaction affects the optimal solution is seen as we now tackle the graphical solution approach.

A key principle of LP is that interactions exist between variables.

7.4   GRAPHICAL SOLUTION TO A LINEAR PROGRAMMING PROBLEM

The easiest way to solve a small LP problem such as that of the Flair Furniture Company is with the graphical solution approach. The graphical procedure is useful only when there are two decision variables (such as number of tables to produce, X_1, and number of chairs to produce, X_2) in the problem. When there are more than two variables, it is not possible to plot the solution on a two-dimensional graph and we must turn to more complex approaches, the topic of Chapter 9. But the graphical method is invaluable in providing us with insights into how other approaches work. For that reason alone, it is worthwhile to spend the rest of this chapter exploring graphical solutions as an intuitive basis for the chapters on mathematical programming that follow.

The graphical method works only when there are two decision variables, but it provides valuable insight into how larger problems are structured.

Graphical Representation of Constraints

To find the optimal solution to a linear programming problem, we must first identify a set, or region, of feasible solutions. The first step in doing so is to plot each of the problem's constraints on a graph. The variable X_1 (tables, in our example) is usually plotted as the horizontal axis of the graph and the variable X_2 (chairs) is plotted as the vertical axis. To obtain meaningful solutions, the values for X_1 and X_2 must be nonnegative numbers. That is, all potential solutions must represent real tables and real chairs. Mathematically, this means that

$X_1 \geq 0$ (number of tables produced is greater than or equal to 0)

$X_2 \geq 0$ (number of chairs produced is greater than or equal to 0)

Adding these *nonnegativity constraints* means that we are always working in the first (or northeast) quadrant of a graph (see Figure 7.1).

Nonnegativity constraints mean we are always in the graphical area when $X_1 \geq 0$ and $X_2 \geq 0$.

FIGURE 7.1

Quadrant Containing All
Positive Values

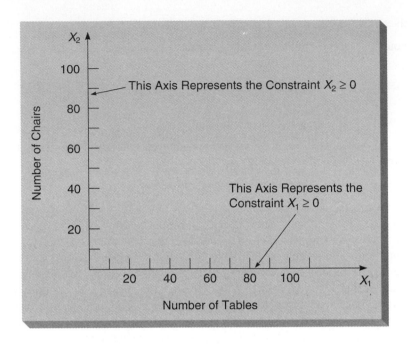

The complete problem may now be restated mathematically as

maximize profit $= \$7X_1 + \$5X_2$

Here is a complete mathematical statement of the LP problem.

subject to the constraints

$4X_1 + 3X_2 \leq 240$ (carpentry constraint)

$2X_1 + 1X_2 \leq 100$ (painting and varnishing constraint)

$\quad X_1 \qquad \geq 0 \quad$ (first nonnegativity constraint)

$\qquad X_2 \geq 0 \quad$ (second nonnegativity constraint)

To represent the first constraint graphically, $4X_1 + 3X_2 \leq 240$, we convert the inequality into an equality, more commonly called an equation, as follows:

$4X_1 + 3X_2 = 240$

As you may recall from elementary algebra, a linear equation in two variables is a straight line. The easiest way to plot the line is to find any two points that satisfy the equation, then draw a straight line through them.

Plotting the first constraint involves finding points at which the line intersects the X_1 and X_2 axes.

The two easiest points to find are generally the points at which the line intersects the X_1 and X_2 axes.

When Flair Furniture produces no tables, namely $X_1 = 0$, it implies that

$4(0) + 3X_2 = 240$

or

$3X_2 = 240$

or

$X_2 = 80$

In other words, if *all* of the carpentry time available is used to produce chairs, 80 chairs *could* be made. Thus, this constraint equation crosses the vertical axis at 80.

To find the point at which the line crosses the horizontal axis, we assume that the firm makes no chairs, that is, $X_2 = 0$. Then

$$4X_1 + (3)(0) = 240$$

or

$$4X_1 = 240$$

or

$$X_1 = 60$$

Hence, when $X_2 = 0$, we see that $4X_1 = 240$, and that $X_1 = 60$.

The carpentry constraint is illustrated in Figure 7.2. It is bounded by the line running from point $A(X_1 = 0, X_2 = 80)$ to point $B(X_1 = 60, X_2 = 0)$.

Recall, however, that the actual carpentry constraint was the *inequality* $4X_1 + 3X_2 \leq 240$. How can we identify all of the solution points that satisfy this constraint? It turns out that there are three possibilities. First, we know that any point that lies on the line $4X_1 + 3X_2 = 240$ satisfies the constraint. Any combination of tables and chairs on the line will use up all 240 hours of carpentry time.[2] We see this by picking a point such as $X_1 = 30$ tables and $X_2 = 40$ chairs (see Figure 7.3). You should be able to see how exactly 240 hours of the carpentry resource are used.

The real question is: Where are the problem points satisfying $4X_1 + 3X_2 \leq 240$? We can answer this question by checking two possible solution points, let's say ($X_1 =$

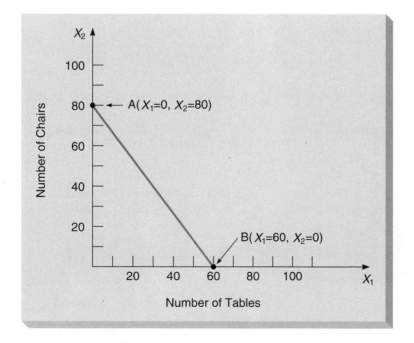

FIGURE 7.2

Graph of Carpentry Constraint Equation $4X_1 + 3X_2 = 240$

---

[2] Thus, what we have done is to plot the constraint equation in its most binding position, that is, using all of the carpentry resource.

30, $X_2 = 20$) and ($X_1 = 70$, $X_2 = 40$). You see in Figure 7.3 that the first point is below the constraint line and the second point lies above it. Let us examine the first solution more carefully. If we substitute the (X_1, X_2) values into the carpentry constraint, the result is

$$4(X_1 = 30) + 3(X_2 = 20) = (4)(30) + (3)(20) = 120 + 60 = 180$$

Since 180 is less than the 240 hours available, the point (30, 20) satisfies the constraint. For the second solution point, we follow the same procedure.

$$4(X_1 = 70) + 3(X_2 = 40) = (4)(70) + (3)(40) = 280 + 120 = 400$$

Four hundred exceeds the carpentry time available and hence violates the constraint. So we now know that the point (70, 40) is an unacceptable production level. As a matter of fact, any point *above* the constraint line violates that restriction. (This is something you may wish to test for yourself with a few other points.) Any point *below* the line does not violate the constraint. In Figure 7.3 the shaded region represents all points that satisfy the original inequality constraint.

Next, let us identify the solution corresponding to the second constraint, which limits the time available in the painting and varnishing department. That constraint was given as $2X_1 + 1X_2 \leq 100$. As before, we start by changing the inequality to an equation:

$$2X_1 + 1X_2 = 100$$

Line *CD* in Figure 7.4 represents all combinations of tables and chairs that use exactly 100 hours of painting and varnishing department time. It is constructed in a fashion similar to the first constraint. When $X_1 = 0$, then

$$2(0) + 1X_2 = 100$$

FIGURE 7.3

Region That Satisfies the Carpentry Constraint

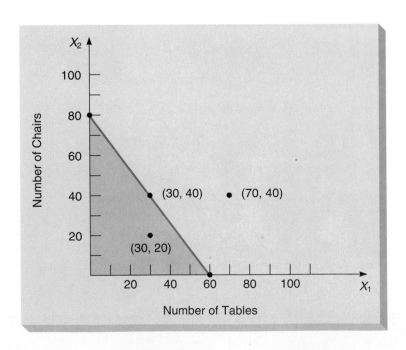

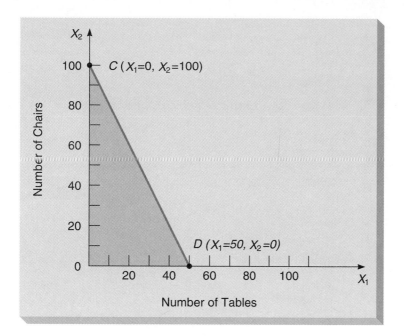

FIGURE 7.4
Region That Satisfies the
Painting and Varnishing
Constraint

or

$X_2 = 100$

When $X_2 = 0$, then

$2X_1 + 1(0) = 100$

or

$2X_1 = 100$

or

$X_1 = 50$

The constraint is bounded by the line between $C(X_1 = 0, X_2 = 100)$ to $D(X_1 = 50, X_2 = 0)$ and the shaded area again contains all possible combinations that do not exceed 100 hours. Thus, the shaded area represents the original inequality $2X_1 + 1X_2 \leq 100$.

Now that each individual constraint has been plotted on a graph, it is time to move on to the next step. We recognize that to produce a chair or a table, both the carpentry and painting and varnishing departments must be used. In an LP problem we need to find that set of solution points that satisfies all of the constraints *simultaneously*. Hence, the constraints should be redrawn on one graph (or superimposed one upon the other). This is shown in Figure 7.5.

In LP problems we are interested in satisfying all inequalities at the same time.

The shaded region now represents the area of solutions that does not exceed either of the two Flair Furniture constraints. It is known by the term *area of feasible solutions* or, more simply, the *feasible region*. The feasible region in a linear programming problem must satisfy *all* conditions specified by the problem's constraints, and is thus the region where all constraints overlap. Any point in the region would be a *feasible solution* to the Flair Furniture problem; any point outside the shaded area would repre-

FIGURE 7.5

Feasible Solution Region for the Flair Furniture Company Problem

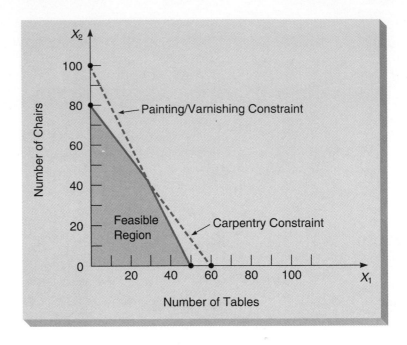

sent an *infeasible solution*. Hence, it would be feasible to manufacture 30 tables and 20 chairs ($X_1 = 30$, $X_2 = 20$) during a production period because both constraints are observed.

The feasible region is the overlapping area of constraints that satisfies all of the restrictions on resources.

Carpentry constraint $4X_1 + 3X_2 \leq 240$ hours available

$(4)(30) + (3)(20) = 180$ hours used ✓

Painting constraint $2X_1 + 1X_2 \leq 100$ hours available

$(2)(30) + (1)(20) = 80$ hours used ✓

But it would violate both of the constraints to produce 70 tables and 40 chairs, as we see here mathematically:

Carpentry constraint $4X_1 + 3X_2 \leq 240$ hours available

$(4)(70) + (3)(40) = 400$ hours used ⊗

Painting constraint $2X_1 + 1X_2 \leq 100$ hours available

$(2)(70) + (1)(40) = 180$ hours used ⊗

Furthermore, it would also be infeasible to manufacture 50 tables and 5 chairs ($X_1 = 50$, $X_2 = 5$). Can you see why?

Carpentry constraint $4X_1 + 3X_2 \leq 240$ hours available

$(4)(50) + (3)(5) = 215$ hours used ✓

Painting constraint $2X_1 + 1X_2 \leq 100$ hours available

$(2)(50) + (1)(5) = 105$ hours used ⊗

This possible solution falls within the time available in carpentry but exceeds the time available in painting and varnishing and thus falls outside the feasible region.

Setting Crew Schedules at American Airlines

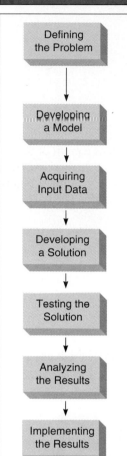

American Airlines (AA) employs more than 8,300 pilots and 16,200 flight attendants to fly more than 5,000 aircraft. Total cost of American's crews exceed $1.4 billion per year, second only to fuel cost. Scheduling crews is one of AA's biggest and most complex problems. The FAA sets work-time limitations designed to ensure that crew members can fulfill their duties safely. And union contracts specify that crews will be guaranteed pay for some number of hours each day or each trip.

American Airlines Decision Technologies (AA's consulting group) spent 15 labor-years in developing an LP model called TRIP (trip reevaluation and improvement program). The TRIP model builds crew schedules that meet or exceed crews' pay guarantee to the maximum extent possible.

Data and constraints are derived from salary information and union and FAA rules that specify maximum duty lengths, overnight costs, airline schedules, and plane sizes.

It takes about 500 hours of mainframe computer time per month to develop crew schedules—these are prepared 40 days prior to the targeted month.

TRIP results were originally compared with crew assignments constructed manually. Since 1971, the model has been improved with new LP techniques, new constraints, and faster hardware and software. A series of what-if? studies have tested TRIP's ability to reach more accurate and optimal solutions.

Each year the LP model improves AA's efficiency and allows the airline to operate with a proportionately smaller work crew. A faster TRIP system now allows sensitivity analysis of the schedule in its first week.

The model, fully implemented, generates annual savings of more than $20 million. AA has also sold TRIP to 10 other airlines and one railroad.

Source: R. Anbil et al. "Recent Advances in Crew Paring Optimization at American Airlines," *Interfaces* 21, 1 (January–February 1991): 62–74.

Isoprofit Line Solution Method

Now that the feasible region has been graphed, we may proceed to find the optimal solution to the problem. The optimal solution is the point lying in the feasible region that produces the highest profit. Yet there are many, many possible solution points in the region. How do we go about selecting the best one, the one yielding the highest profit?

There are a few different approaches that can be taken in solving for the optimal solution when the feasible region has been established graphically. The speediest one to apply is called the *isoprofit line method*.

The isoprofit method is the first method we introduce for finding the optimal solution.

We start the technique by letting profits equal some arbitrary but small dollar amount. For the Flair Furniture problem we may choose a profit of $210. This is a profit level that can be obtained easily without violating either of the two constraints. The objective function can be written as $210 = 7X_1 + 5X_2$.

This expression is just the equation of a line; we call it an *isoprofit line*. It represents all combinations of (X_1, X_2) that would yield a total profit of $210. To plot the profit line, we proceed exactly as we did to plot a constraint line. First, let $X_1 = 0$ and solve for the point at which the line crosses the X_2 axis.

$$\$210 = \$7(0) + \$5X_2$$

$$X_2 = 42 \text{ chairs}$$

Then, let $X_2 = 0$ and solve for X_1.

$$\$210 = \$7X_1 + \$5(0)$$

$$X_1 = 30 \text{ tables}$$

Isoprofit involves graphing parallel profit lines.

We can now connect these two points with a straight line. This profit line is illustrated in Figure 7.6. All points on the line represent feasible solutions that produce a profit of $210.[3]

Now, obviously, the isoprofit line for $210 does not produce the highest possible profit to the firm. In Figure 7.7 we try graphing two more lines, each yielding a higher profit. The middle equation, $\$280 = \$7X_1 + \$5X_2$, was plotted in the same fashion as the lower line. When $X_1 = 0$,

$$\$280 = \$7(0) + \$5X_2$$

$$X_2 = 56$$

When $X_2 = 0$,

$$\$280 = \$7X_1 + \$5(0)$$

$$X_1 = 40$$

Again, any combination of tables (X_1) and chairs (X_2) on this isoprofit line produces a total profit of $280.

FIGURE 7.6

Profit Line of $210 Plotted for the Flair Furniture Company

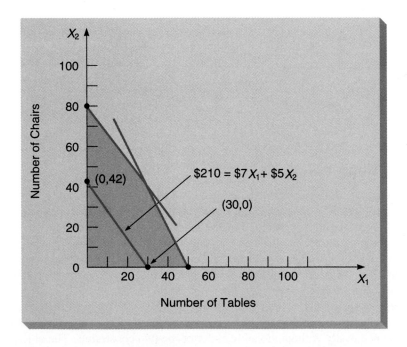

---

[3] *Iso* means "equal" or "similar." Thus, an isoprofit line represents a line with all profits the same, in this case $210.

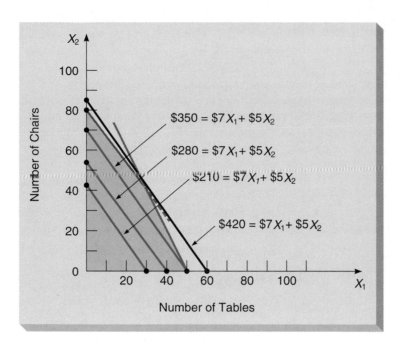

FIGURE 7.7
Four Isoprofit Lines Plotted for the Flair Furniture Company

Note that the third line generates a profit of $350, even more of an improvement. The farther we move from the 0 origin, the higher our profit will be. Another important point to note is that these isoprofit lines are parallel. We now have two clues as to how to find the optimal solution to the original problem. We can draw a series of parallel lines (by carefully moving our ruler in a plane parallel to the first profit line). The highest profit line that still touches some point of the feasible region pinpoints the optimal solution. Notice that the fourth line ($420) is too high to be considered.

The highest possible isoprofit line is illustrated in Figure 7.8. It touches the tip of the feasible region at the corner point ($X_1 = 30$, $X_2 = 40$) and yields a profit of $410.

We draw a series of parallel isoprofit lines until we find the highest isoprofit line, that is, the one with the optimal solution.

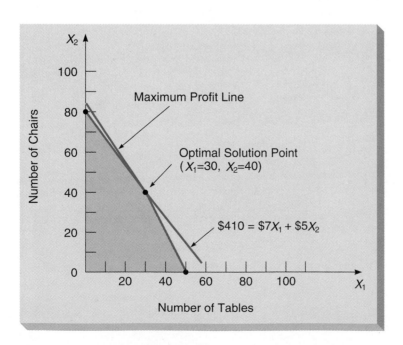

FIGURE 7.8
Optimal Solution to the Flair Furniture Problem

Corner Point Solution Method

A second approach to solving linear programming problems employs the *corner point method*. This technique is simpler conceptually than the isoprofit line approach, but it involves looking at the profit at every corner point of the feasible region.

The mathematical theory behind LP is that the optimal solution must lie at one of the corner points in the feasible region.

The mathematical theory behind linear programming states that an optimal solution to any problem (that is, the values of X_1, X_2 that yield the maximum profit) will lie at a *corner point*, or *extreme point*, of the feasible region. Hence, it is only necessary to find the values of the variables at each corner; the maximum profit or optimal solution will lie at one (or more) of them.

Once again we can see that the feasible region for the Flair Furniture Company problem is a four-sided polygon with four corner, or extreme, points (Figure 7.9). These points are labeled ①, ②, ③, and ④ on the graph. To find the (X_1, X_2) values producing the maximum profit, we find the coordinates of each corner point and test their profit levels.

Testing corner points ①, ②, and ④ is easy because their X_1, X_2 coordinates are quickly identified.

Point ① : $(X_1 = 0, X_2 = 0)$ profit $= \$7(0) + \$5(0) = \$0$

Point ② : $(X_1 = 0, X_2 = 80)$ profit $= \$7(0) + \$5(80) = \$400$

Point ④ : $(X_1 = 50, X_2 = 0)$ profit $= \$7(50) + \$5(0) = \$350$

We skipped corner point ③ momentarily because, to find its coordinates *accurately*, we have to solve for the intersection of the two constraint lines.[4] As you may recall from your last course in algebra, we can apply the *simultaneous equations method* to the two constraint equations:

Solving for corner point ③ requires the use of simultaneous equations, an algebraic technique.

$4X_1 + 3X_2 = 240$ (carpentry line)

$2X_1 + 1X_2 = 100$ (painting line)

FIGURE 7.9

Four Corner Points of the Feasible Region

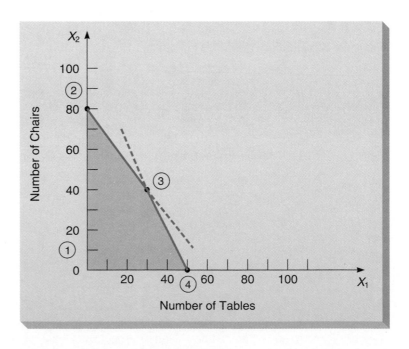

---

[4] Of course, if a graph is perfectly drawn, you can always find point ③ by careful examination of the intersection's coordinates. Otherwise, the algebraic method shown here provides more precision.

To solve these equations simultaneously, we multiply the second equation by -2:

$$-2(2X_1 + 1X_2 = 100) = -4X_1 - 2X_2 = -200$$

and then add it to the first equation:

$$\frac{+4X_1 + 3X_2 = 240}{+ 1X_2 = 40}$$

or

$$X_2 = 40$$

Doing this has enabled us to eliminate one variable, X_1, and to solve for X_2. We can now substitute 40 for X_2 in either of the original equations and solve for X_1. Let's use the first equation. When $X_2 = 40$, then,

$$4X_1 + (3)(40) = 240$$

$$4X_1 + 120 = 240$$

or

$$4X_1 = 120$$

$$X_1 = 30$$

Thus point ③ has the coordinates ($X_1 = 30$, $X_2 = 40$); we can compute its profit level to complete the analysis.

Point ③: ($X_1 = 30$, $X_2 = 40$) profit $= \$7(30) + \$5(40) = \$410$

Because point ③ produces the highest profit of any corner point, the product mix of $X_1 = 30$ tables and $X_2 = 40$ chairs is the optimal solution to Flair Furniture's problem. This solution yields a profit of \$410 per production period, which is the figure that we obtained using the isoprofit line method.

7.5　SOLVING FLAIR FURNITURE'S LP PROBLEM USING QM FOR WINDOWS AND EXCEL

Almost every organization has access to computer programs that are capable of solving enormous LP problems. Although each computer program is slightly different, the approach each takes toward handling LP problems is basically the same. The format of the input data and the level of detail provided in output results may differ from program to program and computer to computer, but once you are experienced in dealing with computerized LP algorithms, you can easily adjust to minor changes.

Using QM for Windows

Let us begin by demonstrating QM for Windows on the Flair Furniture Company problem data. As you can see in Program 7.1A, the input and output from QM for Windows is easy to run and understand. Program 7.1B illustrates the power of the graphical solution and, as we shall see later in this chapter, the software provides sensitivity analysis as well. In Chapter 9, we will illustrate exactly how QM for Windows goes through the solution steps with a procedure called the simplex method of LP.

PROGRAM 7.1A

Sample Linear Programming Computer Run Using QM for Windows Software on the Flair Furniture Company Data

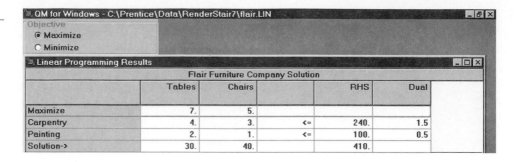

PROGRAM 7.1B

QM for Windows' Graphical Output for the Flair Furniture Company Problem

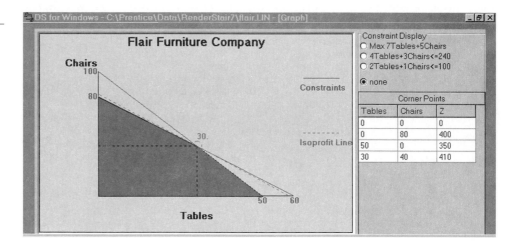

Using Excel's Solver Command to Solve LP Problems

Excel and other spreadsheets offer their users the ability to analyze LP problems using built-in problem solving tools. Excel uses a tool named *Solver* to find the solutions to linear programming related problems (which we use in Chapters 7–9), and integer and non-integer programming problems (the topic of Chapter 11). Excel QM does not contain an LP module, because *Solver* is part of the basic Excel program.

What Are the Limitations of Solver in Solving LP Problems? Solver depends on an algorithmic approach to the optimal solution set, that is, it operates using a series of rules and computations to search for and approximate the optimal solution. Occasionally, Solver may require the user to adjust the rules it uses. Additionally, Solver may be sensitive to the initial values it uses to search for the final solution. In practice, these limitations are rarely encountered.

Solver is limited to 200 changing cells (variables) each with two constraints and up to 100 additional constraints. These capabilities make Solver suitable for the solution of complex, real-world problems.

Using Solver to Solve the Flair Furniture Problem As you recall, this is the formulation for Flair Furniture:

$$\text{Objective Function:} \quad \text{maximize profit} = \$7X_1 + \$5X_2$$

$$\text{subject to} \quad 4X_1 + 3X_2 \leq 240$$

$$2X_1 + 1X_2 \leq 100$$

Program 7.2A shows how to structure this problem using Excel. We use Add, Change, and Delete in the *Subject to the Constraints* box to constrain the LP problem. The constraints may be in the form of a value, formula, or cell reference. The method of constraint assignment shown in Program 7.2A makes it easy to see all the constraints simultaneously.

The Excel screen in Program 7.2B shows Solver's solution to the Flair Furniture Company problem. Note that the optimal solution is now shown in the *changing cells* (Cells B8 and C8, which served as the variables). The "reports selection" in Program 7.2C performs more extensive analysis of the solution. The Answer Report shows that the first two constraints were binding in the solution (no slack).

7.6 SOLVING MINIMIZATION PROBLEMS

Many LP problems involve minimizing an objective such as cost instead of maximizing a profit function. A restaurant, for example, may wish to develop a work schedule to meet staffing needs while minimizing the total number of employees. A manufacturer may seek to distribute its products from several factories to its many regional warehouses in such a way as to minimize total shipping costs. A hospital may want to provide a daily meal plan for its patients that meets certain nutritional standards while minimizing food purchase costs.

PROGRAM 7.2A

Setting up the Flair Furniture Company LP Problem Using Excel and Solver. This Spreadsheet Shows the Formulas Developed by the User.

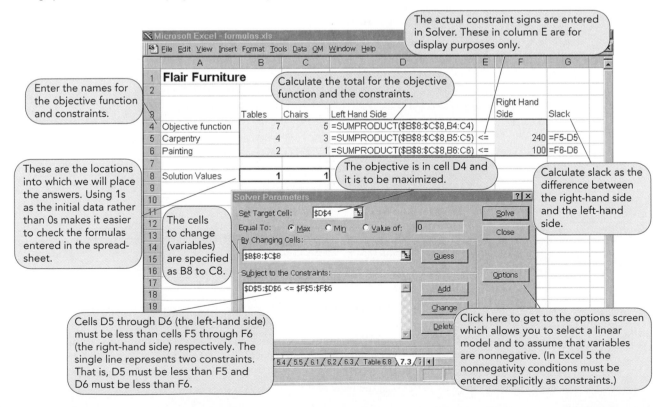

PROGRAM 7.2B

Solution to Flair Furniture Company Problem Using Excel's Solver

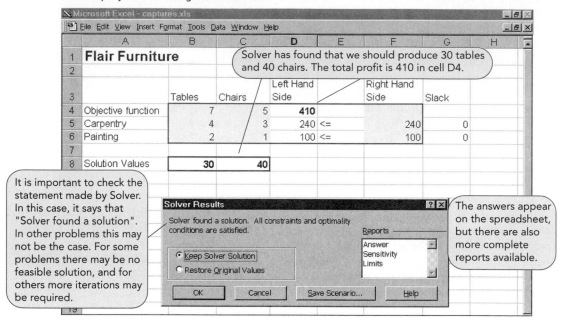

PROGRAM 7.2C

Excel's Answer Report for Flair Furniture Company Problem

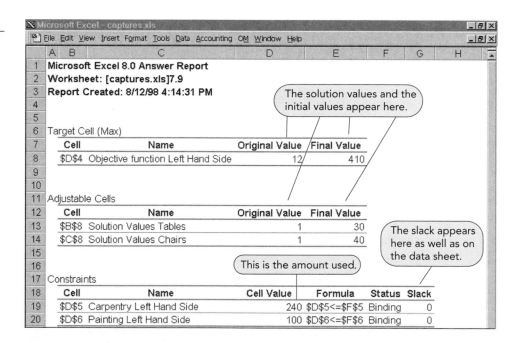

Minimization problems can be solved graphically by first setting up the feasible solution region and then using either the corner point method or an isocost line approach (which is analogous to the isoprofit approach in maximization problems) to find the values of X_1 and X_2 that yield the minimum cost. Let's take a look at a common LP problem referred to as the diet problem. This situation is similar to the one that the hospital faces in feeding its patients at the least cost.

IN ACTION   Using LP to Select Tenants in a Shopping Mall

Homart Development Company is one of the largest shopping-center developers in the United States. When developing a new center, Homart produces a tentative floor plan, or footprint, for the mall. This plan outlines sizes, shapes, and spaces for large department stores. Leasing agreements are reached with the two or three major department stores that will become anchor stores in the mall. The anchor stores are able to negotiate highly favorable occupancy agreements. Typically, they either pay low rent or receive other concessions. Homart's profits come primarily from the rent paid by the nonanchor tenants—the smaller stores that lease space along the aisles of the mall. The decisions allocating space to potential tenants and establishing the tenant mix are therefore crucial to the success of the investment.

The tenant mix describes the desired stores in the mall by their size, general location, and type of merchandise or service provided. For example, the tenant mix might specify two

small jewelry stores in a central section of the mall and a medium-sized shoe store and a large restaurant in one of the side aisles. In the past, Homart developed a plan for tenant mix using "rules of thumb" developed over years of experience in mall development.

Now, to improve its bottom line in an increasingly competitive marketplace, Homart treats the tenant-mix problem as an LP model. First, the model assumes that tenants can be classified into categories according to the type of merchandise or service they provide. Second, the model assumes that for each store type, store sizes can be made into distinct categories. For example, a small jewelry store is said to contain about 700 square feet and a large one about 2,200 square feet. The tenant-mix model is a powerful tool for enhancing Homart's mall planning and leasing activities.

Source: James Bean et al. "Selecting Tenants in a Shopping Mall," *Interfaces*, (March–April 1988): 1–9.

Holiday Meal Turkey Ranch

The Holiday Meal Turkey Ranch is considering buying two different brands of turkey feed and blending them to provide a good, low-cost diet for its turkeys. Each feed contains, in varying proportions, some or all of the three nutritional ingredients essential for fattening turkeys. Each pound of brand 1 purchased, for example, contains 5 ounces of ingredient A, 4 ounces of ingredient B, and ½ ounce of ingredient C. Each pound of brand 2 contains 10 ounces of ingredient A, 3 ounces of ingredient B, but no ingredient C. The brand 1 feed costs the ranch 2 cents a pound, while the brand 2 feed costs 3 cents a pound. The owner of the ranch would like to use LP to determine the lowest-cost diet that meets the minimum monthly intake requirement for each nutritional ingredient.

Table 7.2 summarizes the relevant information. If we let

X_1 = number of pounds of brand 1 feed purchased

X_2 = number of pounds of brand 2 feed purchased

TABLE 7.2 Holiday Meal Turkey Ranch Data

INGREDIENT	COMPOSITION OF EACH POUND OF FEED (OZ)		MINIMUM MONTHLY REQUIREMENT PER TURKEY (OZ)
	BRAND 1 FEED	BRAND 2 FEED	
A	5	10	90
B	4	3	48
C	½	0	1½
Cost per pound	2 cents	3 cents	

then we may proceed to formulate this linear programming problem as follows:

$$\text{minimize cost (in cents)} = 2X_1 + 3X_2$$

subject to these constraints:0

$5X_1 + 10X_2 \geq 90$ ounces	(ingredient A constraint)
$4X_1 + 3X_2 \geq 48$ ounces	(ingredient B constraint)
$\tfrac{1}{2}X_1 \geq 1\tfrac{1}{2}$ ounces	(ingredient C constraint)
$X_1 \geq 0$	(nonnegativity constraint)
$X_2 \geq 0$	(nonnegativity constraint)

Before solving this problem, we want to be sure to note three features that affect its solution. First, you should be aware that the third constraint implies that the farmer *must* purchase enough brand 1 feed to meet the minimum standards for the C nutritional ingredient. Buying only brand 2 would not be feasible because it lacks C. Second, as the problem is formulated, we will be solving for the best blend of brands 1 and 2 to buy per turkey per month. If the ranch houses 5,000 turkeys in a given month, it need simply multiply the X_1 and X_2 quantities by 5,000 to decide how much feed to order overall. Third, we are now dealing with a series of greater-than-or-equal-to constraints. These cause the feasible solution area to be above the constraint lines, a common situation when handling minimization LP problems.

We plot the three constraints to develop a feasible solution region for the minimization problem.

Using the Corner Point Method on a Minimization Problem To solve the Holiday Meal Turkey Ranch problem, we first construct the feasible solution region. This is done by plotting each of the three constraint equations as in Figure 7.10. You may note that the third constraint, $\tfrac{1}{2}X_1 \geq 1\tfrac{1}{2}$, may be rewritten and plotted as $X_1 \geq 3$. (This involves multiplying both sides of the inequality by 2 but does not change the position of the constraint line in any way.) Minimization problems are often unbounded outward (that is, on the right side and on top), but this causes no difficulty in solving them. As long as they are bounded inward (on the left side and the bottom), corner points may be established. The optimal solution will lie at one of the corners as it would in a maximization problem.

Note that minimization problems are often unbounded (that is, open outward).

In this case, there are three corner points: *a, b,* and *c*. For point *a*, we find the coordinates at the intersection of the ingredient C and B constraints, that is, where the line $X_1 = 3$ crosses the line $4X_1 + 3X_2 = 48$. If we substitute $X_1 = 3$ into the B constraint equation, the following sequence of computations may be performed:

$$4X_1 + 3X_2 = 48$$

or

$$4(3) + 3X_2 = 48$$

or

$$12 + 3X_2 = 48$$

or

$$3X_2 = 36$$
$$X_2 = 12$$

Thus, point *a* has the coordinates ($X_1 = 3, X_2 = 12$) and a corresponding

$$\text{cost at point } a = 2X_1 + 3X_2$$
$$= 2(3) + 3(12)$$
$$= 42 \text{ cents}$$

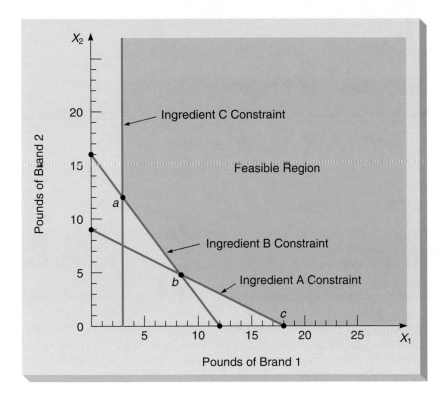

FIGURE 7.10

Feasible Region for the Holiday Meal Turkey Ranch Problem

To find the values of point *b* algebraically, we solve the equations $4X_1 + 3X_2 = 48$ and $5X_1 + 10X_2 = 90$ simultaneously. This can be done by (1) multiplying the first equation (representing the ingredient B constraint) by -5, then (2) multiplying the second equation (the ingredient A constraint line) by 4, and, finally, (3) adding the two new equations together.

We must solve for the three corner points algebraically.

1. $-5(4X_1 + 3X_2 = 48)$ $-20X_1 - 15X_2 = -240$

2. $4(5X_1 + 10X_2 = 90)$ $\underline{20X_1 + 40X_2 = \quad 360}$

3. $+ 25X_2 = \quad 120$

                                          $X_2 = \quad 4.8$

The reason for this procedure was to eliminate one of the variables (X_1) from the equations so that we could solve for the other (X_2). Now that we have a value for X_2, we may substitute $X_2 = 4.8$ into either of the two original equations to solve for X_1. Using the first equation yields

$$4X_1 + (3)(4.8) = 48$$

or

$$4X_1 + 14.4 = 48$$

or

$$4X_1 = 33.6$$

or

$$X_1 = 8.4$$

The cost at point b is now

cost at point $b = 2X_1 + 3X_2$

$$= (2)(8.4) + (3)(4.8)$$

$$= 31.2 \text{ cents}$$

Finally, the cost at point c must be computed. This is much easier, as it is evident that c has the coordinates $(X_1 = 18, X_2 = 0)$:

cost at point $c = 2X_1 + 3X_2$

$$= (2)(18) + (3)(0)$$

$$= 36 \text{ cents}$$

Hence, the minimum cost solution is to purchase 8.4 pounds of brand 1 feed and 4.8 pounds of brand 2 feed per turkey per month. This will yield a cost of 31.2 cents per turkey.

The isocost line method is analogous to the isoprofit line method we used on maximization problems.

Isocost Line Approach As mentioned before, the *isocost line* approach may also be used to solve LP minimization problems such as that of the Holiday Meal Turkey Ranch. As with isoprofit lines, we need not compute the cost at each corner point, but instead draw a series of parallel cost lines. The lowest cost line (that is, the one closest in toward the origin) to touch the feasible region provides us with the optimal solution corner.

For example, we start in Figure 7.11 by drawing a 54-cent cost line, namely $54 = 2X_1 + 3X_2$. Obviously, there are many points in the feasible region that would yield a

FIGURE 7.11

Graphical Solution to the Holiday Meal Turkey Ranch Problem Using the Isocost Line

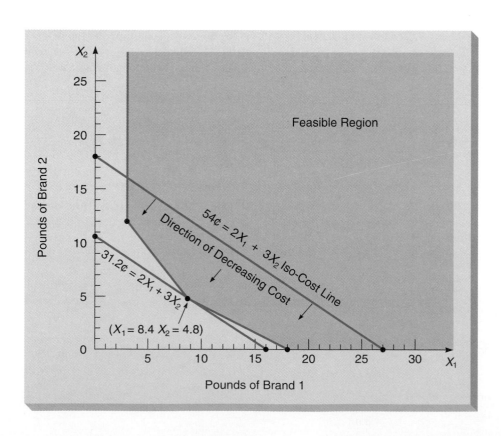

lower total cost. We proceed to move our isocost line toward the lower left, in a plane parallel to the 54-cent solution line. The last point we touch while still in contact with the feasible region is the same as corner point b of Figure 7.10. It has the coordinates $(X_1 = 8.4, X_2 = 4.8)$ and an associated cost of 31.2 cents.

Computer Approach For the sake of completeness, we also solve the Holiday Meal Turkey Ranch problem using the QM for Windows software package (see Program 7.3) and with Excel's Solver function (see Programs 7.4A and 7.4B).

7.7 SUMMARY OF THE GRAPHICAL SOLUTION METHODS

As you saw in the cases of the Flair Furniture Company and the Holiday Meal Turkey Ranch, the graphical method of solving linear programming problems involves several steps. Let's review them briefly before moving on.

1. Formulate the problem in terms of a series of mathematical constraints and an objective function.

2. Graph each of the constraint equations.

3. Identify the feasible solution region, that is, the area that satisfies all of the constraints simultaneously.

4. Select one of the two following graphical solution techniques and proceed to solve.

Corner Point Method	*Isoprofit or Isocost Method*
5. Identify each of the corner, or extreme, points of the feasible region by either visual inspection or the method of simultaneous equations.	**5.** Select a specific profit or cost line and graph it to reveal its slope or angle.
6. Compute the profit or cost at each corner point by substituting that point's coordinates into the objective function.	**6.** If you are dealing with a maximization problem, maintain the same slope, through a series of parallel lines, and move the line up and to the right until it touches the feasible region at only one point. If you have a minimization problem, move down and to the left until it touches only one point in the feasible region.
7. Identify the optimal solution as that corner point with the highest profit, in a maximization problem, or lowest cost, in a minimization problem.	**7.** Identify the optimal solution as the coordinates of that point on the feasible region touched by the highest possible isoprofit line or lowest possible iso-cost line.
	8. Read the optimal (X_1, X_2) coordinates from the graph, or compute their values by using the simultaneous equation method.
	9. Compute the profit or cost.

PROGRAM 7.3

Solving the Holiday Meal
Turkey Ranch Problem Using
QM for Windows Software

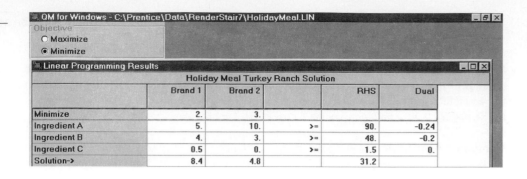

QM for Windows - C:\Prentice\Data\RenderStair7\HolidayMeal.LIN

Objective
- ○ Maximize
- ● Minimize

Linear Programming Results

Holiday Meal Turkey Ranch Solution

	Brand 1	Brand 2		RHS	Dual
Minimize	2.	3.			
Ingredient A	5.	10.	>=	90.	-0.24
Ingredient B	4.	3.	>=	48.	-0.2
Ingredient C	0.5	0.	>=	1.5	0.
Solution->	8.4	4.8		31.2	

PROGRAM 7.4A

Setting up the Holiday Meal Turkey Ranch LP Problem Using Excel and Solver

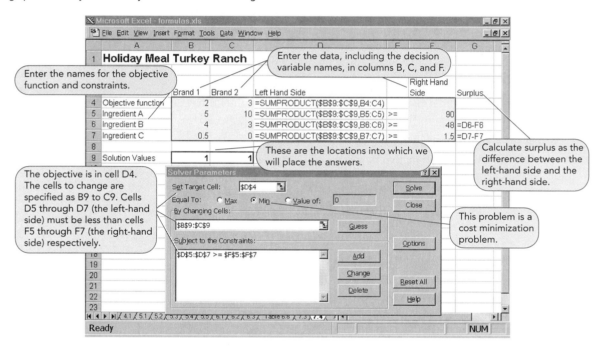

Enter the names for the objective function and constraints.

Enter the data, including the decision variable names, in columns B, C, and F.

	A	B	C	D	E	F	G
1	**Holiday Meal Turkey Ranch**						
		Brand 1	Brand 2	Left Hand Side		Right Hand Side	Surplus
4	Objective function	2	3	=SUMPRODUCT($B$9:$C$9,B4:C4)			
5	Ingredient A	5	10	=SUMPRODUCT($B$9:$C$9,B5:C5)	>=	90	
6	Ingredient B	4	3	=SUMPRODUCT($B$9:$C$9,B6:C6)	>=	48	=D6-F6
7	Ingredient C	0.5	0	=SUMPRODUCT($B$9:$C$9,B7:C7)	>=	1.5	=D7-F7
8							
9	Solution Values	1	1				

These are the locations into which we will place the answers.

Calculate surplus as the difference between the left-hand side and the right-hand side.

The objective is in cell D4. The cells to change are specified as B9 to C9. Cells D5 through D7 (the left-hand side) must be less than cells F5 through F7 (the right-hand side) respectively.

Solver Parameters

Set Target Cell: $D$4

Equal To: ○ Max ● Min ○ Value of: 0

By Changing Cells: $B$9:$C$9

Subject to the Constraints: $D$5:$D$7 >= $F$5:$F$7

This problem is a cost minimization problem.

Solve / Close / Guess / Options / Add / Change / Delete / Reset All / Help

PROGRAM 7.4B

Solution to the Holiday Meal
Turkey Ranch Using Excel's
Solver

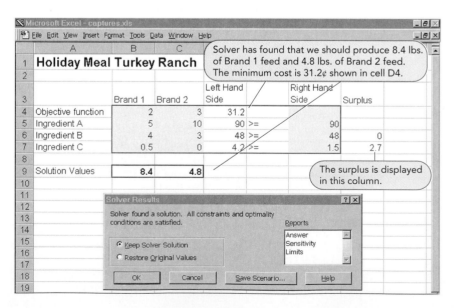

Microsoft Excel - captures.xls

	A	B	C	D	E	F	G
1	**Holiday Meal Turkey Ranch**						
2							
		Brand 1	Brand 2	Left Hand Side		Right Hand Side	Surplus
4	Objective function	2	3	31.2			
5	Ingredient A	5	10	90	>=	90	
6	Ingredient B	4	3	48	>=	48	0
7	Ingredient C	0.5	0	4.2	>=	1.5	2.7
8							
9	Solution Values	8.4	4.8				

Solver has found that we should produce 8.4 lbs. of Brand 1 feed and 4.8 lbs. of Brand 2 feed. The minimum cost is 31.2¢ shown in cell D4.

The surplus is displayed in this column.

Solver Results

Solver found a solution. All constraints and optimality conditions are satisfied.

Reports: Answer / Sensitivity / Limits

● Keep Solver Solution
○ Restore Original Values

OK / Cancel / Save Scenario... / Help

7.8   FOUR SPECIAL CASES IN LINEAR PROGRAMMING

Four special cases and difficulties arise at times when using the graphical approach to solving LP problems. They are called (1) infeasibility, (2) unboundedness, (3) redundancy, and (4) alternate optimal solutions.

Infeasibility

Infeasibility is a condition that arises when there is no solution to a LP problem that satisfies all of the constraints given. Graphically, it means that no feasible solution region exists—a situation that might occur if the problem was formulated with conflicting constraints. This, by the way, is a frequent occurrence in real-life, large-scale LP problems that involve hundreds of constraints. For example, if one constraint is supplied by the marketing manager who states that at least 300 tables must be produced (namely, $X_1 \geq 300$) to meet sales demand, and a second restriction is supplied by the production manager, who insists that no more than 220 tables be produced (namely, $X_1 \leq 220$) because of a lumber shortage, an infeasible solution region results. When the operations research analyst coordinating the LP problem points out this conflict, one manager or the other must revise his or her inputs. Perhaps more raw materials could be procured from a new source, or perhaps sales demand could be lowered by substituting a different model table to customers.

> *Lack of a feasible solution region can occur if constraints conflict with one another. This is called infeasibility.*

As a further graphic illustration of infeasibility, let us consider the following three constraints:

$$X_1 + 2X_2 \leq 6$$
$$2X_1 + X_2 \leq 8$$
$$X_1 \qquad \geq 7$$

As seen in Figure 7.12, there is no feasible solution region for this LP problem because of the presence of conflicting constraints.

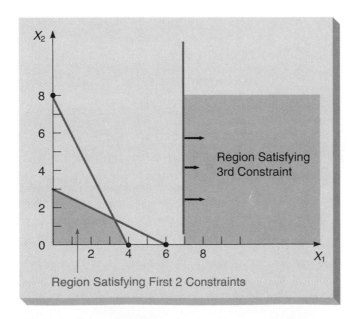

FIGURE 7.12

A Problem with No Feasible Solution

Unboundedness

When the profit in a maximization problem can be infinitely large, the problem is **unbounded** *and is missing one or more constraints.*

Sometimes a linear program will not have a finite solution. This means that in a maximization problem, for example, one or more solution variables, and the profit, can be made infinitely large without violating any constraints. If we try to solve such a problem graphically, we will note that the feasible region is open-ended.

Let us consider a simple example to illustrate the situation. A firm has formulated the following LP problem:

$$\text{maximize profit} = \$3X_1 + \$5X_2$$

$$
\begin{aligned}
\text{subject to:} \quad X_1 \quad &\geq \quad 5 \\
X_2 &\leq \quad 10 \\
X_1 + 2X_2 &\geq \quad 10 \\
X_1, \ X_2 &\geq \quad 0
\end{aligned}
$$

As you see in Figure 7.13, because this is a maximization problem and the feasible region extends infinitely to the right, there is *unboundedness*, or an unbounded solution. This implies that the problem has been formulated improperly. It would indeed be wonderful for the company to be able to produce an infinite number of units of X_1 (at a profit of $3 each!), but obviously no firm has infinite resources available or infinite product demand.

Redundancy

A redundant constraint is one that does not affect the feasible solution region.

The presence of redundant constraints is another common situation that occurs in large LP formulations. *Redundancy* causes no major difficulties in solving LP problems graphically, but you should be able to identify its occurrence. A redundant constraint is simply one that does not affect the feasible solution region. In other words, one constraint may be more binding or restrictive than another and thereby negate its need to be considered.

FIGURE 7.13

A Solution Region That Is Unbounded to the Right

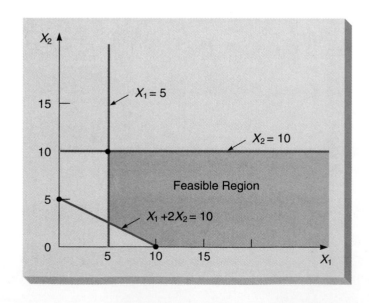

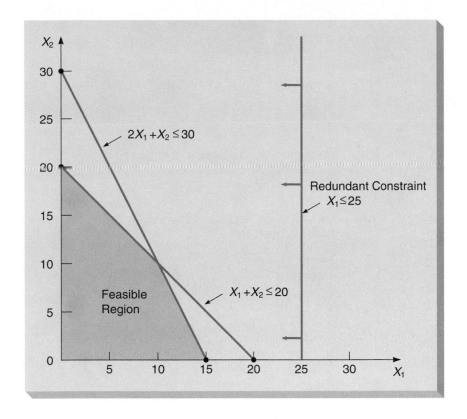

FIGURE 7.14
Problem with a Redundant Constraint

Let's look at the following example of an LP problem with three constraints:

maximize profit = $\$1X_1 + \$2X_2$

subject to:
$$X_1 + X_2 \leq 20$$
$$2X_1 + X_2 \leq 30$$
$$X_1 \leq 25$$
$$X_1, X_2 \geq 0$$

The third constraint, $X_1 \leq 25$, is redundant and unnecessary in the formulation and solution of the problem because it has no effect on the feasible region set from the first two more restrictive constraints (see Figure 7.14).

Alternate Optimal Solutions

A LP problem may, on occasion, have two or more *alternate optimal solutions*. Graphically, this is the case when the objective function's isoprofit or isocost line runs perfectly parallel to one of the problem's constraints—in other words, when they have the same slope.

Multiple optimal solutions are possible in LP problems.

Management of a firm noticed the presence of more than one optimal solution when they formulated this simple LP problem:

maximize profit = $\$3X_1 + \$2X_2$

subject to:
$$6X_1 + 4X_2 \leq 24$$
$$X_1 \leq 3$$
$$X_1, X_2 \geq 0$$

FIGURE 7.15

Example of Alternate Optimal
Solutions

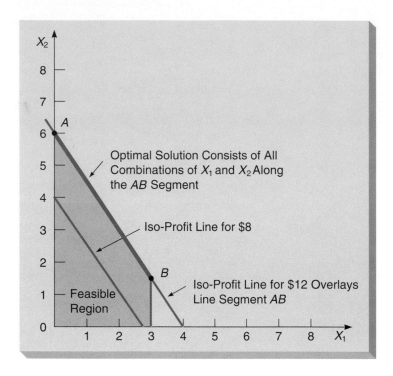

As we see in Figure 7.15, our first isoprofit line of $8 runs parallel to the constraint equation. At a profit level of $12, the isoprofit line will rest directly on top of the segment of the first constraint line. This means that any point along the line between A and B provides an optimal X_1 and X_2 combination. Far from causing problems, the existence of more than one optimal solution allows management great flexibility in deciding which combination to select. The profit remains the same at each alternate solution.

7.9   SENSITIVITY ANALYSIS

Optimal solutions to LP problems have thus far been found under what are called *deterministic assumptions*. This means that we assume complete certainty in the data and relationships of a problem—namely, prices are fixed, resources known, time needed to produce a unit exactly set. But in the real world, conditions are dynamic and changing. How can we handle this apparent discrepancy?

How sensitive is optimal solution to changes in profits, resources, or other input parameters?

One way we can do so is by continuing to treat each particular LP problem as a deterministic situation. However, when an optimal solution is found, we recognize the importance of seeing just how *sensitive* that solution is to model assumptions and data. For example, if a firm realizes that profit per unit is not $5 as estimated but instead is closer to $5.50, how will the final solution mix and total profit change? If additional resources, such as 10 labor hours or three hours of machine time, should become available, will this change the problem's answer? Such analyses are used to examine the effects of changes in three areas: (1) contribution rates for each variable, (2) technological coefficients (the numbers in the constraint equations), and (3) available resources (the right-hand-side quantities in each constraint). This task is alternatively called *sensitivity analysis, postoptimality analysis, parametric programming*, or *optimality analysis*.

The use of sensitivity analysis by management also often involves a series of what-if questions. What if the profit on product 1 increases by 10%? What if less money is available in the advertising budget constraint? What if workers each stay one hour longer every day at 1½-time pay to provide increased production capacity? What if new technology will allow a product to be wired in one-third the time it used to take? So we see that sensitivity analysis can be used to deal not only with errors in estimating input parameters to the LP model but also with management's experiments with possible future changes in the firm that may affect profits.

An important function of sensitivity analysis is to allow managers to experiment with values of the input parameters.

There are two approaches to determining just how sensitive an optimal solution is to changes. The first is simply a trial-and-error approach. This approach usually involves re-solving the entire problem, preferably by computer, each time one input data item or parameter is changed. It can take a long time to test a series of possible changes in this way.

The approach we prefer is the analytic postoptimality method. After an LP problem has been solved, we attempt to determine a range of changes in problem parameters that will not affect the optimal solution or change the variables in the basis. This is done without resolving the whole problem.

Postoptimality analysis means examining changes after the optimal solution has been reached.

Let's investigate sensitivity analysis by developing a small production mix problem. Our goal will be to demonstrate graphically and through the simplex tableau how sensitivity analysis can be used to make linear programming concepts more realistic and insightful.

High Note Sound Company

The High Note Sound Company manufactures quality compact disc (CD) players and stereo receivers. Each of these products requires a certain amount of skilled craftsmanship, of which there is a limited weekly supply. The firm formulates the following LP problem in order to determine the best production mix of CD players (X_1) and receivers (X_2):

maximize profit $= \$50X_1 + \$120X_2$

subject to: $2X_1 + 4X_2 \leq 80$ (hours of available electricians' time)

$\quad\quad\quad\quad 3X_1 + 1X_2 \leq 60$ (hours of audio technicians' time available)

$\quad\quad\quad\quad X_1, X_2 \geq 0$

The solution to this problem is illustrated graphically in Figure 7.16. Given this information and deterministic assumptions, the firm should produce only stereo receivers (20 of them) for a weekly profit of $2,400.

Changes in the Objective Function Coefficient In real-life problems, contribution rates (usually profit or cost) in the objective functions fluctuate periodically, as do most of a firm's expenses. Graphically, this means that although the feasible solution region remains exactly the same, the slope of the isoprofit or isocost line will change. It is easy to see in Figure 7.17 that the High Note Sound Company's profit line is optimal at point *a*. But what if a technical breakthrough just occurred that raised the profit per stereo receiver (X_2) from $120 to $150? Is the solution still optimal? The answer is definitely *yes*, for in this case the slope of the profit line accentuates the profitability at point *a*. The new profit is $3,000 = 0($50) + 20($150).

Changes in contribution rates are examined first.

On the other hand, if X_2's profit coefficient was overestimated and should only have been $80, the slope of the profit line changes enough to cause a new corner point (*b*) to become optimal. Here the profit is $1,760 = 16($50) + 12($80).

Changes in the Technological Coefficients Changes in what are called the *technological coefficients* often reflect changes in the state of technology. If fewer or more resources are needed to produce a product such as a CD player or stereo receiver, coefficients in the

FIGURE 7.16

Hight Note Sound Company
Graphical Solution

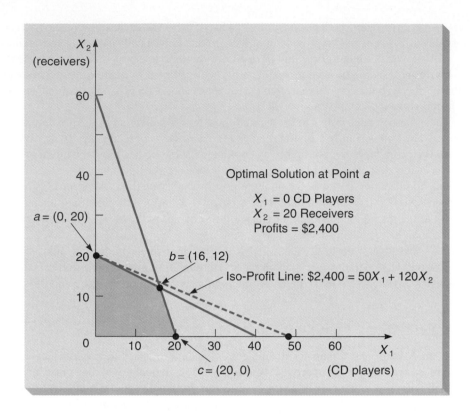

Changes in technological coefficients affect the shape of the feasible solution region.

constraint equations will change. These changes will have no effect on the objective function of an LP problem, but they can produce a significant change in the shape of the feasible solution region, and hence in the optimal profit or cost.

Figure 7.18 illustrates the original High Note Sound Company graphical solution as well as two separate changes in technological coefficients. In Figure 7.18, Part (a), we see that the optimal solution lies at point a, which represents $X_1 = 0$, $X_2 = 20$. You should be able to prove to yourself that point a remains optimal in Figure 7.18, Part (b) despite a constraint change from $3X_1 + 1X_2 \leq 60$ to $2X_1 + 1X_2 \leq 60$. Such a change might take

IN ACTION   **Using LP to Assist AIDS Patients in Italy**

Home care for AIDS patients, in the form of nurses, doctors, and social workers, was introduced by law in Italy in 1990. Organizations that provide home-care work with a limited budget must provide a minimum standard of service. A lack of balance between patient needs and available resources can lead to a low level of service, an excessive workload for the medical and social workers, or both.

To produce an optimal schedule for admitting new patients into the home health care system, Italian researchers turned to LP. Using available quantities of each resource as constraints, the objective is to maximize the sum of the number of patients that can be admitted each week. The LP model

produces an optimal admissions schedule for a given 12-week planning period.

But to complicate the problem, patients fell into various categories of "dependency," ranging from "self-sufficient" to "permanently in bed" to "hospitalized" to "dead." Patients move with predicted probabilities from one category to another, and different classes are given different weights to express priority. This practical and flexible LP tool for public health has also been extended to support centralized decision making by evaluating the impact of different budget assignments.

Source: V. DeAngelis. "Planning Home Assistance for AIDS Patients in the City of Rome, Italy," *Interfaces* 28, 3 (May–June, 1998): 75–83.

FIGURE 7.17

Changes in the Receiver Contribution Coefficients

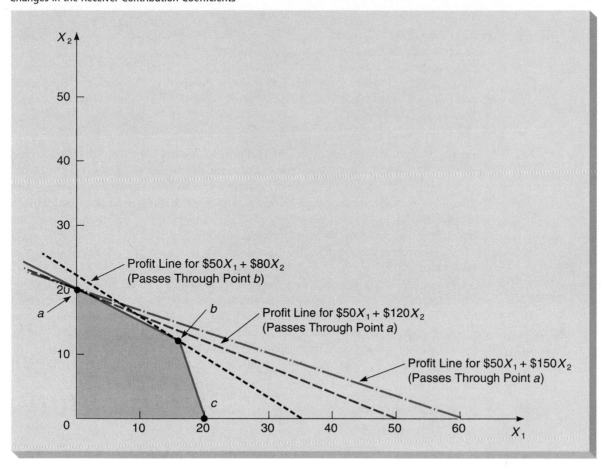

FIGURE 7.18

Change in the Technological Coefficients for the High Note Sound Company

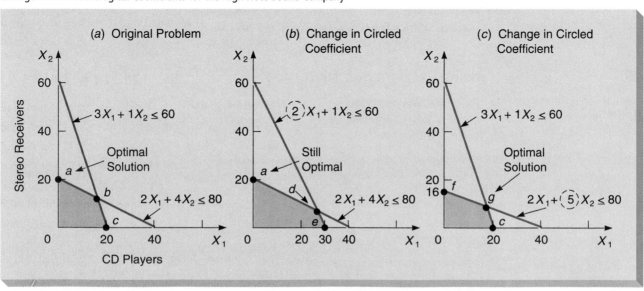

place when the firm discovers that it no longer demands three hours of audio technicians' time to produce a CD player, but only two hours.

In Figure 7.18, Part (c), however, a change in the other constraint changes the shape of the feasible region enough to cause a new corner point (*g*) to become optimal. Before moving on, see if you reach an objective function value of $1,954 profit at point *g* (versus a profit of $1,920 at point *f*).[5]

Changes in the Resources or Right-Hand-Side Values The values on the right-hand-side of linear programming constraints can be considered to represent the resources available to the firm. These resources may be labor hours or machine time available, or perhaps money or production materials available. In the High Note Sound Company example, the two resources are hours of available electricians' time and hours of audio technicians' time. Knowledge of how sensitive the optimal solution is to changes in resources such as these is important because of dynamic marketplace conditions.

Resource changes affect the shape of the feasible region.

Changes in the right-hand-side values result in changes in the feasible region and often in the optimal solution. Figure 7.19 illustrates two resource changes dealing with the number of hours of available electricians' time for each week's production process. An isoprofit line or corner point approach indicates in Figure 7.19 Part (a) and Part (b) that corner point *a* is optimal. However, in Figure 7.19 Part (a) the new resource of 100 electricians' hours (as compared with 80 in the original problem) yields a solution of $X_1 = 0$ CD players, $X_2 = 25$ receivers, and profit = $3,000. Reducing the available resource to 60 hours [Figure 7.19(b)] alters the feasible region again. This time the optimal solution is to produce $X_2 = 0$ CD players and $X_2 = 15$ receivers, for a profit of $1,800.

Using QM for Windows for Sensitivity Analysis

Virtually all LP computer programs have optional outputs for sensitivity analysis. QM for Windows uses the High Note Sound Company data in Programs 7.5A and 7.5B to illustrate objective coefficient ranges and right-hand-side ranges. Program 7.5A shows the input to QM for Windows, and Program 7.5B reveals the output.

Using Excel for Sensitivity Analysis

Program 7.6A provides an Excel spreadsheet analysis of High Note Sound Company. Excel's *Solver* command has an option of providing sensitivity analysis, as we see in Program 7.6B.

---

[5] Note that the values of X_1 and X_2 at point g are fractions. Although the High Note Sound Company cannot produce ⅔, ¾ or ⁹⁄₁₀ of a CD player or stereo, we can assume that the firm can *begin* a unit one week and complete it the next. As long as the production process is fairly stable from week to week, this raises no major problems. If solutions *must* be whole numbers each period, refer to our discussion of integer programming in Chapter 11 to handle the situation.

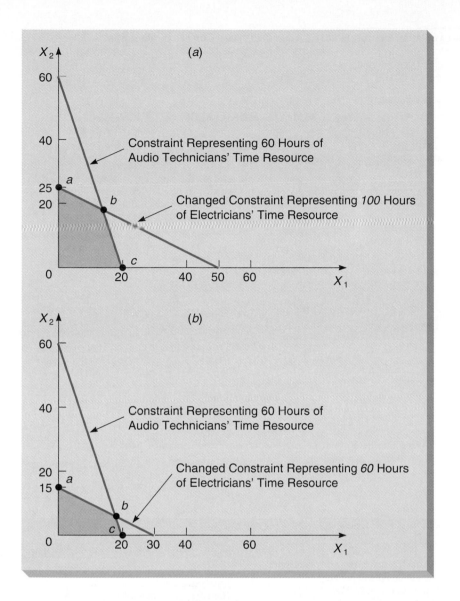

FIGURE 7.19

Changes in the Electricians' Time Resource for the High Note Sound Company

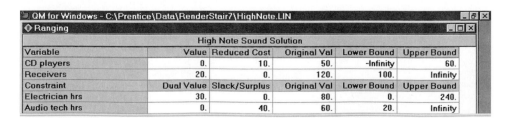

PROGRAM 7.5A

Input to QM for Windows for High Note Sound Company Data

QM for Windows - C:\Prentice\Data\RenderStair7\HighNote.LIN

Objective
- ● Maximize
- ○ Minimize

High Note Sound

	CD players	Receivers		RHS
Maximize	50	120		
Electrician hrs	2	4	<=	80
Audio tech hrs	3	1	<=	60

PROGRAM 7.5B

High Note Sound Company's LP Sensitivity Analysis Output Using Input from Program 7.5A

QM for Windows - C:\Prentice\Data\RenderStair7\HighNote.LIN

◇ Ranging

High Note Sound Solution

Variable	Value	Reduced Cost	Original Val	Lower Bound	Upper Bound
CD players	0.	10.	50.	-Infinity	60.
Receivers	20.		120.	100.	Infinity
Constraint	Dual Value	Slack/Surplus	Original Val	Lower Bound	Upper Bound
Electrician hrs	30.	0.	80.	0.	240.
Audio tech hrs	0.	40.	60.	20.	Infinity

285

PROGRAM 7.6A

Excel Spreadsheet Analysis of High Note Sound Company

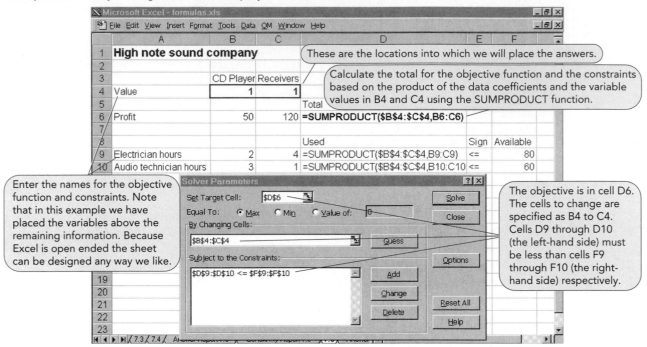

PROGRAM 7.6B

Excel's Sensitivity Analysis Output for High Note Sound Company

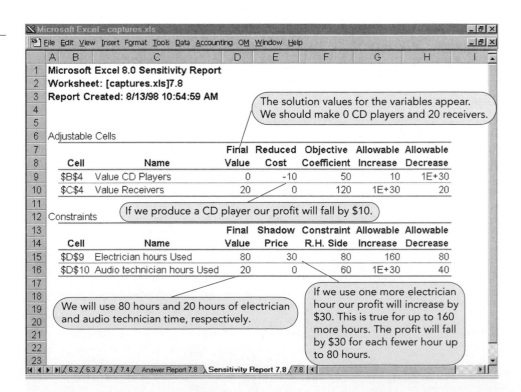

Summary

In this chapter we introduced a mathematical modeling technique called linear programming. It is used in reaching an optimum solution to problems that have a series of constraints binding the objective. We used both the corner point method and the isoprofit/isocost approaches for graphically solving small problems, that is, those with only two decision variables.

The graphical solution approaches of this chapter provide a conceptual basis for tackling larger, more complex problems, some of which are addressed in Chapter 8. To *solve* real-life LP problems with numerous variables and constraints, we need a solution procedure such as the simplex algorithm, the subject of Chapter 9. The simplex algorithm is the method that QM for Windows and Excel use to tackle LP problems.

In this chapter we also presented the important concept of sensitivity analysis. Sometimes referred to as postoptimality analysis, sensitivity analysis is used by management to answer a series of what-if? questions about LP model parameters. It also tests just how sensitive the optimal solution is to changes in profit or cost coefficients, technological coefficients, and right-hand-side resources. We explored sensitivity analysis graphically (that is, for problems with only two decision variables), but we will return to the topic again in Chapter 9 as we see how to conduct sensitivity algebraically through the simplex algorithm.

Glossary

Linear Programming (LP). A mathematical technique used to help management decide how to make the most effective use of an organization's resources.

Mathematical Programming. The general category of mathematical modeling and solution techniques used to allocate resources while optimizing a measurable goal. LP is one type of programming model.

Objective Function. A mathematical statement of the goal of an organization, stated as an intent to maximize or to minimize some important quantity such as profits or costs.

Constraint. A restriction on the resources available to a firm (stated in the form of an inequality or an equation).

Inequality. A mathematical expression containing a greater-than-or-equal-to relation ($\geq$) or a less-than-or-equal-to relation ($\leq$) used to indicate that the total consumption of a resource must be $\geq$ or $\leq$ some limiting value.

Product Mix Problem. A common LP problem involving a decision as to which products a firm should produce given that it faces limited resources.

Nonnegativity Constraints. A set of constraints that requires each decision variable to be nonnegative; that is, each X_i must be greater than or equal to 0.

Feasible Region. The area satisfying all of the problem's resource restrictions; that is, the region where all constraints overlap. All possible solutions to the problem lie in the feasible region.

Feasible Solution. A point lying in the feasible region. Basically, it is any point that satisfies all of the problem's constraints.

Infeasible Solution. Any point lying outside the feasible region. It violates one or more of the stated constraints.

Isoprofit Line. A straight line representing all nonnegative combinations of X_1 and X_2 for a particular profit level.

Corner Point Method. The method of finding the optimal solution to an LP problem by testing the profit or cost level at each corner point of the feasible region. The theory of LP states that the optimal solution must lie at one of the corner points.

Corner Point or Extreme Point. A point that lies on one of the corners of the feasible region. This means that it falls at the intersection of two constraint lines.

Simultaneous Equation Method. The algebraic means of solving for the intersection point of two or more linear constraint equations.

Isocost Line. A straight line representing all combinations of X_1 and X_2 for a particular cost level.

Infeasibility. A condition that arises when there is no solution to an LP problem that satisfies all of the constraints.

Unboundedness. A condition that exists when a solution variable and the profit can be made infinitely large without violating any of the problem's constraints in a maximization process.

Redundancy. The presence of one or more constraints that do not affect the feasible solution region.

Alternate Optimal Solution. A situation when more than one optimal solution is possible. It arises when the angle or slope of the objective function is the same as the slope of a constraint.

Sensitivity Analysis. The study of how sensitive an optimal solution is to model assumptions and to data changes. It is often referred to as postoptimality analysis.

Technological Coefficients. Coefficients of the variables in the constraint equations. The coefficients represent the amount of resources needed to produce one unit of the variable.

Solved Problems

Solved Problem 7-1

Personal Mini Warehouses is planning to expand its successful Orlando business into Tampa. In doing so, the company must determine how many storage rooms of each size to build. Its objective and constraints follow:

$$\text{maximize monthly earnings} = 50X_1 + 20X_2$$

subject to:

$$2X_1 + 4X_2 \leq 400 \quad \text{(advertising budget available)}$$

$$100X_1 + 50X_2 \leq 8{,}000 \quad \text{(square footage required)}$$

$$X_1 \leq 60 \quad \text{(rental limit expected)}$$

$$X_1, X_2 \geq 0$$

where

$$X_1 = \text{number of large spaces developed}$$

$$X_2 = \text{number of small spaces developed}$$

Solution

An evaluation of the five corner points of the accompanying graph indicates that corner point C produces the greatest earnings. Refer to the graph and table.

CORNER POINT	VALUES OF X_1, X_2	OBJECTIVE FUNCTION VALUE ($)
A	(0, 0)	0
B	(60, 0)	3,000
C	(60, 40)	3,800
D	(40, 80)	3,600
E	(0, 100)	2,000

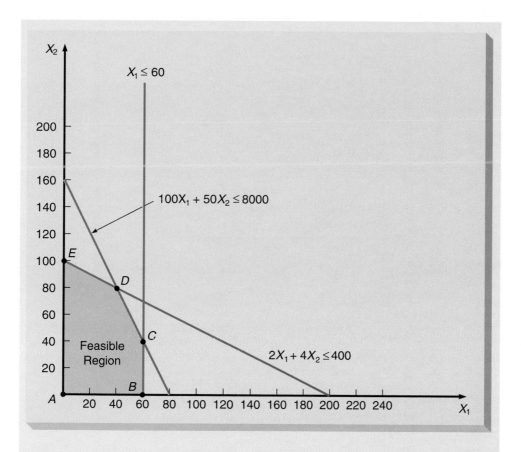

Solved Problem 7-2

Solve the following LP formulation graphically, using the isocost line approach:

$$\text{minimize costs} = 24X_1 + 28X_2$$

$$\text{subject to } 5X_1 + 4X_2 \leq 2{,}000$$

$$X_1 \qquad \geq 80$$

$$X_1 + X_2 \geq 300$$

$$X_2 \geq 100$$

$$X_1, X_2 \geq 0$$

Solution

A graph of the four constraints follows. The arrows indicate the direction of feasibility for each constraint. The next graph illustrates the feasible solution region and plots of two possible objective function cost lines. The first, $10,000, was selected arbitrarily as a starting point. To find the optimal corner point, we need to move the cost line in the direction of lower cost, that is, down and to the left. The last point where a cost line touches the feasible region as it moves toward the origin is corner point D. Thus D, which represents $X_1 = 200$, $X_2 = 100$, and a cost of $7,600, is optimal.

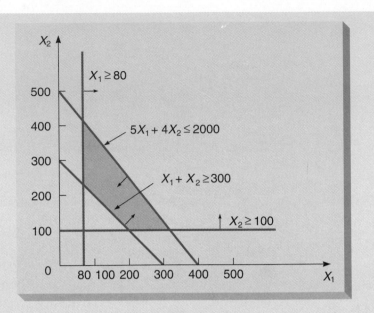

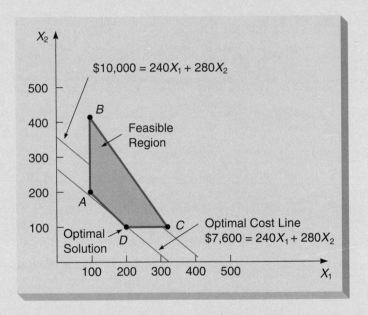

Solved Problem 7-3

Solve the following problems given these constraints and objective function:

$$\text{maximize profit} = 30X_1 + 40X_2$$

$$\text{subject to} \quad 4X_1 + 2X_2 \leq 16$$

$$2X_1 - X_2 \geq 2$$

$$X_2 \leq 2$$

$$X_1, X_2 \geq 0$$

(a) Graph the feasible region.

(b) Evaluate the objective function at each corner point.

(c) Identify the optimal solution.

Solution

(a) The graph appears next with the feasible region shaded.

(b)

CORNER POINT	COORDINATES	PROFIT ($)
A	$X_1 = 1, X_2 = 0$	30
B	$X_1 = 4, X_2 = 0$	120
C	$X_1 = 3, X_2 = 2$	170
D	$X_1 = 2, X_2 = 2$	140

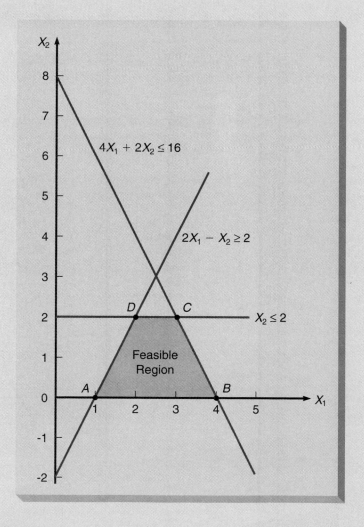

(c) The optimal profit of $170 is at corner point C.

SELF-TEST

- Before taking the self-test, refer back to the learning objectives at the beginning of the chapter, the notes in the margins, and the glossary at the end of the chapter.
- Use the key at the back of the book to correct your answers.
- Restudy pages that correspond to any questions that you answered incorrectly or material you feel uncertain about.

1. When using a graphical solution procedure, the region bounded by the set of constraints is called the
   a. solution.
   b. feasible region.
   c. infeasible region.
   d. maximum profit region.
   e. none of the above.
2. The isoprofit solution method can only be used to solve maximization problems.
   a. True   b. False
3. Sensitivity analysis is also called
   a. dynamic programming.
   b. parametric statistics.
   c. postoptimality analysis.
   d. all of the above.
   e. none of the above.
4. When a technological coefficient changes in sensitivity analysis, the feasible region and optimal solution may change.
   a. True   b. False
5. Using the *graphical solution procedure* to solve a maximization problem requires that we
   a. move the isoprofit line up until it no longer intersects with any constraint equation.
   b. move the isoprofit line down until it no longer intersects with any constraint equation.
   c. apply the method of simultaneous equations to solve for the intersections of constraints.
   d. find the value of the objective functions at the origin.
   e. none of the above.
6. The graphical method of LP can only handle _____ decision variables.
   a. one
   b. two
   c. three
   d. none of the above
7. Types of graphical solutions to LP include all but
   a. isoprofit line solution.
   b. the corner-point solution.

   c. the simplex method.
   d. all are solutions to the graphic approach.
   e. none are solutions to the graphic approach.
8. The graphic method of LP uses
   a. objective equations.
   b. constraint equations.
   c. linear equations.
   d. all of the above.
   e. none of the above.
9. Any LP problem can be solved using the graphical solution procedure.
   a. True   b. False
10. In the term *linear programming*, the word *programming* comes from the phrase "computer programming."
    a. True   b. False
11. The set of solution points that satisfies all of an LP problem's constraints simultaneously is defined as the feasible region in graphical LP.
    a. True   b. False
12. An objective function is necessary in a maximization problem but is not required in a minimization problem.
    a. True   b. False
13. Which of the following is *not* a property of all LP problems?
    a. the presence of restrictions.
    b. optimization of some objective.
    c. a computer program.
    d. alternative courses of action to choose from.
    e. usage of only linear equations and inequalities.
14. A feasible solution to an LP problem
    a. must satisfy all of the problem's constraints simultaneously.
    b. need not satisfy all of the constraints, only some of them.
    c. must be a corner point of the feasible region.
    d. must give the maximum possible profit.

Discussion Questions and Problems

Discussion Questions

7-1 Discuss the similarities and differences between minimization and maximization problems using the graphical solution approaches of LP.

7-2 It is important to understand the assumptions underlying the use of any quantitative analysis model. What are the assumptions and requirements for an LP model to be formulated and used?

7-3 It has been said that each LP problem that has a feasible region has an infinite number of solutions. Explain.

7-4 You have just formulated a maximization LP problem and are preparing to solve it graphically. What criteria should you consider in deciding whether it would be easier to solve the problem by the corner point method or the isoprofit line approach?

7-5 Under what condition is it possible for an LP problem to have more than one optimal solution?

7-6 Develop your own set of constraint equations and inequalities and use them to illustrate graphically each of the following conditions:
  (a) an unbounded problem
  (b) an infeasible problem
  (c) a problem containing redundant constraints

7-7 The production manager of a large Cincinnati manufacturing firm once made the statement, "I would like to use LP, but it's a technique that operates under conditions of certainty. My plant doesn't have that certainty; it's a world of uncertainty. So LP can't be used here." Do you think this statement has any merit? Explain why the manager may have said it.

7-8 The mathematical relationships that follow were formulated by an operations research analyst at the Smith–Lawton Chemical Company. Which ones are invalid for use in an LP problem, and why?

$$\text{maximize profit} = 4X_1 + 3X_1X_2 + 8X_2 + 5X_3$$

$$\text{subject to} \quad 2X_1 + X_2 + 2X_3 \le 50$$

$$X_1 - 4X_2 \ge 6$$

$$1.5X_1^2 + 6X_2 + 3X_3 \ge 21$$

$$19X_2 - \tfrac{1}{3}X_3 = 17$$

$$5X_1 + 4X_2 + 3\sqrt{X_3} \le 80$$

$$-X_1 - X_2 + X_3 = 5$$

7-9 Discuss the role of sensitivity analysis in LP. Under what circumstances is it needed, and under what conditions do you think it is not necessary?

7-10 Is sensitivity analysis a concept applied to LP only, or should it also be used when analyzing other techniques? Provide examples to prove your point.

7-11 What is the value of the computer in solving LP problems today?

7-12 Develop your own original LP problem with two constraints and two real variables.
  (a) Explain the meaning of the numbers on the right-hand side of each of your constraints.
  (b) Explain the significance of the technological coefficients.
  (c) Solve your problem graphically to find the optimal solution.
  (d) Illustrate graphically the effect of increasing the contribution rate of your first variable (X_1) by 50% over the value you first assigned it. Does this change the optimal solution?

7-13 Explain how a change in a technological coefficient can affect a problem's optimal solution. How can a change in resource availability affect a solution?

Problems*

7-14 The Electrocomp Corporation manufactures two electrical products: air conditioners and large fans. The assembly process for each is similar in that both require a certain amount of wiring and drilling. Each air conditioner takes 3 hours of wiring and 2 hours of drilling. Each fan must go through 2 hours of wiring and 1 hour of drilling. During the next production period, 240 hours of wiring time are available and up to 140 hours of drilling time may be used. Each air conditioner sold yields a profit of $25. Each fan assembled may be sold for a $15 profit. Formulate and solve this LP production mix situation to find the best combination of air conditioners and fans that yields the highest profit. Use the corner point graphical approach.

7-15 Electrocomp's management realizes that it forgot to include two critical constraints (see Problem 7-14). In particular, management decides that to ensure an adequate supply of air conditioners for a contract, at least 20 air conditioners should be manufactured. Because Electrocomp incurred an oversupply of fans the preceding period, management also insists that no more than 80 fans be produced during this production period. Resolve this product mix problem to find the new optimal solution.

7-16 The Marriott Tub Company manufactures two lines of bathtubs, called model A and model B. Every tub requires blending a certain amount of steel and zinc; the company has available a total of 25,000 pounds of steel and 6,000 pounds of zinc. Each model A bathtub requires a mixture of 125 pounds of steel and 20 pounds of zinc, and each yields a profit to the firm of $90. Each model B tub produced can be sold for a profit of $70; it in turn requires 100 pounds of steel and 30 pounds of zinc. Find by graphical LP the best production mix of bathtubs.

7-17 The Outdoor Furniture Corporation manufactures two products, benches and picnic tables, for use in yards and parks. The firm has two main resources: its carpenters (labor force) and a supply of redwood for use in the furniture. During the next production cycle, 1,200 hours of labor are available under a union agreement. The firm also has a stock of 3,500 feet of good-quality redwood. Each bench that Outdoor Furniture produces requires 4 labor hours and 10 feet of redwood; each picnic table takes 6 labor hours and 35 feet of redwood. Completed benches will yield a profit of $9 each, and tables will result in a profit of $20 each. How many benches and tables should Outdoor Furniture produce to obtain the largest possible profit? Use the graphical LP approach.

7-18 The dean of the Western College of Business must plan the school's course offerings for the fall semester. Student demands make it necessary to offer at least 30 undergraduate and 20 graduate courses in the term. Faculty contracts also dictate that at least 60 courses be offered in total. Each undergraduate course taught costs the college an average of $2,500 in faculty wages, and each graduate course costs $3,000. How many undergraduate and graduate courses should be taught in the fall so that total faculty salaries are kept to a minimum?

7-19 MSA Computer Corporation manufactures two models of minicomputers, the Alpha 4 and the Beta 5. The firm employs five technicians, working 160 hours each per month, on its assembly line. Management insists that full employment (that is, *all* 160 hours of time) be maintained for each worker during next month's operations. It requires 20 labor hours to assemble each Alpha 4 computer and 25 labor hours to assemble each Beta 5 model. MSA wants to see at least 10 Alpha 4s and at least 15 Beta 5s produced during the production period. Alpha 4s generate a $1,200 profit per unit, and Beta 5s yield $1,800 each. Determine the most profitable number of each model of minicomputer to produce during the coming month.

---

*Note: 🖳 means the problem may be solved with QM for Windows; ✖ means the problem may be solved with Excel; and 🖳 means the problem may be solved with QM for Windows and/or Excel.

: **7-20** The Sweet Smell Fertilizer Company markets bags of manure labeled "not less than 60 pounds dry weight." The packaged manure is a combination of compost and sewage wastes. To provide good-quality fertilizer, each bag should contain at least 30 pounds of compost but no more than 40 pounds of sewage. Each pound of compost costs Sweet Smell 5 cents and each pound of sewage costs 4 cents. Use a graphical LP method to determine the least cost blend of compost and sewage in each bag.

• **7-21** The National Credit Union has $250,000 available to invest in a 12-month commitment. The money can be placed in Treasury notes yielding an 8% return or in municipal bonds at an average rate of return of 9%. Credit union regulations require diversification to the extent that at least 50% of the investment be placed in Treasury notes. Because of defaults in such municipalities as Cleveland and New York, it is decided that no more than 40% of the investment be placed in bonds. How much should the National Credit Union invest in each security so as to maximize its return on investment?

: **7-22** Solve the following LP problem using the corner point graphical method:

maximize profit $= 4X_1 + 4X_2$

subject to $3X_1 + 5X_2 \leq 150$

$X_1 - 2X_2 \leq 10$

$5X_1 + 3X_2 \leq 150$

$X_1, X_2 \geq 0$

: **7-23** Consider this LP formulation:

minimize cost $= \$1X_1 + \$2X_2$

subject to $X_1 + 3X_2 \geq 90$

$8X_1 + 2X_2 \geq 160$

$3X_1 + 2X_2 \geq 120$

$X_2 \leq 70$

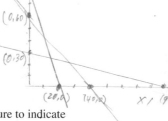

Graphically illustrate the feasible region and apply the isocost line procedure to indicate which corner point produces the optimal solution. What is the cost of this solution?

: **7-24** The stock brokerage firm of Blank, Leibowitz, and Weinberger has analyzed and recommended two stocks to an investors' club of college professors. The professors were interested in factors such as short-term growth, intermediate growth, and dividend rates. These data on each stock are as follows:

	STOCK ($)	
FACTOR	LOUISIANA GAS AND POWER	TRIMEX INSULATION COMPANY
Short-term growth potential, per dollar invested	.36	.24
Intermediate growth potential (over next three years), per dollar invested	1.67	1.50
Dividend rate potential	4%	8%

Each member of the club has an investment goal of (1) an appreciation of no less than $720 in the short term, (2) an appreciation of at least $5,000 in the next three years, and (3) a dividend income of at least $200 per year. What is the smallest investment that a professor can make to meet these three goals?

7-25 The advertising agency promoting the new Breem dishwashing detergent wants to get the best exposure possible for the product within the $100,000 advertising budget ceiling placed upon it. To do so, the agency needs to decide how much of the budget to spend on each of its two most effective media: (1) television spots during the afternoon hours and (2) large ads in the city's Sunday newspaper. Each television spot costs $3,000; each Sunday newspaper ad costs $1,250. The expected exposure, based on industry ratings, is 35,000 viewers for each TV commercial and 20,000 readers for each newspaper advertisement. The agency director, Mavis Early, knows from experience that it is important to use both media in order to reach the broadest spectrum of potential Breem customers. She decides that at least 5 but no more than 25 television spots should be ordered; and that at least 10 newspaper ads should be contracted. How many times should each of the two media be used to obtain maximum exposure while staying within the budget? Use the graphical method to solve.

 7-26 The seasonal yield of olives in a Piraeus, Greece, vineyard is greatly influenced by a process of branch pruning. If olive trees are pruned every two weeks, output is increased. The pruning process, however, requires considerably more labor than permitting the olives to grow on their own and results in a smaller size olive. It also, though, permits olive trees to be spaced closer together. The yield of 1 barrel of olives by pruning requires 5 hours of labor and 1 acre of land. The production of a barrel of olives by the normal process requires only 2 labor hours but takes 2 acres of land. An olive grower has 250 hours of labor available and a total of 150 acres for growing. Because of the olive size difference, a barrel of olives produced on pruned trees sells for $20, whereas a barrel of regular olives has a market price of $30. The grower has determined that because of uncertain demand, no more than 40 barrels of pruned olives should be produced. Use graphical LP to find
(a) the maximum possible profit.
(b) the best combination of barrels of pruned and regular olives.
(c) the number of acres that the olive grower should devote to each growing process.

 7-27 Consider the following four LP formulations. Using a graphical approach, determine
(a) which formulation has more than one optimal solution.
(b) which formulation is unbounded.
(c) which formulation is infeasible.
(d) which formulation is correct as is.

Formulation 1

maximize: $10X_1 + 10X_2$

subject to
$$2X_1 \leq 10$$
$$2X_1 + 4X_2 \leq 16$$
$$4X_2 \leq 8$$
$$X_1 \geq 6$$

Formulation 2

maximize: $X_1 + 2X_2$

subject to
$$X_1 \leq 1$$
$$2X_2 \leq 2$$
$$X_1 + 2X_2 \leq 2$$

Formulation 3

maximize: $3X_1 + 2X_2$

subject to
$$X_1 + X_2 \geq 5$$
$$X_1 \geq 2$$
$$2X_2 \geq 8$$

Formulation 4

maximize: $3X_1 + 3X_2$

subject to
$$4X_1 + 6X_2 \leq 48$$
$$4X_1 + 2X_2 \leq 12$$
$$3X_2 \geq 3$$
$$2X_1 \geq 2$$

7-28 Graph the following LP problem and indicate the optimal solution point:

maximize profit $= \$3X_1 + \$2X_2$

subject to $2X_1 + 1X_2 \leq 150$

$2X_1 + 3X_2 \leq 300$

(a) Does the optimal solution change if the profit per unit of X_1 changes to $4.50?

(b) What happens if the profit function should have been $\$3X_1 + \$3X_2$?

 7-29 Graphically analyze the following problem:

maximize profit $= \$4X_1 + \$6X_2$

subject to $1X_1 + 2X_2 \leq 8$

$6X_1 + 4X_2 \leq 24$

(a) What is the optimal solution?

(b) If the first constraint is altered to $1X_1 + 3X_2 \leq 8$, does the feasible region or optimal solution change?

 7-30 Consider the following LP problem:

maximize profit $= \$1X_1 + \$1X_2$

subject to $2X_1 + 1X_2 \leq 100$

$1X_1 + 2X_2 \leq 100$

(a) What is the optimal solution to this problem? Solve it graphically.

(b) If a technical breakthrough occurred that raised the profit per unit of X_1 to $3, would this affect the optimal solution?

(c) Instead of an increase in the profit coefficient X_1 to $3, suppose that profit was overestimated and should only have been $1.25. Does this change the optimal solution?

 7-31 Consider the LP formulation given in Problem 7-30. If the second constraint is changed from $1X_1 + 2X_2 \leq 100$ to $1X_1 + 4X_2 \leq 100$, what effect will this have on the optimal solution? (Use the same objective function, profit $= 1X_1 + 1X_2$.)

 7-32 Examine the LP formulation in Problem 7-29. The problem's second constraint reads

$6X_1 + 4X_2 \leq 24$ hours   (time available on machine 2)

If the firm decides that 36 hours of time can be made available on machine 2 (namely, an additional 12 hours) at an additional cost of $10, should it add the hours?

7-33 Serendipity[6]

The three princes of Serendip
Went on a little trip.
They could not carry too much weight;
More than 300 pounds made them hesitate.
They planned to the ounce. When they returned to Ceylon
They discovered that their supplies were just about gone
When, what to their joy, Prince William found
A pile of coconuts on the ground.
"Each will bring 60 rupees," said Prince Richard with a grin
As he almost tripped over a lion skin.
"Look out!" cried Prince Robert with glee

---

[6] The word *serendipity* was coined by the English writer Horace Walpole after a fairy tale titled *The Three Princes of Serendip*. Source of problem is unknown.

As he spied some more lion skins under a tree.
"These are worth even more—300 rupees each
If we can just carry them all down to the beach."
Each skin weighed fifteen pounds and each coconut, five,
But they carried them all and made it alive.
The boat back to the island was very small
15 cubic feet baggage capacity—that was all.
Each lion skin took up one cubic foot
While eight coconuts the same space took.
With everything stowed they headed to sea
And on the way calculated what their new wealth might be.
"Eureka!" cried Prince Robert, "Our worth is so great
That there's no other way we could return in this state.
Any other skins or nut that we might have brought
Would now have us poorer. And now I know what—
I'll write my friend Horace in England, for surely
Only he can appreciate our serendipity."

Formulate and *solve* Serendipity by graphical LP in order to calculate "what their new wealth might be."

Problems 7-34, 7-35, and 7-38 test your ability to formulate LP problems that have more than two variables. They cannot be solved graphically but will give you a chance to set up a larger problem.

 7-34 The Feed 'N Ship Ranch fattens cattle for local farmers and ships them to meat markets in Kansas City and Omaha. The owners of the ranch seek to determine the amounts of cattle feed to buy so that minimum nutritional standards are satisfied, and at the same time total feed costs are minimized. The feed mix used can be made up of the three grains that contain the following ingredients per pound of feed:

INGREDIENT	FEED (OZ)		
	STOCK X	STOCK Y	STOCK Z
A	3	2	4
B	2	3	1
C	1	0	2
D	6	8	4

The cost per pound of stocks X, Y, and Z are $2, $4, and $2.50, respectively. The minimum requirement per cow per month is 4 pounds of ingredient A, 5 pounds of ingredient B, 1 pound of ingredient C, and 8 pounds of ingredient D.

The ranch faces one additional restriction: it can only obtain 500 pounds of stock Z per month from the feed supplier regardless of its need. Because there are usually 100 cows at the Feed 'N Ship Ranch at any given time, this means that no more than 5 pounds of stock Z can be counted on for use in the feed of each cow per month.
(a) Formulate this as an LP problem.
(b) Solve using LP software.

 7-35 The Weinberger Electronics Corporation manufactures four highly technical products that it supplies to aerospace firms that hold NASA contracts. Each of the products must pass through the following departments before they are shipped: wiring, drilling, assembly, and inspection. The time requirement in hours for each unit produced and its corresponding profit value are summarized in the following table:

| | DEPARTMENT | | | | |
PRODUCT	WIRING	DRILLING	ASSEMBLY	INSPECTION	UNIT PROFIT ($)
XJ201	0.5	0.3	0.2	0.5	9
XM897	1.5	1	4	1	12
TR29	1.5	2	1	0.5	15
BR788	1	3	2	0.5	11

The production available in each department each month, and the minimum monthly production requirement to fulfill contracts, are as follows:

DEPARTMENT	CAPACITY (HOURS)	PRODUCT	MINIMUM PRODUCTION LEVEL
Wiring	15,000	XJ201	150
Drilling	17,000	XM897	100
Assembly	26,000	TR29	300
Inspection	12,000	BR788	400

The production manager has the responsibility of specifying production levels for each product for the coming month. Help him by formulating (that is, setting up the constraints and objective function) Weinberger's problem using LP.

 7-36 Androgynous Bicycle Company (ABC) has the hottest new products on the upscale toy market—boys' and girls' bikes in bright fashion colors, with oversized hubs and axles, shell design safety tires, a strong padded frame, chrome-plated chains, brackets and valves, and a nonslip handlebar. Due to the seller's market for high-quality toys for the newest baby boomers, ABC can sell all the bicycles it manufactures at the following prices: boys' bikes—$220, girls' bikes—$175. This is the price payable to ABC at its Orlando plant.

The firm's accountant has determined that direct labor costs will be 45% of the price ABC receives for the boys' model and 40% of the price received for the girls' model. Production costs other than labor, but excluding painting and packaging, are $44 per boys' bicycle and $30 per girls' bicycle. Painting and packaging are $20 per bike, regardless of model.

The Orlando plant's overall production capacity is 390 bicycles per day. Each boy's bike requires 2.5 labor hours and each girl's model, 2.4 hours, to complete. ABC currently employs 120 workers, who each put in an 8-hour day. The firm has no desire to hire or fire to affect labor availability, for it believes its stable workforce is one of its biggest assets. Using a graphical approach, determine the best product mix for ABC.

 7-37 Modem Corporation of America (MCA) is the world's largest producer of modem communication devices for microcomputers. MCA sold 9,000 of the regular model and 10,400 of the smart ("intelligent") model this September. Its income statement for the month is shown in the table on the next page. Costs presented are typical of prior months and are expected to remain at the same levels in the near future.

The firm is facing several constraints as it prepares its November production plan. First, it has experienced a tremendous demand and has been unable to keep any significant inventory in stock. This situation is not expected to change. Second, the firm is located in a small Iowa town from which additional labor is not readily available. Workers can be shifted from production of one modem to another, however. To produce the

9,000 regular modems in September required 5,000 direct labor hours. The 10,400 intelligent modems absorbed 10,400 direct labor hours. Third, MCA is experiencing a problem affecting the intelligent modems model. Its component supplier is able to guarantee only 8,000 microprocessors for November delivery. Each intelligent modem requires one of these specially made microprocessors. Alternative suppliers are not available on short notice.

MCA wants to plan the optimal mix of the two modem models to produce in November to maximize profits for MCA.

(a) Formulate, using September's data, MCA's problem as a linear program.
(b) Solve the problem graphically.
(c) Discuss the implications of your recommended solution.

TABLE FOR PROBLEM 7-37
MCA INCOME STATEMENT MONTH ENDED SEPTEMBER 30

		REGULAR MODEMS	**INTELLIGENT MODEMS**
Sales		$450,000	$640,000
Less:	Discounts	10,000	15,000
	Returns	12,000	9,500
	Warranty replacements	4,000	2,500
Net sales		$424,000	$613,000
Sales costs			
	Direct labor	60,000	76,800
	Indirect labor	9,000	11,520
	Materials cost	90,000	128,000
	Depreciation	40,000	50,800
	Cost of sales	$199,000	$267,120
Gross profit		$225,000	$345,880
Selling and general expenses			
	General expenses—variable	30,000	35,000
	General expenses—fixed	36,000	40,000
	Advertising	28,000	25,000
	Sales commissions	31,000	60,000
	Total operating cost	$125,000	$160,000
Pretax income		$100,000	$185,880
Income taxes (25%)		25,000	46,470
Net income		$ 75,000	$139,410

 7-38 Working with chemists at Virginia Tech and George Washington universities, landscape contractor Kenneth Golding blended his own fertilizer, called "Golding-Grow." It consists of four chemical compounds, C-30, C-92, D-21, and E-11. The cost per pound for each compound is indicated as follows:

CHEMICAL COMPOUND	COST PER POUND ($)
C-30	0.12
C-92	0.09
D-21	0.11
E-11	0.04

The specifications for Golding-Grow are as follows: (1) E-11 must constitute at least 15% of the blend; (2) C-92 and C-30 must together constitute at least 45% of the blend; (3) D-21 and C-92 can together constitute no more than 30% of the blend; and (4) Golding-Grow is packaged and sold in 50-pound bags.

(a) Formulate an LP problem to determine what blend of the four chemicals will allow Golding to minimize the cost of a 50-pound bag of the fertilizer.

(b) Solve by computer to find the best solution.

Case Study

Mexicana Wire Works

Ron Garcia felt good about his first week as management trainee at Mexicana Wire Winding, Inc. He had not yet developed any technical knowledge about the manufacturing process, but he had toured the entire facility, located in the suburbs of Mexico City, and had met many people in various areas of the operation.

Mexicana, a subsidiary of Westover Wire Works, a Texas firm, is a medium-sized producer of wire windings used in making electrical transformers. Carlos Alverez, the production control manager, described the windings to Garcia as being of standardized design. Garcia's tour of the plant, laid out by process type (see Figure 7.20), followed the manufacturing sequence for the windings: drawing, extrusion, winding, inspection, and packaging. After inspection, good product is packaged and sent to finished product storage; defective product is stored separately until it can be reworked.

On March 8, Vivian Espania, Mexicana's general manager, stopped by Garcia's office and asked him to attend a staff meeting at 1:00 P.M.

"Let's get started with the business at hand," Vivian said, opening the meeting. "You all have met Ron Garcia, our new management trainee. Ron studied operations management in his MBA program in southern California, so I think he is competent to help us with a problem we have been discussing for a long time without resolution. I'm sure that each of you on my staff will give Ron your full cooperation."

Vivian turned to José Arroyo, production control manager, "José, why don't you describe the problem we are facing?"

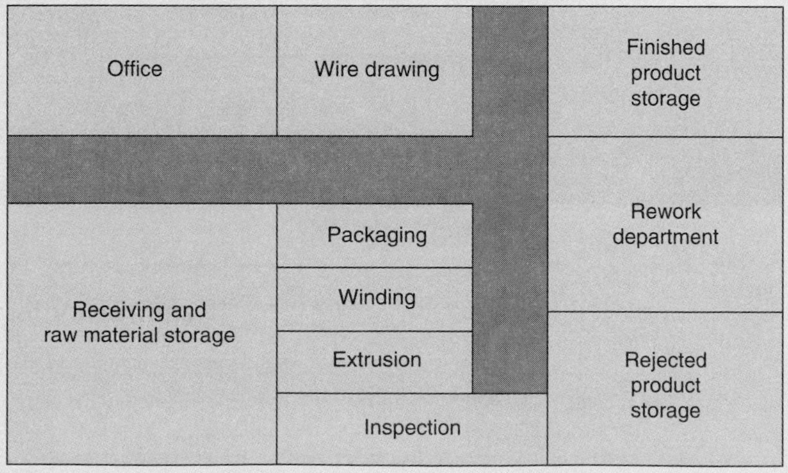

FIGURE 7.20

Mexicana Wire Winding, Inc.

Office	Wire drawing		Finished product storage
Receiving and raw material storage	Packaging		Rework department
	Winding		
	Extrusion		Rejected product storage
	Inspection		

"Well," José said, "business is very good right now. We are booking more orders than we can fill. We will have some new equipment on line within the next several months, which will take care of our capacity problems, but that won't help us in April. I have located some retired employees who used to work in the drawing department, and I am planning to bring them in as temporary employees in April to increase capacity there. Because we are planning to refinance some of our long-term debt, Vivian wants our profits to look as good as possible in April. I'm having a hard time figuring out which orders to run and which to back-order so that I can make the bottom line look as good as possible. Can you help me with this?"

Garcia was surprised and apprehensive to receive such an important, high-profile assignment so early in his career. Recovering quickly, he said, "Give me your data and let me work with it for a day or two."

April Orders

Product W0075C	1,400 units
Product W0033C	250 units
Product W0005X	1,510 units
Product W0007X	1,116 units

Note: Vivian Espania has given her word to a key customer that we will manufacture 600 units of product W0007X and 150 units of product W0075C for him during April.

Standard Cost

PRODUCT	MATERIAL	LABOR	OVERHEAD	SELLING PRICE
W0075C	$33.00	$ 9.90	$23.10	$100.00
W0033C	25.00	7.50	17.50	80.00
W0005X	35.00	10.50	24.50	130.00
W0007X	75.00	11.25	63.75	175.00

Selected Operating Data

Average output per month = 2,400 units

Average machine utilization = 63%

Average percentage of production sent to rework department = 5% (mostly from Winding Department)

Average no. of rejected units awaiting rework = 850 (mostly from Winding Department)

Plant Capacity (Hours)

DRAWING	EXTRUSION	WINDING	PACKAGING
4,000	4,200	2,000	2,300

Note: Inspection capacity is not a problem; we can work overtime as necessary to accommodate any schedule.

Bill of Labor (Hours/Unit)

PRODUCT	DRAWING	EXTRUSION	WINDING	PACKAGING
W0075C	1.0	1.0	1.0	1.0
W0033C	2.0	1.0	3.0	0.0
W0005X	0.0	4.0	0.0	3.0
W0007X	1.0	1.0	0.0	2.0

Discussion Questions

1. What recommendations should Ron Garcia make, with what justification? Provide a detailed analysis with charts, graphs, and computer printouts included.
2. Discuss the need for temporary workers in the drawing department.
3. Discuss the plant layout.

Source: Professor Victor E. Sower, Sam Houston State University. This case material is based on an actual situation, with names and data altered for confidentiality.

INTERNET CASE STUDY

See our Internet home page at **http://www.prenhall.com/render** for this additional case study: Agri Chem Corporation.

Bibliography

Bodington, C. E., and T. E. Baker. "A History of Mathematical Programming in the Petroleum Industry," *Interfaces* 20, 4 (July–August 1990): 117–132.

Eliman, A. A., M. Girgis, and S. Kotob. "A Solution to Post-Crash Debt Entanglements in Kuwait's al-Manakh Stock Market," *Interfaces* 27, (January–February 1997): 89–106.

Farley, A. A. "Planning the Cutting of Photographic Color Paper Rolls for Kodak (Australasia) Pty. Ltd.," *Interfaces* 21, 1 (January–February 1991): 92—106.

Ferris, M. C., and A. B. Philpott. "On the Performance of Karmarkar's Algorithm," *Journal of the Operational Research Society* 39 (March 1988): 257—270.

Gass, S. I. *An Illustrated Guide to Linear Programming*. New York: Dover Publications, Inc., 1990.

Greenberg, H. J. "How to Analyze the Results of Linear Programs—Part 1: Preliminaries," *Interfaces* 23, 4 (July–August 1993): 56–68.

Greenberg, H. J. "How to Analyze the Results of Linear Programs—Part 3: Infeasibility Diagnosis," *Interfaces* 23, 6 (November–December 1993): 120–139.

Hirshfeld, D. S. "Some Thoughts on Math Programming Practice in the '90s," *Interfaces* 20, 4 (July–August 1990): 158–165.

Orden, A. "LP from the '40s to the '90s," *Interfaces* 23, 5 (September–October 1993): 2.

Quinn, P., B. Andrews, and H. Parsons. "Allocating Telecommunications Resources at L. L. Bean, Inc.," *Interfaces* 21, 1 (January–February 1991): 75—91.

Rubin, D. S., and H. M. Wagner. "Shadow Prices: Tips and Traps for Managers and Instructors," *Interfaces* 20, 4 (July–August 1990): 150–157.

Saltzman, M. J. "Survey: Mixed Integer Programming," *OR/MS Today* 21, 2 (April 1994): 42–51.

Schindler, S., and T. Semmel. "Station Staffing at Pan American World Airways," *Interfaces* 23, 3 (May–June 1993): 91.

Sexton, T. R., S. Sleeper, and R. E. Taggart, Jr. "Improving Pupil Transportation in North Carolina," *Interfaces* 24, 1 (January–February 1994): 87–104.

Zappe, C., W. Webster, and I. Horowitz. "Using Linear Programming to Determine Post-Facto Consistency in Performance Evaluations of Major League Baseball Players," *Interfaces* 23, 6 (November–December 1993): 107–119.

Linear Programming Modeling Applications: With Computer Analyses in Excel and QM for Windows

LEARNING OBJECTIVES

After completing this chapter, students will be able to:

1. Model a wide variety of medium to large LP problems.
2. Understand major application areas, including marketing, production, labor scheduling, fuel blending, transportation, and finance.
3. Gain experience in solving LP problems with QM for Windows and Excel Solver Software.

CHAPTER OUTLINE

8.1 Introduction

8.2 Marketing Applications

8.3 Manufacturing Applications

8.4 Employee Scheduling Applications

8.5 Financial Applications

8.6 Transportation Applications

8.7 Ingredient Blending Applications

Summary • Self-Test • Problems • Case Study: Red Brand Canners • Case Study: Chase Manhattan Bank • Bibliography

8.1 INTRODUCTION

The graphical method of linear programming (LP) discussed in Chapter 7 is useful for understanding how to formulate and solve small LP problems. The purpose of this chapter is to go one step further and show how a large number of real-life problems can be modeled using LP. We do this by presenting examples of models in the areas of production mix, labor scheduling, job assignment, production scheduling, marketing research, media selection, shipping and transportation, ingredient mix, and financial portfolio selection. We will solve many of these LP problems using Excel's Solver and QM for Windows.

Although some of these models are relatively small numerically, the principles developed here are definitely applicable to larger problems. Moreover, this practice in "paraphrasing" LP model formulations should help develop your skills in applying the technique to other, less common applications.

8.2 MARKETING APPLICATIONS

Media Selection

Media selection problems can be approached with LP from two perspectives. The objective can be to maximize audience exposure or to minimize advertising costs.

Linear programming models have been used in the advertising field as a decision aid in selecting an effective media mix. Sometimes the technique is employed in allocating a fixed or limited budget across various media, which might include radio or television commercials, newspaper ads, direct mailings, magazine ads, and so on. In other applications, the objective is the maximization of audience exposure. Restrictions on the allowable media mix might arise through contract requirements, limited media availability, or company policy. An example follows.

The Win Big Gambling Club promotes gambling junkets from a large midwestern city to casinos in the Bahamas. The club has budgeted up to $8,000 per week for local advertising. The money is to be allocated among four promotional media: TV spots, newspaper ads, and two types of radio advertisements. Win Big's goal is to reach the largest possible high-potential audience through the various media. The following table presents the number of potential gamblers reached by making use of an advertisement in each of the four media. It also provides the cost per advertisement placed and the maximum number of ads that can be purchased per week.

MEDIUM	AUDIENCE REACHED PER AD	COST PER AD ($)	MAXIMUM ADS PER WEEK
TV spot (1 minute)	5,000	800	12
Daily newspaper (full-page ad)	8,500	925	5
Radio spot (30 seconds, prime time)	2,400	290	25
Radio spot (1 minute, afternoon)	2,800	380	20

Win Big's contractual arrangements require that at least five radio spots be placed each week. To ensure a broad-scoped promotional campaign, management also insists that no more than $1,800 be spent on radio advertising every week.

The problem can now be stated mathematically as follows. Let

X_1 = number of 1-minute TV spots taken each week

X_2 = number of full-page daily newspaper ads taken each week

X_3 = number of 30-second prime-time radio spots taken each week

X_4 = number of 1-minute afternoon radio spots taken each week

Objective:

maximize audience coverage = $5,000X_1 + 8,500X_2 + 2,400X_3 + 2,800X_4$

subject to
$$X_1 \leq 12 \quad \text{(maximum TV spots/week)}$$
$$X_2 \leq 5 \quad \text{(maximum newspaper ads/week)}$$
$$X_3 \leq 25 \quad \text{(maximum 30-second radio spots/week)}$$
$$X_4 \leq 20 \quad \text{(maximum 1-minute radio spots/week)}$$
$$800X_1 + 925X_2 + 290X_3 + 380X_4 \leq \$8,000 \text{ (weekly advertising budget)}$$
$$X_3 + X_4 \geq 5 \quad \text{(minimum radio spots contracted)}$$
$$290X_3 + 380X_4 \leq \$1,800 \text{ (maximum dollars spent on radio)}$$

The solution to this LP formulation, using Excel's Solver (see Programs 8.1A and 8.1B), is found to be

$X_1 = 1.97$ TV spots

$X_2 = 5$ newspaper ads

$X_3 = 6.2$ 30-second radio spots

$X_4 = 0$ one-minute radio spots

This produces an audience exposure of 67,240 contacts. Because X_1 and X_3 are fractional, Win Big would probably round them to 2 and 6, respectively. Problems that demand all-integer solutions are discussed in detail in Chapter 11.

Marketing Research

Linear programming has also been applied to marketing research problems and the area of consumer research. The next example illustrates how statistical pollsters can reach strategy decisions with LP.

Management Sciences Associates (MSA) is a marketing and computer research firm based in Washington, D.C., that handles consumer surveys. One of its clients is a national press service that periodically conducts political polls on issues of widespread interest. In a survey for the press service, MSA determines that it must fulfill several requirements in order to draw statistically valid conclusions on the sensitive issue of new U.S. immigration laws:

1. Survey at least 2,300 U.S. households in total.
2. Survey at least 1,000 households whose heads are 30 years of age or younger.
3. Survey at least 600 households whose heads are between 31 and 50 years of age.
4. Ensure that at least 15% of those surveyed live in a state that borders on Mexico.
5. Ensure that no more than 20% of those surveyed who are 51 years of age or over live in a state that borders on Mexico.

PROGRAM 8.1A

Excel Formulation of Win Big's LP Problem, Using the Solver Command

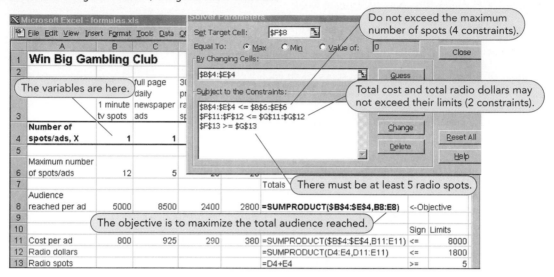

PROGRAM 8.1B

Output from Program 8.1A. Solution to the Win Big Gambling Club LP Model

MSA decides that all surveys should be conducted in person. It estimates that the costs of reaching people in each age and region category are as follows:

	COST PER PERSON SURVEYED ($)		
REGION	AGE ≤ 30	AGE 31–50	AGE ≥ 51
State bordering Mexico	$7.50	$6.80	$5.50
State not bordering Mexico	$6.90	$7.25	$6.10

IN ACTION   **Scheduling Planes at Delta Airlines With Coldstart**

It has been said that an airline seat is the most perishable commodity in the world. Each time an airliner takes off with an empty seat, a revenue opportunity is lost forever. For Delta Airlines, which flies more than 2,500 domestic flight legs per day using about 450 aircraft of 10 different models, its schedule is the very heartbeat of the airline.

One flight leg for Delta might consist of a Boeing 757 jet assigned to fly at 6:21 A.M. from Atlanta to arrive in Boston at 8:45 A.M. Delta's problem, the same as that of every competitor, is to match airplanes such as 747s, 757s, or 767s, to flight legs such as Atlanta–Boston, and fill seats with paying passengers. Recent advances in LP algorithms and computer hardware have made it possible to solve optimization problems of this scope for the first time. Delta calls its huge LP model Coldstart and runs the model every day. Delta is the first airline to solve a problem of this scope.

The typical size of a daily Coldstart model is about 40,000 constraints and 60,000 variables. The constraints are aircraft availability, balancing arrivals and departures at airports, aircraft maintenance needs, and so on. Coldstart's objective is to minimize a combination of operating costs and lost passenger revenue, called spill costs.

The savings from the model so far have been phenomenal, estimated at $220,000 per day over Delta's earlier schedule planning tool, which was nicknamed "Warmstart." Delta expects to save $300 million over the next three years through this use of LP.

Sources: R. Subramanian, et al. *Interfaces* 24, 1 (January–February 1994): 104–120; Peter R. Horner. *OR/MS Today* 22, 4 (August 1995): 14–15.

MSA's goal is to meet the five sampling requirements at the least possible cost. We let

X_1 = number surveyed who are 30 or younger and live in a border state

X_2 = number surveyed who are 31-50 and live in a border state

X_3 = number surveyed who are 51 or older and live in a border state

X_4 = number surveyed who are 30 or younger and do not live in a border state

X_5 = number surveyed who are 31-50 and do not live in a border state

X_6 = number surveyed who are 51 or older and do not live in a border state

Objective function:

$$\text{minimize total interview costs} = \$7.50X_1 + \$6.80X_2 + \$5.50X_3 + \$6.90X_4 + \$7.25X_5 + \$6.10X_6$$

subject to:

$$X_1 + X_2 + X_3 + X_4 + X_5 + X_6 \geq 2{,}300 \quad \text{(total households)}$$

$$X_1 + \qquad\quad X_4 \qquad\qquad \geq 1{,}000 \quad \text{(households 30 or younger)}$$

$$X_2 + \qquad\quad X_5 \qquad \geq 600 \quad \text{(households 31–50 in age)}$$

$$X_1 + X_2 + X_3 \geq 0.15(X_1 + X_2 + X_3 + X_4 + X_5 + X_6) \quad \text{(border states)}$$

$$X_3 \leq 0.2(X_3 + X_6) \quad \text{(limit on age group 51+ who can live in border state)}$$

$$X_1, X_2, X_3, X_4, X_5, X_6 \geq 0$$

PROGRAM 8.2

Using QM for Windows to Solve MSA's LP Problem

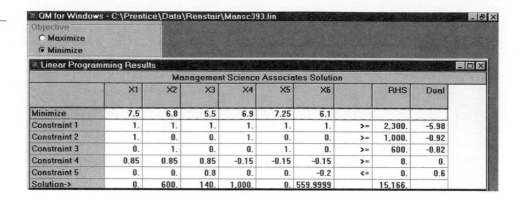

The computer solution to MSA's problem costs $15,166 and is presented in the following table and in Program 8.2, which illustrates the input and output from QM for Windows.

REGION	AGE ⩽ 30	AGE 31–50	AGE ⩾ 51
State bordering Mexico	0	600	140
State not bordering Mexico	1,000	0	560

8.3   MANUFACTURING APPLICATIONS

Production Mix

A fertile field for the use of LP is in planning for the optimal mix of products to manufacture. A company must meet a myriad of constraints, ranging from financial concerns to sales demand to material contracts to union labor demands. Its primary goal is to generate the largest profit possible.

Fifth Avenue Industries, a nationally known manufacturer of menswear, produces four varieties of ties. One is an expensive, all-silk tie, one is an all-polyester tie, and two are blends of polyester and cotton. The following table illustrates the cost and availability (per monthly production planning period) of the three materials used in the production process:

MATERIAL	COST PER YARD ($)	MATERIAL AVAILABLE PER MONTH (YARDS)
Silk	21	800
Polyester	6	3,000
Cotton	9	1,600

The firm has fixed contracts with several major department store chains to supply ties. The contracts require that Fifth Avenue Industries supply a minimum quantity of each tie but allow for a larger demand if Fifth Avenue chooses to meet that demand. (Most of the ties are not shipped with the name Fifth Avenue on their label, incidentally, but with "private stock" labels supplied by the stores.) Table 8.1 summarizes the contract

TABLE 8.1 Data for Fifth Avenue Industries

VARIETY OF TIE	SELLING PRICE PER TIE ($)	MONTHLY CONTRACT MINIMUM	MONTHLY DEMAND	MATERIAL REQUIRED PER TIE (YARDS)	MATERIAL REQUIREMENTS
All silk	6.70	6,000	7,000	0.125	100% silk
All polyester	3.55	10,000	14,000	0.08	100% polyester
Poly–cotton blend 1	4.31	13,000	16,000	0.10	50% polyester–50% cotton
Poly–cotton blend 2	4.81	6,000	8,500	0.10	30% polyester–70% cotton

demand for each of the four styles of ties, the selling price per tie, and the fabric requirements of each variety.

Fifth Avenue's goal is to maximize its monthly profit. It must decide upon a policy
for product mix. Let

X_1 = number of all-silk ties produced per month

X_2 = number of polyester ties

X_3 = number of blend 1 poly–cotton ties

X_4 = number of blend 2 poly–cotton ties

But first the firm must establish the profit per tie.

1. For all-silk ties (X_1), each requires 0.125 yard of silk, at a cost of $21 per yard.
   Therefore, the cost per tie is $2.62. The selling price per silk tie is $6.70, leaving a
   net profit of ($6.70 − $2.62 =) $4.08 per unit of X_1.

2. For all-polyester ties (X_2), each requires 0.08 yard of polyester at a cost of $6 per
   yard. The cost per tie is, therefore, $0.48. The net profit per unit of X_2 is ($3.55 −
   $0.48 =) $3.07.

3. For poly-cotton blend 1 (X_3), each tie requires 0.05 yard of polyester at $6 per yard
   and 0.05 yard of cotton at $9 per yard, for a cost of $0.30 + $0.45 = $0.75 per tie.
   The profit is $3.56.

4. Try to compute the net profit for blend 2. You should calculate a cost of $0.81 per tie
   and a net profit of $4.

The objective function may now be stated as

maximize profit = $4.08X_1 + $3.07X_2 + $3.56X_3 + $4.00X_4

subject to

$$0.125X_1 \leq 800 \quad \text{(yards of silk)}$$

$$0.08X_2 + 0.05X_3 + 0.03X_4 \leq 3,000 \quad \text{(yards of polyester)}$$

$$0.05X_3 + 0.07X_4 \leq 1,600 \quad \text{(yards of cotton)}$$

$$X_1 \geq 6,000 \quad \text{(contract minimum for all silk)}$$

$$X_1 \leq 7,000 \quad \text{(contract maximum)}$$

$$X_2 \geq 10,000 \quad \text{(contract minimum for all polyester)}$$

$$X_2 \leq 14{,}000 \quad \text{(contract maximum)}$$

$$X_3 \geq 13{,}000 \quad \text{(contract minimum for blend 1)}$$

$$X_3 \leq 16{,}000 \quad \text{(contract maximum)}$$

$$X_4 \geq 6{,}000 \quad \text{(contract minimum for blend 2)}$$

$$X_4 \leq 8{,}500 \quad \text{(contract maximum)}$$

$$X_1, X_2, X_3, X_4 \geq 0$$

Using Excel and its Solver command, the computer-generated solution is to produce 6,400 all-silk ties each month; 14,000 all-polyester ties; 16,000 poly–cotton blend 1 ties; and 8,500 poly–cotton blend 2 ties. This produces a profit of $160,020 per production period. See Programs 8.3A and 8.3B for details.

Production Scheduling

Setting a low-cost production schedule over a period of weeks or months is a difficult and important management problem in most plants. The production manager has to consider many factors: labor capacity, inventory and storage costs, space limitations, product demand, and labor relations. Because most companies produce more than one product, the scheduling process is often quite complex.

Basically, the problem resembles the product mix model for each period in the future. The objective is either to maximize profit or to minimize the total cost (production plus inventory) of carrying out the task.

PROGRAM 8.3A

Excel Formulation for Fifth Avenue Industries LP Problem Using Solver

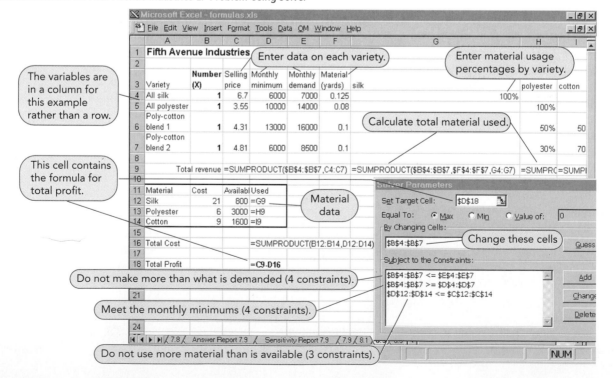

A	B	C	D	E	F	G	H	I
1 Fifth Avenue Industries								
2								
3 Variety	**Number (X)**	Selling price	Monthly minimum	Monthly demand	Material (yards)	silk	polyester	cotton
4 All silk	**6400**	6.7	6000	7000	0.125	100%		
5 All polyester	**14000**	3.55	10000	14000	0.08		100%	
6 Poly-cotton blend 1	**16000**	4.31	13000	16000	0.1		50%	50%
7 Poly-cotton blend 2	**8500**	4.81	6000	8500	0.1		30%	70%
8								
9	Total revenue	202425				800	2175	1395
10								
11 Material	Cost	Available	Used					
12 Silk	21	800	800					
13 Polyester	6	3000	2175					
14 Cotton	9	1600	1395					
15								
16 Total Cost			42405					
17								
18 Total Profit			**160020**					

Production scheduling is amenable to solution by LP because it is a problem that must be solved on a regular basis. When the objective function and constraints for a firm are established, the inputs can easily be changed each month to provide an updated schedule.

Greenberg Motors, Inc., manufactures two different electrical motors for sale under contract to Drexel Corp., a well-known producer of small kitchen appliances. Its model GM3A is found in many Drexel food processors, and its model GM3B is used in the assembly of blenders.

An example of production scheduling: Greenberg Motors

Three times each year, the procurement officer at Drexel contracts Irwin Greenberg, the founder of Greenberg Motors, to place a monthly order for each of the coming four months. Drexel's demand for motors varies each month based on its own sales forecasts, production capacity, and financial position. Greenberg has just received the January–April order and must begin his own four-month production plan. The demand for motors is shown in Table 8.2.

Production planning at Greenberg Motors must consider four factors:

1. The desirability of producing the same number of each motor each month. This simplifies planning and the scheduling of workers and machines.

2. The necessity to keep down inventory carrying, or holding, costs. This suggests producing in each month only what is needed in that month.

TABLE 8.2 Four-Month Order Schedule for Electrical Motors

MODEL	JANUARY	FEBRUARY	MARCH	APRIL
GM3A	800	700	1,000	1,100
GM3B	1,000	1,200	1,400	1,400

3. Warehouse limitations that cannot be exceeded without great additional storage costs.

4. The company's no-layoff policy, which has been effective in preventing a unionization of the shop. This suggests a minimum production capacity that should be used each month.

Although these four factors often conflict, Greenberg has found that LP is an effective tool in setting up a production schedule that will minimize his total costs of per unit production and monthly holding.

Double-subscripted variables are often used in LP. Greenberg Motors is more easily formulated with this approach, as is the next example in this chapter.

Double-subscripted variables can be used here to develop the LP model. We let

$X_{A,i}$ = number of model GM3A motors produced in month i
$\quad\quad$ (i = 1, 2, 3, 4 for January–April)

$X_{B,i}$ = number of model GM3B motors produced in month i

Production costs are currently \$10 per GM3A motor produced and \$6 per GM3B unit. A labor agreement going into effect on March 1 will raise each figure by 10%, however. We can write the part of the objective function that deals with production cost as

$$\text{cost of production} = \$10X_{A1} + \$10X_{A2} + \$11X_{A3} + \$11X_{A4} + \$6X_{B1}$$
$$+ \$6X_{B2} + \$6.60X_{B3} + \$6.60X_{B4}$$

To include the inventory carrying costs in the model, we can introduce a second variable. Let

$I_{A,i}$ = level of on-hand inventory for GM3A motors at end of month i
$\quad\quad$ (i = 1, 2, 3, 4)

$I_{B,i}$ = level of on-hand inventory for GM3B motors at end of month i

Each GM3A motor held in stock costs \$0.18 per month, while each GM3B has a carrying cost of \$0.13 per month. Greenberg's accountants allow monthly ending inventories as an acceptable approximation to the average inventory levels during the month. So the carrying cost part of the LP objective function is

$$\text{cost of carrying inventory} = \$0.18I_{A1} + 0.18I_{A2} + 0.18I_{A3} + 0.18I_{A4}$$
$$+ 0.13I_{B1} + 0.13I_{B2} + 0.13I_{B3} + 0.13I_{B4}$$

The total objective function becomes

$$\text{minimize total costs} = 10X_{A1} + 10X_{A2} + 11X_{A3} + 11X_{A4} + 6X_{B1} + 6X_{B2}$$
$$+ 6.6X_{B3} + 6.6X_{B4} + 0.18I_{A1} + 0.18I_{A2} + 0.18I_{A3} + 0.18I_{A4}$$
$$+ 0.13I_{B1} + 0.13I_{B2} + 0.13I_{B3} + 0.13I_{B4}$$

Inventory constraints set the relationship between closing inventory this month, closing inventory last month, this month's production, and sales this month.

In setting up the constraints, we must recognize the relationship between last month's ending inventory, the current month's production, and the sales to Drexel this month. The inventory at the end of a month is

$$\begin{pmatrix} \text{inventory} \\ \text{at the} \\ \text{end of} \\ \text{this month} \end{pmatrix} = \begin{pmatrix} \text{inventory} \\ \text{at the} \\ \text{end of} \\ \text{last month} \end{pmatrix} + \begin{pmatrix} \text{current} \\ \text{month's} \\ \text{production} \end{pmatrix} - \begin{pmatrix} \text{sales} \\ \text{to Drexel} \\ \text{this month} \end{pmatrix}$$

Suppose that Greenberg is starting the new four-month production cycle with a change in design specifications that left no old motors in stock on January 1. Then, recalling that January's demand for GM3As is 800 and for GM3Bs is 1,000, we can write

$$I_{A1} = 0 + X_{A1} - 800$$

$$I_{B1} = 0 + X_{B1} - 1,000$$

Transposing all unknown variables to the left of the equal sign and multiplying all terms by −1, these January constraints can be rewritten as

$$X_{A1} - I_{A1} = 800$$

$$X_{B1} - I_{B1} = 1,000$$

The constraints on demand in February, March, and April follow:

$$X_{A2} + I_{A1} - I_{A2} = \quad 700 \qquad \text{February GM3A demand}$$

$$X_{B2} + I_{B1} - I_{B2} = 1,200 \qquad \text{February GM3B demand}$$

$$X_{A3} + I_{A2} - I_{A3} = 1,000 \qquad \text{March GM3A demand}$$

$$X_{B3} + I_{B2} - I_{B3} = 1,400 \qquad \text{March GM3B demand}$$

$$X_{A4} + I_{A3} - I_{A4} = 1,100 \qquad \text{April GM3A demand}$$

$$X_{B4} + I_{B3} - I_{B4} = 1,400 \qquad \text{April GM3B demand}$$

If Greenberg also wants to have on hand an additional 450 GM3As and 300 GM3Bs at the end of April, we add the constraints

$$I_{A4} = 450$$

$$I_{B4} = 300$$

The constraints discussed address demand; they do not, however, consider warehouse space or labor requirements. First, we note that the storage area for Greenberg Motors can hold a maximum of 3,300 motors of either type (they are similar in size) at any one time. Then

$$I_{A1} + I_{B1} \leq 3,300$$

$$I_{A2} + I_{B2} \leq 3,300$$

$$I_{A3} + I_{B3} \leq 3,300$$

$$I_{A4} + I_{B4} \leq 3,300$$

Second, we return to the issue of employment. So that no worker is ever laid off, Greenberg has a base employment level of 2,240 labor hours per month. In a busy period, though, the company can bring two skilled former employees on board (they are now retired) to increase capacity to 2,560 hours per month. Each GM3A motor produced requires 1.3 hours of labor, while each GM3B takes a worker 0.9 hour to assemble.

$$1.3X_{A1} + 0.9X_{B1} \geq 2,240 \qquad \text{(January minimum worker hours/month)}$$

$$1.3X_{A1} + 0.9X_{B1} \leq 2,560 \qquad \text{(January maximum labor available/month)}$$

$$1.3X_{A2} + 0.9X_{B2} \geq 2,240 \qquad \text{(February labor minimum)}$$

Employment constraints are set for each month.

TABLE 8.3 Solution to Greenberg Motor Problem

PRODUCTION SCHEDULE	JANUARY	FEBRUARY	MARCH	APRIL
Units of GM3A produced	1,277	1,138	842	792
Units of GM3B produced	1,000	1,200	1,400	1,700
Inventory of GM3A carried	477	915	758	450
Inventory of GM3B carried	0	0	0	300
Labor hours required	2,560	2,560	2,355	2,560

$1.3X_{A2} + 0.9X_{B2} \leq 2,560$ (February labor maximum)

$1.3X_{A3} + 0.9X_{B3} \geq 2,240$ (March labor minimum)

$1.3X_{A3} + 0.9X_{B3} \leq 2,560$ (March labor maximum)

$1.3X_{A4} + 0.9X_{B4} \geq 2,240$ (April labor minimum)

$1.3X_{A4} + 0.9X_{B4} \leq 2,560$ (April labor maximum)

The solution to the Greenberg Motors problem was found by computer and is shown in Table 8.3. The four-month total cost is $76,301.61.

This example illustrates a relatively simple production planning problem in that there were only two products being considered. The 16 variables and 22 constraints may not seem trivial, but the technique can also be applied successfully with dozens of products and hundreds of constraints.

8.4   EMPLOYEE SCHEDULING APPLICATIONS

Assignment Problems

We can assign people to jobs using LP or use a special assignment algorithm discussed in Chapter 10.

Assignment problems involve determining the most efficient assignment of people to jobs, machines to tasks, police cars to city sectors, salespeople to territories, and so on. The objective might be to minimize travel times or costs or to maximize assignment effectiveness. Assignments can be handled with their own special solution procedures (see Chapter 10). Assignment problems are unique because they not only have a coefficient of 1 associated with each variable in the LP constraints; the right-hand side of each constraint is also always equal to 1. The use of LP in solving assignment problems, as illustrated by the following case, yields solutions of either 0 or 1 for each variable in the formulation.

The law firm of Ivan and Ivan maintains a large staff of young attorneys who hold the title of junior partner. Ivan, concerned with the effective utilization of his personnel resources, seeks some objective means of making lawyer-to-client assignments.

On March 1, four new clients seeking legal assistance came to Ivan. Although the current staff is overloaded, Ivan would like to accommodate the new clients. He reviews current case loads and identifies four junior partners who, although busy, could possibly be assigned to the cases. Each young lawyer can handle at most one new client. Furthermore, each lawyer differs in skills and specialty interests.

Seeking to maximize the overall effectiveness of the new client assignments, Ivan draws up the following table, in which he rates the estimated effectiveness (on a scale of 1 to 9) of each lawyer on each new case.

	IVAN'S EFFECTIVENESS RATINGS			
	CLIENT'S CASE			
LAWYER	**DIVORCE**	**CORPORATE MERGER**	**EMBEZZLEMENT**	**EXHIBITIONISM**
Adams	6	2	8	5
Brooks	9	3	5	8
Carter	4	8	3	4
Darwin	6	7	6	4

To solve using LP, we again employ double-subscripted variables. Let

$$X_{ij} = \begin{cases} 1 & \text{if attorney } i \text{ is assigned to case } j \\ 0 & \text{otherwise} \end{cases}$$

Here is another example of double-subscripted variables.

where

$i = 1, 2, 3, 4$ stands for Adams, Brooks, Carter, and Darwin, respectively

$j = 1, 2, 3, 4$ stands for divorce, merger, embezzlement, and exhibitionism, respectively

The LP formulation follows:

$$\text{maximize effectiveness} = 6X_{11} + 2X_{12} + 8X_{13} + 5X_{14} + 9X_{21} + 3X_{22}$$
$$+ 5X_{23} + 8X_{24} + 4X_{31} + 8X_{32} + 3X_{33} + 4X_{34}$$
$$+ 6X_{41} + 7X_{42} + 6X_{43} + 4X_{44}$$

subject to $X_{11} + X_{21} + X_{31} + X_{41} = 1$ (divorce case)

$\qquad X_{12} + X_{22} + X_{32} + X_{42} = 1$ (merger)

$\qquad X_{13} + X_{23} + X_{33} + X_{43} = 1$ (embezzlement)

$\qquad X_{14} + X_{24} + X_{34} + X_{44} = 1$ (exhibitionism)

$\qquad X_{11} + X_{12} + X_{13} + X_{14} = 1$ (Adams)

$\qquad X_{21} + X_{22} + X_{23} + X_{24} = 1$ (Brooks)

$\qquad X_{31} + X_{32} + X_{33} + X_{34} = 1$ (Carter)

$\qquad X_{41} + X_{42} + X_{43} + X_{44} = 1$ (Darwin)

The law firm's problem is solved in Program 8.4 using QM for Windows. There is a total effectiveness rating of 30 by letting $X_{13} = 1$, $X_{24} = 1$, $X_{32} = 1$, and $X_{41} = 1$. All other variables are therefore equal to zero.

QM for Windows – C:\Prentice\Data\RenderStair7\Ivan.LIN

Objective
● Maximize
○ Minimize

Linear Programming Results

Ivan and Ivan Solution

	x11	x12	x13	x14	x21	x22	x23	x24	x31	x32	x33	x34	x41	x42	x43	x44		RHS	Dual
Maximize	6.	2.	8.	5.	9.	3.	5.	8.	4.	8.	3.	4.	6.	7.	6.	4.			
Divorce	1.	1.	1.	1.													=	1.	5.
Merger					1.	1.	1.	1.									=	1.	8.
Embezzlement									1.	1.	1.	1.					=	1.	4.
Exhibitionism													1.	1.	1.	1.	=	1.	5.
Adams	1.				1.				1.				1.				=	1.	1.
Brooks		1.				1.				1.				1.			=	1.	4.
Carter			1.				1.				1.				1.		=	1.	3.
Darwin				1.				1.				1.				1.	=	1.	0.
Solution->	0.	0.	1.	0.	0.	0.	0.	1.	0.	1.	0.	0.	1.	0.	0.	0.		30.	

Labor Planning

Labor planning problems address staffing needs over a specific time period. They are especially useful when managers have some flexibility in assigning workers to jobs that require overlapping or interchangeable talents. Large banks frequently use LP to tackle their labor scheduling.

Hong Kong Bank of Commerce and Industry is a busy bank that has requirements for between 10 and 18 tellers, depending on the time of day. The lunch time, from noon to 2 P.M., is usually heaviest. Table 8.4 indicates the workers needed at various hours that the bank is open.

The bank now employs 12 full-time tellers, but many people are on its roster of available part-time employees. A part-time employee must put in exactly four hours per day, but can start anytime between 9 A.M. and 1 P.M. Part-timers are a fairly inexpensive labor pool, since no retirement or lunch benefits are provided for them. Full-timers, on the other hand, work from 9 A.M. to 5 P.M. but are allowed 1 hour for lunch. (Half of the full-timers eat at 11 A.M., the other half at noon.) Full-timers thus provide 35 hours per week of productive labor time.

TABLE 8.4 **Hong Kong Bank of Commerce and Industry**

TIME PERIOD	NUMBER OF TELLERS REQUIRED
9 A.M.–10 A.M.	10
10 A.M.–11 A.M.	12
11 A.M.–NOON	14
NOON–1 P.M.	16
1 P.M.–2 P.M.	18
2 P.M.–3 P.M.	17
3 P.M.–4 P.M.	15
4 P.M.–5 P.M.	10

By corporate policy, the bank limits part-time hours to a maximum of 50% of the day's total requirement. Part-timers earn $4 per hour (or $16 per day) on average, while full-timers earn $50 per day in salary and benefits, on average. The bank would like to set a schedule that would minimize its total personnel costs. It will release one or more of its full-time tellers if it is profitable to do so.

We can let

F = full-time tellers

P_1 = part-timers starting at 9 A.M. (leaving at 1 P.M.)

P_2 = part-timers starting at 10 A.M. (leaving at 2 P.M.)

P_3 = part-timers starting at 11 A.M. (leaving at 3 P.M.)

P_4 = part-timers starting at noon (leaving at 4 P.M.)

P_5 = part-timers starting at 1 P.M. (leaving at 5 P.M.)

Objective function:

minimize total daily personnel cost = $50F + $16(P_1 + P_2 + P_3 + P_4 + P_5)$

Constraints:

For each hour, the available labor hours must be at least equal to the required labor hours.

$$F + P_1 \geq 10 \quad \text{(9 A.M.–10 A.M. needs)}$$

$$F + P_1 + P_2 \geq 12 \quad \text{(10 A.M.–11 A.M. needs)}$$

$$\tfrac{1}{2}F + P_1 + P_2 + P_3 \geq 14 \quad \text{(11 A.M.–noon needs)}$$

$$\tfrac{1}{2}F + P_1 + P_2 + P_3 + P_4 \geq 16 \quad \text{(noon–1 P.M. needs)}$$

$$F + P_2 + P_3 + P_4 + P_5 \geq 18 \quad \text{(1 P.M.–2 P.M. needs)}$$

$$F + P_3 + P_4 + P_5 \geq 17 \quad \text{(2 P.M.–3 P.M. needs)}$$

$$F + P_4 + P_5 \geq 15 \quad \text{(3 P.M.–4 P.M. needs)}$$

$$F + P_5 \geq 10 \quad \text{(4 P.M.–5 P.M. needs)}$$

Only 12 full-time tellers are available, so

$$F \leq 12$$

Part-time worker hours cannot exceed 50% of total hours required each day, which is the sum of the tellers needed each hour.

$$4(P_1 + P_2 + P_3 + P_4 + P_5) \leq 0.50(10 + 12 + 14 + 16 + 18 + 17 + 15 + 10)$$

or

$$4P_1 + 4P_2 + 4P_3 + 4P_4 + 4P_5 \leq 0.50(112)$$

$$F, P_1, P_2, P_3, P_4, P_5 \geq 0$$

There are several alternate optimal schedules that Hong Kong Bank can follow. The first is to employ only 10 full-time tellers ($F = 10$) and to start two part-timers at 10 A.M. ($P_2 = 2$), 7 part-timers at 11 A.M. ($P_3 = 7$), and 5 part-timers at noon ($P_4 = 5$). No part-timers would begin at 9 A.M. or 1 P.M.

Alternate optimal solutions are common in many LP problems. The sequence you enter the constraints into QM for Windows can affect the solution found.

The second solution also employs 10 full-time tellers, but starts 6 part-timers at 9 A.M. ($P_1 = 6$), 1 part-timer at 10 A.M. ($P_2 = 1$), 2 part-timers at 11 A.M. and 5 at noon ($P_3 = 2$ and $P_4 = 5$), and 0 part-timers at 1 P.M. ($P_5 = 0$). The cost of either of these two policies is $724 per day.

8.5 FINANCIAL APPLICATIONS

Portfolio Selection

Maximizing return on investment subject to a set of risk constraints is a popular financial application of LP.

A problem frequently encountered by managers of banks, mutual funds, investment services, and insurance companies is the selection of specific investments from among a wide variety of alternatives. The manager's overall objective is usually to maximize expected return on investment, given a set of legal, policy, or risk restraints.

For example, the International City Trust (ICT) invests in short-term trade credits, corporate bonds, gold stocks, and construction loans. To encourage a diversified portfolio, the board of directors has placed limits on the amount that can be committed to any one type of investment. ICT has $5 million available for immediate investment and wishes to do two things: (1) maximize the interest earned on the investments made over the next six months, and (2) satisfy the diversification requirements as set by the board of directors.

The specifics of the investment possibilities are as follows:

INVESTMENT	INTEREST EARNED (%)	MAXIMUM INVESTMENT ($ MILLIONS)
Trade credit	7	1.0
Corporate bonds	11	2.5
Gold stocks	19	1.5
Construction loans	15	1.8

In addition, the board specifies that at least 55% of the funds invested must be in gold stocks and construction loans, and that no less than 15% be invested in trade credit.

To formulate ICT's investment decision as an LP problem, we let

X_1 = dollars invested in trade credit

X_2 = dollars invested in corporate bonds

X_3 = dollars invested in gold stocks

X_4 = dollars invested in construction loans

Objective:

maximize dollars of interest earned = $0.07X_1 + 0.11X_2 + 0.19X_3 + 0.15X_4$

subject to:
$$X_1 \leq 1,000,000$$
$$X_2 \leq 2,500,000$$
$$X_3 \leq 1,500,000$$
$$X_4 \leq 1,800,000$$

Few financial markets in recent years have experienced the rapid growth and innovations of the secondary mortgage market. This growth has been spurred by federal agencies whose mandate is to make home ownership easier and more affordable by increasing the flow of funds available. Prudential Securities have entered this $1 trillion market for mortgage-backed securities (MBSs) in a huge way, typically trading $5 billion of MBSs per week. These securities, which are mortgage loans pooled by government agencies, are traded in a somewhat complex market by a network of dealers like Prudential.

To reduce investment risk and to value securities properly and quickly for its investors, Prudential has developed and implemented a number of quantitative analysis models. Its LP model, run hundreds of times per day by Prudential traders, salespeople, and clients, designs an optimal securities portfolio to meet investors' criteria under different interest rate environments. Constraints include the minimum and maximum percentages of a portfolio to invest in any security, the duration of the MBS, and the total amount to be invested. The model helps managers decide how much to invest in each available MBS in order to meet clients' goals.

Source: Yosi Ben-Dov, Lakhbir Hayre, and Vincent Pica. "Mortgage Valuation Models at Prudential Securities," *Interfaces*, 22, 1 (January-February 1992): 55–71.

$$X_3 + X_4 \geq 0.55(X_1 + X_2 + X_3 + X_4)$$

$$X_1 \geq 0.15(X_1 + X_2 + X_3 + X_4)$$

$$X_1 + X_2 + X_3 + X_4 \leq 5{,}000{,}000$$

ICT maximizes its interest earned by making the following investment: $X_1 = \$750{,}000$, $X_2 = \$950{,}000$, $X_3 = \$1{,}500{,}000$, and $X_4 = \$1{,}800{,}000$, and the total interest earned is $712,000.

8.6 TRANSPORTATION APPLICATIONS

Shipping Problem

The transportation or shipping problem involves determining the amount of goods or items to be transported from a number of origins to a number of destinations. The objective usually is to minimize total shipping costs or distances. Constraints in this type of problem deal with capacities at each origin and requirements at each destination. The transportation problem is a very specific case of LP, and in fact, a special algorithm has been developed to solve it. That solution procedure is one of the topics of Chapter 10.

The Top Speed Bicycle Co. manufactures and markets a line of 10-speed bicycles nationwide. The firm has final assembly plants in two cities in which labor costs are low, New Orleans and Omaha. Its three major warehouses are located near the large market areas of New York, Chicago, and Los Angeles.

The sales requirements for the next year at the New York warehouse are 10,000 bicycles, at the Chicago warehouse 8,000 bicycles, and at the Los Angeles warehouse 15,000 bicycles. The factory capacity at each location is limited. New Orleans can assemble and ship 20,000 bicycles; the Omaha plant can produce 15,000 bicycles per year. The cost of shipping one bicycle from each factory to each warehouse differs, and these unit shipping costs are as follows:

Transporting goods from several origins to several destinations efficiently is called the "transportation problem." It can be solved with LP, as we see here, or with a special algorithm introduced in Chapter 10.

	TO		
FROM	**NEW YORK**	**CHICAGO**	**LOS ANGELES**
New Orleans	$2	$3	$5
Omaha	3	1	4

The company wishes to develop a shipping schedule that will minimize its total annual transportation costs.

Double-subscripted variables are again employed in this example.

To formulate this problem using LP, we again employ the concept of double-subscripted variables. We let the first subscript represent the origin (factory) and the second subscript the destination (warehouse). Thus, in general, X_{ij} refers to the number of bicycles shipped from origin i to destination j. We could instead denote X_6 as the variable for origin 2 to destination 3, but we think you will find the double subscripts more descriptive and easier to use. So let

X_{11} = number of bicycles shipped from New Orleans to New York

X_{12} = number of bicycles shipped from New Orleans to Chicago

X_{13} = number of bicycles shipped from New Orleans to Los Angeles

X_{21} = number of bicycles shipped from Omaha to New York

X_{22} = number of bicycles shipped from Omaha to Chicago

X_{23} = number of bicycles shipped from Omaha to Los Angeles

This problem can be formulated as follows:

In a transportation problem, there will be one constraint for each demand source and one constraint for each supply destination.

Minimize total shipping costs = $2X_{11} + 3X_{12} + 5X_{13} + 3X_{21} + 1X_{22} + 4X_{23}$

subject to

$$X_{11} + X_{21} = 10,000 \qquad \text{(New York demand)}$$

$$X_{12} + X_{22} = 8,000 \qquad \text{(Chicago demand)}$$

$$X_{13} + X_{23} = 15,000 \qquad \text{(Los Angeles demand)}$$

$$X_{11} + X_{12} + X_{13} \leq 20,000 \qquad \text{(New Orleans factory supply)}$$

$$X_{21} + X_{22} + X_{23} \leq 15,000 \qquad \text{(Omaha factory supply)}$$

Why are transportation problems a special class of LP problems? The answer is that every coefficient in front of a variable in the constraint equations is always equal to 1. This special trait is also seen in another special category of LP problems, the assignment problem discussed earlier.

Using Excel and its Solver command, the computer-generated solution to Top Speed's problem is shown in the table that follows and in Programs 8.5A and 8.5B. The total shipping cost is $96,000.

	TO		
FROM	**NEW YORK**	**CHICAGO**	**LOS ANGELES**
New Orleans	10,000	0	8,000
Omaha	0	8,000	7,000

PROGRAM 8.5A

Excel Solver Formulation of the Top Speed Bicycle LP Problem

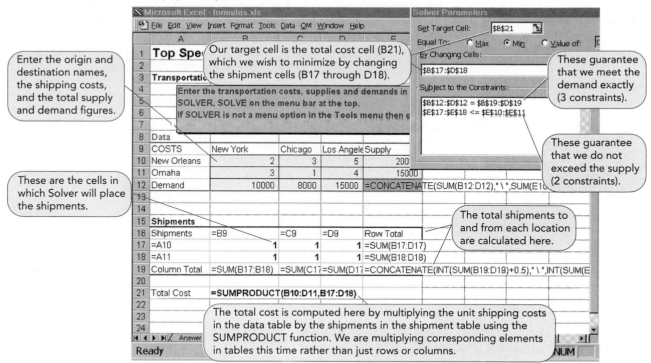

Enter the origin and destination names, the shipping costs, and the total supply and demand figures.

Our target cell is the total cost cell (B21), which we wish to minimize by changing the shipment cells (B17 through D18).

These guarantee that we meet the demand exactly (3 constraints).

These are the cells in which Solver will place the shipments.

These guarantee that we do not exceed the supply (2 constraints).

The total shipments to and from each location are calculated here.

The total cost is computed here by multiplying the unit shipping costs in the data table by the shipments in the shipment table using the SUMPRODUCT function. We are multiplying corresponding elements in tables this time rather than just rows or columns.

PROGRAM 8.5B

Solution to Top Speed's LP Problem Output from Excel Formulation in Program 8.5A

Top Speed Bicycle Company

Transportation

Enter the transportation costs, supplies and demands in the shaded area. Then go to TOOLS, SOLVER, SOLVE on the menu bar at the top.
If SOLVER is not a menu option in the Tools menu then go to TOOLS, ADD-INS.

Data

COSTS	New York	Chicago	Los Angele	Supply
New Orleans	2	3	5	20000
Omaha	3	1	4	15000
Demand	10000	8000	15000	33000 \ 35000

Shipments

Shipments	New York	Chicago	Los Angele	Row Total
New Orleans	10000	0	8000	18000
Omaha	0	8000	7000	15000
Column Total	10000	8000	15000	33000 \ 33000

Total Cost	96000

Truck Loading Problem

The truck loading problem involves deciding which items to load on a truck so as to maximize the value of a load shipped. As an example, we consider Goodman Shipping, an Orlando firm owned by Steven Goodman. One of his trucks, with a capacity of 10,000 pounds, is about to be loaded.[1] Awaiting shipment are the following items:

ITEM	VALUE ($)	WEIGHT (POUNDS)
1	22,500	7,500
2	24,000	7,500
3	8,000	3,000
4	9,500	3,500
5	11,500	4,000
6	9,750	3,500

Each of these six items, we see, has an associated dollar value and weight.

The objective is to maximize the total value of the items loaded onto the truck without exceeding the truck's weight capacity. We let X_i be the proportion of each item i loaded on the truck.

Maximize load value $= \$22,500X_1 + \$24,000X_2 + \$8,000X_3 + \$9,500X_4$
$$+ \$11,500X_5 + \$9,750X_6$$

subject to $7,500X_1 + 7,500X_2 + 3,000X_3 + 3,500X_4 + 4,000X_5$
$$+ 3,500X_6 \leq 10,000 \text{ lb capacity}$$

$$X_1 \leq 1$$

$$X_2 \leq 1$$

$$X_3 \leq 1$$

$$X_4 \leq 1$$

$$X_5 \leq 1$$

$$X_6 \leq 1$$

These final six constraints reflect the fact that at most one "unit" of an item can be loaded onto the truck. In effect, if Goodman can load a *portion* of an item (say, item 1 is a batch of 1,000 folding chairs, not all of which need be shipped together), the X_is will all be proportions ranging from 0 (nothing) to 1 (all of that item loaded).

To solve this LP problem, we turn to Excel's Solver. Program 8.6A shows Goodman's Excel formulation and input data and Program 8.6B shows the solution, which yields a total load value of $31,500.

The answer leads us to an interesting issue that we deal with in detail in Chapter 11. What does Goodman do if fractional values of items cannot be loaded? For example, if luxury cars were the items being loaded, we clearly cannot ship one-third of a Maserati.

If the proportion of item 1 was rounded up to 1.00, the weight of the load would increase to 15,000 pounds. This would violate the 10,000 pounds maximum weight constraint. Therefore, the fraction of item 1 must be rounded down to zero. This would drop

---

[1] Adapted from an example in S. L. Savage, *What's Best!* General Optimization, Inc., and Holden-Day, Oakland, CA, 1985.

PROGRAM 8.7

Solving Whole Food's LP Problem with QM for Windows

QM for Windows - C:\Prentice\Data\RenderStair7\Whole417.lin

Objective
○ Maximize
● Minimize

Linear Programming Results

Whole Food Nutrition Center Solution

	X1	X2	X3		RHS	Dual
Minimize	0.33	0.47	0.38			
Constraint 1	22.	28.	21.	>=	3.	-0.038
Constraint 2	16.	14.	25.	>=	2.	0.
Constraint 3	8.	7.	9.	>=	1.	-0.088
Constraint 4	5.	0.	0.	>=	0.425	0.
Constraint 5	1.	1.	1.	=	0.125	1.21
Solution->	0.025	0.05	0.05		0.05	

grain B, and ⅖ ounce of grain C in each serving. The cost per serving is $0.05. Program 8.7 illustrates this solution using our QM for Windows software package.

Ingredient Mix and Blending Problems

Diet and feed mix problems are actually special cases of a more general class of LP problems known as *ingredient* or *blending problems*. Blending problems arise when a decision must be made regarding the blending of two or more resources to produce one or more products. Resources, in this case, contain one or more essential ingredients that must be blended so that each final product contains specific percentages of each ingredient. The following example deals with an application frequently seen in the petroleum industry, the blending of crude oils to produce refinable gasoline.

The Low Knock Oil Company produces two grades of cut-rate gasoline for industrial distribution. The grades, regular and economy, are produced by refining a blend of two types of crude oil, type $X100$ and type $X220$. Each crude oil differs not only in cost per barrel, but in composition as well. The following table indicates the percentage of crucial ingredients found in each of the crude oils and the cost per barrel for each:

Major oil refineries all use LP for blending crude oils to produce gasoline grades.

CRUDE OIL TYPE	INGREDIENT A (%)	INGREDIENT B (%)	COST/BARREL ($)
$X100$	35	55	30.00
$X220$	60	25	34.80

Weekly demand for the regular grade of Low Knock gasoline is at least 25,000 barrels, while demand for the economy is at least 32,000 barrels per week. *At least* 45% of each barrel of regular must be ingredient A. *At most* 50% of each barrel of economy should contain ingredient B.

The Low Knock management must decide how many barrels of each type of crude oil to buy each week for blending to satisfy demand at minimum cost. To solve this as an LP problem, the firm lets

X_1 = barrels of crude X100 blended to produce the refined regular

X_2 = barrels of crude X100 blended to produce the refined economy

X_3 = barrels of crude X220 blended to produce the refined regular

X_4 = barrels of crude X220 blended to produce the refined economy

This problem can be formulated as follows:

Objective:

$$\text{minimize cost} = \$30X_1 + \$30X_2 + \$34.80X_3 + \$34.80X_4$$

subject to

$$X_1 + X_3 \geqslant 25,000 \qquad \text{(demand for regular)}$$

$$X_2 + X_4 \geqslant 32,000 \qquad \text{(demand for economy)}$$

At least 45% of each barrel of regular must be ingredient A.

$$(X_1 + X_3) = \text{total amount of crude blended to produce the refined regular}$$
$$\text{gasoline demand}$$

Thus,

$$0.45(X_1 + X_3) = \text{minimum amount of ingredient A required}$$

But

$$0.35X_1 + 0.60X_3 = \text{amount of ingredient A in refined regular gas}$$

So

$$0.35X_1 + 0.60X_3 \geqslant 0.45X_1 + 0.45X_3$$

or

$$-0.10X_1 + 0.15X_3 \geqslant 0 \qquad \text{(ingredient A in regular constraint)}$$

Similarly, at most 50% of each barrel of economy should be ingredient B.

$$X_2 + X_4 = \text{total amount of crude blended to produce the refined economy gasoline}$$
$$\text{demanded}$$

Thus,

$$0.50(X_2 + X_4) = \text{maximum amount of ingredient B allowed}$$

But

$$0.55X_2 + 0.25X_4 = \text{amount of ingredient B in refined economy gas}$$

So

$$0.55X_2 + 0.25X_4 \leqslant 0.50X_2 + 0.50X_4$$

or

$$0.05X_2 - 0.25X_4 \leqslant 0 \text{ (ingredient B in economy constraint)}$$

Here is the entire LP formulation:

$$\text{minimize cost} = 30X_1 + 30X_2 + 34.80X_3 + 34.80X_4$$

$$\text{subject to} \quad X_1 \qquad + \quad X_3 \qquad\qquad \geqslant 25,000$$

$$X_2 + \qquad\qquad X_4 \geqslant 32,000$$

$$-0.10X_1 \qquad + \quad 0.15X_3 \qquad\qquad \geqslant 0$$

$$0.05X_2 \qquad\qquad - \ 0.25X_4 \leqslant 0$$

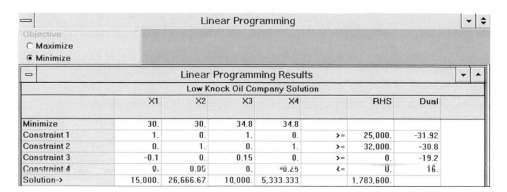

PROGRAM 8.8
Using QM for Windows to Solve Low Knock Oil's LP Problem

Using QM for Windows, the solution to Low Knock Oil's formulation was found to be

X_1 = 15,000 barrels of X100 into regular

X_2 = 26,666⅔ barrels of X100 into economy

X_3 = 10,000 barrels of X220 into regular

X_4 = 5,333⅓ barrels of X220 into economy

The cost of this mix is $1,783,600. Refer to Program 8.8 for details.

Summary

In this chapter, we continued our discussion of LP models. To gain more experience in formulating problems from a variety of disciplines, we examined applications from marketing, production, scheduling, finance, transportation, and ingredient blending. We also solved most of these problems with two computer programs for LP: QM for Windows and Excel's Solver.

SELF-TEST

- Before taking the self-test, refer back to the learning objectives at the beginning of the chapter, the notes in the margins, and the glossary at the end of the chapter.
- Use the key at the back of the book to correct your answers.
- Restudy pages that correspond to any questions that you answered incorrectly or material you feel uncertain about.

1. Linear programming can be used to select effective media mixes, allocate fixed or limited budgets across media, and maximize audience exposure.
   a. True   b. False
2. Blending problems arise when one must decide which of two or more ingredients is to be chosen to produce a product.
   a. True   b. False
3. Using LP to maximize audience exposure in an advertising campaign is an example of the type of LP application known as
   a. marketing research.
   b. media selection.
   c. portfolio assessment.
   d. media budgeting.
   e. all of the above.
4. The following *does not* represent a factor a manager might consider when employing LP for a production scheduling
   a. labor capacity
   b. space limitations
   c. product demand
   d. risk assessment
   e. inventory costs
5. When formulating transportation LP problems, constraints usually deal with
   a. the number of items to be transported.
   b. the shipping cost associated with transporting goods.
   c. the distance goods are to be transported.
   d. the number of origins and destinations.
   e. the capacities of origins and requirements of destinations.
6. Labor planning is a type of LP problem that
   a. is used to address staffing needs over a specific time period.
   b. is useful when there is flexibility in assigning workers to jobs requiring interchangeable talents.
   c. is frequently used by large banks.
   d. might be used to determine teller assignments in banks.
   e. all of the above.

7. When applying LP to diet problems, the objective function is usually designed to
   a. maximize profits from blends of nutrients.
   b. maximize ingredient blends.
   c. minimize production losses.
   d. maximize the number of products to be produced.
   e. minimize the costs of nutrient blends.
8. The diet problem is
   a. also called the feed mix problem in agriculture.
   b. a special case of the ingredient mix problem.
   c. a special case of the blending problem.
   d. all of the above.
9. The following problem type is such a special case of LP that a special algorithm has been developed to solve it:
   a. the transportation problem
   b. the diet problem
   c. the ingredient mix problem
   d. the production mix problem
   e. none of the above
10. Determining the most efficient allocation of people, machines, equipment, and so on, is characteristic of the LP problem type known as
    a. production scheduling.
    b. labor planning.
    c. assignment.
    d. blending.
    e. none of the above.
11. The selection of specific investments from among a wide variety of alternatives is the type of LP problem known as
    a. the product mix problem.
    b. the investment banker problem.
    c. the portfolio selection problem.
    d. the Wall Street problem.
    e. none of the above.
12. A type of LP problem that is used in marketing is called
    a. the 4P problem.
    b. the Madison Avenue problem.
    c. the marketing research problem.
    d. all of the above.

Problems*

8-1 Winkler Furniture manufactures two different types of china cabinets, a French Provincial model and a Danish Modern model. Each cabinet produced must go through three departments: carpentry, painting, and finishing. The accompanying table contains all relevant information concerning production times per cabinet produced and production capacities for each operation per day, along with net revenue per unit produced. The firm has a contract with an Indiana distributor to produce a minimum of 300 of each cabinet per week (or 60 cabinets per day). Owner Bob Winkler would like to determine a product mix to maximize his daily revenue.

(a) Formulate as an LP problem.

(b) Solve using an LP software program or spreadsheet.

Production problem

CABINET STYLE	CARPENTRY (HOURS/ CABINET)	PAINTING (HOURS/ CABINET)	FINISHING (HOURS/ CABINET)	NET REVENUE/ CABINET ($)
French provincial	3	1½	¾	28
Danish modern	2	1	¾	25
Department capacity (hours)	360	200	125	

8-2 The Heinlein and Krampf Brokerage firm has just been instructed by one of its clients to invest $250,000 for her, money obtained recently through the sale of land holdings in Ohio. The client has a good deal of trust in the investment house, but she also has her own ideas about the distribution of the funds being invested. In particular, she requests that the firm select whatever stocks and bonds they believe are well rated, but within the following guidelines:

1. Municipal bonds should constitute at least 20% of the investment.
2. At least 40% of the funds should be placed in a combination of electronics firms, aerospace firms, and drug manufacturers.
3. No more than 50% of the amount invested in municipal bonds should be placed in a high-risk, high-yield nursing home stock.

Investment decision problem

Subject to these restraints, the client's goal is to maximize projected return on investments. The analysts at Heinlein and Krampf, aware of these guidelines, prepare a list of high-quality stocks and bonds and their corresponding rates of return.

INVESTMENT	PROJECTED RATE OF RETURN (%)
Los Angeles municipal bonds	5.3
Thompson Electronics, Inc.	6.8
United Aerospace Corp.	4.9
Palmer Drugs	8.4
Happy Days Nursing Homes	11.8

(a) Formulate this portfolio selection problem using LP.

(b) Solve this problem.

*Note: 🖳 means the problem may be solved with QM for Windows; ✖ means the problem may be solved with Excel; and 🖳 means the problem may be solved with QM for Windows and/or Excel.

8-3 The famous Y. S. Chang Restaurant is open 24 hours a day. Waiters and busboys report for duty at 3 A.M., 7 A.M., 11 A.M., 3 P.M., 7 P.M., or 11 P.M., and each works an 8-hour shift. The following table shows the minimum number of workers needed during the six periods into which the day is divided. Chang's scheduling problem is to determine how many waiters and busboys should report for work at the start of each time period to minimize the total staff required for one day's operation. (*Hint*: Let X_i equal the number of waiters and busboys beginning work in time period i, where $i = 1, 2, 3, 4, 5, 6$.)

Restaurant work scheduling problem.

PERIOD	TIME	NUMBER OF WAITERS AND BUSBOYS REQUIRED
1	3 A.M.–7 A.M.	3
2	7 A.M.–11 A.M.	12
3	11 A.M.–3 P.M.	16
4	3 P.M.–7 P.M.	9
5	7 P.M.–11 P.M.	11
6	11 P.M.–3 A.M.	4

8-4 The Battery Park Stable feeds and houses the horses used to pull tourist-filled carriages through the streets of Charleston's historic waterfront area. The stable owner, an ex-racehorse trainer, recognizes the need to set a nutritional diet for the horses in his care. At the same time, he would like to keep the overall daily cost of feed to a minimum.

Animal feed mix problem

The feed mixes available for the horses' diet are an oat product, a highly enriched grain, and a mineral product. Each of these mixes contains a certain amount of five ingredients needed daily to keep the average horse healthy. The following table shows these minimum requirements, units of each ingredient per pound of feed mix, and costs for the three mixes:

DIET REQUIREMENT (INGREDIENTS)	OAT PRODUCT (UNITS/LB)	ENRICHED GRAIN (UNITS/LB)	MINERAL PRODUCT (UNITS/LB)	MINIMUM DAILY REQUIREMENT (UNITS)
A	2	3	1	6
B	½	1	½	2
C	3	5	6	9
D	1	1½	2	8
E	½	½	1½	5
Cost/lb	$0.09	$0.14	$0.17	

In addition, the stable owner is aware that an overfed horse is a sluggish worker. Consequently, he determines that 6 pounds of feed per day are the most that any horse needs to function properly. Formulate this problem and solve for the optimal daily mix of the three feeds.

8-5 The Dubuque Sackers, a class D baseball team, face a tough four-game road trip against league rivals in Des Moines, Davenport, Omaha, and Peoria. Manager "Red" Revelle faces the task of scheduling his four starting pitchers for appropriate games. Because the games are to be played back to back in less than one week, Revelle cannot count on any pitcher to start in more than one game.

Ballplayer selection problem

Revelle knows the strengths and weaknesses not only of his pitchers, but also of his opponents, and he is able to estimate the probability of winning each of the four games with each of the four starting pitchers. Those probabilities are listed in the following table:

STARTING PITCHER	OPPONENT			
	DES MOINES	DAVENPORT	OMAHA	PEORIA
"Dead-Arm" Jones	0.60	0.80	0.50	0.40
"Spitball" Baker	0.70	0.40	0.80	0.30
"Ace" Parker	0.90	0.80	0.70	0.80
"Gutter" Wilson	0.50	0.30	0.40	0.20

What pitching rotation should manager Revelle set to provide the highest winning probability (i.e., the sum of the probabilities of winning each game) for the Sackers?

(a) Formulate this problem using LP.

(b) Solve the problem.

8-6 The advertising director for Diversey Paint and Supply, a chain of four retail stores on Chicago's North Side, is considering two media possibilities. One plan is for a series of half-page ads in the Sunday *Chicago Tribune* newspaper, and the other is for advertising time on Chicago TV. The stores are expanding their lines of do-it-yourself tools, and the advertising director is interested in an exposure level of at least 40% within the city's neighborhoods and 60% in northwest suburban areas.

Media selection problem

The TV viewing time under consideration has an exposure rating per spot of 5% in city homes and 3% in the northwest suburbs. The Sunday newspaper has corresponding exposure rates of 4% and 3% per ad. The cost of a half-page *Tribune* advertisement is $925; a television spot costs $2,000.

Diversey Paint would like to select the least costly advertising strategy that would meet desired exposure levels.

(a) Formulate using LP.

(b) Solve the problem.

8-7 Capitol Hill Construction Company (CHCC) must complete its current office building renovation as quickly as possible. The first portion of the project consists of six activities, some of which must be finished before others are started. The activities, their precedences, and their estimated times are shown in this table:

ACTIVITY		PRECEDENCE	TIME (DAYS)
Prepare financing options	(A)	—	2
Prepare preliminary sketches	(B)	—	3
Outline specifications	(C)	—	1
Prepare drawings	(D)	A	4
Write specifications	(E)	C and D	5
Run off prints	(F)	B	1

This network of tasks can be drawn shown in Figure 8.1.

Let X_i represent the earliest completion of an activity where i = A, B, C, D, E, F. Formulate and solve CHCC's problem as a linear program.

FIGURE 8.1
Network for Problem 8-7.

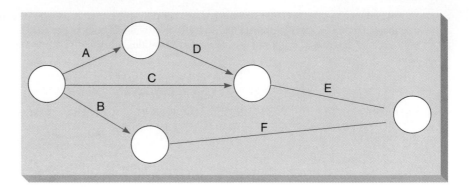

  8-8   The Arden County, Maryland, superintendent of education is responsible for assigning students to the *three* high schools in his county. He recognizes the need to bus a certain number of students, for several sectors of the county are beyond walking distance to a school. The superintendent partitions the county into *five* geographic sectors as he attempts to establish a plan that will minimize the total number of student miles traveled by bus. He also recognizes that if a student happens to live in a certain sector and is assigned to the high school in that sector, there is no need to bus that student because he or she can walk to school. The three schools are located in sectors B, C, and E.

High school busing problem

The accompanying table reflects the number of high-school-age students living in each sector and the distance in miles from each sector to each school.

| | DISTANCE TO SCHOOL | | | |
SECTOR	SCHOOL IN SECTOR B	SCHOOL IN SECTOR C	SCHOOL IN SECTOR E	NUMBER OF STUDENTS
A	5	8	6	700
B	0	4	12	500
C	4	0	7	100
D	7	2	5	800
E	12	7	0	400
				2,500

Each high school has a capacity of 900 students. Set up the objective function and constraints of this problem using LP so that the total number of student miles traveled by bus is minimized. (Note the resemblance to the transportation problem illustrated earlier in this chapter.) Then solve the problem.

  8-9   Bob Bell's fortieth birthday party promised to be the social event of the year in Cookeville. To prepare, Bob stocked up on the following liquors:

Ingredient mix problem

LIQUOR	AMOUNT ON HAND (OUNCES)
Bourbon	52
Brandy	38
Vodka	64
Dry vermouth	24
Sweet vermouth	36

Bob decides to mix four drinks for the party: Chaunceys, Sweet Italians, bourbon on the rocks, and Russian martinis. A Chauncey consists of ¼ bourbon, ¼ vodka, ¼ brandy, and ¼ sweet vermouth. A Sweet Italian contains ¼ brandy, ½ sweet vermouth, and ¼ dry vermouth. Bourbon on the rocks contains only bourbon. Finally, a Russian martini consists of ⅓ dry vermouth and ⅔ vodka. Each drink contains 4 fluid ounces.

Bob's objective is to mix these ingredients in such a way as to make the largest possible number of drinks in advance.

(a) Formulate using LP.

(b) Solve using LP software.

8-10 The I. Kruger Paint and Wallpaper Store is a large retail distributor of the Supertrex brand of vinyl wallcoverings. Kruger will enhance its citywide image in Miami if it can outsell other local stores in total number of rolls of Supertex next year. It is able to estimate the demand function as follows:

Pricing and marketing strategy problem

Number of rolls of Supertrex sold = 20 × dollars spent on advertising + 6.8 × dollars spent on in-store displays + 12 × dollars invested in on-hand wallpaper inventory − 65,000 × percentage markup taken above wholesale cost of a roll.

The store budgets a total of $17,000 for advertising, in-store displays, and on-hand inventory of Supertrex for next year. It decides it must spend at least $3,000 on advertising; in addition, at least 5% of the amount invested in on-hand inventory should be devoted to displays. Markups on Supertrex seen at other local stores range from 20 to 45%. Kruger decides that its markup had best be in this range as well.

(a) Formulate as an LP problem.

(b) Solve the problem.

(c) What is the difficulty with the answer?

(d) What constraint would you add?

8-11 Kathy Roniger, campus dietician for a small Idaho college, is responsible for formulating a nutritious meal plan for students. For an evening meal, she feels that the following five meal-content requirements should be met: (1) between 900 and 1,500 calories; (2) at least 4 milligrams of iron; (3) no more than 50 grams of fat; (4) at least 26 grams of protein; and (5) no more than 50 grams of carbohydrates. On a particular day, Roniger's food stock includes seven items that can be prepared and served for supper to meet these requirements. The cost per pound for each food item and its contribution to each of the five nutritional requirements are given in the accompanying table:

College meal selection problem

TABLE OF FOOD VALUES* AND COSTS

FOOD ITEM	CALORIES/ POUND	IRON (MG/LB)	FAT (GM/LB)	PROTEIN (GM/LB)	CARBOHYDRATES (GM/LB)	COST/ POUND ($)
Milk	295	0.2	16	16	22	0.60
Ground meat	1216	0.2	96	81	0	2.35
Chicken	394	4.3	9	74	0	1.15
Fish	358	3.2	0.5	83	0	2.25
Beans	128	3.2	0.8	7	28	0.58
Spinach	118	14.1	1.4	14	19	1.17
Potatoes	279	2.2	0.5	8	63	0.33

Source: C. F. Church and H. N. Church, Bowes and Church's, *Food Values of Portions Commonly Used*, 12th ed. Philadelphia, J.B. Lippincott, 1975.

What combination and amounts of food items will provide the nutrition Roniger requires at the least total food cost?

(a) Formulate as an LP problem.

(b) What is the cost per meal?

(c) Is this a well-balanced diet?

High tech production problem

8-12 Quitmeyer Electronics Incorporated manufactures the following six microcomputer peripheral devices: internal modems, external modems, graphics circuit boards, floppy disk drives, hard disk drives, and memory expansion boards. Each of these technical products requires time, in minutes, on three types of electronic testing equipment as shown in the following table:

	INTERNAL MODEM	EXTERNAL MODEM	CIRCUIT BOARD	FLOPPY DRIVES	HARD DRIVES	MEMORY BOARDS
Test device 1	7	3	12	6	18	17
Test device 2	2	5	3	2	15	17
Test device 3	5	1	3	2	9	2

The first two test devices are available 120 hours per week. The third (device 3) requires more preventive maintenance and may be used only 100 hours each week. The market for all six computer components is vast, and Quitmeyer Electronics believes that it can sell as many units of each product as it can manufacture. The table that follows summarizes the revenues and material costs for each product:

DEVICE	REVENUE PER UNIT SOLD ($)	MATERIAL COST PER UNIT ($)
Internal modem	200	35
External modem	120	25
Graphics circuit board	180	40
Floppy disk drive	130	45
Hard disk drive	430	170
Memory expansion board	260	60

In addition, variable labor costs are $15 per hour for test device 1, $12 per hour for test device 2, and $18 per hour for test device 3. Quitmeyer Electronics wants to maximize its profits.

(a) Formulate this problem as an LP model.

(b) Solve the problem by computer. What is the best product mix?

(c) What is the value of an additional minute of time per week on test device 1? Test device 2? Test device 3? Should Quitmeyer Electronics add more test device time? If so, on which equipment?

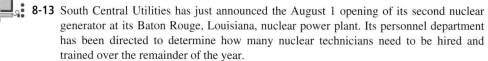

Nuclear plant staffing problem

8-13 South Central Utilities has just announced the August 1 opening of its second nuclear generator at its Baton Rouge, Louisiana, nuclear power plant. Its personnel department has been directed to determine how many nuclear technicians need to be hired and trained over the remainder of the year.

The plant currently employs 350 fully trained technicians and projects the following personnel needs:

MONTH	PERSONNEL HOURS NEEDED
August	40,000
September	45,000
October	35,000
November	50,000
December	45,000

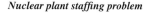

By Louisiana law, a reactor employee can actually work no more than 130 hours per month. (Slightly over one hour per day is used for check-in and check-out, record keeping, and for daily radiation health scans.) Policy at South Central Utilities also dictates that layoffs are not acceptable in those months when the nuclear plant is overstaffed. So, if more trained employees are available than are needed in any month, each worker is still fully paid, even though he or she is not required to work the 130 hours.

Training new employees is an important and costly procedure. It takes one month of one-on-one classroom instruction before a new technician is permitted to work alone in the reactor facility. Therefore, South Central must hire trainees one month before they are actually needed. Each trainee teams up with a skilled nuclear technician and requires 90 hours of that employee's time, meaning that 90 hours less of the technician's time are available that month for actual reactor work.

Personnel department records indicate a turnover rate of trained technicians at 5% per month. In other words, about 5% of the skilled employees at the start of any month resign by the end of that month. A trained technician earns an average monthly salary of $2,000 (regardless of the number of hours worked, as noted earlier). Trainees are paid $900 during their one month of instruction.

(a) Formulate this staffing problem using LP.

(b) Solve the problem. How many trainees must begin each month?

8-14 Margaret Young's family owns five parcels of farmland broken into a southeast sector, north sector, northwest sector, west sector, and southwest sector. Young is involved primarily in growing wheat, alfalfa, and barley crops and is currently preparing her production plan for next year. The Pennsylvania Water Authority has just announced its yearly water allotment, with the Young farm receiving 7,400 acre-feet. Each parcel can only tolerate a specified amount of irrigation per growing season, as specified in the following table:

PARCEL	AREA (ACRES)	WATER IRRIGATION LIMIT (ACRE-FEET)
Southeast	2,000	3,200
North	2,300	3,400
Northwest	600	800
West	1,100	500
Southwest	500	600

Agricultural production planning problem

Each of Young's crops needs a minimum amount of water per acre, and there is a projected limit on sales of each crop. Crop data follow:

CROP	MAXIMUM SALES	WATER NEEDED PER ACRE (ACRE-FEET)
Wheat	110,000 bushels	1.6
Alfalfa	1,800 tons	2.9
Barley	2,200 tons	3.5

Young's best estimate is that she can sell wheat at a net profit of $2 per bushel, alfalfa at $40 per ton, and barley at $50 per ton. One acre of land yields an average of 1.5 tons of alfalfa and 2.2 tons of barley. The wheat yield is approximately 50 bushels per acre.

(a) Formulate Young's production plan.

(b) What should the crop plan be, and what profit will it yield?

(c) The Water Authority informs Young that for a special fee of $6,000 this year, her farm will qualify for an additional allotment of 600 acre-feet of water. How should she respond?

8-15 Amalgamated Products has just received a contract to construct steel body frames for automobiles that are to be produced at the new Japanese factory in Tennessee. The Japanese auto manufacturer has strict quality control standards for all of its component subcontractors and has informed Amalgamated that each frame must have the following steel content:

MATERIAL	MINIMUM PERCENT	MAXIMUM PERCENT
Manganese	2.1	2.3
Silicon	4.3	4.6
Carbon	5.05	5.35

Material blending problem

Amalgamated mixes batches of eight different available materials to produce one ton of steel used in the body frames. The table that follows details these materials:

MATERIAL AVAILABLE	MANGANESE (%)	SILICON (%)	CARBON (%)	POUNDS AVAILABLE	COST PER POUND
Alloy 1	70.0	15.0	3.0	No limit	$0.12
Alloy 2	55.0	30.0	1.0	300	0.13
Alloy 3	12.0	26.0	0	No limit	0.15
Iron 1	1.0	10.0	3.0	No limit	0.09
Iron 2	5.0	2.5	0	No limit	0.07
Carbide 1	0	24.0	18.0	50	0.10
Carbide 2	0	25.0	20.0	200	0.12
Carbide 3	0	23.0	25.0	100	0.09

Formulate and solve the LP model that will indicate how much each of the eight materials should be blended into a 1-ton load of steel so that Amalgamated meets its requirements while minimizing costs.

8-16 Refer to Problem 8-15. Find the cause of the difficulty and recommend how to adjust it. Then solve the problem again.

8-17 Mt. Sinai Hospital in New Orleans is a large, private, 600-bed facility complete with laboratories, operating rooms, and x-ray equipment. In seeking to increase revenues, Mt. Sinai's administration has decided to make a 90-bed addition on a portion of adjacent land currently used for staff parking. The administrators feel that the labs, operating rooms, and x-ray department are not being fully utilized at present and do not need to be expanded to handle additional patients. The addition of 90 beds, however, involves deciding how many beds should be allocated to the medical staff for medical patients and how many to the surgical staff for surgical patients.

Hospital expansion problem

The hospital's accounting medical records departments have provided the following pertinent information. The average hospital stay for a medical patient is 8 days, and the average medical patient generates $2,280 in revenues. The average surgical patient is in the hospital 5 days and receives a $1,515 bill. The laboratory is capable of handling 15,000 tests per year more than it was handling. The average medical patient requires 3.1 lab tests and the average surgical patient takes 2.6 lab tests. Furthermore, the average medical patient uses one x-ray, whereas the average surgical patient requires two x-rays. If the hospital was expanded by 90 beds, the x-ray department could handle up to 7,000 x-rays without significant additional cost. Finally, the administration estimates that up to 2,800 additional operations could be performed in existing operating room facilities. Medical patients, of course, require no surgery, whereas each surgical patient generally has one surgery performed.

Formulate this problem so as to determine how many medical beds and how many surgical beds should be added to maximize revenues. Assume that the hospital is open 365 days a year. Then solve the problem.

8-18 Prepare a written report to the CEO of Mt. Sinai Hospital in Problem 8-17 on the expansion of the hospital. Round off your answers to the nearest *integer*. The format of presentation of results is important. The CEO is a busy person and wants to be able to find your optimal solution quickly in your report. Cover all the areas given in the following sections but do not mention any X's, slack or surplus variables, or shadow prices

(a) What is the maximum revenue per year, how many medical patients/year are there, and how many surgical patients/year are there? How many medical beds and how many surgical beds of the 90-bed addition should be added?

(b) Are there any empty beds with this optimal solution? If so, how many empty beds are there? Discuss the effect of acquiring more beds if needed.

(c) Are the laboratories being used to their capacity? Is it possible to perform more lab tests/year? If so, how many more? Discuss the effect of acquiring more lab space if needed.

(d) Is the x-ray facility being used to its maximum? Is it possible to do more x-rays/year? If so, how many more? Discuss the effect of acquiring more x-ray facilities if needed.

(e) Is the operating room being used to capacity? Is it possible to do more operations/year? If so, how many more? Discuss the effect of acquiring more operating room if needed. (*Source*: Professor Chris Vertullo.)

8-19 Marc Smith's construction firm currently has three projects under way in various counties in Iowa. Each requires a specific supply of gravel. Three gravel pits are available in Iowa to provide for Smith's needs, but shipping costs differ from location to location. The following table summarizes the problem Smith faces. Determine the optimal shipping assignment so as to minimize total costs:

FROM \ TO	JOB 1	JOB 2	JOB 3	TONNAGE ALLOWANCE
Dubuque pit	$6	$8	$10	150
Davenport pit	7	11	11	175
Des Moines pit	4	5	12	275
Job requirements (tons)	200	100	300	600

Gravel transportation problem

8-20 Northwest General, a large hospital in Providence, Rhode Island, has initiated a new procedure to ensure that patients receive their meals while the food is still as hot as possible. The hospital will continue to prepare the food in its kitchen but will now deliver it in bulk (not individual servings) to one of three new serving stations in the building. From there, the food will be reheated and meals will be placed on individual trays, loaded onto a cart, and distributed to the various floors and wings of the hospital.

The three new serving stations are as efficiently located as possible to reach the various hallways in the hospital. The number of trays that each station can serve are as follows:

Hospital food transportation problem

LOCATION	CAPACITY (MEALS)
Station 5A	200
Station 3G	225
Station 1S	275

There are six wings to Northwest General that must be served. The number of patients in each follows:

WING	PATIENTS
1	80
2	120
3	150
4	210
5	60
6	80

The purpose of the new procedure is to increase the temperature of the hot meals that the patient receives. Therefore, the amount of time needed to deliver a tray from a serving station will determine the proper distribution of food from serving station to wing. The following table summarizes the time (minutes) associated with each possible distribution channel.

What is your recommendation for handling the distribution of trays from the three serving stations?

FROM \ TO	WING 1	WING 2	WING 3	WING 4	WING 5	WING 6
Station 5A	12	11	8	9	6	6
Station 3G	6	12	7	7	5	8
Station 1S	8	9	6	6	7	9

Case Study

Red Brand Canners

On Monday, September 13, 1999, Mitchell Gordon, vice president of operations, asked the controller, the sales manager, and the production manager to meet with him to discuss the amount of tomato products to pack that season. The tomato crop, which had been purchased at planting, was beginning to arrive at the cannery, and packing operations would have to be started by the following Monday. Red Brand Canners is a medium-sized company that cans and distributes a variety of fruit and vegetable products under private brands in the western states.

William Cooper, the controller, and Charles Myers, the sales manager, were the first to arrive in Gordon's office. Dan Tucker, the production manager, came in a few minutes later and said that he had picked up Produce Inspection's latest estimate of the quality of the incoming tomatoes. According to the report, about 20% of the crop was grade A quality and the remaining portion of the 3-million-pound crop was grade B.

Gordon asked Myers about the demand for tomato products for the coming year. Myers replied that they could sell all of the whole canned tomatoes they could produce. The expected demand for tomato juice and tomato paste, on the other hand, was limited. The sales manager then passed around the latest demand forecast, which is shown in Table 8.6. He reminded the group that the selling prices had been set in light of the long-term marketing strategy of the company and that the potential sales had been forecast at these prices.

Bill Cooper, after looking at Myers's estimates of demand, said that it looked like the company "should do quite well [on the tomato crop] this year." With the new accounting system that had been set up, he had been able to compute the contribution for each product, and according to his analysis the incremental profit on whole tomatoes was greater than the incremental profit on any other tomato product. In May, after Red Brand had signed contracts agreeing to purchase the grower's production at an average delivered price of 6 cents per pound, Cooper had computed the tomato products' contributions (see Table 8.7).

Dan Tucker brought to Cooper's attention that although there was ample production capacity, it was impossible to pro-

TABLE 8.6 Demand Forecasts

PRODUCT	SELLING PRICE PER CASE ($)	DEMAND FORECAST (CASES)
24—2½ whole tomatoes	4.00	800,000
24—2½ choice peach halves	5.40	10,000
24—2½ peach nectar	4.60	5,000
24—2½ tomato juice	4.50	50,000
24—2½ cooking apples	4.90	15,000
24—2½ tomato paste	3.80	80,000

duce all whole tomatoes because too small a portion of the tomato crop was "grade A" quality. Red Brand used a numerical scale to record the quality of both raw produce and prepared products. This scale ran from 0 to 10, the higher number representing better quality. According to this scale, grade A tomatoes averaged nine points per pound and grade B tomatoes averaged five points per pound. Tucker noted that the minimum average input quality was eight points per pound for canned whole tomatoes and six points per pound for juice. Paste could be made entirely from grade B tomatoes. This meant that whole-tomato production was limited to 800,000 pounds.

TABLE 8.7 Product Item Profitability

PRODUCT	24—2½ WHOLE TOMATOES	24—2½ CHOICE PEACH HALVES	24—2½ PEACH NECTAR	24—2½ TOMATO JUICE	24—2½ COOKING APPLES	24—2½ TOMATO PASTE
Selling price	$4.00	$5.40	$4.60	$4.50	$4.90	$3.80
Variable cost Direct labor	1.18	1.40	1.27	1.32	0.70	0.54
Variable overhead	0.24	0.32	0.23	0.36	0.22	0.26
Variable selling	0.40	0.30	0.40	0.85	0.28	0.38
Packaging material	0.70	0.56	0.60	0.65	0.70	0.77
Fruit*	1.08	1.80	1.70	1.20	0.90	1.50
Total variable costs	3.60	4.38	4.20	4.38	2.80	3.45
Contribution	0.40	1.02	0.40	0.12	1.10	0.35
Less allocated overhead	0.28	0.70	0.52	0.21	0.75	0.23
Net profit	0.12	0.32	(0.12)	(0.09)	0.35	0.12

*Product usage is as follows:

Product	Pounds per Case
Whole tomatoes	18
Peach halves	18
Peach nectar	17
Tomato juice	20
Cooking apples	27
Tomato paste	25

TABLE 8.8 Marginal Analysis of Tomato Products

Z = cost per pound of grade A tomatoes in cents

Y = cost per pound of grade B tomatoes in cents

$$(600{,}000 \text{ lb} \times Z) + (2{,}400{,}000 \text{ lb} \times Y) = (3{,}000{,}000 \text{ lb} \times 6) \qquad (1)$$

$$\frac{Z}{9} = \frac{Y}{5} \qquad (2)$$

Z = 9.32 cents per pound

Y = 5.18 cents per pound

PRODUCT	CANNED WHOLE TOMATOES	TOMATO JUICE	TOMATO PASTE
Selling price	$4.00	$4.50	$3.80
Variable cost (excluding tomato cost)	2.52	3.18	1.95
	$1.48	$1.32	$1.85
Tomato cost	1.49	1.24	1.30
Marginal profit	($0.01)	$0.08	$0.55

Gordon stated that this was not a real limitation. He had been recently solicited to purchase 80,000 pounds of grade A tomatoes at 8½ cents per pound and at that time had turned down the offer. He felt, however, that the tomatoes were still available.

Myers, who had been doing some calculations, said that although he agreed that the company "should do quite well this year," it would not be by canning whole tomatoes. It seemed to him that the tomato cost should be allocated on the basis of quality and quantity rather than by quantity only, as Cooper had done. Therefore, he had recomputed the marginal profit on this basis (see Table 8.8), and from his results had concluded that Red Brand should use 2 million pounds of the grade B tomatoes for paste, and the remaining 400,000 pounds of grade B tomatoes and all of the grade A tomatoes for juice.

If the demand expectations were realized, a contribution of $48,000 would be made on this year's tomato crop.

Discussion Questions

1. Structure this problem verbally, including a written description of the constraints and objective. What are the decision variables?
2. Develop a *mathematical* formulation for Red Brand's objective function and constraints.
3. Solve the problem and discuss the results.

Case Study

Chase Manhattan Bank

The workload in many areas of bank operations has the characteristics of a nonuniform distribution with respect to time of day. For example, at Chase Manhattan Bank in New York, the number of domestic money transfer requests received from customers, if plotted against time of day, would appear to have the shape of an inverted U curve with the peak around 1 P.M. For efficient use of resources, the personnel available should,

therefore, vary correspondingly. Figure 8.2 shows a typical workload curve and corresponding personnel requirements at different hours of the day.

A variable capacity can be achieved effectively by employing part-time personnel. Because part-timers are not entitled to all the fringe benefits, they are often more economical than full-time employees. Other considerations, however, may limit the extent to which part-time people can be hired in a

FIGURE 8.2

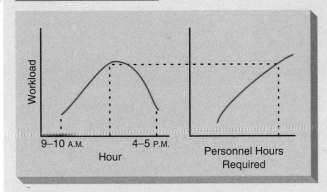

TABLE 8.9	**Workforce Requirements**
TIME PERIOD	**NUMBER OF PERSONNEL REQUIRED**
9–10 A.M.	14
10–11	25
11–12	26
12–1 P.M.	38
1–2	55
2–3	60
3–4	51
4–5	29
5–6	14
6–7	9

given department. The problem is to find an optimum workforce schedule that would meet personnel requirements at any given time and also be economical.

Some of the factors affecting personnel assignment are listed here:

1. By corporate policy, part-time personnel hours are limited to a maximum of 40% of the day's total requirement.
2. Full-time employees work for 8 hours (1 hour for lunch included) per day. Thus, a full-timer's productive time is 35 hours per week.
3. Part-timers work for at least 4 hours per day but less than 8 hours and are not allowed a lunch break.
4. Fifty percent of the full-timers go to lunch between 11 A.M. and noon and the remaining 50% between noon and 1 P.M.
5. The shift starts at 9 A.M. and ends at 7 P.M. (i.e., overtime is limited to 2 hours). Any work left over at 7 P.M. is considered holdover for the next day.
6. A full-time employee is not allowed to work more than 5 hours overtime per week. He or she is paid at the normal rate for overtime hours—*not* at one-and-a-half times the normal rate applicable to hours in excess of 40 per week. Fringe benefits are not applied to overtime hours.

In addition, the following costs are pertinent:

1. The average cost per full-time personnel hour (fringe benefits included) is $10.11.

2. The average cost per overtime personnel hour for full-timers (straight rate excluding fringe benefits) is $8.08.
3. The average cost per part-time personnel hour is $7.82.

The personnel hours required, by hour of day, are given in Table 8.9.

The bank's goal is to achieve the minimum possible personnel cost subject to meeting or exceeding the hourly workforce requirements as well as the constraints on the workers listed earlier.

Discussion Questions

1. What is the minimum-cost schedule for the bank?
2. What are the limitations of the model used to answer question 1?
3. Costs might be reduced by relaxing the constraint that no more than 40% of the day's requirement be met by part-timers. Would changing the 40% to a higher value significantly reduce costs? *(sensitivity analysis)*

Source: Adapted from Shyam L. Moondra, "An L. P. Model for Work Force Scheduling for Banks," *Journal of Bank Research* (Winter 1976).

Bibliography

See the Bibliography at the end of Chapter 7.

CHAPTER 9

Linear Programming: The Simplex Method

LEARNING OBJECTIVES

After completing this chapter, students will be able to:

1. Convert LP constraints to equalities with slack, surplus, and artificial variables.
2. Set up and solve LP problems with simplex tableaus.
3. Interpret the meaning of every number in a simplex tableau.
4. Recognize special cases such as infeasibility, unboundedness and degeneracy.
5. Use the simplex tables to conduct sensitivity analysis.

CHAPTER OUTLINE

9.1 Introduction

9.2 How to Set Up the Initial Simplex Solution

9.3 Simplex Solution Procedures

9.4 The Second Simplex Tableau

9.5 Developing the Third Tableau

9.6 Review of Procedures for Solving LP Maximization Problems

9.7 Surplus and Artificial Variables

9.8 Solving Minimization Problems

9.9 Review of Procedures for Solving LP Minimization Problems

9.10 Special Cases

9.11 Sensitivity Analysis with the Simplex Tableau

9.12 The Dual

9.13 Karmarkar's Algorithm

Summary • Glossary • Key Equation • Solved Problems
• Self-Test • Discussion Questions and Problems • Data
Set Problem • Case Study: Coastal States Chemicals and
Fertilizers • Bibliography

9.1   INTRODUCTION

In Chapter 7 we looked at examples of linear programming (LP) problems that contained two decision variables. With only two variables it was possible to use a graphical approach. We plotted the feasible region and then searched for the optimal corner point and corresponding profit or cost. This approach provided a good way to understand the basic concepts of LP. Most real-life LP problems, however, have more than two variables and are thus too large for the simple graphical solution procedure. Problems faced in business and government can have dozens, hundreds, or even thousands of variables. We need a more powerful method than graphing, so in this chapter we turn to a procedure called the *simplex method*.

Recall that the theory of LP states the optimal solution will lie at a corner point of the feasible region. In large LP problems, the feasible region cannot be graphed because it has many dimensions, but the concept is the same.

How does the simplex method work? The concept is simple, and similar to graphical LP in one important respect. In graphical LP we examined each of the corner points; LP theory told us that the optimal solution lies at one of them. In LP problems containing several variables, we may not be able to graph the feasible region, but the optimal solution will still lie at a corner point of the many-sided, many-dimensional figure (called an *n*-dimensional polyhedron) that represents the area of feasible solutions. The simplex method examines the corner points in a systematic fashion, using basic algebraic concepts. It does so in an *iterative* manner, that is, repeating the same set of procedures time after time until an optimal solution is reached. Each iteration brings a higher value for the objective function so that we are always moving closer to the optimal solution.

The simplex method systematically examines corner points, using algebraic steps, until an optimal solution is found.

Why should we study the simplex method? It is important to understand the ideas used to produce solutions. The simplex approach yields not only the optimal solution to the X_i variables and the maximum profit (or minimum cost), but valuable economic information as well.[1] To be able to use computers successfully and to interpret LP computer printouts, we need to know what the simplex method is doing and why.

We begin by solving a maximization problem using the simplex method. We then tackle a minimization problem and look at a few technical issues that are faced when employing the simplex procedure. From there we examine how to conduct sensitivity analysis using the simplex tables. The chapter concludes with a discussion of the dual, which is an alternative way of looking at any LP problem.

9.2   HOW TO SET UP THE INITIAL SIMPLEX SOLUTION

Let us consider the case of the Flair Furniture Company from Chapter 7. Instead of the graphical solution we used in that chapter, we now demonstrate the simplex method. You may recall that we let

X_1 = number of tables produced

X_2 = number of chairs produced

and that the problem was formulated as

maximize profit = $\$7X_1 + \$5X_2$ (objective function)

subject to $2X_1 + 1X_2 \leq 100$ (painting hours constraint)

$4X_1 + 3X_2 \leq 240$ (carpentry hours constraint)

$X_1, X_2 \geq 0$ (nonnegativity constraints)

---

[1] The simplex method also applies for problems requiring integer solutions, as we see in Chapter 11.

Converting the Constraints to Equations

The first step of the simplex method requires that we convert each inequality constraint in an LP formulation into an equation.[2] Less-than-or-equal-to constraints ($\leq$) such as in the Flair problem are converted to equations by adding a *slack variable* to each constraint. Slack variables represent unused resources; these may be in the form of time on a machine, labor hours, money, warehouse space, or any number of such resources in various business problems.

Slack variables are added to each less-than-or-equal-to constraint. Each slack variable represents an unused resource.

In our case at hand, we can let

S_1 = slack variable representing unused hours in the painting department

S_2 = slack variable representing unused hours in the carpentry department

The constraints to the problem may now be written as

$$2X_1 + 1X_2 + S_1 = 100$$

and

$$4X_1 + 3X_2 + S_2 = 240$$

Thus, if the production of tables (X_1) and chairs (X_2) uses less than 100 hours of painting time available, the unused time is the value of the slack variable, S_1. For example, if $X_1 = 0$ and $X_2 = 0$ (in other words, if nothing is produced), we have $S_1 = 100$ hours of slack time in the painting department. If Flair produces $X_1 = 40$ tables and $X_2 = 10$ chairs, then

$$2X_1 + 1X_2 + S_1 = 100$$

$$2(40) + 1(10) + S_1 = 100$$

$$S_1 = 10$$

and there will be 10 hours of slack, or unused, painting time available.

To include all variables in each equation, which is a requirement of the next simplex step, slack variables not appearing in an equation are added with a coefficient of 0. This means, in effect, that they have no influence on the equations in which they are inserted; but it does allow us to keep tabs on all variables at all times. The equations now appear as follows:

$$2X_1 + 1X_2 + 1S_1 + 0S_2 = 100$$

$$4X_1 + 3X_2 + 0S_1 + 1S_2 = 240$$

$$X_1, X_2, S_1, S_2 \geq 0$$

Because slack variables yield no profit, they are added to the original objective function with 0 profit coefficients. The objective function becomes

$$\text{maximize profit} = \$7X_1 + \$5X_2 + \$0S_1 + \$0S_2$$

---

[2] This is because the simplex is a matrix algebra method that requires all mathematical relationships to be equations, with each equation containing all of the variables.

Finding an Initial Solution Algebraically

Let's take another look at the new constraint equations. We see that there are two equations and four variables. Think back to your last algebra course. When you have the same number of unknown variables as you have equations, it is possible to solve for unique values of the variables. But when there are four unknowns (X_1, X_2, S_1, and S_2, in this case) and only two equations, you can let two of the variables equal 0 and then solve for the other two. For example, if $X_1 = X_2 = 0$, then $S_1 = 100$ and $S_2 = 240$.

Simplex considers only corner points as it seeks the best solution.

The simplex method begins with an initial feasible solution in which all real variables (such as X_1 and X_2) are set equal to 0. This trivial solution always produces a profit of \$0, as well as slack variables equal to the constant (right-hand-side) terms in the constraint equations. It's not a very exciting solution in terms of economic returns, but it is one of the original corner point solutions (see Figure 9.1). As mentioned, the simplex method will start at this corner point (*A*) and then move up or over to the corner point that yields the most improved profit (*B* or *D*). Finally, the technique will move to a new corner point (*C*), which happens to be the optimal solution to the Flair Furniture problem. The simplex method considers only feasible solutions and hence will touch no possible combinations other than the corner points of the shaded region in Figure 9.1.

The First Simplex Tableau

To simplify handling the equations and objective function in an LP problem, we place all of the coefficients into tabular form. The first *simplex tableau* is shown in Table 9.1. An explanation of its parts and how the tableau is derived follows.

FIGURE 9.1

Corner Points of the Flair Furniture Company Problem

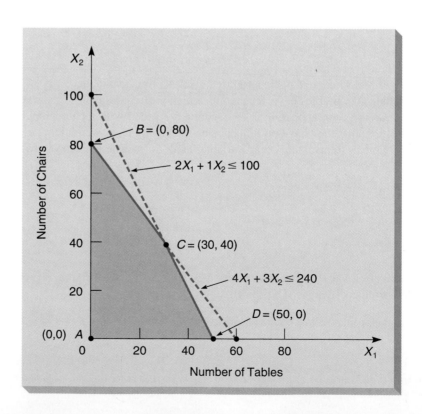

Constraint Equations We see that Flair Furniture's two constraint equations can be expressed as follows:

SOLUTION MIX	X_1	X_2	S_1	S_2	QUANTITY (RIGHT-HAND SIDE)
S_1	2	1	1	0	100
S_2	4	3	0	1	240

Here are the constraints in tabular form.

The numbers (2, 1, 1, 0) in the first row represent the coefficients of the first equation, namely, $2X_1 + 1X_2 + 1S_1 + 0S_2$. The numbers (4, 3, 0, 1) in the second row are the algebraic equivalent of the constraint $4X_1 + 3X_2 + 0S_1 + 1S_2$.

As suggested earlier, we begin the initial solution procedure at the origin, where $X_1 = 0$ and $X_2 = 0$. The values of the other two variables must then be nonzero, so $S_1 = 100$ and $S_2 = 240$. These two slack variables constitute the *initial solution mix*; their values are found in the *quantity* (or right-hand-side—RHS) *column*. Because X_1 and X_2 are not in the solution mix, their initial values are automatically equal to 0.

The initial solution mix begins with real, or decision, variables set equal to zero.

This initial solution is termed a *basic feasible solution* and is described in vector, or column, form as

$$\begin{bmatrix} X_1 \\ X_2 \\ S_1 \\ S_2 \end{bmatrix} = \begin{bmatrix} 0 \\ 0 \\ 100 \\ 200 \end{bmatrix}$$

Here is the basic feasible solution in column form.

Variables in the solution mix, which is called the *basis* in LP terminology, are referred to as basic variables. In this example, the basic variables are S_1 and S_2. Variables

TABLE 9.1   **Flair Furniture's Initial Simplex Tableau**

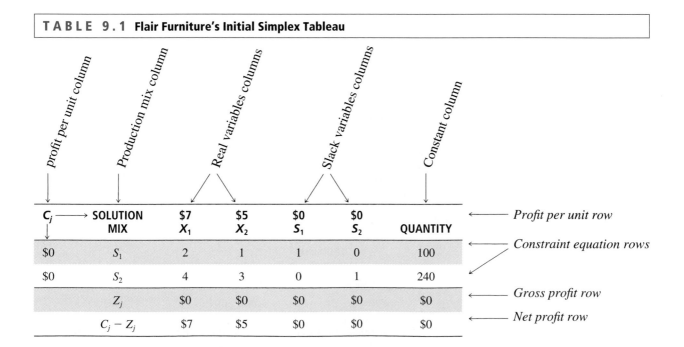

C_j	SOLUTION MIX	$7 X_1	$5 X_2	$0 S_1	$0 S_2	QUANTITY	
$0	S_1	2	1	1	0	100	← Constraint equation rows
$0	S_2	4	3	0	1	240	
	Z_j	$0	$0	$0	$0	$0	← Gross profit row
	$C_j - Z_j$	$7	$5	$0	$0	$0	← Net profit row

Variables in the solution mix are called **basic.** *Those not in the solution are called* **nonbasic.**

not in the solution mix or basis (X_1 and X_2 in this case) are called nonbasic variables. Of course, if the optimal solution to this LP problem turned out to be $X_1 = 30$, $X_2 = 40$, $S_1 = 0$, and $S_2 = 0$, or

$$\begin{bmatrix} X_1 \\ X_2 \\ S_1 \\ S_2 \end{bmatrix} = \begin{bmatrix} 30 \\ 40 \\ 0 \\ 0 \end{bmatrix} \text{ (in vector form)}$$

then X_1 and X_2 would be the final basic variables, while S_1 and S_2 would be the *nonbasic variables.*

Substitution Rates Many students are unsure as to the actual meaning of the numbers in the columns under each variable. We know that the entries are the coefficients for that variable. Under X_1 are the coefficients $\begin{pmatrix} 2 \\ 4 \end{pmatrix}$, under X_2 are $\begin{pmatrix} 1 \\ 3 \end{pmatrix}$, under S_1 are $\begin{pmatrix} 1 \\ 0 \end{pmatrix}$, and under S_2 are $\begin{pmatrix} 0 \\ 1 \end{pmatrix}$.

Substitution rates are numbers in the body of the table. This paragraph explains how to interpret their meaning.

But what is their interpretation? The numbers in the body of the simplex tableau (see Table 9.1) may be thought of as *substitution rates.* For example, suppose we now wish to make X_1 larger than 0, that is, produce some tables. For every unit of the X_1 product introduced into the current solution, 2 units of S_1 and 4 units of S_2 must be removed from the solution. This is so because each table requires 2 hours of the currently unused painting department slack time, S_1. It also takes 4 hours of carpentry time; hence 4 units of variable S_2 must be removed from the solution for every unit of X_1 that enters. Similarly, the substitution rates for each unit of X_2 that enters the current solution are 1 unit of S_1 and 3 units of S_2.

Another point that you are reminded of throughout this chapter is that for any variable ever to appear in the solution mix column, it must have the number 1 someplace in its column and 0s in every other place in that column. We see that column S_1 contains $\begin{pmatrix} 1 \\ 0 \end{pmatrix}$, so variable S_1 is in the solution. Similarly, the S_2 column is $\begin{pmatrix} 0 \\ 1 \end{pmatrix}$, so S_2 is also in the solution.[3]

Adding the Objective Function We now continue to the next step in establishing the first simplex tableau. We add a row to reflect the objective function values for each variable. These contribution rates, called C_j, appear just above each respective variable, as shown in the following table:

$C_j \longrightarrow$		$7	$5	$0	$0	
$\downarrow$	SOLUTION MIX	X_1	X_2	S_1	S_2	QUANTITY
$0	S_1	2	1	1	0	100
$0	S_2	4	3	0	1	240

---

[3] If there had been *three* less-than-or-equal-to constraints in the Flair Furniture problem, there would be three slack variables, S_1, S_2, and S_3. The 1s and 0s would appear like this:

SOLUTION MIX	S_1	S_2	S_3
S_1	1	0	0
S_2	0	1	0
S_3	0	0	1

The unit profit rates are not just found in the top C_j row: in the leftmost column, C_j indicates the unit profit for each variable *currently* in the solution mix. If S_1 were removed from the solution and replaced, for example, by X_2, \$5 would appear in the C_j column just to the left of the term X_2.

The Z_j and $C_j - Z_j$ Rows We may complete the initial Flair Furniture simplex tableau by adding two final rows. These last two rows provide us with important economic information, including the total profit and the answer as to whether the current solution is optimal.

The Z-row entry in the quantity column provides the gross profit.

We compute the Z_j value for each column of the initial solution in Table 9.1 by multiplying the 0 contribution value of each number in the C_j column by each number in that row and the *j*th column, and summing. The Z_j value for the quantity column provides the total contribution (gross profit in this case) of the given solution.

$$Z_j(\text{for gross profit}) = (\text{profit per unit of } S_1) \times (\text{number of units of } S_1)$$
$$+ (\text{profit per unit of } S_2) \times (\text{number of units of } S_2)$$

$$= \$0 \times 100 \text{ units} + \$0 \times 240 \text{ units}$$

$$= \$0 \text{ profit}$$

The Z_j values for the other columns (under the variables X_1, X_2, S_1, and S_2) represent the gross profit *given up* by adding one unit of this variable into the current solution. Their calculations are as follows:

$$Z_j(\text{for column } X_1) = (\$0)(2) + (\$0)(4) = \$0$$

$$Z_j(\text{for column } X_2) = (\$0)(1) + (\$0)(3) = \$0$$

$$Z_j(\text{for column } S_1) = (\$0)(1) + (\$0)(0) = \$0$$

$$Z_j(\text{for column } S_2) = (\$0)(0) + (\$0)(1) = \$0$$

We see that there is no profit *lost* by adding one unit of either X_1 (tables), X_2 (chairs), S_1, or S_2.

The $C_j - Z_j$ row gives the net profit from introducing one unit of each variable into the solution.

The $C_j - Z_j$ number in each column represents the net profit, that is, the profit gained minus the profit given up, that will result from introducing 1 unit of each product or variable into the solution. It is not calculated for the quantity column. To compute these numbers, simply subtract the Z_j total for each column from the C_j value at the very top of that variable's column. The calculations for the net profit per unit (the $C_j - Z_j$ row) in this example follow:

	COLUMN			
	X_1	X_2	S_1	S_2
C_j for column	\$7	\$5	\$0	\$0
Z_j for column	0	0	0	0
$C_j - Z_j$ for column	\$7	\$5	\$0	\$0

It was obvious to us when we computed a profit of \$0 that the initial solution was not optimal. By examining the numbers in the $C_j - Z_j$ row of Table 9.1, we see that the total profit can be increased by \$7 for each unit of X_1 (tables) and by \$5 for each unit of X_2 (chairs) added to the solution mix. A negative number in the $C_j - Z_j$ row would tell us that profits would *decrease* if the corresponding variable were added to the solution mix. An optimal solution is reached in the simplex method when the $C_j - Z_j$ row contains no positive numbers. Such is not the case in our initial tableau.

We reach an optimal solution when the $C_j - Z_j$ row has no positive numbers in it.

9.3   SIMPLEX SOLUTION PROCEDURES

After an initial tableau has been completed, we proceed through a series of five steps to compute all the numbers needed in the next tableau. The calculations are not difficult, but they are complex enough that even the smallest arithmetic error can produce a wrong answer.

Here are the five simplex steps.

We first list the five steps and then carefully explain and apply them in completing the second and third tableaus for the Flair Furniture Company data.

Five Steps of the Simplex Method

1. Variable entering the solution has the largest positive $C_j - Z_j$.

1. Determine which variable to enter into the solution mix next. One way of doing this is by identifying the column, and hence the variable, with the largest positive number in the $C_j - Z_j$ row of the preceding tableau. This means that we will now be producing some of the product contributing the greatest additional profit per unit. The column identified in this step is called the *pivot column*.

2. Variable leaving the solution is determined by a ratio we must compute.

2. Determine which variable to replace. Because we have just chosen a new variable to enter the solution mix, we must decide which basic variable currently in the solution will have to leave to make room for it. Step 2 is accomplished by dividing each amount in the *quantity* column by the corresponding number in the column selected in step 1. The row with the *smallest nonnegative number* calculated in this fashion will be replaced in the next tableau. (This smallest number, by the way, gives the maximum number of units of the variable that may be placed in the solution.) This row is often referred to as the *pivot row*. The number at the intersection of the pivot row and pivot column is referred to as the *pivot number*.

3. New pivot-row calculations are done next.

3. Compute new values for the pivot row. To do this, we simply divide every number in the row by the pivot number.

4. Other new rows are calculated with formula (9-1).

4. Compute the new values for each remaining row. (In our Flair Furniture problem there are only two rows in the LP tableau, but most larger problems have many more rows.) All remaining row(s) are calculated as follows:

(new row numbers) = (numbers in old row)

$$- \left[\begin{pmatrix} \text{number above} \\ \text{or below} \\ \text{pivot number} \end{pmatrix} \times \begin{pmatrix} \text{corresponding number in} \\ \text{the new row, that is, the} \\ \text{row replaced in step 3} \end{pmatrix} \right] \quad \text{(9-1)}$$

5. Finally Z_j and $C_j - Z_j$ rows are recomputed.

5. Compute the Z_j and $C_j - Z_j$ rows, as demonstrated in the initial tableau. If all numbers in the $C_j - Z_j$ row are 0 or negative, an optimal solution has been reached. If this is not the case, return to step 1.

9.4   THE SECOND SIMPLEX TABLEAU

Here we apply the five steps to Flair Furniture.

Now that we have listed the five steps needed to move from an initial solution to an improved solution, we apply them to the Flair Furniture problem. Our goal is to add a new variable to the solution mix, or basis, to raise the profit from its current tableau value of $0.

First, X_1 (tables) enters the solution mix because its $C_j - Z_j$ value of $7 is largest.

Step 1. To decide which of the variables will enter the solution next (it must be either X_1 or X_2, since they are the only two nonbasic variables at this point), we select the one with the largest positive $C_j - Z_j$ value. Variable X_1, tables, has a $C_j - Z_j$ value of $7, implying that each unit of X_1 added into the solution mix will contribute $7 to the overall profit. Variable

TABLE 9.2 Pivot Column Identified in the Initial Simplex Tableau

C_j	SOLUTION MIX	X_1	X_2	S_1	S_2	QUANTITY (RHS)
		$7	$5	$0	$0	
$0	S_1	2	1	1	0	100
$0	S_2	4	3	0	1	240
	Z_j	$0	$0	$0	$0	$0
	$C_j - Z_j$	$7	$5	$0	$0	(total profit)

(Pivot column)

X_2, chairs, has a $C_j - Z_j$ value of only $5. The other two variables, S_1 and S_2, have 0 values and can add nothing more to profit. Hence, we select X_1 as the variable to enter the solution mix and identify its column (with an arrow) as the pivot column. This is shown in Table 9.2.

Step 2. Since X_1 is about to enter the solution mix, we must decide which variable is to be replaced. There can only be as many basic variables as there are constraints in any LP problem, so either S_1 or S_2 will have to leave to make room for the introduction of X_1, tables, into the basis. To identify the pivot row, each number in the quantity column is divided by the corresponding number in the X_1 column.

For the S_1 row:

$$\frac{100 \text{ (hours of painting time available)}}{2 \text{ (hours required per table)}} = 50 \text{ tables}$$

For the S_2 row:

$$\frac{240 \text{ (hours of carpentry time available)}}{4 \text{ (hours required per table)}} = 60 \text{ tables}$$

The smaller of these two ratios, 50, indicates the maximum number of units of X_1 that can be produced without violating either of the original constraints. It also points out that the pivot row will be the first row. This means that S_1 will be the variable to be replaced at this iteration of the simplex method. The pivot row and the pivot number (the number at the intersection of the pivot row and pivot column) are identified in Table 9.3.

S_1 leaves the solution mix because the smaller of the two ratios indicates that the next pivot row will be the first row.

Step 3. Now that we have decided which variable is to enter the solution mix (X_1) and which is to leave (S_1), we begin to develop the second, improved simplex tableau. Step 3 involves computing a replacement for the pivot row. This is done by dividing every number in the pivot row by the pivot number:

$$\frac{2}{2} = 1 \qquad \frac{1}{2} = \frac{1}{2} \qquad \frac{1}{2} = \frac{1}{2} \qquad \frac{0}{2} = 0 \qquad \frac{100}{2} = 50$$

The new pivot row is computed by dividing every number in the pivot row by the pivot number.

The new version of the entire pivot row appears in the accompanying table. Note that X_1 is now in the solution mix and that 50 units of X_1 are being produced. The C_j value is listed as a $7 contribution per unit of X_1 in the solution. This will definitely provide Flair Furniture with a more profitable solution than the $0 generated in the initial tableau.

C_j	SOLUTION MIX	X_1	X_2	S_1	S_2	QUANTITY
$7	X_1	1	½	½	0	50

TABLE 9.3 Pivot Row and Pivot Number Identified in the Initial Simplex Tableau

C_j	→ $7	$5	$0	$0		
SOLUTION MIX	X_1	X_2	S_1	S_2	QUANTITY	
$0 S_1	② ←	1	1	0	100 ← Pivot row	
$0 S_2	4	3	0	1	240	
		Pivot number				
Z_j	$0	$0	$0	$0	$0	
$C_j - Z_j$	→$7	$5	$0	$0		
	Pivot column					

We can now recompute the S_2 row.

Step 4. This step is intended to help us compute new values for the other row in the body of the tableau, that is, the S_2 row. It is slightly more complex than replacing the pivot row and uses the formula (Equation 9.1) shown earlier. The expression on the right side of the following equation is used to calculate the left side.

$\begin{pmatrix} \text{NUMBER IN} \\ \text{NEW } S_2 \text{ ROW} \end{pmatrix}$	=	$\begin{pmatrix} \text{NUMBER IN} \\ \text{OLD } S_2 \text{ ROW} \end{pmatrix}$	−	$\begin{pmatrix} \text{NUMBER BELOW} \\ \text{PIVOT NUMBER} \end{pmatrix}$	×	$\begin{pmatrix} \text{CORRESPONDING NUMBER} \\ \text{IN THE NEW } X_1 \text{ ROW} \end{pmatrix}$
0	=	4	−	(4)	×	(1)
1	=	3	−	(4)	×	($\frac{1}{2}$)
−2	=	0	−	(4)	×	($\frac{1}{2}$)
1	=	1	−	(4)	×	(0)
40	=	240	−	(4)	×	(50)

This new S_2 row will appear in the second tableau in the following format:

C_j	SOLUTION MIX	X_1	X_2	S_1	S_2	QUANTITY
$7	X_1	1	$\frac{1}{2}$	$\frac{1}{2}$	0	50
$0	S_2	0	1	−2	1	40

We note that the X_1 column contains $\begin{pmatrix} 1 \\ 0 \end{pmatrix}$ and the S_2 column contains $\begin{pmatrix} 0 \\ 1 \end{pmatrix}$. These 0's and 1's indicate that X_1 and S_2 are in the basis (the solution mix).

Now that X_1 and S_2 are in the solution mix, take a look at the values of the coefficients in their respective columns. The X_1 column contains $\begin{pmatrix} 1 \\ 0 \end{pmatrix}$, a condition necessary for that variable to be in the solution. Similarly, the S_2 column has $\begin{pmatrix} 0 \\ 1 \end{pmatrix}$, that is, it contains a 1 and a 0.

Basically, the algebraic manipulations we just went through in steps 3 and 4 were simply directed at producing 0's and 1's in the appropriate positions. In step 3 we divided every number in the pivot row by the pivot number; this guaranteed that there would be a 1 in the X_1 column's top row. To derive the new second row, we multiplied the first row (each row is really an equation) by a constant (the number 4 here) and subtracted it from the second equation. The result was the new S_2 row with a 0 in the X_1 column.

Step 5. The final step of the second iteration is to introduce the effect of the objective function. This involves computing the Z_j and $C_j - Z_j$ rows. Recall that the Z_j entry for the quantity column gives us the gross profit for the current solution. The other Z_j values represent the gross profit given up by adding one unit of each variable into this new solution. The Z_j values are calculated as follows:

We find the new profit in the Z row.

$$Z_j(\text{for } X_1 \text{ column}) = (\$7)(1) + (\$0)(0) = \$7$$

$$Z_j(\text{for } X_2 \text{ column}) = (\$7)(\tfrac{1}{2}) + (\$0)(1) = \$\tfrac{7}{2}$$

$$Z_j(\text{for } S_1 \text{ column}) = (\$7)(\tfrac{1}{2}) + (\$0)(-2) = \$\tfrac{7}{2}$$

$$Z_j(\text{for } S_2 \text{ column}) = (\$7)(0) + (\$0)(1) = \$0$$

$$Z_j(\text{for total profit}) = (\$7)(50) + (\$0)(40) = \$350$$

Note that the current profit is $350.

The $C_j - Z_j$ numbers represent the net profit that will result, given our present production mix, if we add one unit of each variable into the solution.

	COLUMN			
	X_1	X_2	S_1	S_2
C_j for column	$7	$5	$0	$0
Z_j for column	$7	$\tfrac{7}{2}$	$\tfrac{7}{2}$	$0
$C_j - Z_j$ for column	$0	$\tfrac{3}{2}$	$-\$\tfrac{7}{2}$	$0

The $C_j - Z_j$ row indicates the net profit, given the current solution, of one more unit of each variable. For example, X_2 has a profit of $1.50 per unit.

The Z_j and $C_j - Z_j$ rows are inserted into the complete second tableau as shown in Table 9.4.

Interpreting the Second Tableau

Table 9.4 summarizes all of the information for the Flair Furniture Company's production mix decision as of the second iteration of the simplex method. Let's briefly look over a few important items.

Current Solution At this point, the solution point of 50 tables and 0 chairs ($X_1 = 50$, $X_2 = 0$) generates a profit of $350. X_1 is a basic variable; X_2 is a nonbasic variable. Using a graphical LP approach, this corresponds to corner point D, as shown in Figure 9.2.

We can look at the current solution as a corner point in the graphical method.

TABLE 9.4 **Completed Second Simplex Tableau for Flair Furniture**

C_j →		$7	$5	$0	$0	
	SOLUTION MIX	X_1	X_2	S_1	S_2	QUANTITY
$7	X_1	1	$\tfrac{1}{2}$	$\tfrac{1}{2}$	0	50
$0	S_2	0	1	-2	1	40
	Z_j	$7	$\tfrac{7}{2}$	$\tfrac{7}{2}$	$0	$350
	$C_j - Z_j$	$0	$\tfrac{3}{2}$	$-\$\tfrac{7}{2}$	$0	

FIGURE 9.2

Flair Furniture Company's
Feasible Region and
Corner Points

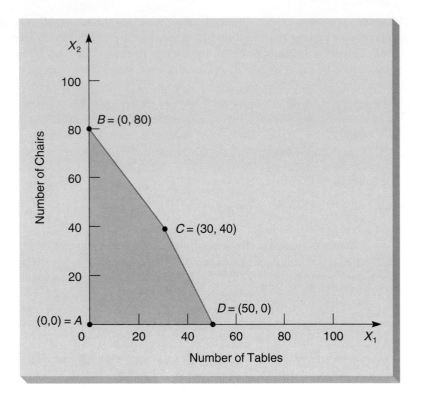

Resource Information We also see in Table 9.4 that slack variable S_2, representing the amount of unused time in the carpentry department, is in the basis. It has a value of 40, implying that 40 hours of carpentry time remain available. Slack variable S_1 is nonbasic and has a value of 0 hours. There is no slack time in the painting department.

Substitution Rates We mentioned earlier that the substitution rates are the coefficients in the heart of the tableau. Look at the X_2 column. If 1 unit of X_2 (1 chair) is added to the current solution, $\frac{1}{2}$ units of X_1 and 1 unit of S_2 must be given up. This is because the solution $X_1 = 50$ tables uses up all 100 hours of time in the painting department. (The original constraint, you may recall, was $2X_1 + 1X_2 + S_1 = 100$.) To capture the 1 painting hour needed to make 1 chair, $\frac{1}{2}$ of a table *less* must be produced. This frees up 1 hour to be used in making 1 chair.

Here is an explanation of the meaning of substitution rates.

But why must 1 unit of S_2 (i.e., 1 hour of carpentry time) be given up to produce 1 chair? The original constraint was $4X_1 + 3X_2 + S_2 = 240$ hours of carpentry time. Doesn't this indicate that 3 hours of carpentry time are required to produce 1 unit of X_2? The answer is that we are looking at *marginal* rates of substitution. Adding 1 chair replaced $\frac{1}{2}$ table. Because $\frac{1}{2}$ table required ($\frac{1}{2} \times 4$ hours per table) = 2 hours of carpentry time, 2 units of S_2 are freed. Thus only 1 *more* unit of S_2 is needed to produce 1 chair.

Just to be sure you have this concept down pat, let's look at one more column, S_1, as well. The coefficients are $\begin{pmatrix} \frac{1}{2} \\ -2 \end{pmatrix}$. These substitution rate values mean that if 1 hour of slack painting time is added to the current solution, $\frac{1}{2}$ of a table (X_1) *less* will be produced. However, note that if 1 unit of S_1 is added into the solution, 2 hours of carpentry time (S_2) will no longer be used. These will be *added* to the current 40 slack hours of carpentry time. Hence, a *negative* substitution rate means that if 1 unit of a column variable is added to the solution, the value of the corresponding solution (or row) variable will be increased. A *positive* substitution rate tells us that if 1 unit of the column variable is added to the solution, the row variable will decrease by the rate.

Can you interpret the rates in the X_1 and S_2 columns now?

Net Profit Row The $C_j - Z_j$ row is important to us for two reasons. First, it indicates whether the current solution is optimal. When there are no positive numbers in the bottom row, an optimum solution to an LP maximization problem has been reached. In the case of Table 9.4, we see that $C_j - Z_j$ values for X_1, S_1, and S_2 are 0 or negative. The value for X_2 ($\frac{3}{2}$) means that the net profit can be increased by $1.50 ($= \frac{3}{2}$) for each chair added into the current solution.

Because the $C_j - Z_j$ value for X_1 is 0, for every unit of X_1 added the total profit will remain unchanged, because we are already producing as many tables as possible. A negative number, such as the $-\frac{7}{2}$ in the S_1 column, implies that total profit will *decrease* by $3.50 if 1 unit of S_1 is added to the solution. In other words, making one slack hour available in the painting department ($S_1 = 0$ currently) means that we would have to produce one-half table less. Since each table results in a $7 contribution, we would be losing $\frac{1}{2} \times \$7 = \$\frac{7}{2}$, for a net loss of $3.50.

Later in this chapter we discuss in detail the subject of *shadow prices*. These relate to $C_j - Z_j$ values in the slack variable columns. Shadow prices are simply another way of interpreting negative $C_j - Z_j$ values; they may be viewed as the potential increase in profit if one more hour of the scarce resource (such as painting or carpentry time) could be made *available*.

The $C_j - Z_j$ row tells us (1) whether the current solution is optimal and (2) if it is not, which variable should enter the solution mix next.

We mentioned previously that there are two reasons to consider the $C_j - Z_j$ row carefully. The second reason, of course, is that we use the row to determine which variable will enter the solution next. Since an optimal solution has not been reached yet, let's proceed to the third simplex tableau.

9.5 DEVELOPING THE THIRD TABLEAU

Since not all numbers in the $C_j - Z_j$ row of the latest tableau are 0 or negative, the previous solution is not optimal, and we must repeat the five simplex steps.

Step 1. Variable X_2 will enter the solution next by virtue of the fact that its $C_j - Z_j$ value of $\frac{3}{2}$ is the largest (and only) positive number in the row. This means that for every unit of X_2 (chairs) we start to produce, the objective function will increase in value by $\$\frac{3}{2}$, or $1.50. The X_2 column is the new pivot column.

X_2 (chairs) will be the next new variable because it has the only positive value in the $C_j - Z_j$ row.

Step 2. The next step involves identifying the pivot row. The question is, which variable currently in the solution (X_1 or S_2) will have to leave to make room for X_2 to enter? Again, each number in the quantity column is divided by its corresponding number in the X_2 column.

For the X_1 row: $\dfrac{50}{\frac{1}{2}} = 100$ chairs

For the S_2 row: $\dfrac{40}{1} = 40$ chairs

The S_2 row has the smallest ratio, meaning that variable S_2 will leave the basis and be replaced by X_2. The new pivot row, pivot column, and pivot number are all shown in Table 9.5.

We replace the variable S_2 because it is in the pivot row.

TABLE 9.5 Pivot Row, Pivot Column, and Pivot Number Identified in the Second Simplex Tableau

C_j		$7	$5	$0	$0	
	SOLUTION MIX	X_1	X_2	S_1	S_2	QUANTITY
$7	X_1	1	½	½	0	50
$0	S_2	0	①	−2	1	40 ← Pivot row
			↖ Pivot number			
	Z_j	$7	$7/2	$7/2	$0	$350
	$C_j − Z_j$	$0	$3/2	−$7/2	$0	(total profit)
		Pivot column ⤴				

The pivot row for the third tableau is replaced here.

Step 3. The pivot row is replaced by dividing every number in it by the (circled) pivot number. Since every number is divided by 1, there is no change.

$$\frac{0}{1} = 0 \qquad \frac{1}{1} = 1 \qquad \frac{-2}{1} = -2 \qquad \frac{1}{1} = 1 \qquad \frac{40}{1} = 40$$

The entire new X_2 row looks like this:

C_j	SOLUTION MIX	X_1	X_2	S_1	S_2	QUANTITY
$5	X_2	0	1	−2	1	40

It will be placed in the new simplex tableau in the same row position that S_2 was in before (see Table 9.5).

Step 4. The new values for the X_1 row may now be computed

$$\begin{pmatrix} \text{number} \\ \text{in new} \\ X_1 \text{ row} \end{pmatrix} = \begin{pmatrix} \text{number} \\ \text{in old} \\ X_1 \text{ row} \end{pmatrix} - \left[\begin{pmatrix} \text{number} \\ \text{above pivot} \\ \text{number} \end{pmatrix} \times \begin{pmatrix} \text{corresponding} \\ \text{number in new} \\ X_2 \text{ row} \end{pmatrix} \right]$$

The new X_1 row is computed here.

1	=	1	−	(½)	×	(0)
0	=	½	−	(½)	×	(1)
3/2	=	½	−	(½)	×	(−2)
−½	=	0	−	(½)	×	(1)
30	=	50	−	(½)	×	(40)

Hence, the new X_1 row will appear in the third tableau in the following position:

C_j	SOLUTION MIX	X_1	X_2	S_1	S_2	QUANTITY
$7	X_1	1	0	3/2	−½	30
$5	X_2	0	1	−2	1	40

Step 5. Finally, the Z_j and $C_j - Z_j$ rows are calculated for the third tableau:

The final step is again computing the Z_j and $C_j - Z_j$ values.

Z_j(for X_1 column) = ($\$7$)(1) + ($\$5$)(0)   = $\$7$

Z_j(for X_2 column) = ($\$7$)(0) + ($\$5$)(1)   = $\$5$

Z_j(for S_1 column) = ($\$7$)($\frac{3}{2}$) + ($\$5$)($-2$) = $\$\frac{1}{2}$

Z_j(for S_2 column) = ($\$7$)($-\frac{1}{2}$) + ($\$5$)(1) = $\$\frac{3}{2}$

Z_j(for total profit) = ($\$7$)(30) + ($\$5$)(40) = $\$410$

The net profit per unit row appears as follows:

	COLUMN			
	X_1	X_2	S_1	S_2
C_j for column	$\$7$	$\$5$	$\$0$	$\$0$
Z_j for column	$\underline{\$7}$	$\underline{\$5}$	$\underline{\$\frac{1}{2}}$	$\underline{\$\frac{3}{2}}$
$C_j - Z_j$ for column	$\$0$	$\$0$	$-\$\frac{1}{2}$	$-\$\frac{3}{2}$

All results for the third iteration of the simplex method are summarized in Table 9.6. Note that since every number in the tableau's $C_j - Z_j$ row is 0 or negative, an optimal solution has been reached.

An optimal solution is reached because all $C_j - Z_j$ values are zero or negative.

That solution is

$X_1 = 30$ tables

$X_2 = 40$ chairs

$S_1 = 0$ slack hours in the painting department

$S_2 = 0$ slack hours in the carpentry department

profit = $\$410$ for the optimal solution

The final solution is to make 30 tables and 40 chairs at a profit of $\$410$. This is the same as the graphical solution presented earlier.

X_1 and X_2 are the final basic variables, while S_1 and S_2 are nonbasic (and thus automatically equal to 0). This solution corresponds to corner point C in Figure 9.2.

It's always possible to make an arithmetic error when you are going through the numerous simplex steps and iterations, so it is a good idea to verify your final solution. This

TABLE 9.6   **Final Simplex Tableau for the Flair Furniture Problem**

C_j		$\$7$	$\$5$	$\$0$	$\$0$	
	SOLUTION MIX	X_1	X_2	S_1	S_2	QUANTITY
$\$7$	X_1	1	0	$\frac{3}{2}$	$-\frac{1}{2}$	30
$\$5$	X_2	0	1	-2	1	40
	Z_j	$\$7$	$\$5$	$\$\frac{1}{2}$	$\$\frac{3}{2}$	$\$410$
	$C_j - Z_j$	$\$0$	$\$0$	$-\$\frac{1}{2}$	$-\$\frac{3}{2}$	

Verifying that the solution does not violate any of the original constraints is a good way to check that no mathematical errors were made.

can be done in part by looking at the original Flair Furniture Company constraints and objective function.

First constraint: $2X_1 + 1X_2 \leq 100$ painting department hours

$$2(30) + 1(40) \leq 100$$

$$100 \leq 100 \checkmark$$

Second constraint: $4X_1 + 3X_2 \leq 240$ carpentry department hours

$$4(30) + 3(40) \leq 240$$

$$240 \leq 240 \checkmark$$

Objective function: profit = $\$7X_1 + \$5X_2$

$$= \$7(30) + \$5(40)$$

$$= \$410$$

9.6   REVIEW OF PROCEDURES FOR SOLVING LP MAXIMIZATION PROBLEMS

Before moving on to other issues concerning the simplex method, we review briefly what we've learned so far for LP maximization problems.

   I. Formulate the LP problem's objective function and constraints.

   II. Add slack variables to each less-than-or-equal-to constraint and to the problem's objective function.

   III. Develop an initial simplex tableau with slack variables in the basis and their variables (the X_is) set equal to 0. Compute the Z_j and $C_j - Z_j$ values for this tableau.

   IV. Follow these five steps until an optimal solution has been reached:

Here is a review of the five simplex steps.

   1. Choose the variable with the greatest positive $C_j - Z_j$ to enter the solution. This is the pivot column.

   2. Determine the row to be replaced by selecting the one with the smallest (nonnegative) quantity-to-pivot column ratio. This is the pivot row.

   3. Calculate the new values for the pivot row.

   4. Calculate the new values for the other row(s).

   5. Calculate the Z_j and $C_j - Z_j$ values for this tableau. If there are any $C_j - Z_j$ numbers greater than 0, return to step 1. If there are no $C_j - Z_j$ numbers that are greater than 0, an optimal solution has been reached.

9.7   SURPLUS AND ARTIFICIAL VARIABLES

To handle $\geq$ and $=$ constraints, the simplex method makes a conversion like it made to $\leq$ constraints.

Up to this point in the chapter, all of the LP constraints you have seen were of the less-than-or-equal-to ($\leq$) variety. Just as common in real-life problems—especially in LP minimization problems—are greater-than-or-equal-to ($\geq$) constraints and equalities. To use the simplex method, each of these must be converted to a special form also. If they are not, the simplex technique is unable to set up an initial feasible solution in the first tableau.

Before moving on to the next section of this chapter, which deals with solving LP minimization problems with the simplex method, we take a look at how to convert a few typical constraints.

Constraint 1: $\qquad 5X_1 + 10X_2 + 8X_3 \geq 210$

Constraint 2: $\qquad 25X_1 + 30X_2 \qquad = 900$

Surplus Variables

Greater-than-or-equal-to ($\geq$) constraints, such as constraint 1 as just described, require a different approach than do the less-than-or-equal-to ($\leq$) constraints we saw in the Flair Furniture problem. They involve the subtraction of a *surplus variable* rather than the addition of a slack variable. The surplus variable tells us how much the solution exceeds the constraint resource. Because of its analogy to a slack variable, surplus is sometimes simply called *negative slack*. To convert the first constraint, we begin by subtracting a surplus variable, S_1, to create an equality.

We subtract a surplus variable to form an equality when dealing with a ≥ constraint.

Constraint 1 rewritten: $5X_1 + 10X_2 + 8X_3 - S_1 = 210$

If, for example, a solution to an LP problem involving this constraint is $X_1 = 20$, $X_2 = 8$, $X_3 = 5$, the amount of surplus, or unused resource, could be computed as follows:

$$5X_1 + 10X_2 + 8X_3 - S_1 = 210$$

$$5(20) + 10(8) + 8(5) - S_1 = 210$$

$$100 + 80 + 40 - S_1 = 210$$

$$-S_1 = 210 - 220$$

$$S_1 = 10 \text{ surplus units of first resource}$$

There is one more step, however, in preparing a $\geq$ constraint for the simplex method.

Artificial Variables

There is one small problem in trying to use the first constraint (as it has just been rewritten) in setting up an initial simplex solution. Since all "real" variables such as X_1, X_2, and X_3 are set to 0 in the initial tableau, S_1 takes on a negative value.

$$5(0) + 10(0) + 8(0) - S_1 = 210$$

$$0 - S_1 = 210$$

$$S_1 = -210$$

All variables in LP problems, be they real, slack, or surplus, *must* be nonnegative at all times. If $S_1 = -210$, this important condition is violated.

To resolve the situation, we introduce one last kind of variable, called an *artificial variable*. We simply add the artificial variable, A_1, to the constraint as follows:

Artificial variables are needed in ≥ and = constraints.

Constraint 1 completed: $5X_1 + 10X_2 + 8X_3 - S_1 + A_1 = 210$

Now, not only the X_1, X_2, and X_3 variables may be set to 0 in the initial simplex solution, but the S_1 surplus variable as well. This leaves us with $A_1 = 210$.

Let's turn our attention to constraint 2 for a moment. This constraint is already an equality, so why worry about it? To be included in the initial simplex solution, it turns out, even an equality must have an artificial variable added to it.

Constraint 2 rewritten: $25X_1 + 30X_2 + A_2 = 900$

The reason for inserting an artificial variable into an equality constraint deals with the usual problem of finding an initial LP solution. In a simple constraint such as number 2, it's easy to guess that $X_1 = 0$, $X_2 = 30$ would yield an initial feasible solution. But what if our problem had 10 equality constraints, each containing seven variables? It would be *extremely* difficult to sit down and "eyeball" a set of initial solutions. By adding artificial variables, such as A_2, we can provide an automatic initial solution. In this case, when X_1 and X_2 are set equal to 0, $A_2 = 900$.

Artificial variables have no physical meaning and drop out of the solution mix before the final tableau.

Artificial variables have no meaning in a physical sense and are nothing more than computational tools for generating initial LP solutions. Before the final simplex solution has been reached, all artificial variables must be gone from the solution mix. This matter is handled through the problem's objective function.

Surplus and Artificial Variables in the Objective Function

Whenever an artificial or surplus variable is added to one of the constraints, it must also be included in the other equations and in the problem's objective function, just as was done for slack variables. Since artificial variables must be forced out of the solution, we can assign a very high C_j cost to each. In minimization problems, variables with *low* costs are the most desirable ones and the first to enter the solution. Variables with *high* costs leave the solution quickly, or never enter it at all. Rather than set an actual dollar figure of $10,000 or $1 million for each artificial variable, however, we simply use the letter $M to represent a very large number.[4] Surplus variables, like slack variables, carry a zero cost.

To make sure that an artificial variable is forced out before the final solution is reached, it is assigned a very high cost.

If a problem we were about to solve had an objective function that read

minimize cost = $5X_1 + $9X_2 + $7X_3$

and constraints such as the two mentioned previously, the completed objective function and constraints would appear as follows:

minimize cost = $5X_1 + $9X_2 + $7X_3 + $0S_1 + $MA_1 + MA_2

subject to $5X_1 + 10X_2 + 8X_3 - 1S_1 + 1A_1 + 0A_2 = 210$

$25X_1 + 30X_2 + 0X_3 + 0S_1 + 0A_1 + 1A_2 = 900$

9.8   **SOLVING MINIMIZATION PROBLEMS**

Now that we have learned how to deal with objective functions and constraints associated with minimization problems, let's see how to use the simplex method to solve a typical problem.

The Muddy River Chemical Company Example   The Muddy River Chemical Corporation must produce exactly 1,000 pounds of a special mixture of phosphate and potassium for a customer. Phosphate costs $5 per pound and potassium costs $6 per pound. No more

---

[4] A technical point: If an artificial variable is ever used in a *maximization* problem (an occasional event), it is assigned an objective function value of $-$M$ to force it from the basis.

A Q IN ACTION   **Optimizing Wood Procurement in Cabinet Manufacturing**

Alabama's Wellborn Cabinet Company is a major producer of cabinet components called "blanks." To make blanks, Wellborn purchases two grades of hardwood logs (no. 1 and no. 2) and two grades of common lumber (no. 1 and no. 2). Common grades of lumber are suitable for construction and general utility purposes. Better quality is indicated by a lower grade number.

Wellborn's management is concerned primarily with the high cost of wood raw materials, which makes up about 45% of the total material cost of producing cabinets. Managers had no way of knowing what the least-cost combination of raw materials should be for processing blanks into cabinets until an LP model of the blank production system was developed. Model inputs included measurements of logs, a tally of the

grades and sizes, the maximum weekly throughput, the delivered cost of logs and lumber, the costs of conversion and drying, and the weekly requirements of blanks.

Results from computer runs with the LP model indicate that Wellborn can minimize the total cost of producing blanks by purchasing only number 2 grade logs and number 2 common lumber. By volume, about 88% of the dry lumber input requirements of the mill should come from number 2 grade logs and the rest should come from purchased number 2 common lumber. By pursuing such a policy, the company can expect to save about $412,000 in raw material costs annually.

Source: Honorio F. Carino and Clinton H. LeNoir, Jr. *Interfaces* 18, 2 (March–April 1988): 10–19.

---

than 300 pounds of phosphate can be used, and at least 150 pounds of potassium must be used. The problem is to determine the least-cost blend of the two ingredients.

This problem may be restated mathematically as

$$\text{minimize cost} = \$5X_1 + \$6X_2$$

subject to $X_1 + X_2 = 1{,}000 \text{ lb}$

$X_1 \le 300 \text{ lb}$

$X_2 \ge 150 \text{ lb}$

$X_1, X_2 \ge 0$

Here is the mathematical formulation of the minimization problem for Muddy River Chemical Corp.

where

X_1 = number of pounds of phosphate

X_2 = number of pounds of potassium

Note that there are three constraints, not counting the nonnegativity constraints; the first is an equality, the second a less-than-or-equal-to, and the third a greater-than-or-equal-to constraint.

Graphical Analysis

To have a better understanding of the problem, a brief graphical analysis may prove useful. There are only two decision variables, X_1 and X_2, so we are able to plot the constraints and feasible region. Because the first constraint, $X_1 + X_2 = 1{,}000$, is an equality, the solution must lie somewhere on the line *ABC* (see Figure 9.3). It must also lie between points *A* and *B* because of the constraint $X_1 \le 300$. The third constraint, $X_2 \ge 150$, is actually redundant (or nonbinding) since X_2 will automatically be greater than 150 pounds if the first two constraints are observed. Hence, the feasible region consists of all points on the line segment *AB*. As you recall from Chapter 7, however, an optimal solution will always lie at a corner point of the feasible region (even if the region is only a straight line). The solution must therefore be either at point *A* or point *B*. A quick analysis reveals that the least-cost solution lies at corner *B*, namely $X_1 = 300$ pounds of phosphate, $X_2 = 700$ pounds of potassium. The total cost is $5,700.

Looking at a graphical solution first will help us understand the steps in the simplex method.

FIGURE 9.3

Muddy River Chemical
Corporation's Feasible
Region Graph

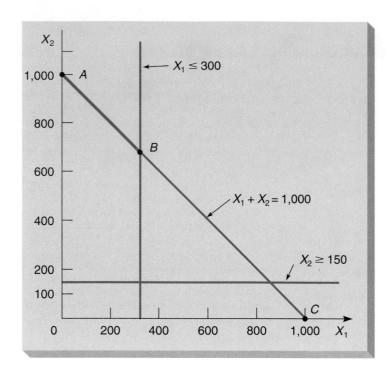

You don't need the simplex method to solve the Muddy River Chemical problem, of course. But we can guarantee you that few problems will be this simple. In general, you can expect to see several variables and many constraints. The purpose of this section is to illustrate the straightforward application of the simplex method to minimization problems.

Converting the Constraints and Objective Function

First, insert slack, surplus, and artificial variables. This makes it easier to set up the initial simplex tableau in Table 9.7.

The first step is to apply what we learned in the preceding section to convert the constraints and objective function into the proper form for the simplex method. The equality constraint, $X_1 + X_2 = 1{,}000$, just involves adding an artificial variable, A_1.

$$X_1 + X_2 + A_1 = 1{,}000$$

The second constraint, $X_1 \leq 300$, requires the insertion of a slack variable—let's call it S_1.

$$X_1 + S_1 = 300$$

The last constraint is $X_2 \geq 150$, which is converted to an equality by subtracting a surplus variable, S_2, and adding an artificial variable, A_2.

$$X_2 - S_2 + A_2 = 150$$

Finally, the objective function, cost $= \$5X_1 + \$6X_2$, is rewritten as

minimize cost $= \$5X_1 + \$6X_2 + \$0S_1 + \$0S_2 + \$MA_1 + \$MA_2$

The complete set of constraints can now be expressed as follows:

$$1X_1 + 1X_2 + 0S_1 + 0S_2 + 1A_1 + 0A_2 = 1{,}000$$

$$1X_1 + 0X_2 + 1S_1 + 0S_2 + 0A_1 + 0A_2 = 300$$

$$0X_1 + 1X_2 + 0S_1 - 1S_2 + 0A_1 + 1A_2 = 150$$

$$X_1, X_2, S_1, S_2, A_1, A_2 \geq 0$$

Rules of the Simplex Method for Minimization Problems

Minimization problems are quite similar to the maximization problems tackled earlier in this chapter. The significant difference involves the $C_j - Z_j$ row. Since our objective is now to minimize cost, the new variable to enter the solution in each tableau (the pivot column) will be the one with the *largest negative* number in the $C_j - Z_j$ row. Thus, we choose the variable that decreases costs the most. In minimization problems, an optimal solution is reached when all the numbers in the $C_j - Z_j$ row are 0 or *positive*—just the opposite from the maximization case.[5] All other simplex steps, as seen in the following, remain the same.

The minimization simplex rules are slightly different. Now, the new variable to enter the solution mix will be in the column with the largest negative $C_j - Z_j$ value.

Steps for Simplex Minimization Problems
1. Choose the variable with the largest negative $C_j - Z_j$ to enter the solution. This is the pivot column.
2. Determine the row to be replaced by selecting the one with the smallest (nonnegative) quantity-to-pivot column ratio. This is the pivot row.
3. Calculate new values for the pivot row.
4. Calculate new values for the other rows.
5. Calculate the Z_j and $C_j - Z_j$ values for this tableau. If there are any $C_j - Z_j$ numbers less than 0, return to step 1.

First Simplex Tableau for the Muddy River Chemical Corporation Problem

Now we solve Muddy River Chemical Corporation's LP formulation using the simplex method. The initial tableau is set up just as in the earlier maximization example. Its first three rows are shown in the accompanying table. We note the presence of the M costs associated with artificial variables A_1 and A_2, but we treat them as if they were any large number. As noted earlier, they have the effect of forcing the artificial variables out of the solution quickly because of their large costs.

C_j	SOLUTION MIX	X_1	X_2	S_1	S_2	A_1	A_2	QUANTITY
$M	A_1	1	1	0	0	1	0	1,000
$0	S_1	1	0	1	0	0	0	300
$M	A_2	0	1	0	−1	0	1	150

[5] We should note that there is a second way to solve minimization problems with the simplex method: It involves a simple mathematical trick. It happens that minimizing the cost objective is the same as *maximizing* the negative of the cost objective function. This means that instead of writing the Muddy River objective function as

minimize cost $= 5X_1 + 6X_2$

we can instead write

maximize $(-\text{cost}) = -5X_1 - 6X_2$

The solution that maximizes $(-\text{cost})$ also minimizes cost. It also means that the same simplex procedure shown earlier for maximization problems can be used if this trick is employed. The only change is that the objective function must be multiplied by (-1).

The numbers in the Z_j row are computed by multiplying the C_j column on the far left of the tableau times the corresponding numbers in each other column. They are then entered into Table 9.7.

$$Z_j(\text{for } X_1 \text{ column}) = \$M(1) \quad + \$0(1) \quad + \$M(0) \quad = \$M$$

$$Z_j(\text{for } X_2 \text{ column}) = \$M(1) \quad + \$0(0) \quad + \$M(1) \quad = \$2M$$

$$Z_j(\text{for } S_1 \text{ column}) = \$M(0) \quad + \$0(1) \quad + \$M(0) \quad = \$0$$

$$Z_j(\text{for } S_2 \text{ column}) = \$M(0) \quad + \$0(0) \quad + \$M(-1) = \$-M$$

$$Z_j(\text{for } A_1 \text{ column}) = \$M(1) \quad + \$0(0) \quad + \$M(0) \quad = \$M$$

$$Z_j(\text{for } A_2 \text{ column}) = \$M(0) \quad + \$0(0) \quad + \$M(1) \quad = \$M$$

$$Z_j(\text{for total cost}) \quad = \$M(1{,}000) + \$0(300) + \$M(150) = \$1{,}150M$$

The $C_j - Z_j$ entries are determined as follows:

	COLUMN					
	X_1	X_2	S_1	S_2	A_1	A_2
C_j for column	$\$5$	$\$6$	$\$0$	$\$0$	$\$M$	$\$M$
Z_j for column	$\underline{\$M}$	$\underline{\$2M}$	$\underline{\$0}$	$\underline{-\$M}$	$\underline{\$M}$	$\underline{\$M}$
$C_j - Z_j$ for column	$-\$M + \$5$	$-\$2M + \$6$	$\$0$	$\$M$	$\$0$	$\$0$

Here is the initial simplex solution.

This initial solution was obtained by letting each of the variables X_1, X_2, and S_2 assume a value of 0. The current basic variables are $A_1 = 1{,}000$, $S_1 = 300$, and $A_2 = 150$. This complete solution could be expressed in vector, or column, form as

$$\begin{bmatrix} X_1 \\ X_2 \\ S_1 \\ S_2 \\ A_1 \\ A_2 \end{bmatrix} = \begin{bmatrix} 0 \\ 0 \\ 300 \\ 0 \\ 1{,}000 \\ 150 \end{bmatrix}$$

T A B L E   9 . 7   Initial Simplex Tableau for the Muddy River Chemical Corporation Problem

C_j		$\$5$	$\$6$	$\$0$	$\$0$	$\$M$	$\$M$	
	SOLUTION MIX	X_1	X_2	S_1	S_2	A_1	A_2	QUANTITY
$\$M$	A_1	1	1	0	0	1	0	1,000
$\$0$	S_1	1	0	1	0	0	0	300
$\$M$	A_2	0	①→	0	−1	0	1	150 ← Pivot row
			Pivot number					
	Z_j	$\$M$	$\$2M$	0	−$\$M$	$\$M$	$\$M$	$\$1,150M$
	$C_j - Z_j$	$-\$M + 5$	$-\$2M + 6$	$\$0$	$\$M$	$\$0$	0	(total cost)
			Pivot column					

An extremely high cost, $1,150M$, is associated with this answer. We know that this can be reduced significantly and now move on to the solution procedures.

Developing a Second Tableau

In the $C_j - Z_j$ row of Table 9.7, we see that there are two entries with negative values, X_1 and X_2. In the simplex rules for minimization problems, this means that an optimal solution does not yet exist. The pivot column is the one with the *largest negative* entry in the $C_j - Z_j$ row—shown in Table 9.7 as the X_2 column, which means that X_2 will enter the solution next.

We examine whether the current solution is optimal by looking at the $C_j - Z_j$ row.

Which variable will leave the solution to make room for the new variable, X_2? To find out, we divide the elements of the quantity column by the respective pivot column values.

For the A_1 row $= \dfrac{1,000}{1} = 1,000$

For the S_1 row $= \dfrac{300}{0}$ (this is an undefined ratio, so we ignore it)

For the A_2 row $= \dfrac{150}{1} = 150$ (smallest quotient, indicating pivot row)

A_2 is the pivot row because 150 is the smallest quotient.

Hence, the pivot row is the A_2 row, and the pivot number (circled) is at the intersection of the X_2 column and the A_2 row.

The entering row for the next simplex tableau is found by dividing each element in the pivot row by the pivot number, 1. This leaves the old pivot row unchanged, except that it now represents the solution variable X_2. The other two rows are altered one at a time by again applying the formula shown earlier in step 4.

(new row numbers) = (numbers in old row)

$$- \left[\left(\frac{\text{number above or below}}{\text{pivot number}} \right) \times \left(\frac{\text{corresponding number}}{\text{in newly replaced row}} \right) \right]$$

A_1 Row	S_1 Row
$1 = 1 - (1)(0)$	$1 = 1 - (0)(0)$
$0 = 1 - (1)(1)$	$0 = 0 - (0)(1)$
$0 = 0 - (1)(0)$	$1 = 1 - (0)(0)$
$1 = 0 - (1)(-1)$	$0 = 0 - (0)(-1)$
$1 = 1 - (1)(0)$	$0 = 0 - (0)(0)$
$-1 = 0 - (1)(1)$	$0 = 0 - (0)(1)$
$850 = 1,000 - (1)(150)$	$300 = 300 - (0)(150)$

The Z_j and $C_j - Z_j$ rows are computed next.

$Z_j(\text{for } X_1)$	$= \$M(1)$	$+ \$0(1)$	$+ \$6(0)$	$= \$M$
$Z_j(\text{for } X_2)$	$= \$M(0)$	$+ \$0(0)$	$+ \$6(1)$	$= \$6$
$Z_j(\text{for } S_1)$	$= \$M(0)$	$+ \$0(1)$	$+ \$6(0)$	$= \$0$
$Z_j(\text{for } S_2)$	$= \$M(1)$	$+ \$0(0)$	$+ \$6(-1)$	$= \$M - 6$

$$Z_j(\text{for } A_1) \qquad = \$M(1) \quad + \$0(0) \quad + \$6(0) \quad = \$M$$

$$Z_j(\text{for } A_2) \qquad = \$M(-1) + \$0(0) \quad + \$6(1) \quad = -\$M + 6$$

$$Z_j(\text{for total cost}) = \$M(850) + \$0(300) + \$6(150) = \$850M + 900$$

	COLUMN					
	X_1	X_2	S_1	S_2	A_1	A_2
C_j for column	$5	$6	$0	$0	$M	$M
Z_j for column	$\underline{\$M}$	$\underline{\$6}$	$\underline{\$0}$	$\underline{\$M - 6}$	$\underline{\$M}$	$-\$M + 6$
$C_j - Z_j$ for column	$-\$M + 5$	$0	$0	$-\$M + 6$	$0	$2M - 6$

All of these computational results are presented in Table 9.8.

The solution after second tableau is still not optimal.

The solution at the end of the second tableau is $A_1 = 850$, $S_1 = 300$, $X_2 = 150$. X_1, S_2, and A_2 are currently the nonbasic variables and have zero value. The cost at this point is still quite high, $\$850M + \$900$. This answer is not optimal because not every number in the $C_j - Z_j$ row is zero or positive.

Developing a Third Tableau

The new pivot column is the X_1 column. To determine which variable will leave the basis to make room for X_1, we check the *quantity column–to–pivot column* ratios again.

The third tableau is developed in this section.

$$\text{For the } A_1 \text{ row} = \frac{850}{1} = 850$$

$$\text{For the } S_1 \text{ row} = \frac{300}{1} = 300 \qquad \textit{smallest ratio}$$

$$\text{For the } X_2 \text{ row} = \frac{150}{0} = \text{undefined}$$

TABLE 9.8   Second Simplex Tableau for the Muddy River Chemical Corporation Problem

C_j →		$5	$6	$0	$0	$M	$M	
	SOLUTION MIX	X_1	X_2	S_1	S_2	A_1	A_2	QUANTITY
$M	A_1	1	0	0	1	1	-1	850
$0	S_1	①	0	1	0	0	0	300 ← Pivot row
		Pivot number						
$6	X_2	0	1	0	-1	0	1	150
	Z_j	$M	$6	$0	$M - 6	$M	$-\$M + 6$	$850M + $900
	$C_j - Z_j$	$-\$M + 5$	$0	$0	$-\$M + 6$	$0	$2M - 6	
		Pivot column						

Hence, variable S_1 will be replaced by X_1.[6] The pivot number, row, and column are labeled in Table 9.8.

To replace the pivot row, we divide each number in the S_1 row by 1 (the circled pivot number), leaving the row unchanged. The new X_1 row is shown in Table 9.9. The other computations for this third simplex tableau are shown below.

A_1 Row	S_1 Row
$0 = 1 - (1)(1)$	$0 = 0 - (0)(1)$
$0 = 0 \quad (1)(0)$	$1 = 1 - (0)(0)$
$-1 = 0 - (1)(1)$	$0 = 0 - (0)(1)$
$1 = 1 - (1)(0)$	$-1 = -1 - (0)(0)$
$1 = 1 - (1)(0)$	$0 = 0 - (0)(0)$
$-1 = -1 - (1)(0)$	$1 = 1 - (0)(0)$
$550 = 850 - (1)(300)$	$150 = 150 - (0)(300)$

The Z_j and $C_j - Z_j$ rows are computed next.

Z_j(for X_1) $= \$M(0) \quad + \$5(1) \quad + \$6(0) \quad = \$5$

Z_j(for X_2) $= \$M(0) \quad + \$5(0) \quad + \$6(1) \quad = \$6$

Z_j(for S_1) $= \$M(-1) + \$5(1) \quad + \$6(0) \quad = -\$M + 5$

Z_j(for S_2) $= \$M(1) \quad + \$5(0) \quad + \$6(-1) = \$M - 6$

Z_j(for A_1) $= \$M(1) \quad + \$5(0) \quad + \$6(0) \quad = \$M$

Z_j(for A_2) $= \$M(-1) + \$5(0) \quad + \$6(1) \quad = -\$M + 6$

Z_j(for total cost) $= \$M(550) + \$5(300) + \$6(150) = \$550M + 2,400$

TABLE 9.9 Third Simplex Tableau for the Muddy River Chemical Corporation Problem

		$5	$6	$0	$0	$M	$M		
C_j $\longrightarrow$									
	SOLUTION MIX	X_1	X_2	S_1	S_2	A_1	A_2	QUANTITY	
$M	A_1	0	0	−1	①	1	−1	550 ⟵	Pivot row
$5	X_1	1	0	1	0	0	0	300	Pivot number
$6	X_2	0	1	0	−1	0	1	150	
	Z_j	$5	$6	−$M + 5	$M − 6	$M	−$M + 6	$550M + 2,400	
	$C_j - Z_j$	$0	$0	$M − 5	−$M + 6	$0	$2M − 6		
				Pivot column ⟶					

[6] At this point, it might appear to be more cost-effective to replace the A_1 row instead of the S_1 row. This would remove the last artificial variable, and its large $\$M$ cost, from the basis. The simplex method, however, does not always pick the most direct route to reaching the final solution. You may be assured, though, that it *will* lead us to the correct answer.

	COLUMN					
	X_1	X_2	S_1	S_2	A_1	A_2
C_j for column	$5	$6	$0	$0	$M	$M
Z_j for column	$5	$6	$-\$M+5$	$\$M-6$	$M	$-\$M+6$
$C_j - Z_j$ for column	$0	$0	$\$M-5$	$-\$M+6$	$0	$\$2M-6$

The third solution is still not optimal.

The solution at the end of the three iterations is still not optimal because the S_2 column contains a $C_j - Z_j$ value that is negative. Note that the current total cost is nonetheless lower than at the end of the second tableau, which in turn is lower than the initial solution cost. We are headed in the right direction but have one more tableau to go!

Fourth Tableau for the Muddy River Chemical Corporation Problem

The pivot column is now the S_2 column. The ratios that determine the row and variable to be replaced are computed as follows:

For the A_1 row: $\dfrac{550}{1} = 550$ row to be replaced

For the X_1 row: $\dfrac{300}{0}$ undefined

For the X_2 row: $\dfrac{150}{-1}$ not considered because it is negative

Here are the computations for the fourth solution.

Each number in the pivot row is divided by the pivot number (again 1, by coincidence). The other two rows are computed as follows and are shown in Table 9.10.

X_1 Row	X_2 Row
$1 = 1 - (0)(0)$	$0 = 0 - (-1)(0)$
$0 = 0 - (0)(0)$	$1 = 1 - (-1)(0)$
$1 = 1 - (0)(-1)$	$-1 = 0 - (-1)(-1)$
$0 = 0 - (0)(1)$	$0 = -1 - (-1)(1)$
$0 = 0 - (0)(1)$	$1 = 0 - (-1)(1)$
$0 = 0 - (0)(-1)$	$0 = 1 - (-1)(-1)$
$300 = 300 - (0)(550)$	$700 = 150 - (-1)(550)$

$Z_j(\text{for } X_1)$ $= \$0(0)$ $+ \$5(1)$ $+ \$6(0)$ $= \$5$

$Z_j(\text{for } X_2)$ $= \$0(0)$ $+ \$5(0)$ $+ \$6(1)$ $= \$6$

$Z_j(\text{for } S_1)$ $= \$0(-1)$ $+ \$5(1)$ $+ \$6(-1) = -\$1$

$Z_j(\text{for } S_2)$ $= \$0(1)$ $+ \$5(0)$ $+ \$6(0)$ $= \$0$

$Z_j(\text{for } A_1)$ $= \$0(1)$ $+ \$5(0)$ $+ \$6(1)$ $= \$6$

$Z_j(\text{for } A_2)$ $= \$0(-1)$ $+ \$5(0)$ $+ \$6(0)$ $= \$0$

$Z_j(\text{for total cost}) = \$0(550) + \$5(300) + \$6(700) = \$5,700$

	COLUMN					
	X_1	X_2	S_1	S_2	A_1	A_2
C_j for column	\$5	\$6	\$0	\$0	\$M	\$M
Z_j for column	\$5	\$6	−\$1	\$0	\$6	\$0
$C_j − Z_j$ for column	\$0	\$0	\$1	\$0	\$M − 6	\$M

On examining the $C_j − Z_j$ row in Table 9.10, only positive or 0 values are found. The fourth tableau therefore contains the optimum solution. That solution is $X_1 = 300$, $X_2 = 700$, $S_2 = 550$. The artificial variables are both equal to 0, as is S_1. Translated into management terms, the chemical company's decision should be to blend 300 pounds of phosphate (X_1) with 700 pounds of potassium (X_2). This provides a surplus (S_2) of 550 pounds of potassium more than required by the constraint $X_2 \geq 150$. The cost of this solution is \$5,700. If you look back to Figure 9.3, you can see that this is identical to the answer found by the graphical approach.

The optimal solution has been reached because only positive or zero values appear in the $C_j − Z_j$ row.

Although small problems such as this can be solved graphically, more realistic product blending problems demand use of the simplex method, usually in computerized form.

9.9 REVIEW OF PROCEDURES FOR SOLVING LP MINIMIZATION PROBLEMS

Just as we summarized the steps for solving LP maximization problems with the simplex method in Section 9.6, let us do so for minimization problems here:

I. Formulate the LP problem's objective function and constraints.

II. Include slack variables in each less-than-or-equal-to constraint, artificial variables in each equality constraint, and both surplus and artificial variables in each greater-than-or-equal-to constraint. Then add all of these variables to the problem's objective function.

III. Develop an initial simplex tableau with artificial and slack variables in the basis and their variables (the X_i's) set equal to 0. Compute the Z_j and $C_j − Z_j$ values for this tableau.

TABLE 9.10 **Fourth and Optimal Solution to the Muddy River Chemical Corporation Problem**

C_j →		\$5	\$6	\$0	\$0	\$M	\$M	
	SOLUTION MIX	X_1	X_2	S_1	S_2	A_1	A_2	**QUANTITY**
\$0	S_2	0	0	−1	1	1	−1	550
\$5	X_1	1	0	1	0	0	0	300
\$6	X_2	0	1	−1	0	1	0	700
	Z_j	\$5	\$6	−\$1	\$0	\$6	\$0	\$5,700
	$C_j − Z_j$	\$0	\$0	\$1	\$0	\$M − 6	\$M	

IV. Follow these five steps until an optimal solution has been reached:

   1. Choose the variable with the greatest negative $C_j - Z_j$ to enter the solution. This is the pivot column.

   2. Determine the row to be replaced by selecting the one with the smallest (nonnegative) quantity-to-pivot column ratio. This is the pivot row.

   3. Calculate the new values for the pivot row.

   4. Calculate the new values for the other row(s).

   5. Calculate the Z_j and $C_j - Z_j$ values for the tableau. If there are any $C_j - Z_j$ numbers less than 0, return to step 1. If there are no $C_j - Z_j$ numbers that are less than 0, an optimal solution has been reached.

9.10 SPECIAL CASES

In Chapter 7 we addressed some special cases that may arise when solving LP problems graphically (see Section 8 of Chapter 7). Here we describe these cases again, this time as they refer to the simplex method.

Infeasibility

A situation with no feasible solution may exist if the problem was formulated improperly.

Infeasibility, you may recall, comes about when there is no solution that satisfies all of the problem's constraints. In the simplex method, an infeasible solution is indicated by looking at the final tableau. In it, all $C_j - Z_j$ row entries will be of the proper sign to imply optimality, but an artificial variable (A_1) will still be in the solution mix.

Table 9.11 illustrates the final simplex tableau for a hypothetical minimization type of LP problem. The table provides an example of an improperly formulated problem, probably containing conflicting constraints. No feasible solution is possible because an artificial variable, A_2, remains in the solution mix, even though all $C_j - Z_j$ are positive or 0 (the criterion for an optimal solution in a minimization case).

Unbounded Solutions

Unboundedness describes linear programs that do not have finite solutions. It occurs in maximization problems, for example, when a solution variable can be made infinitely large without violating a constraint (refer back to Figure 7.13). In the simplex method, the condi-

---

TABLE 9.11 Illustration of Infeasibility

C_j →		$5	$8	$0	$0	$M	$M	
↓	SOLUTION MIX	X_1	X_2	S_1	S_2	A_1	A_2	QUANTITY
$5	X_1	1	0	−2	3	−1	0	200
$8	X_2	0	1	1	2	−2	0	100
$M	A_2	0	0	0	−1	−1	1	20
	Z_j	$5	$8	−$2	$31 − M	−$21 − M	$M	$1,800 + 20M
	$C_j - Z_j$	$0	$0	$2	$M − 31	$2M + 21	$0	

TABLE 9.12 **Problem with an Unbounded Solution**

C_j		$6	$9	$0	$0	
	SOLUTION MIX	X_1	X_2	S_1	S_2	QUANTITY
$9	X_2	− 1	1	2	0	30
$0	S_2	−2	0	−1	1	10
	Z_j	−$9	$9	$18	$0	$270
	$C_j - Z_j$	→$15	$0	−$18	$0	

Pivot column

tion of unboundedness will be discovered prior to reaching the final tableau. We will note the problem when trying to decide which variable to remove from the solution mix. As seen earlier in this chapter, the procedure is to divide each quantity column number by the corresponding pivot column number. The row with the smallest positive ratio is replaced. But if all the ratios turn out to be negative or undefined, it indicates that the problem is unbounded.

Table 9.12 illustrates the second tableau calculated for a particular LP maximization problem by the simplex method. It also points to the condition of unboundedness. The solution is not optimal because not all $C_j - Z_j$ entries are 0 or negative, as required in a maximization problem. The next variable to enter the solution should be X_1. To determine which variable will leave the solution, we examine the ratios of the quantity column numbers to their corresponding numbers in the X_1, or pivot, column.

No finite solution may exist in problems that are not bounded. This means that a variable can be infinitely large without violating a constraint.

Ratio for the X_2 row: $\dfrac{30}{-1}$ ⎫
Ratio for the S_2 row: $\dfrac{10}{-2}$ ⎬ → Negative ratios unacceptable

Since both pivot column numbers are negative, an unbounded solution is indicated.

Degeneracy

Degeneracy is another situation that can occur when solving an LP problem using the simplex method. It may develop when a problem contains a redundant constraint; that is, one or more of the constraints in the formulation makes another unnecessary. For example, if a problem has the three constraints $X_1 \leq 10$, $X_2 \leq 10$, and $X_1 + X_2 \leq 20$, the latter is unnecessary because the first two constraints make it redundant. Degeneracy arises when the ratio calculations are made. If there is a *tie* for the smallest ratio, this is a signal that degeneracy exists.

Table 9.13 provides an example of a degenerate problem. At this iteration of the given maximization LP problem, the next variable to enter the solution will be X_1, since it has the only positive $C_j - Z_j$ number. The ratios are computed as follows:

Tied ratios in the simplex calculations signal degeneracy, that is, the case in which redundant constraints exist.

For the X_2 row: $\dfrac{10}{1/4} = 40$

For the S_2 row: $\dfrac{20}{4} = 5$ ← ⎫ tie for the smallest ratio indicates degeneracy

For the S_3 row: $\dfrac{10}{2} = 5$ ←

TABLE 9.13 Problem Illustrating Degeneracy

C_j		$5	$8	$2	$0	$0	$0	
	SOLUTION MIX	X_1	X_2	X_3	S_1	S_2	S_3	QUANTITY
$8	X_2	$1/4$	1	1	−2	0	0	10
$0	S_2	4	0	$1/3$	−1	1	0	20
$0	S_3	2	0	2	$2/5$	0	1	10
	Z_j	$2	$8	$8	$16	$0	$0	$80
	$C_j - Z_j$	→$3	$0	−$6	−$16	$0	$0	
		└ pivot column						

Cycling **may** *result from degeneracy.*

Theoretically, degeneracy could lead to a situation known as cycling, in which the simplex algorithm alternates back and forth between the same nonoptimal solutions; that is, it puts a new variable in, then takes it out in the next tableau, puts it back in, and so on. One simple way of dealing with the issue is to select either row (S_2 or S_3 in this case) arbitrarily. If we are unlucky and cycling does occur, we simply go back and select the other row.

More Than One Optimal Solution

Alternate optimal solutions may exist if the $C_j - Z_j$ *value = 0 for a real variable not in the solution mix.*

Multiple, or alternate, optimal solutions are spotted when the simplex method is being used by looking at the final tableau. If the $C_j - Z_j$ value is equal to 0 for a variable that is not in the solution mix, more than one optimal solution exists.

Let's take Table 9.14 as an example. Here is the last tableau of a maximization problem; each entry in the $C_j - Z_j$ row is 0 or negative, indicating that an optimal solution has been reached. That solution is read as $X_2 = 6$, $S_2 = 3$, profit = $12. Note, however, that variable X_1 can be brought into the solution mix without increasing or decreasing profit. The new solution, with X_1 in the basis, would become $X_1 = 3$, $X_2 = 3/2$, with profit still at $12. Can you modify Table 9.14 to prove this? You might note, by the way, that this example of an alternate optimal solution corresponds to the graphical solution shown in Figure 7.15.

TABLE 9.14 Problem with Alternate Optimal Solutions

C_j		$3	$2	$0	$0	
	SOLUTION MIX	X_1	X_2	S_1	S_2	QUANTITY
$2	X_2	$3/2$	1	1	0	6
$0	S_2	1	0	$1/2$	1	3
	Z_j	$3	$2	$2	$0	$12
	$C_j - Z_j$	$0	$0	−$2	$0	

9.11 SENSITIVITY ANALYSIS WITH THE SIMPLEX TABLEAU

In Chapter 7 we introduced the topic of sensitivity analysis as it applies to LP problems that we have solved graphically. This valuable concept showed how the optimal solution and the value of its objective function change, given changes in various inputs to the problem. Graphical analysis is useful in understanding intuitively and visually how feasible regions and the slopes of objective functions can change as model coefficients change. Computer programs handling LP problems of all sizes provide sensitivity analysis as an important output feature. Those programs use the information provided in the final simplex tableau to compute ranges for the objective function coefficients and ranges for the right-hand-side values. They also provide "shadow prices," a concept that we introduce in this section.

High Note Sound Company Revisited

In Section 7.9 we used the High Note Sound Company to illustrate sensitivity analysis graphically. High Note is a firm that makes compact disk (CD) players (called X_1's) and stereo receivers (called X_2's). Its LP formulation is repeated here:

maximize profit $= \$50X_1 + \$120X_2$

subject to $\quad 2X_1 + 4X_2 \leq 80 \quad$ (hours of electricians' time available)

$\qquad\qquad 3X_1 + 1X_2 \leq 60 \quad$ (hours of audio technicians' time available)

High Note's graphical solution is also repeated, as we see in Figure 9.4.

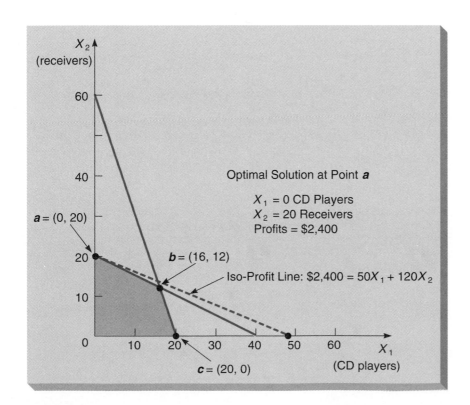

FIGURE 9.4

High Note Sound Company Graphical Solution

Changes in the Objective Function Coefficients

In Chapter 7 we saw how to use graphical LP to examine the objective function coefficients. A second way of illustrating the sensitivity analysis of objective function coefficients is to consider the problem's final simplex tableau. For the High Note Sound Company, this tableau is shown in Table 9.15. The optimal solution is seen to be as follows:

$X_2 = 20$ stereo receivers

$S_2 = 40$ hours of slack time of audio technicians $\Big\}$ *Basic variables*

$X_1 = 0$ CD players

$S_1 = 0$ hours of slack time of electricians $\Big\}$ *Nonbasic variables*

Basic variables (those in the solution mix) and *nonbasic variables* (those set equal to 0) must be handled differently using sensitivity analysis. Let us first consider the case of a nonbasic variable.

Nonbasic variables are variables that have a value of zero.

Nonbasic Objective Function Coefficient Our goal here is to find out how sensitive the problem's optimal solution is to changes in the contribution rates of variables not currently in the basis (X_1 and S_1). Just how much would the objective function coefficients have to change before X_1 or S_1 would enter the solution mix and replace one of the basic variables?

The answer lies in the $C_j - Z_j$ row of the final simplex tableau (as in Table 9.15). Since this is a maximization problem, the basis will not change unless the $C_j - Z_j$ value of one of the nonbasic variables becomes positive. That is, the current solution will be optimal as long as all numbers in the bottom row are less than or equal to 0. It will not be optimal if X_1's $C_j - Z_j$ value is positive, or if S_1's $C_j - Z_j$ value is greater than 0. Therefore, the values of C_j for X_1 and S_1 that do not bring about any change in the optimal solution are given by

The solution is optimal as long as all $C_j - Z_j \leq 0$.

$$C_j - Z_j \leq 0$$

This is the same as writing

$$C_j \leq Z_j$$

Since X_1's C_j value is \$50 and its Z_j value is \$60, the current solution is optimal as long as the profit per CD player does not exceed \$60, or correspondingly, does not increase by more than \$10. Similarly, the contribution rate per unit of S_1 (or per hour of electricians' time) may increase from \$0 up to \$30 without changing the current solution mix.

TABLE 9.15   **Optimal Solution by the Simplex Method**

C_j →		\$50	\$120	\$0	\$0	
↓	SOLUTION MIX	X_1	X_2	S_1	S_2	QUANTITY
\$120	X_2	$\frac{1}{2}$	1	$\frac{1}{4}$	0	20
\$0	S_2	$\frac{5}{2}$	0	$-\frac{1}{4}$	1	40
	Z_j	\$60	\$120	\$30	\$0	\$2,400
	$C_j - Z_j$	$-$\$10	\$0	$-$\$30	\$0	

In both cases, when you are maximizing an objective function, you may increase the value of C_j up to the value of Z_j. You may also *decrease* the value of C_j for a nonbasic variable to negative infinity ($-\infty$) without affecting the solution. This range of C_j values is called the *range of insignificance* for nonbasic variables.

The range over which C_j rates for nonbasic variables can vary without causing a change in the optimal solution mix is called the range of insignificance.

$$-\infty \leqslant C_j(\text{for } X_1) \leqslant \$60$$

$$-\infty \leqslant C_j(\text{for } S_1) \leqslant \$30$$

Basic Objective Function Coefficient Sensitivity analysis on objective function coefficients of variables that are in the basis or solution mix is slightly more complex. We saw that a change in the objective function coefficient for a nonbasic variable affects only the $C_j - Z_j$ value for that variable. But a change in the profit or cost of a basic variable can affect the $C_j - Z_j$ values of *all* nonbasic variables.

Testing basic variables involves reworking the final simplex tableau.

Let us consider changing the profit contribution of stereo receivers in the High Note Sound Company problem. Currently, the objective function coefficient is \$120. The change in this value can be denoted by the Greek capital letter delta (Δ). We rework the final simplex tableau (first shown Table 9.15) and see our results in Table 9.16.

Notice the new $C_j - Z_j$ values for nonbasic variables X_1 and S_1. These were determined in exactly the same way as we did earlier in this chapter. But wherever the C_j value for X_2 of \$120 was seen in Table 9.15, a new value of \$120 + Δ is used in Table 9.16.

Once again, we recognize that the current optimal solution will change only if one or more of the $C_j - Z_j$ row values becomes greater than 0. The question is, how may the value of Δ vary so that all $C_j - Z_j$ entries remain positive? To find out, we solve for Δ in each column.

From the X_1 column:

$$-10 - \tfrac{1}{2}\Delta \leqslant 0$$

$$-10 \leqslant \tfrac{1}{2}\Delta$$

$$-20 \leqslant \Delta \text{ or } \Delta \geqslant -20$$

This inequality means that the optimal solution will not change unless X_2's profit coefficient decreases by at least \$20, which is a change of $\Delta = -\$20$. Hence, variable X_1 will not enter the basis unless the profit per stereo receiver drops from \$120 to \$100 or less. This, interestingly, is exactly what we noticed graphically in Figure 7.17. When the profit per stereo receiver dropped to \$80, the optimal solution changed from corner point *a* to corner point *b*.

T A B L E 9 . 1 6 **Change in the Profit Contribution of Stereo Receivers**

C_j →		$50	$120 + Δ	$0	$0	
↓	SOLUTION MIX	X_1	X_2	S_1	S_2	QUANTITY
$120 + Δ	X_2	$\tfrac{1}{2}$	1	$\tfrac{1}{4}$	0	20
$0	S_2	$\tfrac{5}{2}$	0	$-\tfrac{1}{4}$	1	40
	Z_j	$60 + \tfrac{1}{2}\Delta$	$120 + \Delta$	$30 + \tfrac{1}{4}\Delta$	$0	$2{,}400 + 20\Delta$
	$C_j - Z_j$	$-\$10 - \tfrac{1}{2}\Delta$	$0	$-\$30 - \tfrac{1}{4}\Delta$	$0	

Now we examine the S_1 column:

$$-30 - \tfrac{1}{4}\Delta \le 0$$

$$-30 \le \tfrac{1}{4}\Delta$$

$$-120 \le \Delta \text{ or } \Delta \ge -120$$

This inequality implies that S_1 is less sensitive to change than X_1. S_1 will not enter the basis unless the profit per unit of X_2 drops from \$120 all the way down to \$0.

The range of optimality is the range of values over which a basic variable's coefficient can change without causing a change in the optimal solution mix.

Since the first inequality is more binding, we can say that the *range of optimality* for X_2's profit coefficient is

$$\$100 \le C_j(\text{for } X_2) \le \infty$$

As long as the profit per stereo receiver is greater than or equal to \$100, the current production mix of $X_2 = 20$ receivers and $X_1 = 0$ CD players will be optimal.

In analyzing larger problems, we would use this procedure to test for the range of optimality of every real decision variable in the final solution mix. The procedure helps us avoid the time-consuming process of reformulating and resolving the entire linear programming problem each time a small change occurs. Within the bounds set, changes in profit coefficients would not force a firm to alter its product mix decision or change the number of units produced. Overall profits, of course, will change if a profit coefficient increases or decreases, but such computations are quick and easy to perform.

Changes in Resources or Right-Hand-Side Values

Making changes in the right-hand-side values (the resources of electricians' and audio technicians' time) result in changes in the feasible region and often the optimal solution.

The shadow price is the value of one additional unit of a scarce resource. Shadow pricing provides an important piece of economic information.

The negatives of the numbers in the $C_j - Z_j$ row's slack variable columns are the shadow prices.

Shadow Prices This leads us to the important subject of *shadow prices*. Exactly how much should a firm be willing to pay to make additional resources available? Is one more hour of machine time worth \$1 or \$5 or \$20? Is it worthwhile to pay workers an overtime rate to stay one extra hour each night to increase production output? Valuable management information could be provided if the worth of additional resources was known.

Fortunately, this information is available to us by looking at the final simplex tableau of an LP problem. An important property of the $C_j - Z_j$ row is that the negatives of the numbers in its slack variable (S_i) columns provide us with what we call shadow prices. A *shadow price* is the change in value of the objective function from an increase of one unit of a scarce resource (e.g., by making one more hour of machine time or labor time or other resource available).

The final simplex tableau for the High Note Sound Company problem is repeated as Table 9.17 (it was first shown as Table 9.15). The tableau indicates that the optimal solution is $X_1 = 0$, $X_2 = 20$, $S_1 = 0$, $S_2 = 40$, and that profit = \$2,400. Recall that S_1 represents slack availability of the electricians' resource and S_2 the unused time in the audio technicians' department.

The firm is considering hiring an extra electrician on a part-time basis. Let's say that it will cost \$22 per hour in wages and benefits to bring the part-timer on board. Should the firm do this? The answer is yes; the shadow price of the electrician time resource is \$30. Thus, the firm will *net* \$8 (= \$30 − \$22) for every hour the new worker helps in the production process.

Should High Note also hire a part-time audio technician at a rate of \$14 per hour? The answer is *no*: The shadow price is \$0, implying no increase in the objective function by making more of this second resource available. Why? Because not all of the resource

TABLE 9.17 Final Tableau for the High Note Sound Company

C_j	→	$50	$120	$0	$50	
	SOLUTION MIX	X_1	X_2	S_1	S_2	QUANTITY
$120	X_2	$\frac{1}{2}$	1	$\frac{1}{4}$	1	20
$0	S_2	$\frac{5}{2}$	0	$-\frac{1}{4}$	0	40
	Z_j	$60	$120	$30	$0	$2,400
	$C_j - Z_j$	$-$10	$0	$-$30	$0	

Objective function increases by $30 if 1 additional hour of electricians' time is made available

is currently being used—40 hours are still available. It would hardly pay to buy more of the resource.

Right-Hand-Side Ranging Obviously, we can't add an unlimited number of units of resource without eventually violating one of the problem's constraints. When we understand and compute the shadow price for an additional hour of electricians' time ($30), we will want to determine how many hours we can actually use to increase profits. Should the new resource be added 1 hour per week, 2 hours, or 200 hours? In LP terms, this process involves finding the range over which shadow prices will stay valid. *Right-hand-side* (RHS) *ranging* tells us the number of hours High Note can add or remove from the electrician department and still have a shadow price of $30.

The range over which shadow prices remain valid is called right-hand-side ranging.

Ranging is simple in that it resembles the simplex process we used earlier in this chapter to find the minimum ratio for a new variable. The S_1 column and quantity column from Table 9.17 are repeated in the following table; the ratios, both positive and negative, are also shown.

QUANTITY	S_1	RATIO	
20	$\frac{1}{4}$	$20/(\frac{1}{4}) =$	80
40	$-\frac{1}{4}$	$40/(-\frac{1}{4}) = -160$	

The smallest positive ratio (80 in this example) tells us by how many hours the electricians' time resource can be *reduced* without altering the current solution mix. Hence, we may decrease the RHS resource by as much as 80 hours—basically from the current 80 hours all the way down to 0 hours—without causing a basic variable to be pivoted out of the solution.

The smallest negative ratio (-160) tells us the number of hours that can be added to the resource before the solution mix changes. In this case, we may increase electricians' time by 160 hours, up to 240 ($= 80$ currently $+ 160$ may be added) hours. We have now established the range of electricians' time over which the shadow price of $30 is valid. That range is from 0 to 240 hours.

The audio technician resource is slightly different in that all 60 hours of time originally available have not been used. (Note that $S_2 = 40$ hours in Table 9.17.) If we apply the ratio test, we see that we can reduce the number of audio technicians' hours by only

40 before a shortage occurs. But since we are not using all the hours currently available, we can increase them indefinitely without altering the problem's solution. Hence, the valid range for *this* shadow price would be from 20 (= 60 − 40) hours to an unbounded upper limit.

Sensitivity Analysis by Computer

To confirm our calculations of High Note Sound Company's sensitivity analysis, let us turn to Program 9.1, an Excel computer run of the problem. Note that we had earlier used QM for Windows and Excel to analyze High Note in Chapter 7 when we treated the topic graphically. Program 9.1A repeats the Excel solution and formulation, and Program 9.1B illustrates sensitivity analysis.

PROGRAM 9.1A

Excel Solution to the High Note LP Problem

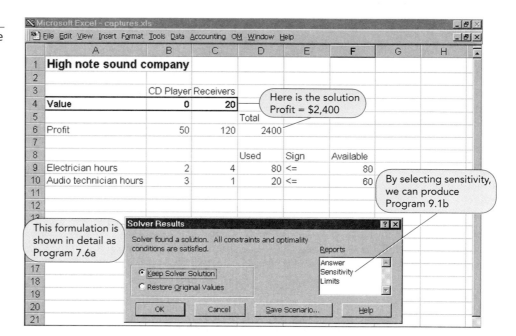

PROGRAM 9.1B

Excel's Sensitivity Analysis Output for High Note Sound Company

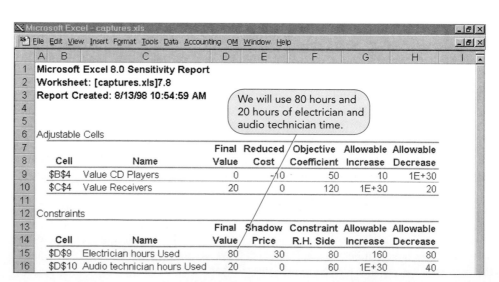

9.12 THE DUAL

Every LP problem has another LP problem associated with it, which is called its *dual*. The first way of stating a linear problem is called the *primal* of the problem; we can view all of the problems formulated thus far as primals. The second way of stating the same problem is called the *dual*. The optimal solutions for the primal and the dual are equivalent, but they are derived through alternative procedures.

Every LP primal has a dual. The dual provides useful economic information.

The dual contains economic information useful to management, and it may also be easier to solve, in terms of less computation, than the primal problem. Generally, if the LP primal involves maximizing a profit function subject to less-than-or-equal-to resource constraints, the dual will involve minimizing total opportunity costs subject to greater-than-or-equal-to product profit constraints. Formulating the dual problem from a given primal is not terribly complex, and once it is formulated, the solution procedure is exactly the same as for any LP problem.

Let's illustrate the *primal–dual relationship* with the High Note Sound Company data. As you recall, the primal problem is to determine the best production mix of CD players (X_1) and stereo receivers (X_2) to maximize profit.

maximize profit = $\$50X_1 + \$120X_2$

subject to $\quad 2X_1 + 4X_2 \leqslant 80 \quad$ (hours of available electrician time)

$\qquad\qquad 3X_1 + 1X_2 \leqslant 60 \quad$ (hours of audio technician time available)

The dual of this problem has the objective of minimizing the opportunity cost of not using the resources in an optimal manner. Let's call the variables that it will attempt to solve for U_1 and U_2. U_1 represents the potential hourly contribution or worth of electrician time; in other words, the dual value of 1 hour of the electricians' resource. U_2 stands for the imputed worth of the audio technicians' time, or the dual technician resource.

The dual variables represent the potential value of resources.

The right-hand-side quantities of the primal *constraints* become the dual's *objective function* coefficients. The total opportunity cost that is to be minimized will be represented by the function $80U_1 + 60U_2$, namely,

minimize opportunity cost = $80U_1 + 60U_2$

The corresponding dual constraints are formed from the transpose[7] of the primal constraints coefficients. Note that if the primal constraints are $\leqslant$, the dual constraints are $\geqslant$.

$2 \, U_1 + 3 \, U_2 \geqslant 50 \longrightarrow$ Primal profit coefficients

$4 \, U_1 + 1 \, U_2 \geqslant 120 \longrightarrow$ Coefficients from the second primal constraint

$\longrightarrow$ Coefficients from the first primal constraint

Let's look at the meaning of these dual constraints. In the first inequality, the right-hand-side constant ($\$50$) is the income from one CD player. The coefficients of U_1 and U_2 are the amounts of each scarce resource (electrician time and audio technician time) that are required to produce a CD player. That is, 2 hours of electricians' time and 3 hours of audio technicians' time are used up in making one CD player. Each CD player produced

---

[7]For example, the transpose of the set of numbers $\begin{pmatrix} a & b \\ c & d \end{pmatrix}$ is $\begin{pmatrix} a & c \\ b & d \end{pmatrix}$. In the case of the transpose of the primal coefficients $\begin{pmatrix} 2 & 4 \\ 3 & 1 \end{pmatrix}$, the result is $\begin{pmatrix} 2 & 3 \\ 4 & 1 \end{pmatrix}$. Refer to CD Module 5, dealing with matrices and determinants, for a review of the transpose concept.

yields $50 of revenue to High Note Sound Company. This inequality states that the total imputed value or potential worth of the scarce resources needed to produce a CD player must be at least equal to the profit derived from the product. The second constraint makes an analogous statement for the stereo receiver product.

Dual Formulation Procedures

The mechanics of formulating a dual from the primal problem are summarized in the following list.

These are the five steps for formulating a dual.

> **Steps to Form a Dual**
> 1. If the primal is a maximization, the dual is a minimization, and vice versa.
> 2. The right-hand-side values of the primal constraints become the dual's objective function coefficients.
> 3. The primal objective function coefficients become the right-hand-side values of the dual constraints.
> 4. The transpose of the primal constraint coefficients become the dual constraint coefficients.
> 5. Constraint inequality signs are reversed.[8]

Solving the Dual of the High Note Sound Company Problem

The simplex algorithm is applied to solve the preceding dual problem. With appropriate surplus and artificial variables, it may be restated as follows:

$$\text{minimize opportunity cost} = 80U_1 + 60U_2 + 0S_1 + 0S_2 + MA_1 + MA_2$$

$$\text{subject to} \qquad 2U_1 + 3U_2 - 1S_1 + 1A_1 = 50$$

$$4U_1 + 1U_2 - 1S_2 + 1A_2 = 120$$

The first and second tableaus are shown in Table 9.18. The third tableau, containing the optimal solution of $U_1 = 30$, $U_2 = 0$, $S_1 = 10$, $S_2 = 0$, opportunity cost = $2,400, appears in Figure 9.5 along with the final tableau of the primal problem.

We mentioned earlier that the primal and dual lead to the same solution even though they are formulated differently. How can this be?

It turns out that in the final simplex tableau of a primal problem, the absolute values of the numbers in the $C_j - Z_j$ row under the slack variables represent the solutions to the dual problem, that is, the optimal U_is (see Figure 9.5). In the earlier section on sensitivity analysis we termed these numbers in the columns of the slack variables *shadow prices*. Thus, the solution to the dual problem presents the marginal profits of each additional unit of resource.

The solution to the dual yields shadow prices.

It also happens that the absolute value of the $C_j - Z_j$ values of the slack variables in the optimal *dual* solution represent the optimal values of the *primal* X_1 and X_2 variables. The minimum opportunity cost derived in the dual must always equal the maximum profit derived in the primal.

Also note the other relationships between the primal and the dual that are indicated in Figure 9.5 by arrows. Columns A_1 and A_2 in the optimal dual tableau may be ignored because, as you recall, artificial variables have no physical meaning.

---

[8] If the jth primal constraint should be an equality, the ith dual variable is unrestricted in sign. This technical issue is discussed on page 170 of *Methods and Applications of Linear Programming*, by L. Cooper and D. Steinberg (Philadelphia: W. B. Saunders, 1974).

TABLE 9.18 First and Second Tableaus of the High Note Dual Problem

	$C_j \rightarrow$	80	60	0	0	M	M	
	SOLUTION MIX	U_1	U_2	S_1	S_2	A_1	A_2	QUANTITY
First tableau $M	A_1	2	3	−1	0	1	0	50
$M	A_2	4	1	0	−1	0	1	120
	Z_j	$6M	$4M	−$M	−$M	$M	$M	$170M
	$C_j - Z_j$	80 − 6M	60 − 4M	M	M	0	0	
Second tableau $80	U_1	1	$\frac{3}{2}$	$-\frac{1}{2}$	0	$\frac{1}{2}$	0	25
$M	A_2	0	−5	2	−1	−2	1	20
	Z_j	$80	$120 − 5M	−$40 + 2M	−$M	$40 − 2M	$M	$2,000 + 20M
	$C_j - Z_j$	0	5M − 60	−2M + 40	M	3M − 40	0	

FIGURE 9.5

Comparison of the Primal and Dual Optimal Tableaus

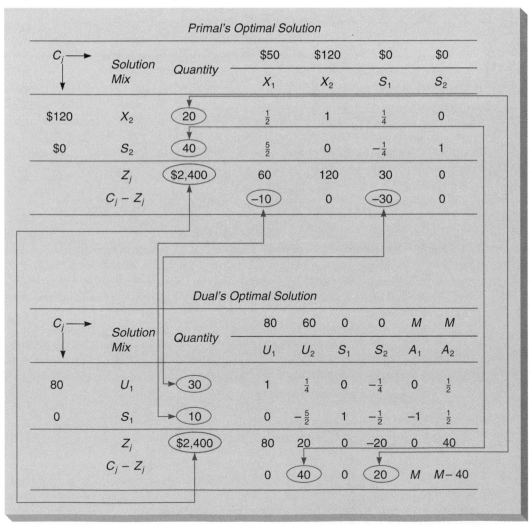

9.13   KARMARKAR'S ALGORITHM

The biggest change to take place in the field of LP solution techniques in four decades was the 1984 arrival of an alternative to the simplex algorithm. Developed by Narendra Karmarkar, the new method, called Karmarkar's algorithm, often takes significantly less computer time to solve very large-scale LP problems.[9]

As we saw, the simplex algorithm finds a solution by moving from one adjacent corner point to the next, following the outside edges of the feasible region. In contrast, Karmarkar's method follows a path of points on the *inside* of the feasible region. Karmarkar's method is also unique in its ability to handle an *extremely* large number of constraints and variables, thereby giving LP users the capacity to solve previously unsolvable problems.

Although it is likely that the simplex method will continue to be used for many LP problems, a new generation of LP software built around Karmarkar's algorithm is already becoming popular. Delta Air Lines became the first commercial airline to use the Karmarkar program, called KORBX, which was developed and is sold by AT&T. Delta found that the program streamlined the monthly scheduling of 7,000 pilots who fly more than 400 airplanes to 166 cities worldwide. With increased efficiency in allocating limited resources, Delta saves millions of dollars in crew time and related costs.

Summary

The simplex systematically improves solutions by algebraically examining corner points and moving toward an optimal solution.

In Chapter 7 we examined the use of graphical methods to solve LP problems that contained only two decision variables. This chapter moved us one giant step further by introducing the simplex method. The simplex method is an iterative procedure for reaching the optimal solution to LP problems of any dimension. It consists of a series of rules that, in effect, algebraically examine corner points in a systematic way. Each step moves us closer to the optimal solution by increasing profit or decreasing cost, while maintaining feasibility.

We saw the procedure for converting less-than-or-equal-to, greater-than-or-equal-to, and equality constraints into the simplex format. These conversions employed the inclusion of slack, surplus, and artificial variables. An initial simplex tableau was developed that portrayed the problem's original data formulations. It also contained a row providing profit or cost information and a net evaluation row. The latter, identified as the $C_j - Z_j$ row, was examined in determining whether an optimal solution had yet been reached. It also pointed out which variable would next enter the solution mix, or basis, if the current solution was nonoptimal.

The simplex method consists of five steps: (1) identifying the pivot column, (2) identifying the pivot row and number, (3) replacing the pivot row, (4) computing new values for each remaining row, and (5) computing the Z_j and $C_j - Z_j$ rows and examining for optimality. Each tableau of this iterative procedure was displayed and explained for a sample maximization and minimization problem.

A few special issues in LP that arise in using the simplex method were also discussed in this chapter. Examples of infeasibility, unbounded solutions, degeneracy, and multiple optimal solutions were presented.

---

[9] For details, see Narendra Karmarkar, "A New Polynomial Time Algorithm for Linear Programming," *Combinatorica* 4, 4 (1984): 373–395, or J. N. Hooker, "Karmarkar's Linear Programming Algorithm," *Interfaces* 16, 4 (July–August 1986): 75–90.

Although large LP problems are seldom, if ever, solved by hand, the purpose of this chapter was to help you gain an understanding of how the simplex method works. Understanding the underlying principles help interpret and analyze computerized linear programming solutions.

Chapter 9 also provided a foundation for another issue: answering questions about the problem after an optimal solution has been found, which is called postoptimality analysis, or sensitivity analysis. Included in this discussion was the analysis of the value of additional resources, called shadow pricing. Finally, the relationship between a primal LP problem and its dual was explored. We illustrated how to derive the dual from a primal and how the solutions to the dual variables are actually the shadow prices.

Glossary

Simplex Method. A matrix algebra method for solving LP problems.

Iterative Procedure. A process (algorithm) that repeats the same steps over and over.

Slack Variable. A variable added to less-than-or-equal-to constraints in order to create an equality for a simplex method. It represents a quantity of unused resource.

Simplex Tableau. A table for keeping track of calculations at each iteration of the simplex method.

Solution Mix. A column in the simplex tableau that contains all the variables in the solution.

Quantity Column. A column in the simplex tableau that gives the numeric value of each variable in the solution mix column.

Basic Feasible Solution. A solution to an LP problem that corresponds to a corner point of the feasible region.

Basis. The set of variables that are in the solution, have positive, nonzero values, and are listed in the solution mix column. They are also called **basic variables.**

Nonbasic Variables. Variables not in the solution mix or basis. Nonbasic variables are equal to zero.

Substitution Rates. The coefficients in the central body of each simplex table. They indicate the number of units of each basic variable that must be removed from the solution if a new variable (as represented at any column head) is entered.

Z_j Row. The row containing the figures for gross profit or loss given up by adding one unit of a variable into the solution.

$C_j - Z_j$ Row. The row containing the net profit or loss that will result from introducing one unit of the variable indicated in that column into the solution.

Pivot Column. The column with the largest positive number in the $C_j - Z_j$ row of a maximization problem, or the largest negative $C_j - Z_j$ value in a minimization problem. It indicates which variable will enter the solution next.

Pivot Row. The row corresponding to the variable that will leave the basis in order to make room for the variable entering (as indicated by the new pivot column). This is the smallest positive ratio found by dividing the quantity column values by the pivot column values for each row.

Pivot Number. The number at the intersection of the pivot row and pivot column.

Current Solution. The basic feasible solution that is the set of variables presently in the solution. It corresponds to a corner point of the feasible region.

Surplus Variable. A variable inserted in a greater-than-or-equal-to constraint to create an equality. It represents the amount of resource usage above the minimum required usage.

Artificial Variable. A variable that has no meaning in a physical sense but acts as a tool to help generate an initial LP solution.

Infeasibility. The situation in which there is no solution that satisfies all of a problem's constraints.

Unboundedness. A condition describing LP maximization problems having solutions that can become infinitely large without violating any stated constraints.

Degeneracy. A condition that arises when there is a tie in the values used to determine which variable will enter the solution next. It can lead to cycling back and forth between two nonoptimal solutions.

Range of Insignificance. The range of values over which a nonbasic variable's coefficient can vary without causing a change in the optimal solution mix.

Range of Optimality. The range of values over which a basic variable's coefficient can change without causing a change in the optimal solution mix.

Shadow Prices. The coefficients of slack variables in the $C_j - Z_j$ row. They represent the value of one additional unit of a resource.

Right-Hand-Side Ranging. A method used to find the range over which shadow prices remain valid.

Primal–Dual Relationship. Alternative ways of stating a LP problem.

Key Equation

(9-1)   (New row numbers) = (numbers in old row)

$$- \left[\left(\frac{\text{number above or below}}{\text{pivot number}} \right) \times \left(\begin{array}{c} \text{corresponding number} \\ \text{in newly replaced row} \end{array} \right) \right]$$

Formula for computing new values for nonpivot rows in the simplex tableau (step 4 of the simplex procedure).

Solved Problems

Solved Problem 9-1

Convert the following constraints and objective function into the proper form for use in the simplex method:

minimize cost $= 4X_1 + 1X_2$

subject to $3X_1 + X_2 = 3$

$4X_1 + 3X_2 \geqslant 6$

$X_1 + 2X_2 \leqslant 3$

Solution

minimize cost $= 4X_1 + 1X_2 + 0S_1 + 0S_2 + MA_1 + MA_2$

subject to $3X_1 + 1X_2 \qquad\qquad + 1A_1 \qquad = 3$

$4X_1 + 3X_2 - 1S_1 \qquad\qquad + 1A_2 = 6$

$1X_1 + 2X_2 \qquad + 1S_2 \qquad\qquad = 3$

Solved Problem 9-2

Solve the following LP problem:

maximize profit $= \$9X_1 + \$7X_2$

subject to $2X_1 + 1X_2 \leqslant 40$

$X_1 + 3X_2 \leqslant 30$

Solution

We begin by adding slack variables and converting inequalities into equalities.

maximize profit $= 9X_1 + 7X_2 + 0S_1 + 0S_2$

subject to $\qquad 2X_1 + 1X_2 + 1S_1 + 0S_2 = 40$

$\qquad\qquad\qquad 1X_1 + 3X_2 + 0S_1 + 1S_2 = 30$

The initial tableau is then as follows:

C_j →		$9	$7	$0	$0	
↓	**SOLUTION MIX**	X_1	X_2	S_1	S_2	**QUANTITY**
$0	S_1	②	1	1	0	40
$0	S_2	1	3	0	1	30
	Z_j	$0	$0	$0	$0	$0
	$C_j - Z_j$	9	7	0	0	

The correct second tableau and third tableau and some of their calculations appear below. The optimal solutions, given in the third tableau, are $X_1 = 18$, $X_2 = 4$, $S_1 = 0$, $S_2 = 0$, and profit $= \$190$.

Steps 1 and 2 To go from the first to the second tableau, we note that the pivot column (in the first tableau) is X_1, which has the highest $C_j - Z_j$ value, $9. The pivot row is S_1 since 40/2 is less than 30/1, and the pivot number is 2.

Step 3 The new X_1 row is found by dividing each number in the old S_1 row by the pivot number, namely, $2/2 = 1$, $1/2 = 1/2$, $1/2 = 1/2$, $0/2 = 0$, and $40/2 = 20$.

Step 4 The new values for the S_2 row are computed as follows:

$$\begin{pmatrix} \text{number in} \\ \text{new } S_2 \text{ row} \end{pmatrix} = \begin{pmatrix} \text{number in} \\ \text{old } S_2 \text{ row} \end{pmatrix} - \left[\begin{pmatrix} \text{number below} \\ \text{pivot number} \end{pmatrix} \times \begin{pmatrix} \text{corresponding} \\ \text{number in} \\ \text{new } X_1 \text{ row} \end{pmatrix} \right]$$

0	=	1	−	[(1)	×	(1)]
$\frac{5}{2}$	=	3	−	[(1)	×	($\frac{1}{2}$)]
$-\frac{1}{2}$	=	0	−	[(1)	×	($\frac{1}{2}$)]
1	=	1	−	[(1)	×	(0)]
10	=	30	−	[(1)	×	(20)]

Step 5 The following new Z_j and $C_j - Z_j$ rows are formed:

$Z_j(\text{for } X_1) = \$9(1) + 0(0) = \$9 \qquad C_j - Z_j = \$9 - \$9 = 0$

$Z_j(\text{for } X_2) = \$9(\frac{1}{2}) + 0(\frac{5}{2}) = \$\frac{9}{2} \qquad C_j - Z_j = \$7 - \frac{9}{2} = \$\frac{5}{2}$

$Z_j(\text{for } S_1) = \$9(\frac{1}{2}) + 0(-\frac{1}{2}) = \$\frac{9}{2} \qquad C_j - Z_j = 0 - \frac{9}{2} = -\$\frac{9}{2}$

$Z_j(\text{for } S_2) = \$9(0) + 0(1) = \$0 \qquad C_j - Z_j = 0 - 0 = 0$

$Z_j(\text{profit}) = \$9(20) + 0(10) = \$180$

C_j →	SOLUTION MIX	$9 X_1	$7 X_2	$0 S_1	$0 S_2	QUANTITY
$9	X_1	1	½	½	0	20
0	S_2	0	⑤⁄₂	−½	1	10 ← Pivot row
	Z_j	$9	$9/2	$9/2	$0	$180
	$C_j − Z_j$	0	5/2	−9/2	0	

Pivot column

The solution above is not optimal, and you must perform steps 1 to 5 again. The new pivot column is X_2, the new pivot row is S_2, and 5/2 (circled in the second tableau) is the new pivot number.

C_j →	SOLUTION MIX	$9 X_1	$7 X_2	$0 S_1	$0 S_2	QUANTITY
$9	X_1	1	0	⅗	−⅕	18
7	X_2	0	1	−⅕	⅖	4
	Z_j	$9	$7	$4	$1	$190
	$C_j − Z_j$	0	0	−4	−1	

The final solution is $X_1 = 18$, $X_2 = 4$, profit = $190.

Solved Problem 9-3

Solve the following LP problem using Excel and answer the questions regarding a firm that manufactures both lawn mowers and snowblowers:

maximize profit = $30 mowers + $80 blowers

subject to

2 mowers + 4 blowers ≤ 1,000 labor hours available

6 mowers + 2 blowers ≤ 1,200 lb of steel available

1 blower ≤ 200 snowblower engines available

(a) What is the best product mix? What is the optimal profit?

(b) What are the shadow prices? When the optimal solution has been reached, which resource has the highest marginal value?

(c) Over what range in each of the RHS values are these shadows valid?

(d) What are the ranges over which the objective function coefficients can vary for each of the two decision variables?

(e) State the dual to this problem. What is its solution?

Solution

(a) The best product mix is 100 lawn mowers and 200 snowblowers, yielding a profit of $19,000. This is found by formulating the model in Program 9.2A and solving using Excel's Solver in Program 9.2B.

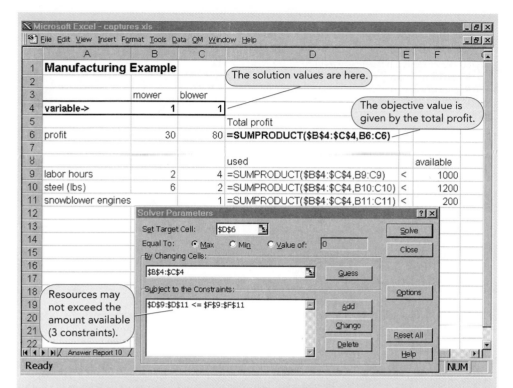

PROGRAM 9.2A

Excel Formulation for Solved Problem 9-3

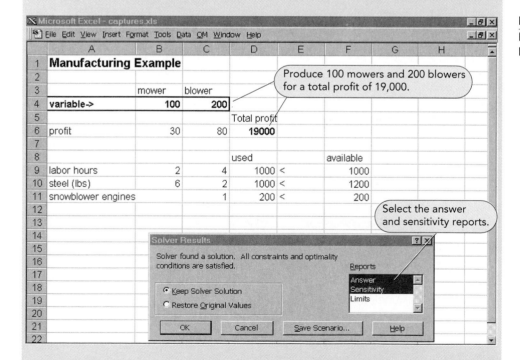

PROGRAM 9.2B

Excel Solution to Solved Problem 9-3

PROGRAM 9.2C

Excel Sensitivity Analysis for
Solved Problem 9-3

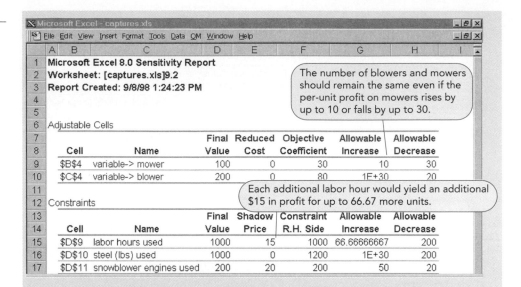

1 **Microsoft Excel 8.0 Sensitivity Report**
2 **Worksheet: [captures.xls]9.2**
3 **Report Created: 9/8/98 1:24:23 PM**

The number of blowers and mowers should remain the same even if the per-unit profit on mowers rises by up to 10 or falls by up to 30.

6 Adjustable Cells

Cell	Name	Final Value	Reduced Cost	Objective Coefficient	Allowable Increase	Allowable Decrease
$B$4	variable-> mower	100	0	30	10	30
$C$4	variable-> blower	200	0	80	1E+30	20

Each additional labor hour would yield an additional $15 in profit for up to 66.67 more units.

12 Constraints

Cell	Name	Final Value	Shadow Price	Constraint R.H. Side	Allowable Increase	Allowable Decrease
$D$9	labor hours used	1000	15	1000	66.66666667	200
$D$10	steel (lbs) used	1000	0	1200	1E+30	200
$D$11	snowblower engines used	200	20	200	50	20

(b) The shadow prices are seen in Program 9.2C. Each constraint has one shadow price associated with it. For labor, the value of one additional hour over the existing 1,000 is $15. There is zero value to an additional pound of steel since the row 3 slack variable currently has a value of 200 pounds. In other words, with 200 unused pounds of steel, there is no point in paying for additional steel. Finally, there is a value of $20 for each additional snowblower engine made available. So snowblower engines have the highest marginal value at the optimal solution.

(c) The shadow price for labor hours is valid from 800 hours to 1,066.66 hours; that is, it can increase by $66\frac{2}{3}$ (or 67) hours or decrease by as much as 200 hours. The shadow price for pounds of steel is valid from 1,000 pounds up to an infinite number of pounds. The shadow price for snowblower engines ranges from 180 engines up to 250 engines.

(d) Without changing the current solution mix, the profit coefficient for the mowers can range from $0 to $40, while the coefficient for the blowers can range from $60 to infinity.

(e) The dual can be written as

$$\text{minimize } 1{,}000\,U_1 + 1{,}200U_2 + 200U_3 \geqslant 30$$

$$\text{subject to} \quad 2U_1 + \quad 6U_2 + \quad 0U_3 \geqslant 30$$

$$4U_1 + \quad 2U_2 + \quad 1U_3 \geqslant 80$$

The solution to the dual will be the shadow prices in the primal. So $U_1 = 15$, $U_2 = 0$, $U_3 = 20$. The dual solution provides the marginal profits of each additional unit of resource.

SELF-TEST

- Before taking the self-test, refer back to the learning objectives at the beginning of the chapter, the notes in the margins, and the glossary at the end of the chapter.
- Use the key at the back of the book to correct your answers.
- Restudy pages that correspond to any questions that you answered incorrectly or material you feel uncertain about.

1. A basic feasible solution is a solution to an LP problem that corresponds to a corner point of the feasible region.
   a. True   b. False
2. A surplus variable is added to a less-than-or-equal-to constraint to create an equality and represents a quantity of unused resource.
   a. True   b. False
3. If all of a resource represented by a slack variable is used, that slack variable will not be in the solution mix column of an LP simplex tableau.
   a. True   b. False
4. Even if an LP problem involves many variables, an optimal solution will always be found at a corner point of the n-dimensional polyhedron forming the feasible region.
   a. True   b. False
5. Surplus variables, unlike slack variables, don't carry a zero cost.
   a. True   b. False
6. To formulate a problem for solution by the simplex method, we must add slack variables to
   a. all inequality constraints.
   b. only equality constraints.
   c. only "greater than" constraints.
   d. only "less than" constraints.
7. If in the optimal tableau of an LP problem an artificial variable is present in the solution mix, this implies
   a. infeasibility.   b. unboundedness.
   c. degeneracy.   d. alternate optimal solutions.
8. If in the final optimal simplex tableau the $C_j - Z_j$ value for a basic variable is zero, this implies
   a. feasibility.   b. unboundedness.
   c. degeneracy.   d. alternate optimal solutions.
9. One thing not true about the initial solution of the simplex method is that
   a. it is a feasible solution.
   b. it represents the situation at the origin.
   c. the real variables are equal to zero.
   d. it rarely produces a profit of zero.
10. A *shadow price* is
    a. the price we must pay for the resource on the black market.

b. the amount we could save by eliminating one unit of resource that we have in excess.
    c. the amount we could earn by providing one more unit of a scarce resource.
    d. the increase in profit if we were to produce one additional unit of each product considered in a problem.
11. A change in the objective function coefficient of a basic variable can affect the $C_j - Z_j$ values of all nonbasic variables.
    a. True   b. False
12. Linear programming has few applications in the real world due to the assumption of certainty in the data and relationships of a problem.
    a. True   b. False
13. The analytic postoptimality method attempts to determine a range of changes in problem parameters that will not affect the optimal solution or change the variables in the basis.
    a. True   b. False
14. For every LP solution, every nonbasic variable has a zero value.
    a. True   b. False
15. Sensitivity analysis on objective function coefficients of variables that are nonbasic to the solution mix are slightly more complex than those of variables that are in the basis or solution mix.
    a. True   b. False
16. The solution to the dual LP problem
    a. presents the marginal profits of each additional unit of resource.
    b. can always be derived by examining the Z_j row of the primal's optimal simplex tableau.
    c. is better than the solution to the primal.
    d. all of the above.
17. The following is not true about slack variables in a simplex tableau:
    a. They are used to convert less-than-or-equal-to constraint inequations to equations.
    b. They represent unused resources.
    c. They require the addition of an artificial variable.
    d. They may represent machine time, labor hours, or warehouse space.
    e. They yield no product.

Discussion Questions and Problems

Discussion Questions

9-1 Explain the purpose and procedures of the simplex method.

9-2 How do the graphical and simplex methods of solving LP problems differ? In what ways are they the same? Under what circumstances would you prefer to use the graphical approach?

9-3 What are slack, surplus, and artificial variables? When is each used, and why? What value does each carry in the objective function?

9-4 You have just formulated an LP problem with 12 decision variables and eight constraints. How many basic variables will there always be? What is the difference between a basic and a nonbasic variable?

9-5 What are the simplex rules for selecting the pivot column? The pivot row? The pivot number?

9-6 How do maximization and minimization problems differ when applying the simplex method?

9-7 What is the reason behind the use of the minimum ratio test in selecting the pivot row? What might happen without it?

9-8 A particular LP problem has the following objective function:

$$\text{maximize profit} = \$8X_1 + \$6X_2 + \$12X_3 - \$2X_4$$

Which variable should enter at the second simplex tableau? If the objective function was

$$\text{minimize cost} = \$2.5X_1 + \$2.9X_2 + \$4.0X_3 + \$7.9X_4$$

which variable would be the best candidate to enter the second tableau?

9-9 What happens if an artificial variable is in the final optimal solution? What should the manager who formulated the LP problem do?

9-10 The great Romanian operations researcher, Dr. Ima Student, proposes that instead of selecting the variable with the largest positive $C_j - Z_j$ value (in a maximization LP problem) to enter the solution mix next, a different approach be used. She suggests that any variable with a positive $C_j - Z_j$ can be chosen, even if it isn't the largest. What will happen if we adopt this new rule for the simplex procedure? Will an optimal solution still be reached?

9-11 What is a shadow price? How does the concept relate to the dual of an LP problem? How does it relate to the primal?

9-12 If a primal problem has 12 constraints and eight variables, how many constraints and variables will its corresponding dual have?

9-13 Explain the relationship between each number in a primal and corresponding numbers in the dual.

9-14 Create your own original LP maximization problem with two variables and three less-than-or-equal-to constraints. Now form the dual for this primal problem.

Problems*

• **9-15** The Dreskin Development Company is building two apartment complexes. It must decide how many units to construct in each complex subject to labor and material con-

---

*Note: ⌨ₐ means the problem may be solved with QM for Windows; ✖ means the problem may be solved with Excel QM; and 🖥ₐ means the problem may be solved with QM for Windows and/or Excel QM.

straints. The profit generated for each apartment in the first complex is estimated at $900, for each apartment in the second complex, $1,500. A partial initial simplex tableau for Dreskin is given in the following table:

C_j		$900	$1,500	$0	$0	
	SOLUTION MIX	X_1	X_2	S_1	S_2	QUANTITY
		14	4	1	0	3,360
		10	12	0	1	9,600
Z_j						
$C_j - Z_j$						

(a) Complete the initial tableau.
(b) Reconstruct the problem's original constraints (excluding slack variables).
(c) Write the problem's original objective function.
(d) What is the basis for the initial solution?
(e) Which variable should enter the solution at the next iteration?
(f) Which variable will leave the solution at the next iteration?
(g) How many units of the variable entering the solution next will be in the basis in the second tableau?

9-16 Consider the following LP problem:

$$\text{maximize earnings} = \$0.80X_1 + \$0.40X_2 + \$1.20X_3 - \$0.10X_4$$

$$\text{subject to} \quad X_1 + 2X_2 + X_3 + 5X_4 \leqslant 150$$

$$X_2 - 4X_3 + 8X_4 = 70$$

$$6X_1 + 7X_2 + 2X_3 - X_4 \geqslant 120$$

$$X_1, X_2, X_3, X_4 \geqslant 0$$

(a) Convert these constraints to equalities by adding the appropriate slack, surplus, or artificial variables. Also, add the new variables into the problem's objective function.
(b) Set up the complete initial simplex tableau for this problem. Do not attempt to solve.

9-17 Solve the following LP problem graphically. Then set up a simplex tableau and solve the problem using the simplex method. Indicate the corner points generated at each iteration by the simplex method on your graph.

$$\text{maximize profit} = \$3X_1 + \$5X_2$$

$$\text{subject to} \quad X_2 \leqslant 6$$

$$3X_1 + 2X_2 \leqslant 18$$

$$X_1, X_2 \geqslant 0$$

9-18 Convert the following LP problem into the proper simplex form and solve by applying the simplex algorithm:

$$\text{maximize profit} = 20X_1 + 10X_2$$

$$\text{subject to} \quad 5X_1 + 4X_2 \leqslant 250$$

$$2X_1 + 5X_2 \leqslant 150$$

$$X_1, X_2 \geqslant 0$$

Also solve the problem graphically and compare your answers.

9-19 Solve the following LP problem first graphically and then by the simplex algorithm:

$$\text{minimize cost} = 4X_1 + 5X_2$$

$$\text{subject to} \quad X_1 + 2X_2 \geq 80$$

$$3X_1 + X_2 \geq 75$$

$$X_1, X_2 \geq 0$$

What are the values of the basic variables at each iteration? Which are the nonbasic variables at each iteration?

• **9-20** The final simplex tableau for an LP maximization problem is shown in the following table:

C_j 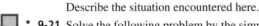	SOLUTION MIX	3 X_1	5 X_2	0 S_1	0 S_2	$-M$ A_1	QUANTITY
$5	X_2	1	1	2	0	0	6
$-M$	A_1	-1	0	-2	-1	1	2
	Z_j	$5 + M$	$5	$10 + 2M$	M	$-$M$	$30 - 2M$
	$C_j - Z_j$	$-2 - M$	0	$-10 - 2M$	$-M$	0	

Describe the situation encountered here.

 9-21 Solve the following problem by the simplex method. What condition exists that prevents you from reaching an optimal solution?

$$\text{maximize profit} = 6X_1 + 3X_2$$

$$\text{subject to} \quad 2X_1 - 2X_2 \leq 2$$

$$-X_1 + X_2 \leq 1$$

$$X_1 + X_2 \geq 0$$

 9-22 Consider the following financial problem:

$$\text{maximize return on investment} = \$2X_1 + \$3X_2$$

$$\text{subject to} \quad 6X_1 + 9X_2 \leq 18$$

$$9X_1 + 3X_2 \geq 9$$

$$X_1, X_2 \geq 0$$

(a) Find the optimal solution using the simplex method.
(b) What evidence indicates that an alternate optimal solution exists?
(c) Find the alternate optimal solution.
(d) Solve this problem graphically as well, and illustrate the alternate optimal corner points.

⋮ **9-23** At the third iteration of a particular LP maximization problem, the following tableau is established:

C_j	SOLUTION MIX	$6 X_1	$3 X_2	$5 X_3	0 S_1	0 S_2	0 S_3	QUANTITY
$5	X_3	0	1	1	1	0	3	5
$6	X_1	1	-3	0	0	0	1	12
$0	S_2	0	2	0	1	1	-1	10
	Z_j	$6	$-$13$	$5	$5	$0	$21	$97
	$C_j - Z_j$	$0	$16	$0	$-$5$	$0	$-$21$	

What special condition exists as you improve the profit and move to the next iteration? Proceed to solve the problem for the optimal solution.

 9-24 A pharmaceutical firm is about to begin production of three new drugs. An objective function designed to minimize ingredient costs and three production constraints are as follows:

$$\text{minimize cost} = 50X_1 + 10X_2 + 75X_3$$

$$\text{subject to} \quad X_1 - X_2 \qquad\qquad = 1{,}000$$

$$2X_2 + 2X_3 = 2{,}000$$

$$X_1 \qquad\qquad\qquad \leq 1{,}500$$

$$X_1, X_2, X_3 \geq 0$$

(a) Convert these constraints and objective function to the proper form for use in the simplex tableau.

(b) Solve the problem by the simplex method. What is the optimal solution and cost?

 9-25 The Bitz-Karan Corporation faces a blending decision in developing a new cat food called Yum-Mix. Two basic ingredients have been combined and tested, and the firm has determined that to each can of Yum-Mix at least 30 units of protein and at least 80 units of riboflavin must be added. These two nutrients are available in two competing brands of animal food supplements. The cost per kilogram of the brand A supplement is $9, and the cost per kilogram of brand B supplement is $15. A kilogram of brand A added to each production batch of Yum-Mix provides a supplement of 1 unit of protein and 1 unit of riboflavin to each can. A kilogram of brand B provides 2 units of protein and 4 units of riboflavin in each can. Bitz-Karan must satisfy these minimum nutrient standards while keeping costs of supplements to a minimum.

(a) Formulate this problem to find the best combination of the two supplements to meet the minimum requirements at the least cost.

(b) Solve for the optimal solution by the simplex method.

 9-26 The Roniger Company produces two products: bed mattresses and box springs. A prior contract requires that the firm produce at least 30 mattresses or box springs, in any combination. In addition, union labor agreements demand that stitching machines be kept running at least 40 hours per week, which is one production period. Each box spring takes 2 hours of stitching time, while each mattress takes 1 hour on the machine. Each mattress produced costs $20, each box spring costs $24.

(a) Formulate this problem so as to minimize total production costs.

(b) Solve using the simplex method.

 9-27 Each coffee table produced by Meising Designers nets the firm a profit of $9. Each bookcase yields a $12 profit. Meising's firm is small, and its resources are limited. During any given production period of one week, 10 gallons of varnish and 12 lengths of high-quality redwood are available. Each coffee table requires approximately 1 gallon of varnish and 1 length of redwood. Each bookcase takes 1 gallon of varnish and 2 lengths of wood. Formulate Meising's production mix decision as an LP problem, and solve using the simplex method. How many tables and bookcases should be produced each week? What will the maximum profit be?

 9-28 Bagwell Distributors packages and distributes industrial supplies. A standard shipment can be packaged in a class A container, a class K container, or a class T container. A single class A container yields a profit of $8; a class K container, a profit of $6; and a class T container, a profit of $14. Each shipment prepared requires a certain amount of packing material and a certain amount of time, as seen in the following table:

CLASS OF CONTAINER	PACKING MATERIAL (POUNDS)	PACKING TIME (HOURS)
A	2	2
K	1	6
T	3	4
Total amount of resource available each week	120 pounds	240 hours

Bill Bagwell, head of the firm, must decide the optimal number of each class of container to pack each week. He is bound by the previously mentioned resource restrictions, but he also decides that he must keep his six full-time packers employed all 240 hours (6 workers, 40 hours) each week. Formulate and solve this problem using the simplex method.

9-29 The Foggy Bottom Development Corporation has just purchased a small hotel for conversion to condominium apartments. The building, in a popular area of Washington, D.C., near the U.S. State Department, will be highly marketable, and each condominium sale is expected to yield a good profit. The conversion process, however, includes several options. Basically, four types of condominiums can be designed out of the former hotel rooms. They are deluxe one-bedroom apartments, regular one-bedroom apartments, deluxe studios, and efficiency apartments. Each will yield a different profit, but each type also requires a different level of investment in carpeting, painting, appliances, and carpentry work. Bank loans dictate a limited budget that may be allocated to each of these needs. Profit and cost data, and cost of conversion requirements, for each apartment are shown in the accompanying table.

	TYPE OF APARTMENT				
RENOVATION REQUIREMENT	DELUXE ONE-BEDROOM ($)	REGULAR ONE-BEDROOM ($)	DELUXE STUDIO ($)	EFFICIENCY ($)	TOTAL BUDGETED ($)
New carpeting	1,100	1,000	600	500	35,000
Painting	700	600	400	300	28,000
New appliances	2,000	1,600	1,200	900	45,000
Carpentry work	1,000	400	900	200	19,000
Profit per unit	8,000	6,000	5,000	3,500	

Thus, we see that the cost of carpeting a deluxe one-bedroom unit will be $1,100, the cost of carpeting a regular one-bedroom unit is $1,000, and so on. A total of $35,000 is budgeted for all new carpeting in the building.

Zoning regulations dictate that the building contain no more than 50 condominiums when the conversion is completed—and no less than 25 units. The development company also decides that to have a good blend of owners, at least 40% but no more than 70% of the units should be one-bedroom apartments. Not all money budgeted in each category need be spent, although profit is not affected by cost savings. But since the money represents a bank loan, under no circumstances may it be exceeded or even shifted from one area, such as carpeting, to another, such as painting.

(a) Formulate Foggy Bottom Development Corporation's decision as a linear program to maximize profits.

(b) Convert your objective function and constraints to a form containing the appropriate slack, surplus, and artificial variables.

9-30 The accompanying initial simplex tableau (see page 397) was developed by Tommy Gibbs, vice president of a large cotton spinning mill. Unfortunately, Gibbs quit before

Simplex Tableau for Problem 9-30

C_j	SOLUTION MIX	$12 X_1	$18 X_2	$10 X_3	$20 X_4	$7 X_5	$8 X_6	$0 S_1	$0 S_2	$0 S_3	$0 S_4	$0 S_5	M A_1	M A_2	M A_3	M A_4	QUANTITY
$M	A_1	1	0	−3	0	0	0	0	0	0	0	0	1	0	0	0	100
0	S_1	0	25	1	2	8	0	1	0	0	0	0	0	0	0	0	900
M	A_2	2	1	0	4	0	1	0	−1	0	0	0	0	1	0	0	250
M	A_3	18	−15	−2	−1	15	0	0	0	−1	0	0	0	0	1	0	150
0	S_4	0	0	0	0	0	25	0	0	0	1	0	0	0	0	0	300
M	A_4	0	0	0	2	6	0	0	0	0	0	−1	0	0	0	1	70
	Z_j	$21M	−$14M	−$5M	$5M	$21M	$M	$0	$0	−$M	$0	−$M	$M	$M	$M	$M	$570M
	$C_j − Z_j$	12 − 21M	18 + 14M	10 + 5M	20 − 5M	7 − 21M	8 − M	0	0	M	0	M	0	0	0	0	0

completing this important LP application. Stephanie Robbins, the newly hired replacement, was immediately given this task of using LP to determine what different kinds of yarn the mill should use to minimize costs. Her first need was to be certain that Gibbs correctly formulated the objective function and constraints. She could find no statement of the problem in the files, so she decided to reconstruct the problem from the initial tableau.

(a) What is the correct formulation, using real decision variables (that is, X_is) only?

(b) Which variable will enter this current solution mix in the second tableau? Which basic variable will leave?

9-31 Consider the following optimal tableau, where S_1 and S_2 are slack variables added to the original problem:

C_j		$10	$30	$0	$0	
	SOLUTION MIX	X_1	X_2	S_1	S_2	QUANTITY
$10	X_1	1	4	2	0	160
$0	S_2	0	6	−7	1	200
	Z_j	$10	$40	$20	$0	$1,600
	$C_j - Z_j$	0	−10	−20	0	

(a) What is the range of optimality for the contribution rate of the variable X_1?

(b) What is the range of insignificance of the contribution rate of the variable X_2?

(c) How much would you be willing to pay for one more unit of the first resource, which is represented by slack variable S_1?

(d) What is the value of one more unit of the second resource? Why?

9-32 The following is the final simplex tableau of an LP problem that has three constraints and four variables:

C_j		$4	$6	$3	$1	$0	$0	$0	
	SOLUTION MIX	X_1	X_2	X_3	X_4	S_1	S_2	X_3	QUANTITY
$3	X_3	$\frac{1}{20}$	0	1	$\frac{1}{2}$	$\frac{3}{10}$	0	$-\frac{1}{5}$	125
0	S_2	$\frac{39}{12}$	0	0	$-\frac{1}{2}$	$-\frac{1}{2}$	1	0	425
6	X_2	$\frac{39}{60}$	1	0	$\frac{1}{2}$	$-\frac{1}{10}$	0	$\frac{3}{5}$	25
	Z_j	$\$8\frac{1}{20}$	$6	$3	$\$\frac{9}{2}$	$\$\frac{3}{10}$	$0	$3	$525
	$C_j - Z_j$	$-\frac{1}{20}$	0	0	$-\frac{7}{2}$	$-\frac{3}{10}$	0	−3	

What are the values of each of the shadow prices? What meaning does a zero shadow price have, and how can it occur?

9-33 Clapper Electronics produces two models of telephone-answering devices, model 102 (X_1) and model H23 (X_2). Jim Clapper, vice president for production, formulates their constraints as follows:

$$2X_1 + 1X_2 \leq 40 \text{ (hours of time available on soldering machine)}$$

$$1X_1 + 3X_2 \leq 30 \text{ (hours of time available in inspection department)}$$

Clapper's objective function is

$$\text{maximize profit} = \$9X_1 + \$7X_2$$

Solving the problem using the simplex method, he produces the following final tableau:

C_j	SOLUTION MIX	$9 X_1	$7 X_2	$0 S_1	$0 S_2	QUANTITY
$9	X_1	1	0	⅗	−⅕	18
7	X_2	0	1	−⅕	⅖	4
	Z_j	$9	$7	$4	$1	$190
	$C_j - Z_j$	0	0	−4	−1	

(a) What is the optimal mix of models 102 and H23 to produce?
(b) What do variables S_1 and S_2 represent?
(c) Clapper is considering renting a second soldering machine at a cost to the firm of $2.50 per hour. Should he do so?
(d) Clapper computes that he can hire a part-time inspector for only $1.75 per hour. Should he do so?

9-34 Refer to Table 9.6, which is the optimal tableau for the Flair Furniture Company problem.
(a) What are the values of the shadow prices?
(b) Interpret the physical meaning of each shadow price in the context of the furniture problem.
(c) What is the range over which the profit per table can vary without changing the optimal basis (solution mix)?
(d) What is the range of optimality for X_2 (number of chairs produced)?
(e) How many hours can Flair Furniture add to or remove from the first resource (painting department time) without changing the basis?
(f) Conduct right-hand-side ranging on the carpentry department resource to determine the range over which the shadow price remains valid.

9-35 Consider the optimal solution to the Muddy River Chemical Corporation problem in Table 9.10.
(a) For each of the two chemical ingredients, phosphate and potassium, determine the range over which their cost may vary without affecting the basis.
(b) If the original constraint that "no more than 300 pounds of phosphate can be used" ($X_1 \leq 300$) were changed to $X_1 \leq 400$, would the basis change? Would the values of X_1, X_2, and S_2 change?

• **9-36** Formulate the dual of this LP problem.

$$\text{maximize profit} = 80X_1 + 75X_2$$

$$1X_1 + 3X_2 \leq 4$$

$$2X_1 + 5X_2 \leq 8$$

Find the dual of the problem's dual.

• **9-37** What is the dual of the following LP problem?

$$\text{Primal: minimize cost} = 120X_1 + 250X_2$$

$$\text{subject to} \quad 12X_1 + 20X_2 \geq 50$$

$$X_1 + 3X_2 \geq 4$$

• **9-38** The third, and final, simplex tableau for the LP problem stated here follows:

$$\text{maximize profit} = 200X_1 + 200X_2$$

$$\text{subject to} \quad 2X_1 + X_2 \leq 8$$

$$X_1 + 3X_2 \leq 9$$

What are the solutions to the dual variables, U_1 and U_2? What is the optimal dual cost?

C_j	SOLUTION MIX	$200 X_1	$200 X_2	$0 S_1	$0 S_2	QUANTITY
$200	X_1	1	0	$\frac{3}{5}$	$-\frac{1}{5}$	3
200	X_2	0	1	$-\frac{1}{5}$	$\frac{2}{5}$	2
	Z_j	$200	$200	$80	$40	$1,000
	$C_j - Z_j$	0	0	-80	-40	

- **9-39** The accompanying tableau provides the optimal solution to this dual:

$$\text{minimize cost} = 120U_1 + 240U_2$$

$$\text{subject to} \quad 2U_1 + 2U_2 \geq 0.5$$

$$U_1 + 3U_2 \geq 0.4$$

C_j	SOLUTION MIX	120 U_1	240 U_2	0 S_1	0 S_2	M A_1	M A_2	QUANTITY
$120	U_1	1	0	$-\frac{3}{4}$	$\frac{1}{2}$	$\frac{3}{4}$	$-\frac{1}{2}$	0.175
240	U_2	0	1	$\frac{1}{4}$	$-\frac{1}{2}$	$-\frac{1}{4}$	$\frac{1}{2}$	0.075
	Z_j	$120	$240	$-$30	$-$60	$30	$60	$39
	$C_j - Z_j$	0	0	30	60	$M - 30$	$M - 60$	

What does the corresponding primal problem look like, and what is its optimal solution?

- **9-40** Given the following dual formulation, reconstruct the original primal problem:

$$\text{minimize cost} = 28U_1 + 53U_2 + 70U_3 + 18U_4$$

$$\text{subject to} \quad U_1 + U_4 \geq 10$$

$$U_1 + 2U_2 + U_3 \geq 5$$

$$- 2U_2 + 5U_4 \geq 31$$

$$5U_3 \geq 28$$

$$12U_1 + 2U_3 - U_4 \geq 17$$

$$U_1, U_2, U_3, U_4 \geq 0$$

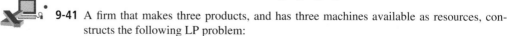

- **9-41** A firm that makes three products, and has three machines available as resources, constructs the following LP problem:

$$\text{maximize profit} = 4X_1 + 4X_2 + 7X_3$$

$$\text{subject to} \quad 1X_1 + 7X_2 + 4X_3 \leq 100 \text{ (hours on machine 1)}$$

$$2X_1 + 1X_2 + 7X_3 \leq 110 \text{ (hours on machine 2)}$$

$$8X_1 + 4X_2 + 1X_3 \leq 100 \text{ (hours on machine 3)}$$

Solve this problem by computer and answer these questions:

(a) Before the third iteration of the simplex method, which machine still has unused time available?

(b) When the final solution is reached, is there any unused time available on any of the three machines?

(c) What would it be worth to the firm to make an additional hour of time available on the third machine?

(d) How much would the firm's profit increase if an extra 10 hours of time were made available on the second machine at no extra cost?

9-42 Management analysts at a Fresno laboratory have developed the following LP primal problem:

$$\text{minimize cost} = 23X_1 + 18X_2$$

$$\text{subject to} \quad 8X_1 + 4X_2 \geq 120$$

$$4X_1 + 6X_2 \geq 115$$

$$9X_1 + 4X_2 \geq 116$$

This model represents a decision concerning number of hours spent by biochemists on certain laboratory experiments (X_1) and number of hours spent by biophysicists on the same series of experiments (X_2). A biochemist costs \$23 per hour, while a biophysicist's salary averages \$18 per hour. Both types of scientists can be used on three needed laboratory operations: test 1, test 2, and test 3. The experiments and their times are as follows:

LAB EXPERIMENT	SCIENTIST TYPE		MINIMUM TEST TIME NEEDED PER DAY
	BIOPHYSICIST	BIOCHEMIST	
Test 1	8	4	120
Test 2	4	6	115
Test 3	9	4	116

This means that a biophysicist can complete 8, 4, and 9 of tests 1, 2, and 3 per hour. Similarly, a biochemist can perform 4 of test 1, 6 of test 2, and 4 of test 3 per hour. The optimal solution to the lab's primal problem is:

$$X_1 = 8.12 \text{ hours and } X_2 = 13.75 \text{ hours}$$

$$\text{total cost} = \$434.37 \text{ per day}$$

The optimal solution to the dual problem is

$$U_1 = 2.07, U_2 = 1.63, U_3 = 0$$

(a) What is the dual of the primal LP problem?

(b) Interpret the meaning of the dual and its solution.

9-43 The Flair Furniture Company first described in Chapter 7, and again in this chapter, manufactures inexpensive tables (X_1) and chairs (X_2). The firm's daily LP formulation is given as

$$\text{maximize profits} = \$7X_1 + 5X_2$$

$$\text{subject to} \quad 4X_1 + 3X_2 \leq 240 \text{ hours of carpentry time available}$$

$$2X_1 + 1X_2 \leq 100 \text{ hours of painting time available}$$

In addition, Flair finds that three more constraints are in order. First, each table and chair must be inspected and may need rework. The following constraint describes the time required on the average for each:

$$\tfrac{1}{2}X_1 + \tfrac{3}{5}X_2 \leq 36 \text{ hours of inspection/rework time available}$$

Second, Flair faces a resource constraint relating to the lumber needed for each table or chair and the amount available each day:

$32X_1 + 10X_2 \leq 1{,}248$ linear feet of lumber available for production

Finally, the demand for tables is found to be a maximum of 40 daily. There are no similar constraints regarding chairs.

$X_1 \leq 40$ maximum table production daily

These data have been entered in the QM for Windows software that is available with this book. The inputs and results are shown in the accompanying printout. Refer to the computer output in Programs 9.3, 9.4, and 9.5 in answering these questions.

(a) How many tables and chairs should Flair Furniture produce daily? What is the profit generated by this solution?

(b) Will Flair use all of its resources to their limits each day? Be specific in explaining your answer.

PROGRAM 9.3

QM for Windows Input Data for Flair Furniture's Revised Problem for Problem 9-43

QM for Windows - C:\Prentice\Data\RenderStair7\Flair.revised.lin

Objective
● Maximize
○ Minimize

	X1	X2		RHS
Maximize	7	5		
Carpentry hours	4	3	<=	240
Painting hours	2	1	<=	100
Inspection hours	0.5	0.6	<=	36
Lumber (linear ft)	32	10	<=	1248
Demand	1	0	<=	40

PROGRAM 9.4

Solution Results for Flair Furniture's Problem 9-43

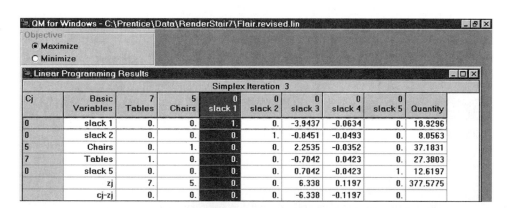

QM for Windows - C:\Prentice\Data\RenderStair7\Flair.revised.lin

Objective
● Maximize
○ Minimize

Linear Programming Results

Simplex Iteration 3

Cj	Basic Variables	7 Tables	5 Chairs	0 slack 1	0 slack 2	0 slack 3	0 slack 4	0 slack 5	Quantity
0	slack 1	0.	0.	1.	0.	-3.9437	-0.0634	0.	18.9296
0	slack 2	0.	0.	0.	1.	-0.8451	-0.0493	0.	8.0563
5	Chairs	0.	1.	0.	0.	2.2535	-0.0352	0.	37.1831
7	Tables	1.	0.	0.	0.	-0.7042	0.0423	0.	27.3803
0	slack 5	0.	0.	0.	0.	0.7042	-0.0423	1.	12.6197
	zj	7.	5.	0.	0.	6.338	0.1197	0.	377.5775
	cj-zj	0.	0.	0.	0.	-6.338	-0.1197	0.	

PROGRAM 9.5

Sensitivity Analysis for Problem 9-43

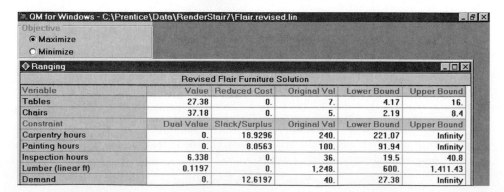

QM for Windows - C:\Prentice\Data\RenderStair7\Flair.revised.lin

Objective
● Maximize
○ Minimize

Ranging

Revised Flair Furniture Solution

Variable	Value	Reduced Cost	Original Val	Lower Bound	Upper Bound
Tables	27.38	0.	7.	4.17	16.
Chairs	37.18	0.	5.	2.19	8.4
Constraint	Dual Value	Slack/Surplus	Original Val	Lower Bound	Upper Bound
Carpentry hours	0.	18.9296	240.	221.07	Infinity
Painting hours	0.	8.0563	100.	91.94	Infinity
Inspection hours	6.338	0.	36.	19.5	40.8
Lumber (linear ft)	0.1197	0.	1,248.	600.	1,411.43
Demand	0.	12.6197	40.	27.38	Infinity

(c) Explain the physical meaning of each shadow price.
(d) Should Flair purchase more lumber if it is available at $0.07 per linear foot? Should it hire more carpenters at $12.75 per hour?
(e) Flair's owner has been approached by a friend whose company would like to use several hours in the painting facility every day. Should Flair sell time to the other firm? If so, how much? Explain.
(f) What is the range within which the carpentry hours, painting hours, and inspection/rework hours can fluctuate before the optimal solution changes?
(g) Within what range for the current solution can the profit contribution of tables and chairs change?

Data Set Problem

9-44 A Chicago manufacturer of office equipment is desperately attempting to control its profit and loss statement. The company currently manufactures 15 different products, each coded with a one-letter and three-digit designation.
(a) How many of each of the 15 products should be produced each month?
(b) Clearly explain the meaning of each shadow price.
(c) A number of workers interested in saving money for the holidays have offered to work overtime next month at a rate of $12.50 per hour. What should the response of management be?
(d) Two tons of steel alloy are available from an overstocked supplier at a total cost of $8,000. Should the steel be purchased? All or part of the supply?

PRODUCT	STEEL ALLOY REQUIRED (LB)	PLASTIC REQUIRED (SQ FT)	WOOD REQUIRED (BD FT)	ALUMINUM REQUIRED (LB)	FORMICA REQUIRED (BD FT)	LABOR REQUIRED (HOURS)	MINIMUM MONTHLY DEMAND (UNITS)	CONTRIBUTION TO PROFIT
A158	—	0.4	0.7	5.8	10.9	3.1	—	$18.79
B179	4	0.5	1.8	10.3	2.0	1.0	20	6.31
C023	6	—	1.5	1.1	2.3	1.2	10	8.19
D045	10	0.4	2.0	—	—	4.8	10	45.88
E388	12	1.2	1.2	8.1	4.9	5.5	—	63.00
F422	—	1.4	1.5	7.1	10.0	0.8	20	4.10
G366	10	1.4	7.0	6.2	11.1	9.1	10	81.15
H600	5	1.0	5.0	7.3	12.4	4.8	20	50.06
I701	1	0.4	—	10.0	5.2	1.9	50	12.79
J802	1	0.3	—	11.0	6.1	1.4	20	15.88
K900	—	0.2	—	12.5	7.7	1.0	20	17.91
L901	2	1.8	1.5	13.1	5.0	5.1	10	49.99
M050	—	2.7	5.0	—	2.1	3.1	20	24.00
N150	10	1.1	5.8	—	—	7.7	10	88.88
P259	10	—	6.2	15.0	1.0	6.6	10	77.01
Availability per month	980	400	600	2,500	1,800	1,000		

(e) The accountants have just discovered that an error was made in the contribution to profit for product N150. The correct value is actually $8.88. What are the implications of this error?

(f) Management is considering the abandonment of five product lines (those beginning with the letters A through E). If no minimum monthly demand is established, what are the implications? Note that there already is no minimum for two of these products. Use the corrected value for N150.

Case Study

Coastal States Chemicals and Fertilizers

In December 1999, Bill Stock, general manager for the Louisiana Division of Coastal States Chemicals and Fertilizers, received a letter from Fred McNair of the Cajan Pipeline Company which notified Coastal States that priorities had been established for the allocation of natural gas. The letter stated that Cajan Pipeline, the primary supplier of natural gas to Coastal States, might be instructed to curtail natural gas supplies to its industrial and commercial customers by as much as 40% during the ensuing winter months. Moreover, Cajan Pipeline had the approval of the Federal Power Commission (FPC) to curtail such supplies.

Possible curtailment was attributed to the priorities established for the use of natural gas:

First priority:	residential and commercial heating
Second priority:	commercial and industrial users whereby natural gas is used as a source of raw material
Third priority:	commercial and industrial users whereby natural gas is used as boiler fuel

Almost all of Coastal State's uses of natural gas were in the second and third priorities. Hence, its plants were certainly subject to brown-outs, or natural gas curtailments. The occurrence and severity of the brown-outs depended on a number of complex factors. First, Cajan Pipeline was part of an interstate transmission network that delivered natural gas to residential and commercial buildings on the Atlantic coast and in northeastern regions of the United States. Hence, the severity of the forthcoming winter in these regions would have a direct impact on the use of natural gas.

Second, the demand for natural gas was soaring because it was the cleanest and most efficient fuel. There were almost no environmental problems in burning natural gas. Moreover, maintenance problems due to fuel-fouling in fireboxes and boilers were negligible with natural gas systems. Also, burners were much easier to operate with natural gas than with oil or coal.

Finally, the supply of natural gas was dwindling. The traditionally depressed price of natural gas had discouraged new exploration for gas wells; hence, shortages appeared imminent.

Stock and his staff at Coastal States had been aware of the possibility of shortages of natural gas and had been investigating ways of converting to fuel oil or coal as a substitute for natural gas. Their plans, however, were still in the developmental stages. Coastal States required an immediate contingency plan to minimize the effect of a natural gas curtailment on its multiplant operations. The obvious question was, what operations should be curtailed, and to what extent could the adverse effect upon profits be minimized? Coastal States had approval from the FPC and Cajan Pipeline to specify which of its plants would bear the burden of the curtailment if such cutbacks were necessary. McNair, of Cajan Pipeline, replied, "It's your 'pie': we don't care how you divide it if we make it smaller."

The Model

Six plants of Coastal States Louisiana Division were to share in the "pie." They were all located in the massive Baton Rouge—Geismar—Gramercy industrial complex along the Mississippi River between Baton Rouge and New Orleans. Products produced at those plants which required significant amounts of natural gas were phosphoric acid, urea, ammonium phosphate, ammonium nitrate, chlorine, caustic soda, vinyl chloride monomer, and hydrofluoric acid.

Stock called a meeting of members of his technical staff to discuss a contingency plan for allocation of natural gas among the products if a curtailment developed. The objective was to minimize the impact on profits. After detailed discussion, the meeting was adjourned. Two weeks later, the meeting reconvened. At this session, the data in Table 9.19 were presented.

Coastal State's contract with Cajan Pipeline specified a maximum natural gas consumption of 36,000 cu ft $\times$ 10^3 per day for all six member plants. With these data, the technical staff proceeded to develop a model that would specify changes in production rates in response to a natural gas curtailment. (Curtailments are based on contracted consumption and not current consumption.)

TABLE 9.19 Contribution to Profit and Overhead

PRODUCT	CONTRIBUTION PER TON ($)	CAPACITY (TONS PER DAY)	MAXIMUM PRODUCTION RATE (PERCENT OF CAPACITY)	NATURAL GAS CONSUMPTION (1,000 CU FT PER TON)
Phosphoric acid	60	400	80	5.5
Urea	80	250	80	7 0
Ammonium phosphate	90	300	90	8.0
Ammonium nitrate	100	300	100	10.0
Chlorine	50	800	60	15.0
Caustic soda	50	1,000	60	16.0
Vinyl chloride monomer	65	500	60	12.0
Hydrofluoric acid	70	400	80	11.0

Discussion Questions

1. Develop a contingency model and specify the production rates for each product for
   a. a 20% natural gas curtailment.
   b. a 40% natural gas curtailment.
2. Explain which of the products in the table should require the most emphasis with regard to energy conservation.
3. What problems do you foresee if production rates are not reduced in a planned and orderly manner?
4. What impact will the natural gas shortage have on company profits?

Source: Professor Jerry Kinard, Western Carolina University.

Bibliography

See the Bibliography at the end of Chapter 7.

Transportation and Assignment Models

After completing this chapter, students will be able to:

1. Structure special LP problems using the transportation and assignment models.
2. Use the N.W. corner, VAM, MODI, and stepping-stone methods.
3. Solve facility location and other application problems with transportation models.
4. Solve assignment problems with the Hungarian (matrix reduction) method.

CHAPTER OUTLINE

10.1 Introduction

10.2 Setting Up a Transportation Problem

10.3 Developing an Initial Solution: Northwest Corner Rule

10.4 Stepping-Stone Method: Finding a Least-Cost Solution

10.5 MODI Method

10.6 Vogel's Approximation Method

10.7 Unbalanced Transportation Problems

10.8 Degeneracy in Transportation Problems

10.9 More Than One Optimal Solution

10.10 Facility Location Analysis

10.11 Approach of the Assignment Model

10.12 Dummy Rows and Dummy Columns

10.13 Maximization Assignment Problems

Glossary • Key Equations • Solved Problems • Self-Test • Discussion Questions and Problems • Data Set Problems • Case Study: Andrew–Carter, Inc. • Case Study: Custom Vans, Inc. • Case Study: Old Oregon Wood Store • Internet Case Study • Bibliography

Appendix 10.1: Using QM for Windows

10.1   INTRODUCTION

In this chapter we explore two special linear programming (LP) models. Because of their structure, these models—called the transportation and assignment models—can be solved using more efficient computational procedures than the simplex method.

Both transportation and assignment problems are members of a category of LP techniques called *network flow problems*. Networks, described in detail in Chapter 12, consist of nodes (or points) and arcs (or lines) that join the modes together. Roadways, telephone systems, and citywide water systems are all examples of networks.

Transportation Model

The first model we examine, the *transportation problem*, deals with the distribution of goods from several points of supply *(sources)* to a number of points of demand *(destinations)*. Usually, we have a given capacity of goods at each source and a given requirement for the goods at each destination. An example of this is shown in Figure 10.1. The objective of such a problem is to schedule shipments from sources to destinations so that total transportation and production costs are minimized.

Transportation models can also be used when a firm is trying to decide where to locate a new facility. Before opening a new warehouse, factory, or sales office, it is good practice to consider a number of alternative sites. Good financial decisions concerning facility location also attempt to minimize total transportation and production costs for the entire system.

Assignment Model

The assignment problem refers to the class of LP problems that involve determining the most efficient assignment of people to projects, salespeople to territories, contracts to bidders, jobs to machines, and so on. The objective is most often to minimize total costs or total time of performing the tasks at hand. One important characteristic of assignment problems is that only one job or worker is assigned to one machine or project.

Special-Purpose Algorithms

The special-purpose transportation and assignment algorithms are more efficient than using LP's simplex method.

Although LP can be used to solve these types of problems (as seen in Chapter 8), more efficient special-purpose algorithms have been developed for the transportation and assignment applications. As in the simplex algorithm, they involve finding an initial feasible

FIGURE 10.1

Example of a Transportation Problem

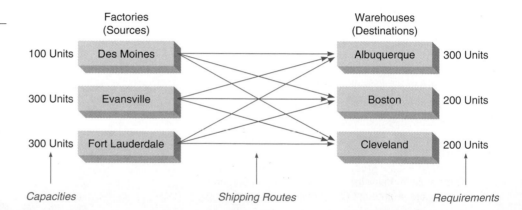

The use of transportation models to minimize the cost of shipping from a number of sources to a number of destinations was first proposed in 1941. This study, called "The Distribution of a Product from Several Sources to Numerous Localities," was written by F. L. Hitchcock. Six years later, T. C. Koopmans independently produced the second major contribution, a report titled "Optimum Utilization of the Transportation System." In 1953, A. Charnes and W. W. Cooper developed the stepping-stone method, an algorithm discussed in detail in this chapter. The modified-distribution (MODI) method, a quicker computational approach, came about in 1955.

solution and then making step-by-step improvements until an optimal solution is reached. Unlike the simplex method, the transportation and assignment methods are fairly simple in terms of computation.

Streamlined versions of the simplex method are important for three reasons:

1. Their computation times are generally 100 times faster than the simplex algorithm.

2. They require less computer memory (and hence can permit larger problems to be solved).

3. They produce integer solutions, which is important because it is hard to ship one-half of a car from a factory or to assign one-third of an astronaut to a shuttle flight.

In the first half of this chapter we take a look at the makeup of a typical transportation problem. Several solution techniques—the northwest corner rule, the stepping-stone method, the modified distribution (MODI) method, and Vogel's approximation method—are discussed. Complications that commonly arise, such as the situation where demand is not exactly equal to supply or the case of a degenerate solution, are also examined.

In the second half of the chapter, we introduce a solution procedure for assignment problems alternatively called the *Hungarian method, Flood's technique,* or the *reduced matrix method.*

10.2 SETTING UP A TRANSPORTATION PROBLEM

Let us begin with an example dealing with the Executive Furniture Corporation, which manufactures office desks at three locations: Des Moines, Evansville, and Fort Lauderdale. The firm distributes the desks through regional warehouses located in Albuquerque, Boston, and Cleveland (see Figure 10.2). An estimate of the monthly production capacity at each factory and an estimate of the number of desks that are needed each month at each of the three warehouses is shown as Figure 10.1.

The firm has found that production costs per desk are identical at each factory, and hence the only relevant costs are those of shipping from each *source* to each *destination.* These costs are shown in Table 10.1. They are assumed to be constant regardless of the volume shipped.[1] The transportation problem may now be described as *how to select the shipping routes to be used and the number of desks shipped on each route so as to minimize total transportation cost.* This, of course, must be done while observing the restrictions regarding factory capacities and warehouse requirements.

Our goal is to select the shipping routes and units to be shipped to minimize total transportation cost.

---

[1] The other assumptions that held for LP problems (see Chapter 7) are still applicable to transportation problems.

FIGURE 10.2

Geographical Locations of
Executive Furniture's Factories
and Warehouses

The transportation table is a
convenient means of
summarizing all the data.

The first step at this point is setting up a *transportation table*; its purpose is to summarize conveniently and concisely all relevant data and to keep track of algorithm computations. (In this respect, it serves the same role as the simplex tableau did for LP problems.) Using the information for the Executive Furniture Corporation displayed in Figure 10.1 and Table 10.1, we proceed to construct a transportation table and to label its various components in Table 10.2.

We see in Table 10.2 that the total factory supply available is exactly equal to the total warehouse demand. When this situation of equal demand and supply occurs (something that is rather unusual in real life) a *balanced problem* is said to exist. Later in this chapter we take a look at how to deal with unbalanced problems, namely, those where destination requirements may be greater than or less than origin capacities.

*Balanced supply and
demand occurs when total
demand equals total supply.*

TABLE 10.1 **Transportation Costs per Desk for Executive Furniture Corp.**

TO FROM	ALBUQUERQUE	BOSTON	CLEVELAND
Des Moines	$5	$4	$3
Evansville	$8	$4	$3
Fort Lauderdale	$9	$7	$5

| **TABLE 10.2** Transanalysis Table for Executive Furniture Corporation | | | | |

TABLE 10.2 Transportation Table for Executive Furniture Corporation

TO / FROM	WAREHOUSE AT ALBUQUERQUE	WAREHOUSE AT BOSTON	WAREHOUSE AT CLEVELAND	FACTORY CAPACITY
DES MOINES FACTORY	$5	$4	$3	100
EVANSVILLE FACTORY	$8	$4	$3	300
FORT LAUDERDALE FACTORY	$9	$7	$5	300
WAREHOUSE REQUIREMENTS	300	200	200	700

Des Moines capacity constraint

Cell representing a source-to-destination (Evansville to Cleveland) shipping assignment that could be made

Cleveland warehouse demand

Total demand and total supply

Cost of shipping 1 unit from Fort Lauderdale factory to Boston warehouse

10.3 DEVELOPING AN INITIAL SOLUTION: NORTHWEST CORNER RULE

When the data have been arranged in tabular form, we must establish an initial feasible solution to the problem. One systematic procedure, known as the *northwest corner rule*, requires that we start in the upper-left-hand cell (or northwest corner) of the table and allocate units to shipping routes as follows:

1. Exhaust the supply (factory capacity) at each row before moving down to the next row.

2. Exhaust the (warehouse) requirements of each column before moving to the right to the next column.

3. Check that all supply and demands are met.

We can now use the northwest corner rule to find an initial feasible solution to the Executive Furniture Corporation problem shown in Table 10.2.

It takes five steps in this example to make the initial shipping assignments (see Table 10.3):

1. Beginning in the upper-left-hand corner, we assign 100 units from Des Moines to Albuquerque. This exhausts the capacity or supply at the Des Moines factory. But it still leaves the warehouse at Albuquerque 200 desks short. Move down to the second row in the same column.

2. Assign 200 units from Evansville to Albuquerque. This meets Albuquerque's demand for a total of 300 desks. The Evansville factory has 100 units remaining, so we move to the right to the next column of the second row.

Here is an explanation of the five steps needed to make an initial shipping assignment for Executive Furniture.

3. Assign 100 units from Evansville to Boston. The Evansville supply has now been exhausted, but Boston's warehouse is still short by 100 desks. At this point, we move down vertically in the Boston column to the next row.

4. Assign 100 units from Fort Lauderdale to Boston. This shipment will fulfill Boston's demand for a total of 200 units. We note, though, that the Fort Lauderdale factory still has 200 units available that have not been shipped.

5. Assign 200 units from Fort Lauderdale to Cleveland. This final move exhausts Cleveland's demand *and* Fort Lauderdale's supply. This always happens with a balanced problem. The initial shipment schedule is now complete.

We can easily compute the cost of this shipping assignment.

| ROUTE | | UNITS | | PER UNIT | | TOTAL |
FROM	TO	SHIPPED	×	COST ($)	=	COST ($)
D	A	100		5		500
E	A	200		8		1,600
E	B	100		4		400
F	B	100		7		700
F	C	200		5		1,000
					Total	4,200

A feasible solution is reached when all demand and supply constraints are met.

This solution is feasible since demand and supply constraints are all satisfied. It was also very quick and easy to reach. However, we would be very lucky if this solution yielded the optimal transportation cost for the problem, because this route-loading method totally ignored the costs of shipping over each of the routes.

TABLE 10.3 **Initial Solution to Executive Furniture Problem Using the Northwest Corner Method**

FROM \ TO	ALBUQUERQUE (A)	BOSTON (B)	CLEVELAND (C)	FACTORY CAPACITY
DES MOINES (D)	100 $5	$4	$3	100
EVANSVILLE (E)	200 $8	100 $4	$3	300
FORT LAUDERDALE (F)	$9	(100) $7	200 $5	300
WAREHOUSE REQUIREMENTS	300	200	200	700

Means that the firm is shipping 100 units along the Fort Lauderdale-to-Boston route

---

| MODELING IN THE REAL WORLD | The Transportation Approach Moves Sand at Brisbane Airport |

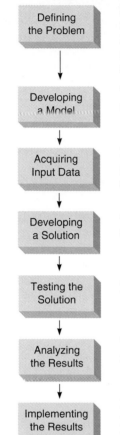

Defining the Problem

Most large construction projects, such as the expansion of the Brisbane International Airport in Australia, require the transportation of gravel, rock, sand, and other materials from one location to another. At Brisbane, sand from nearby bay areas was to be moved to various parts of the airport site and used as fill. In the past, civil engineers usually used their own judgment in deciding how to transport such material from initial reclaimed areas to final locations.

Developing a Model

To solve this classic transportation problem, a mathematical model called the out-of-kilter algorithm (OKA) was chosen. The analysis took only three person-weeks of a consultant's time.

Acquiring Input Data

Input to the model was the cost/distance of transportation between each possible source site and each possible final site, and the maximum and minimum limits on the amount of sand that had to be moved along these paths.

Developing a Solution

OKA determined the least-cost plan of transporting the sand from 26 source sites to 35 final fill sites. It also scheduled the movements month by month.

Testing the Solution

A pilot test of the airport site (using five source and nine fill sites) was used to prove that modeling would be able to save time and money.

Analyzing the Results

The analysis provided a mechanism for altering the solution developed if the amount of sand at source nodes was found to be different than expected.

Implementing the Results

It was originally estimated that 2.5 million cubic meters of sand would have to be moved. The transportation model resulted in a move of only 1.8 million cubic meters, a savings of $802,000, or 27% of the total hauling budget for the project.

Source: M. Lawrence and C. Perry. "Earthmoving on Construction Projects," *Interfaces* 14, 1 (March–April 1984): 84–86.

10.4 STEPPING-STONE METHOD: FINDING A LEAST-COST SOLUTION

The *stepping-stone method* is an iterative technique for moving from an initial feasible solution to an optimal feasible solution. For the stepping-stone method to be applied to a transportation problem, one rule about the number of shipping routes being used must first be observed. The rule is this: *The number of occupied routes (or squares) must always be equal to one less than the sum of the number of rows plus the number of columns.* In the Executive Furniture problem, this means that the initial solution must have $3 + 3 - 1 = 5$ squares used. Thus

$$\text{occupied shipping routes (squares)} = \text{number of rows} + \text{number of columns} - 1$$

$$5 = 3 + 3 - 1$$

When the number of occupied routes is less than this, the solution is called *degenerate*. Later in this chapter we talk about what to do if the number of used squares is less than the number of rows plus the number of columns minus 1.

Testing the Solution for Possible Improvement

The stepping-stone method involves testing each unused route to see if shipping one unit on that route would increase or decrease total costs.

How does the stepping-stone method work? Its approach is to evaluate the cost-effectiveness of shipping goods via transportation routes not currently in the solution. Each unused shipping route (or square) in the transportation table is tested by asking the following question: "What would happen to total shipping costs if one unit of our product (in our example, one desk) were tentatively shipped on an unused route?"

This testing of each unused square is conducted using the following five steps:

Five Steps to Test Unused Squares

1. Select an unused square to be evaluated.

2. Beginning at this square, trace a closed path back to the original square via squares that are currently being used, and moving with only horizontal and vertical moves.

3. Beginning with a plus (+) sign at the unused square, place alternate minus (−) signs and plus signs on each corner square of the closed path just traced.

4. Calculate an *improvement index* by adding together the unit cost figures found in each square containing a plus sign and then subtracting the unit costs in each square containing a minus sign.

5. Repeat steps 1 to 4 until an improvement index has been calculated for all unused squares. If all indices computed are greater than or equal to zero, an optimal solution has been reached. If not, it is possible to improve the current solution and decrease total shipping costs.

To see how the stepping-stone method works, let us apply these steps to the Executive Furniture Corporation data in Table 10.3 to evaluate unused shipping routes. The four currently unassigned routes are Des Moines to Boston, Des Moines to Cleveland, Evansville to Cleveland, and Fort Lauderdale to Albuquerque.

Steps 1 and 2. Beginning with the Des Moines–Boston route, we first trace a closed path using only currently occupied squares (see Table 10.4) and then place alternate plus signs and minus signs in the corners of this path. To indicate more clearly the meaning of a *closed path*, we see that only squares currently used for shipping can be used in turning the corners of the route being traced. Hence the path Des Moines–Boston to Des Moines–Albuquerque to Fort Lauderdale–Albuquerque to Fort Lauderdale–Boston to Des Moines–Boston would not be acceptable since the Fort Lauderdale–Albuquerque square is currently empty. It turns out that *only one* closed route is possible for each square we wish to test.

Closed paths are used to trace alternate plus and minus signs.

Step 3. How do we decide which squares are given plus signs and which minus signs? The answer is simple. Since we are testing the cost-effectiveness of the Des Moines–Boston shipping route, we pretend we are shipping one desk from Des Moines to Boston. This is one more unit than we *were* sending between the two cities, so we place a plus sign in the box. But if we ship one *more* unit than before from Des Moines to Boston, we end up sending 101 desks out of the Des Moines factory.

How to assign + and − signs.

That factory's capacity is only 100 units; hence we must ship one desk *less* from Des Moines–Albuquerque—this change is made to avoid violating the factory capacity constraint. To indicate that the Des Moines–Albuquerque shipment has been reduced, we place a minus sign in its box. Continuing along the closed path, we notice that we are no longer meeting the Albuquerque warehouse requirement for 300 units. In fact, if the Des Moines–Albuquerque shipment is reduced to 99 units, the Evansville–Albu-

TABLE 10.4 **Evaluating the Unused Des Moines-Boston Shipping Route**

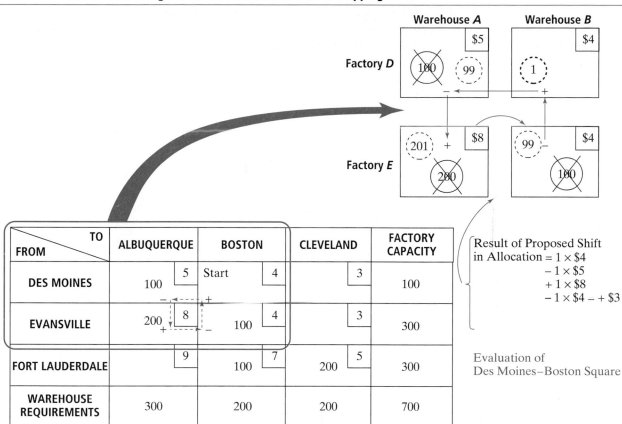

TO FROM	ALBUQUERQUE	BOSTON	CLEVELAND	FACTORY CAPACITY
DES MOINES	100 ⌐5	Start ⌐4	⌐3	100
EVANSVILLE	200 ⌐8	100 ⌐4	⌐3	300
FORT LAUDERDALE	⌐9	100 ⌐7	200 ⌐5	300
WAREHOUSE REQUIREMENTS	300	200	200	700

Result of Proposed Shift
in Allocation = 1 × $4
− 1 × $5
+ 1 × $8
− 1 × $4 − + $3

Evaluation of
Des Moines–Boston Square

querque load has to be increased by 1 unit, to 201 desks. Therefore, we place a plus sign in that box to indicate the increase. Finally, we note that if the Evansville–Albuquerque route is assigned 201 desks, the Evansville–Boston route must be reduced by 1 unit, to 99 desks, to maintain the Evansville factory capacity constraint of 300 units. Thus, a minus sign is placed in the Evansville–Boston box. We observe in Table 10.4 that all four routes on the closed path are hereby balanced in terms of demand-and-supply limitations.

Step 4. An *improvement index* (I_{ij}) for the Des Moines–Boston route is now computed by adding unit costs in squares with plus signs and subtracting costs in squares with minus signs. Hence

Des Moines–Boston index = I_{DB} = +$4 − $5 + $8 − $4 = +$3

This means that for every desk shipped via the Des Moines–Boston route, total transportation costs will *increase* by $3 over their current level.

Step 5. Let us now examine the Des Moines–Cleveland unused route, which is slightly more difficult to trace with a closed path. Again, you will notice that we turn each corner along the path only at squares that represent existing routes. The path can go *through* the Evansville–Cleveland box but cannot turn a corner or place a + or − sign there. Only an occupied square may be used as a stepping stone (Table 10.5).

Improvement index computation involves adding costs in squares with plus signs and subtracting costs in squares with minus signs. I_{ij} is the improvement index on the route from source i to destination j.

TABLE 10.5 Evaluating the Des Moines-Cleveland (D-C) Shipping Route

FROM \ TO	(A) ALBUQUERQUE	(B) BOSTON	(C) CLEVELAND	FACTORY CAPACITY
(D) DES MOINES	$5 — 100	$4	$3 Start +	100
(E) EVANSVILLE	$8 + 200	$4 — 100	$3	300
(F) FORT LAUDERDALE	$9	$7 100 + 100	$5 — 200	300
WAREHOUSE REQUIREMENTS	300	200	200	700

The closed path we use is $+DC - DA + EA - EB + FB - FC$.

Des Moines—Cleveland improvement index $= I_{DC}$

$$= +\$3 - \$5 + \$8 - \$4 + \$7 - \$5$$

$$= +\$4$$

*A path can go **through** any box but can only turn at a box or cell that is occupied.*

Thus, opening this route will also not lower our total shipping costs.

The other two routes may be evaluated in a similar fashion:

Evansville—Cleveland index $= I_{EC} = +\$3 - \$4 + \$7 - \$5$

$$= +\$1$$

(closed path: $+EC - EB + FB - FC$)

Fort Lauderdale—Albuquerque index $= I_{FA} = +\$9 - \$7 + \$4 - \$8$

$$= -\$2$$

(closed path: $+FA - FB + EB - EA$)

Because this last improvement index (I_{FA}) is negative, a cost savings may be attained by making use of the (currently unused) Fort Lauderdale—Albuquerque route.

Obtaining an Improved Solution

To reduce our overall costs, we want to select the route with the largest negative index.

Each negative index computed by the stepping-stone method represents the amount by which total transportation costs could be decreased if 1 unit or product were shipped on that route. We found only one negative index in the Executive Furniture problem, that being −$2 on the Fort Lauderdale factory–Albuquerque warehouse route. If, however, there were more than one negative improvement index, our strategy would be to choose the route (unused square) with the *largest* negative index.

The next step, then, is to ship the maximum allowable number of units (or desks, in our case) on the new route (Fort Lauderdale to Albuquerque). What is the maximum quantity that can be shipped on the money-saving route? That quantity is found by referring to the closed path of plus signs and minus signs drawn for the route and selecting the *smallest number* found in those squares containing *minus signs*. To obtain a new solution, that number is added to all squares on the closed path with plus signs and subtracted from all squares on the path assigned minus signs.

The maximum we can ship on the new route is found by looking at the closed path's minus signs. We select the smallest number found in the squares with minus signs.

Let us see how this process can help improve Executive Furniture's solution. We repeat the transportation table (Table 10.6) for the problem. Note that the stepping-stone route for Fort Lauderdale to Albuquerque (*F–A*) is drawn in. The maximum quantity that can be shipped on the newly opened route (*F–A*) is the smallest number found in squares containing minus signs—in this case, 100 units. Why 100 units? Since the total cost decreases by $2 per unit shipped, we know we would like to ship the maximum possible number of units. Table 10.6 indicates that each unit shipped over the *F–A* route results in an increase of 1 unit shipped from *E* to *B* and a decrease of 1 unit in both the amounts shipped from *F* to *B* (now 100 units) and from *E* to *A* (now 200 units). Hence the maximum we can ship over the *F–A* route is 100. This results in 0 units being shipped from *F* to *B*.

Changing the shipping route involves adding to squares on the closed path with plus signs and subtracting from squares with minus signs.

We add 100 units to the 0 now being shipped on route *F–A*; then proceed to subtract 100 from route *F–B*, leaving 0 in that square (but still balancing the row total for *F*); then add 100 to route *E–B*, yielding 200; and finally, subtract 100 from route *E–A*, leaving 100 units shipped. Note that the new numbers still produce the correct row and column totals as required.

The new solution is shown in Table 10.7.

Total shipping cost has been reduced by (100 units) × ($2 saved per unit) = $200, and is now $4,000. This cost figure can, of course, also be derived by multiplying each unit shipping cost times the number of units transported on its route, namely, (100 × $5) + (100 × $8) + (200 × $4) + (100 × $9) + (200 × $5) = $4,000.

The solution shown in Table 10.7 may or may not be optimal. To determine whether further improvement is possible, we return to the first five steps given earlier to test each

TABLE 10.6 **Stepping-Stone Path Used to Evaluate Route *F–A***

TO / FROM	A	B	C	FACTORY
D	$5 100	$4	$3	100
E	$8 −200	$4 +100	$3	300
F	$9 +	$7 −100	$5 200	300
WAREHOUSE	300	200	200	700

TABLE 10.7 **Second Solution to the Executive Furniture Problem**

FROM \ TO	A	B	C	FACTORY
D	100 $5	$4	$3	100
E	100 $8	200 $4	$3	300
F	100 $9	$7	200 $5	300
WAREHOUSE	300	200	200	700

square that is *now* unused. The four improvement indices—each representing an available shipping route—are as follows:

Improvement indices for each of the four unused shipping routes must now be tested to see if any are negative.

D to $B = I_{DB} = +\$4 - \$5 + \$8 - \$4 = +\$3$

(closed path: $+ DB - DA + EA - EB$)

D to $C = I_{DC} = +\$3 - \$5 + \$9 - \$5 = +\$2$

(closed path: $+ DC - DA + FA - FC$)

E to $C = I_{EC} = +\$3 - \$8 + \$9 - \$5 = -\$1$

(closed path: $+ EC - EA + FA - FC$)

F to $B = I_{FB} = +\$7 - \$4 + \$8 - \$9 = +\$2$

(closed path: $+ FB - EB + EA - FA$)

Hence, an improvement can be made by shipping the maximum allowable number of units from E to C (see Table 10.8). Only the squares $E-A$ and $F-C$ have minus signs in the closed path; because the smallest number in these two squares is 100, we add 100 units to $E-C$ and $F-A$ and subtract 100 units from $E-A$ and $F-C$. The new cost for this third solution of \$3,900 is computed in the following table:

TOTAL COST OF THIRD SOLUTION

ROUTE FROM	TO	DESKS SHIPPED	×	PER UNIT COST ($)	=	TOTAL COST ($)
D	A	100		5		500
E	B	200		4		800
E	C	100		3		300
F	A	200		9		1,800
F	C	100		5		500
						Total 3,900

T A B L E   1 0 . 8   Path to Evaluate the *E–C* Route

FROM \ TO	A	B	C	FACTORY
D	$5 100	$4	$3	100
E	$8 100 −	$4 200	$3 Start +	300
F	$9 100 +	$7	$5 200 −	300
WAREHOUSE	300	200	200	700

Table 10.9 contains the optimal shipping assignments because each improvement index that can be computed at this point is greater than or equal to zero as shown in the following equations. Improvement indices for the table are

$$D \text{ to } B = I_{DB} = +\$4 - \$5 + \$9 - \$5 + \$3 - \$4$$
$$= +\$2 \text{ (path: } +DB - DA + FA - FC + EC - EB)$$
$$D \text{ to } C = I_{DC} = +\$3 - \$5 + \$9 - \$5 = +\$2 \text{ (path: } +DC - DA + FA - FC)$$
$$E \text{ to } A = I_{EA} = +\$8 - \$9 + \$5 - \$3 = +\$1 \text{ (path: } +EA - FA + FC - EC)$$
$$F \text{ to } B = I_{FB} = +\$7 - \$5 + \$3 - \$4 = +\$1 \text{ (path: } +FB - FC + EC - EB)$$

Since all four of these improvement indices are greater than or equal to zero, we have reached an optimal solution.

T A B L E   1 0 . 9   Third and Optimal Solution

FROM \ TO	A	B	C	FACTORY
D	$5 100	$4	$3	100
E	$8	$4 200	$3 100	300
F	$9 200	$7	$5 100	300
WAREHOUSE	300	200	200	700

PROGRAM 10.1A

Excel QM Input Screen and Formulas, Using Executive Furniture Data

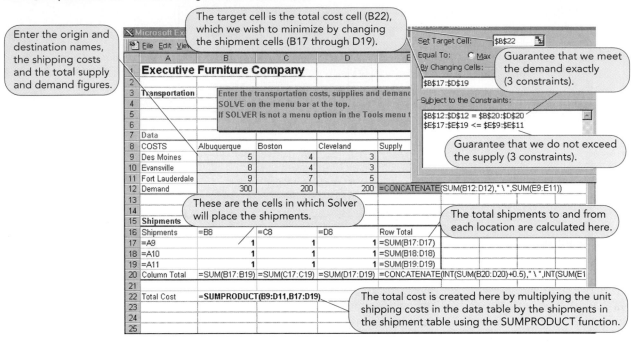

PROGRAM 10.1B

Output from Excel QM with
Optimal Solution to Executive
Furniture Problem

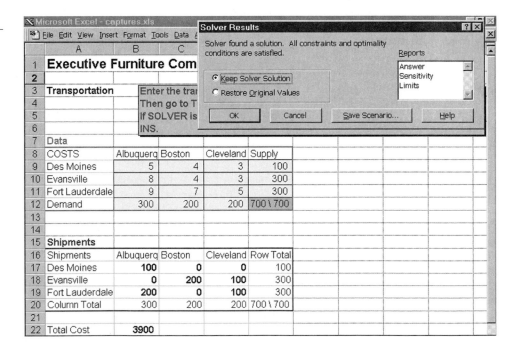

The hardest part in solving problems like this is identifying every stepping-stone path so that we may compute the improvement indices. In Section 10.5, we will introduce an easier way to find the optimal solution to transportation problems, especially larger ones with more sources and destinations. This way is called the MODI method.

Using Excel QM to Solve Transportation Problems Excel QM's Transportation module uses Excel's built-in Solver routine to find optimal solutions to transportation problems such as Executive Furniture. Program 10.1A illustrates the input data and total cost formulas. To reach an optimal solution, we must go to Excel's Tools bar, select Solver, and then select Solve. The output appears in Program 10.1B.

10.5 MODI METHOD

The MODI (*modified distribution*) method allows us to compute improvement indices quickly for each unused square without drawing all of the closed paths. Because of this, it can often provide considerable time savings over the stepping-stone method for solving transportation problems.

MODI has some advantages over the stepping-stone method.

MODI provides a new means of finding the unused route with the largest negative improvement index. Once the largest index is identified, we are required to trace only one closed path. Just as with the stepping-stone approach, this path helps determine the maximum number of units that can be shipped via the best unused route.

How to Use the MODI Approach

In applying the MODI method, we begin with an initial solution obtained by using the northwest corner rule.[2] But now we must compute a value for each row (call the values R_1, R_2, R_3 *if there are three rows) and for each column* (K_1, K_2, K_3) in the transportation table. In general, we let

R_i = value assigned to row i

K_j = value assigned to column j

C_{ij} = cost in square ij (cost of shipping from source i to destination j)

The MODI method then requires five steps:

Five Steps in the MODI Method

1. To compute the values for each row and column, set
   $$R_i + K_j = C_{ij} \qquad \text{(10-1)}$$
   but *only for those squares that are currently used or occupied.* For example, if the square at the intersection of row 2 and column 1 is occupied, we set $R_2 + K_1 = C_{21}$.
2. After all equations have been written, set $R_1 = 0$.
3. Solve the system of equations for all R and K values.
4. Compute the improvement index for each unused square by the formula
   improvement index $(I_{ij}) = C_{ij} - R_i - K_j$. $\qquad \text{(10-2)}$
5. Select the largest negative index and proceed to solve the problem as you did using the stepping-stone method.

Here are the five MODI steps.

---

[2] Note that any initial feasible solution will do: northwest corner rule, Vogel's approximation method solution, or any arbitrary assignment.

Solving the Executive Furniture Corporation Problem with MODI

Let us try out these rules on the Executive Furniture Corporation problem. The initial northwest corner solution is repeated in Table 10.10. MODI will be used to compute an improvement index for each unused square. Note that the only change in the transportation table is the border labeling the R_is (rows) and K_js (columns).

We first set up an equation for each occupied square:

*Solving for **R** and **K** values.*

(1) $R_1 + K_1 = 5$

(2) $R_2 + K_1 = 8$

(3) $R_2 + K_2 = 4$

(4) $R_3 + K_2 = 7$

(5) $R_3 + K_3 = 5$

Letting $R_1 = 0$, we can easily solve, step by step, for K_1, R_2, K_2, R_3, and K_3.

(1) $R_1 + K_1 = 5$

$0 + K_1 = 5$ $K_1 = 5$

(2) $R_2 + K_1 = 8$

$R_2 + 5 = 8$ $R_2 = 3$

(3) $R_2 + K_2 = 4$

$3 + K_2 = 4$ $K_2 = 1$

(4) $R_3 + K_2 = 7$

$R_3 + 1 = 7$ $R_3 = 6$

(5) $R_3 + K_3 = 5$

$6 + K_3 = 5$ $K_3 = -1$

TABLE 10.10	Initial Solution to Executive Furniture Problem in the MODI Format

K_j	K_1	K_2	K_3	
R_i TO FROM	ALBUQUERQUE	BOSTON	CLEVELAND	FACTORY CAPACITY
R_1 DES MOINES	5 100	4	3	100
R_2 EVANSVILLE	8 200	4 100	3	300
R_3 FORT LAUDERDALE	9	7 100	5 200	300
WAREHOUSE REQUIREMENTS	300	200	200	700

You can observe that these R and K values will not always be positive; it is common for zero and negative values to occur as well. We also think that after solving for the Rs and Ks in a few practice problems, you may become so proficient that the calculations can be done in your head instead of by writing the equations out.

The next step is to compute the improvement index for each unused cell. That formula, again, is

$$\text{improvement index} = I_{ij} = C_{ij} - R_i - K_j$$

We have:

These are the same indices calculated by the stepping-stone method, but now we have to trace only one closed path.

Des Moines–Boston index $= I_{DB} = C_{12} - R_1 - K_2 = 4 - 0 - 1$
$$= +\$3$$

Des Moines–Cleveland index $= I_{DC} = C_{13} - R_1 - K_3 = 3 - 0 - (-1)$
$$= +\$4$$

Evansville–Cleveland index $= I_{EC} = C_{23} - R_2 - K_3 = 3 - 3 - (-1)$
$$= +\$1$$

Fort Lauderdale–Albuquerque index $= I_{FA} = C_{31} - R_3 - K_1 = 9 - 6 - 5$
$$= -\$2$$

Note that these indices are exactly the same as the ones calculated when we used the stepping-stone approach (see Tables 10.4 and 10.5). Since one of the indices is negative, the current solution is not optimal. But now it is necessary to trace only the one closed path, for Fort Lauderdale–Albuquerque, in order to proceed with the solution procedures as used in the stepping-stone method.

To improve the solution we follow these four steps.

For your convenience, the steps we follow to develop an improved solution after the improvement indices have been computed are outlined briefly:

1. Beginning at the square with the best improvement index (Fort Lauderdale–Albuquerque), trace a closed path back to the original square via squares that are currently being used.

2. Beginning with a plus (+) sign at the unused square, place alternate minus (−) signs and plus signs on each corner square of the closed path just traced.

3. Select the smallest quantity found in those squares containing minus signs. *Add* that number to all squares on the closed path with plus signs; *subtract* the number from all squares assigned minus signs.

4. Compute new improvement indices for this new solution using the MODI method.

Following this procedure, the second and third solutions to the Executive Furniture Corporation problem can be found. In tabular form, the result of your MODI computations will look identical to Tables 10.7 (second solution using stepping-stone) and 10.9 (optimal solution). With each new MODI solution, we must recalculate the R and K values. These values then are used to compute new improvement indices in order to determine whether further shipping cost reduction is possible.

10.6 VOGEL'S APPROXIMATION METHOD: ANOTHER WAY TO FIND AN INITIAL SOLUTION

In addition to the northwest corner method of setting an initial solution to transportation problems, we talk about one other important technique—*Vogel's approximation method* (VAM). VAM is not quite as simple as the northwest corner approach, but it facilitates a very good initial solution—as a matter of fact, one that is often the *optimal* solution.

Vogel's approximation method tackles the problem of finding a good initial solution by taking into account the costs associated with each route alternative. This is something that the northwest corner rule did not do. To apply the VAM, we first compute for each row and column the penalty faced if we should ship over the *second best* route instead of the *least-cost* route.

The six steps involved in determining an initial VAM solution are illustrated on our now familiar Executive Furniture Corporation data. (We begin with the same layout originally shown in Table 10.2.)

Here are the six steps of VAM.

VAM Step 1. For each row and column of the transportation table, find the difference between the two lowest unit shipping costs. These numbers represent the difference between the distribution cost on the *best* route in the row or column and the *second best* route in the row or column. (This is the *opportunity cost* of not using the best route.)

Step 1 has been done in Table 10.11. The numbers at the heads of the columns and to the right of the rows represent these differences. For example, in row E the three transportation costs are $8, $4, and $3. The two lowest costs are $4 and $3, so their difference is $1.

VAM Step 2. Identify the row or column with the greatest opportunity cost, or difference. In case of Table 10.11, the row or column selected is column A, with a difference of 3.

Assignments in VAM are based on penalty costs.

VAM Step 3. Assign as many units as possible to the lowest-cost square in the row or column selected.

Step 3 has been done in Table 10.12. Under column A, the lowest-cost route is $D-A$ (with a cost of $5) and 100 units have been assigned to that square. No more were placed in the square because doing so would exceed D's availability.

> **TABLE 10.11** **Transportation Table with VAM Row and Column Differences Shown**

	3	0	0	
FROM \ TO	**ALBUQUERQUE** A	**BOSTON** B	**CLEVELAND** C	**TOTAL AVAILABLE**
DES MOINES D	5	4	3	100 1
EVANSVILLE E	8	4	3	300 1
FORT LAUDERDALE F	9	7	5	300 2
TOTAL REQUIRED	300	200	200	700

VAM Step 4. Eliminate any row or column that has just been completely satisfied by the assignment just made. This can be done by placing X's in each appropriate square.

Step 4 has been done in Table 10.12's D row. No future assignments will be made to the D–B or D–C routes.

VAM Step 5. Recompute the cost differences for the transportation table, omitting rows or columns crossed out in the preceding step.

This is also shown in Table 10.12. A's, B's, and C's differences each change. D's row is eliminated, and E's and F's differences remain the same as in Table 10.11.

> **TABLE 10.12** **VAM Assignment with D's Requirements Satisfied**

	3̸ 1	0̸ 3	0̸ 2	
FROM \ TO	**A**	**B**	**C**	**TOTAL AVAILABLE**
D	5 100	4 X	3 X	100 1̸
E	8	4	3	300 1
F	9	7	5	300 2
TOTAL REQUIRED	300	200	200	700

T A B L E 1 0 . 1 3 Second VAM Assignment with *B*'s Requirements Satisfied

FROM \ TO	A (̷3̷ 1)	B (̷∅̷ 3)	C (̷∅̷ 2)	TOTAL AVAILABLE	
D	5 / 100	4 / X	3 / X	100	̷X̷
E	8	4 / 200	3	300	̷X̷ 5
F	9	7 / X	5	300	̷2̷ 4
TOTAL REQUIRED	300	200	200	700	

VAM Step 6. Return to step 2 and repeat the steps until an initial feasible solution has been obtained.

In our case, column *B* now has the greatest difference, which is 3. We assign 200 units to the lowest-cost square in column *B* that has not been crossed out. This is seen to be *E–B*. Since *B*'s requirements have now been met, we place an *X* in the *F–B* square to eliminate it. Differences are once again recomputed. This process is summarized in Table 10.13.

The greatest difference is now in row *E*. Hence, we shall assign as many units as possible to the lowest-cost square in row *E*, that is, *E–C* with a cost of $3. The maximum as-

T A B L E 1 0 . 1 4 Third VAM Assignment with *C*'s Requirements Satisfied

FROM \ TO	A	B	C	TOTAL AVAILABLE
D	5 / 100	4 / X	3 / X	100
E	8 / X	4 / 200	3 / 100	300
F	9	7 / X	5	300
TOTAL REQUIRED	300	200	200	700

TABLE 10.15 **Final Assignments to Balance Column and Row Requirements**

FROM \ TO	A	B	C	TOTAL AVAILABLE
D	100 — 5	X — 4	X — 3	100
E	X — 8	200 — 4	100 — 3	300
F	200 — 9	X — 7	100 — 5	300
TOTAL REQUIRED	300	200	200	700

signment of 100 units depletes the remaining availability at *E*. The square *E–A* may therefore be crossed out. This is illustrated in Table 10.14.

The final two allocations, at *F–A* and *F–C*, may be made by inspecting supply restrictions (in the rows) and demand requirements (in the columns). We see that an assignment of 200 units to *F–A* and 100 units to *F–C* completes the table (see Table 10.15).

The cost of this VAM assignment is = (100 units × \$5) + (200 units × \$4) + (100 units × \$3) + (200 units × \$9) + (100 units × \$5) = \$3,900.

It is worth noting that the use of Vogel's approximation method on the Executive Furniture Corporation data produces the optimal solution to this problem. Even though VAM takes many more calculations to find an initial solution than does the northwest corner rule, it almost always produces a much better initial solution. Hence VAM tends to minimize the total number of computations needed to reach an optimal solution.

VAM may yield an optimal solution with its initial solution, meaning fewer computations than other techniques.

10.7 UNBALANCED TRANSPORTATION PROBLEMS

A situation occurring quite frequently in real-life problems is the case in which total demand is not equal to total supply. These *unbalanced problems* can be handled easily by the preceding solution procedures if we first introduce *dummy sources* or *dummy destinations*. In the event that total supply is greater than total demand, a dummy destination (warehouse), with demand exactly equal to the surplus, is created. If total demand is greater than total supply, we introduce a dummy source (factory) with a supply equal to the excess of demand over supply. In either case, shipping cost coefficients of zero are assigned to each dummy location or route because no shipments will actually be made from a dummy factory or to a dummy warehouse.

Dummy sources or destinations are used to balance problems in which demand is not equal to supply.

Demand Less Than Supply

Considering the original Executive Furniture Corporation problem, suppose that the Des Moines factory increases its rate of production to 250 desks. (That factory's capacity used to be 100 desks per production period.) The firm is now able to supply a total of 850 desks

TABLE 10.16   Initial Solution to an Unbalanced Problem Where Demand is Less Than Supply

FROM \ TO	ALBUQUERQUE A	BOSTON B	CLEVELAND C	DUMMY WAREHOUSE	FACTORY CAPACITY
DES MOINES D	5 250	4	3	0	250
EVANSVILLE E	8 50	4 200	3 50	0	300
FORT LAUDERDALE F	9	7	5 150	0 150	300
WAREHOUSE REQUIREMENTS	300	200	200	150	850

New Des Moines capacity (pointing to Des Moines capacity 250)

Total cost = 250($5) + 50($8) + 200($4) + 50($3) + 150($5) + 150($0) = $3,350

each period. Warehouse requirements, however, remain the same (at 700 desks), so the row and column totals do not balance.

To balance this type of problem, we simply add a dummy column that will represent a fake warehouse requiring 150 desks. This is somewhat analogous to adding a slack variable in solving a linear programming problem. Just as slack variables were assigned a value of zero dollars in the LP objective function, the shipping costs to this dummy warehouse are all set equal to zero.

The northwest corner rule is used once again, in Table 10.16, to find an initial solution to this modified Executive Furniture problem. As you can see, expanding capacity at Des Moines has decreased total cost. If you wanted to complete this task and find an optimal solution, either the stepping-stone or MODI method would now be employed.

Note that the 150 units from Fort Lauderdale to the dummy warehouse represent 150 units that are *not* shipped from Fort Lauderdale.

Demand Greater Than Supply

The second type of unbalanced condition occurs when total demand is greater than total supply. This means that customers or warehouses require more of a product than the firm's factories can provide. In this case we need to add a dummy row representing a fake factory. The new factory will have a supply exactly equal to the difference between total demand and total real supply. The shipping costs from the dummy factory to each destination will be zero.

Let us set up such an unbalanced problem for the Happy Sound Stereo Company. Happy Sound assembles high-fidelity stereophonic systems at three plants and distributes through three regional warehouses. The production capacities at each plant, demand at each warehouse, and unit shipping costs are presented in Table 10.17.

As can be seen in Table 10.18, a dummy plant adds an extra row, balances the problem, and allows us to apply the northwest corner rule to find the initial solution shown.

TABLE 10.17 Unbalanced Transportation Table for Happy Sound Stereo Company

FROM \ TO	WAREHOUSE A	WAREHOUSE B	WAREHOUSE C	PLANT SUPPLY
PLANT W	$6	$4	$9	200
PLANT X	$10	$5	$8	175
PLANT Y	$12	$7	$6	75
WAREHOUSE DEMAND	250	100	150	450 / 500

Totals do not balance

This initial solution shows 50 units being shipped from the dummy plant to warehouse *C*. This means that warehouse *C* will be 50 units short of its requirements. In general, any units shipped from a dummy source represent unmet demand at the respective destination.

TABLE 10.18 Initial Solution to an Unbalanced Problem Where Demand Is Greater Than Supply

FROM \ TO	WAREHOUSE A	WAREHOUSE B	WAREHOUSE C	PLANT SUPPLY
PLANT W	6 — 200	4	9	200
PLANT X	10 — 50	5 — 100	8 — 25	175
PLANT Y	12	7	6 — 75	75
DUMMY PLANT	0	0	0 — 50	50
WAREHOUSE DEMAND	250	100	150	500

Total cost of initial solution = 200($6) + 50($10) + 100($5) + 25($8) + 75($6) + 50($0) = $2,850

10.8 DEGENERACY IN TRANSPORTATION PROBLEMS

We briefly mentioned the subject of *degeneracy* earlier in this chapter. Degeneracy occurs when the number of occupied squares or routes in a transportation table solution is less than the number of rows plus the number of columns minus 1. Such a situation may arise in the initial solution or in any subsequent solution. Degeneracy requires a special procedure to correct the problem. Without enough occupied squares to trace a closed path for each unused route, it would be impossible to apply the stepping-stone method or to calculate the R and K values needed for the MODI technique. You might recall that no problem discussed in the chapter thus far has been degenerate.

Degeneracy arises when the number of occupied squares is less than the number of rows + columns − 1.

To handle degenerate problems, we create an artificially occupied cell—that is, we place a zero (representing a fake shipment) in one of the unused squares and then treat that square as if it were occupied. The square chosen must be in such a position as to allow *all* stepping-stone paths to be closed, although there is usually a good deal of flexibility in selecting the unused square that will receive the zero.

Degeneracy in an Initial Solution

Degeneracy can occur in our application of the northwest corner rule to find an initial solution, as we see in the case of the Martin Shipping Company. Martin has three warehouses from which to supply its three major retail customers in San Jose. Martin's shipping costs, warehouse supplies, and customer demands are presented in Table 10.19. Note that origins in this problem are warehouses and destinations are retail stores. Initial shipping assignments are made in the table by application of the northwest corner rule.

This initial solution is degenerate because it violates the rule that the number of used squares must be equal to the number of rows plus the number of columns minus 1 (i.e., $3 + 3 - 1 = 5$ is greater than the number of occupied boxes). In this particular problem,

TABLE 10.19 Initial Solution of a Degenerate Problem

FROM \ TO	CUSTOMER 1	CUSTOMER 2	CUSTOMER 3	WAREHOUSE SUPPLY
WAREHOUSE 1	100 8	2	6	100
WAREHOUSE 2	10	100 9	20 9	120
WAREHOUSE 3	7	10	80 7	80
CUSTOMER DEMAND	100	100	100	300

degeneracy arose because both a column and a row requirement (that being column 1 and row 1) were satisfied simultaneously. This broke the stair-step pattern that we usually see with northwest corner solutions.

To correct the problem, we may place a zero in an unused square. In this case, those squares representing either the shipping route from warehouse 1 to customer 2 or from warehouse 2 to customer 1 will do. If you treat the new zero square just like any other occupied square, any of the regular solution methods can be used.

Degeneracy during Later Solution Stages

A transportation problem can become degenerate *after* the initial solution stage if adding an unused square results in the elimination of two previously occupied routes, instead of eliminating the usual *one*. Such a problem occurs when two squares assigned minus signs on a closed path both have the same lowest quantity.

Bagwell Paint Example After one iteration of the stepping-stone method, cost analysts at Bagwell Paint produced the transportation table shown as Table 10.20. We observe that the solution in Table 10.20 is not degenerate, but it is also not optimal. The improvement indices for the four currently unused squares are

factory A − warehouse 2 index = +2

factory A − warehouse 3 index = +1

factory B − warehouse 3 index = −15 ← *Only route with a negative index*

factory C − warehouse 2 index = +11

Hence, an improved solution may be obtained by opening the route from factory B to warehouse 3. Let us go through the stepping-stone procedure for finding the next solution

---

TABLE 10.20 Bagwell Paint Transportation Table

FROM \ TO	WAREHOUSE 1	WAREHOUSE 2	WAREHOUSE 3	FACTORY CAPACITY
FACTORY A	8 70	5	16	70
FACTORY B	15 50	10 80	7	130
FACTORY C	3 30	9	10 50	80
WAREHOUSE REQUIREMENT	150	80	50	280

Total shipping cost = $2,700

T A B L E 1 0 . 2 1 **Tracing a Closed Path for the Factory B–Warehouse 3 Route**

FROM \ TO	WAREHOUSE 1	WAREHOUSE 3
FACTORY B	50 — ◄---- ---- +	15 ⬚ 7 ⬚
FACTORY C	30 + ---- ----► − 50	3 ⬚ 10 ⬚

to Bagwell Paint's problem. We begin by drawing a closed path for the unused square representing factory B–warehouse 3. This is shown in Table 10.21, which is an abbreviated version of Table 10.20 and contains only the factories and warehouses necessary to close the path.

The smallest quantity in a square containing a minus sign is 50, so we assign 50 units to the factory B–warehouse 3 and factory C–warehouse 1 routes, and subtract 50 units from the two squares containing minus signs. However, this act causes both formerly occupied squares to drop to 0. It also means that there are not enough occupied squares in the new solution and that it will be degenerate. We will have to place an artificial zero in one of the squares (generally, the one with the lowest shipping cost) to handle the degeneracy problem.

10.9 MORE THAN ONE OPTIMAL SOLUTION

Multiple solutions are possible when one or more improvement indices in the optimal solution stages are equal to zero.

Just as with linear programming problems, it is possible for a transportation problem to have multiple optimal solutions. Such a situation is indicated when one or more of the improvement indices that we calculate for each unused square is zero in the optimal solution. This means that it is possible to design alternative shipping routings with the same total shipping cost. The alternate optimal solution can be found by shipping the most to this unused square. Practically speaking, multiple optimal solutions provide management with greater flexibility in selecting and using resources.

10.10 FACILITY LOCATION ANALYSIS

Locating a new facility within one overall distribution system is aided by the transportation method.

The transportation method has proved to be especially useful in helping a firm decide where to locate a new factory or warehouse. Since a new location is an issue of major financial importance to a company, several alternative locations must ordinarily be considered and evaluated. Even though a wide variety of subjective factors are considered, including quality of labor supply, presence of labor unions, community attitude and appearance, utilities, and recreational and educational facilities for employees, a final decision also involves minimizing total shipping and production costs. This means that each alternative facility location should be analyzed within the framework of one *overall* distribution system. The new location that will yield the minimum cost for the *entire system* will be the one recommended. Let us consider the case of the Hardgrave Machine Company.

Locating a New Factory for Hardgrave Machine Company

The Hardgrave Machine Company produces computer components at its plants in Cincinnati, Salt Lake City, and Pittsburgh. These plants have not been able to keep up with demand for orders at Hardgrave's four warehouses in Detroit, Dallas, New York, and Los Angeles. As a result, the firm has decided to build a new plant to expand its productive capacity. The two sites being considered are Seattle and Birmingham, Alabama; both cities are attractive in terms of labor supply, municipal services, and ease of factory financing.

Table 10.22 presents the production costs and output requirements for each of the three existing plants, demand at each of the four warehouses, and estimated production costs of the new proposed plants. Transportation costs from each plant to each warehouse are summarized in Table 10.23.

TABLE 10.22 Hardgrave's Demand and Supply Data

WAREHOUSE	MONTHLY DEMAND (UNITS)	PRODUCTION PLANT	MONTHLY SUPPLY	COST TO PRODUCE ONE UNIT($)
Detroit	10,000	Cincinnati	15,000	48
Dallas	12,000	Salt Lake	6,000	50
New York	15,000	Pittsburgh	14,000	52
Los Angeles	9,000		35,000	
	46,000			

Supply needed from new plant = 46,000 − 35,000 = 11,000 units per month

ESTIMATED PRODUCTION COST PER UNIT AT PROPOSED PLANTS	
Seattle	$53
Birmingham	$49

TABLE 10.23 Hardgrave's Shipping Costs

FROM \ TO	DETROIT	DALLAS	NEW YORK	LOS ANGELES
CINCINNATI	$25	$55	$40	$60
SALT LAKE	35	30	50	40
PITTSBURGH	36	45	26	66
SEATTLE	60	38	65	27
BIRMINGHAM	35	30	41	50

TABLE 10.24 Birmingham Plant Optimal Solution: Total Hardgrave Cost Is $3,741,000

TO FROM	DETROIT	DALLAS	NEW YORK	LOS ANGELES	MONTHLY SUPPLY
CINCINNATI	73 10,000	103	88 1,000	108 4,000	15,000
SALT LAKE	85	80 1,000	100	90 5,000	6,000
PITTSBURGH	88	97	78 14,000	118	14,000
BIRMINGHAM	84	79 11,000	90	99	11,000
MONTHLY DEMAND	10,000	12,000	15,000	9,000	46,000

TABLE 10.25 Seattle Plant Optimal Solution: Total Hardgrave Cost Is $3,704,000

TO FROM	DETROIT	DALLAS	NEW YORK	LOS ANGELES	MONTHLY SUPPLY
CINCINNATI	73 10,000	103 4,000	88 1,000	108	15,000
SALT LAKE	85	80 6,000	100	90	6,000
PITTSBURGH	88	97	78 14,000	118	14,000
SEATTLE	113	91 2,000	118	80 9,000	11,000
MONTHLY DEMAND	10,000	12,000	15,000	9,000	46,000

The important question that Hardgrave now faces is: Which of the new locations will yield the lowest cost for the firm in combination with the existing plants and warehouses? Note that the cost of each individual plant-to-warehouse route is found by adding the shipping costs (in the body of Table 10.23) to the respective unit production costs (from Table 10.22). Thus, the total production plus shipping cost of one computer component from Cincinnati to Detroit is $73 ($25 for shipping plus $48 for production).

To determine which new plant (Seattle or Birmingham) shows the lowest total systemwide cost of distribution and production, we solve two transportation problems—one for each of the two possible combinations. Tables 10.24 and 10.25 show the resulting two optimum solutions with the total cost for each. It appears that Seattle should be selected as the new plant site: Its total cost of $3,704,000 is less than the $3,741,000 cost at Birmingham.

We solve two transportation problems to find the new plant with lowest system cost.

Using Excel QM as a Solution Tool We can use Excel QM to solve each of the two Hardgrave Machine Company problems. To illustrate, Program 10.2A reflects the Birmingham computer analysis. As we saw earlier in this chapter, the Transportation module of Excel QM uses Solver. The output appears in Program 10.2B.

PROGRAM 10.2A

Excel QM Input Screen, showing formulas. To reach an optimal solution, we use Excel's Tool bar, select Solver, and then choose Solve. Data from Table 10.24 for Birmingham are used.

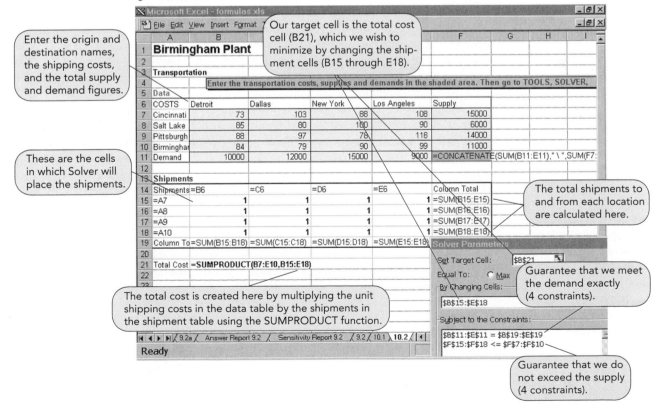

PROGRAM 10.2B

Output from Excel QM Analysis in Program 10.2A with Optimal Solution to Hardgrave machine Problem for Birmingham

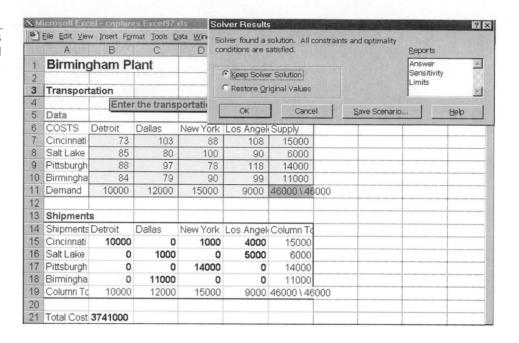

10.11 APPROACH OF THE ASSIGNMENT MODEL

The second special-purpose LP algorithm discussed in this chapter is the assignment method. Each assignment problem has associated with it a table, or matrix. Generally, the rows contain the objects or people we wish to assign, and the columns comprise the tasks or things we want them assigned to. The numbers in the table are the costs associated with each particular assignment.

As an illustration of the assignment method, let us consider the case of the Fix-It Shop, which has just received three new rush projects to repair: (1) a radio, (2) a toaster oven, and (3) a broken coffee table. Three repair persons, each with different talents and abilities, are available to do the jobs. The Fix-It Shop owner estimates what it will cost in wages to assign each of the workers to each of the three projects. The costs, which are shown in Table 10.26, differ because the owner believes that each worker will differ in speed and skill on these quite varied jobs.

The goal is to assign projects to people (one project to one person) so that the total costs are minimized.

The owner's objective is to assign the three projects to the workers in a way that will result in the lowest total cost to the shop. Note that the assignment of people to projects must be on a one-to-one basis; each project will be assigned exclusively to one worker only. Hence the number of rows must always equal the number of columns in an assignment problem's cost table.

One way to solve (small) problems is to enumerate all possible outcomes.

Because the Fix-It Shop problem only consists of three workers and three projects, one easy way to find the best solution is to list all possible assignments and their respective costs. For example, if Adams is assigned to project 1, Brown to project 2, and Cooper to project 3, the total cost will be $11 + $10 + $7 = $28. Table 10.27 summarizes all six assignment options. The table also shows that the least-cost solution would be to assign Cooper to project 1, Brown to project 2, and Adams to project 3, at a total cost of $25.

TABLE 10.26 Estimated Project Repair Costs for the Fix-It Shop Assignment Problem

	PROJECT		
PERSON	**1**	**2**	**3**
Adams	$11	$14	$6
Brown	8	10	11
Cooper	9	12	7

Obtaining solutions by enumeration works well for small problems but quickly becomes inefficient as assignment problems become larger. For example, a problem involving the assignment of four workers to four projects requires that we consider $4! \ (= 4 \times 3 \times 2 \times 1)$ or 24 alternatives. A problem with eight workers and eight tasks, which actually is not that large in a realistic situation, yields $8! \ (= 8 \times 7 \times 6 \times 5 \times 4 \times 3 \times 2 \times 1)$ or 40,320 possible solutions! Since it would clearly be impractical to compare so many alternatives, a more efficient solution method is needed.

The Hungarian Method (Flood's Technique)

The Hungarian method of assignment provides us with an efficient means of finding the optimal solution without having to make a direct comparison of every option. It operates on a principle of *matrix reduction*, which means that by subtracting and adding appropriate numbers in the cost table or matrix, we can reduce the problem to a matrix of *opportunity costs*. Opportunity costs show the relative penalties associated with assigning *any* person to a project as opposed to making the *best* or least-cost assignment. If we can reduce the matrix to the point where there is one zero element in each row and column, it will then be possible to make optimal assignments, that is, assignments in which all of the opportunity costs are zero.

Matrix reduction reduces the table to a set of opportunity costs. These show the penalty of not making the least-cost (or best) assignment.

TABLE 10.27 Summary of Fix-It Shop Assignment Alternatives and Costs

PROJECT ASSIGNMENT				
1	**2**	**3**	**LABOR COSTS ($)**	**TOTAL COSTS ($)**
Adams	Brown	Cooper	11 + 10 + 7	28
Adams	Cooper	Brown	11 + 12 + 11	34
Brown	Adams	Cooper	8 + 14 + 7	29
Brown	Cooper	Adams	8 + 12 + 6	26
Cooper	Adams	Brown	9 + 14 + 11	34
Cooper	Brown	Adams	9 + 10 + 6	25

There are basically three steps in the assignment method[3]:

Here are the three steps of assignment method.

Three Steps of the Assignment Method

1. *Find the opportunity cost table by*

   (a) Subtracting the smallest number in each row of the original cost table or matrix from every number in that row.

   (b) Then subtracting the smallest number in each column of the table obtained in part (a) from every number in that column.

2. *Test the table resulting from step 1 to see whether an optimal assignment can be made.* The procedure is to draw the minimum number of vertical and horizontal straight lines necessary to cover all zeros in the table. If the number of lines equals either the number of rows or columns in the table, an optimal assignment can be made. If the number of lines is less than the number of rows or columns, we proceed to step 3.

3. *Revise the present opportunity cost table.* This is done by subtracting the smallest number not covered by a line from every other uncovered number. This same smallest number is also added to any number(s) lying at the intersection of horizontal and vertical lines. We then return to step 2 and continue the cycle until an optimal assignment is possible.

The assignment method is much easier than using LP.

This assignment "algorithm" is not nearly as difficult to apply as the linear programming algorithm we discussed in Chapters 7 to 9, or even as complex as the transportation procedures we saw earlier in this chapter. All it requires is some careful addition and subtraction and close attention to the three preceding steps. These steps are charted for your convenience in Figure 10.3. Let us now apply them.

Step 1: Find the Opportunity Cost Table. As we mentioned earlier, the opportunity cost of any decision we make in life consists of the opportunities that are sacrificed in making that decision. For example, the opportunity cost of the unpaid time a person spends starting a new business is the salary that person would earn for those hours that he or she could have worked on another job. This important concept in the assignment method is best illustrated by applying it to a problem. For your convenience, the original cost table for the Fix-It Shop problem is repeated in Table 10.28.

Suppose that we decide to assign Cooper to project 2. The table shows that the cost of this assignment is $12. Based on the concept of opportunity costs, this is not the best decision, since Cooper could perform project 3 for only $7. The assignment of Cooper to project 2 then involves an opportunity cost of $5 (= $12 − $7), the amount we are sacrificing by making this assignment instead of the least-cost one. Similarly, an assignment of Cooper to project 1 represents an opportunity cost of $9 – $7 = $2. Finally, because the assignment of Cooper to project 3 is the best assignment, we can say that the opportunity cost of this assignment is zero ($7 – $7). The results of this operation for each of the rows in Table 10.28 are called the row opportunity costs and are shown in Table 10.29.

Row and column opportunity costs reflect the cost we are sacrificing by not making the least-cost selection.

We note at this point that although the assignment of Cooper to project 3 is the cheapest way to make use of Cooper, it is not necessarily the least-expensive approach to completing project 3. Adams can perform the same task for only $6. In other words, if we look at this assignment problem from a project angle instead of a people angle, the *column* opportunity costs may be completely different.

---

[3] The steps apply if we can assume that the matrix is balanced, that is, the number of rows in the matrix equals the number of columns. In Section 10.12 we discuss how to handle unbalanced problems.

FIGURE 10.3

Steps in the Assignment Method

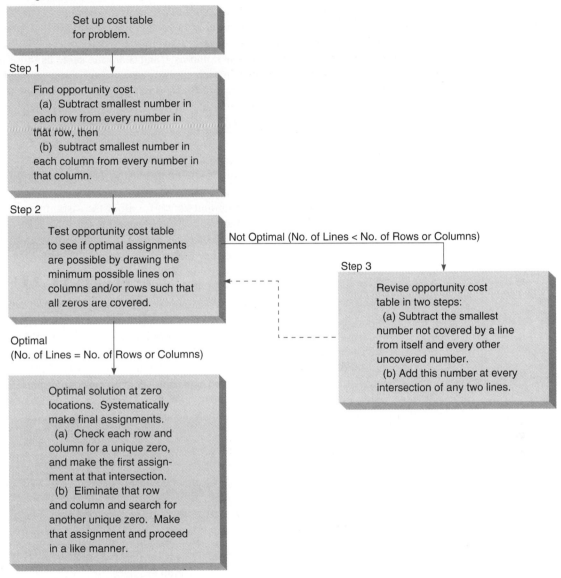

TABLE 10.28	**Cost of Each Person-Project Assignment for the Fix-It Shop Problem**		
	PROJECT		
PERSON	1	2	3
Adams	$11	$14	$6
Brown	8	10	11
Cooper	9	12	7

TABLE 10.29	**Row Opportunity Cost Table for the Fix-It Shop Step 1, Part (a)**		
	PROJECT		
PERSON	1	2	3
Adams	$5	$8	$0
Brown	0	2	3
Cooper	2	5	0

Total opportunity costs reflect the row and column opportunity cost analyses.

What we need to complete step 1 of the assignment method is a *total* opportunity cost table, that is, one that reflects both row and column opportunity costs. This involves following part (b) of step 1 to derive column opportunity costs.[4] We simply take the costs in Table 10.29 and subtract the smallest number in each column from each number in that column. The resulting total opportunity costs are given in Table 10.30.

You might note that the numbers in columns 1 and 3 are the same as those in Table 10.29, since the smallest column entry in each case was zero. Thus it may turn out that the assignment of Cooper to project 3 is part of the optimal solution because of the relative nature of opportunity costs. What we are trying to measure are the relative efficiencies for the entire cost table and to find what assignments are best for the overall solution.

Step 2: Test for an Optimal Assignment. The objective of the Fix-It Shop owner is to assign the three workers to the repair projects in such a way that total labor costs are kept at a minimum. When translated to making assignments using our total opportunity cost table, this means that we would like to have a total assigned opportunity cost of 0. In other words, an optimal solution has zero opportunity costs for all of the assignments.

When a zero opportunity cost is found for all of the assignments, an optimal assignment can be made.

Looking at Table 10.30, we see that there are four possible zero opportunity cost assignments. We could assign Adams to project 3 and Brown to either project 1 or project 2. But this leaves Cooper without a zero opportunity cost assignment. Recall that two workers cannot be given the same task; each must do one and only one repair project, and each project must be assigned to only one person. Hence, even though four zeros appear in this cost table, it is not yet possible to make an assignment yielding a total opportunity cost of zero.

This line test is used to see if a solution is optimal.

A simple test has been designed to help us determine whether an optimal assignment can be made. The method consists of finding the *minimum* number of straight lines (vertical and horizontal) necessary to cover all zeros in the cost table. (Each line is drawn so that it covers as many zeros as possible at one time.) If the number of lines equals the number of rows or columns in the table, then an optimal assignment can be made. If, on the other hand, the number of lines is less than the number of rows or columns, an optimal assignment cannot be made. In the latter case, we must proceed to step 3 and develop a new total opportunity cost table.

Table 10.31 illustrates that it is possible to cover all four zero entries in Table 10.30 with only two lines. Because there are three rows, an optimal assignment may not yet be made.

TABLE 10.30 Total Opportunity Cost Table for the Fix-It Shop Step 1, Part (b)

PERSON	PROJECT 1	2	3
Adams	$5	$6	$0
Brown	0	0	3
Cooper	2	3	0

TABLE 10.31 Test for Optimal Solution to Fix-It Shop Problem

PERSON	PROJECT 1	2	3
Adams	$5	$6	$0
Brown	0	0	3 → Covering line 1
Cooper	2	3	0

Covering line 2

---

[4] Can you think of a situation in which part (b) of step 1 would not be required? See if you can design a cost table in which an optimal solution is possible after part (a) of step 1 is completed.

TABLE 10.32 Revised Opportunity Cost Table for the Fix-It Shop Problem

	PROJECT		
PERSON	1	2	3
Adams	$3	$4	$0
Brown	0	0	5
Cooper	0	1	0

TABLE 10.33 Optimality Test on the Revised Fix-It Shop Opportunity Cost Table

	PROJECT		
PERSON	1	2	3
Adams	$3	$4	$0
Brown	0	0	5	→ Covering line 2
Cooper	0	1	0

Covering line 1   Covering line 3

Step 3: Revise the Opportunity-Cost Table. An optimal solution is seldom obtained from the initial opportunity cost table. Often, we need to revise the table in order to shift one (or more) of the zero costs from its present location (covered by lines) to a new uncovered location in the table. Intuitively, we would want this uncovered location to emerge with a new zero opportunity cost.

This is accomplished by *subtracting* the smallest number not covered by a line from all numbers not covered by a straight line. This same smallest number is then added to every number (including zeros) lying at the intersection of any two lines.

The smallest uncovered number in Table 10.31 is 2, so this value is subtracted from each of the four uncovered numbers. A 2 is also added to the number that is covered by the intersecting horizontal and vertical lines. The results of step 3 are shown in Table 10.32.

To test now for an optimal assignment, we return to step 2 and find the minimum number of lines necessary to cover all zeros in the revised opportunity cost table. Because it requires three lines to cover the zeros (see Table 10.33), an optimal assignment can be made.

Making the Final Assignment

It is apparent that the Fix-It Shop problem's optimal assignment is Adams to project 3, Brown to project 2, and Cooper to project 1. In solving larger problems, however, it is best to rely on a more systematic approach to making valid assignments. One such way is first to select a row or column that contains only one zero cell. Such a situation is found in the first row, Adams's row, in which the only zero is in the project 3 column. An assignment can be made to that cell, and then lines drawn through its row and column (see Table 10.34). From the uncovered rows and columns, we again choose a row or column in which there is only one zero cell. We make that assignment and continue the procedure until each person is assigned to one task.

The total labor costs of this assignment are computed from the original cost table (see Table 10.28). They are as follows:

Making an optimal assignment involves first checking the rows and columns where there is only one zero cell.

ASSIGNMENT	COST ($)
Adams to project 3	6
Brown to project 2	10
Cooper to project 1	9
Total cost	25

TABLE 10.34   Making the Final Fix-It Shop Assignments

(A) FIRST ASSIGNMENT				(B) SECOND ASSIGNMENT				(C) THIRD ASSIGNMENT		
	1	2	3		1	2	3		1	2	3
Adams	3	4	[0]	Adams	3	4	[0]	Adams	3	4	[0]
Brown	0	0	5	Brown	0	0	5	Brown	0	[0]	5
Cooper	0	1	0	Cooper	[0]	1	0	Cooper	[0]	1	0

Using Excel QM for the Fix-It Shop Assignment Problem Excel QM's Assignment module can be used to solve the Fix-It problem. The input screen, using data from Table 10.28 appears first, as Program 10.3A. The constraints are also shown in Program 10.3A. When the data are all entered, we choose the Tools command, followed by the Solver command. Excel's Solver uses LP to optimize assignment problems. We then select the Solve command. The solution appears in Program 10.3B.

10.12   DUMMY ROWS AND DUMMY COLUMNS

The solution procedure to assignment problems just discussed requires that the number of rows in the table equal the number of columns. Often, however, the number of people or objects to be assigned does not equal the number of tasks or clients or machines listed in the columns. When this occurs and we have more rows than columns, we simply add a *dummy column* or task (similar to how we handled unbalanced transportation problems earlier in this chapter). If the number of tasks that need to be done exceeds the number of people available, we add a *dummy row*. This creates a table of equal dimensions and allows us to solve the problem as before. Since the dummy task or person is really nonexistent, it is reasonable to enter zeros in its row or column as the cost or time estimate.

Suppose the owner of the Fix-It Shop realizes that a fourth worker, Davis, is also available to work on one of the three rush jobs that just came in. Davis can do the first project for $10, the second for $13, and the third project for $8. The shop's owner still faces the same basic problem, that is, which worker to assign to which project to minimize total labor costs. We do not have a fourth project, however, so we simply add a dummy column or dummy project. The initial cost table is shown in Table 10.35 on page 444. One of the four workers, you should realize, will be assigned to the dummy project; in other words, the worker will not really be assigned any of the tasks. Problem 10-35 asks you to find the optimal solution for the data in Table 10.35.

10.13   MAXIMIZATION ASSIGNMENT PROBLEMS

Maximization problems can easily be converted to minimization problems. This is done by subtracting each rating from the largest rating in the table.

Some assignment problems are phrased in terms of maximizing the payoff, profit, or effectiveness of an assignment instead of minimizing costs. It is easy to obtain an equivalent minimization problem by converting all numbers in the table to opportunity costs. This is brought about by subtracting every number in the original payoff table from the

PROGRAM 10.3A

Excel QM's Assignment Module. After entering the data, select Tools, then Solver, and then Solve.

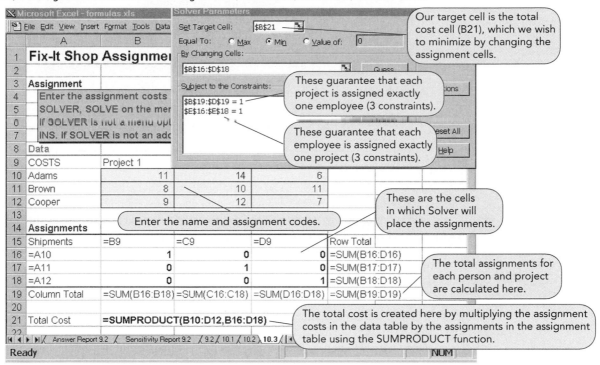

PROGRAM 10.3B

Excel QM Output Screen for the Fix-It Shop Problem

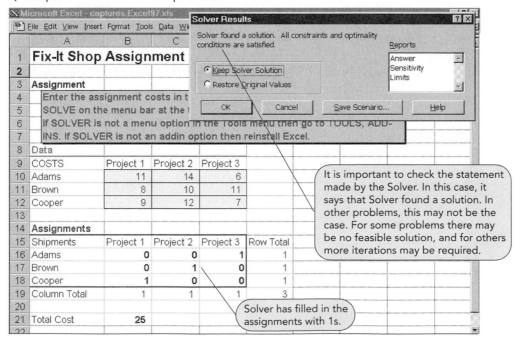

TABLE 10.35   Estimated Project Repair Costs for Fix-It Shop with Davis Included

	PROJECT			
PERSON	1	2	3	DUMMY
Adams	$11	$14	$6	$0
Brown	8	10	11	0
Cooper	9	12	7	0
Davis	10	13	8	0

largest single number in that table. The transformed entries represent opportunity costs; it turns out that minimizing opportunity costs produces the same assignment as the original maximization problem. Once the optimal assignment for this transformed problem has been computed, the total payoff or profit is found by adding the original payoffs of those cells that are in the optimal assignment.

Let us consider the following example. The British navy wishes to assign four ships to patrol four sectors of the North Sea. In some areas ships are to be on the outlook for illegal fishing boats, and in other sectors to watch for enemy submarines, so the commander rates each ship in terms of its probable efficiency in each sector. These relative efficiencies are illustrated in Table 10.36. On the basis of the ratings shown, the commander wants to determine the patrol assignments producing the greatest overall efficiencies.

Step by step, the solution procedure is as follows. We first convert the maximizing efficiency table into a minimizing opportunity cost table. This is done by subtracting each rating from 100, the largest rating in the whole table. The resulting opportunity costs are given in Table 10.37.

Row subtractions: the smallest number in each row is subtracted from every number in that row.

Column subtractions: the smallest number in each column is subtracted from every number in that column.

We now follow steps 1 and 2 of the assignment algorithm. The smallest number in each row is subtracted from every number in that row (see Table 10.38); and then the smallest number in each column is subtracted from every number in that column (as shown in Table 10.39).

The minimum number of straight lines needed to cover all zeros in this total opportunity cost table is four. Hence an optimal assignment can be made already. You should be

TABLE 10.36   Efficiencies of British Ships in Patrol Sectors

	SECTOR			
SHIP	A	B	C	D
1	20	60	50	55
2	60	30	80	75
3	80	100	90	80
4	65	80	75	70

TABLE 10.37   Opportunity Costs of British Ships

	SECTOR			
SHIP	A	B	C	D
1	80	40	50	45
2	40	70	20	25
3	20	0	10	20
4	35	20	25	30

IN ACTION   Scheduling American League Umpires with the Assignment Model

Scheduling umpires in professional baseball is a complex problem that must include a number of criteria. In assigning officials to games, one objective typically is to minimize total travel cost while satisfying a set of frequency-oriented constraints such as limiting the number of times an official or crew is exposed to each team, balancing home and away game exposures, balancing exposures to teams over the course of a season, and so on. These constraints complicate the problem to such an extent that except for the most trivial cases, the use of a computer-based system is essential.

The American League is composed of 14 professional baseball teams organized into Western and Eastern divisions. The Western Division is comprised of Seattle, Oakland, California, Texas, Kansas City, Minnesota, and Chicago. The Eastern Division is comprised of Milwaukee, Detroit, Cleveland, Toronto, Baltimore, New York, and Boston. The game schedule, constructed each winter prior to the start of the baseball season, is a difficult scheduling problem in itself. Consid-

eration must be given to such factors as the number of games played against other teams both within and outside a division, the split between home games and road trips, travel time, and possible conflicts in cities that have teams in the National League.

The objective of balancing crew assignments relatively evenly and minimizing travel costs are by nature conflicting. Attempting to balance crew assignments necessitates considerable airline travel and equipment moves, and hence increased travel costs.

Using an assignment model as part of a microcomputer-based decision support system, the American League was able to reduce travel mileage by about 4% during the first year of use. This not only saved the league $30,000 but improved the crew exposure balance.

Source: J. Evans. "Scheduling American League Umpires" *Interfaces* (November–December 1988): 42–51.

able by now to spot the best solution, namely, ship 1 to sector *D*, ship 2 to sector *C*, ship 3 to sector *B*, and ship 4 to sector *A*.

The overall efficiency, computed from the original efficiency data in Table 10.36, can now be shown:

ASSIGNMENT	EFFICIENCY
Ship 1 to sector *D*	55
Ship 2 to sector *C*	80
Ship 3 to sector *B*	100
Ship 4 to sector *A*	65
Total efficiency	300

TABLE 10.38 Row Opportunity Costs for the British Navy Problem

	SECTOR			
SHIP	A	B	C	D
1	40	0	10	5
2	20	50	0	5
3	20	0	10	20
4	15	0	5	10

TABLE 10.39 Total Opportunity Costs for the British Navy Problem

	SECTOR			
SHIP	A	B	C	D
1	25	0	10	0
2	5	50	0	0
3	5	0	10	15
4	0	0	5	5

Glossary

Transportation Problem. A specific case of LP concerned with scheduling shipments from sources to destinations so that total transportation costs are minimized.

Source. An origin or supply location in a transportation problem.

Destination. A demand location in a transportation problem.

Transportation Table. A table summarizing all transportation data to help keep track of all algorithm computations. It stores information on demands, supplies, shipping costs, units shipped, origins, and destinations.

Balanced Problem. The condition under which total demand (at all destinations) is equal to total supply (at all sources).

Northwest Corner Rule. A systematic procedure for establishing an initial feasible solution to the transportation problem.

Stepping-Stone Method. An iterative technique for moving from an initial feasible solution to an optimal solution in transportation problems.

Improvement Index. The net cost of shipping one unit on a route not used in the current transportation problem solution.

Modified Distribution (MODI) Method. Another algorithm for finding the optimal solution to a transportation problem. It can be used in place of the stepping-stone method.

Vogel's Approximation Method (VAM). An algorithm used to find a relatively efficient initial feasible solution to a transportation problem. This initial solution is often the optimal solution.

Unbalanced Problem. A situation in which total demand is not equal to total supply.

Dummy Source. An artificial source added when total demand is greater than total supply. The supply at the dummy source is set so that total demand and supply are equal. The transportation cost for dummy source cells is zero.

Dummy Destination. An artificial destination added when total supply is greater than total demand. The demand at the dummy destination is set so that total supply and demand are equal. The transportation cost for dummy destination cells is zero.

Degeneracy. A condition that occurs when the number of occupied squares in any solution is less than the number of rows plus the number of columns minus 1 in a transportation table.

Facility Location Analysis. An application of the transportation method to help a firm decide where to locate a new factory, warehouse, or other facility.

Matrix Reduction. The approach of the assignment method which reduces the original assignment costs to a table of opportunity costs.

Opportunity Costs. The costs associated with a sacrificed opportunity to make a particular decision.

Dummy Rows or Columns. Extra rows or columns added in order to "balance" an assignment problem so that the number of rows equals the number of columns.

Key Equations

(10-1) $R_i + K_j = C_{ij}$

An equation used to compute the MODI cost values (R_i, K_j) for each column and row intersection for squares in the solution.

(10-2) Improvement index (I_{ij}) $= C_{ij} - R_i - K_j$

The equation used to compute the improvement index for each unused square by the MODI method. If all improvement indices are greater than or equal to zero, an optimal solution has been reached.

Solved Problems

Solved Problem 10-1

Don Yale, president of Hardrock Concrete Company, has plants in three locations and is currently working on three major construction projects, located at different sites. The shipping cost per truckload of concrete, plant capacities, and project requirements are provided in the accompanying table.

(a) Formulate an initial feasible solution to Hardrock's transportation problem using the northwest corner rule.

(b) Then evaluate each unused shipping route (each empty cell) by applying the stepping-stone method and computing all improvement indices. Remember to:

1. Check that supply and demand are equal.
2. Load the table via the northwest corner method.
3. Check that there are the proper number of occupied cells for a "normal" solution, namely, number of rows + number of columns − 1 = number of occupied cells.
4. Find a closed path to each empty cell.
5. Determine the improvement index for each unused cell.
6. Move as many units as possible to the cell that provides the most improvement (if there is one).
7. Repeat steps 3 through 6 until no further improvement can be found.

TO / FROM	PROJECT A	PROJECT B	PROJECT C	PLANT CAPACITIES
PLANT 1	$10	$4	$11	70
PLANT 2	$12	$5	$8	50
PLANT 3	$9	$7	$6	30
PROJECT REQUIREMENTS	40	50	60	150

Solution

(a) Northwest Corner Solution

Initial cost = 40($10) + 30($4) + 20($5) + 30($8) + 30($6) = $1,040

TO / FROM	PROJECT A	PROJECT B	PROJECT C	PLANT CAPACITIES
PLANT 1	$10 40	$4 30	$11	70
PLANT 2	$12	$5 20	$8 30	50
PLANT 3	$9	$7	$6 30	30
PROJECT REQUIREMENTS	40	50	60	150

(b) Using the stepping-stone method, the following improvement indices are computed:

Path: plant 1 to project $C = \$11 - \$4 + \$5 - \$8 = +\$4$

(closed path: $1C$ to $1B$ to $2B$ to $2C$)

TO⟍FROM	PROJECT A	PROJECT B	PROJECT C	PLANT CAPACITIES
PLANT 1	10	4	11	70
PLANT 2	12	5	8	50
PLANT 3	9	7	6	30
PROJECT REQUIREMENTS	40	50	60	150

Path: plant 1 to project C

Path: plant 2 to project $A = \$12 - \$5 + \$4 - \$10 = +\$1$

(closed path: $2A$ to $2B$ to $1B$ to $1A$)

TO⟍FROM	PROJECT A	PROJECT B	PROJECT C	PLANT CAPACITIES
PLANT 1	10	4	11	70
PLANT 2	12	5	8	50
PLANT 3	9	7	6	30
PROJECT REQUIREMENTS	40	50	60	150

Path: plant 2 to project A

Path: plant 3 to project $A = \$9 - \$6 + \$8 - \$5 + \$4 - \$10 = \$0$

(closed path: $3A$ to $3C$ to $2C$ to $2B$ to $1B$ to $1A$)

TO⟍FROM	PROJECT A	PROJECT B	PROJECT C	PLANT CAPACITIES
PLANT 1	10	4	11	70
PLANT 2	12	5	8	50
PLANT 3	9	7	6	30
PROJECT REQUIREMENTS	40	50	60	150

Path: plant 3 to project A

Path: plant 3 to project B = \$7 − \$6 + \$8 − \$5 = +\$4

(closed path: $3B$ to $3C$ to $2C$ to $2B$)

TO FROM	PROJECT A	PROJECT B	PROJECT C	PLANT CAPACITIES
PLANT 1	10	4	11	70
PLANT 2	12	5	8	50
PLANT 3	9	7	6	30
PROJECT REQUIREMENTS	40	50	60	150

Path: plant 3 to project B

Since all indices are greater than or equal to zero (all are positive or zero), this initial solution provides the optimal transportation schedule, namely, 40 units from 1 to A, 30 units from 1 to B, 20 units from 2 to B, 30 units from 2 to C, and 30 units from 3 to C.

Had we found a path that allowed improvement, we would move all units possible to that cell and then check every empty cell again. Because the plant 3 to project A improvement index was equal to zero, we note that multiple optimal solutions exist.

Solved Problem 10-2

Solve the Hardgrave Machine Company facility location problem shown in Table 10.25 with an LP formulation.

Solution

First we shall formulate this transportation problem as an LP model by introducing double-subscripted decision variables. We let X_{11} denote the number of units shipped from origin 1 (Cincinnati) to destination 1 (Detroit), X_{12} denote shipments from origin 1 (Cincinnati) to destination 2 (Dallas), and so on. In general, the decision variables for a transportation problem having m origins and n destinations are written as

$$X_{ij} = \text{number of units shipped from origin } i \text{ to destination } j$$

where

$$i = 1, 2, \ldots, m \text{ and } j = 1, 2, \ldots, n$$

Because the objective of the transportation model is to minimize total transportation costs, we develop the following cost expression:

$$\begin{aligned}
\text{minimize} = \ &73X_{11} + 103X_{12} + 88X_{13} + 108X_{14} \\
&+ 85X_{21} + 80X_{22} + 100X_{23} + 90X_{24} \\
&+ 88X_{31} + 97X_{32} + 78X_{33} + 118X_{34} \\
&+ 113X_{41} + 91X_{42} + 118X_{43} + 80X_{44}
\end{aligned}$$

Now we establish supply constraints for each of the four plants:

$$X_{11} + X_{12} + X_{13} + X_{14} \leq 15{,}000 \text{ (Cincinnati supply)}$$
$$X_{21} + X_{22} + X_{23} + X_{24} \leq \ 6{,}000 \text{ (Salt Lake supply)}$$
$$X_{31} + X_{32} + X_{33} + X_{34} \leq 14{,}000 \text{ (Pittsburgh supply)}$$
$$X_{41} + X_{42} + X_{43} + X_{44} \leq 11{,}000 \text{ (Seattle supply)}$$

With four warehouses as the destinations, we need the following four demand constraints:

$$X_{11} + X_{21} + X_{31} + X_{41} = 10,000 \text{ (Detroit demand)}$$

$$X_{12} + X_{22} + X_{32} + X_{42} = 12,000 \text{ (Dallas demand)}$$

$$X_{13} + X_{23} + X_{33} + X_{43} = 15,000 \text{ (New York demand)}$$

$$X_{14} + X_{24} + X_{34} + X_{44} = 9,000 \text{ (Los Angeles demand)}$$

In Chapters 7, 8, and 9, we saw how QM for Windows and Excel spreadsheets can be used to solve LP problems. A computer solution will confirm that total shipping costs will be $3,704,000.

Although LP codes can indeed be used on transportation problems, the special transportation module for Excel QM (shown earlier) and QM for Windows (shown in Appendix 10.1) tend to be easier to input, run, and interpret.

Solved Problem 10-3

Prentice Hall, Inc., a publisher headquartered in New Jersey, wants to assign three recently hired college graduates, Jones, Smith, and Wilson to regional sales districts in Omaha, Dallas, and Miami. But the firm also has an opening in New York and would send one of the three there if it were more economical than a move to Omaha, Dallas, or Miami. It will cost $1,000 to relocate Jones to New York, $800 to relocate Smith there, and $1,500 to move Wilson. What is the optimal assignment of personnel to offices?

OFFICE HIREE	OMAHA	MIAMI	DALLAS
JONES	$800	$1,100	$1,200
SMITH	$500	$1,600	$1,300
WILSON	$500	$1,000	$2,300

Solution

(a) The cost table has a fourth column to represent New York. To balance the problem, we add a dummy row (person) with a zero relocation cost to each city.

OFFICE HIREE	OMAHA	MIAMI	DALLAS	NEW YORK
JONES	$800	$1,100	$1,200	$1,000
SMITH	$500	$1,600	$1,300	$800
WILSON	$500	$1,000	$2,300	$1,500
DUMMY	0	0	0	0

(b) Subtract smallest number in each row and cover zeros (column subtraction will give the same numbers and therefore is not necessary).

OFFICE HIREE	OMAHA	MIAMI	DALLAS	NEW YORK
JONES	0	300	400	200
SMITH	0	1,100	800	300
WILSON	0	500	$1,800	$1,000
DUMMY	0	0	0	0

(c) Subtract smallest uncovered number (200), add it to each square where two lines intersect, and cover all zeros.

HIREE \ OFFICE	OMAHA	MIAMI	DALLAS	NEW YORK
JONES	0	100	200	0
SMITH	0	900	600	100
WILSON	0	300	1,600	800
DUMMY	200	0	0	0

(d) Subtract smallest uncovered number (100), add it to each square where two lines intersect, and cover all zeros.

HIREE \ OFFICE	OMAHA	MIAMI	DALLAS	NEW YORK
JONES	0	0	100	0
SMITH	0	800	500	100
WILSON	0	200	1,500	800
DUMMY	300	0	0	100

(e) Subtract smallest uncovered number (100), add it to squares where two lines intersect, and cover all zeros.

HIREE \ OFFICE	OMAHA	MIAMI	DALLAS	NEW YORK
JONES	100	0	100	0
SMITH	0	700	400	0
WILSON	0	100	$1,400	700
DUMMY	400	0	0	100

(f) Since it takes four lines to cover all zeros, an optimal assignment can be made at zero squares. We assign:

   Dummy (no one) to Dallas

   Wilson to Omaha

   Smith to New York

   Jones to Miami

   Cost = $0 + $500 + $800 + $1,100 = $2,400

SELF-TEST

- Before taking the self-test, refer back to the learning objectives at the beginning of the chapter, the notes in the margins, and the glossary at the end of the chapter.
- Use the key at the back of the book to correct your answers.
- Restudy pages that correspond to any questions that you answered incorrectly or material you feel uncertain about.

1. In the transportation technique, the initial solution can be generated in any fashion that one chooses. The only restriction is that
   a. the solution be optimal.
   b. one uses the northwest corner method.
   c. the edge constraints for supply and demand are satisfied.
   d. the solution not be degenerate.
   e. none of the above.

2. The purpose of the stepping-stone method is to
   a. develop the initial solution to a transportation problem.
   b. identify the relevant costs in a transportation problem.
   c. determine whether a given solution is feasible or not.
   d. assist one in moving from an initial feasible solution to the optimal solution.
   e. none of the above.

3. The stepping-stone method can be used only to solve problems requiring the maximization of some criteria.
   a. True   b. False

4. The purpose of a *dummy source* or a *dummy destination* in a transportation problem is to
   a. provide a means of representing a dummy problem.
   b. obtain a balance between total supply and total demand.
   c. prevent the solution from becoming degenerate.
   d. make certain that the total cost does not exceed some specified figure.
   e. none of the above.

5. In a transportation system, a degenerate solution means that
   a. the solution does not provide the correct answer to the real problem.
   b. it becomes impossible to trace a single closed path for each unused square.
   c. the optimal solution has a higher cost than would be the case if the solution were not degenerate.
   d. total supply and total demand are no longer unbalanced.
   e. none of the above.

6. The northwest corner rule is an efficient substitute for the stepping-stone and MODI methods.
   a. True   b. False

7. The solution for degeneracy is to
   a. reformulate the problem.
   b. create additional occupied cells.
   c. solve the problem by the MODI method.
   d. solve the problem by the Vogel's approximation method.
   e. none of the above.

8. The three "steps" in the northwest corner rule are
   1. _____   2. _____
   3. _____

9. The assignment problem
   a. requires that only one job be assigned to each machine.
   b. is a special algorithm of the transportation problem.
   c. cannot be used to minimize total time.
   d. all of the above.
   e. none of the above.

10. The special algorithm used to solve the assignment problem is called
    a. the Hungarian method.
    b. Flood's technique.
    c. the reduced matrix method.
    d. all of the above.
    e. none of the above.

11. In using the assignment problem algorithm, if you have five employees and six machines you
    a. arbitrarily forget one of those machines.
    b. select a slow machine to omit and then solve the problems using a 5 × 5 matrix.
    c. create a dummy employee.
    d. none of the above.

12. In finding the opportunity cost table
    a. part of the first step is to subtract the smallest column value from each cell value in the column.
    b. part of the first step is to subtract the smallest row value from each cell value in the row.
    c. you are finding the relative penalty associated with making a particular assignment as compared to making another assignment.
    d. all of the above.
    e. none of the above.

Discussion Questions and Problems

Discussion Questions

10-1 Is the transportation model an example of decision making under certainty or decision making under uncertainty? Why?

10-2 Why does Vogel's approximation method provide a good initial feasible solution? Could the northwest corner rule ever provide an initial solution with as low a cost?

10-3 What is a *balanced* transportation problem? Describe the approach you would use to solve an *unbalanced* problem.

10-4 How do the MODI and stepping-stone methods differ?

10-5 Develop a *northeast* corner rule and explain how it would work. Set up an initial solution to the Executive Furniture Corporation problem shown in Table 10.2 using your new approach. What comment might you make about this initial solution?

10-6 Explain what happens when the solution to a transportation problem does not have $m + n - 1$ occupied squares (where m = number of rows in the table and n = number of columns in the table).

10-7 What is the enumeration approach to solving assignment problems? Is it a practical way to solve a 5 row $\times$ 5 column problem? A 7×7 problem? Why?

10-8 Think back to the transportation problem at the beginning of this chapter. How could an assignment problem be solved using the transportation approach? Set up the Fix-It Shop problem (shown in Table 10.26) using the transportation approach. What condition will make the solution of this problem difficult?

10-9 You are the plant supervisor and are responsible for scheduling workers to jobs on hand. After estimating the cost of assigning each of five available workers in your plant to five projects that must be completed immediately, you solve the problem using the Hungarian method. The following solution is reached and you post these job assignments:

> Jones to project *A*
>
> Smith to project *B*
>
> Thomas to project *C*
>
> Gibbs to project *D*
>
> Heldman to project *E*

The optimal cost was found to be $492 for these assignments. The plant general manager inspects your original cost estimates and informs you that increased employee benefits mean that each of the 25 numbers in your cost table is too low by $5. He suggests that you immediately rework the problem and post the new assignments.

Is this necessary? Why? What will the new optimal cost be?

10-10 Sue Simmons's marketing research firm has local representatives in all but five states. She decides to expand to cover the whole United States by transferring five experienced volunteers from their current locations to new offices in each of the five states. Simmons's goal is to relocate the five representatives at the least total cost. Consequently, she sets up a 5×5 relocation cost table and prepares to solve it for the best assignment by use of the Hungarian method. At the last moment, Simmons recalls that although the first four volunteers did not pose any objections to being placed in any of the five new cities, the fifth volunteer *did* make one restriction. That person absolutely refused to be assigned to the new office in Tallahassee, Florida—fear of southern roaches, the representative claimed! How should Sue Simmons alter the cost matrix to ensure that this assignment is not included in the optimal solution?

Problems*

10-11 The management of the Executive Furniture Corporation decided to expand the production capacity at its Des Moines factory and to cut back production at its other factories. It also recognizes a shifting market for its desks and revises the requirements at its three warehouses.

NEW WAREHOUSE REQUIREMENTS		NEW FACTORY CAPACITIES	
Albuquerque (A)	200 desks	Des Moines (D)	300 desks
Boston (B)	200 desks	Evansville (E)	150 desks
Cleveland (C)	300 desks	Fort Lauderdale (F)	250 desks

TO FROM	ALBUQUERQUE	BOSTON	CLEVELAND
DES MOINES	5	4	3
EVANSVILLE	8	4	3
FORT LAUDERDALE	9	7	5

(a) Use the northwest corner rule to establish an initial feasible shipping schedule and calculate its cost.

(b) Use the stepping-stone method to test whether an improved solution is possible.

(c) Explain the meaning and implications of an improvement index that is equal to 0. What decisions might management make with this information? Exactly how is the final solution affected?

10-12 The Hardrock Concrete Company has plants in three locations and is currently working on three major construction projects, each located at a different site. The shipping cost per truckload of concrete, daily plant capacities, and daily project requirements are provided in the following table:

TO FROM	PROJECT A	PROJECT B	PROJECT C	PLANT CAPACITIES
PLANT 1	$10	$4	$11	70
PLANT 2	12	5	8	50
PLANT 3	9	7	6	30
PROJECT REQUIREMENTS	40	50	60	150

---

*Note: 🖥, means the problem may be solved with QM for Windows; ✖ means the problem may be solved with Excel QM; and 🖥✖, means the problem may be solved with QM for Windows and/or Excel QM.

(a) Formulate an initial feasible solution to Hardrock's transportation problem using the northwest corner rule. Then evaluate each unused shipping route by computing all improvement indices. Is this solution optimal? Why?

(b) Is there more than one optimal solution to this problem? Why?

 10-13 Hardrock Concrete's owner has decided to increase the capacity at his smallest plant (see Problem 10-12). Instead of producing 30 loads of concrete per day at plant 3, that plant's capacity is doubled to 60 loads. Find the new optimal solution using the northwest corner rule and stepping-stone method. How has changing the third plant's capacity altered the optimal shipping assignment? Discuss the concepts of degeneracy and multiple optimal solutions with regard to this problem.

 10-14 The Saussy Lumber Company ships pine flooring to three building supply houses from its mills in Pineville, Oak Ridge, and Mapletown. Determine the best transportation schedule for the data given in the following table. Use the northwest corner rule and the stepping-stone method.

FROM \ TO	SUPPLY HOUSE 1	SUPPLY HOUSE 2	SUPPLY HOUSE 3	MILL CAPACITY (TONS)
PINEVILLE	$3	$3	$2	25
OAK RIDGE	4	2	3	40
MAPLETOWN	3	2	3	30
SUPPLY HOUSE DEMAND (TONS)	30	30	35	95

 10-15 Using the same Saussy Lumber Company data and the same initial solution you found with the northwest corner rule, resolve Problem 10–14 using the MODI method.

 10-16 The Krampf Lines Railway Company specializes in coal handling. On Friday, April 13, Krampf had empty cars at the following towns in the quantities indicated:

TOWN	SUPPLY OF CARS
Morgantown	35
Youngstown	60
Pittsburgh	25

By Monday, April 16, the following towns will need coal cars as follows:

TOWN	DEMAND FOR CARS
Coal Valley	30
Coaltown	45
Coal Junction	25
Coalsburg	20

Using a railway city-to-city distance chart, the dispatcher constructs a mileage table for the preceding towns. The result is as follows:

	TO			
FROM	COAL VALLEY	COALTOWN	COAL JUNCTION	COALSBURG
Morgantown	50	30	60	70
Youngstown	20	80	10	90
Pittsburgh	100	40	80	30

Minimizing total miles over which cars are moved to new locations, compute the best shipment of coal cars. Use the northwest corner rule and the MODI method.

 10-17 The Jessie Cohen Clothing Group owns factories in three towns (W, Y, and Z) which distribute to three Cohen retail dress shops (in A, B, and C). Factory availabilities, projected store demands, and unit shipping costs are summarized in the table that follows;

FROM \ TO	A	B	C	FACTORY AVAILABILITY
W	$4	$3	$3	35
X	6	7	6	50
Y	8	2	5	50
STORE DEMAND	30	65	40	135

Use Vogel's approximation method to find an initial feasible solution to this transportation problem. Is your VAM solution optimal?

 10-18 The state of Missouri has three major power-generating companies (A, B, and C). During the months of peak demand, the Missouri Power Authority authorizes these companies to pool their excess supply and to distribute it to smaller independent power companies that do not have generators large enough to handle the demand. Excess supply is distributed on the basis of cost per kilowatt hour transmitted. The following table shows the demand and supply in millions of kilowatt hours and the costs per kilowatt hour of transmitting electric power to four small companies in cities W, X, Y, and Z:

FROM \ TO	W	X	Y	Z	EXCESS SUPPLY
A	12¢	4¢	9¢	5¢	55
B	8¢	1¢	6¢	6¢	45
C	1¢	12¢	4¢	7¢	30
UNFILLED POWER DEMAND	40	20	50	20	

Use Vogel's approximation method to find an initial transmission assignment of the excess power supply. Then apply the MODI technique to find the least-cost distribution system.

10-19 Consider the following transportation problem:

FROM \ TO	DESTINATION A	DESTINATION B	DESTINATION C	SUPPLY
SOURCE 1	$8	$9	$4	72
SOURCE 2	5	6	8	38
SOURCE 3	7	9	6	46
SOURCE 4	5	3	7	19
DEMAND	110	34	31	175

Find an initial solution using the northwest corner rule. What special condition exists? Explain how you will proceed to solve the problem.

 10-20 The three blood banks in Franklin County are coordinated through a central office that facilitates blood delivery to four hospitals in the region. The cost to ship a standard container of blood from each bank to each hospital is shown in the next table. Also given are the biweekly number of containers available at each bank and the biweekly number of containers of blood needed at each hospital. How many shipments should be made biweekly from each blood bank to each hospital so that total shipment costs are minimized?

FROM \ TO	HOSPITAL 1	HOSPITAL 2	HOSPITAL 3	HOSPITAL 4	SUPPLY
BANK 1	$8	$9	$11	$16	50
BANK 2	12	7	5	8	80
BANK 3	14	10	6	7	120
DEMAND	90	70	40	50	250

 10-21 The B. Hall Real Estate Investment Corporation has identified four small apartment buildings in which it would like to invest. Mrs. Hall has approached three savings and loan companies regarding financing. Because Hall has been a good client in the past and has maintained a high credit rating in the community, each savings and loan company is willing to consider providing all or part of the mortgage loan needed on each property. Each loan officer has set differing interest rates on each property (rates are affected by the neighborhood of the apartment building, condition of the property, and desire by the individual savings and loan to finance various-size buildings), *and* each loan company has placed a maximum credit ceiling on how much it will lend Hall in total. This information is summarized in the following table.

| SAVINGS AND LOAN COMPANY | PROPERTY (INTEREST RATES) (%) | | | | |
	HILL ST.	BANKS ST.	PARK AVE.	DRURY LANE	MAXIMUM CREDIT LINE ($)
First Homestead	8	8	10	11	80,000
Commonwealth	9	10	12	10	100,000
Washington Federal	9	11	10	9	120,000
Loan required to purchase building	$60,000	$40,000	$130,000	$70,000	

Each apartment building is equally attractive as an investment to Hall, so she has decided to purchase all buildings possible at the lowest total payment of interest. From which savings and loan companies should she borrow to purchase which buildings? More than one savings and loan can finance the same property.

10-22 The J. Mehta Company's production manager is planning for a series of one-month production periods for stainless steel sinks. The demand for the next four months is as follows:

MONTH	DEMAND FOR STAINLESS STEEL SINKS
1	120
2	160
3	240
4	100

The Mehta firm can normally produce 100 stainless steel sinks in a month. This is done during regular production hours at a cost of $100 per sink. If demand in any one month cannot be satisfied by regular production, the production manager has three other choices: (1) he can produce up to 50 more sinks per month in overtime but at a cost of $130 per sink; (2) he can purchase a limited number of sinks from a friendly competitor for resale (the maximum number of outside purchases over the four-month period is 450 sinks, at a cost of $150 each); or (3) he can fill the demand from his on-hand inventory. The inventory carrying cost is $10 per sink per month. Back orders are not permitted. Inventory on hand at the beginning of month 1 is 40 sinks. Set up this "production smoothing" problem as a transportation problem to minimize cost. Use the northwest corner rule to find an initial level for production and outside purchases over the four-month period.

10-23 Ashley's Auto Top Carriers currently maintains plants in Atlanta and Tulsa that supply major distribution centers in Los Angeles and New York. Because of an expanding demand, Ashley has decided to open a third plant and has narrowed the choice to one of two cities—New Orleans or Houston. The pertinent production and distribution costs, as well as the plant capacities and distribution demands, are shown in the following table:

TO DISTRIBUTION CENTERS / FROM PLANTS	LOS ANGELES	NEW YORK	NORMAL PRODUCTION	UNIT PRODUCTION COST ($)
ATLANTA	$8	$5	600	6
TULSA	$4	$7	900	5
NEW ORLEANS	$5	$6	500	4 (anticipated)
HOUSTON	$4	($6)	500	3 (anticipated)
FORECAST DEMAND	800	1,200	2,000	

Existing plants — ATLANTA, TULSA

Proposed locations — NEW ORLEANS, HOUSTON

Indicates distribution cost (shipping, handling, storage) will be $6 per carrier if sent from Houston to New York

Which of the new possible plants should be opened?

 10-24 Marc Smith, vice-president for operations of HHN, Inc., a manufacturer of cabinets for telephone switches, is constrained from meeting the five-year forecast by limited capacity at the existing three plants. These three plants are Waterloo, Pusan, and Bogota. You, as his able assistant, have been told that because of existing capacity constraints and the expanding world market for HHN cabinets, a new plant is to be added to the existing three plants. The real estate department has advised Mr. Smith that two sites seem particularly good because of a stable political situation and tolerable exchange rate: Dublin, Ireland, and Fontainebleau, France. Mr. Smith suggests that you should be able to take the following data and determine where the fourth plant should be located on the basis of production costs and transportation costs. *Note*: This problem is degenerate with the data for both locations.

MARKET AREA	PLANT LOCATION				
	WATERLOO	PUSAN	BOGOTA	FONTAINEBLEAU	DUBLIN
Canada					
Demand 4,000					
Production cost	$ 50	$ 30	$ 40	$ 50	$ 45
Transportation cost	10	25	20	25	25
South America					
Demand 5,000					
Production cost	50	30	40	50	45
Transportation cost	20	25	10	30	30
Pacific Rim					
Demand 10,000					
Production cost	50	30	40	50	45
Transportation cost	25	10	25	40	40
Europe					
Demand 5,000					
Production cost	50	30	40	50	45
Transportation cost	25	40	30	10	20
Capacity	8,000	2,000	5,000	9,000	9,000

10-25 Don Levine Corporation is considering adding an additional plant to its three existing facilities in Decatur, Minneapolis, and Carbondale. Both St. Louis and East St. Louis are being considered. Evaluating only the transportation costs per unit as shown in the table, which site is best?

| TO | FROM EXISTING PLANTS | | | |
	DECATUR	MINNEAPOLIS	CARBONDALE	DEMAND
Blue Earth	$20	$17	$21	250
Ciro	25	27	20	200
Des Moines	22	25	22	350
Capacity	300	200	150	

| TO | FROM PROPOSED PLANTS | |
	EAST ST. LOUIS	ST. LOUIS
Blue Earth	$29	$27
Ciro	30	28
Des Moines	30	31
Capacity	150	150

 10-26 Using the data from Problem 10-25 plus the unit production costs shown in the following table, which locations yield the lowest cost?

LOCATION	PRODUCTION COSTS
Decatur	$50
Minneapolis	60
Carbondale	70
East St. Louis	40
St. Louis	50

 10-27 In a job shop operation, four jobs may be performed on any of four machines. The hours required for each job on each machine are presented in the following table. The plant supervisor would like to assign jobs so that total time is minimized. Use the assignment method to find the best solution.

| JOB | MACHINE | | | |
	W	X	Y	Z
A12	10	14	16	13
A15	12	13	15	12
B2	9	12	12	11
B9	14	16	18	16

10-28 The personnel director of Dollar Finance Corp. must assign three recently hired college graduates to three regional offices. The three new loan officers are equally well qualified, so the decision will be based on the costs of relocating the graduates' families. Cost data are presented in the following table:

| | OFFICE | | |
OFFICER	OMAHA	MIAMI	DALLAS
Jones	$800	$1,100	$1,200
Smith	500	1,600	1,300
Wilson	500	1,000	2,300

Use the assignment algorithm to solve this problem.

10-29 The Orange Top Cab Company has a taxi waiting at each of four cab stands in Evanston, Illinois. Four customers have called and requested service. The distances, in miles, from the waiting taxis to the customers are given in the following table. Find the optimal assignment of taxis to customers so as to minimize total driving distances to the customers.

| | CUSTOMER | | | |
CAB SITE	A	B	C	D
Stand 1	7	3	4	8
Stand 2	5	4	6	5
Stand 3	6	7	9	6
Stand 4	8	6	7	4

10-30 The Burlington Police Department has five detective squads available for assignment to five open crime cases. The chief of detectives wishes to assign the squads so that the total time to conclude the cases is minimized. The average number of days, based on past performance, for each squad to complete each case is as follows:

| | CASE | | | | |
SQUAD	A	B	C	D	E
1	14	7	3	7	27
2	20	7	12	6	30
3	10	3	4	5	21
4	8	12	7	12	21
5	13	25	24	26	8

Each squad is composed of different types of specialists and, as noted, whereas one squad may be very effective in certain types of cases, they may be almost useless in others. Solve the problem by using the assignment method.

10-31 Roscoe Davis, chairman of a college's business department, has decided to apply the Hungarian method in assigning professors to courses next semester. As a criterion for judging who should teach each course, Professor Davis reviews the past two years' teaching evaluations (which were filled out by students). Since each of the four professors taught each of the four courses at one time or another during the two-year period, Davis is able to record a course rating for each instructor. These ratings are shown in the following table. Find the best assignment of professors to courses to maximize the overall teaching rating.

| | COURSE | | | |
PROFESSOR	STATISTICS	MANAGEMENT	FINANCE	ECONOMICS
Anderson	90	65	95	40
Sweeney	70	60	80	75
Williams	85	40	80	60
McKinney	55	80	65	55

10-32 The hospital administrator at St. Charles General must appoint head nurses to four newly established departments: urology, cardiology, orthopedics, and obstetrics. In anticipation of this staffing problem, she had hired four nurses: Hawkins, Condriac, Bardot, and Hoolihan. Believing in the quantitative analysis approach to problem solving, the administrator has interviewed each nurse, considered his or her background, personality, and talents, and developed a cost scale ranging from 0 to 100 to be used in the assignment. A 0 for Nurse Bardot being assigned to the cardiology unit implies that she would be perfectly suited to that task. A value close to 100, on the other hand, would imply that she is not at all suited to head that unit. The accompanying table gives the complete set of cost figures that the hospital administrator felt represented all possible assignments. Which nurse should be assigned to which unit?

| | DEPARTMENT | | | |
NURSE	UROLOGY	CARDIOLOGY	ORTHOPEDICS	OBSTETRICS
Hawkins	28	18	15	75
Condriac	32	48	23	38
Bardot	51	36	24	36
Hoolihan	25	38	55	12

10-33 The Gleaming Company has just developed a new dishwashing liquid and is preparing for a national television promotional campaign. The firm has decided to schedule a series of 1-minute commercials during the peak homemaker audience viewing hours of 1 to 5 P.M. To reach the widest possible audience, Gleaming wants to schedule one commercial on each of four networks and to have one commercial appear during each of the four 1-hour time blocks. The exposure ratings for each hour, which represent the number of viewers per $1,000 spent, are presented in the following table. Which network should be scheduled each hour to provide the maximum audience exposure?

| | NETWORK | | | |
VIEWING HOURS	A	B	C	INDEPENDENT
1–2 P.M.	27.1	18.1	11.3	9.5
2–3 P.M.	18.9	15.5	17.1	10.6
3–4 P.M.	19.2	18.5	9.9	7.7
4–5 P.M.	11.5	21.4	16.8	12.8

10-34 The G. Saussy Manufacturing Company is putting out four new electronic components. Each of Saussy's four plants has the capacity to add one more product to its current line of electronic parts. The unit manufacturing costs for producing the different parts at the four plants are shown in the accompanying table. How should Saussy assign the new products to the plants to minimize manufacturing costs?

ELECTRONIC COMPONENT	PLANT			
	1	2	3	4
C53	$0.10	$0.12	$0.13	$0.11
C81	0.05	0.06	0.04	0.08
D5	0.32	0.40	0.31	0.30
D44	0.17	0.14	0.19	0.15

10-35 As mentioned in Section 10.12 on page 442, the Fix-It Shop has added a fourth repairman, Davis. Solve the accompanying cost table for the new optimal assignment of workers to projects. Why did this solution occur?

WORKER	PROJECT		
	1	2	3
Adams	$11	$14	$6
Brown	8	10	11
Cooper	9	12	7
Davis	10	13	8

10-36 The Patricia Garcia Company is producing seven new medical products. Each of Garcia's eight plants can add one more product to its current line of medical devices. The unit manufacturing costs for producing the different parts at the eight plants are shown in the following table. How should Garcia assign the new products to the plants to minimize manufacturing costs?

ELECTRONIC COMPONENT	PLANT							
	1	2	3	4	5	6	7	8
C53	$0.10	$0.12	$0.13	$0.11	$0.10	$0.06	$0.16	$0.12
C81	0.05	0.06	0.04	0.08	0.04	0.09	0.06	0.06
D5	0.32	0.40	0.31	0.30	0.42	0.35	0.36	0.49
D44	0.17	0.14	0.19	0.15	0.10	0.16	0.19	0.12
E2	0.06	0.07	0.10	0.05	0.08	0.10	0.11	0.05
E35	0.08	0.10	0.12	0.08	0.09	0.10	0.09	0.06
G99	0.55	0.62	0.61	0.70	0.62	0.63	0.65	0.59

Data Set Problems

 10-37 Haifa Instruments, an Israeli producer of portable kidney dialysis units and other medical products, develops an eight-month aggregate plan. Demand and capacity (in units) are forecast as follows:

CAPACITY SOURCE	JAN.	FEB.	MAR.	APR.	MAY	JUNE	JULY	AUG.
Labor								
Regular time	235	255	290	300	300	290	300	290
Overtime	20	24	26	24	30	28	30	30
Subcontract	12	15	15	17	17	19	19	20
Demand	255	294	321	301	330	320	345	340

The cost of producing each dialysis unit is $1,000 on regular time, $1,300 on overtime, and $1,500 on a subcontract. Inventory carrying cost is $100 per unit per month. There is no beginning or ending inventory in stock.

(a) Set up a production plan, using the transportation model, that minimizes cost. What is this plan's cost?

(b) Through better planning, regular time production can be set at exactly the same value, 275, per month. Does this alter the solution?

(c) If overtime costs rise from $1,300 to $1,400, does this change your answer to part (a)? What if they fall to $1,200?

 10-38 NASA's astronaut crew currently includes 10 mission specialists who hold a Ph.D. in either astrophysics or astromedicine. One of these specialists will be assigned to each of the 10 flights scheduled for the upcoming nine months. Mission specialists are responsible for carrying out scientific and medical experiments in space or for launching, retrieving, or repairing satellites. The chief of astronaut personnel, himself a former crew member with three missions under his belt, must decide who should be assigned and trained for each of the very different missions. Clearly, astronauts with medical educations are more suited to missions involving biological or medical experiments, while those with engineering- or physics-oriented degrees are best suited to other types of missions. The chief assigns each astronaut a rating on a scale of 1 to 10 for each possible mission, with a 10 being a perfect match for the task at hand and a 1 being a mismatch. Only one specialist is assigned to each flight, and none is reassigned until all others have flown at least once.

(a) Who should be assigned to which flight?

(b) We have just been notified that Anderson is getting married in February and has been granted a highly sought publicity tour in Europe that month. (He intends to take his wife and let the trip double as a honeymoon.) How does this change the final schedule?

(c) Certo has complained that he was misrated on his January missions. Both ratings should be 10s, he claims to the chief, who agrees and recomputes the schedule. Do any changes occur over the schedule set in part (b)?

(d) What are the strengths and weaknesses of this approach to scheduling?

ASTRONAUT	MISSION									
	JAN. 12	JAN. 27	FEB. 5	FEB. 26	MAR. 26	APR. 12	MAY 1	JUN. 9	AUG. 20	SEP. 19
Vincze	9	7	2	1	10	9	8	9	2	6
Veit	8	8	3	4	7	9	7	7	4	4
Anderson	2	1	10	10	1	4	7	6	6	7
Herbert	4	4	10	9	9	9	1	2	3	4
Schatz	10	10	9	9	8	9	1	1	1	1
Plane	1	3	5	7	9	7	10	10	9	2
Certo	9	9	8	8	9	1	1	2	2	9
Moses	3	2	7	6	4	3	9	7	7	9
Brandon	5	4	5	9	10	10	5	4	9	8
Drtina	10	10	9	7	6	7	5	4	8	8

Case Study

Andrew–Carter, Inc.

Andrew–Carter, Inc. (A–C), is a major Canadian producer and distributor of outdoor lighting fixtures. Its fixture is distributed throughout North America and has been in high demand for several years. The company operates three plants that manufacture the fixture and distribute it to five distribution centers (warehouses).

During the present recession. A–C has seen a major drop in demand for its fixture as the housing market has declined. Based on the forecast of interest rates, the head of operations feels that demand for housing and thus for its product will remain depressed for the foreseeable future. A–C is considering closing one of its plants, as it is now operating with a forecasted excess capacity of 34,000 units per week. The forecasted weekly demands for the coming year are

Warehouse 1	9,000 units
Warehouse 2	13,000 units
Warehouse 3	11,000 units
Warehouse 4	15,000 units
Warehouse 5	8,000 units

TABLE 10.40 **Andrew–Carter, Inc., Variable Costs and Fixed Production Costs per Week**

PLANT	VARIABLE COST	FIXED COST PER WEEK	
		OPERATING	NOT OPERATING
No. 1, regular time	$2.80/unit	$14,000	$6,000
No. 1, overtime	3.52		
No. 2, regular time	2.78	12,000	5,000
No. 2, overtime	3.48		
No. 3, regular time	2.72	15,000	7,500
No. 3, overtime	3.42		

TABLE 10.41   Andrew–Carter, Inc., Distribution Costs per Unit

FROM PLANT	TO DISTRIBUTION CENTER				
	W1	W2	W3	W4	W5
No. 1	$0.50	$0.44	$0.49	$0.46	$0.56
No. 2	0.40	0.52	0.50	0.56	0.57
No. 3	0.56	0.53	0.51	0.54	0.35

The plant capacities in units per week are

Plant 1, regular time	27,000 units
Plant 1, on overtime	7,000 units
Plant 2, regular time	20,000 units
Plant 2, on overtime	5,000 units
Plant 3, on regular time	25,000 units
Plant 3, on overtime	6,000 units

If A–C shuts down any plants any plants, its weekly costs will change, as fixed costs are lower for a nonoperating plant. Table 10.40 shows production costs at each plant, both variable at regular time and overtime, and fixed when operating and shut down. Table 10.41 shows distribution costs from each plant to each warehouse (distribution center).

Discussion Question

1. Evaluate the various configurations of operating and closed plants that will meet weekly demand. Determine which configuration minimizes total costs.
2. Discuss the implications of closing a plant.

Source: Professor Michael Ballot, University of the Pacific.

Case Study

Custom Vans, Inc.

Custom Vans, Inc., specializes in converting standard vans into campers. Depending on the amount of work and customizing to be done, the customizing could cost less than $1,000 to more than $5,000. In less than four years, Tony Rizzo was able to expand his small operation in Gary, Indiana, to other major outlets in Chicago, Milwaukee, Minneapolis, and Detroit.

Innovation was the major factor in Tony's success in converting a small van shop into one of the largest and most profitable custom van operations in the Midwest. Tony seemed to have a special ability to design and develop unique features and devices that were always in high demand by van owners. An example was Shower-Rific, which was developed by Tony only six months after Custom Vans, Inc., was started. These small showers were completely self-contained, and they could be placed in almost any type of van and in a number of different locations within a van. Shower-Rific was made of fiberglass and contained towel racks, built-in soap and shampoo holders, and a unique plastic door. Each Shower-Rific took 2 gallons of fiberglass and 3 hours of labor to manufacture.

Most of the Shower-Rifics were manufactured in Gary in the same warehouse where Custom Vans, Inc., was founded. The manufacturing plant in Gary could produce 300 Shower-Rifics in a month, but this capacity never seemed to be enough. Custom Van shops in all locations were complaining about not getting enough Shower Rifics, and because Min-

neapolis was farther away from Gary than the other locations, Tony was always inclined to ship Shower-Rifics to the other locations before Minneapolis. This infuriated the manager of Custom Vans at Minneapolis, and after many heated discussions, Tony decided to start another manufacturing plant for Shower-Rifics at Fort Wayne, Indiana. The manufacturing plant at Fort Wayne could produce 150 Shower-Rifics per month.

The manufacturing plant at Fort Wayne was still not able to meet current demand for Shower-Rifics, and Tony knew that the demand for his unique camper shower would grow rapidly in the next year. After consulting with his lawyer and banker, Tony concluded that he should open two new manufacturing plants as soon as possible. Each plant would have the same capacity as the Fort Wayne manufacturing plant. An initial investigation into possible manufacturing locations was made, and Tony decided that the two new plants should be located in Detroit, Michigan; Rockford, Illinois; or Madison, Wisconsin. Tony knew that selecting the best location for the two new manufacturing plants would be difficult. Transportation costs and demands for the various locations should be important considerations.

The Chicago shop was managed by Bill Burch. This Custom Van shop was one of the first established by Tony, and it continued to outperform the other locations. The manufacturing plant at Gary was supplying 200 Shower-Rifics each month, although Bill knew that the demand for the showers in

Chicago was 300 units. The transportation cost per unit from Gary was \$10, and although the transportation cost from Fort Wayne was double that amount, Bill was always pleading with Tony to get an additional 50 units from the Fort Wayne manufacturer. The two additional manufacturing plants would certainly be able to supply Bill with the additional 100 showers he needed. The transportation costs would, of course, vary, depending on which two locations Tony picked. The transportation cost per shower would be \$30 from Detroit, \$5 from Rockford, and \$10 from Madison.

Wilma Jackson, manager of the Custom Van shop in Milwaukee, was the most upset about not getting an adequate supply of showers. She had a demand for 100 units, and at the present time, she was only getting half of this demand from the Fort Wayne manufacturing plant. She could not understand why Tony didn't ship her all 100 units from Gary. The transportation cost per unit from Gary was only \$20, while the transportation cost from Fort Wayne was \$30. Wilma was hoping that Tony would select Madison for one of the manufacturing locations. She would be able to get all of the showers needed, and the transportation cost per unit would only be \$5. If not Madison, a new plant in Rockford would be able to supply her total needs, but the transportation cost per unit would be twice as much as it would be from Madison. Because the transportation cost per unit from Detroit would be \$40, Wilma speculated that even if Detroit became one of the new plants, she would not be getting any units from Detroit.

Custom Vans, Inc., of Minneapolis was managed by Tom Poanski. He was getting 100 showers from the Gary plant. Demand was 150 units. Tom faced the highest transportation costs of all locations. The transportation cost from Gary was \$40 per unit. It would cost \$10 more if showers were sent from the Fort Wayne location. Tom was hoping that Detroit would not be one of the new plants, as the transportation cost would be \$60 per unit. Rockford and Madison would have a cost of \$30 and \$25, respectively, to ship one shower to Minneapolis.

The Detroit shop's position was similar to Milwaukee's—only getting half of the demand each month. The 100 units that Detroit did receive came directly from the Fort Wayne plant. The transportation cost was only \$15 per unit from Fort Wayne, whereas it was \$25 from Gary. Dick Lopez, manager of Custom Vans, Inc., of Detroit, placed the probability of having one of the new plants in Detroit fairly high. The factory would be located across town, and the transportation cost would be only \$5 per unit. He could get 150 showers from the new plant in Detroit and the other 50 showers from Fort Wayne. Even if Detroit was not selected, the other two locations were not intolerable. Rockford had a transportation cost per unit of \$35, and Madison had a transportation cost of \$40.

Tony pondered the dilemma of locating the two new plants for several weeks before deciding to call a meeting of all the managers of the van shops. The decision was complicated, but the objective was clear—to minimize total costs. The meeting was held in Gary, and everyone was present except Wilma.

Tony: Thank you for coming. As you know, I have decided to open up two new plants at Rockford, Madison, or Detroit. The two locations, of course, will change our shipping practices, and I sincerely hope that they will supply you with the Shower-Rifics that you have been wanting. I know you could have sold more units, and I want you to know that I am sorry for this situation.

Dick: Tony, I have given this situation a lot of consideration, and I feel strongly that at least one of the new plants should be located in Detroit. As you know, I am now only getting half of the showers that I need. My brother, Leon, is very interested in running the plant, and I know he would do a good job.

Tom: Dick, I am sure that Leon could do a good job, and I know how difficult it has been since the recent layoffs by the auto industry. Nevertheless, we should be considering total costs and not personalities. I believe that the new plants should be located in Madison and Rockford. I am farther away from the other plants than any other shop, and these locations would significantly reduce transportation costs.

Dick: That may be true, but there are other factors. Detroit has one of the largest suppliers of fiberglass, and I have checked prices. A new plant in Detroit would be able to purchase fiberglass for \$2 per gallon less than any of the other existing or proposed plants.

Tom: At Madison, we have an excellent labor force. This is due primarily to the large number of students attending the University of Madison. These students are hard workers, and they will work for \$1 less per hour than the other locations that we are considering.

Bill: Calm down, you two. It is obvious that we will not be able to satisfy everyone in locating the new plants. Therefore, I would like to suggest that we vote on the two best locations.

Tony: I don't think that voting would be a good idea. Wilma was not able to attend, and we should be looking at all of these factors together in some type of logical fashion.

Discussion Question

Where would you locate the two new plants?

Case Study

Old Oregon Wood Store

In 1992, George Brown started the Old Oregon Wood Store to manufacture Old Oregon tables. Each table is carefully constructed by hand using the highest-quality oak. Old Oregon tables can support more than 500 pounds, and since the start of the Old Oregon Wood Store, not one table has been returned because of faulty workmanship or structural problems. In addition to being rugged, each table is beautifully finished using a urethane varnish that George developed over 20 years of working with wood-finishing materials.

The manufacturing process consists of four steps: preparation, assembly, finishing, and packaging. Each step is performed by one person. In addition to overseeing the entire operation, George does all of the finishing. Tom Surowski performs the preparation step, which involves cutting and forming the basic components of the tables. Leon Davis is in charge of the assembly, and Cathy Stark performs the packaging.

Although each person is responsible for only one step in the manufacturing process, everyone can perform any one of the steps. It is George's policy that occasionally everyone should complete several tables on his or her own without any help or assistance. A small competition is used to see who can complete an entire table in the least amount of time. George maintains average total and intermediate completion times. The data are shown in Figure 10.4.

It takes Cathy longer than the other employees to construct an Old Oregon table. In addition to being slower than the other employees, Cathy is also unhappy about her current responsibility of packaging, which leaves her idle most of the day. Her first preference is finishing, and her second preference is preparation.

In addition to quality, George is concerned with costs and efficiency. When one of the employees misses a day, it causes major scheduling problems. In some cases, George assigns another employee overtime to complete the necessary work. At other times, George simply waits until the employee returns to work to complete his or her step in the manufacturing process. Both solutions cause problems. Overtime is expensive, and waiting causes delays and sometimes stops the entire manufacturing process.

To overcome some of these problems, Randy Lane was hired. Randy's major duties are to perform miscellaneous jobs and to help out if one of the employees is absent. George has given Randy training in all phases of the manufacturing process, and he is pleased with the speed at which Randy has

FIGURE 10.4

Manufacturing Time in Minutes

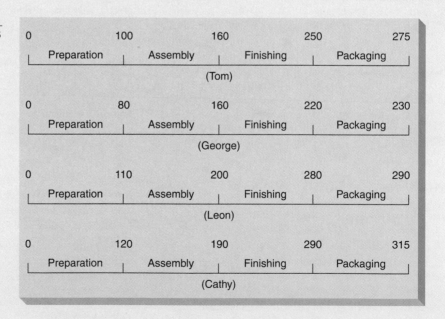

FIGURE 10.5

Randy's Completion Times in Minutes

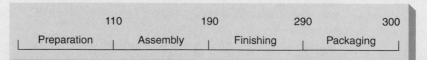

been able to learn how to completely assemble Old Oregon tables. Total and intermediate completion times are given in Figure 10.5.

Discussion Questions

1. What is the fastest way to manufacture Old Oregon tables using the original crew? How many could be made per day?
2. Would production rates and quantities change significantly if George would allow Randy to perform one of

the four functions and make one of the original crew the backup person?
3. What is the fastest time to manufacture a table with the original crew if Cathy is moved to either preparation or finishing?
4. Whoever performs the packaging function is severely underutilized. Can you find a better way of utilizing the four- or five-person crew than either giving each a single job or allowing each to manufacture an entire table? How many tables could be manufactured per day with this scheme?

INTERNET CASE STUDY

See our Internet home page at **http://www.prenhall.com/render** for this additional case study: Northwest General Hospital.

Bibliography

Anbil, R., E. Gelman, B. Patty, and R. Tanga. "Recent Advances in Crew-Pairing Optimization at American Airlines," *Interfaces* 21, 1 (January–February 1991): 62–74.

Bowman, E. "Production Scheduling by the Transportation Method of Linear Programming," *Operations Research* 4 (1956).

Choypeng, P., P. Puakpong, and Richard E. Rosenthal. "Optimal Ship Routing and Personnel Assignment for Naval Recruitment in Thailand," *Interfaces* 16, 4 (July–August 1986): 49–52.

Domich, P. D., K. L. Hoffman, R. H. F. Jackson, and M. A. McClain. "Locating Tax Facilities: A Graphics-Based Microcomputer Optimization Model," *Management Science* 37 (August 1991): 960.

Fitzsimmons, J. A. "A Warehouse Location Model Helps Texas Comptroller Select Out-of-State Audit Officers," *Interfaces* 13 (October 1983): 40–45.

Glassey, C. Roger, and Michael Mizrach. "A Decision Support System for Assigning Classes to Rooms," *Interfaces* 16, 5 (September–October 1986): 92–100.

McKeown, P., and B. Workman. "A Study in Using Linear Programming to Assign Students to Schools," *Interfaces* 6, 4 (August 1976).

Render, B., and R. M. Stair. *Introduction to Management Science*. Boston: Allyn and Bacon, Inc., 1992.

APPENDIX 10.1: USING QM FOR WINDOWS

QM for Windows has both a transportation module and an assignment module in its menu. Both are easy to use in terms of data entry and easy to interpret in terms of output. Program 10.4 uses the sample transportation data of Table 10.42 on the next page as input.

PROGRAM 10.4

QM for Windows Input and
Results for the Transportation
Data in Table 10.42

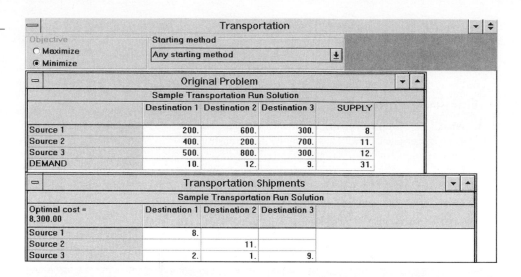

T A B L E 1 0 . 4 2 **Sample Data for QM for Windows Transportation Program**

FROM / TO	WAREHOUSE 1	WAREHOUSE 2	WAREHOUSE 3	AMOUNT AVAILABLE
FACTORY 1	200	600	300	8
FACTORY 2	400	200	700	11
FACTORY 3	500	800	300	12
AMOUNT NEEDED	10	12	9	31

Program 10.5 tackles an assignment problem whose input data are shown in Table 10.43.

PROGRAM 10.5

QM for Windows Input and
Results for the Assignment
Data in Table 10.43

QM for Windows – C:\Prentice\Data\RenderStair7\Crhrt559.ass

Objective
- ○ Maximize
- ◉ Minimize

Assignments

Machine Tool Company Solution			
Optimal cost = $248	Drill 1	Drill 2	Drill 3
Job 1	Assign 100	60.	80.
Job 2	124.	Assign 80	76.
Job 3	140.	96.	Assign 68

TABLE 10.43 Cost Data for a Machine Tool Company

	DRILLING MACHINE		
JOB	**1**	**2**	**3**
1	$100	$60	$80
2	124	80	76
3	140	96	68

Integer Programming, Goal Programming, Nonlinear Programming, and Branch and Bound Models

LEARNING OBJECTIVES

After completing this chapter, students will be able to:

1. Understand the difference between LP and integer programming.
2. Apply the cutting plane method to solve integer programming problems.
3. Understand and solve the three types of integer programming problems.
4. Apply the branch and bound method to solve integer programming problems.
5. Solve goal programming problems graphically and using a modified simplex technique.
6. Formulate nonlinear programming problems and solve using Excel.

CHAPTER OUTLINE

11.1 Introduction

11.2 Integer Programming

11.3 Branch and Bound Method

11.4 Goal Programming

11.5 Nonlinear Programming

Summary • Glossary • Solved Problems • Self-Test • Discussion Questions and Problems • Data Set Problem • Case Study: Schank Marketing Research • Case Study: Oakton River Bridge • Case Study: Puyallup Mall • Bibliography

11.1   INTRODUCTION

We have just seen two special types of linear programming (LP) models—the transportation and assignment models—that were handled by making certain modifications to the general LP approach. This chapter presents a series of other important mathematical programming models that arise when some of the basic assumptions of LP are made more or less restrictive.

Integer programming is the extension of LP that solves problems requiring integer solutions.

For example, one assumption of LP is that decision variables can take on fractional values such as $X_1 = 0.33$, $X_2 = 1.57$, or $X_3 = 109.4$. Yet a large number of business problems can be solved only if variables have *integer* values. When an airline decides how many Boeing 757s or Boeing 777s to purchase, it can't place an order for 5.38 aircraft; it must order 4, 5, 6, 7, or some other integer amount. In Section 11.2 we present the subject of integer programming. We show you how to solve integer programming problems both graphically and by use of an algorithm called the branch and bound method.

Goal programming is the extension of LP that permits more than one objective to be stated.

A major limitation of LP is that it forces the decision maker to state one objective only. But what if a business has several objectives? Management may indeed want to maximize profit, but it might also want to maximize market share, maintain full employment, and minimize costs. Many of these goals can be conflicting and difficult to quantify. South States Power and Light, for example, wants to build a nuclear power plant in Taft, Louisiana. Its objectives are to maximize power generated, reliability, and safety, and to minimize cost of operating the system and the environmental effects on the community. Goal programming is an extension to linear programming that can permit multiple objectives such as these.

Nonlinear programming is the case where objectives or constraints are nonlinear.

Linear programming can, of course, be applied only to cases in which the constraints and objective function are linear. Yet in many situations this is not the case. The price of various products, for example, may be a function of the number of units produced. As more are made, the price per unit decreases. Hence an objective function may read as follows:

$$\text{maximize profit} = 25X_1 - 0.4X_1^2 + 30X_2 - 0.5X_2^2$$

Because of the squared terms, this is a nonlinear programming problem.

Let's examine each of these extensions of LP—integer, goal, and nonlinear programming—one at a time.

11.2   INTEGER PROGRAMMING

Solution values must be whole numbers in integer programming.

An *integer programming* model is a model that has constraints and an objective function identical to that formulated by LP. The only difference is that one or more of the decision variables has to take on an integer value in the final solution. Let's look at a simple example of an integer programming problem and see how to solve it.

Harrison Electric Company Example of Integer Programming

The Harrison Electric Company, located in Chicago's Old Town area, produces two products popular with home renovators: old-fashioned chandeliers and ceiling fans. Both the chandeliers and fans require a two-step production process involving wiring and assembly. It takes about 2 hours to wire each chandelier and 3 hours to wire a ceiling fan. Final assembly of the chandeliers and fans requires 6 and 5 hours, respectively. The production capability is such that only 12 hours of wiring time and 30 hours of assembly time are available. If each chandelier produced nets the firm $7 and each fan $6, Harrison's production mix decision can be formulated using linear programming as follows:

maximize profit = $7X_1 + $6X_2

subject to $2X_1 + 3X_2 \leq 12$ (wiring hours)

$6X_1 + 5X_2 \leq 30$ (assembly hours)

$X_1, X_2 \geq 0$

where

X_1 = number of chandeliers produced

X_2 = number of ceiling fans produced

With only two variables and two constraints, Harrison's production planner, Wes Wallace, employed the graphical linear programming approach (see Figure 11.1) to generate the optimal solution of X_1 = 3.75 chandeliers and X_2 = 1.5 ceiling fans during the production cycle. Recognizing that the company could not produce and sell a fraction of a product, Wes decided that he was dealing with an integer programming problem.

It seemed to Wes that the simplest approach was to round off the optimal fractional solutions for X_1 and X_2 to integer values of X_1 = 4 chandeliers and X_2 = 2 ceiling fans. Unfortunately, rounding can produce two problems. First, the new integer solution may

Rounding off is one way to reach integer solution values, but it often does not yield the best solution.

FIGURE 11.1
Harrison Electric Problem

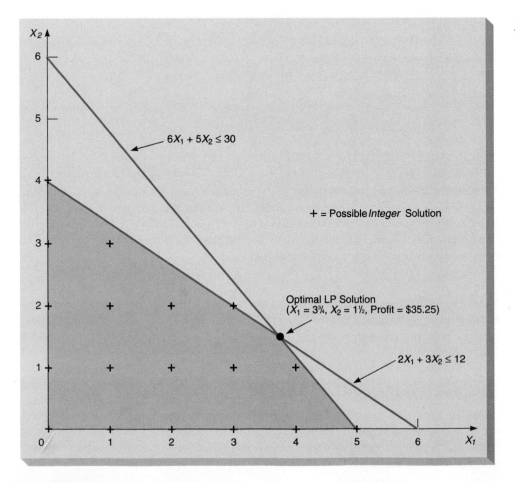

TABLE 11.1   Integer Solutions to the Harrison Electric Company Problem

CHANDELIERS (X_1)	CEILING FANS (X_2)	PROFIT ($\$7X_1 + \$6X_2$)	
0	0	$0	
1	0	7	
2	0	14	
3	0	21	
4	0	28	
5	0	35	← Optimal solution to integer programming problem
0	1	6	
1	1	13	
2	1	20	
3	1	27	
4	1	34	← Solution if rounding off is used
0	2	12	
1	2	19	
2	2	26	
3	2	33	
0	3	18	
1	3	25	
0	4	24	

Although enumeration is feasible for some small integer programming problems, it can be difficult or impossible for large ones.

not be in the feasible region and thus is not a practical answer. This is the case if we round to $X_1 = 4$, $X_2 = 2$. Second, even if we round off to a feasible solution, such as $X_1 = 4$, $X_2 = 1$, it may not be the *optimal* feasible integer solution. Table 11.1 lists the entire set of integer-valued solutions to the Harrison Electric problem. By inspecting the right-hand column, we see that the optimal *integer* solution is

$X_1 = 5$ chandeliers, $X_2 = 0$ ceiling fans, with a profit = $35

An important concept to understand is that an integer programming solution can never be better than the solution to the same LP problem. The integer problem is usually **worse** *in terms of higher cost or lower profit.*

Note that this integer restriction results in a lower profit level than the original optimal linear programming solution. As a matter of fact, an integer programming solution can *never* produce a greater profit than the LP solution to the same problem; *usually,* it means a lesser value.

Cutting Plane Method

Although it is possible to solve simple integer programming problems like Harrison Electric's by inspection or enumeration, several more complicated methods are available to handle larger, more complex problems. Gomory's *cutting plane method* is one such integer programming algorithm.

In applying the cutting plane algorithm, integer requirements are first ignored, and the linear programming problem is solved in the usual way, usually with the simplex method. If the solution has all integer values, then the current answer is also the integer programming answer and no further steps are needed. But if the solution does not have integer values, we must add one or more new constraints to the problem. These new constraints, called *Gomory cuts*, construct a new, smaller area covering all integer values of the feasible region. They exclude the original optimal *noninteger* solution and allow us to converge on the integer solution.

Constraints called Gomory cuts build a new, smaller area that includes all feasible integer values.

Figure 11.2 illustrates the addition of a first cut, the constraint $X_1 + X_2 \leq 5$. This equation was selected as a first cut by observation.[1] It goes through a series of integer points without excluding any that were in the original feasible region. If you look carefully, you will also see that it is the *only* constraint that could be added to cut the size of the feasible region without excluding any integer points.

The cut creates a new feasible region *ABCD*. Once the cut is made, the revised problem can be solved by the simplex method, or graphically. If an integer solution is reached now, we are done. If not, we continue to add Gomory cuts, one at a time. Sooner or later, the optimal integer solution will be found.

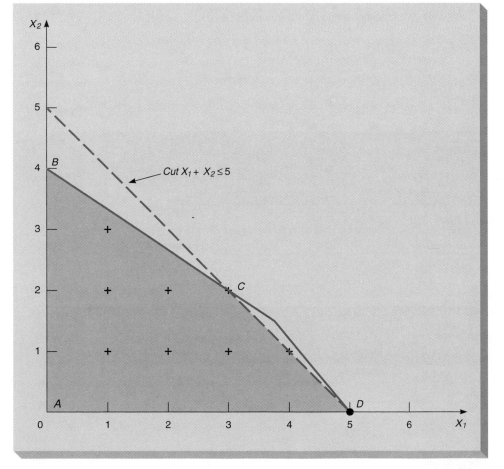

FIGURE 11.2
Harrison Electric Problem with Cut $X_1 + X_2 \leq 5$ Added

---

[1] An algorithm also exists for the simplex method to do the cuts.

Using Software to Solve the Harrison Integer Programming Problem

QM for Windows and Excel spreadsheets are capable of handling integer programming problems such as the Harrison Electric case. Program 11.1A illustrates the input data to QM for Windows, while Program 11.1B provides the results.

Programs 11.2A and B illustrate an Excel spreadsheet approach to the same problem. Program 11.2A formulates the problem for Solver, while Program 11.2B shows the solution. Both QM for Windows and Excel produce the same solution of 5 chandeliers and 0 ceiling fans.

Types of Integer Programming Problems

The Harrison Electric production decision is an example of one of the three types of integer programming problems:

There are three types of integer programs: pure integer programming; mixed-integer programming; and zero–one integer programming.

1. Pure *integer programming* problems, such as Harrison Electric's, are cases in which *all* decision variables must have integer solutions.

2. *Mixed-integer programming* problems are cases in which *some,* but not all, of the decision variables are required to have integer values.

3. *Zero–one integer programming* problems are special cases in which all decision variables must have integer solution values of 0 or 1.

We now look at application examples of the latter two problems.

PROGRAM 11.1A

QM for Windows Analysis of Harrison Electric's Problem Using Integer Programming: Input Screen

QM for Windows – C:\Prentice\Data\Hrrsn587.int

Objective
- ⦿ Maximize
- ○ Minimize

Harrison Electric

	Chandeliers	Ceiling Fans		RHS
Maximize	7	6		
Wiring hours	2	3	<=	12
Assembly hours	6	5	<=	30

PROGRAM 11.1B

Output Screen Using QM for Windows on Harrison Electric's Integer Programming Problem

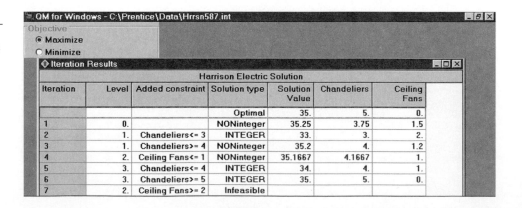

QM for Windows – C:\Prentice\Data\Hrrsn587.int

Objective
- ⦿ Maximize
- ○ Minimize

Iteration Results

Harrison Electric Solution

Iteration	Level	Added constraint	Solution type	Solution Value	Chandeliers	Ceiling Fans
			Optimal	35.	5.	0.
1	0.		NONinteger	35.25	3.75	1.5
2	1.	Chandeliers<= 3	INTEGER	33.	3.	2.
3	1.	Chandeliers>= 4	NONinteger	35.2	4.	1.2
4	2.	Ceiling Fans<= 1	NONinteger	35.1667	4.1667	1.
5	3.	Chandeliers<= 4	INTEGER	34.	4.	1.
6	3.	Chandeliers>= 5	INTEGER	35.	5.	0.
7	2.	Ceiling Fans>= 2	Infeasible			

PROGRAM 11.2A

Using Excel's Solver Command to Formulate Harrison's Integer Programming Model

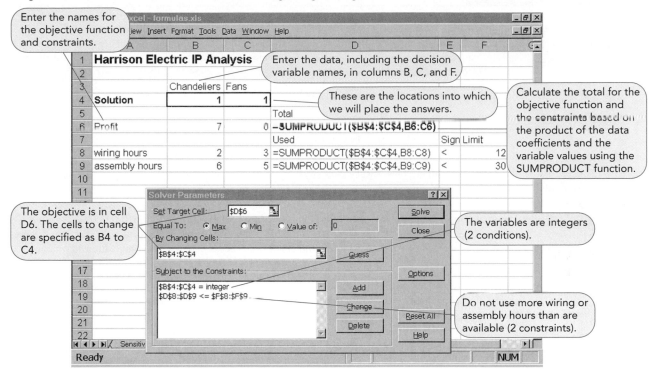

PROGRAM 11.2B

Excel Solution to the Harrison Electric Integer Programming Model

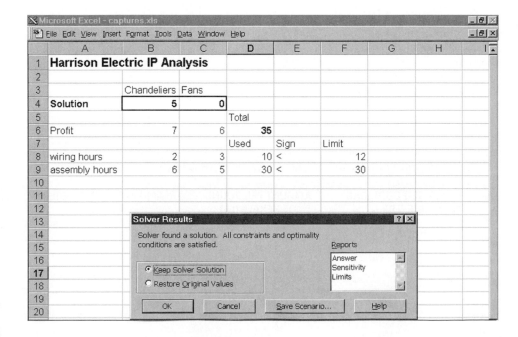

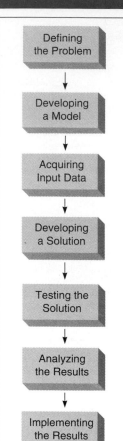

| | MODELING IN THE REAL WORLD | Scheduling Employees at McDonald's |

Defining the Problem

Each week, the managers of Al Boxley's four McDonald's restaurants in Cumberland, Maryland were spending more than 8 hours to prepare manually the schedules for 150 employees. This time-consuming activity was complicated by high turnover, movement of employees among restaurants, and constant change in the availability of student workers.

Developing a Model

Boxley hired two consultants to develop a PC-based integer programming model.

Acquiring Input Data

Boxley prepared the data for each restaurant's three work areas, 150 employees, and 30 possible work shifts needed as input to the integer program.

Developing a Solution

The consultants found that the scheduling problem they formulated resulted in 100,000 decision variables and 3,000 constraints. This clearly was too big to be solved very quickly on a PC. So they subdivided the problem into a number of subproblems (in a process called a "decomposition into network flows").

Testing the Solution

The model was tested with store managers running the program. Initial schedules were favorably received. The consultants then concentrated efforts on developing user-friendly screens so that inexperienced managers could master the inputs and use the outputs successfully.

Analyzing the Results

Managers found that they could use the model for what-if? analysis, to measure the sensitivity of employee schedules to a variety of operating conditions.

Implementing the Results

Managers report an 80% to 90% reduction in the time it takes to generate employee schedules. Costs are now kept down by eliminating overstaffing, and employee morale and efficiency are improved.

Source: R. R. Love and J. M. Hoey. "Management Science Improves Fast Food Operations," *Interfaces* 20, 2 (March–April 1990): 21–29.

Mixed-Integer Programming Problem Example

Bagwell Chemical Company, in Jackson, Mississippi, produces two industrial chemicals. The first product, xyline, must be produced in 50-pound bags; the second, hexall, is sold by the pound in dry bulk and hence can be produced in any quantity. Both xyline and hexall are composed of three ingredients, *A, B,* and *C*, as follows:

AMOUNT PER 50-POUND BAG OF XYLINE (LB)	AMOUNT PER POUND OF HEXALL (LB)	AMOUNT OF INGREDIENTS AVAILABLE
30	0.5	2,000 lb—ingredient A
18	0.4	800 lb—ingredient B
2	0.1	200 lb—ingredient C

Bagwell sells 50-pound bags of xyline for $85 and hexall in any weight for $1.50 per pound.

If we let X_1 = number of 50-pound bags of xyline produced and X_2 = number of pounds of hexall (in dry bulk) mixed, Bagwell's problem can be described with mixed-integer programming:

maximize profit = $\$85X_1 + \$1.50X_2$

subject to $30X_1 + 0.5X_2 \leq 2{,}000$

$\qquad\qquad 18X_1 + 0.4X_2 \leq 800$

$\qquad\qquad 2X_1 + 0.1X_2 \leq 200$

with $X_1, X_2 \geq 0$ and X_1 integer.

Note that X_2 represents bulk weight of hexall and is not required to be integer valued.

Using QM for Windows and Excel to Solve Bagwell's Integer Programming Model

The solution to Bagwell's problem is to produce 44 bags of xyline and 20 pounds of hexall, yielding a profit of $3,770. This is first illustrated in Program 11.3, which uses QM for Windows. Note that variable X_1 is identified as Integer, while X_2 is Real in Program 11.3.

In Programs 11.4A and 11.4B we use Excel to provide an alternative solution method.

DS for Windows - C:\Prentice\Data\RenderStair7\bagwell.MIX

Objective
- ◉ Maximize
- ○ Minimize

◆ Original Problem w/answers

Bagwell Chemical Company Solution

	Xylene	Hexall		RHS
Maximize	85.	1.5		
Ingredient A	30.	0.5	<=	2,000.
Ingredient B	18.	0.4	<=	800.
Constraint 3	2.	0.1	<=	201.
Variable type	Integer	Real		
Solution->	44.	20.	Optimal Z->	3,770.

PROGRAM 11.3

Bagwell's Mixed Integer Program Using QM for Windows

IN ACTION   Selling Seats at American Airlines Using Integer Programming

American Airlines (AA) describes *yield management* as "selling the right seats to the right customers at the right prices." The role of yield management is to determine how much of each product to put on the shelf (make available for sale). American's storefront is the computerized reservations system called SABRE.

The AA yield-management problem is a mixed-integer program that requires data such as passenger demand, cancellations, and other estimates of passenger behavior that are subject to frequent changes. To solve the system-wide yield-management problem would require approximately 250 million decision variables.

To bring this problem down to a manageable size, AA's integer programming model creates three smaller and easier subproblems. The airline looks at:

1. Overbooking, which is the practice of intentionally selling more reservations for a flight than there are actual seats on the aircraft.

2. Discount allocation, which is the process of determining the number of discount fares to offer on a flight.

3. Traffic management, which is the process of controlling reservations by passenger origin and destination to provide the mix of markets that maximizes revenue.

Yield management, much disliked by airline passengers who view it as a way of squeezing the most money out of travelers as possible, has been a big winner for AA and other airlines. In one year, American increased profits by about $1 billion using this approach.

Sources: T. Cook. "SABRE Soars," *OR/MS Today* (June 1998): 26–31 and B. Smith, J. Leimkuhler, and R. Darrow. "Yield Management at American Airlines," *Interfaces* 22, 1 (January–February 1992): 8–31.

PROGRAM 11.4A

Excel Formulation of Bagwell's Integer Programming Problem with Solver

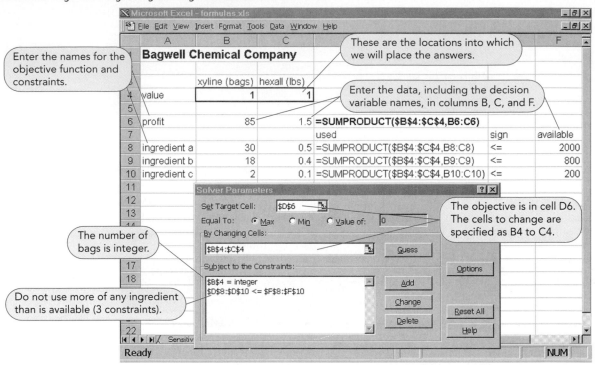

PROGRAM 11.4B

Output from Program 11.4A of Excel's Bagwell Chemical Analysis

Bagwell Chemical Company

	xyline (bags)	hexall (lbs)			
value	44	20			
profit	85	1.5	3770		
			used	sign	available
ingredient a	30	0.5	1330	<=	2000
ingredient b	18	0.4	800	<=	800
ingredient c	2	0.1	90	<=	200

Zero–One Integer Programming Problem Example

Here is an example of stock portfolio analysis with zero–one programming.

The Houston-based investment firm of Simkin, Simkin, and Steinberg specializes in recommending oil stock portfolios for wealthy clients. One such client has made the following specifications: (1) at least two Texas oil firms must be in the portfolio, (2) no more than one investment can be made in foreign oil companies, (3) one of the two California oil stocks must be purchased. The client has up to $3 million available for investments and insists on purchasing large blocks of shares of each company that he invests in. Table 11.2 describes various stocks that Simkin considers. The objective is to maximize annual return on investment subject to the constraints.

TABLE 11.2 Oil Investment Opportunities

STOCK	COMPANY NAME	EXPECTED ANNUAL RETURN ($1,000's)	COST FOR BLOCK OF SHARES ($1,000's)
1	Trans-Texas Oil	50	480
2	British Petroleum	80	540
3	Dutch Shell	90	680
4	Houston Drilling	120	1,000
5	Texas Petroleum	110	700
6	San Diego Oil	40	510
7	California Petro	75	900

To formulate this as a zero–one integer programming problem, Simkin lets X_i be a 0–1 integer variable, where $X_i = 1$ if stock i is purchased and $X_i = 0$ if stock i is not purchased.

maximize return $= 50X_1 + 80X_2 + 90X_3 + 120X_4 + 110X_5 + 40X_6 + 75X_7$

subject to $X_1 + X_4 + X_5 \geq 2$ (Texas constraint)

$X_2 + X_3 \leq 1$ (foreign oil constraint)

$X_6 + X_7 = 1$ (California constraint)

$480X_1 + 540X_2 + 680X_3 + 1,000X_4 + 700X_5 + 510X_6 + 900X_7$
$\leq \$3,000$ ($3 million limit)
All variables must be 0 or 1 in value.

Using Excel to Solve the Simkin Example   To solve this problem by computer, you may use Excel and its Solver function. Programs 11.5A and 11.5B show this approach. As we see in the output screen (Program 11.5B), X_3, X_4, X_5, and X_6 are all equal to 1 in the all-integer solution, while X_1, X_2, and X_7 are 0. This means that Simkin should invest in Dutch Shell, Houston Drilling, Texas Petroleum, and San Diego Oil, and not in the other three oil firms. The expected return is $360,000.

You might also recall that assignment problems solved by linear programming, in Chapter 8, are also actually 0–1 integer programs. All assignments of people to jobs, for example, are presented by either a 1 (person gets job) or a 0 (person not assigned to particular job).

11.3 BRANCH AND BOUND METHOD

The *branch and bound method* is an algorithm that can be used to solve all-integer and mixed-integer linear programs. It searches for an optimal solution by examining only a small part of the total number of possible solutions. This is especially useful when enumeration becomes economically impractical or impossible because there are a large number of feasible solutions.

Branch and bound works by breaking the area of feasible solutions into smaller and smaller parts (subproblems) until the optimal solution is reached. It introduces the concept of feasible and infeasible bounds. Each subproblem that we examine with a total cost or

Branch and bound breaks the feasible solution region into subproblems until an optimal solution is found.

PROGRAM 11.5A

Excel Formulation for Solving Simkin's 0–1 Integer Programming Problem

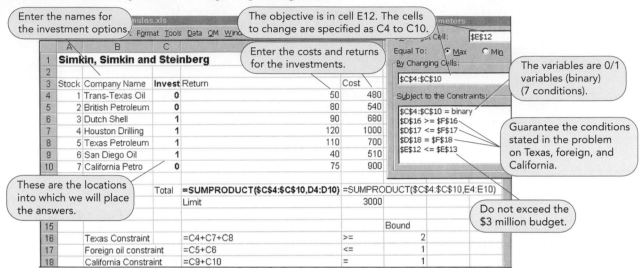

PROGRAM 11.5B

Excel Solution to Simkin's 0–1
Integer Programming Problem

	A	B	C	D	E	F	G	H	I
1	Simkin, Simkin and Steinberg								
2									
3	Stock	Company Name	**Invest**	Return	Cost				
4		1 Trans-Texas Oil	0	50	480				
5		2 British Petroleum	0	80	540				
6		3 Dutch Shell	1	90	680				
7		4 Houston Drilling	1	120	1000				
8		5 Texas Petroleum	1	110	700				
9		6 San Diego Oil	1	40	510				
10		7 California Petro	0	75	900				
11									
12			Total	**360**	2890				
13			Limit		3000				
14									
15					Bound				
16		Texas Constraint		2 >=	2				
17		Foreign oil constraint		1 <=	1				
18		California Constraint		1 =	1				

profit worse than the current feasible bound will be discarded, and we will examine only the remaining subproblems. At the point where no more subproblems can be created, we will find an optimal solution.

Assignment Problem Example

In Chapter 10, we faced the problem of trying to make the best assignment of three workers to three projects. Table 11.3 shows the costs associated with assigning each employee in the Fix-It Shop to a project. For example, it costs the firm $14 for Adams to complete

TABLE 11.3   Cost of Each Person-Project Assignment

PERSON	PROJECT		
	1	2	3
Adams (A)	$11	$14	$6
Brown (B)	8	10	11
Cooper (C)	9	12	7

project 2. The firm's objective is to minimize the total cost of doing all three jobs. We demonstrate the use of the branch and bound method to solve this problem in three steps.

Step 1. First, the lowest possible total-cost bound is found. This is the assignment that yields the lowest cost; it does *not* have to be a feasible solution. This means that we are allowed to assign more than one worker to the same project. We are "bounding" total cost on the low side, saying that no possible assignment of people to projects can cost less.

    The easiest way to set the lower bound is to select the smallest cost from each row. We assign Adams to project 3 (*A*3), Brown to 1 (*B*1) and Cooper to 3 (*C*3), for a total cost of $6 + $8 + $7 = $21.

We first set a lower bound on total cost. This need not be feasible.

LOWER BOUND ASSIGNMENT	COST ($)
A3	6
B1	8
C3	7
Total	21

Because two people were assigned the same project (both *A* and *C* are assigned to 3), this solution is infeasible. If it had been feasible, incidentally, it would also be the optimal solution and we would be done. Since it was not, we begin with this *lower bound* and proceed to find the lowest-cost feasible solution.

Step 2. We now do our first branching and divide the problem to search for solutions. We can change any one assignment in the current infeasible solution of *A*3, *B*1, *C*3 and create three new problems. Suppose that we consecutively assign *A*, *B*, and *C* to project 2 and observe each of the outcomes.

When we branch, we create new subproblems.

    First *A* is assigned to project 2; the other original assignments of *B*1 and *C*3 remain unchanged. This solution is feasible with a cost of $29:

When A is assigned to project 2, the solution is feasible.

ASSIGNMENT	COST ($)
A2	14
B1	8
C3	7
Total	29

Second, *B* is assigned to project 2; *A*'s and *C*'s original assignments of *A*3 and *C*3 are kept. This solution is *infeasible*, with a cost of $23:

When B is assigned to project 2, the solution is not feasible.

ASSIGNMENT	COST ($)
A3	6
B2	10
C3	7
Total	23

Finally, *C* is assigned to project 2; the original assignment of *A*3 and *B*1 are kept. This solution is also feasible and has a $26 cost:

When C is assigned to project 2, the solution is also feasible.

ASSIGNMENT	COST ($)
A3	6
B1	8
C2	12
Total	26

As we can see in Figure 11.3, the original problem has now been partitioned into three new problems. The *best* solution, which is still infeasible, is now $23; this becomes the *new lower bound* and replaces the previous problem's lower bound of $21. Why is $23 best? Because it's the lowest of the three new costs. Notice that the new lower bound is closer to the feasible region than the previous one. Of the two feasible solutions, the one with the lowest value, $26, is the best one. It is set as an *upper feasible bound*. The optimal solution to this assignment problem must lie between the upper bound of $26 and the lower bound of $23. Solution branch *A*2 is dropped from further consideration because it is above the upper bound.

FIGURE 11.3

First Branching: Steps 1 and 2 of Branch and Bound Method

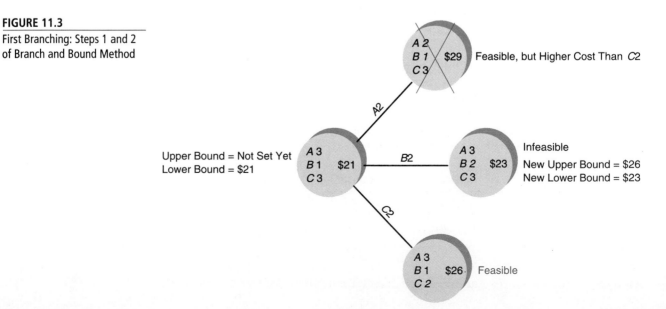

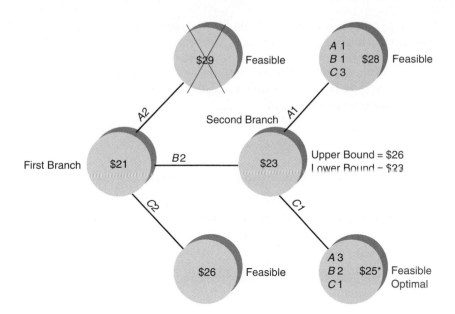

We can see at this point that the branch and bound method evaluates only a portion of the possible solutions, while not eliminating any possible optimal solutions.

Step 3. In the second branching, we start from $B2$ because this is currently the best solution that is infeasible. Even though the $23 cost of $B2$ is not feasible, other higher-cost solutions on this branch *may* be feasible.

This time there are only *two* possible branches from $A3$, $B2$, and $C3$ because $B2$ is already set and we can only change one assignment. Either $A3$ can become $A1$, or $C3$ can become $C1$. Branches $A1$ and $C1$ are shown in Figure 11.4.

Branch $A1$ is dropped because its cost of assigning $A1$, $B2$, and $C3$ is ($11 + 10 + 7 =$) $28, which is greater than the current upper bound of $26. Because both alternatives in step 3 are feasible, and feasible solutions are not partitioned, we see that branch $C1$ provides the optimal solution of $25. The assignment is as follows:

OPTIMAL ASSIGNMENT	COST ($)
A to 3	6
B to 2	10
C to 1	9
Total	25

The branch and bound procedure we followed is very flexible in that we could have looked at the problem from a perspective of column assignment instead of row assignment. This means that we could have selected the smallest number in each column at step 1 and still reached the same answer.

Branch and bound can also be used in maximization problems, of course. We need only rephrase the three steps slightly.

Step 1. Find the maximum possible profit assignment, row by row, disregarding the infeasibility of the assignment. (If the solution is feasible, it means that we have found the optimal solution.)

The 3 steps for using branch and bound for maximization problems.

Step 2. Change any one assignment in this newly established infeasible solution. This partitions the problem into a series of new subproblems—three if there are three people or machines, four if there are four people, and so on. The *new upper bound* is the infeasible solution closer to the lower feasible area value than the previous upper bound was. Of the proposed feasible solutions, the one with the highest value is chosen as the best, and labeled the *new lower (feasible) bound.*

Step 3. We continue branching, if necessary, from the current best feasible solution until no further branches are possible.

Solving an Integer Programming Problem with Branch and Bound

Let us now turn to the familiar Harrison Electric Company integer programming problem again, using the branch and bound method to solve it this time. The approach entails six steps when dealing with a maximization problem:[2]

Six Steps in Solving Integer Programming Maximization Problems by Branch and Bound

1. Solve the original problem using LP. If the answer satisfies the integer constraints, we are done. If not, this value provides an initial upper bound.

2. Find any feasible solution that meets the integer constraints for use as a lower bound. Usually, rounding down each variable will accomplish this.

3. Branch on one variable from step 1 that does not have an integer value. Split the problem into two subproblems based on integer values that are immediately above and below the noninteger value. For example, if $X_2 = 3.75$ was in the final LP solution, introduce the constraint $X_2 \geq 4$ in the first subproblem and $X_2 \leq 3$ in the second subproblem.

4. Create nodes at the top of these new branches by solving the new problems.

5. a. If a branch yields a solution to the LP problem that is *not feasible*, terminate the branch.

   b. If a branch yields a solution to the LP problem that is feasible, but not an integer solution, go to step 6.

   c. If the branch yields a *feasible integer* solution, examine the value of the objective function. If this value equals the upper bound, an optimal solution has been reached. If it is not equal to the upper bound, but exceeds the lower bound, set it as the new lower bound and go to step 6. Finally, if it is less than the lower bound, terminate this branch.

6. Examine both branches again and set the upper bound equal to the maximum value of the objective function at all final nodes. If the upper bound equals the lower bound, stop. If not, go back to step 3.

Harrison Electric Company Revisited

We recall from earlier in this chapter that the Harrison Electric Company's integer programming formulation was

$$\text{maximize profit} = \$7X_1 + \$6X_2$$

$$\text{subject to} \quad 2X_1 + 3X_2 \leq 12$$

$$6X_1 + 5X_2 \leq 30$$

---

[2] Minimization problems involve reversing the roles of the upper and lower bounds.

and both X_1 and X_2 must be nonnegative integers, where

X_1 = number of chandeliers produced

X_2 = number of ceiling fans produced

Figure 11.1 illustrated graphically that the optimal, noninteger solution is

X_1 = 3.75 chandeliers

X_2 = 1.5 ceiling fans

profit = $35.25

Since X_1 and X_2 are not integers, this solution is not valid. The profit value of $35.25 will serve as an initial *upper bound*. We note that rounding down gives $X_1 = 3$, $X_2 = 1$, profit = $27, which is feasible and can be used as a *lower bound*.

The problem is now divided into two subproblems, A and B. We can consider branching on either variable that does not have an integer solution; let us pick X_1 this time.

*We divide the problem into subproblems **A** and **B**.*

Subproblem A	Subproblem B
maximize profit = $7X_1$ + $6X_2$	maximize profit = $7X_1$ + $6X_2$
subject to $\quad 2X_1 + 3X_2 \leqslant 12$	subject to $\quad 2X_1 + 3X_2 \leqslant 12$
$6X_1 + 5X_2 \leqslant 30$	$6X_1 + 5X_2 \leqslant 30$
$X_1 \qquad \geqslant 4$	$X_1 \qquad \leqslant 3$

If you solve both subproblems graphically, you will observe the solutions:

subproblem A's optimal solution = [$X_1 = 4$, $X_2 = 1.2$, profit = 35.20]

subproblem B's optimal solution = [$X_1 = 3$, $X_2 = 2$, profit = 33.00]

This information is presented in branch form in Figure 11.5. We have completed steps 1 to 4 of the branch and bound method.

We may stop the search of the subproblem B branch because it has an all-integer feasible solution (see step 5c). The profit value of $33 becomes the new *lower bound*. Subproblem A's branch is searched further since it has a noninteger solution. The second *upper bound* takes on the value $35.20, replacing $35.25 from the first node.

Subproblem A is now branched into two new subproblems: C and D. Subproblem C has the additional constraint of $X_2 \geqslant 2$. Subproblem D adds the constraint $X_2 \leqslant 1$. The logic for developing these subproblems is that since subproblem A's optimal solution of $X_2 = 1.2$ is not feasible, the integer feasible answer must lie either in the region $X_2 \geqslant 2$ or in the region $X_2 \leqslant 1$.

*Subproblem **A**'s branching yields subproblems **C** and **D**.*

Subproblem C	Subproblem D
maximize profit = $7X_1$ + $6X_2$	maximize profit = $7X_1$ + $6X_2$
subject to $\quad 2X_1 + 3X_2 \leqslant 12$	subject to $\quad 2X_1 + 3X_2 \leqslant 12$
$6X_1 + 5X_2 \leqslant 30$	$6X_1 + 5X_2 \leqslant 30$
$X_1 \qquad \geqslant 4$	$X_1 \qquad \geqslant 4$
$X_2 \geqslant 2$	$X_2 \leqslant 1$

Subproblem C has no feasible solution whatsoever because the first two constraints are violated if the $X_1 \geqslant 4$ and $X_2 \geqslant 2$ constraints are observed. We terminate this branch and do not consider its solution.

FIGURE 11.5

Harrison Electric's First
Branching: Subproblems
A and B

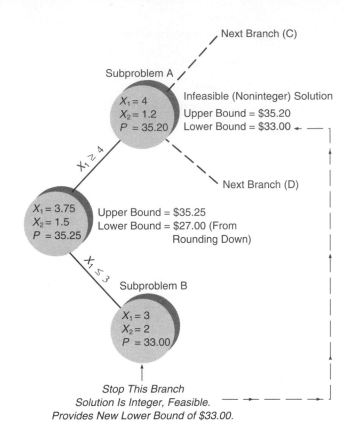

Subproblem D's optimal solution = ($X_1 = 4\frac{1}{6}$, $X_2 = 1$, profit = \$35.16). This noninteger solution yields a *new upper bound* of \$35.16, replacing \$35.20. Subproblems C and D, as well as the final branches for the problem, are shown in Figure 11.6.

Finally, we create subproblems E and F and solve for X_1 and X_2 with the added constraints $X_1 \leq 4$ and $X_1 \geq 5$. The subproblems and their solutions are

Subproblem E	*Subproblem F*
maximize profit = \$7X_1 + \$6X_2	maximize profit = \$7X_1 + \$6X_2
subject to $\quad 2X_1 + 3X_2 \leq 12$	subject to $\quad 2X_1 + 3X_2 \leq 12$
$6X_1 + 5X_2 \leq 30$	$6X_1 + 5X_2 \leq 30$
$X_1 \qquad \geq 4$	$X_1 \qquad \geq 4$
$X_1 \qquad \leq 4$	$X_1 \qquad \geq 5$
$X_2 \leq 1$	$X_2 \leq 1$

Optimal solution to E: Optimal solution to F:

$X_1 = 4$, $X_2 = 1$, profit = \$34 $X_1 = 5$, $X_2 = 0$, profit = \$35

The stopping rule for the branching process is that we continue until the new upper bound is less than or equal to the lower bound *or* no further branching is possible. The latter is the case here since both branches yielded feasible integer solutions. The optimal solution is at subproblem F's node: $X_1 = 5$, $X_2 = 0$, profit = \$35. You can, of course, confirm this by looking back to Table 11.1.

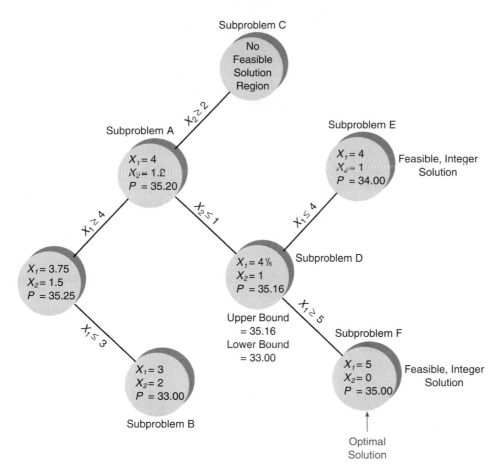

FIGURE 11.6
Harrison Electric's Full Branch and Bound Solution

The branch and bound method has been computerized and does a good job of solving problems with a small to medium number of integer variables. On especially large problems, the analyst must sometimes settle for a near-optimal answer. Much research has been conducted on this subject, and new algorithms that increase the computer's efficiency are constantly under study.

11.4 GOAL PROGRAMMING

In today's business environment, profit maximization or cost minimization are not always the only objectives that a firm sets forth. Often, maximizing total profit is just one of several goals, including such contradictory objectives as maximizing market share, maintaining full employment, providing quality ecological management, minimizing noise level in the neighborhood, and meeting numerous other noneconomic goals.

Firms usually have more than one goal.

Mathematical programming techniques such as linear and integer programming have the shortcoming that their objective function is measured in one dimension only. It's not possible for linear programming to have *multiple goals* unless they are all measured in the same units (such as dollars), a highly unusual situation. An important technique that has been developed to supplement linear programming is called *goal programming.*

Goal programming permits multiple goals.

Goal programming is capable of handling decision problems involving multiple goals. A four-decade old concept, it began with the work of Charnes and Cooper in 1961 and has been refined and extended by Lee and Ignizio in the 1970s (see the Bibliography).

In typical decision-making situations, the goals set by management can be achieved only at the expense of other goals. It is necessary to establish a hierarchy of importance among these goals so that lower-priority goals are tackled only after higher-priority goals are satisfied. Since it is not always possible to achieve every goal to the extent the decision maker desires, goal programming attempts to reach a satisfactory level of multiple objectives. This, of course, differs from linear programming, which tries to find the best possible outcome for a *single* objective. Nobel laureate Herbert A. Simon, of Carnegie-Mellon University, states that modern managers may not be able to optimize, but may instead have to "*satisfice*" or "come as close as possible" to reaching goals. This is the case with models such as goal programming.

Goal programming "satisfices," as opposed to LP, which tries to "optimize." This means coming as close as possible to reaching goals.

How, specifically, does goal programming differ from linear programming? The objective function is the main difference. Instead of trying to maximize or minimize the objective function directly, with goal programming we try to minimize *deviations* between set goals and what we can actually achieve within the given constraints. In the LP simplex approach, such deviations are called *slack variables* and they are used only as dummy variables. In goal programming, these slack terms are either positive or negative, and not only are they real variables, but they are also the only terms in the objective function. The objective is to minimize these *deviational variables*.

The objective function is the main difference between goal programming and LP.

In goal programming we want to minimize deviational variables, which are the only terms in the objective function.

When the goal programming model is formulated, the computational algorithm is almost the same as a minimization problem solved by the simplex method.

Example of Goal Programming: Harrison Electric Company Revisited

To illustrate the formulation of a goal programming problem, let's look back at the Harrison Electric Company case presented earlier in this chapter as an integer programming problem. That problem's LP formulation, you recall, was

$$\text{maximize profit} = \$7X_1 + \$6X_2$$

$$\text{subject to} \quad 2X_1 + 3X_2 \leq 12 \text{ (wiring hours)}$$

$$6X_1 + 5X_2 \leq 30 \text{ (assembly hours)}$$

$$X_1, X_2 \geq 0$$

where

X_1 = number of chandeliers produced

X_2 = number of ceiling fans produced

We saw that if Harrison's management had a single goal, say profit, linear programming could be used to find the optimal solution. But let's assume that the firm is moving to a new location during a particular production period and feels that maximizing profit is not a realistic goal. Management sets a profit level, which would be satisfactory during the adjustment period, of $30. We now have a goal programming problem in which we want to find the production mix that achieves this goal as closely as possible, given the production time constraints. This simple case will provide a good starting point for tackling more complicated goal programs.

We first define two deviational variables:

d_1^- = underachievement of the profit target

d_1^+ = overachievement of the profit target

Now we can state the Harrison Electric problem as a *single-goal* programming model:

minimize under- or overachievement of profit target $= d_1^- + d_1^+$

subject to $\quad \$7X_1 + \$6X_2 + d_1^- - d_1^+ = \$30$ (profit goal constraint)

$$2X_1 + 3X_2 \qquad \leq 12 \quad \text{(wiring hours constraint)}$$

$$6X_1 + 5X_2 \qquad \leq 30 \quad \text{(assembly hours constraint)}$$

$$X_1, X_2, d_1^-, d_1^+ \qquad \geq 0$$

Note that the first constraint states that the profit made, $\$7X_1 + \$6X_2$, plus any underachievement of profit minus any overachievement of profit has to equal the target of $30. For example, if $X_1 = 3$ chandeliers and $X_2 = 2$ ceiling fans, then $33 profit has been made. This exceeds $30 by $3, so d_1^+ must be equal to 3. Since the profit goal constraint was *overachieved*, Harrison did not underachieve and d_1^- will clearly be equal to zero. This problem is now ready for solution by a goal programming algorithm.

If the target profit of $30 is exactly achieved, we see that both d_1^+ and d_1^- are equal to zero. The objective function will also be minimized at zero. If Harrison's management was only concerned with *underachievement* of the target goal, how would the objective function change? It would be as follows: minimize underachievement $= d_1^-$. This is also a reasonable goal since the firm would probably not be upset with an overachievement of its target.

Deviational variables are zero if a goal is completely obtained.

In general, once all goals and constraints are identified in a problem, management should analyze each goal to see if underachievement or overachievement of that goal is an acceptable situation. If overachievement is acceptable, the appropriate d^+ variable can be eliminated from the objective function. If underachievement is okay, the d^- variable should be dropped. If management seeks to attain a goal exactly, both d^- and d^+ must appear in the objective function.

Extension to Equally Important Multiple Goals

Let's now look at the situation in which Harrison's management wants to achieve several goals, each equal in priority.

Goal 1: to produce as much profit above $30 as possible during the production period

Goal 2: to fully utilize the available wiring department hours

Goal 3: to avoid overtime in the assembly department

Goal 4: to meet a contract requirement to produce at least seven ceiling fans

The deviational variables can be defined as follows:

We need a clear definition of deviational variables, such as these.

$d_1^- =$ underachievement of the profit target

$d_1^+ =$ overachievement of the profit target

$d_2^- =$ idle time in the wiring department (underutilization)

$d_2^+ =$ overtime in the wiring department (overutilization)

$d_3^- =$ idle time in the assembly department (underutilization)

$d_3^+ =$ overtime in the assembly department (overutilization)

$d_4^- =$ underachievement of the ceiling fan goal

$d_4^+ =$ overachievement of the ceiling fan goal

Management is unconcerned about whether there is overachievement of the profit goal, overtime in the wiring department, idle time in the assembly department, or more than seven ceiling fans are produced: hence, d_1^+, d_2^+, d_3^-, and d_4^+ may be omitted from the objective function. The new objective function and constraints are:

$$\text{minimize total deviation} = d_1^- + d_2^- + d_3^+ + d_4^-$$

$$\text{subject to} \quad 7X_1 + 6X_2 + d_1^- - d_1^+ = 30 \text{ (profit constraint)}$$

$$2X_1 + 3X_2 + d_2^- - d_2^+ = 12 \text{ (wiring hours constraint)}$$

$$6X_1 + 5X_2 + d_3^- - d_3^+ = 30 \text{ (assembly constraint)}$$

$$X_2 + d_4^- - d_4^+ = 7 \text{ (ceiling fan constraint)}$$

All X_i, d_i variables ≥ 0.

Ranking Goals

A key idea in goal programming is that one goal is more important than another. Priorities are assigned to each deviational variable.

In most goal programming problems, one goal will be more important than another, which in turn will be more important than a third. The idea is that goals can be ranked with respect to their importance in management's eyes. Lower-order goals are considered only after higher-order goals are met. Priorities (P_i's) are assigned to each deviational variable—with the ranking that P_1 is the most important goal, P_2 the next most important, then P_3, and so on.

Let's say Harrison Electric sets the priorities shown in the accompanying table.

GOAL	PRIORITY
Reach a profit as much above $30 as possible	P_1
Fully use wiring department hours available	P_2
Avoid assembly department overtime	P_3
Produce at least seven ceiling fans	P_4

IN ACTION   Planning for a University Lab Using Goal Programming

When the University of Missouri needed help in deciding how to allocate the floor space in its new 5,072-square foot computer-integrated manufacturing (CIM) lab, it turned to goal programming. Although central planners viewed the new facility as a campus-wide resource, debate over the best layout for the lab was contentious. A multidisciplinary task force identified 15 departments, or sections (such as physical simulation lab, robot systems, packaging, production machines, and so on), to be located in the CIM lab. Unfortunately, it would require 6,035 square feet to house all 15. How could the team find a systematic way of allocating the actual space in a manner that met the university's mission?

Consulting with administrators, the team established the following five goals: Priority goal 1 (P_1), increase student use of the CIM facilities; priority goal 2 (P_2), develop new courses

relying on lab facilities; priority goal 3 (P_3), stimulate graduate-level and funded research; priority goal 4 (P_4), heighten industry awareness of CIM concepts; and priority goal 5 (P_5), enhance the university's public image.

Using a goal programming software package called SAS/OR, 9 of the 15 departments obtained space allocations less than 1.0 (suggesting a reduction in the ideal areas originally allocated). The team followed up with a sensitivity analysis on the priority ratings and found the model to be fairly robust in response to priority rankings. This systematic work of the taskforce led to a ready acceptance of its layout proposals for the CIM lab.

Source: Colin O. Benjamin, Ike C. Ehie, and Y. Omurtag. "Planning Facilities at the University of Missouri—Rolla," *Interfaces* 22, 4 (July–August 1992): 95–105.

This means, in effect, that the priority of meeting the profit goal (P_1) is infinitely more important than the wiring goal (P_2), which is, in turn, infinitely more important than the assembly goal (P_3), which is infinitely more important than producing at least seven ceiling fans (P_4).

With ranking of goals considered, the new objective function becomes

$$\text{minimize total deviation} = P_1d_1^- + P_2d_2^- + P_3d_3^+ + P_4d_4^-$$

The constraints remain identical to the previous ones.

Priority 1 is infinitely more important than Priority 2, which is infinitely more important than the next goal, and so on.

Solving Goal Programming Problems Graphically

Just as we solved linear programming problems graphically in Chapter 7, we can analyze goal programming problems graphically. First, we must be aware of three characteristics of goal programming problems: (1) goal programming models are all minimization problems; (2) there is no single objective, but multiple goals to be attained; and (3) the deviation from a high-priority goal must be minimized to the greatest extent possible before the next-highest-priority goal is considered.

Let us use the Harrison Electric Company goal programming problem as an example. The model was formulated as

$$\text{minimize total deviation} = P_1d_1^- + P_2d_2^- + P_3d_3^+ + P_4d_4^-$$

$$\text{subject to} \quad 7X_1 + 6X_2 + d_1^- - d_1^+ = 30 \text{ (profit)}$$

$$2X_1 + 3X_2 + d_2^- - d_2^+ = 12 \text{ (wiring)}$$

$$6X_1 + 5X_2 + d_3^- - d_3^+ = 30 \text{ (assembly)}$$

$$X_2 + d_4^- - d_4^+ = 7 \text{ (ceiling fans)}$$

$$X_1, X_2, d_1^-, d_1^+ \geq 0 \text{ (nonnegativity)}$$

where

X_1 = number of chandeliers produced

X_2 = number of ceiling fans produced

To solve this problem, we graph one constraint at a time, starting with the one that has the highest-priority deviational variables. This is the profit constraint, since d_1^- has priority P_1 in the objective function. Figure 11.7 shows the profit constraint line. Note that in graphing the line, the deviational variables d_1^- and d_1^+ are ignored. To minimize d_1^- (the underachievement of $30 profit), the feasible area is the shaded region. Any point in the shaded region satisfies the first goal because profit exceeds $30.

Figure 11.8 includes the second priority goal of minimizing d_2^-. The region below the constraint line $2X_1 + 3X_2 = 12$ represents the values for d_2^-, while the region above the line stands for d_2^+. To avoid underutilizing wiring department hours, the area below the line is eliminated. But this goal must be attained within the feasible area already defined by satisfying the first goal.

The third goal is to avoid overtime in the assembly department, which means we want d_3^+ to be as close to zero as possible. As we can see in Figure 11.9, this goal can also be fully attained. The area that contains solution points that will satisfy the first three priority goals is bounded by the points *A, B, C, D*. Inside this narrow strip, any solution will meet the three most critical goals.

Graphical constraints are drawn, one at a time.

FIGURE 11.7

Analysis of First Goal

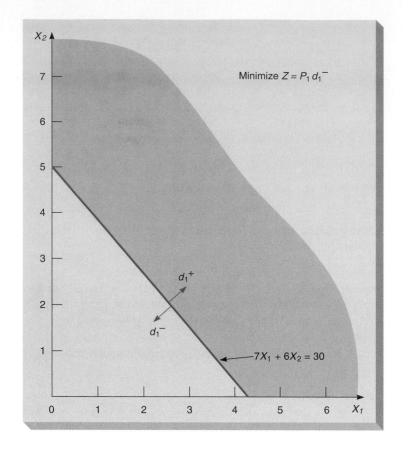

FIGURE 11.8

Analysis of First and
Second Goals

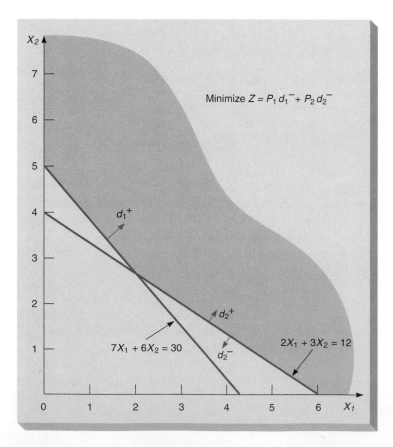

FIGURE 11.9
Analysis of All Four
Priority Goals

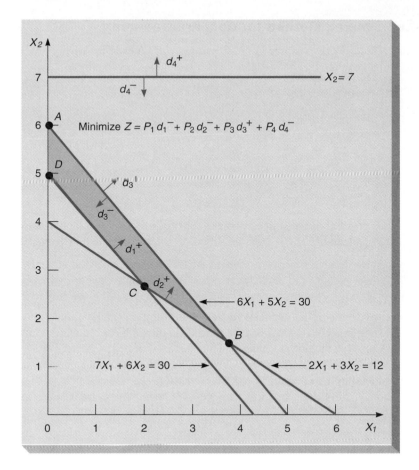

The fourth goal is to produce at least seven ceiling fans, and hence to minimize d_4^-. To achieve this final goal, the area below the constraint line $X_2 = 7$ must be eliminated. But we cannot do this without violating one of the higher-priority goals. We want, then, to find a solution point that still satisfies the first three goals, and also comes as close as possible to achieving the fourth goal. Do you see which point this would be?

Corner point A appears to be the optimal solution. We easily see that its coordinates are $X_1 = 0$ chandeliers and $X_2 = 6$ ceiling fans. Substituting these values into the goal constraints, we find that the other variables are

$$d_1^- = \$0,\ d_1^+ = \$6,\ d_2^- = 0 \text{ hours},\ d_2^+ = 6 \text{ hours}$$

$$d_3^- = 0 \text{ hours},\ d_3^+ = 0 \text{ hours},\ d_4^- = 1 \text{ ceiling fan}$$

$$d_4^+ = 0 \text{ ceiling fans}$$

The solution is found at corner point A, which satisfies the first three goals and comes close to achieving the fourth goal.

Thus the profit goal was met and exceeded by $6 (a $36 profit was attained), the wiring department was fully utilized as 6 hours of overtime were used there, the assembly department had no idle time (or overtime), and the ceiling fan goal was underachieved by only one fan. This was the most satisfactory solution to the problem.

The graphical approach to goal programming has the same drawbacks as it did with linear programming, namely, it can only handle problems with two real variables. By modifying the simplex method of LP, a more general solution to goal programming problems can be found.

Modified Simplex Method for Goal Programming

To demonstrate how the modified simplex method can be used to solve a goal programming problem, we again turn to the Harrison Electric Company example.

$$\text{minimize} = P_1 d_1^- + P_2 d_2^- + P_3 d_3^+ + P_4 d_4^-$$

$$\text{subject to} \quad 7X_1 + 6X_2 + d_1^- - d_1^+ = 30$$

$$2X_1 + 3X_2 + d_2^- - d_2^+ = 12$$

$$6X_1 + 5X_2 + d_3^- - d_3^+ = 30$$

$$X_2 + d_4^- - d_4^+ = 7$$

$$X_1, X_2, d_i^-, d_i^+ \geqslant 0$$

Table 11.4 presents the initial simplex tableau for this problem. We should point out four features of this tableau that differ from the simplex tableaus we saw in Chapter 9:

Here are four differences between LP simplex tableau and GP tableau.

1. The variables in the problem are listed at the top, with the decision variables (X_1 and X_2) first, then the negative deviational variables, and finally, the positive deviational variables. The priority level of each variable is assigned on the very top row.

2. The negative deviational variables for each constraint provide the initial basic feasible solution. This is analogous to the LP simplex tableau, in which slack variables provide the initial solution. (Thus we see that $d_1^- = 30$, $d_2^- = 12$, $d_3^- = 30$, and $d_4^- = 7$.) The priority level of each variable in the current solution mix is entered in the C_j column on the far left. Note that the coefficients in the body of the tableau are set up exactly as they were in the regular simplex approach.

TABLE 11.4   Initial Goal Programming Tableau

C_j →		0	0	P_1	P_2	0	P_4	0	0	P_3	0	
↓	SOLUTION MIX	X_1	X_2	d_1^-	d_2^-	d_3^-	d_4^-	d_1^+	d_2^+	d_3^+	d_4^+	QUANTITY
P_1	d_1^-	7	6	1	0	0	0	−1	0	0	0	30
P_2	d_2^-	2	3	0	1	0	0	0	−1	0	0	12
0	d_3^-	6	5	0	0	1	0	0	0	−1	0	30
P_4	d_4^-	0	1	0	0	0	1	0	0	0	−1	7
P_4	Z_j	0	1	0	0	0	1	0	0	0	−1	7
	$C_j - Z_j$	0	−1	0	0	0	0	0	0	0	+1	
P_3	Z_j	0	0	0	0	0	0	0	0	0	0	0
	$C_j - Z_j$	0	0	0	0	0	0	0	0	1	0	
P_2	Z_j	2	3	0	1	0	0	0	−1	0	0	12
	$C_j - Z_j$	−2	−3	0	0	0	0	0	1	0	0	
P_1	Z_j	7	6	1	0	0	0	−1	0	0	0	30
	$C_j - Z_j$	→−7	−6	0	0	0	0	1	0	0	0	

Pivot column

3. There is a separate Z_j and $C_j - Z_j$ row for each of the P_i priorities. Since profit goals, department hour goals, and production goals are each measured in different units, the four separate priority rows are needed. In goal programming, the bottom row of the simplex tableau contains the highest ranked (P_1) goal, the next row up has the P_2 goal, and so on. The rows are computed exactly as in the regular simplex method, but they are done for each priority level. In Table 11.4, the $C_j - Z_j$ value for column X_1, for example, is read as $-7P_1 - 2P_2 + 0P_3 + 0P_4$.

Each P_i priority has a separate Z_j and $C_j - Z_j$ row.

4. In selecting the variable to enter the solution mix, we start with the highest-priority row, P_1, and select the most negative $C_j - Z_j$ value in it. (The pivot column is X_1 in Table 11.4.) If there was no negative number in the $C_j - Z_j$ row for P_1, we would move up to priority P_2's $C_j - Z_j$ row and select the largest negative number there. A negative $C_j - Z_j$ that has a positive number in a P row underneath it, however, is ignored. This means that deviations from a more important goal (one in a lower row) would be *increased* if that variable were brought into the solution.

Selecting the variable to enter the solution mix next.

After we set up the initial modified simplex tableau, we move toward the optimal solution just as with the regular minimization simplex procedures described in detail in Chapter 9. Keeping in mind the four features just listed, the next step in moving from Table 11.4 to Table 11.5 is to find the pivot row. We do this by dividing the quantity values by their corresponding pivot column (X_1) values and picking the one with the smallest positive ratio. Thus d_1^- leaves the basis in the second tableau and is replaced by X_1.

The new rows of the tableau are computed exactly as they are in the regular simplex method. You may recall that this means first computing a new pivot row, and then using the formula in Section 9.3 to find the other new rows.

TABLE 11.5 Second Goal Programming Tableau

$C_j \rightarrow$		0	0	P_1	P_2	0	P_4	0	0	P_3	0	
	SOLUTION MIX	X_1	X_2	d_1^-	d_2^-	d_3^-	d_4^-	d_1^+	d_2^+	d_3^+	d_4^+	QUANTITY
0	X_1	1	5/7	1/7	0	0	0	-1/7	0	0	0	30/7
P_2	d_2^-	0	9/7	-2/7	1	0	0	2/7	-1	0	0	24/7
0	d_3^-	0	-1/7	-6/7	0	1	0	6/7	0	-1	0	30/7
P_4	d_4^-	0	1	0	0	0	1	0	0	0	-1	7
P_4	Z_j	0	1	0	0	0	1	0	0	0	-1	7
	$C_j - Z_j$	0	-1	0	0	0	0	0	0	0	+1	
P_3	Z_j	0	0	0	0	0	0	0	0	0	0	0
	$C_j - Z_j$	0	0	0	0	0	0	0	0	1	0	
P_2	Z_j	0	9/7	-2/7	1	0	0	2/7	-1	0	0	24/7
	$C_j - Z_j$	0	-9/7	+2/7	0	0	0	-2/7	1	0	0	
P_1	Z_j	0	0	0	0	0	0	0	0	0	0	0
	$C_j - Z_j$	0	0	1	0	0	0	1	0	0	0	

Pivot column

TABLE 11.6   Final Solution to Harrison Electric's Goal Program

C_j	→	0	0	P_1	P_2	0	P_4	0	0	P_3	0	
↓	SOLUTION MIX	X_1	X_2	d_1^-	d_2^-	d_3^-	d_4^-	d_1^+	d_2^+	d_3^+	d_4^+	QUANTITY
0	d_2^+	$8/5$	0	0	-1	$3/5$	0	0	1	$-3/5$	0	6
0	X_2	$6/5$	1	0	0	$1/5$	0	0	0	$-1/5$	0	6
0	d_1^+	$1/5$	0	-1	0	$6/5$	0	1	0	$-6/5$	0	6
P_4	d_4^-	$-6/5$	0	0	0	$-1/5$	1	0	0	$1/5$	-1	1
P_4	Z_j	$-6/5$	0	0	0	$-1/5$	1	0	0	$1/5$	-1	1
	$C_j - Z_j$	$6/5$	0	0	0	$1/5$	0	0	0	$-1/5$	$+1$	
P_3	Z_j	0	0	0	0	0	0	0	0	0	0	0
	$C_j - Z_j$	0	0	0	0	0	0	0	0	**1**	0	
P_2	Z_j	0	0	0	0	0	0	0	0	0	0	0
	$C_j - Z_j$	0	0	0	1	0	0	0	0	0	0	
P_1	Z_j	0	0	0	0	0	0	0	0	0	0	0
	$C_j - Z_j$	0	0	1	0	0	0	0	0	0	0	

We see in the new $C_j - Z_j$ row for priority P_1, in Table 11.5, that there are no negative values. Thus, the first priority's goal has been reached. Priority 2 is the next objective, and we find two negative entries in its $C_j - Z_j$ row. Again, the largest one is selected as the pivot column and X_2 will become the next variable to enter the solution mix.

Let us skip two tableaus and go directly to Table 11.6, which contains the most satisfactory solution to the problem. (One of the homework problems gives you the chance to work through to this final tableau.)

Notice in the final solution that the first, second, and third goals have been totally achieved: there are no negative $C_j - Z_j$ entries in their rows. A negative value appears (in the d_3^+ column) in the priority 4 row, however, indicating that it has not been fully attained. Indeed, d_4^- is equal to 1, meaning that we have underachieved the ceiling fan goal by one fan. But there is a positive number (see the shaded "1") in the d_3^+ column at the P_3 priority level, and thus at a higher-priority level. If we try to force d_3^+ into the solution mix to attain the P_4 goal, it will be at the expense of a more important goal (P_3) which has already been satisfied. We do not want to sacrifice the P_3 goal, so this will be the best possible goal programming solution. The answer is

$X_1 = 0$ chandeliers produced

$X_2 = 6$ ceiling fans produced

$d_1^+ = \$6$ over the profit goal

$d_2^+ = 6$ wiring hours over the minimum set

$d_4^- = 1$ fan less than desired

QM for Windows - C:\Prentice\Data\Renstair\Hrrsn617.goa

Harrison Electric Company

	Wt(d+)	Prty(d+)	Wt(d-)	Prty(d-)	X1	X2		RHS
Constraint 1	0	0	1	1	7	6	=	30
Constraint 2	0	0	1	2	2	3	=	12
Constraint 3	1	3	0	0	6	5	=	30
Constraint 4	0	0	1	4	0	1	=	7

QM for Windows - C:\Prentice\Data\Renstair\Hrrsn617.goa

Final Tableau

Harrison Electric Company Solution

	X1	X2	d- 1	d- 2	d- 3	d- 4	d+ 1	d+ 2	d+ 3	d+ 4	RHS
Constraint 1	1.6	0.	0.	-1.	0.6	0.	0.	1.	-0.6	0.	6.
Constraint 2	1.2	1.	0.	0.	0.2	0.	0.	0.	-0.2	0.	6.
Constraint 3	0.2	0.	-1.	0.	1.2	0.	1.	0.	-1.2	0.	6.
Constraint 4	-1.2	0.	0.	0.	-0.2	1.	0.	0.	0.2	-1.	1.
Priority 4	-1.2	0.	0.	0.	-0.2	0.	0.	0.	0.2	-1.	1.
Priority 3	0.	0.	0.	0.	0.	0.	0.	0.	-1.	0.	0.
Priority 2	0.	0.	0.	-1.	0.	0.	0.	0.	0.	0.	0.
Priority 1	0.	0.	-1.	0.	0.	0.	0.	0.	0.	0.	0.

QM for Windows - C:\Prentice\Data\Renstair\Hrrsn617.goa

Summary

Harrison Electric Company Solution

Item			
Decision variable analysis	Value		
X1	0.		
X2	6.		
Priority analysis	Nonachievement		
Priority 1	0.		
Priority 2	0.		
Priority 3	0.		
Priority 4	1.		
Constraint Analysis	RHS	d+ (row i)	d- (row i)
Constraint 1	30.	6.	0.
Constraint 2	12.	6.	0.
Constraint 3	30.	0.	0.
Constraint 4	7.	0.	1.

Using QM for Windows to Solve Harrison's Problem Our microcomputer software program, QM for Windows, has a goal programming module, which is illustrated in Programs 11.6A, 11.6B, and 11.6C. The input screen appears first, in Program 11.6A. It is followed by the final tableau, which is identical in content to Table 11.6. Finally, the solution is shown in Program 11.6C, which also provides analyses of deviations and goal achievement. Note again that the first two constraints have deviational variables equal to +6 and the fourth constraint has a negative deviation of 1.

11.5 NONLINEAR PROGRAMMING

Linear, integer, and goal programming all assume that a problem's objective function and constraints are linear. That means that they contain no nonlinear terms such as X_1^3, $1/X_2$, $\log X_3$, or $5X_1X_2$. Yet in many mathematical programming problems, the objective function and/or one or more of the constraints are nonlinear.

In this section, we examine three categories of nonlinear programming (NLP) problems and illustrate how Excel can often be used to solve such problems.

IN ACTION Goal Programming Model for Prison Expenditures in Virginia

Prisons across the United States are overcrowded, and there is need for immediate expansion of their capacity and replacement or renovation of obsolete facilities. This study demonstrates how goal programming was used on the capital allocation problem faced by the Department of Corrections of Virginia.

The expenditure items considered by the Virginia corrections department included new and renovated maximum, medium, and minimum security facilities; community diversion programs; and personnel increases. The goal programming technique forced all prison projects to be completely accepted or rejected.

Model variables defined the construction, renovation, or establishment of a particular type of correctional facility for a specific location or purpose and indicated the people required by the facilities. The goal constraints fell into five categories: additional inmate capacity created by new and renovated cor-

rectional facilities; operating and personnel costs associated with each expenditure item; the impact of facility construction and renovation on imprisonment, sentence length, and early releases and parole; the mix of different facility types required by the system; and the personnel requirements resulting from the various capital expenditures for correctional facilities.

The solution results for Virginia were: one new maximum security facility for drug, alcohol, and psychiatric treatment activities; one new minimum security facility for youthful offenders; two new regular minimum security facilities; two new community diversion programs in urban areas, renovation of one existing medium security and one minimum security facility; 250 new correctional officers; four new administrators; 46 new treatment specialist/counselors; and six new medical personnel.

Source: R. Russell, B. Taylor, and A. Keown. *Computer Environmental Urban Systems* 11, 4 (1986): 135–146.

Nonlinear Objective Function and Linear Constraints

Here is an example of a nonlinear objective function.

The Great Western Appliance Company sells two models of toaster ovens, the Microtoaster (X_1) and the Self-Clean Toaster Oven (X_2). The firm earns a profit of \$28 for each Microtoaster regardless of the number sold. Profits for the Self-Clean model, however, increase as more units are sold because of fixed overhead. Profit on this model may be expressed as $21X_2 + 0.25X_2^2$.

Hence the firm's objective function is nonlinear:

$$\text{maximize profit} = 28X_1 + 21X_2 + 0.25X_2^2$$

Great Western's profit is subject to two linear constraints on production capacity and sales time available.

$$X_1 + X_2 \leq 1{,}000 \text{ (units of production capacity)}$$
$$0.5X_1 + 0.4X_2 \leq 500 \text{ (hours of sales time available)}$$
$$X_1, X_2 \geq 0$$

Quadratic programming contains squared terms in the objective function.

When an objective function contains squared terms (such as $0.25X_2^2$) and the problem's constraints are linear, it is called a *quadratic programming* problem. A number of useful problems in the field of portfolio selection fall into this category. Quadratic programs can be solved by a modified method of the simplex method. Such work is outside the scope of this book but can be found in sources listed in the Bibliography.

For purposes of illustration, we can turn to Excel's powerful Solver command to solve Great Western's model. Programs 11.7A and 11.7B provide the input and outputs, respectively.

Both Nonlinear Objective Function and Nonlinear Constraints

An example in which the objective and constraints are both nonlinear.

The annual profit at a medium-sized (200–400 beds) Hospicare Corporation–owned hospital depends on the number of medical patients admitted (X_1) and the number of surgical patients admitted (X_2). The nonlinear objective function for Hospicare is

$$\$13X_1 + \$6X_1 X_2 + \$5X_2 + \$1/X_2$$

PROGRAM 11.7A

An Excel Formulation of Great Western Appliance's Nonlinear Programming Problem

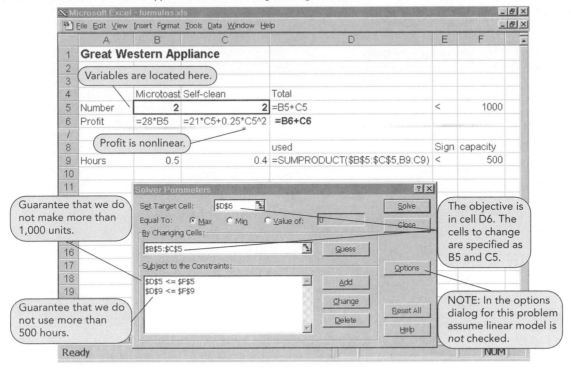

PROGRAM 11.7B

Solution to Great Western Appliance's NLP Problem Using Excel Solver Command Shown in Program 11.7A

The corporation identifies three constraints, two of which are also nonlinear, that affect operations. They are

$$2X_1^2 + 4X_2 \le 90 \text{ (nursing capacity, in thousands of labor-days)}$$

$$X_1 + X_2^3 \le 75 \text{ (x-ray capacity, in thousands)}$$

$$8X_1 - 2X_2 \le 61 \text{ (marketing budget required, in thousands of \$)}$$

An example of nonlinear constraints.

Excel's Solver is capable of formulating such a problem (see Program 11.8A). The optimal solution is provided in Program 11.8B.

PROGRAM 11.8A

An Excel Formulation of Hospicare Corp's NLP Problem

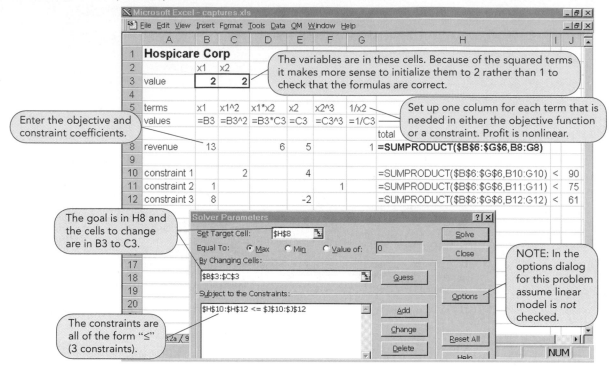

PROGRAM 11.8B

Excel Solution to the Hospicare Corp. NLP Problem, Using Solver

	A	B	C	D	E	F	G	H	I	J
1	**Hospicare Corp**									
2		x1	x2							
3	value	6.066259	4.100253							
4										
5	terms	x1	x1^2	x1*x2	x2	x2^3	1/x2			
6	values	6.066259	36.79949	24.87319	4.100253	68.93374	0.243887			
7								total		
8	revenue	13		6	5		1	**248.85**		
9										
10	constraint 1		2		4			90	<	90
11	constraint 2	1				1		75	<	75
12	constraint 3	8			-2			40.33	<	61

Linear Objective Function with Nonlinear Constraints

Thermlock Corp. produces massive rubber washers and gaskets like the type used to seal joints on the NASA Space Shuttles. To do so, it combines two ingredients: rubber (X_1) and oil (X_2). The cost of the industrial quality rubber used is $5 per pound and the cost of the high viscosity oil is $7 per pound. Two of the three constraints Thermlock faces are nonlinear. The firm's objective function and constraints are

Minimize costs = $5X_1 + $7X_2

Subject to $= 3X_1 + 0.25X_1^2 + 4X_2 + 0.3X_2^2 \geq 125$ (hardness constraint)

$$13X_1 + X_1^3 \geq 80 \text{ (tensile strength)}$$

$$0.7X_1 + X_2 \geq 17 \text{ (elasticity)}$$

To solve this nonlinear programming, we turn again to Excel. Program 11.9A illustrates how to formulate the constraints and how to set up the Solver parameters. The output is provided in Program 11.9B.

PROGRAM 11.9A

Excel Formulation of Thermlock's NLP Problem

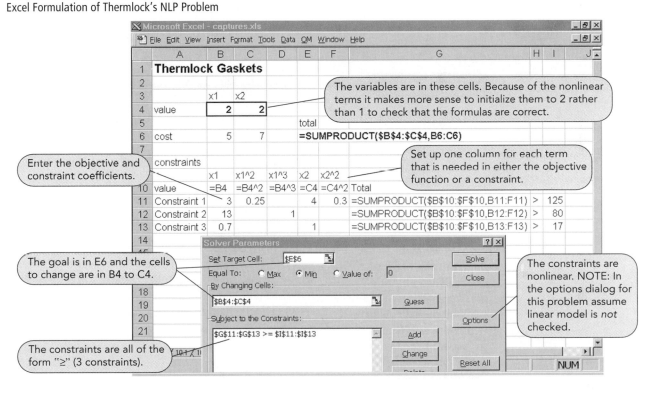

PROGRAM 11.9B

Solution to Thermlock's NLP Problem Using the Excel Solver Formulation in Program 11.9A

Computational Procedures for Nonlinear Programming

We cannot always find an optimal solution to nonlinear programs.

Unlike LP methods, computational procedures to solve many nonlinear problems do not always yield an optimal solution in a finite number of steps. In addition, there is no general method for solving all nonlinear problems. *Classical optimization* techniques, based on calculus, can handle some special cases, usually simpler types of problems. The *gradient method*, sometimes called the *steepest ascent method*, is an iterative procedure that moves from one feasible solution to the next in improving the value of the objective function. It has been computerized and can handle problems with both nonlinear constraints and objectives. But perhaps the best way to deal with nonlinear problems is to try to reduce them into a form that is linear or almost linear. *Separable programming* deals with a class of problems in which the objective and constraints are approximated by linear functions. In this way, the powerful simplex algorithm may again be applied. In general, work in the area of NLP is the least charted and most difficult of all the quantitative analysis models.

Summary

This chapter addressed three special types of linear programming problems. The first, integer programming, examines LP problems that cannot have fractional answers. We saw how to tackle such problems graphically, with the cutting plane method. We also noted that there are three types of integer programming problems: (1) pure or all-integer programs, (2) mixed problems, in which *some* solutions variables need not be integer, and (3) 0–1 problems, in which all solutions are either 0 or 1. QM for Windows and Excel were used to illustrate computer approaches to these problems. The branch and bound method, a popular algorithm for solving all-integer and mixed-integer linear problems, was also described.

The latter part of the chapter dealt with goal programming. This extension of LP allows problems to have multiple goals. We saw how to solve such a problem both graphically and by use of a modified method of the simplex algorithm. Again, software such as QM for Windows is a powerful tool in solving this offshoot of LP. Finally, the advanced topic of NLP was introduced as a special mathematical programming problem. Excel was seen to be a useful tool in solving simple NLP models.

Glossary

Integer Programming. A mathematical programming technique that produces integer solutions to linear programming problems.

Cutting Plane Method. A means of adding one or more constraints to LP problems to help produce an optimum integer solution.

Zero–One Integer Programming. Problems in which all decision variables must have integer values of 0 or 1.

Branch and Bound Method. An algorithm for solving all-integer and mixed-integer linear programs and assignment problems. It divides the set of feasible solutions into subsets that are examined systematically.

Goal Programming. A mathematical programming technique that permits decision makers to set and prioritize multiple objective functions.

Satisficing. The process of coming as close as possible to reaching your set of objectives.

Deviational Variables. Terms that are minimized in a goal programming problem. Like slack variables in LP, they are real. They are the only terms in the objective function.

Nonlinear Programming. A category of mathematical programming techniques that allow the objective function and/or constraints to be nonlinear.

Solved Problem 11-1

Consider the 0–1 integer programming problem that follows:

$$\text{maximize} \quad 50X_1 + 45X_2 + 48X_3$$
$$\text{subject to} \quad 19X_1 + 27X_2 + 34X_3 \le 80$$
$$22X_1 + 13X_2 + 12X_3 \le 40$$
$$X_1, X_2, X_3 \text{ must be either 0 or 1}$$

Now reformulate this problem with additional constraints so that no more than two of the three variables can take on a value equal to 1 in the solution. Further, make sure that if $X_1 = 1$, then $X_2 = 1$ also. Then solve the new problem using Excel.

Solution

Excel can handle all-integer, mixed-integer, and zero–one integer problems. Program 11.10A on page 508 shows two new constraints to handle the reformulated problem. These constraints are:

$$X_1 + X_2 + X_3 \le 2$$
$$\text{and} \quad X_1 - X_2 = 0$$

The output is shown in Program 11.10B on page 508. The optimal solution is $X_1 = 1$, $X_2 = 1$, $X_3 = 0$, with an objective function value of 95.

Solved Problem 11-2

Recall the Harrison Electric Company goal programming problem seen in Section 11.4. Its LP formulation was

$$\text{maximize profit} = \$7X_1 + \$6X_2$$
$$\text{subject to} \quad 2X_1 + 3X_2 \le 12 \text{ (wiring hours)}$$
$$6X_1 + 5X_2 \le 30 \text{ (assembly hours)}$$
$$X_1, X_2 \ge 0$$

where

X_1 = number of chandeliers produced

X_2 = number of ceiling fans produced

Reformulate Harrison Electrical as a goal programming model with the following goals:

Priority 1: Produce at least 4 chandeliers and 3 ceiling fans.
Priority 2: Maximize profit.
Priority 3: Limit overtime in the assembly department to 10 hours and in the wiring department to 6 hours.

Solution

$$\text{minimize} = P_1(d_1^- + d_2^-) + P_2 d_3^- + P_3(d_4^+ + d_5^+)$$
$$\text{subject to} \quad X_1 + d_1^- - d_1^+ = 4 \left.\vphantom{\begin{matrix}1\\1\end{matrix}}\right\} Priority\ 1$$
$$X_2 + d_2^- - d_2^+ = 3$$
$$7X_1 + 6X_2 + d_3^- - d_3^+ = 99{,}999 \} Priority\ 2$$
$$2X_1 + 3X_2 + d_4^- - d_4^+ = 18 \left.\vphantom{\begin{matrix}1\\1\end{matrix}}\right\} Priority\ 3$$
$$6X_1 + 5X_2 + d_5^- - d_5^+ = 40$$

In the priority 2 goal constraint, the 99,999 represents an unrealistically high profit. It is just a mathematical trick to use as a target so that we can get as close as possible to the maximum profit.

PROGRAM 11.10A

Excel Formulation for Solved Problem 11-1's 0–1 Integer Program

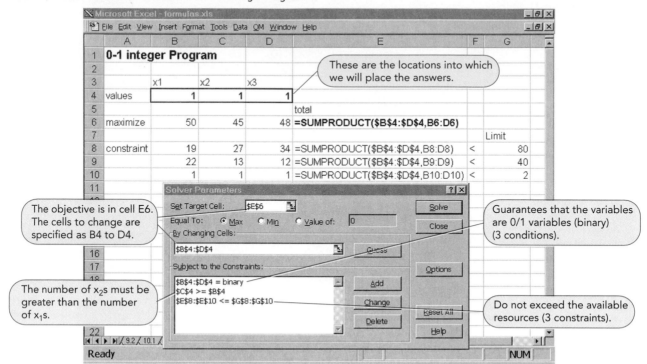

PROGRAM 11.10B

Output from Excel Formulation in Program 11.10A with Solution to Solved Problem 11-1's 0–1 IP Problem.

SELF-TEST

- Before taking the self-test, refer back to the learning objectives at the beginning of the chapter, the notes in the margins, and the glossary at the end of the chapter.
- Use the key at the back of the book to correct your answers.
- Restudy pages that correspond to any questions that you answered incorrectly or material you feel uncertain about.

1. If all of the decision variables require integer solutions, the problem is
   a. a pure integer programming type of problem.
   b. a simplex method type of problem.
   c. a mixed-integer programming type of problem.
   d. a Gorsky type of problem.
2. The cutting plane method
   a. is also called Gomory's method.
   b. is sometimes called the Gorsky approach.
   c. is only useful in the zero–one integer programming problem.
   d. is needed even if the LP algorithm provides an initial integer solution.
3. In a mixed-integer programming problem
   a. some integers must be even while others must be odd.
   b. some decisions variables must require integer results only and some variables must allow for continuous results.
   c. different objectives are mixed together even though they sometimes have relative priorities established.
4. When you apply the cutting plane method
   a. you also use the standard LP approach between each cutting plane application.
   b. you may get a greater result with the integer programming solution than with the standard LP approach because you cut some fat from the feasible region.
   c. you actually reduce the number of constraints in the problem since you cut them off.
5. A model containing a linear objective function and linear constraints but requiring that one or more of the decision variables take on an integer value in the final solution is called
   a. an integer programming problem.
   b. a goal programming problem.
   c. a nonlinear programming problem.
   d. a multiple objective LP problem.
6. An integer programming solution can never produce a greater profit than the LP solution to the same problem.
   a. True   b. False

7. In goal programming if all the goals are achieved, the value of the objective function will always be zero.
   a. True   b. False
8. The quantities that are maximized in a goal programming problem are termed deviation variables.
   a. True   b. False
9. Nobel laureate Herbert A. Simon of Carnegie-Mellon University says that modern managers should always optimize, not satisfice.
   a. True   b. False
10. In applying the branch and bound method to the assignment problem, if the first lowest cost calculated is a feasible solution, an error in calculation has been made.
    a. True   b. False
11. The zero–one integer programming problem
    a. requires the decision variables to have values between zero and 1.
    b. requires that the constraints all have coefficients between zero and 1.
    c. requires that the decision variables have coefficients between zero and 1.
    d. includes the assignment type of problems.
12. Goal programming
    a. requires only that you know whether the goal is direct profit maximization or cost minimization.
    b. allows you to have multiple goals, with or without priorities.
    c. is an algorithm with the goal of a quicker solution to the pure integer programming problem.
    d. is an algorithm with the goal of a quicker solution to the mixed-integer programming problem.
13. Nonlinear programming includes problems
    a. in which the objective function is linear but some constraints are not linear.
    b. in which the constraints are linear but the objective function is not linear.
    c. in which both the objective function and all of the constraints are not linear.
    d. solvable by quadratic programming.
    e. all of the above.

Discussion Questions and Problems

Discussion Questions

11-1 Compare the similarities and differences of linear and goal programming.

11-2 Provide your own examples of five applications of integer programming.

11-3 List the advantages and disadvantages of solving integer programming problems by (a) rounding off, (b) enumeration, (c) the cutting plane method, and (d) the branch and bound method.

11-4 Explain in your own words how the cutting plane method works.

11-5 What is the difference between the three types of integer programming problems? Which do you think is most common, and why?

11-6 What are the meaning and role of the lower bound and upper bound in the branch and bound method?

11-7 What is meant by "satisficing," and why is the term often used in conjunction with goal programming?

11-8 What are deviational variables? How do they differ from decision variables in traditional linear programming problems?

11-9 If you were the president of the college you are attending and were employing goal programming to assist in decision making, what might your goals be? What kinds of constraints would you include in your model?

11-10 What does it mean to rank goals in goal programming? How does this affect the problem's solution?

11-11 How does the solution of goal programming problems with the modified simplex method differ from the use of the regular simplex approach for LP problems?

11-12 Which of the following are nonlinear programming problems, and why?

(a) maximize profit $= 3X_1 + 5X_2 + 99X_3$

subject to
$$X_1 \geqslant 10$$
$$X_2 \leqslant 5$$
$$X_3 \geqslant 18$$

(b) minimize cost $= 25X_1 + 30X_2 + 8X_1X_2$

subject to
$$X_1 \geqslant 8$$
$$X_1 + X_2 \geqslant 12$$
$$0.0005X_1 - X_2 = 11$$

(c) minimize $Z = P_1d_1^- + P_2d_2^+ + P_3d_3^+$

subject to
$$X_1 + X_2 + d_1^- - d_1^+ = 300$$
$$X_2 + d_2^- - d_2^+ = 200$$
$$X_1 + d_3^- - d_3^+ = 100$$

(d) maximize profit $= 3X_1 + 4X_2$

subject to
$$X_1^2 - 5X_2 \geqslant 8$$
$$3X_1 + 4X_2 \geqslant 12$$

(e) minimize cost $= 18X_1 + 5X_2 + X_2^2$

subject to
$$4X_1 - 3X_2 \geqslant 8$$
$$X_1 + X_2 \geqslant 18$$

Are any of these quadratic programming problems?

Problems*

 11-13   Use the cutting plane method to solve the following pure-integer programming problem: Check your answers with QM for Windows or Excel.

$$\text{maximize profit} = 8X_1 + 6X_2$$

subject to
$$4X_1 + 6X_2 \le 16$$
$$15X_1 + 3X_2 \le 27$$
$$X_1, X_2 \text{ integers} \ge 0$$

 11-14   Student Enterprises sells two sizes of wall posters, a large 3- by 4-foot poster and a smaller 2- by 3-foot poster. The profit earned from the sale of each large poster is $3; each smaller poster earns $2. The firm, although profitable, is not large; it consists of one art student, Jan Meising, at the University of Kentucky. Because of her classroom schedule, Jan has the following weekly constraints: (1) up to three large posters can be sold, (2) up to five smaller posters can be sold, (3) up to 10 hours can be spent on posters during the week, with each large poster requiring 2 hours of work and each small one taking 1 hour. With the semester almost over, Jan plans on taking a three-month summer vacation to England and doesn't want to leave any unfinished posters behind. Find the integer solution that will maximize her profit.

 11-15   An airline owns an aging fleet of Boeing 727 jet airplanes. It is considering a major purchase of up to 17 new Boeing model 757 and 767 jets. The decision must take into account numerous cost and capability factors, including the following: (1) the airline can finance up to $400 million in purchases; (2) each Boeing 757 will cost $35 million, while each Boeing 767 will cost $22 million; (3) at least one-third of the planes purchased should be the longer-ranged 757; (4) the annual maintenance budget is to be no more than $8 million; (5) the annual maintenance cost per 757 is estimated to be $800,000, and it is $500,000 for each 767 purchased; and (6), each 757 can carry 125,000 passengers per year, while each 767 can fly 81,000 passengers annually. Formulate this as an integer programming problem to maximize the annual passenger-carrying capability. What category of integer programming problem is this?

 11-16   Solve Problem 11-15 by the cutting plane method.

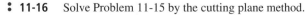 **11-17**   Innis Construction Company specializes in building moderately priced homes in Cincinnati, Ohio. Tom Innis has identified eight potential locations to construct new single-family dwellings, but he cannot put up homes on all of the sites because he has only $300,000 to invest in all projects. The accompanying table shows the cost of constructing homes in each area and the expected profit to be made from the sale of each home. Note that the home-building costs differ considerably due to lot costs, site preparation, and differences in the models to be built. Note also that a fraction of a home cannot be built.

---

*Note: means the problem may be solved with QM for Windows; means the problem may be solved with Excel; and means the problem may be solved with QM for Windows and/or Excel.

LOCATION	COST OF BUILDING AT THIS SITE ($)	EXPECTED PROFIT ($)
Clifton	60,000	5,000
Mt. Auburn	50,000	6,000
Mt. Adams	82,000	10,000
Amberly	103,000	12,000
Norwood	50,000	8,000
Covington	41,000	3,000
Roselawn	80,000	9,000
Eden Park	69,000	10,000

a) Formulate Innis's problem using zero–one integer programming.

b) Solve with QM for Windows or Excel.

11-18 Stockbroker Suzan Shader has made the following recommendations to her client:

TYPE OF INVESTMENT	COST ($)	EXPECTED RETURN ($)
Hanover municipal bonds	500	50
Hamilton city bonds	1,000	100
S.E. Power & Light Co.	350	30
Nebraska Electric Service	490	45
Southern Gas and Electric	700	65
Samuels Products Co.	270	20
Nation Builder Paint Co.	800	90
Hammer Head Hotels Co.	400	35

The client agrees to this list but provides several conditions: (1) no more than $3,000 can be invested, (2) the money is to be spread among at least five investments, (3) no more than one type of bond can be purchased, and (4) at least two utility stocks and at least two regular stocks must be purchased. Formulate this as a zero–one integer programming problem for Ms. Shader to maximize expected return.

11-19 Solve Problem 11-13 using the branch and bound method.

11-20 Solve Problem 11-15 using the branch and bound method.

11-21 Golding Manufacturing has four new jobs that must be assigned to any of four available machines. The cost of doing each job on each machine is as follows:

	MACHINE			
JOB	1	2	3	4
A	$85	$70	$60	$10
B	6	15	90	76
C	50	80	5	75
D	75	84	82	25

Use the branch and bound method to generate the least-total-cost assignment of performing the four jobs.

 11-22 Solve the following integer programming problem using the branch and bound approach.

maximize profit $= \$2X_1 + \$3X_2$

subject to
$$X_1 + 3X_2 \leq 9$$
$$3X_1 + X_2 \leq 7$$
$$X_1 - X_2 \leq 1$$

where both X_1 and X_2 must be nonnegative integer values.

 11-23 Geraldine Shawhan is president of Shawhan File Works, a firm that manufactures two types of metal file cabinets. The demand for her two-drawer model is up to 600 cabinets per week; demand for a three-drawer cabinet is limited to 400 per week. Shawhan File Works has a weekly operating capacity of 1,300 hours, with the two-drawer cabinet taking 1 hour to produce and the three-drawer cabinet requiring 2 hours. Each two-drawer model sold yields a $10 profit, while the profit for the large model is $15. Shawhan has listed the following goals in order of importance:
1. Attain a profit as close to $11,000 as possible each week.
2. Avoid underutilization of the firm's production capacity.
3. Sell as many two and three-drawer cabinets as the demand indicates.

Set this up as a goal programming problem.

11-24 Solve Problem 11-23 graphically. Are any goals unachieved in this solution? Explain.

 11-25 Harris Segal, marketing director for North-Central Power and Light, is about to begin an advertising campaign promoting energy conservation. In trying to budget between television and newspaper advertisements, he sets the following goals in order of importance:
1. The total advertising budget of $120,000 should not be exceeded.
2. There should be a mix of TV and newspaper ads, with at least 10 TV spots (costing $5,000 each) and at least 20 newspaper ads (costing $2,000 each).
3. The total number of people to read or hear the advertisements should be at least 9 million.

Each television spot reaches approximately 300,000 people. A newspaper advertisement is read by about 150,000 persons. Formulate Segal's goal programming problem to find out how many of each type of ad to place.

11-26 Solve Problem 11-25 graphically. How many people, in total, will read or hear the advertisements?

11-27 Hilliard Electronics produces specially coded computer chips for laser surgery in 64MB, 256MB, and 512MB sizes. (1MB means that the chip holds 1 million bytes of information.) To produce a 64MB chip requires 8 hours of labor, a 256MB chip takes 13 hours, and a 512MB chip requires 16 hours. Hilliard's monthly production capacity is 1,200 hours. Mr. Blank, the firm's sales manager, estimates that the maximum monthly sales of the 64MB, 256MB, and 512MB chips are 40, 50, and 60, respectively. The company has the following goals (ranked in order from most important to least important):
1. Fill an order from the best customer for thirty 64MB chips and thirty-five 256MB chips.
2. Provide sufficient chips to at least equal the sales estimates set by Mr. Blank.
3. Avoid underutilization of the production capacity.

Formulate this problem using goal programming.

11-28 The modified simplex method was presented for the Harrison Electric Company example in Tables 11.4, 11.5, and 11.6. Two iterations of the method were skipped between the second tableau in Table 11.5 and the final tableau in Table 11.6. Apply the method to provide the missing third and fourth tableaus. To which corner point (A, B, C, or D) in Figure 11.9 does each of these tableaus correspond?

11-29 An Oklahoma manufacturer produces two products: speaker telephones (X_1) and push-button telephones (X_2). The following goal programming model has been formulated to find the number of each to produce each day to meet the firm's goals:

$$\text{minimize} \qquad P_1 d_1^- + P_2 d_2^- + P_3 d_3^+ + P_4 d_1^+$$

$$\text{subject to} \qquad 2X_1 + 4X_2 + d_1^- - d_1^+ = 80$$

$$8X_1 + 10X_2 + d_2^- - d_2^+ = 320$$

$$8X_1 + 6X_2 + d_3^- - d_3^+ = 240$$

$$\text{all } X_i, d_i \geq 0$$

(a) Set up the complete initial goal programming tableau for this problem.

(b) Find the optimal solution using the modified simplex method.

11-30 Major Bill Bligh, director of the Army War College's new six-month attaché training program, is concerned about how the 20 officers taking the course spend their precious time while in his charge. Major Bligh recognizes that there are 168 hours per week and thinks that his students have been using them rather inefficiently. Bligh lets

X_1 = number of hours of sleep needed per week

X_2 = number of personal hours (eating, personal hygiene, handling laundry, and so on)

X_3 = number of hours of class and studying

X_4 = number of hours of social time off base (dating, sports, family visits, and so on)

He thinks that students should study 30 hours a week to have time to absorb material. This is his most important goal. Bligh feels that students need at most 7 hours sleep per night on average and that this goal is number 2. He believes that goal number 3 is to provide at least 20 hours per week of social time. (a) Formulate this as a goal programming problem. (b) Solve the problem using computer software.

11-31 Hinkel Rotary Engine, Ltd., produces four- and six-cylinder models of automobile engines. The firm's profit for each four-cylinder engine sold during its quarterly production cycle is $1,800 - \$50X_1$, where X_1 is the number sold. Hinkel makes $2,400 - \$70X_2$ for each of the larger engines sold, with X_2 equal to the number of six-cylinder engines sold. There are 5,000 hours of production time available during each production cycle. A four-cylinder engine requires 100 hours of production time, whereas six-cylinder engines take 130 hours to manufacture. Formulate this production planning problem for Hinkel.

11-32 Motorcross of Wisconsin produces two models of snowmobiles, the XJ6 and the XJ8. In any given production-planning week Motorcross has 40 hours available in its final testing bay. Each XJ6 requires 1 hour to test and each XJ8 takes 2 hours. The revenue (in $1,000s) for the firm is nonlinear and is stated as (no. of XJ6s)(4 − 0.1 no. of XJ6s) + (no. of XJ8s)(5 – 0.2 no. of XJ8s).

(a) Formulate this problem.

(b) Solve using Excel.

Data Set Problem

11-33 The following integer programming problem has been developed to help First National Bank decide where, out of 10 possible sites, to locate four new branch offices:

$$\text{maximize expected returns} = 120X_1 + 100X_2 + 110X_3 + 140X_4 + 155X_5$$
$$+ 128X_6 + 145X_7 + 190X_8 + 170X_9 + 150X_{10}$$

subject to

$$20X_1 + 30X_2 + 20X_3 + 25X_4 + 30X_5 + 30X_6 + 25X_7 + 20X_8 + 25X_9 + 30X_{10} \leq 110$$

$$15X_1 + 5X_2 + 20X_3 + 20X_4 + 5X_5 + 5X_6 + 10X_7 + 20X_8 + 5X_9 + 20X_{10} \leq 50$$

$$X_2 + X_6 + X_7 + X_9 + X_{10} \leq 3$$

$$X_2 + X_3 + X_5 + X_8 + X_9 \geq 2$$

$$X_1 + X_3 + X_{10} \geq 1$$

$$\Sigma X_i \leq 4$$

$$\text{all } X_i = 0 \text{ or } 1$$

where X_i represents Winter Park, Maitland, Osceola, Downtown, South Orlando, Airport, Winter Garden, Apopka, Lake Mary, Cocoa Beach for i equals 1 to 10, respectively.

(a) Where should the four new sites be located, and what will be the expected return?

(b) If at least one new branch *must* be opened in Maitland or Osceola, will this change the answers? Add the new constraint and rerun.

(c) The expected return at Apopka was overestimated. The correct value is $160,000 per year (that is, 160). Using the original assumptions (namely, ignoring (b)), does your answer to part (a) change?

Case Study

Schank Marketing Research

Schank Marketing Research has just signed contracts to conduct studies for four clients. At present, three project managers are free for assignment to the tasks. Although all are capable of handling each assignment, the times and costs to complete the studies depend on the experience and knowledge of each manager. Using his judgment, John Schank, the president, has been able to establish a cost for each possible assignment. These costs, which are really the salaries each manager would draw on each task, are summarized in the following table.

Schank is very hesitant about neglecting NASA, which has been an important customer in the past. (NASA has employed the firm to study the public's attitude toward the Space Shuttle and proposed Space Station.) In addition, Schank has promised to try to provide Ruth a salary of at least $3,000 on his next assignment. From previous contracts, Schank also knows that Gardener does not get along well with the management at CBT Television, so he hopes to avoid assigning her to CBT. Finally, as Hines Corporation is also an old and valued client, Schank feels that it is twice as important to assign a project manager immediately to Hines's task as it is to provide one to General Foundry, a brand-new client. Schank wants to minimize the total costs of all projects while considering each of these goals. He feels that all of these goals are important, but if he had to rank them, he would put his concern about NASA first, his worry about Gardener second, his need to keep Hines Corporation happy third, his promise to Ruth fourth, and his concern about minimizing all costs last.

Each project manager can handle, at most, one new client.

Discussion Questions

1. If Schank were not concerned about noncost goals, how would he formulate this problem so that it could be solved quantitatively?

2. Develop a formulation that will incorporate all five objectives.

PROJECT MANAGER	CLIENT			
	HINES CORP.	NASA	GENERAL FOUNDRY	CBT TELEVISION
Gardener	$3,200	$3,000	$2,800	$2,900
Ruth	2,700	3,200	3,000	3,100
Hardgraves	1,900	2,100	3,300	2,100

Case Study

Oakton River Bridge

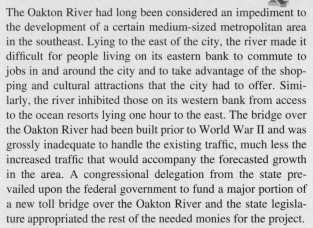

The Oakton River had long been considered an impediment to the development of a certain medium-sized metropolitan area in the southeast. Lying to the east of the city, the river made it difficult for people living on its eastern bank to commute to jobs in and around the city and to take advantage of the shopping and cultural attractions that the city had to offer. Similarly, the river inhibited those on its western bank from access to the ocean resorts lying one hour to the east. The bridge over the Oakton River had been built prior to World War II and was grossly inadequate to handle the existing traffic, much less the increased traffic that would accompany the forecasted growth in the area. A congressional delegation from the state prevailed upon the federal government to fund a major portion of a new toll bridge over the Oakton River and the state legislature appropriated the rest of the needed monies for the project.

Progress in construction of the bridge has been in accordance with what was anticipated at the start of construction. The state highway commission, which will have operational jurisdiction over the bridge, has concluded that opening of the bridge for traffic is likely to take place at the beginning of the next summer, as scheduled. A personnel task force has been established to recruit, train, and schedule the workers needed to operate the toll facility.

The personnel task force is well aware of the budgetary problems facing the state. They have taken as part of their mandate the requirement that personnel costs be kept as low as possible. One particular area of concern is the number of toll collectors that will be needed. The bridge is scheduling three shifts of collectors: shift A from midnight to 8 A.M., shift B from 8 A.M. to 4 P.M., and shift C from 4 P.M. to midnight. Recently, the state employees union negotiated a contract with the state which requires that all toll collectors be permanent, full-time employees. In addition, all collectors must work a five-on, two-off schedule on the same shift. Thus, for example, a worker could be assigned to work Tuesday, Wednesday, Thursday, Friday, and Saturday on shift A, followed by Sunday and Monday off. An employee could not be scheduled to work, say, Tuesday on shift A followed by Wednesday, Thursday, Friday, and Saturday on shift B or on any other mixture of shifts during a five-day block. The employees would choose their assignments in order of their seniority.

The task force has received projections of traffic flow on the bridge by day and hour. These projections are based on extrapolations of existing traffic patterns—the pattern of commuting, shopping, and beach traffic currently experienced with growth projections factored in. Standards data from other state-operated toll facilities have allowed the task force to convert these traffic flows into toll collector requirements, that is, the minimum number of collectors required per shift, per day, to handle the anticipated traffic load. These toll collector requirements are summarized in the following table:

Minimum Number of Toll Collectors Required Per Shift

SHIFT	SUN.	MON.	TUE.	WED.	THU.	FRI.	SAT.
A	8	13	12	12	13	13	15
B	10	10	10	10	10	13	15
C	15	13	13	12	12	13	8

The numbers in the table include one or two extra collectors per shift to fill in for collectors who call in sick and to provide relief for collectors on their scheduled breaks. Note that each of the eight collectors needed for shift A on Sunday, for example, could have come from any of the A shifts scheduled to begin on Wednesday, Thursday, Friday, Saturday, or Sunday.

Discussion Questions

1. Determine the minimum number of toll collectors that would have to be hired to meet the requirements expressed in the table.
2. The union had indicated that it might lift its opposition to the mixing of shifts in a five-day block in exchange for additional compensation and benefits. By how much could the numbers of toll collectors required be reduced if this is done?

Source: B. Render, R.M. Stair, and I. Greenberg. *Cases and Readings in Management Science*, 2nd ed. 1990, pp. 55–56. Reprinted by permission of Prentice Hall, Upper Saddle River, New Jersey.

Case Study

Puyallup Mall

Jane Rodney, president of the Rodney Development Company, was trying to decide what types of stores to include in her new shopping center at Puyallup Mall. She had already contracted for a supermarket, a drugstore, and a few other stores that she considered essential. However, she had available an additional 16,000 square feet of floor space yet to allo-

cate. She drew up a list of the 15 types of stores she might consider (see Table 11.7) including the floor space required by each. Rodney did not think she would have any trouble finding occupants for any type of store.

The lease agreements Rodney used in her developments included two types of payment. The store had to pay a certain annual rent, depending on the size and type of store. In

TABLE 11.7 Characteristics of Possible Leases, Puyallup Mall Shopping Center

TYPE OF STORE	SIZE OF STORE (1000's OF SQ FT)	ANNUAL RENT ($1000's)	PRESENT VALUE ($1000's)	CONSTRUCTION COST ($1000's)
Clothing				
1. Men's	1.0	$4.4	$28.1	$24.6
2. Women's	1.6	6.1	34.6	32.0
3. Variety (both)	2.0	8.3	50.0	41.4
Restaurants				
4. Fancy restaurant	3.2	24.0	162.0	124.4
5. Lunchroom	1.8	19.5	77.8	64.8
6. Cocktail lounge	2.1	20.7	100.4	79.8
7. Candy and ice cream shop	1.2	7.7	45.2	38.6
Hardgoods				
8. Hardware store	2.4	19.4	80.2	66.8
9. Cutlery and variety	1.6	11.7	51.4	45.1
10. Luggage and leather	2.0	15.2	62.5	54.3
Miscellaneous				
11. Travel agency	0.6	3.9	18.0	15.0
12. Tobacco shop	0.5	3.2	11.6	13.4
13. Camera store	1.4	11.3	50.4	42.0
14. Toys	2.0	16.0	73.6	63.7
15. Beauty parlor	1.0	9.6	51.2	40.0

addition, Rodney was to receive a small percentage of the store's sales if the sales exceeded a specified minimum amount. The amount of annual rent from each store is shown in the second column of the table. To estimate the profitability of each type of store, Rodney calculated the present value of all future rent and sales percentage payments. These are given in the third column. Rodney wants to achieve the highest total *present value* over the set of stores she selects. However, she could not simply pick those stores with the highest present values, for there were several restrictions. The first, of course, was that she has available only 16,000 square feet.

In addition, a condition on the financing of the project required that the total annual rent should be at least as much as the annual fixed costs (taxes, management fees, debt service, and so forth). These annual costs were $130,000 for this part of the project. Finally, the total funds available for construction of this part of the project were $700,000, and each type of

store required different construction costs depending on the size and type of store (fourth column in the table).

In addition, Rodney had certain requirements in terms of the mix of stores that she considered best. She wanted at least one store from each of the clothing, hardgoods, and miscellaneous groups, and at least two from the restaurant category. She wanted no more than two from the clothing group. Furthermore, the number of stores in the miscellaneous group should not exceed the total number of stores in the clothing and hardgoods groups combined.

Discussion Question

Which tenants should be selected for the mall?

Source: Adapted from H. Bierman, C. P. Bonini, and W. H. Hausman, *Quantitative Analysis*, 7th ed. (Homewood, IL: Richard D. Irwin, Inc.), pp. 467–468, copyright © 1986.

Bibliography

Arntzen, Bruce C., et al. "Global Supply Chain Management at Digital Equipment Corporation," *Interfaces* 25, 1 (January–February 1995): 69–93.

Bean, James C., Charles E. Noon, Sarah M. Ryan, and Gary J. Salton. "Selecting Tenants in a Shopping Mall," *Interfaces* 18, 2 (March–April 1988): 1–9.

Bohl, Alan H. "Computer Aided Formulation of Silicon Defoamers for the Paper Industry," *Interfaces* 24, 5 (September–October 1994): 41–48.

DeKluyver, Cornelis A., and Herbert Moskowitz. "Assessing Scenario Probabilities via Interactive Goal Programming," *Management Science* 30, 3 (March 1984): 273–278.

Ignizio, J. P. *Goal Programming and Extensions.* Lexington, MA: D.C. Heath and Company, 1976.

Kuby, Michael, et al. "Planning China's Coal and Electricity Delivery System," *Interfaces* 25, 1 (January–February 1995): 41–68.

Lee, Sang M., and Marc J. Schniederjans. "A Multicriterial Assignment Problem: A Goal Programming Approach," *Interfaces* 13, 4 (August 1983): 75–79.

Stowe, J. D. "An Integer Programming Solution for the Optimal Credit Investigation/Credit Granting Sequence," *Financial Management* 14 (Summer 1985): 66–76.

Subramanian, R., et al. "Coldstart: Fleet Assignment at Delta Airlines," *Interfaces* 24, 1 (January–February 1994): 104–120.

Taylor, B. W. "An Integer Nonlinear Goal Programming Model for the Deployment of State Highway Patrol Units," *Management Science* 31, 11 (November 1985): 1335–1347.

Tingley, Kim M., and Judith S. Liebmen. "A Goal Programming Example in Public Health Resource Allocation," *Management Science* 30, 3 (March 1984): 279–289.

Wang, Hongbo. "A Branch and Bound Approach for Sequencing Expansion Projects," *Production and Operations Management* 4, 1 (Winter 1995): 57–75.

Zangwill, W. I. *Nonlinear Programming: A Unified Approach.* Upper Saddle River, NJ: Prentice Hall, 1969.

Analytic Hierarchy Process

LEARNING OBJECTIVES

After completing this supplement students will be able to:

1. Use the multifactor evaluation process in making decisions that involve a number of factors, where importance weights can be assigned.
2. Understand the use of the analytic hierarchy process in decision making.
3. Contrast multifactor evaluation with the analytic hierarchy process.

SUPPLEMENT OUTLINE

S11.1 Introduction

S11.2 Multifactor Evaluation Process

S11.3 Analytic Hierarchy Process

S11.4 Comparison of MFEP and AHP

Summary • Glossary • Key Equations • Solved Problems • Self-Test • Discussion Questions and Problems • Bibliography

S11.1 INTRODUCTION

Many decisions involve a large number of factors.

Many decision-making problems involve a number of factors. For example, if you are considering a new job, factors might include starting salary, career advancement opportunities, work location, the people you'll be working with on the job, the type of work you will be doing, and assorted fringe benefits. If you are considering the purchase of a personal computer, there are a number of important factors to consider as well: price, memory, compatibility with other computers, flexibility, brand name, software availability, the existence of any user groups, and the support of the computer manufacturer and the local computer store. In buying a new or used car, such factors as color, style, make and model, year, number of miles (if it's a used car), price, dealership or person you are purchasing the car from, warranties, and cost of insurance may be important factors to consider.

In *multifactor decision making*, individuals subjectively and intuitively consider the various factors in making their selection. For difficult decisions, a quantitative approach is recommended. All of the important factors can then be given appropriate weights and each alternative, such as a car, a computer, or a new job prospect, can be evaluated in terms of these factors. This approach is called the *multifactor evaluation process* (MFEP).

In other cases we may not be able to quantify our preferences for various factors and alternatives. We then use the analytic hierarchy process. This process uses pairwise comparisons and then computes the weighting factors and evaluations for us. We begin with a discussion of the multifactor evaluation process.

S11.2 MULTIFACTOR EVALUATION PROCESS

With the multifactor evaluation process, we start by listing the factors and their relative importance on a scale from 0 to 1.

Let's consider an example. Steve Markel, an undergraduate business major, is looking at several job opportunities. After discussing the employment situation with his academic advisor and the director of the placement center, Steve has determined that the only three factors really important to him are salary, career advancement opportunities, and location of the new job. Furthermore, Steve has decided that career advancement opportunities are the most important to him. He has given this a weight of 0.6. Steve has placed salary next, with a weight of 0.3. Finally, Steve has given location an importance weight of 0.1. As with any MFEP problem, the importance weights for factors must sum to 1 (see Table S11.1).

At this time, Steve feels confident that he will get offers from AA Company, EDS, Ltd., and PW, Inc. For each of these jobs, Steve evaluated, or rated, the various factors on a 0 to 1 scale. For AA Company, Steve gave salary an evaluation of 0.7, career advance-

TABLE S11.1 Factor Weights

FACTOR	IMPORTANCE (WEIGHT)
Salary	0.3
Career advancement	0.6
Location	0.1

TABLE S11.2 Factor Evaluations

FACTOR	AA CO.	EDS, LTD.	PW, INC.
Salary	0.7	0.8	0.9
Career advancement	0.9	0.7	0.6
Location	0.6	0.8	0.9

ment an evaluation of 0.9, and location an evaluation of 0.6. For EDS, Steve evaluated salary as 0.8, career advancement as 0.7, and location as 0.8. For PW, Inc., Steve gave salary an evaluation of 0.9, career advancement an evaluation of 0.6, and location an evaluation of 0.9. The results are shown in Table S11.2.

Given this information, Steve can determine a total weighted evaluation for each of the alternatives or job possibilities. Each company is given a factor evaluation for the three factors, and then the factor weights are multiplied times the factor evaluation and summed to get a total weighted evaluation for each company. As you can see in Table S11.3, AA Company has received a total weighted evaluation of 0.81. The same type of analysis is done for EDS, Ltd., and PW, Inc., in Tables S11.4 and S11.5. As you can see from the analysis, AA Company received the highest total weighted evaluation. EDS, Ltd., was next with a total weighted evaluation of 0.74. Using the multifactor evaluation process, Steve's decision was to go with AA Company because it had the highest total weighted evaluation.

The company with the highest total weighted evaluation is selected.

T A B L E S 1 1 . 3 Evaluation of AA Co.

FACTOR NAME	FACTOR WEIGHT		FACTOR EVALUATION		WEIGHTED EVALUATION
Salary	0.3	×	0.7	=	0.21
Career	0.6	×	0.9	=	0.54
Location	0.1	×	0.6	=	0.06
Total	1				0.81

T A B L E S 1 1 . 4 Evaluation of EDS, Ltd.

FACTOR NAME	FACTOR WEIGHT		FACTOR EVALUATION		WEIGHTED EVALUATION
Salary	0.3	×	0.8	=	0.24
Career	0.6	×	0.7	=	0.42
Location	0.1	×	0.8	=	0.08
Total	1				0.74

T A B L E S 1 1 . 5 Evaluation of PW, Inc.

FACTOR NAME	FACTOR WEIGHT		FACTOR EVALUATION		WEIGHTED EVALUATION
Salary	0.3	×	0.9	=	0.27
Career	0.6	×	0.6	=	0.36
Location	0.1	×	0.9	=	0.09
Total	1				0.72

S11.3   ANALYTIC HIERARCHY PROCESS

AHP uses pairwise comparisons.

In situations where we can assign evaluations and weights to the various decision factors, the multifactor evaluation process described previously works fine. In other cases, decision makers may have difficulties in accurately determining the various factor weights and evaluations. In this case, the *analytic hierarchy process* (AHP) can be used. AHP was developed by Thomas L. Saaty and published in his 1980 book, *The Analytic Hierarchy Process*.

This process involves pairwise comparisons. The decision maker starts by laying out the overall hierarchy of the decision. This hierarchy reveals the factors to be considered as well as the various alternatives in the decision. Then, a number of pairwise comparisons are done, which result in the determination of *factor weights* and *factor evaluations*. They are the same types of weights and evaluations discussed in the preceding section and shown in Tables S11.1 through S11.5. As before, the alternative with the highest total weighted score is selected as the best alternative.

Judy Grim's Computer Decision

As an example of this process, we take the case of Judy Grim, who is looking for a new computer system for her small business. She has determined that the most important overall factors are hardware, software, and vendor support. Furthermore, Judy has narrowed down her alternatives to three possible computer systems. She has labeled these SYSTEM-1, SYSTEM-2, and SYSTEM-3. To begin, Judy has placed these factors and alternatives into a decision hierarchy (see Figure S11.1).

The decision hierarchy for the computer selection has three different levels. The top level describes the overall decision. As you can see in Figure S11.1, this overall decision is to select the best computer system. The middle level in the hierarchy describes the factors that are to be considered: hardware, software, and vendor support. Judy could decide to use a number of additional factors, but for this example we keep our factors to only three to show you the types of calculations that are to be performed using AHP. The lower level of the decision hierarchy reveals the alternatives. (Alternatives have also been called *items* or *systems*.) As you can see, the alternatives include the three different computer systems.

 IN ACTION   **R&D at Air Products and Chemicals, Inc.**

Without new ideas and products, a company can lose its competitive edge and profitability. A lack of research and development can mean a loss of business and even bankruptcy for some organizations. Yet, spending money on R&D does not guarantee success. How scarce resources are allocated among diverse R&D projects can help a company develop leading products and sustain high profitability for years.

Realizing its importance, Air Products and Chemicals, Inc., identifies key issues for successful R&D investments. These issues are then communicated to those involved in R&D to improve project proposals and help increase the likelihood of successful R&D results. To determine the best R&D projects for funding, Air Products selects and weights criteria in a structured framework, using the analytic hierarchy process (AHP) discussed in this supplement. AHP is used to determine the real strengths and weaknesses of proposed R&D projects. In addition, AHP allows decision makers to determine a project ranking for each project. With AHP, Air Products fully funds the strong projects, denies funding to weak projects, and funds intermediate projects to some extent to resolve and overcome any weaknesses.

Source: Brenner Merrill, "Practical R&D Project Prioritization," *Research-Technology Management* (September 1994): 38.

FIGURE S11.1

Decision Hierarchy for Computer System Selection

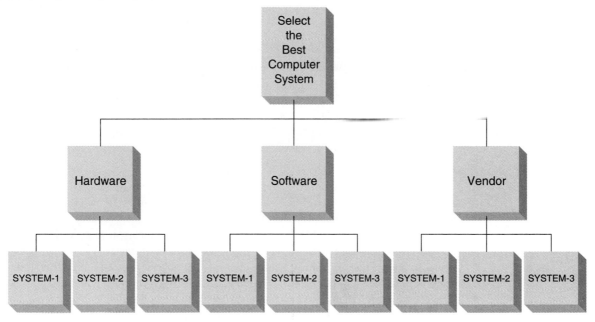

The key to using AHP is pairwise comparisons. The decision maker, Judy Grim, needs to compare two different alternatives using a scale that ranges from equally preferred to extremely preferred.

We use the following for pairwise comparison:

1—Equally preferred

2—Equally to moderately preferred

3—Moderately preferred

4—Moderately to strongly preferred

5—Strongly preferred

6—Strongly to very strongly preferred

7—Very strongly preferred

8—Very to extremely strongly preferred

9—Extremely preferred

Using Pairwise Comparisons

Judy begins by looking at the hardware factor and by comparing computer SYSTEM-1 with computer SYSTEM-2. Using the scale above, Judy determines that the hardware for computer SYSTEM-1 is moderately preferred to computer SYSTEM-2. Thus, Judy uses the number 3, representing moderately preferred. Next, Judy compares the hardware for SYSTEM-1 to SYSTEM-3. She believes that the hardware for computer SYSTEM-1 is extremely preferred to computer SYSTEM-3. This is a numerical score of 9. Finally, Judy considers the only other pairwise comparison, which is the hardware for computer SYSTEM-2 compared to the hardware for computer SYSTEM-3. She be-

Pairwise comparisons are performed for hardware.

lieves that the hardware for computer SYSTEM-2 is strongly to very strongly preferred to the hardware for computer SYSTEM-3, a score of 6. With these pairwise comparisons, Judy constructs a pairwise comparison matrix for hardware. This is shown in the following table:

HARDWARE	SYSTEM-1	SYSTEM-2	SYSTEM-3
SYSTEM-1		3	9
SYSTEM-2			6
SYSTEM-3			

This pairwise comparison matrix reveals Judy's preferences for hardware concerning the three computer systems. From this information, using AHP, we can determine the evaluation factors for hardware for the three computer systems.

Look at the upper left corner of the pairwise comparison matrix. This upper left corner compares computer SYSTEM-1 to itself for hardware. When comparing anything to itself, the evaluation scale must be 1, representing equally preferred. Thus, we can place the number 1 in the upper left corner (see below), which compares SYSTEM-1 to itself. The same can be said for comparing SYSTEM-2 to itself and comparing SYSTEM-3 to itself. Each of these must also get a score of 1, which represents equally preferred.

In general, for any pairwise comparison matrix, we will place 1s down the diagonal from the upper left corner to the lower right corner. To finish such a table, we make the observation that if alternative A is twice as preferred to alternative B, we can conclude that alternative B is preferred only one half as much as alternative A. Thus, if alternative A receives a score of 2 relative to alternative B, then alternative B should receive a score of ½ when compared with alternative A. We can use this same logic to complete the lower left side of the matrix of pairwise comparisons:

Finishing the pairwise comparisons matrix.

HARDWARE	SYSTEM-1	SYSTEM-2	SYSTEM-3
SYSTEM-1	1	3	9
SYSTEM-2	⅓	1	6
SYSTEM-3	⅑	⅙	1

Look at this newest matrix of pairwise comparisons. You will see that there are 1s down the diagonal from the upper left to the lower right corner. Then, look at the lower left part of the table. In the second row and first column of this table, you can see that SYSTEM-2 received a score of ⅓ compared to SYSTEM-1. This is because SYSTEM-1 received a score of 3 over SYSTEM-2 from the original assessment. Now look at the third row. The same has been done. SYSTEM-3 compared to SYSTEM-1, in row 3 column 1 of the table, received a score of ⅑. This is because SYSTEM-1 compared to SYSTEM-3 received a score of 9 in the original pairwise comparison. In a similar fashion, SYSTEM-3 compared to SYSTEM-2 received a score of ⅙ in the third row and second column of the table. This is because when comparing SYSTEM-2 to SYSTEM-3 in the original pairwise comparison, the score of 6 was given.

Evaluations for Hardware

Now that we have the completed matrix of pairwise comparisons, we can start to compute the evaluations for hardware. We start by converting the numbers in the matrix of pairwise comparisons to decimals to make them easier to work with. We then get column totals:

HARDWARE	SYSTEM-1	SYSTEM-2	SYSTEM-3
SYSTEM-1	1	3	9
SYSTEM-2	0.333	1	6
SYSTEM-3	0.1111	0.1677	1
Column totals	1.444	4.1667	16.0

Once the column totals have been determined, the numbers in the matrix are divided by their respective column totals as follows:

HARDWARE	SYSTEM-1	SYSTEM-2	SYSTEM-3
SYSTEM-1	0.6923	0.7200	0.5625
SYSTEM-2	0.2300	0.2400	0.3750
SYSTEM-3	0.0769	0.0400	0.0625

To determine the priorities for hardware for the three computer systems, we simply find the average of the various rows from the matrix of numbers as follows:

HARDWARE

$$\text{Row Averages} \begin{bmatrix} 0.6583 \\ 0.2819 \\ 0.0598 \end{bmatrix} \begin{matrix} = & (0.6923 + 0.7200 + 0.5625)/3 \\ = & (0.2300 + 0.2400 + 0.3750)/3 \\ = & (0.0769 + 0.0400 + 0.0625)/3 \end{matrix}$$

The results are displayed in Table S11.6. As you can see, the factor evaluation for SYSTEM-1 is 0.6583. For SYSTEM-2 and SYSTEM-3, the factor evaluations are 0.2819 and 0.0598. The same procedure is used to get the factor evaluations for all the other factors, which are software and vendor support in this case. But before we do this, we need to determine whether our responses are consistent by determining a *consistency ratio*.

Determining the Consistency Ratio

To arrive at the consistency ratio, we begin by determining the weighted sum vector. This is done by multiplying the factor evaluation number for the first system times the first column of the original pairwise comparison matrix. We multiply the second factor evaluation

TABLE S11.6 Factor Evaluation for Hardware

FACTOR	SYSTEM-1	SYSTEM-2	SYSTEM-3
Hardware	0.6583	0.2819	0.0598

times the second column, and the third factor times the third column of the original matrix of pairwise comparisons. Then we sum these values over the rows.

Weighted sum vector =

Computing the weighted sum vector and the consistency vector.

$$
\begin{bmatrix}
(0.6583)(1) & + & (0.2819)(3) & + & (0.0598)(9) \\
(0.6583)(0.3333) & + & (0.2819)(1) & + & (0.0598)(6) \\
(0.6583)(0.1111) & + & (0.2819)(0.1677) & + & (0.0598)(1)
\end{bmatrix}
=
\begin{bmatrix}
2.0423 \\
0.8602 \\
0.1799
\end{bmatrix}
$$

The next step is to determine the consistency vector. This is done by dividing the weighted sum vector by the factor evaluation values determined previously.

$$
\text{Consistency vector} =
\begin{bmatrix}
2.0423/0.6583 \\
0.8602/0.2819 \\
0.1799/0.0598
\end{bmatrix}
=
\begin{bmatrix}
3.1025 \\
3.0512 \\
3.0086
\end{bmatrix}
$$

Computing Lambda and the Consistency Index   Now that we have found the consistency vector, we need to compute values for two more terms, lambda (λ) and the consistency index (CI), before the final consistency ratio can be computed. The value for lambda is simply the average value of the consistency vector. The formula for CI is

$$
\text{CI} = \frac{\lambda - n}{n - 1}
\tag{S11-1}
$$

where n is the number of items or systems being compared. In this case, $n = 3$, for three different computer systems being compared. The results of the calculations are as follows:

$$
\lambda = \frac{3.1025 + 3.0512 + 3.0086}{3}
$$

$$
= 3.0541
$$

$$
\text{CI} = \frac{\lambda - n}{n - 1}
$$

$$
= \frac{3.0541 - 3}{3 - 1} = 0.0270
$$

Computing the Consistency Ratio   Finally, we are now in a position to compute the consistency ratio. The consistency ratio (CR) is equal to the consistency index divided by the random index (RI), which is determined from a table. The random index is a direct function of the number of alternatives or systems being considered. This table is shown, followed by the final calculation of the consistency ratio.

n	RI	n	RI
2	0.00	6	1.24
$n \longrightarrow$ 3 $\longrightarrow$ 0.58		7	1.32
4	0.90	8	1.41
5	1.12		

In general,

$$CR = \frac{CI}{RI} \tag{S11-2}$$

In this case,

$$CR = \frac{CI}{RI} = \frac{0.0270}{0.58} = 0.0466$$

The consistency ratio tells us how consistent we are with our answers. A higher number means we are less consistent, while a lower number means that we are more consistent. In general, if the consistency ratio is 0.10 or less, the decision maker's answers are relatively consistent. For a consistency ratio that is greater than 0.10, the decision maker should seriously consider reevaluating his or her responses during the pairwise comparisons that were used to obtain the original matrix of pairwise comparisons.

The consistency ratio tells us how consistent we are.

As you can see from the analysis, we are relatively consistent with our responses, so there is no need to reevaluate the pairwise comparison responses. If you look at the original pairwise comparison matrix, this makes sense. The hardware for SYSTEM-1 was moderately preferred to the hardware for SYSTEM-2. The hardware for SYSTEM-1 was extremely preferred to the hardware for SYSTEM-3. This implies that the hardware for SYSTEM-2 should be preferred over the hardware for SYSTEM-3. From our responses, the hardware for SYSTEM-2 was strongly to very strongly preferred over the hardware for SYSTEM-3, as indicated by the number 6. Thus, our original assessments of the pairwise comparison matrix seem to be consistent, and the consistency ratio that we computed supports our observations.

Although the calculations to compute the consistency ratio are fairly involved, they are an important step in using the analytical hierarchy process.

Evaluations for the Other Factors

So far, we have determined the factor evaluations for hardware for the three different computer systems along with a consistency ratio for these evaluations. Now, we can make the same calculations for the other factors, namely software and vendor support. As before, we start with the matrix of pairwise comparisons. We perform the same calculations and end up with the various factor evaluations for both software and vendor support. We begin by presenting the matrix of pairwise comparisons for both software and vendor support.

Next, we perform pairwise comparisons for software and vendor support.

SOFTWARE	SYSTEM-1	SYSTEM-2	SYSTEM-3
SYSTEM-1			
SYSTEM-2	2		
SYSTEM-3	8	5	

VENDOR SUPPORT	SYSTEM-1	SYSTEM-2	SYSTEM-3
SYSTEM-1		1	6
SYSTEM-2			3
SYSTEM-3			

TABLE S11.7 **Factor Evaluations**

FACTOR	SYSTEM-1	SYSTEM-2	SYSTEM-3
Hardware	0.6583	0.2819	0.0598
Software	0.0874	0.1622	0.7504
Vendor	0.4967	0.3967	0.1066

With the matrices shown, we can perform the same types of calculations to determine the factor evaluations for both software and vendor support for the three computer systems. The data for the three different systems are summarized in Table S11.7. We also need to determine the consistency ratios for both software and support. As it turns out, both consistency ratios are under 0.10, meaning that the responses to the pairwise comparison are acceptably consistent.

You should note that the factor evaluations for the three factors and three different computer systems shown in Table S11.7 are similar to the factor evaluations in Table S11.2 for the job selection problem. The major difference is that we had to use the analytic hierarchy process to determine these factor evaluations using pairwise comparisons, because we were not comfortable in our abilities to assess these factors subjectively without some assistance.

Determining Factor Weights

AHP can be used to set the factor weights.

Next, we need to determine the various factor weights. When we used the multifactor evaluation process, it was assumed that we could simply determine these values subjectively. Another approach is to use the AHP and pairwise comparisons to determine the factor weights for hardware, software, and vendor support.

In comparing the three factors, we determine that software is the most important. Software is very to extremely strongly preferred over hardware (number 8). Software is moderately preferred over vendor support (number 3). In comparing vendor support to hardware, we decide that vendor support is more important. Vendor support is moderately preferred to hardware (number 3). With these values, we can construct the pairwise comparison matrix and then compute the weights for hardware, software, and support. We also need to compute a consistency ratio to make sure that our responses are consistent. As with software and vendor support, the actual calculations for determining the factor weights are left for you to make on your own. After making the appropriate calculations, the factor weights for hardware, software, and vendor support are shown in Table S11.8.

Overall Ranking

Finally, the overall ranking is determined by multiplying the factor evaluations times the factor weights.

After the factor weights have been determined, we can multiply the factor evaluations in Table S11.7 times the factor weights in Table S11.8. This is the same procedure that we used for the job selection decision in section S11.2. It will give us the overall ranking for the three computer systems, which is shown in Table S11.9. As you can see, SYSTEM-3 received the highest final ranking and is selected as the best computer system.

TABLE S11.8 Factor Weights	
FACTOR	FACTOR WEIGHT
Hardware	0.0820
Software	0.6816
Vendor	0.2364

TABLE S11.9 Total Weighted Evaluations	
SYSTEM OR ALTERNATIVE	TOTAL WEIGHTED EVALUATION
SYSTEM-1	0.2310
SYSTEM-2	0.2275
SYSTEM-3*	0.5416

* SYSTEM-3 is selected.

Using the Computer to Solve AHP Problems

As you can see from the previous pages, solving AHP problems can involve a large number of calculations. Fortunately, computer programs are available to make AHP easier. A commercial package called Expert Choice for Windows can be used to solve the types of AHP problems discussed in this supplement. Program S11.1 shows the evaluation and choice component of Expert Choice that allows decision makers to make pairwise comparisons. It is also possible to use AHP with group decision making. Team Expert Choice helps groups brainstorm ideas, structure their decisions, and evaluate alternatives.

S11.4 COMPARISON OF MFEP AND AHP

Multifactor decision making has a number of useful and important applications. If you know or can determine with confidence and accuracy the factor weights and factor evaluations, MFEP is preferred. If not, you should use AHP. As it turns out, AHP also gives the factor weights and factor evaluations from which the final selection can be made. The

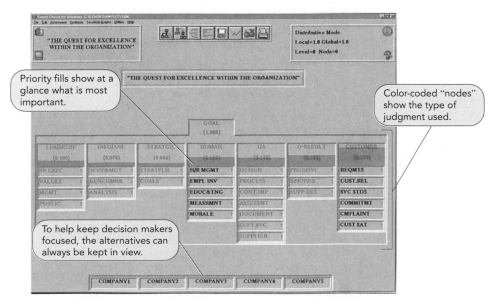

PROGRAM S11.1

Evaluation and Choice Window to Make Pairwise Comparisons Using a Computer Program Called Expert Choice for Windows

IN ACTION   Using AHP in a Pilot Study of Organ Transplantation

Getting organs for transplantation and deciding who gets scarce organs has been a topic of discussion for decades. There have been cases of celebrities, retired athletes, and movie stars receiving organs, perhaps ahead of more deserving people. Some believe the decision as to who gets organs can be political instead of medical. There have also been charges that some countries harvest organs from living and healthy prisoners.

At the Hospital for Sick Children (HSC) in Toronto, AHP has been used in a pilot study to help determine who should get organs. The goal of the pilot study was to develop a set of consistent and broadly acceptable criteria. Developing good criteria was difficult. For example, what priority should a child with Down's Syndrome be given to receive an organ transplant? Using pairwise comparisons, a set of criteria for children receiving organ transplants was evaluated using the AHP framework. The criteria included intelligence, survival expectations, physical independence on others, the need for long-term financial support, the need for long-term health support, parent activities required, the ability of the child to return to a full schedule of school activities, and other similar factors.

The results of the AHP study differed from standard surveys conducted in Canada and the U.S. The AHP study, for example, determined that such factors as the ability to pay, the presence of medical insurance, or a patient's financial or economic status should not be considered in making a transplant decision. This may have been a result of Canada's national health care system, which assures health care for all Canadian citizens. It was also determined that physical limitations, such as being disabled, should not be a determining factor for an organ transplant. A low intelligence, such as an IQ of 70 or lower, was also not as important in the AHP study as it had been in earlier surveys. The AHP study determined that the most important criteria was the organ transplant patient's ability to survive the difficult transplant process, accept the difficult transition process following organ transplant, and lead a relatively normal life after organ transplant. Overall, the study was able to take into account ethical, qualitative, and quantitative factors to determine who should receive organ transplants.

Source: Tom Koch et al. "A Pilot Study on Transplant Eligibility Criteria," *Pediatric Nursing* (March 13, 1997): 160.

only difference is that with AHP we compute the factor weights and factor evaluations from a number of pairwise comparison matrices. We also compute a consistency ratio to make sure that our responses to the original pairwise comparison matrix are consistent and acceptable. If they are not, we should go back and perform the pairwise comparison again. Although AHP involves a larger number of calculations, it is preferred to MFEP in cases where we do not feel confident or comfortable in determining factor weights or factor evaluations without making pairwise comparisons.

Summary

Multifactor decision making is appropriate when an individual, group, or organization faces a number of factors in a decision-making situation. With the multifactor evaluation process (MFEP), a decision maker assigns an importance weight to each factor. The weights can, for example, range from 0 to 1. Then, for each alternative, all factors are evaluated. The factor weights are multiplied times each factor evaluation for a given alternative and summed. The alternative with the highest overall score is selected.

With the AHP, the decision maker performs a number of pairwise comparisons between each pair of alternatives for each factor to determine the factor evaluations. A pairwise comparison is also performed between each pair of factors to determine the factor weights. This information is used to determine a total weighted evaluation for each alternative. The alternative with the highest total weighted evaluation is selected. The AHP approach also allows for the computation of a consistency ratio to help decision makers determine if their pairwise comparisons are consistent.

Glossary

Multifactor Decision Making. A decision-making environment where multiple factors are to be considered in making the final selection.

Multifactor Evaluation Process (MFEP). A multifactor decision-making approach in which the factor weights and factor evaluations can be accurately determined and used in the decision-making process.

Analytic Hierarchy Process (AHP). A process that uses pairwise comparisons to determine factor evaluations and factor weights in a multifactor decision-making environment.

Factor Evaluations. These are evaluations that indicate our preference for a particular factor for a particular alternative or item.

Factor Weights. These are weights that give the relative importance of one factor to another.

Key Equations

(S11-1) $CI = \dfrac{\lambda - n}{n - 1}$

Consistency index.

(S11-2) $CR = \dfrac{CI}{RI}$

Consistency ratio.

Solved Problems

Solved Problem S11-1

Tom Schmid is thinking about buying a Nordic ski machine. The three factors important to him are price, ease of use, and the ability to store the exercise equipment in a closet when he is done using it. Given the following data, help Tom determine the best machine for him:

FACTOR WEIGHTS

FACTOR	IMPORTANCE WEIGHT
Price	0.9
Ease of use	0.75
Storage	0.6

FACTOR EVALUATIONS

FACTOR	PROFESSIONAL NORDIC SKIER	ECONO NORDIC SKIER
Price	0.5	0.8
Ease of use	0.95	0.6
Storage	0.9	0.7

Solution

Given these data, we can multiply the weights times the evaluations for each skier and then sum the results. The results are shown in the following table.

FINAL EVALUATIONS

FACTOR	PROFESSIONAL NORDIC SKIER	ECONO NORDIC SKIER
Price	(0.5)(0.9) = 0.45	(0.8)(0.9) = 0.72
Ease of use	(0.95)(0.75) = 0.7125	(0.6)(0.75) = 0.45
Storage	(0.9)(0.6) = 0.54	(0.7)(0.6) = 0.42
Total	1.70	1.59

Given the above analysis, Tom should select the Professional Nordic Skier.

Solved Problem S11-2

Gretchen Little has used AHP to determine factor evaluations. The consistency index for her problem is 0.0988. The number of factors in her problem is four. Can you draw any conclusions from these data?

Solution

Using a value of 4 for n, we look in the table in this supplement to get the random index (RI). From the table with a value of 4 for n, we see that RI is 0.90. From this information we can compute the consistency ratio as follows:

$$CR = \frac{CI}{RI} = \frac{0.0988}{0.9} = 0.10978$$

Because CR is close to but greater than 0.10, her pairwise comparisons may not have been consistent. It is recommended that she resolve the problem carefully and recompute the consistency ratio.

SELF-TEST

- Before taking the self-test, refer back to the learning objectives at the beginning of the supplement and the glossary at the end of the supplement.
- Use the key at the back of the book to correct your answers.
- Restudy pages that correspond to any questions that you answered incorrectly or material you feel uncertain about.

1. In the multifactor evaluation process,
   a. factor weights are multipled times factor evaluations.
   b. probability values are multipled times factor evaluations.
   c. probability values are multipled times factor weights.
   d. weighted evaluations are multiplied times probability values.
   e. weighted evaluations are multiplied times factor weights.
2. Pairwise comparisons are used with
   a. multifactor evaluation process.
   b. analytic hierarchy process.
   c. all-purpose evaluation process.
   d. multipurpose decision process.
   e. none of the above.
3. In using pairwise comparisons, an evaluation of 1 is given for
   a. extremely preferred.
   b. very strongly preferred.
   c. strongly preferred.
   d. not preferred.
   e. none of the above.
4. The weighted sum vector is used to calculate
   a. factor weights.
   b. factor evaluations.
   c. the consistency ratio.
   d. factor probabilities.
   e. final evaluations.
5. What is used to indicate how consistent people are with their AHP evaluations?
   a. factor index
   b. factor ratio
   c. pairwise index
   d. consistency ratio
   e. none of the above
6. What value of CR is desirable when using AHP?
   a. less than 0.10
   b. less than 0.50
   c. more than 0.50
   d. more than 1.0
   e. more than 100
7. Important factors can be given weights by decision makers in using _____ .
8. Thomas Saaty developed a decision-making technique called _____ .

Discussion Questions and Problems

Discussion Questions

S11-1 Describe decision situations in which multifactor decision making is appropriate. What decision-making situations do you face that could benefit from the multifactor decision-making approach?

S11-2 Briefly describe the multifactor evaluation process.

S11-3 When should the analytic hierarchy process be used compared to the multifactor evaluation process?

Problems

S11-4 George Lyon is about to buy a compact stereo cassette player. He is currently considering three brands—Sun, Hitek, and Surgo. The important factors to George are the price, color, warranty, size of the unit, and brand name. George has determined factor weights of 0.4, 0.1, 0.1, 0.1, and 0.3, respectively. Furthermore, George has determined factor evaluations for all of the factors for the three different manufacturers of the unit he is considering. The Sun unit has factor evaluations of 0.7, 0.9, 0.8, 0.8, and 0.9 for the price, color, warranty, size, and brand-name factors. The Hitek unit has factor evaluations of 0.6, 0.9, 0.9, 0.8, and 0.9 for these factors. Finally, Surgo has factor evaluations of 0.8, 0.4, 0.4, 0.2, and 0.6 for the same factors of price, color, warranty, size, and brand name. Determine the total weighted evaluation for the three manufacturers. Which one should George select?

S11-5 Linda Frieden is thinking about buying a new car. There are three different car models she is considering: car 1, car 2, or car 3. An important factor for Linda is the price. She has determined that car 1 is equally to moderately preferred to car 2. Car 1 is very strongly preferred to car 3, and car 2 is moderately to strongly preferred to car 3. Determine the priorities or factor evaluations for the three cars for price. What is the consistency ratio?

S11-6 Linda Frieden (Problem S11-5) is also concerned about the warranty for the three cars she is considering. The second car is moderately preferred to the first car in terms of warranty. The third car is very to extremely strongly preferred over the first car, and the third car is strongly preferred over the second car. Determine the factor evaluations or priorities for the three cars for car warranty. Compute the consistency ratio.

S11-7 Linda Frieden (Problems S11-5 and S11-6) would like to consider style as an important factor in making a decision to purchase a new car. Car 2 is moderately preferred to car 1 in terms of style, but car 1 is moderately preferred to car 3 in terms of style. Furthermore, car 2 is very to extremely strongly preferred over car 3. Determine the factor evaluations for style concerning the three cars and compute the consistency ratio.

S11-8 Linda Frieden (Problems S11-5 to S11-7) now must determine the relative weights for the three factors of price, warranty, and style. She believes that the price is equally to moderately preferred over warranty, and that price is extremely preferred to style. She also believes that the car warranty is strongly to very strongly preferred over the style. Using this information, determine the weights for these three factors. Also determine the consistency ratio to make sure that the values above are consistent enough to use in the analysis. In Problems S11-5 to S11-7, Linda has determined factor evaluations for price, warranty, and style for the three cars. Using the information you determined in this problem along with the solutions to the three problems above, determine the final rankings for each car. Which car should be selected?

S11-9 Jim Locke, an undergraduate student in the E.S.U. College of Business, is trying to decide which microcomputer to purchase with the money his parents gave him for Christmas. He has reduced the number of computers he has been considering to three, calling them system 1 (S1), system 2 (S2), and system 3 (S3). For each computer, he would like to consider the price, the brand name, the memory capacity, speed, flexibility, and compatibility with IBM PCs.

In order to make the correct decision, he has decided to make pairwise comparisons for all the factors. For price, the first computer system is equally to moderately preferred over the second computer system and very to extremely strongly preferred over the third computer system. The second computer system is strongly preferred over the third computer system.

For brand name, the first computer system is equally preferred to the second computer system, and the first computer system is strongly to very strongly preferred over the third computer system. The second computer system is moderately to strongly preferred over the third computer system.

When it comes to memory, the second computer is equally to moderately preferred over the first computer system, and the third computer system is very strongly preferred over the first computer system. Furthermore, the third computer system is strongly to very strongly preferred over the second computer system.

For speed, the second computer system is moderately preferred to the first computer system, but the first computer system is equally to moderately preferred over the third computer system. Furthermore, the second computer system is strongly preferred over the third computer system.

For the flexibility factor, the third computer system is very to extremely strongly preferred over the first computer system, and the second computer system is equally to moderately preferred over the first computer system. The third computer system is also moderately to strongly preferred over the second computer system.

Finally, Jim has used pairwise comparisons to look at how compatible each computer system is with the IBM PC. Using this analysis, he has determined that the first computer system is very to extremely strongly preferred over the second computer system when it comes to compatibility. The first computer system is moderately to strongly preferred over the third computer system, and the third computer system is moderately preferred over the second computer system.

When it comes to comparing the factors, Jim has used pairwise comparisons to look at price, brand name, memory, speed, flexibility, and compatibility. Here are the results of the analysis. Price is extremely preferred to brand name, moderately to strongly preferred to memory, strongly preferred to speed, moderately preferred to flexibility, and equally to moderately preferred to PC compatibility. In other words, price is a very important factor. The computer's memory is equally to moderately preferred to brand name, speed is equally preferred to brand name, flexibility is moderately to strongly preferred to brand name, and PC compatibility is strongly preferred to brand name. In looking at memory, Jim has determined that memory is equally to moderately preferred to speed. PC compatibility, however, is strongly to very strongly preferred to memory, and overall flexibility is equally to moderately preferred to the computer's memory. PC compatibility is strongly to very strongly preferred to speed, and flexibility is moderately preferred to speed. Finally, Jim has determined that PC compatibility is equally to moderately preferred to flexibility.

Using all of these preferences for pairwise comparisons, determine the priorities or factor evaluations, along with the appropriate consistency ratios for price, brand name, memory, speed, flexibility, and PC compatibility for the three different computer systems. In addition, determine the overall weights for each of the factors. Which computer system should be selected?

Bibliography

Durso, A., and S. Donahue. "An Analytic Approach to Reshaping the United States Army," *Interfaces* 25, 1 (January–February 1995): 109.

Goh, Chon. "AHP for Robot Selection," *Journal of Manufacturing Systems*, (January 1997): 14.

Islei, Gerd, Geoff Lockett, Barry Cox, Steve Gisbourne, and Mike Stratford. "Modeling Strategic Decision Making and Performance Measurements at ICI Pharmaceuticals," *Interfaces* 21, 6 (November–December 1991): 4–22.

Koch, Tom et al. "A Pilot Study on Transplant Eligibility Criteria," *Pediatric Nursing* (March 13, 1997): 160.

Kang, Moonsig, et al. "PAHAP: A Pairwise Aggregated Hierarchical Analysis of Ration-Scale Preferences," *Decision Sciences* (July 1994): 607.

Saaty, Thomas. *The Analytic Hierarchy Process*. New York: McGraw-Hill Book Company, 1980.

Saaty, Thomas. "How to Make a Decision: The Analytic Hierarchy Process," *Interfaces* 24 (November–December 1994): 19.

Saaty, Thomas, and K. Kearn. *Analytical Planning: The Organization of Systems*. Oxford: Pergamon Press Ltd., 1985.

Stam, Antonie, et al. "Stochastic Judgements in the AHP," *Decision Sciences* (July 1997).

Network Models

CHAPTER OUTLINE

12.1 Introduction

12.2 Minimal-Spanning Tree Technique

12.3 Maximal-Flow Technique

12.4 Shortest-Route Technique

Summary • Glossary • Solved Problems • Self-Test • Discussion Questions and Problems • Data Set Problem • Case Study: Ranch Development Project • Case Study: Binder's Beverage • Bibliography

Appendix 12.1: Network Models with QM for Windows

12.1   INTRODUCTION

Three network models are covered in this chapter.

This chapter covers three network models that can be used to solve a variety of problems: the minimal-spanning tree technique, the maximal-flow technique, and the shortest-route technique. The *minimal-spanning tree technique* determines the path through the network that connects all the points while minimizing total distance. When the points represent houses in a subdivision, the minimal-spanning tree technique can be used to determine the best way to connect all of the houses to electrical power, water systems, and so on, in a way that minimizes the total distance or length of power lines or water pipes. The *maximal-flow technique* finds the maximum flow of any quantity or substance through a network. This technique can determine, for example, the maximum number of vehicles (cars, trucks, and so forth) that can go through a network of roads from one location to another. Finally, the *shortest-route technique* can find the shortest path through a network. For example, this technique can find the shortest route from one city to another through a network of roads.

All of the examples used to describe the various network techniques in this chapter are small and simple compared to real problems. This is done to make it easier for you to understand the techniques. In many cases, these smaller network problems can be solved by inspection or intuition. For larger problems, however, finding a solution can be very difficult and requires the use of these powerful network techniques. Larger problems may require hundreds, or even thousands, of iterations. To computerize these techniques, it is necessary to use the systematic approach we present.

12.2   MINIMAL-SPANNING TREE TECHNIQUE

This minimal-spanning tree technique connects nodes at a minimum distance.

The minimal-spanning tree technique seeks to connect all the points of a network together while minimizing the distance between them. It has been applied, for example, by telephone companies to connect a number of phones together while minimizing the total length of telephone cable.

Let us consider the Lauderdale Construction Company, which is currently developing a luxurious housing project on Panama City Beach. Melvin Lauderdale, owner and president of Lauderdale Construction, must determine the least expensive way to provide water and power to each house. The network of houses is shown in Figure 12.1.

As seen in Figure 12.1, there are eight houses on the gulf. The distance between each house in hundreds of feet is shown on the network. The distance between houses 1 and 2, for example, is 300 feet. (The number 3 is between nodes 1 and 2.) Now, the minimal-spanning tree technique will be used to determine the minimum distance that can be used to connect all of the nodes. The approach is outlined as follows:

There are five steps for the minimal-spanning tree problem.

Steps for the Minimal-Spanning Tree Technique

1. Select any node in the network.
2. Connect this node to the nearest node that minimizes the total distance.
3. Considering all of the nodes that are now connected, find and connect the nearest node that is not connected.
4. Repeat the third step until all nodes are connected.
5. If there is a tie in the third step and two or more nodes that are not connected are equally near, select one arbitrarily and continue. A tie suggests that there might be more than one optimal solution.

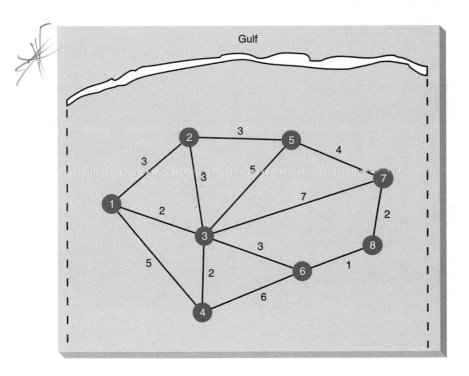

FIGURE 12.1
Network for Lauderdale
Construction

Now, we solve the network in Figure 12.1 for Melvin Lauderdale. We start by arbitrarily selecting node 1. Since the nearest node is the third node at a distance of 2 (200 feet), we connect node 1 to node 3. This is shown in Figure 12.2.

Considering nodes 1 and 3, we look for the next-nearest node. This is node 4, which is the closest to node 3. The distance is 2 (200 feet). Again, we connect these nodes (see Figure 12.3a).

Step 1: We select node 1.

Step 2: We connect node 1 to node 3.

FIGURE 12.2
First Iteration for Lauderdale
Construction

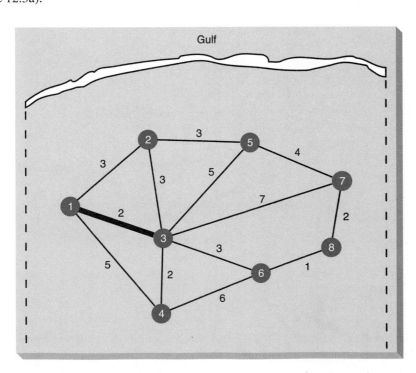

FIGURE 12.3
Second and Third Iterations

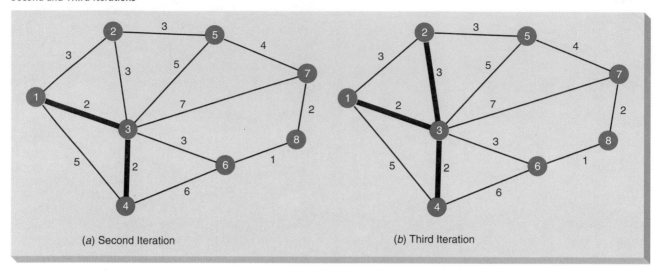

(a) Second Iteration   (b) Third Iteration

Step 3: We connect the next nearest node.

Step 4: We repeat the process.

We continue, looking for the nearest unconnected node to nodes 1, 3, and 4. This is node 2 or node 6, both at a distance of 3 from node 3. We will pick node 2 and connect it to node 3 (see Figure 12.3b).

We continue the process. There is another tie for the next iteration with a minimum distance of 3 (node 2–node 5 and node 3–node 6). You should note that we do not consider node 1–node 2 with a distance of 3 because both nodes 1 and 2 are already connected. We arbitrarily select node 5 and connect it to node 2 (see Figure 12.4a). The next nearest node is node 6, and we connect it to node 3 (see Figure 12.4b).

FIGURE 12.4
Fourth and Fifth Iterations

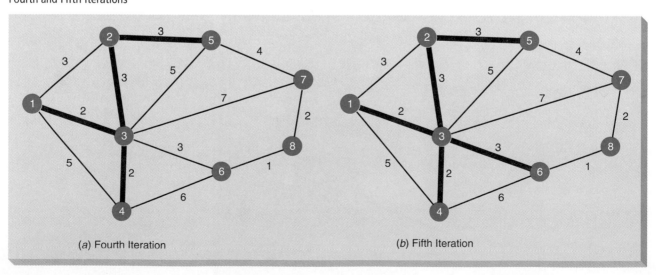

(a) Fourth Iteration   (b) Fifth Iteration

FIGURE 12.5

Sixth and Final Iterations

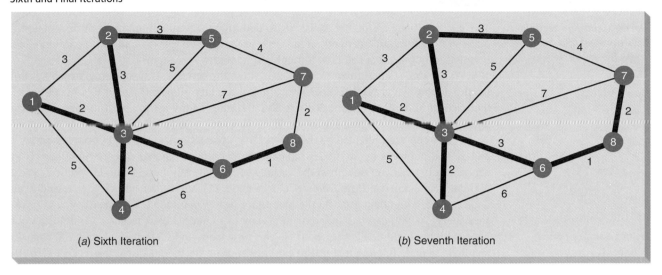

(*a*) Sixth Iteration   (*b*) Seventh Iteration

At this stage, we have only two unconnected nodes left. Node 8 is the nearest to node 6 with a distance of 1 and we connect it (see Figure 12.5a). Then the remaining node 7 is connected to node 8 (see Figure 12.5b).

The final solution can be seen in the seventh and final iteration (see Figure 12.5b). Nodes 1, 2, 4, and 6 are all connected to node 3. Node 2 is connected to node 5. Node 6 is connected to node 8, and node 8 is connected to node 7. All of the nodes are now connected.

 **IN ACTION**   **Spanning Tree Analysis of a Telecommunications Network**

Network models have been used to solve a variety of problems for many different companies. In telecommunications, there is always a need to connect computer systems and devices together in an efficient and effective manner. Digital Equipment Corporation (DEC) for example, was concerned about how computer systems and devices were connected to a local area network (LAN) using a technology called Ethernet. The DECnet routing department was responsible for this and other network and telecommunications solutions.

Because of a number of technical difficulties, it was important to have an effective way to transport packets of information throughout the LAN. The solution was to use a spanning tree algorithm. The success of this approach can be seen in a poem written by one of the developers:

"I think I shall never see a graph more lovely than a tree.

A tree whose critical property is loop-free connectivity.

A tree that must be sure to span, so packets can reach every LAN.

First the route must be selected, by ID it is elected.

Least-cost paths from the root are traced.

In the tree these paths are placed.

A mesh is made for folks by me, then bridges find a spanning tree."

Source: Radia Perlman et al. "Spanning the LAN," *Data Communications* (October 21, 1997): 68.

12.3   MAXIMAL-FLOW TECHNIQUE

The maximal-flow technique finds the most that can flow through a network.

The *maximal-flow technique* allows us to determine the maximum amount of a material that can flow through a network. It has been used, for example, to find the maximum number of automobiles that can flow through a state highway system.

Waukesha, a small town in Wisconsin, is in the process of developing a road system for the downtown area. Bill Blackstone, one of the city planners, would like to determine the maximum number of cars that can flow through the town from west to east. The road network is shown in Figure 12.6.

Traffic can flow in both directions.

The streets are indicated by their respective nodes. Look at the street between nodes 1 and 2. The numbers by the nodes indicate the maximum number of cars (in hundreds of cars per hour) that can flow *from* the various nodes. The number 3 by node 1 indicates that 300 cars per hour can flow *from* node 1 to node 2. Look at the numbers 1, 1, and 2 by node 2. These numbers indicate the maximum flow *from* node 2 to nodes 1, 4, and 6, respectively. As you can see, the maximum flow from node 2 back to node 1 is 100 cars per hour (1). One hundred cars per hour (1) can flow from node 2 to node 4, and 200 cars (2) can flow to node 6. Note that traffic can flow in both directions down a street. A zero (0) means no flow or a one-way street.

The maximal-flow technique is not difficult. It involves the following steps:

The four maximal-flow technique steps.

> **Four Steps of the Maximal-Flow Technique**
> 1. Pick any path (any street from west to east) with some flow.
> 2. Increase the flow (number of cars) as much as possible.
> 3. Adjust the flow capacity numbers on the path (or street, in this case).
> 4. Repeat these steps until an increase in flow is no longer possible.

We start by arbitrarily picking a path and adjusting the flow.

We start by arbitrarily picking the path 1–2–6, which is at the top of the network. What is the maximum flow from west to east? It is 2 because only 2 units (200 cars) can flow from node 2 to node 6. Now we adjust the flow capacities (see Figure 12.7). As you

FIGURE 12.6

Road Network for Waukesha

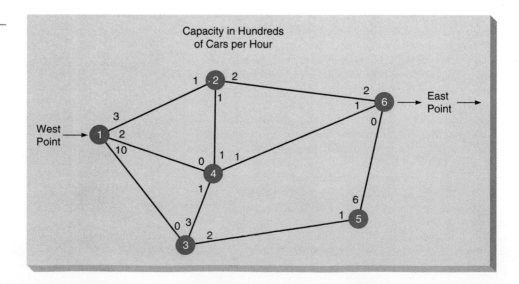

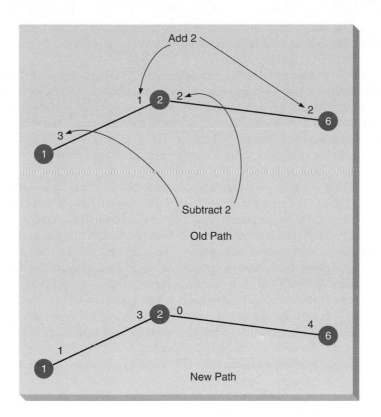

FIGURE 12.7
Capacity Adjustment for Path
1–2–6 Iteration 1

IN ACTION **Traffic-Control System on the Hanshin Expressway**

The Hanshin expressway started with a 2.3-kilometer section of road in Osaka City, Japan, in the 1960s. This small stretch of highway was the first urban toll expressway in Osaka City. The traffic flow was approximately 5,000 cars per day. Today, the expressway includes about 200 kilometers of roadway in a system that connects Osaka and Kobe, Japan. The traffic flow in the early 1990s was more than 800,000 vehicles per day, with peak traffic flows that exceeded 1 million cars per day.

As discussed in this chapter, maximizing the flow of traffic through a network involves an investigation of current and future capacity of the various branches in the network. In addition to capacity analysis, Hanshin decided to use an automated traffic control system to maximize the flow of traffic through the existing expressway and to reduce congestion and bottlenecks caused by accidents, and by road maintenance or disabled cars. It was hoped that the control system would also increase income from the expressway.

Hanshin's management investigated the number of accidents and breakdowns on the expressway to help reduce prob-

lems and further increase traffic flow. The traffic control system provides both direct and indirect control. Direct control includes controlling the number of vehicles entering the expressway at the various on-ramps. Indirect control involves providing comprehensive and up-to-the-minute information concerning traffic flows and the general traffic conditions on the expressway. Information on general traffic conditions is obtained using vehicle detectors, TV cameras, ultrasonic detectors, and automatic vehicle identifiers that read information on license plates. The data gathered from these devices gives people at home and driving the information they need to determine if they will use the Hanshin expressway.

This application reveals that a solution to a problem involves a variety of components, including quantitative analysis, equipment, and other elements, such as providing information to riders.

Source: T. Yoshino, et al. "The Traffic-Control System on the Hanshin Expressway," *Interfaces* 25 (January—February 1995): 94.

can see, we subtracted the maximum flow of 2 along the path 1–2–6 in the direction of the flow (west to east) and added 2 to the path in the direction against the flow (east to west). The result is the new path in Figure 12.7.

It is important to note that the new path in Figure 12.7 reflects the new relative capacity at this stage. The flow number by any node represents two factors. One factor is the flow that can come *from* that node. The second factor is flow that can be *reduced* coming *into* the node. First consider the flow from west to east. Look at the path that goes from node 1 to node 2. The number 1 by node 1 tells us that 100 cars can flow *from* node 1 to node 2. Looking at the path from node 2 to node 6, we can see that the number 0 by node 2 tells us that 0 cars can flow *from* node 2 to node 6. Now consider the flow from east to west shown in the new path in Figure 12.7. First, consider the path from node 6 to node 2. The number 4 by node 6 tells us that we can reduce the flow *into* node 6 by 2 (or 200 cars) and that there is a capacity of 2 (or 200 cars) that can come *from* node 6. These two factors total 4. Looking at the path from node 2 to node 1, we see the number 3 by node 2. This tells us that we can reduce the flow *into* node 2 by 2 (or 200 cars) and that we have a capacity of 1 (or 100 cars) *from* node 2 to node 1. At this stage, we have a flow of 200 cars through the network from node 1 to node 2 to node 6. We have also reflected the new relative capacity, as shown in Figure 12.7.

Now we repeat the process by picking another path with existing capacity. We will arbitrarily pick path 1–2–4–6. The maximum capacity along this path is 1. In fact, the capacity at every node along this path (1–2–4–6) going from west to east is 1. Remember, the capacity of branch 1–2 is now 1 because 2 units (200 cars per hour) are now flowing through the network. Thus, we increase the flow along path 1–2–4–6 by 1 and adjust the capacity flow (see Figure 12.8).

Now we have a flow of 3 units (300 cars): 200 cars per hour along path 1–2–6 plus 100 cars per hour along path 1–2–4–6. Can we still increase the flow? Yes, along path 1–3–5–6. This is the bottom path. The maximum flow is 2 because this is the maximum from node 3 to node 5. The increased flow along this path is shown in Figure 12.9.

Again we repeat the process, trying to find a path with any unused capacity through the network. If you carefully check the last iteration in Figure 12.9, you will see that there are no more paths from node 1 to node 6 with unused capacity, even though several other

The process is repeated.

We continue until there are no more paths with unused capacity.

FIGURE 12.8

Second Iteration for Waukesha Road System

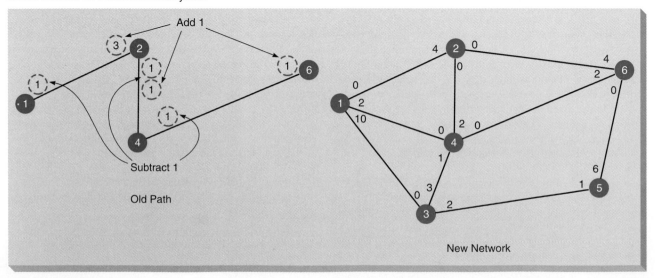

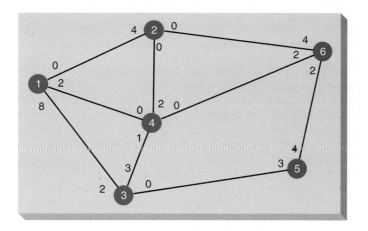

FIGURE 12.9
Third and Final Iteration for
Waukesha Road System

branches in the network do have unused capacity. The maximum flow of 500 cars per hour is summarized in the following table:

PATH	FLOW (CARS PER HOUR)
1–2–6	200
1–2–4–6	100
1–3–5–6	200
	Total 500

You can also compare the original network to the final network to see the flow between any of the nodes.

12.4 SHORTEST-ROUTE TECHNIQUE

The *shortest-route technique* finds how a person or item can travel from one location to another while minimizing the total distance traveled. In other words, it finds the shortest route to a series of destinations.

The shortest-route technique minimizes the distance through a network.

Every day, Ray Design, Inc., must transport beds, chairs, and other furniture items from the factory to the warehouse. This involves going through several cities. Ray would like to find the route with the shortest distance. The road network is shown in Figure 12.10.

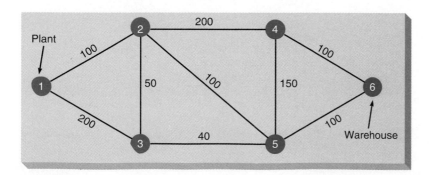

FIGURE 12.10
Roads from Ray's Plant
to Warehouse

IN ACTION   Improving Pupil Transportation

In the early 1990s, North Carolina was spending almost $150 million on transporting students to schools. The state's student transportation system involved some 13,000 buses, 100 school districts, and 700,000 students. In 1989, the General Assembly of the state decided to investigate ways that could be used to save money by developing a better way of transporting students. The General Assembly was committed to funding school districts that transported students efficiently, while only reimbursing justifiable expenses for those districts that were not efficient in terms of how they transported students to and from public schools.

The input data to North Carolina's network model included the number of buses used and total operating expenses. Total operating expenses included driver salaries, salaries to other transportation personnel, payments to local governments,

fuel costs, parts and repair costs, and other related costs. These input values were used to compute an efficiency score for the various districts. These efficiency scores were then used to help in allocating funds to the districts. Those districts with an efficiency score of 0.9 or higher received full funding. Converting efficiency scores to funding was originally received with skepticism. After several years, however, more state officials realized the usefulness of the approach. In 1994–1995, the efficiency-based funding approach was used alone to determine funding.

The use of efficiency-based funding resulted in the elimination of hundreds of school buses, with savings over a three-year period greater than $25 million.

Source: T. Sexton, et al. "Improving Pupil Transportation in North Carolina," *Interfaces* 24 (January—February 1994): 87.

The shortest-route technique can be used to minimize total distance from any starting node to a final node. The technique is summarized in the following steps:

The steps of the shortest-route technique.

> **Steps of the Shortest-Route Technique**
> 1. Find the nearest node to the origin (plant). Put the distance in a box by the node.
> 2. Find the next-nearest node to the origin (plant), and put the distance in a box by the node. In some cases, several paths will have to be checked to find the nearest node.
> 3. Repeat this process until you have gone through the entire network. The last distance at the ending node will be the distance of the shortest route. You should note that the distance placed in the box by each node is the shortest route to this node. These distances are used as intermediate results in finding the next-nearest node.

Looking at Figure 12.10, we can see that the nearest node to the plant is node 2, with a distance of 100 miles. Thus we will connect these two nodes. This first iteration is shown in Figure 12.11.

We look for the nearest node to the origin.

Now we look for the next-nearest node to the origin. We check nodes 3, 4, and 5. Node 3 is the nearest, but there are two possible paths. Path 1–2–3 is nearest to the origin, with a total distance of 150 miles (see Figure 12.12).

FIGURE 12.11

First Iteration for Ray Design

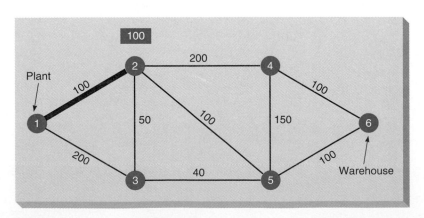

FIGURE 12.12
Second Iteration for Ray Design

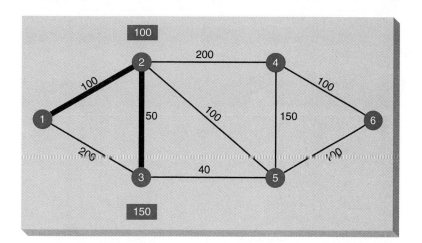

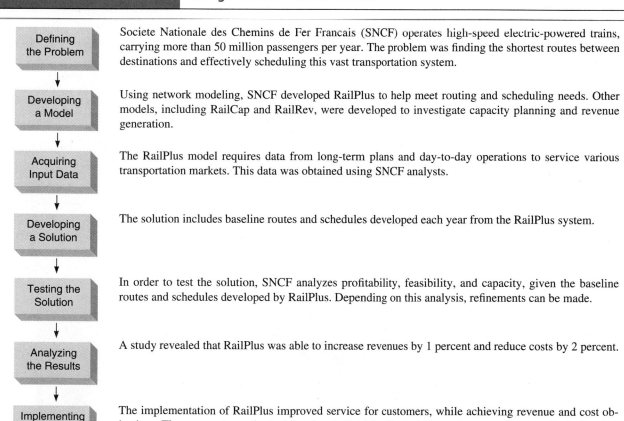

MODELING IN THE REAL WORLD   Using a Network Model at SNCF

Defining the Problem

Societe Nationale des Chemins de Fer Francais (SNCF) operates high-speed electric-powered trains, carrying more than 50 million passengers per year. The problem was finding the shortest routes between destinations and effectively scheduling this vast transportation system.

Developing a Model

Using network modeling, SNCF developed RailPlus to help meet routing and scheduling needs. Other models, including RailCap and RailRev, were developed to investigate capacity planning and revenue generation.

Acquiring Input Data

The RailPlus model requires data from long-term plans and day-to-day operations to service various transportation markets. This data was obtained using SNCF analysts.

Developing a Solution

The solution includes baseline routes and schedules developed each year from the RailPlus system.

Testing the Solution

In order to test the solution, SNCF analyzes profitability, feasibility, and capacity, given the baseline routes and schedules developed by RailPlus. Depending on this analysis, refinements can be made.

Analyzing the Results

A study revealed that RailPlus was able to increase revenues by 1 percent and reduce costs by 2 percent.

Implementing the Results

The implementation of RailPlus improved service for customers, while achieving revenue and cost objectives. The new routes and schedules do a better job of matching customer preferences, including frequency, departure times, and itineraries.

Source: Nejib Ben-Khedher et al. "Schedule Optimization at SNCF from Conception to Day of Departure," *Interfaces* (January–February 1998): 6.

FIGURE 12.13

Third Iteration for Ray Design

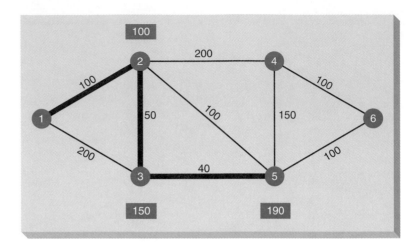

The process is repeated.

We repeat the process. The next-nearest node is either node 4 or node 5. Node 4 is 200 miles from node 2, and node 2 is 100 miles from node 1. Thus, node 4 is 300 miles from the origin. There are two paths for node 5, 2–5 and 3–5, to the origin. Note that we don't have to go all the way back to the origin because we already know the shortest route from node 2 and node 3 to the origin. The minimum distances are placed in boxes by these nodes. Path 2–5 is 100 miles, and node 2 is 100 miles from the origin. Thus, the total distance is 200 miles. In a similar fashion, we can determine that the path from node 5 to the origin through node 3 is 190 (40 miles between node 5 and 3 plus 150 miles from node 3 to the origin). Thus, we pick node 5 going through node 3 to the origin (see Figure 12.13).

The next-nearest node will be either node 4 or node 6, as the last remaining nodes. Node 4 is 300 miles from the origin (300 = 200 from node 4 to node 2 plus 100 from node 2 to the origin). Node 6 is 290 miles from the origin (290 = 100 + 190). Node 6 has the minimum distance, and because it is the ending node, we are done (refer to Figure 12.14). The shortest route is path 1–2–3–5–6, with a minimum distance of 290 miles.

FIGURE 12.14

Fourth and Final Iteration for Ray Design

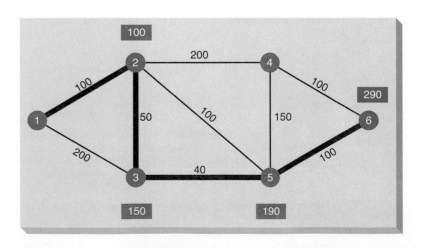

Summary

We presented three important network techniques in this chapter. First, we discussed the minimal-spanning tree technique, which determines the path through the network that connects all of the nodes while minimizing total distance. Then the maximal-flow technique was discussed, which finds the maximum flow of any quantity or substance that can go through a network. Finally, the shortest-route technique, which finds the shortest path through a network, was examined.

Glossary

Minimal-Spanning Tree Technique. Determines the path through the network that connects all of the nodes while minimizing total distance.

Maximal-Flow Technique. Finds the maximum flow of any quantity or substance through a network.

Shortest-Route Technique. Determines the shortest path through a network.

Solved Problems

Solved Problem 12-1

Roxie LaMothe, owner of a large horse breeding farm near Orlando, is planning to install a complete water system connecting all of the various stables and barns. The location of the facilities and the distances between them is given in the network shown in Figure 12.15. Roxie must determine the least expensive way to provide water to each facility. What do you recommend?

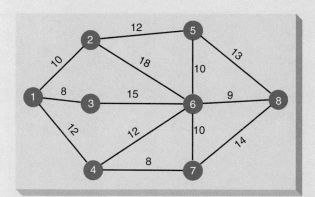

FIGURE 12.15

Solution

This is a typical minimum-spanning tree problem that can be solved by hand. We begin by selecting node 1 and connecting it to the nearest node, which is node 3. Nodes 1 and 2 are the next to be connected, followed by nodes 1 and 4. Now we connect node 4 to node 7 and node 7 to node 6. At this point, the only remaining points to be connected are node 6 to node 8 and node 6 to node 5. The final solution can be seen in Figure 12.16.

FIGURE 12.16

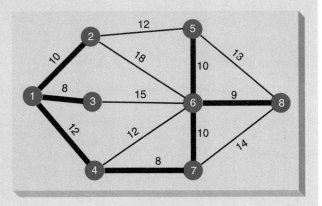

Solved Problem 12-2

PetroChem, an oil refinery located on the Mississippi River south of Baton Rouge, Louisiana, is designing a new plant to produce diesel fuel. Figure 12.17 shows the network of the main processing centers along with the existing rate of flow (in thousands of gallons of fuel). The management at PetroChem would like to determine the maximum amount of fuel that can flow through the plant, from node 1 to node 7.

FIGURE 12.17

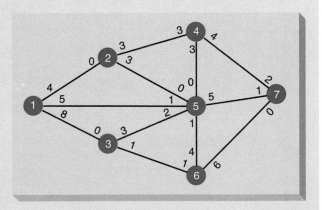

Solution

This problem can be solved using the steps outlined in the chapter on the maximal-flow technique. We start by arbitrarily picking path 1–2–5–7. The maximum flow is 3 along this path. The next path we choose is 1–2–4–7. The maximum flow possible, considering the 1–2–5–7 flow, is 1. The 1–7 flow is 4, and the 1–5–6–7 flow is 1. Finally, the 1–3–6–7 flow is 1. The total flow is 10 (10 = 3 + 1 + 4 + 1 + 1). The network of Figure 12.18, showing only the flow in thousands of gallons, details the by-hand solution.

FIGURE 12.18

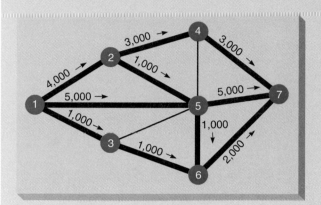

Solved Problem 12-3

The network of Figure 12.19 shows the highways and cities surrounding Leadville, Colorado. Leadville Tom, a bicycle helmet manufacturer, must transport his helmets to a distributor based in Dillon, Colorado. To do this, he must go through several cities. Tom would like to find the shortest way to get from Leadville to Dillon. What do you recommend?

FIGURE 12.19

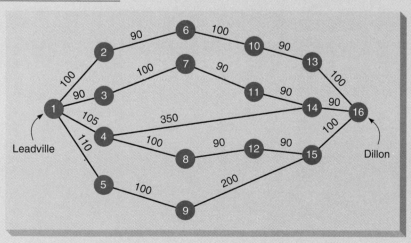

Solution

This problem can be solved using the shortest-route technique discussed in the chapter. The nearest node to the origin (Leadville) is node 3, with a distance of 90 miles. Thus, we put 90 in a box by node 3. The next-nearest node to the origin is node 7 at 190 miles. Again, we put 190 in a box by node 7. Next is node 11 at 280 miles and then node 14 at 370 miles. Finally, we see that the next-nearest (and final) node is node 16 at 460 miles. See Figure 12.20 for the solution.

FIGURE 12.20

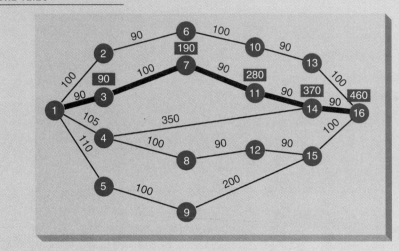

SELF-TEST

- Before taking the self-test, refer back to the learning objectives at the beginning of the chapter, the notes in the margins, and the glossary at the end of the chapter.
- Use the key at the back of the book to correct your answers.
- Restudy pages that correspond to any questions that you answered incorrectly or material you feel uncertain about.

1. Which technique is used to connect all points of a network together while minimizing the distance between them?
   a. maximal flow
   b. minimal flow
   c. minimal-spanning tree
   d. shortest route
   e. longest span

2. The first step of the minimal-spanning tree technique is to
   a. select the node with the highest distance between it and any other node.
   b. select the node with the lowest distance between it and any other node.
   c. select the node that is closest to the origin.
   d. select any arc that connects two nodes.
   e. select any node.

3. The first step of the maximal-flow technique is to
   a. select any node.
   b. pick any path with some flow between two nodes.
   c. pick the path with the maximum flow.
   d. pick the path with the minimal flow.
   e. maximal flow is not a technique discussed in this chapter.

4. In which technique do you connect the nearest node to the existing solution that is not currently connected?
   a. maximal tree
   b. shortest route
   c. minimal-spanning tree
   d. maximal flow
   e. minimal flow

5. The first step of the minimal-flow technique is to
   a. select any node.
   b. pick any path with some flow between two nodes.
   c. pick the path with the maximum flow.
   d. pick the path with the minimal flow.
   e. minimal flow is not a technique discussed in this chapter.

6. Adjusting the flow capacity numbers on a path is an important step in which techniques?
   a. maximal flow
   b. minimal flow
   c. maximal-spanning tree

   d. minimal spanning tree
   e. shortest route

7. Which technique involves finding the nearest node to the origin?
   a. maximal flow
   b. minimal flow
   c. maximal-spanning tree
   d. minimal-spanning tree
   e. shortest route

8. The fire chief was not satisfied with the amount of water put on the warehouse fire by pumper 3. With two hydrant connections and a number of different (known) hose capacities due to leakage of repairs, the chief could determine the best combination by several uses of
   a. the minimal-spanning tree technique.
   b. the maximal-flow technique.
   c. the shortest-route technique.

9. The fire chief is on a very tight budget and the price of gasoline has just gone up again. She wants to minimize the distance traveled by all the fire trucks to each fire hydrant in case of a fire call. She should use
   a. the minimal-spanning tree technique.
   b. the maximal-flow technique.
   c. the shortest-route technique.

10. Tearing up city streets is expensive. The fire chief wants to convince the city council, using the smallest-distance figures, to put in a new water main connecting eight vital spots downtown. She should use
    a. the minimal-spanning tree technique.
    b. the maximal-flow technique.
    c. the shortest-route technique.

11. _____ is a technique that is used to find how a person or item can travel from one location to another while minimizing the total distance traveled.

12. The technique that allows us to determine the maximum amount of a material that can flow through a network is called _____ .

13. The _____ technique can be used to connect all of the points of a network together while minimizing the distance between them.

Discussion Questions and Problems

Discussion Questions

12-1   What is the minimal-spanning tree technique? What types of problems can be solved using this quantitative analysis technique?

12-2   Describe the steps of the maximal-flow technique.

12-3   Give several examples of problems that can be solved using the maximal-flow technique.

12-4   What are the steps of the shortest-route technique?

12-5   Describe a problem that can be solved by the shortest-route technique.

12-6   Is it possible to get alternate optimal solutions with the shortest-route technique? Is there an automatic way of knowing if you have an alternate optimal solution?

Problems*

12-7   Bechtold Construction is in the process of installing power lines to a large housing development. Steve Bechtold wants to minimize the total length of wire used, which will minimize his costs. The housing development is shown as a network in Figure 12.21. Each house has been numbered, and the distances between houses is given in hundreds of feet. What do you recommend?

FIGURE 12.21

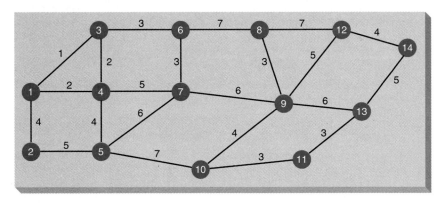

12-8   The city of New Berlin is considering making several of its streets one-way. What is the maximum number of cars per hour that can travel from east to west? The network is shown in Figure 12.22.

FIGURE 12.22

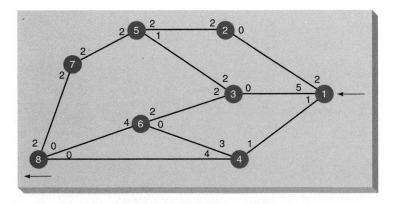

---

*Note: ⌨ means the problem may be solved with QM for Windows.

12-9 Transworld Moving has been hired to move the office furniture and equipment of Cohen Properties to their new headquarters. What route do you recommend? The network of roads is shown in Figure 12.23.

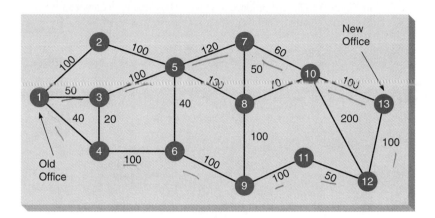

FIGURE 12.23

12-10 Because of a sluggish economy, Bechtold Construction has been forced to modify their plans for the housing development in Problem 12-7. The result is that the path from node 6 to 7 now has a distance of 7. What impact does this have on the total length of wire needed to install the power lines?

12-11 Due to increased property taxes and an aggressive road development plan, the city of New Berlin has been able to increase the road capacity of two of its roads (see Problem 12-8). The capacity along the road represented by the path from node 1–2 has been increased from 2 to 5. In addition, the capacity from node 1–4 has been increased from 1 to 3. What impact do these changes have on the number of cars per hour that can travel from east to west?

12-12 The director of security wants to connect security video cameras to the main control site from five potential trouble locations. Ordinarily, cable would simply be run from each location to the main control site. However, because the environment is potentially explosive, the cable must be run in a special conduit that is continually air purged. This conduit is very expensive but large enough to handle five cables (the maximum that might be needed). Use the minimal-spanning tree technique to find a minimum distance route for the conduit between the locations noted in Figure 12.24. (Note that it makes no difference which one is the main control site.)

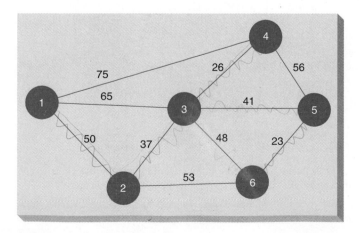

FIGURE 12.24

12-13 One of our best customers has had a major plant breakdown and wants us to make as many widgets for him as possible during the next few days, until he gets the necessary repairs done. With our general-purpose equipment there are several ways to make widgets (ignoring costs). Any sequence of activities that takes one from node 1 to node 6 in Figure 12.25, will produce a widget. How many widgets can we produce per day? Quantities given are number of widgets per day.

FIGURE 12.25

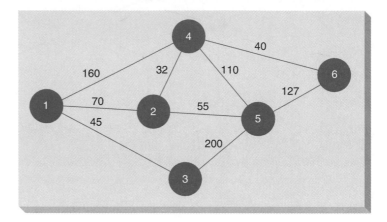

12-14 Transworld Moving, like other moving companies, closely follows the impact of road construction to make sure that its routes remain the most efficient. Unfortunately, there has been unexpected road construction due to a lack of planning for road repair around the town of New Haven, represented by node 9 in the network. (See Problem 12-9.) All roads leading to node 9, except the road from node 9 to node 11, can no longer be traveled. Does this have any impact on the route that should be used to ship the office furniture and equipment of Cohen Properties to their new headquarters?

12-15 Solve the minimal-spanning tree problem in the network shown in Figure 12.26. Assume that the numbers in the network represent distance in hundreds of yards.

FIGURE 12.26

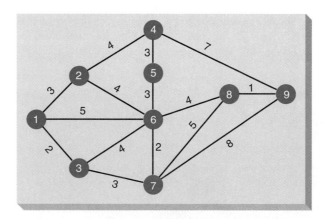

12-16 Refer to Problem 12-15. What impact would changing the value for path 6–7 to 500 yards have on the solution to the problem and the total distance?

12-17 The road system around the hotel complex on International Drive (node 1) to Disney World (node 11) in Orlando, Florida, is shown in the network of Figure 12.27. The numbers by the nodes represent the traffic flow in hundreds of cars per hour. What is the maximum flow of cars from the hotel complex to Disney World?

FIGURE 12.27

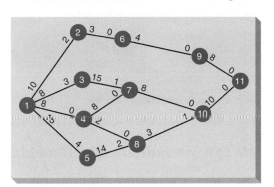

12-18 A road construction project would increase the road capacity around the outside roads from International Drive to Disney World by 200 cars per hour (see Problem 12-17). The two paths affected would be 1–2–6–9–11 and 1–5–8–10–11. What impact would this have on the total flow of cars? Would the total flow of cars increase by 400 cars per hour?

12-19 Solve the maximal-flow problem presented in the network of Figure 12.28. The numbers in the network represent thousands of gallons per hour as they flow through a chemical processing plant.

FIGURE 12.28

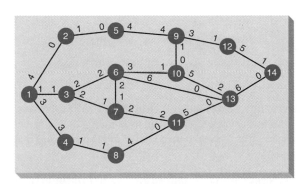

12-20 Two terminals in the chemical processing plant, represented by nodes 6 and 7, require emergency repair (see Problem 12-19). No material can flow into or out of these nodes. What impact does this have on the capacity of the network?

12-21 Solve the shortest-route problem presented in the network of Figure 12.29, going from node 1 to node 16. All numbers represent kilometers between German towns near the Black Forest.

FIGURE 12.29

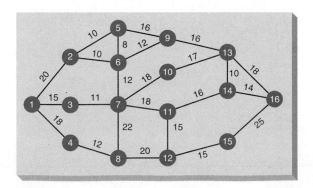

12-22 Due to bad weather, the roads represented by nodes 7 and 8 have been closed (see Problem 12-21). No traffic can get onto or off of these roads. Describe the impact that this will have (if any) on the shortest route through this network.

12-23 Grey Construction would like to determine the least expensive way of connecting houses it is building with cable TV. It has identified 11 possible branches or routes that could be used to connect the houses. The cost in hundreds of dollars and the branches are summarized in the following table.

(a) What is the least expensive way to run cable to the houses?

BRANCH	START NODE	END NODE	COST (HUNDREDS OF DOLLARS)
Branch 1	1	2	5
Branch 2	1	3	6
Branch 3	1	4	6
Branch 4	1	5	5
Branch 5	2	6	7
Branch 6	3	7	5
Branch 7	4	7	7
Branch 8	5	8	4
Branch 9	6	7	1
Branch 10	7	9	6
Branch 11	8	9	2

(b) After reviewing cable and installation costs, Grey Construction would like to alter the costs for installing cable TV between its houses. The first branches need to be changed. The changes are summarized in the following table. What is the impact on total costs?

BRANCH	START NODE	END NODE	COST (HUNDREDS OF DOLLARS)
Branch 1	1	2	5
Branch 2	1	3	1
Branch 3	1	4	1
Branch 4	1	5	1
Branch 5	2	6	7
Branch 6	3	7	5
Branch 7	4	7	7
Branch 8	5	8	4
Branch 9	6	7	1
Branch 10	7	9	6
Branch 11	8	9	2

12-24 In going from Quincy to Old Bainbridge, there are 10 possible roads that George Olin can take. Each road can be considered a branch in the shortest-route problem.

(a) Determine the best way to get from Quincy (Node 1) to Old Bainbridge (Node 8) that will minimize total distance traveled. All distances are in hundreds of miles.

BRANCH	START NODE	END NODE	DISTANCE (IN HUNDREDS OF MILES)
Branch 1	1	2	3
Branch 2	1	3	2
Branch 3	2	4	3
Branch 4	3	5	3
Branch 5	4	5	1
Branch 6	4	6	4
Branch 7	5	7	2
Branch 8	6	7	2
Branch 9	6	8	3
Branch 10	7	8	6

(b) George Olin made a mistake in estimating the distances from Quincy to Old Bainbridge. The new distances are in the following table. What impact does this have on the shortest route from Quincy to Old Bainbridge?

BRANCH	START NODE	END NODE	DISTANCE (IN HUNDREDS OF MILES)
Branch 1	1	2	3
Branch 2	1	3	2
Branch 3	2	4	3
Branch 4	3	5	1
Branch 5	4	5	1
Branch 6	4	6	4
Branch 7	5	7	2
Branch 8	6	7	2
Branch 9	6	8	3
Branch 10	7	8	6

12-25 South Side Oil and Gas, a new venture in Texas, has developed an oil pipeline network to transport oil from exploration fields to the refinery and other locations. There are 10 pipelines (Branches) in the network. The oil flow in hundreds of gallons and the network of pipelines is given in the following table.

(a) What is the maximum that can flow through the network?

	START NODE	END NODE	CAPACITY	REVERSE CAPACITY	FLOW
Branch 1	1	2	10	4	10
Branch 2	1	3	8	2	5
Branch 3	2	4	12	1	10
Branch 4	2	5	6	6	0
Branch 5	3	5	8	1	5
Branch 6	4	6	10	2	10
Branch 7	5	6	10	10	0
Branch 8	5	7	5	5	5
Branch 9	6	8	10	1	10
Branch 10	7	8	10	1	5

(b) South Side Oil and Gas needs to modify its pipeline network flow patterns. The new data is in the following table. What impact does this have on the maximum flow through the network?

	START NODE	END NODE	CAPACITY	REVERSE CAPACITY	FLOW
Branch 1	1	2	10	4	10
Branch 2	1	3	8	2	5
Branch 3	2	4	12	1	10
Branch 4	2	5	0	0	0
Branch 5	3	5	8	1	5
Branch 6	4	6	10	2	10
Branch 7	5	6	10	10	0
Branch 8	5	7	5	5	5
Branch 9	6	8	10	1	10
Branch 10	7	8	10	1	5

Data Set Problem

12-26 Northwest University is in the process of completing a computer bus network that will connect computer facilities throughout the university. The prime objective is to string a main cable from one end of campus to the other (nodes 1–25) through underground conduits. These conduits are shown in the network of Figure 12.30; the distance be-

FIGURE 12.30

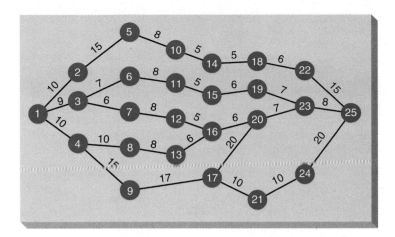

tween them is in hundreds of feet. Fortunately, these underground conduits have remaining capacity through which the bus cable can be placed.

(a) Given the network for this problem, how far (in hundreds of feet) is the shortest route from node 1 to node 25?

(b) In addition to the computer bus network, a new phone system is also being planned. The phone system would use the same underground conduits. If the phone system were installed, the following paths along the conduit would be at capacity and would not be available for the computer bus network: 6–11, 7–12, and 17–20. What changes (if any) would you have to make to the path used for the computer bus if the phone system were installed?

(c) The university *did* decide to install the new phone system before the cable for the computer network. Because of unexpected demand for computer networking facilities, an additional cable is needed for node 1 to node 25. Unfortunately, the cable for the first or original network has completely used up the capacity along its path. Given this situation, what is the best path for the second network cable?

Ranch Development Project

One hundred years ago, a high plains area near the continental divide in Colorado was used as a working ranch. The views were majestic, although the winters could be harsh. As a result of the boom in skiing, snowmobiling, and other winter sports, the area quickly became a major tourist attraction. The result was a higher population base to support tourism and increased property values. During the late 1960s and 1970s, the area experienced dramatic growth. Many people from states such as Oklahoma and Texas vacationed here, and so purchased land, houses, or condominiums. Many property developers who finished their projects before the mid-1980s and early 1990s did very well financially. The success of other developers led to the organization of the Ranch Development Project.

The Ranch Development Project was undertaken by two real estate companies in the Colorado high country and several investors from Oklahoma. The idea was to convert the working ranch into a luxury single-family development. The project became known as The Ranch. The average home price was $475,000, and it was not uncommon to have homes valued at more than $1 million. The center of the development was a first-class 18-hole golf course. Green fees could approach $100 per day, depending on services required. Some have claimed that the course is one of the best in Colorado. The Ranch also had a four-star restaurant located in a beautiful and spacious log cabin, which included a fireplace big enough for a 6-foot-tall person to walk into without hitting his head. Other amenities included a heated pool, lighted tennis courts, and a complete workout center. Free shuttle service was provided to the ski slopes a few miles away.

To preserve the beauty of the area and to enhance property values, each home site varied from 1 acre to more than

FIGURE 12.31

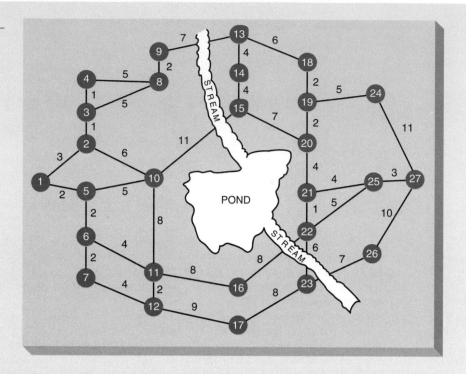

20 acres. There were numerous building restrictions. Every home and structure had to be approved by the Ranch Development Board. Approval required developing a scale model of all buildings on the property and a complete set of blueprints. The average cost of preparing the necessary plans was $25,000. The concept of a footprint was also used. A *footprint* is a relatively small circular area on each plot of land. Homes and all structures had to be placed inside the footprint. Although the homeowner held title to the entire property, all structures had to be placed in the footprint unless special permission was given by the Ranch Development Board (a rare occurrence).

Each homeowner had to pay monthly fees, depending on the location and value of the land. The fees could vary from $450 to more than $1,250 per month. These fees included water, sewer, cable TV, and access to the pool, tennis courts, and exercise facility. Golf and restaurant fees were additional.

One of the developments in The Ranch is outlined in Figure 12.31. The development was not as close to the golf course as some of the others, but it had a beautiful trout stream and pond in the center. The footprints are shown in the network. Distances between footprints are given in hundreds of feet.

Discussion Questions

1. What is the least expensive way to connect all homes with water and sewer lines? Assume that minimizing total distance will also minimize total costs.
2. The Ranch Development Board is considering the possibility of expanding the pond area. This would allow for boating, including sailing and water skiing. This would increase property values, but some distances would change. The distance for path 11–16 would be 9, and the distance for path 16–22 would be 12. What impact would this have on the plan for the water and sewer system?

Case Study

Binder's Beverage

Bill Binder's business nearly went under when Colorado almost passed the bottle bill. Binder's Beverage produced soft drinks for many of the large grocery stores in the area. After the bottle bill failed, Binder's Beverage flourished. In a few short years, the company had a major plant in Denver with a warehouse in east Denver. The problem was getting the finished product to the warehouse. Although Bill was not good with distances, he was good with times. Denver is a big city with numerous roads that could be taken from the plant to the warehouse.

The soft drink plant is located at the corner of North Street and Columbine Street. High Street also intersects North and Columbine Street at the plant. Twenty minutes due north of the plant on North Street is I-70, the major east-west highway in Denver.

North Street intersects I-70 at Exit 135. It takes five minutes driving east on I-70 to reach Exit 136. This exit connects I-70 with High Street and 6th Avenue. Ten minutes east on I-70 is Exit 137. This exit connects I-70 with Rose Street and South Avenue.

From the plant, it takes 20 minutes on High Street, which goes in a north-east direction, to reach West Street. It takes another 20 minutes on High Street to reach I-70 and Exit 136.

It takes 30 minutes on Columbine Street to reach West Street from the plant. Columbine Street travels east and slightly north.

West Street travels east and west. From High Street, it takes 15 minutes to get to 6th Avenue on West Street. Columbine Street also comes into this intersection. From this intersection, it takes an additional 20 minutes on West Street to get to Rose Street, and another 15 minutes to get to South Avenue.

From Exit 136 on 6th Avenue, it takes 5 minutes to get to West Street. Sixth Avenue continues to Rose Street, requiring 25 minutes. Sixth Avenue then goes directly to the warehouse. From Rose Street, it takes 40 minutes to get to the warehouse on 6th Avenue.

At Exit 137, Rose Street travels southwest. It takes 20 minutes to intersect with West Street, and another 20 minutes to get to 6th Avenue. From Exit 137, South Street goes due south. It takes 10 minutes to get to West Street and another 15 minutes to get to the Warehouse.

Discussion Question

1. What route do you recommend?

Street map for Binder's Beverage case

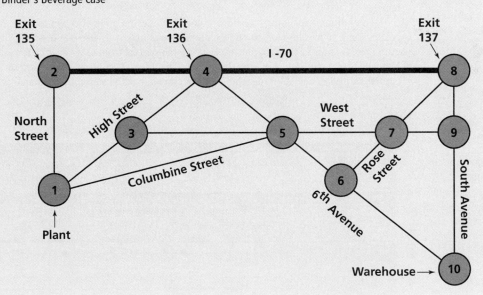

Bibliography

Bentley, Jon. "Faster And Faster And Faster," *UNIX Review*, (June 1997): 59.

Cipra, Barry. "Taking Hard Problems to the Limit: Mathematics," *Science* (March 4, 1997): 1570.

Current, J. "The Minimum-Covering/Shortest Path Problem," *Decision Sciences* 19 (Summer 1988): 490–503.

Jain, A., and J. W. Mamer. "Approximations for the Random Minimal Spanning Tree with Application to Network Provisioning," *Operations Research* 36 (July–August 1988): 575–584.

Onal, Hayri et al. "Two Formulations of the Vehicle Routing Problem," *The Logistics and Transportation Review* (June 1996): 117.

Perlman, Radia et al. "Spanning the LAN," *Data Communications* (October 21, 1997): 68.

Render, B., and R. M. Stair. *Cases and Readings in Management Science*, 2nd ed. Boston: Allyn and Bacon, Inc., 1990.

Sancho, N. G. F. "On the Maximum Expected Flow in a Network," *Journal of Operational Research Society* 39 (May 1988): 481–485.

Williams, Martyn. "When Does the Shortest Route Between Tokyo and Singapore Include a Stop in New York?" *Data Communications* (December 19, 1997): 45.

William, Carlton et al. "Solving the Traveling-Salesman Problem with Time Windows Using Tabu Search," *IEEE Transactions* (August 1996): 617.

APPENDIX 12.1: NETWORK MODELS WITH QM FOR WINDOWS

Network models, including the minimal-spanning tree, maximal-flow, and shortest-route techniques were covered in this chapter. QM for Windows can be used to solve each of these network problems.

The minimal-spanning technique connects nodes on a network while minimizing distance or costs. The Lauderdale Construction Company example was used to describe the overall procedure (see Section 12.2). Program 12.1 shows the output from QM for Windows for this problem. Note that all input data are also displayed. The *Include* column shows which branches are included as part of the solution. The solution shows that the minimum distance is 16 (16 hundred feet).

PROGRAM 12.1

QM for Windows for the Minimum-Spanning Tree Method

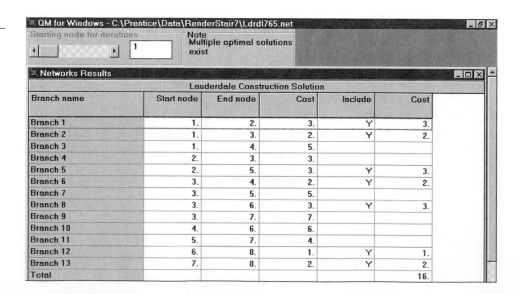

Branch name	Start node	End node	Cost	Include	Cost
Branch 1	1.	2.	3.	Y	3.
Branch 2	1.	3.	2.	Y	2.
Branch 3	1.	4.	5.		
Branch 4	2.	3.	3.		
Branch 5	2.	5.	3.	Y	3.
Branch 6	3.	4.	2.	Y	2.
Branch 7	3.	5.	5.		
Branch 8	3.	6.	3.	Y	3.
Branch 9	3.	7.	7.		
Branch 10	4.	6.	6.		
Branch 11	5.	7.	4.		
Branch 12	6.	8.	1.	Y	1.
Branch 13	7.	8.	2.	Y	2.
Total					16.

The maximal-flow problem determines the maximum flow of cars, chemicals, or other items through an existing network. The Waukesha Road example was explained in Section 12.3. Program 12.2 shows the input data for this problem. Program 12.3 shows how QM for Windows can be used to solve this problem.

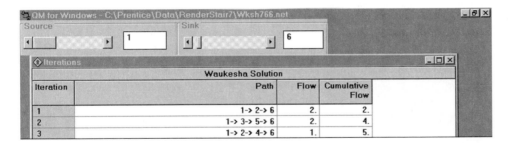

PROGRAM 12.2

QM for Windows for the Maximal-Flow Model

Branch name	Start node	End node	Capacity	Reverse capacity
Branch 1	1	2	3	1
Branch 2	1	3	10	0
Branch 3	1	4	2	0
Branch 4	2	4	1	1
Branch 5	2	6	2	2
Branch 6	3	4	3	1
Branch 7	3	5	2	1
Branch 8	4	6	1	1
Branch 9	5	6	6	0

PROGRAM 12.3

Output from the Maximal-Flow Model

Source 1   Sink 6

Waukesha Solution

Iteration	Path	Flow	Cumulative Flow
1	1-> 2-> 6	2.	2.
2	1-> 3-> 5-> 6	2.	4.
3	1-> 2-> 4-> 6	1.	5.

The shortest-route problem determines how a person or item can travel from one location to another while minimizing total distance traveled. In this chapter we explored the Ray Design problem (see Section 12.4). To illustrate the use of QM for Windows, let's use these data to solve a typical shortest-route problem. The input data are shown in Program 12.4. The output results are shown in Program 12.5.

PROGRAM 12.4

QM for Windows Input for the Shortest-Route Model

Network Models / Shortest Route

Network type: ● Undirected ○ Directed

Origin: 0   Destination: 0

Shortest Route Example

	Start node	End node	Distance
Branch 1	1.	2.	100.
Branch 2	1.	3.	200.
Branch 3	2.	3.	50.
Branch 4	2.	4.	200.
Branch 5	2.	5.	100.
Branch 6	3.	5.	40.
Branch 7	4.	5.	150.
Branch 8	4.	6.	100.
Branch 9	5.	6.	100.

PROGRAM 12.5

QM for Windows Results for
the Shortest-Route Model

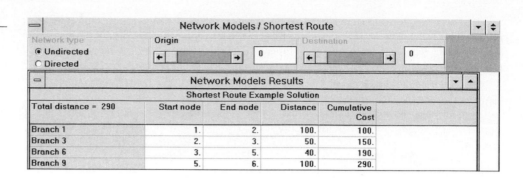

Project Management

LEARNING OBJECTIVES

After completing this chapter, students will be able to:

1. Understand how to plan, monitor, and control projects with the use of PERT.

2. Determine earliest start, earliest finish, latest start, latest finish, and slack times for each activity, along with the total project completion time.

3. Reduce total project time at the least total cost by crashing the network using manual or linear programming techniques.

4. Understand the important role of software in project management.

CHAPTER OUTLINE

13.1 Introduction

13.2 PERT

13.3 PERT/Cost

13.4 Critical Path Method

Summary • Glossary • Key Equations • Solved Problems • Self-Test • Discussion Questions and Problems • Data Set Problem • Case Study: Haygood Brothers Construction Company • Case Study: Family Planning Research Center of Nigeria • Internet Case Studies • Bibliography

Appendix 13.1: Project Management with QM for Windows

13.1   INTRODUCTION

Project management can be used to manage complex projects.

Most realistic projects that organizations like Microsoft, General Motors, or the U.S. Defense Department undertake are large and complex. A builder putting up an office building, for example, must complete thousands of activities costing millions of dollars. NASA must inspect countless components before it launches a rocket. Avondale Shipyards in New Orleans requires tens of thousands of steps in constructing an ocean-going tugboat. Almost every industry worries about how to manage similar large-scale, complicated projects effectively. It is a difficult problem, and the stakes are high. Millions of dollars in cost overruns have been wasted due to poor planning of projects. Unnecessary delays have occurred due to poor scheduling. How can such problems be solved?

The *program evaluation and review technique* (PERT) and the *critical path method* (CPM) are two popular quantitative analysis techniques that help managers plan, schedule, monitor, and control large and complex projects. They were developed because there was a critical need for a better way to manage (see the History box).

Framework of PERT and CPM

There are six steps common to both PERT and CPM. The procedure follows:

Six Steps of PERT and CPM

1. Define the project and all of its significant activities or tasks.
2. Develop the relationships among the activities. Decide which activities must precede and follow others.
3. Draw the network connecting all of the activities.
4. Assign time and/or cost estimates to each activity.
5. Compute the longest time path through the network; this is called the *critical path*.
6. Use the network to help plan, schedule, monitor, and control the project.

The critical path is important because activities on the critical path can delay the entire project.

Finding the critical path is a major part of controlling a project. The activities on the critical path represent tasks that will delay the entire project if they are delayed. Managers derive flexibility by identifying noncritical activities and replanning, rescheduling, and reallocating resources such as personnel and finances.

Although PERT and CPM are similar in their basic approach, they do differ in the way activity times are estimated. For every PERT activity, three time estimates are combined to determine the expected activity completion time and its variance. Thus PERT is a *probabilistic* technique; it allows us to find the probability that the entire project will be completed by any given date. CPM, on the other hand, is called a *deterministic* approach. It uses two time estimates, the *normal time* and the *crash time*, for each activity. The normal completion time is the time we estimate it will take under normal conditions to complete the activity. The crash completion time is the shortest time it would take to finish an activity if additional funds and resources were allocated to the task.

PERT is probabilistic, while CPM is deterministic.

In this chapter we investigate not only PERT and CPM, but also a technique called PERT/Cost that combines the benefits of both PERT and CPM.

HISTORY   How PERT and CPM Started

Managers have been planning, scheduling, monitoring, and controlling large-scale projects for hundreds of years, but it has only been in the past 50 years that QA techniques have been applied to major projects. One of the earliest techniques was the *Gantt chart*. This type of chart shows the start and finish times of one or more activities, as shown in the accompanying chart.

In 1958, the Special Projects Office of the U.S. Navy developed the Program Evaluation and Review Technique (PERT) to plan and control the Polaris missile program. This project involved the coordination of thousands of contractors. Today PERT is still used to monitor countless government contract schedules. At about the same time (1957), the Critical Path Method (CPM) was developed by J. E. Kelly of Remington Rand and M. R. Walker of du Pont. Originally, CPM was used to assist in the building and maintenance of chemical plants at du Pont.

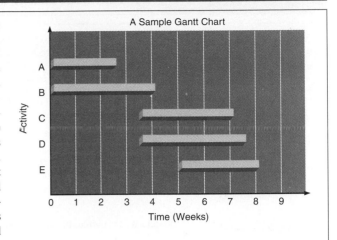

13.2   PERT

Almost any large project can be subdivided into a series of smaller activities or tasks that can be analyzed with PERT. When you recognize that projects can have thousands of specific activities, you see why it is important to be able to answer such questions as the following:

1. When will the entire project be completed?

2. What are the *critical* activities or tasks in the project, that is, the ones that will delay the entire project if they are late?

3. Which are the *noncritical* activities, that is, the ones that can run late without delaying the entire project's completion?

4. What is the probability that the project will be completed by a specific date?

5. At any particular date, is the project on schedule, behind schedule, or ahead of schedule?

6. On any given date, is the money spent equal to, less than, or greater than the budgeted amount?

7. Are there enough resources available to finish the project on time?

8. If the project is to be finished in a shorter amount of time, what is the best way to accomplish this at the least cost?

PERT (or PERT/Cost) can help answer each of these questions.

Questions answered by PERT.

General Foundry Example of PERT

General Foundry, Inc., a metalworks plant in Milwaukee, has long been trying to avoid the expense of installing air pollution control equipment. The local environmental protection group has recently given the foundry 16 weeks to install a complex air filter system

MODELING IN THE REAL WORLD   PERT Helps Change the Face of British Airways

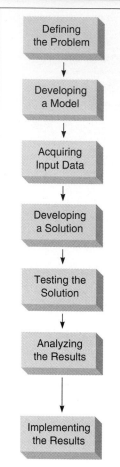

Defining the Problem

British Airways (BA) wanted to rejuvenate its image using international design consultants to help develop a new identity. The "makeover" was to be completed in all areas of BA's public image as quickly as possible.

Developing a Model

Using a computerized project management package—PERTMASTER from Abex Software—a BA team constructed a PERT model of all tasks involved.

Acquiring Input Data

Data were collected from each department involved. Printers were asked to develop time estimates for new company stationery, tickets, timetables, baggage tags; clothing suppliers for uniforms; and Boeing Corp. for all the tasks involved in remaking the inside and outside of BA's jets.

Developing a Solution

All the data were entered into PERTMASTER for a schedule and critical path.

Testing the Solution

The resulting schedule did not please BA management. Boeing could not prepare a huge 747 in time for a December 4 gala launch date. Uniform designs were also going to delay the entire project.

Analyzing the Results

An analysis of the earliest possible date that all items for a refurbished airplane could be ready (new paint, upholstery, carpets, trim, and so on) revealed that there were just sufficient materials to totally convert a smaller Boeing 737 that was available in the Seattle plant. Critical path analysis also showed that uniforms—the work of British designer Roland Klein—would have to be launched six months later in a separate ceremony.

Implementing the Results

The smaller 737 was outfitted just in time for a brilliant light show in an auditorium specially built in a Heathrow Airport hangar. Ground vehicles were also prepared in time.

Source: *Industrial Management and Data Systems* (March–April 1986): 6–7.

The first step is to define the project and all project activities.

on its main smokestack. General Foundry was warned that it will be forced to close unless the device is installed in the allotted period. Lester Harky, the managing partner, wants to make sure that installation of the filtering system progresses smoothly and on time.

When the project begins, the building of the internal components for the device (activity A) and the modifications that are necessary for the floor and roof (activity B) can be started. The construction of the collection stack (activity C) can begin once the internal components are completed, and pouring of the new concrete floor and installation of the frame (activity D) can be completed as soon as the roof and floor have been modified. After the collection stack has been constructed, the high-temperature burner can be built (activity E), and the installation of the pollution control system (activity F) can begin. The air pollution device can be installed (activity G) after the high-temperature burner has been built, the concrete floor has been poured, and the frame has been installed. Finally, after the control system and pollution device have been installed, the system can be inspected and tested (activity H).

All of these activities seem rather confusing and complex until they are placed in a network. First, all of the activities must be listed. This information is shown in Table 13.1.

TABLE 13.1 Activities and Immediate Predecessors for General Foundry, Inc.

ACTIVITY	DESCRIPTION	IMMEDIATE PREDECESSORS
A	Build internal components	—
B	Modify roof and floor	—
C	Construct collection stack	A
D	Pour concrete and install frame	B
E	Build high-temperature burner	C
F	Install control system	C
G	Install air pollution device	D, E
H	Inspect and test	F, G

We see in the table that before the collection stack can be constructed (activity C), the internal components must be built (activity A). Thus activity A is the immediate predecessor of activity C. Similarly, both activities D and E must be performed just prior to installation of the air pollution device (activity G).

Immediate predecessors are determined in the second step.

Drawing the PERT Network

Once the activities have all been specified (step 1 of the PERT procedure) and management has decided which activities must precede and follow others (step 2), the network can be drawn (step 3).

Activities and events are drawn and connected in the third step.

An *activity* carries the arrow symbol: →. This represents a task or subproject that uses time or resources. The only other piece needed to create a network is called an *event*. An event marks the start or completion of a particular activity. It is denoted by the symbol ○, which contains a number that helps identify its location. For example, activity A can be drawn as follows:

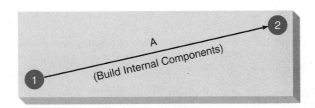

It begins with event 1 and ends with event 2. Activity C's only *immediate predecessor* is activity A, so it can be drawn like this:

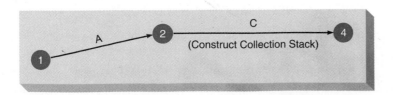

FIGURE 13.1

Network for General Foundry, Inc.

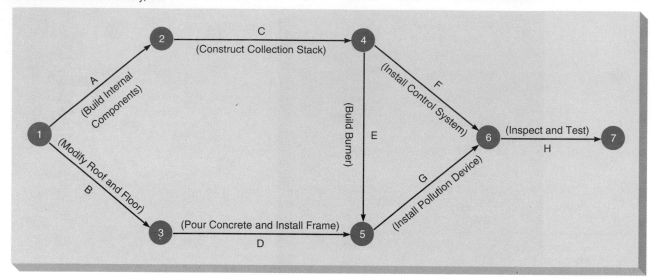

The number inside the event is used to identify the beginning or ending of an activity more easily.

Now we are ready to draw the entire *network* for General Foundry. This is shown in Figure 13.1.

You should note that drawing a PERT network takes some time and experience. You start with the beginning node, node 1. You then draw the activities from this node that do not have any immediate predecessor activities (in this case, A and B). Successive nodes and activities are drawn, making sure that the appropriate relationships between activities and nodes are maintained. You must take care that all immediate predecessor activities are appropriately reflected in the network. When you first draw the network, it is usually impossible to draw all the activities as straight lines. It is good to first get a rough draft version of the network, making sure that all of the appropriate relationships are intact. Then you can redraw the network to make all of the activity lines straight.

Activity Times

The fourth step is to assign activity times.

The next step in the PERT procedure is to assign estimates of the time required to complete each activity. Time is usually given in units of weeks. For one-of-a-kind projects or for new jobs, providing *activity time estimates* is not always an easy task. Without solid historical data, managers are often uncertain as to activity times. For this reason, the developers of PERT employed a probability distribution based on three time estimates for each activity:

Optimistic time (a) = time an activity will take if everything goes as well as possible. There should be only a small probability (say, $\frac{1}{100}$) of this occurring.

Pessimistic time (b) = time an activity would take assuming very unfavorable conditions. There should also be only a small probability that the activity will really take this long.

Most likely time (m) = most realistic time estimate to complete the activity.

FIGURE 13.2

Beta Probability Distribution with Three Time Estimates

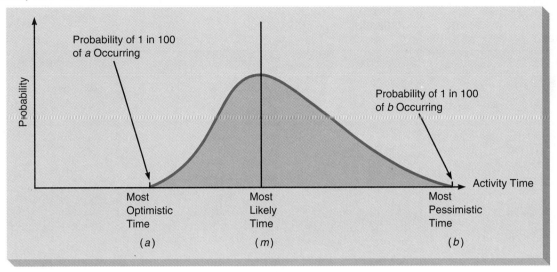

PERT often assumes that time estimates follow the *beta probability distribution* (see Figure 13.2). This continuous distribution has been found to be appropriate, in many cases, for determining an expected value and variance for activity completion times.

The beta probability distribution is often used.

To find the *expected activity time (t)*, the beta distribution weights the estimates as follows:

$$t = \frac{a + 4m + b}{6} \qquad \text{(13-1)}$$

To compute the dispersion or *variance of activity completion time*, we use the formula[1]

$$\text{variance} = \left(\frac{b - a}{6}\right)^2 \qquad \text{(13-2)}$$

Table 13.2 shows General Foundry's optimistic, most likely, and pessimistic time estimates for each activity. It also reveals the expected time *(t)* and variance for each of the activities, as computed with Equations 13-1 and 13-2.

How to Find the Critical Path

Once the expected completion time for each activity has been determined, we accept it as the actual time of that task. Variability in times will be considered later.

Although Table 13.2 indicates that the total expected time for all eight of General Foundry's activities is 25 weeks, it is obvious in Figure 13.3 that several of the tasks can be taking place simultaneously. To find out just how long the project will take, we perform the critical path analysis for the network.

---

[1] This formula is based on the statistical concept that from one end of the beta distribution to the other is 6 standard deviations (± 3 standard deviations from the mean). Because $b - a$ is 6 standard deviations, one standard deviation is $(b - a)/6$. Thus the variance is $[(b - a)/6]^2$.

TABLE 13.2   Time Estimates (Weeks) for General Foundry, Inc.

ACTIVITY	OPTIMISTIC, a	MOST PROBABLE, m	PESSIMISTIC, b	EXPECTED TIME, $t = [(a + 4m + b)/6]$	VARIANCE, $[(b - a)/6]^2$
A	1	2	3	2	$\left(\dfrac{3 - 1}{6}\right)^2 = \dfrac{4}{36}$
B	2	3	4	3	$\left(\dfrac{4 - 2}{6}\right)^2 = \dfrac{4}{36}$
C	1	2	3	2	$\left(\dfrac{3 - 1}{6}\right)^2 = \dfrac{4}{36}$
D	2	4	6	4	$\left(\dfrac{6 - 2}{6}\right)^2 = \dfrac{16}{36}$
E	1	4	7	4	$\left(\dfrac{7 - 1}{6}\right)^2 = \dfrac{36}{36}$
F	1	2	9	3	$\left(\dfrac{9 - 1}{6}\right)^2 = \dfrac{64}{36}$
G	3	4	11	5	$\left(\dfrac{11 - 3}{6}\right)^2 = \dfrac{64}{36}$
H	1	2	3	<u>2</u>	$\left(\dfrac{3 - 1}{6}\right)^2 = \dfrac{4}{36}$
	12	23	46	25	

12+23+46 =   81=6

FIGURE 13.3

General Foundry's Network with Expected Activity Times

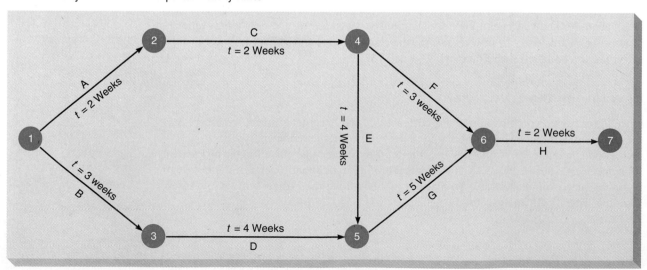

The *critical path* is the longest time path route through the network. If Lester Harky wants to reduce the total project time for General Foundry, he will have to reduce the length of some activity on the critical path. Conversely, any delay of an activity on the critical path will delay completion of the entire project.

The fifth step is to compute the longest path through the network—the critical path.

To find the critical path, we need to determine the following quantities for each activity in the network:

1. *Earliest start time* (ES): the earliest time an activity can begin without violation of immediate predecessor requirements
2. *Earliest finish time* (EF): the earliest time at which an activity can end
3. *Latest start time* (LS): the latest time an activity can begin without delaying the entire project
4. *Latest finish time* (LF): the latest time an activity can end without delaying the entire project

We begin at the network's origin, event 1, to compute the earliest start time (ES) and earliest finish time (EF) for each activity. For the first event, the starting time is always set equal to zero. Since activity A has an expected time of 2 weeks, its earliest finish time is 2, as seen here:

We begin by computing earliest start and finish times for each activity.

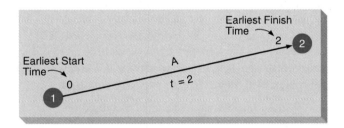

The earliest finish time can be computed by

earliest finish time = earliest start time + expected activity time

$$EF = ES + t \qquad\qquad (13\text{-}3)$$

Earliest Start Time Rule   There is one basic rule to follow as you find ES and EF for all activities in the network. Before any activity can be started, *all* of its predecessor activities must be completed. In other words, we search for the *longest* path to an activity in determining ES. For example, we see that ES for activity C is 2 weeks. Its only predecessor activity is A, which has an EF of 2 weeks.

All predecessor activities must be completed before an activity can be started.

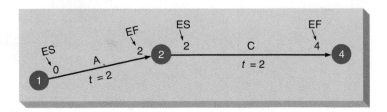

Earliest start time for activity G, however, is 8 weeks. It has two predecessor activities, D and E. Since activity D has an EF of 7 weeks and activity E's EF is 8 weeks, the earliest time that activity G can begin is at the 8-week mark.

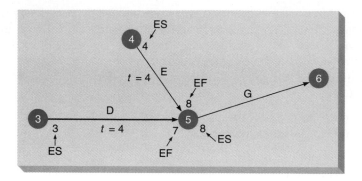

A forward pass through the network is completed.

To complete the ES and EF times for all activities, we make what is called a *forward pass* through the network. Figure 13.4 illustrates the results. At each step we see that EF = ES + t. Note that the earliest the *entire project can be finished is 15 weeks*. This is because activity H cannot be started until 13 weeks (ES = 13) and its expected time is 2 weeks; hence EF = 13 + 2 = 15 weeks. So the best Lester Harky can expect to do is have the air pollution control device installed and tested in 15 weeks.

A backward pass through the network is done next.

Latest Finish Time Rule The next step in finding the critical path is to compute the latest start time (LS) and latest finish time (LF) for each activity. We do this by making a *backward pass* through the network, that is, starting at the last activity and working backward to the first activities. This means assigning a latest finish time of 15 weeks to activity H.

Recall that latest finish time is the latest an activity can end without delaying the project. To compute the latest start time, we apply the following formula:

Compute the latest start time by using the formula LS = LF − t.

latest start time = latest finish time − expected activity time

$$LS = LF - t$$

(13-4)

FIGURE 13.4

General Foundry's Earliest Start (ES) and Earliest Finish (EF) Times

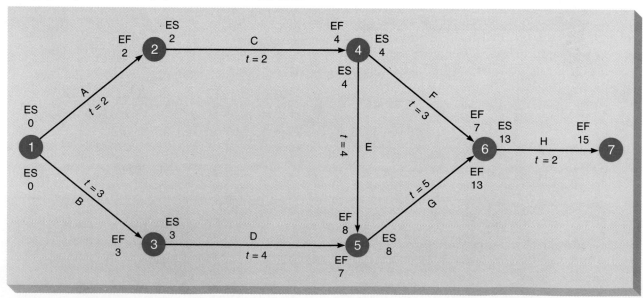

For example, with LF = 15 for activity H, the latest start time for activity H is

LS = 15 − 2 = 13 weeks

In general, the rule we apply is that the latest finish time for an activity equals the *smallest* latest starting time for all activities leaving that same event. Thus, LF for activity C is 4 weeks, which is the smaller of the LS times for the two activities leaving event 4.

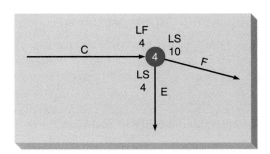

LS and LF times for all activities in the General Foundry case are shown in Figure 13.5.

Concept of Slack in Critical Path Computations. When ES, LS, EF, and LF have been determined, it is a simple matter to find the amount of *slack time*, or free time, that each activity has. Slack is the length of time an activity can be delayed without delaying the whole project. Mathematically,

Slack time is free time for an activity.

slack = LS − ES   or   slack = LF − EF   **(13-5)**

Table 13.3 summarizes the ES, EF, LS, LF, and slack times for all of General Foundry's activities. Activity B, for example, has 1 week of slack time since LS − ES = 1 − 0 = 1 (or, similarly, LF − EF = 4 − 3 = 1). This means that it can be delayed up to 1 week without causing the project to run any longer than expected.

On the other hand, activities A, C, E, G, and H have *no* slack time; this means that none of them can be delayed without delaying the entire project. Because of this, they are

FIGURE 13.5

General Foundry's Latest Start (LS) and Lastest Finish (LF) Times

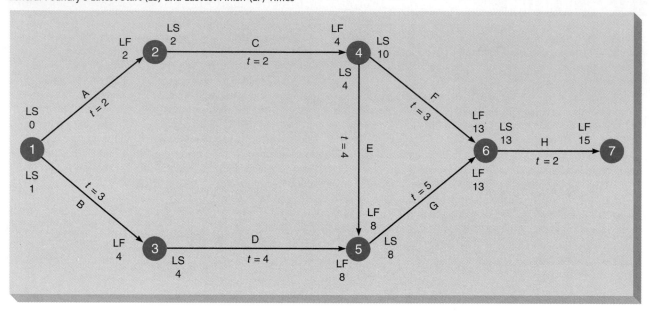

Critical activities have no slack time.

called *critical activities* and are said to be on the *critical path*. Lester Harky's critical path is shown in network form in Figure 13.6. The total project completion time, 15 weeks, is seen as the largest number in the EF or LF columns of Table 13.3. Industrial managers call this a boundary timetable.

Probability of Project Completion

The *critical path analysis* helped us determine that the foundry's expected project completion time is 15 weeks. Harky knows, however, that if the project is not completed in 16 weeks, General Foundry will be forced to close by environmental controllers. He is also

TABLE 13.3 General Foundry's Schedule and Slack Times

ACTIVITY	EARLIEST START, ES	EARLIEST FINISH, EF	LATEST START, LS	LATEST FINISH, LF	SLACK, LS – ES	ON CRITICAL PATH?
A	0	2	0	2	0	Yes
B	0	3	1	4	1	No
C	2	4	2	4	0	Yes
D	3	7	4	8	1	No
E	4	8	4	8	0	Yes
F	4	7	10	13	6	No
G	8	13	8	13	0	Yes
H	13	15	13	15	0	Yes

FIGURE 13.6

General Foundry's Critical Path (A–C–E–G–H)

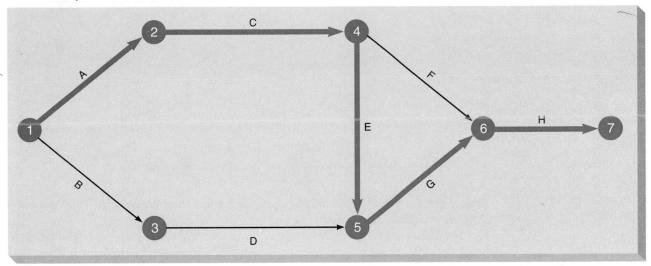

aware that there is significant variation in the time estimates for several activities. Variation in activities that are on the critical path can impact on overall project completion—possibly delaying it. This is one occurrence that worries Harky considerably.

PERT uses the variance of critical path activities to help determine the variance of the overall project. Project variance is computed by summing variances of critical activities:

Computing project variance is done by summing activity variances along the critical path.

project variance = Σ variances of activities on the critical path   **(13-6)**

From Table 13.2 we know that

CRITICAL ACTIVITY	VARIANCE
A	$\frac{4}{36}$
C	$\frac{4}{36}$
E	$\frac{36}{36}$
G	$\frac{64}{36}$
H	$\frac{4}{36}$

Hence the project variance is

project variance = $\frac{4}{36} + \frac{4}{36} + \frac{36}{36} + \frac{64}{36} + \frac{4}{36} = \frac{112}{36} = 3.111$

We know that the standard deviation is just the square root of the variance, so

project standard deviation = $\sigma_T = \sqrt{\text{project variance}}$

$= \sqrt{3.11} = 1.76$ weeks

Computing the standard deviation.

How can this information be used to help answer questions regarding the probability of finishing the project on time? PERT makes two more assumptions: (1) total project completion times follow a normal probability distribution; and (2) activity times are statistically independent. With these assumptions, the bell-shaped curve shown in Figure 13.7 can be used to represent project completion dates. It also means that there is a 50%

FIGURE 13.7

Probability Distribution for
Project Completion Times

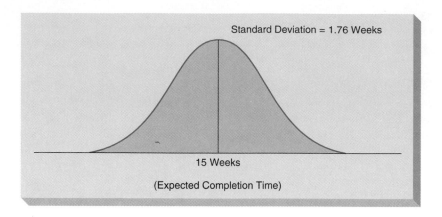

chance that the entire project will be completed in less than the expected 15 weeks and a 50% chance that it will exceed 15 weeks.[2]

For Harky to find the probability that his project will be finished on or before the 16-week deadline, he needs to determine the appropriate area under the normal curve. The standard normal equation can be applied as follows:

Computing the probability of project completion.

$$Z = \frac{\text{due date} - \text{expected date of completion}}{\sigma_T}$$

$$= \frac{16 \text{ weeks} - 15 \text{ weeks}}{1.76 \text{ weeks}} = 0.57$$

(13-7)

where

Z is the number of standard deviations the due date or target date lies from the mean or expected date.

Referring to the normal table in Appendix A, we find a probability of 0.71566. Thus, there is a 71.6% chance that the pollution control equipment can be put in place in 16 weeks or less. This is shown in Figure 13.8.

FIGURE 13.8

Probability of General
Foundry's Meeting the
16-Week Deadline

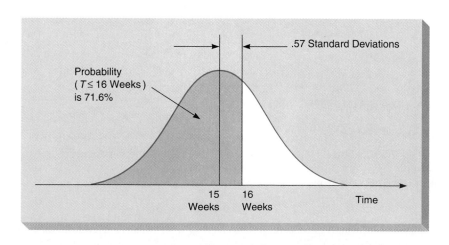

---

[2] You should be aware that noncritical activities also have variability (as seen in Table 13.2). This means that it is possible for a noncritical path to have a higher probability of completion in a shorter time than the probability of completion along the critical path. In fact, a different critical path can evolve because of the probabilistic situation.

What PERT Was Able to Provide

PERT has thus far been able to provide Lester Harky with several valuable pieces of management information:

1. The project's expected completion date is 15 weeks.

2. There is a 71.6% chance that the equipment will be in place within the 16-week deadline. PERT can easily find the probability of finishing by any date Harky is interested in.

3. Five activities (A, C, E, G, H) are on the critical path. If any one of them is delayed for any reason, the entire project will be delayed.

4. Three activities (B, D, F) are not critical but have some slack time built in. This means that Harky can borrow from their resources, if needed, possibly to speed up the entire project.

5. A detailed schedule of activity starting and ending dates has been made available (see Table 13.3).

The sixth and final step is to monitor and control the project using the information provided by PERT.

Dummy Activities in PERT

Before leaving the basics of PERT, we should point out that it is sometimes necessary to use dummy activities to draw a network. A *dummy activity* is an imaginary activity that consumes no time; it is inserted for the sole purpose of preserving the precedence logic of the network.

This can be illustrated by assuming that General Foundry has one more restriction in installing its air pollution control equipment. Recall that activity D (pour concrete/install frame) had only one activity preceding it (B) in the original network. What would happen if activity A also had to be completed before D could begin? A beginning student might try to draw an arrow for activity A from node 1 to node 3 where activity D starts. This would result in two arrows (or two activities) being drawn from node 1 to node 3. This would make drawing the rest of the network extremely difficult, and it would make solving the network a nightmare. Another mistake that some beginning students make is to do nothing and leave the network the way it is. The solution will probably be wrong. If activity A took 6 weeks instead of 2 weeks, what would happen if you did not change the network? The solution to the network, shown in Table 13.3, reveals that activity D can be started after week 3 (ES = 3 for activity D). But because activity A takes 6 weeks and must be completed before activity D can be started, the entire solution is incorrect. One of the best solutions to these problems is to use a dummy activity. A dummy activity will allow you to draw and solve the network correctly. Here is how it is done.

In this case a dummy activity, shown in Figure 13.9 as a dashed line, must be inserted between events 2 and 3 to make the diagram reflect the actual situation. Although the dummy activity has a time of 0 weeks, it is possible for it to have an impact on the critical path analysis. Check for yourself to see if this occurs in the example. Is the path A–C–E–G–H still critical, or has it changed because of the dummy activity in Figure 13.9?

Adding a dummy activity to the network may be necessary.

Sensitivity Analysis and Project Management

During any project, the time required to complete an activity can vary from the projected or expected time. If the activity is on the critical path, the total project completion time will change as discussed previously. In addition to having an impact on the total project

FIGURE 13.9

Dummy Activity in General Foundry's PERT Network

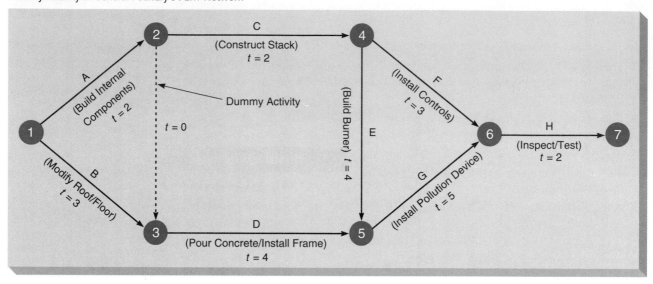

completion time, there is also an impact on the earliest start, earliest finish, latest start, latest finish, and slack times for other activities. The exact impact depends on the relationship between the various activities.

In previous sections we have defined an immediate predecessor activity as an activity that comes immediately before a given activity. In general, a *predecessor activity* is one that must be completed before the given activity can be started. Consider activity G (install pollution device) for the General Foundry example. As seen previously, this activity is on the critical path. Predecessor activities are A, B, C, D, and E. All of these activities must be completed before activity G can be started. A *successor activity* is an activity that can be started only after the given activity is finished. Activity H is the only successor activity for activity G. A *parallel activity* is an activity that does not directly depend on the given activity. Again consider activity G. Are there any parallel activities for this activity? Looking at the network for General Foundry, it can be seen that activity F is a parallel activity of activity G.

Once predecessor, successor, and parallel activities have been defined, we can explore the impact that an increase (decrease) in an activity time for a critical path activity would have on other activities in the network. The results are summarized in Table 13.4. If the time it takes to complete activity G increases, there will be an increase in the earliest start, earliest finish, latest start, and latest finish times for all successor activities. Because these activities follow activity G, these times will also increase. Because slack time is equal to latest finish time minus the earliest finish time (or the latest start time minus earliest start time; LF $-$ EF or LS $-$ ES), there will be no change in the slack for successor activities. Because activity G is on the critical path, an increase in activity time will increase the total project competition time. This would mean that the latest finish, latest start, and slack time will also increase for all parallel activities. You can prove this to yourself by completing a backward pass through the

TABLE 13.4 Impact of an Increase (Decrease) in an Activity Time for a Critical Path Activity

ACTIVITY TIME	SUCCESSOR ACTIVITY	PARALLEL ACTIVITY	PREDECESSOR ACTIVITY
Earliest start	Increase (decrease)	No Change	No change
Earliest finish	Increase (decrease)	No Change	No change
Latest start	Increase (decrease)	Increase (decrease)	No change
Latest finish	Increase (decrease)	Increase (decrease)	No change
Slack	No change	Increase (decrease)	No change

network using a higher total project competition time. There are no changes for predecessor activities.

13.3 PERT/COST

Although PERT is an excellent method of monitoring and controlling project length, it does not consider another very important factor, project *cost*. *PERT/Cost* is a modification of PERT that allows a manager to plan, schedule, monitor, and control cost as well as time.

Using PERT/Cost to plan, schedule, monitor, and control project cost helps accomplish the sixth and final step of PERT.

We begin this section by investigating how costs can be planned and scheduled. Then we see how costs can be monitored and controlled.

 IN ACTION   Costing Projects at Nortel

Many companies, including Nortel, a large telecommunications company, are benefiting from project management. With more than 20,000 active projects worth a total of more than $2 billion, effectively managing projects at Nortel has been challenging. Getting the needed input data, including times and costs, can be difficult.

Like most companies, Nortel used standard accounting practices to monitor and control costs. This typically involves allocating costs to each department. Most projects, however, span multiple departments. This can make it very difficult to get timely cost information. Project managers often get project cost data later than they wanted. Because the cost data are allocated to departments, the data are often not detailed enough to help manage projects and get an accurate picture of true project costs.

To get more accurate cost data for project management, Nortel adopted an Activity-Based-Costing (ABC) method often used in manufacturing operations. In addition to standard cost data, each project activity was coded with a project identification number and a regional R&D location number. This greatly improved the ability of project managers to control costs. Because some of the month-end costing processes were simplified, the approach also lowered project costs in most cases. Project managers also were able to get more detailed costing information. Because the cost data were coded for each project, getting timely feedback was also possible. In this case, getting good input data reduced project costs, reduced the time needed to get critical project feedback, and made project management more accurate.

Source: Chris Dorey. "The ABCs of R&D at Nortel," *CMA Magazine* (March 1998): 19.

Planning and Scheduling Project Costs: Budgeting Process

The overall approach in the budgeting process of a project is to determine how much is to be spent every week or month. This is accomplished as follows:

Four Steps of the Budgeting Process

1. Identify all costs associated with each of the activities. Then add these costs together to get one estimated cost or budget for each activity.

2. If you are dealing with a large project, several activities may be combined into larger work packages. A *work package* is simply a logical collection of activities. Since the General Foundry project we have been discussing is small, one activity will be a work package.

3. Convert the budgeted cost per activity into a cost per time period. To do this, we assume that the cost of completing any activity is spent at a uniform rate over time. Thus, if the budgeted cost for a given activity is $48,000 and the activity's expected time is four weeks, the budgeted cost per week is $12,000 (= $48,000/4 weeks).

4. Using the earliest and latest start times, find out how much money should be spent during each week or month to finish the project by the date desired.

Budgeting for General Foundry   Let us apply this budgeting process to the General Foundry problem. Lester Harky has carefully computed the costs associated with each of his eight activities. He has also divided the total budget for each activity by the activity's expected completion time to determine the weekly budget for the activity. The budget for activity A, for example, is $22,000 (see Table 13.5). Since its expected time (t) is 2 weeks, $11,000 is spent each week to complete the activity. Table 13.5 also provides two pieces of data we found earlier using PERT: the earliest start time (ES) and latest start time (LS) for each activity.

Looking at the total of the budgeted activity costs, we see that the entire project will cost $308,000. Finding the weekly budget will help Harky determine how the project is progressing on a week-to-week basis.

TABLE 13.5 **Activity Cost for General Foundry, Inc.**

ACTIVITY	EARLIEST START TIME, ES	LATEST START TIME, LS	EXPECTED TIME, t	TOTAL BUDGETED COST ($)	BUDGETED COST PER WEEK ($)
A	0	0	2	22,000	11,000
B	0	1	3	30,000	10,000
C	2	2	2	26,000	13,000
D	3	4	4	48,000	12,000
E	4	4	4	56,000	14,000
F	4	10	3	30,000	10,000
G	8	8	5	80,000	16,000
H	13	13	2	16,000	8,000
			Total	308,000	

The weekly budget for the project is developed from the data in Table 13.5. The earliest start time for activity A, for example, is 0. Because A takes 2 weeks to complete, its weekly budget of $11,000 should be spent in weeks 1 and 2. For activity B, the earliest start time is 0, the expected completion time is 3 weeks, and the budgeted cost per week is $10,000. Thus, $10,000 should be spent for activity B in each of weeks 1, 2, and 3. Using the earliest start time, we can find the exact weeks during which the budget for each activity should be spent. These weekly amounts can be summed for all activities to arrive at the weekly budget for the entire project. This is shown in Table 13.6.

A budget is computed using ES.

Do you see how the weekly budget for the project (total per week) is determined in Table 13.6? The only two activities that can be performed during the first week are activities A and B because their earliest start times are 0. Thus, during the first week, a total of $21,000 should be spent. Because activities A and B are still being performed in the second week, a total of $21,000 should also be spent during that period. The earliest start time for activity C is at the end of week 2 (ES = 2 for activity C). Thus $13,000 is spent on activity C in both weeks 3 and 4. Because activity B is also being performed during week 3, the total budget in week 3 is $23,000. Similar computations are done for all activities to determine the total budget for the entire project for each week. Then these weekly totals can be added to determine the total amount that should be spent to date (total to date). This information is displayed in the bottom row of the table.

Those activities along the critical path must spend their budgets at the times shown in Table 13.6. The activities that are *not* on the critical path, however, can be started at a later date. This concept is embodied in the latest starting time, LS, for each activity. Thus, if *latest starting times* are used, another budget can be obtained. This budget will delay the expenditure of funds until the last possible moment. The procedures for computing the budget when LS is used are the same as when ES is used. The results of the new computations are shown in Table 13.7.

Another budget is computed using LS.

T A B L E 1 3 . 6 Budgeted Cost (Thousand of Dollars) for General Foundry, Inc., Using Earliest Start Times

ACTIVITY	WEEK 1	2	3	4	5	6	7	8	9	10	11	12	13	14	15	TOTAL
A	11	11														22
B	10	10	10													30
C			13	13												26
D				12	12	12	12									48
E					14	14	14	14								56
F					10	10	10									30
G									16	16	16	16	16			80
H														8	8	16
																308
Total per week	21	21	23	25	36	36	36	14	16	16	16	16	16	8	8	
Total to date	21	42	65	90	126	162	198	212	228	244	260	276	292	300	308	

TABLE 13.7   Budgeted Cost (Thousand of Dollars) for General Foundry, Inc., Using Latest Start Times

ACTIVITY	1	2	3	4	5	6	7	8	9	10	11	12	13	14	15	TOTAL
A	11	11														22
B		10	10	10												30
C			13	13												26
D					12	12	12	12								48
E					14	14	14	14								56
F											10	10	10			30
G									16	16	16	16	16			80
H														8	8	16
																308
Total per week	11	21	23	23	26	26	26	26	16	16	26	26	26	8	8	
Total to date	11	32	55	78	104	130	156	182	198	214	240	266	292	300	308	

Compare the budgets given in Tables 13.6 and 13.7. The amount that should be spent to date (total to date) for the budget in Table 13.7 uses fewer financial resources in the first few weeks. This is because this budget is prepared using the latest start times. Thus the budget in Table 13.7 shows the *latest* possible time that funds can be expended and still finish the project on time. The budget in Table 13.6 reveals the *earliest* possible time that funds can be expended. Therefore, a manager can choose any budget that falls between the budgets presented in these two tables. These two tables form feasible budget ranges. This concept is illustrated in Figure 13.10.

The budget ranges for General Foundry were established by plotting the total-to-date budgets for ES and LS. Lester Harky can use any budget between these feasible ranges and still complete the air pollution project on time. Budgets like the ones shown in Figure 13.10 are normally developed before the project is started. Then, as the project is being completed, funds expended should be monitored and controlled.

Monitoring and Controlling Project Costs

Is the project on schedule and within its budget?

The purpose of monitoring and controlling project costs is to ensure that the project is progressing on schedule and that cost overruns are kept to a minimum. The status of the entire project should be checked periodically.

Lester Harky wants to know how his air pollution project is going. It is now the sixth week of the 15-week project. Activities A, B, and C have been finished. These activities incurred costs of $20,000, $36,000, and $26,000, respectively. Activity D is only 10% completed and so far the cost expended has been $6,000. Activity E is 20% completed with an incurred cost of $20,000, and activity F is 20% completed with an incurred cost of $4,000. Activities G and H have not been started. Is the air pollution project on schedule? What is the value of work completed? Are there any cost overruns?

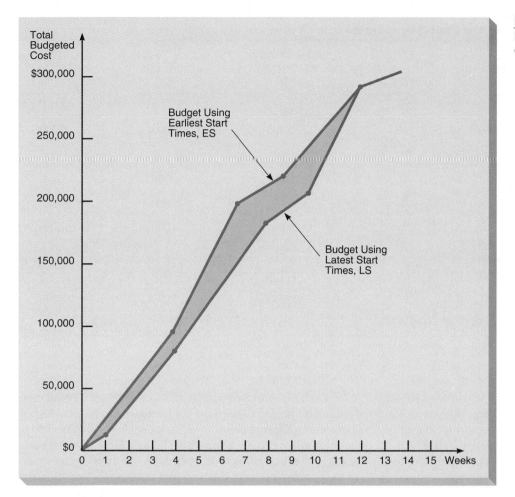

FIGURE 13.10
Budget Ranges for
General Foundry

The value of work completed, or the cost to date for any activity, can be computed as follows:

$$\text{value of work completed} = (\text{percent of work completed}) \times (\text{total activity budget}) \quad \text{(13-8)}$$

The activity difference is also of interest:

$$\text{activity difference} = \text{actual cost} - \text{value of work completed} \quad \text{(13-9)}$$

If an activity difference is negative, there is a cost underrun, but if the number is positive, there has been a cost overrun.

Table 13.8 provides this information for General Foundry. The second column contains the total budgeted cost (from Table 13.6), while the third column contains the percent of completion. With these data and the actual cost expended for each activity, we can compute the value of work completed and the overruns or underruns for every activity.

One way to measure the value of the work completed is to multiply the total budgeted cost times the percent of completion for every activity.[3] Activity D, for example, has a value

Compute the value of work completed by multiplying budgeted cost times percent of completion.

---

[3] The percent of completion for each activity can be measured in other ways as well. For example, one might examine the ratio of labor hours expended to total labor hours estimated.

TABLE 13.8 **Monitoring and Controlling Budgeted Cost**

ACTIVITY	TOTAL BUDGETED COST ($)	PERCENT OF COMPLETION	VALUE OF WORK COMPLETED ($)	ACTUAL COST ($)	ACTIVITY DIFFERENCE ($)
A	22,000	100	22,000	20,000	−2,000
B	30,000	100	30,000	36,000	6,000
C	26,000	100	26,000	26,000	0
D	48,000	10	4,800	6,000	1,200
E	56,000	20	11,200	20,000	8,800
F	30,000	20	6,000	4,000	−2,000
G	80,000	0	0	0	0
H	16,000	0	0	0	0
		Total	100,000	112,000	12,000
					Overrun

of work completed of $4,800 (= $48,000 times 10%). To determine the amount of overrun or underrun for any activity, the value of work completed is subtracted from the actual cost. These differences can be added to determine the overrun or underrun for the project. As you see, at week 6 there is a $12,000 cost overrun. Furthermore, the value of work completed is only $100,000, and the actual cost of the project to date is $112,000. How do these costs compare with the budgeted costs for week 6? If Harky had decided to use the budget for earliest start times (see Table 13.6) we can see that $162,000 should have been spent. Thus the project is behind schedule and there are cost overruns. Harky needs to move faster on this project to finish on time, and he must control future costs carefully to try to eliminate the

IN ACTION   **Project Management and Software Development**

While computers have revolutionized how companies conduct business and allowed some organizations to achieve a long-term competitive advantage in the marketplace, the software that controls these computers is often more expensive than intended and takes longer to develop than expected. In some cases, large software projects are never fully completed. The London Stock Exchange, for example, had an ambitious software project called TAURUS that was intended to improve computer operations at the exchange. The TAURUS project, which cost hundreds of millions of dollars, was never completed. After numerous delays and cost overruns, the project was finally halted. The FLORIDA system, an ambitious software development project for the Department of Health and Rehabilitative Services (HRS) for the state of Florida, was also delayed, cost more than expected, and didn't operate as

everyone had hoped. Although not all software development projects are delayed or over budget, it has been estimated that more than half of all software projects cost more than 189% of their original projections.

To control large software projects, many companies are now using project management techniques. Ryder Systems, Inc., American Express Financial Advisors, and United Airlines have all created project management departments for their software and information systems projects. These departments have the authority to monitor large software projects and make changes to deadlines, budgets, and resources used to complete software development efforts.

Source: Julia King. "Tough Love Reins in IS Projects," *Computerworld* (June 19, 1995): 25.

current cost overrun of $12,000. To monitor and control costs, the budgeted amount, the value of work completed, and the actual costs should be computed periodically.

In the next section we see how a project can be shortened by spending additional money. The technique is called the critical path method (CPM).

13.4 CRITICAL PATH METHOD

As mentioned earlier, CPM is a *deterministic* network model. This means it assumes that both the time to complete each activity and the cost of doing so are known with certainty. Unlike PERT, it does not employ probability concepts. Instead, CPM uses two sets of time and cost estimates for activities: a normal time and cost and a crash time and cost. The *normal time* estimate is like PERT's expected time. The *normal cost* is an estimate of how much money it will take to complete an activity in its normal time. The *crash time* is the shortest possible activity time. *Crash cost* is the price of completing the activity on a crash or deadline basis. The critical path calculations for a CPM network follow the same steps as used in PERT; you just find the early start times (ES), late start times (LS), early finish (EF), late finish (LF), and slack as shown earlier.

CPM is deterministic.

Project Crashing with CPM

Suppose that General Foundry had been given 14 weeks instead of 16 weeks to install the new pollution control equipment or face a court-ordered shutdown. As you recall, the length of Lester Harky's critical path was 15 weeks. What can he do? We see that Harky cannot possibly meet the deadline unless he is able to shorten some of the activity times. This process of shortening a project, called *crashing*, is usually achieved by adding extra resources (such as equipment or people) to an activity. Naturally, crashing costs more money, and managers are usually interested in speeding up a project at the *least additional cost*.

Project crashing with CPM involves four steps:

Shortening a project is called **crashing.**

Four Steps of Project Crashing

1. Find the normal critical path and identify the critical activities.
2. Compute the crash cost per week (or other time period) for all activities in the network. This process uses the following formula[4]:

$$\text{crash cost/time period} = \frac{\text{crash cost} - \text{normal cost}}{\text{normal time} - \text{crash time}} \qquad \textbf{(13-10)}$$

3. Select the activity on the critical path with the smallest crash cost per week. Crash this activity to the maximum extent possible or to the point at which your desired deadline has been reached.
4. Check to be sure that the critical path you were crashing is still critical. Often, a reduction in activity time along the critical path causes a noncritical path or paths to become critical. If the critical path is still the longest path through the network, return to step 3. If not, find the new critical path and return to step 3.

General Foundry's normal and crash times and normal and crash costs are shown in Table 13.9. Note, for example, that activity B's normal time is 3 weeks (this estimate was

[4] This formula assumes that crash costs are linear. If they are not, the approach will not work.

T A B L E   1 3 . 9   Normal and Crash Data for General Foundry, Inc.

ACTIVITY	TIME (WEEKS)		COST ($)		CRASH COST PER WEEK ($)	CRITICAL PATH?
	NORMAL	CRASH	NORMAL	CRASH		
A	2	1	22,000	23,000	1,000	Yes
B	3	1	30,000	34,000	2,000	No
C	2	1	26,000	27,000	1,000	Yes
D	4	3	48,000	49,000	1,000	No
E	4	2	56,000	58,000	1,000	Yes
F	3	2	30,000	30,500	500	No
G	5	2	80,000	86,000	2,000	Yes
H	2	1	16,000	19,000	3,000	Yes

also used for PERT) and its crash time is 1 week. This means that the activity can be shortened by 2 weeks if extra resources are provided. The normal cost is $30,000, while the crash cost is $34,000. This implies that crashing activity B will cost General Foundry an additional $4,000. CPM assumes that crashing costs are linear. As shown in Figure 13.11, activity B's crash cost per week is $2,000. Crash costs for all other activities can be computed in a similar fashion. Then steps 3 and 4 may be applied to reduce the project's completion time.

Activities A, C, and E are on the critical path and each have a minimum crash cost per week of $1,000. Harky can crash Activity A by 1 week to reduce the project completion time to 14 weeks. The cost is an additional $1,000.

At this stage, there are two critical paths. The original critical path consists of Activities A, C, E, G, and H, with a total completion time of 14 weeks. The new critical path consists of Activities B, D, G, and H, also with a total completion time of 14 weeks. Any

FIGURE 13.11

Crash and Normal Times and Costs for Activity B

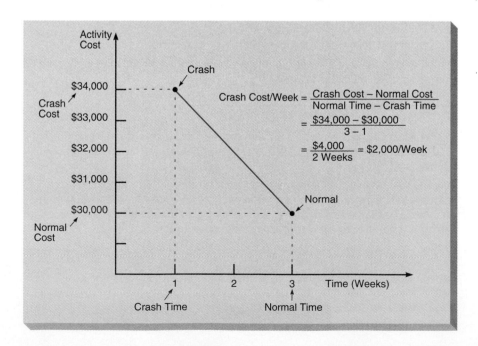

further crashing must be done to both critical paths. For example, if Harky wants to reduce the project completion time by an additional 2 weeks, both paths must be reduced. This can be done by reducing Activity G, which is on both critical paths, by two weeks for an additional cost of $2,000 per week. The total completion time would be 12 weeks, and total crashing cost would be $5,000 ($1,000 to reduce Activity A by one week and $4,000 to reduce Activity G by two weeks).

There are now two critical paths.

For small networks, such as General Foundry's, it is possible to use the four-step procedure to find the least cost of reducing the project completion dates. For larger networks, however, this approach is difficult and impractical, and more sophisticated techniques, such as linear programming, must be employed.

Project Crashing with Linear Programming

Linear programming (see Chapters 7 to 9) is another approach to finding the best-project crashing schedule. We illustrate its use on General Foundry's network. The data needed are derived from Table 13.9 and Figure 13.12.

We begin by defining the decision variables. If X is the time an event will occur, measured since the beginning of the project, then

The first step is to define decision variables for the linear program.

X_1 = time event 1 will occur

X_2 = time event 2 will occur

X_3 = time event 3 will occur

X_4 = time event 4 will occur

X_5 = time event 5 will occur

X_6 = time event 6 will occur

X_7 = time event 7 will occur

Y is defined as the number of weeks that each activity is crashed. Y_A is the number of weeks we decide to crash activity A, Y_B the amount of crash time used for activity B, and so on, up to Y_H.

FIGURE 13.12

General Foundry's Network with Activity Times

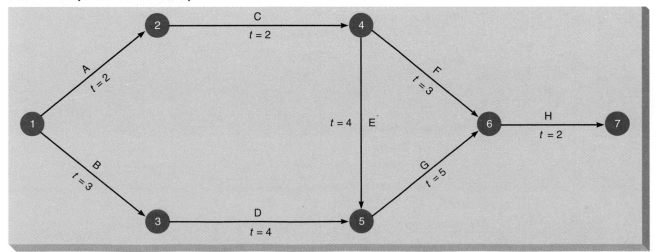

The next step is to determine the objective function.

Objective Function Since the objective is to minimize the cost of crashing the total project, our LP objective function is

$$\text{minimize crash cost} = 1{,}000Y_A + 2{,}000Y_B + 1{,}000Y_C + 1{,}000Y_D + 1{,}000Y_E + 500Y_F + 2{,}000Y_G + 3{,}000Y_H$$

(These cost coefficients were drawn from the sixth column of Table 13.9.)

Crash Time Constraints Constraints are required to ensure that each activity is not crashed more than its maximum allowable crash time. The maximum for each Y variable is the difference between the normal time and the crash time (from Table 13.9):

Crash constraints are determined next.

$$Y_A \leqslant 1$$

$$Y_B \leqslant 2$$

$$Y_C \leqslant 1$$

$$Y_D \leqslant 1$$

$$Y_E \leqslant 2$$

$$Y_F \leqslant 1$$

$$Y_G \leqslant 3$$

$$Y_H \leqslant 1$$

Project Completion Constraint This constraint specifies that the last event must take place before the project deadline date. If Harky's project must be crashed down to 12 weeks, then

$$X_7 \leqslant 12$$

Constraints Describing the Network The final set of constraints describes the structure of the network. There will be one or more constraints for each event. We begin by setting the event-occurrence time for event 1 to be $X_1 = 0$.

For event 2,

X_2	$\geqslant$	normal time for A	$-$	Y_A	$+$	0
Occurrence time for event 2		*Two weeks it takes for activity A*		*Number of weeks A is crashed*		*Start time for activity A* $(X_1 = 0)$

The final step is to determine event constraints.

$$X_2 \geqslant 2 - Y_A$$

or

$$X_2 + Y_A \geqslant 2$$

For event 3,

$$X_3 \geqslant 3 - Y_B + 0$$

or

$$X_3 + Y_B \geqslant 3$$

For event 4, we note that activity C begins with event 2, X_2, not 0:

$$X_4 \geqslant 2 - Y_C + X_2$$

or

$$X_4 - X_2 + Y_C \geq 2$$

For event 5, we need two constraints. The first represents the path from activity D:

$$X_5 \geq 4 - Y_D + X_3$$

or

$$X_5 - X_3 + Y_D \geq 4$$

The second constraint is the path along activity E.

$$X_5 \geq 4 - Y_E + X_4$$

or

$$X_5 - X_4 + Y_E \geq 4$$

For event 6, again two constraints are needed:

$$X_6 \geq 3 - Y_F + X_4$$

or

$$X_6 - X_4 + Y_F \geq 3$$

The second constraint is

$$X_6 \geq 5 - Y_G + X_5$$

or

$$X_6 - X_5 + Y_G \geq 5$$

For event 7,

$$X_7 \geq 2 - Y_H + X_6$$

or

$$X_7 - X_6 + Y_H \geq 2$$

After adding nonnegativity constraints, this linear programming problem can be solved for the optimal Y values. This can be done with QM for Windows or Excel.

Summary

The fundamentals of PERT and CPM have been presented in this chapter. Both of these techniques are excellent for controlling large and complex projects.

PERT is probabilistic and allows three time estimates for each activity. These estimates are used to compute the project's expected completion time, variance, and the probability that the project will be completed by a given date. PERT/Cost, an extension of standard PERT, can be used to plan, schedule, monitor, and control project costs. Using PERT/Cost, it is possible to determine if there are cost overruns or underruns at any point in time. It is also possible to determine whether the project is on schedule.

CPM, although similar to PERT, has the ability to crash projects by reducing their completion time through additional resource expenditures. Finally, we saw that linear programming can also be used to crash a network by a desired amount at a minimum cost.

Glossary

PERT. Program Evaluation and Review Technique. A network technique that allows three time estimates for each activity in a project.

Activity. A time-consuming job or task that is a key subpart of the total project.

Event. A point in time that marks the beginning or ending of an activity.

Immediate Predecessor. An activity that must be completed before another activity can be started.

Network. A graphical display of a project that contains both activities and events.

Activity Time Estimates. Three time estimates that are used in determining the expected completion time and variance for an activity in a PERT network.

Optimistic Time (a). The shortest amount of time that could be required to complete the activity.

Pessimistic Time (b). The greatest amount of time that could be required to complete the activity.

Most Likely Time (m). The amount of time that you would expect it would take to complete the activity.

Beta Probability Distribution. A probability distribution that is often used in computing the expected activity completion times and variances in networks.

Variance of Activity Completion Time. A measure of dispersion of the activity completion time. Variance $= [(b - a)/6]^2$.

Expected Activity Time. The average time that it should take to complete an activity. $t = (a + 4m + b)/6$.

Earliest Start Time (ES). The earliest time that an activity can start without violation of precedence requirements.

Earliest Finish Time (EF). The earliest time that an activity can be finished without violation of precedence requirements.

Latest Start Time (LS). The latest time that an activity can be started without delaying the entire project.

Latest Finish Time (LF). The latest time that an activity can be finished without delaying the entire project.

Forward Pass. A procedure that moves from the beginning of a network to the end of the network. It is used in determining earliest activity start times and earliest finish times.

Backward Pass. A procedure that moves from the end of the network to the beginning of the network. It is used in determining the latest finish and start times.

Slack Time. The amount of time that an activity can be delayed without delaying the entire project. Slack is equal to the latest start time minus the earliest start time, or the latest finish time minus the earliest finish time.

Critical Path. The series of activities that have a zero slack. It is the longest time path through the network. A delay for any activity that is on the critical path will delay the completion of the entire project.

Critical Path Analysis. An analysis that determines the total project completion time, the critical path for the project, slack, ES, EF, LS, and LF for every activity.

Dummy Activity. A fictitious activity that consumes no time and is inserted into a network to make the network display the proper predecessor relationships between activities.

PERT/Cost. A technique that allows a decision maker to plan, schedule, monitor, and control project *cost* as well as project time.

CPM. Critical path method. A deterministic network technique that is similar to PERT but allows for project crashing.

Crashing. The process of reducing the total time that it takes to complete a project by expending additional funds.

Key Equations

(13-1) $t = \dfrac{a + 4m + b}{6}$

Expected activity completion time.

(13-2) $\text{Variance} = \left(\dfrac{b - a}{6}\right)^2$

Activity variance.

(13-3) $EF = ES + t$

Earliest finish time.

(13-4) $LS = LF - t$

Latest start time.

(13-5) $\text{Slack} = LS - ES \quad or \quad \text{slack} = LF - EF$

Slack time in an activity.

(13-6) Project variance $= \Sigma$ variances of activities on critical path.

(13-7) $Z = \dfrac{\text{due date} - \text{expected date of completion}}{\sigma_T}$

Number of standard deviations the target date lies from the expected date, using the normal distribution.

(13-8) Value of work completed = (percent of work completed) $\times$ (total activity budget)

(13-9) Activity difference = actual cost $-$ value of work completed

(13-10) crash cost/time period $= \dfrac{\text{crash cost} - \text{normal cost}}{\text{normal time} - \text{crash time}}$

The cost in CPM of reducing an activity's length per time period.

Solved Problems

Solved Problem 13-1

To complete the wing assembly for an experimental aircraft, Scott DeWitte has laid out the major steps and seven activities involved. These activities have been labeled A through G in the following table, which also shows their estimated completion times (in weeks) and immediate predecessors. Determine the expected time and variance for each activity.

ACTIVITY	a	m	b	IMMEDIATE PREDECESSORS
A	1	2	3	—
B	2	3	4	—
C	4	5	6	A
D	8	9	10	B
E	2	5	8	C, D
F	4	5	6	B
G	1	2	3	E

Solution

Although not required for this problem, a diagram of all the activities can be useful. A PERT diagram for the wing assembly is shown in Figure 13.13.

FIGURE 13.13

PERT Diagram for Scott DeWitte (Solved Problem 13-1)

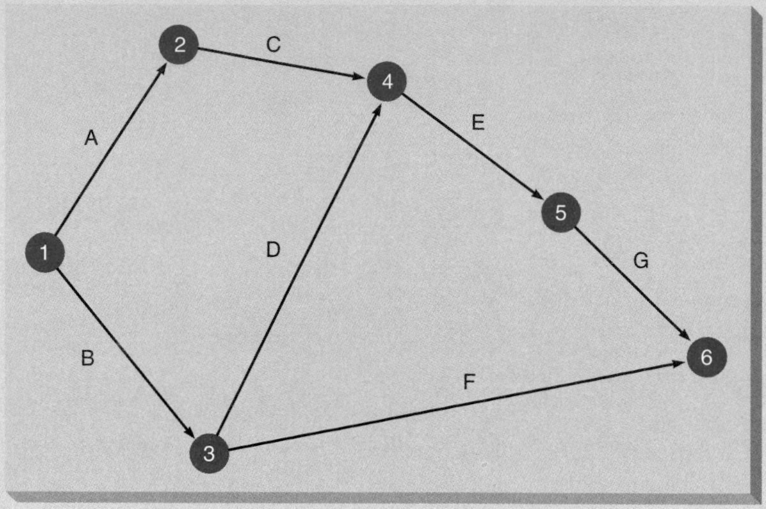

Expected times and variances can be computed using the formulas presented in the chapter. The results are summarized in the following table:

ACTIVITY	NODES	EXPECTED TIME (in weeks)	VARIANCE
A	1–2	2	$\frac{1}{9}$
B	1–3	3	$\frac{1}{9}$
C	2–4	5	$\frac{1}{9}$
D	3–4	9	$\frac{1}{9}$
E	4–5	5	1
F	3–6	5	$\frac{1}{9}$
G	5–6	2	$\frac{1}{9}$

Solved Problem 13-2

Referring to Solved Problem 13-1, now Scott would like to determine the critical path for the entire wing assembly project as well as the expected completion time for the total project. In addition, he would like to determine the earliest and latest start and finish times for all activities.

Solution

The critical path, earliest start times, earliest finish times, latest start times, and latest finish times can be determined using the procedures outlined in the chapter. The results are summarized in the following table.

		ACTIVITY TIME				
ACTIVITY	**NODES**	**ES**	**EF**	**LS**	**LF**	**SLACK**
A	1-2	0	2	5	7	5
B	1–3	0	3	0	3	0
C	2–4	2	7	7	12	5
D	3–4	3	12	3	12	0
E	4–5	12	17	12	17	0
F	3–6	3	8	14	19	11
G	5–6	17	19	17	19	0

Expected project length = 19 weeks

Variance of the critical path = 1.333

Standard deviation of the critical path = 1.155 weeks

The activities along the critical path are B, D, E, and G. These activities have zero slack, as shown in the table. The expected project completion time is 19. The earliest and latest start and finish times are shown in the table.

SELF-TEST

- Before taking the self-test, refer back to the learning objectives at the beginning of the chapter, the notes in the margins, and the glossary at the end of the chapter.
- Use the key at the back of the book to correct your answers.
- Restudy pages that correspond to any questions that you answered incorrectly or material you feel uncertain about.

1. Network models such as PERT and CPM are used to
   a. manage complex projects.
   b. save time.
   c. save money.
   d. all of the above.
   e. none of the above.
2. PERT is an acronym for
   a. Practical Evaluation and Research Technique.
   b. Program Evaluation and Review Technique.
   c. Performance Elevation and Restoration Time.
   d. Promotion Effectiveness and Retail Trial.
   e. none of the above.
3. In PERT, if the most pessimistic time was 14 weeks, the most optimistic time was 8 weeks, and the most likely time was 11 weeks,
   a. the variance would be 1 week.
   b. the variance would be 11 weeks.
   c. the expected time would be 6 weeks.
   d. the expected time would be 5 ½ weeks.
   e. not enough information.
   f. none of the above.
4. The critical path is
   a. the least-slack path.
   b. the longest time path through the network.
   c. that series of activities whose delay is most likely to delay the entire project.
   d. one or more paths through a network whose last activity EF time is the largest for any activity in the project.
   e. all of the above.
   f. none of the above.
5. PERT never uses
   a. activities with probabilistic times.
   b. deterministic activities.
   c. dummy activities.
   d. activity variance estimates.
   e. none of the above.
6. In PERT, the time estimate b represents
   a. the most optimistic time.
   b. the most likely time.
   c. the most pessimistic time.
   d. the expected time.
   e. none of the above.
7. In PERT, slack time equals
   a. $ES + t$.
   b. $LS - ES$.

   c. zero.
   d. $EF - ES$.
   e. none of the above.
8. The standard deviation for the PERT project is approximately
   a. the square root of the sum of the variances along the critical path.
   b. the sum of the critical path activity standard deviations.
   c. the square root of the sum of the variances of the project activities.
   d. all of the above.
   e. none of the above.
9. For PERT/Cost the values needed include
   a. normal time.
   b. normal time cost.
   c. crash time.
   d. crash time cost.
   e. all of the above.
   f. none of the above.
10. In CPM, the crash cost per week
    a. is the difference in costs divided by the difference in times (crash and normal).
    b. is considered to be linear in the range between normal and crash.
    c. needs to be determined so that the smallest values on the critical path may be considered for time reduction first.
    d. all of the above.
    e. none of the above.
11. _____ activities are ones that will delay the entire project if they are late or delayed.
12. PERT stands for _____ .
13. Project crashing can be performed using the _____ .
14. PERT requires both a _____ and a _____ to determine the slack for every activity.
15. The _____ technique allows a person to crash a project at minimal cost.
16. PERT can use three estimates for activity time. These three estimates are _____ , _____ , and _____ .
17. The latest start time minus the earliest start time is called the _____ time for any activity.
18. The percent of project completion, value of work completed, and actual activity costs are used to _____ projects.

Discussion Questions and Problems

Discussion Questions

13-1 What are some of the questions that can be answered with PERT and CPM?

13-2 What are the major differences between PERT and CPM?

13-3 What is an activity? What is an event? What is an immediate predecessor?

13-4 Describe how expected activity times and variances can be computed in a PERT network.

13-5 Briefly discuss what is meant by critical path analysis. What are critical path activities, and why are they important?

13-6 What are the earliest activity start time and latest activity start time? How are they computed?

13-7 Describe the meaning of slack and discuss how it can be determined.

13-8 How can we determine the probability that a project will be completed by a certain date? What assumptions are made in this computation?

13-9 Briefly describe PERT/Cost and how it is used.

13-10 What is crashing, and how is it done by hand?

13-11 Why is linear programming useful in CPM crashing?

Problems*

13-12 Sid Davidson is the personnel director of Babson and Willcount, a company that specializes in consulting and research. One of the training programs that Sid is considering for the middle-level managers of Babson and Willcount is leadership training. Sid has listed a number of activities that must be completed before a training program of this nature could be conducted. The activities and immediate predecessors appear in the following table:

ACTIVITY	IMMEDIATE PREDECESSORS
A	—
B	—
C	—
D	B
E	A, D
F	C
G	E, F

Develop a network for this problem.

---

*Note: 🖥 means the problem may be solved with QM for Windows; ✖ means the problem may be solved with Excel; and 🖥 means the problem may be solved with QM for Windows and/or Excel.

13-13 Sid Davidson was able to determine the activity times for the leadership training program. He would like to determine the total project completion time and the critical path. The activity times appear in the following table (see Problem 13-12):

ACTIVITY	TIME (DAYS)
A	2
B	5
C	1
D	10
E	3
F	6
G	8
	35

13-14 Monohan Machinery specializes in developing weed-harvesting equipment that is used to clear small lakes of weeds. George Monohan, president of Monohan Machinery, is convinced that harvesting weeds is far better than using chemicals to kill weeds. Chemicals cause pollution, and the weeds seem to grow faster after chemicals have been used. George is contemplating the construction of a machine that would harvest weeds on narrow rivers and waterways. The activities that are necessary to build one of these experimental weedharvesting machines are listed in the following table. Construct a network for these activities.

ACTIVITIES	IMMEDIATE PREDECESSORS
A	—
B	—
C	A
D	A
E	B
F	B
G	C, E
H	D, F

13-15 After consulting with Butch Radner, George Monohan was able to determine the activity times for constructing the weed-harvesting machine to be used on narrow rivers. George would like to determine ES, EF, LS, LF, and slack for each activity. The total project completion time and the critical path should also be determined. (See Problem 13-14 for details.) The activity times are shown in the following table:

ACTIVITY	TIME (WEEKS)
A	6
B	5
C	3
D	2
E	4
F	6
G	10
H	7

13-16 Zuckerman Wiring and Electric is a company that installs wiring and electrical fixtures in residential construction. John Zuckerman has been concerned with the amount of time that it takes to complete wiring jobs. Some of his workers are very unreliable. A list of activities and their optimistic, their pessimistic, and their most likely completion times in days are given in the following table:

	DAYS			
IMMEDIATE ACTIVITY	*a*	*m*	*b*	PREDECESSORS
A	3	6	8	—
B	2	4	4	—
C	1	2	3	—
D	6	7	8	C
E	2	4	6	B, D
F	6	10	14	A, E
G	1	2	4	A, E
H	3	6	9	F
I	10	11	12	G
J	14	16	20	C
K	2	8	10	H, I

Determine the expected completion time and variance for each activity.

13-17 John Zuckerman would like to determine the total project completion time and the critical path for installing electrical wiring and equipment in residential houses. See Problem 13-16 for details. In addition, determine ES, EF, LS, LF, and slack for each activity.

13-18 What is the probability that Zuckerman will finish the project described in Problems 13-16 and 13-17 in 40 days or less?

13-19 Tom Schriber, director of personnel of Management Resources, Inc., is in the process of designing a program that their customers can use in the job-finding process. Some of the activities include preparing résumés, writing letters, making appointments to see prospective employers, researching companies and industries, and so on. Some of the information on the activities appears in the following table:

ACTIVITY	DAYS a	DAYS m	DAYS b	IMMEDIATE PREDECESSORS
A	8	10	12	—
B	6	7	9	—
C	3	3	4	—
D	10	20	30	A
E	6	7	8	C
F	9	10	11	B, D, E
G	6	7	10	B, D, E
H	14	15	16	F
I	10	11	13	F
J	6	7	8	G, H
K	4	7	8	I, J
L	1	2	4	G, H

(a) Construct a network for this problem.
(b) Determine the expected times and variances for each activity.
(c) Determine ES, EF, LS, LF, and slack for each activity.
(d) Determine the critical path and project completion time.
(e) Determine the probability that the project will be finished in 70 days.
(f) Determine the probability that the project will be finished in 80 days.
(g) Determine the probability that the project will be finished in 90 days.

13-20 Using PERT, Ed Rose was able to determine that the expected project completion time for the construction of a pleasure yacht is 21 months, and the project variance is 4.
(a) What is the probability that the project will be completed in 17 months?
(b) What is the probability that the project will be completed in 20 months?
(c) What is the probability that the project will be completed in 23 months?
(d) What is the probability that the project will be completed in 25 months?

13-21 The air pollution project discussed in the chapter has progressed over the past several weeks and it is now the end of week 8. Lester Harky would like to know the value of the work completed, the amount of any cost overruns or underruns for the project, and the extent to which the project is ahead of schedule or behind schedule by developing a table like Table 13.8. The revised cost figures appear in the following table:

ACTIVITY	PERCENT OF COMPLETION	ACTUAL COST ($)
A	100	20,000
B	100	36,000
C	100	26,000
D	100	44,000
E	50	25,000
F	60	15,000
G	10	5,000
H	10	1,000

13-22 Fred Ridgeway has been given the responsibility of managing a training and development program. He knows the earliest start time, the latest start time, and the total costs for each activity. This information is given in the following table:

ACTIVITY	ES	LS	t	Total Cost ($1,000's)
A	0	0	6	10
B	1	4	2	14
C	3	3	7	5
D	4	9	3	6
E	6	6	10	14
F	14	15	11	13
G	12	18	2	4
H	14	14	11	6
I	18	21	6	18
J	18	19	4	12
K	22	22	14	10
L	22	23	8	16
M	18	24	6	18

(a) Using earliest start times, determine Fred's total monthly budget.
(b) Using latest start times, determine Fred's total monthly budget.

13-23 General Foundry's project crashing data were shown in Table 13.9. Crash this project to 13 weeks using CPM. What are the final times for each activity after crashing?

13-24 Bowman Builders manufactures steel storage sheds for commercial use. Joe Bowman, president of Bowman Builders, is contemplating producing sheds for home use. The activities necessary to build an experimental model and related data are given in the accompanying table.
(a) What is the project completion date?
(b) Formulate a linear programming problem to crash this project to 10 weeks.

ACTIVITY	NORMAL TIME	CRASH TIME	NORMAL COST ($)	CRASH COST ($)	IMMEDIATE PREDECESSORS
A	3	2	1,000	1,600	—
B	2	1	2,000	2,700	—
C	1	1	300	300	—
D	7	3	1,300	1,600	A
E	6	3	850	1,000	B
F	2	1	4,000	5,000	C
G	4	2	1,500	2,000	D, E

13-25 Software Development Specialists (SDS) is involved with developing software for customers in the banking industry. SDS breaks a large programming project into teams that perform the necessary steps. Team A is responsible for going from general systems design all the way through to actual systems testing. This involves 18 separate activities. Team B is then responsible for the final installation.

To determine cost and time factors, optimistic, most likely, and pessimistic time estimates have been made for all of the 18 activities involved for team A. The first step that this team performs is general systems design. The optimistic, most likely, and pessimistic times are 3 weeks, 4 weeks, and 5 weeks. Following this, a number of activities can begin. Activity 2 is involved with procedures design. Optimistic, most likely, and pessimistic times for completing this activity are 4, 5, and 7 weeks. Activity 3 is developing detailed report designs. Optimistic, most likely, and pessimistic time estimates are 6, 8, and 9 weeks. Activity 4, detailed forms design, has optimistic, most likely, and pessimistic time estimates of 2, 3, and 5 weeks.

The fifth and sixth activities involve writing detailed program specifications and developing file specifications. The three time estimates for activity 5 are 6, 7, and 9 weeks, and the three time estimates for activity 6 are 3, 4, and 5 weeks. Activity 7 is to specify system test data. Before this is done, activity 6, involving file specifications, must be completed. The time estimates for activity 7 are 2, 4, and 5 weeks. Activity 8 involves reviewing forms. Before activity 8 can be conducted, detailed forms design must be completed. The time estimates for activity 8 are 3, 4, and 6 weeks. The next activity, activity 9, is reviewing the detailed report design. This requires that the detailed report design, activity 3, be completed first. The time estimates for activity 9 are 1, 2, and 4 weeks, respectively.

Activity 10 involves reviewing procedures design. Time estimates are 1, 3, and 4 weeks. Of course, procedures design must be done before activity 10 can be started. Activity 11 involves the system design checkpoint review. A number of activities must be completed before this is done. These activities include reviewing the forms, reviewing the detailed report design, reviewing the procedures design, writing detailed program specs, and specifying system test data. The optimistic, most likely, and pessimistic time estimates for activity 11 are 3, 4, and 6 weeks. Performing program logic design is activity 12. This can only be started after the system design checkpoint review is completed. The time estimates for activity 12 are 4, 6, and 7 weeks.

Activity 13, coding the programs, is done only after the program logic design is completed. The time estimates for this activity are 6, 8, and 10 weeks. Activity 14 is involved in developing test programs. Activity 13 is the immediate predecessor. Time estimates for activity 14 are 3, 4, and 6 weeks. Developing a system test plan is activity 15. A number of activities must be completed before activity 15 can be started. These activities include specifying system test data, writing detailed program specifications, and reviewing procedure designs, the detailed report design, and forms.

The time estimates for activity 15 are 3, 4, and 5 weeks. Activity 16, creating system test data, has time estimates of 2, 4, and 6 weeks. Activity 15 must be done before activity 16 can be started. Activity 17 is reviewing program test results. The immediate predecessor to activity 17 is to test the programs (activity 14). The three time estimates for activity 17 are 2, 3, and 4 weeks. The final activity is conducting system tests. This is activity 18. Before activity 18 can be started, activities 16 and 17 must be complete. The three time estimates for conducting these system tests are 3, 5, and 6 weeks.

a) How long will it take for team A to complete their programming assignment?

b) What would happen if activity 5, writing detailed program specifications, had larger time estimates? Assume that these larger time estimates are 12, 14, and 15.

T A B L E   1 3 . 1 0   Data for Problem 13-26, Bender Construction Company, on the next page

| ACTIVITY | TIME REQUIRED (WEEKS) | | | DESCRIPTION OF ACTIVITY | IMMEDIATE PREDECESSORS |
	a	m	b		
1	1	4	5	Drafting legal documents	—
2	2	3	4	Preparation of financial statements	—
3	3	4	5	Draft of history	—
4	7	8	9	Draft demand portion of feasibility study	—
5	4	4	5	Review and approval of legal documents	1
6	1	2	4	Review and approval of history	3
7	4	5	6	Review feasibility study	4
8	1	2	4	Draft final financial portion of feasibility study	7
9	3	4	4	Draft facts relevant to the bond transaction	5
10	1	1	2	Review and approval of financial statements	2
11	18	20	26	Firm price received of project	—
12	1	2	3	Review and completion of financial portion of feasibility study	8
13	1	1	2	Draft statement completed	6, 9, 10, 11, 12
14	.10	.14	.16	All material sent to bond rating services	13
15	.2	.3	.4	Statement printed and distributed to all interested parties	14
16	1	1	2	Presentation to bond rating services	14
17	1	2	3	Bond rating received	16
18	3	5	7	Marketing of bonds	15, 17
19	.1	.1	.2	Purchase contract executed	18
20	.1	.14	.16	Final statement authorized and completed	19
21	2	3	6	Purchase contract	19
22	.1	.1	.2	Bond proceeds available	20
23	0	.2	.2	Sign construction contract	21, 22

13-26 The Bender Construction Co. is involved in constructing municipal buildings and other structures that are used primarily by city and state municipalities. This requires developing legal documents, drafting feasibility studies, obtaining bond ratings, and so forth. Recently, Bender was given a request to submit a proposal for the construction of a municipal building. The first step is to develop legal documents and to perform all steps necessary before the construction contract is signed. This requires more than 20 separate activities that must be completed. These activities, their immediate predecessors, and time requirements are given in Table 13.10 on the previous page.

As you can see, optimistic (a), most likely (m), and pessimistic (b) time estimates have been given for all of the activities described in the table. Using the data, determine the total project completion time for this preliminary step, the critical path, and slack time for all activities involved.

13-27 Getting a degree from a college or university can be a long and difficult task. Certain courses must be completed before other courses may be taken. Develop a network diagram, in which every activity is a particular course that must be taken for a given degree program. The immediate predecessors will be course prerequisites. Don't forget to include all university, college, and departmental course requirements. Then try to group these courses into semesters or quarters for your particular school. How long do you think it will take you to graduate? Which courses, if not taken in the proper sequence, could delay your graduation?

13-28 Dream Team Productions was in the final design phases of its new film, *Killer Worms*, to be released next summer. Market Wise, the firm hired to coordinate the release of *Killer Worm* toys, identified 16 critical tasks to be completed before the release of the film.

(a) How many weeks in advance of the film release should Market Wise start its marketing campaign? What are the critical paths? The tasks are as follows:

	START NODE	END NODE	OPTIMISTIC TIME	MOST LIKELY TIME	PESSIMISTIC TIME
Task 1	1	2	1	2	4
Task 2	1	3	3	3.5	4
Task 3	1	4	10	12	13
Task 4	1	5	4	5	7
Task 5	1	6	2	4	5
Task 6	2	7	6	7	8
Task 7	3	7	2	4	5.5
Task 8	4	7	5	7.7	9
Task 9	4	9	9.9	10	12
Task 10	4	8	2	4	5
Task 11	5	8	2	4	6
Task 12	6	8	2	4	6
Task 13	7	9	5	6	6.5
Task 14	8	10	1	1.1	2
Task 15	9	11	5	7	8
Task 16	10	11	5	7	9

(b) If Tasks 9 and 10 were not necessary, what impact would this have on the critical path and the number of weeks needed to complete the marketing campaign?

Data Set Problem

13-29 Sager Products has been in the business of manufacturing and marketing toys for toddlers for the past two decades. Jim Sager, president of the firm, is considering the development of a new manufacturing line to allow it to produce high-quality plastic toys at reasonable prices. The development process is long and complex. Jim estimates that there are five phases involved and multiple activities for each phase.

Phase 1 of the development process involves the completion of four activities. These activities have no immediate predecessors. Activity A has an optimistic completion time of 2 weeks, a probable completion time of 3 weeks, and a pessimistic completion time of 4 weeks. Activity B has estimated completion times of 5, 6, and 8 weeks; these represent optimistic, probable, and pessimistic time estimates. Similarly, activity C has estimated completion times of 1 week, 1 week, and 2 weeks; and activity D has expected completion times of 8 weeks, 9 weeks, and 11 weeks.

Phase 2 involves six separate activities. Activity E has activity A as an immediate predecessor. Time estimates are 1 week, 1 week, and 4 weeks. Activity F and activity G both have activity B as their immediate predecessor. For activity F, the time estimates are 3 weeks, 3 weeks, and 4 weeks. For activity G, the time estimates are 1 week, 2 weeks, and 2 weeks. The only immediate predecessor for activity H is activity C. Time estimates for activity H are 5 weeks, 5 weeks, and 6 weeks. Activity D must be performed before activity I and activity J can be started. Activity I has estimated completion times of 9 weeks, 10 weeks, and 11 weeks. Activity J has estimated completion times of 1 week, 2 weeks, and 2 weeks.

Phase 3 is the most difficult and complex of the entire development project. It also consists of six separate activities. Activity K has three time estimates of 2 weeks, 2 weeks, and 3 weeks. The immediate predecessor for this activity is activity E. The immediate predecessor for activity L is activity F. The time estimates for activity L are 3 weeks, 4 weeks, and 6 weeks. Activity M has 2 weeks, 2 weeks, and 4 weeks for the estimates of the optimistic, probable, and pessimistic time estimates. The immediate predecessor for activity M is activity G. Activities N and O both have activity I as their immediate predecessor. Activity N has 8 weeks, 9 weeks, and 11 weeks for its three time estimates. Activity O has 1 week, 1 week, and 3 weeks as its time estimates. Finally, activity P has time estimates of 4 weeks, 4 weeks, and 8 weeks. Activity J is its only immediate predecessor.

Phase 4 involves five activities. Activity Q requires activity K to be completed before it can be started. The three time estimates for activity Q are 6 weeks, 6 weeks, and 7 weeks. Activity R requires that both activity L and activity M be completed first. The three time estimates for activity R are 1, 2, and 4 weeks. Activity S requires activity N to be completed first. Its time estimates are 6 weeks, 6 weeks, and 7 weeks. Activity T requires that activity O be completed. The time estimates for activity T are 3 weeks, 3 weeks, and 4 weeks. The final activity for phase 4 is activity U. The time estimates for this activity are 1 week, 2 weeks, and 3 weeks. Activity P must be completed before activity U can be started.

Phase 5 is the final phase of the development project. It consists of only two activities. Activity V requires that activity Q and activity R be completed before it can be started. Time estimates for this activity are 9 weeks, 10 weeks, and 11 weeks. Activity W is the final activity of the process. It requires three activities to be completed before it can be started. These are activities S, T, and U. The estimated completion times for activity W are 2 weeks, 4 weeks, and 5 weeks.

(a) Given this information, determine the expected completion time for the entire process. Also determine those activities along the critical path. Jim hopes that the total project will take less than 40 weeks. Is this likely to occur?

(b) Jim has just determined that activity D has already been completed and that no additional work is required. What is the impact of this change on the activities along the critical path?

(c) What is the impact on the critical path and the total project completion time if both activity D and activity I have been completed?

(d) What would happen if the immediate predecessor activity changed? For example, activity F may have an immediate predecessor of activity A instead of activity B.

Case Study

Haygood Brothers Construction Company

George and Harry Haygood are building contractors who specialize in the construction of private home dwellings, storage warehouses, and small businesses (less than 20,000 sq. ft. of floor space). Both George and Harry entered a carpenter union's apprenticeship program in the early 1990s and, upon completion of the apprenticeship, became skilled craftsmen in 1996. Before going into business for themselves, they worked for several local building contractors in the Detroit area.

Typically, the Haygood Brothers submit competitive bids for the construction of proposed dwellings. Whenever their bids are accepted, various aspects of the construction (electrical wiring, plumbing, brick laying, painting, and so forth) are subcontracted. George and Harry, however, perform all carpentry work. In addition, they plan and schedule all construction operations, frequently arrange interim financing, and supervise all construction activities.

The philosophy under which the Haygood Brothers have always operated can be simply stated: "Time is money." Delays in construction increase the costs of interim financing and postpone the initiation of their building projects. Consequently, they deal with all bottlenecks promptly and avoid all delays whenever possible. To minimize the time consumed in a construction project, the Haygood Brothers use PERT.

First, all construction activities and events are itemized and properly arranged (in parallel and sequential combinations) in a network. Then time estimates for each activity are made, the expected time for completing each activity is determined, and the critical (longest) path is calculated. Finally, earliest times, latest times, and slack values are computed. Having made these calculations, George and Harry can place their resources in the critical areas to minimize the time of completing the project.

The following are the activities that constitute an upcoming project (home dwelling) of the Haygood Brothers:

1. Arrange financing (AB).

2. Let subcontracts (BC).

3. Set and pour foundations (CD).

4. Plumbing (CE).

5. Framing (DF).

6. Roofing (FG).

7. Electrical wiring (FH).

8. Installation of windows and doors (FI).

9. Ductwork and insulation (including heating and cooling units) (FJ).

10. Sheetrock, paneling, and paper hanging (JK).

11. Installation of cabinets (KL).

FIGURE 13.14

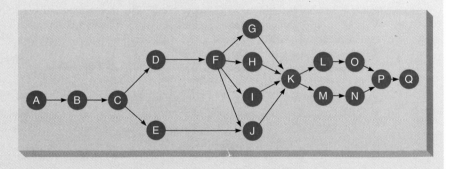

	DAYS		
T A B L E 1 3 . 1 1 **Haygood Brothers Construction Co.**			
ACTIVITY	**a**	**m**	**b**
AB	4	5	6
BC	2	5	8
CD	5	7	9
CE	4	5	6
DF	2	4	6
FG	3	5	9
FH	4	5	6
FI	3	4	7
FJ	5	7	9
JK	10	11	12
KL	4	6	8
KM	7	8	9
MN	4	5	10
LO	5	7	9
OP	5	6	7
PQ	2	3	4

12. Bricking (KM).

13. Outside trim (MN).

14. Inside trim (including fixtures) (LO).

15. Painting (OP).

16. Flooring (PQ).

The PERT diagram is shown in Figure 13.14, and the optimistic (*a*), most likely (*m*), and pessimistic (*b*) time estimates, are shown in Table 13.11.

Any activities in the network, but not in Table 13.11, are dummy activities that consume no time.

Discussion Questions

1. What is the time length of the critical path? What is the significance of the critical path?
2. Compute the amount of time that the completion of each activity can be delayed without affecting the overall project.
3. The project was begun August 1. What is the probability that the project can be completed by September 30? (Note: Scheduled completion time = 60 days.)

Source: Professor Jerry Kinard, Western Carolina University.

Case Study

Family Planning Research Center of Nigeria

Dr. Adinombe Watage, deputy director of the Family Planning Research Center in Nigeria's Over-The-River Province, was assigned the task of organizing and training five teams of field workers to perform educational and outreach activities as part of a large project to demonstrate acceptance of a new method of birth control. These workers already had training in family planning education but must receive specific training regarding the new method of contraception. Two types of materials must also be prepared: (1) those for use in training the workers, and (2) those for distribution in the field. Training faculty must be brought in and arrangements made for transportation and accommodations for the participants.

Dr. Watage first called a meeting of his office staff. Together they identified the activities that must be carried out, their necessary sequences, and the time that they would require. Their results are displayed in Table 13.12.

Louis Odaga, the chief clerk, noted that the project had to be completed in 60 days. Whipping out his solar-powered calculator, he added up the time needed. It came to 94 days. "An impossible task, then," he noted. "No," Dr. Watage replied, "some of these tasks can go forward in parallel." "Be careful, though," warned Mr. Oglagadu, the chief nurse, "there aren't that many of us to go around. There are only 10 of us in this office."

"I can check whether we have enough heads and hands once I have tentatively scheduled the activities," Dr. Watage responded. "If the schedule is too tight, I have permission from the Pathminder Fund to spend some funds to speed it up, just so long as I can prove that it can be done at the least cost necessary. Can you help me prove that? Here are the costs for the activities with the elapsed time that we planned and the costs and times if we shorten them to an absolute minimum." Those data are given in Table 13.13.

TABLE 13.12 Family Planning Research Center Activities

ACTIVITY	MUST FOLLOW	TIME (DAYS)	STAFFING NEEDED
A. Identify faculty and their schedules	—	5	2
B. Arrange transport to base	—	7	3
C. Identify and collect training materials	—	5	2
D. Arrange accommodations	A	3	1
E. Identify team	A	7	4
F. Bring in team	B, E	2	1
G. Transport faculty to base	A, B	3	2
H. Print program material	C	10	6
I. Have program materials delivered	H	7	3
J. Conduct training program	D, F, G, I	15	0
K. Perform fieldwork training	J	30	0

TABLE 13.13 Family Planning Research Center Costs

ACTIVITY	NORMAL		MINIMUM		AVERAGE COST
	TIME	COST ($)	TIME	COST ($)	PER DAY SAVED ($)
A. Identify faculty	5	400	2	700	100
B. Arrange transport	7	1,000	4	1,450	150
C. Identify materials	5	400	3	500	50
D. Make accommodations	3	2,500	1	3,000	250
E. Identify team	7	400	4	850	150
F. Bring team in	2	1,000	1	2,000	1,000
G. Transport faculty	3	1,500	2	2,000	500
H. Print materials	10	3,000	5	4,000	200
I. Deliver materials	7	200	2	600	80
J. Train team	15	5,000	10	7,000	400
K. Do fieldwork	30	10,000	20	14,000	400

Discussion Questions

1. Some of the tasks in this project can be done in parallel. Prepare a diagram showing the required network of tasks and define the critical path. What is the length of the project without crashing?

2. At this point, can the project be done given the personnel constraint of 10 persons?

3. If the critical path is longer than 60 days, what is the least amount that Dr. Watage can spend and still achieve this schedule objective? How can he prove to Pathminder Foundation that this is the minimum-cost alternative?

Source: Professor Curtis P. McLaughlin, Kenan-Flagler Business School, University of North Carolina at Chapel Hill.

INTERNET CASE STUDIES

See our Internet home page at **http://www.prenhall.com/render** for these additional case studies: Alpha Beta Gamma Record, Bay Community Hospital, Cranston Construction Company, and Shale Oil Company.

Bibliography

Charoenngam, Chotchai et al. "Cost/Schedule Information System," *Cost Engineering*, (September 1997): 29.

Dorey, Chris. "The ABCs of R&D at Nortel," *CMA Magazine* (March 1998): 19.

Graham, Robert et al. "Creating an Environment for Successful Projects," *Research Technology Management* (February 1998): 60.

Nibletto, Paolo. "Historical Data Needed to See into Harley Davidson's Future," *Info Canada* (July 1992): 42.

Render, B., and R. M. Stair. *Cases and Readings in Management Science,* 2nd ed. Boston: Allyn and Bacon, Inc., 1990.

Roe, Justin. "Bringing Discipline to Project Management," *Harvard Business Review* (April 1998): 153.

Sander, Wayne. "The Projects Manager's Guide," *Quality Progress* (January 1998): 109.

Sivathanu, Pillai. "Enhanced PERT for Program Analysis, Control, and Evaluation,"

International Journal of Project Management (February 1993): 39.

Weist, J., and F. Levy. *Management Guide to PERT-CPM*, 2nd ed. Upper Saddle River, NJ: Prentice Hall, 1977.

APPENDIX 13.1: PROJECT MANAGEMENT WITH QM FOR WINDOWS

PERT is one of the most popular project management techniques. In this chapter we explored the General Foundry, Inc., example. When expected times and variances have been computed for each activity, we can use the data to determine slack, the critical path, and the total project completion time. Program 13.1 shows the results from the QM for Windows program. Note that those activities with no slack are on the critical path.

PROGRAM 13.1

QM for Windows Results for Project Management at General Foundry, Inc.

Project Management (CPM/PERT) / Triple time estimate

Network type
○ Precedence list
◉ Start/end node number

Method
Triple time estimate

Project Management (CPM/PERT) Results

General Foundry Solution

	Start node	End node	Activity time	Early Start	Early Finish	Late Start	Late Finish	slack	Activity std dev
Project			15.						1.7638
Task 1	1.	2.	2.	0.	2.	0.	2.	0.	0.3333
Task 2	1.	3.	3.	0.	3.	1.	4.	1.	0.3333
Task 3	2.	4.	2.	2.	4.	2.	4.	0.	0.3333
Task 4	3.	5.	4.	3.	7.	4.	8.	1.	0.6667
Task 5	4.	5.	4.	4.	8.	4.	8.	0.	1.
Task 6	4.	6.	3.	4.	7.	10.	13.	6.	1.3333
Task 7	5.	6.	5.	8.	13.	8.	13.	0.	1.3333
Task 8	6.	7.	2.	13.	15.	13.	15.	0.	0.3333

In addition to basic project management, QM for Windows also allows for project crashing, where additional resources are used to reduce project completion time. Program 13.2 shows how project crashing can be accomplished using General Foundry's data from Table 13.9.

PROGRAM 13.2

QM for Windows Results from Project Crashing the Data for General Foundry in Table 13.9

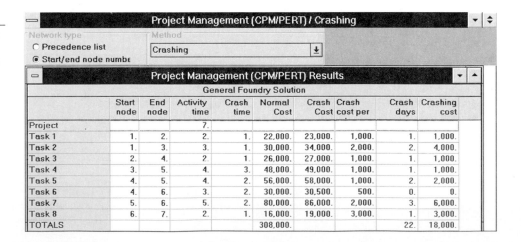

Project Management (CPM/PERT) / Crashing

Network type
○ Precedence list
◉ Start/end node number

Method
Crashing

Project Management (CPM/PERT) Results

General Foundry Solution

	Start node	End node	Activity time	Crash time	Normal Cost	Crash Cost	Crash cost per	Crash days	Crashing cost
Project			7.						
Task 1	1.	2.	2.	1.	22,000.	23,000.	1,000.	1.	1,000.
Task 2	1.	3.	3.	1.	30,000.	34,000.	2,000.	2.	4,000.
Task 3	2.	4.	2.	1.	26,000.	27,000.	1,000.	1.	1,000.
Task 4	3.	5.	4.	3.	48,000.	49,000.	1,000.	1.	1,000.
Task 5	4.	5.	4.	2.	56,000.	58,000.	1,000.	2.	2,000.
Task 6	4.	6.	3.	2.	30,000.	30,500.	500.	0.	0.
Task 7	5.	6.	5.	2.	80,000.	86,000.	2,000.	3.	6,000.
Task 8	6.	7.	2.	1.	16,000.	19,000.	3,000.	1.	3,000.
TOTALS					308,000.			22.	18,000.

Monitoring and controlling projects is always an important aspect of project management. In this chapter you saw how to construct budgets using the earliest and latest start times. Programs 13.3 and 13.4 show how QM for Windows can be used to develop budgets using earliest and latest starting times for a project. The data come from the General Foundry example in Tables 13.6 and 13.7.

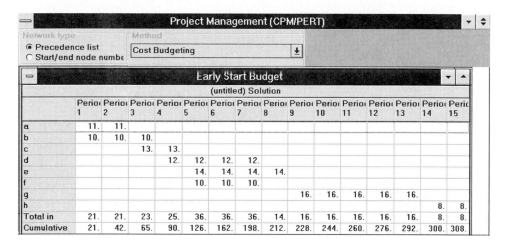

PROGRAM 13.3

QM for Windows for Budgeting with Earliest Start Times for General Foundry

Project Management (CPM/PERT)

Network type: ◉ Precedence list ○ Start/end node number
Method: Cost Budgeting

Early Start Budget

(untitled) Solution

	Period 1	Period 2	Period 3	Period 4	Period 5	Period 6	Period 7	Period 8	Period 9	Period 10	Period 11	Period 12	Period 13	Period 14	Period 15
a	11.	11.													
b	10.	10.	10.												
c			13.	13.											
d				12.	12.	12.	12.								
e					14.	14.	14.	14.							
f					10.	10.	10.								
g									16.	16.	16.	16.	16.		
h														8.	8.
Total in	21.	21.	23.	25.	36.	36.	36.	14.	16.	16.	16.	16.	16.	8.	8.
Cumulative	21.	42.	65.	90.	126.	162.	198.	212.	228.	244.	260.	276.	292.	300.	308.

PROGRAM 13.4

QM for Windows for Budgeting with Latest Start Times for General Foundry

Project Management (CPM/PERT) / Cost Budgetting - [Late Start Budget]

Network type: ◉ Precedence list ○ Start/end node number
Method: Cost Budgeting

(untitled) Solution

	Period 1	Period 2	Period 3	Period 4	Period 5	Period 6	Period 7	Period 8	Period 9	Period 10	Period 11	Period 12	Period 13	Period 14	Period 15
a	11.	11.													
b		10.	10.	10.											
c			13.	13.											
d					12.	12.	12.	12.							
e					14.	14.	14.	14.							
f											10.	10.	10.		
g									16.	16.	16.	16.	16.		
h														8.	8.
Total in	11.	21.	23.	23.	26.	26.	26.	26.	16.	16.	26.	26.	26.	8.	8.
Cumulative	11.	32.	55.	78.	104.	130.	156.	182.	198.	214.	240.	266.	292.	300.	308.

Waiting Lines and Queuing Theory Models

LEARNING OBJECTIVES

After completing this chapter, students will be able to:

1. Describe the trade-off curves for cost-of-waiting time and cost of service.
2. Understand the three parts of a queuing system: the calling population, the queue itself, and the service facility.
3. Describe the basic queuing system configurations.
4. Understand the assumptions of the common models dealt with in this chapter.
5. Analyze a variety of operating characteristics of waiting lines.

CHAPTER OUTLINE

14.1 Introduction

14.2 Waiting Line Costs

14.3 Characteristics of a Queuing System

14.4 Single-Channel Queuing Model with Poisson Arrivals and Exponential Service Times

14.5 Multiple-Channel Queuing Model with Poisson Arrivals and Exponential Service Times

14.6 Constant Service Time Model

14.7 Finite Population Model

14.8 More Complex Queuing Models and the Use of Simulation

Summary • Glossary • Key Equations • Solved Problems • Self-Test • Discussion Questions and Problems • Case Study: New England Castings • Case Study: Winter Park Hotel • Internet Case Study • Bibliography

Appendix 14.1: Using QM for Windows

14.1   INTRODUCTION

The study of *waiting lines*, called *queuing theory*, is one of the oldest and most widely used quantitative analysis techniques. Waiting lines are an everyday occurrence, affecting people shopping for groceries, buying gasoline, making a bank deposit, or waiting on the telephone for the first available airline reservationist to answer. Queues,[1] another term for waiting lines, may also take the form of machines waiting to be repaired, trucks in line to be unloaded, or airplanes lined up on a runway waiting for permission to take off. The three basic components of a queuing process are arrivals, service facilities, and the actual waiting line.

In this chapter we discuss how analytical models of waiting lines can help managers evaluate the cost and effectiveness of service systems. We begin with a look at waiting line costs and then describe the characteristics of waiting lines and the underlying mathematical assumptions used to develop queuing models. We also provide the equations needed to compute the operating characteristics of a service system and show examples of how they are used. Later in the chapter, you will see how to save computational time by applying queuing tables and by running waiting line computer programs.

14.2   WAITING LINE COSTS

One of the goals of queuing analysis is finding the best level of service for an organization.

Most waiting line problems are centered about the question of finding the ideal level of services that a firm should provide. Supermarkets must decide how many cash register checkout positions should be opened. Gasoline stations must decide how many pumps should be opened and how many attendants should be on duty. Manufacturing plants must determine the optimal number of mechanics to have on duty each shift to repair machines that break down. Banks must decide how many teller windows to keep open to serve customers during various hours of the day. In most cases, this level of service is an option over which management has control. An extra teller, for example, can be borrowed from another chore or can be hired and trained quickly if demand warrants it. This may not always be the case, though. A plant may not be able to locate or hire skilled mechanics to repair sophisticated electronic machinery.

When an organization *does* have control, its objective is usually to find a happy medium between two extremes. On the one hand, a firm can retain a large staff and provide *many* service facilities. This may result in excellent customer service, with seldom more than one or two customers in a queue. Customers are kept happy with the quick response and appreciate the convenience. This, however, can become expensive.

The other extreme is to have the *minimum* possible number of checkout lines, gas pumps, or teller windows open. This keeps the *service cost* down but may result in customer dissatisfaction. How many times would you return to a large discount department store that had only one cash register open during the day you shop? As the average length of the queue increases and poor service results, customers and goodwill may be lost.

Managers must deal with the trade-off between the cost of providing good service and the cost of customer waiting time. The latter may be hard to quantify.

Most managers recognize the trade-off that must take place between the cost of providing good service and the cost of customer waiting time. They want queues that are short enough so that customers don't become unhappy and either storm out without buying or buy but never return. But they are willing to allow some waiting in line if it is balanced by a significant savings in service costs.

---

[1] The word *queue* is pronounced like the letter *Q*, that is, "kew."

One means of evaluating a service facility is thus to look at a *total expected cost*, a concept illustrated in Figure 14.1. Total expected cost is the sum of expected *service costs* plus expected *waiting costs*.

Total expected cost is the sum of service plus waiting costs.

Service costs are seen to increase as a firm attempts to raise its level of service. For example, if three teams of stevedores, instead of two, are employed to unload a cargo ship, service costs are increased by the additional price of wages. As service improves in speed, however, the cost of time spent waiting in lines decreases. This waiting cost may reflect lost productivity of workers while their tools or machines are awaiting repairs, or may simply be an estimate of the costs of customers lost because of poor service and long queues.

Three Rivers Shipping Company Example   As an illustration, let's look at the case of the Three Rivers Shipping Company. Three Rivers runs a huge docking facility located on the Ohio River near Pittsburgh. Approximately five ships arrive to unload their cargoes of steel and ore during every 12-hour work shift. Each hour that a ship sits idle in line waiting to be unloaded costs the firm a great deal of money, about $1,000 per hour. From experience, management estimates that if one team of stevedores is on duty to handle the unloading work, each ship will wait an average of 7 hours to be unloaded. If two teams are working, the average waiting time drops to 4 hours; for three teams, it's 3 hours; and for four teams of stevedores, only 2 hours. But each additional team of stevedores is also an expensive proposition, due to union contracts.

Three Rivers's superintendent would like to determine the optimal number of teams of stevedores to have on duty each shift. The objective is to minimize total expected costs. This analysis is summarized in Table 14.1. To minimize the sum of service costs and waiting costs, the firm makes the decision to employ two teams of stevedores each shift.

The goal is to find the service level that minimizes total expected cost.

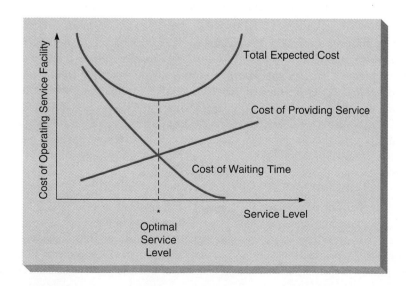

FIGURE 14.1

Queuing Costs and Service Levels

TABLE 14.1 Three Rivers Shipping Company Waiting Line Cost Analysis

	NUMBER OF TEAMS OF STEVEDORES WORKING			
	1	**2**	**3**	**4**
(a) Average number of ships arriving per shift	5	5	5	5
(b) Average time each ship waits to be unloaded (hours)	7	4	3	2
(c) Total ship hours lost per shift (a × b)	35	20	15	10
(d) Estimated cost per hour of idle ship time	$1,000	$1,000	$1,000	$1,000
(e) Value of ship's lost time or waiting cost (c × d)	$35,000	$20,000	$15,000	$10,000
(f) Stevedore team salary,* or service cost	$6,000	$12,000	$18,000	$24,000
(g) Total expected cost (e + f)	$41,000	$32,000	$33,000	$34,000

Optimal cost

*Stevedore team salaries are computed as the number of people in a typical team (assumed to be 50), times the number of hours each person works per day (12 hours), times an hourly salary of $10 per hour. If two teams are employed, the rate is just doubled.

14.3 CHARACTERISTICS OF A QUEUING SYSTEM

In this section we take a look at the three parts of a queuing system: (1) the arrivals or inputs to the system (sometimes referred to as the *calling population*), (2) the queue or the waiting line itself, and (3) the service facility. These three components have certain characteristics that must be examined before mathematical queuing models can be developed.

Arrival Characteristics

The input source that generates arrivals or customers for the service system has three major characteristics. It is important to consider the *size* of the calling population, the *pattern* of arrivals at the queuing system, and the *behavior* of the arrivals.

Unlimited (or infinite) calling populations are assumed for most queuing models.

Size of the Calling Population Population sizes are considered to be either *unlimited* (essentially *infinite*) or *limited (finite)*. When the number of customers or arrivals on hand at any given moment is just a small portion of potential arrivals, the calling population is considered unlimited. For practical purposes, examples of unlimited populations include cars arriving at a highway tollbooth, shoppers arriving at a supermarket, or students arriving to register for classes at a large university. Most queuing models assume such an infinite calling population. When this is not the case, modeling becomes much more complex. An example of a finite population is a shop with only eight machines that might break down and require service.

Arrivals are random when they are independent of one another and cannot be predicted exactly.

Pattern of Arrivals at the System Customers either arrive at a service facility according to some known schedule (for example, one patient every 15 minutes or one student for advising every half hour) or else they arrive *randomly*. Arrivals are considered random when they are independent of one another and their occurrence cannot be predicted exactly. Frequently in queuing problems, the number of arrivals per unit of time can be estimated by a probability distribution known as the *Poisson distribution*. For any given arrival rate, such as two customers per hour, or four trucks per minute, a discrete Poisson distribution can be established by using the formula

$$P(X) = \frac{e^{-\lambda}\lambda^{X}}{X!} \quad \text{for } X = 0, 1, 2, 3, 4, \ldots \tag{14-1}$$

where

$P(X)$ = probability of X arrivals

X = number of arrivals per unit of time

λ = average arrival rate

e = 2.7183

With the help of the table in Appendix C, these values are easy to compute. Figure 14.2 illustrates the Poisson distribution for $\lambda = 2$ and $\lambda = 4$. This means that if the average arrival rate is $\lambda = 2$ customers per hour, the probability of 0 customers arriving in any random hour is about 13%, probability of 1 customer is about 27%, 2 customers about 27%, 3 customers about 18%, 4 customers about 9%, and so on. The chances that 9 or more will arrive are virtually nil. Arrivals, of course, are not always Poisson (they may follow some other distribution) and should be examined to make certain that they are well approximated by Poisson before that distribution is applied. This usually involves observing arrivals, plotting the data, and applying statistical measures of goodness of fit, a topic discussed in more advanced texts.

The Poisson probability distribution is used in many queuing models to represent arrival patterns.

Behavior of the Arrivals Most queuing models assume that an arriving customer is a patient customer. Patient customers are people or machines that wait in the queue until they are served and do not switch between lines. Unfortunately, life and quantitative analysis are complicated by the fact that people have been known to balk or renege. *Balking* refers to customers who refuse to join the waiting line because it is too long to suit their needs or interests. *Reneging* customers are those who enter the queue but then become impatient

The concepts of balking and reneging.

FIGURE 14.2

Two Examples of the Poisson Distribution for Arrival Times

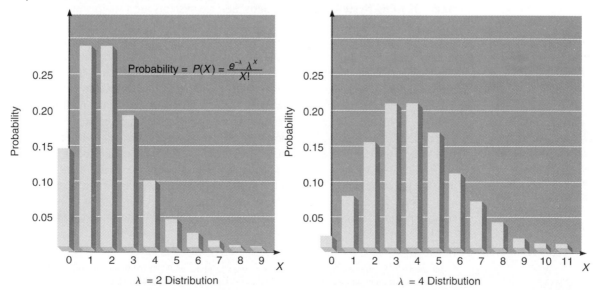

$\lambda = 2$ Distribution

$\lambda = 4$ Distribution

Probability = $P(X) = \dfrac{e^{-\lambda}\lambda^{X}}{X!}$

and leave without completing their transaction. Actually, both of these situations just serve to accentuate the need for queuing theory and waiting line analysis. How many times have you seen a shopper with a basket full of groceries, including perishables such as milk, frozen food, or meats, simply abandon the shopping cart before checking out because the line was too long? This expensive occurrence for the store makes managers acutely aware of the importance of service-level decisions.

Waiting Line Characteristics

The models in this chapter assume unlimited queue length.

The waiting line itself is the second component of a queuing system. The length of a line can be either *limited* or *unlimited*. A queue is limited when it cannot, by law of physical restrictions, increase to an infinite length. This may be the case in a small restaurant that has only 10 tables and can serve no more than 50 diners an evening. Analytic queuing models are treated in this chapter under an assumption of *unlimited* queue length. A queue is unlimited when its size is unrestricted, as in the case of the tollbooth serving arriving automobiles.

Most queuing models use the first-in, first-out rule. This is obviously not appropriate in all service systems, especially those dealing with emergencies.

A second waiting line characteristic deals with *queue discipline*. This refers to the rule by which customers in the line are to receive service. Most systems use a queue discipline known as the *first-in, first-out rule* (FIFO). In a hospital emergency room or an express checkout line at a supermarket, however, various assigned priorities may preempt FIFO. Patients who are critically injured will move ahead in treatment priority over patients with broken fingers or noses. Shoppers with fewer than 10 items may be allowed to enter the express checkout queue but are *then* treated as first-come, first-served. Computer programming runs are another example of queuing systems that operate under priority scheduling. In most large companies, when computer-produced paychecks are due out on a specific date, the payroll program has highest priority over other runs.[2]

Service Facility Characteristics

The third part of any queuing system is the service facility. It is important to examine two basic properties: (1) the configuration of the service system and (2) the pattern of service times.

Number of service channels in a queuing system is the number of servers.

Basic Queuing System Configurations   Service systems are usually classified in terms of their number of channels, or number of servers, and number of phases, or number of service stops, that must be made. A *single-channel system*, with one server, is typified by the drive-in bank that has only one open teller, or by the type of drive-through fast-food restaurant that has become so popular in the United States. If, on the other hand, the bank had several tellers on duty and each customer waited in one common line for the first available teller, we would have a *multiple-channel system* at work. Many banks today are multichannel service systems, as are most large barber shops and many airline ticket counters.

Single-phase means the customer receives service at only one station before leaving the system. Multiphase implies two or more stops before leaving the system.

A *single-phase system* is one in which the customer receives service from only one station and then exits the system. A fast-food restaurant in which the person who takes your order also brings you the food and takes your money is a single-phase system. So is a driver's license agency in which the person taking your application also grades your test and collects the license fee. But if the restaurant requires you to place your order at one station, pay at a second, and pick up the food at a third service stop, it becomes a *multi-*

---

[2] The term *FIFS* (*first in, first served*) is often used in place of FIFO. Another discipline, LIFS (*last in, first served*), is common when material is stacked or piled and the items on top are used first.

phase system. Similarly, if the driver's license agency is large or busy, you will probably have to wait in a line to complete the application (the first service stop), then queue again to have the test graded (the second service stop), and finally go to a third service counter to pay the fee. To help you relate the concepts of channels and phases, Figure 14.3 presents four possible configurations.

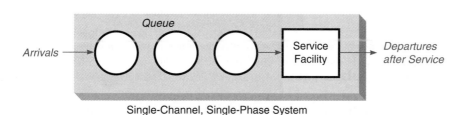

Single-Channel, Single-Phase System

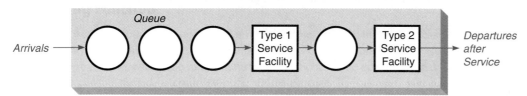

Single-Channel, Multiphase System

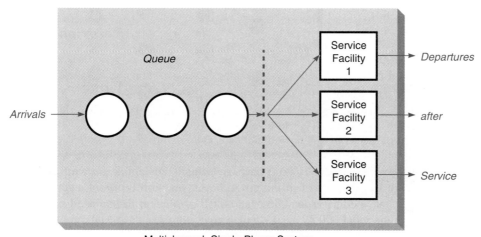

Multichannel, Single-Phase System

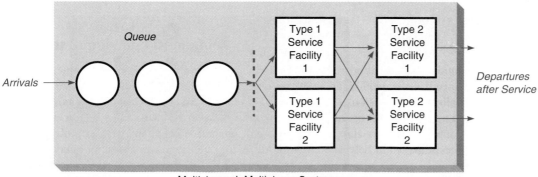

Multichannel, Multiphase System

FIGURE 14.3

Four Basic Queuing System Configurations

Service Time Distribution Service patterns are like arrival patterns in that they may be either constant or random. If service time is constant, it takes the same amount of time to take care of each customer. This is the case in a machine-performed service operation such as an automatic car wash. More often, service times are randomly distributed. In many cases it can be assumed that random service times are described by the *negative exponential probability distribution*. This is a mathematically convenient assumption if arrival rates are Poisson distributed.

Service times often follow the negative exponential distribution.

Figure 14.4 illustrates that if service times follow an exponential distribution, the probability of any very long service time is low. For example, when an average service time is 20 minutes, seldom if ever will a customer require more than 90 minutes in the service facility. If the mean service time is one hour, the probability of spending more than 180 minutes in service is virtually zero.

It is important to confirm that the queuing assumptions of Poisson arrivals and exponential services are valid before applying the model.

The exponential distribution is important to the process of building mathematical queuing models because many of the models' theoretical underpinnings are based on the assumption of Poisson arrivals and exponential services. Before they are applied, however, the quantitative analyst can and should observe, collect, and plot service time data to determine if they fit the exponential distribution.

FIGURE 14.4

Two Examples of the Exponential Distribution for Service Times

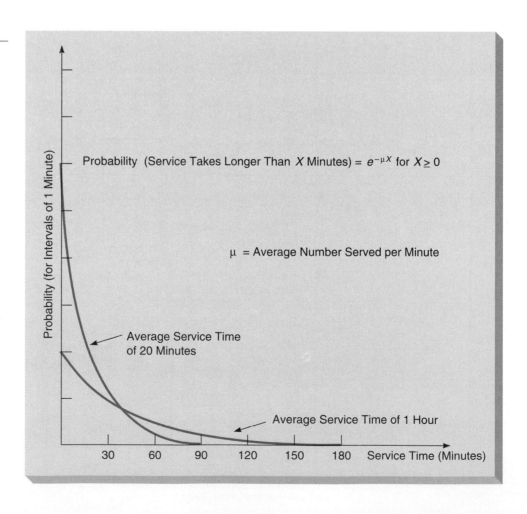

| MODELING IN THE REAL WORLD | New Haven Fire Department |

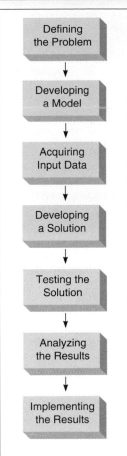

Defining the Problem

Facing severe budget restrictions, the city of New Haven, Connecticut, decided to investigate whether its fire department could close one or more firehouses with an acceptably small risk to public safety.

Developing a Model

Two consultants, Arthur Swersey (from Yale) and Louis Goldring, developed a series of hour-by-hour queuing models that estimated the average time a person calling would have to wait for emergency service. The models were based on Poisson arrivals and exponential service times.

Acquiring Input Data

A grid map of the city of New Haven was developed to measure travel times/distances. Consultants also collected data on utilization of each of the 10 engine companies and five truck companies. 1990 emergency medical equipment and fire alarm data were employed.

Developing a Solution

Two alternative configurations for closing/merging firehouses that appeared to be reasonable and feasible were developed.

Testing the Solution

Using a mathematical probability analysis of fires occurring in each census tract area, the solutions were tested. They predicted the average emergency travel time to reach each of New Haven's 28 census tracts. One plan showed a response rate more than a half-minute faster than the other.

Analyzing the Results

The Fire Department analyzed the trade-offs of the various plans and submitted them to public hearings and to the Board of Aldermen for a vote.

Implementing the Results

On Sept. 27, 1991, New Haven Fire Chief Earl D. Geyer announced the implementation of the selected plan and its projected savings of $1.4 million/year, 10% of the department's budget.

Source: A. J. Swersey, L. Goldring, and E. D. Geyer. "Improving Fire Department Productivity," *Interfaces* 23, 1 (January–February 1993): 109–129.

14.4 SINGLE-CHANNEL QUEUING MODEL WITH POISSON ARRIVALS AND EXPONENTIAL SERVICE TIMES[3]

In this section we present an analytical approach to determine important measures of performance in a typical service system. After these numeric measures have been computed, it will be possible to add in cost data and begin to make decisions that balance desirable service levels with waiting line service costs.

---

[3] In the technical terminology of the operations research world, this model is also referred to as the M/M/1 queuing model.

IN ACTION   L.L. Bean Turns to Queuing Theory

L. L. Bean faced severe problems. It was the peak selling season, and the service level to incoming calls was simply unacceptable. Widely known as a high-quality outdoor goods retailer, about 65% of L.L. Bean's sales volume is generated through telephone orders via its toll-free service centers located in Maine.

Here is how bad the situation was: During certain periods, 80% of the calls received a busy signal, and those that did not often had to wait up to 10 minutes before speaking with a sales agent. L.L. Bean estimated that it lost $10 million in profit because of the way it allocated telemarketing resources. Keeping customers waiting "in line" (on the phone) was costing $25,000 per day. On exceptionally busy days, the total orders lost because of queue problems approached $500,000 in gross revenues.

Developing queuing models similar to those presented here, L.L. Bean was able to set the number of phone lines and the number of agents to have on duty for each half-hour of every day of the season. Within a year, use of the model resulted in 24% more calls answered, 17% more orders taken, and 16% more revenues. It also meant 81% fewer abandoned callers and 84% faster answering time. The percent of calls spending less than 20 seconds in the queue increased from 25% to 77%. Queuing theory changed the way L.L. Bean thinks about telecommunications.

Source: Phil Quinn, Bruce Andrews, and Henry Parsons, *Interfaces* 21, 1 (January–February 1991): 75–91.

Assumptions of the Model

The single-channel, single-phase model considered here is one of the most widely used and simplest queuing models. It assumes that seven conditions exist:

1. Arrivals are served on a FIFO basis.
2. Every arrival waits to be served regardless of the length of the line; that is, there is no balking or reneging.
3. Arrivals are independent of preceding arrivals, but the average number of arrivals (the arrival rate) does not change over time.
4. Arrivals are described by a Poisson probability distribution and come from an infinite or very large population.

These seven assumptions must be met if the single-channel, single-phase model is to be applied.

5. Service times also vary from one customer to the next and are independent of one another, but their average rate is known.
6. Service times occur according to the negative exponential probability distribution.
7. The average service rate is greater than the average arrival rate.

When these seven conditions are met, we can develop a series of equations that define the queue's *operating characteristics*. The mathematics used to derive each equation is rather complex and outside the scope of this book, so we will just present the resulting formulas here.

Queuing Equations

We let

λ = mean number of arrivals per time period (for example, per hour)

μ = mean number of people or items served per time period

The queuing equations follow.

These seven queuing equations for the single-channel, single-phase model describe the important operating characteristics of the service system.

1. The average number of customers or units in the system, L, that is, the number in line plus the number being served:

$$L = \frac{\lambda}{\mu - \lambda}$$

(14-2)

2. The average time a customer spends in the system, W, that is, the time spent in line plus the time spent being served:

$$W = \frac{1}{\mu - \lambda}$$ (14-3)

(handwritten: $\frac{1}{30-20} = \frac{1}{10} = .1\mathbb{D}$)

3. The average number of customers in the queue, L_q:

$$L_q = \frac{\lambda^2}{\mu(\mu - \lambda)}$$ (14-4)

4. The average time a customer spends waiting in the queue, W_q:

$$W_q = \frac{\lambda}{\mu(\mu - \lambda)}$$ (14-5)

5. The *utilization factor* for the system, ρ (the Greek lowercase letter rho), that is, the probability that the service facility is being used:

$$\rho = \frac{\lambda}{\mu}$$ (14-6)

6. The percent idle time, P_0, that is, the probability that no one is in the system:

$$P_0 = 1 - \frac{\lambda}{\mu}$$ (14-7)

7. The probability that the number of customers in the system is greater than k, $P_{n>k}$:

$$P_{n>k} = \left(\frac{\lambda}{\mu}\right)^{k+1}$$ (14-8)

Arnold's Muffler Shop Case

We now apply these formulas to the case of Arnold's Muffler Shop in New Orleans. Arnold's mechanic, Reid Blank, is able to install new mufflers at an average rate of 3 per hour, or about 1 every 20 minutes. Customers needing this service arrive at the shop on the average of 2 per hour. Larry Arnold, the shop owner, studied queuing models in an MBA program and feels that all seven of the conditions for a single-channel model are met. He proceeds to calculate the numerical values of the preceding operating characteristics.

$\lambda = 2$ cars arriving per hour

$\mu = 3$ cars serviced per hour

$L = \dfrac{\lambda}{\mu - \lambda} = \dfrac{2}{3 - 2} = \dfrac{2}{1}$ = 2 cars in the system on the average

$W = \dfrac{1}{\mu - \lambda} = \dfrac{1}{3 - 2}$ = 1 hour that an average car spends in the system

$L_q = \dfrac{\lambda^2}{\mu(\mu - \lambda)} = \dfrac{2^2}{3(3 - 2)} = \dfrac{4}{3(1)} = \dfrac{4}{3} = 1.33$ cars waiting in line on the average

$W_q = \dfrac{\lambda}{\mu(\mu - \lambda)} = \dfrac{2}{3(3 - 2)} = \dfrac{2}{3}$ hour = 40 minutes = average waiting time per car

$\rho = \dfrac{\lambda}{\mu} = \dfrac{2}{3} = 0.67$ = percent of time mechanic is busy, or the probability that the server is busy

$P_0 = 1 - \dfrac{\lambda}{\mu} = 1 - \dfrac{2}{3} = 0.33$ = probability that there are 0 cars in the system

PROBABILITY OF MORE THAN *k* CARS IN THE SYSTEM

k	$P_{n>k} = (2/3)^{k+1}$
0	(0.667) ← *Note that this is equal to* $1 - P_0 = 1 - 0.33 = 0.667$.
1	0.444
2	0.296
3	(0.198) ← *Implies that there is a 19.8% chance that more than 3 cars are in the system.*
4	0.132
5	0.088
6	0.058
7	0.039

Using Excel QM on the Arnold's Muffler Shop Queue Excel QM easily handles Arnold's single-channel, single-phase model. Using the equations shown in Program 14.1A, Excel QM provides the results in Program 14.1B.

Conducting an economic analysis is the next step. It permits cost factors to be included.

Introducing Costs into the Model Now that the characteristics of the queuing system have been computed, Arnold decides to do an economic analysis of their impact. The waiting line model was valuable in predicting potential waiting times, queue lengths, idle times, and so on. But it did not identify optimal decisions or consider cost factors. As stated earlier, the solution to a queuing problem may require management to make a trade-off between the increased cost of providing better service and the decreased waiting costs derived from providing that service.

Customer waiting time is often considered the most important factor.

Arnold estimates that the cost of customer waiting time, in terms of customer dissatisfaction and lost goodwill, is $10 per hour of time spent *waiting* in line. (After customers' cars are actually being serviced on the rack, customers don't seem to mind waiting.) Because on the average a car has a $2/3$ hour wait and there are approximately 16 cars serviced per day (2 per hour times 8 working hours per day), the total number of hours that customers spend waiting for mufflers to be installed each day is $2/3 \times 16 = {}^{32}/_3$, or $10\frac{2}{3}$ hours. Hence, in this case,

customer waiting cost = ($10/hour) × ($10\frac{2}{3}$ hours/day) = $106 per day

Waiting costs plus service costs equal total cost.

The only other major cost that Larry Arnold can identify in the queuing situation is the pay rate of Reid Blank, the mechanic. Blank is paid $7 per hour, or $56 per day. Total anticipated costs, then, are $106 + $56 = $162 per day.

Now comes a decision. Arnold finds out through the muffler business grapevine that the Rusty Muffler, a crosstown competitor, employs a mechanic named Jimmy Smith who can efficiently install new mufflers at the rate of 4 per hour. Larry Arnold contacts Smith and inquires as to his interest in switching employers. Smith says that he would consider leaving the Rusty Muffler but only if he were paid a $9 per hour salary. Arnold, being a crafty businessman, decides that it may be worthwhile to fire Blank and replace him with the speedier but more expensive Smith.

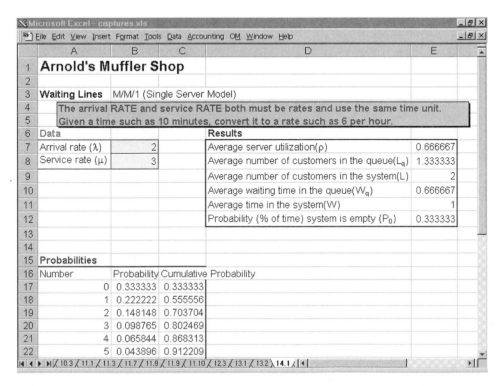

He first recomputes all the operating characteristics using a new service rate of 4 mufflers per hour.

λ = 2 cars arriving per hour

μ = 4 cars serviced per hour

$$L = \frac{\lambda}{\mu - \lambda} = \frac{2}{4 - 2} = 1 \text{ car in the system on the average}$$

$$W = \frac{1}{\mu - \lambda} = \frac{1}{4 - 2} = \frac{1}{2} \text{ hour in the system on the average}$$

$$L_q = \frac{\lambda^2}{\mu(\mu - \lambda)} = \frac{2^2}{4(4 - 2)} = \frac{4}{8} = \frac{1}{2} \text{ cars waiting in line on the average}$$

$$W_q = \frac{\lambda}{\mu(\mu - \lambda)} = \frac{2}{4(4 - 2)} = \frac{2}{8} = \frac{1}{4} \text{ hour} = 15 \text{ minutes average waiting time per car in the queue}$$

$$\rho = \frac{\lambda}{\mu} = \frac{2}{4} = 0.5 = \text{percent of time mechanic is busy}$$

$$P_0 = 1 - \frac{\lambda}{\mu} = 1 - 0.5 = 0.5 = \text{probability that there are 0 cars in the system}$$

PROBABILITY OF MORE THAN k CARS IN THE SYSTEM

k	$P_{n>k} = (\frac{2}{4})^{k+1}$
0	0.5
1	0.25
2	0.125
3	0.062
4	0.031
5	0.016
6	0.008
7	0.004

It is quite evident that Smith's speed will result in considerably shorter queues and waiting times. For example, a customer would now spend an average of $\frac{1}{2}$ hour in the system and $\frac{1}{4}$ hour waiting in the queue, as opposed to 1 hour in the system and $\frac{2}{3}$ hour in the queue with Blank as mechanic. Total hours customers spend *waiting* if Smith is on duty = (16 cars/day) $\times$ ($\frac{1}{4}$ hour/car) = 4 hours.

Here is a comparison for total costs using the two different mechanics.

Customer waiting cost = $10/hour $\times$ 4 hours = $40 per day

Service cost of Smith = 8 hours/day $\times$ $9/hour = $72 per day

Total expected cost = waiting cost + service cost = $40 + $72

= $112 per day

Because the total daily expected cost with Blank as mechanic was $162, Arnold may very well decide to hire Smith and reduce costs by $162 − $112 = $50 per day.

14.5 MULTIPLE-CHANNEL QUEUING MODEL WITH POISSON ARRIVALS AND EXPONENTIAL SERVICE TIMES[4]

The next logical step is to look at a multiple-channel queuing system, in which two or more servers or channels are available to handle arriving customers. Let us still assume that customers awaiting service form one single line and then proceed to the first available server. An example of such a multichannel, single-phase waiting line is found in many banks today. A common line is formed and the customer at the head of the line proceeds to the first free teller. (Refer back to Figure 14.3 for a typical multichannel configuration.)

The multiple-channel system presented here again assumes that arrivals follow a Poisson probability distribution and that service times are distributed exponentially. Service is first come, first served, and all servers are assumed to perform at the same rate. Other assumptions listed earlier for the single-channel model apply as well.

The multiple-channel model also assumes Poisson arrivals and exponential services.

Equations for the Multichannel Queuing Model

If we let M = number of channels open,

λ = average arrival rate, and

μ = average service rate at each channel

the following formulas may be used in the waiting line analysis.

NOT on Final exam

1. The probability that there are zero customers or units in the system:

$$P_0 = \frac{1}{\left[\sum_{n=0}^{n=M-1} \frac{1}{n!}\left(\frac{\lambda}{\mu}\right)^n\right] + \frac{1}{M!}\left(\frac{\lambda}{\mu}\right)^M \frac{M\mu}{M\mu - \lambda}} \quad \text{for} \quad M\mu > \lambda \quad (14\text{-}9)$$

2. The average number of customers or units in the system:

$$L = \frac{\lambda\mu(\lambda/\mu)^M}{(M-1)!(M\mu - \lambda)^2} P_0 + \frac{\lambda}{\mu} \quad (14\text{-}10)$$

3. The average time a unit spends in the waiting line or being serviced (namely, in the system):

$$W = \frac{\mu(\lambda/\mu)^M}{(M-1)!(M\mu - \lambda)^2} P_0 + \frac{1}{\mu} = \frac{L}{\lambda} \quad (14\text{-}11)$$

4. The average number of customers or units in line waiting for service:

$$L_q = L - \frac{\lambda}{\mu} \quad (14\text{-}12)$$

5. The average time a customer or unit spends in the queue waiting for service:

$$W_q = W - \frac{1}{\mu} = \frac{L_q}{\lambda} \quad (14\text{-}13)$$

6. Utilization rate:

$$\rho = \frac{\lambda}{M\mu} \quad (14\text{-}14)$$

---

[4] This model is also known by the technical name of the M/M/m model.

These equations are obviously more complex than the ones used in the single-channel model, yet they are used in exactly the same fashion and provide the same type of information as did the simpler model.

Arnold's Muffler Shop Revisited

For an application of the multichannel queuing model, let's return to the case of Arnold's Muffler Shop. Earlier, Larry Arnold examined two options. He could retain his current mechanic, Reid Blank, at a total expected cost of $162 per day; or he could fire Blank and hire a slightly more expensive but faster worker named Jimmy Smith. With Smith on board, service system costs could be reduced to $112 per day.

The muffler shop considers opening a second muffler service channel that operates at the same speed as the first one.

A third option is now explored. Arnold finds that at minimal after-tax cost he can open a *second* garage bay in which mufflers can be installed. Instead of firing his first mechanic, Blank, he would hire a second worker. The new mechanic would be expected to install mufflers at the same rate as Blank—about $\mu = 3$ per hour. Customers, who would still arrive at the rate of $\lambda = 2$ per hour, would wait in a single line until one of the two mechanics is free. To find out how this option compares with the old single-channel waiting line system, Arnold computes several operating characteristics for the $M = 2$ channel system.

$$P_0 = \frac{1}{\left[\sum_{n=0}^{1} \frac{1}{n!}\left(\frac{2}{3}\right)^n\right] + \frac{1}{2!}\left(\frac{2}{3}\right)^2\left(\frac{2(3)}{2(3) - 2}\right)}$$

$$= \frac{1}{1 + \frac{2}{3} + \frac{1}{2}\left(\frac{4}{9}\right)\left(\frac{6}{6 - 2}\right)} = \frac{1}{1 + \frac{2}{3} + \frac{1}{3}} = \frac{1}{2} = 0.5$$

= probability of 0 cars in the system

$$L = \left(\frac{(2)(3)(2/3)^2}{1![2(3) - 2]^2}\right)\left(\frac{1}{2}\right) + \frac{2}{3} = \frac{8/3}{16}\left(\frac{1}{2}\right) + \frac{2}{3} = \frac{3}{4} = 0.75$$

= average number of cars in the system

$$W = \frac{L}{\lambda} = \frac{3/4}{2} = \frac{3}{8} \text{ hours } = 22\frac{1}{2} \text{ minutes}$$

= average time a car spends in the system

$$L_q = L - \frac{\lambda}{\mu} = \frac{3}{4} - \frac{2}{3} = \frac{1}{12} = 0.083$$

= average number of cars in the queue

$$W_q = \frac{L_q}{\lambda} = \frac{0.083}{2} = 0.0415 \text{ hour } = 2\frac{1}{2} \text{ minutes}$$

= average time a of car spends in the queue

Dramatically lower waiting time results from opening the second service bay.

These data are compared with earlier operating characteristics in Table 14.2. The increased service from opening a second channel has a dramatic effect on almost all characteristics. In particular, time spent waiting in line drops from 40 minutes with one mechanic (Blank) or 15 minutes with Smith down to only $2\frac{1}{2}$ minutes! Similarly, the av-

OPERATING CHARACTERISTIC	LEVEL OF SERVICE		
	ONE MECHANIC (REID BLANK) $\mu = 3$	TWO MECHANICS $\mu = 3$ FOR EACH	ONE FAST MECHANIC (JIMMY SMITH) $\mu = 4$
Probability that the system is empty (P_0)	0.33	0.50	0.50
Average number of cars in the system (L)	2 cars	0.75 car	1 car
Average time spent in the system (W)	60 minutes	22.5 minutes	30 minutes
Average number of cars in the queue (L_q)	1.33 cars	0.083 car	0.50 car
Average time spent in the queue (W_q)	40 minutes	2.5 minutes	15 minutes

erage number of cars in the queue falls to 0.083 (about $\frac{1}{12}$ of a car).[5] But does this mean that a second bay should be opened?

To complete his economic analysis, Arnold assumes that the second mechanic would be paid the same as the current one, Blank, namely, $7 per hour. Total time customers will now spend waiting will be = (16 cars/day) × (0.0415 hour/car) = 0.664 hour.

$$\text{Customer waiting cost} = \$10/\text{hour} \times 0.664 \text{ hour} = \$6.64 \text{ per day}$$

$$\text{Service cost of 2 mechanics} = 2 \times 8 \text{ hours each/day} \times \$7/\text{hour} = \$112 \text{ per day}$$

$$\text{Total expected cost} = \text{waiting cost} + \text{service cost}$$

$$= \$6.64 + \$112.00 = \$118.64 \text{ per day}$$

As you recall, total cost with just Blank as mechanic was found to be $162 per day. Cost with just Smith was just $112. Although opening a second channel would be likely to have a positive effect on customer goodwill and hence lower the cost of waiting time, it means an increase in the cost of providing service. Look back to Figure 14.1 and you will see that such trade-offs are the basis of queuing theory. Arnold's decision is to replace his present worker with the speedier Smith and *not* to open a second service bay.

Using Excel QM for Analysis of Arnold's Multichannel Queuing Model Just as we used Excel QM to model Arnold's single-channel queue (in Program 14.1), we can model the multichannel case with Excel as well. Programs 14.2A and 14.2B provide the input/formulas and output, respectively.

---

[5] You might note that adding a second mechanic does not cut queue waiting time and length just in half, but makes it even smaller. This is because of the *random* arrival and service processes. When there is only one mechanic and two customers arrive within a minute of each other, the second will have a long wait. The fact that the mechanic may have been idle for 30 to 40 minutes before they both arrive does not change this average waiting time. Thus, single-channel models often have high wait times relative to multichannel models.

PROGRAM 14.2A

Input Data and Formulas for Arnold's Multichannel Queuing Decision Using Excel QM

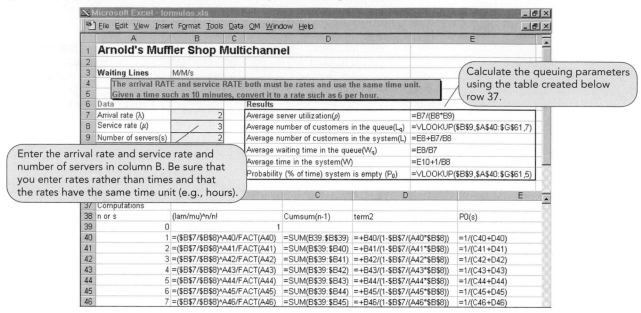

PROGRAM 14.2B

Output from Excel QM Analysis in Program 14.2A

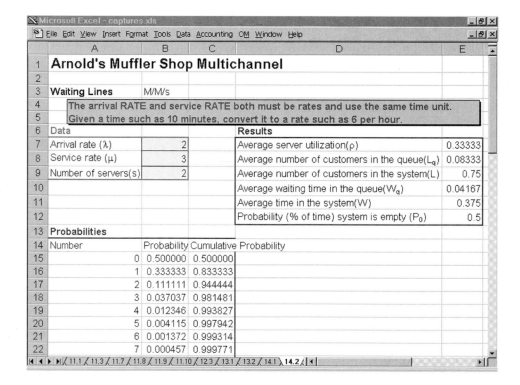

 **IN ACTION** Shortening the Arrest-to-Arraignment Time in New York City's Police Department

On March 23, 1990, the *New York Times* ran a front-page story on a woman who spent 45 hours in prearraignment detention in that city under the headline "Trapped in the terror of New York's holding pens." Indeed, people arrested in New York City at that time averaged a 40-hour wait (some more than 70 hours) prior to arraignment. These people were held in crowded, noisy, stressful, unhealthy, and often dangerous holding facilities, and in effect, denied a speedy court appearance. That same year, the New York Supreme Court ruled that the city was to attempt to arraign in 24 hours or to release the prisoner.

The arrest-to-arraignment (ATA) process, which has the general characteristics of a large queuing system, involves these steps: arrest of suspected criminal, transport to a police precinct, search/fingerprinting, paperwork for arrest, transport to a central booking facility, additional paperwork, processing of fingerprints, a bail interview, transport to either the courthouse or an outlying precinct, checks for a criminal record, and finally, an assistant district attorney drawing up a complaint document.

To solve the very complex problem of improving this system, the city hired Queues Enforth Development, Inc., a Massachusetts consulting firm. Their Monte Carlo simulation of the ATA process included single- and multiple-server queuing models. The modeling approach successfully reduced the average ATA time to 24 hours and resulted in an annual cost savings of $9.5 million for the city and state.

Source: R. C. Larson, M. F. Colan, and M. C. Shell. "Improving the New York Arrest-to-Arraignment System," *Interfaces* 23, 1 (January–February 1993): 76–96.

14.6 CONSTANT SERVICE TIME MODEL[6]

Some service systems have constant service times instead of exponentially distributed times. When customers or equipment are processed according to a fixed cycle, as in the case of an automatic car wash or an amusement park ride, constant service rates are appropriate. Because constant rates are certain, the values for L_q, W_q, L, and W are always less than they would be in the models we have just discussed, which have variable service times. As a matter of fact, both the average queue length and the average waiting time in the queue are *halved* with the constant service rate model.

Constant service rates speed the process compared to exponentially distributed service times with the same value of μ.

Equations for the Constant Service Time Model

Constant service model formulas follow:

1. Average length of the queue:

$$L_q = \frac{\lambda^2}{2\mu(\mu - \lambda)}$$

(14-15)

2. Average waiting time in the queue:

$$W_q = \frac{\lambda}{2\mu(\mu - \lambda)}$$

(14-16)

3. Average number of customers in the system:

$$L = L_q + \frac{\lambda}{\mu}$$

(14-17)

4. Average time in the system:

$$W = W_q + \frac{1}{\mu}$$

(14-18)

[6] In the operations research literature, this is also referred to as the M/D/1 model.

Garcia-Golding Recycling, Inc.

Garcia-Golding Recycling, Inc., collects and compacts aluminum cans and glass bottles in New York City. Their truck drivers, who arrive to unload these materials for recycling, currently wait an average of 15 minutes before emptying their loads. The cost of the driver and truck time wasted while in queue is valued at $60 per hour. A new automated compactor can be purchased that will process truck loads at a constant rate of 12 trucks per hour (that is, 5 minutes per truck). Trucks arrive according to a Poisson distribution at an average rate of 8 per hour. If the new compactor is put in use, its cost will be amortized at a rate of $3 per truck unloaded. A summer intern from a local college did the following analysis to evaluate the costs versus benefits of the purchase.

$$\textit{Current} \text{ waiting cost/trip} = (\text{¼ hour waiting now}) (\$60/\text{hour cost})$$
$$= \$15/\text{trip}$$

$$\textit{New} \text{ system: } \lambda = 8 \text{ trucks/hour arriving,}$$
$$\mu = 12 \text{ trucks/hour served}$$

Cost analysis for the recycling example.

$$\text{Average waiting time in queue} = W_q = \frac{\lambda}{2\mu(\mu - \lambda)} = \frac{8}{2(12)(12 - 8)}$$

$$= \frac{1}{12} \text{ hour}$$

$$\text{Waiting cost/trip with new compactor} = (\tfrac{1}{12} \text{ hour wait}) (\$60/\text{hour cost}) = \$5/\text{trip}$$

$$\text{Savings with new equipment} = \$15 \text{ (current system)} - \$5 \text{ (new system)}$$
$$= \$10/\text{trip}$$

$$\text{Cost of new equipment amortized} = \underline{\$3/\text{trip}}$$

$$\text{Net savings} = \$7/\text{trip}$$

Using Excel QM for Garcia-Golding's Constant Service Time Model To help solve this constant service time model with Excel QM, we refer to Programs 14.3A and 14.3B. The former provides an input screen and Excel formulas, and the latter contains the computed model parameters, including W_q.

14.7 FINITE POPULATION MODEL[7]

When there is a limited population of potential customers for a service facility, we need to consider a different queuing model. This model would be used, for example, if you were considering equipment repairs in a factory that has five machines, if you were in charge of maintenance for a fleet of 10 commuter airplanes, or if you ran a hospital ward that has 20 beds. The limited population model permits any number of repair people (servers) to be considered.

The reason this model differs from the three earlier queuing models is that there is now a *dependent* relationship between the length of the queue and the arrival rate. To illustrate the extreme situation, if your factory had five machines and all were broken and awaiting re-

---

[7] In the operations research literature, this is called the M/M/1 finite source model.

PROGRAM 14.3A

Input Data and Formulas for Excel QM's Constant Service Time Queuing Model Applied to Garcia-Golding Recycling, Inc.

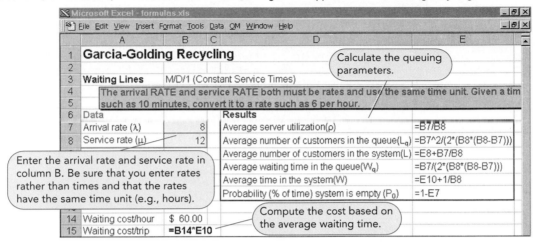

PROGRAM 14.3B

Output from Excel QM Constant Service Time Model in Program 14.3A

pair, the arrival rate would drop to zero. In general, as the waiting line becomes longer in the limited population model, the arrival rate of customers or machines drops lower.

In this section we describe a finite calling population model that has the following assumptions:

1. There is only one server.
2. The population of units seeking service is finite.[8]
3. Arrivals follow a Poisson distribution, while service times are exponentially distributed.
4. Customers are served on a first-come, first-served basis.

---

[8] Although there is no definite number that we can use to divide finite from infinite populations, the general rule of thumb is this: If the number in the queue is a significant proportion of the calling population, use a finite queuing model. *Finite Queuing Tables*, by L. G. Peck and R. N. Hazelwood (New York: John Wiley & Sons, Inc., 1958), eliminates much of the mathematics involved in computing the operating characteristics for such a model.

Equations for the Finite Population Model

Using

$$\lambda = \text{mean arrival rate}, \quad \mu = \text{mean service rate}, \quad N = \text{size of the population}$$

the operating characteristics for the finite population model with a single channel or server on duty are as follows:

1. Probability that the system is empty:

$$P_0 = \frac{1}{\displaystyle\sum_{n=0}^{N} \frac{N!}{(N-n)!}\left(\frac{\lambda}{\mu}\right)^n} \tag{14-19}$$

2. Average length of the queue:

$$L_q = N - \left(\frac{\lambda + \mu}{\lambda}\right)(1 - P_0) \tag{14-20}$$

3. Average number of customers (units) in the system:

$$L = L_q + (1 - P_0) \tag{14-21}$$

4. Average waiting time in the queue:

$$W_q = \frac{L_q}{(N-L)\lambda} \tag{14-22}$$

5. Average time in the system:

$$W = W_q + \frac{1}{\mu} \tag{14-23}$$

6. Probability of n units in the system:

$$P_n = \frac{N!}{(N-n)!}\left(\frac{\lambda}{\mu}\right)^n P_0 \qquad \text{for } n = 0, 1, \ldots, N \tag{14-24}$$

Department of Commerce Example

Past records indicate that each of the five high-speed "page" printers at the U.S. Department of Commerce, in Washington, DC, needs repair after about 20 hours of use. Breakdowns have been determined to be Poisson distributed. The one technician on duty can service a printer in an average of 2 hours, following an exponential distribution.

To compute the system's operation characteristics we first note that the mean arrival rate is $\lambda = \frac{1}{20} = 0.05$ printer/hour. The mean service rate is $\mu = \frac{1}{2} = 0.50$ printer/hour. Then

1. $P_0 = \dfrac{1}{\displaystyle\sum_{n=0}^{5} \frac{5!}{(5-n)!}\left(\frac{0.05}{0.5}\right)^n} = 0.564$ (we leave these calculations for you to confirm)

2. $L_q = 5 - \left(\dfrac{0.05 + 0.5}{0.05}\right)(1 - P_0) = 5 - (11)(1 - 0.564) = 5 - 4.8$

   $= 0.2$ printer

3. $L = 0.2 + (1 - 0.564) = 0.64$ printer

4. $W_q = \dfrac{0.2}{(5 - 0.64)(0.05)} = \dfrac{0.2}{0.22} = 0.91$ hour

5. $W = 0.91 + \dfrac{1}{0.50} = 2.91$ hours

If printer downtime costs \$120 per hour and the technician is paid \$25 per hour, we can also compute the total cost per hour:

total hourly cost = (average number of printers down) (cost per downtime hour)
    + cost per technician hour

$$= (0.64) (\$120) + \$25 = \$76.80 + \$25.00 = \$101.80$$

Solving the Department of Commerce Finite Population Model with Excel QM Program 14.4A shows the input data and formulas used to help solve this problem using Excel QM. The results are provided in Program 14.4B. Note that the computer calculations are slightly more accurate because there is less rounding than we did in our calculations in the preceding section.

PROGRAM 14.4A

Excel QM Input Data and Formulas for Solving the Department of Commerce Finite Population Queuing Model

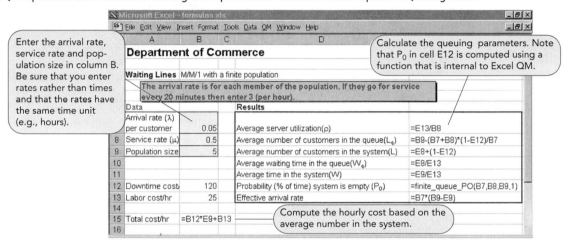

PROGRAM 14.4B

Output from Excel QM's Program 14.4A

14.8   MORE COMPLEX QUEUING MODELS AND THE USE OF SIMULATION

Many practical waiting line problems that occur in production and operations service systems have characteristics like those of Arnold's Muffler Shop, Garcia-Golding Recycling Inc., or the Department of Commerce. This is true when the situation calls for single- or multiple-channel waiting lines, with Poisson arrivals and exponential or constant service times, an infinite calling population, and first-in, first-out service.

More sophisticated models exist to handle variations of basic assumptions, but when even these do not apply we can turn to computer simulation, the topic of Chapter 15.

Often, however, *variations* of this specific case are present in an analysis. Service times in an automobile repair shop, for example, tend to follow the normal probability distribution instead of the exponential. A college registration system in which seniors have first choice of courses and hours over all other students is an example of a first-come, first-served model with a preemptive priority queue discipline. A physical examination for military recruits is an example of a multiphase system—one that differs from the single-phase models discussed in this chapter. A recruit first lines up to have blood drawn at one station, then waits to take an eye exam at the next station, talks to a psychiatrist at the third, and is examined by a doctor for medical problems at the fourth. At each phase, the recruit must enter another queue and wait his or her turn.

Models to handle these cases have been developed by operations researchers. The computations for the resulting mathematical formulations are somewhat more complex than the ones covered in this chapter,[9] and many real-world queuing applications are too complex to be modeled analytically at all. When this happens, quantitative analysts usually turn to *computer simulation.*

Simulation, the topic of Chapter 15, is a technique in which random numbers are used to draw inferences about probability distributions (such as arrivals and services). Using this approach, many hours, days, or months of data can be developed by a computer in a few seconds. This allows analysis of controllable factors, such as adding another service channel, without actually doing so physically. Basically, whenever a standard analytical queuing model provides only a poor approximation of the actual service system, it is wise to develop a simulation model instead.

Summary

A review of the assumptions underlying queuing models is discussed.

Waiting lines and service systems are important parts of the business world. In this chapter we described several common queuing situations and presented mathematical models for analyzing waiting lines following certain assumptions. Those assumptions were that (1) arrivals come from an infinite or very large population, (2) arrivals are Poisson distributed, (3) arrivals are treated on a first-in, first-out basis and do not balk or renege, (4) service times follow the negative exponential distribution or are constant, and (5) the average service rate is faster than the average arrival rate.

The models illustrated in this chapter were for single-channel, single-phase and multiple-channel, single-phase problems. After a series of operating characteristics were com-

---

[9] Often, the *qualitative* results of queuing models are as useful as the quantitative results. Results show that it is inherently more efficient to pool resources, use central dispatching, and provide single multiple-server systems rather than multiple single-server systems.

puted, total expected costs were studied. As shown graphically in Figure 14.1, total cost is the sum of the cost of providing service plus the cost of waiting time.

Key operating characteristics for a system were shown to be (1) utilization rate, (2) percent idle time, (3) average time spent waiting in the system and in the queue, (4) average number of customers in the system and in the queue, and (5) probabilities of various numbers of customers in the system.

It was emphasized that a variety of queuing models exist that do not meet all of the assumptions of the traditional models. In these cases we use more complex mathematical models or turn to a technique called computer simulation. The application of simulation to problems of queuing systems, inventory control, machine breakdown, and other quantitative analysis situations is the topic discussed in Chapter 15.

Here is a listing of the key system characteristics

Glossary

Waiting Line. One or more customers or objects waiting to be served.

Queuing Theory. The mathematical study of waiting lines or queues.

Service Cost. The cost of providing a particular level of service.

Waiting Cost. The cost to the firm of having customers or objects waiting in line to be serviced.

Calling Population. The population of items from which arrivals at the queuing system come.

Unlimited or Infinite Population. A calling population that is very large relative to the number of customers currently in the system.

Limited or Finite Population. A case in which the number of customers in the system is a significant proportion of the calling population.

Poisson Distribution. A probability distribution that is often used to describe random arrivals in a queue.

Balking. The case in which arriving customers refuse to join the waiting line.

Reneging. The case in which customers enter a queue but then leave before being serviced.

Limited Queue Length. A waiting line that cannot increase beyond a specific size.

Unlimited Queue Length. A queue that can increase to an infinite size.

Queue Discipline. The rule by which customers in a line receive service.

FIFO. A queue discipline (meaning first-in, first-out) in which the customers are served in the strict order of arrival.

Single-Channel Queuing System. A system with one service facility fed by one queue.

Multiple-Channel Queuing System. A system that has more than one service facility, all fed by the same single queue.

Single-Phase System. A queuing system in which service is received at only one station.

Multiphase System. A system in which service is received from more than one station, one after the other.

Negative Exponential Probability Distribution. A probability distribution that is often used to describe random service times in a service system.

M/M/1. Another name for the single-channel model with Poisson arrivals and exponential service times.

Operating Characteristics. Descriptive characteristics of a queuing system, including the average number of customers in a line and in the system, the average waiting times in a line and in the system, and percent idle time.

Utilization Factor (ρ). The proportion of the time that service facilities are in use.

M/M/m. A technical name for the multichannel queuing model (with m servers) and Poisson arrivals and exponential service times.

M/D/1. A technical name for the constant service time model.

Simulation. A technique for representing queuing models that are complex and difficult to model analytically.

Key Equations

λ = mean number of arrivals per time period

μ = mean number of people or items served per time period

(14-1) $P(X) = \dfrac{e^{-\lambda}\lambda^X}{X!}$

Poisson probability distribution used in describing arrivals.

Equations 14-2 through 14-8 describe operating characteristics in the single-channel model that has Poisson arrival and exponential service rates.

(14-2) L = average number of units (customers) in the system

$= \dfrac{\lambda}{\mu - \lambda}$

(14-3) W = average time a unit spends in the system (waiting time + service time)

$= \dfrac{1}{\mu - \lambda}$

(14-4) L_q = average number of units in the queue $= \dfrac{\lambda^2}{\mu(\mu - \lambda)}$

(14-5) W_q = average time a unit spends waiting in the queue $= \dfrac{\lambda}{\mu(\mu - \lambda)}$

(14-6) ρ = utilization factor for the system $= \dfrac{\lambda}{\mu}$

(14-7) P_0 = probability of 0 units in the system (that is, the service unit is idle)

$= 1 - \dfrac{\lambda}{\mu}$

(14-8) $P_{n>k}$ = probability of more than k units in the system $= \left(\dfrac{\lambda}{\mu}\right)^{k+1}$

Equations 14-9 through 14-14 describe operating characteristics in multiple-channel models that have Poisson arrival and exponential service rates, where M = the number of open channels.

(14-9) $P_0 = \dfrac{1}{\left[\displaystyle\sum_{n=0}^{n=M-1} \dfrac{1}{n!}\left(\dfrac{\lambda}{\mu}\right)^n\right] + \dfrac{1}{M!}\left(\dfrac{\lambda}{\mu}\right)^M \dfrac{M\mu}{M\mu - \lambda}}$ for $M\mu > \lambda$

The probability that there are no people or units in the system.

(14-10) $L = \dfrac{\lambda\mu(\lambda/\mu)^M}{(M-1)!(M\mu - \lambda)^2}P_0 + \dfrac{\lambda}{\mu}$

The average number of people or units in the system.

(14-11) $W = \dfrac{\mu(\lambda/\mu)^M}{(M-1)!(M\mu - \lambda)^2}P_0 + \dfrac{1}{\mu} = \dfrac{L}{\lambda}$

The average time a unit spends in the waiting line or being serviced (namely, in the system).

(14-12) $L_q = L - \dfrac{\lambda}{\mu}$

The average number of people or units in line waiting for service.

(14-13) $W_q = W - \dfrac{1}{\mu} = \dfrac{L_q}{\lambda}$

The average time a person or unit spends in the queue waiting for service.

(14-14) $\rho = \dfrac{\lambda}{M\mu}$

Utilization rate.

Equations 14-15 through 14-18 describe operating characteristics in single-channel models that have Poisson arrivals and constant service rates.

(14-15) $L_q = \dfrac{\lambda^2}{2\mu(\mu - \lambda)}$

The average length of the queue.

(14-16) $W_q = \dfrac{\lambda}{2\mu(\mu - \lambda)}$

The average waiting time in the queue.

(14-17) $L = L_q + \dfrac{\lambda}{\mu}$

The average number of customers in the system.

(14-18) $W = W_q + \dfrac{1}{\mu}$

The average waiting time in the system.

Equations 14-19 through 14-24 describe operating characteristics in single-channel models that have Poisson arrivals and exponential service rates and a finite calling population.

(14-19) $P_0 = \dfrac{1}{\displaystyle\sum_{n=0}^{N} \dfrac{N!}{(N - n)!} \left(\dfrac{\lambda}{\mu}\right)^n}$

The probability that the system is empty.

(14-20) $L_q = N - \left(\dfrac{\lambda + \mu}{\lambda}\right)(1 - P_0)$

Average length of the queue.

(14-21) $L = L_q + (1 - P_0)$

Average number of units in the system.

(14-22) $W_q = \dfrac{L_q}{(N - L)\lambda}$

Average time in the queue.

(14-23) $W = W_q + \dfrac{1}{\mu}$

Average time in the system.

(14-24) $P_n = \dfrac{N!}{(N - n)!} \left(\dfrac{\lambda}{\mu}\right)^n P_0 \qquad \text{for} \qquad n = 0, 1, \ldots, N$

Probability of n units in the system.

Solved Problems

Solved Problem 14-1

The Maitland Furniture store gets an average of 50 customers per shift. The manager of Maitland wants to calculate whether she should hire 1, 2, 3, or 4 salespeople. She has determined that average waiting times will be 7 minutes with one salesperson, 4 minutes with two salespeople, 3 minutes with three salespeople, and 2 minutes with four salespeople. She has estimated the cost per minute that customers wait at $1. The cost per salesperson per shift (including fringe benefits) is $70.

How many salespeople should be hired?

Solution

The manager's calculations are as follows:

	NUMBER OF SALESPEOPLE			
	1	**2**	**3**	**4**
(a) Average number of customers per shift	50	50	50	50
(b) Average waiting time per customer (minutes)	7	4	3	2
(c) Total waiting time per shift ($a \times b$) (minutes)	350	200	150	100
(d) Cost per minute of waiting time (estimated)	$1.00	$1.00	$1.00	$1.00
(e) Value of lost time ($c \times d$) per shift	$350	$200	$150	$100
(f) Salary cost per shift	$ 70	$140	$210	$280
(g) Total cost per shift	$420	$340	$360	$380

Because the minimum total cost per shift relates to two salespeople, the manager's optimum strategy is to hire two salespeople.

Solved Problem 14-2

Marty Schatz owns and manages a chili dog and soft drink store near the campus. While Marty can service 30 customers per hour on the average (μ), he only gets 20 customers per hour (λ). Because Marty could wait on 50% more customers than actually visit his store, it doesn't make sense to him that he should have any waiting lines.

Marty hires you to examine the situation and to determine some characteristics of his queue. After looking into the problem, you make the seven assumptions listed in Section 14.4. What are your findings?

Solution

$$L = \frac{\lambda}{\mu - \lambda} = \frac{20}{30 - 20} = 2 \text{ customers in the system on the average}$$

$$W = \frac{1}{\mu - \lambda} = \frac{1}{30 - 20} = 0.1 \text{ hour (6 minutes) that the average customer spends in the total system}$$

$$L_q = \frac{\lambda^2}{\mu(\mu - \lambda)} = \frac{20^2}{30(30 - 20)} = 1.33 \text{ customers waiting for service in line on the average}$$

$$W_q = \frac{\lambda}{\mu(\mu - \lambda)} = \frac{20}{30(30 - 20)} = \frac{1}{15} \text{ hour} = (4 \text{ minutes}) = \text{average waiting time of a customer in the queue awaiting service}$$

$$\rho = \frac{\lambda}{\mu} = \frac{20}{30} = 0.67 = \text{percent of the time that Marty is busy waiting on customers}$$

$$P_0 = 1 - \frac{\lambda}{\mu} = 1 - \rho = 0.33 = \text{probability that there are no customers in the system (being waited on or waiting in the queue) at any given time}$$

PROBABILITY OF *k* OR MORE CUSTOMERS WAITING IN LINE AND/OR BEING WAITED ON

k	$P_{n>k} = \left(\frac{\lambda}{\mu}\right)^{k+1}$
0	0.667
1	0.444
2	0.296
3	0.198

Solved Problems 14-3

Refer to the preceding Solved Problem. Marty agreed that these figures seemed to represent his approximate business situation. You are quite surprised at the length of the lines and elicit from him an estimated value of the customer's waiting time (in the queue, not being waited on) at 10 cents per minute. During the 12 hours that he is open he gets $(12 \times 20) = 240$ customers. The average customer is in a queue 4 minutes, so the total customer waiting time is $(240 \times 4$ minutes$) = 960$ minutes. The value of 960 minutes is $(\$0.10)$ (960 minutes) $= \$96$. You tell Marty that not only is 10 cents per minute quite conservative, but he could probably save most of that $96 of customer ill will if he hired another salesclerk. After much haggling, Marty agrees to provide you with all the chili dogs you can eat during a week-long period in exchange for your analysis of the results of having two clerks wait on the customers.

Assuming that Marty hires one additional salesclerk whose service rate equals Marty's rate, complete the analysis.

Solution

With two cash registers open, the system becomes two-channel, or $M = 2$. The computations yield

$$P_0 = \frac{1}{\left[\displaystyle\sum_{n=0}^{n=M-1} \frac{1}{n!}\left[\frac{20}{30}\right]^n\right] + \frac{1}{2!}\left[\frac{20}{30}\right]^2 \left[\frac{2(30)}{2(30) - 20}\right]}$$

$$= \frac{1}{(1)(2/3)^0 + (1)(2/3)^1 + (1/2)(4/9)(6/4)} = 0.5$$

$= \text{probability of no customers in the system}$

$$L = \left[\frac{(20)(30)(20/30)^2}{(2-1)![(2)(30-20)]^2}\right]0.5 + \frac{20}{30} = 0.75 \text{ customer in the system on the average}$$

$$W = \frac{L}{\lambda} = \frac{3/4}{20} = \frac{3}{80} \text{ hours} = 2.25 \text{ minutes that the average customer spends in the total system}$$

$$L_q = L - \frac{\lambda}{\mu} = \frac{3}{4} - \frac{20}{30} = \frac{1}{12} = 0.083 \text{ customer waiting for service in line on the average}$$

$$W_q = \frac{L_q}{\lambda} = \frac{\frac{1}{12}}{20} = \frac{1}{240} \text{ hour} = \frac{1}{4} \text{ minute} = \text{ average waiting time of a customer in the queue itself (not being serviced)}$$

$$\rho = \frac{\lambda}{M\mu} = \frac{20}{2(30)} = \frac{1}{3} = 0.33 = \text{ utilization rate}$$

You now have (240 customers) × (1/240 hour) = 1 hour total customer waiting time per day.

Total cost of 60 minutes of customer waiting time is (60 minutes) ($0.10 per minute) = $6.

Now you are ready to point out to Marty that the hiring of one additional clerk will save $96 − $6 = $90 of customer ill will per 12-hour shift. Marty responds that the hiring should also reduce the number of people who look at the line and leave as well as those who get tired of waiting in line and leave. You tell Marty that you are ready for two chili dogs, extra hot.

SELF-TEST

- Before taking the self-test, refer back to the learning objectives at the beginning of the chapter, the notes in the margins, and the glossary at the end of the chapter.
- Use the key at the back of the book to correct your answers.
- Restudy pages that correspond to any questions that you answered incorrectly or material you feel uncertain about.

1. Most systems use the queue discipline known as the first-in, first-out rule.
   a. True   b. False
2. Before using exponential distributions to build queuing models, the quantitative analyst should determine if the service-time data fit the distribution.
   a. True   b. False
3. In a multichannel, single-phase queuing system, the arrival will pass through at least two different service facilities.
   a. True   b. False
4. Which of the following is *not* an assumption in common queuing mathematical models?
   a. arrivals come from an infinite or very large population
   b. arrivals are Poisson distributed
   c. arrivals are treated on a first-in, first-out basis and do not balk or renege
   d. service times follow the exponential distribution
   e. the average arrival rate is faster than the average service rate
5. Which of the following is *not* a key operating characteristic for a queuing system?
   a. utilization rate
   b. percent idle time
   c. average time spent waiting in the system and in the queue
   d. average number of customers in the system and in the queue
   e. none of the above
6. Three parts of a queuing system are
   a. the inputs, the queue, and the service facility.
   b. the calling population, the queue, and the service facility.
   c. the calling population, the waiting line, and the service facility.
   d. all of the above.

7. The utilization factor for a system is defined as
   a. mean number of people served divided by the mean number of arrivals per time period.
   b. the average time a customer spends waiting in a queue.
   c. proportion of the time the service facilities are in use.
   d. the percent idle time.
   e. none of the above.
8. If everything else remains constant, including the mean arrival rate and service rate, except that the service time becomes constant instead of exponential,
   a. the average queue length will be halved.
   b. the average waiting time will be doubled.
   c. the average queue length will increase.
   d. none of the above.
9. Customers enter the waiting line at a cafeteria on a first-come, first-served basis. The arrival rate follows a Poisson distribution, while service times follow an exponential distribution. If the average number of arrivals is 6 per minute and the average service rate of a single server is 10 per minute, what is the average number of customers in the system?
   a. 0.6
   b. 0.9
   c. 1.5
   d. 0.25
   e. none of the above
10. In the standard queuing model, we assume that the queue discipline is _____ .
11. The service *time* in the basic queuing model is assumed to be _____ .
12. When managers find standard queuing formulas inadequate or the mathematics unsolvable, they often resort to _____ to obtain their solutions.
13. In the basic queuing model, the number of arrivals is assumed to be _____ .

Discussion Questions and Problems

Discussion Questions

14-1 What is the waiting line problem? What are the components in a waiting line system?

14-2 What are the assumptions underlying common queuing models?

14-3 Describe the important operating characteristics of a queuing system.

14-4 Why must the service rate be greater than the arrival rate in a single-channel queuing system?

14-5 Briefly describe three situations in which the FIFO discipline rule is not applicable in queuing analysis.

14-6 Provide examples of four situations in which there is a limited, or finite, waiting line.

14-7 What are the components of the following systems? Draw and explain the configuration of each.
 (a) Barbershop
 (b) Car wash
 (c) Laundromat
 (d) Small grocery store

14-8 Do doctors' offices generally have random arrival rates for patients? Are service times random? Under what circumstances might service times be constant?

14-9 Do you think the Poisson distribution, which assumes independent arrivals, is a good estimation of arrival rates in the following queuing systems? Defend your position in each case.
 (a) Cafeteria in your school
 (b) Barbershop
 (c) Hardware store
 (d) Dentist's office
 (e) College class
 (f) Movie theater

Problems*

‡ 14-10 The Golding Discount Department Store has approximately 300 customers shopping in its store between 9 A.M. and 5 P.M. on Saturdays. In deciding how many cash registers to keep open each Saturday, Golding's manager considers two factors: customer waiting time (and the associated waiting cost) and the service costs of employing additional checkout clerks. Checkout clerks are paid an average of $4 per hour. When only one is on duty, the waiting time per customer is about 10 minutes (or ⅙ of an hour); when two clerks are on duty, the average checkout time is 6 minutes per person; 4 minutes when three clerks are working; and 3 minutes when four clerks are on duty.

Golding's management has conducted customer satisfaction surveys and has been able to estimate that the store suffers approximately $5 in lost sales and goodwill for every *hour* of customer time spent waiting in checkout lines. Using the information provided, determine the optimal number of clerks to have on duty each Saturday to minimize the store's total expected cost.

  14-11 The Rockwell Electronics Corporation retains a service crew to repair machine breakdowns that occur on an average of $\lambda = 3$ per day (approximately Poisson in nature).

---

*Note: means the problem may be solved with QM for Windows; ✗ means the problem may be solved with Excel QM; and 🖥 means the problem may be solved with QM for Windows and/or Excel QM.

The crew can service an average of $\mu = 8$ machines per day, with a repair time distribution that resembles the exponential distribution.

(a) What is the utilization rate of this service system?

(b) What is the average downtime for a machine that is broken?

(c) How many machines are waiting to be serviced at any given time?

(d) What is the probability that more than one machine is in the system? Probability that more than two are broken and waiting to be repaired or being serviced? More than three? More than four?

14-12 From historical data, Harry's Car Wash estimates that dirty cars arrive at the rate of 10 per hour all day Saturday. With a crew working the wash line, Harry figures that cars can be cleaned at the rate of one every 5 minutes. One car at a time is cleaned in this example of a single-channel waiting line.

Assuming Poisson arrivals and exponential service times, find the

(a) average number of cars in line.

(b) average time a car waits before it is washed.

(c) average time a car spends in the service system.

(d) utilization rate of the car wash.

(e) probability that no cars are in the system.

14-13 Mike Dreskin manages a large Los Angeles movie theater complex called Cinema I, II, III, and IV. Each of the four auditoriums plays a different film; the schedule is set so that starting times are staggered to avoid the large crowds that would occur if all four movies started at the same time. The theater has a single ticket booth and a cashier who can maintain an average service rate of 280 movie patrons per hour. Service times are assumed to follow an exponential distribution. Arrivals on a typically active day are Poisson distributed and average 210 per hour.

To determine the efficiency of the current ticket operation, Mike wishes to examine several queue operating characteristics.

(a) Find the average number of moviegoers waiting in line to purchase a ticket.

(b) What percentage of the time is the cashier busy?

(c) What is the average time that a customer spends in the system?

(d) What is the average time spent waiting in line to get to the ticket window?

(e) What is the probability that there are more than two people in the system? More than three people? More than four?

14-14 A university cafeteria line in the student center is a self-serve facility in which students select the food items they want and then form a single line to pay the cashier. Students arrive at a rate of about four per minute according to a Poisson distribution. The single cashier ringing up sales takes about 12 seconds per customer, following an exponential distribution.

(a) What is the probability that there are more than two students in the system? More than three students? More than four?

(b) What is the probability that the system is empty?

(c) How long will the average student have to wait before reaching the cashier?

(d) What is the expected number of students in the queue?

(e) What is the average number in the system?

(f) If a second cashier is added (who works at the same pace), how will the operating characteristics computed in parts (b), (c), (d), and (e) change? Assume that customers wait in a single line and go to the first available cashier.

14-15 The wheat harvesting season in the American Midwest is short, and most farmers deliver their truckloads of wheat to a giant central storage bin within a two-week span. Because of this, wheat-filled trucks waiting to unload and return to the fields have been known to back up for a block at the receiving bin. The central bin is owned cooperatively, and it is to every farmer's benefit to make the unloading/storage process as efficient as possible. The cost of grain deterioration caused by unloading delays and the cost of truck rental and idle driver time are significant concerns to the cooperative

$\lambda = 30$

$\mu = 35$

members. Although farmers have difficulty quantifying crop damage, it is easy to assign a waiting and unloading cost for truck and driver of $18 per hour. The storage bin is open and operated 16 hours per day and 7 days per week during the harvest season and is capable of unloading 35 trucks per hour according to an exponential distribution. Full trucks arrive all day long (during the hours the bin is open) at a rate of about 30 per hour, following a Poisson pattern.

To help the cooperative get a handle on the problem of lost time while trucks are waiting in line or unloading at the bin, find the

(a) average number of trucks in the unloading system.
(b) average time per truck in the system.
(c) utilization rate for the bin area.
(d) probability that there are more than three trucks in the system at any given time.
(e) total daily cost to the farmers of having their trucks tied up in the unloading process.
(f) The cooperative, as mentioned, uses the storage bin only two weeks per year. Farmers estimate that enlarging the bin would cut unloading costs by 50% next year. It will cost $9,000 to do so during the off-season. Would it be worth the cooperative's while to enlarge the storage area?

$\lambda = 4$

$\mu = 12$

14-16 Ashley's Department Store in Kansas City maintains a successful catalog sales department in which a clerk takes orders by telephone. If the clerk is occupied on one line, incoming phone calls to the catalog department are answered automatically by a recording machine and asked to wait. As soon as the clerk is free, the party that has waited the longest is transferred and answered first. Calls come in at a rate of about 12 per hour. The clerk is capable of taking an order in an average of 4 minutes. Calls tend to follow a Poisson distribution, and service times tend to be exponential. The clerk is paid $5 per hour, but because of lost goodwill and sales, Ashley's loses about $25 per hour of customer time spent waiting for the clerk to take an order.

(a) What is the average time that catalog customers must wait before their calls are transferred to the order clerk?   W
(b) What is the average number of callers waiting to place an order?   Q
(c) Ashley is considering adding a second clerk to take calls. The store would pay that person the same $5 per hour. Should it hire another clerk? Explain.

14-17 Sal's International Barbershop is a popular haircutting and styling salon near the campus of the University of New Orleans. Four barbers work full-time and spend an average of 15 minutes on each customer. Customers arrive all day long at an average rate of 12 per hour. When they enter, they take a number to wait for the first available barber. Arrivals tend to follow the Poisson distribution, and service times are exponentially distributed.

(a) What is the probability that the shop is empty?
(b) What is the average number of customers in the barbershop?
(c) What is the average time spent in the shop?
(d) What is the average time that a customer spends waiting to be called to the barber chair?
(e) What is the average number waiting to be served?
(f) What is the shop's utilization factor?
(g) Sal's is thinking of adding a fifth barber. How will this affect the utilization rate?

14-18 The medical director of a large emergency clinic faces a problem of providing treatment for patients who arrive at different rates during the day. There are four doctors available to treat patients when needed. If not needed, they can be assigned to other responsibilities (for example, lab tests, reports, x-ray diagnoses) or else rescheduled to work at other hours.

It is important to provide quick and responsive treatment, and the medical director feels that, on average, patients should not have to sit in the waiting area for more than 5 minutes before being seen by a doctor. Patients are treated on a first-come, first-served basis and see the first available doctor after waiting in the queue. The arrival pattern for a typical day is as follows:

TIME	ARRIVAL RATE (PATIENTS/HOUR)
9 A.M.–3 P.M.	6
3 P.M.–8 P.M.	4
8 P.M.–midnight	12

These arrivals follow a Poisson distribution, and treatment times, 12 minutes on the average, follow the exponential pattern.

How many doctors should be on duty during each period to maintain the level of patient care expected?

14-19 Juhn and Sons Wholesale Fruit Distributors employ one worker whose job it is to load fruit on outgoing company trucks. Trucks arrive at the loading gate at an average of 24 per day, or 3 per hour, according to a Poisson distribution. The worker loads them at a rate of 4 per hour, following approximately the exponential distribution in service times.

Determine the operating characteristics of this loading gate problem. What is the probability that there will be more than three trucks either being loaded or waiting? Discuss the result of your queuing model computation.

14-20 Juhn believes that adding a second fruit loader will substantially improve the firm's efficiency. He estimates that a two-person crew, still acting like a single-server system, at the loading gate will double the loading rate from 4 trucks per hour to 8 trucks per hour. Analyze the effect on the queue of such a change and compare the results with those found in Problem 14-19.

14-21 Truck drivers working for Juhn and Sons (see Problems 14-19 and 14-20) are paid a salary of $10 per hour on average. Fruit loaders receive about $6 per hour. Truck drivers waiting in the queue or at the loading gate are drawing a salary but are productively idle and unable to generate revenue during that time. What would be the *hourly* cost savings to the firm associated with employing two loaders instead of one?

14-22 Juhn and Sons Wholesale Fruit Distributors (of Problem 14-19) are considering building a second platform or gate to speed the process of loading their fruit trucks. This, they think, will be even more efficient than simply hiring another loader to help out the first platform (as in Problem 14-20).

Assume that workers at each platform will be able to load 4 trucks per hour each and that trucks will continue to arrive at the rate of 3 per hour. Then apply the preceding equations to find the waiting line's new operating conditions. Is this new approach indeed speedier than the other two considered?

14-23 Customers arrive at an automated coffee vending machine at a rate of four per minute, following a Poisson distribution. The coffee machine dispenses a cup of coffee at a constant rate of 10 seconds.
(a) What is the average number of people waiting in line?
(b) What is the average number in the system?
(c) How long does the average person wait in line before receiving service?

14-24 The average number of customers in the system in the single-channel, single-phase model described in Section 14.4 is

$$L = \frac{\lambda}{\mu - \lambda}$$

Show that for $M = 1$ server, the multichannel queuing model in Section 14.5,

$$L = \frac{\lambda \mu \left(\frac{\lambda}{\mu}\right)^M}{(M - 1)!(M\mu - \lambda)^2} P_0 + \frac{\lambda}{\mu}$$

is identical to the single-channel system. Note that the formula for P_0 (Equation 14-9) must be utilized in this highly algebraic exercise.

14-25 One mechanic services five drilling machines for a steel plate manufacturer. Machines break down on an average of once every six working days, and breakdowns tend to follow a Poisson distribution. The mechanic can handle an average of one repair job per day. Repairs follow an exponential distribution.

(a) How many machines are waiting for service, on average?
(b) How many are currently being served?
(c) How many drills are in running order, on average?
(d) What is the average waiting time in the queue?
(e) What is the average wait in the system?

14-26 A technician monitors a group of five computers that run an automated manufacturing facility. It takes an average of 15 minutes (exponentially distributed) to adjust a computer that develops a problem. The computers run for an average of 85 minutes (Poisson distributed) without requiring adjustments. What is the:

(a) average number of computers waiting for adjustment?
(b) average number of computers not in working order?
(c) probability the system is empty?
(d) average time in the queue?
(e) average time in the system?

14-27 The typical subway station in Washington, DC, has six turnstiles, each of which can be controlled by the station manager to be used for either entrance or exit control—but never for both. The manager must decide at different times of the day just how many turnstiles to use for entering passengers and how many to be set up to allow exiting passengers.

At the Washington College Station, passengers enter the station at a rate of about 84 per minute between the hours of 7 and 9 A.M. Passengers exiting trains at the stop reach the exit turnstile area at a rate of about 48 per minute during the same morning rush hours. Each turnstile can allow an average of 30 passengers per minute to enter or exit. Arrival and service times have been thought to follow Poisson and exponential distributions, respectively. Assume riders form a common queue at both entry and exit turnstile areas and proceed to the first empty turnstile.

The Washington College Station manager does not want the average passenger at his station to have to wait in a turnstile line for more than 6 seconds, nor does he want more than eight people in any queue at any average time.

(a) How many turnstiles should be opened in each direction every morning?
(b) Discuss the assumptions underlying the solution of this problem using queuing theory.

Case Study

New England Castings

For more than 75 years, New England Castings, Inc., has manufactured wood stoves for home use. In recent years, with increasing energy prices, George Mathison, president of New England Castings, has seen sales triple. This dramatic increase in sales has made it even more difficult for George to maintain quality in all the wood stoves and related products.

Unlike other companies manufacturing wood stoves, New England Castings is *only* in the business of making stoves and stove-related products. Their major products are the Warmglo I, the Warmglo II, the Warmglo III, and the Warmglo IV. The Warmglo I is the smallest wood stove, with a heat output of 30,000 Btu, while the Warmglo IV is the largest, with a heat output of 60,000 Btu. In addition, New England Castings, Inc., produces a large array of products that have been designed to be used with one of their four stoves. These products include warming shelves, surface thermometers, stovepipes, adaptors, stove gloves, trivets, mitten racks, andirons, chimneys, and heat shields. New England Castings also publishes a newsletter and several paperback books on stove installation, stove operation, stove maintenance, and wood sources. It is George's belief that their wide assortment of products was a major contributor to the sales increases.

The Warmglo III outsells all the other stoves by a wide margin. The heat output and available accessories are ideal for the typical home. The Warmglo III also has a number of outstanding features that make it one of the most attractive and heat-efficient stoves on the market. Each Warmglo III has a thermostatically controlled primary air intake valve that allows the stove to adjust itself automatically to produce the correct heat output for varying weather conditions. A secondary air opening is used to increase the heat output in case of very cold weather. The internal stove parts produce a horizontal flame path for more efficient burning, and the output gases are forced to take an S-shaped path through the stove. The S-shaped path allows more complete combustion of the gases and better heat transfer from the fire and gases through the cast iron to the area to be heated. These features, along with the accessories, resulted in expanding sales and prompted George to build a new factory to manufacture Warmglo III stoves. An overview diagram of the factory is shown in Figure 14.5.

The new foundry uses the latest equipment, including a new Disamatic that helps in manufacturing stove parts. Regardless of new equipment or procedures, casting operations have remained basically unchanged for hundreds of years. To begin with, a wooden pattern is made for every cast-iron piece in the stove. The wooden pattern is an exact duplication of the cast-iron piece that is to be manufactured. New England Castings has all of its patterns made by Precision Patterns, Inc., and these patterns are stored in the pattern shop and maintenance room. Then a specially formulated sand is molded around the wooden pattern. There can be two or more sand molds for each pattern. Mixing the sand and making the molds are done in the molding

FIGURE 14.5
Overview of Factory

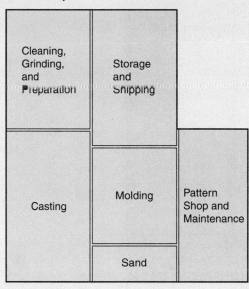

room. When the wooden pattern is removed, the resulting sand molds form a negative image of the desired casting. Next, the molds are transported to the casting room, where molten iron is poured into the molds and allowed to cool. When the iron has solidified, the molds are moved into the cleaning, grinding, and preparation room. The molds are dumped into large vibrators that shake most of the sand from the casting. The rough castings are then subjected to both sandblasting to remove the rest of the sand and grinding to finish some of the surfaces of the castings. The castings are then painted with a special heat-resistant paint, assembled into workable stoves, and inspected for manufacturing defects that may have gone undetected thus far. Finally, the finished stoves are moved to storage and shipping, where they are packaged and shipped to the appropriate locations.

At present, the pattern shop and the maintenance department are located in the same room. One large counter is used by both maintenance personnel to get tools and parts and by sand molders that need various patterns for the molding operation. Pete Nawler and Bob Bryan, who work behind the counter, are able to service a total of 10 people per hour (or about 5 per hour each). On the average, 4 people from maintenance and 3 people from the molding department arrive at the counter per hour. People from the molding department and from maintenance arrive randomly, and to be served they form a single line. Pete and Bob have always had a policy of first come, first served. Because of the location of the pattern shop and maintenance department, it takes about 3 minutes for a person from the maintenance department to walk to the pattern and maintenance room, and it takes about 1 minute for a person to walk from the molding department to the pattern and maintenance room.

FIGURE 14.6

Overview of Factory after Changes

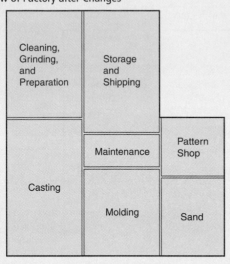

After observing the operation of the pattern shop and maintenance room for several weeks, George decided to make some changes to the layout of the factory. An overview of these changes appears in Figure 14.6.

Separating the maintenance shop from the pattern shop had a number of advantages. It would take people from the maintenance department only 1 minute instead of 3 to get to the new maintenance department. Using time-and-motion studies, George was also able to determine that improving the layout of the maintenance department would allow Bob to serve 6 people from the maintenance department per hour, and improving the layout of the pattern department would allow Pete to serve 7 people from the molding shop per hour.

Discussion Questions

1. How much time would the new layout save?
2. If maintenance personnel were paid $9.50 per hour and molding personnel were paid $11.75 per hour, how much could be saved per hour with the new factory layout?

Case Study

Winter Park Hotel

Donna Shader, manager of the Winter Park Hotel, is considering how to restructure the front desk to reach an optimum level of staff efficiency and guest service. At present, the hotel has five clerks on duty, each with a separate waiting line, during the peak check-in time of 3:00 P.M. to 5:00 P.M. Observation of arrivals during this time show that an average of 90 guests arrive each hour (although there is no upward limit on the number that could arrive at any given time). It takes an average of 3 minutes for the front-desk clerk to register each guest.

Ms. Shader is considering three plans for improving guest service by reducing the length of time guests spend waiting in line. The first proposal would designate one employee as a quick-service clerk for guests registering under corporate accounts, a market segment that fills about 30% of all occupied rooms. Because corporate guests are preregistered, their registration takes just 2 minutes. With these guests separated from the rest of the clientele, the average time for registering a typical guest would climb to 3.4 minutes. Under plan 1, noncorporate guests would choose any of the remaining four lines.

The second plan is to implement a single-line system. All guests could form a single waiting line to be served by whichever of five clerks became available. This option would require sufficient lobby space for what could be a substantial queue.

The use of an automatic teller machine (ATM) for check-ins is the basis of the third proposal. This ATM would provide approximately the same service rate as would a clerk. Given that initial use of this technology might be minimal, Shader estimated that 20% of customers, primarily frequent guests, would be willing to use the machines. (This might be a conservative estimate if the guests perceive direct benefits from using the ATM, as bank customers do. Citibank reports that some 80% of its Manhattan customers use its ATMs.) Ms. Shader would set up a single queue for customers who prefer human check-in clerks. This would be served by the five clerks, although Shader is hopeful that the machine will allow a reduction to four.

Discussion Questions

1. Determine the average amount of time that a guest spends checking in. How would this change under each of the state options?
2. Which option do you recommend?

INTERNET CASE STUDY

See our Internet home page at **http://www.prenhall.com/render** for this additional case study: Pantry Shopper.

Bibliography

Cooper, R. B. *Introduction to Queuing Theory*, 2nd ed. New York: Elsevier—North Holland, 1980.

Grassmann, Winfried, K. "Finding the Right Number of Servers in Real-World Queuing Systems," *Interfaces* 18, 2 (March–April 1988): 94–104.

Kaplan, Edward H. "A Public Housing Queue with Reneging and Task-Specific Servers," *Decision Sciences* 19 (1988): 383–391.

Katz, K., B. Larson, and R. Larson. "Prescription for the Waiting-in-Line Blues," *Sloan Management Review* (Winter 1991): 44–53.

Panico, J. A. *Queuing Theory: A Study of Waiting Lines for Business, Economics and Sciences*. Englewood Cliffs, NJ: Prentice Hall, 1969.

Prabhu, N. U. *Foundations of Queuing Theory*. Klewer Academic Publishers, 1997.

Quinn, Phil, Bruce Andrews, and Henry Parsons. "Allocating Telecommunications Resources at L.L.Bean, Inc.," *Interfaces* 21, 1 (January–February 1991): 75–91.

Swersey, Arthur J., et al. "Improving Fire Department Productivity," *Interfaces* 23, 1 (January–February 1993): 109–129.

Sze, D. "A Queuing Model for Telephone Operator Staffing," *Operations Research* 32, 2 (March–April 1984): 229–249.

Worthington, D. J. "Queuing Models for Hospital Waiting Lists," *Journal of the Operational Research Society* 38, 5 (May 1987): 413–422.

APPENDIX 14.1: USING QM FOR WINDOWS

This appendix illustrates the ease of use of the QM for Windows in solving queuing problems. Program 14.5 represents the Arnold's Muffler Shop analysis, with 2 servers. The only required inputs were a title, selection of the proper model, the arrival rate (2 cars per hour), the service rate (3 cars per hour), and the number of servers (2). System and queue times are available in hours, minutes (in the value * 60 column) and seconds (in the value * 60 * 60 column).

Waiting Lines / Single-channel system					
Waiting Lines Results					
(untitled) Solution					
Parameter	Value	Parameter	Value	Value * 60	Value * 60 * 60
Single-channel		Average server utilization	0.6667		
arrival rate(lambda)	2.	Average number in the queue	1.3333		
service rate(mu)	3.	Average number in the system	2.		
number of servers	1.	Average time in the queue(Wq)	0.6667	40.	2,400.
		Average time in the system(Ws)	1.	60.	3,600.

PROGRAM 14.5

Using QM for Windows to Solve a Multichannel Queuing Model (Arnold Muffler Shop Data)

Program 14.6 reflects a constant service time model, illustrated in the chapter by Garcia-Golding Recycling, Inc. The other queuing models can also be solved by QM for Windows, which additionally provides cost/economic analysis.

Waiting Lines / Constant service times					
Waiting Lines Results					
Garcia-Golding Recycling Inc. Solution					
Parameter	Value	Parameter	Value	Value * 60	Value * 60 * 60
Constant service		Average server utilization	0.6667		
arrival rate(lambda)	8.	Average number in the queue	0.6667		
service rate(mu)	12.	Average number in the system	1.3333		
number of servers	1.	Average time in the queue(Wq)	0.0833	5.	300.
		Average time in the system(Ws)	0.1667	10.	600.

PROGRAM 14.6

Using QM for Windows to Solve a Constant Service Time Model (Garcia-Golding Data)

CHAPTER 15

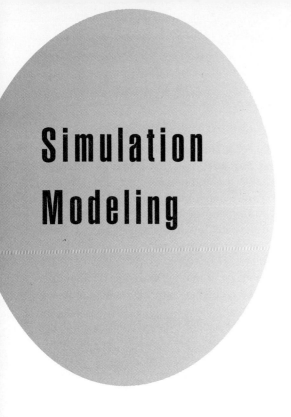

Simulation Modeling

LEARNING OBJECTIVES

After completing this chapter, students will be able to:

1. Tackle a wide variety of problems by simulation.
2. Understand the seven steps of conducting a simulation.
3. Explain the advantages and disadvantages of simulation.
4. Develop random number intervals and use them to generate outcomes.
5. Understand alternative computer simulation packages available.

CHAPTER OUTLINE

15.1 Introduction

15.2 Advantages and Disadvantages of Simulation

15.3 Monte Carlo Simulation

15.4 Simulation and Inventory Analysis

15.5 Simulation of a Queuing Problem

15.6 Simulation Model for a Maintenance Policy

15.7 Two Other Types of Simulation Models

15.8 Role of Computers in Simulation

Summary • Glossary • Solved Problems • Self-Test • Discussion Questions and Problems • Case Study: Alabama Airlines • Case Study: Abjar Transport Company • Internet Case Studies • Bibliography

Appendix 15.1: Using the Crystal Ball Excel Add-In

15.1 INTRODUCTION

We are all aware to some extent of the importance of simulation models in our world. Boeing Corporation and Airbus Industries, for example, commonly build *simulation* models of their proposed jet aircraft and then test the aerodynamic properties of the models. Your local civil defense organization may carry out rescue and evacuation practices as it simulates the natural disaster conditions of a hurricane or tornado. The U.S. Army simulates enemy attacks and defense strategies in war games played on a computer. Business students take courses that use management games to simulate realistic competitive business situations. And thousands of business, government, and service organizations develop simulation models to assist in making decisions concerning inventory control, maintenance scheduling, plant layout, investments, and sales forecasting.

As a matter of fact, simulation is one of the most widely used quantitative analysis tools. Various surveys of the largest U.S. corporations reveal that over half use simulation in corporate planning.

Simulation sounds like it may be the solution to all management problems. This is, unfortunately, by no means true. Yet we think you may find it one of the most flexible and fascinating of the quantitative techniques in your studies. Let's begin our discussion of simulation with a simple definition.

To *simulate* is to try to duplicate the features, appearance, and characteristics of a real system. In this chapter we show how to simulate a business or management system by building a *mathematical model* that comes as close as possible to representing the reality of the system. We won't build any *physical* models, as might be used in airplane wind tunnel simulation tests. But just as physical model airplanes are tested and modified under experimental conditions, so our mathematical models are experimented with to estimate the effects of various actions. The idea behind simulation is to imitate a real-world situation mathematically, then to study its properties and operating characteristics, and finally, to draw conclusions and make action decisions based on the results of the simulation. In this way, the real-life system is not touched until the advantages and disadvantages of what may be a major policy decision are first measured on the system's model.

The idea behind simulation is to imitate a real-world situation with a mathematical model that does not affect operations. The seven steps of simulation are illustrated in Figure 15.1.

Using simulation, a manager should (1) define a problem, (2) introduce the variables associated with the problem, (3) construct a numerical model, (4) set up possible courses of action for testing, (5) run the experiment, (6) consider the results (possibly deciding to modify the model or change data inputs), and (7) decide what course of action to take. These steps are illustrated in Figure 15.1.

The problems tackled by simulation may range from very simple to extremely complex, from bank teller lines to an analysis of the U.S. economy. Although very small simulations may be conducted by hand, effective use of this technique requires some automated means of calculation, namely, a computer. Even large-scale models, simulating perhaps years of business decisions, can be handled in a reasonable amount of time by computer. Though simulation is one of the oldest quantitative analysis tools (see the History box on page 658), it was not until the introduction of computers in the mid-1940s and early 1950s that it became a practical means of solving management and military problems.

The explosion of personal computers has created a wealth of computer simulation languages and broadened the use of simulation. Now, even spreadsheet software can be used to conduct fairly complex simulations (see Appendix 15.1).

We begin this chapter with a presentation of the advantages and disadvantages of simulation. An explanation of the Monte Carlo method of simulation follows. Three sample simulations, in the areas of inventory control, queuing, and maintenance planning, are presented. Other simulation models besides the Monte Carlo approach are also discussed briefly. Finally, the important role of computers in simulation is illustrated.

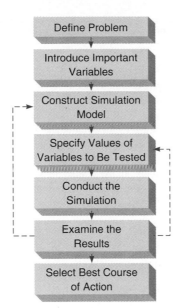

FIGURE 15.1

Process of Simulation

15.2 ADVANTAGES AND DISADVANTAGES OF SIMULATION

Simulation is a tool that has become widely accepted by managers for several reasons:

1. It is relatively straightforward and flexible.

2. It can be used to analyze large and complex real-world situations that cannot be solved by conventional quantitative analysis models. For example, it may not be possible to build and solve a mathematical model of a city government system that incorporates important economic, social, environmental, and political factors. Simulation has been used successfully to model urban systems, hospitals, educational systems, national and state economies, and even world food systems.

3. Simulation allows what-if? types of questions. Managers like to know in advance what options are attractive. With a computer, a manager can try out several policy decisions within a matter of minutes.

4. Simulations do not interfere with the real-world system. It may be too disruptive, for example, to experiment with new policies or ideas in a hospital, school, or manufacturing plant. With simulation, experiments are done with the model, not on the system itself.

5. Simulation allows us to study the interactive effect of individual components or variables to determine which ones are important.

6. "Time compression" is possible with simulation. The effect of ordering, advertising, or other policies over many months or years can be obtained by computer simulation in a short time.

7. Simulation allows for the inclusion of real-world complications that most quantitative analysis models cannot permit. For example, some queuing models require exponential or Poisson distributions; some inventory and network models require normality. But simulation can use *any* probability distribution that the user defines; it does not require standard distributions.

These seven advantages of simulation make it one of the most widely used quantitative analysis techniques in corporate America.

HISTORY   Simulation

The history of simulation goes back 5,000 years to Chinese war games, called *weich' i*, and continues through 1780, when the Prussians used the games to help train their army. Since then, all major military powers have used war games to test out military strategies under simulated environments.

From military or operational gaming, a new concept, *Monte Carlo simulation*, was developed as a quantitative technique by the great mathematician John von Neumann during World War II. Working with neutrons at the Los Alamos Scientific Laboratory, von Neumann used simulation to solve physics problems that were too complex or expensive to analyze by hand or by physical model. The random nature of the neutrons suggested the use of a roulette wheel in dealing with probabilities. Because of the gaming nature, von Neumann called it the Monte Carlo model of studying laws of chance.

With the advent and common use of business computers in the 1950s, simulation grew as a management tool. Specialized computer languages were developed in the 1960s (GPSS and SIMSCRIPT) to handle large-scale problems more effectively. In the 1980s, prewritten simulation programs to handle situations ranging from queuing to inventory were developed. They have such names as Xcell, SLAM, Witness, and MAP/1.

The four disadvantages of simulation are cost, its trial-and-error nature, the need to generate answers to tests, and uniqueness.

The main disadvantages of simulation are:

1. Good simulation models can be very expensive. It is often a long, complicated process to develop a model. A corporate planning model, for example, may take months or even years to develop.

2. Simulation does not generate optimal solutions to problems as do other quantitative analysis techniques such as EOQ, linear programming, or PERT. It is a trial-and-error approach that may produce different solutions in repeated runs.

3. Managers must generate all of the conditions and constraints for solutions that they want to examine. The simulation model does not produce answers by itself.

4. Each simulation model is unique. Its solutions and inferences are not usually transferable to other problems.

15.3   MONTE CARLO SIMULATION

When a system contains elements that exhibit chance in their behavior, the *Monte Carlo method* of simulation may be applied. The basis of Monte Carlo simulation is experimentation on the chance (or *probabilistic*) elements through random sampling. The technique breaks down into five simple steps:

Five Steps of Monte Carlo Simulation
1. Setting up a probability distribution for important variables
2. Building a cumulative probability distribution for each variable in step 1
3. Establishing an interval of random numbers for each variable
4. Generating random numbers
5. Actually simulating a series of trials

The Monte Carlo method can be used with variables that are probabilistic.

This section examines each of these steps in turn.

Step 1: Establishing Probability Distributions. The basic idea in Monte Carlo simulation is to generate values for the variables making up the model being studied. There are a lot of variables in real-world systems that are probabilistic in nature and that we might want to simulate. A few of these variables are:

1. Inventory demand on a daily or weekly basis

2. Lead time for inventory orders to arrive

3. Times between machine breakdowns

4. Times between arrivals at a service facility

5. Service times

6. Times to complete project activities

7. Number of employees absent from work each day

Variables we may want to simulate abound in business problems because very little in life is certain.

One common way to establish a *probability distribution* for a given variable is to examine historical outcomes. The probability, or relative frequency, for each possible outcome of a variable is found by dividing the frequency of observation by the total number of observations.

Harry's Auto Tire Example   The daily demand for radial tires, for example, at Harry's Auto Tire over the past 200 days is shown in Table 15.1. We can convert these data to a probability distribution, if we assume that past demand rates will hold in the future, by dividing each demand frequency by the total demand, 200. This is illustrated in Table 15.2.

To establish a probability distribution for tires we assume that historical demand is a good indicator of future outcomes.

Probability distributions, we should note, need not be based solely on historical observations. Often, managerial estimates based on judgment and experience are used to create a distribution. Sometimes, a sample of sales, machine breakdowns, or service rates is used to create probabilities for those variables. And the distributions themselves can be either empirical, as in Table 15.1, or based on the commonly known normal, binomial, Poisson, or exponential patterns.

Step 2: Building a Cumulative Probability Distribution for Each Variable. The conversion from a regular probability distribution, such as in the right-hand column of Table 15.2, to a *cumulative distribution* is an easy job. In Table 15.3 we see that the cumulative probability for each level of demand is the sum of the number in the probability column (middle column) added to the previous cumulative probability (rightmost column). The cumulative probability, graphed in Figure 15.2, is used in step 3 to help assign random numbers.

Step 3: Setting Random Number Intervals. After we have established a cumulative probability distribution for each variable included in the simulation, we must assign a set of numbers to represent each possible value or outcome. These are referred to as *random*

TABLE 15.1 Historical Daily Demand for Radial Tires at Harry's Auto Tire	
DEMAND FOR TIRES	FREQUENCY (DAYS)
0	10
1	20
2	40
3	60
4	40
5	30
	200

TABLE 15.2 Probability of Demand for Radial Tires	
DEMAND VARIABLE	PROBABILITY OF OCCURRENCE
0	10/200 = 0.05
1	20/200 = 0.10
2	40/200 = 0.20
3	60/200 = 0.30
4	40/200 = 0.20
5	30/200 = 0.15
	200/200 = 1.00

Cumulative probabilities are found by summing all the previous probabilities up to the current demand.

TABLE 15.3 **Cumulative Probabilities for Radial Tires**

DAILY DEMAND	PROBABILITY	CUMULATIVE PROBABILITY
0	0.05	0.05
1	0.10	0.15
2	0.20	0.35
3	0.30	0.65
4	0.20	0.85
5	0.15	1.00

number intervals. Random numbers are discussed in detail in step 4. Basically, a *random number* is a series of digits (say, two digits from 01, 02, . . . , 98, 99, 00) that have been selected by a totally random process.

Random numbers can actually be assigned in many different ways—as long as they represent the correct proportion of the outcomes.

If there is a 5% chance that demand for a product (such as Harry's radial tires) is 0 units per day, we want 5% of the random numbers available to correspond to a demand of 0 units. If a total of 100 two-digit numbers is used in the simulation (think of them as being numbered chips in a bowl), we could assign a demand of 0 units to the first five random numbers: 01, 02, 03, 04, and 05.[1] Then a simulated demand for 0 units would be created every time one of the numbers 01 to 05 was drawn. If there is also a 10% chance that

FIGURE 15.2

Graphical Representation of the Cumulative Probability Distribution for Radial Tires

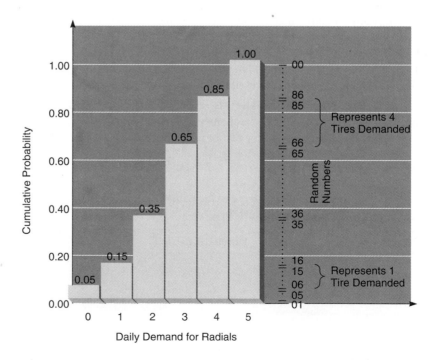

---
[1] Alternatively, we could have assigned the random numbers 00, 01, 02, 03, 04 to represent a demand of 0 units. The two digits 00 can be thought of as either 0 or 100. As long as 5 numbers out of 100 are assigned to the 0 demand, it doesn't make any difference which 5 they are.

TABLE 15.4	Assignment of Random Number Intervals for Harry's Auto Tire		
DAILY DEMAND	PROBABILITY	CUMULATIVE PROBABILITY	INTERVAL OF RANDOM NUMBERS
0	0.05	0.05	01 to 05
1	0.10	0.15	06 to 15
2	0.20	0.35	16 to 35
3	0.30	0.65	36 to 65
4	0.20	0.85	66 to 85
5	0.15	1.00	86 to 00

demand for the same product is 1 unit per day, we could let the next 10 random numbers (06, 07, 08, 09, 10, 11, 12, 13, 14, and 15) represent that demand—and so on for other demand levels.

In general, using the cumulative probability distribution computed and graphed in step 2, we can set the interval of random numbers for each level of demand in a very simple fashion. You will note in Table 15.4 that the interval selected to represent each possible daily demand is very closely related to the cumulative probability on its left. The top end of each interval is always equal to the cumulative probability percentage.

The relation between intervals and cumulative probability is that the top end of each interval is equal to the cumulative probability percentage.

Similarly, we can see in Figure 15.2 and in Table 15.4 that the length of each interval on the right corresponds to the probability of one of each of the possible daily demands. Hence, in assigning random numbers to the daily demand for three radial tires, the range of the random number interval (36 to 65) corresponds *exactly* to the probability (or proportion) of that outcome. A daily demand for three radial tires occurs 30% of the time. Any of the 30 random numbers greater than 35 up to and including 65 are assigned to that event.

Step 4: Generating Random Numbers. Random numbers may be generated for simulation problems in several ways. If the problem is very large and the process being studied involves thousands of simulation trials, computer programs are available to generate the random numbers needed.

If the simulation is being done by hand, as in this book, the numbers may be selected by the spin of a roulette wheel that has 100 slots, by blindly grabbing numbered chips out of a hat, or by any method that allows you to make a random selection.[2] The most commonly used means is to choose numbers from a table of random digits such as Table 15.5.

Table 15.5 was itself generated by a computer program. It has the characteristic that every digit or number in it has an equal chance of occurring. In a very large random number table, 10% of digits would be 1s, 10% 2s, 10% 3s, and so on. Because *everything* is random, we can select numbers from anywhere in the table to use in our simulation procedures in step 5.

There are several ways to pick random numbers— random number generators (which are a built-in feature in spreadsheets and many computer languages), tables (such as Table 15.5), a roulette wheel, etc.

---

[2] One more method of generating random numbers is called the von Neumann midsquare method, developed in the 1940s. Here's how it works: (1) select any arbitrary number with n digits (for example, $n = 4$ digits), (2) square the number, (3) extract the middle n digits as the next random number. As an example of a four-digit arbitrary number, use 3,614. The square of 3,614 is 13,060,996. The middle four digits of this new number are 0609. Thus 0609 is the next random number and steps 2 and 3 are repeated. The midsquare method is simple and easily programmed, but sometimes the numbers repeat quickly and are *not* random. For example, try using the method starting with 6,100 as your first arbitrary number!

T A B L E 1 5 . 5 **Table of Random Numbers**

52	06	50	88	53	30	10	47	99	37	66	91	35	32	00	84	57	07
37	63	28	02	74	35	24	03	29	60	74	85	90	73	59	55	17	60
82	57	68	28	05	94	03	11	27	79	90	87	92	41	09	25	36	77
69	02	36	49	71	99	32	10	75	21	95	90	94	38	97	71	72	49
98	94	90	36	06	78	23	67	89	85	29	21	25	73	69	34	85	76
96	52	62	87	49	56	59	23	78	71	72	90	57	01	98	57	31	95
33	69	27	21	11	60	95	89	68	48	17	89	34	09	93	50	44	51
50	33	50	95	13	44	34	62	64	39	55	29	30	64	49	44	30	16
88	32	18	50	62	57	34	56	62	31	15	40	90	34	51	95	26	14
90	30	36	24	69	82	51	74	30	35	36	85	01	55	92	64	09	85
50	48	61	18	85	23	08	54	17	12	80	69	24	84	92	16	49	59
27	88	21	62	69	64	48	31	12	73	02	68	00	16	16	46	13	85
45	14	46	32	13	49	66	62	74	41	86	98	92	98	84	54	33	40
81	02	01	78	82	74	97	37	45	31	94	99	42	49	27	64	89	42
66	83	14	74	27	76	03	33	11	97	59	81	72	00	64	61	13	52
74	05	81	82	93	09	96	33	52	78	13	06	28	30	94	23	37	39
30	34	87	01	74	11	46	82	59	94	25	34	32	23	17	01	58	73
59	55	72	33	62	13	74	68	22	44	42	09	32	46	71	79	45	89
67	09	80	98	99	25	77	50	03	32	36	63	65	75	94	19	95	88
60	77	46	63	71	69	44	22	03	85	14	48	69	13	30	50	33	24
60	08	19	29	36	72	30	27	50	64	85	72	75	29	87	05	75	01
80	45	86	99	02	34	87	08	86	84	49	76	24	08	01	86	29	11
53	84	49	63	26	65	72	84	85	63	26	02	75	26	92	62	40	67
69	84	12	94	51	36	17	02	15	29	16	52	56	43	26	22	08	62
37	77	13	10	02	18	31	19	32	85	31	94	81	43	31	58	33	51

Source: Excerpted from *A Million Random Digits with 100,000 Normal Deviates* (New York: Free Press, 1955), p. 7, with permission of the Rand Corporation.

Step 5: Simulating the Experiment. We may simulate outcomes of an experiment by simply selecting random numbers from Table 15.5. Beginning anywhere in the table, we note the interval in Table 15.4 or Figure 15.2 into which each number falls. For example, if the random number chosen is 81 and the interval 65 to 85 represents a daily demand for four tires, we select a demand of four tires.

We now illustrate the concept further by simulating 10 days of demand for radial tires at Harry's Auto Tire (see Table 15.6). We select the random numbers needed from Table 15.5, starting in the upper left-hand corner and continuing down the first column.

TABLE 15.6 Ten-Day Simulation of Demand for Radial Tires		
DAY	**RANDOM NUMBER**	**SIMULATED DAILY DEMAND**
1	52	3
2	37	3
3	82	4
4	69	4
5	98	5
6	96	5
7	33	2
8	50	3
9	88	5
10	90	5
		39 = total 10-day demand
		3.9 = average daily demand for tires

It is interesting to note that the average demand of 3.9 tires in this 10-day simulation differs significantly from the *expected* daily demand, which we may compute from the data in Table 15.2.

Simulated results can differ from analytical results in a short simulation.

$$\text{Expected daily demand} = \sum_{i=0}^{5} (\text{probability of } i \text{ tires}) \times (\text{demand of } i \text{ tires})$$
$$= (0.05)(0) + (0.10)(1) + (0.20)(2) + (0.30)(3)$$
$$+ (0.20)(4) + (0.15)(5)$$
$$= 2.95 \text{ tires}$$

If this simulation were repeated hundreds or thousands of times, it is much more likely that the average *simulated* demand would be nearly the same as the *expected* demand.

Naturally, it would be risky to draw any hard and fast conclusions regarding the operation of a firm from only a short simulation. It is also unlikely that anyone would actually want to go to the effort of simulating such a simple model containing only one variable. Simulating by hand does, however, demonstrate the important principles involved and *may* be useful in small-scale studies. As you might expect, the computer can be a very helpful tool in carrying out the tedious work in larger simulation undertakings.

Using QM for Windows for Simulation

Program 15.1 is a Monte Carlo simulation using our accompanying software, QM for Windows. It reveals that after 250 runs the average daily demand is 2.852 tires. If even more repetitions occurred, we would clearly come closer to the expected valve of 2.95 tires.

PROGRAM 15.1

Monte Carlo Computer
Simulation of Harry's Auto Tire
Using QM for Windows

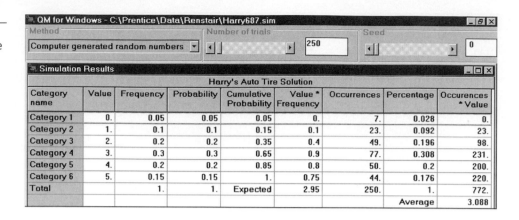

Simulation With Excel Spreadsheets

The ability to generate random numbers and then "look up" these numbers in a table in order to associate them with a specific event makes spreadsheets excellent tools for conducting simulations. Excel QM does not have a simulation module, because we are able to model all simulation problems directly in Excel. Program 15.2A illustrates an Excel simulation for Harry's Auto Tire.

Notice that the cumulative probabilities are calculated in column D of Program 15.2A. This procedure reduces the chance of error and is useful in larger simulations involving more levels of demand.

The = VLOOKUP function in column I looks up the random number (generated in column H) in the leftmost column of the defined lookup table ($C$3:$E$8). It moves downward through this column until it finds a cell that is bigger than the random number. It then goes to the previous row and gets the value from column E of the table.

In the output screen of Program 15.2B, for example, the first random number shown is .585. Excel looked down the left-hand column of the lookup table ($C$3:$E$8) of Program 15.2A until it found .65. From the previous row it retrieved the value in column E which is 3. Pressing the [**F9**] function key recalculates the random numbers and the simulation.

15.4 SIMULATION AND INVENTORY ANALYSIS

In Chapter 6 we introduced the subject of "deterministic" inventory models. These commonly used models are based on the assumption that both product demand and reorder lead time are known, constant values. In many real-world inventory situations, though, demand and lead time are variables, and accurate analysis becomes extremely difficult to handle by any means other than simulation.

In this section we present an inventory problem with two decision variables and two probabilistic components. The owner of the hardware store we are about to describe would like to establish *order quantity* and *reorder point* decisions for a particular product that has probabilistic (uncertain) daily demand and reorder lead time. He wants to make a series of simulation runs, trying out various order quantities and reorder points, to minimize his total inventory cost for the item. Inventory costs in this case include an ordering, holding, and stockout cost.

Simulation is useful when demand and lead time are probabilistic—in this case the inventory models like EOQ (of Chapter 6) can't be used.

PROGRAM 15.2A

Using Excel to Simulate Tire Demand for Harry's Auto Tire Shop

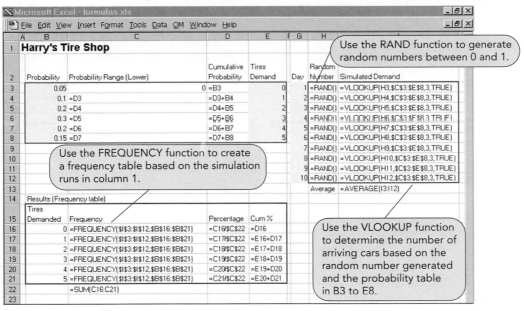

PROGRAM 15.2B

Excel Simulation Results for Harry's Auto Tire Shop. The Spreadsheet Output in Program 15.2B Shows a Simulated Average of 2.8 tires per day.

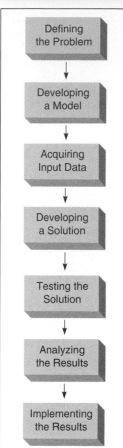

MODELING IN THE REAL WORLD — **U.S. Postal Service Simulates Automation**

Defining the Problem

The U.S. Postal Service (USPS) recognizes that automation technology is the only way to handle increases in mail volume, stay price competitive, and satisfy service goals. To do so, it needs to evaluate automation options: (1) on other automated or semiautomated equipment, (2) on the workforce, (3) on facilities, and (4) on other costs of operation.

Developing a Model

Kenan Systems Corporation was hired to develop a national simulation model called META (model for evaluating technology alternatives) to quantify the effects of different automation strategies. The initial version of META took three months to develop.

Acquiring Input Data

Data needed were collected from the USPS technology resource and delivery services departments. They included a nationwide survey that measured 3,200 of the 150,000 city carrier routes.

Developing a Solution

Users specify inputs for the quantity and type of mail to be processed, the people/equipment used to sort the mail, the flow of mail, and unit costs. META models how the entire nationwide mail system will function with these scenarios or inputs. META is not an optimization model, but allows users to examine changes in output that result from modifying inputs.

Testing the Solution

META's simulations were submitted to a three-month period of testing and validation to ensure that scenarios run produced reliable outputs. Hundreds of META scenarios were run.

Analyzing the Results

USPS uses META to analyze the effect of rate discounts, technology changes or advances, and changes to current processing operations.

Implementing the Results

The U.S. Postal Service estimates savings starting in 1995 at 100,000 work years annually, which translates into more than $4 billion. The simulation model also ensures that future technologies will be implemented in a timely and cost-effective manner.

Sources: M. E. Debry, A. H. DeSilva, and F. J. DiLisio. *Interfaces* 22, 1 (January–February 1992): 110–130 and M. D. Lasky and C. T. Balbach. *OR/MS Today* 23, 6 (December 1996): 38–41.

Simkin's Hardware Store

Simkin's Hardware sells the Ace model electric drill. Daily demand for the drill is relatively low but subject to some variability. Over the past 300 days, Simkin has observed the sales shown in column 2 of Table 15.7. He converts this historical frequency data into a probability distribution for the variable daily demand (column 3). A cumulative probability distribution is formed in column 4. Finally, Simkin establishes an interval of random numbers to represent each possible daily demand (column 5).

When Simkin places an order to replenish his inventory of Ace electric drills, there is a delivery lag of from one to three days. This means that lead time may also be considered a probabilistic variable. The number of days it took to receive the past 50 orders is presented in Table 15.8. In a fashion similar to that for the demand variable, Simkin establishes a probability distribution for the lead time variable (column 3 of Table 15.8),

TABLE 15.7 Probabilities and Random Number Intervals for Daily Ace Drill Demand

(1) DEMAND FOR ACE DRILL	(2) FREQUENCY (DAYS)	(3) PROBABILITY	(4) CUMULATIVE PROBABILITY	(5) INTERVAL OF RANDOM NUMBERS
0	15	0.05	0.05	01 to 05
1	30	0.10	0.15	06 to 15
2	60	0.20	0.35	16 to 35
3	120	0.40	0.75	36 to 75
4	45	0.15	0.90	76 to 90
5	30	0.10	1.00	91 to 00
	300	1.00		

TABLE 15.8 Probabilities and Random Number Intervals for Reorder Lead Time

(1) LEAD TIME (DAYS)	(2) FREQUENCY (ORDERS)	(3) PROBABILITY	(4) CUMULATIVE PROBABILITY	(5) RANDOM NUMBER INTERVAL
1	10	0.20	0.20	01 to 20
2	25	0.50	0.70	21 to 70
3	15	0.30	1.00	71 to 00
	50	1.00		

computes the cumulative distribution (column 4), and assigns random number intervals for each possible time (column 5).

The first inventory policy that Simkin's Hardware wants to simulate is an order quantity of 10 with a reorder point of 5. That is, every time the on-hand inventory level at the end of the day is 5 or less, Simkin will call his supplier and place an order for 10 more drills. If the lead time is one day, by the way, the order will not arrive the next morning but at the beginning of the following working day.

A delivery lag is the lead time in receiving an order— the time it was placed until it was received.

The logic of the simulation process is presented in Figure 15.3. Such a *flow diagram* or *flowchart* is useful in the logical coding procedures for programming this simulation process. The entire process is simulated for a 10-day period in Table 15.9. We can assume that beginning inventory is 10 units on day 1. (Actually, it makes little difference in a long simulation what the initial inventory level is. Since we would tend in real life to simulate hundreds or thousands of days, the beginning values will tend to be averaged out.) Random numbers for Simkin's inventory problem are selected from the second column of Table 15.5.

FIGURE 15.3

Flow Diagram for Simkin's Inventory Example

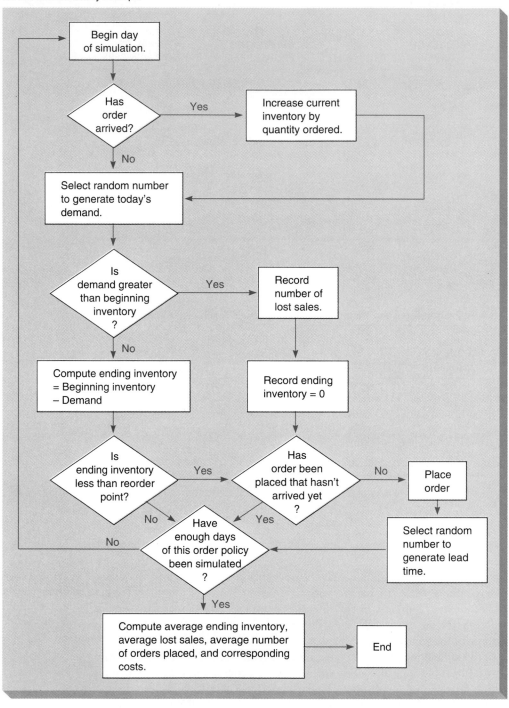

TABLE 15.9	Simkin Hardware's First Inventory Simulation

ORDER QUANTITY = 10 UNITS   **REORDER POINT = 5 UNITS**

(1) DAY	(2) UNITS RECEIVED	(3) BEGINNING INVENTORY	(4) RANDOM NUMBER	(5) DEMAND	(6) ENDING INVENTORY	(7) LOST SALES	(8) ORDER?	(9) RANDOM NUMBER	(10) LEAD TIME
1	...	10	06	1	9	0	No		
2	0	9	63	3	6	0	No		
3	0	6	57	3	(3)[a]	0	Yes	(02)[b]	1
4	0	3	(94)[c]	5	0	2	No[d]		
5	(10)[e]	10	52	3	7	0	No		
6	0	7	69	3	4	0	Yes	33	2
7	0	4	32	2	2	0	No		
8	0	2	30	2	0	0	No		
9	(10)[f]	10	48	3	7	0	No		
10	0	7	88	4	3	0	Yes	14	1
				Totals	41	2			

[a] This is the first time inventory dropped to the reorder point of 5 drills. Because no prior order was outstanding, an order is placed.

[b] The random number 02 is generated to represent the first lead time. It was drawn from column 2 of Table 15.5 as the next number in the list being used. A separate column could have been used to draw lead time random numbers from if we had wanted to do so, but in this example we did not do so.

[c] Again, notice that the random digits 02 were used for lead time (see footnote b). So the next number in the column is 94.

[d] No order is placed on day 4 because there is one outstanding from the previous day that has not yet arrived.

[e] The lead time for the first order placed is one day, but as noted in the text, an order does not arrive the next morning but at the beginning of the following working day. Thus the first order arrives at the start of day 5.

[f] This is the arrival of the order placed at the close of business of day 6. Fortunately for Simkin, no lost sales occurred during the two-day lead time until the order arrived.

Table 15.9 is filled in by proceeding one day (or line) at a time, working from left to right. It is a four-step process:

1. Begin each simulated day by checking whether any ordered inventory has just arrived (column 2). If it has, increase the current inventory (in column 3) by the quantity ordered (10 units, in this case).

2. Generate a daily demand from the demand probability distribution in Table 15.7 by selecting a random number. This random number is recorded in column 4. The demand simulated is recorded in column 5.

3. Compute the ending inventory every day and record it in column 6. Ending inventory equals beginning inventory minus demand. If on-hand inventory is insufficient to meet the day's demand, satisfy as much as possible and note the number of lost sales (in column 7).

4. Determine whether the day's ending inventory has reached the reorder point (5 units). If it has and if there are no outstanding orders, place an order (column 8). Lead time for a new order is simulated by first choosing a random number from Table 15.5 and recording it in column 9. (We may continue down the same string of the random number table that we were using to generate numbers for the demand variable.) Finally, we convert this random number into a lead time by using the distribution set in Table 15.8.

Here is how we simulated the Simkin Hardware example.

Analyzing Simkin's Inventory Costs

Simkin's first inventory simulation yields some interesting results. The average daily ending inventory is

$$\text{average ending inventory} = \frac{41 \text{ total units}}{10 \text{ days}} = 4.1 \text{ units per day}$$

We also note the average lost sales and number of orders placed per day:

$$\text{average lost sales} = \frac{2 \text{ sales lost}}{10 \text{ days}} = 0.2 \text{ unit per day}$$

$$\text{average number of orders placed} = \frac{3 \text{ orders}}{10 \text{ days}} = 0.3 \text{ order per day}$$

These data are useful in studying the inventory costs of the policy being simulated.

Simkin's store is open for business 200 days per year. He estimates that the cost of placing each order for Ace drills is $10. The cost of holding a drill in stock is $6 per drill per year, which can also be viewed as 3 cents per drill per day (over a 200-day year). Finally, Simkin estimates that the cost of each shortage, or lost sale, is $8. What is Simkin's total daily inventory cost for the ordering policy of order quantity, $Q = 10$ and reorder point, ROP = 5?

Let us examine the three cost components:

$$\text{daily order cost} = (\text{cost of placing one order})$$
$$\times (\text{number of orders placed per day})$$
$$= \$10 \text{ per order} \times 0.3 \text{ order per day} = \$3$$

$$\text{daily holding cost} = (\text{cost of holding one unit for one day})$$
$$\times (\text{average ending inventory})$$
$$= \$0.03 \text{ per unit per day} \times 4.1 \text{ units per day}$$
$$= \$0.12$$

$$\text{daily stockout cost} = (\text{cost per lost sale})$$
$$\times (\text{average number of lost sales per day})$$
$$= \$8 \text{ per lost sale} \times 0.2 \text{ lost sales per day}$$
$$= \$1.60$$

$$\text{total daily inventory cost} = \text{daily order cost} + \text{daily holding cost}$$
$$+ \text{daily stockout cost} = \$4.72$$

Thus the total daily inventory cost for this simulation is $4.72. Annualizing this daily figure to a 200-day working year suggests that this inventory policy's cost is approximately $944.

It is important to remember that the simulation should be conducted for many, many days before it is legitimate to draw any solid conclusions.

Now once again we want to emphasize something very important. This simulation should be extended many more days before we draw any conclusions as to the cost of the inventory policy being tested. If a hand simulation is being conducted, 100 days would provide a better representation. If a computer is doing the calculations, 1,000 days would be helpful in reaching accurate cost estimates.

Let's say that Simkin *does* complete a 1,000-day simulation of the policy that order quantity = 10 drills, reorder point = 5 drills. Does this complete his analysis? The answer is *no*—this is just the beginning! Simkin must now compare *this* potential strategy to

IN ACTION   **Using Simulation at Mexico's Largest Truck Manufacturer**

The manufacturing world has gone global. To remain competitive, firms have made strategic and cultural alliances. Mexico is the United States' third-largest trading partner ($27 billion), after Canada and Japan. Trading breakthroughs, such as the North American Economic Community (NAEC), have fundamental implications for industries in the United States and Mexico, including the truck manufacturer Vilpac headquartered in Mexicali, Mexico.

Vilpac developed a comprehensive simulation model for the analysis and design of its manufacturing operation using SIMNET II (a network-based simulation language on an IBM 3090 supercomputer). The idea was to allow manufacturing engineers to experiment with alternative systems and strategies to seek the best overall factory performance.

Ninety-five machines and 1,900 parts were included in the model, which performed a wide variety of experiments. SIMNET II was used to study the effects of policies on (1) the flexibility of the factory to adapt to change in the demand and product mix, (2) the factory's responsiveness to customer orders, (3) product quality, and (4) total cost. Benefits of the simulation approach included a 260% increase in production, a 70% decrease in work-in-process, and an increase in market share.

Source: J. P. Nuno, et al. "Mexico's Vilpac Truck Company Uses a CIM Implementation to Become a World Class Manufacturer," *Interfaces* 23, 1 (January–February 1993): 59–75.

other possibilities. For example, what about $Q = 10$, ROP $= 4$; or $Q = 12$, ROP $= 6$; or $Q = 14$, ROP $= 5$? Perhaps every combination of values of Q from 6 to 20 drills and ROP from 3 to 10 should be simulated. After simulating all reasonable combinations of order quantities and reorder points, Simkin would probably select the pair yielding the lowest total inventory cost.

15.5   SIMULATION OF A QUEUING PROBLEM

An important area of simulation application has been in the analysis of waiting line problems. As mentioned earlier, the assumptions required for solving queuing problems analytically are quite restrictive. For most realistic queuing systems, simulation may actually be the only approach available.

This section illustrates the simulation at a large unloading dock and its associated queue. Arrivals of barges at the dock are not Poisson distributed, and unloading rates (service times) are not exponential or constant. As such, the mathematical waiting line models of Chapter 14 cannot be used.

Port of New Orleans

Fully loaded barges arrive at night in New Orleans following their long trips down the Mississippi River from industrial midwestern cities. The number of barges docking on any given night ranges from 0 to 5. The probability of 0, 1, 2, 3, 4, or 5 arrivals is displayed in Table 15.10. In the same table, we establish cumulative probabilities and corresponding random number intervals for each possible value.

A study by the dock superintendent reveals that because of the nature of their cargo, the number of barges unloaded also tends to vary from day to day. The superintendent provides information from which we can create a probability distribution for the variable *daily unloading rate* (see Table 15.11). As we just did for the arrival variable, we can set up an interval of random numbers for the unloading rates.

Barge arrivals and unloading rates are both probabilistic variables. Unless they follow the queuing probability distributions of Chapter 14, we must turn to a simulation approach.

TABLE 15.10 Overnight Barge Arrival Rates and Random Number Intervals

NUMBER OF ARRIVALS	PROBABILITY	CUMULATIVE PROBABILITY	RANDOM NUMBER INTERVAL
0	0.13	0.13	01 to 13
1	0.17	0.30	14 to 30
2	0.15	0.45	31 to 45
3	0.25	0.70	46 to 70
4	0.20	0.90	71 to 90
5	0.10	1.00	91 to 00

TABLE 15.11 Unloading Rates and Random Number Intervals

DAILY UNLOADING RATE	PROBABILITY	CUMULATIVE PROBABILITY	RANDOM NUMBER INTERVAL
1	0.05	0.05	01 to 05
2	0.15	0.20	06 to 20
3	0.50	0.70	21 to 70
4	0.20	0.90	71 to 90
5	0.10	1.00	91 to 00
	1.00		

Barges are unloaded on a first-in, first-out basis. Any barges that are not unloaded the day of arrival must wait until the following day. Tying up a barge in dock is an expensive proposition, and the superintendent cannot ignore the angry phone calls from barge line owners reminding him that "time is money!" He decides that before going to the Port of New Orleans's controller to request additional unloading crews, a simulation study of arrivals, unloadings, and delays should be conducted. A 100-day simulation would be ideal, but for purposes of illustration, the superintendent begins with a shorter 15-day analysis. Random numbers are drawn from the top row of Table 15.5 to generate daily arrival rates. They are drawn from the second row of Table 15.5 to create daily unloading rates. Table 15.12 shows the day-by-day port simulation.

The superintendent will probably be interested in at least three useful and important pieces of information:

Here are the simulation results regarding average barge delays, average nightly arrivals, and average unloadings.

$$\text{average number of barges delayed to the next day} = \frac{20 \text{ delays}}{15 \text{ days}}$$
$$= 1.33 \text{ barges delayed per year}$$

$$\text{average number of nightly arrivals} = \frac{41 \text{ arrivals}}{15 \text{ days}} = 2.73 \text{ arrivals}$$

$$\text{average number of barges unloaded each day} = \frac{39 \text{ unloadings}}{15 \text{ days}} = 2.60 \text{ unloadings}$$

TABLE 15.12 Queuing Simulation of Port of New Orleans Barge Unloadings						
(1) **DAY**	**(2)** **NUMBER DELAYED** **FROM PREVIOUS DAY**	**(3)** **RANDOM** **NUMBER**	**(4)** **NUMBER** **NIGHTLY ARRIVALS**	**(5)** **TOTAL TO BE** **UNLOADED**	**(6)** **RANDOM** **NUMBER**	**(7)** **NUMBER** **UNLOADED**
1	(—)[a]	52	3	3	37	3
2	0	06	0	0	63	(0)[b]
3	0	50	3	3	28	3
4	0	88	4	4	02	1
5	3	53	3	6	74	4
6	2	30	1	3	35	3
7	0	10	0	0	24	(0)[c]
8	0	47	3	3	03	1
9	2	99	5	7	29	3
10	4	37	2	6	60	3
11	3	66	3	6	74	4
12	2	91	5	7	85	4
13	3	35	2	5	90	4
14	1	32	2	3	73	(3)[d]
15	0	00	5	5	59	3
	20		41			39
	Total delays		Total arrivals			Total unloadings

[a] We can begin with no delays from the previous day. In a long simulation, even if we started with 5 overnight delays, that initial condition would be averaged out.

[b] Three barges *could* have been unloaded on day 2. But because there were no arrivals and no backlog existed, zero unloadings took place.

[c] The same situation as noted in footnote b takes place.

[d] This time 4 barges could have been unloaded, but since only 3 were in the queue, the number unloaded is recorded as 3.

When these data are analyzed in the context of delay costs, idle labor costs, and the cost of hiring extra unloading crews, it will be possible for the dock superintendent and port controller to make a better staffing decision. They may even elect to resimulate the process assuming different unloading rates that would correspond to increased crew sizes. Although simulation is a tool that cannot guarantee an optimal solution to problems such as this, it can be helpful in recreating a process and identifying good decision alternatives.

Using Excel to Simulate the Port of New Orleans Queuing Problem

As we saw earlier in this chapter, simulation problems can be modeled in Excel directly (Excel QM does not contain a simulation module). To illustrate the Port of New Orleans problem, Program 15.3A provides the formulas needed. For a review of the VLOOKUP function refer back to Program 15.2A. The results of the Excel simulation are shown in Program 15.3B.

PROGRAM 15.3A

An Excel Model for the Port of New Orleans Queuing Simulation

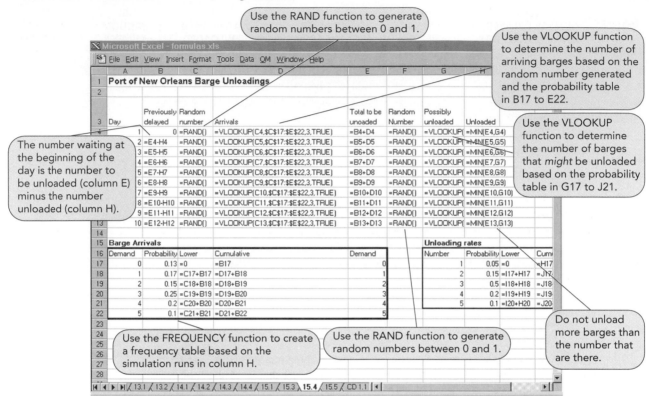

Use the RAND function to generate random numbers between 0 and 1.

Use the VLOOKUP function to determine the number of arriving barges based on the random number generated and the probability table in B17 to E22.

Use the VLOOKUP function to determine the number of barges that *might* be unloaded based on the probability table in G17 to J21.

The number waiting at the beginning of the day is the number to be unloaded (column E) minus the number unloaded (column H).

Use the FREQUENCY function to create a frequency table based on the simulation runs in column H.

Use the RAND function to generate random numbers between 0 and 1.

Do not unload more barges than the number that are there.

PROGRAM 15.3B

Output from the Excel Formulas in Program 15.3A

	A	B	C	D	E	F	G	H	I	J	K	L
1	Port of New Orleans Barge Unloadings											
2												
3	Day	Previously delayed	Random number	Arrivals	Total to be unloaded	Random Number	Possibly unloaded	Unloaded				
4	1	0	0.990073	5	5	0.715591	4	4				
5	2	1	0.02753	0	1	0.581144	3	1				
6	3	0	0.624446	3	3	0.897867	4	3				
7	4	0	0.166571	1	1	0.104936	2	1				
8	5	0	0.784053	4	4	0.392847	3	3				
9	6	1	0.361456	2	3	0.072112	2	2				
10	7	1	0.422756	2	3	0.101345	2	2				
11	8	1	0.522196	3	4	0.694828	3	3				
12	9	1	0.113926	0	1	0.074691	2	1				
13	10	0	0.753562	4	4	0.944656	5	4				
14												
15	Barge Arrivals						Unloading rates					
16	Demand	Probability	Lower	Cumulative	Demand		Number	Probability	Lower	Cumulative	Unloading	
17	0	0.13	0	0.13	0		1	0.05	0	0.05	1	
18	1	0.17	0.13	0.3	1		2	0.15	0.05	0.2	2	
19	2	0.15	0.3	0.45	2		3	0.5	0.2	0.7	3	
20	3	0.25	0.45	0.7	3		4	0.2	0.7	0.9	4	
21	4	0.2	0.7	0.9	4		5	0.1	0.9	1	5	
22	5	0.1	0.9	1	5							

15.6 SIMULATION MODEL FOR A MAINTENANCE POLICY

Simulation is a valuable technique for analyzing various maintenance policies before actually implementing them. A firm can decide whether to add additional maintenance staff based on machine downtime costs and costs of additional labor. It can simulate replacing parts that have not yet failed in exploring ways to prevent future breakdowns. Many companies use computerized simulation models to decide if and when to shut down an entire plant for maintenance activities. This section provides an example of the value of simulation in setting maintenance policy.

Maintenance problems are an area in which simulation is widely used.

Three Hills Power Company

The Three Hills Power Company provides electricity to a large metropolitan area through a series of almost 200 hydroelectric generators. Management recognizes that even a well-maintained generator will have periodic failures or breakdowns. Energy demands over the past three years have been consistently high, and the company is concerned over downtime of generators. It currently employs four highly skilled and highly paid ($30 per hour) repairpersons. Each works every fourth 8-hour shift. In this way there is a repairperson on duty 24 hours a day, seven days a week.

As expensive as the maintenance staff salaries are, breakdown expenses are even more costly. For each hour that one of its generators is down, Three Hills loses approximately $75. This amount is the charge for reserve power that Three Hills must "borrow" from the neighboring utility company.

Stephanie Robbins has been assigned to conduct a management analysis of the breakdown problem. She determines that simulation is a workable tool because of the probabilistic nature of two important maintenance system components.

First, the time between successive generator breakdowns varies historically from as little as one-half hour to as much as three hours. For the past 100 breakdowns Robbins

 IN ACTION | **Simulating Canadian National Railways Line Capacity**

The Canadian National Railway is one of the largest and oldest companies owned by the federal government of Canada. Geographically, the Canadian National Railway operates in areas that range all the way from Thunder Bay, Ontario, to Prince Rupert, in British Columbia. Included in this stretch are the beautiful Rocky Mountains that go through such areas as Jasper and Blue River. The railway originally started in 1923 from a collection of Canadian railways that were near bankruptcy. Since then, many changes have been made. In the 1970s, estimates were made that traffic and volume over Canada's National Railway would double. Any significant increase in traffic requires a lot of planning and a large investment in new equipment, tracks, and so forth.

To handle this new traffic, very large amounts of capital were needed to improve railway service, equipment, and personnel. These costs were projected to be approximately 3.5 billion Canadian dollars between 1985 and 1989. This represented a projected increase of traffic ranging from 60 to 75 million gross tons by 1990, up from 40 to 50 million gross tons in 1980.

To plan for this expansion, a number of simulation models were developed and used. A Signal Wake model was used to determine the minimum train headway that should be established for a given fleet or number of trains that are following each other. Another simulation model, the Route Capacity Model, investigated such important variables as train delay and overall efficiency as a function of specified track maintenance activities.

The overall result was a proposal for future capacity expansion. Using computer simulation, Canadian National Railway was able to defer spending approximately 350 million Canadian dollars.

Source: N. Welch and J. Gusso. "Expansion of Canadian National Railways Line Capacity," *Interfaces* 16, 1 (January–February 1986): 51–64.

TABLE 15.13 Time Between Generator Breakdown at Three Hills Power

TIME BETWEEN RECORDED MACHINE FAILURES (HOURS)	NUMBER OF TIMES OBSERVED	PROBABILITY	CUMULATIVE PROBABILITY	RANDOM NUMBER INTERVAL
½	5	0.05	0.05	01 to 05
1	6	0.06	0.11	06 to 11
1½	16	0.16	0.27	12 to 27
2	33	0.33	0.60	28 to 60
2½	21	0.21	0.81	61 to 81
3	19	0.19	1.00	82 to 00
Total	100	1.00		

TABLE 15.14 Generator Repair Times Required

REPAIR TIME REQUIRED (HOURS)	NUMBER OF TIMES OBSERVED	PROBABILITY	CUMULATIVE PROBABILITY	RANDOM NUMBER INTERVAL
1	28	0.28	0.28	01 to 28
2	52	0.52	0.80	29 to 80
3	20	0.20	1.00	81 to 00
Total	100	1.00		

tabulates the frequency of various times between machine failures (see Table 15.13). She also creates a probability distribution and assigns random number intervals to each expected time range.

Robbins then notes that the people who do repairs log their maintenance time in one-hour time blocks. Because of the time it takes to reach a broken generator, repair times are generally rounded to one, two, or three hours. In Table 15.14 she performs a statistical analysis of past repair times, similar to that conducted for breakdown times.

Robbins's objective is to determine (1) the service maintenance cost, (2) the simulated machine breakdown cost, and (3) the total simulated maintenance cost of the current system. She does this by selecting a series of random numbers to generate simulated times between generator breakdowns and a second series to simulate repair times required. A simulation of 15 machine failures is presented in Table 15.15. We now examine the elements in the table, one column at a time.

Column 1: Breakdown Number. This is just the count of breakdowns as they occur, going from 1 to 15.

Column 2: Random Number for Breakdowns. This is a number used to simulate time between breakdowns. The numbers in this column have been selected from Table 15.5 on page 662, from the second column from the right hand side of the table.

TABLE 15.15 Simulation of Generator Breakdowns and Repairs

(1) BREAKDOWN NUMBER	(2) RANDOM NUMBER FOR BREAKDOWNS	(3) TIME BETWEEN BREAKDOWNS	(4) TIME OF BREAKDOWN	(5) TIME REPAIRPERSON IS FREE TO BEGIN THIS REPAIR	(6) RANDOM NUMBER FOR REPAIR TIME	(7) REPAIR TIME REQUIRED	(8) TIME REPAIR ENDS	(9) NUMBER OF HOURS MACHINE DOWN
1	57	2	02:00	02:00	07	1	03:00	1
2	17	1½	03:30	03:30	60	2	05:30	2
3	36	2	05:30	05:30	77	2	07:30	2
4	72	2½	08:00	08:00	49	2	10:00	2
5	85	3	11:00	11:00	76	2	13:00	2
6	31	2	13:00	13:00	95	3	16:00	3
7	44	2	15:00	16:00	51	2	18:00	3
8	30	2	17:00	18:00	16	1	19:00	2
9	26	1½	18:30	19:00	14	1	20:00	1½
10	09	1	19:30	20:00	85	3	23:00	3½
11	49	2	21:30	23:00	59	2	01:00	3½
12	13	1½	23:00	01:00	85	3	04:00	5
13	33	2	01:00	04:00	40	2	06:00	5
14	89	3	04:00	06:00	42	2	08:00	4
15	13	1½	05:30	08:00	52	2	10:00	4½

Total 44

677

Column 3: Time between Breakdowns. This number is generated from column 2 random numbers and the random number intervals defined in Table 15.13. The first random number, 57, falls in the interval 28 to 60, implying a time of 2 hours since the prior breakdown.

Column 4: Time of Breakdown. This converts the data in column 3 into an actual time of day for each breakdown. This simulation assumes that the first day begins at midnight (00:00 hours). Since the time between zero breakdowns and the first breakdown is 2 hours, the first recorded machine failure is at 02:00 on the clock. The second breakdown, you note, occurs 1½ hours later, at a calculated clock time of 03:30 (or 3:30 A.M.).

Column 5: Time Repairperson Is Free to Begin Repair. This is 02:00 hours for the first breakdown if we assume that the repairperson began work at 00:00 hours and was not tied up from a previous generator failure. Before recording this time on the second and all subsequent lines, however, we must check column 8 to see what time the repairperson finishes the previous job. Look, for example, at the seventh breakdown. The breakdown occurs at 15:00 hours (or 3:00 P.M.). But the repairperson does not complete the previous job, the sixth breakdown, until 16:00 hours. Hence the entry in column 5 is 16:00 hours.

One further assumption is made to handle the fact that each repairperson works only an 8-hour shift. It is that when each person is replaced by the next shift, he or she simply hands the tools over to the new worker. The new repairperson continues working on the same broken generator until the job is completed. There is no lost time and no overlap of workers. Hence, labor costs for each 24-hour day are exactly 24 hours × \$30 per hour = \$720.

Column 6: Random Number for Repair Time. This is a number selected from the rightmost column of Table 15.5. It helps simulate repair times.

Column 7: Repair Time Required. This is generated from column 6's random numbers and Table 15.14's repair time distribution. The first random number, 07, represents a repair time of 1 hour since it falls in the random number interval 01 to 28.

Column 8: Time Repair Ends. This is the sum of the entry in column 5 (time repairperson is free to begin) plus the required repair time from column 7. Since the first repair begins at 02:00 and takes one hour to complete, the time repair ends is recorded in column 8 as 03:00.

Column 9: Number of Hours the Machine Is Down. This is the difference between column 4 (time of breakdown) and column 8 (time repair ends). In the case of the first breakdown, that difference is 1 hour (03:00 minus 02:00). In the case of the tenth breakdown, the difference is 23:00 hours minus 19:30 hours, or 3½ hours.

Cost Analysis of the Simulation

The simulation of 15 generator breakdowns in Table 15.15 spans a time of 34 hours of operation. The clock began at 00:00 hours of day 1 and ran until the final repair at 10:00 hours of day 2.

The critical factor that interests Robbins is the total number of hours that generators are out of service (from column 9). This is computed to be 44 hours. She also notes that toward the end of the simulation period, a backlog is beginning to appear. The thirteenth breakdown occurred at 01:00 hours but could not be worked on until 04:00 hours. The fourteenth and fifteenth breakdowns experienced similar delays. Robbins is determined to write a computer program to carry out a few hundred more simulated breakdowns, but first wants to analyze the data she has collected thus far.

She measures her objectives as follows:

$$\text{service maintenance cost} = 34 \text{ hours of worker service time} \\ \times \$30 \text{ per hour}$$

$$= \$1,020$$

$$\text{simulated machine breakdown cost} = 44 \text{ total hours of breakdown} \\ \times \$75 \text{ lost per hour of downtime}$$

$$= \$3,300$$

$$\begin{aligned} \text{total simulated maintenance} \\ \text{cost of the current system} &= \text{service cost} + \text{breakdown cost} \end{aligned}$$

$$= \$1,020 + \$3,300$$

$$= \$4,320$$

A total cost of $4,320 is reasonable only when compared with other more attractive or less attractive maintenance options. Should, for example, the Three Hills Power Company add a second full-time repairperson to each shift? Should it add just one more worker and let him or her come on duty every fourth shift to help catch up on any backlogs? These are two alternatives that Robbins may choose to consider through simulation. You may help by solving Problem 15-19 at the end of the chapter.

As mentioned at the outset of this section, simulation can also be used in other maintenance problems, including the analysis of *preventive maintenance*. Perhaps the Three Hills Power Company should consider strategies for replacing generator motors, valves, wiring, switches, and other miscellaneous parts that typically fail. It could (1) replace all parts of a certain type when one fails on any generator, or (2) repair or replace all parts after a certain length of service based on an estimated average service life. This would again be done by setting probability distributions for failure rates, selecting random numbers, and simulating past failures and their associated costs.

Preventive maintenance policies can also be simulated.

Building an Excel Simulation Model for Three Hills Power Company

Programs 15.4A and 15.4B provide an Excel spreadsheet approach to simulating the Three Hills Power maintenance problem. Formulas are shown in Program 15.4A and the results in Program 15.4B.

15.7 TWO OTHER TYPES OF SIMULATION MODELS

Simulation models are often broken into three categories. The first, the Monte Carlo method just discussed, uses the concepts of probability distribution and random numbers to evaluate system responses to various policies. The other two categories are operational gaming and systems simulation. Although in theory the three methods are distinctly different, the growth of computerized simulation has tended to create a common basis in procedures and blur these differences.[3]

---

[3] Theoretically, random numbers are used only in Monte Carlo simulation. However, in some complex gaming or systems simulation problems in which all relationships cannot be defined exactly, it may be necessary to use the probability concepts of the Monte Carlo method.

PROGRAM 15.4A

An Excel Spreadsheet Model for Simulating Three Hills Power Company Maintenance Problem

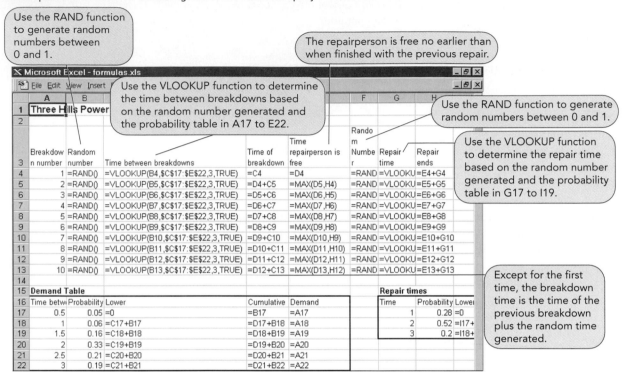

PROGRAM 15.4B

Output from Excel Spreadsheet in Program 15.4A

Operational Gaming

Operational gaming refers to simulation involving two or more competing players. The best examples are military games and business games. Both allow participants to match their management and decision-making skills in hypothetical situations of conflict.

Military games are used worldwide to train a nation's top military officers, to test offensive and defensive strategies, and to examine the effectiveness of equipment and armies. Business games, first developed by the firm Booz, Allen and Hamilton in the 1950s, are popular with both executives and business students. They provide an opportunity to test business skills and decision-making ability in a competitive environment. The person or team that performs best in the simulated environment is rewarded by knowing that his or her company has been most successful in earning the largest profit, grabbing a high market share, or perhaps increasing the firm's trading value on the stock exchange.

During each period of competition, be it a week, month, or quarter, teams respond to market conditions by coding their latest management decisions with respect to inventory, production, financing, investment, marketing, and research. The competitive business environment is simulated by computer, and a new printout summarizing current market conditions is presented to players. This allows teams to simulate years of operating conditions in a matter of days, weeks, or a semester.

Systems Simulation

Systems simulation is similar to business gaming in that it allows users to test various managerial policies and decisions to evaluate their effect on the operating environment. This variation of simulation models the dynamics of large *systems*. Such systems include corporate operations,[4] the national economy, a hospital, or a city government system.

In a *corporate operating system*, sales, production levels, marketing policies, investments, union contracts, utility rates, financing, and other factors are all related in a series of mathematical equations that are examined by simulation. In a simulation of an *urban government*, systems simulation may be employed to evaluate the impact of tax increases, capital expenditures for roads and buildings, housing availability, new garbage routes, immigration and out-migration, locations of new schools or senior citizen centers, birth and death rates, and many more vital issues. Simulations of *economic systems*, often called econometric models, are used by government agencies, bankers, and large organizations to predict inflation rates, domestic and foreign money supplies, and unemployment levels. Inputs and outputs of a typical economic system simulation are illustrated in Figure 15.4.

Econometric models are huge simulations involving thousands of regression equations tied together by economic factors. They use what-if? questions to test out various policies.

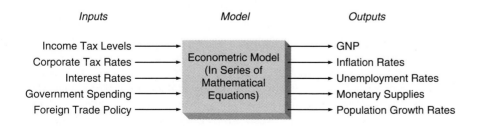

FIGURE 15.4

Inputs and Outputs of a Typical Economic System Simulation

---

[4] This is sometimes referred to as *industrial dynamics*, a term coined by Jay Forrester. Forrester's goal was to find a way "to show how policies, decisions, structure, and delays are interrelated to influence growth and stability" in industrial systems. See J. W. Forrester, *Industrial Dynamics* (Cambridge, MA: The MIT Press, 1961).

IN ACTION | **Simulating Taco Bell's Restaurant Operation**

Determining how many employees to schedule each 15 minutes to perform each function in a Taco Bell restaurant is a complex and vexing problem. So Taco Bell, the $5 billion giant with 6,500 U.S. and foreign locations, decided to build a simulation model. It selected MOSDIM as its software to develop a new labor-management system called LMS.

To develop and use a simulation model, Taco Bell had to collect quite a bit of data. Almost everything that takes place in a restaurant, from customer arrival patterns to the time it takes to wrap a taco, had to be translated into reliable, accurate data. Just as an example, analysts had to conduct time studies and data analysis for every task that is part of preparing every

item on the menu. To the researcher's surprise, the hours devoted to collecting data greatly exceeded those it took to actually build the LMS model.

Inputs to LMS include staffing, such as number of people and positions. Outputs are performance measures, such as mean time in the system, mean time at the counter, people utilization and equipment utilization. The model paid off. More than $53 million in labor costs were saved in LMS's first four years of use.

Source: J. Hueter and W. Swart. "An Integrated Labor-Management System for Taco Bell," *Interfaces* 28, 1 (January–February 1998): 75–91.

The value of systems simulation lies in its allowance of what-if? questions to test the effects of various policies. A corporate planning group, for example, can change the value of any input, such as an advertising budget, and examine the impact on sales, market share, or short-term costs. Simulation can also be used to evaluate different research and development projects or to determine long-range planning horizons.

15.8 ROLE OF COMPUTERS IN SIMULATION

We recognize that computers are critical in simulating complex tasks. They can generate random numbers, simulate thousands of time periods in a matter of seconds or minutes, and provide management with reports that make decision making easier. As a matter of fact, a computer approach is almost a necessity for us to draw valid conclusions from a simulation. Because we require a very large number of simulations, it would be a real burden to rely on pencil and paper alone.

Special purpose simulation languages have several advantages over general purpose languages like BASIC.

Three types of computer programming languages are available to help the simulation process. The first type, *general-purpose languages*, includes BASIC, C^{++}, and Pascal. The second type, *special-purpose simulation languages* have three advantages: (1) they require less programming time for large simulations, (2) they are usually more efficient and easier to check for errors, and (3) they have random number generators already built in as subroutines. The major special-purpose languages are GPSS, SIMSCRIPT, DYNAMO, and GASP.

Simulation has proven so popular that a third type, commercial, easy-to-use *prewritten simulation programs*, are also available. Some are generalized to handle a wide variety of situations, ranging from queuing to inventory. These include Extend, Witness, MicroSaint, Taylor II, Arena, Simfactory, Xcell, MAP/1, and SLAM. These programs all run on personal computers and have graphic capabilities.

As we saw in Programs 15.2, 15.3, and 15.4, spreadsheet software such as Excel can be used to develop simulations quickly and easily. There are a number of Excel add-ins, such as Crystal Ball (which is provided on the CD-Rom with this text), that make this process easier.

Crystal Ball

Crystal Ball is a very popular forecasting and risk analysis program, published by Decisioneering Corp., which uses Monte Carlo simulation to develop a range of possible statistical results. Crystal Ball allows us to extend beyond problems that have discrete probability distributions. So far, each example in this chapter could be solved with Excel spreadsheets fairly easily because they did not contain complex probability distributions, such as the normal distribution. The Crystal Ball add-in, which can solve the applications discussed in this chapter as well as more complex ones, is described in detail in Appendix 15.1.

Summary

The purpose of this chapter was to discuss the concept and approach of simulation as a problem-solving tool. Simulation involves building a mathematical model that attempts to describe a real-world situation. The model's goal is to incorporate important variables and their interrelationships in such a way that we can study the impact of managerial changes upon the total system. The approach has many advantages over other quantitative analysis techniques and is especially useful when a problem is too complex or difficult to solve by other means.

The Monte Carlo method of simulation is developed through the use of probability distributions and random numbers. Random number intervals are established to represent possible outcomes for each probabilistic variable in the model. Random numbers are then either selected from a random number table or generated by computer to simulate variable outcomes. The simulation procedure is conducted for many time periods to evaluate the long-term impact of each policy value being studied. Monte Carlo simulation was illustrated by hand on problems of inventory control, queuing, and machine maintenance.

Operational gaming and systems simulation, two other categories of simulation, were also presented in this chapter. We concluded with a discussion of the important role of the computer in the simulation process.

Glossary

Simulation. A quantitative analysis technique that involves building a mathematical model that represents a real-world situation. The model is then experimented with to estimate the effects of various actions and decisions.

Monte Carlo Simulation. Simulations that experiment with probabilistic elements of a system by generating random numbers to create values for those elements.

Random Number Interval. A range of random numbers assigned to represent a possible simulation outcome.

Random Number. A number whose digits are selected completely at random.

Flow Diagram or Flowchart. A graphical means of presenting the logic of a simulation model. It is a tool that helps in writing a simulation computer program.

Operational Gaming. The use of simulation in competitive situations such as military games and business or management games.

Systems Simulation. Simulation models dealing with the dynamics of large organizational or governmental systems.

General-Purpose Languages. Computer programming languages, such as, BASIC, C^{++}, or PASCAL, that are used to simulate a problem.

Special-Purpose Simulation Languages. Programming languages especially designed to be efficient in handling simulation problems. The category includes GPSS, SIMSCRIPT, GASP, and DYNAMO.

Prewritten Simulation Programs. These graphical programs are prestructured to handle a variety of situations.

Solved Problems

Solved Problem 15-1

Higgins Plumbing and Heating maintains a stock of 30-gallon hot water heaters that it sells to homeowners and installs for them. Owner Jerry Higgins likes the idea of having a large supply on hand to meet customer demand, but he also recognizes that it is expensive to do so. He examines hot water heater sales over the past 50 weeks and notes the following:

HOT WATER HEATER SALES PER WEEK	NUMBER OF WEEKS THIS NUMBER WAS SOLD
4	6
5	5
6	9
7	12
8	8
9	7
10	3
	Total 50

(a) If Higgins maintains a constant supply of 8 hot water heaters in any given week, how many times will he be out of stock during a 20-week simulation? We use random numbers from the seventh column of Table 15.5, beginning with the random digits 10.

(b) What is the average number of sales per week (including stockouts) over the 20-week period?

(c) Using an analytic nonsimulation technique, what is the expected number of sales per week? How does this compare with the answer in part (b)?

Solution

HEATER SALES	PROBABILITY	RANDOM NUMBER INTERVALS
4	0.12	01 to 12
5	0.10	13 to 22
6	0.18	23 to 40
7	0.24	41 to 64
8	0.16	65 to 80
9	0.14	81 to 94
10	0.06	95 to 00
	1.00	

(a) WEEK	RANDOM NUMBER	SIMULATED SALES	WEEK	RANDOM NUMBER	SIMULATED SALES
1	10	4	11	08	4
2	24	6	12	48	7
3	03	4	13	66	8
4	32	6	14	97	10
5	23	6	15	03	4
6	59	7	16	96	10
7	95	10	17	46	7
8	34	6	18	74	8
9	34	6	19	77	8
10	51	7	20	44	7

With a supply of 8 heaters, Higgins will be out of stock three times during the 20-week period (in weeks 7, 14, and 16).

(b) Average sales by simulation $= \dfrac{\text{total sales}}{20 \text{ weeks}} = \dfrac{135}{20} = 6.75$ per week.

(c) Using expected values,

$$E(\text{sales}) = 0.12(4 \text{ heaters}) + 0.10(5) + 0.18(6) + 0.24(7)$$
$$+ 0.16(8) + 0.14(9) + 0.06(10)$$

$$= 6.88 \text{ heaters}$$

With a longer simulation, these two approaches will lead to even closer values.

Solved Problem 15-2

The manager of Denton Savings and Loan is attempting to determine how many tellers are needed at the drive-in window during peak times. As a general policy, the manager wishes to offer service such that average customer waiting time does not exceed 2 minutes. Given the existing service level, as shown in the following data, does the drive-in window meet this criterion?

DATA FOR SERVICE TIME

SERVICE TIME (MINUTES)	PROBABILITY (FREQUENCY)	CUMULATIVE PROBABILITY	RANDOM NUMBER INTERVAL
0	0.00	0.00	(impossible)
1.0	0.25	0.25	01 to 25
2.0	0.20	0.45	26 to 45
3.0	0.40	0.85	46 to 85
4.0	0.15	1.00	86 to 00

TIME BETWEEN SUCCESSIVE CUSTOMER ARRIVALS	PROBABILITY (FREQUENCY)	CUMULATIVE PROBABILITY	RANDOM NUMBER INTERVAL
0	0.10	0.10	01 to 10
1.0	0.35	0.45	11 to 45
2.0	0.25	0.70	46 to 70
3.0	0.15	0.85	71 to 85
4.0	0.10	0.95	86 to 95
5.0	0.05	1.00	96 to 00

Solution

(1) CUSTOMER NUMBER	(2) RANDOM NUMBER	(3) INTERVAL TO ARRIVAL	(4) TIME OF ARRIVAL	(5) RANDOM NUMBER	(6) SERVICE TIME	(7) START SERVICE	(8) END SERVICE	(9) WAIT TIME	(10) IDLE TIME
1	50	2	9:02	52	3	9:02	9:05	0	2
2	28	1	9:03	37	2	9:05	9:07	2	0
3	68	2	9:05	82	3	9:07	9:10	2	0
4	36	1	9:06	69	3	9:10	9:13	4	0
5	90	4	9:10	98	4	9:13	9:17	3	0
6	62	2	9:12	96	4	9:17	9:21	5	0
7	27	1	9:13	33	2	9:21	9:23	8	0
8	50	2	9:15	50	3	9:23	9:26	8	0
9	18	1	9:16	88	4	9:26	9:30	10	0
10	36	1	9:17	90	4	9:30	9:34	13	0
11	61	2	9:19	50	3	9:34	9:37	15	0
12	21	1	9:20	27	2	9:37	9:39	17	0
13	46	2	9:22	45	2	9:39	9:41	17	0
14	01	0	9:22	81	3	9:41	9:44	19	0
15	14	1	9:23	66	3	9:44	9:47	21	0

Read the data as in the following example for the first row:

Column 1: Number of customer.

Column 2: From third column of random number Table 15.5.

Column 3: Time interval corresponding to random number (random number of 50 implies a 2-minute interval).

Column 4: Starting at 9 A.M. the first arrival is at 9:02.

Column 5: From the first column of the random number Table 15.5.

Column 6: Teller time corresponding to random number 52 is 3 minutes.

Column 7: Teller is available and can start at 9:02.

Column 8: Teller completes work at 9:05 (9:02 + 0:03).

Column 9: Wait time for customer is 0 as the teller was available.

Column 10: Idle time for the teller was 2 minutes (9:00 to 9:02).

The drive-in window clearly does not meet the manager's criteria for an average wait time of 2 minutes. As a matter of fact, we can observe an increasing queue buildup after only a few customer simulations. This observation can be confirmed by expected value calculations on both arrival and service rates.

SELF-TEST

- Before taking the self-test, refer back to the learning objectives at the beginning of the chapter, the notes in the margins, and the glossary at the end of the chapter.
- Use the key at the back of the book to correct your answers.
- Restudy pages that correspond to any questions that you answered incorrectly or material you feel uncertain about.

1. Simulation is a technique usually reserved for studying only the simplest and most straightforward of problems.
   a. True   b. False
2. A simulation model is designed to arrive at a single specific numerical answer to a given problem.
   a. True   b. False
3. Simulation typically requires a familiarity with statistics to evaluate the results.
   a. True   b. False
4. With regard to inventory problems, one reason for using simulation rather than an analytical model is that the simulation model is able to handle probabilistic demand and lead times.
   a. True   b. False
5. Simulation is best thought of as a technique to
   a. give concrete numerical answers.
   b. increase understanding of a problem.
   c. provide rapid solutions to relatively simple problems.
   d. provide optimal solutions to complex problems.
6. Specialized computer languages have been developed that allow one to readily simulate specific types of problems.
   a. True   b. False
7. Simulation is perhaps the only technique that can be applied to the study of virtually *any* problem.
   a. True   b. False
8. The seven steps we should perform when using simulation to analyze a problem are
   (1) _____ , (2) _____ ,
   (3) _____ , (4) _____ ,
   (5) _____ , (6) _____ ,
   (7) _____ .
9. The five steps required to implement the Monte Carlo simulation technique are
   (1) _____ , (2) _____ ,
   (3) _____ , (4) _____ ,
   (5) _____ .
10. Advantages of simulation include
   (1) _____ , (2) _____ ,
   (3) _____ , (4) _____ ,
   (5) _____ , (6) _____ ,
   (7) _____ .
11. Disadvantages of simulation include
   (1) _____ , (2) _____ ,
   (3) _____ , (4) _____ .

12. When simulating the Monte Carlo experiment, the average simulated demand over the long run should approximate the
   a. real demand.   b. expected demand.
   c. sampled demand.   d. daily demand.
13. The idea behind simulation is to
   a. imitate a real-world situation.
   b. study the properties and operating characteristics of a real-world situation.
   c. draw conclusions and make action decisions based on simulation results.
   d. all of the above.
14. Using simulation for a queuing problem
   a. would be rare in a realistic situation.
   b. is an unreasonable alternative if the arrival rate is not Poisson distributed but can be plotted on a curve.
   c. would be appropriate if the service time was not exponential or constant.
   d. all of the above.
15. Special-purpose simulation languages include
   a. C++   b. BASIC   c. GPSS
   d. PASCAL   e. all of the above
16. In assigning random numbers in Monte Carlo simulation,
   a. it is important to develop a cumulative probability distribution.
   b. it is not important to assign the exact range of random number interval as the probability.
   c. it is important to assign the particular appropriate random numbers.
   d. all of the above.
17. In a Monte Carlo simulation, a variable that we might want to simulate is
   a. lead time for inventory orders to arrive.
   b. times between machine breakdowns.
   c. time between arrivals at a service facility.
   d. number of employees absent from work each day.
   e. all of the above.
18. Use the following random numbers to simulate *yes* and *no* answers to 10 questions by starting in the first *row* and letting
   a. the double-digit number 00-49 represent *yes* and 50-99 represent *no*.
   b. the double-digit even numbers represent *yes* and the odd numbers represent *no*.
   Random Numbers: 52 06 50 88 53 30 10 47 99 37 66 91 35 32 00 84 57 00

Discussion Questions and Problems

Discussion Questions

15-1 What are the advantages and limitations of simulation models?

15-2 Why might a manager be forced to use simulation instead of an analytical model in dealing with a problem of
(a) Inventory ordering policy?
(b) Ships docking in a port to unload?
(c) Bank teller service windows?
(d) The U.S. economy?

15-3 What types of management problems can be solved more easily by quantitative analysis techniques other than simulation?

15-4 What are the major steps in the simulation process?

15-5 What is Monte Carlo simulation? What principles underlie its use, and what steps are followed in applying it?

15-6 List three ways in which random numbers may be generated for use in a simulation.

15-7 In the simulation of an order policy for drills at Simkin's Hardware, would the results (Table 15.9) change significantly if a longer period were simulated? Why is the 10-day simulation valid or invalid?

15-8 Why is a computer necessary in conducting a real-world simulation?

15-9 What is operational gaming? What is systems simulation? Give examples of how each may be applied.

15-10 Do you think the application of simulation will increase strongly in the next 10 years? Why or why not?

15-11 Why would an analyst ever prefer a general-purpose language such as BASIC in a simulation when there are advantages to using special-purpose languages such as GPSS, SIMSCRIPT, Xcell, or SLAM?

Problems*

The problems that follow involve simulations that are to be done by hand. You are aware that to obtain accurate and meaningful results, long periods must be simulated. This is usually handled by computer. If you are able to program some of the problems using a spreadsheet (see Programs 15.2, 15.3, and 15.4) or QM for Windows (see Program 15.1) we suggest that you try to do so. If not, the hand simulations will still help you in understanding the simulation process.

 15-12 Clark Property Management is responsible for the maintenance, rental, and day-to-day operation of a large apartment complex on the east side of New Orleans. George Clark is especially concerned about the cost projections for replacing air conditioner compressors. He would like to simulate the number of compressor failures each year over the next 20 years. Using data from a similar apartment building he manages in a New Orleans suburb, Clark establishes a table of relative frequency of failures during a year as shown in table on top of next page:

---

*Note: ▢ₐ means the problem may be solved with QM for Windows; ✗ means the problem may be solved with Excel; and ✗▢ₐ means the problem may be solved with QM for Windows and/or Excel.

NUMBER OF A.C. COMPRESSOR FAILURES	PROBABILITY (RELATIVE FREQUENCY)
0	0.06
1	0.13
2	0.25
3	0.28
4	0.20
5	0.07
6	0.01

He decides to simulate the 20-year period by selecting two-digit random numbers from the third column of Table 15.5, starting with the random number 50.

Conduct the simulation for Clark. Is it common to have three or more consecutive years of operation with two or less compressor failures per year?

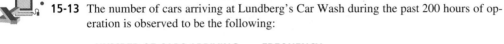 **15-13** The number of cars arriving at Lundberg's Car Wash during the past 200 hours of operation is observed to be the following:

NUMBER OF CARS ARRIVING	FREQUENCY
3 or less	0
4	20
5	30
6	50
7	60
8	40
9 or more	0
Total	200

(a) Set up a probability and cumulative probability distribution for the variable of car arrivals.
(b) Establish random number intervals for the variable.
(c) Simulate 15 hours of car arrivals and compute the average number of arrivals per hour. Select the random numbers needed from the first column of Table 15.5, beginning with the digits 52.

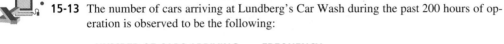 **15-14** Refer to the data in Solved Problem 15-1, which deals with Higgins Plumbing and Heating. Higgins has now collected 100 weeks of data and finds the following distribution for sales:

HOT WATER HEATER SALES PER WEEK	NUMBER OF WEEKS THIS NUMBER WAS SOLD	HOT WATER HEATER SALES PER WEEK	NUMBER OF WEEKS THIS NUMBER WAS SOLD
3	2	8	12
4	9	9	12
5	10	10	10
6	15	11	5
7	25		

(a) Resimulate the number of stockouts incurred over a 20-week period (assuming Higgins maintains a constant supply of 8 heaters).

(b) Conduct this 20-week simulation two more times and compare your answers with those in part (a). Did they change significantly? Why or why not?

(c) What is the new expected number of sales per week?

 15-15 An increase in the size of the barge unloading crew at the Port of New Orleans (see Section 15.5) has resulted in a new probability distribution for daily unloading rates. In particular, Table 15.11 may be revised as shown here:

DAILY UNLOADING RATE	PROBABILITY
1	0.03
2	0.12
3	0.40
4	0.28
5	0.12
6	0.05

(a) Resimulate 15 days of barge unloadings and compute the average number of barges delayed, average number of nightly arrivals, and average number of barges unloaded each day. Draw random numbers from the bottom row of Table 15.5 to generate daily arrivals and from the second-from-the-bottom row to generate daily unloading rates.

(b) How do these simulated results compare to those in the chapter?

 15-16 Simkin's Hardware Store simulated an inventory ordering policy for Ace electric drills that involved an order quantity of 10 drills with a reorder point of 5. The first attempt to develop a cost-effective ordering strategy was illustrated in Table 15.9. The brief simulation resulted in a total daily inventory cost of $4.72. Simkin would now like to compare this strategy with one in which he orders 12 drills, with a reorder point of 6. Conduct a 10-day simulation for him and discuss the cost implications.

15-17 Draw a flow diagram to represent the logic and steps of simulating barge arrivals and unloadings at the Port of New Orleans (see Section 15.5). For a refresher in flow-charts, see Figure 15.3.

15-18 Draw a flow diagram for the simulation of generator maintenance by the Three Hills Power Company (Section 15.6).

15-19 Stephanie Robbins is the Three Hills Power Company management analyst assigned to simulate maintenance costs. In Section 15.6 we described the simulation of 15 generator breakdowns and the repair times required when one repairperson is on duty per shift. The total simulated maintenance cost of the current system was $4,320.

Robbins would now like to examine the relative cost-effectiveness of adding one more worker per shift. The new repairperson would be paid $30 per hour, the same rate as the first is paid. The cost per breakdown hour is still $75. Robbins makes one vital assumption as she begins—that repair times with two workers will be exactly one-half the times required with only one repairperson on duty per shift. Table 15.14 can then be restated as follows:

REPAIR TIME REQUIRED (HOURS)	PROBABILITY
½	0.28
1	0.52
1½	0.20
	1.00

(a) Simulate this proposed maintenance system change over a 15-generator break-down period. Select the random numbers needed for time between breakdowns from the second-from-the-bottom row of Table 15.5 (beginning with the digits 69). Select random numbers for generator repair times from the last row of the table (beginning with 37).

(b) Should Three Hills add a second repairperson each shift?

15-20 Vincent Maruggi, an MBA student at Northern Massachusetts University, has been having problems balancing his checkbook. His monthly income is derived from a graduate research assistantship; however, he also makes extra money in most months by tutoring undergraduates in their quantitative analysis course. His chances of various income levels are shown here:

MONTHLY INCOME* ($)	PROBABILITY
350	0.40
400	0.20
450	0.30
500	0.10

* Assume that this income is received at the beginning of each month.

Maruggi's expenditures also vary from month to month, and he estimates that they will follow this distribution:

MONTHLY EXPENSES ($)	PROBABILITY
300	0.10
400	0.45
500	0.30
600	0.15

He begins his final year with $600 in his checking account. Simulate the entire year (12 months) and discuss Maruggi's financial picture.

15-21 The Brennan Aircraft Division of TLN Enterprises operates a large number of computerized plotting machines. For the most part, the plotting devices are used to create line drawings of complex wing airfoils and fuselage part dimensions. The engineers operating the automated plotters are called loft lines engineers.

The computerized plotters consist of a minicomputer system connected to a 4- by 5-foot flat table with a series of ink pens suspended above it. When a sheet of clear plastic or paper is properly placed on the table, the computer directs a series of horizontal and vertical pen movements until the desired figure is drawn.

The plotting machines are highly reliable, with the exception of the four sophisticated ink pens that are built in. The pens constantly clog and jam in a raised or lowered position. When this occurs, the plotter is unusable.

Currently, Brennan Aircraft replaces each pen as it fails. The service manager has, however, proposed replacing all four pens every time one fails. This should cut down the frequency of plotter failures. At present, it takes one hour to replace one pen. All four pens could be replaced in two hours. The total cost of a plotter being unusable is $50 per hour. Each pen costs $8.

If only one pen is replaced each time a clog or jam occurs, the following break-down data are thought to be valid:

HOURS BETWEEN PLOTTER FAILURES IF ONE PEN IS REPLACED DURING A REPAIR	PROBABILITY
10	0.05
20	0.15
30	0.15
40	0.20
50	0.20
60	0.15
70	0.10

Based on the service manager's estimates, if all four pens are replaced each time one pen fails, the probability distribution between failures is as follows:

HOURS BETWEEN PLOTTER FAILURES IF ALL FOUR PENS ARE REPLACED DURING A REPAIR	PROBABILITY
100	0.15
110	0.25
120	0.35
130	0.20
140	0.05

(a) Simulate Brennan Aircraft's problem and determine the best policy. Should the firm replace one pen or all four pens on a plotter each time a failure occurs?

(b) Develop a second approach to solving this problem, this time without simulation. Compare the results. How does it affect Brennan's policy decision using simulation?

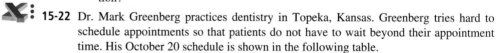 **15-22** Dr. Mark Greenberg practices dentistry in Topeka, Kansas. Greenberg tries hard to schedule appointments so that patients do not have to wait beyond their appointment time. His October 20 schedule is shown in the following table.

SCHEDULED APPOINTMENT AND TIME		EXPECTED TIME NEEDED
Adams	9:30 A.M.	15
Brown	9:45 A.M.	20
Crawford	10:15 A.M.	15
Dannon	10:30 A.M.	10
Erving	10:45 A.M.	30
Fink	11:15 A.M.	15
Graham	11:30 A.M.	20
Hinkel	11:45 A.M.	15

Unfortunately, not every patient arrives exactly on schedule, and expected times to examine patients are just that, *expected*. Some examinations take longer than expected, while some take less time.

Greenberg's experience dictates the following:

(a) 20% of the patients will be 20 minutes early.
(b) 10% of the patients will be 10 minutes early.
(c) 40% of the patients will be on time.
(d) 25% of the patients will be 10 minutes late.
(e) 5% of the patients will be 20 minutes late.

He further estimates that
(a) 15% of the time he will finish in 20% less time than expected.
(b) 50% of the time he will finish in the expected time.
(c) 25% of the time he will finish in 20% more time than expected.
(d) 10% of the time he will finish in 40% more time than expected.

Dr. Greenberg has to leave at 12:15 P.M. on October 20 to catch a flight to a dental convention in New York. Assuming that he is ready to start his workday at 9:30 A.M. and that patients are treated in order of their scheduled exam (even if one late patient arrives after an early one), will he be able to make the flight? Comment on this simulation.

 15-23 The Pelnor Corporation is the nation's largest manufacturer of industrial-size washing machines. A main ingredient in the production process is 8- by 10-foot sheets of stainless steel. The steel is used for both interior washer drums and outer casings.

Steel is purchased weekly on a contractual basis from the Smith-Layton Foundry, which, because of limited availability and lot sizing, can ship either 8,000 or 11,000 square feet of stainless steel each week. When Pelnor's weekly order is placed, there is a 45% chance that 8,000 square feet will arrive and a 55% chance of receiving the larger size order.

Pelnor uses the stainless steel on a stochastic (nonconstant) basis. The probabilities of demand each week follow:

STEEL NEEDED PER WEEK (SQ FT)	PROBABILITY
6,000	0.05
7,000	0.15
8,000	0.20
9,000	0.30
10,000	0.20
11,000	0.10

Pelnor has a capacity to store no more than 25,000 square feet of steel at any time. Because of the contract, orders *must* be placed each week regardless of the on-hand supply.

(a) Simulate stainless steel order arrivals and use for 20 weeks. (Begin the first week with a starting inventory of 0 stainless steel.) If an end-of-week inventory is ever negative, assume that back orders are permitted and fill the demand from the next arriving order.

(b) Should Pelnor add more storage area? If so, how much? If not, comment on the system.

15-24 Milwaukee's General Hospital has an emergency room that is divided into six departments: (1) the initial exam station, to treat minor problems or make diagnoses; (2) an x-ray department; (3) an operating room; (4) a cast-fitting room; (5) an observation room for recovery and general observation before final diagnoses or release; and (6) an out-processing department where clerks check patients out and arrange for payment or insurance forms.

The probabilities that a patient will go from one department to another are presented in the following table:

FROM	TO	PROBABILITY
Initial exam at emergency room entrance	X-ray department	0.45
	Operating room	0.15
	Observation room	0.10
	Out-processing clerk	0.30
X-ray department	Operating room	0.10
	Cast-fitting room	0.25
	Observation room	0.35
	Out-processing clerk	0.30
Operating room	Cast-fitting room	0.25
	Observation room	0.70
	Out-processing clerk	0.05
Cast-fitting room	Observation room	0.55
	X-ray department	0.05
	Out-processing clerk	0.40
Observation room	Operating room	0.15
	X-ray department	0.15
	Out-processing clerk	0.70

(a) Simulate the trail followed by 10 emergency room patients. Proceed one patient at a time from each one's entry at the initial exam station until he or she leaves through out-processing. You should be aware that a patient can enter the same department more than once.

(b) Using your simulation data, what are the chances that a patient enters the x-ray department twice?

 15-25 Management of the First Syracuse Bank is concerned over a loss of customers at its main office downtown. One solution that has been proposed is to add one or more drive-through teller stations to make it easier for customers in cars to obtain quick service without parking. Chris Carlson, the bank president, thinks the bank should only risk the cost of installing one drive-through. He is informed by his staff that the cost (amortized over a 20-year period) of building a drive-through is $12,000 per year. It also costs $16,000 per year in wages and benefits to staff each new teller window.

The director of management analysis, Beth Shader, believes that the following two factors encourage the immediate construction of two drive-through stations, however. According to a recent article in *Banking Research* magazine, customers who wait in long lines for drive-through teller service will cost banks an average of $1 per minute in loss of goodwill. Also, adding a second drive-through will cost an additional $16,000 in staffing, but amortized construction costs can be cut to a total of $20,000 per year if two drive-throughs are installed together instead of one at a time. To complete her analysis, Shader collected one month's arrival and service rates at a competing downtown bank's drive-through stations. These data are shown as observation analyses 1 and 2 in the following tables.

(a) Simulate a one-hour time period, from 1 to 2 P.M., for a single-teller drive-through.

(b) Simulate a one-hour time period, from 1 to 2 P.M., for a two-teller system.

(c) Conduct a cost analysis of the two options. Assume that the bank is open 7 hours per day and 200 days per year.

OBSERVATION ANALYSIS 1: INTERARRIVAL TIMES FOR 1,000 OBSERVATIONS

TIME BETWEEN ARRIVALS (MINUTES)	NUMBER OF OCCURRENCES
1	200
2	250
3	300
4	150
5	100

OBSERVATION ANALYSIS 2: CUSTOMER SERVICE TIME FOR 1,000 CUSTOMERS

SERVICE TIME (MINUTES)	NUMBER OF OCCURRENCES
1	100
2	150
3	350
4	150
5	150
6	100

15-26 The Alfredo Fragrance Company produces only one product, a perfume called Hint of Elegance. Hint of Elegance consists of two secret ingredients blended into an exclusive fragrance which is marketed in Zurich. An economic expression referred to as the Cobb–Douglas function describes the production of Hint of Elegance as follows:

$$X = \sqrt{(\text{ingredient 1})(\text{ingredient 2})}$$

where X is the amount of perfume produced.

The company operates at a level where ingredient 1 is set daily at 25 units and ingredient 2 at 36 units. Although the price Alfredo pays for ingredient 1 is fixed at $50 per unit, the cost of ingredient 2 and the selling price for the final perfume are both probabilistic. The sales price for Hint of Elegance follows this distribution:

SALES PRICE ($)	PROBABILITY
300	0.2
350	0.5
400	0.3

The cost for ingredient 2 is

INGREDIENT 2 COST ($)	PROBABILITY
35	0.1
40	0.6
45	0.3

(a) What is the profit equation for Alfredo Fragrance Company?

(b) What is the expected profit to the firm?

(c) Simulate the firm's profit for a period of nine days, using these random numbers from Table 15.5: 52, 06, 50, 88, 53, 30, 10, 47, 99, 37, 66, 91, 35, 32, 00, 84, 57, 07.

(d) What is the expected daily profit as simulated in part (c)?

 15-27 Julia Walters owns and operates one of the largest Mercedes-Benz auto dealerships in Washington, DC. In the past 36 months her sales of this luxury car have ranged from a low of 6 new cars to a high of 12 new cars, as reflected in the following table:

SALES OF NEW CARS PER MONTH	FREQUENCY
6	3
7	4
8	6
9	12
10	9
11	1
12	1
	Total 36 months

Walters believes that sales will continue during the next 24 months at about the same historical rates and that delivery times will also continue to follow this pace (stated in probability form):

DELIVERY TIME (MONTHS)	PROBABILITY
1	0.44
2	0.33
3	0.16
4	0.07
	1.00

Walters's current policy is to order 14 cars at a time (two full truckloads, with 7 autos on each truck) and to place a new order whenever the stock on hand reaches 12 autos. What are the results of this policy when simulated over the next two years?

15-28 Referring to Problem 15-27, Julia Walters establishes the following relevant costs: (1) the carrying cost per Mercedes per month is $600, (2) the cost of a lost sale averages $4,350, and (3) the cost of placing an order is $570. What is the total inventory cost of the policy simulated ($Q = 14$, ROP $= 12$) in Problem 15-27?

15-29 Julia Walters (see Problems 15-27 and 15-28) wishes to try a new simulated policy, ordering 21 cars per order, with a reorder point of 10 autos. Which policy is better, this one or the one formulated in Problems 15-27 and 15-28?

Case Study

Alabama Airlines

Alabama Airlines opened its doors in June 1995 as a commuter service with its headquarters and only hub located in Birmingham. A product of airline deregulation, Alabama Air joined the growing number of successful short-haul, point-to-point airlines, including Lone Star, Comair, Atlantic Southeast, Skywest, and Business Express.

Alabama Air was started and managed by two former pilots, David Douglas (who had been with the defunct Eastern Airlines) and Michael Hanna (formerly with Pan Am). It acquired a fleet of 12 used prop-jet planes and the airport gates vacated by Delta Airlines' 1994 downsizing.

With business growing quickly, Douglas turned his attention to Alabama Air's toll-free reservations system. Between

TABLE 15.16 Incoming Call Distribution

TIME BETWEEN CALLS (MINUTES)	PROBABILITY
1	0.11
2	0.21
3	0.22
4	0.20
5	0.16
6	0.10

TABLE 15.17 Service Time Distribution

TIME TO PROCESS CUSTOMER ENQUIRIES (MINUTES)	PROBABILITY
1	0.20
2	0.19
3	0.18
4	0.17
5	0.13
6	0.10
7	0.03

TABLE 15.18 Incoming Call Distribution

TIME BETWEEN CALLS (MINUTES)	PROBABILITY
1	0.22
2	0.25
3	0.19
4	0.15
5	0.12
6	0.07

midnight and 6:00 A.M., only one telephone reservations agent had been on duty. The time between incoming calls during this period is distributed as shown in Table 15.16. Douglas carefully observed and timed the agent and estimated that the time taken to process passenger inquiries is distributed as shown in Table 15.17.

All customers calling Alabama Air go on hold and are served in the order of the calls unless the reservations agent is available for immediate service. Douglas is deciding whether a second agent should be on duty to cope with customer demand. To maintain customer satisfaction, Alabama Air does not want a customer on hold for more than 3 to 4 minutes and also wants to maintain a "high" operator utilization.

Further, the airline is planning a new TV advertising campaign. As a result, it expects an increase in toll-free line phone inquiries. Based on similar campaigns in the past, the incoming call distribution from midnight to 6 A.M. is expected to be as shown in Table 15.18. (The same service time distribution will apply.)

Discussion Questions

1. What would you advise Alabama Air to do for the current reservation system based on the original call distribution? Create a simulation model to investigate the scenario. Describe the model carefully and justify the duration of the simulation, assumptions, and measures of performance.

2. What are your recommendations regarding operator utilization and customer satisfaction if the airline proceeds with the advertising campaign?

Source: Professor Zbigniew H. Przasnyski, Loyola Marymount University.

Case Study

Abjar Transport Company

In 1998, Samir Khaldoun, after receiving an MBA degree from a leading university in the United States, returned to Jeddah, Saudi Arabia, where his family has extensive business holdings. Samir's first assignment was to stabilize and develop a newly formed, family-owned transport company—Abjar Transport.

An immediate problem facing Samir was the determination of the number of trucks needed to handle the forecasted freight volume. Heretofore, trucks were added to the fleet on an "as-needed" basis without comprehensive capacity planning. This approach created problems of driver recruitment, truck service and maintenance, and excessive demurrage (that is, port fees) because of delays at unloading docks and retention of cargo containers.

Samir forecasts that Abjar's freight volume should average 160,000 tons per month with a standard deviation of 30,000 tons. Freight is unloaded on a uniform basis throughout the month. Based on past experience, the amount handled per month is assumed to be normally distributed, as seen in the following table:

LESS THAN (TONS)	PROBABILITY
100,000	0.02
130,000	0.16
160,000	0.50
190,000	0.84
220,000	0.98

After extensive investigation, Samir concluded that the fleet should be standardized to 40-foot Mercedes 2624 2 × 4 tractor-trailer rigs, which are suitable for carrying two 20-foot containers, one 30-foot container, or one 40-foot container. Cargo capacity is approximately 60 tons per rig. Each tractor-trailer unit is estimated to cost 240,000 riyals. Moreover, they must meet Saudi Arabian specifications—double cooling fans, oversized radiators, and special high-temperature tires. Historical evidence suggests that these Mercedes rigs will operate 96% of the time.

Approximately 25% of the freight handled by these tractor-trailer rigs is containerized in container lengths of 20, 30, and 40 feet. (The balance of the freight—75%—is not containerized.) The 20-foot containers hold approximately 20 tons of cargo, the 30-foot containers hold 45 tons, and the 40-foot containers hold 60 tons of freight. Approximately 60% of the containerized freight is shipped in 40-foot units, 20% is shipped in 30-foot units, and 20% is transported in 20-foot units.

Abjar Transport picks up freight at the dock and delivers it directly to customers, or warehouses it for later delivery. Based on his study of truck routing and scheduling patterns, Samir concluded that each rig should pick up freight at the dock three times each day.

Discussion Question

How many tractor-trailer rigs should make up the Abjar Transport fleet?

Bibliography

Abdou, G., and S. P. Dutta. "A Systematic Simulation Approach for the Design of JIT Manufacturing Systems," *Journal of Operations Management* 11, 3 (September 1993): 25–38.

Banks, J, and V. Norman. "Justifying Simulation in Today's Manufacturing Environment," *IIE Solutions* (November 1995).

———. "Second Look at Simulation Software," *OR/MS Today* 23, 4 (August 1996): 55–57.

Brennan, J. E., B. L. Golden, and H. K. Rappoport. "Go with the Flow: Improving Red Cross Bloodmobiles Using Simulation Analysis," *Interfaces* 22, 5 (September–October 1992): 1.

Buchanan, E., and R. Keeler. "Simulating Health Expenditures Under Alternative Insurance Plans," *Management Science* (September 1991): 1069–1088.

Evans, J. R. and D. L. Olson. *Introduction to Simulation and Risk Analysis.* Upper Saddle River, NJ: Prentice Hall, 1998.

Fishman, G. S., and V. G. Kulkarni. "Improving Monte Carlo Efficiency by Increasing Variance," *Management Science* 38, 10 (October 1992): 1432.

Greenwood, A. G., L. P. Rees, and I. W. M. Crouch. "Separating the Art and Science of Simulation Optimization: A Knowledge-Based Architecture Providing for Machine Learning," *IIE Transactions* 25, 6 (November 1993): 70.

Harris, Carl M., Karla L. Hoffman, and Patsy B. Saunders. "Modeling the IRS Telephone Taxpayer Information System," *Operations Research* 35, 4 (July–August 1987): 504–522.

Hutchinson, J., G. K. Leong, and P. T. Ward. "Improving Delivery Performance in Gear Manufacturing at Jeffrey Division of Dresser Industries," *Interfaces* 23, 2 (March–April 1993): 69–79.

Law, A. M., and W. D. Kelton. *Simulation Modeling and Analysis*. 2nd ed. New York: McGraw-Hill, 1991.

Lev, B. "Simulation of Manufacturing Systems," *Interfaces* 20, 3 (May–June 1990): 99.

Main, Linda. "Computer Simulation and Library Management," *Journal of Information Science* 13 (1987): 285–296.

Pegden, C. D., R. E. Shannon, and R. P. Sadowski. *Introduction to Simulation Using SIMAN*, New York: McGraw-Hill, 1995.

INTERNET CASE STUDY

See our Internet home page at **http://www.prenhall.com/render** for these additional case studies: Bialis Waste Disposal, and Buffalo Alkali and Plastics.

APPENDIX 15.1: USING THE CRYSTAL BALL EXCEL ADD-IN

In Chapter 1 we introduced a simple break-even example as a way of demonstrating the quantitative modeling approach. The formula shown in Equation (1-1) was as follows:

Profit = (Price/unit)(Number of units sold) − Fixed Costs − (Variable costs/unit)(Number of units sold)

To demonstrate Crystal Ball, we are going to expand on this model with an example of a publisher who wishes to conduct a profit analysis for a new textbook. First, let us describe how to install Crystal Ball.

Installing and Starting Crystal Ball

The setup file for Crystal Ball is on the CD-ROM that accompanies this book in the directory named Crystal. Run that program and follow the installation directions.

To start the program, select **Start**, **Program**, **Crystal Ball**, and then **Crystal Ball** again. Or, you may load the file **cb.xla** into Excel. Note that a toolbar has been added to Excel and that two menus, **Cell** and **Run**, have been added to the main menu.

Textbook Profitability Analysis Model

Let us first create an Excel spreadsheet for the textbook publisher, one that contains *no* random variables. Programs 15.5A and 15.5B provide a straightforward spreadsheet analysis of the data, and the formulas leading to total profit.

But now let us introduce three random variables into this model. First, we are going to assume that demand is a random variable defined by the Normal distribution with a mean of 25,000 units and a standard deviation of 2,500 units. We will further assume that printing cost per page is not fixed but is also uncertain and follows a uniform probability distribution from 3.5 cents to 4.5 cents per page. Finally, we assume that the selling price is discrete and given in the following distribution:

PRICE	PROBABILITY
$60	0.4
61	0.3
62	0.2
63	0.1

PROGRAM 15.5A

Data Screen for Textbook Publisher's Excel Spreadsheet Analyzing the Profit on a New Textbook

PROGRAM 15.5B

Excel Formulas for Textbook Publisher's Profit Analysis Using Data from Program 15.5A

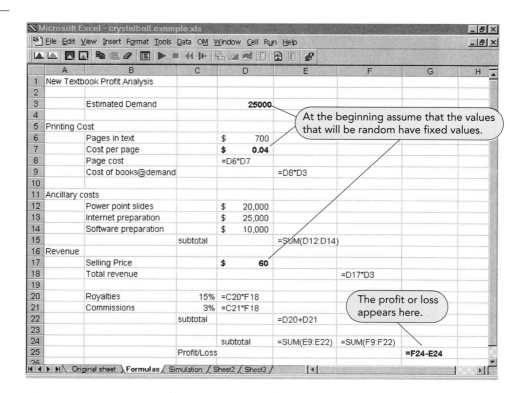

Steps in Using Crystal Ball

Step 1. For each item (cell) that has randomness, we click on that cell and then use the menu **Cell** and **Define Assumption** (which is also the first tool in the toolbar). In Program 15.6, we have done this for demand, printing cost per page, and selling price per book. The selling price distribution appears at the top right of Program 15.6.

	A	B	C	D	E	F	G	H	
1	New Textbook Profit Analysis								
2							$	60.0	0.4
3		Estimated Demand		25000	(mean=25000, std=2500)		$	61.0	0.3
4							$	62.0	0.2
5	Printing Cost						$	63.0	0.1
6		Pages in text	$	700					
7		Cost per page	$	0.04	(uniform between .035 and .045)				
8		Page cost	$	28					
9		Cost of books@demand			$	700,000			
10									
11	Ancillary costs								
12		Power point slides	$	20,000					
13		Internet preparation	$	25,000					
14		Software preparation	$	10,000					
15			subtotal		$	55,000			
16	Revenue								
17		Selling Price	$	60	(distribution in h2:i4)				
18		Total revenue				$	1,500,000		
19									
20		Royalties	15%	$	225,000				
21		Commissions	3%	$	45,000				
22			subtotal		$	270,000			
23									
24			subtotal		$ 1,025,000	$ 1,500,000			
25			Profit/Loss				$	475,000	
26									
27									

PROGRAM 15.6
Text book Analysis with Three Probability Distributions Identified

When we select **Define Assumption** from the menu, the **Distribution Gallery** shown in Program 15.7 is displayed. A variety of different probability distributions are available.

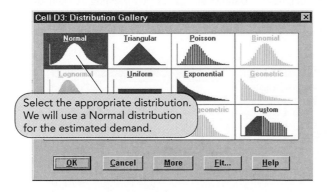

PROGRAM 15.7
Distribution Gallery Choices

Because we indicated that demand for cell D3 is normally distributed, we click on the **Normal** box and then **OK**. Program 15.8 is displayed. After typing in the standard deviation of 2,500, we click on the **Enter** button, and then **OK**.

PROGRAM 15.8

Identifying the Normal
Distribution, With a Mean of
25,000 and a Standard
Deviation of 2,500 for Demand
in Cell D3

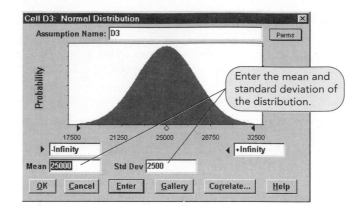

We repeat the same process for the random variable **cost per page**, which follows the uniform distribution, in Program 15.9. When cell D7 is activated, we click on **Cell** and then **Define Assumption** from the menu. When the **Distribution Gallery** is displayed, we click on the uniform distribution and then on **OK**.

PROGRAM 15.9

Selecting the Uniform
Distribution to Describe
Printing Cost per Page

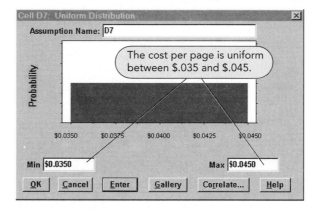

Finally, to select a **custom distribution** for the random variable **selling price**, we repeat this process for cell D17. Program 15.10 shows the first screen for setting a custom distribution. We click on **Data** in the lower right to access Program 15.11's screen, which allows a range (G2:H5) to be entered on the lower left. Having selected distributions for our three random variables, we have completed Step 1.

PROGRAM 15.10

Selecting a Custom Distribution
for the Random Variable
Selling Price

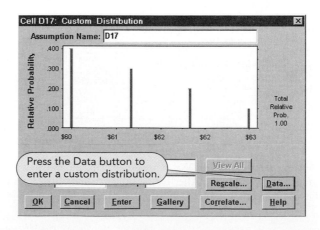

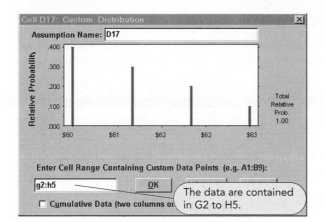

PROGRAM 15.11
Second Screen in Selecting a
Custom Distribution for Selling
Price with Range Identified in
Cells G2:H5

Step 2. We now define the forecast by clicking on **Cell** menu and selecting **Define Forecast** (or selecting the second tool). The forecast is the measurement to be monitored in simulations. There may be more than one. Program 15.12 identifies Profits, in cell G25, as our measurement.

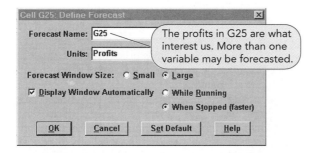

PROGRAM 15.12
Defining Profit as the
Measurement to Be Monitored
in this Simulation

Step 3. We set run preferences by accessing the **Run** menu, which results in Program 15.13. Then click on **Run Preferences** (or the eighth tool on the toolbar).

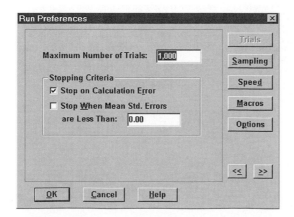

PROGRAM 15.13
Running the Simulation. The
maximum number of trials are
entered as 1,000.

Step 4. To run the actual simulation, we go to the **Run** menu and click on **Run** (or the ninth tool in the toolbar), which begins the simulation. Program 15.14 shows a graph of the forecast value after the simulation has been completed for 1,000 trials. A statistical summary can be obtained by clicking on **View** and then selecting **Statistics**. This is illustrated in Program 15.15.

PROGRAM 15.14

Forecast of Profit Values for a
Simulation of 1,000 Trials

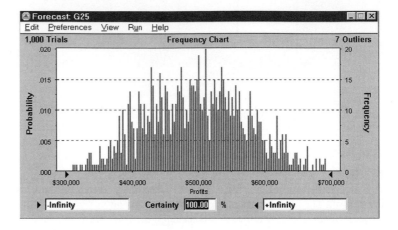

PROGRAM 15.15

A Statistical Summary of Data
from the Simulation of Profit
after 1,000 Trials

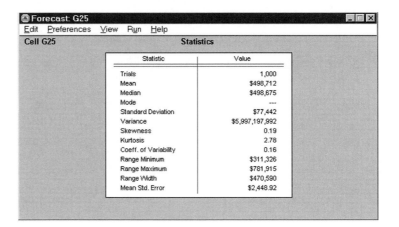

Crystal Ball can handle much more complex examples than the textbook publisher we just described. This demonstration is only intended as a starting point to understanding some of the program's basic features.

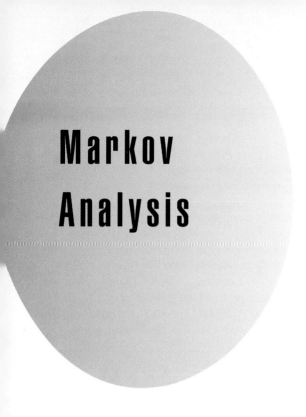

CHAPTER 16

Markov Analysis

LEARNING OBJECTIVES

After completing this chapter, students will be able to:

1. Determine future states or conditions using Markov analysis.
2. Compute long-term or steady-state conditions using only the matrix of transition.
3. Understand the use of absorbing state analysis in predicting future conditions.

CHAPTER OUTLINE

16.1 Introduction

16.2 States and State Probabilities: Grocery Store Example

16.3 Matrix of Transition Probabilities

16.4 Predicting Future Market Shares

16.5 Markov Analysis of Machine Operations

16.6 Equilibrium Conditions

16.7 Absorbing States and the Fundamental Matrix: Accounts Receivable Application

Summary • Glossary • Key Equations • Solved Problems • Self-Test • Discussion Questions and Problems • Data Set Problems • Case Study: Rentall Trucks • Internet Case Studies • Bibliography

Appendix 16.1: Markov Analysis with QM for Windows

16.1 INTRODUCTION

Markov analysis is a technique that deals with the probabilities of future occurrences by analyzing presently known probabilities.[1] The technique has numerous applications in business, including market share analysis, bad debt prediction, university enrollment predictions, and determining whether a machine will break down in the future.

The matrix of transition probabilities shows the likelihood of change.

Markov analysis makes the assumption that the system starts in an initial state or condition. For example, two competing manufacturers might have 40% and 60% of the market sales, respectively, as initial states. Perhaps in two months the market shares for the two companies will change to 45% and 55% of the market, respectively. Predicting these future states involves knowing the system's likelihood or probability of changing from one state to another. For a particular problem, these probabilities can be collected and placed in a matrix or table. This *matrix of transition probabilities* shows the likelihood that the system will change from one time period to the next. This is the Markov process, and it enables us to predict future states or conditions.

Like many other quantitative techniques, Markov analysis can be studied at any level of depth and sophistication. Fortunately, the major mathematical requirements are just that you know how to perform basic matrix manipulations and solve several equations with several unknowns. If you are not familiar with these techniques, you may wish to review Module 5 on the CD that accompanies this book, which covers matrices and other useful mathematical tools, before you begin this chapter.

Because the level of this course prohibits a detailed study of Markov mathematics, we limit our discussion to Markov processes that follow four assumptions:

There are four assumptions of Markov analysis.

1. There are a limited or finite number of possible states.

2. The probability of changing states remains the same over time.

3. We can predict any future state from the previous state and the matrix of transition probabilities.

4. The size and makeup of the system (for example, the total number of manufacturers and customers) do not change during the analysis.

16.2 STATES AND STATE PROBABILITIES: GROCERY STORE EXAMPLE

States are used to identify all possible conditions of a process or a system. For example, a machine can be in one of two states at any point in time. It can be either functioning correctly or not functioning correctly. We can call the proper operation of the machine the first state, and we can call the incorrect functioning the second state. Indeed, it is possible to identify specific states for many processes or systems. If there are only three grocery stores in a small town, a resident can be a customer of any one of the three at any point in time. Therefore, there are three states corresponding to the three grocery stores. If students can take one of three specialties in the management area (let's say management science, management information systems, or general management), each of these areas can be considered a state.

In Markov analysis we also assume that the states are both *collectively exhaustive* and *mutually exclusive*. Collectively exhaustive means that we can list all of the possible states

---

[1] The founder of the concept was A. A. Markov, whose 1905 studies of the sequence of experiments connected in a chain were used to describe the principle of Brownian motion.

of a system or process. Our discussion of Markov analysis assumes that there is a finite number of states for any system. Mutually exclusive means that a system can be in only one state at any point in time. A student can be in only one of the three management specialty areas and *not* in two or more areas at the same time. It also means that a person can only be a customer of *one* of the three grocery stores at any point in time.

Collectively exhaustive and mutually exclusive states are two additional assumptions of Markov analysis.

After the states have been identified, the next step is to determine the probability that the system is in this state. Such information is then placed into a *vector of state probabilities*.

$\pi(i)$ = vector of state probabilities for period i

$$= (\pi_1, \pi_2, \pi_3, \ldots, \pi_n) \tag{16-1}$$

where

n = number of states

$\pi_1, \pi_2, \ldots, \pi_n$ = probability of being in state 1, state 2, . . . , state n

In some cases, where we are only dealing with one item, such as one machine, it is possible to know with complete certainty what state this item is in. For example, if we are investigating only one machine, we may know that at this point in time the machine is functioning correctly. Then the vector of states can be represented as follows:

$\pi(1) = (1, 0)$

where

$\pi(1)$ = vector of states for the machine in period 1

$\pi_1 = 1$ = probability of being in the first state

$\pi_2 = 0$ = probability of being in the second state

This shows that the probability the machine is functioning correctly, state 1, is 1, and the probability that the machine is functioning incorrectly, state 2, is 0 for the first period. In most cases, however, we are dealing with more than one item.

The Vector of State Probabilities for Three Grocery Store Example   Let's look at the vector of states for people in the small town with the three grocery stores. There could be a total of 100,000 people that shop at the three grocery stores during any given month. Forty thousand people may be shopping at American Food Store, which will be called state 1. Thirty thousand people may be shopping at Food Mart, which will be called state 2, and 30,000 people may be shopping at Atlas Foods, which will be called state 3. The probability that a person will be shopping at one of these three grocery stores is as follows:

State 1—American Food Store: 40,000/100,000 = 0.40 = 40%

State 2—Food Mart: 30,000/100,000 = 0.30 = 30%

State 3—Atlas Foods: 30,000/100,000 = 0.30 = 30%

These probabilities can be placed in the vector of state probabilities shown as follows:

$\pi(1) = (0.4, 0.3, 0.3)$

where

$\pi(1)$ = vector of state probabilities for the three grocery stores for period 1

$\pi_1 = 0.4$ = probability that a person will shop at American Food, state 1

$\pi_2 = 0.3$ = probability that a person will shop at Food Mart, state 2

$\pi_3 = 0.3$ = probability that a person will shop at Atlas Foods, state 3

The vector of state probabilities represents market shares.

You should also notice that the probabilities in the vector of states for the three grocery stores represent the *market shares* for these three stores for the first period. Thus American Food has 40% of the market, Food Mart has 30%, and Atlas Foods has 30% of the market in period 1. When we are dealing with market shares, the market shares can be used in place of probability values.

When the initial states and state probabilities have been determined, the next step is to find the matrix of transition probabilities. This matrix is used along with the state probabilities in predicting the future.

16.3   MATRIX OF TRANSITION PROBABILITIES

The matrix of transition allows us to get from a current state to a future state.

The concept that allows us to get from a current state, such as market shares, to a future state is the *matrix of transition probabilities*. This is a matrix of conditional probabilities of being in a future state given a current state. The following definition is helpful:

Let P_{ij} = conditional probability of being in state j in the future given the current state of i

For example, P_{12} is the probability of being in state 2 in the future given the event was in state 1 in the period before.

Let P = matrix of transition probabilities

$$P = \begin{bmatrix} P_{11} & P_{12} & P_{13} & \cdots & P_{1n} \\ P_{21} & P_{22} & P_{23} & \cdots & P_{2n} \\ \vdots & & & & \\ P_{m1} & & \cdots & & P_{mn} \end{bmatrix} \qquad \text{(16-2)}$$

Individual P_{ij} values are usually determined empirically. For example, if we have observed over time that 10% of the people currently shopping at store 1 (or state 1) will be shopping at store 2 (state 2) next period, then we know that $P_{12} = 0.1$ or 10%.

Transition Probabilities for the Three Grocery Stores

Let's say we can determine the matrix of transition probabilities for the three grocery stores by using historical data. The results of our analysis appear in the following matrix:

$$P = \begin{bmatrix} 0.8 & 0.1 & 0.1 \\ 0.1 & 0.7 & 0.2 \\ 0.2 & 0.2 & 0.6 \end{bmatrix}$$

Recall that American Food represents state 1, Food Mart is state 2, and Atlas Foods is state 3. The meaning of these probabilities can be expressed in terms of the various states, as follows:

Row 1

$0.8 = P_{11}$ = probability of being in state 1 after being in state 1 the preceding period

$0.1 = P_{12}$ = probability of being in state 2 after being in state 1 the preceding period

$0.1 = P_{13}$ = probability of being in state 3 after being in state 1 the preceding period

Row 2

$0.1 = P_{21} =$ probability of being in state 1 after being in state 2 the preceding period

$0.7 = P_{22} =$ probability of being in state 2 after being in state 2 the preceding period

$0.2 = P_{23} =$ probability of being in state 3 after being in state 2 the preceding period

Row 3

$0.2 = P_{31} =$ probability of being in state 1 after being in state 3 the preceding period

$0.2 = P_{32} =$ probability of being in state 2 after being in state 3 the preceding period

$0.6 = P_{33} =$ probability of being in state 3 after being in state 3 the preceding period

Note that the three probabilities in the top row sum to 1. The probabilities for any row in a matrix of transition probabilities will also sum to 1.

The probability values for any row must sum to 1.

After the state probabilities have been determined along with the matrix of transition probabilities, it is possible to predict future state probabilities.

16.4 PREDICTING FUTURE MARKET SHARES

One of the purposes of Markov analysis is to predict the future. Given the vector of state probabilities and the matrix of transition probabilities, it is not very difficult to determine the state probabilities at a future date. With this type of analysis, we are able to compute the probability that a person will be shopping at one of the grocery stores in the future. Because this probability is equivalent to market share, it is possible to determine future market shares for American Food, Food Mart, and Atlas Foods. When the current period is 1, calculating the state probabilities for the next period (period 2) can be accomplished as follows:

$$\pi(2) = \pi(1)P \qquad \text{(16-3)}$$

Computing future market shares.

Furthermore, if we are in any period n, we can compute the state probabilities for period $n + 1$ as follows:

$$\pi(n + 1) = \pi(n)P \qquad \text{(16-4)}$$

Equation 16-3 can be used to answer the question of next period's market shares for the grocery stores. The computations are

$$\pi(2) = \pi(1)P$$

$$= (0.4, 0.3, 0.3) \begin{bmatrix} 0.8 & 0.1 & 0.1 \\ 0.1 & 0.7 & 0.2 \\ 0.2 & 0.2 & 0.6 \end{bmatrix}$$

$$= [(0.4)(0.8) + (0.3)(0.1) + (0.3)(0.2) , (0.4)(0.1)$$
$$+ (0.3)(0.7) + (0.3)(0.2) , (0.4)(0.1) + (0.3)(0.2) + (0.3)(0.6)]$$

$$= (0.41, 0.31, 0.28)$$

As you can see, the market share for American Food and Food Mart has increased while the market share for Atlas Foods has decreased. Will this trend continue in the future? Will Atlas eventually lose all of its market share? Or will a stable condition be reached for all three grocery stores? Questions such as these can be answered with a discussion of equilibrium conditions. To help introduce the concept of equilibrium, we present a second application of Markov analysis—machine breakdowns.

16.5   MARKOV ANALYSIS OF MACHINE OPERATIONS

Paul Tolsky, owner of Tolsky Works, has recorded the operation of his milling machine for several years. Over the past two years, 80% of the time the milling machine functioned correctly during the current month if it had functioned correctly in the preceding month. This also means that only 20% of the time did the machine not function correctly for a given month when it was functioning correctly during the preceding month. In addition, it has been observed that 90% of the time the machine remained incorrectly adjusted for any given month if it was incorrectly adjusted the preceding month. Only 10% of the time did the machine operate correctly in a given month when it did *not* operate correctly during the preceding month. In other words, this machine *can* correct itself when it has not been functioning correctly in the past, and this happens 10% of the time. These values can now be used to construct the matrix of transition probabilities. Again, state 1 is a situation in which the machine is functioning correctly, and state 2 is a situation in which the machine is not functioning correctly. The matrix of transition probabilities for this machine is

$$P = \begin{bmatrix} 0.8 & 0.2 \\ 0.1 & 0.9 \end{bmatrix}$$

where

$P_{11} = 0.8 =$ probability that the machine will be *correctly* functioning this month given it was *correctly* functioning last month

$P_{12} = 0.2 =$ probability that the machine will *not* be correctly functioning this month given it was *correctly* functioning last month

$P_{21} = 0.1 =$ probability that the machine will be functioning *correctly* this month given it was *not* correctly functioning last month

$P_{22} = 0.9 =$ probability that the machine will *not* be correctly functioning this month given that it was *not* correctly functioning last month

The row probabilities must sum to 1 because the events are mutually exclusive and collectively exhaustive.

Look at this matrix for the machine. The two probabilities in the top row are the probabilities of functioning correctly and not functioning correctly given that the machine was functioning correctly in the last period. Because these are mutually exclusive and collectively exhaustive, the row probabilities again sum to 1.

What is the probability that Tolsky's machine will be functioning correctly one month from now? What is the probability that the machine will be functioning correctly in two months? To answer these questions, we again apply Equation 16-3:

$$\pi(2) = \pi(1)P$$

$$= (1,0) \begin{bmatrix} 0.8 & 0.2 \\ 0.1 & 0.9 \end{bmatrix}$$

$$= [(1)(0.8) + (0)(0.1) , (1)(0.2) + (0)(0.9)]$$

$$= (0.8, 0.2)$$

Therefore, the probability that the machine will be functioning correctly one month from now, given that it is now functioning correctly, is 0.80. The probability that it will *not* be functioning correctly in one month is 0.20. Now we can use these results to determine the probability that the machine will be functioning correctly two months from now. The analysis is exactly the same:

$\pi(3) = \pi(2)P$

$$= (0.8, 0.2) \begin{bmatrix} 0.8 & 0.2 \\ 0.1 & 0.9 \end{bmatrix}$$

$$= [(0.8)(0.8) + (0.2)(0.1) , (0.8)(0.2) + (0.2)(0.9)]$$

$$= (0.66, 0.34)$$

This means that in the third period, or month, there is a probability of 0.66 that the machine will still be functioning correctly. The probability that the machine will not be functioning correctly is 0.34. Of course, we could continue this analysis as many times as we want in computing state probabilities for future months.

16.6 EQUILIBRIUM CONDITIONS

Looking at the Tolsky machine example, it is easy to think that eventually all market shares or state probabilities will be either 0 or 1. This is usually not the case. *Equilibrium share* of the market values or probabilities are normally encountered.

One way to compute the equilibrium share of the market, or equilibrium state probabilities, is to use Markov analysis for a large number of periods. It is possible to see if the future values are approaching a stable value. For example, it is possible to repeat Markov analysis for 15 periods for Tolsky's machine. This is not too difficult to do by hand. The results for this computation appear in Table 16.1.

The machine starts off functioning correctly (in state 1) in the first period. In period 5, there is only a 0.4934 probability that the machine is still functioning correctly, and by period 10, this probability is only 0.360235. In period 15, the probability that the machine is still functioning correctly is about 0.34. The probability that the machine will be functioning correctly at a future period is decreasing—but it is decreasing at a decreasing rate. What would you expect in the long run? If we made these calculations for 100 periods, what would happen? Would there be an equilibrium in this case? If the answer is *yes*, what would it be? Looking at Table 16.1, it appears that there will be an equilibrium at 0.333333 or ⅓. But how can we be sure?

By definition, an *equilibrium condition* exists if the state probabilities or market shares do not change after a large number of periods. Thus, at equilibrium, the state probabilities for a future period must be the same as the state probabilities for the current period. This fact is the key to solving for the equilibrium state probabilities. This relationship can be expressed as follows:

Equilibrium conditions exist if state probabilities do not change after a large number of periods.

At equilibrium,

$$\pi(\text{next period}) = \pi(\text{this period})P$$

or

$$\pi = \pi P \qquad\qquad\qquad \textbf{(16-5)}$$

Equation 16-5 states that at equilibrium, the state probabilities for the *next* period are the same as the state probabilities for the *current* period. For Tolsky's machine, this can be expressed as follows:

At equilibrium, state probabilities for the next period equal the state probabilities for this period.

$$\pi = \pi P$$

$$(\pi_1, \pi_2) = (\pi_1, \pi_2) \begin{bmatrix} 0.8 & 0.2 \\ 0.1 & 0.9 \end{bmatrix}$$

TABLE 16.1	State Probabilities for the Machine Example for 15 Periods	
PERIOD	STATE 1	STATE 2
1	1.0	0.0
2	0.8	0.2
3	0.66	0.34
4	0.562	0.438
5	0.4934	0.5066
6	0.44538	0.55462
7	0.411766	0.588234
8	0.388236	0.611763
9	0.371765	0.628234
10	0.360235	0.639754
11	0.352165	0.647834
12	0.346515	0.653484
13	0.342560	0.657439
14	0.339792	0.660207
15	0.337854	0.662145

Using matrix multiplication, we get

$$(\pi_1, \pi_2) = [(\pi_1)(0.8) + (\pi_2)(0.1) , (\pi_1)(0.2) + (\pi_2)(0.9)]$$

The *first term* on the left-hand side, π_1, is equal to the *first term* on the right-hand side $(\pi_1)(0.8) + (\pi_2)(0.1)$. In addition, the *second term* on the left-hand side, π_2, is equal to the *second term* on the right-hand side $(\pi_1)(0.2) + (\pi_2)(0.9)$. This gives us the following:

$$\pi_1 = 0.8\pi_1 + 0.1\pi_2 \tag{a}$$

$$\pi_2 = 0.2\pi_1 + 0.9\pi_2 \tag{b}$$

We also know that the state probabilities, π_1 and π_2 in this case, must sum to 1. (Looking at Table 16.1, you note that π_1 and π_2 sum to 1 for all 15 periods.) We can express this property as follows:

$$\pi_1 + \pi_2 + \cdots + \pi_n = 1 \tag{c}$$

For Tolsky's machine, we have

$$\pi_1 + \pi_2 = 1 \tag{d}$$

We drop one equation in solving for equilibrium conditions.

Now, we have three equations for the machine (**a**, **b**, and **c**). We know that Equation **d** must hold. Thus we can drop either Equation **a** or **b** and solve the remaining two equations for π_1 and π_2. It is necessary to drop one of the equations so that we end up with two

MODELING IN THE REAL WORLD   **Use of Markov Analysis in Tracing People with AIDS**

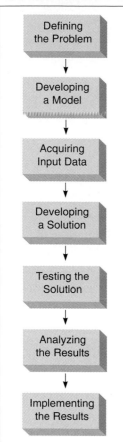

Defining the Problem

For more than a decade, the AIDS epidemic has caused great pain to individuals, families, and society in general. When it comes to federal funding, one problem is predicting the patterns of Medicaid enrollment among people with AIDS.

Developing a Model

A Markov model was developed to trace people with AIDS as they move between assistance categories in Medicaid.

Acquiring Input Data

To use the Markov model, data on how patients flowed between care categories was obtained. In addition, beginning states or conditions provided the needed data for the vector of state probabilities.

Developing a Solution

It was found that most Medicaid-eligible people with AIDS were Medicaid recipients prior to their AIDS diagnosis. These people shifted significantly between various Medicaid eligibility categories in distinct and predictable ways.

Testing the Solution

The model was tested by comparing the Markov analysis with actual patterns and trends. One result was that the number of people with AIDS enrolling in Medicaid is increasing by about 4% annually.

Analyzing the Results

Knowing how AIDS-infected persons are likely to move from one assistance category to another through the use of Markov analysis can help health agencies plan for the resources they need to provide adequate care.

Implementing the Results

The Medicaid program in Maryland was able to predict funding requirements for persons with AIDS as they moved through the Medicaid program.

Source: Linda M. Bartnyska. "Patterns in Maryland Medicaid Enrollment among Persons with AIDS," *Inquiry* 32, 2 (Summer 1995): 184–195.

unknowns and two equations. If we were solving for equilibrium conditions that involved three states, we would end up with four equations. Again, it would be necessary to drop one of the equations so that we end up with three equations and three unknowns. In general, when solving for equilibrium conditions, it will always be necessary to drop one of the equations such that the total number of equations is the same as the total number of variables for which we are solving. The reason that we can drop one of the equations is that they are interrelated mathematically. In other words, one of the equations is redundant in specifying the relationships between the various equilibrium equations.

Let us arbitrarily drop Equation **a**. Thus we will be solving the following two equations:

$$\pi_2 = 0.2\pi_1 + 0.09\pi_2$$

$$\pi_1 + \pi_2 = 1$$

Rearranging the first equation, we get

$$0.1\pi_2 = 0.2\pi_1$$

or

$$\pi_2 = 2\pi_1$$

Substituting this into Equation **d**, we have

$$\pi_1 + \pi_2 = 1$$

or

$$\pi_1 + 2\pi_1 = 1$$

or

$$3\pi_1 = 1$$

$$\pi_1 = \frac{1}{3} = 0.33333333$$

Thus

$$\pi_2 = \frac{2}{3} = 0.66666667$$

Initial-state probability values do not influence equilibrium conditions.

Compare these results with Table 16.1. As you can see, the equilibrium state probability for state 1 is 0.33333333, and the equilibrium state probability for state 2 is 0.66666667. These values are what you would expect by looking at the tabled results. This analysis indicates that it is only necessary to know the matrix of transition in determining the equilibrium market shares. The initial values for the state probabilities or the market shares do not influence the equilibrium state probabilities. The analysis for determining equilibrium state probabilities or market shares is the same when there are more states. If there are three states (as in the grocery store example), we have to solve three equations for the three equilibrium states; if there are four states, we have to solve four simultaneous equations for the four unknown equilibrium values, and so on.

You may wish to prove to yourself that the equilibrium states we have just computed are, in fact, equilibrium states. This can be done by multiplying the equilibrium states times the original matrix of transition. The results will be the same equilibrium states. Performing this analysis is also an excellent way to check your answers to end-of-chapter problems or examination questions.

16.7 ABSORBING STATES AND THE FUNDAMENTAL MATRIX: ACCOUNTS RECEIVABLE APPLICATION

If you are in an absorbing state, you cannot go to another state in the future.

In the examples discussed thus far, we assumed that it is possible for the process or system to go from one state to any other state between any two periods. In some cases, however, if you are in a state, you cannot go to another state in the future. In other words, when you are in a given state, you are "absorbed" by it, and you will remain in that state. Any state that has this property is called an *absorbing state*. An example of this is the accounts receivable application.

An accounts receivable system normally places debts or receivables from its customers into one of several categories or states depending on how overdue the oldest unpaid bill is. Of course, the exact categories or states depend on the policy set by each company. Four typical states or categories for an accounts receivable application follow:

State 1 (π_1): paid, all bills

State 2 (π_2): bad debt, overdue more than three months

State 3 (π_3): overdue less than one month

State 4 (π_4): overdue between one and three months

At any given period, in this case one month, a customer can be in one of these four states.[2] For this example it will be assumed that if the oldest unpaid bill is over three months due, it is automatically placed in the bad debt category. Therefore, a customer can be paid in full (state 1), have the oldest unpaid bill overdue less than one month (state 3), have the oldest unpaid bill overdue between one and three months inclusive (state 4), or have the oldest unpaid bill overdue more than three months, which is a bad debt (state 2).

Like any other Markov process, we can set up a matrix of transition probabilities for these four states. This matrix will reflect the propensity of customers to move among the four accounts receivable categories from one month to the next. The probability of being in the paid category for any item or bill in a future month, given that a customer is in the paid category for a purchased item this month, is 100% or 1. It is impossible for a customer to completely pay for a product one month and to owe money on it in a future month. Another absorbing state is the bad debts state. If a bill is not paid in three months, we are assuming that the company will completely write it off and not try to collect it in the future. Thus, once a person is in the bad debt category, that person will remain in that category forever. For any absorbing state, the probability that a customer will be in this state in the future is 1, and the probability that a customer will be in any other state is 0.

If a person is in an absorbing state now, the probability of being in an absorbing state in the future is 100%.

These values will be placed in the matrix of transition probabilities. But before we construct this matrix, we need to know the probabilities for the other two states—a debt of less than one month and a debt that is between one and three months old. For a person in the less than one month category, there is a 0.60 probability of being in the paid category, a 0 probability of being in the bad debt category, a 0.20 probability of remaining in the less than one month category, and a probability of 0.20 of being in the one to three month category in the next month. Note that there is a 0 probability of being in the bad debt category the next month because it is impossible to get from state 3, less than one month, to state 2, more than three months overdue, in just one month. For a person in the one to three month category, there is a 0.40 probability of being in the paid category, a 0.10 probability of being in the bad debt category, a 0.30 probability of being in the less than one month category, and a 0.20 probability of remaining in the one to three month category in the next month.

How can we get a probability of 0.30 of being in the one to three month category for one month, and in the one month or less category in the next month? Because these categories are determined by the oldest unpaid bill, it is possible to pay one bill that is one to three months old and still have another bill that is one month or less old. In other words, any customer may have more than one outstanding bill at any point in time.

---

[2] You should also be aware that the four states can be placed in any order you choose. For example, it might seem more natural to order this problem with the states:

1. Paid
2. Overdue less than one month
3. Overdue one to three months
4. Overdue more than three months; bad debt

This is perfectly legitimate and the only reason this ordering is not used is to facilitate some matrix manipulations you will see shortly.

With this information, it is possible to construct the matrix of transition probabilities of the problem.

| | NEXT MONTH | | | |
THIS MONTH	PAID	BAD DEBT	<1 MONTH	1 TO 3 MONTHS
Paid	1	0	0	0
Bad debt	0	1	0	0
Less than 1 month	0.6	0	0.2	0.2
1 to 3 months	0.4	0.1	0.3	0.2

Thus

$$P = \begin{bmatrix} 1 & 0 & 0 & 0 \\ 0 & 1 & 0 & 0 \\ 0.6 & 0 & 0.2 & 0.2 \\ 0.4 & 0.1 & 0.3 & 0.2 \end{bmatrix}$$

If we know the fraction of the people in each of the four categories or states for any given period, we can determine the fraction of the people in these four states or categories for any future period. These fractions are placed in a vector of state probabilities and multiplied times the matrix of transition probabilities. This procedure was described in Section 16.4.

In the long run, everyone will be either in the paid or bad debt category.

Even more interesting are the equilibrium conditions. Of course, in the long run, everyone will be either in the paid or bad debt category. This is because the categories are absorbing states. But how many people, or how much money, will be in each of these categories? Knowing the total amount of money that will be in either the paid or bad debt category will help a company manage its bad debts and cash flow. This analysis requires the use of the *fundamental matrix*.

To obtain the fundamental matrix, it is necessary to *partition* the matrix of transition, *P*. This can be done as follows:

$$P = \begin{bmatrix} 1 & 0 & 0 & 0 \\ 0 & 1 & 0 & 0 \\ \hline 0.6 & 0 & 0.2 & 0.2 \\ 0.4 & 0.1 & 0.3 & 0.2 \end{bmatrix} \quad \begin{matrix} I & O \\ \downarrow & \downarrow \\ \\ \uparrow & \uparrow \\ A & B \end{matrix}$$

(16-6)

$$I = \begin{bmatrix} 1 & 0 \\ 0 & 1 \end{bmatrix} \qquad O = \begin{bmatrix} 0 & 0 \\ 0 & 0 \end{bmatrix}$$

$$A = \begin{bmatrix} 0.6 & 0 \\ 0.4 & 0.1 \end{bmatrix} \qquad B = \begin{bmatrix} 0.2 & 0.2 \\ 0.3 & 0.2 \end{bmatrix}$$

where

  I = an identity matrix (that is, a matrix with 1s on the diagonal and 0s everyplace else)

  0 = a matrix with all 0s

The fundamental matrix can be computed as follows:

  $$F = (I - B)^{-1}$$ **(16-7)**   **F** *is the fundamental matrix.*

In Equation 16 7, $(I - B)$ means that we subtract matrix B from matrix I. The superscript -1 means that we take the inverse of the result of $(I - B)$. Here is how we can compute the fundamental matrix for the accounts receivable application:

  $$F = (I - B)^{-1}$$

or

  $$F = \left(\begin{bmatrix} 1 & 0 \\ 0 & 1 \end{bmatrix} - \begin{bmatrix} 0.2 & 0.2 \\ 0.3 & 0.2 \end{bmatrix} \right)^{-1}$$

Subtracting B from I, we get

  $$F = \begin{bmatrix} 0.8 & -0.2 \\ -0.3 & 0.8 \end{bmatrix}^{-1}$$

Taking the inverse, -1, involves several steps, described in the Module 5 on your textbook's CD-ROM. The results of these steps are

  $$F = \begin{bmatrix} 1.38 & 0.34 \\ 0.52 & 1.38 \end{bmatrix}$$

Now we are in a position to use the fundamental matrix in computing the amount of bad debt money that we could expect in the long run. First we need to multiply the fundamental matrix, F, times the matrix A. This is accomplished as follows:

  $$FA = \begin{bmatrix} 1.38 & 0.34 \\ 0.52 & 1.38 \end{bmatrix} \times \begin{bmatrix} 0.6 & 0 \\ 0.4 & 0.1 \end{bmatrix}$$

or

  $$FA = \begin{bmatrix} 0.97 & 0.03 \\ 0.86 & 0.14 \end{bmatrix}$$

The new *FA* matrix has an important meaning. It indicates the probability that an amount in one of the nonabsorbing states will end up in one of the absorbing states. The top row of this matrix indicates the probabilities that an amount in the less than one month category will end up in the paid and the bad debt category. The probability that an amount that is less than one month overdue will be paid is 0.97, and the probability that an amount that is less than one month overdue will end up as a bad debt is 0.03. The second row has a similar interpretation for the other nonabsorbing state, which is the one to three month category. Therefore, 0.86 is the probability that an amount that is one to three months overdue will eventually be paid, and 0.14 is the probability that an amount that is one to three months overdue will never be paid but will become a bad debt.

The **FA** *matrix indicates the probability that an amount will end up in an absorbing state.*

The matrix M *represents the money in the absorbing states—paid or bad debt.*

This matrix can be used in a number of ways. If we know the amount of the less than one month category and the one to three month category, we can determine the amount of money that will be paid and the amount of money that will become bad debts. We let the matrix M represent the amount of money that is in each of the nonabsorbing states as follows:

$$M = (M_1, M_2, M_3, \ldots, M_n)$$

where

$n =$ number of nonabsorbing states

$M_1 =$ amount in the first state or category

$M_2 =$ amount in the second state or category

$M_n =$ amount in the nth state or category

Assume that there is $2,000 in the less than one month category and $5,000 in the one to three month category. Then M would be represented as follows:

$$M = (2,000, 5,000)$$

The amount of money that will end up as being paid and the amount that will end up as bad debts can be computed by multiplying the matrix M times the FA matrix that was computed previously. Here are the computations:

amount paid and amount in bad debts $= MFA$

$$= (2,000, \ 5,000) \begin{bmatrix} 0.97 & 0.03 \\ 0.86 & 0.14 \end{bmatrix}$$

$$= (6,240, \ 760)$$

Thus, out of the total of $7,000 ($2,000 in the less than one month category and $5,000 in the one to three month category), $6,240 will be eventually paid, and $760 will end up as bad debts.

 **IN ACTION** **Markov Analysis for Credit Risk Management**

Some companies believe that using Markov analysis to determine expected default frequencies is very beneficial, if not a necessity. Determining credit risk is important for all banks and other financial institutions involved in making loans. In the sixth annual survey on bank credit risk management performed by KPMG, it was reported that 51% of all banks use migration analysis and that 70% of banks with assets of $10 billion or more use this analysis in managing credit risk. Migration analysis is a combination of average loss rate (ALR) and Markov models.

In the past, Markov-supported migration analysis was used primarily for determining credit risk and loss factors.

Today, this analysis is also used to support the allocation of bank assets, risk-based pricing of products, and general portfolio management. Markov analysis can also be used to determine the effectiveness of various risk-rating systems. For example, this approach can be used to compare a corporate risk-rating system of an investment with the risk-rating system of an outside rater, such as Standard & Poor's or Moody's.

Source: Mike Shearer et al. "Migration Analysis: Combining Approaches for Better Results," *Journal of Lending and Credit Risk Management* (April 1, 1998): 52.

Summary

With the assumptions discussed in this chapter, it was possible to use Markov analysis to predict future states and to determine equilibrium conditions. We also explored a special case of Markov analysis in which there were one or more absorbing states. This involved using the fundamental matrix to determine equilibrium conditions.

In this chapter only three applications of Markov analysis were explored. We investigated Tolsky's machine, the market shares for three grocery stores, and an accounts receivable system. The applications of the method are far reaching, and any dynamic system that meets the model's assumptions can be analyzed by the Markov approach.

Glossary

Markov Analysis. A type of analysis that allows us to predict the future by using the state probabilities and the matrix of transition probabilities.

State Probability. The probability of an event occurring at a point in time. Examples include the probability that a person will be shopping at a given grocery store during a given month.

Vector of State Probabilities. A collection or vector of all state probabilities for a given system or process. The vector of state probabilities could be the initial state or future state.

Market Share. The fraction of the population that shops at a particular store or market. When expressed as a fraction, market shares can be used in place of state probabilities.

Transition Probability. The conditional probability that we will be in a future state given a current or existing state.

Matrix of Transition Probabilities. A matrix containing all transition probabilities for a certain process or system.

Equilibrium Condition. A condition that exists when the state probabilities for a future period are the same as the state probabilities for a previous period.

Absorbing State. A state that, when entered, cannot be left. The probability of going from an absorbing state to any other state is 0.

Fundamental Matrix. A matrix that is the inverse of the I minus B matrix. It is needed to compute equilibrium conditions when absorbing states are involved.

Key Equations

(16-1) $\pi(i) = (\pi_1, \pi_2, \pi_3, \ldots, \pi_n)$

The vector of state probabilities for period i.

(16-2) $P = \begin{bmatrix} P_{11} & P_{12} & P_{13} & \cdots & P_{1n} \\ P_{21} & P_{22} & P_{23} & \cdots & P_{2n} \\ \vdots & & & & \vdots \\ P_{m1} & P_{m2} & P_{m3} & & P_{mn} \end{bmatrix}$

The matrix of transition probabilities, that is, the probability of going from one state into another.

(16-3) $\pi(2) = \pi(1)P$

Formula for calculating the state 2 probabilities given state 1 data.

(16-4) $\pi(n + 1) = \pi(n)P$

Formula for calculating the state probabilities for the period $n + 1$ if we are in period n.

(16-5) $\pi = \pi P$ at equilibrium

The equilibrium state equation used to derive equilibrium probabilities.

(16-6) $P = \begin{bmatrix} I & | & 0 \\ \hline A & | & B \end{bmatrix}$

The partition of the matrix of transition for absorbing state analysis.

(16-7) $F = (I - B)^{-1}$

The fundamental matrix, used in computing probabilities of ending up in an absorbing state.

Solved Problems

Solved Problem 16-1

George Walls, president of Bradley School, is concerned about declining enrollments. Bradley School is a technical college that specializes in training computer programmers and computer operators. Over the years, there has been a lot of competition among Bradley School, International Technology, and Career Academy. The three schools compete in providing education in the areas of programming, computer operations, and basic secretarial skills.

To gain a better understanding of which of these schools is emerging as a leader, George decided to conduct a survey. His survey looked at the number of students who transferred from one school to the other during their academic careers. On the average, Bradley School was able to retain 65% of those students it originally enrolled. Twenty percent of the students originally enrolled transferred to Career Academy and 15% transferred to International Technology. Career Academy had the highest retention rate: 90% of its students remained at Career Academy for their full academic program. George estimated that about half the students who left Career Academy went to Bradley School, while the other half went to International Technology. International Technology was able to retain 80% of its students after they enrolled. Ten percent of the originally enrolled students transferred to Career Academy and the other 10% percent enrolled in Bradley School.

Currently, Bradley School has 40% of the market. Career Academy, a much newer school, has 35% of the market. The remaining market share—25%—consists of students attending International Technology. George would like to determine the market share for Bradley for the next year. What are the equilibrium market shares for Bradley School, International Technology, and Career Academy?

Solution

The data for this problem are summarized as follows:

State 1 initial share = 0.40—Bradley School

State 2 initial share = 0.35—Career Academy

State 3 initial share = 0.25—International Technology

The transition matrix values are

| | | TO | |
FROM	1 BRADLEY	2 CAREER	3 INTERNATIONAL
1 Bradley	0.65	0.20	0.15
2 Career	0.05	0.90	0.05
3 International	0.10	0.10	0.80

For George to determine market share for Bradley School for next year, he has to multiply the current market shares times the matrix of transition probability. Here is the overall structure of these calculations:

$$(0.40 \ 0.35 \ 0.25) \begin{bmatrix} 0.65 & 0.20 & 0.15 \\ 0.05 & 0.90 & 0.05 \\ 0.10 & 0.10 & 0.80 \end{bmatrix}$$

Thus the market shares for Bradley School, International Technology, and Career Academy can be computed by multiplying the current market shares times the matrix of transition probabilities as shown. The result will be a new matrix with three numbers, each representing the market share for one of the schools. The detailed matrix computations follow:

market share for Bradley School = (0.40)(0.65) + (0.35)(0.05) + (0.25)(0.10)
= 0.303

market share for Career Academy = (0.40)(0.20) + (0.35)(0.90) + (0.25)(0.10)
= 0.420

market share for International Technology = (0.40)(0.15) + (0.35)(0.05) + (0.25)(0.80)
= 0.278

Now George would like to compute the equilibrium market shares for the three schools. At equilibrium conditions, the future market share is equal to the existing or current market share times the matrix of transition probabilities. By letting the variable X represent various market shares for these three schools, it is possible to develop a general relationship that will allow us to compute equilibrium market shares:

Let X_1 = market share for Bradley School

X_2 = market share for Career Academy

X_3 = market share for International Technology

At equilibrium,

$$(X_1, X_2, X_3) = (X_1, X_2, X_3) \begin{bmatrix} 0.65 & 0.20 & 0.15 \\ 0.05 & 0.90 & 0.05 \\ 0.10 & 0.10 & 0.80 \end{bmatrix}$$

The next step is to make the appropriate multiplications on the right-hand side of the equation. Doing this will allow us to obtain three equations with the three unknown X values. In addition, we know that the sum of the market shares for any particular period must equal 1. Thus we are able to generate four equations, which are now summarized:

$X_1 = 0.65X_1 + 0.05X_2 + 0.10X_3$

$X_2 = 0.20X_1 + 0.90X_2 + 0.10X_3$

$X_3 = 0.15X_1 + 0.05X_2 + 0.80X_3$

$X_1 + X_2 + X_3 = 1$

Because we have four equations and only three unknowns, we are able to delete one of the top three equations, which will give us three equations and three unknowns. These equations can then be solved using standard algebraic procedures to obtain the equilibrium market share values for Bradley School, International Technology, and Career Academy. The results of these calculations are shown in the following table:

SCHOOL	MARKET SHARE
X_1 (Bradley)	0.158
X_2 (Career)	0.579
X_3 (International)	0.263

Solved Problem 16-2

Central State University administers computer competency examinations every year. These exams allow students to "test out" of the introductory computer class held at the university. Results of the exams can be placed in one of the following four states:

State 1: pass all of the computer exams and be exempt from the course
State 2: do not pass all of the computer exams on the third attempt and be required to take the course
State 3: fail the computer exams on the first attempt
State 4: fail the computer exams on the second attempt

The course coordinator for the exams has noticed the following matrix of transition probabilities:

$$\begin{bmatrix} 1 & 0 & 0 & 0 \\ 0 & 1 & 0 & 0 \\ 0.8 & 0 & 0.1 & 0.1 \\ 0.2 & 0.2 & 0.4 & 0.2 \end{bmatrix}$$

Currently, there are 200 students who did not pass all of the exams on the first attempt. In addition, there are 50 students who did not pass on the second attempt. In the long run, how many students will be exempted from the course by passing the exams? How many of the 250 students will be required to take the computer course?

Solution

The transition matrix values are summarized as follows:

FROM	TO 1	2	3	4
1	1	0	0	0
2	0	1	0	0
3	0.8	0	0.1	0.1
4	0.2	0.2	0.4	0.2

The first step in determining how many students will be required to take the course and how many will be exempt from it is to partition the transition matrix into four matrices. These are the I, 0, A, and B matrices:

$$I = \begin{bmatrix} 1 & 0 \\ 0 & 1 \end{bmatrix}$$

$$0 = \begin{bmatrix} 0 & 0 \\ 0 & 0 \end{bmatrix}$$

$$A = \begin{bmatrix} 0.8 & 0 \\ 0.2 & 0.2 \end{bmatrix}$$

$$B = \begin{bmatrix} 0.1 & 0.1 \\ 0.4 & 0.2 \end{bmatrix}$$

The next step is to compute the fundamental matrix, which is represented by the letter F. This matrix is determined by subtracting the B matrix from the I matrix and taking the inverse of the result:

$$F = (I - B)^{-1}$$

$$= \begin{bmatrix} 1.176 & 0.147 \\ 0.588 & 1.324 \end{bmatrix}$$

Now multiply the F matrix by the A matrix. This step is needed to determine how many students will be exempt from the course and how many will be required to take it. Multiplying the F matrix times the A matrix is fairly straightforward:

$$FA = \begin{bmatrix} 1.176 & 0.147 \\ 0.588 & 1.324 \end{bmatrix} \begin{bmatrix} 0.8 & 0 \\ 0.2 & 0.2 \end{bmatrix}$$

$$= \begin{bmatrix} 0.971 & 0.029 \\ 0.735 & 0.265 \end{bmatrix}$$

The final step is to multiply the results from the FA matrix by the M matrix, as shown here:

$$MFA = (200 \quad 50) \begin{bmatrix} 0.971 & 0.029 \\ 0.735 & 0.265 \end{bmatrix}$$

$$= (231 \quad 19)$$

As you can see, the MFA matrix consists of two numbers. The number of students who will be exempt from the course is 231. The number of students who will eventually have to take the course is 19.

SELF-TEST

- Before taking the self-test, refer back to the learning objectives at the beginning of the chapter, the notes in the margins, and the glossary at the end of the chapter.
- Use the key at the back of the book to correct your answers.
- Restudy pages that correspond to any questions that you answered incorrectly or material you feel uncertain about.

1. The probabilities in any vector of state probabilities
   a. must be mutually exclusive.
   b. must be collectively exclusive.
   c. must each represent one of the finite number of states of nature represented in the system.
   d. all of the above.
   e. none of the above.
2. The product of a vector of state probabilities and the matrix of transition probabilities will yield
   a. another vector of state probabilities.
   b. a meaningless mess.
   c. the inverse of the equilibrium state matrix.
   d. all of the above.
   e. none of the above.
3. In the long run, the state probabilities will be 0 and 1
   a. in no instances.
   b. in all instances.
   c. in some instances.
4. To find equilibrium conditions
   a. the first vector of state probabilities must be known.
   b. the matrix of transition probabilities is unnecessary.
   c. the general terms in the vector of state probabilities are used on two occasions.
   d. the matrix of transition probabilities must be squared before it is inverted.
   e. none of the above.
5. Which of the following is not one of the assumptions of Markov analysis?
   a. There is a limited number of possible states.
   b. There is a limited number of possible future periods.
   c. A future state can be predicted from the previous state and the matrix of transition.
   d. The size and makeup of the system do not change during the analysis.
   e. All of the above are assumptions of Markov analysis.

6. In Markov analysis, the state probabilities must
   a. sum to 1.
   b. be less than 1.
   c. be less than 0.01.
   d. be greater than 1.
   e. be greater than 0.01.
7. Equilibrium conditions
   a. do not exist.
   b. approach 0.3333 and 0.6667.
   c. must sum to 1.
   d. must be less than 0.01.
   e. none of the above.
8. The A and B matrices are used with
   a. equilibrium conditions.
   b. the matrix of transition probabilities.
   c. the state probabilities.
   d. absorbing states.
   e. none of the above.
9. In absorbing state analysis, the amount of money that is in each of the nonabsorbing states is contained in which matrix?
   a. FA
   b. M
   c. B
   d. A
   e. none of the above
10. In Markov analysis, the _____ allows us to get from a current state to a future state.
11. In Markov analysis, we assume that the state probabilities are both _____ and _____ .
12. The _____ is the probability that the system is in a particular state.

Discussion Questions and Problems

Discussion Questions

16-1 List the assumptions that are made in Markov analysis.

16-2 What are the vector of state probabilities and the matrix of transition probabilities, and how can they be determined?

16-3 Describe how we can use Markov analysis to make future predictions.

16-4 What is an equilibrium condition? How do we know that we have an equilibrium condition, and how can we compute equilibrium conditions given the matrix of transition probabilities?

16-5 What is an absorbing state? Give several examples of absorbing states.

16-6 What is the fundamental matrix, and how is it used in determining equilibrium conditions?

Problems*

16-7 Ray Cahnman is the proud owner of a 1955 sports car. On any given day, Ray never knows whether or not his car will start. Ninety percent of the time it will start if it started the previous morning, and 70% of the time it will not start if it did not start the previous morning.

(a) Construct the matrix of transition probabilities.

(b) What is the probability that it will start tomorrow if it started today?

(c) What is the probability that it will start tomorrow if it did *not* start today?

16-8 Alan Resnik, a friend of Ray Cahnman, bet Ray $5 that Ray's car would not start five days from now (see Problem 16-7).

(a) What is the probability that it will not start five days from now if it started today?

(b) What is the probability that it will not start five days from now if it did not start today?

(c) What is the probability that it will start in the long run if the matrix of transition probabilities does not change?

16-9 Over any given month, Dress-Rite loses 10% of its customers to Fashion, Inc., and 20% of its market to Luxury Living. But Fashion, Inc., loses 5% of its market to Dress-Rite and 10% of its market to Luxury Living each month; and Luxury Living loses 5% of its market to Fashion, Inc., and 5% of its market to Dress-Rite. At the present time, each of these clothing stores has an equal share of the market. What do you think the market shares will be next month? What will they be in three months?

16-10 Goodeating Dog Chow Company produces a variety of brands of dog chow. One of their best values is the 50-pound bag of Goodeating Dog Chow. George Hamilton, president of Goodeating, uses a very old machine to load 50 pounds of Goodeating Chow automatically into each bag. Unfortunately, because the machine is old, it occasionally over- or under-fills the bags. When the machine is *correctly* placing 50 pounds of dog chow into each bag, there is a 0.10 probability that the machine will only put 49 pounds in each bag the following day, and there is a 0.20 probability that 51 pounds will be placed in each bag the next day. If the machine is currently placing 49 pounds of dog chow in each bag, there is a 0.30 probability that it will put 50

---

*Note: ⌨ means the problem may be solved with QM for Windows; ✖ means the problem may be solved with Excel QM; and ⌨ means the problem may be solved with QM for Windows and/or Excel QM.

pounds in each bag tomorrow and a 0.20 probability that it will put 51 pounds in each bag tomorrow. In addition, if the machine is placing 51 pounds in each bag today, there is a 0.40 probability that it will place 50 pounds in each bag tomorrow and a 0.10 probability that it will place 49 pounds in each bag tomorrow.

(a) If the machine is loading 50 pounds in each bag today, what is the probability that it will be placing 50 pounds in each bag tomorrow?

(b) Resolve part (a) when the machine is only placing 49 pounds in each bag today.

(c) Resolve part (a) when the machine is placing 51 pounds in each bag today.

16-11 The University of South Wisconsin has had steady enrollments over the past five years. The school has its own bookstore, called University Book Store, but there are also three private bookstores in town: Bill's Book Store, College Book Store, and Battle's Book Store. The university is concerned about the large number of students who are switching to one of the private stores. As a result, South Wisconsin's president, Andy Lange, has decided to give a student three hours of university credit to look into the problem. The following matrix of transition probabilities was obtained:

	UNIVERSITY	BILL'S	COLLEGE	BATTLE'S
University	0.6	0.2	0.1	0.1
Bill's	0	0.7	0.2	0.1
College	0.1	0.1	0.8	0
Battle's	0.05	0.05	0.1	0.8

At the present time, each of the four bookstores has an equal share of the market. What will the market shares be for the next period?

16-12 Resolve Problem 16-10 (Goodeating Dog Chow) for five periods.

16-13 Andy Lange, president of the University of South Wisconsin, is concerned with the declining business at the University Book Store. (See Problem 16-11 for details.) The students tell him that the prices are simply too high. Andy, however, has decided not to lower the prices. If the same conditions exist, what long-run market shares can Andy expect for the four bookstores?

16-14 During the day, the traffic on North Monroe Street in Quincy is fairly steady, but the traffic conditions can vary considerably from one hour to the next due to slow drivers and traffic accidents. As one driver said, "The traffic conditions on Monroe can be either fair, tolerable, or miserable." If the traffic conditions are fair in one hour, there is a 20% chance that they will be tolerable in the next hour and a 10% chance that they will be miserable. If the traffic conditions are tolerable, there is a 20% chance that they will be fair in the next hour and a 5% chance that they will be miserable. In addition, if the traffic conditions are miserable, there is a 60% chance that they will remain that way and a 30% chance that they will be fair in the next hour. If the traffic conditions are miserable at this time, what is the probability that they will be fair in two hours? What is the probability that they will be tolerable in two hours?

16-15 Greg Cracker, mayor of Quincy, is alarmed about the traffic conditions on Monroe Street (see Problem 16-14). In the long run, what percent of the time will traffic conditions be fair, tolerable, and miserable on Monroe Street?

16-16 The tiger minnow, which can be found in Lake Jackson and in Lake Bradford, is a small meat-eating fish. At the present time, there are 900 tiger minnows in Lake Jackson and 100 tiger minnows in Lake Bradford, but a new 10-foot-wide canal between these two lakes will soon change these numbers. Because tiger minnows eat other fish and themselves, the total population remains about the same. Bob Brite, an Eagle Scout from Troop B, has done nothing but watch the tiger minnows going through the canal. During the past month Bob has observed 90 tiger minnows go from Lake Jackson to Lake Bradford, and he has observed 5 tiger minnows go from Lake Bradford to Lake Jackson. Assuming that these migration patterns will remain the same, how many tiger minnows will be in each lake in the long run?

16-17 The residents of Lake Bradford are angry about the canal between Lake Bradford and Lake Jackson. This canal has allowed too many tiger minnows into Lake Bradford, and, as a result, the value of the lake property on Lake Bradford has gone down considerably. One solution would be to place a one-way dam in the canal. This would only reduce the fraction of the tiger minnows migrating from Lake Jackson to Lake Bradford. (See Problem 16-16 for details.) In other words, the dam would have the effect of reducing the probability of a tiger minnow migrating from Lake Jackson to Lake Bradford. What would this probability have to be to restore the original number of tiger minnows in each lake?

16-18 In Section 16.7 we investigated an accounts receivable problem. How would the paid category and the bad debt category change with the following matrix of transition probabilities?

$$P = \begin{bmatrix} 1 & 0 & 0 & 0 \\ 0 & 1 & 0 & 0 \\ 0.7 & 0 & 0.2 & 0.1 \\ 0.4 & 0.2 & 0.2 & 0.2 \end{bmatrix}$$

16-19 Professor Green gives two-month computer programming courses during the summer term. Students must pass a number of exams to pass the course, and each student is given three chances to take the exams. The following states describe the possible situations that could occur:

1. *State 1*: pass all of the exams and pass the course
2. *State 2*: do not pass all of the exams by the third attempt and flunk the course
3. *State 3*: fail an exam in the first attempt
4. *State 4*: fail an exam in the second attempt

After observing several classes, Professor Green was able to obtain the following matrix of transition probabilities:

$$P = \begin{bmatrix} 1 & 0 & 0 & 0 \\ 0 & 1 & 0 & 0 \\ 0.6 & 0 & 0.1 & 0.3 \\ 0.3 & 0.3 & 0.2 & 0.2 \end{bmatrix}$$

At the present time there are 50 students who did not pass all exams on the first attempt, and there are 30 students who did not pass all remaining exams on the second attempt. How many students in these two groups will pass the course, and how many will fail the course?

16-20 Hicourt Industries is a commercial printing outfit in a medium-sized town in central Florida. Its only competitors are the Printing House and Gandy Printers. Last month, Hicourt Industries had approximately 30% of the market for the printing business in the area. The Printing House had 50% of the market, and Gandy Printers had 20% of the market. The association of printers, a locally run association, had recently determined how these three printers and smaller printing operations not involved in the commercial market were able to retain their customer base. Hicourt was the most successful in keeping its customers. Eighty percent of its customers for any one month remained customers for the next month. The Printing House, on the other hand, had only a 70% retention rate. Gandy Printers was in the worst condition. Only 60% of the customers for any one month remained with the firm. In one month, the market share had significantly changed. This was very exciting to George Hicourt, president of Hicourt

Industries. This month Hicourt Industries was able to obtain a 38% market share. The Printing House, on the other hand, lost market share. This month, it only had 42% of the market share. Gandy Printers remained the same; it kept its 20% of the market. Just looking at market share, George concluded that he was able to take 8% per month away from the Printing House. George estimated that in a few short months, he could basically run the Printing House out of business. His hope was to capture 80% of the total market, representing his original 30% along with the 50% share that the Printing House started off with. Will George be able to reach his goal? What do you think the long-term market shares will be for these three commercial printing operations? Will Hicourt Industries be able to run the Printing House completely out of business?

16-21 John Jones of Bayside Laundry has been providing cleaning and linen service for rental condominiums on the Gulf coast for over 10 years. Currently, John is servicing 26 condominium developments. John's two major competitors are Cleanco, which currently services 15 condominium developments, and Beach Services, which performs laundry and cleaning services for 11 condominium developments.

Recently, John contacted Bay Bank about a loan to expand his business operations. To justify the loan, John has kept detailed records of his customers and the customers that he received from his two major competitors. During the past year, he was able to keep 18 of his original 26 customers. During the same period, he was able to get 1 new customer from Cleanco and 2 new customers from Beach Services. Unfortunately, John lost 6 of his original customers to Cleanco and 2 of his original customers to Beach Services during the same year. John has also learned that Cleanco has kept 80% of its current customers. He also knows that Beach Services will keep at least 50% of its customers. For John to get the loan from Bay Bank, he needs to show the loan officer that he will maintain an adequate share of the market. The officers of Bay Bank are concerned about the recent trends for market share, and they have decided not to give John a loan unless he will keep at least 35% of the market share in the long run. What types of equilibrium market shares can John expect? If you were an officer of Bay Bank, would you give John a loan?

16-22 Set up both the vector of state probabilities and the matrix of transition probabilities given the following information:

Store 1 currently has 40% of the market, store 2 currently has 60% of the market.
In each period, store 1 customers have an 80% chance of returning, 20% of switching to store 2.
In each period, store 2 customers have a 90% chance of returning, 10% of switching to store 1.

16-23 Find $\pi(2)$ for Problem 16-22.

16-24 Find the equilibrium conditions for Problem 16-23. Explain what it means.

16-25 As a result of a recent survey of students at the University of South Wisconsin, it was determined that the university owned bookstore currently has 40% of the market. See Problem 16-11. The other three bookstores, Bill's, College, and Battle's, each split the remaining initial market share. Given that the state probabilities are the same, what is the market share for the next period given the initial market shares? What impact do the initial market shares have on each store next period? What is the impact on the steady state market shares?

Data Set Problems

16-26 Sandy Sprunger is part-owner in one of the largest quick-oil-change operations for a medium-sized city in the Midwest. Currently, the firm has 60% of the market. There are a total of 10 quick lubrication shops in the area. After performing some basic marketing research, Sandy has been able to capture the initial probabilities, or market shares, along with the matrix of transition, which represents probabilities that customers will switch from one quick lubrication shop to another. These values are shown in the following table:

FROM	TO									
	1	2	3	4	5	6	7	8	9	10
1	0.60	0.10	0.10	0.10	0.05	0.01	0.01	0.01	0.01	0.01
2	0.01	0.80	0.01	0.01	0.01	0.10	0.01	0.01	0.01	0.03
3	0.01	0.01	0.70	0.01	0.01	0.10	0.01	0.05	0.05	0.05
4	0.01	0.01	0.01	0.90	0.01	0.01	0.01	0.01	0.01	0.02
5	0.01	0.01	0.01	0.10	0.80	0.01	0.03	0.01	0.01	0.01
6	0.01	0.01	0.01	0.01	0.01	0.91	0.01	0.01	0.01	0.01
7	0.01	0.01	0.01	0.01	0.01	0.10	0.70	0.01	0.10	0.04
8	0.01	0.01	0.01	0.01	0.01	0.10	0.03	0.80	0.01	0.01
9	0.01	0.01	0.01	0.01	0.01	0.10	0.01	0.10	0.70	0.04
10	0.01	0.01	0.01	0.01	0.01	0.10	0.10	0.05	0.00	0.70

Initial probabilities, or market share, for shops 1 through 10 are 0.6, 0.1, 0.1, 0.1, 0.05, 0.01, 0.01, 0.01, 0.01, and 0.01.

(a) Given these data, determine market shares for the next period for each of the 10 shops.

(b) What are the equilibrium market shares?

(c) Sandy believes that the original estimates for market shares were wrong. She believes that shop 1 has 40% of the market, and shop 2 has 30%. All other values are the same. If this is the case, what is the impact on market shares for next-period and equilibrium shares?

(d) A marketing consultant believes that shop 1 has tremendous appeal. She believes that this shop will retain 99% of its current market share; 1% may switch to shop 2. If the consultant is correct, will shop 1 have 90% of the market in the long run?

16-27 During a recent trip to her favorite restaurant, Sandy (owner of shop 1) met Chris Talley (owner of shop 7) (see Problem 16-26). After an enjoyable lunch, Sandy and Chris had a heated discussion about market share for the quick-oil-change operations in their city. Here is their conversation:

Sandy: My operation is so superior that after someone changes oil at one of my shops, they will never do business with anyone else. On second thought, maybe 1 person out of 100 will try your shop after visiting one of my shops. In a month, I will have 99% of the market and you will have 1% of the market.

Chris: You have it completely reversed. In a month, I will have 99% of the market and you will only have 1% of the market. In fact, I will treat you to a meal at a restaurant of your choice if you are right. If I am right, you will treat me to one of those big steaks at David's Steak House. Do we have a deal?

Sandy: Yes! Get your checkbook or your credit card. You will have the privilege of paying for two very expensive meals at Anthony's Seafood Restaurant.

(a) Assume that Sandy is correct about customers visiting one of her quick-oil-change shops. Will she win the bet with Chris?

(b) Assume that Chris is correct about customers visiting one of his quick-oil-change shops. Will he win the bet?

(c) Describe what would happen if both Sandy and Chris are correct about customers visiting their quick-oil-change operations.

16-28 The first quick-oil change store in Problem 16-26 retains 73% of its market share. This represents a probability of .73 in the first row and first column of the matrix of transition probabilities. The other probability values in the first row are equally distributed across the other stores (namely, 3% each). What impact does this have on the steady-state market shares for the quick-oil stores?

Case Study

Rentall Trucks

Jim Fox, an executive for Rentall Trucks, could not believe it. He had hired one of the town's best law firms, Folley, Smith, and Christensen. Their fee for drawing up the legal contracts was over $50,000. Folley, Smith, and Christensen had made one important omission from the contracts, and this blunder would more than likely cost Rentall Trucks millions of dollars. For the hundredth time, Jim carefully reconstructed the situation and pondered the inevitable.

Rentall Trucks was started by Robert (Bob) Renton more than 10 years ago. It specialized in renting trucks to businesses and private individuals. The company prospered, and Bob increased his net worth by millions of dollars. Bob was a legend in the rental business and was known all over the world for his keen business abilities.

Only a year and a half ago some of the executives of Rentall and some additional outside investors offered to buy Rentall from Bob. Bob was close to retirement, and the offer was unbelievable. His children and their children would be able to live in high style off the proceeds of the sale. Folley, Smith, and Christensen developed the contracts for the executives of Rentall and other investors, and the sale was made.

Being a perfectionist, it was only a matter of time until Bob was marching down to the Rentall headquarters, telling everyone the mistakes that Rentall was making and how to solve some of their problems. Pete Rosen, president of Rentall, became extremely angry about Bob's constant interference, and in a brief 10-minute meeting, Pete told Bob never to enter the Rentall offices again. It was at this time that Bob decided to reread the contracts, and it was also at this time that Bob and his lawyer discovered that there was no clause in the contracts that prevented Bob from competing directly with Rentall.

The brief 10-minute meeting with Pete Rosen was the beginning of Rentran. In less than six months, Bob Renton had lured some of the key executives away from Rentall and into his new business, Rentran, which would compete directly with

Rentall Trucks in every way. After a few months of operation, Bob estimated that Rentran had about 5% of the total national market for truck rentals. Rentall had about 80% of the market, and another company, National Rentals, had the remaining 15% of the market.

Rentall's Jim Fox was in total shock. In a few months, Rentran had already captured 5% of the total market. At this rate, Rentran might completely dominate the market in a few short years. Pete Rosen even wondered if Rentall could maintain 50% of the market in the long run. As a result of these concerns, Pete hired a marketing research firm that analyzed a random sample of truck rental customers. The sample consisted of 1,000 existing or potential customers. The marketing research firm was very careful to make sure that the sample represented the true market conditions. The sample, taken in August, consisted of 800 customers of Rentall, 60 customers of Rentran, and the remainder National customers. The same sample was then analyzed the next month concerning the customers' propensity to switch companies. Of the original Rentall customers, 200 switched to Rentran, and 80 switched to National. Rentran was able to retain 51 of their original customers. Three customers switched to Rentall, and 6 customers switched to National. Finally, 14 customers switched from National to Rentall, and 35 customers switched from National to Rentran.

The board of directors meeting was only two weeks away, and there would be some difficult questions to answer—what happened, and what can be done about Rentran? In Jim Fox's opinion, nothing could be done about the costly omission made by Folley, Smith, and Christensen. The only solution was to take immediate corrective action that would curb Rentran's ability to lure customers away from Rentall.

After a careful analysis of Rentran, Rentall, and the truck rental business in general, Jim concluded that immediate changes would be needed in three areas: rental policy, advertising, and product line. Regarding rental policy, a number of changes were needed to make truck rental both easier and faster. Rentall could implement many of the techniques used by Hertz and other car rental agencies. In addition, changes in the product line were needed. Rentall's smaller trucks had to be more comfortable and easier to drive. Automatic transmission, comfortable bucket seats, air conditioners, quality radio and tape stereo systems, and cruise control should be included. Although expensive and difficult to maintain, these items could make a significant difference in market shares. Finally, Jim knew that additional advertising was needed. The advertising had to be immediate and aggressive. Television and journal advertising had to be increased, and a good advertising company was needed. If these new changes were implemented now, there would be a good chance that Rentall would be able to maintain close to its 80% of the market. To confirm Jim's perceptions, the same marketing research firm was employed to analyze the effect of these changes, using the same sample of 1,000 customers.

The marketing research firm, Meyers Marketing Research, Inc., performed a pilot test on the sample of 1,000 cus-

tomers. The results of the analysis revealed that Rentall would only lose 100 of its original customers to Rentran and 20 to National if the new policies were implemented. In addition, Rentall would pick up customers from both Rentran and National. It was estimated that Rentall would now get 9 customers from Rentran and 28 customers from National.

Discussion Questions

1. What will the market shares be in one month if these changes are made? If no changes are made?

2. What will the market shares be in three months with the changes?

3. If market conditions remain the same, what market share would Rentall have in the long run? How does this compare with the market share that would result if the changes were not made?

INTERNET CASE STUDIES

See our Internet home page at **http://www.prenhall.com/render** for these additional case studies: St. Pierre Salt Company and University of Texas-Austin.

Bibliography

Bowers, J. A. "Weather Risk in Offshore Projects," *Journal of the Operational Research Society* 45, 4 (April 1994): 409–418.

Ching, Wai. "Markov-Modulated Poisson Processes for Multi-Location Inventory Problems," *International Journal of Production Economics* (November 20, 1997).

Derman, C. *Finite State Markov Decision Process*. New York: Academic Press, Inc., 1970.

Freedman, D. *Markov Chains*. San Francisco: Holden-Day, Inc., 1971.

Gates, David. "Replacement of Train Wheels: An Application of Dynamic Reversal of a Markov Process," *Journal of Applied Probability* 31, 1 (March 1994): 1–8.

Martin, J. *Bayesian Decision Problems and Markov Chains*. New York: John Wiley & Sons, Inc., 1967.

Render, B., R. M. Stair, and Irwin Greenberg. *Cases and Readings in Quantitative Analysis*, 2nd ed. Boston: Allyn and Bacon, Inc., 1990.

Rodrigo, V. et al. "A New Markov Description of the M/G/1 Retrial Queue," *European Journal of Operations Research* (January 1, 1998).

Shearer, Mike et al. "Migration Analysis: Combining Approaches for Better Results," *Journal of Lending and Credit Risk Management* (April 1, 1998): 52.

APPENDIX 16.1: MARKOV ANALYSIS WITH QM FOR WINDOWS

Markov analysis can be used for a variety of practical problems, including market share, equilibrium conditions, and tracing patients through a medical system (see the QA in Action box). The grocery store example was used to show how Markov analysis can be used to determine future market-share conditions. Programs 16.1 and 16.2 reveal how QM for Windows is used to compute market shares and equilibrium conditions. Note that the initial conditions and the ending market share (probabilities) are also displayed.

PROGRAM 16.1

QM for Windows for Markov Analysis for the Three Grocery Stores

PROGRAM 16.2

Markov Analysis Results for Grocery Example

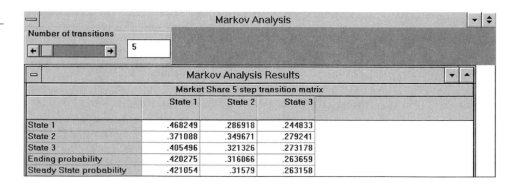

Absorbing state analysis was also discussed in this chapter. A bill-paying example was used. Program 16.3 shows how QM for Windows is used to compute the amount paid and the amount of bad debt using absorbing state analysis.

Markov Analysis - [Matrices]

Number of transitions: 2

Accounts Receivable Solution

Markov Matrix (sorted if	Paid	Bad Debt	Due < 1	Due 1-3
Paid	1.	0.	0.	0.
Bad Debt	0.	1.	0.	0.
Due < 1 month	0.6	0.	0.2	0.2
Due 1-3 months	0.4	0.1	0.3	0.2
B matrix	Due < 1	Due 1-3		
Due < 1 month	0.2	0.2		
Due 1-3 months	0.3	0.2		
F matrix (I-B)^-1	Due < 1	Due 1-3		
Due < 1 month	1.3793	0.3448		
Due 1-3 months	0.5172	1.3793		
FA matrix	Paid	Bad Debt		
Due < 1 month	0.9655	0.0345		
Due 1-3 months	0.8621	0.1379		

PROGRAM 16.3

Output from Absorbing State Analysis on the Accounts Receivable Example of Section 16.7

Appendices

A. Areas under the Standard Normal Curve

B. Unit Normal Loss Integral

C. Values of $e^{-\lambda}$ for Use in the Poisson Distribution

D. Using QM for Windows

E. Using Excel QM

F. Solutions to Selected Problems

G. Solutions to Self-Tests

APPENDIX A: AREAS UNDER THE STANDARD NORMAL CURVE

Example: To find the area under the normal curve, you must know how many standard deviations that point is to the right of the mean. Then the area under the normal curve can be read directly from the normal table. For example, the total area under the normal curve for a point that is 1.55 standard deviations to the right of the mean is .93943.

	00	.01	.02	.03	.04	.05	.06	.07	.08	.09
0.0	.50000	.50399	.50798	.51197	.51595	.51994	.52392	.52790	.53188	.53586
0.1	.53983	.54380	.54776	.55172	.55567	.55962	.56356	.56749	.57142	.57535
0.2	.57926	.58317	.58706	.59095	.59483	.59871	.60257	.60642	.61026	.61409
0.3	.61791	.62172	.62552	.62930	.63307	.63683	.64058	.64431	.64803	.65173
0.4	.65542	.65910	.66276	.66640	.67003	.67364	.67724	.68082	.68439	.68793
0.5	.69146	.69497	.69847	.70194	.70540	.70884	.71226	.71566	.71904	.72240
0.6	.72575	.72907	.73237	.73536	.73891	.74215	.74537	.74857	.75175	.75490
0.7	.75804	.76115	.76424	.76730	.77035	.77337	.77637	.77935	.78230	.78524
0.8	.78814	.79103	.79389	.79673	.79955	.80234	.80511	.80785	.81057	.81327
0.9	.81594	.81859	.82121	.82381	.82639	.82894	.83147	.83398	.83646	.83891
1.0	.84134	.84375	.84614	.84849	.85083	.85314	.85543	.85769	.85993	.86214
1.1	.86433	.86650	.86864	.87076	.87286	.87493	.87698	.87900	.88100	.88298
1.2	.88493	.88686	.88877	.89065	.89251	.89435	.89617	.89796	.89973	.90147
1.3	.90320	.90490	.90658	.90824	.90988	.91149	.91309	.91466	.91621	.91774
1.4	.91924	.92073	.92220	.92364	.92507	.92647	.92785	.92922	.93056	.93189
1.5	.93319	.93448	.93574	.93699	.93822	.93943	.94062	.94179	.94295	.94408
1.6	.94520	.94630	.94738	.94845	.94950	.95053	.95154	.95254	.95352	.95449
1.7	.95543	.95637	.95728	.95818	.95907	.95994	.96080	.96164	.96246	.96327
1.8	.96407	.96485	.96562	.96638	.96712	.96784	.96856	.96926	.96995	.97062
1.9	.97128	.97193	.97257	.97320	.97381	.97441	.97500	.97558	.97615	.97670
2.0	.97725	.97784	.97831	.97882	.97932	.97982	.98030	.98077	.98124	.98169
2.1	.98214	.98257	.98300	.98341	.98382	.98422	.98461	.98500	.98537	.98574
2.2	.98610	.98645	.98679	.98713	.98745	.98778	.98809	.98840	.98870	.98899
2.3	.98928	.98956	.98983	.99010	.99036	.99061	.99086	.99111	.99134	.99158
2.4	.99180	.99202	.99224	.99245	.99266	.99286	.99305	.99324	.99343	.99361
2.5	.99379	.99396	.99413	.99430	.99446	.99461	.99477	.99492	.99506	.99520

	00	.01	.02	.03	.04	.05	.06	.07	.08	.09
2.6	.99534	.99547	.99560	.99573	.99585	.99598	.99609	.99621	.99632	.99643
2.7	.99653	.99664	.99674	.99683	.99693	.99702	.99711	.99720	.99728	.99736
2.8	.99744	.99752	.99760	.99767	.99774	.99781	.99788	.99795	.99801	.99807
2.9	.99813	.99819	.99825	.99831	.99836	.99841	.99846	.99851	.99856	.99861
3.0	.99865	.99869	.99874	.99878	.99882	.99886	.99899	.99893	.99896	.99900
3.1	.99903	.99906	.99910	.99913	.99916	.99918	.99921	.99924	.99926	.99929
3.2	.99931	.99934	.99936	.99938	.99940	.99942	.99944	.99946	.99948	.99950
3.3	.99952	.99953	.99955	.99957	.99958	.99960	.99961	.99962	.99964	.99965
3.4	.99966	.99968	.99969	.99970	.99971	.99972	.99973	.99974	.99975	.99976
3.5	.99977	.99978	.99978	.99979	.99980	.99981	.99981	.99982	.99983	.99983
3.6	.99984	.99985	.99985	.99986	.99986	.99987	.99987	.99988	.99988	.99989
3.7	.99989	.99990	.99990	.99990	.99991	.99991	.99992	.99992	.99992	.99992
3.8	.99993	.99993	.99993	.99994	.99994	.99994	.99994	.99995	.99995	.99995
3.9	.99995	.99995	.99996	.99996	.99996	.99996	.99996	.99996	.99997	.99997

Source: Reprinted from Robert O. Schlaifer, *Introduction to Statistics for Business Decisions,* published by McGraw-Hill Book Company, 1961, by permission of the copyright holder, the President and Fellows of Harvard College.

APPENDIX B: UNIT NORMAL LOSS INTEGRAL

D	.00	.01	.02	.03	.04	.05	.06	.07	.08	.09
.0	.3989	.3940	.3890	.3841	.3793	.3744	.3697	.3649	.3602	.3556
.1	.3509	.3464	.3418	.3373	.3328	.3284	.3240	.3197	.3154	.3111
.2	.3069	.3027	.2986	.2944	.2904	.2863	.2824	.2784	.2745	.2706
.3	.2668	.2630	.2592	.2555	.2518	.2481	.2445	.2409	.2374	.2339
.4	.2304	.2270	.2236	.2203	.2169	.2137	.2104	.2072	.2040	.2009
.5	.1978	.1947	.1917	.1887	.1857	.1828	.1799	.1771	.1742	.1714
.6	.1687	.1659	.1633	.1606	.1580	.1554	.1528	.1503	.1478	.1453
.7	.1429	.1405	.1381	.1358	.1334	.1312	.1289	.1267	.1245	.1223
.8	.1202	.1181	.1160	.1140	.1120	.1100	.1080	.1061	.1042	.1023
.9	.1004	.09860	.09680	.09503	.09328	.09156	.08986	.08819	.08654	.08491
1.0	.08332	.08174	.08019	.07866	.07716	.07568	.07422	.07279	.07138	.06999
1.1	.06862	.06727	.06595	.06465	.06336	.06210	.06086	.05964	.05844	.05726
1.2	.05610	.05496	.05384	.05274	.05165	.05059	.04954	.04851	.04750	.04650
1.3	.04553	.04457	.04363	.04270	.04179	.04090	.04002	.03916	.03831	.03748
1.4	.03667	.03587	.03508	.03431	.03356	.03281	.03208	.03137	.03067	.02998
1.5	.02931	.02865	.02800	.02736	.02674	.02612	.02552	.02494	.02436	.02380
1.6	.02324	.02270	.02217	.02165	.02114	.02064	.02015	.01967	.01920	.01874
1.7	.01829	.01785	.01742	.01699	.01658	.01617	.01578	.01539	.01501	.01464
1.8	.01428	.01392	.01357	.01323	.01290	.01257	.01226	.01195	.01164	.01134
1.9	.01105	.01077	.01049	.01022	$.0^2 9957$	$.0^2 9698$	$.0^2 9445$	$.0^2 9198$	$.0^2 8957$	$.0^2 8721$
2.0	$.0^2 8491$	$.0^2 8266$	$.0^2 8046$	$.0^2 7832$	$.0^2 7623$	$.0^2 7418$	$.0^2 7219$	$.0^2 7024$	$.0^2 6835$	$.0^2 6649$
2.1	$.0^2 6468$	$.0^2 6292$	$.0^2 6120$	$.0^2 5952$	$.0^2 5788$	$.0^2 5628$	$.0^2 5472$	$.0^2 5320$	$.0^2 5172$	$.0^2 5028$
2.2	$.0^2 4887$	$.0^2 4750$	$.0^2 4616$	$.0^2 4486$	$.0^2 4358$	$.0^2 4235$	$.0^2 4114$	$.0^2 3996$	$.0^2 3882$	$.0^2 3770$
2.3	$.0^2 3662$	$.0^2 3556$	$.0^2 3453$	$.0^2 3352$	$.0^2 3255$	$.0^2 3159$	$.0^2 3067$	$.0^2 2977$	$.0^2 2889$	$.0^2 2804$
2.4	$.0^2 2720$	$.0^2 2640$	$.0^2 2561$	$.0^2 2484$	$.0^2 2410$	$.0^2 2337$	$.0^2 2267$	$.0^2 2199$	$.0^2 2132$	$.0^2 2067$
2.5	$.0^2 2004$	$.0^2 1943$	$.0^2 1883$	$.0^2 1826$	$.0^2 1769$	$.0^2 1715$	$.0^2 1662$	$.0^2 1610$	$.0^2 1560$	$.0^2 1511$
2.6	$.0^2 1464$	$.0^2 1418$	$.0^2 1373$	$.0^2 1330$	$.0^2 1288$	$.0^2 1247$	$.0^2 1207$	$.0^2 1169$	$.0^2 1132$	$.0^2 1095$
2.7	$.0^2 1060$	$.0^2 1026$	$.0^3 9928$	$.0^3 9607$	$.0^3 9295$	$.0^3 8992$	$.0^3 8699$	$.0^3 8414$	$.0^3 8138$	$.0^3 7870$
2.8	$.0^3 7611$	$.0^3 7359$	$.0^3 7115$	$.0^3 6879$	$.0^3 6650$	$.0^3 6428$	$.0^3 6213$	$.0^3 6004$	$.0^3 5802$	$.0^3 5606$
2.9	$.0^3 5417$	$.0^3 5233$	$.0^3 5055$	$.0^3 4883$	$.0^3 4716$	$.0^3 4555$	$.0^3 4398$	$.0^3 4247$	$.0^3 4101$	$.0^3 3959$
3.0	$.0^3 3822$	$.0^3 3689$	$.0^3 3560$	$.0^3 3436$	$.0^3 3316$	$.0^3 3199$	$.0^3 3087$	$.0^3 2978$	$.0^3 2873$	$.0^3 2771$

D	.00	.01	.02	.03	.04	.05	.06	.07	.08	.09
3.1	$.0^3$2673	$.0^3$2577	$.0^3$2485	$.0^3$2396	$.0^3$2311	$.0^3$2227	$.0^3$2147	$.0^3$2070	$.0^3$1995	$.0^3$1922
3.2	$.0^3$1852	$.0^3$1785	$.0^3$1720	$.0^3$1657	$.0^3$1596	$.0^3$1537	$.0^3$1480	$.0^3$1426	$.0^3$1373	$.0^3$1322
3.3	$.0^3$1273	$.0^3$1225	$.0^3$1179	$.0^3$1135	$.0^3$1093	$.0^3$1051	$.0^3$1012	$.0^4$9734	$.0^4$9365	$.0^4$9009
3.4	$.0^4$8666	$.0^4$8335	$.0^4$8016	$.0^4$7709	$.0^4$7413	$.0^4$7127	$.0^4$6852	$.0^4$6587	$.0^4$6331	$.0^4$6085
3.5	$.0^4$5848	$.0^4$5620	$.0^4$5400	$.0^4$5188	$.0^4$4984	$.0^4$4788	$.0^4$4599	$.0^4$4417	$.0^4$4242	$.0^4$4073
3.6	$.0^4$3911	$.0^4$3755	$.0^4$3605	$.0^4$3460	$.0^4$3321	$.0^4$3188	$.0^4$3059	$.0^4$2935	$.0^4$2816	$.0^4$2702
3.7	$.0^4$2592	$.0^4$2486	$.0^4$2385	$.0^4$2287	$.0^4$2193	$.0^4$2103	$.0^4$2016	$.0^4$1933	$.0^4$1853	$.0^4$1776
3.8	$.0^4$1702	$.0^4$1632	$.0^4$1563	$.0^4$1498	$.0^4$1435	$.0^4$1375	$.0^4$1317	$.0^4$1262	$.0^4$1208	$.0^4$1157
3.9	$.0^4$1108	$.0^4$1061	$.0^4$1016	$.0^5$9723	$.0^5$9307	$.0^5$8908	$.0^5$8525	$.0^5$8158	$.0^5$7806	$.0^5$7469
4.0	$.0^5$7145	$.0^5$6835	$.0^5$6538	$.0^5$6253	$.0^5$5980	$.0^5$5718	$.0^5$5468	$.0^5$5227	$.0^5$4997	$.0^5$4777
4.1	$.0^5$4566	$.0^5$4364	$.0^5$4170	$.0^5$3985	$.0^5$3807	$.0^5$3637	$.0^5$3475	$.0^5$3319	$.0^5$3170	$.0^5$3027
4.2	$.0^5$2891	$.0^5$2760	$.0^5$2635	$.0^5$2516	$.0^5$2402	$.0^5$2292	$.0^5$2188	$.0^5$2088	$.0^5$1992	$.0^5$1901
4.3	$.0^5$1814	$.0^5$1730	$.0^5$1650	$.0^5$1574	$.0^5$1501	$.0^5$1431	$.0^5$1365	$.0^5$1301	$.0^5$1241	$.0^5$1183
4.4	$.0^5$1127	$.0^5$1074	$.0^5$1024	$.0^6$9756	$.0^6$9296	$.0^6$8857	$.0^6$8437	$.0^6$8037	$.0^6$7655	$.0^6$7290
4.5	$.0^6$6942	$.0^6$6610	$.0^6$6294	$.0^6$5992	$.0^6$5704	$.0^6$5429	$.0^6$5167	$.0^6$4917	$.0^6$4679	$.0^6$4452
4.6	$.0^6$4236	$.0^6$4029	$.0^6$3833	$.0^6$3645	$.0^6$3467	$.0^6$3297	$.0^6$3135	$.0^6$2981	$.0^6$2834	$.0^6$2694
4.7	$.0^6$2560	$.0^6$2433	$.0^6$2313	$.0^6$2197	$.0^6$2088	$.0^6$1984	$.0^6$1884	$.0^6$1790	$.0^6$1700	$.0^6$1615
4.8	$.0^6$1533	$.0^6$1456	$.0^6$1382	$.0^6$1312	$.0^6$1246	$.0^6$1182	$.0^6$1122	$.0^6$1065	$.0^6$1011	$.0^7$9588
4.9	$.0^7$9096	$.0^7$8629	$.0^7$8185	$.0^7$7763	$.0^7$7362	$.0^7$6982	$.0^7$6620	$.0^7$6276	$.0^7$5950	$.0^7$5640

Example of table notation: $.0^4$5848 = .00005848.

Source: Reprinted from Robert O. Schlaifer, *Introduction to Statistics for Business Decisions,* published by McGraw-Hill Book Company, 1961, by permission of the copyright holder, the President and Fellows of Harvard College.

APPENDIX C: VALUES OF $e^{-\lambda}$ FOR USE IN THE POISSON DISTRIBUTION

λ	$e^{-\lambda}$	λ	$e^{-\lambda}$
0.0	1.0000	3.1	0.0450
0.1	0.9048	3.2	0.0408
0.2	0.8187	3.3	0.0369
0.3	0.7408	3.4	0.0334
0.4	0.6703	3.5	0.0302
0.5	0.6065	3.6	0.0273
0.6	0.5488	3.7	0.0247
0.7	0.4966	3.8	0.0224
0.8	0.4493	3.9	0.0202
0.9	0.4066	4.0	0.0183
1.0	0.3679	4.1	0.0166
1.1	0.3329	4.2	0.0150
1.2	0.3012	4.3	0.0136
1.3	0.2725	4.4	0.0123
1.4	0.2466	4.5	0.0111
1.5	0.2231	4.6	0.0101
1.6	0.2019	4.7	0.0091
1.7	0.1827	4.8	0.0082
1.8	0.1653	4.9	0.0074
1.9	0.1496	5.0	0.0067
2.0	0.1353	5.1	0.0061
2.1	0.1225	5.2	0.0055
2.2	0.1108	5.3	0.0050
2.3	0.1003	5.4	0.0045
2.4	0.0907	5.5	0.0041
2.5	0.0821	5.6	0.0037
2.6	0.0743	5.7	0.0033
2.7	0.0672	5.8	0.0030
2.8	0.0608	5.9	0.0027
2.9	0.0550	6.0	0.0025
3.0	0.0498		

APPENDIX D: USING QM FOR WINDOWS

Introduction

Welcome to QM for Windows. Along with its companion, Excel QM (see Appendix E), you have available to you the most user-friendly software available for the field of quantitative analysis/quantitative methods (QA/QM). QM for Windows is a package that has been designed to help you to better learn and understand this field. The software can be used to either solve problems or check answers that have been derived by hand. You will find that this free software is exceptionally friendly due to the following features.

- Anyone familiar with any standard spreadsheet or word processor in Windows will easily be able to use QM for Windows. All modules have help screens that can be accessed at any time.

- Even though QM for Windows contains 18 modules and 40 submodules, the screens for every module are consistent, so that after you become accustomed to using one module you will have an easy time with the other modules.

- The spreadsheet-type data editor allows full screen editing.

- Files are opened and saved in the usual Windows fashion, and in addition, files are named by module, which makes it easy to find files saved previously.

- It is easy to change from one solution method to another to compare methods and answers.

- Graphs are easily displayed and printed.

Installing QM for Windows

For all Windows installations, including this one, it is best to be certain that no programs, including virus protection programs are running while you are installing a new one:

1. Insert the Render/Stair CD into the CD-ROM drive, which we assume is drive D:.
2. From the Windows 95/98 Start button, select Run, Browse.
3. Change to the QM4win directory.
4. Select QM Setup.7RS for Windows 95/98.
5. Press [**Return**] or click on [**OK**].
6. Follow the setup instructions on the screen.

Default values have been assigned in the setup program, but you may change them if you like. The default values are that the program will be installed to a directory on the c: drive named C:\Program Files\QMwin32 and that the program group will be named QM for Windows 2.0.

QM for Windows requires some general information in order to operate. The first screen at registration is a software licensing agreement. In the second registration screen you should enter your name, university, course, and professor. The name is required. When you are finished, press [**OK**].

After the registration is complete, you will have a program group added to your program manager. The group will be called QM for Windows 2. In addition, a shortcut to the program will be placed on the desktop. To use the QM for Windows program, double-click on the shortcut on the desktop or use Start, QM for Windows 2, QM for Windows.

The screen that is displayed is the basic screen for the software and contains the assorted components that are part of most of the screens. This screen was displayed in chapter 1 as Program 1.1. The top of that screen is the standard Windows title bar for the window. Below the title bar is a standard Windows menu bar. The menu bar should be easy to use. The details of the seven menu options of File, Edit, View, Module, Format, Tools, Window, and Help are explained in this appendix. At the beginning of the program the only enabled menu options are File (to open a previously saved file or to exit the program), Module (to select the module), and Help. The other options will become enabled as a module is chosen or as a problem is started.

Solving a problem
There are several ways to solve a problem. The easiest way is to press the Solve button on the standard toolbar. Alternatively, the function key [F9] may be used. Finally, if you enter the data by using the enter key, after the last piece of data is entered the problem will be solved. After solving a problem, to return to editing the data press the Edit button, which has replaced the Solve button on the Standard toolbar, or use [F9].

Below the menu are two toolbars: a standard toolbar and a format toolbar. The toolbars contain standard shortcuts for several of the menu commands. If you move the mouse over the button for about two seconds, an explanation of the button will be displayed on the screen.

The next bar contains an instruction. There is always an instruction here trying to help you to figure out what to do or what to enter. Currently, the instruction indicates to select a module or open a file. When data are to be entered into the data table, this instruction will explain what type of data (integer, real, positive, etc.) are to be entered.

In Program 1.1 in chapter 1 we showed the module list after clicking on Module. In some cases after selecting one of these modules a second menu of submodules will appear. The module list has 19 options, consisting of 18 QM modules and an Exit option.

Creating a New Problem

At this point the first option that will be chosen is File, followed by either New or Open to create a new data set or to load a previously saved data set. This is an option which will be chosen very often.

The top line of the creation screen contains a text box in which the title of the problem can be entered. For many modules it is necessary to enter the number of rows in the problem. Rows will have different names depending on the modules. For example, in linear programming, rows are constraints, whereas in forecasting, rows are past periods. At any rate, the number of rows can be chosen with either the scroll bar or the text box. In general, the maximum number of rows in any module is 90.

QM for Windows has the capability to allow you different options for the default row and column names. Select one of the radio buttons to indicate which style of default naming should be used. In most modules the row names are not used for computations, but you should be careful because in some modules (most notably, Project Management) the names might relate to precedences.

Many modules require you to enter the number of columns. This is given in the same way as the number of rows. All row and column names can be changed in the data table.

Some modules will have an extra option box, such as for choosing minimize or maximize or selecting whether distances are symmetric. Select one of these options. In most cases this option can later be changed on the data screen.

When you are satisfied with your choices, click on the **[OK]** button or press the **[Return/Enter]** key. At this point a blank data screen will be displayed. Screens will differ module by module.

[Return/Enter]
This key moves from cell to cell in the order from left to right, from top to bottom, skipping the first column (which usually contains names). Therefore, when entering a table of data, if you start at the upper left and work your way to the lower right row by row, this key is exceptionally useful.

Entering and Editing Data

After a new data set has been created or an existing data set has been loaded, the data can be edited. Every entry is in a row and column position. You navigate through the spreadsheet using the cursor movement keys. These keys function in a regular way with one exception—the **[Return/Enter]** key.

The instruction bar on the screen will contain a brief instruction describing what is to be done. There are essentially three types of cells in the data table. One type is a regular data cell into which you enter either a name or a number. A second type is a cell that cannot be changed. A third type is a cell that contains a drop-down box. For example, the signs in a linear programming constraint are chosen from this type of box. To see all of the options, press the box with the arrow.

There is one more aspect to the data screen that needs to be considered. Some modules need extra data above that in the table. In most of these cases the data are contained in text/scrollbar combinations that appear on top of the data table.

Solution Displays

Numerical Formatting
Formatting is handled by the program automatically. For example, in most cases the number 1000 will automatically be formatted as 1,000. Do not type the comma. The program will prevent you from doing so!

At this point you can press the **[Solve]** button to begin the solution process. A new screen will be displayed.

An important thing to notice is that there is more solution information available. This can be seen by the icons given at the bottom. Click on these to view the information. Alternatively, notice that the Window option in the main menu is now enabled. It is always enabled at solution time. Even if the icons are covered by a window the Window option will always allow you to view the other solution windows.

Now that we have examined how to create and solve a problem we explain all of the Menu options that are available.

File

File contains the usual options that one finds in Windows 95 or Windows 98.

New   As demonstrated before, this is chosen to begin a new problem/file.

Open   This is used to open/load a previously saved file. File selection is the standard Windows common dialog type. Notice that the extension for files in the QM for Windows system is given by the first three letters of the module name. For example, all linear programming files have the extension *.lin. When you go to the open dialog, the default value is for the program to look for files of the type in this module. This can be changed at the bottom left where it says "Files of Type."

The names that are legal are standard Windows 95 file names. Case (upper or lower) does not matter. In addition to the file name, you may preface the name with a drive letter (with its colon) or path designation. Examples of legal file names are

sample, test, a:sample, linear programming problem, chapter8.problem1.

You may type them in as uppercase, lowercase, or mixed. In all of the examples, QM for Windows will add the three-letter extension to the end of the file name. For example, linear programming problem will become linear programming problem.lin (assuming that it is indeed a linear programming problem).

In the event that there is a problem with the drive or file, an error message will be displayed to that effect.

Save   Save will replace the file without asking you if you care about overwriting the previous version of this file. If you try to save and have not previously named the file, you will be asked to name this file.

Save as   Save as will prompt you for a file name before saving. You can also specify the drive, such as C: or A:. This option is very similar to the option to load a data file. When you choose this option, the Windows Common Dialog Box for Files will be displayed. It is essentially identical to the one shown previously.

Save as Excel File   Save as Excel File saves a file as an excel file with both the data and appropriate formulas for the solutions and is available for some but not all of the modules.

Save as HTML   Save as HTML saves the table as an HTML formatted file that can immediately be placed on the Internet.

Print   Print will display a print menu screen with four tabs. The Information tab allows you to select which of the output tables should be printed. The Page Header tab allows you to control the information displayed at the top of the page. The Layout tab controls the printing style. Information may be printed as plain ASCII text or as a table (grid) resembling the table on the screen. Try both types of printing and see which one you/your instructor prefers. The Printer tab allows certain print settings to be changed.

Exit the Program   The last option on the File menu is Exit. This will exit the program if you are on the data screen or exit the solution screen and return to the data screen if you are on the solution screen. This can also be achieved by pressing the Edit command button on the solution screen.

Edit

The commands under Edit have three purposes. The first four commands are used to insert or delete rows or columns. The next command is used to copy an entry from one cell to all cells below it in the column. This is not often useful, but when it is useful it saves a great deal of work. The last two entries can be used to copy the data table to other Windows programs.

View

View has several options that enable you to customize the appearance of the screen. The toolbar can be displayed or not. The Instruction bar can be displayed at its default location above the data or below the data, as a floating window, or not at all. The Status bar can be displayed or not.

Colors can be set to monochrome (black and white) or from this state to their original colors.

Deleting files
It is not possible to delete a file using QM for Windows. Use the Windows file manager to do so.

Module

Module has been shown in chapter 1 as Program 1.1. The Module selection contains a list of programs available with this book.

Format

Format also has several options for the display. The colors for the entire screen can be set, and the font type and size for the table can be set. Zeros can be set to display as blanks rather than zeros. The problem title that is displayed in the data table and was created at the creation screen can be changed. The table can be squeezed or expanded. That is, the column widths can be decreased or increased. The input can be checked or not.

Tools

The Tools menu option is an area available to annotate problems. If you want to write a note to yourself about the problem select annotation; the note will be saved with the file if you save the file.

A normal distribution calculator is found in the Tools menu option.

A calculator is available for simple calculations, including square root. There is a normal distribution calculator that can be used for finding confidence intervals and the like.

Window

The Window menu option is enabled only at the solution screen.

Help

The first help option, module help, will give a small description of the module, the data required for input, the output results, and the options available in the module. It is worthwhile to look at this screen at least one time to be certain that there are no differences between your assumptions and the assumptions of the program. If there is anything to be warned about regarding the option, it will appear on the help screen as well as in the appropriate chapter of this book.

Help also contains a pointer to an online manual that is available for this software through www.prenhall.com/weiss. If you send mail, be sure to include the name of the program (QM for Windows), the version of the program (from Help, About), the module in which the problem is occurring, and a detailed explanation of the problem, and to attach the data file for which the problem occurs.

APPENDIX E: USING EXCEL QM

Excel QM

Excel QM has been designed to help you to better learn and understand both quantitative analysis and Excel. Even though the software contains many modules and submodules, the screens for every module are consistent and easy to use. The modules were illustrated in Program 1.2. This software is provided by means of the CD ROM in the back of this book at no cost to purchasers. No floppy disk drive is required, but Excel version 5 or better must be on your PC.

To install Excel QM, exit and reenter Windows; then follow these steps:

1. Insert the Render/Stair CD into the CD-ROM drive, which we assume is drive D:.
2. From the Windows 95/98 Start button, select Run, Browse.
3. Change to the Excel/QM folder. Go to the directory Excel QM.
4. Run Excel QM.exe. There are several ways to do this. For example, from the Windows Program Manager (Win 3.1), select File, Run, or in Windows 95/98, use Start, Run. Alternatively, from File Manager (Win 3.1) or Explorer (Windows 95/98), double-click on the file name—ExcelQM.exe.
5. Follow the setup instructions on the screen.

Default values have been assigned in the setup program, but you may change them if you like. For Windows 3.1 the default values are that the program will be installed to a directory on the C: drive named C:\ExcelQM and that the program group will be named Excel QM. For Windows 95, the default folder is C:\Program Files\ExcelQM. Generally speaking, it is simply necessary to click Next each time that the installation program asks a question.

The Program Group

Under Windows 3.1 you will have a program group added to your program manager. The group will be called Excel QM, and after you open the group it will be displayed with five icons. Under Windows 95 a program group with four options will be added to the Start menu. Prior to starting the program, you should check the README file by clicking on the Readme icon in the program group.

The Excel QM icon is the option that is used to begin the program. Help is available from within the program, but if you want to read some information about the program without starting it first, use the Excel QM Help icon.

Under either Win 95 or Win 3.1, the program group contains one icon named Prentice Hall Web Site Gateway. If you have an association for HTM files with a Web browser (e.g., Netscape or Internet Explorer), this document will point you to program upgrades.

Starting the Program

If you do not already have Excel open, then to start Excel QM under Windows 3.1, double click on the Excel QM program icon. For Windows 95, click on Start, Programs, and then the Excel QM icon in order to use the software. In addition, under Windows 95 the installation will create a short-cut and place it on your desktop. This can be used to start Excel QM. If you already have Excel open, then simply load the file ExcelQM.xla, which is in the default directory (C:ExcelQM or C:\Program Files\ExcelQM) if you did not change this at the time of installation.

It is also possible to install Excel QM as an add-in. This will load *Excel QM* each time that you start Excel. To do this, simply go to Tools, Addins, Browse and select Excel QM.xla.

Excel QM serves two purposes in the learning process. First, it can simply help you solve homework problems. You enter the appropriate data, and the program provides numerical solutions. QM for Windows operates on the same principal. But Excel QM allows for a second approach, that is, noting the Excel *formulas* used to develop solutions and modifying them to deal with a wider variety of problems. This "open" approach allows you to observe, understand, and even charge the formulas underlying the Excel calculations, conveying Excel's power as a quantitative analysis tool.

Technical Support

If you have technical problems with either QM for Windows or Excel QM that your instructor cannot answer, send email to hweiss@sbm.temple.edu. If you send email be sure to include the name of the program (QM for Windows or Excel QM), the version of the program (from Help, About in QM for Windows; from QM About in Excel QM), the module in which the problem is occurring, and a detailed explanation of the problem, and to attach the data file for which the problem occurs (if appropriate).

APPENDIX F: SOLUTIONS TO SELECTED PROBLEMS

Supplement 1

S1-5 Strategy for $X:X_2$; strategy for $Y:Y_2$; value of the game = 6

S1-7 $X_1 = {}^{35}\!/_{57}$; $X_2 = {}^{22}\!/_{57}$; $Y_1 = {}^{32}\!/_{57}$; $Y_2 = {}^{25}\!/_{57}$; value of game = 66.70

S1-10 $A_1 = {}^{41}\!/_{72}$; $A_2 = {}^{31}\!/_{72}$; $B_1 = {}^{55}\!/_{72}$; $B_2 = {}^{17}\!/_{72}$; value of game = −1.32; would rather be *B*.

Chapter 2

2-14 0.30

2-16 (a) 0.10   (b) 0.04   (c) 0.25   (d) 0.40

2-18 (a) 0.20   (b) 0.09   (c) 0.31   (d) dependent

2-19 0.54

2-21 Into Abu Ilan 0.384; into El Kamin 0.616

2-23 0.947   ,855

2-26 (a) 0.995   (b) 0.885
     (c) Assumed events are independent

2-28 0.78

2-30 2.85

2-31 $E(X) = 5.45$; variance = 4.047

2-32 0.8849

2-34 0.3413

2-36 P(oven causes defect) = 0.1587; $P(460°–470°) = 0.1327$

2-38 0.0668

2-39 1829.27

2-40 (b) 0.6125

2-41 0.7365

Chapter 3

3-9 Maximin criterion: best alternative is Texan.
3-11 Best decision: deposit $10,000 in bank
3-14 (a) $200   (b) Yes, $80
3-15 (b) Large wing   (c) No
3-17 (b) Medium sized facility
3-20 (b) Back roads   (c) 3⅓ minutes
3-21 Produce 300 cases and stock them
3-24 62 bottles
3-27 3016 reports
3-29 Option 3, $20,000

Chapter 4

4-12 Construct clinic.
4-13 The survey should be taken; EVSI = $11,140.
4-15 If the survey is favorable, build large shop. Otherwise, do not build.
4-17 P(successful shop | unfavorable study) = 0.25
4-18 Do not gather information but build quadplex.
4-21 (b) Use supplier A   (c) $60 less than supplier A
4-24 Do not conduct survey and do not construct clinic. They are risk avoiders.
4-27 Yes. He would not conduct the study but he would build the large plant.
4-28 (a) Broad street, 27.5 minutes   (b) Expressway   (c) Lynn is a risk avoider.
4-30 Jack should accept his kids' bet.
4-32 (b) Stock 1,500 gallons   (c) EVPI = $1,500
4-33 Do not conduct survey. Build medium-sized facility; EMV = $670,000.

Chapter 5

5-10 (a) 337   (b) 380   (c) 423
5-12 3-month MAD = 6.48; 4-month MAD = 7.78
5-13 Weighted M.A. is slightly more accurate.
5-15 MAD for 2-year M.A. = 2.22, which is lowest.
5-17 Year 1, 410.0; year 2, 422.0; year 3, 443.9; year 4, 466.1; year 5, 495.2; year 6, 521.8
5-19 MAD for α = 0.3 is 74.56; MAD for α = 0.6 is 51.8; MAD for α = 0.9 is 38.1.
5-21 $Y = 522 + 33.6X$ if years are coded $-2, -1, 0, +1, +2$; next years sales = 622.8. If years are coded 1–5, $Y = 421.2 + 33.6X$.
5-23 (b) $Y = 1.0 + 1.0X$ (c) 10
5-31 (a) $Y = 1 + 1X; r = 0.845$
5-32 (b) $Y = 5.06 + 1.593X$ (c) 2,099,000 people
5-36 $130,000, $108,000, $98,000, $184,000
5-38 $Y = 0.972 + 0.0035X, r^2 = 0.479$ $Y = 2.197, Y = 3.77$

Chapter 6

6-17 $Q^* = $ 20,000 screws
6-18 ROP = 4,000 screws
6-21 D = 8 million loads of plywood
6-25 Yes; total cost = $41,416

6-26 Expand to 10,000 cu ft to hold 100 motors; expansion worth $250 per year
6-28 $1,920 on a yearly basis
6-31 $Q_p^* = $ 2,697 scissors
6-32 1,217 wheel bearings
6-33 Take the discount; cost = $49,912.50
6-34 30 units of safety stock
6-36 Item 33CP needs strict control; no strict control for the others.
6-37 Maintain a safety stock of 400.
6-40 Order quantity = 852; total cost = $176
6-42 Order quantity = 51; total cost = $1,901.22
6-43 Order 300 units; total cost = $9,066.83

Chapter 7

7-14 40 air conditioners, 60 fans, profit = $1,900
7-16 200 model A tubs, 0 model B tubs, $18,000 profit
7-18 40 undergraduate, 20 graduate, $160,000
7-19 10 Alpha 4's, 24 Beta 5's, $55,200
7-22 $X_1 = 18\frac{3}{4}, X_2 = 18\frac{3}{4}$, profit = $150
7-23 $X_1 = 25.71, X_2 = 21.43$, cost = $68.57
7-25 5 TV spots, 68 ads, exposure of 1,535,000
7-28 (a) Yes   (b) Doesn't change
7-29 (b) $X_1 = 2, X_2 = 3$ (b) Yes
7-30 (b) $X_1 = 33.33, X_2 = 33.33$ (b) Yes   (c) No
7-33 24 coconuts, 12 skins; profit = 5,040 rupees
7-37 Make all MCA regular modems (27,750 of them)

Chapter 8

8-1 Max. $R = 28X_1 + 25X_2$
$$3X_1 + 2X_2 \leqslant 360$$
$$1\frac{1}{2}X_1 + 1X_2 \leqslant 200$$
$$\frac{3}{4}X_1 + \frac{3}{4}X_2 \leqslant 125$$
$$X_1 \geqslant 60$$
$$X_2 \geqslant 60$$
$X_1 = 60, X_2 = 90, P = $3,930$
8-6 Min. $C = 925X_1 + 2,000X_2$
$$0.04X_1 + 0.05X_2 \geqslant 0.40$$
$$0.03X_1 + 0.03X_2 \geqslant 0.60$$
$X_1 = 20, X_2 = 0, C = $18,500$
8-9 $X_1 = 26, X_2 = 5, X_3 = 6.5, X_4 = 14.25$, 51.75 drinks
8-10 Min. rolls = $20X_1 + 6.8X_2 + 12X_3 - 65,000X_4$
$$X_1 + X_2 + X_3 \leqslant 17,000$$
$$X_1 \geqslant 3,000$$
$$X_2 - 0.05X_3 \geqslant 0$$
$$X_4 \geqslant 0.20$$
$$X_4 \leqslant 0.45 \quad \text{Sell 327,000 rolls}$$
8-11 $X_1 = 0, X_2 = 0.499, X_3 = 0.173, X_4 = 0, X_5 = 0, X_6 = 0.105, X_7 = 0.762, C = 1.75
8-12 $X_1 = 497, X_2 = 1,241, P = $195,505$
8-14 1,250 wheat in N parcel, 500 wheat in NW, 312.5 wheat in W, 137.5 wheat in SW, 131 alfalfa in SW, 600 barley in SE, 400 barley in N, profit = $337,862.10
8-17 61 medical beds, 29 surgical beds; revenue = $9,551,656 per year.

Chapter 9

9-15 (b) $14X_1 + 4X_2 \leq 3,360$; $10X_1 + 12X_2 \leq 9,600$
(d) $S_1 = 3,360$, $S_2 = 9,600$ (e) X_2 (f) S_2
(g) 800 units of X_2

9-17 $X_1 = 2$, $X_2 = 6$, $S_1 = 0$, $S_2 = 0$, $P = \$36$

9-18 $X_1 = 50$, $X_2 = 0$, $P = \$1,000$

9-19 $X_1 = 14$, $X_2 = 33$, $C = \$221$

9-23 Degeneracy; $X_1 = 27$, $X_2 = 5$, $X_3 = 0$, $P = \$177$

9-25 (a) Min. $C = 9X_1 + 15X_2$
$$X_1 + 2X_2 \geq 30$$
$$X_1 + 4X_2 \geq 80$$
(b) $X_1 = 0$, $X_2 = 20$, $C = \$300$

9-26 (a) Min. $C = 20X_1 + 24X_2$
$$X_1 + X_2 \geq 30$$
$$X_1 + 2X_2 \geq 40$$
(b) $X_1 = 20$, $X_2 = 10$, $C = \$640$

9-28 $X_1 = 0$, $X_2 = 17.14$, $X_3 = 34.29$, $P = \$582.86$

9-30 (b) X_5 will enter; A_3 will leave

9-31 (a) $\$7\frac{1}{2}$ to infinity   (b) Negative infinity to $\$40$
(c) $\$20$ (d) $\$0$

9-32 30 cents, 0, $\$3.00$

9-35 (a) Negative infinity to $\$6$ for phosphate; $\$5$ to infinity for potassium
(b) Basis won't change; but X_1, X_2, and S_2 will change.

9-37 max $P = 50U_1 + 4U_2$
$$12U_1 + 1U_2 \leq 120$$
$$20U_1 + 3U_2 \leq 250$$

Chapter 10

10-14 Oak Ridge to House 2 = 30; Oak Ridge to House 3 = 10; Pineville to House 3 = 25; Mapletown to House 1 = 30; cost = $\$230$

10-16 Morgantown to Coaltown = 35; Youngstown to Coal Valley = 30; Youngstown to Coaltown = 5; Youngstown to Coal Junction = 25; Pittsburgh to Coaltown = 5; Pittsburgh to Coalsburg = 20; cost = 3,100 miles

10-19 Degeneracy; need to place a zero in an empty cell (such as 2-C)

10-23 New Orleans' systems cost = $\$20,000$; Houston's is $\$19,500$, so Houston should be selected.

10-27 $A12$ to W, $A15$ to Z, $B2$ to Y, $B9$ to X, 50 hours

10-29 Stand 1 to C, stand 2 to B, stand 3 to A, stand 4 to D, 18 miles

10-31 Total rating = 335

10-32 Total "cost" = 86

10-33 Overall rating = 75.5

10-34 $C53$ at plant 1, $C81$ at plant 3, $D5$ at plant 4, $D44$ at plant 2, 58 cents.

10-36 Total cost = $\$1.18$

10-38 (a) 96   (b) 92   (c) Yes, score = 93

Chapter 11

11-13 $X_1 = 1$, $X_2 = 2$, $P = \$20$

11-14 $X_1 = 3$, $X_2 = 4$, $P = \$17$

11-16 $X_1 = 5$, $X_2 = 8$, $Z = 1,273,000$ passengers

11-21 $A4$, $B1$, $C3$, $D2$ or $A4$, $B2$, $C3$, $D1$; both cost $\$105$

11-22 $X_1 = 0$, $X_2 = 3$, $P = \$9$

11-24 $X_1 = 500$, $X_2 = 400$, $d_3^- = 100$

11-26 $X_1 = 10$ TV spots, $X_2 = 35$ ads, exposure = 8,250,000

11-29 (b) $X_1 = 15$, $X_2 = 20$, $d_1^+ = 30$

11-32 (b) $X_1 = 18.3$, $X_2 = 10.8$, Revenue = $\$70,420$

Supplement 11

S11-4 SUN $- 0.80$

S11-8 Car 1, 0.4045

S11-9 System 1, 0.4928

Chapter 12

12-7 One solution is 1–2, 1–3, 1–4, 3–6, 4–5, 6–7, 7–9, 8–9, 9–12, 9–10, 10–11, 11–13, and 12–14.

12-9 1–3–5–7–10–13; distance is 430 miles.

12-11 New flow is 7 cars per hour.

12-15 The total length is 21. One solution is 1–2, 1–3, 3–7, 4–5, 5–6, 6–8, 6–7, and 8–9.

12-16 The minimal spanning tree length is 23.

12-18 The maximal flow is 17.

12-20 The maximal flow is 2,000 gallons.

12-21 The shortest route is 74. The path is 1–3–7–11–14–16.

12-26 (a) The shortest distance is 49.
(b) The shortest distance is 55.
(c) The shortest distance is 64.

Chapter 13

13-13 26 days; critical path is 1–2–3–5–6.

13-15 Completion time is 19; there are two critical paths: A–C–G and B–E–G.

13-17 36.33 days; critical path is C–D–E–F–H–K.

13-18 0.9463

13-20 (a) 0.0228   (b) 0.3085
(c) 0.8413   (d) 0.9772

13-21 $\$181,600$; cost underrun = $\$9,600$; behind schedule

13-25 44; completion time increases to 47.8 weeks.

13-26 34 weeks; critical path activities are 11, 13, 14, 16, 17, 18, 19, 21, and 23.

13-29 (a) Project completion time is 38 weeks.
(b) Activity D is still on critical path; project completion time is 29.
(c) Completion time is 26.
(d) Completion time is 23.

Chapter 14

14-11 (a) 0.375   (b) 0.2 days or 1.6 hours
(c) 0.225   (d) 0.141, 0.053, 0.020, 0.007

14-12 (a) 4.167 cars   (b) .4167 hours   (c) 0.5 hours
(d) 0.8333   (e) 0.1667

14-15 (a) 6   (b) 12 minutes   (c) 0.857
(d) 0.54   (e) $\$1,728$/day   (f) yes

14-18 3, 2, 4

14-21 $36 with 1 loader, $18 with 2 loaders; saving $18 with 2 loaders

14-22   No

14-27   4 entrances, 2 exits

Chapter 15

15-12   No

15-14   (a) 3 times
(b) 6.95/week if we ignore the fact that sales cannot exceed 8 per week
(c) 7.16 heaters

15-19   (a) From the 15 breakdown simulation, there are 14½ hours of machine down time $\times$ $75/hour = $1,087.50. Cost of labor is 29½ hours $\times$ $60/hour = $1,770. Total cost = $2,857.50.
(b) Hire second worker; one repair person costs $4,320.

15-21   (a) Cost/hour is generally more expensive replacing 1 pen each time.
(b) Expected cost/hour with 1 pen policy = $1.38 (or $58/breakdown); expected cost/hour with 4-pen policy = $1.12 (or $132/breakdown).

Chapter 16

16-7   (b) 90%   (c) 30%

16-8   (a) 23.056%   (b) 30.832%   (c) 75%

16-10   (a) 70%   (b) 30%   (c) 40%

16-11   25% for Battles; 18.75% for University; 26.25% for Bill's; 30% for College

16-14   41% that conditions will be fair; 19.5% that conditions will be tolerable

16-16   333 in Lake Jackson and 667 in Lake Bradford

16-18   New MFA = (5,645.16, 1,354.84)

16-19   61 will pass and 19 will fail.

CD Module 1

M1-6   45.034 to 46.966 for $\bar{x}$
0 to 4.008 for R

M1-8   16.814 to 17.187 for $\bar{x}$
0.068 to 0.932 for R

M1-10   2.236 to 3.728 for $\bar{x}$
0 to 2.336 for R
In control

M1-13   62.36 to 64.54 for $\bar{x}$
0 to 3.423 for R

M1-15   0.0081 to 0.0581

M1-17   6.6 to 33.4
Out of control

CD Module 2

M2-6   1–2–6–7 with a total distance of 10 miles.

M2-8   Shortest route is 1–2–5–7 with a total distance of 14 miles.

M2-10   The shortest route is 1–2–4–8–11.

M2-13   Ship 6 units of item 1, 1 unit of item 2, and 1 unit of item 3.

M2-15   The shortest route is 1–3–6–11–15–17–19–20.

CD Module 3

M3-5   (a) 20,000 books   (b) $320,000

M3-9   No effect

M3-13 $999.60

M3-15 $249

CD Module 4

M4-6   Number of B's = 50, number of C's = 150, number of D's = 100, number of E's = 300, and number of F's = 300.

CD Module 5

M5-1   (a) 27   (b) 16

M5-2 $X = -\frac{3}{2}, Y = \frac{1}{2}, Z = \frac{7}{2}$

M5-5 $380, $440, $260

M5-7
$$\begin{pmatrix} -48 & 6 & 12 \\ 6 & -12 & 6 \\ 32 & 6 & -8 \end{pmatrix} = \text{matrix of cofactors}$$

$$\begin{pmatrix} -48 & 6 & 32 \\ 6 & -12 & 6 \\ 12 & 6 & -8 \end{pmatrix} = \text{adjoint of matrix}$$

M5-8
$$\begin{pmatrix} -\frac{48}{60} & \frac{6}{60} & \frac{32}{60} \\ \frac{6}{60} & -\frac{12}{60} & \frac{6}{60} \\ \frac{12}{60} & \frac{6}{60} & -\frac{8}{60} \end{pmatrix}$$

CD Module 6

M6-4   .8125, .03125, .03125

M6-5   .327, .410, .205, .051, .0064, .00032

M6-7   (b) 2.5, 1.875   (c) $312.50

APPENDIX G: SOLUTIONS TO SELF-TESTS

Chapter 1

1. c
2. d
3. b
4. c
5. a
6. d
7. a
8. a
9. Quantitative analysis
10. Defining the problem
11. schematic model
12. algorithm

Supplement 1

1. b
2. c

3. a
4. e
5. Zero sum
6. pure strategy

Chapter 2

1. b
2. a
3. c
4. d
5. b
6. discrete distribution
7. adding the individual probabilities
8. finding the total area of the probability distribution
9. one
10. d
11. two
12. a
13. d
14. b
15. a

Chapter 3

1. a
2. e
3. a
4. a
5. d
6. e
7. e
8. b
9. e
10. b
11. c
12. c
13. e
14. b
15. a

Chapter 4

1. b
2. d
3. e
4. a
5. f
6. d
7. a
8. d
9. c
10. decision trees
11. posterior probabilities
12. standard gamble

Chapter 5

1. d
2. c
3. d
4. b
5. b
6. b
7. b
8. a
9. d
10. b
11. b
12. a
13. a
14. a
15. a
16. independent variable is said to cause variations in the dependent variable
17. (1) naive approach, (2) moving average, (3) exponential smoothing, (4) trend projection, (5) linear regression
18. (1) trend, (2) seasonality, (3) cycles, (4) random variation
19. (1) jury of executive opinion, (2) sales force composite, (3) Delphi method, (4) consumer market survey
20. alert the user of a forecasting tool to periods in which the forecast was significantly in error
21. exponential smoothing is a weighted moving average model in which all previous values are weighted with a set of weights that decline exponentially

Chapter 6

1. c
2. d
3. b
4. e
5. d
6. d
7. a
8. b
9. d
10. Safety stock
11. Service level
12. ABC analysis

Chapter 7

1. b
2. b

3. c
4. a
5. a
6. b
7. c
8. d
9. b
10. b
11. a
12. b
13. c
14. a

Chapter 8

1. a
2. b
3. b
4. d
5. e
6. e
7. e
8. d
9. a
10. c
11. c
12. c

Chapter 9

1. a
2. b
3. a
4. a
5. b
6. d
7. a
8. d
9. d
10. c
11. a
12. b
13. a
14. a
15. b
16. a
17. c

Chapter 10

1. c
2. d
3. b
4. b
5. b
6. b
7. b

8. (1) exhaust the supply of each row before moving down to the next row, (2) exhaust the demand requirements of each column before moving to the next column on the right, (3) check that all supply and demand constraints are met.

9. a
10. d
11. c
12. d

Chapter 11

1. a
2. a
3. b
4. a
5. a
6. a
7. a
8. b
9. b
10. b
11. d
12. b
13. e

Supplement 11

1. a
2. b
3. e
4. c
5. d
6. a
7. multifactor evaluation process
8. analytic hierarchy process

Chapter 12

1. c
2. e
3. b
4. c
5. e
6. a
7. e
8. b
9. c
10. a
11. Shortest route
12. maximal flow
13. minimal spanning tree

Chapter 13

1. d
2. b
3. a

4. e
5. b
6. c
7. b
8. a
9. f
10. d
11. Critical path
12. program evaluation and review technique
13. linear programming
14. forward pass, backward pass
15. CPM
16. most optimistic, most likely, and most pessimistic
17. slack
18. monitor and control

Chapter 14

1. a
2. a
3. b
4. e
5. e
6. c
7. c
8. a
9. c
10. first-come, first-served
11. negatively exponentially distributed
12. simulation
13. unlimited

Chapter 15

1. b
2. b
3. a
4. a
5. b
6. a
7. b
8. (1) define the problem, (2) introduce the important variables associated with the problem, (3) construct a numerical model, (4) set up possible courses of action for testing, (5) run the experiment, (6) consider the results, (7) decide what course of action to take.
9. (1) set up a probability distribution for each of the important variables, (2) build a cumulative probability distribution for each of the important variables, (3) estab-

lish an interval of random numbers for each variable, (4) generate sets of random numbers, (5) actually simulate a set of trials.

10. (1) it is relatively straightforward and flexible, (2) it can be used to analyze large and complex real-world situations that cannot be solved by conventional management science models, (3) it allows for the inclusion of real-world complications that most models cannot permit, (4) it allows "time compression," (5) it allows the user to ask what if questions, (6) it does not interfere with the real system, (7) it allows us to study the interactive effect of individual components or variables in order to determine which ones are important.

11. (1) it can be very expensive and complex, (2) it does not generate optimal solutions to problems, (3) managers must generate all of the conditions and constraints for solutions that they want to examine, (4) in-depth understanding of the results of a simulation does require knowledge of statistics.

12. b
13. d
14. c
15. c
16. a
17. e
18. (a) no, yes, no, no, no, yes, yes, yes, no, yes
(b) no, yes, yes, yes, no, yes, yes, yes, no, no

Chapter 16

1. d
2. a
3. c
4. c
5. b
6. a
7. e
8. d
9. b
10. matrix of transition probabilities
11. collectively exhaustive and mutually collective
12. vector of state probabilities

CD Module 1

1. the degree to which the product or service meets specifications
2. d
3. e
4. a
5. a
6. a
7. b
8. dispersion or variability
9. 2 standard deviations
10. $\bar{x}$ chart, R chart

CD Module 2

1. c
2. b
3. e
4. c
5. e
6. a
7. c
8. e

9. a
10. a
11. c
12. c
13. e
14. b

CD Module 3

1. c
2. c
3. a
4. b
5. e
6. d
7. a
8. unit normal loss integral

CD Module 4

1. e
2. b
3. c
4. e

5. b
6. just-in-time
7. net material requirements
8. dependent

CD Module 5

1. a square array of numbers arranged in rows and columns.
2. c
3. multiply the numbers on the primary diagonal and subtract from that product the numbers on the secondary diagonal.
4. e
5. number of columns in the first matrix equals the number of rows in the second matrix.
6. e
7. interchange the rows with the columns.
8. d

Index

Note: Any page number preceded by the letter M means that the topic is located on your CD-ROM.

ABC analysis, 231–232
  definition of, 234
Abdou, G. 698
Absorbing states, 714–720
  definition of, 719
Ackoff, R.L., 19
Activity, 571
  definition of 594
Activity time estimates, 572–573
  definition of, 594
Adaptive smoothing, 184
Additivity, LP problems and, 255
Adjoint of a matrix, M5.9
  definition of, M5.11
Ahlbrecht, Martin, 114
AHP, *See* Analytic Hierarchy Process
Air Products and Chemicals, Inc., 522, 530
Algorismus, 5
Algorithm, 5, 17
  Karmarkar's. *See* Karmarar's
    algorithm
  special purpose, 408–409
Allnoch, Allen, M4.15
Alternate optimal solutions, LP and
    279–280
Alternatives, decision making and, 82, 100
American Airlines, 179, 263
American League of Umpires, 445
Analytic Hierarchy Process (AHP),
    519–536
  comparison with MFEP, 530
  computer solving problems, 529
  computer systems for, 522–529
  consistency ratio, 525–527
  definition of, 531
  factor weights, 528
  hardware evaluations, 525

multifactor evaluation process,
    520–521
  pairwise comparisons, 523–524
  software and vendor supports, 527–528
Anbil, R., 263n, 469
Andrews, B., 303, 624n, 653
Annual holding cost, 208, 216–217
Annual ordering cost, 208, 216–217
Annual setup cost, 215–217
  definition of, 234
Arcs, dynamic programming and, M2.2
Area of feasible solution, 261, 287
Arntzen, Bruce C., 518
Arrival behavior, queuing system and,
    618–620
Artificial variable, 360–362
  definition of, 385
  objective function and, 362
Assignable variations, control charts and,
    M.1.4-M.1.5, M1.14
Assignment modules, transportation and,
    406–471, *See* transportation
    models
  approach of, 436
  dummy columns in, 442
  dummy rows, 442
  Hungarian method in, 437–441
  maximization problems, 442–445
  three steps of, 438
Attributes. *See* control charts
Average inventory, 210, 234

Backward pass, 576,
  definition of, 594
Badinetti, Ralph D., 250
Baker, T.E., 303

Balanced problem, 410
  definition of, 446
Balbach, C.T., 666n
Balking, 619
  definition of, 639
Ballot, Michael, 466n
Banks, J. 698
Bartnyska, Linda M., 713n
Basic feasible solution, 349
  definition of, 385
Basic objective function coefficient,
    377–378
Basic variables, 349, 376
  definition of, 385
Bayes' Law. *See* Bayes's Theorem
Bayes' Theorem, 47, 48–50, 68
  derivation of, 80
  general form, 50
  posterior probabilities, 48–49, 125
  prior probability assessments, 49, 126
  probability values and, 125–128
Bayes, Thomas, 47
Bavuso, R. J., 200
Bayus, Barry, 158n
Bean, James C., 271m, 518
Bellcore, 222
Bell Laboratories, M1.3
Bellman, R. E., M2.24
Ben-Dov, Yosi, 321n
Benjamin, Colin, 494n
Ben-Khedher, Nejib, 547n
Bentley, Jon 563
Bernoulli process, M6.2
Berry, L.L., M1.24
Besterfield, D.H., M1.24
Beta probability distribution of, 573
  definition of, 594

Bias, 167, 186
Bierman, H., 517n
Binomial Distribution M6.1-M6.7
  introduction, M6.2
  solving problems with binomial
    formula, M6.2-M6.3
  solving problems with binomial table,
    M6.4-M6.5
Binomial distribution tables,
  M6.4-M6.5
Binomial formula, M6.2-M6.3
Binomial probability distribution, M6.2
Binomial probability formula, M6.2
BIOMED, 184
Bistritz, Nancy, 92n, 114
Blair, Thomas, 99
Blending problems, L.P. and, 326–329
Blue Bell, 232
Bodington, C.E., 303
Bohl, Alan H., 518
Bonini, C. P., 517n
Borison, Adam, 114, 122n, 152
Bourland, Karla, M2.24
Bower, Kenneth Credson, 37
Bowman, E., 469
Branch and bound method, 483–491
  assignment problem and, 484–488
  definition of, 506
  integer programming and, 488–491
Bradenburger, A., 26n, 37
Break-even analysis, M3.8
  normal distribution and, M3.2-M3.6
Break-even point, 8, M3.2
  derivation of, M3.13
Brennen, J.E., 698
Brenner, Merill, 522n
Brown, R., 114
Brown, R.V., 114
Brucker, H.D., M4.15
Buchanan, E., 698
Bushko, David, 37

C-charts, M1.11, M1.14
Cj-Zj rows, 351
  definition of, 385
Cahill May Roberts Co., 442
Calling population, 618
  definition of, 639
Campell, S., 80
Canadian National Railway, 675
Carino, Honorio F., 363n

Carr, L.P., M1.24
Carraway, R.L., M2.24
Carrying cost, inventory and, 208
Causal forecasting methods, 157,
  176–182, 185
  correlation coefficient for regression
    lines, 180–181
  dependent variable, 176
  independent variable, 176
  multiple regression, 181–182
  regression analysis, 176–177, 186
  standard error of the estimate, 178–180
Causal models, definition of, 185
Central Limit Theorem, M1.5-M1.8,
  M1.14
Central tendency, probability
  distributions and, 55
Certainty, LP problems and, 255
Chambers, J.C., 200
Chang, T., M1.24
Changing cells, Excel and, 269
Charnes, A., 409, 492
Charoenngam, Chotchai, 611n
Childress, R.l., M5.14
Choypeng, P., 469
Churchman, C.W., 14, 14n, 19
Cipra, Barry, 563
Classical method, probability and, 42, 68
Classical optimization techniques, 506
Clements, Dale, 19, 200
Closed path, 414
Coefficient of correlation, 180–181, 186
Coefficient of determination, 181
Coefficient of realism, 92–93, 100
Cofactors of matrix, M5.9
COGS, Consumer Goods Program, 184
Colan, M.F. 632n
Coldstart, L.P. and, 309
Collectively exhaustive events, 42–45
  Markov analysis and, 706
Compaq, M4.6
Components, material structure tree and,
  M4.2
Computer
  AHP problems and, 529
  forecasting and, 184
  simulation and, 682–683
Computer simulation, 638
Conditional probabilities, 46, 47, 68, 120
Conditional value, 83, 100
Consistency ratio, analytic hierarchy
  process and, 525–527

Constant service time model (M/D/I),
  632–634
  definition, 640
Constraints, converting and objective
  function, 364
  definition of, 287
  graphical representation of, 257–267
  nonlinear, 502–504
  nonnegativity and, 257–258
  linear programming and, 254–255, 287
  project management and, 592
  simplex method and, 349–350
Consumer market survey, qualitative
  forecasting and, 158
Continuous random variable, 52–54,
  57–58, 68
Control. See Inventory control
Control charts, M1.3
  for attributes, M1.9-M1.13
  building of, M1.4
  C-Charts, M1.11, M1.14
  Central Limit Theorem, M1.5-M1.8,
    M1.14
  P-Charts, M1.10-M1.11, M1.14
  R-Chart (Range chart), M1.5, M1.8-
    M1.9, M1.14
  X-Bar Charts, M1.5-M1.8, M1.14
  five steps in using, X and R charts
    and, M.1.10
  for variables, M1.5-M1.9
Complete enumeration, 5
Controllable variable, 4
Cook, T., 481n
Cooper, L., 382n
Cooper, R.B., 653
Cooper, W.W., 409, 492
Corner point, 266
Corner point method, 266–267, 275
  definition of, 287
  minimization problems and,
    272–275
Corporate operating system simulation
  and, 681
Correlation coefficient for regression
  lines, 180–181
Cosares, S., 15n, 19
Cost. See PERT/Cost
Costin, H., M1.24
Cost-volume analysis, M3.2
Cox, Barry, 536
Cox, J.F., 250
CPM. See Critical Path Method

Crash cost, 589
Crashing, and Critical Path Method, 589–591
 constraints and, 592
 definition of, 594
 linear programming and, 591–593
 objective function and, 592
Crash time, 568
Crawford-Mason, C., M1.24
 steps in analyzing, 100–101
 symbols used in, 100
Criterion of realism, 92–93, 100
Critical activities, 578
Critical path, 573–578
 definition of, 594
 probability of project completion, 578–580
Critical path analysis, 573–578
Critical Path Method (CPM), 568, 589–593
 crashing and, 589–593
 definition of, 594
 framework of, 568
 history of, 569
Crosby, Philip, M1.3, M1.24
Crouch, I.W.M., 698
Crystal Bell, 10, 683, 699–704
Cumulative binomial distribution table, M6.4-M6.5
Cumulative probability distribution, 659
Current, J., 563
Current solution, 355
 definition of, 385
Cutting plane method, 476–477
 definition of, 506
Cycles (C), time series forecasting models and, 159, 161

Dantzig, G.B., 114, 255
Darrow, Ross, 481n
Davis, D., 185n
Davis, Joyce, 19
Davis, M., 37
DeAngelis, V. 282n
Debry, M.E., 666n
Decision, dynamic programming and, M2.7-M2.9
Decision criterion, dynamic programming and, M2.6, M2.17
Decision-making criterion, 132–133
Decision-making, multifactor, 560
Decision-making group 158, 186
Decision-making under certainty, 84, 90, 100

Decision-making under risk, 85–90, 100
Decision-making under uncertainty, 85, 90–94, 100
 criterion of realism, 92–93, 100
 equally likely, 91–92, 100
 maximax, 90–91, 100
 maximum, 91, 100
 minimax, 93, 100
Decision nodes, 118
Decision points, 118
Decision Support Systems (DSS), 15
Decision Theory Models, 81–115
 decision-making under certainty, 84, 85, 90, 100
 decision-making under risk, 85–90, 100
 decision-making under uncertainty, 90–94, 100
 definition, 82
 environment types, 84–85
 EWV (Expected Monetary Value), 85–86, 100
 EOL (Expected Opportunity Loss), 88, 100
 EVPI (Expected Value of Perfect Information), 87, 100
 Excel QM and, 93
 marginal analysis, 95–99, 100
 Opportunity loss, 88–89
 QM for Windows, 114–115
 sensitivity analysis, 88–89
Decision Theory and Normal Distribution
 Break-even analysis and normal distribution, M3.2-M3.6
 EVPI and the normal distribution, M3.6-M3.8
 Introduction, M3.2
Decision trees and utility theory, 117–154
 Bayesian analysis and probability values, 125–128
 Decision trees, 118–124
 Excel and decision tree problems, 153
 Expected Value of Sample Information, 123–124
 Five steps of analysis, 118
 Probability values and Bayesian analysis, 125–128
 QM for Windows, 152–153
 Sensitivity analysis, 134–135
 Utility theory, 129–133
Decision variables, dynamic programming and, M2.6, M2.17
Decoupling function, inventory control and, 205

Degeneracy, 373–374
 definition of, 386, 446
 inital solution and, 430–431
 later solution stages and, 431–432
 transportation problems and, 430–432
DeKluyver, Comelis, A., 518
Delphi method, qualitative forecasting and, 158, 185
Delta Airlines, Coldstart and, 309
DeLurgio, S.A., 200
Deming, Edward, W., M1.3, M1.24
Dennison, Basile A., M1.7
Denton, D.K., M1.24
Department of Corrections of Virginia, 502
Dependent demand, material requirements planning and, M4.2-M4.8
Dependent events, probability and, 45, 47–48
Dependent variable, 176
Derfler, Frank, 152
Derivation of break-even point, M3.13
DeSilva, A.H., 666n
Destination, transportation model and, 408
 definition, 446
Determinants, M5.2-M5.4
 definition of, M5.11
Deterministic approach, 568, 589
Deterministic assumptions, 280
Deviational variables, 492
 definition of, 506
DeVor, R.E., M1.24
Diagram, Venn, 44
Diebold, F.C., 200
Dietrich, D., M1.24
Digital Equipment Corp., 565
Dijkstra, M., 86
DiLisio, F.J., 666n
Ding, F., M4.15
Discrete probability distribution, 54–56, 68
Discrete random variable, 52–56, 68
Divisibility, LP problems and, 255
Dobyns, L., M1.24
Dodge, H.F., M1.3
Domich, P.D., 469
Dominance, game theory and, 29–30, 31
Donahue, S., 536
Dorey, Christ, 583n, 611n
Double smoothing, 169
Dual in linear programming, simplex method and, 381–383
 computational advantage of, 420–421
 formulation procedures, 382

Dummy activities, 581–582
Dummy columns, 442
    definition of, 446
Dummy destinations, 426
    definition of, 446
Dummy rows, 442
    definition of, 446
Dummy sources, 426
    definition of, 446
Duopoly, 22
DuPont, M1.4, 569
Durso, A., 536
Dutta, S.P., 698
Dwinells, E.E., M.14
Dynamic programming, M2.1-M2.25
    definition of, M2.2, M2.16
    four steps in using, M2.2
    introduction, M2.2
    Knapsack problem, M2.9-M2.16
    and shortest-route problem, M2.2-
        M2.5
    programming notation, M2.7-M2.9
    programming terminology, M2.5-
        M2.7
DYNAMO, 682

Earliest Finish time (EF), 575, 594
Earliest Start time (ES), 575, 594
Earliest Start Time Rule, 575–576
Economic Order Quantity (EOQ),
        208–213, 234
    four steps in finding, 210–212
    inventory costs, 209–210
    purchase cost of inventory items,
        212
Economic systems, simulation and,
        681
Edds, Daniel, 250
Edwards, J.R., 232n
EE, See Earliest Finish Time
Ehie, Ike, C., 494n
Eliman, A.A., 303
Elmaghraby, Salah, M2.24
El-Rayes, Khaled, M2.24
Elsayed, E.A., M1.24
Emmons, Hamilton, 250
Employee scheduling applications of
        linear programming, 316–320
    assignment problems, 316–318
    labor planning, 318–320
EMV. See Expected Monetary Value

EOL. See Expected Opportunity Loss
EOQ. See Economic Order Quantity
Equally likely, 91–92, 100
Equilibrium conditions, Markov analysis
        and, 711–714
    definition of, 719
Erland, A.K., 617
Erwin, S., M2.10
ES. See Earliest Start Time
Evans, J., 445n
Evans, J.R., 698
Events
    collectively exhaustive, 42–45, 68
    dependent, 45, 47–48, 68
    independent, 45–46, 68
    mutually exclusive, 42–45, 68
    not mutually exclusive, 45
    PERT, 571, 594
EVPI. See Expected Value of Perfect
        Information
EVSI. See Expected Value of Sample
        Information
Excel
    analytical hierarchy problems,
        572–573
    Crystal Ball, 699–704
    decision trees, 153
    forecasting, 163–164
    integer programming problems,
        478–479, 482, 483, 484, 508
    linear programming problems,
        267–269, 307–308, 312, 322–323,
        324–326
    nonlinear programming problem,
        503–505
    queuing problem, 673–674
    sensitivity analysis, 5–6, 17, 284, 286,
        380
    simulation, 644–655, 679–680
    Solver. See linear programming
        problems
Excel QM
    Assignment problems, 442–443
    Constant Service time model 634–635
    Exponential smoothing, 168–169
    Finite Population model, 637–638
    How to use, 744–745
    Inventory problems, 212–213
    Production run models, 218–219
    Quantitative models, 10
    Quantity discount problems,
        223–224

Queuing and, 626–627, 631, 633
Regression analysis, 177–178
Solution tool, 435–436
Statistical Quality Control, M1.11
Theory Problems, 93–94
Transportation problems, 421,
        435–436
Trend analysis, 173
Expected activity time (t), 573
    definition of, 594
Expected Monetary Value (EVM)
    decision theory models and, 85–86,
        100, 122–123, M3.5-M3.6
    decision theory and normal
        distribution and, M3.5-M3.6
Expected Opportunity Loss (EOL),
        88–89, 100
    normal distribution and, M3.7
Expected value probability distribution
        and, 56, 69
    probability distribution of demand,
        M3.3-M3.5
Expected value of sample information
        (EVSI), 123
Expected value with perfect information
        (EVPI), 87–88, 100
    normal distribution and, M3.6
Expert Choice for Windows, 529
Exponential distribution, 66
Exponential smoothing, 163–169
    definition of, 186
    trend adjustment and, 169
Extreme point, 266, 288

Facility location analysis, 432–435
    definition of, 446
Factor evaluations, 522
    definition of, 531
Factor weights, 522, 528
    definition of, 531
Factorial M6.2
Farley, A.A., 303
Favorable Market (FM), decision trees
        and, 126
FCST 1, 184
FCST 2, 184
Feasible region, 261
    definition of, 287
Feasible solution, 261
    definition of, 287
Feller, W., 80

Feigenbaum, A.V., M1.3, M1.24
Feinstein, Charles D., 152
Ferland, J., 114
Ferris, M.C ., 303
FIFO. *See* First-in, First-out rule
FIFS (First In, First Served), 620n
Financial applications of linear
    programming, portfolio selection,
    320–321
Finite population model, 618, 634–638
    definition of, 639
    equations for, 636
First simplex tableau, 348–351
First-in, First-out rule (FIFO), 620
    definition of, 639
First order smoothing, 169
Fishman, G.S., 698
Fitzsimmons, J.A., 469
Fleurent, C., 114
Flood's technique, 409, 437–441
Flowchart, 667–668
    definition of, 683
Flow diagram, 667–668
    definition of, 683
Flowers, G.A., M4.15
FM. *See* Favorable Market (FM)
Fordyce, Kenneth, 114, 207
Forecasting. *See* also Time series models
    Causal models, 176–177, 186
    controlling of, 182–184
    eight steps to, 156
    exponential smoothing, 163–169
    introduction to, 156
    monitoring of, 182–184
    moving averages, 161–163, 186
    qualitative models, 157–158, 185
    quantitative, 156
    scatter diagrams, 158–159, 186
    seasonal variations, 159, 161,
        173–175
    steps in, 174
    time series models, 159
    transforming time variables,
        171–172
    trend projections, 169–178\
    types of, 157–158
    use of computers in, 184
Forrestor, Joy, 681n
Forward pass, 576
    definition of, 594
Fryar, E.O., 152n
Freedman, J.S., 152
Fundamental matrix, 714–720
    definition of, 719
Funk, Jeffrey L., M4.9n, M4.15

Fundamental concepts, probability and,
    41–42
    objective probability, 42
    subjective probability, 42
    two laws of probability, 41
Future market shares, Markov analysis
    and, 709

Gale, J.R., 152
Gamble, standard. *See* Standard gamble
Game theory, 21–37
    2x2 games, 22–23, 31
    definition of, 22
    dominace, 29–30, 31
    introduction, 22
    language of, 22–23
    minimax criterion, 25, 31
    mixed strategy games, 25–29, 31
    pure strategy, 24, 31
    QM for Windows and, 37
    saddle point, 24, 31
    value of the game, 25, 31
    zero sum game, 22, 31
Garbage-in, Garbage-out (GIGO), 4
Gardner, E.S., 169n, 200
GASP, 682
Gass, S.I., 114, 303
Gelman, E., 469
General Motors, 26
General purpose languages, 682
    definition of, 683
    and simulation, 682
Georgeoff, D.M., 200
Geyer, E.D., 623n
Girgis, M., 303
Gisbourne, Steve, 536
Ginzberg, M.J., 19
Glassy, C. Roger, 469
Goal programming, 491–501
    definition of, 506
    example of, 492
    extention to equally important
        multiple goals, 493–494
    graphical solutions in, 495–497
    multiple goals, 493–494
    programming tableau, 498–499
    ranking of, 494–495
    simplex method for, 498–501
Goal Seek, 10
Goh, Chon, 536
Golden, B.L., 698
Goldring, L., 623n
Gomory cuts, 477
Gorban, Lonny R., 4n, 19, 114

Gould, Eppen, 250
GPSS, 682
Gradient method, 506
Graham, Robert, 611n
Graphical analysis, simplex method and,
    363–364
Graphical solutions in goal
    programming, 495–497
Graphical solutions in LP problems
    computer approach, 275–276
    corner point solution, 266 267
    isoprofit line solution method, 263–267
    representation of constraints, 257–263
    summary of, 275
Grassmann, Winfried, K., 653
Grayson, C.J., 19
Green, A.E.S., 114
Greenberg, H.J., 303
Greenberg, T., 516n
Greenwood, A.G., 698
Greis, Noel, 250
Gross material requirements plan, M4.3-
    M4.6
Gusso, James, 675n

Hamburg, Morris, 80
Hammond, J.S., 114, 152, M3.13
Hanke, J.E., 80, 179n, 200
Hanshin Expressway, 541
Harpell, J.L, 114
Harris, Carl M., 19, 698
Harris, Ford W., 208
Harris, Janet, 37
Harrison, H., 422n
Harsanui, John, 22
Hasbro, Inc., 218
Hausman, W.H., 517n
Hayre, Lakhbir, 321n
Hazelwood, R.N., 635n
Heian, B.C., 152
Heizer, J., 200
Hess S.W., 114, 119
Hewlett-Packard, 206
Hillard, Michael R., M2.24
Hirshfield, D.S., 303
History boxes critical path method, 603
    linear programming, 289
    Program Evaluation Review
        Technique (PERT), 602
    quality control evaluation, 149
    quantitative analysis, 2
    queuing, 651
    simulation, 694
    transportation methods, 449

Hitchock, F.L., 409

Hoey, J.M., 480n

Hoffman, K.L., 469, 698

Holder, Roy, M4.9n, M4.15

Holding cost inventory and, 208

Homart Development Co., 271

Hong Kong Bank of Commerce and Industry, 318–320

Hooker, J.N., 384n

Horowitz, I., 303

Horner, Peter, 309n

Howard, R.A., M2.24

Hosseini, Jinoos, 64

Hueter, J., 171n

Huff, D., 80

Hungarian method, 409, 437–441

Hurwicz criterion, decision making and, 92–93

Hutchinson, J., 699

IBM, 207

Ibarake, Toshihide, M2.25

Ichiishi, Tatsuro, 37

Idem, Fideles, M2.25

Identity matrix, M5.9
  definition of, M5.11

Ignizio, J.P., 492, 518

Imai, Masakki, M4.15

Immediate predecessor, 571

IMPACT, 184

Improvement index, 414–416
  definition of, 446

Independent events, probability and, 45–46, 68
  definition of, 89

Independent variable, 176

Indifference, utility curve and, 131

Inequality, linear programming and, 255
  definition of, 287

Infeasibility, L.P. and, 277, 372
  definition of, 288, 385

Infeasible solution, 262
  definition of, 287

Infinite population, 618
  definition of, 639

Ingredient blending applications, linear programming and, 326–329
  diet problems, 326–327
  ingredient mix and blending problems, 327–329

Initial solution mix, simplex method and, 349

Inland Steel, 215

Input, dynamic programming and M2.7-M2.9

Input date, 4,17

Instantaneous inventory receipt, 215–220
  annual carrying cost, 216
  ordering cost, 216–217
  annual setup cost, 216–217
  definition of, 234
  optimal order quantity, 217–218
  optimal production quantity 217–218

Integer programming, 474–483
  assignment problems and, 484–488
  branch and bound method and, 483–491
  cutting plane method, 476–477
  definition of, 506
  Excel and, 325
  software for, 478
  types of, 478

Inventory control models, 203–251.
  See also specific inventory models
  ABC analysis, 231–232
  decisions in, 207–208
  Economic Order Quantity (EOQ), 208–213, 234
  importance of, 205–207
  introduction to, 204–205
  quantity discount models, 220–223, 234
  reorder point, 214, 234
  safety stock, 223–231, 234
  sensitivity analysis, 232, 234
  without instantaneous receipt assumption, 215–220, 234

Inverse of a matrix, M5.9
  definition, M5.11

Irregular supply and demand, inventory control and, 205

Islei, Gerd, 536

Iso-cost line, definition of, 288

Iso-cost line approach, 274–275
  minimization problems and, 307

Iso-profit line, definition of, 287

Iso-profit line solution method, 263–267, 275

Items, analytic hierarchy process and, 522

Iterative procedure, 346, 385

Jackson, H.F., 469

Jacobs, F.R., M4.15

Jain, A., 563

Jbuedj, Coden, 114

Jankins, G.M., 169n

JIT inventory. *See* Just-in-time (JIT) inventory

Joint probability, 46,48,68

Judgmental models, 175

Juran, J.M., M1.3, M1.24

Jury of executive opinion, qualitative forecasting and, 158

Just-in-time (JIT) inventory, M4.8-M4.10
  definition of, M4.10

Kanban, M4.8-M4.9, M4.10
  four steps of, M4.8

Kang, Moonsig, 536

Kantorovisch, Leonid, 255

Kaplan, Edward H., 653

Karmarkar, N., 255, 384n

Karmarkar's algorithm, 255, 384

Katz, K., 653

Katz, P., 222n

Keaton, M., M3.13

Keeler, R., 698

Keller, Gerald, 250

Kelly, J.E., 569

Kelton, W.D., 699

Kenny, R.L., 114, 152, M3.13

Keown, A., 502n

Kinard, Jerry, 405n, 609n, M1.23, M1.24n

King, Julia, 588

Kirkpatrick, Charles A., 62n

Kirkwood, C.W., 114

KLM Royal Dutch Airlines, 86

Knapsack problems, dynamic planning and, M2.9-M2.16

Koch, Tom, 530n, 536

Kolmogorov, A.N., 255

Koopmans, T.C., 409

KORBX, 384

Koselka, Rita, 22n, 37

Kotob, S., 303

Krishnan, R., 170

Note: Any page number preceded by the letter M means that the topic is located on your CD-ROM.

Krzysztofowizz, Roman, 185n
Kuby, M., 6n, 19, 518
Kulkarni, V.G., 698

Labor planning, employee scheduling
   applications, L.P. and, 316–320
Lan, Lim, 37
Lancaster, Hal, 19
Lane, M.S., 114
Laplace, equally likely and, 91–92
Larson, B., 653
Larson, R.C., 632n, 653
Lasky, M.D., 666n
Latest Finish time (LF), 575, 594
Latest Finish time rule (LF), 576–577
Latest Start time (LS), 575, 594
Law, A.M., 699
Lawrence, M., 413n
Lead time (L), 208
   definition of, 234
Least squares method, fund projections
   and, 169–171,186
Lee, D.R., 216
Lee, H., 206
Lee, Sang M., 518
Leimkukler, John, 481n
LeNoir, Clinton H., Jr., 363n
Leong, G.K., 699
Levin, Richard, 63n, 80
Lev, B., 114, 699
Levy, F., 612
LF. See Latest Finish time (LF)
Liebmen, Judith S., 518
LIFS (Last in-first served), 620n
Limited population, 618
   defnition of, 639
Limited queue length, 620
   definition of, 639
LINDO software package, linear
   programming and, 302–303, 353,
   358, 428
   integer programming, 523
   sensitivity analysis and, 417
Linear equations, 255
Linear Programming (LP), 252–303. See
   also Simplex method
   basic assumptions of, 255
   computer applications, 275–276
   definition of, 286
   formulation of problems, 256–257
   graphical solutions to, 257–267
   introduction, 254
   minimization problems, 269–275
   requirements of LP problem, 254–255

sensitivity analysis, 280–286
special cases in, 277–280
Linear Programming, crashing and,
   591–593
Linear Programming Modeling
   applications with computer
   analyses, 304–343
   employee scheduling applications,
   316–320
   financial applications, 320–321
   ingredient blending applications,
   326–329
   introduction, 306
   manufacturing applications, 310–316
   marketing applications, 306–310
   transportation applications, 321–325
Linear Programming: the simplex
   method, 344–405. See also
   Simplex method
   artificial variables, 360–362
   dual, 381–383
   introduction, 346
   Karmarkar's algorithm, 384
   maximization problems solution
   review, 360
   minimization problems solved,
   362–371
   second simplex tableau, 352–357
   sensitivity analysis with simplex
   tableau, 375–380
   simplex solution, initial set up,
   346–351
   simplex solution procedures, 352
   special cases, 372–374
   surplus variables, 360–362
   third tableau, 357–360
L.L. Bean, 624
Lockett, Geoff, 536
Logical method, probability and, 42,68
Love, R.R., 480n
LP. See Linear Programming (LP)
LS. See Latest Start time (LS)
Lucas, W., 37
Luce, R.D., 37, 114

Machine operations, Markov analysis of,
   710–711
Machol, Robert, 52n
MAD. See Mean Absolute Deviation
Main, Linda, 699
Maintenance policy, simulation model
   for, 675–679
Malcolm Baldrige National Quality
   Award, M1.3

Mamer, J.W., 563
Management science, 3,17
   programming and, 254
Management Sciences Associates,
   (MSA), 307
Mansour, A.H., 114
Manufacturing applications of linear
   programming, 310–316
   production mix, 310–312
   production scheduling, 312–316
MAPE. See Mean Absolute Percent
   Error, (MAPE)
MAP/I, 658
Marginal analysis, 95–99, 100
   with discrete distributions, 95–97
   with normal distribution, 98–99
Marginal Loss (ML), 95, 100
Marginal probability, 46, 47
   definition of, 89
Marginal Profit (MP), 100
Marketing applications of linear
   programming, 306–310
   marketing research, 307
   media selection, 306–307
Market shares, Markov analysis and, 708
   definition of, 719
Markov, A.A., 706n
Markov analysis, 705–729
   accounts receivable application,
   714–720
   assumptions of, 738
   definition of, 719
   equilibrium conditions, 711–714
   introduction, 706
   machine operations and, 710–711
   matrix of transition probabilities,
   708–709
   predicting future market shares, 709
   states and state probabilities, 706–709
Material Requirements Planning (MRP),
   M4.2-M4.8
   benefits of, M4.2
   definition of, M4.10
   dependent demand, M4.2-M4.8
Material Structure tree, M4.2-M4.3
Mathematical model, 4, 17, 656
   advantage of, 8
   categorized by risk, 9
Mathematical programming, 254
   definition of, 287
Mathematical tools, Determinants and
   matrices, M5.1-M5.11
   determinants, M5.2-M5.4
   matrices, M5.4-M5.9
Matrices. See Matrix

Matrix, M5.4-M5.9
  addition, M5.5
  adjoint of, M5.9
  cofactors, M5.9
  definition of, M5.11
  inverses of, M5.9
  multplication, M5.5-M5.6
  subtraction, M5.5
  transpose, M5.8
Matrix of cofactors, six steps in, M5.9
  definition of, M5.11
Matrix reduction, assignment method
      and, 437
  definition of, 446
Matrix of transition probabilities, 706,
      708–709
  definition of, 719
Maximal-flow techniques, network
      models, and, 542–545, 550
  definition of, 548
  steps in, 542
Maximax, 90–91,100
Maximin, 91, 100
Maximization problems, assignment
      problems and, 442–445
  linear programming and, 254, 360
McClain, M.A., 469
McDonald, John, 152
McKeown, P., 469
McLaughlin, Curtis, R., 611n
M/D/I model (constant service time
      model), 632–634
  definition of, 640
Mean Absolute Deviation (MAD), 166,
      186
Mean Absolute Percent Error (MAPE),
      167, 186
Mean (in) control charts and, M1.5
Mean Squared Error (MSE), 167, 186
MFEP. See Multifactor Evaluation
      Process
Miller, Craig, 152
Millet, Ido, 250
Minimal-spanning tree technique,
      538–541, 549
  definition of, 548
  steps in, 538
Minimax, 93, 100
Minimax criterion, 25,31
Minimization problems, 269–275
  corner point method and, 272–275
  iso-cost line approach and, 307

linear programming and, 254
  Simplex method and, 362–371, 365
Minitab, 184
Mitra, A., M1.24, 250
Mixed-integer programming, 478,
      480–482
Mixed strategy game, 25–29, 31
Mizrach, Michael, 469
M/M/M model (Multiple-channel
      queuing model with Poisson
      arrivals and exponential service
      times), 629–631
  definition of, 640
  queuing equations, 629–630
  random numbers, 697–698
  random numbers intervals, 695–697
  steps of, 694
  probability distributions, 694–695
M/M/I model (Single-channel queuing
      model with Poisson arrivals and
      exponential service times), 623–628
  assumption of, 624
  definition of, 639
  queuing equations, 624–625
Model. See also Forecasting, time series
      models, and other specific kinds of
      models
  definition of, 3,17
  types of, 4
Modeling in the Real World
  decision theory models, 84
  decision tree analysis, 119
  dynamic programming, M2.10
  forecasting, 165
  integer programming, 480
  inventory model, 206
  linear programming problem, 263
  Markov analysis, 713
  network models, 547
  Poisson arrivals and exponential
      service time, 623
  project management, 570
  quantitative analysis and, 7
  simulation, 666
  statistical process control, M1.7
  transportation problem, 413
Modified distribution (MODI) method,
      421–424
  definition of, 446
  five steps in, 421
MODI method. See Modified distribution
      (MODI) method

Modules. See Dynamic programming,
      Game theory, Mathematical tools
Mondschein, et al., 12n
Monte Carlo simulation, 658–664
  five steps of, 658
Moondra, Shyam L., 343n
Moore, William E., Jr., 4n, 19, 114
Morgenstren, Oscar, 22, 22n, 37
Moskowitz, Herbert, 518
Most likely time (M), 572
  definition of, 594
Moving averages, time series forecasting
      and, 161–163, 186
MRR. See Material Requirements
      Planning
MSE. See Mean Squared Error
Mullick, S.K., 200
Multifactor decision making, 520
  definition of, 531
Multifactor Evaluation Process (MFEP),
      520–521
  comparison with AHP, 530
  definition of, 531
Multiphase system, 620–621
  definition of, 639
Multi-channel queuing system, 620
Multiple-channel queuing model with
      Poisson arrivals and exponential
      service times, 629–631. See
      M/M/M
Multiple goals, 491, 493–494
Multiple regression analysis, 181–182
Munching, Philip Van, 23n
Murdick R.G., 200
Mutually exclusive events, 42–45
  definition of, 42
  Markov analysis and, 706–707

Nash, John, 22
Natural Oceanic and Atmospheric
      Administration, 185
Natural variations, control charts and,
      M1.4-M1.5, M1.14
Nebike, R., 16n
Negative exponential probability
      distribution, 66, 69, 622
  definition of, 639
Negative slack, 361
Net material requirements plan, M4.3-
      M4.6
Net profit row, 357

Network, PERT and, 572
  definition of, 594
  project management, constraints and, 592–593
Network flow problems, 408
Network models, 537–565
  introduction, 538
  maximal-flow technique, 542–545, 550
  minimal-spanning tree technique, 538–541, 549
  shortest route technique, 545–547, 551
Neumann, John Von, 22, 22n, 37
New Haven Fire Department, 623
New York City Police Department, 632
Nibletto, Paolo, 611n
Nobel Prize in Economics, 22
Nodes, dynamic programming and, M2.2
Nonbasic objective function coefficient, 376–377
Nonbasic variables, 350, 376
  definition of, 385
Non-cooperative game theory, 22
Non-linear programming, 501–508
  definition of, 506
  computational procedures, 506
  linear objective function with non-linear constraints, 504–505
  non-linear objective function with linear constraints, 502
  non-linear objective function with non-linear constraints, 502–503
Nonnegative constraints, 257–258
Nonnegativity, linear programming and, 255
Noon, Charles, E., 518
Nooris, A. Hamid, 250
Normal curve, 736–737
Normal distribution, 58–65
  area under normal curve, 58–60
  and break-even analysis, M3.2
  definition of, 69
  standard normal table, 60–65
  EMV (Expected Monetary Value), M3.5-M3.6
  EVPI (Expected Value of Perfect Information), M3.6
  EOL (Expected Opportunity Loss), M3.7
  exponential distribution, 66
  with marginal analysis, 98–99
  opportunity loss function, M3.6
  probability distribution of demand, M3.3-M3.5

Nortel, 583
Norman V., 698
Northwest corner rule, 411–412
  definition of, 446
Numbers of players, games and, 22
Numbers of strategies, games and, 22
Nuno, J.P., 671n

Objective probability, 42
Objective function and crashing
  converting constraints and, 364
  crashing and, 592
  of linear programming problem, 254, 287, 350–351
Objective function coefficient, changes in, 281, 376–378
Oglethorpe Power Corp., 122
Olson, D.L., 698
Omurtag Y., 494n
Omal, Hayri, 563
Operating characteristics, queuing systems and, 624
  definition of, 639
Operational gaming, 681
  definition of, 683
Operations research, 3
Opportunity costs, 437
  definition of, 446
  table and, 438–441
Opportunity loss function, M3.6, M3.8
Optimality analysis, 280
Optimal order quantity, 217–218
  four steps in determining, 217
Optimal policy, dynamic programming and, M2.6, M2.17
  definition of, 795
Optimal production quantity, 217–218
  four steps in determining, 217
Optimistic decision criterion, 90
Optimistic time, 572
  definition of, 594
Orden, A., 303
Order quantity, 664
Ordering cost, inventory and, 208
Output, dynamic programming and, M2.7-M2.9

P-charts, M1.10-M1.11, M1.14
Pairwise comparisons, Analytic Hierarchy Process and, 520–521
Panico, J.A., 653
Parallel activity, 583
Parameter, 4

Parametric programming, 280
Parasuraman, A., M1.24
Parents, material structure tree and, M4.2-M4.3
Parker, G.C., 200
Parsons, H., 303, 624n, 653
Payoffs, 83, 100
Payoff table, 83
Peck, L.G., 635n
Peck, R.D., M4.15
Pogdon, C.D., 699
Penlesky, R.J., M1.5
Perlman, Radia, 541n
Perry, C., 413n
PERT. *See* Program Evaluation and Review Technique (PERT)
PERT/Cost, 568, 583–589
  budgeting process, 584–586
  definition of, 594
  monitoring and controlling project costs, 586–589
Pessimistic decision criterion, 91
Pessimistic time, 572
  definition of, 594
Philpott, A.B., 303
Physical model, 4, 656
Pica, Vincent, 321n
Pivot columns, 352
  definition of, 385
Pivot numbers, 352
  definition of, 385
Pivot rows, 352
  definition of , 385
Plosal, George, 183, 183n
Point estimate, 178
Poisson distribution, 66–67, 69, 619, 740,
  definition of, 639
Poisson, Simeon, 66n
Positive substitution rate, 393
Posterior probabilities, 48–51
  definition of, 88–89
Postoptimality analysis, 5, 280–281
Prabhu, N.U., 653
Pratt, J.W., 114
Predecessor activity, 582
Prewritten simulation programs, 682
  definition of, 684
Primal-dual relationships, 381
  definition of, 386
Prior Probability, 50, 68
  definition of, 89
Pritsker, Alan B., 43
Probabilistic models, 9
Probabilistic technique, 568

Probability concepts and applications, 39–80
  Bayes's theorem or law, 47,48 -50, 68, 80
  classical method, 42, 68
  collectively exhaustive events, 42–45, 68
  conditional, 46, 47, 68
  definition of, 40, 68
  dependent events, 45, 47–48, 68
  fundamental concepts, 41
  independent events, 45–46, 68
  introduction, 40
  joint, 46, 48, 68
  logical method, 42, 68
  marginal probability, 46, 47, 68
  mutually exclusive events, 42–45, 68
  objective method, 42
  posterior, 48–50, 68
  prior, 50, 68
  random variables, discrete and continuous, 52–58
  revised, 48–51, 68
  simple, 46
  statistically independent events, 45–46
  subjective approach, 42, 68
  types of, 42
Probability density function, 57, 69
Probability distribution of demand. *See* Normal distribution
Probability distributions, 54–58. *See also* Continuous random variable, Discrete random variable, Discrete probability distribution
  continuous random variable, 52–54, 57–58
  definition of, 68
  discrete random variable, 52–56
  discrete probability distribution, 54–56
  expected value of discrete probability distributions, 55–56
  exponential distribution, 66
  Monte Carlo simulation and, 658–659
  negative exponential distribution, 66, 69
  Poisson distribution, 66–67, 69
  variance of discrete probability distribution, 56–57
Probability function, 57
Probability values, Bayesian analysis and, 125–128

Problem, definition of, 3, 17
Problem possibilities in QA approach, 12–15
  acquiring input data, 14
  analyzing results, 15
  defining problem, 13
  developing a model, 13–14
  developing a solution, 14–15
  testing the solution, 15
Production run model, 215–216
  definition of, 234
Product mix problem, 256–257
  definition of, 287
Program Evaluation and Review Technique (PERT), 566–613
  activity times, 572–573
  critical path and, 573–578
  definition of, 594
  drawing the network for, 571–572
  dummy activities in, 581–582
  framework of, 568
  history of, 569
  sensitivity analysis, 582–583
Programming. *See* Linear programming, dynamic programming, and other specific types of programming
Project completion constraint, 592
Project cost. *See* PERT/Cost
Project crashing. *See* crashing
Project management
  introduction to, 568
  sensitivity analysis and, 616–617
Proportionality, LP problems and, 255
Przasnyski, Zbigniew H., 697n
Puakpong, P. 469
Pure integer programming, 478
Pure strategy, 24, 31

QA in Action
  Aids assistance, linear programming and, 282
  Airline safety, probability analysis and, 52
  Air Products and Chemicals, Inc., 522, 530
  American Airlines, 179, 263, 481
  American League Umpires, assignment model and, 445
  Bellcore, quantity discounts and, 222
  Bellcore's SONET Decision Support System, 15

Blue Bell, inventory and, 232
British Columbia, Canada, Long Term Care, 750
Cahill May Roberts, Co., transportation problem and, 422
Canadian National Railway, 657
Chile, QA and pollution control, 12
Compaq, material resource planning and, M4.6
Delta Airlines scheduling, 309, 577
Department of Corrections of Virginia, 502
Digital Equipment Corp., 541
DuPont, statistical quality control and, M1.4
Game theory, brewing business and, 23
General Motors, game theory and, 26
Hasbro Inc. production speed and quality, 218
Hanshin Expressway, 543
HDTV (higher definition TV), forecastings and, 158
Homart Development Co., linear programming and, 271
IBM, inventory management and, 207
Inland Steel, inventory costs and, 215
KLM Royal Dutch Airlines, decision theory and maintenance, 86
L.L. Bean, 624
Markov analysis, 718
National Oceanic and Atmospheric Administration (NOAA) forecasting and, 185
New York City Police Departments, 632
Nortel, 583
North Carolina School Transportation, 546
Nursery production, dynamic programming and, M2.6
Oglethorpe Power Corp., decision trees and, 122
Probability distributions, sunken gold search and, 59
Project management, software development and, 588
Prudential Securities, L.P. for portfolio selection, 321
Reynolds Metals Co., management science and, 4
Rio Bravo Electronics, MRP and JIT and, M4.9

Note: Any page number preceded by the letter M means that the topic is located on your CD-ROM.

Taco Bell, 200, 682
United Kingdom, decision analysis, healthcare and, 92
University of Missouri, 494
Vilpac, 671
Weapons of mass destruction, decision modes and, 128
Wellborn Cabinet Co., 363
QM for Windows
  decision theory, 114–115
  decision trees, 152–153
  forecasting, 200–202
  game theory, 37
  goal planning, 501
  how to use, 741–744
  integer programming, 478, 481
  inventory control, 250–251
  linear programming problems, 267–268
  linear programming modular application, 317–318
  Markov analysis, 764–765
  network models, 563–565
  project management 612–613
  quantitative analysis, 9–10
  queuing models, 653
  sensitivity analysis, 284–285
  simulation and, 663–664
  Statistical quality control, M1.25
  transportation and assignment methods, 469–470
Quadratic programming, 502
Qualitative factors, 2
Qualitative models, 157–158, 185
  Delphi method, 158, 185
  Jury of Executive opinion, 158
  sales force composite, 158
Quality and TQM, M1.2-M1.3
  definition of, M1.2, M1.4
Quantitative analysis, 1–19
  analysts lack of commitment, 16
  analyzing solution results, 5–6
  approach to, 2–3
  acquiring input data, 4–5, 17
  commitment to cheap, 16
  defining problems, 3, 17
  definition of, 2,17
  development of a model, 3–4, 7–9
  development of a solution, 5
  GIGO (Garbage-in, Garbage-out), 4
  history of, 3
  implementing the results, 6,16
  introduction, 2
  computers and, 9–12

problems in approach, 12–15
problems in acquiring input data, 14
problems in analyzing results, 15
problems in defining problem, 13
QM for Windows and, 9–10
  developing a model, 13–14
  developing a solution, 14–15
  testing the solution, 15
  resistance to change, 16
  sensitivity analysis and, 5–6, 17
  spreadsheets and, 9–12
  testing solution, 5
Quantity column, 349
  definition of, 385
Quantity discount models, inventory control and, 206, 220–223, 234
  definition of, 234
  four steps in, 221
Queue discipline, 620
  definition of, 639
Queuing models, and exponential service times, 657–667
  Poisson distribution and, 619
Queuing problem simulation and, 671–674
Queuing system characteristics of, 618–623
  arrival characteristics, 618–620
Queuing theory, 616–653. *See* Waiting lines
  constant service time model, 632–634
  definition of, 639
  finite population model, 634–638
  multiple-channel with Poisson arrivals and exponential service times, 629-632
  single-channel with Poisson arrivals and exponential service times, 623–628
Quinn, P., 303, 624n, 653

R-chart (Range chart), M1.5, M1.8-M1.9, M1.14
  four steps to use, M1.10
Raiffa, H., 37, 114, 152, M3.13
Random arrivals, queuing system and, 652
Random number intervals, 659–662
  definition of, 683
Random numbers, 660
  definition of, 683
  table of, 662
Random variables probability and, 52–53, 68

continuous, 52–53, 54, 57–58, 68
  definition of, 52, 68
  discrete, 52–53, 68
Random variations (R), time series forecasting model and, 159, 161
Range of insignificance, 377
  definition of, 386
Range of optimalitiy, 378
  definition of, 386
Rappoport, H.K., 698
Reduced matrix method, 409
Redundancy, L.P. and, 278–279
  definition of, 288
Rees, L.P. 698
Regression analysis, 176–177, 186
Reid, Richard A., 200
Reinsel, G.C., 169n
Reiner, L., M5.14
Reitsch, A.G., 80, 179n, 200
Relative frequency probability and, 42, 68
Remington Rand, 569
Render, Barry, 114, 200, 469, 612, 516n, 563
Reneging, 619–620
  definition of, 639
Reorder point (ROP), 214, 234, 664
  known stockout costs and, 242–244
Return, dynamic programming and, M2.7-M2.9
Revised probabilities, 48–51, 126–128
Reynolds Metal Co., 4
RHS (right-hand-side) column, 349
RHS ranging. *See* Right-hand-side ranging.
Right-hand-side column, 349
Right-hand-side (RHS) ranging, 379–380
Right-hand-side values, 284, 378–379
Rio Bravo Electronics, M4.9
Risk avoider, utility curve and, 131, 135
Risk seeker, utility curve and, 131, 135
Roe, Justin, 612n
Romig, H.G., M1.3
ROR. *See* Reorder point
Rosenthal, Richard E., 469
Roundy, Robin, 250
Royal Swedish Academy of Sciences, 22
RSFE. *See* Running Sum of the Forecast Errors
Rubin, D.S., 80, 303
Running sum of the forecast errors (RSFE), 182–184
Russell, R., 502n
Ryan, Sarah M., 518

Saaty, Thomas, L., 521, 536
Saddle point, 24
Saddle point game, 24, 31
Sadowsky, R.P., 699
Safety stock, 223–231
  definition of, 234
  reorder point and, 223, 225–227
Safety stock with known stockout costs,
    225–227
  definition of, 234
Safety stock with unknown stockout
    costs, 228–231
  definition of, 234
Sales force composite, qualitative
    forecasting and, 158
Salton, Gary, J., 518
Saltzman, M.J., 303
Salveson, Melvin, 19
Sancho, N.G.F, 563
Sander, Wayne, 612
SAS, 199
Satinder, C., 200
Satisficing, 492, 506
Saunders, Patsy, B., 698
Scale models, 4
Scatter diagrams, 158, 160, 186
Schematic model, 4
Schindler, S., 303
Schlaifer, R., 114, M6.5, 737, 739
Schnaars, Steven P., 200
Schniederjans, Marc J., 518
Seasonality (s) time series forecasting
    model and, 159, 161, 173–175
Second simplex tableau, 352–357,
    367–368
  interpreting of, 355–357
Second order smoothing, 169
Selten, Reinhard, 22
Semmel, T., 303
Sensitivity analysis, 5–6, 17, 89–90,
    134–135
  computer and, 380
  inventory control models and, 232,
    234
  linear programming and, 280–286
  project management and, 616–617
  simplex tableau and, 375–380
Separable programming, 506
Sequential decision, 119–123, 135. *See
    also* Decision tree analysis
  definition of, 671
Service cost, waiting line and, 616

Service facility characteristics, queuing
    system and, 620–622
  basic configurations, 620
  service time distribution, 622
Service level, 228–231
  definition of, 234
  normal distribution and, 229
Setup cost, inventory control and,
    215–217, 234
Sexton, T.R., 303, 546
Shadow prices, 357, 375, 378–379
Shannon, R.E., 699
Shearer, Mike, 178n
Sheffer, J.P., M1.4
Shell, M.C., 632n
Shewart, W., M1.3
Shipping assignment, five steps to make,
    411–412
Shortages, inventory control and
    avoidance of, 206
Shortest-route problem, dynamic
    programming and, 780–784
Shortest-route technique, 545–547, 551
  dynamic programming and, M2.2-
    M2.5
  definition of, 548
  steps in, 546
Shubik, M., 37
Shyrock,E.G., 175n
SIMNETTII, 671
Simon, Herbert, A., 492
Simple probability, 46
Simplex method, 346. *See* also specific
    types
  algebraic initial solution, 348
  converting constraints to equations,
    347
  definition of, 385
  dual, 318–383
  first tableau of, 348–351, 365–367
  five steps in, 352
  fourth tableau of, 370–371
  in goal programming, 498–501
  initial solution of, 346–351
  interpreting second tableau, 355–357
  Karmarkar's algorithm, 384
  minimization problems in, 362–371
  second tableau of, 352–357,
    367–368
  solution procedures of, 352
  special cases in using, 372–374
  third tableau of, 357–360, 368–370

Simplex tableau
  definition of, 385
  first, 348–351
  fourth, 370–371
  interpreting the second, 355–357
  second, 352–357
  sensitivity analysis and, 375–380
  third, 357–360
SIMSCRIPT, 682
Simulation, modeling, 656–704. *See* also
    Monte Carlo simulation
  advantages of, 657–658
  and computers, 682
  and cost analysis, 678–679
  definition of, 656, 683
  disadvantages of, 657–658
  general purpose languages, 682
  introduction to, 656
  inventory analysis and, 664
  maintenance policy and, 657–679
  Monte Carlo, 658–664
  operational gaming and, 681
  queuing model and, 638
  queuing problem and, 671–674
  systems and, 681
Simultaneous equation method,
    266–267
  definition of, 288
Simultaneous equations, M5.3-M5.4
  definition of, M5.11
Single-channel queuing model with
    Poisson arrivals and exponential
    service times, 623–628
  assumptions of, 624
  queuing equations, 624–625
Single-channel queuing system, 620
  definition of, 639
Single-phase system, 620
  definition of, 639
Sinha, Arunava, 37
Sivathanu, Pillai, 612
Slack time, 577–578
  definition of, 594
Slack variables, 347, 385
SLAM, 658
Sleeper, S., 303
Smith, B., 481n
Smith, D.D., 200
Smock, Doug, 218n, 250
Smoothing constant, 163, 165–169, 186
Solomon, S.L., 733
Solution, 5–6

Note: Any page number preceded by the letter M means that the topic is located on your CD-ROM.

Solution mix, 385
    definition of, 423
Solutions to selected problems, 745–748
Solutions to self-tests, 748–751
Solver, 10
    L.P. problems and, 268, 307–308,
        312, 322–323, 324–326, 436
Source, transportation model and, 408
    definition of, 446
Sower, Victor, E., 302n
Sox, Charles, 250
Special purpose algorithms, 408–409
Special purpose simulation languages, 682
    definition of, 684
Special simulation languages. *See also*
        GPSS language, MAPI language.
SPSS, 184
Stafira, Stanley, 128, 152
Stage, dynamic programming and, M2.5,
        M2.16
Stair, Ralph M., 114, 469, 516n, 563, 612
Stam, Antonie, 536
Standard deviation distributions, control
        charts and, M1.5
Standard deviation of the regression,
        178–180.
Standard error of the estimate, 178–180,
        186
Standard gamble, utility theory and, 129
Standard normal curve, 736
Standard normal distribution, 58–60
Standard normal table, 60–65
State-of-nature, decision theory and, 83,
        100
State-of-nature points, 118
State probabilities, 706–709
    definition of, 719
States, 706
State variables, dynamic programming
        and, M2.5, M2.16
Statistical Process Control (SPC) M1.3,
        M1.5
    variability in, M1.3-M1.5
Statistical quality control, M1.1-M1.24
    control chart for attributes, M1.9-
        M1.13
    control chart for variables, M1.5-
        M1.9
    defining quality and TQM, M1.2-
        M1.3
    QM for Windows, M1.25
    statistical process control (SPC),
        M1.3
Steepest ascent method, 506
Steinberg, D., 383n

Stepping-stone method, 413–421
    definition of, 446
    five steps testing unused squares, 414
    obtaining an improved solution,
        416–421
Sterk, W.E., 175n
Stockouts, 204, 206, 234
    avoiding of, 206
    definition of, 234
Stokes, Jeffrey, M2.6n, M2.25
Stone, Lawrence D., 59n, 152
Storing resources, inventory control and,
        205
Stowe, J.D., 518
Strait, Scott, 114
Stratford, Mike, 536
Strum, Jay E., 421n
Subjective probability, 412
Subramanian, R., 309n, 518
Substitution rates, 350, 356
    definition of, 385
Successor activity, 582
Sullivan, Gerald, 114, 207
Sum of all payoffs, 22
Surplus variable, 360–362
    definition of, 385
    objective function and, 362
Sutherland, J.W., M1.24
Swart, W., 171n
Swersey, A.J., 623n, 653
Symbols in decision trees, 118
SYSTAB, 184
Systems, Analytic Hierarchy Process
        and, 522–529
Systems simulation, 681
    definition of, 683
Sze, D., 653

Tableau. *See* Simplex tableau
Taco Bell, 200, 682
Taggart, Jr., R.E., 303
Tanga, R., 469
Taylor, B., III, 502n
Taylor, B.W., 518
Taylor, Frederick, W., 3
Technological coefficients, change in
        and, 281–284
    definition of, 288
Tedone, Mark J., 179n
The Analytic Hierarchy Process, 521
Theory of Games and Economic
        Behavior, 22
Third simplex tableau, 357–360,
        368–370

Time series forecasting models, 157, 159
    components of, 159, 161
    decomposition of, 159–161
    definition of, 185
    exponential smoothing, 163–169, 186
    moving averages, 161–163
    seasonal variation, 173–175
Tingley, Kim M., 518
Toelle, Richard, M2.25
Total Quality Management (TQM),
        M1.2-M1.3, M1.14
Tracking signal, 182, 186
Transformation, dynamic programming
        and, M2.6, M2.17
Transition probability, 708–709
    definition of, 719
Transportation applications and linear
        programming, 321–325
    shipping problem, 321–323
    truck loading problem, 324–325
Transportation and assignment models,
        406–471. *See* Assignment models
    degeneracy in, 430–432
    facility location analysis, 432–435
    improvement index in, 454–455, 483
    introduction, 408
    modified distribution (MODI) method
        in, 421–424
    multiple solutions, 432
    northwest corner rule in, 411–412
    problem, 408, 446
    setting up transportation problem,
        409–411
    stepping stone method, 413–421
    unbalanced transportation problems,
        426–430
    Vogel's Approximation Method
        (VAM) in, 424–426
        six steps in, 424–425
Transportation table, 410
    definition of, 446
Transpose of matrix, M5.8
    definition of, M5.11
Treeplan, 10
Trend (T), time series forecasting models
        and, 159, 161
Trend projections forecasting and,
        169–173
    transporting time variables, 171–172
Trial and error, 5
Two or more end products, MRP and,
        M4.6-M4.8
Two-person game, 22, 31
Types of probability, 42
Types of integer programming, 478

Unbalanced problems, transportation and, 426–430
   definition of, 446
     demand less than supply, 427–428
     demand greater than supply, 428–430
Unboundedness, L.P. and, 278
   definition of, 288
   simplex method and, 372–373
Uncontrollable variable, 4
Unfavorable Market (UM), decision trees and, 126
Unit normal loss integral, M3.7, M3.8, 738–739
University of Missouri, 494
Unlimited population, 618
   definition of, 639
Unlimited queue length, 620
   definition of, 639
Urban government, simulation and, 681
Utility assessment, 129, 135
Utility curve, 129–132, 135
   decision-making criterion, 132–134
Utility theory and decision trees. *See* Decision Trees and Utility Theory
Utilization factor, 625
   definition of, 640

Valid model, 8
Value of the game, 25, 31
vander Duyn Schouten, Frank, 250
Variable. *See* Dependent variable, Independent variable, Random variable: control charts
   definition of, 4
Variance, probability distributions and, 55, 69

Variance of activity completion time, PERT and, 573
   definition of, 594
Variations. *See* natural and assignable variations
Vazsoni, Andrew, 19
Vector of state probabilities, 706
   definition of, 719
Venn diagram, 44
Venkatakrishnan, C.C., 19
Vogel's approximation method (VAM), 424–426
   definition of, 446
VonNeuman, John, 658
VonNeuman midsquare method, 661n

Wagner, H.M., 232n, 303
Waiting costs, 617
   definition of, 639
Waiting lines, 616–653. *See* queue models, queuing system
   characteristics of, 620
   costs, 616
   definition of, 639
   introduction, 616
Walker, M.R., 569
Walpole, Horace, 297n
Wang, Hongbo, 518
Ward, P.T., 699
Warmke, Janice M., 4n, 19, 114
Webster, W., 303
Weighted moving averages, forecasting and, 162–163, 186
Weinberg, Charles, B., 200
Weist, J., 612
Welch, Norma, 675n

Wellborn Cabinet Co., 363
Wheeler, D.J., M1.24
Whybark, D.C., M4.15
Wight, Oliver, 183, 183n
William, Carlton, 563
Williams, Martyn, 563
Winterdeldt, Detlof von, 84n
WITNESS, 658
Wood, W.P., 232n
Woolsey, Gene, 14
Woolsey, R.E.D., 14n
Workman, B., 469
Worthington, D.J., 653

XCell, 658
X-Barchart, M1.5-M1.8, M1.14
   five steps to use, M1.10
   setting limits and, M1.6-M1.8

Yield management, 481
Yoshino, T., 543n
Young, Margaret, 80
Yuen, M., M4.15
Yurkiewicz, J., 200

Zangwill, W.I., 518
Zappe, C., 303
Zeithaml, V.A., M1.24
Zero-one integer programming, 478, 482–483
   definition of, 506
Zero sum game, 22, 31
Z; row, 351
   definition of 385

Note: Any page number preceded by the letter M means that the topic is located on your CD-ROM.

SITE LICENSE AGREEMENT AND LIMITED WARRANTY